lonely planet

Southwest

Jeff Campbell
Rob Rachowiecki
Jennifer Rasin Denniston

LONELY PLANET PUBLICATIONS
Melbourne • Oakland • London • Paris

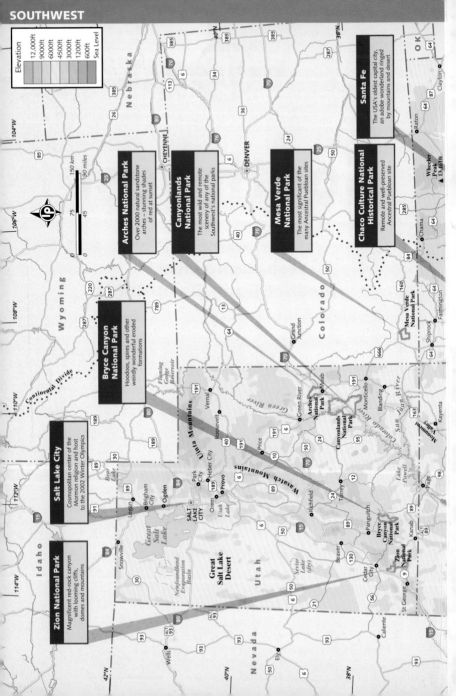

SOUTHWEST

Elevation
12,000ft
9000ft
6000ft
4500ft
3000ft
1200ft
600ft
Sea Level

Zion National Park
Magnificent red-rock canyon with looming cliffs, domes and mountains

Salt Lake City
Cosmopolitan center of the Mormon religion and host to the 2002 Winter Olympics

Bryce Canyon National Park
Hoodoos, spires and other weirdly wonderful eroded formations

Arches National Park
Over 2000 natural sandstone arches – stunning shades of red at sunset

Canyonlands National Park
The most wild and remote scenery of any of the Southwest's national parks

Mesa Verde National Park
The most significant of the many Ancestral Puebloan sites

Chaco Culture National Historical Park
Remote and well-preserved Ancestral Puebloan site

Santa Fe
The USA's oldest capital city, an adobe wonderland ringed by mountains and desert

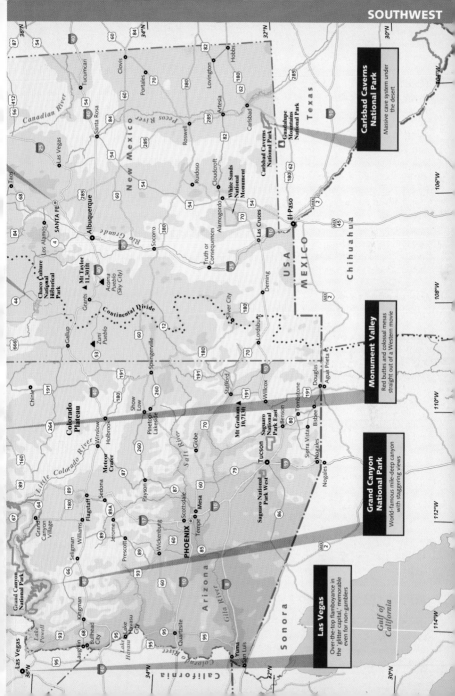

Carlsbad Caverns National Park
Massive cave system under the desert

Monument Valley
Red buttes and colossal mesas straight out of a Western movie

Grand Canyon National Park
World-famous mile-deep canyon with staggering views

Las Vegas
Over-the-top flamboyance in the glitter capital; memorable even for non-gamblers

Texas

USA
MEXICO

Chihuahua

Arizona

New Mexico

Sonora

California

Gulf of California

Colorado Plateau

Continental Divide

Canadian River

Pecos River

Rio Grande

Salt River

Gila River

Little Colorado River

Colorado River

Lake Powell

Lake Mead

Lake Havasu

PHOENIX
SANTA FE

Albuquerque
Las Vegas
Taos
Los Alamos
Gallup
Grants
Acoma Pueblo (Sky City)
Zuni Pueblo
Mt Taylor 11,301ft
Chaco Culture National Historical Park
Socorro
Truth or Consequences
Deming
Silver City
Lordsburg
Las Cruces
El Paso
Deming
Alamogordo
White Sands National Monument
Cloudcroft
Ruidoso
Roswell
Carlsbad
Carlsbad Caverns National Park
Guadalupe Mountains National Park
Artesia
Lovington
Hobbs
Portales
Clovis
Santa Rosa
Tucumcari
Las Vegas

Grand Canyon National Park
Grand Canyon Village
Williams
Flagstaff
Sedona
Jerome
Prescott
Wickenburg
Seligman
Kingman
Bullhead City
Laughlin
Las Vegas
Havasu City
Lake Havasu City
Quartzsite
Yuma
San Luis
Nogales
Nogales
Sierra Vista
Bisbee
Tombstone
Douglas
Agua Prieta
Benson
Willcox
Safford
Mt Graham 10,713ft
Saguaro National Park West
Saguaro National Park East
Tucson
Mesa
Tempe
Scottsdale
Payson
Show Low
Pinetop-Lakeside
Springerville
Globe
Holbrook
Winslow
Meteor Crater
Chinle

Sierra
Nogales

Southwest
3rd edition – April 2002
First published – November 1995

Published by
Lonely Planet Publications Pty Ltd ABN 36 005 607 983
90 Maribyrnong St, Footscray, Victoria 3011, Australia

Lonely Planet Offices
Australia Locked Bag 1, Footscray, Victoria 3011
USA 150 Linden St, Oakland, CA 94607
UK 10a Spring Place, London NW5 3BH
France 1 rue du Dahomey, 75011 Paris

Photographs
Many of the images in this guide are available for licensing from
Lonely Planet Images.
email: lpi@lonelyplanet.com.au
Web site: www.lonelyplanetimages.com

Front cover photograph
Lipan Point, Grand Canyon National Park (John Elk III)

Title page photographs
Utah – Slot Canyon, Zion National Park (Richard Cummins)
Arizona – Antelope Canyon, Page (Michael Aw)
New Mexico – Chiles hanging out to dry (John Hay)

ISBN 1 86450 376 9

Printed by SNP SPrint (M) Sdn Bhd
Printed in Malaysia

Contents

SOUTHEASTERN UTAH

LAS VEGAS

FACTS ABOUT ARIZONA

PHOENIX & AROUND

GRAND CANYON & LAKE POWELL

4 Contents

SOUTHEASTERN ARIZONA

SOUTHWESTERN COLORADO

FACTS ABOUT NEW MEXICO

ALBUQUERQUE AREA

SANTA FE & TAOS

NORTHWESTERN NEW MEXICO

6   Contents

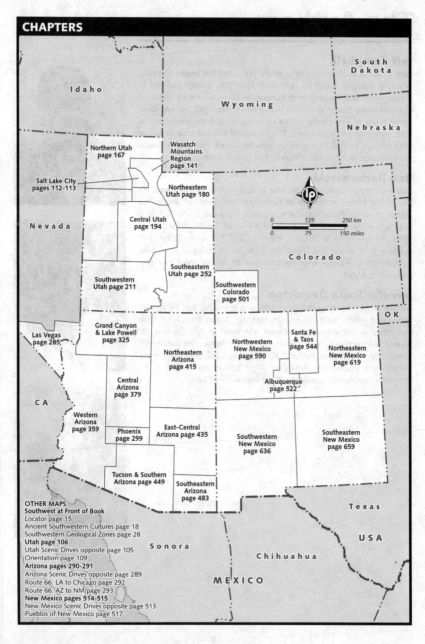

CHAPTERS

Idaho

Wyoming

South Dakota

Nebraska

Northern Utah
page 167

Wasatch Mountains Region
page 141

Salt Lake City
pages 112-113

Northeastern Utah page 180

Nevada

Central Utah
page 194

Colorado

Southeastern Utah page 252

Southwestern Utah page 211

Southwestern Colorado
page 501

OK

Las Vegas
page 285

Grand Canyon & Lake Powell
page 325

Northeastern Arizona
page 415

Northwestern New Mexico
page 590

Santa Fe & Taos
page 544

Northeastern New Mexico
page 619

CA

Central Arizona
page 379

Albuquerque
page 522

Western Arizona
page 359

Phoenix
page 299

East-Central Arizona page 435

Southwestern New Mexico
page 636

Southeastern New Mexico
page 659

Tucson & Southern Arizona page 449

Southeastern Arizona
page 483

Texas

USA

OTHER MAPS
Southwest at Front of Book
Locator page 15
Ancient Southwestern Cultures page 18
Southwestern Geological Zones page 28
Utah page 106
Utah Scenic Drives opposite page 105
Orientation page 109
Arizona pages 290-291
Arizona Scenic Drives opposite page 289
Route 66: LA to Chicago page 292
Route 66: AZ to NM page 293
New Mexico pages 514-515
New Mexico Scenic Drives opposite page 513
Pueblos of New Mexico page 517

Sonora

Chihuahua

MEXICO

0   125   250 km
0   75   150 miles

The Authors

Jeff Campbell

Born in Texas and raised in New Jersey, Jeff Campbell began traveling when he dropped out of his cold, rainy New York college and fled to Europe – winding his way from London to Crete, where he spent an idyllic summer teaching windsurfing. Forever changed, he has since mixed bouts of world travel with a varied career in book publishing, as both an editor and writer. In 2001, he toured the red rock desert of Utah for this, his first writing assignment for Lonely Planet. Jeff lives in San Francisco with his wife, Deanna, and son, Jackson.

Rob Rachowiecki

Rob was born in London and became an avid traveler as a teenager. He has visited places as diverse as Greenland and Thailand and is the author of Lonely Planet's guides to Ecuador, Peru and Costa Rica. Rob is an active member of the Society of American Travel Writers. Since 1989, he has lived in Tucson, Arizona, with his wife, Cathy, and children, Julia, Alison and David. He finds Tucson to be an ideal base from which to explore what he considers to be the most beautiful region of the USA.

Jennifer Rasin Denniston

Jennifer began traveling independently as a teenager, and by age 21 had visited Africa, Australia, Europe, Vietnam, Japan and China. Born and raised in the American Midwest, she lived in Albuquerque for several years and calls New Mexico her second home. She lives in Mt Vernon, Iowa, with her husband Rhawn, dog Cyril, and baby Anna Salinas, and studies the American West and visual culture as an American Studies PhD candidate at the University of Iowa.

FROM THE AUTHORS

Jeff Campbell First and foremost, I thank my coauthors, for their support and good cheer, and the editors at Lonely Planet, especially David Zingarelli, who guided us with a sure and steady hand. Rangers and information bureaus were unfailingly helpful throughout Utah. Many thanks to Susan Stordahl, Theresa Hallerin, Michael Cawley, Naomi Silverstone, Gene Hansen and James Beebe for sharing their insights, tips and favorite places. Thanks to Christine and David Hale for their friendly Mormon welcome, to Ashley at A Cup of Joe for his boundless enthusiasm, and to Tom Wharton for being kind and generous with a first-timer. For great steaks, long walks and a home away from home, a million thanks to Rachel Blackham, Brian Mischo and Morgan. And I am forever grateful to my wife, Deanna, for her infinite patience, love and support, and to wee Jackson, who was always ready for a hike.

Rob Rachowiecki I dedicate my sections of the book to my son, David, who loves to play in the desert.

I thank the staffers at chambers of commerce throughout Arizona and southwestern New Mexico who provided information about their towns. Claire Heywood of the Hopi tribe made numerous helpful suggestions both about the Hopi people and the Hopi Indian Reservation. Information officers at federal and state parks were unfailingly helpful with checking my information. Many readers of the 2nd edition sent in suggestions and updates – their names are listed at the back of this book. I really do appreciate all of your input.

I especially thank my family for enabling me to travel for many weeks to update this book, and for being supportive of my work. I love you.

Jennifer Rasin Denniston I thank Rob Rachowiecki and Jeff Campbell for their inspiration, support, patience, kindness and sense of humor – I can't imagine better guys to work with. Thanks to David Zingarelli, who is always willing to answer just one more question. I appreciate the excellent work of several Lonely Planet editors and cartographers, especially Rachel Bernstein – thank you for your painstaking attention to detail and consistency. And to Rhawn, thanks for taking the time from your own work to spend months driving around New Mexico with me and our newborn baby. I wouldn't have been able to do this research without you.

This Book

This is the 3rd edition of Lonely Planet's *Southwest*. The 1st and 2nd editions of the book were researched and written by Rob Rachowiecki. Nicko Goncharoff, Steve McLaughlin, Scott McNeely and Jennifer Rasin Denniston also contributed to the early editions.

This 3rd edition was researched and updated by Rob and fellow authors Jeff Campbell and Jennifer Rasin Denniston. Jeff was the coordinating author of this edition, and he updated the Utah chapters. Rob researched and updated the introductory chapters, all of the Arizona chapters and Southwestern New Mexico; Jennifer Rasin Denniston did the same for the rest of the New Mexico chapters. Maria Mack covered Las Vegas, and Pelin Thornhill updated the Southwestern Colorado chapter from material originally contributed by Mason Florence for Lonely Planet's *Rocky Mountains*.

FROM THE PUBLISHER

This edition of *Southwest* was produced in the Oakland, California, office of Lonely Planet. Rachel Bernstein and Susan Malloy edited the book, with lots of help from Rebecca Northen, Wade Fox and Paul Sheridan. Michael Johnson, Tammy Fortin and Eleanor Renner Brown proofed the text and Margaret Livingston created the index. Michele Posner and Robert Reid pitched in at layout. Thanks to senior editor David Zingarelli for his calm, cool and collected nature and to managing editor Kate Hoffman.

Unflappable Justin Colgan was the lead cartographer, heading up a cast of thousands that included Don Patterson, Narinder Bansal, Rachel Jereb, Anneka Imkamp, Carole Nuttall, David Ryder, Dion Good, Gina Gillich, Graham Neale, Kat Smith, Marji Hamm, Patrick Phelan, Brad Lodge, Buck Cantwell, Eric Thomsen, John Culp, Patrick Huerta and Tessa Rottiers. The senior cartographers were Tracey Croom and Bart Wright, and Alex Guilbert managed it all.

The book was designed and laid out in record time by Henia Miedzinski and Lora Santiago. Henia designed color pages that attracted oohs and aahs from everyone and a cover that made us all happy. The illustrations were drawn by Hugh D'Andrade, John Fadeff, Hayden Foell and Lara Sox Harris. Special thanks to Justin Marler, who contributed several creative and hilarious illustrations to the book and coordinated the illustration process. Thanks also to Susan 'Nerves of Steel' Rimerman for her help with the scenic drives maps.

We couldn't have done it without the authors, Jeff, Rob and Jennifer, who took on an enormous task and made it look easy.

Foreword

ABOUT LONELY PLANET GUIDEBOOKS

The story begins with a classic travel adventure: Tony and Maureen Wheeler's 1972 journey across Europe and Asia to Australia. Useful information about the overland trail did not exist at that time, so Tony and Maureen published the first Lonely Planet guidebook to meet a growing need.

From a kitchen table, then from a tiny office in Melbourne (Australia), Lonely Planet has become the largest independent travel publisher in the world, an international company with offices in Melbourne, Oakland (USA), London (UK) and Paris (France).

Today Lonely Planet guidebooks cover the globe. There is an ever-growing list of books, and there's information in a variety of forms and media. Some things haven't changed. The main aim is still to help make it possible for adventurous travelers to get out there – to explore and better understand the world.

At Lonely Planet we believe travelers can make a positive contribution to the countries they visit – if they respect their host communities and spend their money wisely. Since 1986 a percentage of the income from each book has been donated to aid projects and human-rights campaigns.

Updates Lonely Planet thoroughly updates each guidebook as often as possible. This usually means there are around two years between editions, although for more unusual or more stable destinations the gap can be longer. Check the imprint page (following the title page at the beginning of the book) for publication dates.

Between editions, up-to-date information is available in two free newsletters – the paper *Planet Talk* and email *Comet* (to subscribe, contact any Lonely Planet office) – and on our Web site at www.lonelyplanet.com. The *Upgrades* section of the Web site covers a number of important and volatile destinations and is regularly updated by Lonely Planet authors. *Scoop* covers news and current affairs relevant to travelers. And, lastly, the *Thorn Tree* bulletin board and *Postcards* section of the site carry unverified, but fascinating, reports from travelers.

Correspondence The process of creating new editions begins with the letters, postcards and emails received from travelers. This correspondence often includes suggestions, criticisms and comments about the current editions. Interesting excerpts are immediately passed on via newsletters and the Web site, and everything goes to our authors to be verified when they're researching on the road. We're keen to get more feedback from organizations or individuals who represent communities visited by travelers.

> Lonely Planet gathers information for everyone who's curious about the planet – and especially for those who explore it firsthand. Through guidebooks, phrasebooks, activity guides, maps, literature, newsletters, image library, TV series and Web site, we act as an information exchange for a worldwide community of travelers.

Research Authors aim to gather sufficient practical information to enable travelers to make informed choices and to make the mechanics of a journey run smoothly. They also research historical and cultural background to help enrich the travel experience and allow travelers to understand and respond appropriately to cultural and environmental issues.

Authors don't stay in every hotel because that would mean spending a couple of months in each medium-size city and, no, they don't eat at every restaurant because that would mean stretching belts beyond capacity. They do visit hotels and restaurants to check standards and prices, but feedback based on readers' direct experiences can be very helpful.

Many of our authors work undercover; others aren't so secretive. None of them accept freebies in exchange for positive write-ups. And none of our guidebooks contain any advertising.

Production Authors submit their manuscripts and maps to offices in Australia, the USA, the UK or France. Editors and cartographers – all experienced travelers themselves – then begin the process of assembling the pieces. When the book finally hits the shops, some things are already out of date, we start getting feedback from readers and the process begins again....

WARNING & REQUEST

Things change – prices go up, schedules change, good places go bad and bad places go bankrupt – nothing stays the same. So, if you find things better or worse, recently opened or long since closed, please tell us and help make the next edition even more accurate and useful. We genuinely value all the feedback we receive. Julie Young coordinates a well-traveled team that reads and acknowledges every letter, postcard and email and ensures that every morsel of information finds its way to the appropriate authors, editors and cartographers for verification.

Everyone who writes to us will find their name in the next edition of the appropriate guidebook. They will also receive the latest issue of *Planet Talk*, our quarterly printed newsletter, or *Comet*, our monthly email newsletter. Subscriptions to both newsletters are free. The very best contributions will be rewarded with a free guidebook.

Excerpts from your correspondence may appear in new editions of Lonely Planet guidebooks, the Lonely Planet Web site, *Planet Talk* or *Comet*, so please let us know if you *don't* want your letter published or your name acknowledged.

Send all correspondence to the Lonely Planet office closest to you:

Australia: Locked Bag 1, Footscray, Victoria 3011
USA: 150 Linden St, Oakland, CA 94607
UK: 10A Spring Place, London NW5 3BH
France: 1 rue du Dahomey, 75011 Paris

Or email us at: talk2us@lonelyplanet.com.au

For news, views and updates, see our Web site: www.lonelyplanet.com

HOW TO USE A LONELY PLANET GUIDEBOOK

The best way to use a Lonely Planet guidebook is any way you choose. At Lonely Planet, we believe the most memorable travel experiences are often those that are unexpected, and the finest discoveries are those you make yourself. Guidebooks are not intended to be used as if they provided a detailed set of infallible instructions!

Contents All Lonely Planet guidebooks follow the same format. The Facts about the Country chapters or sections give background information ranging from history to weather. Facts for the Visitor gives practical information on issues like visas and health. Getting There & Away gives a brief starting point for researching travel to and from the destination. Getting Around gives an overview of the transport options available when you arrive.

The peculiar demands of each destination determine how subsequent chapters are broken up, but some things remain constant. We always start with background, then proceed to sights, places to stay, places to eat, entertainment, getting there and away, and getting around information – in that order.

Heading Hierarchy Lonely Planet headings are used in a strict hierarchical structure that can be visualized as a set of Russian dolls. Each heading (and its following text) is encompassed by any preceding heading that is higher on the hierarchical ladder.

Entry Points We do not assume guidebooks will be read from beginning to end, but that people will dip into them. The traditional entry points are the list of contents and the index. In addition, however, some books have a complete list of maps and an index map illustrating map coverage.

There may also be a color map that shows highlights. These highlights are dealt with in greater detail later in the book, along with planning questions. Each chapter covering a geographical region usually begins with a locator map and another list of highlights. Once you find something of interest in a list of highlights, turn to the index.

Maps Maps play a crucial role in Lonely Planet guidebooks and include a huge amount of information. A legend is printed on the back page. We seek to have complete consistency between maps and text, and to have every important place in the text captured on a map. Map key numbers usually start in the top left corner.

Although inclusion in a guidebook usually implies a recommendation, we cannot list every good place. Exclusion does not necessarily imply criticism. In fact, there are a number of reasons why we might exclude a place – sometimes it is simply inappropriate to encourage an influx of travelers.

Introduction

Mention the Southwest and distinct images leap to mind: thick arms of the saguaro cactus, towering red-rock outcrops of Monument Valley, howling coyotes, stunning ancient Indian sites tucked against cliffs, the changing colors of the Grand Canyon. Deserts, grasslands, mountain ranges and high mesas and plateaus are all engulfed in the vast sky. Yet, more than a magnificent geographical terrain, the Southwest also exists as a cultural phenomenon.

The first people in the region were the ancestors of today's Native Americans. Archaeologists have excavated fragments of their villages, hunting sites and irrigation ditches, and have found petroglyphs and pictographs – many of which can be seen in protected national monuments and in museums. Today's Southwestern tribes –

the Navajo, Apache, Pueblo and Tohono O'odham, among others – relate oral histories that shed light on their ancestors, and their vibrant cultures and languages reveal traces of their forebears.

The first Europeans in the region were Spanish conquistadors and missionaries searching for gold, land, slaves and converts. But the Indian tribes had no gold and held land communally. They rebelled against forced labor and resented the new religion. After centuries of overt and covert resistance, many tribes succeeded in maintaining their cultural identity, and all learned the lessons they would rely upon when confronted with the next wave of newcomers – the Anglo Americans.

After Mexico won its independence from Spain, the USA was quick to fight for the

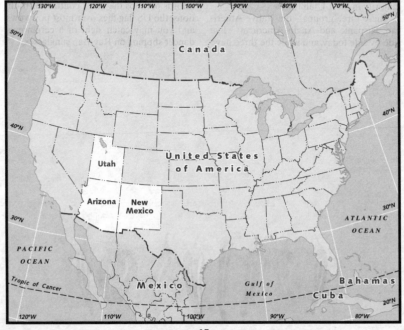

new territory. After the Mexican War of 1846 to 1847, the US assumed control over what was to be called the New Mexico Territory, which included most of Arizona and New Mexico. Traders continued to travel west from Missouri to New Mexico along the Santa Fe Trail, but the best route to California lay south of the territorial border. In 1853 the Gadsden Purchase brought southern Arizona into US hands. The government soon sent troops to 'clear' the lands of the Native Americans, establishing massive reservations that still cover large parts of the Southwest.

Meanwhile to the north, members of a new Christian sect, the Church of Jesus Christ of Latter-day Saints (LDS), had reached the Great Salt Lake, where their leader, Brigham Young, announced 'this is the place' where they would settle. Under Young's orders, small bands of Mormons, as LDS members were called, established communities throughout what is now Utah. The progeny of those pioneers still form the majority in most Utah towns.

These three groups – the Native American, Hispanic and Anglo American – live side by side today, and while the three have assimilated aspects of each other's cultures, they remain quite distinct. Phoenix, Tucson, Santa Fe and Albuquerque all have districts where one culture or another is more prevalent, and many smaller towns still reflect the ethnicity of their founders in their residents and architecture. In Salt Lake City, the Mormon influence is still strong, but even there economic growth has lured newcomers of various races and religions.

As you raft through the Grand Canyon of the Colorado River or mountain bike on slickrock trails outside Moab, watch for the evidence of other eras: lacy fossils of sea creatures, footprints of dinosaurs, pottery shards and rusting mining rigs. As you hike through Canyon de Chelly or Monument Valley, contemplate the harmonious lives of the Indians disrupted by the Spaniards and US Cavalry. When you drive in the warmth of your car to ski slopes covered in Utah's world-famous snow, imagine Mormon pioneers digging their wagons out of those deep drifts. A visit to any Indian reservation affords perhaps the finest contrast of traditions: the US flag flies over most powwows, and you may catch sight of a ceremonial dancer slipping on Ray-Ban sunglasses.

Facts about the Southwest

HISTORY
The First Americans

The history of the sun-baked Southwest begins not with sun but with ice. For it was during the last ice age, roughly 25,000 years ago, that the first people reached the North American continent from Asia by way of the Bering Strait. These first Americans were hardy nomadic hunters who, armed with little more than pointed sticks and the courage born of hunger, pursued Ice Age mammals such as mammoths, cave bears and giant sloths.

As the climate warmed, the glaciers that covered much of North America receded and the nomads began moving south. In the 1920s, workers in Folsom and Clovis, New Mexico, found stone spear points embedded in the bones of extinct mammals dated to over 11,000 years ago. This is the earliest evidence of the first inhabitants of the Southwest, although people probably arrived earlier.

Indian oral histories offer various other scenarios. One cosmic origin myth describes how the first arrivals, four men and three women, came from the Man Carrier (an Indian name for the Big Dipper constellation) 50,000 years ago. There are many other tribal beliefs.

After many large Ice Age mammals became extinct, people began hunting smaller animals such as deer and rabbits. Hunters built simple traps and used a throwing device called an *atlatl* to propel hunting spears. Gathering wild food (berries, seeds, roots and fruits) bolstered diets. Baskets used to collect food were so tightly woven that they held water and could be used for cooking when heated stones were dropped into the water. Stone *metates* were developed to grind hard seeds and roots. Archaeological sites near Cochise County in southeastern Arizona have yielded the remains of baskets and stone cooking implements, so Southwestern hunter-gatherers of this early period (7000 BC to 500 BC) have been named the Cochise people.

After 3000 BC, contacts with farmers from farther south (now central Mexico) led to the beginnings of agriculture in the Southwest. The first crops were minor additions to diets of people continuing their nomadic hunter-gatherer lifestyles. Eventually, people started reusing the same plots of land for their crops and spending more time in these areas. Primitive corn was one of the first crops. By 500 BC, beans and squash were also being cultivated, and cotton followed soon afterward. Finally, around 300 BC to AD 100, distinct groups began to settle in semipermanent villages in the Southwest.

Ancient Southwestern Cultures

By about AD 100, three dominant cultures were emerging in the Southwest: the Hohokam of the desert, the Mogollon of the central mountains and valleys, and the Ancestral Puebloan (formerly known as the Anasazi) of the northern plateaus. In addition, several other groups were either blendings of or offshoots from the three main cultures – these smaller groups are still the subject of controversy among archaeologists. Examples are the Hakataya, Fremont, Salado and Sinagua traditions.

These groups are discussed below, but there is debate and disagreement about these matters. Clearly, neither the three dominant cultures nor the smaller ones existed in isolation, and much blending and fusion of lifestyles took place. By the mid-15th century, and earlier in some cases, most of these cultures had disappeared, their villages abandoned. The reasons for this are unclear, although many theories have been suggested. Most likely was a combination of factors including a devastating drought near the end of the 12th century, climate changes, overhunting, soil erosion, disease and the arrival of new groups.

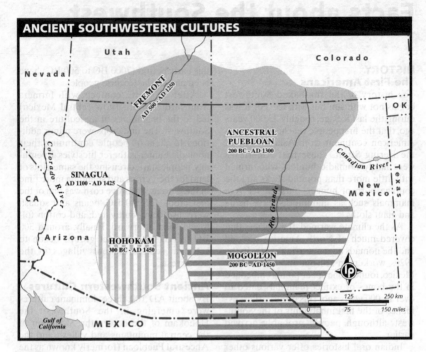

ANCIENT SOUTHWESTERN CULTURES

Hohokam This culture existed in the southern and central deserts of Arizona from 300 BC to AD 1450. These people created an advanced irrigation system based on the Gila, Salt and Verde Rivers and became well adapted to desert life. Apart from farming, they collected wild desert food such as saguaro cactus fruit and mesquite tree beans – a practice that can still be observed among desert Indians such as the Tohono O'odham tribe.

Their irrigation system was quite incredible. Using stone tools the people dug many miles of canals, some of which were 15 feet deep and twice as wide.

The people lived in simple mud or stick shelters over shallow depressions in the earth. As time passed, this culture developed low earthen pyramids, which may have been temples, and sunken ball courts with earthen walls in which games were played. These features clearly point to a Hohokam connection with the cultures of

Mexico and Guatemala. The dead were cremated, and so archaeologists today learn comparatively little by excavating burial sites. A rich heritage of pottery, however, attests to Hohokam artistry, and their ceramics and other artifacts can be seen in such places as the Arizona State Museum in Tucson. Hohokam sites can be visited in the Pueblo Grande Museum, Phoenix, and the Casa Grande Ruins National Monument, between Phoenix and Tucson.

Around 1450, the Hohokam disappeared. Why? We don't know. Today's Pima and Tohono O'odham (formerly called Papago) Indians appear to be descended from the Hohokam, but the links are not clear. This is but one of the many mysteries that make the Southwest a fascinating place.

Mogollon The Mogollon (pronounced 'mo-guh-YOHN') culture is named after the mountains of the same name in western New Mexico and the Mogollon Rim in eastern Arizona. The region south of these mountainous areas as far as the Mexican border and east to the flatlands of eastern New Mexico was the province of the Mogollon culture, which existed here from 200 BC to AD 1450.

The Mogollon people settled in small communities, often elevated on an isolated mesa or ridge top. Their houses were simple pit dwellings. They did some farming, but depended more on hunting and foraging than did their contemporaries of other cultures. As the Mogollon people developed, their villages grew bigger and often featured a *kiva* (a circular, underground chamber used for ceremonies and other purposes).

Later, the Mogollon people began to depend on farming to a greater extent. There are many signs that by about the 13th or 14th century the Mogollon were being peacefully incorporated by the Ancestral Puebloan groups from the north. The beautiful black-on-white Mimbres pottery (from the Mimbres River area in southwestern New Mexico) has distinctive animal and human figures executed in a geometric style reminiscent of Puebloan ware. The Gila Cliff Dwellings National Monument, near the Mimbres area, is a late Mogollon site with Puebloan features. In fact, most of today's Pueblo Indians trace their ancestry to the Mogollon or Ancestral Puebloan culture.

Ancestral Puebloan These people inhabited the Colorado Plateau (also called the Four Corners area) comprising parts of northeastern Arizona, northwestern New Mexico, southwestern Colorado and southeastern Utah. This culture left us by far the richest heritage of archaeological sites and ancient settlements that are still inhabited in the Southwest. Until recently, this culture was called the 'Anasazi,' a Navajo term meaning 'enemy ancestors.' The Navajo, however, were late arrivals on the scene (see Later Cultures, below) and modern Pueblo people prefer the more accurate term Ancestral Puebloan. Texts written prior to the mid-1990s used Anasazi.

Like the Hohokam and Mogollon cultures, the earliest Ancestral Puebloans were

Petroglyphs

Throughout the Southwest, rocks, boulders and cliffs may be darkened with a blue-black layer called desert varnish. The dark color is caused by iron and manganese oxides that leach out of the rock over many centuries, leaving a thin and slightly shiny polish that sometimes streaks cliffs from top to bottom. Ancient Indians chipped away the varnish to expose the lighter rock beneath, thus creating the rock art known as petroglyphs.

hunter-gatherers who slowly added farming to their repertoire of methods of obtaining food. The people lived in pit houses. They gathered food in baskets, and the excellence of their basket weaving has led archaeologists to refer to these as the Basket Maker periods. Toward the end of the Basket Maker III period (AD 400 to AD 700), pottery became increasingly important.

The Pueblo periods, which followed the Basket Maker periods, saw much development in pottery and architecture. Larger villages, some with over 100 rooms, were built, many of them in shallow caves under overhanging cliffs. Important Ancestral Puebloan sites can be seen at Mesa Verde National Park; Navajo National Monument; Canyon de Chelly National Monument; Bandelier National Monument; Aztec Ruins National Monument; Chaco Culture National Historic Park; and many other places.

Today, descendants of the Ancestral Puebloans are found in the Pueblo Indian groups along New Mexico's Rio Grande, and in the Acoma, Zuni and Laguna pueblos of New Mexico's northwestern corner. The oldest links with the Ancestral Puebloans are found among the Hopi tribe of northern Arizona. Here, perched on a mesa top, the village of Old Oraibi has been inhabited since the 1100s, making it the oldest continuously inhabited settlement in North America. The living pueblos at Acoma and Taos in northwestern New Mexico may be as old.

By about AD 1450, the Hohokam had mysteriously disappeared and the Mogollon people had been more or less incorporated into the Ancestral Puebloans, who themselves began to leave many of their ancient pueblos in the 1400s and, by the 1500s, had mainly moved to the pueblos now found along the Rio Grande.

Smaller Groups The Hakataya is the general term for several small groups that once lived in western and central Arizona and were contemporaries of the Ancestral Puebloans. The best known of these groups is the Sinagua, who left various interesting and attractive sites such as those at the Montezuma Castle, Tuzigoot, Walnut Canyon and Wupatki National Monuments in central Arizona. Lesser-known groups existed west of the Sinagua and included the Prescott, Cohonina, Cerbat and Laquish peoples.

The Salado culture exhibits influences from both the Ancestral Puebloan and Mogollon peoples, and the culture appears to have influenced some late Hohokam sites. Salado remains are found in central Arizona, in an area where all three of the major cultural groups overlapped to some extent. The best Salado site is seen at the Tonto National Monument.

The Fremont culture took hold north of the Ancestral Puebloan, in south and central Utah. The Fremont were marginally related to the Puebloan but their culture possessed several distinct features. Among these were a unique form of pottery, made from a coarse sand/clay mixture, and a greater reliance on hunting. A good place to see artifacts from this culture is in Fremont Indian State Park.

Later Cultures

The cultures described above can be traced back in the Southwest for two millennia or longer. Many of the tribes living in the Southwest today, however, are comparatively recent arrivals. Nomadic bands of Indians from two distinct language groups, the Shoshonean and the Athapaskan, straggled into the Southwest from the north between AD 1300 and AD 1600.

Shoshonean tribes found in the Southwest today live mainly in Utah and make up only a small part of the population. They include the Shoshone in northern Utah (and into Idaho and Wyoming), Utes in central and eastern Utah (and into Colorado), Goshutes in western Utah (and into Nevada) and Southern Paiutes in southwestern Utah (and into Nevada and Arizona).

The Navajo and various Apache tribes are of Athapaskan descent; they now make up a substantial part of Arizona's and New Mexico's populations. The Navajos moved into the Four Corners area, especially northeastern Arizona. The Apaches consisted of several distinct groups, of which the most important were the Jicarilla Apaches in the north-central mountains of New Mexico, the Mescalero Apaches in New Mexico's south-central mountains and various other groups, together referred to as the Western Apaches, in southeastern Arizona.

These late arrivals didn't conquer the Pueblo and Hopi descendants of the Ancestral Puebloans but rather coexisted with them. Certainly, there were occasional skirmishes and raids, but generally the Pueblo peoples took advantage of the hunting skills of the newcomers, while the Apache and Navajo learned about pottery, weaving and agriculture from the Pueblo tribes. Then the Europeans arrived in the Southwest, bringing a lifestyle completely foreign to the Native Americans. Mother Earth and Father Sky, bows and arrows, ritual dances and sweatlodges, foot travel, spiritual oneness with the land – all these were to be challenged by the new concepts of Christ and conquest, gunpowder and sword, European civilization and education, horses, and a grasping desire for land.

The Spaniards

For the next three centuries, it was the Spanish who wrought the greatest changes in the region. Most of Arizona and New Mexico became a Spanish colony and, much later, part of Mexico. It wasn't until the 1840s that the Southwest became part of the USA. Utah, however, remained almost unexplored by Europeans until the arrival of the Mormons in the 19th century.

After brief incursions into the Southwest by small Spanish groups in 1536 and 1539, a major expedition was launched in 1540 led by Francisco Vásquez de Coronado. He set off from Mexico City with 336 Europeans, 1000 Indians and 1100 pack and riding animals. The expedition's goal was the fabled, immensely rich 'Seven Cities of Cibola.'

For two years, they traveled through Arizona, New Mexico and as far east as Kansas, but instead of gold and precious gems, the expedition found Indian pueblos of adobe bricks. Some of the leaders took contingents to explore the Hopi mesas and the Grand Canyon, among other areas. During the harsh winters, the expedition expropriated some of the pueblos for its own use, burned one, and killed dozens of Indians. This ferocity was to prove typical of the behavior of many of the Europeans who were yet to come. Finally, the expedition returned home, penniless and broken. Coronado had failed to become rich or find the fabled cities and, for the next 50 years, Spanish exploration focused on areas outside the Southwest.

The dreams of fabulously rich cities were revived periodically by small groups making minor forays, especially along the Rio Grande. Then, in 1598, a large force of 400 European men and an unknown number of Indians, women and children, accompanied by 7000 head of various livestock and 83 oxcarts, headed north from Mexico and up the Rio Grande. Their leader was a fortune-seeker named Juan de Oñate, a Spaniard born in Mexico whose deceased wife had been a descendant of both the conquistador Hernán Cortés and the Aztec emperor, Moctezuma. Oñate was accompanied by his 12-year-old son and two nephews.

Near what is now El Paso, Texas, Oñate stopped. He called the land to the north New Mexico, claimed it for Spain and became governor of this land. Then he headed north and, as the Rio Grande began to swing westward, he continued north through the dry and inhospitable desert that became named *Jornada del Muerto* or the 'Journey of the Dead.' (This is where the USA chose to detonate the first nuclear bomb, which gives an idea of how desolate this Jornada del Muerto is.)

After a desperate journey, Oñate reached San Juan Pueblo near the confluence of the Rio Chama and Rio Grande. After a brief stop, he crossed the Rio Grande and set up the first capital of New Mexico, San Gabriel. Apart from some church ruins, nothing remains of San Gabriel today. This route along the Rio Grande and Jornada del Muerto became known as *El Camino Real* (the royal road) and was the standard trail linking Mexico with northern New Mexico. For most of the 17th century, there was little European exploration of other parts of the Southwest.

During the Spaniards' first few years in northern New Mexico, they tried to subdue the pueblos, which led to much bloodshed. The fighting started in Acoma Pueblo when a Spanish contingent of 30 men led by Juan de Zaldívar, one of Oñate's nephews, demanded payment of taxes in the form of food. The Acoma Indians responded by killing Zaldívar and about half of his force. Oñate then sent 70 soldiers led by his other nephew, Vicente de Zaldívar, to punish the inhabitants of Acoma. This was accomplished with the Spaniards' usual ruthlessness: several hundred Indians were killed, and hundreds more were taken prisoner and subjected to punishments such as amputation of a foot or slavery. By 1601, three other pueblos were ransacked and many hundreds of Indians were killed or enslaved.

Meanwhile, San Gabriel fared poorly as the capital of New Mexico. Tense relations with the Indians, poor harvests, harsh weather and accusations of Oñate's cruelty led to many desertions among the colonizers. By 1608, Oñate had been recalled to Mexico and, on the journey south, lost his son to an Indian attack. When he arrived, he was stripped of his governorship.

A new governor, Pedro de Peralta, was sent north to found a new capital, which he did in 1609. This was Santa Fe, and it remains the capital of New Mexico today, the oldest capital in what is now the USA. In 1610, Peralta built the Palace of the Governors on the Plaza in Santa Fe. It is the oldest non-Indian building in the USA still in use today. (The first British colony was founded in Jamestown, Virginia, in 1607. The second British colony was founded in 1620 at Plymouth, Massachusetts, by the famous Pilgrims.)

A steady trickle of colonists, accompanied by soldiers and Franciscan priests, moved from Mexico to the Santa Fe area over the next 50 years. Their aim was to settle and farm the land and bring the Indians into the Catholic Church. Most of the Pueblo groups had little interest in being converted, although some blended Catholicism with their own beliefs. Neither were the Indians much inclined to help the Spanish build churches in their pueblos nor to work for the new colonists. For the most part, the Spanish treated the recalcitrant Pueblo people brutally at any sign of resistance: imprisonment, beatings, torture and executions were common.

A particularly destructive Spanish campaign in 1675 was aimed at destroying the Pueblo kivas and powerful ceremonial objects such as prayer sticks and kachina dolls. The horrified Indians tried to protect their heritage but were punished harshly. This was the last straw for them. In 1680, the united northern Pueblos rose up in the Pueblo Revolt and succeeded in driving some 2400 Spaniards back down the Rio Grande to El Paso. The Pueblo people took over Santa Fe's Palace of the Governors and held it until 1692.

The northern Pueblo people were a mix of many different tribes, languages and beliefs, so they didn't remain united for long. In 1692, the Spaniards, led by Diego de Vargas, again took over Santa Fe and, over the succeeding years, subdued all the pueblos in the area. During the 18th century, the colony grew slowly but steadily, and the Spaniards lived uneasily but relatively peacefully alongside the Pueblo peoples.

Meanwhile, less brutal incursions were made into Arizona by the Jesuit priest

Eusebio Kino, who has garnered almost mythical status as the bringer of God to what is now (mainly) southern Arizona. He began his travels in Mexico in 1687 and spent over two decades in the Arizona-Sonora area. His approach to being a missionary was, certainly by the standards of the day, humane, and this distinguished him from many of his contemporaries. He established missions at Tumacácori and San Xavier del Bac (both south of Tucson); these sites can be visited today, although the present buildings were erected about a century after Kino was there.

After Kino's departure, conditions for the Indians deteriorated and led to the short-lived Pima Revolt of 1751 and the Yuma Massacre of 1781, when the Yuma killed colonizers in their area.

Throughout the Southwest, Apaches, Comanches, Navajos and Hopis were alternately fighting with one another or with the Spaniards, and it was this warfare that limited further Spanish expansion in the area during the 18th century.

In an attempt to link Santa Fe with the newly established port of San Francisco and to avoid Indian raids, the Spanish priests Francisco Atanasio Domínguez and Silvestre Vélez de Escalante led a small group of explorers into what is now Utah, but they were turned back by the rugged and arid terrain. The 1776 Domínguez-Escalante expedition was the first to survey Utah, but no attempt was made to settle there.

Although the historically important events outlined above provide a sketch of Hispanic-Indian relations during the 16th to the 18th century, one crucial point is missing. The Europeans brought with them diseases to which the Indians had no resistance and which caused terrible epidemics within the tribes. By some accounts, 80% of Native Americans died from disease in the 16th century, and the history of North America may have been very different if epidemics had not taken such a terrible toll.

The Anglos

In 1803, the Louisiana Purchase resulted in the USA's acquiring a huge tract of land (from Louisiana to the Rocky Mountains) from the French, doubling the size of the young country. The Spanish colonies of the Southwest now abutted, for the first time, US territory, and the two countries maintained an uneasy peace.

During the winter of 1806–1807, a small contingent of US soldiers led by Lieutenant Zebulon Montgomery Pike reached the upper Rio Grande and were taken by Spanish soldiers to Santa Fe for lengthy interrogation before being allowed to return to the USA. In 1810, Pike published a book about his experiences. He described New Mexican life, including details of the high cost of merchandise in Santa Fe because of the great distances from the rest of New Mexico. This induced several groups of US traders and entrepreneurs to make the difficult journey to Santa Fe with trade goods, but the Spanish repudiated their efforts, jailing the Americans and confiscating their goods.

This situation changed in 1821, when Mexico became independent from Spain. The next party of US traders who arrived in Santa Fe were welcomed by the newly independent Mexicans, and a major trade route was established. This was the famous Santa Fe Trail between Missouri and Santa Fe, a trail traversed by thousands of people until the railway arrived in 1879.

Politically, the Southwest had changed, but for a couple of decades, life continued much as before. The Spanish soldiers and missionaries left and were replaced by a Mexican army. Santa Fe grew and thrived, but the Hispanic inhabitants continued to be hampered by raiding Indians, especially Apaches and Comanches (a nomadic prairie tribe known for their hunting and riding skills). Few Anglos (as non-Hispanic whites from the USA were called) ventured beyond the Santa Fe Trail. Some who did were the 'mountain men' – hunters and trappers who explored all over the West. These men were the first Europeans to explore Utah since the 1776 Domínguez-Escalante expedition.

In 1846, the USA declared war on Mexico and, two years later, Mexico gave

up all the land between Texas and the Pacific. The border roughly followed the present one, except for 30,000 sq miles in southern Arizona and New Mexico, which the USA bought from the Mexicans in 1853 with the 'Gadsden Purchase.' The Mormons, led by Brigham Young, founded Salt Lake City, still technically part of Mexico, in 1847. A Mormon battalion was sent to help US forces in the Mexican War effort, although it saw no action.

The Territory Years

After the Mexican War, most of present-day Arizona and New Mexico became the New Mexico Territory of the United States, while most of Utah and Nevada became the Utah Territory. It was not until 1861 that Nevada became a separate territory, and in 1863 Arizona became a separate territory.

Territories differed from states in that they were not allowed to elect their own senators and representatives to the US Congress in Washington, DC. Territories were headed by an elected governor, with little power in the nation's capital.

Utah's territorial capital was briefly in Fillmore but was relocated to Salt Lake City in 1858, where it has remained. Arizona's first capital was Prescott, but was moved quickly to Tucson in 1867, returned to Prescott in 1877 and finally moved to the present location, Phoenix, in 1889. New Mexico's capital has been Santa Fe since its foundation in 1609. Statehood came first to Utah, in 1896, and much later to New Mexico and Arizona, in 1912.

The history of the Southwest during territorial years and the gaining of statehood is complex and colorful. It is beyond the scope of this book to probe deeply into it, and readers are directed to the Books section in Facts for the Visitor for suggestions for further study. Also see the Recent History sections beginning the Facts About chapter for each state. Following are overviews of some of the more important historical topics.

Indian Wars & Reservations The Americans settled the new territories much more aggressively than the Spaniards had. For decades, US forces pushed west across the continent, killing or forcibly moving whole tribes of Indians who were in their way. All of the many tribes in the Southwest resisted the westward growth of the USA to a greater or lesser extent.

The best-known incident is the forceful relocation of many Navajos in 1864. US forces, led by Kit Carson, destroyed Navajo fields, orchards and houses and forced the people into surrendering or withdrawing into remote parts of the Canyon de Chelly in Arizona. Eventually, they were starved out and 9000 Navajos were rounded up and marched 400 miles east to a camp at Bosque Redondo, near Fort Sumner in New Mexico. Hundreds of Indians died from sickness, starvation or gunshot along the way. The Navajos call this 'The Long Walk,' and it remains an important part of their history.

Life at Bosque Redondo was harsh, with inadequate resources for 9000 people; over 2000 Navajos died. Even from the Anglo point of view, this relocation was not working and, after four years, the surviving Navajos were allowed to return to their lands in northeastern Arizona and allotted over 5000 sq miles for their reservation. Since the 1868 treaty, the reservation has grown to encompass over 20,000 sq miles in Arizona, New Mexico and Utah; it is the largest in the USA and the Navajo people are the largest tribe.

The last serious conflicts were between US troops and Apaches. This was partly because raiding was the essential and honorable path to manhood for Apaches. Young Apache men had to demonstrate raiding skills in order to marry well, and then to provide for an extended family and to be considered a leader. As US forces and settlers moved into Apache land, they became obvious targets for the raids that were part of the Apache way of life. These continued under the leadership of Mangas Coloradas,

Cochise, Victorio and, finally, Geronimo, who surrendered in 1886 after being promised that he and the Apaches would be imprisoned for two years and then allowed to return to their homeland. As with many promises made during these years, this one, too, was broken. The Apaches spent the next 27 years as prisoners of war.

By the time of Geronimo's surrender, there were many Indian reservations in the Southwest, each belonging to one or sometimes a few tribes. Although the wars were over, Indian people continued to be treated like second-class citizens for many decades. Non-Indians used legal loopholes and technicalities to take over reservation land. Many children were removed from reservations and shipped off to boarding schools where they were taught in English and punished for speaking their own languages or behaving 'like Indians' – this practice continued into the 1930s. Older Indians were encouraged to lose their culture and customs. Despite the history of cultural oppression, Indians today still practice spiritual customs and other beliefs that predate US expansion. Many native languages are still spoken, and a majority of Navajos learn their tribal language before English.

Indians fought alongside Americans in WWI but were not extended US citizenship until 1924 and were not given voting rights until 1948 in Arizona and New Mexico, and 1957 in Utah. Most tribes have their own governments and laws that are applicable to people living on or visiting their reservations. Federal laws are also applicable to reservations, but normally state and other local laws do not apply.

WWII prompted the first large exodus of Indians from the reservations, when they joined the US war effort. The most famous unit was the Navajo Code Talkers – 420 Navajo marines

Geronimo

who used a code based on their language for vital messages in the Pacific arena. This code was never broken by the Japanese. Today, the surviving code talkers are among the most revered of Navajo elders and are often honored in public events.

Currently, about half of the Indians in the US live off reservations, but many maintain strong ties with their tribes.

Transportation The history of the Southwest during the 19th century is strongly linked to the development of transportation. During early territorial days, movement of goods and people from the East to the Southwest was very slow. Horses, mule trains and stagecoaches were state-of-the-art transportation in those days.

Major trails included the Santa Fe Trail, which linked Missouri with Santa Fe from the 1820s to the 1870s, and the Old Spanish Trail, from Santa Fe into central Utah and across Nevada to Los Angeles, California. Regular stagecoach service along the Santa Fe Trail began in 1849.

The Mormon Trail reached Salt Lake City in 1847. In succeeding years, thousands of Mormon settlers followed this route, many pulling their possessions for hundreds of miles in handcarts.

The Butterfield Overland Mail Company opened in 1858 and linked St Louis, Missouri, with San Francisco, California, via southwestern New Mexico, Tucson and Yuma. Butterfield offered two stagecoaches a week that completed the journey in 25 days – an exhausting trip.

Cattle trails, along which cowboys drove many thousands of head of cattle, letting them feed as they went, sprang up in the 1860s and 1870s; among these, the most important were the Goodnight-Loving Trail for moving cattle from Texas through eastern New Mexico into Colorado, and the Chisholm Trail, which branched off from the Goodnight-Loving Trail near Roswell, New Mexico, and directed cattle west into Arizona. Clearly, ranching was already important business; it has remained so to this day.

More people arrived with the advent of the railroads. The first transcontinental line

was completed in northern Utah in 1869 and led to an influx of non-Mormons into Utah. The Atchison, Topeka and Santa Fe Railroad reached Santa Fe in 1879, linking that city with the east. Meanwhile, the Southern Pacific Railroad had been pushed inland from Los Angeles through Yuma and Tucson as far as Deming, New Mexico. A few years later, this was linked up to the Santa Fe line. The Atlantic and Pacific Railroad, built in 1883, went from near Albuquerque across northern Arizona to Los Angeles.

The arrival of more people and resources via the railroad led to further exploration of the land, and the frequent discovery of mineral deposits. The 1870s and 1880s saw the foundation of many mining towns; some of these are now ghost towns, while others (for example Tombstone and Silver City) remain active today. Gold, copper and silver mining all boomed, although silver mining busted suddenly with the crash of 1893. Mining, particularly for copper, continues to be a significant part of the Southwest's economy today.

The Wild West Desperate tales of gunslingers and cattle rustlers, outlaws and train robbers, are all part of the legend of the Wild West. The good guys and the bad guys were designations often in flux – a tough outlaw in one state might become a sheriff in another. New mining towns, mushrooming overnight near the richest mines, often had more saloons and bordellos than any other kind of building. Newly rich miners would come into town to brawl, drink and gamble, sometimes being fleeced by professional cardsharps. It is no surprise that law and order were practically nonexistent in many parts of the Southwest during the latter part of the 19th century.

The most legendary figures in the Southwest include Billy the Kid and Sheriff Pat Garrett, who were involved in the infamous Lincoln County War in New Mexico in the late 1870s. Billy the Kid reputedly shot and killed over 20 men in a brief career as a gunslinger – he himself was shot and killed by Garrett at the tender age of 21. In 1881,

Wyatt Earp, along with his brothers Virgil and Morgan and Doc Holliday, shot dead Billy Clanton and the McLaury brothers in a blazing gunfight at the OK Corral in Tombstone, Arizona – the showdown took less than a minute. Both sides accused the other of cattle rustling, but the real story will never be known. Today, reenactments of the gunfight take place regularly in Tombstone.

Such reenactments are the closest you'll get to those lawless frontier days. Several towns have them daily or for annual festivals. One chilling event that you won't see reenacted is the hanging of notorious train robber Black Jack Ketchum in Clayton in 1901 – an error by the hangman caused Ketchum to literally lose his head. Other names inextricably linked with the Southwest are Butch Cassidy and the Sundance Kid, who roamed over much of Utah and other parts of the West. Cassidy, a Mormon, robbed banks and trains with his Wild Bunch gang during the 1890s, but he never killed anyone.

By the dawn of the 20th century, some semblance of law and order had arrived in the Southwest, and the days of gunslingers were over.

GEOGRAPHY

Travelers find that vast canyons and steep bluffs, buttes, mesas and mountains often make it difficult to get from here to there. Although the varied topography may hinder travel, it is also one of the attractions that lure travelers to the region in the first place. The scenery is literally breathtaking.

The central part of the Southwest is the Colorado Plateau, often called the Four Corners region because Arizona, New Mexico, Utah and Colorado share a common boundary point here, the only place where four US states meet. Much of this area is part of the Navajo Indian Reservation, the largest in the USA.

The Colorado Plateau is a series of plateaus between 5000 and 8000 feet in elevation, separated by deep canyons, among them the world-famous Grand Canyon. The plateaus are topped by distinctive buttes, mesas and other topographical features that

give the landscape its Southwestern character. Erosion has played with these features, resulting in natural arches, bridges, spires and towers. These characteristics led to the foundation of many national parks and other scenic sites.

Southwest of the Colorado Plateau, Arizona's terrain drops in a rugged cliff called the Mogollon Rim, reaching a height of 2000 feet in some places and stretching a third of the way across Arizona. Beyond lies a broad belt of mountain ranges, getting progressively lower to the southwest.

The southwestern and south-central parts of Arizona belong to the desert Basin and Range province. Desert basins alternate with mountain ranges, many topped by forests and most running north to south. It's in these arid basins that Arizona's major cities, Phoenix and Tucson, are found, supported by massive irrigation projects from the Colorado, Gila and Salt Rivers. This is part of the **Arizona-Sonora Desert**.

Basin and Range country continues northwest into Nevada and swings back into Utah. In Utah, northwest of the Colorado Plateau, the Basin and Range province forms part of the **Great Basin Desert**. Where the Great Basin Desert abuts the Wasatch Mountains (part of the Rocky Mountain Region) in north-central Utah lies a fertile valley where Salt Lake City and other important Utah towns are found. The northeastern corner of Utah pertains more to the Rocky Mountains than to the Southwestern deserts. This region includes the unusual Uinta Mountains, one of the few US mountain ranges that trends from west to east.

Southeast of the Colorado Plateau, heading into New Mexico, the traveler again encounters the Rocky Mountains, whose Continental Divide snakes through the western part of the state. The Southwest's highest peaks belong to the Rocky Mountains in north-central New Mexico, including Wheeler Peak at 13,161 feet. These highland areas are home to many of the state's inhabitants today, as they were in earlier centuries to the Ancestral Puebloans. New Mexico's biggest city, Albuquerque, is on the edge of the Rockies, and the state capital of Santa Fe is, at 6950 feet, the nation's highest capital.

Farther south, the Rockies are split by New Mexico's most important river valley, that of the Rio Grande. To the west is the beginning of the Basin and Range province.

East of the Continental Divide are the high plains of the Llano Estacado (pronounced 'yah-no esta-CAH-doe,' it means 'Staked Plain'), the westernmost parts of the Great Plains. About a third of New Mexico falls into this area, which is mainly pancake-flat ranching country, with some oil production in the south. This area is watered by the Pecos River and the recently discovered Ogallala Aquifer.

By way of comparison, the Southwest lies within about the same latitudes as Spain, Greece, Turkey, and northern China and Japan.

GEOLOGY

The Southwest owes its unusual and dramatic landscape to the interaction of two processes: large-scale forces that have stretched the earth's crust, uplifted mountain ranges, and erupted volcanoes; and less powerful forces eroding the rocks away. It's easy to visualize wind and rain slowly wearing down hillsides and carrying away loose sediment. Harder to grasp are the movements of the crust, called plate tectonics, that have pushed and pulled the Southwest into geologic provinces including the Basin and Range, Colorado Plateau, Rocky Mountains, and Rio Grande Rift. The basic idea behind plate tectonics (also called continental drift), is that the earth's crust is divided into a dozen or so large pieces (plus several smaller ones), called plates, that fit together like a jigsaw puzzle but move independently of one another. Although the plates travel at only millimeters per year, collisions between them fold and buckle their edges; their interiors, meanwhile, remain largely untouched. As a result, mountains, volcanoes and earthquakes are generally found along plate boundaries while the centers of continents, far removed from this activity, are worn flat by millions of years of erosion.

In order to discuss the sequence of events that led to present-day Arizona, New Mexico and Utah, it is necessary to understand geologic time. The appearance of fossils in the geologic record marks the beginning of the **Paleozoic** (ancient life) **Era**, the oldest segment of which is the **Cambrian Period**. The rapid evolution of marine invertebrates is named the Cambrian Explosion; earth's four-billion-year history prior to this, when little but bacteria and other primitive creatures existed, is lumped together as the **Precambrian Era**. The **Mesozoic** (middle life) **Era** began 245 million years ago with the appearance of dinosaurs and ended 65 million years ago with their sudden extinction. The **Cenozoic** (recent life) **Era** witnessed the proliferation of mammals.

Because little evidence remains exposed today, we know only the highlights of the Southwest's earliest geologic history. Approximately 1.7 billion years ago, during the Precambrian Era, what is now the Southwest formed the western edge of the North American continent (tectonic plates would later mash themselves onto western North America, extending it to the west). Tectonic plates crashed against North America, buckling the crust, raising Himalayan-sized mountain ranges, erupting huge volumes of volcanic ash and lava, and producing molten magma deep in the earth that rose into the crust and cooled to form large bodies of granite. Millions of years later, sea levels rose and flooded the region, depositing thick sequences of marine sediments that formed shales, siltstones and sandstones.

Then, about 1.4 billion years ago, numerous granite bodies again intruded into the crust during a new round of mountain-building. As the Precambrian ended, the seas gradually withdrew, and for hundreds of millions of years the region was slowly beveled by erosion. Now called the **Great Unconformity**, this erosion removed over one billion years of geologic history from much of the Southwest.

At the start of the Paleozoic, North America was joined with Europe, Asia, Africa and Antarctica into a supercontinent

SOUTHWESTERN GEOLOGICAL ZONES

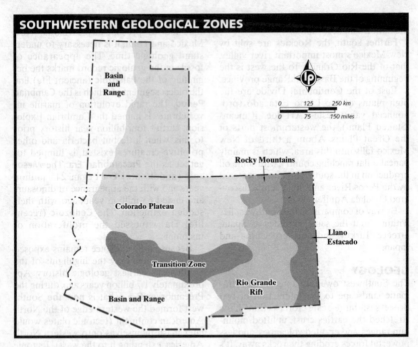

named **Pangaea**. Early in the Cambrian, a sea advanced across western Pangaea and began depositing another thick sequence of sediments. As the Paleozoic progressed, sea levels rose and fell, alternating fossil-rich marine rocks with continental deposits that formed on floodplains and in deltas. In what is now the Colorado Plateau, these seas laid down horizontal layers of sandstone and limestone exposed strikingly today in the Grand Canyon. During the late Paleozoic, 200 million years later, mountains rose in north-central New Mexico – ancestors of today's Rocky Mountains. At the same time, southern New Mexico lay under a shallow, tropical sea teeming with life, including a barrier reef that would later host Carlsbad Caverns.

During the early Mesozoic, much of the Southwest may have looked like northern Egypt: floodplains and deltas surrounded by expanses of desert. Rising mountains in the west shut off moisture from the ocean while mountains in central and eastern Arizona collected what rain did fall and channeled it toward the west. However, the climate become more humid as the Mesozoic progressed; meandering rivers dissected floodplains and swamps filled lowlands – an ideal climate for dinosaurs. Fossil remains of *Coelophysis*, the earliest known dinosaur, tell us that they roamed the Southwest from the start of the Mesozoic, and *Seismosaurus*, the largest dinosaur ever discovered, shook New Mexican ground.

During the final segment of the Mesozoic, or the **Cretaceous Period**, the ocean swept in again, forming a long, north-south trending sea called the Cretaceous Seaway, which extended as far north as Canada. At this time, a series of tectonic microplates began crunching into the western coast of North America, folding and shortening the crust by up to 60 miles, and uplifting Utah's Sevier Mountains. Meanwhile, North America had broken away from Europe and begun drifting west. The resulting gap between the continents formed the Atlantic Ocean. As North America moved, it rode over a piece of crust called the East Pacific plate. This collision, named the **Laramide Orogeny**, resulted in the birth of the modern Rocky Mountains, uplifted the Colorado Plateau and led to another round of volcanic eruptions throughout the Southwest. In Arizona, magma rich in precious metals intruded into the crust. Circulating groundwater then concentrated this gold, silver and copper into valuable veins.

The Cenozoic is a geologically complex era. Uplift of the Rockies continued well into the Cenozoic, leading to powerful volcanic eruptions in Utah 40 million years ago. About 10 million years later, an unusual event began: In contrast to the compression that uplifted the Rockies, the crust began to stretch to the east and west. In response to this pulling, the crust cracked along two long parallel fractures that extended from Colorado through New Mexico and into Texas. As the stretching continued, the area between these faults dropped down and the rocks on either side tilted outward; this was the beginning of the **Rio Grande Rift**. East of the rift, tilted blocks of crust formed a series of mountain ranges that helped channel the Rio Grande. Magma rose along the rift's fractures and erupted in a chain of volcanoes. East from the mountains that flank the Rio Grande Rift, the ground is flat, with most of the relief due to erosion by the Pecos and Canadian Rivers, a small number of sinkholes and a scattering of early and late Cenozoic volcanoes. This is the **Llano Estacado** – the western edge of North America's stable interior. Largely unaffected by the tectonic activity that pushed and pulled the crust farther to the west, the rocks in this zone remain horizontal, just as they were originally deposited.

Between 15 and 8 million years ago, the crust throughout western Arizona, western Utah, and southern New Mexico began stretching as well. And just as in the Rio Grande Rift, cracks in the crust formed long, north-south trending mountains

(ranges) and valleys (basins). This geologic province, called the **Basin and Range**, forms a distinctive Southwestern landscape. By the time it finished, rifting had thinned and extended the crust approximately 50 miles to the east and west. Separating the Basin and Range from the Colorado Plateau is a northwest/southeast band of mountains, called the **Central Highlands**, that crosscuts Arizona and western New Mexico. Also called the Transition Zone, this area shares the northeast-southwest mountains and valleys of the Basin and Range with the flat-lying sedimentary rocks of the Colorado Plateau. Uplifted by the Laramide Orogeny and stretched with the Basin and Range, the Central Highlands were also intruded by granite several times in the early Cenozoic. In Utah, runoff from the rising Rockies fed large lakes that teemed with alligators, fish, and turtles, many of which are preserved as fossils in the **Green River Formation**.

Although rifting, volcanism and uplift have occurred within the last few million years, wind and rain have played a more important role in sculpting most of today's Southwestern landscape. Much of the Southwest is desert today, but climate has fluctuated greatly throughout the Cenozoic. Evidence of wetter times includes massive amounts of sediment, often thousands of meters thick, shed by mountain ranges and carried into adjacent valleys by a network of streams. Changing climate is also recorded in the dry lake basins scattered throughout the Southwest. By 20,000 years ago, massive glaciers, some over a mile thick, had moved south from Canada into the upper Midwest. As a result, the jet stream, which today flows west to east across the northwestern US, was split in two, one arm going farther north and the other swinging south to cross over the Southwest. This southern jet stream carried moisture-laden air from the Pacific, increasing cloud cover and precipitation. Isolated basins filled and finally overflowed, merging together into **Lake Bonneville**, the Great Salt Lake's ancestor, which once covered 20,000 sq miles. Around 10,000 years ago, the glaciers retreated, returning the jet stream to its normal route and the area to desert.

Weathering and erosion beautified the landscape by carving flat-lying rocks into plateaus, mesas, buttes and spires. In areas with tilted strata, hills develop sharp ridge tops called hogbacks and *cuestas*. Sandstone is occasionally sculpted into natural bridges and arches, some of the most dramatic examples of which are found in Utah's Canyonlands and Arches National Parks. Erosion has also exposed the plumbing of ancient volcanoes, called volcanic necks, such as Shiprock in northwestern New Mexico. Rainwater reacts with chemical elements in some rocks to produce a wide range of colors, making the Southwest one of North America's most visually stunning landscapes. Iron and manganese oxides rust to red, pink, yellow and purple; unrusted

iron oxides may look blue or green. In addition, black lavas, tan volcanic ash and white limestones are often painted with patches of orange, green and brown lichens. These areas are popularly called painted deserts.

CLIMATE

The Southwest conjures up images of searing desert heat, and this is certainly true in many parts of the region (see the accompanying charts). An excellent rule of thumb, however, is to gauge the climate by the altitude. The lower you are, the hotter and drier it will be. As you climb, temperatures drop 3° to 5°F for every 1000 feet of elevation gain.

Southwestern and south-central Arizona is below 3000 feet in elevation and is often the hottest part of the USA. High temperatures exceed 100°F for weeks on end and occasionally surpass 120°F. The humidity is

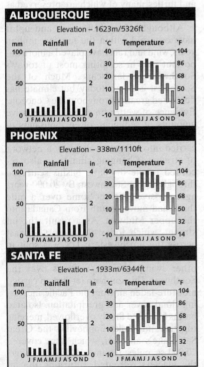

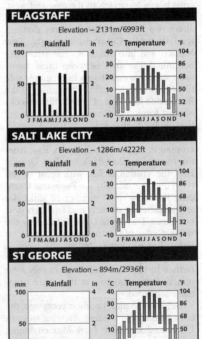

low, however, and evaporation helps to cool the body. As the locals say, 'It's a dry heat.' Dry air does not hold heat like humid air does, and so nighttime temperatures drop by 20° or 30°F. Winter temperatures occasionally will drop below freezing but only for a few hours. Yuma, at 200 feet in the southwestern corner of Arizona, is the driest part of the region covered in this book. The rest of Arizona is higher and cooler; the state's average elevation is 4100 feet.

Almost 90% of New Mexico is over 4000 feet, with the exception being the lower Rio Grande and Pecos River valleys, which are the hottest parts of the state. The average elevation of New Mexico is 5700 feet, rather higher and slightly cooler than the 5000 feet at Albuquerque. Utah is generally higher and cooler still, with an average elevation of 6100 feet (the third highest state in the USA). The far southwestern corner of Utah is the lowest and hottest part of that state.

Over 90% of the Southwest receives less than 20 inches of precipitation annually and about 30% receives less than 10 inches a year. In the driest areas of southwestern Arizona, almost no rain falls from April to June. The highest rainfall here is during the monsoons of July and August, when rains tend to be brief, heavy downpours falling mainly in the afternoon. In the wetter areas, it can rain at any time, but even so, few areas have more than five wet days in any month.

The areas of greatest precipitation (more than 20 inches) are mostly in the high mountains of central Arizona, the Wasatch and Uinta Mountains of northern Utah and the mountains north of Albuquerque. These areas receive the most snowfall in winter and have excellent skiing.

Conditions can be extreme, and every year people die from lightning, dehydration and flash floods. For more information, see Dangers & Annoyances in the Facts for the Visitor chapter, and the Flash Floods boxed text in the Outdoor Activities chapter.

ECOLOGY & ENVIRONMENT

The current ecology and environment of the arid Southwest are closely linked with the history of modern settlement and the accompanying development of water use. The region's most important river is the 1450-mile-long Colorado, the ninth longest in North America. The Rio Grande, at about 1900 miles, is longer but has less water. Other important rivers are the Salt, Gila, Green and Little Colorado, all tributaries of the Colorado, and the Pecos River.

The climate, dry for months and then subject to sudden heavy rainstorms, made the rivers difficult to control for early settlers. Reduced to a trickle or drying completely during the dry months, rivers could change into tremendous torrents in a matter of hours after a monsoon storm. Interestingly enough, the ancient Hohokam people had learned how to irrigate large parts of central and southern Arizona, but their system is long abandoned and silted up.

From the 1870s until the early 1900s, Mormon pioneers along the Little Colorado River, ranchers along the Salt and Pecos Rivers and settlers in river valleys throughout the Southwest built makeshift dams to control and divert the waters for irrigation. Time after time, floods swept away the dams, which would be rebuilt. In 1905, a huge flood along the lower Colorado River resulted in a permanent alteration of its course.

To control the rivers, the Reclamation Act of 1902 was passed, which led to the building of huge federally funded dams, constructed to resist the wildest of floods. The first was the Theodore Roosevelt Dam on the Salt River, completed in 1911, soon followed by the Strawberry River Dam in Utah in 1913, the Rio Grande's Elephant Butte Dam in 1916 and the Coolidge Dam, finished in 1929 on the Gila River.

Constant disagreements and rancorous debates raged within each state as to who should be allowed to use the dammed river water. Colorado River water rights, however, were an even bigger matter – seven states and Mexico had claims to the water. In 1922, US secretary of commerce (later president) Herbert Hoover united the states in the Colorado River Compact and engineered a scheme to divide water rights, with California getting the largest share.

Although Arizona refused to ratify the compact until 1944, the 1922 legislation laid the groundwork for a series of major dams on the Colorado River, particularly the Hoover Dam. Built between 1931 and 1936, the Hoover Dam was then the largest ever built and is still the second highest in the USA. Its reservoir, Lake Mead, has the largest capacity in the USA, followed closely by Lake Powell, which was formed in 1966 by the construction of Glen Canyon Dam, also on the Colorado River.

Despite this seeming bounty of water created by modern technology, there were and are many water problems, not the least of which were ethical ones – the huge lakes formed by the dams flooded canyons containing hundreds of ancient Indian sites that are now lost. Technical problems have included the inaccurate measurement of water flow by early gauges; what to do with the silt that drops out of the water when it comes to a halt behind a dam; and how to deal with drought.

Nevertheless, water has become available in the Southwest and, with it, towns have grown. More water means more people who need more water still – a vicious cycle that has reached crisis proportions. Phoenix is a noteworthy example. Founded in 1870, the city had 5500 inhabitants in 1900. It has more than 1.3 million today, making it the sixth largest city in the country. Including those in adjoining towns, 3.3 million people live in the metropolitan area. There is simply not enough water to continue supplying all these people.

Recent additions to the Southwest's water supply are underground water reserves, or aquifers, which have been discovered in west-central Arizona, southwestern Utah and elsewhere. The most important of these is the Ogallala Aquifer of the Great Plains, which provides water for large parts of New Mexico and five other plains states.

These aquifers are 'mined' – in other words, water is extracted from them at a faster rate than it can naturally be replenished. Despite legislative attempts to avoid losing the aquifers, providing water to the ever-growing population of the Southwest

remains the region's most serious problem. Water-thirsty golf courses (about 200 in the Phoenix area alone) and irrigated farms have played a part in making water the Southwest's major ecological concern. Agriculture requires a huge volume of water for irrigation. Before dams, irrigation was limited, but water can now reach extensive areas. In the 1990s, the Central Arizona Project (CAP) enabled Tucson and southeastern Arizona to receive water from the Colorado River.

Cattle ranching is also a concern. Many federal lands are leased inexpensively to ranchers to graze cattle. This can result in degradation of riparian areas when cattle trample the edges of streams in efforts to find water. This trampling doesn't allow plants to grow and deteriorates the banks so that they are washed away. Over 90% of riparian habitats have disappeared in Arizona over the past century. Although questionable ranching and agricultural practices have led to environmental deterioration, some ranchers are figuring out more sustainable techniques. The Malpais Borderlands Group, with about 25 environmentally minded ranchers on the southern New Mexican-Arizona border, has pushed for sound ranching techniques in this area. They are led by William McDonald, a fifth-generation rancher from Douglas, Arizona, who won major recognition with a MacArthur Foundation Genius Award in 1998.

One of the few remaining riparian areas is along the San Pedro River in southeastern Arizona, with a phenomenal diversity of species. Almost half of the birds in North America have been recorded here (which is partly why southeastern Arizona is considered one of the premier birding regions in the continent), as well as large numbers of amphibians, reptiles, mammals and other wildlife. Despite being protected as a BLM Conservation Area, parts of the San Pedro dry up during certain times of year, and the water levels are dropping annually, due mainly to burgeoning growth in nearby Sierra Vista and Fort Huachuca.

The mining industry also plays a controversial environmental role. Huge copper mines scar the earth's surface (the Bingham Canyon mine near Salt Lake City is proudly called 'the biggest hole on earth') and strip-mining for coal is also a contentious issue. Uranium mines in the Moab area have become unproductive, but their tailings continue to pollute the environment long after the mines have gone out of business. The Atlas site causes the worst of the nation's uranium tailings pollution, with almost 11 million gallons of pollutants annually leaking out of the tailings into the Colorado River.

Perhaps the most contentious mining issue at this time is what to do with all the radioactive waste left as a legacy of the Cold War. One solution, which has been two decades in the making, is to bury it in deep underground salt beds near Carlsbad, New Mexico. The Waste Isolation Pilot Plant (WIPP) has been accepting waste since March 1999; Citizens for Alternatives to Radioactive Dumping, a volunteer group, has been monitoring the plant's activities. Unfortunately, even if WIPP continues to operate safely, it will only take care of a tiny fraction of the nation's nuclear waste.

FLORA & FAUNA

Southwestern wildlife is unique and fascinating, and much of it can easily be seen and experienced. Forests of the giant saguaro (pronounced 'sa-WA-roh') cactus cover many slopes of southern Arizona. The road-runner, the state bird of New Mexico, and the coyote, the wily trickster of Navajo legend, are often seen darting across the highways or skulking off the road. Vultures wheel through the air, poisonous lizards and venomous snakes are occasionally glimpsed, tarantulas and scorpions scuttle along the ground and jackrabbits bound along with prodigious leaps. Southeastern Arizona is a mecca for birders, with 16 species of hummingbirds recorded (eight are commonly seen). This area also has many other exotic species and people fly thousands of miles to record an unusual bird here.

Clearly, there is plenty of life in this desert – the question is, which desert? What was once called the Great Southwestern Desert by early travelers is now divided into four different deserts. Each has characteristic flora, fauna, climate and physical geography to distinguish it from the others, although some features are common to all four deserts as well as other areas. In addition, highland regions in all three Southwestern states, and the plains of eastern New Mexico, have distinct ecologies, with unique plants and animals.

A brief overview of these regions introduces you to the diversity of plants and animals in the Southwest. Note that many of the species mentioned below are found, to a greater or lesser extent, in areas other than those under which they are mentioned.

Packrats – Today's Pest, Yesterday's Historian

Packrats (or, more properly, woodrats, genus *Neotoma*) are large rodents, related to mice, that have an incredible ability to dig and burrow through the hard desert soil. The nickname packrat arose out of their habit of collecting and hoarding almost anything in large and often inaccessible nests. Plants and pennies, bones and bottle caps are all collectibles for the packrat. Tales abound in the Southwest of packrats ruining air-conditioning systems or collapsing patios with their endeavors. I once left a refrigerator in storage for six months and returned to find a packrat nest inside and the wiring stripped away.

The dry conditions of the Southwest preserve packrat nests remarkably well. Scientists have discovered nests thousands of years old. Microscopic scrutiny of the contents has revealed much about the ancient history of the region. Plant materials found inside the nests show that the environment was much wetter and greener when the first people arrived in the Southwest, at least 11,000 years ago.

The Arizona-Sonora Desert

This area covers most of southern Arizona and much of the northern part of Mexico's state of Sonora, most of Baja California, and the southeastern corner of California. It is a subtropical desert with two distinct wet seasons: the summer monsoons and the winter rains. Generally low-lying and extremely hot, it has a greater diversity of wildlife than the other deserts. This is partly because the rainfall pattern allows for two flowering seasons and also because tropical regions have more species than do temperate ones. The spring flowering season, in particular, can sometimes be incredibly spectacular, though short-lived. If winter rainfall and temperature are just right, yellow, orange, blue, violet and pink flowers bloom by the billions.

More than any other region, the Arizona-Sonora Desert is characterized by cacti, especially the giant saguaro cactus that is found in southern Arizona but nowhere else in the USA. These huge columnar cacti with their uplifted arms are part of almost everyone's image of the Southwest. The organpipe cactus and the senita cactus are other giants found in southern Arizona near the Mexican border. Dozens of other species are here too: prickly pear, barrel, fishhook, hedgehog and teddybear cholla are the most typical cacti of this desert.

The Arizona-Sonora Desert also has the greatest variety of trees, which tend to be short and spiny with small leaves. The Arizona state tree, the blue paloverde, as well as the yellow and Mexican paloverdes are common here. *Paloverde* is Spanish for 'green stick' and refers to the color of the bark, which is capable of photosynthesis. The ironwood, a tree with very dense wood that sinks in water, is also typical of this

Cacti of the Southwest

My mother always had a couple of small cacti surviving desperately in tiny pots on the sunless windowsills of our suburban London house. I'll never forget the spring day when one of those hopelessly decrepit specimens suddenly burst into a florid bloom, exotically overwhelming all the surrounding houseplants. And exotic it certainly was – every one of the world's more than 2000 species of cactus is native to the Americas.

Researchers cannot agree on exact numbers, but more than a hundred species of cactus are found in the Southwest. They are superbly adapted to survival in the arid environment. The succulent pads that form the body of the plant are actually modified stems, and their waxy 'skin' helps retard moisture loss. The leaves, which in other plants normally allow a lot of water to escape through transpiration, have been modified into spines that not only lose little moisture, but also protect the plant against herbivores looking for water. Evaporation is further reduced by the plant keeping its pores closed during the day and open only at night. These remarkable plants are further enhanced by their often splendid flowers.

Identification It is fairly easy to identify the six most common types of Southwestern cactus. These are prickly pear, pincushion, cholla, giant columnar, barrel and hedgehog cacti.

Prickly pears are often of the genus *Opuntia* and are distinguished by the flattened cross-section of their pads. If the pads are cylindrical, read on.

Pincushion cacti, often of the genus *Mammilaria*, are small and cylindrical in cross-section, and don't have ribs running from top to bottom. Spine clusters grow out of nipplelike bumps on the stems – hence the scientific name. Many species have hooked spines.

Cholla (pronounced 'CHOY-uh') cacti are also cylindrical and lack ribs, but are much taller and have branches. Like the prickly pears, they belong to the genus *Opuntia*. They can range from pencil chollas, with extremely thin branches; to teddybear chollas, which look warm and fuzzy but

desert. Mesquite trees are common but not confined to this region.

Animals are easily seen, especially many species of lizards and, sometimes, several snake species including various rattlesnakes and the highly venomous Arizona coral snake. Commonly seen mammals are coyotes, several rabbit species and various species of ground, rock and antelope squirrels. (These mammals are common throughout most of the Southwest.) Birds include the quaint Gambel's quail, with its question-mark-shaped head plume, the roadrunner and the ubiquitous cactus wren.

The superb Arizona-Sonora Desert Museum in Tucson provides visitors with an excellent introduction to this region.

The Chihuahua Desert

This desert is found in southern New Mexico, western Texas, the extreme south-eastern corner of Arizona and the Mexican state of Chihuahua. Although at a similar latitude to the Arizona-Sonora Desert, it lies at a generally higher elevation and is therefore cooler. On average, more rain falls in summer, and most flowers bloom in late summer and early fall.

The desert's most striking plants are the agaves (pronounced 'a-GAH-vees') and yuccas. The agaves, of which there are several species (some found in the other desert regions), have a rosette of large, tough, spiny swordlike leaves out of which shoots an amazing flowering stalk, often reaching as high as 15 feet, covered with thousands of tiny flowers. This stalk can grow as much as a foot a day and the energy required to produce this huge reproductive body is so great that it is a one-time occurrence. After flowering for a few weeks, the plant dies.

Cacti of the Southwest

have wickedly barbed spines; to large jumping chollas, which have fruits hanging in loose chains. Brushing a jumping cholla lightly often results in part of the chain becoming attached to your body – almost as if it had jumped onto you. Jumping chollas often grow in thick stands. The chollas have some of the sharpest and most difficult to remove spines – if you are stuck, it may be easier to cut the spines with scissors and then remove them one by one with tweezers.

The remaining three main types are all cylindrical in cross-section and ribbed. If they are also very tall (from 15 to 50 feet high), they are giant columnar cacti and most likely to be a saguaro cactus (Cereus giganteus), which has branches high off the ground (and is found only in southern Arizona and northern Mexico). In a few places in southern Arizona, you might see large cacti branching from the ground. These are either organ-pipe or senita cacti. (Organ-pipes have 10 or more ribs, and lack the white or gray hairs of the senita. You can see them at Organ Pipe Cactus National Monument.) There are many more species of columnar cacti across the border in Mexico.

Finally, smaller cylindrical cacti with ribs are likely to be hedgehog or barrel cacti. Hedgehog cacti, often of the genus Echinocereus, are small, with the main pad less than 4 inches in diameter. When they bloom, the flowers grow from the sides. Barrel cacti, often of the genus Ferocactus, are over 5 inches in diameter and their flowers grow from the top. The largest examples can grow to 10 feet in height, although this is unusual.

All six types are commonly found in southern Arizona. The other Southwestern deserts lack the giant columnar cacti. The Great Basin Desert tends to have just the smaller species.

Protection Cacti are legally protected. You need a permit to collect any kind of cactus from the wild. It is also illegal to damage or destroy a cactus. A famous (and true) story you may hear is of a man who was shooting at a saguaro from close range. One of the huge arms of the cactus toppled over and killed him.

Some yuccas resemble agaves with rosettes of tough leaves and tall flower stalks; others are more shrublike. Unlike the agave, however, the yucca flowers annually. There are some 15 species of yucca in the Southwest; the soaptree yucca is New Mexico's state flower. The flowers are pollinated at night by yucca moths, which lay their eggs inside the flowers. The moth larvae then feed on the developing fruit and thus both plant and animal benefit.

Creosote bush dominates the ground cover of the Chihuahua Desert, and is found in the Arizona-Sonora and Mojave Deserts as well. Although this low, straggly bush is not much to look at, it produces complex oils and resins that make it taste bad to most animals. When it rains, these chemicals are released and give the air a characteristically astringent but not unpleasant smell.

The ocotillo is a common plant of both the Chihuahua and Arizona-Sonora Deserts. During dry months, this plant looks like a bunch of skinny, spiny stems. After rain, the stems are covered by many tiny green leaves and tipped by clusters of small, bright red flowers.

Both the Chihuahua and Arizona-Sonora Deserts are home to mammals that are typical of Mexico but not frequently seen by visitors to the USA. If you enjoy hiking and backcountry camping, you may well see javelina or coati. Javelinas are pig-like mammals that travel in small groups or occasionally herds of up to 60, feeding on cacti and making quiet grunting sounds. They are most easily seen in early morning or late afternoon. Coatis are members of the raccoon family and live primarily in subtropical regions of Central and South America. They have made inroads northward and are sighted fairly often both in the deserts and in the mountains as far as the Mogollon Rim in Arizona.

One of the best places to learn more about this area's biology is the Living Desert State Park in Carlsbad, New Mexico.

The Mojave Desert

This desert spreads across parts of southern Nevada, southeastern California, north-western Arizona and extreme southwestern Utah, so only a small portion falls within the area covered by this book. The Mojave is the smallest, driest and hottest of the country's deserts, and it is also thought of as a transition desert between the Arizona-Sonora and Great Basin Deserts.

Much of this desert is low-lying. It includes the lowest point in the Western Hemisphere: Death Valley (282 feet below sea level). The lowest areas are characterized by widely spread shrubby vegetation or empty sand dunes and dry lakebeds. In Arizona and Utah the elevations are higher and the dominant plants are the eerie Joshua trees. These 30- to 40-foot-high plants, believed to live up to 1000 years, are the largest species of yucca and are members of the lily family.

After the right amount of rainfall in winter, spring can bring a carpet of about 250 species of flowers, of which 80% are endemic to the Mojave Desert. Cacti are quite common, although they are generally smaller than the ones of the Arizona-Sonora Desert. Creosote bushes are seen in great and odorous quantities and many lizards and desert birds are present.

The Great Basin Desert

This is the continent's most northerly desert, covering most of Nevada, western Utah and the Colorado Plateau, and stretching on into Idaho and Oregon. The name derives from the fact that the Great Basin is an area of interior drainage, where most of the waterways drain into desert flats, not into the sea.

This is generally a high desert, with most of the basins at over 4000 feet. The high latitude and elevation make this a cooler desert with less wildlife. Cacti, agaves and yuccas are fewer and smaller. Instead, miles of low, rather nondescript shrubs such as saltbrush and sagebrush cover the ground.

Here, the big sagebrush, which can reach more than 6 feet in height, replaces the creosote of the hot desert. It, too, has volatile oils, making it less appetizing to potential herbivores and giving off a pleasantly pungent odor after rain or when crushed. So pervasive is this plant that, in some areas, it provides 70% of the ground cover and an astonishing 90% of the plant biomass.

Generally, wildlife is either scarce or hard to observe. A bird that is closely associated with big sagebrush is the sage grouse, which feeds mainly on this plant. Males make a resonant booming call and dance around in specific places (called leks) to attract females during the early spring breeding season, when they are the most noticeable. Sage sparrow and sage thrashers are small, secretive and hard to spot.

Raptors, particularly red-tailed hawks and kestrels, are often seen as they search for lizards and snakes. Otherwise, rabbits are the most likely animals to catch your eye. Badgers and pronghorns might be seen browsing among the sagebrush.

Grasslands

Grasslands once covered extensive areas of the Southwest, particularly in the river basins of Arizona and New Mexico. Millions of head of cattle and sheep were introduced into these fine grazing areas in the 1870s and 1880s. The animals overgrazed the grasslands, and many of these areas quickly became extensions of the deserts. Today, the grassland areas are found in eastern New Mexico, especially in the northeastern part of the state. Here, the observant traveler can spot small herds of pronghorn, with small forked horns and graceful bodies.

Higher Life Zones

As you climb into the mountain ranges, you'll pass plants and animals evocative of the northern parts of the continent. A rough rule of thumb is that a 1000-foot elevation gain is equivalent to a drive of several hundred miles to the north; in other words, the vegetation of the Southwest's high mountains is comparable to that of Canada.

Biologists divide the elevations of the mountains into a series of life zones that, despite being somewhat arbitrary and imprecise in regards to their altitude, are useful tools for making sense of the sudden changes in flora and the associated fauna. The following is a popular zonation.

The lower elevations (below 4500 feet) are called the Lower Sonoran Zone, followed by the Upper Sonoran Zone (4500 to 6500 feet). These encompass most of the deserts discussed above. The Upper Sonoran Zone also supports evergreen trees such as small junipers and the piñon pine.

The Transition Zone (6500 to 8000 feet) falls between the desert basins and the high mountains. Much of the Colorado Plateau appears to be in this zone, although many biologists include it in the Great Basin Desert. The most notable vegetation is the ponderosa pine, of which there are large stands, especially in New Mexico, where it is extensively logged. Other plants found here are Gambel's oak and various shrubs. There are fewer species of reptiles, but squirrels and chipmunks are common. Black bears and mountain lions live here, but you are unlikely to see them. White-tailed deer are more often sighted and, in some places, you may see elk.

From about 8000 to 9500 feet, the predominant trees are Douglas firs and aspens in what is called the Canadian Forest Zone (also called the Montane Forest Zone). Other trees include white fir and juniper, and the shading of these thick forests precludes the growth of many other plants. From 9500 to 11,500 feet, in the Hudsonian Zone (also called Subalpine Forest Zone), other conifers tend to predominate, including Engelmann spruce, subalpine fir and bristlecone pine. This zone receives heavy winter snows, and few mammals are found here in winter. Above the tree line (11,500 feet) is the Alpine zone, characterized by small tundra-like plants.

GOVERNMENT & POLITICS

Elections are often hotly contested, and politicians and parties spend many millions of dollars on political campaigns that often become acrimonious. Despite this, barely half of eligible voters cast ballots. All US citizens over the age of 18 (except for felons) are eligible to vote.

The two main parties are the Republicans and the Democrats. Other parties exist, but are usually too small to play a significant part in government. Traditionally, Republicans are conservative, and Democrats are liberal. The fact that two parties with opposing views are both strongly represented in Congress means that it is sometimes difficult to pass laws considered beneficial to the country by one party but not by the other.

The federal government has three branches: the legislative branch makes the laws of the land, the executive branch executes these laws, and the judicial branch studies and interprets both the Constitution and the laws.

The legislative branch is made up of the bicameral Congress, composed of the Senate and the House of Representatives. The Senate has two senators from each of the 50 states, while the House has several members from each state, depending on the size of that state's population. Arizona has six representatives, while sparsely populated New Mexico and Utah each have three. In contrast, California, the most populous state, has 52 representatives.

The executive branch consists of the President, the 14-member Cabinet and various assistants. The President has the power to veto the laws passed by Congress, although a presidential veto can be overturned by two-thirds of the members of Congress. The President serves four years and may serve only two terms.

The judicial branch is headed by the Supreme Court, with nine justices who are appointed for life by presidents and approved by the Senate.

Each of the 50 states has its own government, run along similar lines to the national government with some differences. The head of each state is the governor, and the bicameral legislature consists of a senate and a house delegation.

National (federal) laws apply to all states, although there are often conflicts between federal and state interests. Additionally, each state enacts its own laws that visitors should be aware of. States have different laws about driving, alcohol use and taxes, described in each state's introduction.

Traditionally, most Western states are Republican. Utah and Arizona are generally conservative, New Mexico is more middle-of-the-road. In a land where water is a scarce resource and the population is increasing more rapidly than in the country as a whole, it is not surprising that the most contentious issues in the region concern the use of water and land.

ECONOMY

Traditionally, mining and agriculture (especially ranching) were the backbone of the Southwest's economy and major factors in the settling of the southwest. Some laws enacted in the 19th century to regulate these industries are still in force. Recent moves to modernize this legislation have met with strong resistance from the industries involved. Miners and ranchers consider the old laws to be reasonable; others find that current concerns about fair price for the use of public lands, conservation, water quality and pollution necessitate a modernization of the laws. One of the most contentious issues is that of ranchers' traditional rights to graze on public land for a small fraction of the current cost of a grazing lease on private land. Modern ranching is a far cry from the rough-and-tumble 19th century, but still sparks the interest of many visitors who stay on 'dude ranches' or take part in cowboy-led horse packing trips.

In modern times, manufacturing, tourism, government and service industries have become increasingly important sectors in the Southwest's economy.

POPULATION & PEOPLE

The US Census Bureau takes a census of the population every 10 years. The last census was in April 2000. The Southwest is one of the fastest-growing regions in the USA, with the warm weather attracting large numbers of retirees. From 1990 to 2000, Nevada, Arizona, Colorado and Utah experienced the greatest population growth of all the states. Despite this, the Southwestern states are sparsely populated. Arizona's comparatively high population density is skewed by the presence of the greater Phoenix metropolitan area, which accounts for over 60% of the state's inhabitants. Similarly, the Salt Lake City region accounts for three-quarters of Utah's population.

Arizona is the 20th most populous state with 5,130,632 inhabitants, Utah's 2,233,169 people rank it 34th, and New Mexico is 36th with 1,819,046. New Mexico and Arizona have a rich Hispanic heritage and these states also have large populations of Native Americans, over half of which are Navajo. Other tribes include various Apache groups, Havasupai, Hopi, Hualapai, various Pueblo tribes, Tohono O'odham, Ute and a host of smaller groups. Arizona and New Mexico have the third- and fourth-largest Native American populations of the 50 states (Oklahoma and California have the largest). The Southwest's African American population, on the other hand, is very small, as is the Asian/Pacific Islander group. Utah, with its strong Mormon heritage, is predominantly white.

The Southwest is commonly perceived as having a tricultural mix of Indian, Hispanic and Anglo cultures. Only in northwestern and north-central New Mexico can you see clear evidence of all three cultures – ancient Indian pueblos, historic Hispanic churches and Anglo atomic bomb laboratories coexist in an intricate and unique alliance.

In the rest of the Southwest, all three cultures make their mark in differing degrees depending on the region. The Indians predominantly live in the Four Corners area, especially on the Navajo and Hopi Reservations of northeastern Arizona, and in the pueblos of northwestern New Mexico. There are large Apache reservations in mountainous eastern Arizona, the Tohono O'odham Reservation in the southern desert of Arizona and a scattering of smaller reservations elsewhere in the region. With the exception of the pueblo areas, none of these places can be considered tricultural! However, reservation culture is definitely bicultural – Indian and Anglo – in most respects.

New Mexico has the highest proportion of Hispanics, with the Rio Grande Valley and Santa Fe being historically the center of that culture. Southern Arizona, too, has much Hispanic influence. The most obvious signs of this may be the huge number of Mexican restaurants in Tucson and the fact that telephone directories and government documents have Spanish translations, but there are subtler manifestations as well. The architecture and arts often reflect this heritage. In the border areas, many Hispanic people are of Mexican-American heritage and proudly call themselves Chicano. Some still do not recognize the legality of the US claim of Mexican land in 1848 after the US-Mexican war and the Gadsden Purchase in 1853; they refer to the land affected as Aztlan.

Anglos dominate the scene in most of Mormon Utah and in many fast-growing cities of Arizona, particularly the Phoenix metropolitan area and the towns along the Colorado River in western Arizona. In rural areas of the Southwest, many off-reservation ranches and mines are Anglo-owned, although workers may be Hispanic or Indian.

The Southwest's unique flavor does not stem simply from its triculturalism. That must be combined with the land and climate – beautifully desolate, splendidly harsh, incredibly varied and rarely forgiving. People's survival in these extreme conditions has shaped what may be perceived as the culture of the Southwest.

ARTS

Albuquerque, Salt Lake City, Phoenix and Tucson have their own symphony orchestras. Major opera companies include the Arizona Opera Company, which performs in Tucson and Phoenix; the Santa Fe Opera; and the Utah Opera in Salt Lake City. The famous Mormon Tabernacle Choir has performed in weekly radio broadcasts since 1929. Notable dance companies include Ballet Arizona in Phoenix; Ballet West and the Repertory Dance Theater in Salt Lake City; and the Maria Benitez Teatro Flamenco in Santa Fe. Every city of any size has theaters, art galleries and museums.

Hispanic and Native American influences have helped create a distinctive local arts scene. Much of this aesthetic is evident

Native American Dance & Music

Swirling dancers bedecked in headdresses and facepaint, wearing intricately beaded clothing and stomping to the beat of a circle of drummers – this spectacle is one that many travelers to the region want to see. Here are suggestions on how to best enjoy the various dances that are held throughout the year all over the Southwest.

From the visitor's point of view, Native American dances can be grouped into three categories, although there is certainly overlap between them.

Religious First, there are the ceremonial or ritual religious dances that take place on Indian reservations at traditionally specified times of the year. Some of these are celebratory occasions that mark stages of life (for instance, a girl's puberty rite), and others, such as rain dances, revere specific gods. Precise dates and locations vary from year to year and are often not known until a few weeks before the event. Because of the strong religious and traditional motive, access to ceremonial dances is usually strictly controlled.

Some ceremonials are open to the public, but photography or recording of any kind is completely prohibited. It is important for tourists to respect this rule. Occasionally, a tourist might try to sneak a quick and unobtrusive photo. In this case, a tribal police officer may confiscate the camera, or an irate tribal elder may simply grab the camera and hurl it over the nearest cliff! Other rules for watching ceremonial dances are to refrain from applauding and asking many questions, to follow instructions about where to stand or sit, to wear appropriate clothing (no shorts or tank tops) and generally to behave in a quiet and respectful way. Alcohol is not permitted during dances or anywhere on most Indian reservations. Increasing numbers of ceremonial dances are being closed to the general public because the Indians are fed up with non-Indians' behavior.

For information about dances and performance dates, contact the tribal offices listed in the relevant parts of the text.

Social Social dances can be very traditional or relatively modern, and are danced for competition, display, to tell a story, as an honor, or just for fun and getting together with other families, clans or tribes. The dancers are accompanied by drum groups and singers. Usually, songs are in one of the Native American languages, or they are vocables (songs made up of sounds that are not words). An emcee calls each dance, often with an inside joke or two, and usually at least some of the dances are called in English, especially the intertribals, when anyone, including members of the tourist tribe, can go out and dance.

For visitors, these are the best kind of dances because you can enjoy them, participate if you wish, and let go of your worries about interfering in a religious ceremony. Social dances occur throughout the Southwest during powwows or at various festivities with names like 'Indian Days.' They also occur during fairs, rodeos and other gatherings in Indian reservations. Details are given in appropriate places in the text.

Often, a small admission fee is charged; Indian food, arts and crafts, and cassettes or CDs are sold; and photography may be permitted. Photographers can usually take general pictures of the festivities but should always ask permission to take photographs of individuals. A small tip may be requested in this case.

Performances The third category of dances is purely performance dancing, where you sit in a theater (often outdoors) and watch. These dances are usually of the social kind and are very colorful. It's performance art, but it's also authentic – the dancers don't just make up non-Indian dances for tourists! One of the best places to see dance performances is during the summer at Red Rock State Park just outside of Gallup, New Mexico.

in the region's pottery, paintings, weavings, jewelry, sculpture, woodcarving and leatherworking. You'll find that Southwestern art can be very traditional or cutting-edge contemporary.

Perhaps the region's most famous artist is Georgia O'Keeffe (1887–1986), whose Southwestern landscapes and motifs are found in major museums throughout the world. Also highly regarded is the Navajo artist RC Gorman (born 1932), whose sculptures and paintings of Navajo women are becoming increasingly famous worldwide. Gorman has made his home in Taos for many years. Both Taos and Santa Fe have large and active artist communities considered seminal in the development of Southwestern art.

Many visitors are eager to see Native American art. The Southwest has a wide diversity: Navajo rugs, Hopi kachina dolls, Zuni silverware, Tohono O'odham basketry and Pueblo pottery are some of the best known. Maria Martinez (1887–1980) of the San Ildefonso Pueblo led a revival of traditional pottery making during the 1920s; her 'black on black' pots are some of the finest ever made and are now worth thousands of dollars. Excellent examples of Southwestern Native American art can be seen in many museums, especially Phoenix's Heard Museum. Contemporary Native American art is eminently buyable, and both traditional and modern work is available in hundreds of galleries.

The Southwest's music scene, too, has its Hispanic and Native American influences. Of course, you can hear anything from jazz to hip-hop in the major cities, but you can also catch *mariachis* (typically dressed in dark, ornately sequined, body-hugging costumes and playing predominantly brass instruments and guitars), especially in towns close to the Mexican border. Native American dances and music are performed throughout the Southwest. A couple of noteworthy musicians are Carlos R Nakai and Perry Silver Bird, both flute players. Nakai is a Navajo-Ute who has played his traditional cedar flute with classically trained musicians.

RELIGION

Christians make up the religious majority, with Catholics having the numerical edge in New Mexico and Mormons being by far the majority in Utah. New Mexico and Utah have very few Jews, while Arizona's Jewish population is about 2%, the national average.

Native American tribes have the oldest North American religions, which may have changed since contact with Europeans. Some, like the Native American Church, which uses hallucinatory peyote buttons as a sacrament, are partly pan-Indian responses to encroachment by Anglo culture.

Various Native American religions are closely followed by tens of thousands of people. In any discussion of Indian religious beliefs, several points are worth bearing in mind. First, different tribes often have particular creation stories, rituals and practices, which means that there are dozens of unique and carefully prescribed spiritual ways of life. Second, Indians usually maintain a strict sense of privacy about their most important ceremonies and thus books written by even the most respected outsiders, such as anthropologists, usually contain some inaccuracies when describing Indian religion. Third, the Indian ways are beliefs that Indians feel and know essentially because they are Indians – it's not something that non-Indians can properly understand or convert to.

Travelers will find that members of almost every religion, belief, faith or sect can be found in major cities. Even small towns have several religious groups to choose from. For further information, look in the telephone yellow pages under Churches, Mosques or Synagogues.

LANGUAGE

Although American English is spoken throughout the USA, there are regional variations. Over a third of New Mexico's population (over the age of five) speaks a language other than English at home – more than in any other US state. In Arizona, over 20% speak a language other than English at home, but in Utah it's less than 10%. In New Mexico and Arizona, non-English languages spoken at home are usually Spanish or one of numerous Indian languages.

Particularly in New Mexico and Arizona, you are likely to hear 'Spanglish,' in which speakers switch smoothly between Spanish and English, even within the same sentence. You might be invited to 'vamos a mi house' (come to my house), or hear Spanglish patter on the radio.

Although English is spoken many places that travelers go, you can also hear Spanish and Indian languages spoken. There are plenty of Spanish-language radio stations in the southern parts of New Mexico and Arizona, many broadcasting from Mexico. In the Four Corners area, KTTN radio station, broadcasting out of Window Rock on 660 AM, has many programs in Navajo. One word you might hear frequently in this area is the Navajo greeting *ya'at'eeh*.

Visitors to Indian reservations should remember that silence is almost like a statement. If you say something to an Indian and are met by silence, this doesn't indicate that the person you are talking to is ignoring you. Indians speak their minds when they disagree with the speaker and may remain silent when they agree with the speaker or have no special opinion. This can be strange to non-Indians used to interjecting 'uh huh' and 'really' after almost every sentence they hear.

Finally, visitors to the major national parks will often find introductory brochures printed in Spanish, German, French or Japanese. Although speakers of the last three languages are among the most frequent foreign visitors to the Southwest, they will find that few Americans here speak these languages.

Facts for the Visitor

PLANNING

When to Go

The best season to visit the Southwest is January to December.

In northern Arizona, New Mexico and Utah, summer is the high season, coinciding with school vacations in both North America and Europe. Traditionally, Memorial Day weekend (end of May) to Labor Day weekend (beginning of September) is the vacation season; expect higher prices and more crowds except in hot southern Arizona, where luxury resorts cut their prices in half.

Winter visitors flock to the highlands for great skiing. Utah has world-class skiing and New Mexico is pretty good. If you don't enjoy hurtling down snow-covered mountains, head to southern Arizona. Hotels in Phoenix, Tucson and other southern Arizona towns consider winter (Christmas to May) their high (and more expensive) season. While the rest of the country is buried under snowdrifts, southern Arizonans enjoy T-shirt weather most days.

Spring and fall is less crowded, but some services may not be available then.

Maps

Free state maps are available from state tourist information offices and welcome centers. Members of the American Automobile Association (AAA) and its foreign affiliates (see Useful Organizations, later in this chapter) can receive free state maps from AAA offices, as well as their *Indian Country* map, which covers the Four Corners area in excellent detail. AAA also has maps of major cities. AAA maps are available to nonmembers for a few dollars. City maps are often provided by chambers of commerce for free or at nominal cost.

National parks provide free maps after you pay the entrance fee. US Forest Service (USFS) ranger stations sell maps of their national forest lands. Topographic maps published by the US Geological Survey (USGS) are sold at camping stores, US National Park visitor centers and USFS ranger stations. 1:62,500 (approximately 1 inch= 1 mile) or 1:24,000 maps are ideal for backcountry use.

Many outdoor equipment stores sell the DeLorme Mapping series of individual state atlases that contain detailed topographic and highway maps at a scale of 1:250,000.

What to Bring

The Southwest generally has a casual attitude, and people's clothing reflects that. Few restaurants expect men to wear ties or jackets. Southern Arizonans wear shorts and T-shirts all summer long, but if you are heading into the highlands, you'll need some warmer clothes for the evening, even in midsummer. Use the climate charts in this book to help you decide what to pack for your visit.

For much of the year, severe sunburn is a real possibility, so bring plenty of sunblock. A broad-brimmed hat and sunglasses are important, too. Bring a water bottle if you plan on doing any walking outside of towns; the heat will prostrate you very quickly. Don't forget prescription medicines, spare contact lenses or glasses, and copies of your prescriptions.

If you are staying in the cheapest motels, a travel alarm clock is useful. (Wake-up calls can be arranged in better hotels.) Some travelers bring a small immersion heater and a cup to heat up water for instant coffee or soup in their room.

TOURIST OFFICES

Many towns don't have tourist offices per se – this function is often performed by local chambers of commerce. They can provide local information about what to see and where to stay, but their degree of usefulness is far from uniform. Reference sections of public libraries are also useful sources of local information.

State tourist offices can send you informative, colorful brochures about their states' main attractions. These free brochures are updated annually and contain addresses and telephone numbers of chambers of commerce, hotel lists and other useful information. State tourist offices may be able to answer specific questions or refer you to the appropriate office. The Utah Travel Council also publishes an annual *Winter Vacation Planner* brochure with detailed information about each ski area. These brochures are available in many chambers of commerce and tourist offices, including the state tourist offices listed below.

Arizona Office of Tourism (☎ 602-230-7733, 800-842-8257, 888-520-3433), 2702 N Third St, Suite 4015, Phoenix, AZ 85004
website: www.arizonaguide.com

New Mexico Dept of Tourism (☎ 505-827-7400, 800-545-2040, 800-733-6396), 491 Old Santa Fe Trail, Santa Fe NM 87501
website: www.newmexico.org

Utah Travel Council (☎ 801-538-1030, 800-200-1160), Council Hall/Capitol Hill, Salt Lake City, UT 84114
website: www.utah.com

VISAS & DOCUMENTS
Passport & Visas

Canadians must have proper proof of Canadian citizenship, such as a citizenship card with photo ID, or a passport. Visitors from other countries must have valid passports and many visitors also must have a US visa.

There is a reciprocal visa-waiver program in which citizens of certain countries may enter the USA for stays of 90 days or less with a passport but without first obtaining a US visa. Currently these countries are Andorra, Argentina, Australia, Austria, Belgium, Brunei, Denmark, Finland, France, Germany, Iceland, Ireland, Italy, Japan, Liechtenstein, Luxembourg, Monaco, the Netherlands, New Zealand, Norway, San Marino, Spain, Sweden, Switzerland and the UK. Under this program you must have a roundtrip ticket that is nonrefundable in the USA, and you will not be allowed to extend your stay beyond 90 days.

HIV & Entering the USA

Everyone entering the USA who isn't a US citizen is subject to the authority of the Immigration & Naturalization Service (INS). The INS can keep someone from entering or staying in the USA by excluding or deporting them. This is especially relevant to travelers with HIV. Though being HIV-positive is not grounds for deportation, it is 'grounds for exclusion' and the INS can invoke it to refuse admission.

Although the INS doesn't test people for HIV at customs, it may try to exclude anyone who answers yes to this question on the non-immigrant visa application form: 'Have you ever been afflicted with a communicable disease of public health significance?' INS officials may also stop people if they seem sick, are carrying AIDS/HIV medicine or, sadly, if the officer happens to think the person 'looks gay,' though sexual orientation is not legally grounds for exclusion.

It's imperative that visitors know and assert their rights. Immigrants and visitors who may face exclusion should discuss their rights and options with a trained immigration advocate before applying for a visa. For legal immigration information and referrals to immigration advocates, contact the National Immigration Project of the National Lawyers Guild (☎ 617-227-9727), 14 Beacon St, Suite 506, Boston, MA 02108; or Immigrant HIV Assistance Project, Bar Association of San Francisco (☎ 415-267-0795), 685 Market St, Suite 700, San Francisco, CA 94105.

Other travelers will need to obtain a visa from a US consulate or embassy. In some countries the process can be done by mail.

Your passport should be valid for at least six months longer than your intended stay in the USA. You will need to submit a recent photo 1½ inches square (37mm x 37mm) with the application. Documents showing financial stability and/or guarantees from a US resident may be required, particularly if you are coming from a developing country.

Visa applicants may be required to 'demonstrate binding obligations' that will ensure their return to their countries. Because of this requirement, those planning to travel through other countries before arriving in the USA are generally better off applying for their US visa while they are still in their home country – rather than while on the road.

The validity period for US visitor visas depends on what country you're from. The length of time you'll be allowed to stay in the USA is ultimately determined by US immigration authorities at the port of entry.

The US State Dept has a Visa Services page online that contains a good deal of information on various kinds of visas: http://travel.state.gov/visa_services.html. It also includes a list of embassy phone and fax numbers and addresses.

Although Canadians do not need their passports to visit the US, they and US citizens may want to bring them along to the Southwest, in the event they're tempted to extend their travels into Mexico or beyond. All visitors should bring their driver's licenses and any health-insurance or travel-insurance cards.

You'll need a picture ID to show that you are over 21 to buy alcohol or gain admission to bars or clubs (make sure your driver's license has a photo on it, or else get some other form of ID).

For information on work visas and employment in the US, see Work, later in this chapter.

Visa Extensions & Re-Entry If you want, need or hope to stay in the USA longer than the date stamped on your passport, go to the local Immigration & Naturalization Service (INS) office *before* the stamped date to apply for an extension. (To locate the nearest INS office, look in the blue section of the local white pages telephone directory under 'US Government' or call ☎ 800-755-0777). Applying late usually will lead to an unamusing conversation with an INS official who will assume you want to work illegally. If you find yourself in that situation, it's a good idea to bring a US citizen with you to vouch for your character. It's also a good idea to have some verification that you have enough money to support yourself.

Travel Insurance

No matter how you're traveling, make sure you take out travel insurance. This should cover you not only for medical expenses and luggage theft or loss, but also for cancellations or delays in your travel arrangements, and everyone should be covered for the worst possible case, such as an accident that requires hospital treatment and a flight home. Coverage depends on your insurance and type of ticket, so ask both your insurer and your ticket-issuing agency to explain the finer points. STA Travel and Council Travel offer travel insurance options at reasonable prices. Ticket loss is also covered by travel insurance. Make sure you have a separate record of all your ticket details – or better still, a photocopy of it. Also make a copy of your policy, in case the original is lost.

Buy travel insurance as early as possible. If you buy it the week before you fly, you may find, for instance, that you're not covered for delays to your flight caused by strikes or other industrial action that may have been in force before you took out the insurance.

International Driving Permit

An International Driving Permit is a useful accessory for foreign visitors in the USA. Local traffic police are more likely to accept it as valid identification than an unfamiliar document from another country. Your national automobile association can provide one for a nominal fee. They're usually valid for one year.

Other Documents

If you plan on doing a lot of driving in the USA, it would be beneficial to join your national automobile association. See Useful Organizations, later in this chapter, for more information.

Most hostels in the USA are members of Hostelling International-American Youth Hostel (HI-AYH). HI is managed by the International Youth Hostel Federation (IYHF). You can purchase membership on the spot when checking in, or purchase it before you leave home.

If you're a student, get an international student ID or bring along a school or university ID card to take advantage of the discounts available to students.

All people over the age of 65 get discounts throughout the USA. All you need is ID with proof of age. In some cases, people over 60 or 62 are considered seniors, so ask. There are organizations, such as the AARP (see Senior Travelers later), that offer membership cards for discounts and extend coverage to citizens of other countries.

Copies

Before you leave home, you should photocopy all important documents (passport data page and visa page, credit cards, travel insurance policy, air/bus/train tickets, driver's license, etc). Leave one copy with someone at home and keep another with you, separate from the originals.

It's also a good idea to store details of your vital travel documents in Lonely Planet's free online Travel Vault in case you lose the photocopies or can't be bothered with them. Your password-protected Travel Vault is accessible online anywhere in the world – create it at www.ekno.lonely-planet.com.

EMBASSIES & CONSULATES
US Embassies & Consulates

Some US diplomatic offices abroad include the following:

Australia
(☎ 2-6270-5900), 21 Moonah Place, Yarralumla ACT 2600
(☎ 2-9373-9200), Level 59 MLC Centre 19-29 Martin Place, Sydney NSW 2000
(☎ 3-9526-5900), 553 St Kilda Rd, Melbourne, Victoria

Canada
(☎ 613-238-5335), 490 Sussex Dr, Ottawa, Ontario K1N 1G8

(☎ 604-685-4311), 1095 W Pender St, Vancouver, BC V6E 2M6
(☎ 514-398-9695), 1155 rue St-Alexandre, Montreal, Quebec

France
(☎ 01 43 12 48 76), 2 rue Saint Florentin, 75001 Paris

Germany
(☎ 30-8305-0), Neustädtische Kirchstr.4-5, 100117 Berlin

Ireland
(☎ 1-668-8777), 42 Elgin Rd, Ballsbridge, Dublin 4

Israel
(☎ 3-519-7575), 71 Hayarkon St, Tel Aviv 63903

Japan
(☎ 3-224-5000), 10-5 Akasaka Chome, Minato-ku, Tokyo 107-8420

Mexico
(☎ 5-209-9100), Paseo de la Reforma 305, Colonia Cuauhtémoc, 06500 Mexico City

Netherlands
(☎ 70-310-9209), Lange Voorhout 102, 2514 EJ, The Hague
(☎ 20-575-5309), Museumplein 19, 1071 DJ Amsterdam

New Zealand
(☎ 644-722-2068), 29 Fitzherbert Terrace, Thorndon, Wellington

United Kingdom
(☎ 20-7499-2000), 24 Grosvenor Sq, London W1A 1AE
(☎ 31-556-8315), 3 Regent Terrace, Edinburgh EH7 5BW
(☎ 28-9032-8239), Queens House, 14 Queen St, Belfast BT1 6EQ

Foreign Embassies & Consulates in the US

Most nations' main consuls or embassies are in Washington, DC. To find the telephone number of your embassy or consul, call Washington, DC, directory assistance (☎ 202-555-1212).

There are a few foreign consular offices in the Southwest. Albuquerque has Mexican and German consuls; Salt Lake City has Mexican, Guatemalan, New Zealand, Swiss, French, Norwegian and Italian consuls; Phoenix has Mexican, Dutch, German and Swiss consuls; and Tucson has a Mexican consul. These lists change often and are found in the yellow pages of telephone directories under 'Consulates.' There is a

Your Own Embassy

It's important to realize what your own embassy – the embassy of the country of which you are a citizen – can and can't do to help you if you get into trouble. Generally speaking, it won't be much help in emergencies if the trouble you're in is remotely your own fault. Remember that you are bound by the laws of the country you are in. Your embassy will not be sympathetic if you end up in jail after committing a crime locally, even if such actions are legal in your own country.

In genuine emergencies, you might get some assistance, but only if other channels have been exhausted. If you need to get home urgently, a free ticket home is exceedingly unlikely – the embassy would expect you to have insurance. If all your money and documents are stolen, it might assist you with getting a new passport, but a loan for onward travel is out of the question.

Some embassies used to keep letters for travelers or have a small reading room with home newspapers, but these days most of the mail-holding services have been stopped and even newspapers tend to be out of date.

consulate for the UK in Los Angeles (☎ 310-477-3322).

CUSTOMS

US Customs allows each person over the age of 21 to bring 1 liter of liquor and 200 cigarettes duty-free into the USA. US citizens are allowed to import, duty-free, $400 worth of gifts from abroad, and non-US citizens are allowed to bring in $100 worth. Should you be carrying more than $10,000 in US and foreign cash, traveler's checks, money orders or the like, you need to declare the excess amount. There is no legal restriction on the amount that may be imported, but undeclared sums in excess of $10,000 may be subject to confiscation. Agricultural inspection stations at the Arizona-California border may ask you to surrender fruit when entering California, in an attempt to halt the spread of pests associated with the fruit.

MONEY
Currency & Exchange Rates

The US dollar ($) is divided into 100 cents (¢). Coins come in denominations of 1¢ (penny), 5¢ (nickel), 10¢ (dime), 25¢ (quarter), 50¢ (half-dollar) and $1 (dollar); the latter two are infrequently seen. Quarters are the most useful in vending machines and parking meters.

Bills (paper currency) are all the same size and color, regardless of denomination; bills come in $1, $2 (rare), $5, $10, $20, $50 and $100. Many places won't accept bills larger than $20.

At press time, exchange rates were:

country	unit		US dollar
Australia	A$1	=	$0.50
Canada	C$1	=	$0.63
euro	€1	=	$0.90
France	FF1	=	$0.14
Germany	DM1	=	$0.46
Hong Kong	HK$1	=	$0.13
Japan	¥10	=	$0.80
New Zealand	NZ$1	=	$0.41
United Kingdom	UK£1	=	$1.46

Exchanging Money

Some banks exchange cash or traveler's checks in major foreign currencies, though banks in outlying areas do this infrequently and it may take them some time. It's easier to exchange foreign currency in larger cities. Additionally, Thomas Cook, American Express and exchange windows in international airports offer exchange (although you'll get a better rate at a bank or at home).

Cash & Traveler's Checks Though carrying cash is more risky, it's still a good idea to travel with some for the convenience; it's useful for tips and some smaller places may not accept credit cards or traveler's checks. Traveler's checks offer greater protection from theft or loss and in many places they can be used as cash. American Express and

Thomas Cook are widely accepted and have efficient replacement policies.

Keeping a record of the check numbers and the checks you have used is vital to replace lost checks. Keep this record separate from the checks themselves.

You'll save yourself trouble and expense if you buy traveler's checks in US dollars. The savings you *might* make on exchange rates by carrying traveler's checks in a foreign currency doesn't make up for the hassle of exchanging them at banks and other facilities. Restaurants, hotels and most stores accept US-dollar traveler's checks as if they were cash, so if you're carrying traveler's checks in US dollars, the odds are you'll rarely have to use a bank or pay an exchange fee.

Take large-denomination checks. It's only toward the end of a stay that you may want to change a small check so that you aren't left with too much local currency.

Credit & Debit Cards Major credit and charge cards are widely accepted by car-rental agencies and most hotels, restaurants, gas stations, shops and larger grocery stores. The most commonly accepted cards are Visa, MasterCard and, to a lesser extent, American Express.

It's virtually impossible to rent a car without a credit card and they are useful for hotel reservations and ticket agencies.

Places that accept Visa and MasterCard are also likely to accept debit cards. Unlike a credit card, a debit card deducts payment directly from the user's bank account. Sometimes a minimal fee is charged for the transaction. Check with your bank to confirm that your debit card will be accepted in other states; debit cards from large commercial banks can often be used worldwide. Check with your bank or credit card company about which toll-free number you should call if you need to report a card lost or stolen.

ATMs Most banks, airports, shopping malls, and some grocery stores have ATMs, usually open 24 hours a day. There are various ATM networks and most banks are affiliated with several. Some of the most common are Cirrus, Plus, Star and Interlink. For a nominal service charge, you can withdraw cash from an ATM using a credit or debit card. Credit card companies usually charge a 2% fee ($2 minimum), but cards linked to your personal checking account usually give fee-free cash advances from any branch of your bank. Check with your bank or credit card company for detailed information.

Security Be cautious – but not paranoid – about carrying money. If your hotel has a safe, keep your valuables and excess cash in it. It's best not to display large amounts of cash in public. A money belt worn under your clothes is a good place to carry excess currency when you're on the move or otherwise unable to stash it in a safe. Avoid carrying your wallet in a back pocket of your pants. This is a prime target for pickpockets, as are handbags and the outside pockets of day packs and fanny packs (bum bags). See Dangers & Annoyances later in this chapter.

Costs The best way to get around is by car, because intercity buses, trains and planes are not very cheap, nor do they go to the out-of-the-way places. Car rental is available in most towns of any size, and rates can be as cheap as $100 a week for the smallest (subcompact) cars – these are off-season rates. More often, though, rentals begin around $140 for a week. A midsize car is about $40 more and jeeps or 4WD vehicles can be as high as $90 a day. Insurance, if you are not already covered by a credit card or personal insurance policy, is usually another $7 to $12 a day. Gas (petrol) is cheap, ranging from about $1.40 to over $2 for a US gallon, depending on the location, grade of fuel and international economic factors.

Those on a very tight budget can camp for free on public lands in many places and cook for themselves. Maintained campgrounds range from about $6 for basic places with cooking grills and pit toilets to over $20 for some full-service campgrounds with RV (recreational vehicle) hookups.

Youth hostels are few and charge around $12 to $18 per person. Cheap and basic motels from about $20 a double are often a better deal for budget travelers. Some towns (for example, Gallup, Tucumcari and Flagstaff) are known for their motel strips full of places advertising rooms for about $20. Most other towns have basic motels beginning at around $30 for a double room and going up from there.

Travelers looking for more than a basic room can find satisfactory mid-range accommodations for $40 to $80 a double in most places, and some towns have luxury hotels with rooms over $100. World-class resorts, spas and dude ranches charge $200 to $400 a day. Some Southwestern towns are relatively expensive – Sedona, Santa Fe, Taos and Park City are among these. High demand for rooms in national park lodges pushes rates to $80 and more. B&Bs (bed & breakfasts) are not for budget travelers; most are in the $90 to $200 range.

Meals also vary tremendously in price. Cheap fast-food joints are ubiquitous. Mexican restaurants abound in the Southwest and offer great meals for well under $10. A large pizza – enough for two – can be had for $10 and up. You can eat well in any town for less than $25 per person for a complete meal with wine. For a splurge, try first-class restaurants in bigger cities, where dinner for two will go well over $100.

Tipping Tips are expected in restaurants and better hotels. You also should tip taxi drivers, hairdressers and baggage carriers. In restaurants and bars, wait staff are paid minimal wages and rely upon tips for their livelihoods. Tip 15% unless the service is terrible (in which case a complaint to the manager is warranted) or up to 20% if the service is great. Don't tip in fast-food, take-out or buffet-style restaurants where you serve yourself.

Taxi drivers expect 10% to 15%; hairdressers get 15% if their service is satisfactory. Baggage carriers (skycaps in airports, bellboys in hotels) receive $1 for the first bag and 50¢ for each additional bag carried, or more if they go a long way. In better

hotels, housekeeping staff get $1 or $2 a day, and parking valets get $1 or $2 upon delivering your car.

Taxes Almost everything you pay for in the USA is taxed. Occasionally, the tax is included in the advertised price (eg, gas, drinks in a bar, transportation tickets and museum or theater entrance tickets). Restaurant meals and drinks, motel rooms and most other purchases are taxed, and this is added to the advertised cost.

You'll pay different taxes in every town. Most restaurants add 6% to 8% to the bill, most hotels add 9% to 14%, and most car-rental companies add 10% to 15%, though those at airports add over 20%. The prices given in this book do not reflect local taxes; always ask.

POST & COMMUNICATIONS
Postal Rates
Postage rates increase every few years. At the time of this writing, 1st-class mail within the USA cost 34¢ for letters up to 1 ounce (23¢ for each additional ounce) and 21¢ for postcards.

International airmail rates (except to Canada and Mexico) are 60¢ for a half-ounce letter and 40¢ for each additional half ounce. International postcard rates are 50¢. Letters to Canada are 48¢ for a half-ounce letter and 45¢ for a postcard. Letters to Mexico are 40¢ for a half-ounce letter, 40¢ for a postcard. Aerogrammes are 60¢.

The cost for parcels airmailed anywhere within the USA is $3.20 for 2lb or less, increasing up to $6.50 for 5lb. For heavier items, rates differ according to the distance mailed. Books, periodicals and computer disks can be sent by a cheaper 4th-class rate. For rates, office address and zip code information, call ☎ 800-275-8777 or check www.usps.com.

Sending Mail
If you have the correct postage, you can drop your mail into any blue mailbox. However, to send a package of more than 16 ounces, to buy stamps or weigh your mail go to a post office. The address of each

town's main post office is given in the text. Larger towns have branch post offices and post-office centers in some supermarkets and drugstores.

Usually, post offices in main towns are open from 8 am to 5 pm Monday to Friday and 8 am to 3 pm on Saturday.

Receiving Mail

You can have mail sent to you care of General Delivery at any post office that has its own 5-digit zip (postal) code. Mail is usually held for 10 days before it's returned to sender; you might request that your correspondents write 'hold for arrival' on their letters. Mail should be addressed like this:

Name
c/o General Delivery
Caballo, NM 87931

Alternatively, have mail sent to the local American Express or Thomas Cook representative. Both companies provide mail service for their customers.

Telephone

All phone numbers within the USA consist of a three-digit area code followed by a seven-digit local number. If you are calling locally, just dial the seven-digit number. If you are calling long distance, dial 1 + the three-digit area code + the seven-digit number. If you're calling from abroad, the international country code for the USA is '1.'

For local directory assistance, dial ☎ 411. For directory assistance outside your area code, dial 1 + the three-digit area code of the place you want to call + 555-1212. Area codes for places outside the region are listed in telephone directories. If you aren't sure of the area code of the place you want to call, try 1 + 411, which can give you numbers nationwide from many phones in the Southwest. Directory assistance calls cost up to 95¢.

Due to skyrocketing demand for phone numbers (for faxes, cellular phones, etc), many areas are being divided into multiple new area codes. These changes are not reflected in older phone books. Operators can help in these cases.

The 800, 888 or 877 area codes are for toll-free numbers within the USA, and may work from Canada. These might not be available if dialing locally. Call ☎ 800-555-1212 to request a company's toll-free number.

The 900 area code is for numbers for which the caller pays a premium rate.

Rates Local calls usually cost 50¢ at pay phones. Many mid-range and top-end hotels add a service charge of 50¢ to $1 for local calls made from a room phone and also have hefty surcharges for long-distance calls. Public pay phones, found in many hotel lobbies, are cheaper. You can pump in quarters, use a phone card or make collect calls from pay phones. A new long-distance alternative is phone debit cards, which allow purchasers to pay $5, $10, $20 or $50 in advance, with access through an 800 number.

Long-distance rates vary depending on the destination and which telephone company you use – call the operator (☎ 0) for rates information. Don't ask the operator to put your call through, however, because operator-assisted calls are much more expensive than direct-dial calls. Generally, nights (11 pm to 8 am), all day Saturday and from 8 am to 5 pm Sunday are the cheapest (60% discount) times to call. A 35% discount applies in the evenings from 5 to 11 pm Sunday to Friday. Daytime calls (8 am to 5 pm Monday to Friday) are full-price calls within the USA.

eKno There's a wide range of local and international phone cards. Lonely Planet's eKno Communication Card is aimed specifically at independent travelers and provides budget international calls, a range of messaging services, free email and travel information – for local calls, you're usually better off with a local card. You can join online at www.ekno.lonelyplanet.com or by phone by dialing ☎ 800-707-0031. To use eKno from the US once you have joined, dial ☎ 800-706-1333.

Check the eKno website for membership information, access numbers from other countries, and updates on super budget local access numbers and other new features.

International Calls To make an international call direct, dial ☎ 011, then the country code, followed by the area code and the phone number. You may need to wait as long as 45 seconds for the ringing to start. International rates vary depending on the time of day, telephone company used and the destination. Call the operator (☎ 0) for rates. The first minute is always more expensive than extra minutes.

Fax
Fax machines are easy to find in the US at shipping companies like Mail Boxes Etc, photocopy stores and hotel business service centers, but be prepared to pay high prices (over $1 a page).

Email & Internet Access
Free Internet access is available at most public libraries during library hours. In large towns, photocopy centers such as Kinko's are open 24 hrs and charge 20¢ per minute. Internet cafés are limited to larger or popular towns and charge around 10¢ a minute. Hotel business centers and major airports charge about $4 for 15 minutes. If you have a laptop and modem, you can connect with the Internet from most hotel rooms.

INTERNET RESOURCES
The World Wide Web is a rich resource for travelers. You can research your trip, hunt down bargain airfares, book hotels, check on weather conditions and chat with locals and other travelers about the best places to visit (or avoid!).

There's no better place to start your Web explorations than the Lonely Planet website (www.lonelyplanet.com). Here you'll find succinct summaries on traveling to most places on earth, postcards from other travelers and the Thorn Tree bulletin board, where you can ask questions before you go or dispense advice when you get back. You can also find travel news and updates for many of our most popular guidebooks. The subWWWay section links you to the most

useful travel resources available elsewhere on the Web.

Thousands of Southwestern businesses, hotels and other organizations have websites; many are mentioned in appropriate parts of the book. Good starting points for travelers are websites sponsored by state travel organizations (see Tourist Offices, earlier in this chapter) which have links to hundreds of other Internet resources that feature anything from cities to hotels to ski resorts.

The National Park Service has a website with links to sites for every park and monument at www.nps.gov. To make reservations for any US Forest Service campground, go to www.reserveusa.com. Lonely Planet's website (www.lonelyplanet.com) has summaries to travel everywhere on earth, as well as postcards from readers, the Thorn Tree bulletin board, Scoop travel news and many other updates and links.

Don't forget to add 'http://' to the beginning of the URLs given throughout this book.

BOOKS
Most books are published in different editions by different publishers in different countries. As a result, a book might be a hardcover rarity in one country but readily available in paperback in another. Fortunately, bookstores and libraries can search by title or author, so your local bookstore or library is best placed to advise you on the availability of the following recommendations.

Tens of thousands of books have been written about the Southwest, and many have comprehensive indexes that will lead you as far as you want to go. Some are updated periodically; check that you are getting the most recent edition. For books dealing specifically with outdoor activities, see the recommendations under the appropriate headings in the Outdoor Activities chapter.

Lonely Planet
Rocky Mountains and *USA* will give plenty of information for travels outside of the Southwest, and *Las Vegas* is full of details

about that gritty and glamorous city. Outdoorsy types should check out *Hiking in the USA*. If you're heading south, get a copy of *Mexico*.

Archaeology & History

Those Who Came Before by Robert H and Florence C Lister is an excellent source of readable information about the prehistory of the Southwest and about the archaeological sites of the national parks and monuments of this area. It is extensively indexed.

The best general history is *The Southwest* by David Lavender. It has a detailed (if dated) index. *The Smithsonian Guide to Historic America – The Desert States* by Michael S Durham is a beautifully illustrated guide to the historic sites of the region.

New Mexico by Calvin A and Susan A Roberts is probably the best book on that state's history through the early 1980s. *Arizona: A History* by Thomas E Sheridan covers the area from prehistoric times through the early 1990s. *The Gathering of Zion* by Wallace Stegner is an evocative history of the Mormon migration to Utah.

Geology

Basin and Range by John McPhee is as much a journey as a popular geological text. It covers Nevada as well as Utah, and is a recommended read. An introduction for the nonspecialist is *The Colorado Plateau: A Geologic History* by Donald L Baars.

Roadside Geology of Arizona, Roadside Geology of New Mexico and *Roadside Geology of Utah,* all by Halka Chronic, are good guides for the curious nongeologist. They describe the geology along major roads and are well illustrated.

Natural History

A tremendous variety of books will help you identify Southwestern plants and animals, tell you where you can see them and give you insight into their biology. The Peterson Field Guide series has over forty titles and is recommended. The Golden Field Guide series is known for its simple approach and is often preferred by begin-

ners. The National Geographic Society's *Field Guide to the Birds of North America* is well done and one of the most detailed. The series of Audubon Society Field Guides covers birds, plants and animals, arranged by color and using photos – a departure from the standard field guides, which are arranged in biological sequence and are illustrated by color paintings. The Audubon Society Nature Guide *Deserts,* by James A MacMahon, gives a fine overview of all four Southwestern deserts, as well as being a field guide to the most important plants and animals of these regions. An excellent series of pocket books published by the Southwest Parks & Monuments Association in Tucson helps you identify the region's plants.

Birders may want to supplement their field guides with *Birds in Southeastern Arizona* by William A Davis and Stephen M Russell, which describes the seasonal distribution and abundance of birds in what is one of the premier birding 'hot spots' in the country, and gives directions on how to travel to scores of the best birding areas.

Utah Wildlife Viewing Guide by Jim Cole, *Arizona Wildlife Viewing Guide* by John N Carr and *New Mexico Wildlife Viewing Guide* by Jane S MacCarter list scores of places to see wildlife. They include information on access, and on the probability of seeing the most important species at specific sites.

Several excellent books about Southwestern natural history are designed to be read rather than used as field guides. These include John Alcock's excellent and very readable *Sonoran Desert Spring* and *Sonoran Desert Summer. Gathering the Desert* by Gary Paul Nabhan describes in splendid and fascinating detail 12 desert plants and their importance to Native Americans.

Ann Zwinger writes eloquently in *The Mysterious Lands: A Naturalist Explores the Four Great Deserts of the Southwest.* In her *Run, River, Run: A Naturalist's Journey down One of the Great Rivers of the American West* she describes her journey down the Green River from its headwaters in

Wyoming to its confluence with the Colorado River in southeastern Utah.

Native Americans

The best introduction for the serious student is the 20-volume Handbook of North American Indians (Smithsonian Institution). The volumes that cover this region are *Volume 9: Southwest* and *Volume 10: Southwest* edited by Alfonso Ortiz, and *Volume 11: Great Basin* edited by Warren L D'Azevedo.

An even better introduction for the generalist is *The People: Indians of the Southwest* by Stephen Trimble. The author traveled among the area's many tribes, photographing and interviewing them for almost a decade. Much of the book is in the words of the Indians themselves. It is a remarkable and satisfying work. The excellent 14-page annotated bibliography will lead you to many other books.

Some introductions to Southwestern Indian arts and crafts include *Navajo Rugs: How to Find, Evaluate, Buy and Care for Them* by Don Dedera; *Hopi Kachinas: The Complete Guide to Collecting Kachina Dolls* by Barton Wright; and *Hopi Silver: The History and Hallmarks of Hopi Silversmithing* by Margaret Wright.

Though it covers only sites in Utah, *Guide to Rock Art of the Utah Region* by Dennis Slifer is an authoritative overview of our current knowledge about prehistoric Indian cultures and their petroglyphs and pictographs.

Native Roads by Fran Kosik, subtitled *The Complete Motoring Guide to the Navajo and Hopi Nations,* does an excellent job describing the history, and native cultures to be experienced, along the highways through and around these reservations.

Native American writers are mentioned in the section on fiction.

Fiction

It comes as some surprise that one of the earliest novels about the Southwest is Arthur Conan Doyle's first Sherlock Holmes mystery, *A Study in Scarlet* (1887). Half the book is set in the 'Alkali Plains' of Mormon Utah. Another surprise is that the author of *Ben Hur,* written in 1880, was New Mexico Governor Lew Wallace. Other early novels of note include Zane Grey's westerns, of which *Riders of the Purple Sage* is the best known. Grey spent years living in Arizona. *Death Comes for the Archbishop* by Willa Cather is a 1927 novel based on the life of Bishop Jean Baptiste Lamy, who was the first archbishop of Santa Fe. It gives insights into New Mexican life during territorial days. Oliver La Farge won a Pulitzer Prize for his 1929 *Laughing Boy,* a somewhat romantic portrayal of Navajo life.

House Made of Dawn won Kiowa novelist and poet N Scott Momaday a Pulitzer Prize. His theme of a Pueblo Indian's struggle to return physically and spiritually to his home after fighting in WWII is echoed in another superb book, *Ceremony,* by Leslie Marmon Silko. Silko, herself a Pueblo Indian, is one of the best Southwestern novelists. Some other critically acclaimed novels by Silko include *Almanac of the Dead* and *Storyteller.*

Tony Hillerman, an Anglo, writes award-winning mystery novels that take place on the Navajo, Hopi and Zuni Reservations. Even Indians find his writing true to life. Following the adventures of Navajo policemen Jim Chee and Joe Leaphorn is a lot of fun, particularly when you are driving around the reservations of the Four Corners area. Hillerman's first mystery novel was *The Blessing Way* in 1970, and he has written over a dozen since then.

The Monkey Wrench Gang, by Edward Abbey, is hugely fun to read, which is more than can be said of many classic novels, and this one certainly is a classic. It's a fictional and comic account of real people who become 'eco-warriors'; their plan is to blow up Glen Canyon Dam before it floods Glen Canyon. You don't have to believe in industrial sabotage to enjoy this book, or any of his others. *The Milagro Beanfield War* by John Nichols tells the story of bean growers trying to protect their New Mexican lands against developers. It's a good book, and a good movie, too (directed by Robert Redford).

An acclaimed recent Southwestern novelist is Barbara Kingsolver, whose novels are superb portrayals of people living in the Southwest. *The Bean Trees* echoes the author's own life – a young woman from rural Kentucky moves to Tucson. *Animal Dreams* gives wonderful insights into the lives of people from a small Hispanic village near the Arizona–New Mexico border and from an Indian pueblo. Don't miss these books.

Author Picks
Desert Solitaire: Season in the Wilderness by Edward Abbey describes the author's job as a park ranger in Arches National Park in the 1950s, when the park was still a monument reached by a dirt road and locals easily outnumbered tourists in nearby Moab. Abbey shares his philosophy and passions about the desert, the mismanagement of the Southwest, and the problems of mass tourism – which he foresaw with striking clarity. This book is a classic.

Another important book is *Grizzly Years: In Search of the American Wilderness* by Doug Peacock. The author was a friend of Edward Abbey's (one of the Monkey Wrench Gang members was based on Peacock) and is one of the world's experts on grizzly bears. Although much of the action takes place in the northern Rockies, with Vietnam flashbacks, the narrative occasionally returns to Tucson, where the author lives. Another Abbey protégé is Charles Bowden, who wrote eloquent essays about Arizona in *Blue Desert* and *Frog Mountain Blues*.

The curiously named *Jack Ruby's Kitchen Sink* by Tom Miller is accurately subtitled *Offbeat Travels Through America's Southwest*. It's a quirky read that will satisfyingly accompany your own Southwestern odyssey. Other insightful essays on the Southwest are found in *The Telling Distance* by Bruce Berger.

Also consider reading *Cadillac Desert: The American West and Its Disappearing Water* by Marc Reisner, a thorough account of how the exploding populations of Western states have utilized every possible

drop of available water. *The Man Who Walked Through Time* by Colin Fletcher tells the story of the author's many weeks backpacking the length of the Grand Canyon – the first account of such a trip and a seminal book on the modern 'sport' of backpacking.

Naturalist Terry Tempest Williams writes from the perspective of an avowedly liberal Mormon woman; her first book, *Refuge,* is an evocative, complex personal portrait of family, Mormons and nature. To learn more about the Southwest's dubious environmental record, particularly as it pertains to Utah, read *Canaries on the Rim: Living Downwind in the West* by Chip Ward.

NEWSPAPERS
Of over 1500 daily newspapers published in the USA, those with the highest circulation include the *Wall Street Journal* (with an emphasis on financial and business news), *USA Today* (general US and world news), the *New York Times* and the *Los Angeles Times,* all of which are available in main cities.

Major Southwestern newspapers are published in Salt Lake City, Albuquerque, Phoenix and Tucson – see those cities for details. These papers are generally available in many other towns in their respective states.

RADIO & TV
All rental cars have radios. In the southern parts of the region, stations broadcasting from Mexico (in Spanish) can easily be picked up. In and near major cities, you have scores of stations to choose from, with a wide variety of music and entertainment. In rural areas, be prepared for a predominance of country & western music, Christian programming, local news and 'talk radio.' National Public Radio features a more level-headed approach to news, discussion, music and more. NPR stations usually broadcast on the lower end of the FM dial.

All the major TV networks have affiliated stations throughout the USA. These include ABC, CBS, NBC, FOX (all commercial stations) and PBS (noncommercial

Public Broadcasting System). Cable News Network (CNN), a cable channel, provides almost continuous news coverage. There are many other cable stations such as ESPN (sports), HBO (mainly movies) and the Weather Channel. Almost all hotel rooms have TVs (most with cable), but many B&Bs do not.

PHOTOGRAPHY & VIDEO
Film & Equipment
Film can be damaged by excessive heat, so don't leave your camera and film in the car on a hot summer's day and avoid placing your camera on the dashboard while you are driving. Carry a spare battery for your camera to avoid disappointment when your camera dies in the middle of nowhere. If you're buying a new camera for your trip, do so several weeks before you leave and practice using it.

Color print film is widely available, but slide and black & white film is found only in larger towns. Acceptable, fast print-film developing is available in many drugstores, but professionals prefer to bring their work home to be developed in a lab they know for reliable results.

Video Systems
Overseas visitors who are considering purchasing videos should remember that the USA uses the National Television System Committee (NTSC) color TV standard, which is incompatible with other standards (PAL or SECAM) used in Africa, Europe, Asia and Australasia.

Photographing People & Places
Most Indian reservations have photography restrictions. In some, no photography of any kind is allowed. In others, you need to buy a tribal camera permit. Photographing Indians is either not allowed or allowed only with permission, and then a tip is expected. More details are given in appropriate parts of the text.

Airport Security
All passengers have to pass their luggage through X-ray machines. Most machines don't damage lower-speed film, but it's best to hand-carry film (in a see-through plastic bag) and cameras with you and ask the X-ray inspector for a visual inspection to be sure.

TIME
The Southwest is on Mountain Time, which is seven hours behind Greenwich Mean Time. Daylight saving time begins on the first Sunday in April, when clocks are put forward one hour, and ends on the last Sunday in October, when the clocks are turned back one hour.

Arizona does not use daylight saving time, and so during that period it is eight hours behind Greenwich Mean Time and one hour behind the rest of the Southwest. The Navajo Indian Reservation, most of which lies in Arizona, does use daylight saving time, but the small Hopi Indian Reservation, which is surrounded by the Navajo Indian Reservation, doesn't.

ELECTRICITY
The USA uses 110 V and 60 cycles and the plugs have two (flat) or three (two flat, one round) pins. Most European appliances will require voltage converters and plug adapters.

WEIGHTS & MEASURES
Distances are in feet (ft), yards (yds) and miles (m or mi). Three feet equal 1 yard; 1760 yards or 5280 feet equal 1 mile (1.61 kilometers). In southern Arizona and New Mexico, distances are also marked in kilometers to aid Mexican drivers on trips into the USA.

Dry weights are in ounces (oz), pounds (lb) and tons (16 ounces are one pound; 2000 pounds are one ton), but liquid measures differ from dry measures. One pint equals 16 fluid ounces; 2 pints equal 1 quart, a common measure for liquids like milk, which is also sold in gallons (4 quarts). Gasoline is dispensed in US gallons, about 20% less than Imperial gallons. Pints and quarts are also 20% less than Imperial ones. There is a conversion chart on the inside back cover of this book.

LAUNDRY

Visitors will find self-service, coin-operated laundry facilities in most towns of any size and in better campgrounds and many hotels. Washing a load costs about $1 and drying it another $1. Laundries and dry-cleaners are listed under 'Laundries' or 'Cleaners' in the yellow pages of the telephone directory.

TOILETS

Public toilets are normally free and found in shopping malls and parks. People often use the facilities in restaurants and gas stations when necessary. Toilets are commonly called bathrooms or restrooms.

HEALTH

Generally speaking, the USA is a healthy place to visit and the country is well-served by hospitals. However, because of the high cost of health care, international travelers should take out comprehensive travel insurance (see below) before they leave.

Immunizations are rarely required unless you are arriving from a country with cholera or yellow fever outbreaks.

Predeparture Preparations

Health Insurance A travel insurance policy to cover medical problems (as well as theft or loss) is recommended. Even the most cursory visit to a doctor will cost around $50, and hospitalization for two days may cost more than your entire vacation. Get insurance!

Policies vary significantly and your travel agent will have recommendations. International student travel policies handled by STA Travel or other student travel organizations are usually a good value. Some policies offer lower and higher medical expenses options. The higher one is for countries like the USA with extremely high medical costs. Check the small print.

Some policies specifically exclude 'dangerous activities' like motorcycling. Some policies pay doctors or hospitals directly. Others reimburse you after you pay, in which case keep *all* documentation. Some policies require a collect (reverse charge) call for an immediate assessment of your problem. Few policies cover emergency evacuations, body repatriation or flights home requiring two or three seats to stretch out on. This may require a separate policy.

Health Preparations Before leaving on a long trip, get a dental checkup and make sure your immunizations are up-to-date. Take spare glasses and your prescription. New spectacles are made for under $100 (except for difficult prescriptions or better frames). Take an adequate supply of necessary medications, along with prescriptions in case you lose your supply.

Everyday Health Normal body temperature is 98.6°F or 37°C; more than 2°C or 4°F higher indicates a 'high' fever. Normal adult pulse rate is 60 to 80 beats per minute (children 80 to 100, babies 100 to 140). Between 12 and 20 breaths/minute is normal for adults and older children (up to 30 for younger children, 40 for babies). People with high fever or serious respiratory illness breathe more quickly.

Travel- & Climate-Related Problems

Sunburn In the desert or at high altitude you can get sunburned in an hour, even through cloud cover. Use a sunscreen (protection factor 30+) and take extra care to cover areas not normally exposed to sun.

Heat Exhaustion Dehydration or salt deficiency can cause heat exhaustion. Take time to acclimatize to high temperatures and make sure you get enough liquids. Salt deficiency is characterized by fatigue, lethargy, headaches, giddiness and muscle cramps. Salt tablets may help. Vomiting or diarrhea can also deplete your liquid and salt levels. Anhydrotic heat exhaustion, caused by the inability to sweat, is quite rare. Unlike other forms of heat exhaustion, it may strike people who have been in a hot climate for some time, rather than newcomers. Always use water bottles on long trips. Four quarts per person per day is recommended if hiking. It's a good idea to carry jugs of drinking water in your car in case it should break down.

Heat Stroke Long, continuous exposure to high temperatures can lead to this serious, sometimes fatal, condition, which occurs when the body's heat-regulating mechanism breaks down and body temperature rises to dangerous levels. Avoid excessive alcohol intake or strenuous activity when you first arrive in a hot climate.

Symptoms include feeling unwell, lack of perspiration, and a high body temperature. Hospitalization is essential for extreme cases, but meanwhile get out of the sun, remove clothing, cover with a wet sheet or towel, and fan continually.

Hypothermia Skiers and winter hikers will find that temperatures in the mountains or desert can quickly drop below freezing. A sudden soaking or even high winds can lower your body temperature rapidly. Travel with a partner whenever possible.

Seek shelter when bad weather is unavoidable. Woolen clothing and synthetics, which retain warmth even when wet, are superior to cottons. Carry a good-quality sleeping bag and high-energy, easily digestible snacks like chocolate or dried fruit.

Get hypothermia victims out of bad weather and into dry, warm clothing. Give hot liquids (not alcohol) and high-calorie, easily digestible food. In advanced stages place victims in warm sleeping bags and get in with them. Do not rub victims.

Fungal Infections Fungal infections occur with greater frequency in hot weather. Minimize them by wearing loose, comfortable clothes, avoiding artificial fibers, washing frequently and drying carefully. If you are infected, wash the area daily with a disinfectant or medicated soap and water, rinse and dry well. Apply antifungal powder, air the infected area when possible, wash towels and underwear in hot water and change them often.

Altitude Sickness This can happen when ascending too quickly to high altitude, such

Medical Kit Check List

The following is a list of items you should consider including in your medical kit – consult your pharmacist for brands available in your country.

❏ **Aspirin or paracetamol** (acetaminophen in the USA) – for pain or fever

❏ **Antihistamine** – for allergies, (eg, hay fever); to ease the itch from insect bites or stings; and to prevent motion sickness

❏ **Cold and flu tablets, throat lozenges and nasal decongestant**

❏ **Multivitamins** – consider for long trips, when dietary vitamin intake may be inadequate

❏ **Antibiotics** – consider including these if you're traveling well off the beaten track; see your doctor, as they must be prescribed, and carry the prescription with you

❏ **Loperamide or diphenoxylate** –'blockers' for diarrhea

❏ **Prochlorperazine or metaclopramide** – for nausea and vomiting

❏ **Rehydration mixture** – to prevent dehydration, which may occur, for example, during bouts of diarrhea; particularly important when traveling with children

❏ **Insect repellent, sunscreen, lip balm and eye drops**

❏ **Calamine lotion, sting relief spray or aloe vera** – to ease irritation from sunburn and insect bites or stings

❏ **Antifungal cream or powder** – for fungal skin infections and thrush

❏ **Antiseptic (such as povidone-iodine)** – for cuts and grazes

❏ **Bandages, Band-Aids (plasters) and other wound dressings**

❏ **Water purification tablets or iodine**

❏ **Scissors, tweezers and a thermometer** – note that mercury thermometers are prohibited by airlines

as driving up to a ski resort. Lack of oxygen at high elevations causes headaches, nausea, shortness of breath, physical weakness and other symptoms that can be fatal (though rarely at Southwestern elevations). Most people recover within a day or two. If symptoms persist, descent to lower elevations is the only effective remedy. For mild cases, aspirin (or something similar) will relieve symptoms until the body adapts. Avoid smoking, alcohol, sedatives, eating heavily or exercising strenuously. Drink extra fluids. Ascend slowly where possible and sleep at lower altitudes than those reached during the day.

Motion Sickness Eating lightly before and during a trip reduces the chances of motion sickness. Those prone to motion sickness should find a place that minimizes disturbance: near the wing on aircraft, near the center on buses. Fresh air usually helps; reading, or cigarette smoke, doesn't. Commercial antimotion sickness preparations, which can cause drowsiness, should be taken before the trip commences; when you're feeling sick, it's too late. Ginger, a natural preventative, is available in capsule form.

Jet Lag This is experienced when a person flies across more than three time zones. It occurs because many body functions (temperature, pulse rate and emptying of the bladder and bowels) are regulated by internal 24-hour cycles (circadian rhythms). During jet lag, our bodies are adjusting to the 'new time' of our destination, and we may experience fatigue, disorientation, insomnia, anxiety, impaired concentration and loss of appetite. These effects usually disappear within three days of arrival.

To minimize jet lag, rest well on the days prior to departure. Select flight schedules that minimize sleep deprivation; arrive late in the day and sleep after you arrive. For very long flights, arrange a stopover. Avoid excessive eating, alcohol and smoking on flights. Drink plenty of juice or water. Wear comfortable loose clothing.

Infectious Diseases

Diarrhea Changes in water or food can cause the runs; diarrhea from contaminated food or water (uncommon in the USA) is more serious. Use bottled water if you are susceptible, and never drink from streams or lakes.

Despite precautions you may still have a mild bout of travelers' diarrhea, but this is rarely serious. Dehydration is the main danger, particularly for children, where dehydration can occur quite quickly. Fluid replacement is important. Weak black tea with a little sugar, soda water or soft drinks allowed to go flat and diluted 50% with water are all good. With severe diarrhea, a rehydrating solution is necessary to replace minerals and salts. Commercially available ORS (oral rehydration salts) are useful.

Lomotil or Imodium relieve the symptoms, but do not cure the problem. Use them only if absolutely necessary – eg, if you *must* travel.

Giardiasis Also called Giardia, this intestinal parasite is present in apparently pristine backcountry streams. Giardia can appear weeks after you have ingested contaminated water; symptoms may recur repeatedly, disappearing for a few days and then returning.

Symptoms are stomach cramps, nausea, bloated stomach, watery, foul-smelling diarrhea and frequent gas. Tinidazole (Fasigyn) or metronidazole (Flagyl) are the recommended drugs; antibiotics are useless.

HIV/AIDS Any exposure to infected blood, blood products or bodily fluids may put an individual at risk for HIV. Infection can come from practicing unprotected sex with somebody who is infected or sharing contaminated needles. Apart from abstinence, the most effective preventative is to practice safe sex using condoms. It is impossible to detect the HIV status of an otherwise healthy-looking person without a blood test.

A good resource for help and information is the US Centers for Disease Control AIDS hotline (☎ 800-342-2437).

Cuts, Bites & Stings

Cuts & Scratches Skin punctures can become infected in hot climates and may heal slowly. Treat cuts with an antiseptic such as Betadine. Where possible avoid bandages and Band-Aids, which can keep wounds wet.

Bites & Stings Bee and wasp stings are usually painful rather than dangerous. Calamine lotion gives relief, and ice packs reduce pain and swelling.

Some spiders have dangerous bites, and scorpion stings are very painful, but both are rarely fatal. Avoid bites by not using bare hands to turn over rocks or pieces of wood.

Bites from snakes do not cause instantaneous death, and antivenins are usually available. Seek medical help. The Arizona Poison Control System reports that half of reported snake bites result from people picking up the snake, either out of bravado or mistakenly assuming that the animal was dead. Keep a healthy distance away from snakes and watch where you step.

If you are bitten or stung, call Poison Control (see below). After a snake bite, avoid slashing and sucking the wound, avoid tight tourniquets (a light constricting band above the bite can help), avoid ice, keep the affected area below the level of the heart and move it as little as possible. Don't ingest alcohol or drugs. Stay calm and get to a medical facility promptly.

There are no special first-aid techniques for spider or scorpion injuries. A black widow spider bite may be barely noticeable, but their venom can be dangerous. Conenose bug bites may also require medical assistance. Bites or stings from a centipede, bee, wasp or ant may be relieved by application of ice (but don't use ice for the other critters mentioned above).

If you are hiking far from help and you are bitten or stung, hike out and get help, particularly in the case of snake and spider bites. Often, reactions are delayed for up to 12 hours and you can hike out before then. Hiking with a companion is recommended.

Also see Dangers & Annoyances later in this chapter.

Poison Control Centers These are staffed 24 hours a day and advise about bites, stings and ingested poisons of all kinds. Call (☎ 800-222-1222) anywhere in the Southwest for the one nearest you.

WOMEN TRAVELERS

If you are a woman traveler, especially traveling alone, it's a good idea to travel with a little extra awareness of your surroundings. Conducting yourself in a common-sense manner will help you to avoid most problems. For example, you're more vulnerable if you've been drinking or using drugs than if you're sober; you're more vulnerable to some dangers alone than if you're with company; and you're more vulnerable in a high-crime urban area than in a lower-crime district.

In general, exercise more vigilance in large cities than in rural areas. Try to avoid the 'bad' or unsafe neighborhoods or districts; if you must go into or through these areas, use a private vehicle (car or taxi). It's more dangerous at night, but crime can occur even in the daytime. If you are unsure which areas are considered unsafe, ask at your hotel or telephone the tourist office for advice. Tourist maps can sometimes be deceiving, compressing areas that are not tourist attractions and making the distances look shorter than they are.

While there is less to beware of in rural areas, women may still be harassed by men unaccustomed to seeing women traveling solo. Try to avoid hiking or camping alone, especially in unfamiliar places. Use the 'buddy system,' not only for protection from other humans, but also for aid in case of unexpected falls, snakebites or other injuries.

In any emergency, call the police (☎ 911). In some rural areas where 911 is not active, dial ☎ 0 for the operator. Cities and larger towns have crisis centers and women's shelters that provide help and support; these are listed in the telephone directory, or the police can refer you to them.

Men may interpret a woman drinking alone in a bar as a bid for male company, whether you intend it that way or not. If you don't want the company, most men will respect a firm but polite 'no thank you.'

At night avoid leaving your car to flag down help; turn on your hazard lights and wait for the police to arrive. Consider renting a cell phone (major car-rental companies have them) if you plan on a lot of long-distance driving. Be extra careful at night on public transit, and remember to check the time of the last bus or train before you go out.

To deal with potential dangers, many women protect themselves with a whistle, mace, cayenne pepper spray or some self-defense training. If you do decide to purchase a spray, contact a police station to find out about regulations and training classes. Laws regarding sprays vary from state to state and town to town, so be informed based on your destination. It is a federal offense to carry defensive sprays on airplanes.

The headquarters for the National Organization for Women (NOW; ☎ 202-331-0066), 1000 16th St NW, Suite 700, Washington, DC 20036, is a good resource for any woman-related information and can refer you to state and local chapters; its website is www.now.org. Planned Parenthood (☎ 212-541-7800), 810 7th Ave, New York, NY 10019, can refer you to clinics throughout the country and offer advice on medical issues. Check the yellow pages under 'Women's Organizations & Services' for local resources.

GAY & LESBIAN TRAVELERS

There are out gay people throughout the USA, but by far the most visible gay communities are in the major cities. In large coastal metropolises it is easier for gay men and women to live their lives with a certain amount of openness. As you travel into the middle of the country, it is much harder to be open. Gay travelers should be careful, *especially* in the predominantly rural areas – holding hands might get you bashed.

In the Southwest, the most active gay community is in the Phoenix area, which is hardly surprising when you consider that the Phoenix urban area has a far larger population than either of the states of Utah or New Mexico. Utah, conservative and Mormon, has almost no visible gay life outside of Salt Lake City.

Resources & Organizations

A couple of good national guidebooks are *Women's Traveller*, providing listings for lesbians, and *Damron's Address Book* for men, both published by the Damron Company (☎ 800-462-6654, 415-255-0404); information is available at www.damron.com. *Men's Travel* and *Women's Travel*, both published by Ferrari (☎ 602-863-2408) are international in scope, but also useful. All these are available from good bookstores or the publishers. The Ferrari website, www.ferrariguides .com, is especially useful for gay travel in the Southwest and anywhere.

Another good resource is the Gay Yellow Pages (☎ 212-674-0120), PO Box 533, Village Station, NY 10014-0533, which has a national edition as well as regional editions.

National resource numbers include the National Gay and Lesbian Task Force (☎ 202-332-6483 in Washington, DC), and the Lambda Legal Defense Fund (☎ 212-995-995-8585 in New York City, ☎ 213-937-2728 in Los Angeles).

In the Southwest, there are few gay organizations compared to coastal cities. They are listed under Gay & Lesbian Organizations in the yellow pages of major cities' telephone directories.

DISABLED TRAVELERS

Public buildings (including hotels, restaurants, theaters and museums) are now required by law to be wheelchair accessible and to have available restroom facilities. Public transportation services (buses, trains and taxis) must be made accessible to all, including those in wheelchairs, and telephone companies are required to provide relay operators for the hearing impaired. Many banks now provide ATM instructions in Braille, and you will find audible crossing signals as well as dropped curbs at busier roadway intersections.

Larger private and chain hotels (see Accommodations, later in this chapter, for listings) have suites for disabled guests. Main car-rental agencies offer hand-controlled models at no extra charge. All major airlines, Greyhound buses and Amtrak trains allow service animals to accompany passengers and frequently sell two-for-one packages when attendants for seriously disabled passengers are required. Airlines also provide assistance for connecting, boarding and deplaning – just ask for assistance when making your reservation. (Note: Airlines must accept wheelchairs as checked baggage and have an onboard chair available, though some advance notice may be required on smaller aircraft.) Of course, the more populous the area, the greater the likelihood of facilities for the disabled, so it's important to call ahead to see what is available.

Organizations & Resources

Access-Able Travel Source
(☎ 303-232-2979, fax 239-8486), PO Box 1796, Wheat Ridge, CO 80034
Access-Able has an excellent website with many links.
website: www.access-able.com

Mobility International USA (MIUSA)
(☎ 541-343-1284, fax 541-343-6812), PO Box 10767, Eugene, OR 97440
MIUSA primarily runs educational exchange programs, both in the USA and overseas.
website: www.miusa.org

Moss Rehabilitation Hospital's Travel Information Service
(☎ 215-456-9600, TTY 456-9602)

Society for the Advancement of Travel for the Handicapped (SATH)
(☎ 212-447-7284, fax 725-8253), 347 Fifth Ave No 610, New York, NY 10016
email: sathtravel@aol.com

SENIOR TRAVELERS

Though the age when the benefits begin varies with the attraction, travelers aged 50 years and older can expect to receive cut rates and benefits. Be sure to inquire about such rates at hotels, museums and restaurants.

The National Park Service (see Useful Organizations, below) issues Golden Age Passports that cut costs greatly for seniors.

Organizations & Resources

American Association of Retired Persons
(AARP; ☎ 800-424-3410), 601 E St NW, Washington DC 20049
AARP is an advocacy group for Americans 50 years and older and is a good resource for travel bargains. US residents pay US$10 for annual membership (spouse included). Foreign residents should ask about membership.
website: www.aarp.org

Elderhostel
(☎ 617-426-8056), 75 Federal St, Boston, MA 02110-1941
This is a nonprofit organization that offers seniors the opportunity to attend academic college courses and tours throughout the USA and Canada. The programs last one to three weeks and include meals and accommodations. They are open to people 55 years and older and their companions.
website: www.elderhostel.org

Grand Circle Travel
(☎ 617-350-7500, 800-350-7500), 347 Congress St, Boston, MA 02210
This group offers escorted tours and travel information in a variety of formats, mainly for mature travelers.
website: www.gct.com

TRAVEL WITH CHILDREN

Children receive discounts on anything ranging from motel stays to museum admissions. The definition of 'child' varies widely from under 18 to under six.

Many hotels allow children to share a room with their parents for free or for a modest fee, though B&Bs rarely do and some don't allow children at all. More expensive hotels can arrange babysitting services or have 'kids' clubs' for younger children. Restaurants offer inexpensive children's menus with a limited selection of kid-friendly foods at cheap prices, only for patrons under 10 or 12 years of age.

Children's tickets on airlines are often more expensive than the cheapest APEX adult tickets. Most buses and tours have discounted children's prices, though the discounts aren't substantial. Car-rental companies provide infant seats for their cars on request.

Various children's activities are mentioned in appropriate places in the text. For more information read *Travel With Children* by Cathy Lanigan.

USEFUL ORGANIZATIONS
American Automobile Association (AAA)

AAA, with offices in major cities and many smaller towns, provides useful information, free maps and routine road services like tire repair, towing (free within a limited radius) and locksmith service to its members. The membership card can often be used to obtain car-rental and sightseeing admission discounts. Members of AAA's foreign affiliates, like the Automobile Association in the UK, are entitled to the same services; for others, the basic membership fee starts at $59 for the first year and $44 for following years (still an excellent investment for the maps alone, even for nonmotorists). Its nationwide toll-free roadside assistance number is ☎ 800-222-4357 (☎ 800-AAA-HELP).

National Park Service (NPS)

The NPS, part of the Dept of the Interior, administers almost all national parks, monuments and historic sites, and a few other areas. Visitors often can camp and hike in the bigger areas, but hunting and commercial activities like logging are prohibited in these protected sites. All have visitor centers with information (exhibits, films, park ranger talks, etc) about why that particular site has been preserved for posterity.

National parks often surround spectacular natural features and cover hundreds of square miles. The many Southwestern NPS sites (including the famous Grand Canyon, Zion, Arches and Canyonlands National Parks) are fully described in detail in the text. National park campground and reservations information can be obtained by telephone (☎ 800-365-2267) or online at http://reservations.nps.gov. Lodges within parks, and motels and campgrounds near them, are privately owned. Details are given in the text.

Most NPS areas charge entrance fees, valid for seven days, of $6 to $20 per vehicle (usually half-price for walk-in or biking visitors). A few are free, and some don't collect entrance fees during periods of low visitation (usually late fall to early spring). Additional fees are charged for camping and some other activities, depending on each park.

Passes Various passes can be obtained at the first park you visit. The **National Parks Pass** costs $50 annually and offers one-year entry into all national parks to the holder and anyone in the holder's vehicle. **Golden Age Passports** cost $10 and allow permanent US residents aged 62 years and older unlimited free entry to all NPS sites, plus 50% discounts on camping and other fees. **Golden Access Passports** are free and give free admission to US residents who are legally blind or permanently disabled. **Golden Eagle Passports** cost $65 and are similar to National Park Passes but also allow entrance to BLM, USFS and USFWS with entrance fees. The passes are not transferable, and pass-holders may be asked for a picture ID.

US Forest Service (USFS)

The USFS is part of the Dept of Agriculture. National forests are less protected than parks, allowing commercial logging or privately owned recreational facilities in some areas. Forests are multi-use, with recreational activities such as hunting, fishing, snowmobiling, 4WD use and mountain biking permitted in many areas, unlike the NPS parks, where these activities are infrequently permitted. There are many forest campgrounds, which vary from simple sites with a fire-ring and a pit toilet but no water to campgrounds with showers and sometimes limited RV hookups. Most sites are $6 to $14; a few without water are free.

Entrance into national forests is often free, although some of the most popular roads through the forest cost $2 to $5 (per vehicle) to drive through. Golden Eagle Passports are usually accepted.

Current information about national forests can be obtained from ranger stations, which are listed in the text. National forest campground and reservation information can be obtained by calling ☎ 800-280-2267 (☎ 800-280-CAMP).

Bureau of Land Management (BLM)

The BLM, within the Dept of the Interior, manages public use of many federal lands outside of the parks and forests. This includes grazing and mining leases as well as recreational uses. They may offer no-frills camping, often in untouched settings. Entrance fees are charged for a small number of BLM sites, and Golden Passports may be valid in some cases. Local information offices are detailed in the text.

State Fish & Game Departments

Unlike the above organizations, fish & game departments are run by state governments. Information about seasons, licenses and other regulations is available from the following agencies:

Arizona Fish & Game Dept
(☎ 602-942-3000), 2222 W Greenway Rd, Phoenix, AZ 85023-4313

New Mexico Fish & Game Dept
(☎ 505-827-7911), Villagra Building, State Capitol, Santa Fe, NM 87503-0001

Utah Wildlife Resources Division
(☎ 801-596-8660), 1594 W North Temple, Salt Lake City, UT 84114-6301

DANGERS & ANNOYANCES
Crime

Southwestern cities generally have lower levels of violent crime than larger, better known cities such as New York, Los Angeles and Washington, DC. Nevertheless, violent crime is certainly present, and you should take the usual precautions.

Always lock cars and put valuables out of sight, whether leaving the car for a few minutes or for longer, and whether you are in towns or backcountry. Rent a car with a lockable trunk. If your car is bumped from behind by another vehicle, keep going to a well-lit area, service station or even a police station.

Be aware of your surroundings and who may be watching you. Avoid walking dimly lit streets at night, particularly if you are alone. Walk purposefully. Exercise particular caution in large parking lots or parking structures at night. Avoid unnecessary displays of money or jewelry. Split up your money and credit cards to avoid losing everything, and try to use ATM machines in well-trafficked areas.

In hotels, don't leave valuables lying around your room. Use safety deposit boxes or at least place valuables in a locked bag. Don't open your door to strangers – check the peephole or call the front desk if unexpected people are trying to enter.

Weather

Summer storms can be dangerous in the Southwest. Lightning is common and you should avoid being in the open, especially on canyon rims or hilltops, or next to tall or metallic objects. During heavy rain, flash floods occur regularly (see the boxed text 'Flash Floods – A Deadly Danger in the Desert' in the Outdoor Activities chapter).

The Southwest is very dry, and people die of dehydration every year. Dehydration occurs rapidly in 100°F weather. Tourists on short day hikes have become disoriented and lost – what starts off as an hour or two of hiking can turn into a fatal accident without water. Don't attempt any hike, however short, without carrying plenty of water. A minimum of four quarts per person per day is needed in the summer. Also remember to carry containers of water in the car, in case you break down on a rural road.

Dust storms are brief but can be temporarily blinding. If caught in a dust storm while driving, pull over as far to the side of the road as you can, turn off your lights and wait it out. It will blow over in a few minutes.

Wildlife Big & Small

Drivers should watch for livestock on highways, especially on Indian reservations, which are generally unfenced, and in areas signed as 'Open Rangelands.' Hitting a cow (or a deer) at 65mph can total your car and kill the animal, and it might kill you as well. When camping in highlands where bears are present, follow instructions about not placing your food inside your tent. Use a food box (one is often provided by the campground).

Despite the large numbers of snakes, spiders, scorpions and other venomous creatures in the South-west, fatalities are very rare. This is partly because these animals tend to avoid humans and partly because their venom is designed to kill small animals rather than big ones like ourselves. If you are bitten or stung by one of these critters, refer to the Health section, earlier.

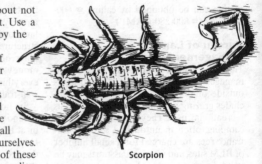

Scorpion

When hiking, watch where you are stepping, particularly on hot summer afternoons and evenings when rattlesnakes like to bask on the trail. These snakes are most easily identified by the 'rattle' of scales at the tip of the tail, which emit a rapid rattling sound when the snake is disturbed. Most rattlesnakes have roughly diamond-shaped patterns along their backs and vary in length from two to six feet. They are found all over the western USA. If you are bitten, you will experience rapid swelling, very severe pain and possible temporary paralysis, but rarely do victims die. Antivenin is available in Southwestern hospitals.

Black widow spiders (identified by a red hourglass shape on the underneath of the abdomen) make very messy webs, so avoid these. Bites are very painful but rarely fatal, except in young children. Again, antivenin is available. The large and hairy tarantulas rarely bite unless harassed; their bites are painful but not serious. Scorpions spend their days under rocks or woodpiles, so use caution when handling these. The long stinger curving up and around the back is characteristic of these animals. The stings can be very painful but are almost never fatal; again, small children are at highest risk. Centipedes bite occasionally, resulting in a painfully inflamed wound that lasts for about a day.

EMERGENCIES

If you need any kind of emergency assistance, such as police, ambulance or firefighters, call ☎ 911. This is a free call from any phone. A few rural phones might not have this service, in which case dial ☎ 0 for the operator and ask for emergency assistance.

LEGAL MATTERS

If you are stopped by the police for any reason, remember that there is no system of paying fines on the spot. For traffic offenses, the police officer will explain your options to you. Attempting to pay the fine to the officer is frowned upon at best and may lead to a charge of bribery to compound your troubles.

If you are arrested for more serious offenses, you are allowed to remain silent and are presumed innocent until proven guilty. Apart from identifying yourself, there is no legal mandate to speak to a police officer if you don't wish to. All persons who are arrested are legally allowed the right to make one phone call. If you don't have a lawyer or family member to help you, call your embassy. The police will give you the number upon request.

Driving & Drinking Laws Each state has its own laws, and what may be legal in one state may be illegal in others.

Some general rules are that you must be at least 16 years of age to drive (older in some states). Speed limits are normally 55 to 75mph on interstates and freeways. Speed limits on other highways are 60mph or less, and in cities can vary from 25 to 45mph. Watch for school zones, where the speed limit can be as low as 15mph during school hours – these limits are strictly enforced. Seat belts must be worn in most states. Motorcyclists must wear helmets.

The drinking age is 21 and you need a photo ID to prove your age. You could incur stiff fines, jail time and penalties if you are caught driving under the influence of alcohol. During festive holidays and special events, road blocks are sometimes set up to deter drunk drivers. See also Driving Laws and Drinking Laws in the introductory chapter for each state.

For more information on other car-related topics, see the Getting Around chapter.

BUSINESS HOURS & PUBLIC HOLIDAYS

Generally speaking, business hours are from 9 am to 5 pm, but there are certainly no hard and fast rules. In large cities, a few supermarkets, restaurants and the main post office lobby are open 24 hours a day. Shops are usually open from 9 or 10 am to 5 or 6 pm, or until 9 pm in shopping malls, except on Sunday, when hours are approximately noon to 5 pm. Post offices are open from 8 am to 4 or 5:30 pm Monday to Friday, and some are open from 8 am to 3 pm on Saturday. Banks are usually open from either 9 or 10 am to 5 or 6 pm Monday to Friday. A few banks are open from 9 am to 2 or 4 pm on Saturday. Call individual banks for exact hours.

National public holidays are celebrated throughout the USA. Banks, schools and government offices (including post offices) are closed and ground transportation, some museums and other services are on a Sunday schedule. Holidays falling on a Sunday are usually observed on the following Monday. Air travel is especially difficult around these holidays, with Thanksgiving, Christmas, and Memorial and Labor Days being the busiest.

January
New Year's Day January 1
Martin Luther King Jr Day Third Monday

February
Presidents' Day Third Monday

April
Easter A Sunday in early April, sometimes in late March

May
Memorial Day Final Monday (honors the war dead; the unofficial beginning of the summer tourist season)

July
Independence Day July 4

September
Labor Day First Monday (honors working people; the unofficial end of the summer tourist season)

October
Columbus Day Second Monday in October (a federal holiday, though celebrating Columbus' 'discovery' of America has become controversial)

November
Veterans Day November 11
Thanksgiving Fourth Thursday in November

December
Christmas Day December 25

SPECIAL EVENTS

From highbrow arts festivals to down-home country fairs, from American Indian ceremonial dances to chile-cooking competitions, from duck races to hot-air balloon ascents, the Southwest has literally hundreds of holidays, festivals and sporting events. As dates for these vary slightly from year to year, it's best to check local papers or chambers of commerce for precise dates. In larger cities with diverse cultures, traditional holidays of other countries are also celebrated with as much, if not more, fanfare. Some of these are also public holidays (see above) and therefore banks, schools and government buildings are closed. Many more local festivals are listed under individual towns.

January
Utah
Sundance Film Festival – second half of January in Park City, Utah

Visitors' Etiquette in Pueblos & on Reservations

Indian pueblos and reservations are governed by both federal and tribal law. Each tribe is independent and visitors should be aware that what is permitted on one reservation may be banned on another. Language, customs and religious ceremonies differ from one reservation to the next. Many Indians prefer to speak their own language and some don't speak English. Privacy is cherished, both on an individual and community level. Visitors to pueblos and reservations are generally welcome, but they should behave in an appropriately courteous and respectful manner. Tribal rules are often clearly posted at the entrance to each reservation, but here are a few guidelines.

Photography & Other Recording Many tribes ban all forms of recording be it photography, videotaping, audiotaping or drawing. Others permit these activities in certain areas only if you pay the appropriate fee. If you wish to photograph a person, do so only after obtaining his or her permission. This also holds true for children. A posing tip is usually expected. Photographers who disregard these rules can expect tribal police officers to confiscate their cameras and then escort them off the reservation.

Private Property Do not walk into houses or climb onto roofs unless invited. Do not climb on ruins. Kivas are always off-limits to visitors. Do not remove any kind of artifact. Off-road travel (foot, horse or vehicle) is not allowed without a permit.

Verbal Communication It is considered polite to listen without comment, particularly when an elder is speaking. Silent listening does not mean that the listener is ignoring the speaker; to the contrary, intent listening is considered respectful. Be prepared for long silences in the middle of conversations; such silences often indicate that a topic is under serious consideration.

Ceremonials & Powwows These are either open to the public or exclusively for tribal members. Ceremonials are religious events. Applauding, chatting, asking questions or trying to talk to the performers is rude. Photography and other recording are rarely permitted. While powwows also hold spiritual significance, they are usually more informal. Many ceremonials and powwows don't have a fixed date and are arranged a couple of weeks ahead of time. The tribal office can inform you of upcoming events.

Clothing Modest dress is customary. Especially when watching ceremonials, you should dress conservatively. Halter or tank tops and miniskirts or short shorts are inappropriate.

Alcohol Most reservations ban the sale or use of alcohol. The Apache reservations are notable exceptions. Drugs are banned on all reservations.

Eating There are few restaurants. Especially during public ceremonials, visitors may be invited into a house for a meal. Courteous behavior includes enjoying the food (of course!) but not lingering at the table after your meal, because others are waiting. Tipping is not customary.

Recreation Activities such as backpacking, camping, fishing and hunting require tribal permits. On Indian lands, state fishing or hunting licenses are not valid.

Arizona

Fiesta Bowl January 1 – a major post-season college football game, Tempe, Arizona

Professional Golf – men's PGA (Professional Golfer's Association) tournaments include the Tucson Open in mid-January and the Phoenix Open in late January

New Mexico

Various Dances January 1 and 6 – public dances and performances at most Indian pueblos in New Mexico

Animal Dances January 22 – performances in the evening and throughout the next day in San Ildefonso Pueblo, New Mexico

February
Arizona

Quartzsite Gem & Mineral Show – from late January to mid-February. Draws thousands of gem fans to this small Arizona town – be prepared to camp

Tucson Gem & Mineral Show – first two weeks. One of the biggest in the country

La Fiesta de los Vaqueros – last Thursday to Sunday of February in Tucson. Begins with the world's largest nonmotorized parade, followed by a rodeo and other cowboy events – even the city's schools close for the last two days of what is locally called 'Rodeo Week'

New Mexico

Candelaria Day February 2 – ceremonial dances in Santo Domingo, San Felipe and Acoma Pueblos, New Mexico

March
Arizona

Wa:k Powwow Conference – early March; hosted by the Tohono O'odham tribe in San Xavier del Bac Mission, near Tucson, is attended by members of many Southwestern Indian tribes; highlights include several days of dances, singing, food and other entertainment

Professional Golf – women's PGA tournaments include the Tucson Open in mid-March, and the Turquoise Classic, held in Phoenix in late March

April
New Mexico

Gathering of Nations Powwow – a weekend in late April (or early May); consists of a Miss Indian World contest, dances and arts and crafts at the University of New Mexico Arena in Albuquerque; preceded by American Indian Week

May
Arizona

Santa Cruz Day May 3 – dances at Cochiti and Taos Pueblos

New Mexico

San Felipe Day May 1 – dances at San Felipe and other New Mexican pueblos

Throughout the Southwest

Cinco de Mayo May 5 – the anniversary of Mexico's 1862 victory over the French in the Battle of Puebla, celebrated in many Southwestern towns, especially those with a strong Hispanic heritage. Parades, dances, music, arts and crafts, street fairs and Mexican food are the order of the day

June
Utah

Mormon Miracle Pageant – two weeks in mid-June. Huge Mormon gathering in Manti, Utah

New Mexico

St Anthony's Day, San Juan Day, St Peter's and St Paul's Day June 13, 24 & 29 – celebrated with dances and other events at several Indian pueblos and villages in New Mexico

July
Utah

Utah Shakespearean Festival – late June through late August. Professional quality performances in Cedar City, Utah

Days of '47 (or Pioneer Days) – two weeks up to July 24. The arrival of pioneering Mormon leader Brigham Young on July 24, 1847, is celebrated in Salt Lake City and other Utah towns

Arizona

Frontier Days – first week. Prescott, Arizona, hosts one of the world's oldest professional rodeos plus other entertainment

New Mexico

Santiago and Santa Ana Days July 25 and 26 – celebrated with dances at several Indian pueblos and a big traditional fiesta in Taos, New Mexico

Throughout the Southwest

Independence Day July 4 – American independence is celebrated in most Southwestern towns with events including races, rodeos, arts and crafts fairs, ceremonial Indian dances, pageants, music festivals, pancake breakfasts, barbecues, picnics, country & western dancing and the obligatory parades and fireworks

August
Arizona

Payson Rodeo – mid-August; another of the world's oldest rodeos is held in Payson, Arizona

New Mexico

Inter-Tribal Indian Ceremonial – second week. Held in Red Rock State Park, Gallup, draws members of dozens of tribes and includes rodeos, dances, powwows, parades, races, food, arts and crafts and much more

San Lorenzo Day August 10 – celebrated with dances at Acoma, Laguna and Picuris Pueblos, New Mexico

September
Arizona

Navajo Nation Fair – mid-September; held in Window Rock, it's the largest Indian fair in the country and offers a rodeo, parade, dances, songs, arts and crafts, food and more

New Mexico

All American Futurity – Labor Day; Ruidoso Downs, New Mexico, hosts a quarter-horse race worth $2 million

Fiesta de Santa Fe – first (occasionally second) weekend; held in Santa Fe, it's one of the oldest annual fiestas in the country

New Mexico State Fair and Rodeo – two weeks mid-month; held in Albuquerque, it ranks as one of the largest state fairs in the USA

October
New Mexico

Whole Enchilada Festival – first weekend; held in Las Cruces, it showcases the world's biggest enchilada; other draws include local food, entertainment, arts and crafts and races

International Balloon Fiesta – second week; Albuquerque hosts the world's biggest gathering of hot-air balloons

Halloween (All Hallows Day) October 31 – kids dress in costumes and, in safer neighborhoods, go 'trick-or-treating' for candy; some adults go to parties to act out their alter egos; ceremonies and dances take place at most New Mexico Indian pueblos

November
New Mexico

All Saint's Day November 1 – more ceremonies and dances in New Mexico pueblos.

San Diego Day November 12 – involves ceremonial dances at Tesuque and Jemez Pueblos, New Mexico

Throughout the Southwest

Day of the Dead November 2 – a traditional Mexican celebration for families to honor dead relatives; often, breads and sweets are made resembling skeletons, skulls and such, and graveyard visits are made

Thanksgiving – third Thursday; this important family gathering is celebrated with a bounty of food (traditionally a turkey dinner with fall harvest vegetables) and, more recently, American football games on TV; the following day is considered the biggest shopping day of the year

December
New Mexico

Fiesta of Our Lady of Guadalupe December 10 to 12 – celebrated with traditional dances and a pilgrimage in Tortugas, Las Cruces, New Mexico

Throughout the Southwest

Christmas – festivities occur all month, including Nativity pageants and festivals of lights in many Southwestern towns.

WORK

Seasonal work is possible in national parks and other tourist sites, especially ski areas; for information, contact park concessionaires or local chambers of commerce.

If you're coming from abroad and want to work in the USA, you need to apply for a work visa from the US embassy in your home country before you leave. The type of visa varies depending on how long you're staying and the kind of work you plan to do. Generally, you need either a J-1 visa, which you can obtain by joining a visitor-exchange program, or an H-2B visa, which you get when being sponsored by a US employer. The latter is not easy to obtain (since the employer has to prove that no US citizen or permanent resident is available to do the job); the former is issued mostly to students for work in summer camps.

ACCOMMODATIONS

The Southwest has a comprehensive range of accommodations, including free camping, developed campsites for tents and

RVs, youth hostels, cheap and midrange motels, B&Bs, expensive hotels, guest ranches and luxury resorts. For information on lodging taxes, see Money, earlier in this chapter.

Camping

Public Campgrounds These are on public lands such as national forests, state and national parks and BLM land. Some of them are managed by private concessionaires. The more developed areas may accept or require reservations. For USFS campground reservations, call ☎ 800-280-2267; for national parks call ☎ 800-365-2267. Credit cards are required.

Free dispersed camping (meaning you can camp almost anywhere) is permitted in many public backcountry areas in national forests and BLM lands, less so in national parks. Sometimes you can camp right from your car along a dirt road, and sometimes you can backpack your gear in. Information on where camping is permitted, and detailed maps, are available from many local ranger stations (contact details are in the text) and may be posted along the road. Sometimes a camping permit is required. The less-developed sites are often on a first-come, first-served basis, and can fill up on Friday night.

Camping in undeveloped areas, whether from your car or backpacking, entails basic responsibility. Choose a campsite at least 100 yards from water, and wash up at camp, not in the stream. Dig a 6-inch-deep hole to bury your feces, and burn your toilet paper (unless fires are prohibited because of high forest-fire danger). Carry out all trash. Use a portable charcoal grill or camping stove; do not build new fires. If there already is a fire ring, use only dead and down wood or wood you have carried in yourself. Leave the campsite as you found it.

Developed areas usually have toilets, drinking water, fire pits (or charcoal grills) and picnic benches. Some don't have drinking water. At any rate, it is always a good idea to have a few gallons of water in the vehicle if you are going to be out in the boonies. These basic campgrounds usually cost about $6 to $12 a night. More developed areas may have showers or recreational vehicle (RV) hookups. These cost more.

Costs given in the text for public campgrounds are per site. A site is normally for up to six people (or one vehicle). If there are more of you, you'll need two sites. Public campgrounds often have seven- or 14-night limits.

Private Campgrounds These are on private property and are usually close to or in towns. Most are designed with recreational vehicles (RVs) in mind; tenters can camp but fees are higher than in public campgrounds. Also, fees given in the text are for two people per site. There is usually a charge of $1 to $3 per extra person and state and city taxes apply. However, they may offer discounts for weeklong or month-long stays. Private campgrounds often have many facilities lacking in public ones. These include hot showers, a coin laundry, a swimming pool, full RV hookups, a games area, a playground and a convenience store. Kampgrounds of America (KOA) (☎ 406-248-7444) is a national network of private campgrounds with sites averaging $20; visit www.koa.com.

Hostels

The US hostel network is less widespread than in Canada, the UK, Europe and Australia, and is predominately in the coastal parts of the country. Not all hostels are affiliated with Hostelling International-American Youth Hostels (HI-AYH). Those that are offer discounts to HI-AYH members and allow nonmembers to stay for $3 more. Dormitory beds cost about $10 to $14 per person a night. Rooms are in the $20s for one or two people, sometimes more. Annual membership is $25 for 18- to 54-year-olds, free for youths and $15 for seniors.

HI-AYH hostels expect you to rent or carry a sleeping sheet or sleeping bag to keep the beds clean. Dormitories are segregated by sex and curfews may exist. Kitchen and laundry privileges are usually available in return for light housekeeping duties. Information and advertising boards, TV rooms and lounge areas are common. Alcohol may be banned.

Reservations are advised during the high season, when there may be a three-night limit. Get further information from HI-AYH (☎ 202-783-6161, www.hiayh.org), 733 15th St NW, Suite 840, Washington, DC 20005. There are nine hostels in the region covered by this book.

There are many more independent hostels in the Southwest which have comparable rates and conditions to HI-AYH hostels and may sometimes be better. They often have a few private single/double rooms available, sometimes with private bathrooms. Kitchen, laundry, notice board and TV facilities are available. The Internet Guide to Hostelling (www.hostels.com) lists hostels throughout the world.

B&Bs

If you've only experienced B&Bs (bed and breakfasts) in Britain, then you're probably in for a surprise when you stay at US B&Bs. B&Bs all have breakfast included in their prices, but similarities stop there. A few establishments, with rooms in the $50s, may have clean but unexciting rooms with a shared bathroom. Most B&Bs are pricier and have rooms with private baths and, perhaps, amenities such as fireplaces, balconies and dining rooms with enticingly delicious breakfasts. Other places may be in historical buildings, quaint country houses or luxurious urban homes.

Many B&Bs fall in the $75 to $120 price range, but some go over $200. The best are distinguished by a friendly attention to detail by owner/hosts who can provide you with local information, contacts and a host of other amenities. B&B hosts should, and usually do, lend a personal touch to your stay.

Most B&Bs in this book are fairly well established, but some may come and go quickly or are only seasonal, so call ahead to make sure the inn is still in operation; check the local chamber of commerce for new B&Bs that might have opened. Most B&Bs

prefer reservations over walk-in customers, and many don't accept children, pets or smokers.

Motels & Hotels

The cheapest motel rooms are around $20 for a double. Prices vary tremendously from season to season. A double room for $50 in the high season may drop to $25 in the low and may raise its rates to $60 for a special event when the town is overflowing. A $290/night luxury resort may offer special weekend packages for $89 in the low season. So be aware that the prices in this book are only an approximate guideline at best. Also, be prepared to add room tax to prices. Rates given are usually for one or two people; extra people are charged anywhere between $3 and $10 per person. A single room refers to one person, not two people in one bed.

Although high seasons and special events (when prices may rise) are indicated in the text, you never know when a convention may take over several hundred rooms and make beds temporarily hard to find.

Children are often allowed to stay free with their parents, but rules vary. Some hotels allow free stays for children under 18, others allow only children under 12 and others may charge a few dollars per child. Call and inquire if traveling with a family.

The prices advertised by hotels are called 'rack rates' and are not written in stone. If you simply ask about any specials that might apply, you can often save quite a bit of money. Members of AARP and AAA can qualify for a 'corporate' rate at several hotel chains.

Making phone calls directly from your hotel room may be expensive. Many motels allow free local calls, but fancier hotels may charge for them. Long-distance rates may be inflated 100% to 200%.

Budget Motels Motels with $20 rooms are found especially in small towns on major highways and in the motel strips of some larger towns. A quick drive through one of these will yield a selection of neon-lit signs such as '$19.95 for Two.' Take your pick. A few towns that may currently be experiencing great popularity just won't have rock-bottom budget motels. These towns include Santa Fe, Taos, Moab and Sedona, where a room close to $50 is rock-bottom budget. Therefore, what is called a bottom-end motel in one town may pass for a mid-range hotel in another. Utah, on the whole, has budget rooms starting in the high $20s rather than around $20.

Rooms are usually small, beds may be soft or saggy, but the sheets are usually clean. A minimally acceptable level of cleanliness is maintained, but expect scuffed walls, atrocious decor, old furniture and strange noises from your shower. Even these places, however, normally have a private shower and toilet and a TV in each room. Most have air-conditioning and heat. Some of even the cheapest motels may advertise kitchenettes. These may cost a few dollars more but give you the chance to cook a simple meal for yourself if you are fed up with restaurants. Kitchenettes vary from a two-ring burner to a spiffy little mini-kitchen and may or may not have utensils.

In smaller towns, cheap rooms may be acceptable 'mom-and-pop' type places, but in larger towns, the cheap motels may be in the least salubrious areas. Don't leave valuables out in your car, and exercise caution. Budget travelers shouldn't shun these $20-a-night cheapies, though single women may want to think twice about them.

Motel & Hotel Chains The many motel and hotel chains in the USA maintain a certain level of quality and style throughout the chain. It's partially true that 'If you've stayed in one, you've stayed in them all!' but, depending on location, there are certainly individual variations in both standards and, especially, prices. Some travelers like a particular chain and stay there repeatedly, generally receiving the level of comfort they've come to expect. These travelers should investigate the chain's frequent-guest program – discounts and guaranteed reservations are offered to faithful guests. Many motels have at-the-

door parking, with exterior doors. These are convenient, though some folks, especially single women, may prefer the more expensive places with safer interior corridors.

The cheapest national chain is Motel 6, and they are a fair value. Rooms are small, clean, white and spartan, but the beds are OK, every room has a closet shower, table, cable TV and phone (local calls are free). Free coffee is offered in the mornings and most properties have a swimming pool. Rooms start around $30 for a single in smaller towns, in the $40s or $50s in larger towns, and the $60s and $70s in some pricier destinations. They usually charge a flat $6 for each extra person.

Several motel chains compete with one another at the next price level, with rooms perhaps $5 to $20 more than a Motel 6. The main differences are that the rooms are larger, decor a little more attractive, and little extras like a light continental breakfast, a refrigerator, or a bathtub with your shower may be offered. If these sorts of things are worth the extra cost, then you'll be happy with the Super 8 Motel, Econo Lodge, Howard Johnson and the less-common (and cheaper) Budget Host and Red Roof motels. Not all of these have pools, however.

Stepping up to chains with rooms in the $45 to $90 range (or more, depending on location), you'll find noticeably nicer rooms; cafés, restaurants or bars may be on the premises or adjacent to them; and the swimming pool may be indoors with a Jacuzzi or exercise room also available. The Best Western chain consistently has properties in almost every town of any size and offers good rooms in this price range. Often they are the best available in a given town. Best Westerns are individually owned and quality tends to vary a bit more between properties. Days Inn properties are also a good choice in this price range and usually include a continental breakfast.

The Choice Hotel network (www.choicehotels.com) operates Sleep Inns, Comfort Inns or Suites, Quality Inns and Clarion Hotels. A convenient feature of reserving these is that if one isn't available in the town you are visiting, you will automatically be offered rooms in one of the others. Rooms are consistently spacious (Comfort Suites' are especially large) and well-appointed, and continental-plus breakfasts are offered. These rooms tend to be in the $50 to $120 range, depending on season.

Both the Holiday Inn and Ramada Inn chains now have midrange 'Express' hotels that are comparable to the Choice Hotel network. Other more expensive and consistently reliable hotels are less widespread in the Southwest, usually found only in large towns, and include Courtyard or Fairfield Inn by Marriott, Hampton Inn, Hilton, Holiday Inn, La Quinta, Marriott, Radisson, Ritz Carlton and Sheraton.

Private Hotels & Cabins There are, of course, nonchain establishments in all these price ranges. Some of them are funky historical hotels, full of turn-of-the-century furniture. Others are privately run establishments that just don't want to be a part of a chain. In smaller towns, complexes of cabins are available – these often come complete with fireplace, kitchen and an outdoor area with trees and maybe a stream a few steps away.

Another choice is self-contained condo units, which are apartments (flats) with kitchen and laundry facilities. They often have two or more bedrooms, and are designed for longer stays for groups or families. These places don't always have hotel services such as daily maids.

Full-Service Hotels If you want bellhops and doormen, restaurants and bars, exercise rooms and saunas, room service and concierge, splurge when you hit the big urban areas because they are otherwise few and far between.

Lodges
In national parks, you can either camp or stay in park lodges operated as concessions. Lodges are often rustic-looking but are usually quite comfortable inside. Restaurants are on the premises, and tour services

are often available. National park lodges are not cheap, with most rooms going for around $100 or more for a double during the high season, but they are your only option if you want to stay inside the park without camping. A lot of people want to do that, so many lodges are fully booked in advance. Want a room today? Call anyway – you might be lucky and hit on a cancellation. But your best bet for national park lodges, especially in the high season, is to make reservations well ahead.

Resorts & Guest Ranches
Luxury resorts and dude ranches really require a stay of several days to be appreciated and are often destinations in themselves. Guests at a luxury resort can start the day with a round of golf, then continue with a choice of tennis, massage, horseback riding, shopping, beauty treatments, swimming, sunbathing, hot tubbing, drinking and dancing. Guest ranches are even more like 'whole vacations,' with busy schedules of horseback riding and maybe cattle roundups, rodeo lessons, cookouts and other Western activities. Ranches in the desert lowlands may close in summer, while those in the mountains may close in winter or convert into skiing centers.

There is decent skiing in all three Southwestern states, with Utah definitely offering the best. Skiing resorts may charge $200 or more for a condo in midseason; prices drop to less than half in the snowless summer.

Reservations
The cheapest budget places may not accept reservations, but at least you can call them and see if they have a room, which they'll often hold for an hour or two.

Chain hotels take reservations days or months ahead. Normally, you have to give a credit card number to hold the room if you plan a late arrival. If you don't show and don't call to cancel, you will be charged the first night's rental. Cancellation policies vary – some let you cancel at no charge 24 hours or 72 hours in advance; others are less forgiving. Find out about cancellation penalties when you book. Chains often have a toll-free reservation number or website (see below), but their central reservation system might not be aware of local special discounts. Booking ahead, however, gives you the peace of mind of a guaranteed room when you arrive.

Some places, especially B&Bs and some cabins, won't accept credit cards and want a check as a deposit before they'll reserve a room.

Chain hotels are listed and marked on city maps in this book for your convenience, but other details are not given. Contact them as follows:

Best Western   ☎ 800-937-8376
www.bestwestern.com

Budget Host   ☎ 800-283-4678
www.budgethost.com

Clarion Hotel   ☎ 800-252-7466
www.clarionhotel.com

Comfort Inn   ☎ 800-228-5150
www.comfortinn.com

Courtyard by Marriott   ☎ 800-321-2211
www.courtyard.com

Days Inn   ☎ 800-329-7666
www.daysinn.com

Econo Lodge   ☎ 800-553-2666
www.econolodge.com

Fairfield Inn by Marriott   ☎ 800-228-2800
www.fairfieldinn.com

Hampton Inn   ☎ 800-426-7866
www.hampton-inn.com

Hilton   ☎ 800-445-8667
www.hilton.com

Holiday Inn   ☎ 800-465-4329
www.holiday-inn.com

Howard Johnson   ☎ 800-446-4656
www.hojo.com

La Quinta   ☎ 800-531-5900
www.laquinta.com

Marriott   ☎ 800-228-9290
www.marriott.com

Motel 6   ☎ 800-466-8356
www.motel6.com

Quality Inn   ☎ 800-228-5151
www.qualityinn.com

Radisson   ☎ 800-333-3333
www.radisson.com

Ramada   ☎ 800-272-6232
www.ramada.com

Red Roof Inn   ☎ 800-843-7663
www.redroof.com

Ritz-Carlton   ☎ 800-241-3333
www.ritzcarlton.com

Sheraton   ☎ 800-325-3535
www.sheraton.com

Sleep Inn   ☎ 800-753-3746
www.sleepinn.com

Super 8 Motel   ☎ 800-800-8000
www.super8.com

Travel Lodge   ☎ 800-578-7878
www.travelodge.com

FOOD

Whatever your eating preference, you'll be able to find it in the Southwest. From fast food to fancy French, it's all here.

This book's restaurant listings provide a good cross-section of possibilities for everybody, including 24-hour restaurants (the food is bland but quite acceptable, especially if you need a 4 am breakfast or arrive late in town), funky local places where townsfolk gather for breakfast, ice cream parlors, restaurants with an interesting history, and, of course, the various ethnic, Mexican, nouvelle Southwestern and swank uptown possibilities. You can count on every town having several fast-food places, usually on the main drag, their neon-lit logos visible from many blocks away; the Denny's chain serves food 24 hours a day. Supermarkets, many open late or for 24 hours, are shown on city maps for the convenience of travelers.

Many authentic, inexpensive restaurants serve delicious Mexican fare. In small towns, your best choice is often between Mexican and American food – only in the bigger cities and resort areas will you find large varieties of ethnic dining and fine Continental cuisine.

Mexican food is often hot and spicy, but it doesn't have to be. If you don't like spicy food, go easy on the salsa and you'll find plenty to choose from (see the glossary below). There are distinct regional variations. In Arizona, Mexican food is of the

Sonoran type, with dishes like *carne seca* being a specialty. Meals are usually served with refried beans, rice, and flour or corn tortillas, and the chiles used are relatively mild. Tucsonans call their home the 'Mexican food capital of the universe,' which, although hotly contested by a few other towns, is a statement with some ring of truth to it.

New Mexico's food is different from, but reminiscent of, Mexican food. Tortillas may be made from blue corn; pinto beans are served whole instead of refried; and *pozole* may replace rice. Chiles are used not so much as part of a condiment (like salsa) but more as an essential ingredient in almost every dish. Some can be eye-wateringly hot – ask your waiter for advice if you want a mild meal. One dish that is more likely to be found here than in other parts of the Southwest is *carne adobada*.

And then, of course, there's *nouvelle* Southwestern cuisine, an eclectic mix of Mexican and Continental (especially French) traditions that began to flourish in the 1970s. This is your chance to try innovative combinations such as chiles stuffed with lobster or barbecued duck tacos. But don't expect any bargains here. Mexican and New Mexico cooking is usually inexpensive; tack on nouvelle and you'll pay big bucks for your gourmet meal.

What about non-nouvelle Southwestern cooking? Head into one of the many steak houses and get a juicy slab of beef with a baked potato and beans. There won't be much here for a vegetarian.

Native American food is not readily available in restaurants. More often, you'll be able to sample it from food stands at state fairs, powwows, rodeos and other outdoor events in the region. The variety is quite limited. The most popular is fry bread (deep-fried cakes of flattened dough), which may be topped with honey or other delights. Navajo tacos are fry bread topped with a combination of beans, cheese, tomato, lettuce, onion or chile – and sometimes with ground beef.

Generally speaking, Arizona and New Mexico have the most Mexican and nou-velle Southwestern restaurants. Utah doesn't have a tradition of Mexican-influenced food. Here, the influence is mainly Mormon – good, old-fashioned American food like chicken, steak, potatoes and vegetables, homemade pies and ice cream. Salt Lake City, of course, is large and cosmopolitan enough to have a good range of ethnic restaurants.

Southwestern Food Glossary

The items listed below have regional variations – if you like Mexican food, part of the fun of traveling around the Southwest will be figuring out the variations.

burrito (or *burro*) – a soft flour tortilla folded around a choice of chicken, beef, chile, bean or cheese filling. A breakfast burrito is stuffed with scrambled eggs, potatoes and ham. (A burro is a large burrito.)

carne adobada – pork chunks marinated in spicy chile and herb sauce, then baked.

carne seca – beef that has been dried in the sun before cooking.

chile relleno – chile stuffed with cheese and deep-fried in a light batter.

chimichanga – a burrito that is deep-fried to make the tortilla crisp.

enchilada – a rolled corn tortilla stuffed with a choice of sour cream and cheese, beans, beef or chicken, and smothered with a red (or green) chile sauce and melted cheese.

fajitas – marinated beef or chicken strips, grilled with onions and bell peppers, and served with tortillas, salsa, beans and guacamole.

flauta – similar to a burrito but smaller and tightly rolled rather than folded, and then fried.

guacamole – mashed avocado seasoned with lime juice and cilantro, and optionally spiced with chopped chiles and other condiments.

huevos rancheros – fried eggs on a soft tortilla, covered with chile sauce and melted cheese, and served with beans.

menudo – spicy tripe soup; a hangover remedy.

mole – a mildly spicy, dark sauce of chiles flavored with chocolate, usually served with chicken.

nachos – tortilla chips covered with melted cheese and other toppings.

pozole – a corn stew (similar to hominy in other states), which may be spicy and have meat.

refried beans – a thick paste of mashed, cooked pinto beans fried with lard.

salsa – a cold dip or sauce of chopped chiles, pureed tomatoes, onions and other herbs and spices.

sopaipilla – deep-fried puff pastry served with honey as a dessert, or, in New Mexico, plain as an accompaniment to the main course.

taco – a crispy, fried tortilla, folded in half and stuffed with a combination of beans, ground beef, chiles, onions, tomatoes, lettuce, grated cheese and guacamole.

tamale – slightly sweet corn dough *(masa)* stuffed with a choice of pork, beef, chicken, chile or olives (or nothing) and wrapped in a corn husk before being steamed.

tortilla – a pancake made of unleavened wheat or corn flour. They stay soft when baked, become crisp when fried, and form the basis of most Mexican dishes. Small pieces, deep-fried, become the crispy tortilla chips served with salsa as an appetizer (often at no extra cost) in many Mexican restaurants.

tostada – a flat (ie, open-faced) taco.

Meals

Usually served between about 6 and 10 am, standard American breakfasts are large and filling, often including eggs any style, bacon, sausage or ham, fried potatoes, toast with butter and jam and coffee or tea. Continental breakfasts are often pale imitations of their European counterparts and can be as simple as coffee with a donut. Some hotels include a continental breakfast in their rates, but don't expect anything fancy in most of them.

Lunch is available between 11 am and 2 pm. One strategy for enjoying good restaurants on a budget is to frequent them for lunch, when inexpensive fixed-price specials are common. Many towns have American or ethnic restaurants (particularly Chinese and Indian) with all-you-can-eat buffet lunches for about $5 – a good deal for the impecunious.

Dinners, served anytime between about 5 and 9 pm, are more expensive but often very reasonably priced, and portions are usually large. Specials may also be available, but they will usually be more expensive than lunch specials. Some of the better restaurants require reservations.

DRINKS
Nonalcoholic

Restaurants provide customers with free ice water (tap water is safe to drink). All the usual flavors of soft drinks are available, although you may be asked to accept Coke instead of Pepsi and vice versa. Many restaurants offer milk or juices; a few have a wide variety of fruit juices. British travelers should remember that 'lemonade' is a lemon-sugar-ice water mix rather than the carbonated variety. (If you want the fizzy kind, ask for a Sprite or Seven-Up, mate.)

Coffee is served much more often than tea. Most restaurants offer several free coffee refills to customers eating a meal. Drinkers of English-style tea will be disappointed. Tea is usually a cup of hot water with a tea bag next to it – milk is not normally added but a slice of lemon often is. Herb teas are offered in better restaurants and coffee shops.

Alcoholic

The laws for obtaining alcoholic drinks vary by state and are outlined in our introductory chapter for each state.

Bland and boring 'name brand' domestic beers are available everywhere alcohol is sold. Most stores, restaurants and bars also offer much tastier but lesser known local brews, which may cost more than a Bud, but are worth it. Imported beers, especially Mexican brands, are also easily available and, although a little more expensive, offer a wider choice of flavors than do domestic brands.

Wine drinkers will find that California wines compete well with their European and Australian counterparts. For those interested in experimenting, there are little-known wineries in Arizona and New Mexico. A few of these offer tours and wine tasting and are mentioned in the text.

Alcohol & Drinking Age

Persons under the age of 21 (minors) are prohibited from consuming alcohol. Carry a

Rodeo: A Western Ritual

Rodeo, from the Spanish word meaning 'roundup,' began with the cowboys of the Old West. As they used to say, 'There was never a horse that couldn't be rode – and never a rider that couldn't be throwed.' Naturally, cowboys riding half-wild horses eventually competed to determine who was the best. The speed with which they could rope a calf also became a competitive skill.

Rodeo as we know it today began in the 1880s. The first rodeo to offer prize money was held in Texas in 1883, and the first to begin charging admission to the event was in Prescott, Arizona, in 1888. Since then, rodeo has developed into both a spectator and professional sport under the auspices of the Professional Rodeo Cowboys Association (PRCA). Despite rodeo's recognition as a professional sport, very few cowboys earn anywhere near as much as other professional athletes.

For the first-time spectator, the action is full of thrills and spills but may be a little hard to understand. Within the arena, the main participants are cowboys and cowgirls, judges (who are usually retired rodeo competitors) and clowns. Although the clowns perform amusing stunts, their function is to help out the cowboys when they get into trouble. During the bull riding, they are particularly important if a cowboy gets thrown. Then clowns immediately rush in front of the bull to distract the animal, while the winded cowboy struggles out of the arena.

While men are the main contenders in a rodeo, women also compete, mainly in barrel racing, team roping and calf roping.

Each rodeo follows the same pattern, and once you know a few pointers, it all begins to make sense. The first order of the day is the Grand Entry, during which all contestants, clowns and officials parade their horses around the arena, raise the US flag and sing the national anthem. The rodeo then begins, and usually includes seven events, which are often in the following order:

Bareback Bronc Riding A rider must stay on a randomly assigned bucking bronco (a wild horse) for eight seconds. This might not seem long from a comfortable seat in the stands, but from the back of a horse it can seem like an eternity. The cowboy holds on with one hand to a handle strapped around the horse just behind its shoulders. His other hand is allowed to touch nothing but air; otherwise he's disqualified. His spurs must be up at the height of the horse's shoulders when the front hooves hit the ground on the first jump out of the chute, and he must keep spurring the horse during the ride. Two judges give up to 25 points to each the horse and the rider, for a maximum possible total of 100. A good ride is one in which the horse bucks wildly and the rider stays on with style – a score of over 70 is good.

Calf Roping This is a timed event. A calf races out of a chute, followed closely by a mounted cowboy with a rope loop. The cowboy ropes the calf (usually by throwing the loop over its head,

---

driver's license or passport as proof of age to enter a bar, order alcohol at a restaurant or buy alcohol. Servers have the right to ask to see your ID and may refuse service without it. Minors are not allowed in most bars and pubs, even to order nonalcoholic beverages. Unfortunately, this means that most dance clubs are also off-limits to minors, although a few clubs have solved the under-age problem with a segregated drinking area. Minors are, however, welcome in the dining areas of restaurants where alcohol is served.

ENTERTAINMENT
Cinemas

Most sizable towns have multiscreen cinemas showing a variety of first-run Hollywood flicks on two to eight screens. Only the bigger towns have one or two cinemas screening foreign, alternative or underground films.

Rodeo: A Western Ritual

although a leg catch is legal), hooks the rope to the saddle horn, and dismounts, keeping the rope tight all the way to the calf. Watch the horse as the cowboy goes to the calf. A well-trained horse will stand still and hold the rope taut to make the cowboy's job less difficult. When he reaches the calf, the cowboy throws the animal down, ties three of its legs together with a 6-foot-long 'piggin string' and throws up his hands to show he's done. A good roper can do the whole thing in under eight seconds.

Saddle-Bronc Riding This has similar rules to the bareback event and is scored the same way. In addition to starting with the spurs up above the horse's shoulders and keeping one hand in the air, the cowboy must keep both feet in the stirrups. Dismounting from the saddle of a bucking bronco is not easy – watch the two pickup men riding alongside to help the contestant off. This demands almost as much skill as the event itself.

Steer Wrestling In this event (also called bull-dogging), a steer that may weigh as much as 700lb runs out of a chute, tripping a barrier line, which is the signal for two cowboys to pursue the animal. One cowboy – the hazer – tries to keep the steer running in a straight line, while the other cowboy – the wrestler – rides alongside the steer and jumps off his horse trying to grip the steer's head and horns – all of this happens at speeds approaching 40mph! The wrestler must then wrestle the enormous steer to the ground. The best cowboys can accomplish this feat in under five seconds.

Barrel Racing Three large barrels are set up in a triangle, and the rider must race around them in a cloverleaf pattern. The turns are incredibly tight, and the racer must come out of them at full speed to do well. There's a five-second penalty for tipping over a barrel. Good times are around 15 to 17 seconds.

Team Roping A team of two horseback ropers pursues a steer running out of the chute. The first roper must catch the steer by the head or horns and then wrap the rope around the saddle horn. The second team member then lassos the steer's two rear legs in one throw. Good times are under seven seconds.

Bull Riding Riding a bucking and spinning 2000lb bull is wilder and more dangerous than bronc riding, and it is often the crowd's favorite event. Using one heavily gloved hand, the cowboy holds on to a rope that is wrapped around the bull. And that's it – nothing else to hold on to, and no other rules apart from staying on for eight seconds and not touching the bull with your free hand. Scoring is the same as for bronc riding.

Bars

In small Southwestern towns, a bar might be the best place in town to have a beer, meet some locals, shoot a game of pool or listen to a country & western band. Patrons usually take an interest upon hearing a foreign accent, so if you have one, this is a good opportunity to meet people. Bars in bigger towns offer anything from big TV screens showing sporting events to live music of various genres.

Theater & Performances

The main cultural centers are mentioned under Arts in the Facts about the Southwest chapter. In addition, smaller towns may have local amateur theatrical performances. These include Indian pageants, Mormon pageants, vaudeville shows with audience participation (boo the villain, cheer the hero), mystery crime weekends (where a hotel becomes the scene of a hideous 'crime' and guests are both suspects and sleuths) as well as standard dramatic performances.

SPECTATOR SPORTS

Sports in the USA developed separately from the rest of the world, and baseball (with its clone, softball), American football and basketball dominate the sports scene, both for spectators and participants. Football and basketball, in particular, are quite popular. Both are sponsored by high schools and universities, which gives them a community foundation that reinforces their popularity. Basketball has the additional advantages of needing only limited space and equipment, making it a popular pastime in the cities. Soccer has made limited inroads, and remains a relatively minor diversion.

The Southwest has a few nationally ranked teams playing the big three US professional sports. Tickets for these events are hard to get, although you might be lucky. Scalpers sell overpriced tickets outside the stadiums before a game. The only Southwestern major league football team is the Arizona Cardinals of Phoenix. The Arizona Diamondbacks of Phoenix are a major league baseball team. Several other major league baseball teams come from the wintry north in February and March for training seasons in the warm climate of Arizona.

Professional basketball is better represented, with the Phoenix Suns (men) and Phoenix Mercury (women) and the Utah Jazz (out of Salt Lake City). College basketball is always popular – fans seem to enjoy watching the students as much as they do the pros. Currently, the University of Arizona Wildcats (from Tucson) are the highest-ranked Southwestern team, consistently placing among the top 25 college teams in the nation; they won the national college championship in 1997 and were runners-up in 2001.

Rodeo is popular in the Southwest – after all, rodeo as a paying spectator sport started here. From late spring to early fall, there are rodeos almost every week somewhere in the Southwest. Rodeo circuits sponsored by the Professional Rodeo Cowboy Association (PRCA) draw competitors from many western states.

SHOPPING

The main items of interest to travelers are Indian, Hispanic and Southwestern arts and crafts. Often, the dividing line between traditional tribal or Hispanic crafts and Southwestern art is a hazy one, with the latter often being heavily influenced by the former. Tribal crafts, too, have changed somewhat in response to what travelers want to buy.

Buying Indian crafts on reservations, directly from the makers, is often substantially cheaper than buying in off-reservation gift shops. However, the latter afford the buyer a much greater selection and, in the best stores, knowledgeable sales staff who have chosen only the finest quality work and can tell you about it. Buying from roadside stands in reservations can be fun, and you know that you are avoiding the middleman, but it's definitely a case of 'buyer beware' – the quality will vary tremendously.

Various tribes are especially known for particular crafts, though, again, there is much overlap between them. Just about all of them make beautiful jewelry, for example. Navajo weavings are highly sought after (see the boxed texts 'Navajo Weaving' in the Northeastern Arizona chapter and 'Rug Auction' in Northwestern New Mexico). The Hopis are famed for their kachina dolls (see 'Kachinas' in the Northeastern Arizona chapter). The Zuni are accomplished silversmiths and make wonderful fetishes (see the Zuni Pueblo section of Northwestern New Mexico). Most of the New Mexico pueblos produce distinctive ceramics and pots, which vary from tribe to tribe. The Tohono O'odham of southern Arizona and the Jicarilla Apache of northwestern New Mexico are both famed for their intricate basketwork, which requires many days of labor and is therefore not cheap.

Hispanic art includes religious paintings and altarpieces called *retablos*, brightly painted handmade wooden furniture, metal work (especially tin, copper and wrought iron) and fine art such as paintings and sculptures.

Off the reservations, gift shops and trading posts in all the major and many of the smaller cities have good selections of Indian and Hispanic crafts and their spinoff, Southwestern art. This can vary from tacky to breathtaking, from purely utilitarian to completely decorative. Themes include Southwestern wildlife and plants (cacti in

Arizona, chile peppers in New Mexico), the landscape, Native American people and their legends, cowboy art (especially bronzes and oil paintings) and much more. Towns renowned for art galleries include Scottsdale, Sedona, Tubac and Bisbee in Arizona; Santa Fe and Taos in New Mexico; and (to a lesser extent) Moab in Utah. However, every town will have Southwestern art galleries – see the Shopping sections throughout the book.

Outdoor Activities

For many of the millions of people who visit the Southwest, especially for the first time, the sheer scale and grandeur of the scenery viewed from vehicle windows and scenic overlooks is reward enough in itself. Locals, however, know that the Southwest offers a multitude of world-class outdoor activities, some of which, such as skiing or boating, may not be the first things that come to mind when one thinks about desert states. This chapter highlights the myriad outdoor activities possible in the Southwest.

GENERAL BOOKS & RESOURCES

Of the thousands of books about hiking, climbing, river running, canyoneering, bicycling and other activities in the Southwest, some general ones are mentioned in relevant parts of this chapter. Books about a specific place are mentioned in the appropriate parts of the text. Most of the books have extensive bibliographies. Outdoor equipment stores, as well as bookstores, will have many of these and other books.

Adventuring in Arizona by John Annerino gives a selection of hikes, car tours, river expeditions, climbs and canyoneering adventures all around that state. *Utah's National Parks: Hiking, Camping and Vacationing in Utah's Canyon Country* by Ron Adkison is a thorough and useful book with good historical background text.

Many outdoor activities are described on the Internet. One of the most wide-ranging sites is Great Outdoors Recreation Pages at www.gorp.com. For information about activities and permits in national parks, browse the National Park Service (NPS) website at www.nps.gov (with links to every park). Other lands are managed by the US Forest Service (USFS), Bureau of Land Management (BLM) and state wildlife and fisheries departments. The Federal Government has a website – www.recreation.gov – with detailed information about federally owned public lands, including forests, BLM areas and national wildlife refuges. See Useful Organizations in the Facts for the Visitor chapter for more details.

HIKING & BACKPACKING

If you have transportation, you can find perfect hiking and backpacking at any time of year. When highland trails are blanketed in snow, southern Arizona delights in balmy weather, and when temperatures hit the hundreds during Phoenix summers, cooler mountain trails beckon. Utah and New Mexico are generally higher in elevation than southern Arizona. Parts of those states, however, such as the parks near St George in southwestern Utah, offer pleasant hiking possibilities even in mid-winter. Of course, hardy and experienced backpackers can don cross-country skis or snowshoes and head out into the mountains in winter as well.

Planning

Perhaps the most attractive backpacking trip for many visitors is the descent into the Grand Canyon. This trip in particular requires careful advance planning because the number of backpackers is limited by the number of campsites available. Reservations are essential for most months of the year and details are given in the Grand Canyon chapter. Backpacking in Canyonlands National Park is also by reservation in the busy spring and fall months. Visitors without reservations may want to consider the less heavily used Bryce Canyon National Park for a backpacking trip in canyon country during the spring to fall months.

Visitors can also hike and backpack in many other public areas, especially in national forests, BLM lands and state parks. Addresses and phone numbers of individual state parks and USFS or BLM ranger stations are given in the text. These places are less famous than the national parks and usually there is no problem with just showing up and going backpacking. These areas are generally less restricted for wilderness camping than the national parks.

Books & Maps

Arizona Day Hikes: A Guide to the Best Trails from Tucson to the Grand Canyon by Dave Ganci covers day hikes in Arizona. For suggestions about hiking the desert as safely and comfortably as possible, read Ganci's *Desert Hiking.* Falcon Press publishes a series of hiking guides including *The Hiker's Guide to Arizona* by Stewart Aitchison and Bruce Grubbs, and *The Hiker's Guide to New Mexico* by Laurence Parent. Lonely Planet's *Hiking in the USA* covers the whole country and includes a section on major hikes in the Southwest. There are hundreds of books about smaller areas, covering one national park or mountain range, for example. The best are mentioned in the text.

A good map is essential for any hiking trip. NPS visitor centers and USFS ranger stations usually stock topographical maps that cost from $3 to $7. Apart from these, local bookstores and outdoor equipment stores often sell maps. There are many free planning maps available from the national parks that may not be adequate for the trip itself.

Longer hikes require two types of maps: USGS quadrangles and USFS maps. To order a map index and price list, contact the US Geological Survey (☎ 888-275-8747), PO Box 25286, Denver, CO 80225. The website www.usgs.gov has links to map stores throughout the US. For general information on maps, see the Facts for the Visitor chapter; for information regarding specific maps of forests, wilderness areas or national parks, see the appropriate geographic entry.

Minimizing Your Impact

Backcountry areas are composed of fragile environments and cannot support an inundation of human activity, especially any insensitive and careless activity. A new code of backcountry ethics is evolving to deal with the growing numbers of people in the wilderness. Most conservation organizations and hikers' manuals have their own set of backcountry codes, all of which outline the same important principles: minimizing the impact on the land, leaving no trace and taking nothing but photographs and memories. To avoid erosion and, in many desert areas, damage to the cryptobiotic crust (see the boxed text 'The Desert's Delicate Skin' in Southeastern Utah), stay on the main trail.

Wilderness Camping

Camping in undeveloped areas is rewarding for its peacefulness but raises special concerns. Take care to ensure that the area you choose can comfortably support your presence, and leave the surroundings in at least as good condition as when you arrived. The following list of guidelines should help:

• Camp below timberline, since alpine areas are generally more fragile. Good campsites are found, not made. Altering a site shouldn't be necessary.

• Camp at least 200 feet (70 adult steps) away from the nearest lake, river or stream.

• Bury human waste in cat holes dug 6 to 8 inches deep, at least 200 feet from water, camp or trails. The salt and minerals in urine attract deer; use a tent-bottle (funnel attachments are available for women) if you are prone to middle-of-the-night calls by Mother Nature. Camouflage the cat hole when finished.

• Use soaps and detergents sparingly or not at all, and never allow these things to enter streams or lakes. When washing yourself (a backcountry luxury, not a necessity), lather up (with biodegradable soap) and rinse yourself with cans of water 200 feet away from your water source. Scatter dishwater after removing all food particles.

• Some folks recommend carrying a lightweight stove for cooking and using a lantern instead of a campfire.

• If a fire is allowed and appropriate, dig out the native topsoil and build a fire in the hole. Gather sticks no larger than an adult's wrist from the ground. Do not snap branches off live, dead or downed trees. Pour wastewater from meals around the perimeter of the campfire to prevent the fire from spreading, and thoroughly douse it before leaving or going to bed.

• Burn cans to remove odors, then take them from the ashes and pack them out.

• Pack out what you pack in, including all trash. Make an effort to carry out trash left by others, as well.

• In bear country, do not bring food inside your tent. Either place it in supplied bear-proof containers, or hang it at least 10 feet off the ground between two trees.

Safety

The major forces to be reckoned with while hiking and camping are the weather (which is uncontrollable) and your own frame of mind. Be prepared for some unpredictable weather, such as heavy downpours that can cause deadly flash floods (see the boxed text 'Flash Floods – A Deadly Danger in the Desert'). In the Southwest, the most frequent weather problem is the heat. A gallon of water per person per day is the recommended minimum in hot weather; more if you are working up a real sweat. This will have to be carried in waterless areas. Sun protection (brimmed hats, dark glasses and sunblock) are all basic parts of a desert hiker's equipment. A positive attitude is helpful in any situation. If a hot shower, comfortable mattress, and clean clothes are essential to your well-being, don't head out into the wilderness for five days – stick to day hikes.

The most stringent safety measures suggest never hiking alone, but solo travelers should not be discouraged, especially if they value solitude. The important thing is to always let someone know where you are going and how long you plan to be gone. Use sign-in boards at trailheads or ranger stations. Travelers looking for hiking companions can inquire or post notices at ranger stations, outdoors stores, campgrounds, and youth hostels.

People with little hiking or backpacking experience should not attempt to do too much too soon or they might end up being nonhikers for the wrong reasons. Know your limitations, know the route you are planning to take and pace yourself accord-

Flash Floods – A Deadly Danger in the Desert

A flash flood can occur when a very large amount of rain falls suddenly and quickly. This is most common in the Southwest during the 'monsoon months' of mid-July to early September, although heavy precipitation in late winter can also cause these floods. They occur with little warning and reach a raging peak in a matter of minutes. Rainfall occurring miles away is funneled into a normally dry wash or canyon from the surrounding mountains, and a wall of water several feet high can appear seemingly out of nowhere. There are few warning signs – perhaps some distant rain clouds – and if you see a flash flood coming, the only recommendation is to reach higher ground as quickly as possible.

A swiftly moving wall of water is much stronger than it appears. At only a foot high, it will easily knock over a strong adult. A 2-foot-high flood sweeps away vehicles. Floods carry a battering mixture of rocks and trees and can be extremely dangerous. August 1997 was a particularly bad month for flash floods. One event, in Antelope Canyon on the Arizona–Utah border, killed 11 hikers. Another, near Kingman, Arizona, was strong enough to derail an Amtrak passenger train. In a third, several hundred locals and visitors were evacuated by helicopter from the village of Supai in the Havasupai Indian Reservation. The following September, a Capitol Reef National Park ranger had his pickup truck swept away and completely submerged in a flood (the ranger jumped out in time). There were many other flash floods during this period.

Especially during the monsoon season, heed local warnings and weather forecasts, and avoid camping in sandy washes and canyon bottoms – the likeliest spots for flash floods. Campers and hikers are not the only victims; every year foolhardy drivers attempt to drive across flooded roads and are swept away. Flash floods usually subside fairly quickly. A road that is closed will often be passable later on the same day.

ingly. Remember, there is absolutely nothing wrong with turning back or not going as far as you originally planned. Beginners should refer to one of the many books available about how to go backpacking. Chris Townsend's *The Backpacker's Handbook* is a beefy collection of tips for the trail. More candid is *A Hiker's Companion*, by Cindy Ross and Todd Gladfelter, who hiked 12,000 miles before sitting down to write. An excellent overview is *Hiking & Backpacking: A Complete Guide* by Karen Berger. *How to Shit in the Woods* is Kathleen Meyer's explicit, comic and useful manual on wilderness 'toilet' training for adults.

Canyoneering

At its simplest, canyoneering is visiting canyons under your own power. A canyoneer's adventures can vary from a pleasant day hike to a multi-day walking excursion stretching the length of a canyon. Longer trips may involve rock climbing with ropes, swimming across pools and down waterfalls, and camping; many experienced canyoneers bring inflatable mattresses to float their backpacks on as well as to sleep on. Some canyon areas designated as 'wilderness' are very remote, as no development is allowed. Canyoneers must reach the edges of these areas by dirt roads and then continue on foot over poor or barely existent trails to canyon bottoms.

Arizona, the Grand Canyon State, along with its northern neighbor Utah provides some of the best canyoneering anywhere. The first canyoneers in the huge gashes of the Colorado Plateau were Native Americans, whose abandoned cliff dwellings and artifacts mark their passage. Adventurers and explorers in the 19th and 20th centuries sought to unravel the many secrets of the canyons. The most famous was John Wesley Powell, the one-armed geologist who led the first boat descent of the Colorado River.

Today the Grand Canyon is the most popular place for canyoneering, with thousands of hikers descending from the rim every year. Many other canyons, however, are more difficult to access and provide uncrowded and equally scenic challenges. One

The Arizona Trail

Proposed by Flagstaff hiker and teacher Dale Shelwater in the mid-1980s, this 790-mile trail running from the Mexican border to the Utah state line is finally becoming a reality. About 600 miles of the trail have been completed and most of it is open, though some work, such as signing, remains to be done. This is a non-motorized trail, designed mainly for hikers and, in some spots, cross-country skiers or snowshoers in winter.

Meanwhile, most of the trail remains quite an adventure because no trail guide, as such, exists. Bits and pieces of the trail are described in various hiking books, but the best single source of information is the Arizona Trail Association (☎ 602-252-4794), PO Box 36736, Phoenix, AZ 85067; visit www.aztrail.org. There are 44 sections of trail, each with a trailhead that can be reached by vehicle, and the ATA has planning maps and information sheets about those sections that are open.

The trail varies from desert to pine forest and from canyon to mountain. (A side trail reaches Arizona's highest point, Humphreys Peak, at 12,633 feet.) Depending on the time of year, there is always a part of the trail where weather conditions are ideal for hiking. Parts of the trail, such as crossing the Grand Canyon via the Bright Angel and North Kaibab Trail, can be quite busy and require advance permits, while other areas are remote and lightly traveled, and don't require a permit. There's something for everyone.

of the most remote and lovely areas is the rarely visited **Sycamore Canyon Wilderness**, about 16 miles due west of the heavily traveled Oak Creek Canyon near Sedona. It takes three days to hike, scramble and wade the canyon's 25-mile length; Coconino National Forest rangers in Sedona or Flagstaff can provide information. In the same forest, the **Wet Beaver Creek Wilderness** (east of Camp Verde) provides an even more challenging three-day canyoneering adventure; you'll need to swim through more than 20 ponds, so be sure to bring a flotation device; rangers will have details about these remote, difficult trips.

Then there are the slot canyons, hundreds of feet deep and only a few feet wide. These must be negotiated during the dry months, because summer monsoon rains can cause deadly flash floods that may raise the height of the river by many feet in mere minutes. Always check with the appropriate rangers for weather and safety information. The **Paria Canyon**, a tributary of the Colorado River on the Arizona-Utah border, includes the amazing Buckskin Gulch, a stretch of canyon 12 miles long, hundreds of feet deep and only 15 feet wide for most of its length (see the boxed text 'Paria Canyon–Vermilion Cliffs Wilderness Area' in Southwestern Utah). Perhaps the best-known slot canyon is Antelope Canyon (also called Corkscrew Canyon) outside Page near Lake Powell.

Adventures in these and other canyons are described in Annerino's *Adventuring in Arizona*. One of the greatest canyoneering challenges, however, is to get topo maps and set out on your own to explore side canyons of the better-known areas, or to find new canyons that aren't described in guidebooks or elsewhere.

BICYCLING

As with hiking and backpacking, perfect cycling weather can be found at any time of year if you travel to different parts of the Southwest. Southern Arizona is a perfect winter destination, and Tucson is considered a bicycle-friendly city with many bike lanes and some parks with bike trails. In spring and fall, Moab in southeastern Utah is an incredibly popular destination for mountain bikers wanting to spin their wheels on the many scenic slickrock trails in that area. In the searing heat of summer, the high elevations around Brian Head in southwestern Utah attract an increasing number of bikers looking for a scenic destination that beats the heat. More details about these places are given in the text.

Local bike shops in all major and many minor cities rent bikes and provide local maps and information. Bicycle shops are listed in the text. Most bicycle rentals automatically come with a helmet. State and city visitor information offices and chambers of commerce often have brochures about trails in their areas.

Books

Several books detail road and trail rides in the Southwest. *Bicycling America's National Parks: Arizona and New Mexico,* by Sarah Bennett Alley and Dennis Coello, is subtitled *The Best Road and Trail Rides from the Grand Canyon to Carlsbad Caverns.* Along the same vein is *Bicycling America's National Parks: Utah and Colorado* by Sarah Bennett Alley, et al, subtitled *The Best Road and Trail Rides from Canyonlands to Rocky Mountain National Park.* Also read *The Mountain Biker's Guide to Arizona* by Sarah L Bennett, *Arizona Mountain Bike Trail Guide: Fat Tire Tales & Trails* by Cosmic Ray and *Mountain Biking Utah* by Gregg Bromka.

Transporting Your Bike

Bicycles can be transported by air. You *can* disassemble them and put them in a bike bag or box, but it's much easier simply to wheel your bike to the check-in desk, where it should be treated as a piece of baggage, although airlines often charge an additional fee. You may have to remove the pedals and front tire so that it takes up less space in the aircraft's hold. Check any regulations or restrictions on the transportation of bicycles with the airline well in advance, preferably before you pay for your ticket. Bear in mind that while some airlines welcome bicycles, others consider them a nuisance and do everything possible to discourage them.

You can also take bicycles on Greyhound buses and Amtrak trains, but again, check with them in advance. For full protection, bicycles must be boxed.

Bikes are often allowed on metropolitan public transportation, but the number of buses or other types of transport able to accommodate bikes may be limited. Call the local transit authorities for information.

Safety
On the road, bicyclists are generally treated courteously by motorists. You may, though, encounter the occasional careless one who passes too closely or too fast (or both). Helmets should always be worn to reduce the risk of head injury; in most states they are required by law. Always keep at least one hand on the handlebars. Stay close to the edge of roads and don't wear anything, such as headphones, that can reduce your ability to hear. Bicyclists should always lock their bicycles securely and be cautious about leaving bags on the bike, particularly in larger towns or more touristed locations.

Bicyclists should carry at least a gallon of water and refill bottles at every opportunity. Dehydration is a major problem in the arid Southwest.

Laws & Regulations
Cycling has increased in popularity so much in recent years that concerns have risen over damage to the environment, especially from unchecked mountain biking. Know your environment and regulations before you ride.

Bikes are restricted from entering wilderness areas and some designated trails but may otherwise ride in NPS sites, state parks, national and state forests and BLM single-track trails. In many NPS sites, there are no bicycle trails and cyclists are limited to paved roads only. In other areas, off-road trails are shared with other users. Trail etiquette requires that cyclists yield to horses and hikers.

Bikes aren't normally allowed on interstate highways (freeways) and are expected to use the frontage roads paralleling the freeway. On stretches where frontage roads are lacking, bicycles may be permitted on the interstates. In cities, obey traffic lights and signs and other road rules; yield to pedestrians; in downtown areas don't ride on the sidewalk unless there's a sign saying otherwise and don't ride two abreast unless in a cycle lane or path.

RIVER RUNNING
Although it is possible to run rivers privately, most visitors who want to go rafting will take a guided tour. Many companies run the Colorado River through the Grand Canyon – they are listed in that chapter. Bear in mind that most Grand Canyon trips are fully booked a year or more in advance. However, most of these companies offer other rafting options on several other rivers in the Southwest and beyond. Not all rafting trips have to be white-water; many companies run scenic float trips. Trips through the Grand Canyon and some other rivers are multi-day affairs with camping on beaches. For half-day and one-day trips on the Colorado River in and beyond Canyonlands National Park, the Moab area has many companies, most of which do multi-day trips as well. See the Grand Canyon & Lake Powell chapter and the Moab section in Southeastern Utah for details. Other recommended river-running options include the Green and Yampa Rivers out of Vernal (see Northeastern Utah) and the Rio Grande out of Santa Fe and Taos.

BOATING
Despite its desert location, Arizona has more boats per capita than any other state. The main reason for this is the region's many dams, which form huge artificial lakes providing boaters with relief from summer heat.

Arizona's 'West Coast' is a series of dammed lakes on the lower Colorado River on the California–Arizona state line. These lakes are described in detail in the Western Arizona chapter. This is the lowest and hottest part of the Southwest and the lakes are thronged with boaters for much of the year. You can rent canoes, fishing boats, speed boats, water-skiing boats, jet skis and windsurfers at the marinas on those lakes. On the biggest lakes, especially Lake Powell in the Glen Canyon National Recreation Area and Lakes Mead and Mojave in the Lake Mead National Recreation Area, you can also rent houseboats that will sleep from six to 12 people and allow you to explore remote areas that are hard to reach on foot. Many smaller lakes throughout the Southwest offer at least basic fishing and rowing boat rentals. Details are given in pertinent sections of the text.

In addition, the rivers suitable for rafting are also often suitable for kayaking or canoeing, and many of the companies at the Grand Canyon and in Moab, Vernal, Santa Fe and Taos will either arrange guided kayaking or canoeing excursions or rent you the equipment and tell you where to go (this latter option is not available in the Grand Canyon where noncommercial private trips must be booked many years in advance). If you have a kayak or canoe with you, the visitor centers or chambers of commerce in those towns and others with access to water have information about good put-in spots.

Safety

The many lakes and marinas offer boat-rental opportunities to the general public, but many folks are not very knowledgeable about watercraft. Accidents, sometimes fatal, do happen. The main contributing factors to accidents include alcohol and speed – two things that don't mix. You should take the same precautions with alcohol as when you are driving a car. Have a designated sober person to pilot the boat if you are having a party. Check local regulations about speed limits – in some places you should not leave a wake. This not only

limits your speed but also cuts down on erosion of the banks caused by waves. Always use lifejackets, even if you know how to swim. If you have an accident, a bump on the head can render your swimming skills useless.

A recently recognized and insidious threat is carbon monoxide, emitted by houseboat engines. This colorless, odorless and deadly gas is heavier than air and so it gathers at water level, sometimes underneath diving or swimming decks situated immediately above the engine exhausts. Several swimmers have drowned because of this in recent years.

FISHING

The many popular boating lakes also give rise to excellent fishing. Frequent species caught in lakes include bass (striped, largemouth and smallmouth), bluegill, catfish, crappie and walleye, while river anglers go for a variety of trout and salmon. Fish hatcheries are used to stock many lakes and rivers and Southwestern fishing compares favorably with any landlocked area in the contiguous USA. Bass fishing is especially good. San Carlos Lake in Arizona and Elephant Butte Lake in New Mexico are two of the best bass-fishing lakes in the country. Although you can eat what you catch, you should check locally about limits in number and size as well as for possible health problems in some places. Many anglers practice 'catch and release.'

Fishing is regulated by the individual states rather than by the federal government and anglers require a state license for each state that they fish in. The exception is on Indian reservations, where tribal permits are normally required. Licenses are widely available from the Fish & Game Depts of each state, as well as from numerous outdoor outfitting stores and guide services, and often in gas stations, marinas and state or national parks on or near good lakes and rivers. The cost of licenses varies from about $10 to $50 depending on how many days you want to fish (normally, licenses are available for one day, one year, and various intermediate lengths like a week or a season). Residents of each state get substantial discounts. In some federal areas, additional permits that cost a few dollars may be required, such as 'Habitat Improvement Stamps.'

DOWNHILL SKIING & SNOWBOARDING

Southwestern mountain ranges have numerous resorts offering great opportunities for skiing as well as other snow-related sports. Facilities range from day-only ski areas to resorts that are self-contained minicities, from gentle slopes for the learner to trails that challenge the most expert skier.

Snowboarding has swept the nation's ski culture and taken on a following of its own. Many Southwestern ski areas are developing half-pipes, renting the necessary equipment in ski shops and offering introductory lessons. Most at least permit snowboarding. Snowboarders stand sideways, strapped to a board 4 or 5 feet long, to cruise down the mountains. The motion is comparable to surfing or skateboarding rather than skiing.

The best skiing is undoubtedly in Utah, which boasts 'the greatest snow on earth.' It's good enough that Salt Lake City and nearby towns hosted the 2002 Winter Olympics. Pick up a free copy of the Utah *Winter Vacation Planner* for details of the 14 main areas, most of which are near Salt Lake City or in the Wasatch Mountains.

The skiing in New Mexico, especially in the mountains of northern New Mexico and Ski Apache near Ruidoso, is generally pretty good. Taos is considered the best area for its challenging runs and pleasantly low-key atmosphere.

Arizona has four ski areas, with Snowbowl near Flagstaff and Sunrise on the White Mountain Apache Reservation near Pinetop-Lakeside considered the best. There's also a small area in Williams. Mt Lemmon near Tucson is the southernmost ski area in the USA. Snow conditions in Arizona are more variable than in other states and Arizona ski season may be just a few weeks in some years.

Skiing is most expensive in Utah, where day lift tickets at the best resorts are in the

$50s and $60s for adults. Weekend tickets are always the most expensive. Rates drop into the $40s or even $30s in many resorts in New Mexico and Arizona.

Planning

The skiing season lasts from about late November to early April, depending on the area (some have shorter seasons). State tourist offices have information on resorts, and travel agents can arrange full-package tours that include transport and accommodations. Many of the resorts are close to towns so it's quite feasible to travel on your own to the slopes for the day and return to town at night. If you have travel insurance, make sure that it covers you for winter sports.

Ski areas are often well equipped with accommodations, eateries, shops, entertainment venues, child-care facilities (both on and off the mountain) and transport. In fact, it's possible to stay a week at some of the bigger places without leaving the slopes.

Equipment rentals are available at or near even the smallest ski areas, though renting equipment in a nearby town can be cheaper if you can transport it to the slopes.

Recreational programs for handicapped people are offered by Disabled Sports USA (☎ 301-217-0960, TDD 301-217-0963), 451 Hungerford Dr, Suite 100, Rockville, MD 20850. Its website is www.dsusa.org and they have state branches across the country. In Utah, the National Ability Center (☎ 435-649-3991), PO Box 682799, Park City, UT 84068, has its headquarters in Park City. They have year-round sports programs; visit www.nationalabilitycenter.org. Skiers 70 years of age and over can contact the 70+ Ski Club (☎ 518-346-5505), 1633 Albany St, Schenectady, NY 12304, or email RTL70plus@aol.com.

In the recommended *Ski America and Canada,* Charles A Leocha has compiled facts and figures about the USA's big ski resorts. This book is updated every couple of years. *Ski* (www.skimag.com) and *Skiing* (www.skiingmag.com) are year-round magazines available in most newsstands, airports and sporting-goods stores. Their websites are full of useful information about snow conditions, resorts, events etc. Another useful website is www.snocountry .com, detailing snow conditions, pass rates, types of runs and accommodations in resorts throughout the world.

Ski Schools

Visitors planning on taking lessons should rent equipment on the mountain since the price of a lesson usually includes equipment rentals, with no discount for having your own gear. Children's ski schools are popular places to stash the kids for a day, offering lessons, day-care facilities and providing lunch.

OTHER WINTER ACTIVITIES

Both cross-country skiing and snowmobiling are popular, and often conflict with one another. Anywhere that there is substantial snowfall, you'll find groomed tracks designed for both activities, and equipment rental readily available. Snowshoeing is another activity for which equipment rental is available in higher areas with lots of snow. A useful book is *Cross-Country Ski Vacations: A Guide to the Best Resorts, Lodges, and Groomed Trails in North America* by Jonathan Wiesel and Diana Delling.

Lakes often freeze hard in the mountains, where both ice-skating and ice fishing are possible. Ice-skating is also featured in various towns with ice-skating rinks including, surprisingly, Tucson, Arizona, where a year-round indoor ice-skating rink remains open even when summer temperatures soar into the 100s°F.

Park City, Utah, the headquarters of the US Olympic ski team, is also one of the few places where you can try the Olympic sports of ski jumping, bobsledding and luge – details are given in the text.

BIRD WATCHING

The Southwest has a great variety of different habitats, which leads to many different species of birds. Southeastern Arizona, in particular, has great avian biodiversity, with species from Mexico flying in to add to the many birds found in the deserts, mountains,

forests and riparian zones of that area. Sixteen hummingbird species have been recorded in southeastern Arizona, of which eight are quite commonly seen. This attracts avid birders from around the world. The Tucson Audubon Society is a great resource for this area. More information can be found in the Tucson & Southern Arizona and Southeastern Arizona chapters of this book. The Great Salt Lake in Utah is also a major flyway for migratory shorebirds and waterfowl.

For general information, log on to the Audubon Society website at www.audubon .org or call the national office at ☎ 212-979-3000. Each southwestern state has several chapters of the Audubon Society.

HORSEBACK RIDING

Cowboys and Indians, the Pony Express, stagecoaches, cattle drives and rodeo riding – horse legends are legion in the Southwest. This continues to the present day with Bob Baffert, the horse trainer from Nogales, Arizona, whose *Real Quiet* won the Kentucky Derby and Preakness Stakes of the USA's leading 'Triple Crown' horseraces in 1998 and came in second (literally by a nose) in the third race, the Belmont Stakes. (This was the closest that a horse has come to winning the 'Triple Crown' since 1978.)

OK. You probably aren't looking at winning the Derby, but horseback riding is a popular attraction in the Southwest. This ranges from one-hour rides for complete beginners (or experienced riders who just want to get on a horse again) to multi-night horsepacking trips with wranglers, cooks, guides and backcountry camping. Another possibility is staying at a ranch where the main activity is horseback riding on a daily basis, and the comforts of a bed and shower await at the end of the day.

Many towns have stables and offer horseback rides. In a few locations, such as on the South Rim of the Grand Canyon, only mules are available, and these must be booked months in advance. During the winter, southern Arizona has delightful weather for riding. When the weather warms up, head up to Sedona and Pinetop-

Lakeside in Arizona, Chama in New Mexico or Moab in Utah for horseback riding. More places are listed in the text.

If your idea of a southwestern vacation is a week in a comfortable ranch in the country, with cozy log cabins, excellent food, and well-maintained horses available for daily riding, then an excellent resource is *Ranch Vacations* by Gene Kilgore. Updated every two years, this book describes many ranches in detail, including some that include fly-fishing and hunting among their activities. However, most of the ranches have horseback riding as the main focus. Check out Kilgore's website at www.ranch web.com. Another useful resource is the Dude Ranchers' Association (☎ 970-223-8440), PO Box F-471 LaPorte, Colorado 80535, which lists dozens of ranches throughout the Southwest, as well as the whole country; get details at www.duderanch.org. The commercial www.duderanches.com is also worth a look.

ROCK CLIMBING

There are many rock-climbing areas, some of which have become quite famous, such as Mt Lemmon near Tucson and the Fischer Towers near Moab. Many of the red-rock national parks in southern Utah permit rock climbing. There is also good climbing in the Sedona area – in fact almost anywhere that there are mountains. Some cities, such as Flagstaff and Tucson, have indoor rock-climbing gyms where the public is welcome to practice for a small fee.

Outdoor equipment stores sell guide-books, some for large areas and others covering a small local area. Some useful books include *Rock Climbing New Mexico & Texas* by Dennis Jackson, *Rock Climbing Arizona* by Stewart M Green and *Rock Climbing Utah's Wasatch Range* by Bret and Stuart Ruckman.

HOT-AIR BALLOONING

Dozens of companies offer scenic hot-air balloon flights over many parts of the Southwest. Flights usually lift off in the calm morning air, drift for about an hour and finish with a traditional champagne brunch;

costs are in the low $100s per person. Most companies can arrange flights on a day's notice, but flights may be canceled in windy weather and in summer.

Cities especially known for this activity include Albuquerque, with what may be the world's biggest hot-air ballooning festival held every October, as well as Tucson, Phoenix and Sedona in Arizona and Park City in Utah.

ROCKHOUNDING

Rockhounding – the search for semi-precious or just plain pretty rocks, minerals and crystals – is a passion for some people in the Southwest. Tucson has an annual Gem & Mineral Show in February that is one of the biggest in the world. Also in Arizona, the area around Quartzsite is a famous gathering ground for hundreds of thousands of rockhounds and collectors during January and February.

Near Deming, New Mexico, Rockhound State Park is one of the few parks that not only permit collecting, but also actually were established to allow rockhounds to search for their quarry. Most parks, such as the Petrified Forest National Park, famous for its fossilized wood specimens, do not permit any collecting at all, though there are plenty of shops in nearby Holbrook that legally sell samples. Western Utah has several remote areas that are popular for rockhounding, including the House Range along Hwy 6/50 and along the Pony Express Trail.

JEEP TOURING

Taking to the backcountry in a 4WD vehicle, whether just for a half-day or equipped with camping gear, water and food for several days, is a popular activity. In some areas, such as Moab, numerous companies offer 4WD tours or rentals. Especially interesting in the Moab area is an extended 4WD camping trip in the remote reaches of Canyonlands National Park. Sedona is another good center for 4WD activities if you need to rent a vehicle.

Little Sahara Recreation Area in Utah (see the Central Utah chapter) is especially designed for OHVs (off-highway vehicles). The Skyline Drive in central Utah is a beautiful high-altitude drive for which 4WD is recommended. Canyon de Chelly in northeastern Arizona is famous for its Navajo-guided tours in 6WD vehicles – scenic and interesting.

You can drive on dirt roads in many federally owned lands, such as national forests and BLM areas. However, there are some restrictions and certain roads are periodically closed.

GOLFING

Just about every sizeable town in the Southwest has a golf course, and the bigger cities have dozens of courses, a few of which are listed in the text. The Phoenix area alone has almost 200 courses! In many desert areas, golf courses are viewed as a welcome green amenity but the greenness comes at a high price – it has to be irrigated. Conservationists decry the use of this most precious of desert resources for golf courses, but this

hasn't stopped the development of this activity throughout the area.

Golf can be an expensive habit. Some courses don't allow golfers to walk from hole to hole. A round of 18 holes on the best courses, often in upscale resorts that specialize in golf vacations, can cost close to $200 (including use of a golf cart) in the balmy days of a southern Arizona winter. During the heat of summer, rates can drop to under $100 for the same resort. If you don't have that kind of money, try the public city courses where rounds are much more reasonable. Most chambers of commerce will tell you about local city courses charging $30 to $50 for 18 holes, or even less in small towns. It is beyond the scope of this book to list the many hundreds of greens in the Southwest.

For further information, including details on state gold associations, contact the United States Golf Association (☎ 908-234-2300), PO Box 708, Far Hills, NJ 07931; its website is www.usga.org.

Getting There & Away

Most travelers to the Southwest arrive by air, bus or private vehicle. Train service is a little-used fourth option. The landlocked Southwest can't be reached by sea, but the lack of ports has been remedied somewhat by naming the Phoenix International Airport 'Sky Harbor.'

This chapter focuses on getting to the major transport hubs in the Southwest from the major US ports of entry and other parts of the world.

AIR

Unless you live in or near the Southwest, flying there and renting a car is the most time-efficient option. If time is not a problem, drive – and enjoy the rest of the country.

Airports

Sky Harbor Airport in Phoenix, Arizona, and McCarran International Airport in Las Vegas, Nevada, each handle over 30 million passengers arriving or departing every year. Although they are among the busiest international airports in the USA and the region's most important, many international visitors arrive elsewhere in the US (eg, Los Angeles, New York, Miami or Dallas/Fort Worth) and take onward flights to the Southwest.

The Salt Lake City (Utah) airport, with about half as many flights as Phoenix, is the third most important airport in the region, and the Albuquerque (New Mexico) and Tucson (Arizona) airports are fairly distant fourth and fifth places. The many other airports in the Southwest are small and used for regional transportation. More details are given under individual cities.

Denver International Airport (Colorado) is busier than Phoenix, and if you rent a car in Denver, you can be in northeastern New Mexico in four hours. Los Angeles, busier than any of these, is an easy day's drive from western Arizona or southwestern Utah via Las Vegas. El Paso, Texas,

Warning

The information in this chapter is particularly vulnerable to change: prices for international travel are volatile, routes are introduced and canceled, schedules change, special deals come and go, and rules and visa requirements are amended. Airlines and governments seem to take a perverse pleasure in making price structures and regulations as complicated as possible. You should check directly with the airline or a travel agent to make sure you understand how a fare (and any ticket you may buy) works. In addition, the travel industry is highly competitive, and there are many lurks and perks.

The upshot of this is that you should get opinions, quotes and advice from as many airlines and travel agents as possible before you part with your hard-earned cash. The details given in this chapter should be regarded as pointers and are not a substitute for your own careful, up-to-date research.

a few miles from the New Mexico border, is a possible minor gateway.

Airlines

Phoenix is an important hub for America West and Southwest Airlines. Las Vegas is a hub for America West. (Continental Airlines shares these America West hubs.) Salt Lake City is a Delta hub, and Denver is a United Airlines hub. Many other major airlines fly into one or more of these cities. Mesa Air is a small local company with service between ten New Mexican towns and Denver, Colorado or Dallas/Fort Worth, Texas.

The main domestic airlines serving the Southwest include the following:

Alaska ☎ 800-426-0333
www.alaskaair.com

America West ☎ 800-235-9292
www.americawest.com

American www.aa.com	☎ 800-433-7300
Continental www.continental.com	☎ 800-523-3273
Delta www.delta.com	☎ 800-221-1212
Frontier www.flyfrontier.com	☎ 800-432-1359
Hawaiian www.hawaiianair.com	☎ 800-367-5320
Mesa Air www.mesa-air.com	☎ 800-637-2247
Midwest Express www.midwestexpress.com	☎ 800-452-2022
Northwest www.nwa.com	☎ 800-225-2525
Southwest www.southwest.com	☎ 800-435-9792
TWA www.twa.com	☎ 800-221-2000
United www.ual.com	☎ 800-241-6522
US Airways www.usairways.com	☎ 800-428-4322

Some US carriers have different phone numbers for their international desk:

Air Canada www.aircanada.ca	☎ 888-247-2262
Air France www.airfrance.com	☎ 800-237-2747
Air New Zealand www.airnewzealand.com	☎ 800-262-1234
American www.aa.com	☎ 800-433-7300
British Airways www.britishairways.com	☎ 800-247-9297
Continental www.continental.com	☎ 800-231-0856
Delta www.delta.com	☎ 800-221-4141
Japan Air Lines www.japanair.com	☎ 800-525-3663
KLM www.klm.com	☎ 800-374-7747
Lufthansa www.lufthansa.com	☎ 800-645-3880
LTU www.ltu.com	☎ 800-888-0200
Northwest www.nwa.com	☎ 800-447-4747

Qantas Airways www.qantas.com	☎ 800-227-4500
TWA www.twa.com	☎ 800-892-4141
United www.ual.com	☎ 800-538-2929
US Airways www.usairways.com	☎ 800-622-1015

Buying Tickets

Your plane ticket may well be the single most expensive item in your budget, and buying it can be intimidating. It is always worth putting aside a few hours to research the current state of the market. Numerous airlines fly to the USA, and many fares are available – from straightforward roundtrip tickets to Round-the-World (RTW) tickets. So rather than just walking into the nearest travel agent or airline office, you should do a bit of research and shop around first. Start shopping for a ticket early – some of the cheapest tickets must be bought months in advance, and some popular flights sell out early.

Fares within the USA are incredibly varied. An economy roundtrip ticket from Phoenix to the West Coast can cost $100 or four times as much, and these disparities occur almost wherever you fly in the USA. The cheapest flights are often (but not always) those booked 21 days or more in advance and with a Saturday night stopover. Nothing determines fares more than demand, and when things are slow, airlines lower their fares to fill empty seats. Competition is stiff, and at any given time any of the airlines could have the cheapest fare.

The most expensive fares are those booked at the last minute; cheap standby fares are not normally offered. One-way tickets usually cost as much as an economy roundtrip ticket with major airlines; smaller airlines such as America West and Southwest are the best places to look for one-way flights.

Once you have your ticket, write down its number, together with the flight number and other details, and keep the information somewhere separate. If the ticket is lost or stolen, this will help you get a replacement.

Air Travel Glossary

Cancellation Penalties If you have to cancel or change a discounted ticket, there are often heavy penalties involved; insurance can sometimes be taken out against these penalties. Some airlines impose penalties on regular tickets as well, particularly against 'no-show' passengers.

Courier Fares Businesses often need to send urgent documents or freight securely and quickly. Courier companies hire people to accompany the package through customs and, in return, offer a discount ticket which is sometimes a phenomenal bargain. However, you may have to surrender all your baggage allowance and take only carry-on luggage.

Full Fares Airlines traditionally offer 1st class (coded F), business class (coded J) and economy class (coded Y) tickets. These days, so many promotional and discounted fares are available that few passengers pay full economy fare.

Lost Tickets If you lose your airline ticket, an airline will usually treat it like a traveler's check and, after inquiries, issue you with another one. Legally, however, an airline is entitled to treat it like cash: if you lose it, it's gone forever. Take good care of your tickets.

Onward Tickets An entry requirement for many countries is a ticket out of the country. If you're unsure of your next move, the easiest solution is to buy the cheapest onward ticket to a neighboring country or a ticket from a reliable airline that can later be refunded if you do not use it.

Open-Jaw Tickets These are return tickets that permit you to fly into one place but return from another. If available, these tickets can save you backtracking to your arrival point.

Overbooking Because almost every flight has some passengers that fail to show up, airlines often book more passengers than they have seats. Usually excess passengers make up for the no-shows, but occasionally somebody gets 'bumped' onto the next available flight. Guess who it is most likely to be? The passengers who check in late.

Promotional Fares These are officially discounted fares, available from travel agencies or direct from the airline.

Reconfirmation If you don't reconfirm your flight at least 72 hours prior to departure, the airline may delete your name from the passenger list. Call to find out if your airline requires reconfirmation.

Restrictions Discounted tickets often have various restrictions – for example, they may need to be paid for in advance, or altering them may incur a penalty. Other restrictions include minimum and maximum periods you must be away.

Round-the-World Tickets RTW tickets give you a limited period (usually a year) in which to circumnavigate the globe. You can go anywhere the carrying airlines go as long as you don't backtrack. The number of stopovers or total number of separate flights is decided before you set off, and these tickets usually cost a bit more than a basic return flight.

Transferred Tickets Airline tickets cannot be transferred from one person to another. Travelers sometimes try to sell the return half of a ticket, but officials can ask you to prove that you are the person named on the ticket. On an international flight, tickets are compared with passports.

Travel Periods Ticket prices vary with the time of year. There is a low (off-peak) season and a high (peak) season, and often a low-shoulder season and a high-shoulder season as well. Usually the fare depends on your outward flight – if you depart in the high season and return in the low season, you pay the high-season fare.

Remember to buy travel insurance as early as possible.

Discount Tickets The cheapest tickets are non-refundable and require an extra fee for changing the date of travel.

Student travel agencies found in many countries worldwide include Council Travel (☎ 800-226-8624), www.counciltravel.com, and STA (☎ 800-781-4040), www.statravel .com. They not only provide cheap tickets to students, they often have some of the best deals for the general public as well.

Look at the travel ads in newspapers and magazines, and watch for special offers. Often, bucket shops (discount travel agencies) and consolidators offer excellent deals. In some places, especially the UK, some of the newest ones haven't yet reached the telephone directory. Most are honest, though occasional rogues appear. If you are suspicious, don't pay all your money in advance until receiving the ticket.

The Internet is a source of discounted tickets but, as always, shop around. New sites appear every month. Internet buying involves paying by credit card, which is generally secure. Many of these sites will also provide hotel reservations, car rental and other services. Apart from the airlines' sites (some of which do offer discounted tickets occasionally), look at:

www.atevo.com
www.cheaptickets.com
www.discounttickets.com
www.expedia.com
www.lowestfare.com
www.orbitz.com
www.travelocity.com

Seasons High season in the USA is mid-June to mid-September (summer) and the days around major holidays (Thanksgiving is one of the busiest times of year, and Christmas, New Year's, Easter, and Memorial Day and Labor Day weekends are all very busy with few cheap fares). The best rates for travel to and within the USA are found November through March (except for the holidays).

Visit USA Passes Most domestic carriers offer Visit USA passes to non-US citizens. The passes are a book of coupons – each coupon equals a flight. Typically, the minimum number of coupons is three or four and the maximum is eight or ten, and they must be purchased in conjunction with an international airline ticket anywhere outside the USA except Canada and Mexico. Coupons cost anywhere from $100 to $160, depending on how many you buy. Airlines may require you to plan your itinerary in advance and to complete your flights within 60 days of arrival, but rules vary among individual airlines. A few airlines may allow you to use coupons on standby, in which case call the airline a day or two before the flight.

Baggage & Other Restrictions

Many but not all airlines will allow a bicycle or other specialized oversized items as checked luggage. It's best to check with the individual airline about this. On some international flights the luggage allowance is based on weight, not size; again, check with the airline.

If your luggage is delayed upon arrival (which is rare), some airlines will give a cash advance to purchase necessities. If sporting equipment is misplaced, the airline may pay for rentals. If your luggage is lost, it is important to submit a claim. The airline doesn't have to pay the full amount of the claim; rather, it can estimate the value of your lost items. It may take the airline anywhere from six weeks to three months to process the claim and pay you.

Smoking Smoking is prohibited on all domestic flights in the USA, and some international flights. Many airports in the USA also ban smoking; some allow it in designated 'smoking rooms' only.

Illegal Items Items that are illegal to take on a plane, either checked or as carry-on, include weapons, aerosols, tear gas and pepper spray, camp stoves with fuel and divers' tanks that are full. Matches should not be checked.

Items permitted in checked baggage but not on your person or in carry-on luggage include knives and cutting instruments of any kind, anything with a folding or retractable blade, straight razors, metal scissors, metal nail files or clippers and corkscrews.

Travelers with Special Needs

If you have special needs of any sort – dietary restrictions, a broken leg, wheelchair use, responsibility for a baby, fear of flying – airports and airlines can be surprisingly helpful, but do let them know as soon as possible so that they can make arrangements accordingly. You should remind them when you reconfirm your booking (at least 72 hours before departure) and again when you check in at the airport. It may also be worth calling around before you make your booking to find out how the airlines will handle your particular needs.

Guide dogs for the blind often have to travel away from their owners in a specially pressurized baggage compartment with other animals, though smaller guide dogs may be admitted to the cabin. Guide dogs are not subject to quarantine as long as they have proof of being vaccinated against rabies.

Deaf travelers can ask for airport and in-flight announcements to be written down for them. Most international airports can provide escorts from check-in desk to plane where needed, and there should be ramps, elevators, accessible toilets and reachable phones. Aircraft toilets, on the other hand, may present a problem; travelers should discuss this with the airline at an early stage.

Children under two travel for 10% of the standard fare (or free, on some airlines), as long as they don't occupy a seat. (They don't get a baggage allowance either.) 'Skycots' should be provided by the airline if requested in advance; these will take a child weighing up to about 22 pounds. Chil-dren between two and 12 can usually occupy a seat for half to two-thirds of the full fare, and do get a baggage allowance. Folding strollers can often be taken on as hand luggage; larger ones can be checked at the door of the aircraft and are returned to you when you land.

Arriving in the USA

You must complete customs and immigration formalities at the airport where you first land, even if you are continuing immediately to another city. Choose the proper immigration line: either US citizens/residents or non-US citizens. After immigration, recover your luggage in the customs area and proceed to an officer who will ask a few questions and perhaps check your luggage. Dogs trained to detect drugs, explosives and restricted food products might sniff your bags.

If you are continuing to another city, you must recheck your baggage. Airline representatives outside the customs area will assist you.

Departure Taxes

Departure taxes are normally included in the cost of your ticket and you don't have to pay any extra taxes flying from any US airport.

Canada

Travel CUTS (☎ 866-246-9762) has offices in all major cities and online at www.travelcuts.com. They have good deals for students and deal with the general public as well. The Toronto *Globe and Mail* and *Vancouver Sun* carry travel agents' ads.

Many connections between the Southwest and Canada are through Vancouver, BC. Both Phoenix and Salt Lake City have frequent and inexpensive flights to/from Vancouver, which is serviced by Air Canada and many domestic US airlines.

The UK & Ireland

Discount ticket agencies ('bucket shops') generally provide the cheapest fares from London. Agencies usually advertise in the classifieds of Sunday newspapers, magazines such as *Time Out* and many free papers at newsstands everywhere.

Most British travel agents are registered with the Association of British Travel Agents (ABTA). If you have purchased a ticket from an ABTA-registered agent who then goes out of business, ABTA will guarantee a refund or an alternative. Unregistered bucket shops are riskier but sometimes cheaper.

London is arguably the world's headquarters for bucket shops, which are well advertised and can usually beat published airline fares. Good, reliable agents for cheap tickets in the UK include the student agencies mentioned under discount tickets. Among the numerous others is Trailfinders (☎ 020-7938-3939), 194 Kensington High St, London, W8 7RG, at www.trailfinders.com and in many other cities. Try also Flightbookers (☎ 020-7437-7767), 177 Tottenham Court Rd, London, W1. Internet agencies include www.flynow.com (☎ 020-7835-2000, 0870-444-0045), www.cheapflights.co.uk, and www.lastminute.co.uk.

A daily nonstop flight from London to Phoenix is available on British Airways, but this popular route is more expensive than connecting flights. Several carriers fly nonstop to Los Angeles. Round-trip fares from London booked a few months in advance for the low season can be as low as £250; conversely, an economy fare booked a few days ahead in the summer high season can run £700.

Continental Europe

There are no direct flights to the Southwest from Europe. Flying straight to the West Coast is quicker than transferring in a city such as New York or Chicago. Nonstop flights to Los Angeles are available from Amsterdam with Northwest and KLM; from Frankfurt with Delta, United and Lufthansa; from Paris with Air France; and from Rome with Delta. For San Francisco there are nonstop flights from Paris with United and Air France and from Frankfurt with United and Lufthansa. These flights are the most convenient, but they usually cost more than flights that require stops or connections.

European travelers will find that the cheapest flights from London may be about $200 cheaper than flights from European cities. You may want to give London a quick visit before heading over the Atlantic.

Council Travel has several locations in Paris, as well as in the French towns of Aix-en-Provence, Lyon and Nice. The main travel office in Paris is at 22, rue des Pyramides, 75001 (☎ 01-44-55-55-44). Other Council Travel offices include the following in Germany: Düsseldorf (☎ 211-36-30-30), at Graf Adolph Strasse 18, 42112, and Munich (☎ 089-39-50-22), Adalbert Strasse 32, 80799. STA Travel is at Bergerstrasse 118, 60316 Frankfurt 1, Germany (☎ 069-43-01-91). STA is also in a dozen other German cities – call the Frankfurt office for details.

Australia & New Zealand

Flights to Los Angeles and/or San Francisco leave from Sydney, Melbourne, Cairns and Auckland.

STA Travel in Australia (☎ 1-300-360-960) and New Zealand (☎ 0800-874-773) has many offices in the major cities and online at www.statravel.com. Tickets are sold to everyone but there are special deals for students and travelers under 30. Flight Centres International is another major dealer in cheap air fares; check the travel agents' ads in the yellow pages and call around.

The cheapest tickets often have a 21-day advance-purchase requirement, a minimum stay of seven days and a maximum stay of 60 days. Depending on time of year, round-trip flights to Los Angeles run from AUS$1300 to AUS$2100.

Asia

Hong Kong is the discount plane ticket capital of the region, but its bucket shops can be unreliable. Ask the advice of other travelers before buying a ticket. STA Travel, which is dependable, has branches in Japan, Singapore, Thailand, and Malaysia. Council Travel, also reliable, has branches in Japan, Singapore and Thailand. Singapore and

Bangkok seem to be reliable places for cheap flights, many of which go via Honolulu, Hawaii. Sometimes, a free stopover can be included.

Non-stop flights to the West Coast go from several Japanese cities with various airlines.

Mexico, Central & South America

Most flights from Central and South America to the Southwest go via Miami, New Orleans, Houston, Dallas/Fort Worth or Los Angeles. Most countries' international flag carriers and/or privatized airlines, as well as US airlines like United, American and Continental, serve these destinations from Latin America, with onward connections to cities in the Southwest.

America West, Continental and Aero-Mexico have flights from Phoenix and Tucson to numerous Mexican cities.

BUS

Greyhound (☎ 800-231-2222) is the main bus system in the USA, and plays an important transportation role in the Southwest. Parts of New Mexico are served by the TNM&O (Texas, New Mexico & Oklahoma) bus line in conjunction with Greyhound. A few minor regional bus lines, detailed in the text, link minor towns with major cities. However, bus lines don't serve most national parks or some important, off-track tourist towns such as Moab; these can be reached by tour buses only. Traveling by car is definitely recommended as more convenient, although bus services are described in the text if you can't drive or prefer bus travel. Long-distance buses can get you to the region, and then you could rent a car.

Meal stops, usually in inexpensive and unexciting cafes, are made on long trips; you pay for your own food. Buses have onboard lavatories and seats recline for sleeping. Smoking is not permitted aboard Greyhound buses. Long-distance bus trips are often available at bargain prices if you purchase or reserve tickets in advance. At time of writing, tickets ranging in cost from $49 for any journey under 1000 miles to $99 for any journey over 3000 miles were sold 14 days in advance. Journeys of about 100 to 250 miles cost about $20 to $40. For fare and route details, see www.greyhound.com.

Bus terminals are often in poorer or more dangerous areas of town – take a cab to your hotel if you arrive after dark.

Bus Passes

Greyhound Discovery Passes cost between $209 for seven days and $599 for 60 days. Students and seniors receive discounts. These tickets can be bought in advance and use begins from the date of your first trip. You can get on and off at any Greyhound stop or terminal, and the pass is available at every Greyhound terminal.

Foreign tourists can buy International Discovery Passes, which are about 20% cheaper, or a four-day Monday to Thursday pass. The International Pass is usually bought abroad at a travel agency, or it can be bought in the USA through the Greyhound International depot in New York City (☎ 212-971-0492, 800-246-8572) or online, 21 days in advance.

TRAIN

Three Amtrak services cross the south, central and northern part of the Southwest, but are unconnected with one another. Use them to reach the region, not for touring around. Sleeping cabins with private baths and hot showers are available.

The *Southwest Chief* has daily service between Chicago and Los Angeles via Kansas City. The stations in New Mexico and Arizona are Raton, Las Vegas, Lamy, Albuquerque, Gallup, Winslow, Flagstaff, Williams and Kingman.

The *California Zephyr* has daily service between Chicago and San Francisco via Denver. Stations in Utah are Green River, Helper, Provo and Salt Lake City.

The *Sunset Limited* runs thrice weekly from Los Angeles to New Orleans. Stations in Arizona and New Mexico are Yuma, Tucson, Benson, Lordsburg and Deming.

Tickets should be booked in advance with Amtrak (☎ 800-872-7245), online at www.amtrak.com or through a travel agent.

Small stations have no facilities, and trains stop there only if you have bought a ticket in advance.

For non-US citizens, Amtrak offers various USA Rail Passes that must be purchased outside the US (check with a travel agent).

CAR & MOTORCYCLE

Foreign motorists and motorcyclists (traveling with their own foreign vehicles) will need the vehicle's registration papers, liability insurance and an international driver's permit in addition to their domestic license. Canadian and Mexican driver's licenses are accepted.

For information on buying or renting a car, see the Getting Around chapter.

Drive-Aways

Drive-aways are a cheap way to get to the Southwest if you like long-distance driving and meet eligibility requirements. In a typical drive-away, somebody might move from Boston to Phoenix, for example, and elect to fly rather than drive; he or she would then hire a drive-away agency to get the car to Phoenix. The agency will find a driver and take care of all necessary insurance and permits. If you happen to want to

drive from Boston to Phoenix, have a valid driver's license and a clean driving record, you can apply to drive the car. Normally, you have to pay a small refundable deposit. You pay for the gas (though sometimes a gas allowance is given). You are allowed a set number of days to deliver the car – usually based on driving eight hours a day. You are also allowed a limited number of miles, based on the best route and allowing for reasonable side trips, so you can't just zigzag all over the country. There is usually a minimum-age requirement as well.

Drive-away companies often advertise in the classified sections of newspapers under 'Travel.' They are also listed in the yellow pages of telephone directories under 'Auto Transporters & Drive-away Companies.' A well-known company that has been providing this service since 1952 and operates about 75 offices throughout the country is Auto Driveaway Co.

You need to be flexible about dates and destinations when you call. If you are going to a popular area, you may be able to leave within two days or less, or you may have to wait over a week before a car becomes available. The routes most easily available are coast to coast, although intermediate trips are certainly possible.

Getting Around

Once you reach the Southwest, traveling by car is usually the best way of getting around. A car will get you to rural areas not served by air, bus or train. However, you can use public transport to reach towns and cities, then rent a car locally to get to places not served by public transport. This option is usually more expensive than just renting a car and driving yourself everywhere, but it can cut down on long-distance driving trips if you don't relish them.

AIR

Phoenix is the hub of America West Express, which serves small towns throughout Arizona, northwestern New Mexico and southwestern Colorado. Albuquerque is the hub of Mesa Air, which serves small towns throughout New Mexico. Salt Lake City is the hub for Delta Connection, serving St George, Cedar City and Vernal in Utah and some Colorado towns. These short-hop flights tend to be used mainly by local residents and businesspeople, and fares are not very cheap, but they are an option for tourists with money.

America West, Southwest and Delta are the main carriers linking Phoenix, Salt Lake City, Las Vegas, Tucson and Albuquerque. See the Getting There & Away chapter for their toll-free numbers and websites.

Regular fares on these routes can be expensive if you don't have advance booking, but fares can drop by about half if you are able to fly very early in the morning, late at night or on specific flights. Ask about special fares when making reservations.

If you are arriving from overseas or from another major airport in the USA, it is usually much cheaper to buy a through ticket to small airports as part of your fare rather than separately, unless your travel plans are so spontaneous as to preclude doing so.

Another alternative is an air pass, available from the major airlines that fly between the USA and Europe, Asia and Australia. Air passes are particularly valuable if you're flying between widely separated destinations. (See Air Passes in Getting There & Away.)

BUS

Greyhound is the main carrier to and within the Southwest (see the Getting There & Away chapter for more information). They run buses several times a day along major highways between large towns, only stopping at smaller towns that happen to be along the way. Greyhound has reduced or eliminated services to smaller rural communities it once served efficiently. In many small towns Greyhound no longer maintains terminals but merely stops at a given location, such as a grocery store parking lot. In these unlikely terminals, boarding passengers usually pay the driver with exact change.

Towns not on major routes are often served by local carriers. Greyhound usually has information about the local carriers – the name, phone number and, sometimes, fare and schedule information. Information about the many local bus companies is given in the text.

In New Mexico, a major carrier that serves or replaces Greyhound routes is TNM&O (Texas, New Mexico and Oklahoma) lines.

Buying Tickets

Tickets can be bought over the phone with a credit card (MasterCard, Visa or Discover) and mailed to you if purchased 10 days in advance, or they can be picked up at the terminal with proper identification. Greyhound terminals also accept American Express, traveler's checks and cash. Reservations are made with ticket purchases only. Many bus stops are just that – a stop next to a McDonald's restaurant or a gas station. Look for the blue and red Greyhound symbol. You may have to pay the driver when you board. Only larger towns have proper bus stations or terminals.

Fares vary tremendously. Sometimes, but not always, you can get discounted tickets if you purchase them three, seven or 21 days in advance. It's best to call Greyhound for current details or check its website at www.greyhound.com.

TRAIN

Amtrak's three routes through the Southwest are not convenient options for touring the region (see the Getting There & Away chapter).

Several other lines provide service using historic steam trains and are mainly for sightseeing, although the Williams to Grand Canyon run is a destination in itself. These are detailed in the text under Williams, Benson, Cottonwood, Yuma (all in Arizona) and Chama, New Mexico.

CAR

The US highway system is very extensive, and since distances are great and buses can be infrequent, traveling by automobile is worth considering despite the expense. Officially, you must have an International or Inter-American Driving Permit to supplement your national or state driver's license, but US police are more likely to want to see your national, provincial or state driver's license.

Safety

Read the Dangers & Annoyances section in the Facts for the Visitor chapter for general safety rules regarding driving and traveling in the Southwest, and the Legal Matters section for information on drinking and driving laws.

Also bear in mind that Gallup, New Mexico, has built up an unfortunate reputation for careless and drunken driving. Hwy 666 north to Shiprock has an especially high accident rate. New Mexico has one of the highest ratios of fatal car accidents to miles driven in the whole country. Be extra defensive while driving in the Southwest, especially in New Mexico.

Distances are great in the Southwest, and there are long stretches of road without gas stations. Running out of gas on a hot and desolate stretch of highway can be hazardous to your health, so pay close attention to signs that caution 'Next Gas 68 Miles.'

American Automobile Association

The American Automobile Association (AAA, or 'Triple A;' ☎ 800-874-7532) has hundreds of offices throughout the USA and Canada. Annual membership varies from state to state but costs about $40 (plus a one-time initiation fee of about $20) for one driver and $20 for each additional driver in the same household. Reciprocal member services for residents of one state are available in all other states. Members of many similar foreign organizations also receive reciprocal member services.

AAA provides free and detailed state and city maps and will help you plan your trip. If you're a member and break down, get a flat tire, run out of gas or have a dead battery, call their toll-free number (☎ 800-222-4357) and they will send out a reputable towing company at costs lower than if you had called the towing company yourself. They'll make minor repairs (changing a tire, jump-starting a car etc) for free or tow you to the nearest repair shop. Normally, the first three miles of towing are free, or you can buy a more expensive membership with free towing up to 100 miles. Benefits apply when you are driving rented or borrowed cars as well. The AAA travel agency will also book car rentals, air tickets and hotel rooms at discount prices.

The main full-service offices in the Southwest are in Phoenix and Salt Lake City. Maps and many other services are available at the smaller branches in Tucson, Yuma, Albuquerque, Santa Fe, Las Cruces, Ogden and some other towns. Hours are 8:30 am to 5 pm Monday to Friday and Saturday mornings in some towns. Emergency breakdown services are available 24 hours a day. website: www.aaa.com

Rental

Major international rental agencies have offices throughout the region. To rent a car, you must have a valid driver's license, meet minimum age requirements (25 years in many cases, or an extra fee applies) and present a major credit card (some companies will accept a large cash deposit).

Exact details vary from city to city, company to company, and depend on the time of year, so call around to find what you need. Also try calling some of the smaller, lesser known local agencies, which are more likely to allow people under 25 to rent a car with no age surcharge. Very few companies will rent cars to drivers under 21, and those that do charge significantly higher rates.

Many rental agencies have bargain rates for weekend or week-long rentals, especially outside the peak summer season or in conjunction with airline tickets. Prices vary greatly depending on the region, the season and the type or size of the car you'd like to rent. In the off-season, compact cars rent as cheaply as $99 a week, but rates of $129 to $169 a week are more common in the high season. Larger, more comfortable cars are available at higher rates. Taxes are extra and average around 10% (Utah is higher; see 'Car Rental' in the Salt Lake City chapter). If you rent a car for a week and return it sooner, many rental companies will recalculate the rate you were charged at a daily rate, rather than prorate the weekly rate, and you may end up spending more than you were originally quoted.

If you want to rent a car for less than a week, daily rates will be more expensive: $30 a day is a good price but closer to $40 is not unusual. You can get discounts if you are a member of AAA or another travel club. Although $150 or more a week may seem high for travelers on a tight budget, if you split the rental between two or three (or squeeze in a fourth!), it works out much cheaper than going by bus.

Rates usually include unlimited mileage, but make sure they do. If there is a mileage charge, your costs will go up quickly and disconcertingly as you drive the long distances of the Southwest. Be aware that some major rental agencies no longer offer unlimited mileage in noncompetitive markets – this greatly increases the cost of renting a car.

A Crash Course

Accidents do happen – especially in such an auto-dependent country as the USA. It's important for a visitor to know the appropriate protocol when involved in a 'fender-bender.'

- *Don't try to drive away!* Remain at the scene of the accident; otherwise, you may spend time in the local jail.

- Call the police (and an ambulance, if needed) immediately, and give the operator as much specific information as you can (your exact location, if there are any injuries etc). The emergency phone number is ☎ 911.

- Get the other driver's name, address, driver's license number, license plate and insurance information. Be prepared to provide any documentation you have, such as your passport, international driver's license and insurance documents.

- Tell your story to the police carefully. Refrain from answering any questions until you feel comfortable doing so (with a lawyer present, if need be). That's your right under the law. The only insurance information you need to reveal is the name of your insurance carrier and your policy number.

- Always agree to an alcohol breathalyzer test. If you take the option not to, you'll almost certainly find your driving privileges automatically suspended.

- If you're driving a rental car, call the rental company promptly.

You are expected to return the car to the same place where you picked it up. You can sometimes arrange to drop the car off elsewhere, but there is often a large surcharge. Be aware that the person who rents the car is the only legal driver, and in the event of an accident, only the legal driver is covered. However, when you rent the car, additional drivers may be signed on as legal drivers for a fee, usually $3 per day per person.

Basic liability insurance, which will cover damage you may cause to another vehicle, is required by law and comes with the price of renting the car. Liability insurance is also called third-party coverage.

Collision insurance, also called the Collision Damage Waiver (CDW) or Loss Damage Waiver, is optional; it covers the full value of the vehicle in case of an accident, except when caused by acts of nature or fire. For a midsized car the cost for this extra coverage is around $15 per day. You don't need to buy this waiver to rent the car, though you are responsible for covering the cost of repairs in the event of a collision. It may be advisable to buy CDW unless you have some other kind of insurance.

Many credit cards will cover collision insurance if you rent for 15 days or less and charge the full cost of rental to your card. If you have collision insurance on your personal car insurance policy, this will often cover rented vehicles. The credit card will cover the large deductible. To find out if your credit card offers such a service, and the extent of the coverage, contact the credit card company.

Note that many rental agencies stipulate that damage a car suffers while being driven on unpaved roads is not covered by the insurance they offer. Check with the agent when you make your reservation. It never hurts to read the fine print when you get the contract, either.

The following companies rent cars throughout the Southwest. The large cities have the best selection of companies, cars and rates. You can rent subcompact to luxury cars, pickup trucks, 4WDs, vans or moving trucks. Smaller cities have less selection and often charge a little more. Small companies serving just one or two towns are not listed below.

Advantage ☎ 800-777-5500
www.arac.com

Alamo ☎ 800-327-9633
www.goalamo.com

Avis ☎ 800-831-2847
www.avis.com

Budget ☎ 800-527-0700
www.budgetrentacar.com

Dollar ☎ 800-800-4000
www.dollarcar.com

Enterprise ☎ 800-325-8007
www.pickenterprise.com

Hertz ☎ 800-654-3131
www.hertz.com

National ☎ 800-227-7368
www.nationalcar.com

Payless ☎ 800-729-5377
www.800-payless.com

Rent-A-Wreck ☎ 800-944-7501
www.rent-a-wreck.com

Thrifty ☎ 800-847-4389
www.thrifty.com

Purchase

If you're spending several months in the USA, purchasing a car is worth considering, but buying one requires some research.

It's possible to purchase a working car in the USA for about $2000, but you can't expect to go too far before you'll need some repair work that could cost several hundred dollars or more. It doesn't hurt to spend more to get a quality vehicle. It's also worth spending $75 or so to have a mechanic check it for defects (some AAA offices have diagnostic centers where they can do this on the spot for its members and those of foreign affiliates).

You have to register your car with the Department of Motor Vehicles, which will cost several hundred dollars (less for a cheap old clunker, more for a new car), and buy insurance, which will be several hundred dollars for six months. You also have to allow time at the end of your trip to sell the car. Generally, it's more hassle than it's worth unless you are spending six months or more traveling in the USA.

Inspect the title (as the ownership document is called) carefully before purchasing the car; the owner's name that appears on the title must match the identification of the person selling you the car.

BICYCLE

Cycling is a cheap, convenient, healthy, environmentally sound and, above all, fun way of traveling. A note of caution: Before leaving home, go over your bike with a fine-toothed comb, and fill your repair kit with every imaginable spare part in case you break down in the back of beyond. Know how to change tires and do basic repair/maintenance. Carry and use the toughest bicycle padlock available and always carry extra water.

Bicycles can travel by air. You can take them apart and put them in a bike bag or box, but it's much easier simply to wheel your bike to the check-in desk, where it should be treated as a piece of baggage. You may have to remove the pedals and turn the handlebars sideways so that it takes up less space in the aircraft's hold; check all this with the airline well in advance, preferably before you pay for your ticket.

If you'd rather rent a bike when you get there, look under 'Bicycles – Rental' in the telephone directory yellow pages. There are several places to choose from in larger towns. In smaller towns, options for bicycle rentals are mentioned in the text. For a long-term rental, you might want to consider buying a new or used bike and then re-selling it. Call around bike stores in the town where you start from and explore these options.

Bicycles are generally prohibited on interstate highways if there is a frontage road. However, where a suitable frontage road or other alternative is lacking, bicyclists are permitted on some interstates. Note that some scenic areas have cycling restrictions.

HITCHHIKING

Hitching is never entirely safe in any country in the world, and we don't recommend it. Travelers who decide to hitch should understand that they are taking a small but serious risk. You may not be able to identify the local rapist/murderer before you get into the vehicle. People who do choose to hitch will be safer if they travel in pairs and let someone know where they are planning to go. Ask the driver where he or she is going rather than telling the person where you want to go.

LOCAL TRANSPORTATION

Salt Lake City in Utah has the only urban train system in the Southwest; it is a simple two-line system.

Cities and some larger towns have local bus systems that will get you around. These generally run on very limited schedules on Sunday and at night. Telephone numbers of urban bus systems are given in the text.

Taxis will get you around, but are not cheap. Expect to pay around $2 a mile, which makes them very expensive for long distances. Check the yellow pages under 'Taxi' for phone numbers and services. Drivers expect a tip of about 10% to 15% of the fare. In most cities, you have to telephone for a taxi, as there are few to hail on the streets.

Mountain reflections in Emerald Pools, Zion National Park, UT

Hiking in the amphitheater, Bryce Canyon NP, UT

A lonely life, Zion National Park, UT

Eroded sandstone pinnacles, Bryce Canyon National Park, UT

The distinctive Moenkopi sandstone of Capitol Reef National Park, UT

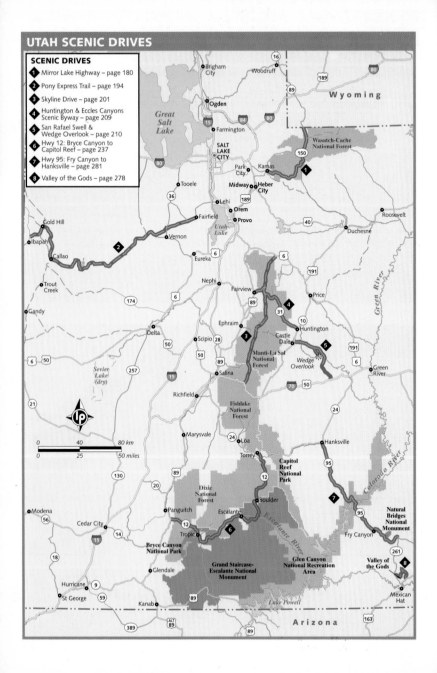

UTAH SCENIC DRIVES

SCENIC DRIVES

① Mirror Lake Highway – page 180
② Pony Express Trail – page 194
③ Skyline Drive – page 201
④ Huntington & Eccles Canyons Scenic Byway – page 209
⑤ San Rafael Swell & Wedge Overlook – page 210
⑥ Hwy 12: Bryce Canyon to Capitol Reef – page 237
⑦ Hwy 95: Fry Canyon to Hanksville – page 281
⑧ Valley of the Gods – page 278

Facts about Utah

Every story in Utah begins and ends with the land, much of which remains just as wild and untamed as it was when humans first stumbled across it about 7000 years ago. For millennia, Indians adapted to the harsh desert terrain, leaving behind mysterious, clearly sacred etchings and paintings on the rock. When the Mormon pioneers reached this country, they too felt a spiritual response and claimed it as their new home (their Zion). And it is impossible today to gaze for any length of time at the sometimes heartbreakingly desolate canyons and cliffs, the wildly eroded buttes and spires and pinnacles, without a sense of awe stealing upon you. At times, Utah provides an experience of nature so elemental and overwhelming it takes your breath away.

Not surprisingly, it's this unique scenery that draws most visitors to the state, and it's the main reason most residents give for staying. But while Utah's famous red rock desert and its Great Salt Lake get most of the press, the state contains the equally rugged and wild Uinta Mountains in the north, a portion of the vast Great Basin in the west, and running down its spine, the snow-covered Wasatch Range. These mountains have now achieved their own measure of fame as the site of the 2002 Winter Olympics, an event that Utah pursued as a way to establish itself not just as a major tourist destination for outdoor adventure, but as an important state with a unique heritage and an international capital, Salt Lake City.

Recent History

Salt Lake City was founded by Mormon pioneers in 1847, marking the beginning of the state's modern era. The region was part of Mexico until 1848, after which it became part of the State of Deseret, which means 'honeybee' according to the Book of Mormon. In 1850 the name was changed to Utah Territory (after the indigenous Ute Indians) because non-Mormons objected to the religious implications of Deseret.

Highlights

- Capitol Reef National Park – the 100-mile-long Waterpocket Fold arches like a dragon's back.

- Hovenweep National Monument – see remote, unrestored Ancestral Puebloan buildings.

- Moki Dugway – the world seems to end here, but the road doesn't.

- Logan Canyon – hike or drive in fall, when brilliant colors splash the steep canyon walls.

- Dinosaur National Monument – visit a unique dinosaur fossil quarry with 1600 exposed fossils.

- Nine Mile Canyon – explore the 'longest art gallery in the world.'

Scenic Drives

The map opposite this page is a sampling of favorite routes through Utah. Some are designated 'Scenic Byways' and some are quiet dirt trails; some are alternative highways and some are rewarding detours. The text includes many more recommended roads for exploring this scenic country.

Church leader Brigham Young (see 'The Church of Jesus Christ of Latter-Day Saints' boxed text in the Salt Lake City chapter) was the first governor.

As Mormons founded more towns in the 1850s, they came into conflict with the Ute Indians and several minor wars ensued, which the Utes lost. However, the relations between the Utes and the Mormons were friendlier than Indian-white relations elsewhere. Brigham Young preferred to coexist with the Indians – and try to convert them – rather than to try and wipe them out. The Utes were eventually settled on a reservation in the Uinta Mountains in 1872.

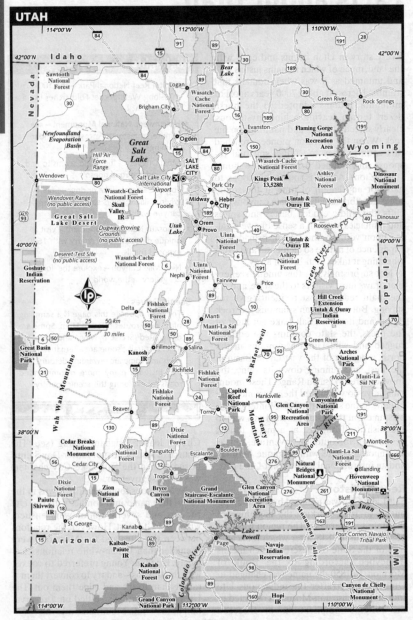

As Mormonism gained a solid foothold in Utah, the rest of the country began to have misgivings about this new power on the Western frontier. Anti-Mormon feelings were strong in the eastern USA, particularly in response to the early Mormon practice of polygamy.

The Mormons petitioned Congress for statehood six times, the first as far back as 1856, but the first five petitions were consistently rejected due to polygamy. The practice was outlawed by the US government in 1862, but the law was not enforced by the Mormons. Church leaders considered the practice protected by the First Amendment (which guarantees freedom of religion), but the US Supreme Court ruled against them in 1879. With the coming of more non-Mormons to Utah, the polygamy issue became more difficult to ignore, and more than a thousand Mormon men were jailed in the 1880s for the practice. The relationship between the territory and the federal government deteriorated steadily, and some congressmen proposed a bill to withdraw voting rights from all Mormon men.

The tense situation was suddenly settled in 1890 when Mormon Church President Wilford Woodruff announced that God had told him that Mormons should abide by US law, and polygamy was discontinued. Soon after, Utah's sixth attempt at statehood was successful; it was admitted to the Union in 1896 as the 45th state. The young state was still very much Mormon, but it resolutely supported US policies at home and abroad. By the early 1900s, political control was increasingly shared with non-Mormons, but politics continued to run as much along religious lines as party ones.

Today, Utah is overwhelmingly Republican and conservative, though liberal Democrats are elected occasionally (such as Salt Lake City's current mayor, Rocky Anderson). Many critics call Utah a de facto 'theocracy,' with the Mormon Church exerting a powerful behind-the-scenes influence. More telling is the growing urban/rural split: About 75% of residents live along the urbanized Wasatch front, but 75% of politicians represent rural areas. These divergent factions are often at odds over how to tackle the major questions facing Utah today – how to control the rampant urban development around Salt Lake City, how to address the environmental degradation of the Wasatch front, how to clean up a legacy of toxic industries and military testing, and whether the state needs to 'liberalize' its image (and specifically, do away with its liquor laws) to attract more high-tech and other industries.

Economy

The pioneering Mormons based their economy on crop agriculture, but today less than 1% of Utah's revenues are from farming. The leading sectors of the economy are now the service industry, government and manufacturing, especially the manufacture of electronic and computer components, medical instruments, metals, transportation equipment and food products; together, these accounted for $17 billion in 1999. Along with Arizona and New Mexico, Utah is one of the nation's three leading producers of copper, although many other substances are also mined. Tourism is also a major industry, bringing in over $4 billion annually. However, six of Utah's nine top employers are universities and educational institutions, and Utah has one of the nation's highest high school graduation rates.

Provo is the center of Utah's growing computer industry, and scientists at the University of Utah in Salt Lake City have pioneered medical and energy techniques of international significance, including the first artificial human heart implant in 1982. Though it lasted only two weeks, the 2002 Olympics were expected to add an additional $1.7 billion to the economy that year.

Utah's population increased by 29.6% from 1990 to 2000, making it the nation's fourth fastest growing state behind Nevada, Arizona and Colorado. It is also the youngest state, with over 32% of the population under 18 years old, and families tend to be large; the average household size was 3.13 in 2000 (it is 2.59 nationally). The average annual salary in 2000 was $27,884, and the average cost of a home was $168,000.

The 2002 Winter Olympics

From February 8 to 24, 2002, Utah hosted the XIX Olympic Games, which brought over 2000 athletes from 85 countries who competed in 75 medal events at 10 different venues. The Olympics also brought Utah a level of international attention heretofore unknown, and for which it prepared with the earnest industriousness Utahns are now, most likely, famous for.

While the Olympics are over (and occurred after this book went to press), they left in their wake a number of first-class skate and ski facilities. All can be visited, and most can be used by the public. All of the sites are within an hour's drive of Salt Lake City, where the opening and closing ceremonies were performed and all of the figure skating, speed skating and most of the ice hockey events were held. Provo hosted a few hockey events, and Ogden hosted curling and a few alpine skiing events at nearby Snowbasin. The rest of the downhill, cross-country, ski jump and sled events were held at outdoor venues in and around Park City.

All of these sites are described further in the text and provide visitors with a chance to relive the drama and ski (and skate) in the tracks of champions.

Information

The Utah Travel Council (☎ 801-538-1030, 800-200-1160), Council Hall, Capitol Hill, Salt Lake City, UT 84114, publishes the helpful free *Utah Travel Guide* and offers a useful website at www.utah.com. It is housed in a historic building in downtown Salt Lake City with the Utah Tourism & Recreation Information Center, which operates 8 am to 5 pm Monday to Friday, and from 10 am to 5 pm on some weekends. The council's bookstore (☎ 801-538-1398), in the same building, has a good selection of Utah histories and guides as well as topographic maps.

New in 2001, the Discover! Public Lands Information Center (☎ 801-466-6411, discoverpubliclands@excite.com), 3285 E 3300 South, inside of REI's Salt Lake City store, is now the central source of information for the National Park Service (NPS), US USFS (USFS), Bureau of Land Management (BLM) and Utah State Parks. The individual public lands agencies created this entity to handle the public for them. Hours are 10:30 am to 7 pm Tuesday to Saturday. However, Discover! only sells the Golden Age national parks pass; all other passes must be purchased at the USFS in the Salt Lake City Federal Building.

While the Discover! desk at REI has the most comprehensive information, the following statewide offices are open to the public. The USFS (☎ 801-524-3900), 8th Floor, Federal Building, 125 S State, Salt Lake City, UT 84138, has maps and sells national parks passes. The US Geological Survey (☎ 801-975-3742), 222 W 2300 South in Salt Lake City (hard to find, call for directions), has the best selection of topographic and other maps in the Southwest.

The BLM (☎ 801-539-4001) is at 324 S State, Suite 400. Their Salt Lake field office (☎ 977-4300), 2370 S 2300 West, covers Bonneville and other western areas.

Utah State Parks & Recreation (☎ 801-538-7220), 1594 W North Temple, sells an annual permit ($65) valid for day use in all state parks. Camping reservations can also be made (☎ 801-322-3770, 800-322-3770) for a $6.25 reservation fee; for most areas, you must reserve three days in advance.

See specific chapters for tourist information for that region.

Telephone Salt Lake City and County use the 801 area code, along with some adjacent communities. In March 2002, the surrounding counties changed to a new 385 area code; boundaries were still being settled at press time, but it includes much of Davis, Morgan, Utah and Weber Counties (which include Ogden and Provo). The rest of Utah uses the 435 area code. For emergencies dial ☎ 911 or 0.

Internet Resources For travel information throughout Utah, go to www.utah.com, while www.utah.gov is the state government's official website. To make camping reservations at any state park and for fishing and hunting updates and regulations, go to www.nr.utah.gov. For access to the Utah yellow pages, go to www.qwestdex.com. Utah's public library has an excellent website with links to the major daily newspapers at www.pioneer.lib.ut.us. The Utah Avalanche Center has updated snow and weather reports at www.avalanche.org/~uac. The official website of the Church of Jesus Christ of Latter-day Saints is www.lds.org.

Time The state is on Mountain Time. When it is noon in Utah, it is 11 am on the West Coast, 2 pm on the East Coast, and 7 pm in London.

Orientation Throughout Utah, towns and cities use the same street layout. The system is more complicated to explain than it is to learn, and once learned, you can use it all over Utah.

Normally, there is a zero point in the town center, at the intersection of two major streets (which are often called Main St and Center St). Addresses and street names radiate out from this zero point, rising by 100 with each city block. Thus an address of 500 South 400 East (**A** on the map above) will be at the intersection of 500 South St and 400 East St, or five blocks south and four blocks east of the zero point. The first cardinal point is usually abbreviated, but the second cardinal point is abbreviated less frequently – 500 S 400 East would be the most likely designation. (The 'St' is often dropped.) An address such as 270 S 300 East (**B**) is a building on 300 East St between 200 South and 300 South St.

Some cities have areas where streets don't follow the same pattern, but the general numbering system remains the same. 500 N 600 East will always be to the northeast of the zero point.

Note that a few maps (and locals) might refer to 1st North, 2nd North etc, instead of 100 North, 200 North. It's the same thing.

Driving Laws You must be at least 16 years old to obtain a driver's license. Drivers and

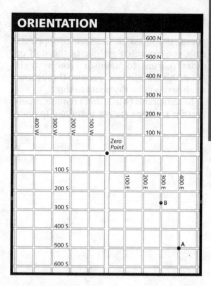

front-seat passengers are required to wear safety belts. Children under age eight must use child restraints. You must be over 16 to obtain a motorcycle license; motorcycle helmets are required for rider and passenger if they are under 18. The blood alcohol concentration over which you are legally considered drunk while driving is 0.08 (lower than the 0.10 of most other states). It is illegal to have an open container of alcohol in your car while driving.

Drinking Laws Due to its Mormon influence, Utah has the strangest liquor laws in the country. However, they sound more complex and discouraging than they wind up being in practice. As in all of the USA, you must be 21 to buy alcohol. Grocery stores can sell beer of not more than 3.2% alcohol content every day of the week. Stronger beer, wine and spirits are sold in state-run liquor stores (also called package stores) that are closed on Sunday.

Lounges and taverns sell only 3.2% beer – stronger drinks can be sold only in restaurants or 'private clubs.' To enter a private club, you must be a member; a temporary visitor's membership costs $5 and is valid for two weeks. All members (including temporary ones) can invite in up to five guests. If you ask at the door of a private club, you can often get one of the staff or other patrons to 'sponsor' you as their guest; this is a common practice throughout Utah, so don't be shy about asking.

In restaurants (which don't require 'membership'), servers are not permitted to offer you a drink or even show you a menu with drinks unless you specifically ask for one. You must order food to buy a drink, but it can be just a snack. At any establishment, you cannot buy two drinks for yourself at any one time (this is known affectionately as Utah's 'slammin' rule,' since you must finish up before ordering the next round). Alcohol is prohibited on Indian reservations.

Salt Lake City

☎ 801 • pop 181,743; metro area 1.7 million
• elevation 4330 feet

Salt Lake City, the capital of Utah, is by far the largest city in the state. It is also the headquarters of the Mormon Church. The Great Salt Lake and the impressive architecture and culture of the Mormon Church are the two most famous attractions for visitors. There is much more to see, however, not the least of which is the city's spectacular setting at the foot of the Wasatch Mountains. The mountains offer great recreational opportunities: beautiful hiking in summer, lovely fall colors and some of the country's best skiing in winter and spring.

Salt Lake City (popularly called Salt Lake) is the heart of a metropolitan area along the Wasatch front, extending from Ogden to Provo, that contains about three-quarters of Utah's population. The city's climate is relatively mild year-round, with summer highs occasionally rising into the 90°s F and winter highs usually staying above freezing.

HISTORY

The city's history is linked inextricably with the remarkable history of the Mormons (see 'The Church of Jesus Christ of Latter-Day Saints' boxed text). Within a few weeks of the city's founding on July 24, 1847, the pioneers' numbers had swelled to 2000. Streets were built 132 feet wide, so that four oxen pulling a wagon could turn around. Each city block was 10 acres in size, which gave rise to a spaciousness that is still evident in downtown Salt Lake and in many other of Utah's Mormon towns.

In 1847, Great Salt Lake City ('Great' was dropped in 1868) was a long way from anywhere. The Mormon settlers struggled hard to survive during the first years, especially in 1848 when a late frost followed by a plague of grasshoppers threatened to wipe out the crops. What happened next is still regarded as miraculous by the Mormons: A flock of gulls flew in, ate the grasshoppers

and saved the remaining crop. (That is why Utah's official state bird is the California gull.)

By 1849, there were some 7500 Mormons in Salt Lake. The California gold rush of that year drew a flood of travelers and prospectors from across the country. The Mormons seized the opportunity to sell food, lodging and supplies to the '49ers,' and from then on the city flourished. By the mid-1850s about 60,000 Mormons had arrived.

However, many US citizens felt threatened by the beliefs and practices of the Mormon Church, especially polygamy, and feared the intentions of its leader, Brigham Young. In 1857, President Buchanan sent hundreds of troops to Salt Lake City to squash a supposed 'Mormon rebellion' and thus began the so-called Utah War. The army marched into the city in 1858, only to find it abandoned except for a few men with orders to burn the town to the ground if the soldiers tried to occupy it. The troops continued through the city and made camp 40 miles away at Camp Floyd, avoiding conflict altogether.

Salt Lake City remained almost 100% Mormon until 1869, when the completion of the transcontinental railway brought a flood of non-Mormons (whom the Mormons called 'Gentiles') to northern Utah. By the late 1800s, only half of the inhabitants of Salt Lake were Mormons and the figure is about the same today (though most other Utah cities are predominantly Mormon).

After polygamy was abolished by the Mormon Church, Utah was granted statehood in 1896, and Salt Lake City became the state capital. The magnificent capitol building was finished in 1915.

The history of Salt Lake in the 20th century is similar to that of many other US cities. A period of economic growth in the first decades of the century was followed by the Depression in the 1930s. The economy revitalized with WWII and industry blossomed. When prices and production of minerals fell a new economic mainstay was found: tourism and related industries, which still play a vital part in Utah's economy. To maintain the integrity of downtown, shopping malls and renovation projects were developed, and the center remains vibrant.

New industries related to computer development and biomedicine are becoming important, and Salt Lake hopes that hosting the 2002 Winter Olympics will increase its stature..

ORIENTATION

Salt Lake City (as with most Mormon towns) is laid out in a spacious grid (for the most part) with streets aligned north-south or east-west. The most important block is Temple Square; the corner of S Temple (running east-west) and Main (north-south) is the zero point for streets and addresses in the city (see Orientation in the Facts about Utah chapter). N Temple, westbound, goes to the airport just 6 convenient miles from downtown.

Two major interstates intersect at Salt Lake City. I-15 heads north-south and I-80 east-west. I-215 is a loop that skirts the city to the east, south and west.

Note that because streets are so long and wide, there are mid-block pedestrian crossings downtown. Orange flags are available at these crossings for increased visibility.

INFORMATION

The Visitor Information Center (☎ 944-4240) and the Salt Lake Convention & Visitors Bureau (☎ 521-2822, 800-541-4955), 90 S West Temple, Salt Lake City, UT 84101, are both in the modern Salt Palace Convention Center. The information center is open daily. The bureau publishes the useful, free *Salt Lake Visitors Guide* and offers information online at www.visitsaltlake.com. There is a gift shop. The local Salt Lake Ranger Station (☎ 733-2660), 6944 S 3000 East, covers the Wasatch-Cache National Forest. Although it no longer handles walk-in visitors, information will be given over the telephone. See the Facts about Utah chapter for resources for statewide information.

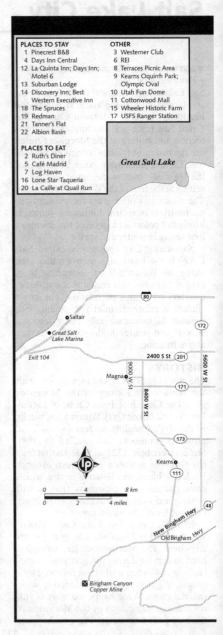

PLACES TO STAY	OTHER
1 Pinecrest B&B	3 Westerner Club
4 Days Inn Central	6 REI
12 La Quinta Inn; Days Inn; Motel 6	8 Terraces Picnic Area
13 Suburban Lodge	9 Kearns Oquirrh Park; Olympic Oval
14 Discovery Inn; Best Western Executive Inn	10 Utah Fun Dome
18 The Spruces	11 Cottonwood Mall
19 Redman	15 Wheeler Historic Farm
21 Tanner's Flat	17 USFS Ranger Station
22 Albion Basin	

PLACES TO EAT
2 Ruth's Diner
5 Café Madrid
7 Log Haven
16 Lone Star Taqueria
20 La Caille at Quail Run

Great Salt Lake

Saltair

Great Salt Lake Marina

Exit 104

Magna

Kearns

2400 S St

New Bingham Hwy

Old Bingham Hwy

Bingham Canyon Copper Mine

0   4   8 km
0   2   4 miles

UTAH

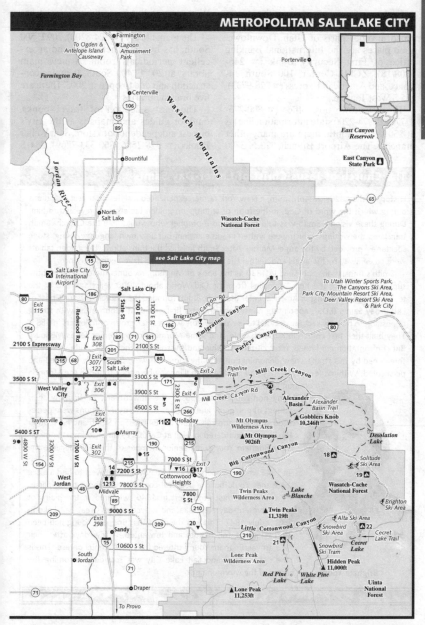

METROPOLITAN SALT LAKE CITY

To Ogden &
Antelope Island
Causeway

Farmington

Lagoon
Amusement
Park

Porterville

Farmington Bay

Centerville

106

Wasatch Mountains

East Canyon
Reservoir

East Canyon
State Park

15
89

Bountiful

65

North
Salt Lake

Wasatch-Cache
National Forest

Jordan River

see Salt Lake City map

15   89

Salt Lake City
International
Airport

Salt Lake City

1

To Utah Winter Sports Park,
The Canyons Ski Area,
Park City Mountain Resort Ski Area,
Deer Valley Resort Ski Area
& Park City

80   Exit
115

186

State St

700 E St

1300 E St

Emigration Canyon Rd

2

154

Exit
308

89   71   181

201

2100 S St

186

Emigration Canyon

Parleys Canyon

80

2100 S Expressway

215   68

Exit
307/
122

South
Salt Lake

80

Exit 2

3500 S St

3300 S St

171

Pipeline
Trail

7

Mill Creek Canyon

West Valley
City

3   Exit
306

4

3900 S St

2300 E St

Exit 4

Mill Creek Canyon Rd

8

Alexander
Basin

Alexander
Basin Trail

4500 S St

5

266

Taylorsville

Exit
302

11   Holladay

Mt Olympus
Wilderness Area

Gobblers Knob
10,246ft

5400 S ST

10

Murray

190

Mt Olympus
9026ft

Desolation
Lake

9

4800 W St

3200 W St

1700 W St

154

Exit
302

215

Big Cottonwood Canyon

18

Solitude
Ski Area

West
Jordan

48

14   7200 S St

215

7000 S St

Exit 7

16   17

19

Midvale

1213

7800 S St

Cottonwood
Heights

7800
S St

Wasatch-Cache
National Forest

Brighton
Ski Area

89

9000 S St

210

Twin Peaks
Wilderness Area

Lake
Blanche

Alta Ski Area

209

South
Jordan

Exit
298

Sandy

20

Twin Peaks
11,319ft

Little Cottonwood Canyon

Snowbird
Ski Area

22

Cecret
Lake Trail

15

10600 S St

209

210

21

Snowbird
Ski Tram

Cecret
Lake

71

Lone Peak
Wilderness Area

Hidden Peak
11,000ft

Draper

Red Pine
Lake

White Pine
Lake

Uinta
National
Forest

71

To Provo

Lone Peak
11,253ft

Exchange foreign currency at the airport or downtown banks because it is difficult to do so in other parts of Utah. Downtown, good places are the International Banking office of First Security Bank (☎ 246-5308/18), ZCMI Center, 100 South entrance, and American Express (☎ 328-9733), 175 S West Temple.

The downtown post office (☎ 800-275-8777, 801-974-2200 state information line) is at 230 W 200 South; there are many other branches. The Airport Branch, 320 N 3700 West (near to, but not in the terminals), has 24-hour service.

The main library (☎ 524-8200), 209 E 500 South, has free Internet access and an excellent periodicals room. A new main library, at 200 E 400 South, is under construction and due to open in 2003. There are five branch libraries.

The best selection of travel books, outdoor guides and maps is at the city's biggest independent bookstore, Sam Weller Books (☎ 328-2586, 800-333-7269), 254 S

The Church of Jesus Christ of Latter-Day Saints

History In the 1820s, Joseph Smith, a New York farmer, experienced a series of angelic visitations during which the word of God, in the form of writings on golden tablets, was revealed to him. During these visions, Smith was told that he was a prophet who would lead the Church. Smith translated the writings, which were written in some ancient but unknown language, using 'stone spectacles' provided by the angel Moroni. After Smith finished the translations, the golden tablets were taken away by the angel and neither the tablets nor the angel have been seen since.

Smith's translation, published in 1830 as the Book of Mormon, recounts the epic story of the supposed arrival of the first Americans from the Old World about 4000 years ago and of the teachings of Jesus Christ in America. Later that year, Smith founded the Church of Jesus Christ of Latter-day Saints (LDS), appointing himself the church's first president. Confronted with strong opposition to his new sect, he decided to leave New York with a small group of followers in 1831. They built their first church in Kirtland, Ohio, and some Mormons moved on as far as Missouri. But confrontation continued; most citizens of Ohio and Missouri felt their way of life was being threatened by this strange new denomination, and the Mormons were continually harassed and persecuted. Within a few years, they had pushed on to Illinois, where they founded the Mormon community of Nauvoo.

Many non-Mormons opposed the newcomers, particularly their teachings of polygamy and religious superiority. Mormons were persecuted, attacked and killed, and in 1844 Joseph Smith and his brother Hyrum were murdered in a jail at Carthage, Illinois. Almost immediately Brigham Young, the senior member of the LDS, became the second president.

In 1845, church leaders decided to move farther west to find a place where they could build a peaceful community without being persecuted. The first group left in 1846, wintered in the plains of present-day Nebraska and arrived at the Great Salt Lake in July 1847. This was the place that Brigham Young had been looking for, remote and unwanted. A few days after their arrival, Brigham Young uttered the now-famous phrase 'This is the right place,' and Salt Lake City was founded, becoming the center of the Mormon faith.

Brigham Young

Main. The King's English (☎ 484-9100, 800-658-7928), 1511 S 1500 East, is another first-rate independent bookseller, and BiblioTect (☎ 236-1010), 329 W Pierpont Ave, has Southwestern art and architecture books. Deseret Book (☎ 328-8191), downtown in ZCMI Shopping Center and several other locations, has the best selection of books for and about Mormons.

The two city newspapers are the fairly conservative morning *Salt Lake Tribune*, with the largest circulation, and the even more conservative, Mormon-run, afternoon *Deseret News*.

Physician referral (☎ 581-2897, 800-662-0052) is provided by the University of Utah Hospital and Clinics. Insurance is advised. Hospitals providing 24-hour emergency care near downtown include the LDS Hospital (☎ 408-1100), 8th Ave at C St; Paracelsus Salt Lake Regional Hospital and Medical Center (☎ 350-4111/631), 1050 E South Temple; and the University Hospital (☎ 581-2121/291), 50 N Medical Drive.

The Church of Jesus Christ of Latter-Day Saints

Religion Church doctrine was originally derived from the Book of Mormon, and most of these original tenets remain integral to Mormon life today. Leadership is through the Church President and 12 elected laymen called the Twelve Apostles. Members are required to be strongly supportive of their families, and the families supportive of one another. A woman marries a man 'into eternity,' and all their relatives (including deceased ancestors) and offspring automatically become Mormons – hence, the Mormon interest in genealogy. Hard work, tithing (donating 10% of one's annual income) and a strict obedience to church leaders are important. Smoking and drinking alcohol, tea or coffee are forbidden, because they do not promote a healthy or moral lifestyle. During the early decades of the church, polygamy was encouraged, particularly within the upper ranks, but this practice was renounced in the 1890s (although isolated pockets of polygamists still exist in a few remote settlements).

The LDS has attracted large numbers of followers who like the strong sense of community, the healthy lifestyle and the fact that Mormons consider themselves God's chosen people. Mormons consider the LDS the one true Christian Church.

The religion is practiced in public and in private. Public services, complete with hymns and sermons, are often held in tabernacles. Private ceremonies, including weddings and baptisms, are usually held in temples and are open only to practicing Mormons who vow to keep the secrets of the faith. Historically, Church practice is to open new temples upon completion to outside visitors for a short period, and then to close them to all but worshipping Mormons.

The LDS Church is very conservative. African American men were not allowed to become church leaders until 1978. Women are still not allowed to take on leadership roles. In Mormon schools and colleges, dress codes are very strict – no shorts or skirts above the knee, for example. Mormon men are not allowed to grow beards. The LDS Church is strongly supportive of the conservative Republican Party. Voluntary missionary work is an important aspect of the church. About 75% of missionaries are young men, called Elders, between the ages of 19 and 26. Their missions are for two years; women, called Sisters, go on missions of 18 months. Over 60,000 missionaries are in 162 countries. South and Central America contain over 3 million Mormon converts to date, the most by far outside of the USA.

The Mormon Church has more than doubled in the last 20 years, with over 11 million members worldwide in 2000, making it one of the world's fastest growing religions. Only about 1.5 million members live in Utah.

The police station (☎ 799-3000) is at 315 E 200 South.

DOWNTOWN
Temple Square

The city's most famous sight, Temple Square (☎ 240-2534, 800-537-9703) is a 10-acre block enclosed by 15-foot-high walls, within which are some of the most important Mormon buildings. Near the two entrances on S and N Temple (or by the central flag-pole), friendly Mormon missionaries will advise you on what to see or take you on a free **guided tour**. Tours last about 40 minutes and are available in many languages. All questions about Mormon faith and history are welcome.

You can also walk around on your own. Two **visitor centers**, remodeled for the 2002 Olympics, house religious paintings. The South Visitor Center has an exhibit about the Book of Mormon, and the North Visitor Center has a small theater showing the 53-minute film *Legacy*, about the Mormons' historical journey to Salt Lake.

Temple Square is open daily from 9 am to 9 pm and from 8 am to 10 pm in the summer. Admission to the square, buildings and performances is free.

The Temple The most impressive building inside Temple Square is the 210-foot-high Temple; atop the tallest spire stands a golden statue of the angel Moroni who appeared to LDS founder Joseph Smith. Built between 1853 and 1893, the Temple was opened upon completion to all visitors for a few days and then closed to everybody except Mormons engaged in secret sacred ceremonies.

The Tabernacle You should make every effort to visit the Tabernacle, opposite the Temple, when the world-famous Mormon Tabernacle Choir is singing or an organ recital is being given. This domed building, constructed between 1863 and 1867, has stunning acoustics. You literally can hear a pin drop on the stage from the back row. The organ has 11,623 pipes, and 30-minute recitals are given at noon Monday to Saturday and at 2 pm on Sunday. In summer, there are additional 2 pm recitals from Monday to Saturday. The Mormon Tabernacle Choir rehearses every Thursday at 8 pm and gives a live, half-hour radio/TV broadcast at 9:30 am every Sunday (arrive by 9 am for seats). Check times as there are occasional changes.

Assembly Hall South of the Tabernacle lies Assembly Hall, built between 1877 and

---

What's in a Name?

Prior to the 2002 Winter Olympics, the Church of Jesus Christ of Latter-day Saints attempted to discourage the international news media from using the nickname the 'Mormon Church.' Church leaders felt that 'Mormon' is a cultural term, not a proper name for the Church itself, and that it still carries pejorative connotations. As well, church leaders wanted to emphasize (to the watching world at large) that theirs is a Christian religion – just like all the other mainstream Christian denominations. While the church has gained the respect of any major religion, its unique teachings about Jesus Christ are generally not accepted among other Christians, which leads to confusion. For instance, the United Methodist Church and the Catholic Church have both declared that converts from Mormonism must be rebaptized.

And the news media? By and large, they demured, mainly for practical reasons. The full name is too unwieldy to repeat often, and the Church's suggestion for a shorthand name – 'The Church of Jesus Christ' – was too vague. (For the same reasons, this book also continues to use 'Mormon' and 'LDS.')

But finally, 'Mormon' carries the weight of 150 years of usage, which is not easily tossed aside. Even Brigham Young embraced the term, believing the living proof of Church members was enough to redeem a word that, much like 'Jew,' was originally used as a slur.

Mormon Genealogy

Genealogy is of great importance to the Mormons because they believe that all family members are united within the LDS Church and therefore ancestors and relatives can be baptized and saved. Mormons have amassed the world's most thorough genealogical collection and research facility in Salt Lake City's **Family History Library** (☎ 240-2331, 800-346-6044), 35 N West Temple, Salt Lake City, UT 84150, and also in the nearby **Joseph Smith Memorial Building** (☎ 240-1266), 14 E South Temple, as well as in numerous other facilities all over the United States, linked with the main library by computer. Non-Mormons are permitted to use the facilities to research their own roots.

In the Family History Library, an orientation center instructs visitors on how to use the facilities, which include 90,000 books, census data and genealogical records on microfilm and microfiche. Library hours are 7:30 am to 5 pm on Monday, to 10 pm Tuesday to Saturday. The 1st and 4th floors of the Joseph Smith Memorial Building house a powerful computer system, called Family-Search, that has information on hundreds of millions of deceased people from around the world from AD 1500 onwards. Hours are 9 am to 9 pm Monday to Saturday. Use of both facilities is free and staff members can assist you.

If you just want to see what's already been collected on your family, start with the computer system and make sure to have the place and date of at least one deceased relative's birth, marriage or death.

1882. It houses a smaller organ. A concert series (☎ 240-3323) is performed here in summer and December, and on many weekends.

Near Temple Square

The streets surrounding Temple Square have several other important Mormon buildings and monuments. The **Museum of Church History and Art** (☎ 240-3310), 45 N West Temple, has impressive exhibits of pioneer history and fine art. Guided tours are available only by reservation two weeks in advance. Hours are 9 am to 9 pm Monday to Friday, 10 am to 7 pm weekends and holidays. Admission is free.

Next door is the **Family History Library** (☎ 240-2331), 35 N West Temple (see the 'Mormon Genealogy' boxed text). Hours are 7:30 am to 10 pm Tuesday to Saturday, till 5 pm Monday.

On Main at South Temple the **Brigham Young Monument** marks the zero point for the city. East of the monument is the **Joseph Smith Memorial Building** (☎ 240-1266), 15 E South Temple. From 1911 to 1987 this was the elaborate old Hotel Utah, and there are free tours of the elegant lobby. Hours are

8 am to 10 pm Monday to Saturday. There is a 10th-floor observation deck and a large-screen theater (☎ 240-4383) with nine free daily screenings of the 65-minute-long *The Testaments,* about Mormon beliefs concerning Jesus Christ; call ahead for tickets. Also here is **FamilySearch** (see the 'Mormon Genealogy' boxed text).

The 28-story **LDS Office Building** (☎ 240-2190), 50 E North Temple, is the tallest building in Salt Lake City. Free 30-minute tours begin in the lobby and go up to the 26th floor observation deck. It's open during weekday business hours, plus Saturday in summer.

Completed in 2000, the church's **LDS Conference Center** (☎ 240-0075), 60 W North Temple, is a daunting granite edifice with walkways and waterfalls cascading down the front; from the four-acre rooftop garden you can take the measure of Temple Square and the entire valley. Free half-hour tours leave continually from the lobby and include a second-floor gallery of religious art. The 1000-seat theater has various religious performances year-round (☎ 240-0080). The building is open 9 am to 9 pm Monday to Saturday.

UTAH

SALT LAKE CITY

PLACES TO STAY
3 Radisson Hotel
4 Holiday Inn Express
5 Motel 6 – Airport
6 Chateau Motel
7 Days Inn
9 Salt Lake City KOA
10 Gateway Inn
12 Econo Lodge
13 Saltair B&B
23 Marriott University Park
27 Holiday Inn
28 Ute Hostel
41 Scenic Motel
43 Skyline Inn

PLACES TO EAT
11 Red Iguana
15 Pie Pizzeria
25 Cafe Trang
29 House of Tibet
33 Coffee Garden
34 Guru's
38 Kyoto
39 Fresco Italian Café;
   The King's English
40 Bangkok Thai
42 Bombay House
46 Snelgrove Ice Cream
   Parlor
47 Salt Lake Pizza & Pasta
48 Michelangelo Ristorante;
   Blue Boutique
49 Blue Plate Diner

OTHER
1 Jordan River State Park
   Ranger Station
2 Children's Museum of
   Utah
8 Utah State Parks &
   Recreation Office
14 Paracelsus Salt Lake
   Regional Hospital &
   Medical Center
16 Utah Museum of Natural
   History
17 Pioneer Theater
   Company
18 Rice-Eccles Stadium
19 Utah Museum of Fine
   Arts
20 University Hospital
21 Red Butte Gardens &
   Arboretum
22 Military Museum; Fort
   Douglas
24 International Peace
   Gardens
26 Burt's Tiki Lounge
30 Chase Home Museum of
   Utah Folk Art
31 Tracy Aviary
32 Tower Theater
35 This Is The Place
   Monument; Old Deseret
   Village
36 Hogle Zoo
37 Franklin Covey Field
44 Raging Waters
45 US Geological Survey
50 E Center
51 Hollywood Connections;
   Hale Centre Theatre

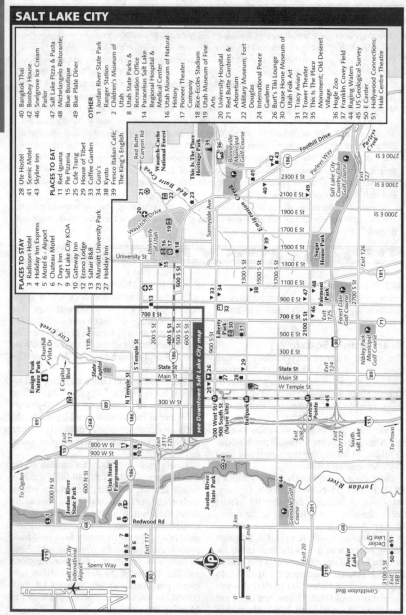

The **Beehive House** (☎ 240-2671), 67 E South Temple, was built in 1854 for Brigham Young, who lived here until his death in 1877. At the time it was the most elegant house in Salt Lake City and it has been meticulously maintained with period furnishings and artwork. As for the house's name, the beehive, with its hard-working, highly organized bees, was adopted as a symbol of industry by the Mormons, and Utah is now nicknamed the Beehive State. Free guided tours are available 9:30 am to 4:30 pm Monday to Saturday (later in summer) and 10 am to 1 pm on Sunday and holidays.

Next door is the **Lion House**, 63 E South Temple, which was built in 1855 as additional living space for Brigham Young's many wives. The building is closed to the public but the Lion House Pantry Restaurant is open for public dining (see Places to Eat, below). Nearby, at the intersection of State and S Temple, stands the impressive **Eagle Gate**, which was originally the entrance to Brigham Young's property. Walk north on State St and east on 1st Ave to reach **Brigham Young's Grave**, where he and several family members are buried.

Hansen Planetarium

The planetarium (☎ 538-2104), 15 S State, will be moving in 2002 (possibly 2003) to the new Gateway complex at 400 West between S Temple and 200 South. Plans are for the planetarium to expand to nearly twice its current size, adding a large-format theater (such as IMAX) in addition to museum exhibits, a gift shop and dome theater, which will be upgraded with projection equipment similar to that of the Hayden Planetarium in New York City. Museum admission is free; it's open daily (call for hours).

The domed theater offers a variety of astronomical (☎ 532-7827), laser/rock music (☎ 363-0559) and live performances. Prices may rise, but at press time were $4.50 to $7.50 for adults and $3.50 to $6 for children. website: www.hansenplanetarium.org

Note that over the next few years, the expansive Gateway complex, currently under construction, will become home to shops, restaurants and various attractions, including the Children's Museum and the restored Union Pacific Railroad Depot.

Salt Lake Art Center

Salt Lake City has a lively fine arts scene. At its center is the nonprofit Art Center (☎ 328-4201), 20 S West Temple (on the north side of Salt Palace), which has changing exhibits of contemporary art, plus classes and lectures, a hands-on kids center and a film series. Hours are 10 am to 5 pm Tuesday to Saturday, till 9 pm on Friday and 1 to 5 pm on Sunday. Admission is by donation.

A free evening gallery stroll occurs the third Friday of every month; the Art Center has information.

Utah Historical Society

Housed in the refurbished 1910 Rio Grande Railroad Depot, the Historical Society (☎ 533-3500), 300 S Rio Grande, has exhibits about local and state history, an excellent bookstore and a research and historic photo library. Hours are 8 am to 5 pm weekdays and 10 am to 3 pm on Saturday. Admission is free.

Gallivan Center

The John W. Gallivan Utah Center (☎ 532-0459), on 200 South between State and Main Sts, has sculpture gardens, an amphitheater and, in winter, an ice skating rink ($4/3 adults/children), which becomes a reflecting pond in summer. Many city events and festivals are held here, and throughout summer there are free concerts and movies.

South Temple Street

South Temple is lined with historic buildings, in addition to those in and around Temple Square. The grand 1909 **Union Pacific Railroad Depot**, 400 W South Temple, will be refurbished as part of the new Gateway complex. Two beautiful, non-Mormon churches in the area are the elaborate, Roman Catholic **Cathedral of the Madeleine** (☎ 328-8941), 331 E South Temple, and the red-sandstone **First Presbyterian Church** (☎ 363-3889), 12 C St at E South Temple. Nearby, the 19th-century

UTAH

DOWNTOWN SALT LAKE CITY

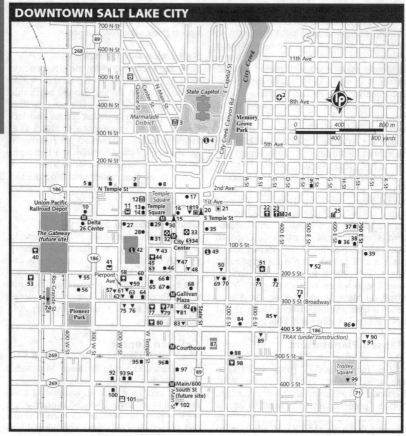

Enos A Wall Mansion, 411 E South Temple, now houses the LDS Business College. The lavish **Kearns Mansion** (☎ 538-1005), 603 E South Temple, is the governor's official residence. Tours are offered on Tuesday and Thursday afternoon April to November.

Pioneer Memorial Museum

Run by the Daughters of Utah Pioneers (DUP), this museum (☎ 538-1050), 300 N Main, is a vast treasure trove of pioneer artifacts. You'll find many DUP museums and monuments throughout Utah, but this is the organization's best by far. Four floors and 38

rooms are packed with, as the brochure notes, 'the world's largest collection of artifacts on one particular subject,' all of it painstakingly and lovingly displayed and labeled. No other Utah museum evokes the pioneer experience as well as this one, and it does so by sheer volume: you'll see scads of old photographs and portraits, crafts, furniture, toys, medical equipment, pioneer Bibles and letters, kitchen implements, wagons, firearms, walking sticks, a gleaming 1902 fire truck and much, much more. Hours are 9 am to 5 pm Monday to Saturday, year-round, and 1 to 5 pm Sunday June

DOWNTOWN SALT LAKE CITY

PLACES TO STAY
5   Howard Johnson's Express
    Inn
6   City Creek Inn
7   Travelodge-Temple Square
9   Avenues Youth Hostel
14 Best Western Salt Lake Plaza
29 The Inn at Temple Square
31 Marriott Hotel
36 Anton Boxrud B&B
37 Anniversary Inn
38 Armstrong Mansion B&B
60 Shilo Inn
64 Peery Hotel
65 Hilton; Spencer's
66 Hotel Monaco; Bambara
92 Wasatch Inn;
    Ramada Inn Downtown
93 Motel 6
94 Quality Inn - City Center;
    Utah Ski & Golf
95 Travelodge - City Center
96 Little America Hotel
97 Grand America
100 Super 8 Motel

PLACES TO EAT
18 Lion House Pantry
    Restaurant
43 Mikado
47 Lamb's Restaurant
48 Kenji's
50 Star of India
52 Oasis Café
54 Rio Grande Cafe
55 A Cup of Joe
57 Red Rock Brewing Company
59 Pierpont Cantina
61 Marmot Mesa
62 PF Chang's China Bistro
69 Cedars of Lebanon
73 Sage's Café

75 Metropolitan
76 Squatter's Pub Brewery
79 Market Street Grill;
    Market Street Oyster Bar;
    New Yorker
81 Shogun
83 Baba Afghan
85 Ichiban Sushi
89 Salt Lake Roasting Company
90 Chuck-A-Rama
91 Hires Big H
99 Old Spaghetti Factory;
    Desert Edge Brewery
102 Millcreek Coffee Roasters

OTHER
1   Salt Lake Acting Company
2   LDS Hospital
3   Pioneer Memorial Museum
4   Utah Tourism & Recreation
    Information Center;
    Council Hall
8   LDS Conference Center
10 Triad Center
11 Greyhound Bus Depot
12 Museum of Church History
    & Art
13 Family History Library
15 Brigham Young Monument
16 Joseph Smith Memorial
    Building
17 LDS Office Building
19 Beehive House
20 Eagle Gate
21 Brigham Young's Grave
22 Cathedral of the Madeleine
23 First Presbyterian Church
24 Enos A Wall Mansion
25 Kearns Mansion
26 Delta Center
27 Abravanel Hall
28 Salt Lake Art Center

30 Mormon Handicrafts
32 Crossroads Plaza
33 ZCMI Shopping Center
34 First Security Bank
35 Hansen Planetarium
39 Wasatch Touring
40 Axis
41 Post Office
42 Salt Lake Convention &
    Visitors Bureau;
    Visitor Information Center;
    Salt Palace Convention
    Center
44 Dead Goat Saloon;
    DV8
45 American Express
46 Capitol Theater
49 USFS Office
51 Police
53 Bricks
56 BiblioTect
58 Zipperz
63 Rose Wagner Performing
    Arts Center
67 Sam Weller Books
68 Gallivan Center
70 Guthrie Bicycle
71 Peter Prier & Sons Violins
72 Albertson's
74 Rio Grande Depot & Utah
    Historical Society
77 Zephyr
78 Ya'Buts
80 Port-O-Call
82 BLM Office
84 Main Library (future site)
86 Wild Oats Community
    Market
87 City & County Building
88 Library
98 Junior's Tavern
101 Brewvies

to August. Admission is free; tours are conducted several times a day.

Marmalade District

Just north of the Pioneer Memorial Museum and west of the State Capitol is an area of steep little streets angled away from the grid pattern of the city. The triangular area, bounded by 300 North to the south, 500 North to the north, Center to the east and Quince to the west, is a residential area with a number of notable, historic late-

19th-century buildings. Visit the nearby Travel Council office for a free, informative walking-tour brochure.

Utah State Capitol

Modeled after the national Capitol in Washington, DC, this impressive structure (☎ 538-3000, tour information 538-1563) stands at the north end of State on the appropriately named Capitol Hill. Inside, the rooms are spacious and elegant, and the walls are covered with WPA murals of

Utah's history. The beautifully landscaped grounds contain several interesting monuments and great views of the city.

Just east of the Capitol, **City Creek Canyon** contains Memory Grove Park, a monument to Utah veterans. Open dawn to dusk, the park is a favorite spot for local walkers, runners and bicyclists; to drive there, take City Creek Canyon Rd off of 2nd Ave.

The Capitol is open daily 6 am to 8 pm in the summer and 6 am to 6 pm during the rest of the year. Free tours depart every half-hour 9 am to 3:30 pm weekdays.

Ensign Peak Nature Park
This peak is where Brigham Young and his party surveyed the region in 1847 and Young declared, 'This is the place,' establishing Salt Lake City as the Mormons' new home. Informative plaques describe the events, and a steep, partially paved, half-mile trail leads to the inspiring views. Open dawn to dusk; to get there, take State St north to E Capitol, and take a left on Churchill Vista Drive.

BEYOND DOWNTOWN
University of Utah
The 'U of U' (☎ 581-7200), 2 miles east of downtown on 200 South, is the oldest and largest university in Utah and comprises more than 30,000 students and faculty. For the 2002 Winter Olympics, the campus became the 'Olympic Village,' housing most of the athletes, and Rice-Eccles Stadium held the opening and closing ceremonies.

In 2001, the excellent **Utah Museum of Fine Arts** (☎ 581-7332), 410 Campus Center Dr, moved into a grand new building worthy of its permanent collection, which extends from the classical age to the present. New galleries focus on Western and Utah art, and changing exhibits feature works by major artists such as Rodin. Hours are 10 am to 5 pm Monday to Friday, noon to 5 pm on weekends. Admission is free. website: www.utah.edu/umfa

The **Utah Museum of Natural History** (☎ 801-581-6927) is on President's Circle, just east of 200 South and University. This

fine museum features the ever-popular paleontology (dinosaurs!), plus some nice hands-on activities for kids. There is a gift shop. Hours are 9:30 am to 5:30 pm Monday to Saturday, noon to 5 pm Sunday. Admission is $4 for adults; $2.50 for three- to 12-year-olds and seniors. Ask inside for a free parking pass.
website: www.umnh.utah.edu

The lovely **Red Butte Gardens and Arboretum** (☎ 581-4747), at the end of Wakara Way east of the university, encompasses 150 acres with trails into the Wasatch foothills and 25 acres of well-tended gardens. Nature and gardening talks occur year-round. Visitor center hours are 9 am to 8 pm daily May to October and 10 am to 5 pm the rest of the year; grounds are open till dusk. Admission is $5; $3 for seniors and children.

Fort Douglas
& Military Museum
Fort Douglas, just east of the university off Wasatch Drive, was built in 1862 to protect telegraph and overland routes from Indian attacks, and was designated a historic landmark in 1975. The Fort Douglas Military Museum (☎ 581-1710) has exhibits pertaining to Utah's military history. (The fort is still in use and some sections are off-limits.) Museum hours are noon to 4 pm Tuesday to Saturday; closed in January. Admission is free.

This Is The Place Heritage Park
This historic state park (☎ 582-1847), 2601 E Sunnyside Ave (the eastern extension of 800 South), has day-use picnicking areas and the huge **This Is The Place Monument**, which was dedicated in 1947 to mark the 100th anniversary of the arrival of the Mormons. Park hours are dawn to dusk. The visitor center has exhibits and is open 9 am to 5 pm. Admission to the visitor center, monument and park is free.

Within the park is **Old Deseret Village**, a living-history museum with actors in mid-19th-century clothes working among buildings typical of the early Mormon settlements. Some buildings are replicas; others are renovated originals, including

Kids' Stuff

Apart from the usual favorites like the zoo and natural history museum, Salt Lake offers several attractions especially for children.

Children's Museum of Utah Fun interactive exhibits at this museum (☎ 328-3383), 840 N 300 West, stimulate the imagination and the senses – from the 'color factory' and artists' workshop to a re-creation of Nine-Mile Canyon. Hours are 10 am to 6 pm Monday to Saturday (until 8 pm on Fridays). Admission is $3.75 for anyone over two. Note that the museum will be moving to the new Gateway complex in 2003 or 2004, expanding to more than twice its current size; check the website for details at www.childmuseum.org.

Wheeler Historic Farm This delightful farm (☎ 264-2241), 6351 S 900 East, dates from 1886 and is located in South Cottonwood Regional Park. Friendly, relaxed and free of 'hype,' it is worked in the traditional manner of a century ago: Farmhands milk cows, churn milk into butter, feed animals or collect chicken eggs – and all allow hands-on 'helping' if you're part of a tour. Other demonstrations, mainly in summer, include blacksmithing, gardening and quilting, and hay rides are offered. The visitor center has exhibits of WPA art and antique farm machinery. The park and grounds are open dawn to dusk, and admission is free. Tours and wagon rides are $1.50 for all ages, and they are offered when the visitor center is open, 9:30 am to 5:30 pm Monday to Saturday; for information, see www.wheelerfarm.com.

Raging Waters If your children are threatening to throw up if they have to suffer another historic museum, cool them off at Raging Waters (☎ 977-8300, 972-3300), 1700 S 1200 West. It has the world's first water roller coaster, a giant wave-making pool, over 20 water slides and 10 heated pools. There are picnic areas and food concessions. From Memorial Day to Labor Day, the park is open 10:30 am to 7:30 pm Monday to Saturday and noon to 7:30 pm on Sunday. Admission is $16.50 for kids over 12, $12.50 for kids three to 11, and $6 for seniors.

Amusement Centers The pre-teen set will love **Hollywood Connection** (☎ 973-4386), 3217 S Decker Lake Dr in West Valley. This small indoor amusement park has various rides as well as bumper cars, mini-golf, roller-skating, laser tag and a play area for toddlers. In the same building is a 15-screen multiplex cinema for any teenagers who want to escape the madness. Or, let the older kids loose in the **Utah Fun Dome** (☎ 265-3866, 263-8769), 4998 S 360 West in Murray. It has 30 bowling lanes, roller-skating, laser tag, a 70-foot bungee-jumping tower, a 3-D theater and rides; see it online at www.fundome.com. Both centers are open daily; call for hours, which change by activity and time of year. Generally, weekday hours don't begin till the afternoon, and weekends start around 11 am and go to midnight. Admission to both centers is free, but bring plenty of change and small bills for the attractions.

Outside the City Also read about the Lagoon Amusement Park and Kearns Oquirrh Park and Olympic Oval.

Brigham Young's farmhouse. Old Deseret is open daily 10 am to 5 pm Memorial Day to Labor Day only. Admission is $6; $4 for seniors and children three to 11. In April, May, September and October, there is no acting, but guided tours are offered for $1. website: www.thisistheplace.org

Hogle Zoo

The small state zoo (☎ 582-1631), 2600 E Sunnyside Ave (opposite This Is The Place Heritage Park), allows an intimate experience of tigers, wolves, gorillas and more in appropriate nature settings. There is a children's petting zoo and a miniature train ride

($1, summers only). The zoo is open daily, 9 am to 6:30 pm Memorial Day to Labor Day, 9 am to 5:30 pm the rest of the year. Admission is $5; $3 for children (four to 14) and seniors over 65.

Liberty Park

This ideal city park (☎ 972-7800) is bounded by 500 and 700 East and 900 and 1300 South. During the summer you'll find a swimming pool, tennis courts, children's amusement park, playground, pond with rental boats, horseshoe pits and formal flower gardens.

Since 1938, **Tracy Aviary** (☎ 322-2473, 596-8500), in the park's southwest corner, has been delighting bird lovers with displays of hundreds of birds from all over the world. Kids can feed the ducks and colorful lories. The aviary can guide you to the area's best birding spots. It's open daily year-round. Admission is $3; $2 for four- to 12-year-olds and seniors.

Recently spruced up, the **Chase Home Museum of Utah Folk Art** (☎ 533-5760) is an 1850s adobe house in the middle of the park. The museum displays such things as quilts, saddles, rugs, needlework and woodcarving. Hours are noon to 5 pm weekends from mid-April to mid-October and daily from Memorial Day to Labor Day. Admission is free.

Jordan River State Park

This state park (☎ 533-4496), 1084 N Redwood Rd, follows both banks of the Jordan River from 1700 South northward for about 8½ miles The ranger station has maps showing boating and fishing areas, picnic sites, jogging, bicycling, equestrian and wheelchair exercise trails, a golf course and a model airplane field; station hours are 8 am to 5 pm weekdays. Most activities (golf and model-plane field excepted) are free. There is no overnight camping.

Within the park lie the **International Peace Gardens** (☎ 972-7800, 974-2411), 1000 S 900 West, where floral displays pay tribute to the cultures of countries from all over the world.

Kearns Oquirrh Park & Olympic Oval

Southwest of downtown, Oquirrh Park (☎ 966-5555), 5624 S 4800 West, in Kearns, contains a gorgeous modern fitness center with extensive indoor and outdoor pools, tennis courts, gym, weight room and sauna and hot tubs.

The park was also the site of the speed skating events of the 2002 Winter Olympics in the Olympic Oval (☎ 968-6825), which is the home of the US National Speed Skating Team. The cavernous, cable-suspended building is itself a marvel, and the public can skate on the oval year-round, nightly in winter (call for times). Ask about their learn to speed skate programs.

The park is open daily. Admission to the fitness center is $5.50 for adults, $5 for kids four to 17, and $4 for seniors. Public skate fees are $4 for adults, and $3 for kids 12 and under; skate rentals are $2.

METROPOLITAN SALT LAKE CITY
Saltair & Great Salt Lake State Marina

Seventeen miles west of Salt Lake City at I-80 exit 104 (Magna), Saltair (☎ 250-4400, 355-5522 for concerts) was once a fashionable resort. Now rebuilt on a smaller scale, it has concessions, a small public exhibit about the lake, and a concert venue. It is ostensibly open year-round, but ownership changes frequently, so call first.

At the same exit is the Great Salt Lake State Marina (☎ 250-1822/98). Formerly a state park, it still has a ranger on duty. The marina is run by Salt Island Adventures (☎ 252-9336), which offers sail boat charters as well as a variety of scenic cruises that are a great way to experience the lake (for details, see Organized Tours below). The marina store has boating supplies and light snacks.

Near the marina and Saltair are beaches where you can float in the water and see what it's like to be unsinkable. Both have showers to wash off the briny water, though the marina beaches are cleaner. The water is pretty cold except in summer.

The Great Salt Lake

The huge lake that gave the city its name lies about 10 miles northwest of downtown. It is the largest lake in the USA west of the Great Lakes. How big is it? That's hard to answer, because since 1873 the lake has varied in size from 900 to 2500 sq miles. Maximum lake depths have ranged from 24 to 45 feet – it is large and shallow like a plate. Variations are caused by spring runoff raising lake levels and summer heat evaporating the water. A series of dry winters and hot summers will cause extremely low levels, and, conversely, wet winters and cooler summers will lead to high water levels. Evaporation, the main cause of water loss, is what has made the lake so salty. The salinity is not uniform, however, but ranges from 6% to 27% depending on location and weather (compared to 3.5% for seawater).

The prehistoric variation in lake levels was much greater. Sixteen thousand years ago the lake was part of Lake Bonneville, which was 900 feet higher and covered almost 20,000 sq miles. Then it suddenly dropped 350 feet when it burst through Red Rock Pass into the Snake River in Idaho. It receded to its present size about 8000 years ago. If you look at the nearby mountains, you can see terraces marking these ancient levels etched into the slopes about 900 and 550 feet above present lake levels.

In the 1980s the Great Salt Lake underwent devastating changes. In 1963, the record low depth of the lake left the surface only 4191 feet above sea level. During that time, several miles of I-80, the main interstate west of Salt Lake City, were built at 4207 feet above sea level. Then, in the '80s, levels increased suddenly and dramatically. The winters of 1982-83 and 1983-84 both had record-breaking snowfalls. Skiers loved it, but the ensuing snowmelts flooded the interstate. Crews worked feverishly to raise the freeway 7 feet, to 4214 feet above sea level. By the winter of 1986-87, lake levels had reached nearly 4212 feet, breaking the 1873 record by several inches. Then, barely averting disaster, the lake began to recede.

For the time being, the interstate is safe again. But many other changes resulted from the sudden increase of water. The salinity dropped from 20% to 6% in some parts of the lake. Hardworking Utahns spent countless volunteer hours sandbagging creeks and rivers, building dikes and fighting the floods. Nevertheless, farmlands surrounding the lake were flooded and washed away. Evaporation ponds used for potash production were inundated. Many beaches, state parks, bird and wildlife refuges, and shoreline buildings were damaged or destroyed. If not for the timely actions of the locals, the toll would have been far greater.

The lake's wildlife was also hard hit. Before the flood, the lake had always been too saline for fish (except for a few areas near the mouths of rivers). Bacteria and small green algae grew in the salty water and became food for brine shrimp. Brine flies lived in great clouds on rotting vegetation in the marshes along the shoreline. The shrimp and the flies attracted great numbers of migrating birds. However, the flooding of coastal marshes caused a huge decline in the shrimp and fly populations, which in turn led to a massive decline in the number of migratory birds. Fortunately, the lake's bird populations have almost recovered to pre-flood levels. For a moving, personal account of the flood, told from the perspective of a naturalist and avowedly liberal Mormon woman, read *Refuge* by Terry Tempest Williams.

The Great Salt Lake has been declared a World Heritage bird sanctuary because of its importance to millions of migratory shorebirds, waders, gulls, ducks and waterfowl that pass through the lake area year-round. Some 150,000 California gulls, Utah's state bird, nest here. In addition, marshes on the east side of the lake contain one of the world's largest populations of nesting white-faced ibis, and Gunnison Island's nesting white pelican colony is one of North America's largest. The height of the fall and spring migrations are not-to-be-missed wildlife pageants.

Lagoon Amusement Park & Pioneer Village

This is the second-oldest amusement park (☎ 385-451-8000, 800-748-5246) in the country (opened in 1886), and it has a wealth of entertainment: several roller coasters and dozens of other rides, a water park with slides and pools, live musical entertainment, and a Pioneer Village. Visitors can ride stagecoaches or steam trains and watch gunslingers shooting it out. There is an old-time restaurant, food booths, pleasant gardens and a campground (see Places to Stay).

The park is open weekends from mid-April to late September and daily Memorial Day to Labor Day. Hours are 11 am to midnight on busy days, earlier on quiet days. All-day park passes for ages five to 64 are $30 and include all attractions and entertainment. Parking is $6.

To get there, take I-15 north to the Lagoon Drive exit, 17 miles north of downtown Salt Lake in the town of Farmington.

Bingham Canyon Copper Mine

Billed as 'The Richest Hole on Earth,' this open-air mine (☎ 252-3234) is a 2½-mile-wide, three-quarter-mile-deep gash that has yielded more than 16 million tons of copper; in all, 6 billion tons of rock have been removed since 1906. This and the Great Wall of China are said to be the only man-made objects that can be seen from space. It is also an environmental disaster. The hazardous wastewater it has emitted over decades poses a threat to Salt Lake City's drinking water. The mine is operated by the Kennecott Corporation (traditionally the state's largest polluter), which has taken steps to clean up the area and improve its mining practices. Government and other authorities, however, still worry that it won't be enough.

The visitor center, which includes a museum, film presentation and overlook of the mine, is open 8 am till dusk daily April to October. Admission is $4 per car, $2 per motorcycle.

The mine is 25 miles southwest of Salt Lake City. Take I-15 south to exit 301, then follow Hwy 48 west to the mine.

ACTIVITIES
Equipment Rentals

Utah Ski & Golf (☎ 355-9088), 134 W 600 South, rents skis, golf equipment, snowboards, ski clothing, mountain bikes and in-line skates. The knowledgeable staff at Wasatch Touring (☎ 359-9361) 702 E 100 South, can rent you mountain bikes, kayaks, climbing shoes, and ski equipment. The well-regarded Guthrie Bicycle (☎ 363-3727), 156 E 200 South, rents bikes. REI (☎ 486-2100), 3285 E 3300 South, can rent you camping equipment, climbing shoes, kayaks, and pretty much all winter sports equipment.

Hiking

Summer hikers and campers head in droves for **Little Cottonwood Canyon**. Take exit 7 off the southeastern corner of the I-215 loop and follow Hwy 190 south to Hwy 210, which climbs up into the canyon – a steep and spectacular 11-mile drive. The canyon has two USFS campgrounds and the Snowbird and Alta ski areas (see Skiing & Snowboarding, below); in summer, Snowbird offers scenic tram rides ($14) and hiking and biking trails.

Good, though strenuous, hiking trails include the **White Pine Lake Trail** and **Red Pine Lake Trail**. White Pine Lake (10,000 feet) is just over 3 miles away. Watch rocky slopes around the lake for the unique pika, a small, short-eared, tailless lagomorph (the order of mammals that includes rabbits). At the end of the road is the **Cecret Lake Trail**, an easy 1-mile trail with spectacular summer wildflowers (July and August).

Another favorite spot for summer hikers is **Big Cottonwood Canyon**. Take exit 7 off the I-215 loop and follow Hwy 190 into the canyon. Along this road are nine picnic areas, two USFS campgrounds and the Brighton and Solitude ski areas (see Skiing & Snowboarding below). Solitude is open in summer with lift-serviced hiking and biking ($15). The paved road ends at Brighton, but an unpaved road goes over a 9800-foot pass and continues to Park City and Heber City. This road is closed by snow from October to May. Many hiking trails leave from various trailheads along Hwy 190. Look for trailhead signs. One of the most attractive hikes is the 2-mile **Lake Blanche Trail**, beginning at the Mill B South Fork trailhead, about 5 miles into the canyon.

The next canyon north of Big Cottonwood Canyon is **Mill Creek Canyon**, which is intimate, lovely and very popular. Take exit 4 off the I-215 loop and follow the signs for Mill Creek. (There are no ski resorts here.) The USFS maintains 10 summer picnic areas here, and there is a $2.25 per vehicle fee to go up this road. There are over a dozen well-signed hiking trails: two of the more difficult and scenic are the 1.75-mile Alexander Basin Trail to Gobblers Knob mountain (10,246 feet) and the 5½-mile trail from the Terraces picnic area to Gobblers Knob. An easier trail is the 5½-mile Pipeline, which leads to great views of Salt Lake; it is popular with mountain bikers and cross-country skiers. Near the end of the road, which is only open from July to November, you can pick up a section of the Great Western Trail.

These brief descriptions will get you started on walking in the Wasatch. For trail maps, advice, and backcountry camping regulations in the Wasatch-Cache National Forest, go to the Discover! desk in REI (see Information). John Veranth's *Hiking the Wasatch* is a good guide.

Mountain Biking

Several books (see the Outdoor Activities chapter) give detailed descriptions of rides in the area and information offices in Salt Lake have useful brochures. The lifts at Snowbird and Solitude (see Hiking above) take bikes. In the city, City Creek Canyon is popular with cyclists, and the Bonneville Shoreline Trail is open to mountain bikes; it can be picked up in several places, such as Red Butte Gardens.

Skiing & Snowboarding

Utah likes to brag that it has 'The Greatest Snow on Earth.' One of the reasons the snow is so good is because the high desert country keeps the snow very dry. Utah would not have hosted the 2002 Winter Olympics if the skiing weren't truly world-class, and it couldn't be easier to get to from Salt Lake: 11 ski resorts are within an hour's drive, and four are only half an hour away.

An entire book could be written about Utah's skiing – this guide isn't it. If you're looking for a ski vacation, your best bet is to get the *Utah Winter Vacation Planner*. This free and recommended booklet is published each winter by Ski Utah (☎ 534-1779, 800-754-8824), 150 W 500 South, Salt Lake City, UT 84101, or from the visitors bureau. It lists up-to-date prices and details of all nearby resorts and amenities, plus hotel packages in Salt Lake City. For current ski conditions, call ☎ 801-521-8102.

website: www.skiutah.com

The Cottonwood Canyons on the Salt Lake City side of the Wasatch Range contain four resorts: Snowbird, Alta, Solitude and Brighton. These resorts receive almost twice as much snow as the slopes on the Park City side of the mountains, but the Park City ski resorts are bigger and posher (see the Wasatch Mountains Region chapter). All the Olympic skiing events were held at the Park City resorts (with the exception of a few at Ogden). While all the resorts have lodging, it's very expensive, and it is easy to use Salt Lake City as a base and still ski at a different resort every day of the week! There is public transportation (with ski racks) from Salt Lake to the Cottonwood Canyon ski resorts. Skiers driving should note that snow tires or chains are often required as early as November and as late as May, which is how long the ski season stretches.

UTA Ski Buses (☎ 287-4636, 743-3882) collect passengers from several downtown hotels. Service begins between 6 and 7 am and buses depart every 20 minutes until 10 am, when they go every hour. One-way fare is $1.75. Lewis Bros Stages (☎ 359-8677, 800-826-5844) has roundtrip shuttles from downtown to the local ski areas and Park City for $28.

Snowbird This ski area (☎ 742-2222, 800-385-2002) is only 25 miles east of Salt Lake City in Little Cottonwood Canyon. It is the

UTAH

highest in northern Utah at 11,000 feet, dropping to 7760 feet at the base. The 2500-acre ski area has 89 runs serviced by seven lifts and a tram that carries up to 250 skiers to the top in about eight minutes. About 25% of the runs are beginner and 30% are intermediate. Snowbird not only allows snowboarding but encourages it – this is one of the best snowboarding areas in the country.

Adult all-day chair lift passes are $56 including the tram or $47 for chairs only. Kids 12 and under ski free on the lifts (two per adult) and seniors over 62 pay $43 or $35. Ski rentals, child care, children's programs and a ski school are available.
website: www.snowbird.com

Alta Alta, an 1870s mining town, became Utah's first ski resort in 1937. Only 2 miles past Snowbird, Alta (☎ 742-3333, 359-1078) is in many ways a throwback to that earlier age. It is the first choice for local skiers for a number of reasons – snowboards aren't allowed, lifts tickets are cheaper, slopes are less crowded – but mainly it's the vibe. Alta is just about skiing, without all the hype of the more expensive resorts. Alta has 2200 acres from 10,550 to 8530 feet, eight chair lifts, five tows and 40 runs. About 25% are for beginners and 40% for intermediate skiers. All-day chair lift passes are $38 for all chair lifts or $22 for beginner chair lifts. People over 80 ski free. Alta and Snowbird also offer a combined ticket for both resorts for $68. Ski rentals, child care and a ski school are available.
website: www.alta.com

Solitude This area (☎ 534-1400, 800-748-4754) is 28 miles from Salt Lake City in Big Cottonwood Canyon. There are 1200 skiable acres between 10,035 and 7,988 feet. Seven chair lifts service 63 runs, of which 20% are for beginners and 50% for intermediate skiers. Snowboards are allowed. All-day lift passes are $39; those over 70 and under 11 (two kids per adult) ski free.

Just beyond the downhill area is the **Solitude Nordic Center** (☎ 536-5774), which features 13 miles of prepared cross-country ski

trails. All-day trail use is $10 for 11- to 69-year-olds.

Rentals and lessons are available, but no child care.
website: www.skisolitude.com

Brighton Just 2 miles beyond Solitude, Brighton (☎ 532-4731, 800-873-5512) has 850 acres between 10,500 and 8755 feet. Seven chair lifts service 66 runs, of which 21% are for beginners and 40% are for intermediate skiers. Their half pipe is very popular with snowboarders. All-day passes are $37, and children under 10 ski free with an adult (two kids per adult). People over 70 also ski free. Brighton offers night skiing from 4 to 9 pm for $22. Both skiing and snowboarding lessons and rentals are available; no child care.
website: www.skibrighton.com

Golf & Tennis
The Salt Lake City Visitors Bureau (or the yellow pages) can give you an exhaustive list of Salt Lake's public and private golf courses. The following Salt Lake City municipal courses (☎ 484-3333 for tee times for all municipal courses) are easily accessible and have 18 holes: Bonneville (☎ 583-9513), 954 Conner St; Glendale (☎ 974-2403), 1630 W 2100 South; Mountain Dell (two courses, ☎ 582-3812), Parleys Canyon; and Rose Park (☎ 596-5030), 1386 N Redwood Rd.

The Salt Lake City Parks & Recreation Department (☎ 972-7800) has information about tennis and other activities in the city's many parks. Liberty Park has the biggest selection of tennis courts in one spot.

ORGANIZED TOURS
Gray Line (☎ 521-7060), in the Shiloh Inn at 206 S West Temple, has 3½-hour city tours that cost $18/9 for adults/children. Innsbruck Tours (☎ 534-1001) has five-hour city tours for $19. Salt Island Adventures (☎ 583-4400, 888-725-8475) runs one-hour scenic cruises on the lake twice daily in summer (reservations required). Adults/children 12 and under and seniors are $12/10. Also ask about sunset dinner cruises and all-day cruises.

SPECIAL EVENTS

The following is a selection of the city's most important annual events. The Visitor Information Center has an exhaustive listing.

The **Utah Arts Festival** is held in the Triad Center, 350 W South Temple, in the last week of June. It is a juried event with hundreds of entries. The **Highlands Festival** with Scottish dancing, bagpipes, crafts, food booths and highland games is held at Fort Douglas on the second Saturday of June. The **Days of '47** commemorates the arrival of Brigham Young's band of Mormon pioneers in 1847. For several days leading up to July 24 there are rodeo competitions, an arts festival and other events. July 24 itself, also celebrated as 'Pioneer Day' in most Mormon towns, features fireworks, picnics, a marathon and a huge parade that is purported to be one of the largest in the country.

The **Utah State Fair** occurs in early to mid-September at the fairgrounds on N Temple near the Jordan River. For over a week there are rodeos, carnival rides, livestock shows and entertainment. During September weekends and ending the first weekend in October, **Oktoberfest** comes to the Snowbird resort with beer, live music and dancing.

Christmas festivities begin in late November with the Christmas Lighting of Temple Square. In December, various Christmas events take place, such as performances of the *Nutcracker* ballet and Dickens' *A Christmas Carol*.

PLACES TO STAY

There are well over 100 places to stay in Salt Lake City and the immediate surroundings. The following represents a large selection – but there are more. Summer and winter are the high seasons and prices may be lower in late spring and fall. Winter rates in the middle and top-end price ranges may include access to UTA buses to the ski slopes and various ski packages. Because of heavy weekday business travel, many downtown hotels have lower weekend rates.

Salt Lake Reservations (☎ 355-4754, 800-847-5810) is a free service run by the Convention & Visitors Bureau; they can help you find an affordable room anywhere in the Salt Lake Valley and at the ski resorts. website: www.visitsaltlake.com

Camping

Two miles west of Temple Square, the *Salt Lake City KOA* (☎ 328-0224, 800-226-7752, 1400 W North Temple) charges $19 for tents, $27 for RV hookups and has over 400 sites; Kamping Kabins are $39. (Despite this, it can fill in summer.) There are two pools, a spa, convenience store, car wash, coin laundry and showers. The well-maintained *Mountain Shadows RV Park* (☎ 571-4024), 13275 S Minute Man Drive in Draper (east of I-15 exit 294, 16 miles south of downtown), charges about the same.

At the Lagoon Amusement Park (see Outside the City, earlier in this chapter) a campground (☎ 800-748-5246 for reservations) is open from May to October. Tents/RVs are $19/25. Showers and a coin laundry are available.

The USFS (☎ 524-5042) maintains four campgrounds (about 200 total sites) in the Wasatch Mountains. In Little Cottonwood Canyon there is *Tanner's Flat* (7100 feet) and *Albion Basin* (9700 feet). Big Cottonwood Canyon has *The Spruces* (7400 feet) and *Redman* (8300 feet). All have water and vault toilets; none have showers or RV hookups. Rates run $10 to $14, and reservations are recommended on weekends (☎ 877-444-6777). Depending on snow conditions, the campgrounds are open late May to October.

Budget

Near Downtown The *Avenues Youth Hostel* (☎ 359-3855, 888-884-4752, 107 F St) has adequately clean dormitory beds for $14/17 for members/nonmembers and 15 private rooms with funky furniture ($25 to $40); there are weekly and monthly discounts. There are a total of 57 beds in 19 rooms with 13 bathrooms. Two kitchens, laundry, big-screen-TV lounge and Internet access ($3 for 30 minutes) are available; guests are mainly young international travelers. Office hours are 7:30 am to 12:30 pm and 4 to 10:30 pm; there is no curfew. Credit card reservations are accepted, and they are especially advised in winter, when the hostel fills up with skiers.

website: www.citysearch.com/slc/hostel

At the south end of downtown is the smaller and homier *Ute Hostel* (☎ 595-1645, 363-8137, 21 E Kelsey Ave). It has 18 dorm beds in three rooms for $15, and two private rooms for $35. There are kitchen facilities and no curfew. They'll pick you up from the airport, bus or train station but won't take credit card reservations; you must mail a check or money order.

website: www.infobytes.com/utehostel

There is a dearth of good cheap motels – most bottom-end places are just that, especially in the downtown area. One exception is *City Creek Inn* (☎ 533-9100, 230 W North Temple), which is a block from Temple Square and one of the best deals in town. Its 33 rooms are small but very clean and attractive; climbing rose bushes around the interior courtyard are a welcome touch. Summer singles/doubles are $48/58.

The downtown *Motel 6* (☎ 531-1252, 176 W 600 South) charges $46/52 for singles/doubles, which is high for a Motel 6! It has more than 100 no-frills rooms, as do all the Motel 6s in the Salt Lake area. Across the street, the *Wasatch Inn* (☎ 355-4402, 230 W 600 South) has decent rooms for $30 to $60, depending on demand. However, rooms have floor-to-ceiling glass fronts (with drapes), which may be a privacy/security concern.

Beyond Downtown W North Temple on the way to the airport is lined with a variety of motels. A half dozen rough cheapies vie for your dollar, of which the most reliable are *Gateway Inn* (☎ 533-0603, 819 W North Temple); *Chateau Motel* (☎ 596-7240, 1999 W North Temple); and *Motel 6-Airport* (☎ 364-1053, 1990 W North Temple). The first two have very simple but adequately clean singles/doubles for $35/40; the Motel 6 is $10 more.

On the east side of downtown, *Scenic Motel* (☎ 582-1527, 1345 S Foothill Drive) charges $38/48 for decent, clean rooms.

Check out State St, south of 1700 South, for more rough budget motels if the above are all booked.

Mid-Range

Near Downtown Mid-range lodgings in Salt Lake consist almost entirely of *chain hotels*. Double rooms range from a low of $50 to highs in the $90s, depending on demand and the chain. The closest to Temple Square are *Howard Johnson's Express Inn* (☎ 521-3450, 800-446-4656, 121 N 300 West) and *Travelodge-Temple Square* (☎ 533-8200, 144 W North Temple). Other chains close to downtown include Econo Lodge, Super 8, Quality Inn and Ramada Inn.

Beyond Downtown There are several mid-range *chain hotels* in the airport area, especially along W North Temple. Rates are a little higher, ranging from $70 to $100. All have pools and hot tubs, and some have restaurants. They include Super 8, Days Inn, Comfort Inn and Holiday Inn Express.

Almost 2 miles south of the university on the east side of town, *Skyline Inn* (☎ 582-5350, 2475 E 1700 South), is a small, clean, attractive motel with an indoor pool and hot tub; singles are $52 to $61, doubles are $66 to $70.

A cluster of hotels in Midvale – near exit 301 off I-15, about 11 miles south of Temple Square – cater to skiers wanting affordable lodgings with easy highway access to the Cottonwood Canyons. As such, winter rates are highest – ask about ski packages. The Motel 6 here charges $40 to $50. For $55 to $80, try La Quinta Inn, Days Inn and Best Western. *Discovery Inn* (☎ 561-2256, 800-380-1415, 380 W 7200 South) has comfortable rooms for $67 to $80. If you'll be staying for a week, your best deal will be at the *Suburban Lodge* (☎ 567-0312, 150 W 7200 South), which is in the $60s per night and under $300 by the week.

Top End

Near Downtown The attractive *Peery Hotel* (☎ 521-4300, 800-331-0073, 110 W 300 South) was completely renovated in 1999.

The formal, elegant lobby of the 1910 building now sparkles, and the 73 tidy rooms are graciously appointed, with the requisite chocolate on every pillow. Full breakfast at Christopher's next door is included. Singles/doubles are $102/117 during the week, and $15 less on weekends. A few suites are $150 and up.

Despite its faded exterior, the **Shilo Inn** (☎ 521-9500, 800-222-2244, 206 S West Temple), opposite the visitor center, has 200 perfectly nice, well-kept rooms that, on weekends, are the best value of the large, full-service downtown hotels. Rooms are $122 during the week, dropping to $72 on the weekends for one or two people.

If you're splurging on a luxury hotel, why not stay at the most outrageous? Funky, arty, over the top, **Hotel Monaco** (☎ 595-0000, 877-294-9710, 15 W 200 South) is like the eccentric aunt of staid Salt Lake. Thankfully, the 225 rooms live up to the gaudy promise of the lobby. Downstairs is a well-regarded new bar and restaurant, Bambara. The hotel is very pet-friendly; they will even bring you, on request, your own companion bowl of goldfish. Rates vary with demand, but are generally $160 to $170 midweek, $100 to $120 weekends, with suites ranging from $200 to $325; all include complimentary evening wine hour and massage.

Taking up an entire city block, the huge **Little America Hotel** (☎ 363-6781, 800-453-9450, 500 S Main) is a good full-service hotel with 850 large rooms and suites ranging from $130 to $235, depending on size, views and amenities. Across the street, and also taking up a city block, is **Grand America** (☎ 258-6000, 800-621-4505, 555 S Main). This sister property opened in 2001, and is attempting to set a new standard for luxury in Salt Lake. The chandeliers are from Venice, the carpets from England and the rates astronomical. Deluxe rooms and suites (there is no 'standard') run $225 to $375, and if these don't satisfy, luxury suites are a mere $1000 to $3500.

The Inn at Temple Square (☎ 531-1000, 800-843-4668, 71 W South Temple) is in a lovely 1930 Edwardian building across the street from its namesake. Many of the 90 rooms and suites have good views of the square, and all are attractive and elegantly old-fashioned. Smoking is not permitted, and no liquor is served. Rates include buffet breakfast and start at $115/85 midweek/weekends. Suites range from $170 to $270.

Other full-service luxury hotels downtown include **Marriott** (☎ 531-0800, 800-228-9290, 75 S West Temple) and **Hilton** (☎ 328-2000, 800-445-8667, 255 S West Temple). Standard rack rates are $190/100 midweek/weekend, but these vary with demand and discounts.

Beyond Downtown Top-end, full-service **chain hotels** include the Holiday Inn, 1½ miles south of Temple Square, and Hilton and Radisson near the airport; spacious rooms range from $100 to $140.

Near the university, and convenient for the Cottonwood Canyons, **Marriott University Park** (☎ 581-1000, 800-637-4390, 480 Wakara Way), has over 200 rooms for $130/70 midweek/weekend in summer, $170/130 in winter.

B&Bs

Salt Lake City has several exceptional B&Bs in historic homes; contact the visitor center for a complete list. Reserve these accommodations well in advance.

Anton Boxrud B&B (☎ 363-8035, 800-524-5511, 57 S 600 East) attracts European guests, who enjoy its emphasis on caring personal service, excellent homemade breakfasts and comfortable but not overly lavish rooms. This historic 1901 home is furnished with antiques and has five nonsmoking rooms with private baths ($98 to $140) and two with shared bath ($69 and $78). There's also an outdoor hot tub, and complimentary evening refreshments; for details, see www.bbiu.org/antonboxrud. Nearby, **Saltair B&B** (☎ 533-8184, 800-733-8184, 164 S 900 East) has expanded to five properties with 17 rooms that appeal to a range of travelers. All make a cozy home away from home. The historic main house (Salt Lake's first B&B) has five pretty rooms (two with private bath) for $55 to $110; full breakfast and evening refreshments are included.

Next door are three cottage rooms, each with kitchen, fireplace, sitting room and continental breakfast included ($130 to $150). Another nine fully equipped suites, suitable for families, are plainer but still nice; most are $100 to $130 (no breakfast). Ask about weekly rates and discount packages or check online at www.saltlakebandb.com.

In an 1893 home that was once the mayoral mansion, the *Armstrong Mansion B&B* (☎ 531-1333, 800-708-1333, 667 E 100 South) exudes ornate Victorian luxury. All 13 antique-filled rooms have private baths and most have hot tubs or fireplaces. Rates are $99 to $209, including full buffet breakfast and afternoon refreshment; the website is www.armstrong-bb.com. The *Pinecrest B&B* (☎ 583-6663, 800-359-6663, 6211 Emigration Canyon) is a 1915 country residence in the Wasatch foothills, about 12 miles east of downtown. It has a large and peaceful garden and six nonsmoking rooms with private bath ($100 to $195); two 'rooms' are cabins that can accommodate families. Full breakfast is included.

The 14 theme rooms at the *Anniversary Inn* (☎ 363-4900, 800-324-4152, 678 E South Temple) are meant to dazzle and entertain – and they succeed to a Disney-esque degree. Each room is thoroughly unique, many dominated by floor-to-ceiling murals, such as the underground catacombs in 'Phantom of the Opera.' Enjoy the whimsical rock waterfall shower and pump faucet of 'Mountain Hideaway' or sleep with a menacing octopus in 'Neptune's Cave.' Weekday rates range from $119 to $259; $20 higher on weekends. All rooms have jetted tubs, free movies and in-room continental breakfast. website: www.Anniversaryinn.com

Ski Resorts

Both the Snowbird/Alta area in Little Cottonwood Canyon and the Solitude/Brighton area in Big Cottonwood Canyon have ski resorts, condos and lodges. Of the ski areas, Snowbird/Alta offers the greatest choice of accommodations. Some of these remain open in summer, when rooms are cheaper.

Ski-season rates vary throughout the low, regular and holiday periods. The low

periods are normally the beginning and end of the ski season, when snowfall is least predictable. The regular season runs from January through March. The Christmas holiday season is the most expensive, but there's a post-holiday lull in January with somewhat lower rates. Note that a sales tax of about 10% is added to the prices given and that lodges offering meals-inclusive packages add a further 15% service charge. Ask your travel agent about airline/resort package deals.

Budget travelers will not find any bargains at the ski resorts. The free and very useful *Utah Winter Vacation Planner* (see Skiing in Activities above) provides both skiing and accommodations information. See also Places to Stay in Park City; many of the reservations services there can arrange lodgings and ski packages at the Cottonwood Canyons resorts.

Snowbird The *Snowbird Resort* (☎ 800-385-2002) operates the *Cliff Lodge*, with more than 500 rooms, as well as three condo complexes. These places house the majority of skiers, as all are within walking and skiing distance of the slopes and have every amenity you might want, including pools, full-service spas, child care, restaurants and bars. A variety of studios, suites and fully furnished condos range from $169 to $599 in the low season and $299 to $989 in the regular season.

Alta There are more than a dozen places to stay in or near Alta, and many can be reserved through *Alta Area Reservations* (☎ 942-0404, 888-782-9257, 3332 East Little Cottonwood Rd). This service also books Snowbird accommodations.

Listed below are a few of the largest lodges; all are close to the chair lifts. They have dorm rooms for around $95 per person and a range of other rooms and suites from $110 to $190; deluxe suites are much more. Most rates include breakfast and dinner (add 10% tax and 15% service charge). Options include *Alta Lodge* (☎ 742-3500, 800-707-2582) or www.altalodge.com; *Alta Peruvian Lodge* (☎ 742-3007, 800-453-8488) or www.altaperuvian.com; the **Goldminer's Daughter Lodge** (☎ 742-2300, 800-453-4573); and **Rustler Lodge** (☎ 742-2200, 888-532-2582) or www.rustlerlodge.com.

If you are looking for more elegant accommodations, **Canyon Services** (☎ 943-1842, 800-562-2888) can set you up with various amenity-packed condos for $310 to over $1,000.
website: www.canyonservices.com

Brighton/Solitude The Brighton/Solitude ski areas have far fewer places to stay. Two places to try are the 20-room **Brighton Lodge** (☎ 800-873-5512), right by the lifts, and **Brighton Chalets** (☎ 942-8824, 800-748-4824), www.brightonchalets.com, a quarter-mile away. Both places have rates beginning around $110.

The **Village at Solitude** (☎ 536-5700, 800-748-4754) has 46 rooms and condos ranging from $210 to $620.

PLACES TO EAT

Salt Lake City has a wide and interesting range of restaurants, with notable choices for all budgets. Make sure to enjoy the city's diverse selection of good ethnic cuisine; this combination of diversity and quality isn't repeated elsewhere in the state.

For grocery shopping, **Albertson's** (☎ 364-5594, 370 E 200 South) is the closest to downtown, and **Wild Oats Community Market** (see Budget below) is an excellent health food store. For a quick, no-regrets lunch downtown, there are fast-food courts at **Crossroads Plaza**, 50 S Main, and **ZCMI**, 36 S State. South of downtown, **Trolley Square**, 600 S 700 East, has a food court and a good selection of restaurants (some are described below).

Days of operation or meals served are listed below, but not specific hours unless they are notable or unusual. Always call ahead to confirm opening and closing times, as these often change.

Coffeehouses

Mormons don't drink coffee but good coffeehouses, serving all the usual espresso drinks, are easy to find. The oldest, and still the best, is **Salt Lake Roasting Company** (☎ 363-7572, 320 E 400 South), open till midnight Monday to Saturday. It serves fine baked goods, homemade soups, quiches and sandwiches. Upstairs are enormous wall maps of Utah, so you can chart your course. Also good is **Millcreek Coffee Roasters** (☎ 323-9174, 657 S Main), which serves muffins, bagels and soup. It's open till mid-afternoon daily.

At the hip 9th and 9th corner, **Coffee Garden** (☎ 355-3425, 898 S 900 East) is a relaxed hangout that's open all day, every day. In the center of the informal arts district, **A Cup of Joe** (☎ 363-8322, 353 W 200 South), features local artists and has live acoustic music and poetry. Order Italian gelato or a slice of pie with your latte. Open daily.

Brewpubs

The upscale and friendly **Squatter's Pub Brewery** (☎ 363-2739, 147 W 300 South) has the classic brewpub look: gleaming fermentation tanks behind the bar, exposed brick and high beamed ceilings. They also brew some of the best beer in Utah (with the awards to prove it); their cream stout is quite commendable. The menu ranges from Asian stir-fries to juicy burgers and bangers and mash ($7-10). Fireplaces blaze in winter and there's a beer garden for summer. It is open till midnight daily, till 1 am Friday and Saturday.

Also vying for, and sometimes winning, 'best brewpub' honors is **Red Rock Brewing Company** (☎ 521-7446, 254 S 200 West). The menu is somewhat more extensive and includes wood-fired pizzas ($9). The pub can be a true 'scene' on weekends, when it's open till midnight. Open daily.

Another spot popular among twenty-somethings is the **Desert Edge Brewery** (☎ 521-8917), in Trolley Square, with an unusual, hangar-like interior and very long bar. Open daily, till 1 am on weekends.

Newest on the scene is the unpretentious **Marmot Mesa** (☎ 994-2800, 163 W Pierpont Ave), which draws students and other budget-minded types. The pub grub is more basic, the brew less expensive; it's a nice place to hang out and play one of the many board games. Open till 2 am daily.

Restaurants

Budget Visit the **Blue Plate Diner** (☎ 463-1151, 2041 S 2100 East) to experience a retro '50s diner with modern sensibilities: A free jukebox plays jazz, the clocks tell time backward and daily all-you-can-eat specials are $5-10 for breakfast, lunch and dinner. That's right: all you can eat for five bucks. And the food's good! This is the rare place where both vegetarian stir-fries and chicken fried steak are equally delicious. The omelettes and pancakes ($4-6) are great, too. No one can replace Bill & Nada's Café (a favorite that closed after many years), but the Blue Plate Diner is a worthy successor. It's open from 7 am to 10 pm daily.

Limited funds go far at **Chuck-A-Rama** (☎ 531-1123, 744 E 400 South), which features all-you-can-eat buffets for lunch ($7) and dinner ($9) daily. The food's not bad, and every day is a new theme cuisine. Nearby, **Hires Big H** (☎ 364-4582, 425 S 700 East) is a very popular '50s-style drive-in. The menu is long, but don't look farther than the Big H Combo: a decent burger, fresh cut fries and the famous root beer in a real frosty glass mug. It's work to spend $8. Both restaurants are local chains with several locations.

Savvy locals head to **Red Iguana** (☎ 322-1489, 736 W North Temple) for reasonably priced, well-prepared Mexican food Monday to Saturday. It doesn't look like much, but never mind. For nicer ambiance, **Rio Grande Cafe** (☎ 364-3302, 270 S Rio Grande) serves good, basic Mexican ($4-8) in the historic Rio Grande Railway Depot. It's open daily.

Few people will drive across town for a humble taco, but if you're one of them, drop everything and run to **Lone Star Taqueria** (☎ 944-2300, 2265 E Fort Union Blvd). The fish tacos are legendary-fresh, piquant, juicy. Look for the wrecked station wagon and the hubcap fence.

In addition to being the city's premiere organic produce and health food store, **Wild Oats Community Market** (☎ 355-7401, 645 E 400 South) makes a great selection of fresh, delicious sandwiches. There are vegetarian and deli-meat sandwiches, salads and juice drinks to take with you or eat upstairs in a relaxed reading area. Open daily. In a converted residential home, **Sage's Café** (☎ 322-3790, 473 East Broadway) serves a completely vegetarian, mostly vegan menu that changes daily. Sandwiches run $6-7, and pastas are $9.50. Wednesday night is all-you-can-eat pizza ($6); be sure to sample the root beer made here too. Open for lunch and dinner Wednesday to Sunday, plus breakfast on weekends.

Bright, clean and cheap, **Guru's** (☎ 355-4878, 912 E 900 South), is a local chain serving a mix of Mexican, Asian and Italian ($4-7). Not only that, but profits go to a foundation that funds youth-centered programs. Housed in an old drive-through hamburger stand, **Kenji's** (☎ 519-2378, 45 E 200 South) is what every city needs: fast-food sushi. It's one of downtown's best lunches, when it's packed. It's open for dinner, too, Monday to Saturday.

For authentic Tibetan cuisine, there's the unassuming **House of Tibet** (☎ 364-1376, 145 E 1300 South, Space 409). Open for lunch and dinner Monday to Saturday; most dishes run $5-7.

Cafe Trang (☎ 539-1638, 818 S Main), is one of the city's old favorites. A lively and popular Vietnamese restaurant, it has a 200-item menu, so there's always new things to try. It's open daily for lunch and dinner.

A university rathskeller, **Pie Pizzeria** (☎ 582-0193, 1320 E 200 South), makes what has deservedly been voted the 'best pizza in Utah' – it's thick with cheese and delicious ($8-18). Called simply 'The Pie,' the lively restaurant has graffiti-covered walls and is always crowded with students. It's open daily, till 3 am Friday and Saturday. Slices are available only for lunch and late at night, but the pies are so good you'll eat the whole thing.

The **Old Spaghetti Factory** (☎ 521-0424, 189 Trolley Square) is very popular and inexpensive. A variety of spaghetti dinners go for $5.50 to $9. The ornate, bright red Victorian interior and a historic trolley car make it a fun place to bring kids. It's open for lunch and dinner daily.

For a cheap meal in a historic spot, there's *Lion House Pantry Restaurant* (☎ 363-5466, 63 E South Temple). The 1855 Lion House was built as quarters for some of Brigham Young's many wives. Hearty American food is served cafeteria-style for weekday lunches (11 am to 2 pm) and dinner Friday and Saturday. Meals range from $6 to $10.

Utahns love their ice cream, and it doesn't get much better than *Snelgrove Ice Cream Parlor* (☎ 485-8932, 850 E 2100 South), where they've been dishing out generous scoops of rich homemade ice cream since 1929. Open Monday to Saturday, till 11 pm Friday and Saturday.

Mid-Range Founded in 1919, *Lamb's Restaurant* (☎ 364-7166, 169 S Main) is Utah's oldest continually operating restaurant. In 2000, it won a 'lifetime achievement' award for its dependable quality and traditional, distinctive ambiance, which with its counter-and-booth seating and homey service remains a time-warp to the 1930s. Breakfast is recommended (and cheap); traditional American dinners run $12-20. Open 7 am to 9 pm Monday to Saturday.

Utah's second oldest restaurant is in Emigration Canyon, about 4 miles east of the university. In the 1930s, *Ruth's Diner* (☎ 582-5807, 2100 Emigration Canyon), was a beat-up trolley car across from a bordello, but today its outdoor patio in this pleasant canyon makes this an ideal spot on a sunny day or warm evening. Locals make the drive for the well-prepared comfort food – chicken fried steak, meat loaf, liver and onions – excellent diner breakfasts and Mexican-inspired dishes. Prices run $5-15, and it's open 7 am to 10 pm daily.

Michelangelo Ristorante (☎ 466-0961, 2156 E 2100 South), near 1100 East, is highly recommended for its authentic Italian cooking (pastas $11-16). The friendly Italian staff make you quickly forget the mall basement location. Dinner is served 5:45 to 9 pm Tuesday to Saturday. Nearby, *Salt Lake Pizza & Pasta* (☎ 484-1804, 1063 E 2100 South) serves reasonably priced pizza and pasta ($7-11), and they have a variety of microbrews to wash it down with; open daily.

The specialty is grilled skewered meats at *Rodizio* (☎ 220-0500) in Trolley Square. This Brazilian restaurant is lively and fun with a modern, open interior. They prepare other traditional Brazilian dishes and have a good salad bar; dinner entrees run $13-17. Open daily for lunch and dinner.

For good Mexican food in an equally festive environment, try *Pierpont Cantina* (☎ 364-1222, 122 W Pierpont Ave). You can dine on the sidewalk outside or surrounded by piñatas and Mexican music inside. Plates run $9-17. It's open for lunch Monday to Friday, dinner daily.

Cedars of Lebanon (☎ 364-4096, 152 E 200 South) has inexpensive Middle Eastern lunches (the all-you-can-eat weekday lunch buffet is $7) and pricier dinners ($10-14). Belly dancers entertain on Friday and Saturday nights. It's open for lunch weekdays and dinner Monday to Saturday. You can also shop at the adjoining deli for Middle Eastern groceries.

Across the street, *Star of India* (☎ 363-7555, 177 E 200 South) prepares good curries and tandoori specialties ($8-14). Open for lunch weekdays and dinner Monday to Saturday. Another excellent choice for Indian meals is *Bombay House* (☎ 581-0222, 1615 S Foothill Drive). Arrive early, as it can get extremely crowded. Open for dinner from 4 to 10:30 pm Monday to Saturday.

Bangkok Thai (☎ 582-8424, 1400 S Foothill Drive), in the Foothill Village shopping center, is generally considered one of the region's best Thai restaurants. However, don't worry – dishes ($9-13) are not as spicy as its ski slope ratings system would lead you to believe. Open Monday to Saturday for lunch and daily for dinner.

P F Chang's China Bistro (☎ 539-0500, 174 West 300 South) serves well-prepared classic Chinese cuisine in an atmospheric dining room complete with imposing statuary. It's a great deal for the price ($6-13), and is consequently packed out on weekends.

Reservations aren't accepted, so arrive early. Open daily till 11 pm.

For genuine and well-prepared Afghan food, the place to go is *Baba Afghan* (☎ 596-0786, 55 E 400 South). Buffet lunches are served Monday to Saturday and dinner ($11-17) Tuesday to Sunday.

The family-owned *Kyoto* (☎ 487-3525, 1080 E 1300 South) has authentic Japanese meals, a sushi bar and private tatami rooms. Lunches (served Monday to Saturday) are $6.50-7.50; dinners (served daily) are $12.50-17.

Oasis Café (☎ 322-0404, 151 S 500 East), and its adjoining Golden Braid bookstore (☎ 322-1162), will keep you healthy in mind, body and spirit with its mostly vegetarian offerings. An outdoor patio with an indoor/outdoor fireplace is a nice spot to enjoy breakfast, lunch ($6-9) or dinner ($16-20), which includes a few fish items. Open daily.

Top End Salt Lake City isn't generally regarded as a gourmet capital, but it can surprise you. Foodies won't be disappointed with a tour of the city's better restaurants.

For the best in fresh seafood, head for *Market Street Grill* (☎ 322-4668, 48 W Market). Daily specials ($22-30) range widely from local trout to Louisiana catfish, mahi mahi to Atlantic salmon, plus crab, lobster, shrimp and premium oysters – all flown in daily. The best deal is their early bird special – arrive before 7 pm and enjoy prime rib or perfectly grilled salmon or halibut for $15. It's open for breakfast, lunch and dinner daily (brunch on Sunday). Breakfasts (from 6:30 am) are excellent and only $5-10. In the same building – the historic 1906 New York Hotel – is the *Market Street Oyster Bar* (☎ 531-6044), a private club with the same food for lunch and dinner (for a description of private clubs, see Entertainment). At both places, prime mealtimes can get hectic and loud.

Next door, the *New Yorker* (☎ 363-0166, 60 Market), is a more formal and elegant private club and restaurant; it's where businessfolk come to wine and dine. Dinner entrées range from $25 to $35, or you can

drop $50 for abalone. Lunch is served weekdays and dinner Monday to Saturday. Reservations are recommended.

In recent years, top honors have gone to *Metropolitan* (☎ 364-3472, 173 W Broadway), which puts it all together with modern urban ambiance, polished service and superior cuisine. The fancier restaurant side serves entrees ($24-34) such as roasted loin of caribou and fricasee of ostrich in addition to more traditional fare. The bistro side serves upscale mac and cheese and squash and truffle ravioli for half the price. You can enjoy the good life for a modest outlay by eating light and ordering a martini at the attractive bar while listening to live jazz music on Saturday evenings. It's open from 5:30 pm Tuesday to Saturday; reservations are recommended.

A few years ago, the esteemed *Ichiban Sushi* (532-7522, 336 S 400 East) moved from Park City to Salt Lake. It remodeled an old Lutheran church – leaving the peaked roof exposed, replacing the stained-glass rose with a modern design, gracing another wall with tumbling sumo wrestlers and adding quiet tatami rooms – to create an environment as unique and inventive as its high-quality sushi and Japanese meals ($16-18). Sushi rolls ($5.50-12) can be elaborate works of art. They are open nightly from 4 pm and don't take reservations; weekend waits can be an hour. Become a regular and you, too, can store your personal set of chopsticks behind the sushi bar.

Salt Lake has two other noteworthy Japanese restaurants. *Mikado* (☎ 328-0929, 67 W 100 South), has authentic Japanese dining in a traditional ambiance, and the sushi bar is particularly good. Dinners range from $14-24. It's open nightly from 6 pm. *Shogun* (☎ 364-7142, 321 S Main) has similar prices for a full range of Japanese meals or a sushi bar, and is open for lunch weekdays and dinner nightly.

Fresco Italian Café (☎ 486-1300, 1513 S 1500 East) is intimate and slightly formal, with an attractive, romantic courtyard in warm weather. They serve gourmet versions of traditional Italian dishes: the 'bolognese' is braised veal, pork and a red wine meat sauce. Main courses are $18-23; open daily for dinner.

The local cognoscenti know and love *Café Madrid* (☎ 273-0837, 2080 E 3900 South). Tucked in an unassuming mall on the south end of town, it serves authentic Spanish cuisine that is the envy of Spain's capital. The owner is passionate about her cooking, and it shows; eschew the formal menu (which she prints 'only because I have to') and order any of her daily specials, which include a range of tapas ($5-10) and entrees ($14-25), all generously proportioned. The small, cozy dining room can get lively, as diners get into the spirit of things (and it makes reservations essential). It is open for dinner from 5:30 pm Monday to Saturday.

In the Hotel Monaco, *Bambara* (☎ 364-5454, 202 S Main) serves upscale contemporary cuisine in funky modern surroundings. It's a popular place to sit at the bar and enjoy a drink.

Spencer's (☎ 238-4748, 255 S West Temple), in the Hilton, is a well-regarded, old-style steakhouse with a men's club atmosphere. A private club, it is open for lunch and dinner, when steaks and other chops run $20 to $33.

A local favorite for its romantic wooded setting and fine creative cuisine is *Log Haven* (☎ 272-8255), 4 miles up Mill Creek Canyon. Entrees such as pomegranate-cinnamon braised lamb shanks and duck confit are $26. Open nightly for dinner; reservations are highly recommended.

Finally, imagine, if you will, a fantasy of an 18th-century French country chateau surrounded by 22 acres of flower gardens and gurgling ponds, the province of white swans and regal peacocks. Inside, expect hearty French meals fit for a king, and you will come close to the wonderland that is *La Caille at Quail Run* (☎ 942-1751, 9665 Wasatch Blvd), near the beginning of Little Cottonwood Canyon. The price for such opulent dreams? From $45 to $62 (and more!) for entrées such as filet mignon and sea scallops. Only the bourgeois would

protest. Dinner is served from 6 pm nightly; reservations are required.

ENTERTAINMENT
Cinemas
You can see first-run Hollywood films at dozens of movie theaters around town, but there's only one place where you can watch a movie while enjoying a beer and burger at the same time, and that's *Brewvies* (☎ 355-5500, 677 S 200 West). This lively, fun place also has pool tables and a regular bar; you have to be 21 to enter.

For alternative movies, call the *Tower Theater* (☎ 412-1824, 876 E 900 South), or try the *Utah Film & Video Center* (☎ 534-1158) in the Salt Lake Art Center, which has avant-garde movies every Friday and runs a festival for Utah filmmakers.

Nightlife
The best listing of bars, concerts and nightclubs is in the free *City Weekly*, published on Thursday and available at hundreds of outlets. The free biweekly *Event* is also a good information source, as are the two city dailies.

Many nightclubs – including all of those below – are private clubs. This means you can buy a temporary two-week membership for $5 (which allows you to bring five guests) or ask at the entrance for a member who might sponsor you for the night (see Drinking Laws in Facts about Utah for more on Utah's liquor laws). You have to be 21 to get into most places and IDs are often checked.

Salt Lake's nightclub scene is very active and varied and below is just a short list of hot spots; see also the brewpubs listed earlier in Places to Eat. S West Temple has several recommended places. *Dead Goat Saloon* (☎ 328-4628, 165 S West Temple) is down a funky-looking iron stairwell and behind a formidable metal door. Inside, it's one of Salt Lake's most popular bars for live music (since 1965). Someone is playing nearly every night; it's mainly blues, but also folk, reggae and rock, usually with a $3 to $6 cover. Open mike nights, poetry slams and

'Goat Jams,' when anyone can join the band on stage, round out the entertainment. It's open till 1 am daily.

More alternative, also with live music or DJs nearly every night, is *DV8* (☎ *539-8400, 115 S West Temple*). The cover can get steep, and the attitude a little thick, but it's always packed.

Zephyr (☎ *355-5646, 301 S West Temple*) is Salt Lake's oldest club, and it books an interesting, eclectic lineup of musicians and DJs, both local and nationally known groups. It's a friendly place with a busy dance floor. It's open till 2 am daily.

The city's premiere dance clubs are *Bricks* (☎ *328-0255, 579 W 200 South*) and, a few blocks away, *Axis* (☎ *519-2947, 100 S 500 West*). Both are huge, with several dance floors (including nonalcohol, underage areas) and different theme nights all week, such as hip-hop, gay night and so on. Covers range from $3 to $7, and increasingly, dress codes are enforced.

Salt Lake City has the only gay club scene in Utah. The largest and best is *Zipperz* (☎ *521-8300, 155 W 200 South*). It's homey and friendly with karaoke, DJs and other entertainment weekly. In addition to Bricks and Axis, above, check the listings in the free monthly *Pillar,* which is the city's gay newspaper. There are at least a half a dozen other gay and lesbian bars.

For country & western bands and dancing, head on over to the *Westerner Club* (☎ *972-5447, 3360 S Redwood Rd*), which offers free dance lessons two or three nights a week.

Popular bars include *Junior's Tavern* (☎ *322-0318, 200 E 500 South*), a neighborhood place with a jukebox, pool table and live jazz and blues on some nights, and *Port-O-Call* (☎ *521-0589, 78 W 400 South*), primarily a sports bar with the requisite big-screen TVs; it draws a college crowd.

Hipsters rack 'em at *Ya'buts* (☎ *359-1200, 45 W 300 South*). This pool hall rents tables by the hour ($5) and has live music on weekends. As the sign says, 'Shoot pool... not people.' *Burt's Tiki Lounge* (☎ *521-0572, 726 S State*) is a popular bar with the tattoo-and-piercing crowd.

Performing Arts

See Nightlife (above) for entertainment information sources. The best new plays or musicals are presented year-round by the *Salt Lake Acting Company* (☎ *363-7522, 168 W 500 North*). The *Pioneer Theater Company* (☎ *581-6961, 300 S 1400 East*), at the university, has performances throughout the September-to-May school year. *Hale Centre Theatre* (☎ *984-9000, 3333 S Decker Lake Dr*), in West Valley City, is a family theater that presents plays and musicals year-round.

Several professional and acclaimed companies share the elegant *Capitol Theater* (☎ *355-2787, 50 W 200 South*). These include the Utah Opera Company (☎ 736-6868) and Ballet West (☎ 323-6901), each of which stages four classical productions during the season (fall to spring). Modern dance is presented by the Ririe-Woodbury Dance Company (☎ 328-1062) and the Repertory Dance Theatre (☎ 534-1000), which both make their home at the intimate *Rose Wagner Performing Arts Center* (☎ *323-6800, 138 W 300 South*). Rose Wagner also hosts plays and concerts by touring groups.

The Utah Symphony Orchestra performs year-round at *Abravanel Hall* (☎ *533-6683, 533-5626, 123 W South Temple*), which is next to the Salt Palace and lays claim to the best acoustics of any modern concert hall in the world.

The Salt Lake City Arts Council (☎ 596-5000) has information about various local cultural events. You can get tickets for most venues from ArtTix (☎ 355-2787, 888-451-2787) or online at www.arttix.org.

SPECTATOR SPORTS

The Delta Center (☎ 325-2500), 301 W South Temple, hosts National Basketball Association (NBA) and Women's National Basketball Association (WNBA) games; the Delta Center, called the Salt Lake Ice Center during the 2002 Olympics, was the site of figure skating and short-track speed skating events. The E Center (☎ 988-8800/88), 3200 Decker Lake Drive, hosts American Hockey League (AHL) games; the center was used as the site of most of the men's ice hockey competitions during the Olympics. The NBA Utah Jazz (☎ 355-7328), WNBA Utah Starzz (☎ 325-7827), and the AHL Utah Grizzlies (☎ 988-7825, 988-8000) are the home teams. The Jazz and the Grizzlies have both been doing well in recent years, and seats for the most important games are sold out well in advance, but call anyway – you might get lucky. Otherwise, scalpers may be found near the center offering tickets for the best games at exorbitant prices.

Franklin Covey Field (☎ 485-3800), 77 W 1300 South, hosts the Salt Lake Buzz baseball team. The Buzz is the Minnesota Twins' AAA team (AAA being the highest level of professional minor league baseball play). Tickets are easier to come by for baseball games.

For University of Utah sports (football and basketball are very popular), contact the Athletics Department (☎ 585-6779) or check www.utahutes.com.

SHOPPING

Conventional shopping is available at a number of good malls. Downtown, ZCMI (Zions Cooperative Mercantile Institution) (☎ 321-8745), 35 S Main, and Crossroads Plaza (☎ 531-1799), 50 S Main, are right next to each other and have about 250 shops and restaurants between them. They are open daily. Free two-hour validated parking is available if you spend over $10 at any mall establishment.

One place in Crossroads Plaza stands out for its typical handicrafts. Simply called Mormon Handicraft (☎ 355-2141, 800-843-1480), it sells beautiful handmade quilts, dolls and stuffed animals, clothes (especially baby clothes) and a host of other traditional crafts. This is *the* place for quilt-making supplies or to hook up with classes.

Trolley Square (☎ 521-9877), 600 S 700 East, is another popular mall with upscale stores. It used to be the trolley-car depot, giving it some historical cachet.

The area around Highland Ave and 2100 South has several hip, funky clothing boutiques. The funkiest of them all is Blue Boutique (☎ 485-2072), 1080 E 2100 South,

which advertises 'nasty stuff' – that is, lingerie, skimpy leopard skirts and various punk attire.

REI (☎ 486-2100), 3285 E 3300 South, is a reliable source of high quality outdoor guidebooks and gear of all kinds. Rentals are available, and the Discover! Public Lands Information Center is here.

Lovers of handmade instruments won't want to miss Peter Prier & Sons Violins (☎ 364-3651, 800-801-3651), 308 E 200 South. This internationally renowned violin maker runs a school next to his shop, and you can watch students making violins. If you play, he sells the best.

GETTING THERE & AWAY
Air

The Salt Lake City International Airport (☎ 575-2400), about 6 miles west of downtown, is by far the most important airport in Utah. Several major carriers, including America West, American, Continental, Delta, Southwest, TWA, United and others, fly out of state; Skywest/Delta Connection flies to the Utah cities of St George, Cedar City and Vernal.

The airport has two national terminals and a third terminal for international flights. Facilities include a tourist information office, money exchange, restaurants, lounge, car rentals, baggage lockers and shops.

Bus

Greyhound (☎ 355-9579), 160 W South Temple, provides long-distance bus service. There are several buses a day heading south on I-15 through Provo, St George and Cedar City to Las Vegas, Nevada, and Los Angeles. There are also several buses a day west to San Francisco, east to Denver, Colorado, and north to Portland, Oregon, and Seattle, Washington.

UTA (Utah Transit Authority) (☎ 287-4636, 888-743-3882) provides services to the nearby cities of Provo, Tooele, Ogden and the towns and suburbs in between. Fares are a very reasonable $2. Weekday departures are frequent to Ogden and Provo; Saturday and Sunday buses run once an hour.
website: www.rideuta.com

Train
Amtrak (☎ 531-0188) is in the Rio Grande Depot at 320 S Rio Grande near downtown. The *California Zephyr* runs daily to Chicago ($215; 36 hours) via Helper ($25; 3 hours), Green River ($39; 4½ hours) and Denver ($86; 15½ hours). The westbound train continues to Oakland, California ($110; 17 hours). Call Amtrak for information on other services available.

GETTING AROUND
To/From the Airport
A taxi downtown will cost about $15. The UTA Bus 50 goes downtown for $1 (exact change required) between about 6 am and 7 pm. Weekday departures are frequent, while weekends are sporadic. UTA Bus 150 has five night buses from Monday to Saturday until about 11 pm. There is no holiday service. See below for local bus information.

Several shuttle services can take you to and from anywhere in the Salt Lake City/Wasatch Front area. Call the airport transportation desk (☎ 575-2477) for information.

Trax
An aboveground light rail line, UTA Trax (287-7245) began carrying passengers' in December 1999. It has two lines: one goes from the Delta Center along South Temple to Main Street, from where it runs straight south to 10000 South in Sandy. The other line runs from Main St along 400 South to the university; plans are to extend this line to the university hospital. There is a free fare zone downtown that includes Trax and all UTA buses: It extends from the state capitol in the north to 500 South, and from 400 West to 200 East. If you enter and exit between these streets, the ride is free.

Trax runs daily beginning around 5 am and ending just before midnight; trains run every fifteen minutes. Sundays and holidays have more limited service. You can get free transfers good on either buses or the train for up to two hours. Trax stops have vending machines where you purchase tickets before boarding. For both Trax and the bus, the fare is $1; an all-day pass is $2.

Bus
The Utah Transit Authority (UTA; ☎ 287-4636) provides comprehensive bus services throughout Salt Lake City and the surrounding areas. Sunday services are limited to buses to the airport, Provo and Ogden. There is no holiday service.

See Trax, above, for fare and free fare zone details. The most useful free fare bus is the No 23, which goes from 325 S West Temple to the State Capitol. Many buses are wheelchair accessible or have bike racks. Seniors and disabled passengers get discounts.

Detailed bus maps and timetables are available from the visitors bureau, public libraries, shopping malls, and city and municipal buildings, or online at www.rideuta.com.

Car
All the major car rental companies have offices in Salt Lake City and at the airport. Note that Utah car rental taxes are high; it's about 16% across the state, and if you rent through offices at the Salt Lake City International Airport or any hotel, another 10% fee will be added on top of this. You can avoid the additional fee by booking through a downtown office.

Parking downtown costs $1 an hour, or $10 all day, in parking lots or 25¢ for 20 minutes at parking meters; metered parking is free on Sunday, and Saturday is free two-hour parking. Finding a spot is rarely a problem. The downtown malls offer two-hour validation in their lots if you make a $10 purchase at any mall merchant.

Taxi
There are three main taxi companies, all with 24-hour service. Try Yellow Cab (☎ 521-2100), Ute Cab (☎ 359-7788) and also City Cab (☎ 363-5550).

Wasatch Mountains Region

Salt Lake City is but one of several towns running north to south along the western front of the Wasatch Mountains. The towns combine into an urban chain stretching roughly from Ogden, 35 miles north of Salt Lake City, to Provo, 45 miles south – three out of four Utah residents live in this metropolitan area. The steep-sided, forested mountains form a splendid backdrop to the cities and, perhaps more to the point, provide a reliable source of water. Historically, nomadic Ute and Shoshone Indians roamed this valley, and it became the first region to be settled by the Mormon pioneers of the mid-1800s.

Today, the Wasatch Mountains provide the winter visitor with 11 ski resorts within 55 miles of Salt Lake City: Four are best reached from Salt Lake City, three are near Park City, three are northeast of Ogden, and the last is north of Provo. Summer has an equally abundant range of outdoor activities, and the towns themselves have a variety of interesting historical buildings,

museums, festivals and plenty of good places to stay and eat.

This chapter first covers the Ogden area north of Salt Lake City, continues with Park City and Heber City to the east, and finishes with the Provo area to the south.

ANTELOPE ISLAND STATE PARK

This pretty, 15-mile-long island, the largest in the Great Salt Lake, is connected to the mainland by a 7-mile causeway. Now a state park, the island's beaches are perhaps the best place to experience the Great Salt Lake, but it is most famous for being the home of one of the largest bison (often called buffalo) herds in the country. People also come for the spring and fall bird migrations. (See the 'Where the Buffalo Roam' boxed text.)

Another attraction is the Fielding Garr ranch, which was established in 1848 and inhabited until 1981, when it was taken over by the state park. At the end of an 11-mile paved road, the pleasant ranch includes several short nature trails, a shaded picnic area and guided horse rides daily in summer (☎ 801-782-4946 for reservations).

Nineteen miles of hiking trails provide many opportunities to view wildlife; indeed, some trails are closed during mating and birthing seasons. Rangers also lead star parties from spring to fall, and a small marina offers cruises from Salt Islands Adventures (☎ 801-252-9336) in summer.

The park is open year-round from dawn till dusk; the visitor center (☎ 801-725-9263) has exhibits and a gift shop. Day use is $4 per bicyclist and $7 per car. A year-round campground ($10; ☎ 800-322-3770 for reservations) offers water and pit toilets; the nearby beach has showers and flush toilets. A simple restaurant (☎ 801-776-6734) is open daily in summer, limited hours in other months.

To get to the park, head west from I-15 exit 335 (25 miles north of Salt Lake City; 10 miles south of Ogden) and follow signs for

MAP INDEX

Idaho

Wasatch Mountains Region page 142

● Ogden page 144

Wyoming

Park City Area page 150

Park City page 152

● Provo page 162

UTAH

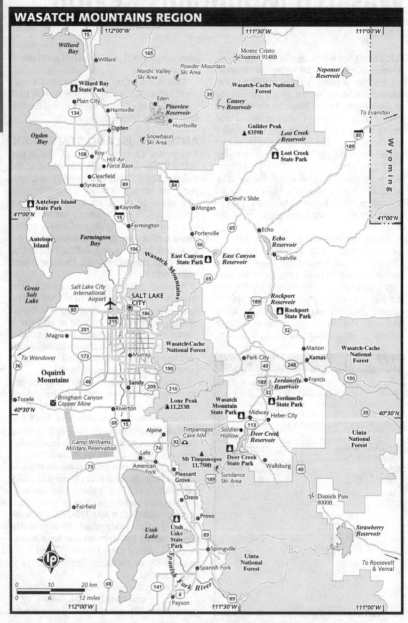

WASATCH MOUNTAINS REGION

Where the Buffalo Roam

Once, tens of millions of bison roamed much of the western part of the continent; now, the 600- to 700-strong herd on Antelope Island is one of the biggest of the few that remain.

Bison calves are normally born in March, April and May, and this is when the population is at its highest. Because of the finite food resources on the island, the herd is rounded up in late October, allowed to rest for a few days, then passed through corrals for veterinary inspection and tagging. A few animals are removed to keep the population stable, and the rest of the bison are allowed to roam freely throughout most of the island for the remainder of the year. Some are always kept at the corrals so visitors can get a close look. The fall herding and corralling of these animals is one of the area's famous wildlife spectacles.

Another wildlife spectacle is the spring and fall bird migration, when hundreds of thousands of shorebirds, waterfowl and seabirds use the island and causeway shorelines as a protected feeding place on their way to distant lands. One of the main food sources is the tiny brine shrimp, which are dense along the shoreline. In August, as many as 250,000 Wilson's phalaropes have been recorded, along with large numbers of other species. In addition, the island itself is the home of burrowing owls, several species of raptors and many other birds.

The visitor may also see one of the several dozen pronghorn antelope, bighorn sheep and deer, which share the island with badgers, porcupines, and numerous coyotes, jackrabbits, cottontails and various rodents.

about 7 miles to the park entrance (☎ 801-773-2941). From here, the causeway leads to the island. State park headquarters (☎ 801-550-6165) are at 4528 W 1700 South, Syracuse, UT 84075.

OGDEN

☎ 385 • pop 77,226 • elevation 4300 feet

This city is named after Peter Skene Ogden, a trapper who arrived in the Ogden river valley in 1826 and traded with the local Shoshone Indians. The area was the site of multiple rendezvous among the Indians, trappers and mountain men of the area during the 1820s and 1830s; the town itself was founded by Mormons in 1850 under Brigham Young's direction.

After the completion of the first transcontinental railway in 1869, Ogden became an important railway town, and a wild one at that. The railway brought many non-Mormon settlers, and their gambling, drinking and cavorting often created tension with the sober Mormon inhabitants.

Since then, Ogden has seen the opening of Weber State University (in 1889) and Hill Air Force Base (in 1939), still an economic mainstay. Today, Ogden is an important agricultural and manufacturing center, but ever since the train stopped running, it has been trying to regain its status as a tourist destination. The historic downtown is being revitalized, and the city is hoping to capitalize on the attention paid to the 2002 Winter Olympics, which held several events here.

Orientation & Information

Although laid out in the typical Mormon wide-avenued grid pattern, the city's street names differ somewhat from the usual. The east-west streets begin at 1st in the north and continue to about 40th in the south; the north-south streets are named mainly after American presidents. I-15 skirts the city to the west.

The visitors bureau (☎ 627-8288, 800-255-8824), 2501 Wall Ave (in Union Station), is open weekdays. Between Memorial Day and Labor Day, the bureau is also open on Saturday; it's online at www.ogdencvb.org. Also in Union Station is the National Forest Information Center (☎ 625-5306), which has maps, passes and national forest information. Another resource is the Wasatch

UTAH

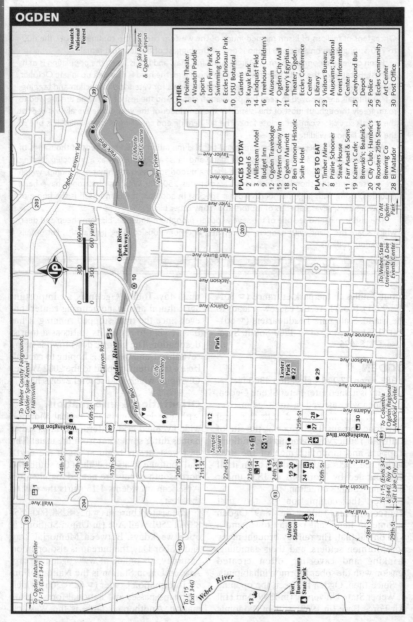

OGDEN

OTHER
1 Pointe Theater
4 Wasatch Paddle Sports
5 Lorin Farr Park & Swimming Pool
6 Eccles Dinosaur Park
10 USU Botanical Gardens
13 Kayak Park
14 Lindquist Field
16 Treehouse Children's Museum
17 Ogden City Mall
21 Peery's Egyptian Theater; Ogden Eccles Conference Center
22 Library
23 Visitors Bureau; Museums; National Forest Information Center
25 Greyhound Bus Depot
26 Police
29 Eccles Community Art Center
30 Post Office

PLACES TO STAY
2 Motel 6
3 Millstream Motel
9 Budget Inn
12 Ogden Travelodge
15 Western Colony Inn
18 Ogden Marriott
27 Ben Lomond Historic Suite Hotel

PLACES TO EAT
7 Timber Mine
8 Prairie Schooner Steak House
11 Farr Asael & Sons
19 Karen's Cafe; Brewski's; Beatnik's
20 City Club; Hambric's
24 Roosters 25th Street Brewing Co
28 El Matador

National Forest Ogden Ranger Station
(☎ 801-625-5112).

The local daily newspaper is the *Standard-Examiner*. Other services include the library (☎ 337-2632) 2464 Jefferson Ave; downtown post office (☎ 627-4184), 2730 Washington Blvd; McKay-Dee Hospital (☎ 627-2800), 3939 Harrison Blvd; Columbia Ogden Regional Medical Center (☎ 479-2111), 5475 S 500 East; and police (☎ 629-8221), 2549 Washington Blvd.

Union Station

Built in the 1920s, the station (☎ 629-8444), 2501 Wall Ave, contains several well-done small museums in addition to the tourist information offices mentioned above. The **Browning-Kimball Car Museum** displays a classic collection of vintage American cars; the **Browning Firearms Museum** has many guns developed by Ogden native John M Browning (1855-1926); and the **Railroad Museum** has historic locomotives as well as an extensive, authentic model train system. There's also a natural history museum, an art gallery, a gift shop and a restaurant. Hours are 10 am to 5 pm Monday to Saturday, plus 11 am to 3 pm on Sunday in summer. One admission is good for all exhibits; it's $3 for adults and $1 for children under 12.

Weber State University

This university, pronounced 'WEE-ber,' (☎ 626-6975), 3750 Harrison Blvd, has a gymnasium, a small natural history museum and an art gallery (free admission). The performing arts center (☎ 626-7000/6800) features Ballet West and the Utah Symphony during the winter season. For further information, contact the information desk at the Shepherd Union (☎ 626-6367), the student center, or check www.weber.edu.

South of campus, the **Dee Events Center** (☎ 626-8500) hosts various concerts, athletic contests and other events. Next to it is the **Ice Sheet** (☎ 399-8750), 4390 Harrison Blvd, which was the site of the men's and women's curling events in the 2002 Olympics. Ogden has embraced this obscure sport with its own league, and curling lessons are

offered. The public can also skate most days ($3.25 for adults, $2.75 for those under 18 or over 55). Call for times – there are usually two sessions a day.

Other Attractions

Since 1959, the non-profit **Eccles Community Art Center** (☎ 392-6935), 2580 Jefferson Ave, has showcased Utah artists in its gorgeous 1893 mansion. It's open Monday to Saturday; free admission.

Temple Square, between Washington and Grant and 20th and 22nd Sts, contains the Mormon tabernacle (which can be visited) and temple, as well as a DUP museum (☎ 393-4460), 2148 Grant Ave. Admission to these sites is free.

You'll wish you were a kid again at the **Treehouse Children's Museum** (☎ 394-9663), 2255 B Ogden City Mall, which features a labyrinth of well-done rooms with hands-on activities focused on the humanities: reading, storytelling, plays, art and music. It's open 10 am to 6 pm Monday to Saturday; admission is $3.50 for kids 15 and under, $2 for adults.

The small **Fort Buenaventura State Park** (☎ 621-4808), 2450 A Ave, contains an accurate, full-size replica of the original fort built in 1846. Open daily March to November; admission is $4 per car.

Eccles Dinosaur Park (☎ 393-3466), 1544 E Park Blvd in Ogden River Parkway, will be impossible to bypass if you have children. Over 100 life-size replicas of dinosaurs are posed outside among the trees, with hidden loudspeakers emitting authentic-sounding grunts and roars. It is open daily (weather permitting) April through October; admission is $3.50 for adults, $2.50 for seniors and $2 for three- to 17-year-olds.

The **Hill Air Force Base Museum** (☎ 777-6868) in Roy (drive 4 miles south on I-15 to exit 341 and follow signs) has several dozen historic military aircraft on display. It's open daily; free admission.

Activities

There are three ski resorts east of Ogden; see Ogden Area Ski Resorts, below. You can do easy **cross-country skiing** on groomed tracks at the Mount Ogden Golf Course (☎ 629-8333), 3000 Taylor at 30th; the USFS can recommend more difficult terrain in the national forest. For rentals, go to Black Diamond (☎ 627-5733), 3701 Washington Blvd, or Miller's Ski & Cycle Haus (☎ 392-3911), 834 Washington Blvd, which also rents bikes.

The pretty, 3-mile **Ogden River Parkway** (☎ 629-8284), between Washington Blvd and the mouth of Ogden Canyon, offers opportunities for picnicking, bicycling, swimming, running and playing tennis and golf. There's also the **USU Botanical Gardens** to visit. Ogden Parks Division (☎ 629-8284), 1875 Monroe Blvd, can lead you to other public pools and tennis courts. For more information on **golfing** in the area and **hiking**, especially on the trails that lead from town into the Wasatch Mountains, contact the visitors bureau.

Ogden now boasts its own **kayak park**, a specially designed spot on the Weber River (from 24th St, turn north on B Ave); water levels are best in spring. Rent what you need from Wasatch Paddle Sports (☎ 392-0862), 1810 Washington Blvd.

Special Events

Ogden hosts an abundance of events all year. The biggest annual event is **Pioneer Days** (☎ 629-8214), during the week leading up to July 24 (but not on Sunday), which includes a rodeo, fireworks, music, antique cars, a street festival, a parade and more. The **Weber County Fair** (☎ 399-8798), held in mid-August, takes place at the Weber County Fairgrounds and Golden Spike Arena (☎ 399-8544), 1000 N 1200 West, about 4 miles north of town.

Places to Stay

The best camping is about 10 to 20 miles east of town along scenic Ogden Canyon (Hwy 39). Maps and details are available from the National Forest Information Center (see Information, above). There are about 10 summer-only campgrounds ($12); most have water but no showers. Sites fill up on weekends (☎ 877-444-6777 for reservations). The closest to Ogden are on Pineview Reservoir.

Rates are slightly higher at many of Ogden's lodgings in summer, and many cheaper places offer weekly discounts.

Washington Blvd has several run-down, low-end motels with rates in the $30s; make sure to see your room first. *Budget Inn (☎ 393-8667, 1956 Washington Blvd)* is frayed but acceptably clean; singles/doubles are $35/40. The only true standout is *Millstream Motel (☎ 394-9425, 1450 Washington Blvd)*. Its 50 rooms are in good repair and retain some of the 1940s character of the motel's heyday. Rates run from $36 to $44. Ask to see the car museum, which is a labor of true automotive love.

Western Colony Inn (☎ 627-1332, 234 24th) charges $47/55 for singles/doubles in summer; rooms are perfectly clean and spacious. The *Ogden Travelodge (☎ 394-4563, 2110 Washington Blvd)* has similar rates and is convenient for downtown.

The Ogden exits off of I-15 are packed with mostly *chain hotels*, such as Motel 6, Comfort Suites and Holiday Inn Express. *Best Rest Inn (☎ 393-8644, 800-343-8644)*, at I-15 exit 346 (take 21st St from Ogden), is the better value. It has pleasant, clean rooms for $45 to $70, depending on demand.

Downtown Ogden has two top-flight, full-service hotels: the *Ogden Marriott (☎ 627-1190, 800-228-9290, 247 24th)*, with rooms for $109 midweek, $69 to $79 on weekends; and the even nicer *Ben Lomond Historic Suite Hotel (☎ 627-1900, 2510 Washington Blvd)*, with suites for $129 midweek, $89 weekends.

Places to Eat

Ogden has a decent selection of eateries. On summer Saturdays, a farmer's market takes over the historic section of 25th Street east of Union Station, which is lined with attractive restaurants and bars.

Jeremiah's (☎ 394-3273, 1335 W 12th St) at the Best Western High Country Inn (at I-15 exit 347) is open daily and has been well recommended for the heartiest breakfasts in Ogden. Western-themed *Karen's Café (☎ 392-0345, 242 25th St)* serves great, inexpensive diner fare for breakfast and lunch only; open daily.

Good American food is served at *Ye Lion's Den* (☎ 399-5804, *3607 Washington Blvd)*, a stalwart for over three decades. It's open for lunch weekdays and dinner nightly. Also recommended is the attractive, 50-year-old *Gray Cliff Lodge* (☎ 392-6775), 5 miles east on Ogden Canyon Rd. The menu features local trout. It's open for dinner only Tuesday to Sunday, plus Sunday brunch.

For good steaks and seafood ($13-25) with a heaping helping of overbaked atmosphere, you can circle the wagons at *Prairie Schooner Steak House* (☎ 392-2712, *445 Park Blvd)* or drop down an Old West mine at *Timber Mine* (☎ 393-2155, *1701 Park Blvd)*.

Roosters 25th Street Brewing Co (☎ 627-6171, *253 25th St)* is an upscale microbrewery with a fancy menu ($10 to $18). Zip into *Hambric's* (☎ 393-1051, *290 25th St)* for homemade soup at lunchtime; open Monday to Saturday.

Near the university is the *Pie Pizzeria* (☎ 627-1920), at 42nd and Harrison Blvd, which serves the same great pizza as the Salt Lake original. It's open daily, till 1 am on weekends. Nearby is the popular *Bavarian Chalet* (☎ 479-7561, *4387 Harrison Blvd)* which dishes up authentic German platters for dinner only Tuesday to Saturday.

El Matador (☎ 393-3151, *2564 Ogden Ave)* is considered Ogden's best Mexican restaurant. It is open daily.

For ice cream, everyone goes to *Farr Asael & Sons* (☎ 393-8629, *274 21st St)*. This old-fashioned ice-cream parlor was established in 1920.

Entertainment

Junction is the free monthly arts paper. There are several first-run movie theaters; the closest to downtown is the *Pointe Theatre* (☎ 392-7474, *151 12th)*.

Ballet, theater, symphony recitals and other performing arts are featured at Weber State University (see above). Also call the Ogden Symphony Ballet Association (☎ 399-9214/0453), 2580 Jefferson Ave, for its performance schedules and information. Part of the Ogden Eccles Conference Center, *Peery's Egyptian Theater* (☎ 395-

3227/05, *2415 Washington Blvd)* dates from the 1920s and has been renovated in sumptuous style. Various cultural events, including a summer musical theater season, are held here.

In summer, the Ogden Raptors play minor league baseball at *Lindquist Field* (☎ 392-2450), 2330 Lincoln Ave.

Harkening back to wilder days, Ogden has a number of private clubs, mainly in the historic hotels above or along 25th. The *City Club* (☎ 392-4447, *264 25th)* has an extensive Beatles collection. *Brewski's* (☎ 394-1713, *244 25th)* is a popular college hangout, and *Beatniks* (☎ 395-2859, *240 25th)* has live jazz.

Getting There & Away

Greyhound (☎ 394-5573), 2501 Grant Ave, has five daily buses to Salt Lake City (45 minutes) and two daily to Las Vegas (10 hours). It also has buses north, east and west out of the state.

UTA (☎ 621-4636) has local services to Salt Lake City and intermediate points as well as services around Weber County. An important UTA bus stop is at 25th and Washington Blvd – there is an information booth here. Buses for Salt Lake City leave frequently (at least once an hour) Monday to Saturday, and three times on Sunday. There is no service on major holidays. The fare is $2; see www.rideuta.com for details.

Ogden plans to add an intermodal transport hub on Wall Ave north of Union Station that will include taxis and all buses. The nearest passenger train station is in Salt Lake City.

OGDEN AREA SKI RESORTS

There are three ski resorts in the mountains east of Ogden, all accessed via the scenic, steep-walled Ogden Canyon. Whether you are going to the ski resorts or not, this is a pretty drive, especially in fall; it continues for about 40 miles to Monte Cristo Summit (9148 feet), and chains or snow tires are required from November through March. Apart from Ogden, you can stay at Powder Mountain or in the villages of Eden and Huntsville. (Eden and Huntsville are on the banks of Pineview Reservoir, a popular spot for boating, fishing, swimming and water-skiing in summer.) All the resorts have ski shops, instructors and places to eat, and they all allow snowboarding.

Nordic Valley

This tiny 85-acre resort (☎ 745-3511) is the closest to Ogden (15 miles) and offers the cheapest skiing in the state. The elevation goes from 5400 to 6400 feet, with two double lifts and 19 runs. All-day lift passes are $18; $5 for those over 65. Lighted night skiing from 5:30 to 10 pm is $10.

Powder Mountain

This resort (☎ 745-3771/2) is 19 miles from Ogden. The elevation goes from 6895 to 8900 feet, and the 2800 acres of skiing include 81 runs serviced by four lifts and three tows. This ski resort lives up to its name, with tons of expert powder and back-country skiing: 700 acres of powder skiing are serviced by snowcat, 800 acres are open for guided tours, and another 1200 acres are backcountry. Only 10% of the terrain is for beginners and 50% is for intermediate skiers. All-day lift passes are $33/26/19 for adults/seniors over 65/children 12 and under. Lighted night skiing (4:30 to 10 pm) is $16/14/11.

There are slope-side rooms and suites at the resort's small **Columbine Inn** and condos through its **Sundown Condos**; rates are $75 to $215. Four lodges provide snacks and meals during the day and one remains open until 10 pm.
website: www.powdermountain.net

Snowbasin

This 3200-acre resort (☎ 399-1135) hosted the downhill and super G skiing events in the 2002 Winter Olympics. The elevation is 6400 to 9350 feet. The Olympic downhill run, with a vertical drop of 2770 feet, is considered one of the best in the world. Nine lifts service 55 runs; terrain is 20% for beginners and 50% for intermediate skiers. All-day lift passes are $39/27/24 for adults/kids/seniors.
website: www.snowbasin.com

Places to Stay & Eat

For camping near Pineview Reservoir and Huntsville, see Places to Stay in Ogden, above.

Eden The **Snowberry Inn** (☎ 745-2634, 1315 N Hwy 158), 8 miles from Powder Mountain, has five rustic rooms with private bath and spa. Rates with full breakfast are $55 to $115. Ski packages are available.

The new **Valley Junction Inn** (☎ 745-1259, 800-406-2383, 2547 N Valley Junction Dr) has 28 nice rooms from $89 to $189. Four miles from the slopes and north of Eden, **Wolf Lodge** (☎ 745-2621, 800-345-8824, 3615 N Wolf Creek Rd) has 50 condos with kitchens for $110 to $155.

Huntsville The **Jackson Fork Inn** (☎ 745-0051, 800-255-0672, 7345 E 900 South) has eight rooms, most with private two-person spas. There is a restaurant (dinner and Sunday brunch only). Rates are from $80/120 without/with spa.

The **Valley House Inn** (☎ 745-8259, 888-791-8259, 7318 E 200 South) is in an 1872 home; theme suites are $84 to $179, including breakfast. Across the street, the **Shooting Star Saloon** (☎ 745-2002, 7350 E 200 South) has been in operation since 1879, making it Utah's oldest continually running saloon. It's a simple but friendly place that's worth searching out – the cheeseburgers are recommended, and the clientele comes from around the globe. Ask to see, and sign, the guestbook.

For an unusual treat, try the homemade peanut butter and honey sold by the Trappist monks at the **Abbey of Our Lady of the Holy Trinity** (☎ 745-3784), 4 miles east of Huntsville.

WILLARD BAY STATE PARK

This state park (☎ 734-9494), 900 W 650 North, PO Box A, Willard, UT 84340, lies on a small bay on the northwest shore of the Great Salt Lake. The park includes mud flats hosting thousands of migrating shorebirds in spring and fall. In summer, locals arrive for boating and fishing.

The park has two sections. To reach the north unit, take exit 360 off I-15 (at Willard,

14 miles north of Ogden) and head a short way west; to reach the south unit, take exit 354 from I-15 and head 3 miles west – there are signs.

The north unit is larger, nicer and more popular; it has a sandy beach and boat rentals. Both units have boat launch areas. The north unit has over 60 shaded campsites ($12-16, showers available) and the south about 30 unshaded ones ($10); bring mosquito repellent (☎ 800-322-3770 for reservations). Day use is $6.

PARK CITY
☎ 435 • pop 7371 • elevation 6900 feet

Surrounded by three of Utah's preeminent ski resorts and with five more within an hour's drive, Park City is the Southwest's most important ski town. The United States Ski Team has its headquarters here, and during the 2002 Winter Olympics, all but a handful of the outdoor skiing, jumping and sledding events were staged at area slopes and venues.

Park City started as a booming mining town after silver was discovered here in 1868. Though most of the town burned down in 1898, it was quickly rebuilt. When the mining boom went bust in the early 20th century, the town faded until locals began building the first ski areas in the 1960s. The rest, as they say, is history. Today, the affluent town is growing by leaps and bounds, as subdivisions sprawl across the hillsides and the rich and famous build enormous vacation homes. Salt Lake City residents flock here in winter to escape the 'winter inversion' (when smog gets trapped in the valley and lowers air quality) and to enjoy conservative Utah's most liberal town – full of lively bars, gourmet restaurants and attractive turn-of-the-19th-century buildings.

Snow blankets the town all winter. In summer, daytime temperatures average in the upper 70s°F, but nights can be chilly. Park City is 5 miles south of I-80 exit 145 and 32 miles west of Salt Lake City.

Information
There are two very helpful Visitor Information Centers (☎ 800-453-1360). One is in the Park City Museum, 528 Main (☎ 649-6104); the other is at 750 Kearns Blvd (☎ 658-4541). From Memorial Day to Labor Day and during ski season, hours are 10 am to 7 pm weekdays, till 6 pm on weekends. During off-season months, hours are 11 am to 5 pm daily or try www.parkcityinfo.com. The local weekly newspaper is the *Park Record*. Other services include the library (☎ 615-5600), 1255 Park Ave; post office (☎ 649-9191), 450 Main; Park City Family Health & Emergency Center (☎ 649-7640), 1665 Bonanza Drive; and police (☎ 615-5500), 445 Marsac Ave.

Things to See & Do
The visitor center has self-guided walking tour brochures of the historic town center.

The free **Park City Museum** (☎ 649-6104), 528 Main, has interesting exhibits of mining and local history.

The **Alf Engen Ski Museum** (☎ 435-658-4200), at the Utah Winter Sports Park off Hwy 224, was scheduled to open in 2002 after the Olympics. It is 'dedicated to preserving and promoting the rich history of winter sports in the Intermountain Region.' Call for hours and fees or check online at www.engenmuseum.org.

Activities
Downhill Skiing The free and recommended *Park City Winter Vacation Planner*, published each winter, is available from visitors bureaus and information centers and is comprehensively detailed. Skiing in the area starts in mid- to late November and ends in mid-April most years, depending on snow conditions.

In town, the main place to rent downhill skis is Jans (☎ 649-4949, 800-745-1020), which has eight locations, including 1600 Park Ave.

At all three resorts listed below, approximately 15% of the runs are for beginners, 45% for intermediate skiers. All-day lift tickets are $58 to $65 for adults, $29 to $34 for kids, and $29 to $44 for seniors; Deer Valley has the most expensive tickets, and The Canyons has the cheapest. All offer rentals and lessons.

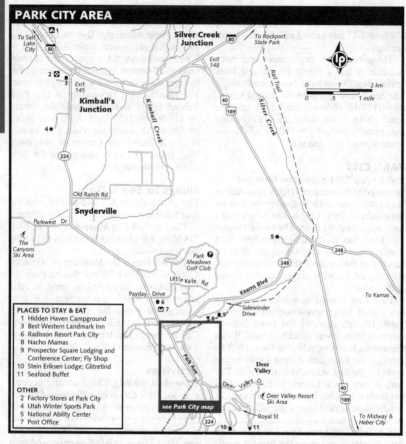

PARK CITY AREA

To Salt Lake City

Silver Creek Junction

To Rockport State Park

Exit 148

Kimball's Junction

Exit 145

Kimball Creek

Rail Trail

Silver Creek

0   1   2 km
0   .5   1 mile

Old Ranch Rd

Snyderville

Parkwest Dr

The Canyons Ski Area

Park Meadows Golf Club

Little Kate Rd

Payday Drive

Kearns Blvd

Sidewinder Drive

To Kamas

PLACES TO STAY & EAT
1   Hidden Haven Campground
3   Best Western Landmark Inn
6   Radisson Resort Park City
8   Nacho Mamas
9   Prospector Square Lodging and
    Conference Center; Fly Shop
10 Stein Eriksen Lodge; Glitretind
11 Seafood Buffet

OTHER
2   Factory Stores at Park City
5   Utah Winter Sports Park
5   National Ability Center
7   Post Office

Park Ave

see Park City map

Deer Valley

Deer Valley Dr

Deer Valley Resort Ski Area

Royal St

To Midway & Heber City

The **Park City Mountain Resort** (☎ 649-8111) offers 3300 skiable acres over seven peaks and was the site of the Olympic giant slalom and snowboarding events in 2002. It unveiled a spiffy and spacious new lodge in 2001. The resort offers 100 runs and 14 lifts, one of which begins in downtown Park City. The resort can handle over 27,000 passengers an hour, so lift lines tend to be short! Elevations range from 6900 to 10,000 feet. Night skiing (4 to 9 pm) includes a lighted halfpipe ($22 for adults, $12 for kids). There is no child care.
website: www.parkcitymountain.com

On the southeastern outskirts of Park City, the skiers-only **Deer Valley Resort** (☎ 649-1000, 800-424-3337) strives to be the most luxurious ski resort in the USA; many would say it succeeds. Nineteen lifts service 88 carefully groomed runs covering 1750 acres between 6570 and 9570 feet. Deer Valley was the site of the Olympic slalom, freestyle mogul and aerial events in 2002. There are child-care facilities.
website: www.deervalley.com

Four miles north of Park City on Hwy 224 (there are free town buses), **The Canyons** (☎ 435-649-5400) has experienced the most growth of any resort, and it is now the largest in Utah and just as upscale as its neighbors. It has 14 lifts (including one eight-person gondola and five high-speed quads) servicing 134 runs on 3625 acres between 6800 and 9990 feet. The Canyons has a very popular half pipe for snowboarding. Day care is offered.

website: www.thecanyons.com

Cross-Country Skiing White Pine Touring (☎ 649-8710), 201 Heber Ave, has ski rentals, cross-country and telemark lessons, and guides on its 13 miles of groomed trails in and around Park City. Day passes are $12 for 13- to 64-year-olds, $6 for kids six to 12, and free to others. The agency also specializes in backcountry ski and snowshoe trips; call for details.

website: www.whitepinetouring.com

Norwegian Outdoor Exploration Center (☎ 649-5322, 800-649-5322), on the second floor of the Main Street Mall, is a nonprofit educational organization that leads customized cross-country ski and snowshoe trips in the Uinta Mountains. Guides are knowledgeable about the area's flora and fauna. Rates, which include equipment rental, depend on group size: one person is $45 an hour, two people $25, and three or more people $20.

website: www.outdoorcenter.org

Sledding & Ski Jumping On Hwy 224 north of Park City, the **Utah Winter Sports Park** (☎ 658-4200) was the site of the Olympic ski jumping, bobsledding, skeleton, nordic combined and luge events in 2002, and it will continue to be a site for national competitions. There are 5-, 10-, 20-, 40-, 64-, 90- and 120-meter nordic ski jumping hills as well as a bobsled and luge run. Admission is $5 per car or $15 per van (during competitions, entry fees are higher). The US Ski Team practices here year-round – in summer, freestyle jumpers land in a bubble-filled pool, and nordic jumpers land on a hillside covered in plastic! Call for a schedule; there is no extra fee to watch practices.

Nordic ski jumping lessons are offered every few days in winter. These last two hours and cost $28 for adults, $19 for 13- to 17-year-olds and $15 for children 12 and under. Helmets are provided, but you need your own skis. In summer, one-day aerial freestyle-jumping 'camps' are $75; these include skis, training and the chance to jump into the pool over a dozen times.

For a bigger thrill, recreational rides on the bobsled runs are also available in winter by advance reservation. It costs $175 for a ride that lasts about a minute and reaches 80mph! Still, tickets, which go on sale each year on September 1, sell out fast; call at least three months in advance. The park plans to add a wheeled-bobsled run in summer.

Year-round, 'rocket rides' – which simulate a luge run – are $40 and also last about a minute. Because this is a training facility, the Sports Park may be closed to recreational use on some days, so call as early as possible for hours and rates.

In summer, the Park City Mountain Resort (see above) operates a similar 'alpine slide,' in which a wheeled sled zips down a cement track ($8).

Snowmobiling If you would rather motor than glide over the snow, some companies with rentals and tours include Park City Snowmobile Adventures (☎ 645-7256, 800-303-7256), ABC Reservations Central (☎ 649-2223, 800-820-2223) and Snowest Snowmobile Tours (☎ 645-7669, 800-499-7660, ext 2000).

UTAH

PARK CITY

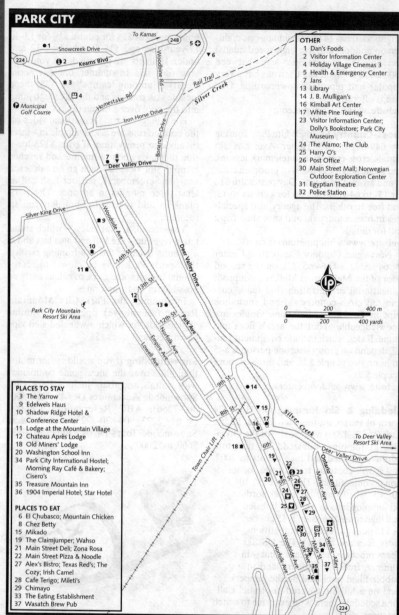

To Kamas

OTHER
1 Dan's Foods
2 Visitor Information Center
4 Holiday Village Cinemas 3
5 Health & Emergency Center
7 Jans
13 Library
14 J. B. Mulligan's
16 Kimball Art Center
17 White Pine Touring
23 Visitor Information Center;
    Dolly's Bookstore; Park City
    Museum
24 The Alamo; The Club
25 Harry O's
26 Post Office
30 Main Street Mall; Norwegian
    Outdoor Exploration Center
31 Egyptian Theatre
32 Police Station

PLACES TO STAY
3 The Yarrow
9 Edelweis Haus
10 Shadow Ridge Hotel &
    Conference Center
11 Lodge at the Mountain Village
12 Chateau Après Lodge
18 Old Miners' Lodge
20 Washington School Inn
34 Park City International Hostel;
    Morning Ray Café & Bakery;
    Cisero's
35 Treasure Mountain Inn
36 1904 Imperial Hotel; Star Hotel

PLACES TO EAT
6 El Chubasco; Mountain Chicken
8 Chez Betty
15 Mikado
19 The Claimjumper; Wahso
21 Main Street Deli; Zona Rosa
22 Main Street Pizza & Noodle
27 Alex's Bistro; Texas Red's; The
    Cozy; Irish Camel
28 Cafe Terigo; Mileti's
29 Chimayo
33 The Eating Establishment
37 Wasatch Brew Pub

Hot-Air Ballooning Another popular activity is hot-air balloon rides, which cost about $150 per person per hour, though companies sometimes offer 'specials.' Try Park City Adventure Center/Balloon Affaire (☎ 649-1217, 649-3343), Park City Balloon Adventures (☎ 645-8787, 800-396-8787) or Great Balloon Escape (☎ 645-9400, 800-287-9401).

Fishing The Provo and Weaver Rivers attract fly-fishers. Call or visit Jans (see Downhill Skiing) and the Fly Shop (☎ 645-8382, 800-324-6778), 2065 Sidewinder Drive, for equipment and guides.

Golfing Play 18 holes of golf at the Municipal Golf Course (☎ 649-8701), 1541 Thaynes Canyon Drive, or the highly rated Park Meadows Golf Club (☎ 649-2460), 2000 Meadows Drive, designed by Jack Nicklaus.

Mountain Biking & Hiking The visitors centers have a trail map for Park City and the nearby mountains; the Rail Trail is an easy and popular route that leads from town. Jans (see Downhill Skiing) and White Pine Touring (see Cross-Country Skiing) offer bicycle and helmet rentals, maps and tours. In summer, Deer Valley Resort has over 50 miles of hiking and bike trails. They host the National Off-Road Biking Association championship races every July and have lift-served mountain biking and full rentals. Park City Mountain Resort also has lift-served biking and hiking. The Canyons keeps its gondola open in the summer for scenic rides and has hiking; they may have lift-served biking in the future (call to check).

Also, White Pine Touring and the Norwegian Outdoor Exploration Center (see Cross-Country Skiing) both lead backcountry nature hikes; rates vary depending on group size.

Horseback Riding Park City Stables (☎ 435-645-7256), at the Park City Mountain Resort, rents horses for guided trail rides; Deer Valley and The Canyons also offer horseback riding.

The **National Ability Center** (NAC; ☎ 649-3991), PO Box 682799, Park City, UT 84068, near the junction of Hwys 248 and 40, is a nonprofit organization that runs a year-round adapted sports program for people with disabilities and their families; the facilities, trails and lessons are also open to the nondisabled public. Horseback riding is by far the most popular program; call for prices and schedules. Other programs include downhill and cross-country skiing, water sports, rafting, rock climbing and bicycling. NAC is the world leader in recreational therapy, and Park City is its headquarters. website: www.nationalabilitycenter.org

Special Events

Besides skiing, perhaps nothing has brought more attention to Park City in recent years than the **Sundance Film Festival** (☎ 801-328-3456), which lasts two weeks at the end of January; check the website for dates at www.sundance.org. The premiere showcase for independent filmmakers, Sundance has inspired a slew of competing, concurrent festivals – the largest of which is Slamdance (☎ 323-466-1786) or www.slamdance.com. Tickets usually sell out well in advance, so call early.

Late February **Winterfest** features a snow sculpture contest and other events. During the ski season, all sorts of prestigious **competitions** take place. Symphony, chamber music, bluegrass, jazz and other music events take place during various **summer concert** series. The **Art Festival** (☎ 649-8882), during the first weekend in August, features more than 200 artists and attracts over 100,000 visitors. **Miners Day** with a parade and contests is held over Labor Day weekend. Contact the visitor center to find out about other events.

Places to Stay

The Park City area experienced a mini-boom in new hotels for the 2002 Olympics; even before that it had about twice as many beds as permanent residents. None of the accommodations are cheap, not even the few chains, especially during the peak winter season from around mid-November to mid-April. You will pay the top prices around Christmas and New Year's.

That said, rates can vary a good deal during winter (for instance, there is a lull right after New Year's) and from midweek to weekend; shoulder rates apply early and late in the ski season, when weather is least reliable; and in summer prices can drop by half. If you're watching your budget, avoid the major festivals and holidays at all costs, and be flexible with your dates. In addition, most lodgings offer a wide variety of accommodations options, with multiple rooms, kitchens, fireplaces, spa tubs etc; be very specific about what you want to avoid paying for amenities you don't need.

As a result of Park City's high prices, more and more budget travelers are choosing to stay at Heber City (19 miles south) or Salt Lake City.

Prices quoted below reflect high winter season rack rates, but they are only an approximate guide. Using a reservation service is a convenient option.

Vacation Packages A dozen or so companies can put together entire packages for you, including accommodations, lift passes, ski rentals, flights, car rentals or transfers and other services. Here are a few of the operators specializing in the Park City area:

Deer Valley Central Reservations (☎ 435-649-1000, 800-558-3337) www.deervalley.com

Lynx Ski and Golf Vacations (☎ 303-355-4775, 800-422-5969) www.lynxskivacations.com

Park City Mountain Vacations (☎ 435-649-0493, 800-222-7275) www.parkcitymountain.com

Park City Reservations (☎ 435-649-9598, 800-453-5789) www.parkcityres.com

Park City Travel and Lodging (☎ 801-487-1300, 800-421-9741) www.parkcitytravel.com

Utah Ski Reservations (☎ 649-6493, 800-882-4754) www.deervalleylodging.com

Reservation Services Park City has no central reservations service with access to all accommodations, but the Visitor Information Centers (see Information) will help suggest places to meet your needs (though

they aren't able to book rooms). The services listed below specialize mainly in the Park City area, but have access to only a portion of available lodgings. They can also arrange lift tickets on request. Room rates range from lows of $70 to $80 to highs of over $1200; the choice is yours.

Skiers should check carefully about all aspects of the rooms offered, especially the distance to the nearest resort (you can walk from some locations but from others you'll need to take a bus or drive). The following is just a selection; the *Park City Winter Vacation Planner* and *Ski Utah* list dozens more.

ABC Reservations (☎ 649-2223, 800-820-2223)

Central Reservations of Park City (☎ 649-6606, 800-519-4764) www.parkcityski.com

David Holland's Resort Lodging (☎ 655-3315, 800-754-2002) www.davidhollands.com

MTA Resorts (☎ 800-272-8824) www.mtaresorts.com

R&R Properties (☎ 649-6175, 800-348-6759) www.parkcitylodging.com

Places to Stay – Camping
The nearest campsite is the *Hidden Haven Campground* (☎ 649-8935, 2200 Rasmussen Rd), 1 mile northwest of I-80 exit 145 along the north frontage road (6 miles north of Park City). Open year-round, it has about 40 tent sites for $20, and about 60 RV sites for $22.50 to $25. There are showers, a playground, and fishing in the stream.

Also see the campgrounds and state parks near Heber City (below).

Places to Stay – Budget
At its perfect location downtown, the new-in-2001 *Park City International Hostel* (☎ 655-7244, 268 Main St) offers 17 sparkling-clean four-bed dorms; all are non-smoking and come with jugs of spring water. Beds are $30 a night; a private room is $100 (two-week maximum stay). Among its many facilities are laundry, comfortable kitchen, smoking deck, free all-night parking, ski lockers and the pièce de résistance: the surround-sound 'media room' with DVD movies and satellite TV. It would be

an attractive, if expensive, hostel anyplace, but in this town, it can't be beat.
website: www.parkcityhostel.com

The only other budget choice is *Chateau Après Lodge (☎ 649-9372, 800-357-3556, 1299 Norfolk Ave)*, which has frayed men's and women's dormitories for $28 per person. Its 32 equally worn private rooms with bath are $82 to $102 for two to four people. You're paying to be walking distance from the Park City lifts.

Places to Stay – Mid-Range

The *Star Hotel (☎ 649-5746, 888-649-8333, 227 Main)* has 10 rooms sharing three bathrooms in an older house. Rates are $85/150 (single/double), including home-cooked breakfast and dinner during the ski season.

Park City has several attractive, non-smoking B&Bs; all have hot tubs, antique furnishings and full breakfast. The *1904 Imperial Hotel (☎ 649-1904, 800-669-8824, 221 Main)* has 10 cozy rooms for $90 to $130 in summer and $150 to $225 in winter; for information, see www.1904Imperial.com. The *Old Miners' Lodge (☎ 645-8068, 800-648-8068, 615 Woodside Ave)* is right next to the town chair lift. Nine rooms and three suites run $70 to $130 in summer, $105 to $245 in winter; see www.oldminerslodge.com. The *Washington School Inn (☎ 649-3800, 800-824-1672, 543 Park Ave)* has 12 rooms and three suites for $125 to $175 in summer, $225 to $375 in winter; www.washington schoolinn.com.

Edelweis Haus (☎ 649-5100, 800-245-6417, 1482 Empire Ave) is less than a quarter-mile from Park City lifts. This is a condo-hotel with about 50 rooms. Hotel-style rooms are $100 in winter (only available early and late in season), and one- and two-bedroom condos with full kitchens are $190 to $395 in winter.

Park City has a number of upscale hotels that would be top end anywhere else. At all of them you can expect high-quality rooms, very helpful staff and excellent facilities that include pools, hot tubs, exercise rooms, restaurants and more. Summer rates are half the winter rates quoted below. The *Best*

Western Landmark Inn (☎ 649-7300, 800-548-8824, 6560 N Landmark Drive), I-80 exit 145, is 5 miles north of Park City, but free buses take you to ski areas. Winter rates are $120 to $169.

The *Radisson Resort Park City (☎ 649-5000, 800-333-3333, 2121 Park Ave)* has 131 rooms for $100 to $325 in winter. *Treasure Mountain Inn (☎ 658-1417, 800-344-2460, 255 Main)* is right downtown and has studios ($160) and one- and two-bedroom condos ($260 and $340).

Prospector Square Lodging and Conference Center (☎ 649-7100, 800-453-3812, 2200 Sidewinder Dr) has rooms for $175 to $190, and one-, two- and three-bedroom condos for $199 to $400.

The *Lodge at the Mountain Village (☎ 649-0800, 800-824-5331, 1415 Lowell Ave)* is right at the base of the Park City lifts. Hotel rooms are $180, studios are $250 to $355 and one- to four-bedroom condos run from $440 to $1030; three-day minimums are preferred in winter. *Shadow Ridge Hotel & Conference Center (☎ 649-4300, 800-451-3031, 50 Shadow Ridge Rd)* is a block from the ski area. In winter, hotel rooms and one- and two-bedroom condos go for $220 to $480; in summer rates drop by over half.

The *Yarrow (☎ 649-7000, 800-927-7694, 1800 Park Ave)*, a full-service resort hotel and conference center, has hotel rooms, efficiencies and one-bedroom condos for $119 to $579.

Places to Stay – Top End

For the very best top-end places, the reservation services will be able to help. One lodge stands above the rest, however. The *Stein Eriksen Lodge (☎ 649-3700, 800-453-1302, 7700 Stein Way)* is at 8200 feet, mid-mountain on the slopes of the Deer Valley ski area. It is the most luxurious ski lodge with the most attentive staff in Park City, which is saying something. How much is the best? Winter rates start at $575 for rooms, and at $1100 for suites. However, summer rates start at under $200!
website: www.steinlodge.com

Places to Eat

Gourmets and gourmands love Park City, which has scores of excellent restaurants, with more opening (and changing) all the time. Reservations are recommended during ski season, and in summer many cut back operations; call ahead for hours. As with everything here, prices are higher, but so is the quality. From July to October, Park City Mountain Resort hosts a **Farmers Market** (☎ 649-6100) every Wednesday from 2 to 6 pm. A good grocery store is **Dan's Foods** (☎ 645-7139, 1500 Snow Creek Dr).

Resort Restaurants At Deer Valley in the Stein Eriksen Lodge is the elegant **Glitretind** (☎ 645-6455), which is fairly regarded as the most romantic gourmet restaurant in Utah. The restaurant serves fresh continental cuisine for breakfast, lunch and dinner, and Sunday brunch (with live jazz); dinner entrees run $22 to $34. During winter only, an adjacent dining room is famed for its game menu – venison, caribou, bison and other meats ($28-39). Reservations are recommended.

Also at Deer Valley, Snow Park Lodge's **Seafood Buffet** (☎ 645-6632) puts the best that Vegas offers to shame. For $45 (children $20), you can have your fill of Dungeness crab, Pacific oysters, seared tuna, poached salmon, roast quail, prime rib and much more. It's open for dinner only from 6:30 to 9:30 pm Monday to Saturday; reservations required.

Main Street The following is just a selection of the many restaurants along Park City's historic Main St (heading approximately south to north).

The **Wasatch Brew Pub** (☎ 649-0900, 250 Main St) is an excellent microbrewery that enjoys tweaking local sensibilities in its ads (such as those proclaiming Wasatch beer is 'Utah's other local religion'). Good pub grub, a variety of dinners ($8-16), a sports bar, pool table and dart board keep everyone happy. New owners at **Morning Ray Café & Bakery** (☎ 649-5686, 268 Main St) achieve the miraculous: they bake real New York bagels (par-baked from the legendary

H&H Bagels) in Utah. Belly up to the bagel bar, or enjoy their large selection of omelettes, pancakes, sandwiches (on fresh bagels, natch), gourmet coffees, soups and salads (all under $10). They open at 7 am and don't stop serving till midnight (till 2 am on weekends).

Cisero's (☎ 649-5044, 306 Main St) is a reasonably priced and popular Italian restaurant. **The Eating Establishment** (☎ 649-8284, 317 Main) is one of the area's most enduring and reasonably priced places to eat. Come for the hearty breakfasts and lunch specialties ($4-8). For upscale Southwestern cuisine, there's **Chimayo** (☎ 649-6222, 368 Main St).

Family-run **Mileti's** (☎ 649-8211, 412 Main St) has been a favorite since 1973. It serves up good pastas ($13-20) and Italian specialties ($17-28) for dinner only. The popular **Cafe Terigo** (☎ 645-9555, 424 Main) serves nouvelle American café cuisine for lunch and dinner.

The oddly named **Irish Camel** (☎ 649-5650, 434 Main St) serves Mexican meals with real spice ($6 to $16) in an Irish pub atmosphere. **Texas Red's** (☎ 649-7337, 440 Main) serves chili ($3.50 and up), barbecue ($8-17) and Texas-style catfish and chicken-fried steak, while next door **Alex's Bistro** (☎ 649-5252, 442 Main St) is a dinner restaurant with live jazz and blues.

Take your pick of interesting, fresh salsas at **Zona Rosa** (☎ 645-0700, 501 Main St) which prepares a mélange of Latin cuisines for lunch and dinner ($8-19). **Main Street Deli** (☎ 649-1110, 525 Main St) is recommended for inexpensive breakfasts, sandwiches and baked goods. Budgeteers can also walk across the street to **Main Street Pizza & Noodle** (☎ 645-8878, 530 Main St); lunches and dinners are $7 to $11. **The Claimjumper** (☎ 649-8051, 573 Main St) is a straightforward steak-and-seafood place (about $12 -25).

The highly regarded **Wahso** (☎ 615-0300, 577 Main St) serves a heady fusion of Asian cuisines nightly from 5:30 pm. Also open only for dinner, **Mikado** (☎ 655-7100, 738 Main St) serves Japanese dinners and has a sushi bar.

Other Eateries Consistently voted one of Park City's best restaurants, *Chez Betty* (☎ 649-8181), in the Copperbottom Inn on Deer Valley Dr, serves French country cuisine, where the 'surf-n-turf' is pan-seared scallops and duck breast with a sun-dried cherry demi-glaze (entrées $20-32). This spot is open for dinner only; call for hours and reservations.

The Park City Plaza at 1890 Bonanza Dr has two good budget choices ($6 and under): *El Chubasco* (☎ 645-9114) serves authentic, fresh Mexican food, and *Mountain Chicken* (☎ 645-8483) serves juicy roast chicken.

Some say *Nacho Mama's* (☎ 645-8226, 888-845-8226, 1821 Sidewinder Dr) has the best Mexican food in town ($10-14); if not, it's certainly fun. Open for dinner only.

Entertainment
During the summer, weekly concerts of all kinds take place in the various resorts and other venues around town, many of which are free; for details, call the visitor center or contact Mountain Town Stages (☎ 901-7664). *Egyptian Theatre Company* (☎ 649-9371, 328 Main St) puts on plays or musicals during summer in the historic, nicely restored Egyptian Theater; information is online at www.egyptiantheatrecompany.org. The *George S and Dolores Dore Eccles Center for the Performing Arts* (☎ 655-3114) hosts an eclectic program of local performers year-round; the schedule can be found at www.ecclescenter.org.

The *Kimball Art Center* (☎ 649-8882, www.kimball-art.org, 638 Park Ave) is an exhibition space for Utah artists and the main resource for fine arts information. The first Friday of every month is an open gallery walk through the many commercial galleries on Main St and Park Ave.

Holiday Village Cinemas 3 (☎ 649-6541, 1776 Park Ave) has first-run movies. The Park City Film Series (☎ 615-8291) screens foreign and independent movies at the Jim Santy Auditorium in the library at 8 pm on Friday and Saturday.

When Salt Lake City's bar and discos close, the young and the restless head to Park City's private clubs, where the fun lasts just a little bit later. As elsewhere in Utah, you must either obtain a guest membership or be sponsored by a member to get in, but both are easy to do. The majority of clubs are on Main St.

Harry O's (☎ 647-9494, 427 Main St) is the largest and hottest dance club in town, with mostly live music. It has six pool tables in addition to a wide dance floor. Next door to each other, *The Club* (☎ 649-6693, 449 Main) and *The Alamo* (☎ 649-2380, 447 Main) are both very popular. Two of the best places for live music are *The Cozy* (☎ 649-6038, 438 Main St), which is very eclectic, and *Cisero's* (☎ 649-6800, 306 Main St), which has mainly blues and rock adjacent to the restaurant. *J. B. Mulligans* (658-0717, 804 Main St) is an Irish pub with a fireplace, darts and bands playing everything from bluegrass to reggae to jazz.

Check out the Diversions section of the *Park Record* on Thursday, or pick up a copy of the free monthly *Park City's EAR* for entertainment, arts and recreation news.

Shopping
The best bookstore for local outdoor guides is Dolly's Bookstore (☎ 649-8062), 510 Main St. The Factory Stores at Park City (☎ 645-7078, 888-746-7333), near I-80 exit 145, has dozens of factory-outlet stores, open daily, selling everything from boots to kid's clothes. Also, Park City's Main St is chock-ablock with antique stores, art galleries, craft shops and boutiques.

Getting There & Around
Lewis Bros Stages (☎ 649-2256 in Park City, 801-359-8677 in Salt Lake City, 800-826-5844,) provides vans between Salt Lake City Airport and Park City several times a day for $22 to $26 one way. They'll pick up and drop off at many Park City hotels; reservations are required. They also provide service to Snowbird and Alta in Little Cottonwood Canyon.

website: www.lewisbros.com

Park City Transit (☎ 615-5350) runs free buses two or three times an hour from about 6 am to 2:30 am. This excellent system

UTAH

covers most of Park City, including all the ski resorts, and makes it easy not to rent a car. Schedules and bus maps are available from the Visitor Information Center, or ask any bus driver.

If you do have a car, note that Park City recently instituted a year-round "pay and display" parking system on and around Main St ($1 per hour). Free lots are available, but require short walks.

HEBER CITY & MIDWAY AREA
☎ 435 • pop 7291 • elevation 5593 feet
Founded in 1859, the agricultural center of Heber City makes a good, affordable base from which to visit the area's ski resorts and other attractions and recreations. The Swiss-founded town of Midway (population 2121) nearby has natural hot springs.

Orientation & Information
Main St (Hwy 40) runs north-south and is Heber City's main commercial street and 100 South St westbound takes you to Midway.

Get area information at the chamber of commerce (☎ 654-3666), 475 N Main or www.hebervalleycc.org, and the Uinta National Forest Heber Ranger Station (☎ 654-0470), 2460 S Hwy 40. Other services include the library (☎ 654-1511), 188 S Main; post office (☎ 654-0881), 125 E 100 North; County Hospital (☎ 654-2500), 55 S 500 E; and police (☎ 654-3040), 75 N Main.

In Midway, a good bookstore is Books & Beyond (☎ 657-2665), 103 E Main St.

Things to See & Do
Known locally as the 'Heber Creeper,' the Heber Valley Historic Railroad (☎ 654-5601, 801-581-9980 in Salt Lake), 450 S 600 West, uses a 1904 steam locomotive and two old diesel engines for slow, very scenic, family-oriented sightseeing trips (from 1½ to 3½ hours). In summer, there are several trips daily, and in winter they are on weekends only, except around the Christmas holidays. Call ahead for times and reservations. Fares range from $12 to $19 for adults (depending on trip length); children and seniors are a few dollars less.

About 15 miles southwest of Heber City along Hwy 189 is the beginning of scenic and steep-walled Provo Canyon, which you drive through en route to Provo.

One of the first sights you'll see, a few miles after the canyon begins, is the 600-foot-high double Bridal Veil Falls. (The aerial tramway to it, damaged in an avalanche, no longer runs.)

On the north side of Hwy 189 near the entrance to Provo Canyon is the paved, 16-mile Alpine Loop Road (Hwy 92), an extremely scenic, steep, narrow and twisting road – not recommended for long RVs or trailers. The road passes Sundance Resort, Timpanogos Cave National Monument (both described later in this chapter) and 11,750-foot Mt Timpanogos, as well as two campgrounds and hiking trails. Fall colors are spectacular. The middle of the loop is closed by snow in winter. Near either end of the road, a USFS tollbooth charges $3 per car (national passes accepted). Contact the Uinta National Forest ranger stations in Heber City (see above), Provo (☎ 385-377-5780) or Pleasant Grove (☎ 385-785-3563) for maps, camping regulations and hiking information.

Special Events
In early February there is dogsled and snowmobile racing. The Wasatch County Fair is held in Heber City in early or mid-August. Midway celebrates its European heritage during Swiss Days, over Labor Day weekend.

Places to Stay
Camping Six miles north of town, near the Provo River at Jordanelle Reservoir, the year-round Heber Valley RV Park (☎ 654-4049) has showers and tent/RV sites for $15/24.

The Uinta National Forest has more than 30 campgrounds open, with few exceptions, during the summer only; most have water and are $12. The closest campgrounds lie along or just off the Alpine Loop Rd (Hwy 92). You can call the Provo ranger (☎ 385-377-5780) or Pleasant Grove ranger (☎ 385-785-3563) for information.

Also see Around Heber City, below, as well as Mirror Lake Hwy and Wolf Creek Pass, which are both east of here, in the Northeastern Utah chapter.

Budget & Mid-Range Hotel prices are much cheaper than Park City, but they tend to get inflated on summer weekends. Ask about weekly discounts and ski packages. Addresses given below are in Heber City, unless otherwise indicated.

Two very simple places with rooms in the $40s are *Mac's Motel* (☎ 654-0612, 670 S Main St) and *Alpine Lodge* (☎ 654-0231, 800-371-0232, 90 N Main St).

Beaver Mountain Motel (☎ 654-2150, 800-932-0355, 425 S Main St) is well run and a good value; its 22 rooms run $40 to $60. *National 9 High Country Inn* (☎ 654-0201, 800-345-9198, 1000 S Main St) is another decent choice for $40 to $54. *Danish Viking Lodge* (☎ 654-2202, 800-544-4066, 989 S Main St) is a little more expensive ($50-65) for about the same quality. The most recommended place is the quaint *Swiss Alps Inn* (☎ 654-0722, 167 S Main St), which has 14 clean and attractive rooms for $50 to $80.

The newest and largest property in town is *Holiday Inn Express* (☎ 654-9990, 800-465-4329, 1268 S Main St). It appeals to skiers with 75 spacious, chain-typical rooms (rates start at $80).

Top End The two top spots in this area are in Midway. The *Homestead Resort* (☎ 654-1102, 800-327-7220, 700 N Homestead Dr) is the area's premier year-round resort, and it offers a wide array of activities: Depending on the season, there's an 18-hole golf course; cross-country ski trails; horse, mountain bike, and snowmobile rentals; horse-drawn buggy and sleigh rides; and natural hot springs in a crater so large it allows for scuba diving! Most activities and some facilities are available to the public (call for rates and schedules). If you're having too much fun to leave, nicely decorated, antique-furnished rooms (from $119), suites (from $189) and condos (from $269) come with a variety of amenities. Ask about vacation packages. website: www.homesteadresort.com

Blue Boar Inn (☎ 654-1400, 888-650-1400, 1235 Warm Springs Rd) is a newer and perhaps even more luxurious hideaway. Plushly decorated rooms (from $150 to $225) are named after literary figures and include breakfast; ask about discounts for longer stays. The quiet country setting is most relaxing.
website: www.theblueboarinn.com

Places to Eat
Besides greasy spoons and average restaurants, Heber has the tiny *Sidetrack Café* (☎ 654-0563, 94 S Main St), ideal for an espresso and a bagel or sandwich.

Kneaders (☎ 654-7021, 680 S Main St) would be perfect if it served coffee; instead, you'll have to make do with the best fresh-baked pastries, sandwiches (under $5) and fruit smoothies in town. At *Granny's Drive-In* (☎ 654-3097, 511 S Main St) they specialize in 57 flavors of thick and delicious milkshakes.

At the other end of the scale, *Snake Creek Grill* (☎ 654-2133, 650W 100 South) dishes up reasonably priced gourmet fare. Entrées such as cornmeal-crusted trout and ten-spice salmon run $12.50 to $16. Open for dinner only Wednesday to Sunday. In addition, the upscale restaurants located at the Homestead Resort and the Blue Boar Inn in Midway (see Places to Stay above) compete for top honors. At both places, reservations are recommended.

Getting There & Away
Greyhound passes through Heber City (the flag stop is at 610 S Main St at McDonald's) on its daily run along Hwy 40 between Salt Lake City and Denver, Colorado. Most people drive.

AROUND HEBER CITY
Wasatch Mountain State Park
This large (34 sq miles) and very popular state park is known for its gorgeous mountain scenery, which makes a splendid backdrop for its top-notch 27-hole golf course (☎ 654-9532) in summer and its 75 miles of snowmobile trails in winter. In addition, the adjacent **Soldier Hollow** was the site of 18

cross-country ski events in the 2002 Olympics, and its 16 miles of trails are open to the public for cross-country skiing and snowshoeing in winter, and for hiking in summer. Plans are to add another golf course, equestrian center, more campgrounds and a platform stop for the Heber Valley Railroad. Call the park for up-to-date information and about rentals.

The park (☎ 654-1791), PO Box 10, Midway, UT 84049, is 2 miles northwest of Midway. It has 122 campsites in several campgrounds; the fees for tents/RVs are $10/16 (call ☎ 800-322-3770 for reservations). Day use is $4.

Jordanelle State Park

This new state park (established in 1995) is one of Utah's nicest and largest 'reservoir parks.' Popular for boating, fishing, wind surfing and hiking, it has two sections: the Hailstone Recreation Site, on the reservoir, has the main visitor center (☎ 649-9540), boat ramps, store, small laundromats and two campgrounds. The walk-in campground ($13) has restrooms; the more developed campground (tents/RVs $15/17) also has showers (☎ 800-322-3770 for reservations). Ten miles away, on the Provo River below the dam, Rock Cliff Recreation Site has the Rock Cliff Nature Center (☎ 783-3030), a pretty boardwalk leading into restored wetlands and a walk-in campground ($15) with showers. Hiking trails lead past beaver dams and nesting osprey, and there is great birdwatching in spring and fall. Ranger programs are offered in summer.

The park, SR 319 No 515, Box 4, Heber City, UT 84032, is about 10 miles north of Heber City on Hwy 40. Day use is $6 per car, $4 for walk-in.

Deer Creek State Park

Also surrounding a reservoir, this state park has all the same boating and water attractions as Jordanelle, above, though it is not as large. Deer Creek (☎ 654-0171), PO Box 257, Midway, UT 84049, is 9 miles southwest of Heber City via Hwy 189. Camping ($10) is available from April to October (call ☎ 800-322-3770); there are showers, a

grocery store and a boat launch. A marina rents boats in summer. Day use is $4.

Sundance Resort

Owned and developed by well known actor/director Robert Redford, this year-round resort (☎ 385-225-4107, 800-892-1600) is a sepia-toned mountain dream come to rough-hewn life. Tucked under Mt Timpanogos, it makes an elegant, upscale getaway or an ideal day trip from Salt Lake City for outdoor recreation.

In winter, the resort offers excellent downhill and cross-country skiing. Three lifts service 41 runs in 450 acres between 6100 and 8250 feet. All-day lift passes are $32/27 for adults on weekends/midweek; passes for children under 12 are $16. The resort also has 9 miles of groomed cross-country ski tracks ($9). Ski rentals and lessons are available.

In summer, there are participatory theater programs as well as other performances and films, kids' camps, hiking, mountain biking (with lift service on weekends), guided horseback trips and fly fishing on the Provo River. Year-round, the resort runs a fine arts and crafts program. Call the resort for information on schedules and prices for all these activities.

Sundance has about 90 upscale-rustic wooden cottages/cabins and a number of sumptuous two- to five-bedroom mountain homes ($660 to $1100 in winter). Rates for cabins range from $205 to $380 in winter to $195 to $300 in spring (the cheapest season). Packages are available; call up to six months in advance. In addition, there are two restaurants (one gourmet, one more relaxed), a private club, slope-side fast food in winter and a fancy grocery for all your picnicking needs.

The resort is 2½ miles along Hwy 92 from the north end of Provo Canyon (Hwy 189). To get here, you can take the Utah Transit Authority's Sundance Ski bus, No 880, from Provo/Orem, or call the resort (☎ 385-225-4107) for its shuttle service, which goes to both Salt Lake International Airport and Park City.
website: www.sundanceresort.com

Moonrise over the Wasatch Mountains and Salt Lake City, UT

Blue skies and snowy peaks in the Wasatch Mountains, UT

RICHARD CUMMINS

Standing tall at the Utah state capitol

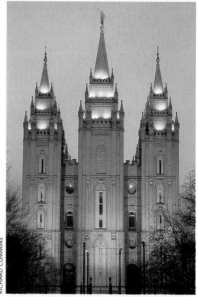

RICHARD CUMMINS

Mormon Temple, Salt Lake City

RICHARD CUMMINS

Historic facade, downtown Salt Lake City

Timpanogos Cave National Monument

The three beautiful caves of this national monument, at an elevation of 6730 feet in the foothills of Mt Timpanogos, are a popular stop for those driving the Alpine Scenic Loop. The caves, studded with lovely geological formations, are reached by a 1½-mile trail that gains 1000 feet in elevation (no wheelchair or stroller access). All cave visitors must be part of a ranger-led guided tour. The caves are open only from mid-May to mid-October.

The hour-long tours, limited to 20 people, are frequent, but afternoon tours are often filled by late morning, so arrive early, preferably midweek, for the shortest waits. You will be assigned a specific time to be at the cave entrance; allow an hour for the hike. Also, cave temperatures are 43°F year-round, so bring a sweater. Visitor center hours are 7 am to 5:30 pm, and it has exhibits, a 20-minute film, a gift shop, snack bar and rangers who can suggest local hikes to help pass the time. Tickets cost $6; $5 for six- to 15-year-olds and $3 for those under six.

Tickets can be purchased in advance at the visitor center or by mail, prepaid, two weeks in advance. Contact Timpanogos Cave National Monument (☎ 385-756-5238), RR 3, Box 200, American Fork, UT 84003. website: www.nps.gov/tica

PROVO

☎ 385 • pop 105,166 • elevation 4490 feet

Provo, 44 miles south of Salt Lake City along I-15, is the Utah County seat and the third largest city in the state. Provo is named after Canadian fur trapper Etienne Provost, who trapped here in 1824-1825. Despite other brief visits by European explorers, the land remained under Ute Indian control until Brigham Young sent 150 settlers to the valley in 1849. Short wars were fought between the Mormons and the Utes, but the settlers prevailed and several more towns were quickly founded nearby.

Provo rapidly grew into the leading Mormon town in the area. In 1875, the Brigham Young Academy (now Brigham Young University) opened, and it has grown into the world's largest church-established university. Most of the 30,000 students are strict Mormons, and the school and city have a squeaky-clean feel to them. More than other Utah cities, Provo has held on to its early Mormon heritage; the population is largely white, conservative and middle class. The university and schools are the town's biggest employers.

For travelers, Provo's main attractions are its many historic buildings (notably the county courthouse, Mormon tabernacle and main library), the university and its museums, the proximity of the Wasatch Mountains and its good selection of reasonably priced hotels.

Orientation & Information

University Ave (Hwy 189), running north from I-15 exit 266, is the main drag. Center St, running east from I-15 exit 268, crosses University Ave at Provo's meridian (or zero) point. (Don't confuse University Ave with University Parkway, which leaves I-15 at exit 272, crosses University Ave at about 1600 N and leads to the university.)

The Utah Valley Visitors Bureau (☎ 370-8393, 800-222-8824,), in the gorgeous, historic courthouse at 51 S University Ave, is open weekdays year-round and on weekends seasonally; it has a historic walking-tour brochure and information online at www.utahvalley.org/cvb. The Uinta National Forest Ranger Station (☎ 377-5780) is at 88 W 100 North. The local newspaper is the *Daily Herald*. Other services include the library (☎ 852-6650), 550 N University, with free Internet access; post office (☎ 374-2000), 95 W 100 South; medical center (☎ 373-7850), 1034 N 500 West; and police (☎ 852-6210), 351 W Center.

The BYU Bookstore (☎ 378-3584), on the campus, is recommended.

Brigham Young University (BYU)

This campus (☎ 378-4636) is huge and known for its sober student dress code – no cutoffs, long hair, bikinis or beards here! Visitor parking is available off Campus Drive south of the Marriott Center, reached

UTAH

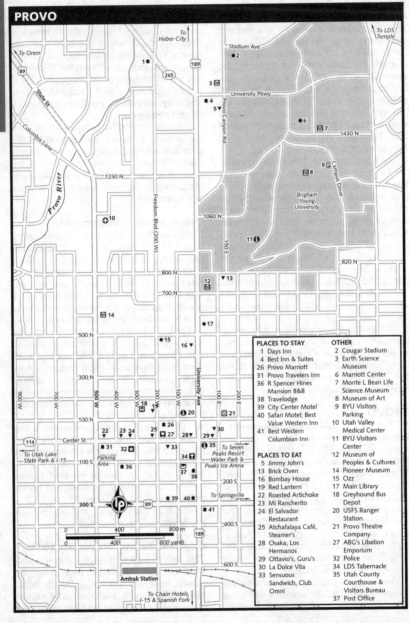

PROVO

PLACES TO STAY
1 Days Inn
4 Best Inn & Suites
26 Provo Marriott
31 Provo Travelers Inn
36 R Spencer Hines
   Mansion B&B
38 Travelodge
39 City Center Motel
40 Safari Motel; Best
   Value Western Inn
41 Best Western
   Columbian Inn

PLACES TO EAT
5 Jimmy John's
13 Brick Oven
16 Bombay House
19 Red Lantern
22 Roasted Artichoke
23 Mi Rancherito
24 El Salvador
   Restaurant
25 Atchafalaya Café,
   Steamer's
28 Osaka, Los
   Hermanos
29 Ottavio's, Guru's
30 La Dolce Vita
33 Sensuous
   Sandwich, Club
   Omni

OTHER
2 Cougar Stadium
3 Earth Science
   Museum
6 Marriott Center
7 Monte L Bean Life
   Science Museum
8 Museum of Art
9 BYU Visitors
   Parking
10 Utah Valley
   Medical Center
11 BYU Visitors
   Center
12 Museum of
   Peoples & Cultures
14 Pioneer Museum
15 Ozz
17 Main Library
18 Greyhound Bus
   Depot
20 USFS Ranger
   Station
21 Provo Theatre
   Company
27 ABG's Libation
   Emporium
32 Police
34 LDS Tabernacle
35 Utah County
   Courthouse &
   Visitors Bureau
37 Post Office

from University Parkway along 450 East. The visitor center (☎ 378-4678) has campus information and gives tours at 11 am and 2 pm, or hourly by appointment.

All the university's museums are free. The beautiful, sophisticated **Museum of Art** (☎ 378-2787) is one of the biggest in the Southwest and makes a rewarding visit. It concentrates on American and Southwest art; there's a fee for the high-quality special exhibits. Hours are 10 am to 6 pm, Monday to Friday (until 9 pm on Monday and Thursday) and noon to 5 pm on Saturday.

The small but well-done **Museum of Peoples & Cultures** (☎ 378-6112), 700 N 100 East in Allen Hall, concentrates on the ancient peoples who populated the Southwest; open weekdays. Also small but worth a look are the **Monte L Bean Life Science Museum** (☎ 378-5051) for dioramas of wildlife from Utah and elsewhere, and the **Earth Science Museum** (☎ 378-3680), where you can see dinosaur remains and watch graduate students clean bones. Both are open Monday to Saturday.

The university sponsors many artistic (☎ 378-4322) and athletic (☎ 378-2981) events, including concerts, theater, dance, football, basketball, baseball and other sports.

website: www.byu.edu

The Peaks Ice Arena

Built for the 2002 Olympics, this ice skating rink (☎ 377-8777), 100 N Seven Peaks Blvd, was the site of the men's and women's hockey competitions. It has two ice sheets and an indoor soccer field. It's open to the public year-round Monday to Saturday; call for the public skating schedule, which is usually two-hour sessions several times a day. Adults are $4, children under 11 and seniors over 63 are $3.50.

Seven Peaks Resort Water Park

This is the state's largest water park (☎ 373-8777), 1330 E 300 North. It has dozens of wave-makers, slides, tubes, twists, and pools, plus picnic areas. Hours are 11 am to 8 pm Monday to Saturday from Memorial Day to Labor Day. Admission is $16.50 for 10- to 62-year-olds, $12.50 for four- to nine-year-olds. Babies and seniors are free. Half-day after 4 pm is $8.50.

Utah Lake State Park

The largest freshwater body in the state, Utah Lake offers fishing, boating and swimming in its 150 sq miles, as well as canoeing in the Provo River; for rentals, call 373-8897. It's open in winter, but is very quiet. The state park (☎ 375-0731, 800-322-3770) is at 4400 W Center (the west end of Center). There is a visitor center and showers. Day use is $6; camping from April to October costs $15 (☎ 800-322-3770 for reservations).

Provo Bay, on the east side of Utah Lake south of the state park, has an important wetlands habitat for migrating birds (spring and fall are best). Ask for directions at the state park to the best areas to view white pelicans, white-faced ibis, ducks, geese and herons.

Golfing

You can play a round at several public courses: East Bay Golf Course (☎ 373-6262), 1860 S East Bay Blvd (27 holes); Cascade Fairways (☎ 225-6677), 1313 E 800 North, Orem (nine holes); and the highly regarded Thanksgiving Point (☎ 768-7400), 3003 North Thanksgiving Way, Lehi (18 holes).

Special Events

The year's main event is the Freedom Festival, which begins about the third week in June. Festivities include sports contests, a carnival, music and arts events and a parade, and culminate with a grand fireworks display on the Fourth of July. Call 370-8019 for an events schedule.

Places to Stay

Camping In addition to the campgrounds listed, see Utah Lake State Park above.

Provo KOA (☎ 375-2994, 320 N 2050 West) charges from $18/24.50 for tent/RV sites. The year-round *Lakeside Campground* (☎ 373-5267, 4000 W Center), near Utah Lake State Park, charges $16/23 for tents/RVs. Both have a pool, showers, coin laundry and play areas.

The Uinta National Forest Pleasant Grove Ranger Station (☎ 785-3563), 390 N 100 East, in Pleasant Grove, UT 84062, 10 miles north of Provo, administers most of the local USFS campgrounds northeast of Provo. The nearest is *Hope Campground* ($12), about 10 miles northwest of Provo off Hwy 189.

About 10 miles south of Provo, the Spanish Fork Ranger Station (☎ 798-3571), 44 W 400 North, Spanish Fork, UT 84660, has information about three USFS campgrounds ($12) in Hobble Creek Canyon east of Springville (within 13 miles). All these USFS campgrounds are open late May to late September, with water but no showers or hookups. The Spanish Fork office also has information about camping along the Nebo Loop (see Nephi in Central Utah). For reservations, call 877-444-6777.

Budget Hotel prices tend to be a little higher in summer. Nearly every place in town has a seasonal pool.

For basic budget accommodations, with musty but adequately clean rooms in the $30s, try *Motel 6* (☎ 375-5064, 1600 S University Ave); *Provo Travelers Inn* (☎ 373-8248, 469 W Center); *City Center Motel* (☎ 373-8489, 150 W 300 South); and *Best Value Western Inn* (☎ 373-0660, 800-500-5003, 40 W 300 South). A step up is the *Safari Motel* (☎ 373-9672, 800-723-2742, 250 S University Ave), with some newer rooms in the mid-$40s.

Mid-Range National *hotel chains* make up the bulk of mid-range options. For rooms from the mid-$40s to the high $50s, try National 9 Colony Inn Suites, Super 8 and Travel Lodge. For rooms from $55 to $75, try Days Inn, Howard Johnson and Best Western. Near BYU, *Best Inn & Suites* (☎ 374-6020, 1555 Provo Canyon Rd) is set in pleasant grounds and has very nice rooms. Rates go up for BYU events, and a few suites are $99 to $129; book online at www.hotels-west.com.

Top End The large *Provo Marriott* (☎ 377-4700, 800-777-7144, 101 W 100 North) is a comfortable full-service hotel with complete facilities. Rates are $90 and up for spacious rooms and suites.

The historic *R Spencer Hines Mansion B&B* (☎ 374-8400, 800-428-5636, 383 W 100 South) features nine elegant, Victorian-style rooms, each with a jetted tub and full breakfast. Weekend and holiday rates range from $99 to $199; weekdays all rooms are $95. Smoking is prohibited.
website: www.hinesmansion.com

Places to Eat

Provo's restaurants, which cover a range of cuisines, are modest and reasonably priced. Unless otherwise noted, all are closed on Sunday. Many good choices are around the historic Provo Town Square (Center St at University Ave).

Budget Friendly and nonthreateningly hip, *Steamer's* (☎ 370-0889, 230 W Center) is the place to enjoy a latte and bagel while checking your email. Open daily, till 1 am on Friday and Saturday.

Good sandwiches can be had at the *Sensuous Sandwich* (☎ 377-9244, 163 W Center) and *Jimmy John's* (☎ 818-3900, 1545 N Provo Canyon Rd), which is near BYU and promises 'subs so fast you'll freak.'

The bright, modern *Guru's* (☎ 377-6980, 45 E Center) serves inexpensive, healthy Asian and Mexican dishes ($5-7), while *Atchafalaya Café* (☎ 373-9014, 204 W Center) serves up spicy cajun cookin'.

Provo has several good Mexican restaurants. Best known is the lively and fun *Los Hermanos* (☎ 375-5732, 16 W Center); most entrees are $6 to $11. Simpler but also recommended are *Mi Rancherito* (☎ 373-1503, 368 W Center) and *El Salvador Restaurant* (☎ 377-9411, 332 W Center), which serves *pupusas*, the typical El Salvadoran snack.

Red Lantern (☎ 356-8866, 175 N 200 West) is pleasant and locally recommended. Its all-day, all-you-can-eat Chinese-food buffet is $10; open daily.

True believers will make the trek to Orem's Krispy Kreme (☎ 222-9995, 417 W 1300 South). It's a paltry 10-minute drive north on University Parkway for the freshest glazed donuts possible. Or for dessert, join the locals at the *Carousel Ice Cream Parlor* (☎ 374-6667, 2250 N University Parkway); open till midnight Friday and Saturday.

Mid-Range Good Italian can be had at *La Dolce Vita* (☎ 373-8482, 61 N 100 East), which serves good-value, traditional meals ($10 or less), and *Ottavio's* (☎ 377-9555, 77 E Center), which is brighter and more upscale, with a full range of pastas ($10-12), entrees ($10-15) and pizza. Near BYU, the *Brick Oven* (☎ 374-8800, 111 E 800 North) is a good choice.

Roasted Artichoke (☎ 427-1558, 480 W Center) serves interesting pastas ($9-$10) in a spacious room with occasional live music.

Osaka (☎ 373-1060, 46 W Center) serves traditional Japanese meals ($8-12) and sushi; private 'shoji rooms' are available. It's open daily.

Voted Provo's best overall restaurant, *Bombay House* (☎ 373-6677, 463 N University Ave) serves good Indian food ($7.50-12).

Entertainment

For films, the Provo Towne Centre shopping mall, at University Ave and 1200 South, has the 16-screen *Cinemark* (☎ 852-2872).

In a renovated church, the *Provo Theatre Company* (☎ 379-0600, 105 N 100 East) has a year-round season of sometimes wacky original and off-Broadway plays and musicals. See also BYU, above, for events.

Bars are not big in this strict Mormon town, but alcoholic drinks and live music can be found at *ABG's Libation Emporium* (☎ 373-1200, 190 W Center) and *Atchafalaya Café* (☎ 373-9014, 204 W Center). Both are friendly places with pool tables and bar food. For nonalcoholic fun catering to a young crowd, *Club Omni* (☎ 375-0011, 153 W Center) has three huge dance floors and *Ozz* (☎ 818-9000, 490 N Freedom Blvd) has 25 pool tables and over 20 TVs tuned to sports channels.

Getting There & Around

Greyhound (☎ 373-4211), 124 N 300 West, has two to four buses a day north and south along I-15.

UTA (☎ 888-743-3882) has buses ($1) along University Ave that go around Provo and to Salt Lake City and other local towns; service is frequent Monday to Saturday and intermittent on Sunday. The BYU Bookstore has free schedules.

Amtrak (☎ 800-872-7245) has an early-morning train to Denver, Colorado ($85; 14½ hours) and points east, and a late-evening train to Salt Lake City ($9, one hour) with connections to Los Angeles and Oakland, California ($124, 19 hours). The train station is at 600 S 300 West.

AROUND PROVO
Peppermint Place

A must for kids (of all ages), this working candy factory (☎ 385-756-7400), 155 E 200 North in Alpine north of Provo (off Hwy 92; take exit 287 off I-15), will conjure visions of Willie Wonka. Watch them making colorful lollipops and intricate sugar animals, and then shop the treat-laden tables in the outlet store – the chocolates are first-rate. Admission is free.

Thanksgiving Point

This complex (385-768-2300), 3003 N Thanksgiving Way, in Lehi (exit 287 off I-15), first opened in 1995 and continues to expand. It has a museum (see below), restaurant, gift shop and golf course, but the reason for its creation is the extensive, tranquil **Thanksgiving Garden**, within which is a children's garden with shrub mazes, model trains and a petting zoo ($2). Admission to both gardens is $8/5 for adults/children three to 12. It's open Monday to Saturday; hours vary with season and venue.

North American Museum of Ancient Life

Completed in 2001, this 2½-acre museum (☎ 385-766-5000) may be the quintessential example of 'infotainment.' The cavernous main gallery re-creates earliest time, its high point being in situ displays of about 60 standing dinosaur skeletons, perhaps the largest such collection in the world. Interactive exhibits, a window to watch scientists scrape real bones, and an Iwerks movie theater, plus the inevitable gift shop and café, round out the experience. Gallery admission is $9/7 for adults/children three to 12; gallery and movie is $14/11. Hours are generally noon to 8 pm Monday to Saturday; call to confirm.

website: www.dinosaurpoint.com

Springville Museum of Art

The town of Springville (7 miles south of Provo on Hwy 89) bills itself as 'Art City,' but its main claim to fame is this museum

(☎ 385-489-2727), 126 E 400 South. Housed in a WPA-built, Spanish colonial-style building, the engaging collection is considered one of Utah's best. It's strong in contemporary Utah art and has the largest collection of Soviet paintings in the USA. A soon-to-be-completed new wing will double the available exhibition space. Hours are 10 am to 5 pm Tuesday to Saturday (till 9 pm on Wednesday) and from 3 to 6 pm on Sunday. Admission is free (except for special events).

Northern Utah

Geographically, northern Utah has two distinct regions – the area west and north of the Great Salt Lake is very arid, saline and extremely barren, while the area north of Ogden and east of I-84 is mountainous and forested. Even desert lovers are stunned by the sheer unlivability of Utah's northwest corner. Except for visitors to Wendover's casinos and Golden Spike National Historic Site, the remote area attracts few visitors.

In sharp contrast, the northeast corner attracts Utahns year-round, who flock to the smaller but no less scenic northern portion of the Wasatch Mountains here for winter snowmobiling and cross-country skiing and summer hiking, camping and fishing. In addition, Brigham City and Logan are charming, quintessential Mormon towns.

WENDOVER

☎ 435 (Utah) 775 (Nevada) • pop 1537 (Utah) 5000 (Nevada) • elevation 4232 feet

Less than two hours west of Salt Lake City along the plumb-straight I-80, Wendover straddles the Nevada/Utah border and is actually composed of two municipalities whose fates are contrasted almost as sharply as a US/Mexico border town: on one side are the prosperous Nevada suburbs and casinos, while in upright Utah the rundown homes and hotels struggle to survive. The situation has become so bad that in 2001 Utah's governor offered to amend the border so that all of Wendover would be in Nevada, but it remains to be seen whether Nevada will accept the 'gift' of the other half of town.

Wendover's primary attraction is its five casinos, which give northern Utahns a taste of the glitter and gambling Nevada is famous for. In addition, Wendover is remembered as the place where the crew of the *Enola Gay* trained before they dropped the first atomic bomb on Japan in WWII.

Orientation & Information

Wendover Blvd, parallel to and south of I-80, is the main thoroughfare. Utah addresses are E Wendover Blvd and Nevada addresses are W Wendover Blvd.

The new Welcome Center (☎ 775-664-3138, 866-299-2489), 937 W Wendover Blvd, is open daily and has a display on the *Enola Gay;* the actual plane is at the municipal airport. Wendover is on Utah time, but the rest of Nevada is one hour behind Utah.

Greyhound (☎ 435-665-2322) stops at 215 E Wendover Blvd, and there's a casino-loop shuttle bus ($1).

Places to Stay & Eat

Behind the Red Garter Casino is a *KOA* (☎ *775-664-3221*) with shadeless, windy tent/RV sites for $19/21. Kamping Kabins are $33 to $37.

Because gamblers descend on the town on weekends, hotels and casinos double or even triple their rates on Fridays, Saturdays, holidays and for special events. Otherwise, it's a buyer's market. Just about every place has a pool.

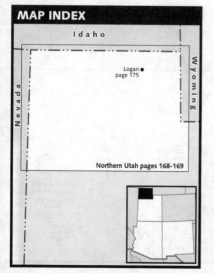

MAP INDEX

Idaho

Wyoming

Nevada

Logan ●
page 175

Northern Utah pages 168-169

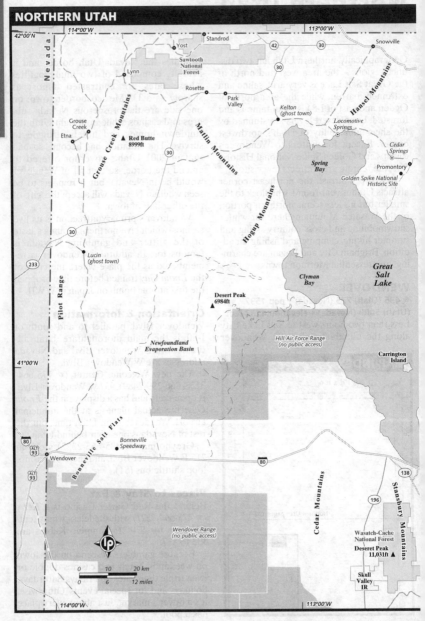

NORTHERN UTAH

42°00'N

114°00'W   113°00'W

Nevada

Snowville

Standrod

Yost

Sawtooth
National
Forest

Lynn

Rosette

Park Valley

Kelton
(ghost town)

Locomotive
Springs

Hansel Mountains

Cedar
Springs

Grouse
Creek

Etna

Red Butte
8999ft

Grouse Creek Mountains

Matlin Mountains

Spring
Bay

Promontory

Golden Spike National
Historic Site

Hogup Mountains

Lucin
(ghost town)

Pilot Range

Clyman
Bay

Great
Salt
Lake

Desert Peak
6984ft

41°00'N

Newfoundland
Evaporation Basin

Hill Air Force Range
(no public access)

Carrington
Island

Wendover

Bonneville
Speedway

Bonneville Salt Flats

Cedar Mountains

Stansbury Mountains

Wendover Range
(no public access)

Wasatch-Cache
National Forest

Deseret Peak
11,031ft

Skull
Valley
IR

0   10   20 km
0   6   12 miles

114°00'W   113°00'W

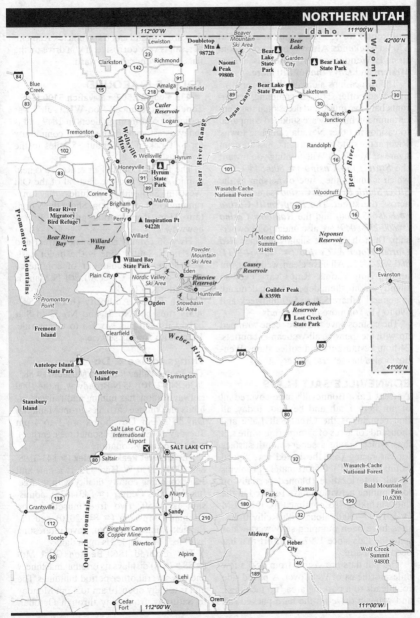

NORTHERN UTAH

Idaho

112°00'W · 111°00'W · 42°00'N

Wyoming

Lewiston

Doubletop Mtn ▲ 9872ft

Beaver Mountain Ski Area

Bear Lake

Clarkston

Richmond 23

142

Naomi Peak 9980ft ▲

Bear Lake State Park

Garden City

Bear Lake State Park

84
Blue Creek

91
Amalga
218 Smithfield
89

Bear Lake State Park

Laketown

83

Cutler Reservoir

Logan Canyon

30

Saga Creek Junction

Tremonton

Mendon

Wellsville Mtns

Logan

Bear River Range

Randolph

16

Bear River

102

Honeyville
Wellsville

Hyrum

101

83

Corinne

69
91
89

Hyrum State Park

Wasatch-Cache National Forest

39

Woodruff

16

Brigham City
Perry

Mantua

Bear River Migratory Bird Refuge

Bear River Bay

Willard Bay

Willard

▲ Inspiration Pt 9422ft

Monte Cristo Summit 9148ft

Neponset Reservoir

89

Powder Mountain Ski Area

Causey Reservoir

Evanston

Willard Bay State Park

Plain City

Nordic Valley Ski Area

Eden

Pineview Reservoir

Guilder Peak ▲ 8359ft

Huntsville

Promontory Mountains

Ogden

Snowbasin Ski Area

Lost Creek Reservoir

Lost Creek State Park

Promontory Point

Weber River

Fremont Island

Clearfield

84

80

189

41°00'N

Antelope Island State Park

Antelope Island

Farmington

80

Stansbury Island

Salt Lake City International Airport

32

Wasatch-Cache National Forest

Bald Mountain Pass 10,620ft

SALT LAKE CITY

150

80
Saltair

Grantsville

138

Murry

180

Park City

Kamas

16

112

Oquirrh Mountains

Sandy

210

Tooele

36

Bingham Canyon Copper Mine

Riverton

Midway

Heber City

Wolf Creek Summit 9480ft

Alpine

189

40

Lehi

Cedar Fort

112°00'W

Orem

111°00'W

E Wendover Blvd, on the Utah side, is lined with half a dozen cheap, frayed motels with rooms for $25 to $35 midweek, $50 to $70 on weekends. Always check your room first. E Wendover Blvd also has a *Best Western* and *Days Inn* for $10 more.

The five casinos along W Wendover Blvd in Nevada offer 24-hour gambling, restaurants, bars, live music and occasional stage entertainment, but they are subdued compared to casinos in other Nevada gambling towns. Right at the state line, you can't miss the giant figure of Wendover Will pointing you toward the *State Line Casino* (☎ 800-848-7300), which is under the same ownership as the *Silver Smith Resort & Casino* (same phone) across the street. The *Peppermill Casino* (☎ 800-648-9660) and the *Rainbow Casino* (☎ 800-217-0049) are also under joint ownership. Then there's the slightly cheaper *Red Garter Hotel & Casino* (☎ 775-664-2111, 800-982-2111). All have clean, well-kept, but unsurprising rooms. Rates vary ever so slightly among them depending on demand; in general, all are $30 to $40 midweek and $90 to $100 or more on weekends.

The casinos have the food scene wrapped up, with inexpensive all-you-can-eat buffets, 24-hour restaurants and coffee shops. Wendover also has several grocery stores.

BONNEVILLE SALT FLATS

Ancient Lake Bonneville once covered all of northern Utah and beyond. Today, all that remains is the Great Salt Lake and thousands of acres of shimmering white salt flats, which create a super-smooth surface for car racing (see the boxed text 'Speed Limit: 763 MPH'). Unfortunately, problems of salt deterioration (blamed partially on local mining activities) have resulted in the flats shrinking. To combat this, the BLM (☎ 801-977-4300), along with Reilly Industries, have been pumping salty wastewater onto the flats since 1997, an effort that has been successful.

The salt flats are visible from I-80 a few miles northeast of Wendover. A paved side road leads to a parking area (no facilities), and you can drive on the hard-packed salt

during late summer and fall (it is too wet at other times). Obey all signs – parts of the flats are thin and can trap vehicles. Remember, salt is very corrosive. If you drive on the flats, wash your car afterward.

TOOELE & AROUND
☎ 435 • pop 22,502 • elevation 5100 feet

Tooele (pronounced 'too-WILL-uh') was settled by Mormon pioneers in 1849 and is today a fast-growing bedroom community for Salt Lake City (about 35 miles to the northeast).

The Tooele County Fair & Rodeo is held in mid-August, and the Festival of the Old West in September includes the long-running Gem and Mineral Show, the Mountain Man Rendezvous and an Indian powwow.

Hwy 36 (Main) is the major street and runs north-south; Vine is the major east-west street. The chamber of commerce (☎ 882-0690, 800-378-0690), 201 N Main, is above the Key Bank.

Utah Transit Authority (UTA; ☎ 882-9031) runs bus No 51 and No 53 to Salt Lake City and bus No 338 to Grantsville. There is no Sunday service.

Things to See & Do
The **Tooele Valley Railroad Museum** (☎ 882-2836, 843-2110), 35 N Broadway, in the 1909 railway station, has mining and railway exhibits and vintage carriages. From Memorial Day to Labor Day, hours are 1 to 4 pm Tuesday to Saturday (sometimes earlier). Admission is by donation.

The **Deseret Peak Complex** (☎ 843-3198, 843-4000), 2930 W Hwy 112, is a new and still-expanding county facility with a large, fun Aquatics Center (☎ 843-4035); admission is $3.50. Two free museums, the Fireman's Museum (☎ 843-2020) and the Barrick Mining Museum, have interesting exhibits. The complex is open daily.

The restored 1860 **Benson Grist Mill** (☎ 882-7678) displays its original machinery and has several other period buildings. The mill is usually open 10 am to 4 pm Monday to Saturday, from May through October.

Speed Limit: 763 MPH

Cars, tents and entire garages mushroom on the flats in the third week of August during the **Bonneville National Speed Trials**. Other speed trials occur from July to October, usually sponsored by the Southern California Timing Association (☎ 805-526-1805) or the Utah Salt Flats Racing Association (☎ 435-785-5364). (Also call the Wendover Welcome Center or BLM for details.) The speed trials have been threatened by salt deterioration, particularly after higher than average rainfall, and some events have been canceled.

The first records made at Bonneville were in 1914, when Teddy Tezlaff unofficially reached 141.73 mph in a Blitzen Benz. English racing driver Sir Malcolm Campbell was the first person to drive over 300 mph, in his *Bluebird Special* on September 3, 1935 on a perfectly groomed, 1-mile course laid on the salt flats. Since then, American Craig Breedlove, driving *Spirit of America*, broke the 400, 500 and 600 mph barriers at Bonneville – the last on November 15, 1965.

Jet-powered cars have recently been breaking records in the Black Rock Desert in neighboring Nevada. Here, in 1996, Breedlove unofficially reached 675 mph before crashing. He was watching on October 15, 1997 (50 years and a day after the first aircraft broke the sound barrier) when Englishman Andy Green caused a sonic boom by driving the jet-car *ThrustSSC* to 763.035 mph – the first-ever supersonic world land-speed record.

The mill is 8 miles north of Tooele, just west of Hwy 36 on Hwy 138.

Eleven miles northwest of Tooele in Grantsville, the **Donner-Reed Memorial Museum**, 90 N Cooley, remembers the famous story of the tragic Donner-Reed Party wagon train, which resorted to cannibalism when it became trapped in the mountains during the winter of 1847. The museum is open only on request; call ahead to the chamber of commerce (☎ 884-3411), 429 E Main.

The **Stansbury Mountains**, a few miles west of Grantsville, include 11,031-foot Deseret Peak; a 4-mile trail to the top has superb views and there are several free, seasonal USFS campgrounds. For more information, contact the USFS in Salt Lake (☎ 801-524-5042).

Places to Stay & Eat

The friendly, family-run *Villa Motel* (☎ 882-4551, 475 N Main) has eight quiet rooms for $37 to $45. Otherwise, *chain motels*, such as Comfort Inn, Hampton Inn and Best Western, have doubles in the $70s.

For a meal, you'll find plenty of modest restaurants along Main St.

BRIGHAM CITY

☎ 435 • pop 17,411 • elevation 4315 feet

Settled in 1851 by Mormons and originally named Box Elder, this town was soon renamed to honor leader Brigham Young. Brigham City today serves as an agricultural center, and it offers a rewarding taste of small-town Mormon life. The tree-lined main street has a number of restored historic buildings, and the turn-of-the-19th-century train station contains a small museum. The village of Willard, 4 miles south, is known for its many late-19th-century Welsh stone houses.

The stretch of Hwy 89 south of town is known as the 'Golden Spike Fruitway' – from July through September it is crowded with fruit stands proudly displaying the abundant local harvest.

Orientation & Information

Brigham City is 2 miles east of I-15, about 50 miles north of Salt Lake City. Main St runs north-south and is the main thoroughfare; Forest St is the main east-west street. To reach downtown, take exit 364 off I-15, which becomes 1100 South, and turn north on Main St.

For information, contact the chamber of commerce (☎ 723-3931), 6 N Main St, or the Box Elder County Tourism office (☎ 734-2634,), 102 E Forest St or www.boxelder.com/tourismcouncil.html. Other services include the library (☎ 723-5850), 26 E Forest St; post office (☎ 723-5234), 16 S 100 West; hospital (☎ 734-9471), 950 S 500 West; and police station (☎ 723-3421), 20 N Main St.

Brigham City Museum Gallery
This nice museum (☎ 723-6769), 24 N 300 West, has changing art shows and permanent exhibits of local history. They also sell a historic walking tour booklet ($4). Hours are 11 am to 6 pm Tuesday to Friday and 1 to 5 pm on Saturday. Admission is free.

Mormon Tabernacle
Built in 1896, with 16 spires and a steeple sweeping skyward, the city's tabernacle (☎ 723-5376), 251 S Main St, is considered one of Utah's finest. It's open daily 9 am to 9 pm; free tours are given May to October.

Bear River Migratory Bird Refuge
Sixteen miles west of Brigham City, this refuge encompasses almost 74,000 acres of marshes on the northeastern shores of the Great Salt Lake and is a must for birders. The refuge is extremely important for millions of waterfowl, shorebirds and other birds, especially during migrations from August to November and March to May. Birds banded here have been recovered as far away as Siberia and Colombia.

Floods topped dikes in 1983, wreaking havoc generally and destroying all the buildings within the refuge. Though the buildings are being rebuilt, visitor facilities are minimal; there's only a pit toilet, covered picnic area and information board. A 12-mile-loop road is open for birding (bring binoculars) daily from 8 am to dusk. Duck hunters use the refuge from October to December. Snow may close the road from January to mid-March.

Further information is available from the headquarters (☎ 723-5887), 58 S 950 West, Brigham City, UT 84302.

Inspiration Point
From Mantua (3 miles north on Hwy 89/91), USFS Rd 84 is a 14-mile dirt road heading south to Inspiration Point (9422 feet); spectacular views encompass the Great Salt Lake and extend, weather permitting, to Nevada and Idaho. Ask for directions in Mantua. Four-wheel drive is recommended, though high-clearance vehicles make it in dry weather.

Crystal Hot Springs
These natural hot springs include several developed soaking pools and a picnic area; a café and convenience store are open during summer weekends. The springs (☎ 435-279-8104, 801-547-0777), 10 miles north at 8215 N Hwy 38 in Honeyville, are open daily year-round from late morning to evening; hours vary. Admission is $9, or about half if you don't use the water slide. If you want to stay overnight, there's a large campground with showers ($9/18 for tents/RVs).

Special Events
Held annually since 1904, Peach Days is the area's main event. It's the weekend after Labor Day and includes a parade, carnival, antique car show and entertainment.

Places to Stay
For camping, the ***Golden Spike RV Park*** (☎ 435-723-8858, 905 W 1075 South) charges $13/22 for tents/full hookups; two cabins are $12. ***KOA*** (☎ 435-723-5503, 800-562-0903), 4 miles south on Hwy 89, charges $19/25. Facilities at both include showers, playground, coin laundry and a store. Also see Crystal Hot Springs, above.

Motel rates drop in winter. The decent ***Galaxie Motel*** (☎ 723-3439, 800-577-4315, 740 S Main St) charges $29/33 to 37 for singles/doubles in summer. The ***Bushnell Motel*** (☎ 723-8575, 115 E 700 South) has similar rates. The ***Howard Johnson Inn*** (☎ 723-8511, 800-446-4656, 1167 S Main St) has an adjoining restaurant and rooms in the $50s. The nicest place is the ***Crystal Inn*** (☎ 723-0440, 800-408-0440, 480 Westland Drive), which has a pool, spa, exercise room, guest laundry and 52 spacious rooms with data ports. Rates are $80 for a double, $100 to 110 for Jacuzzi suites.

About 10 miles northeast on Hwy 89/91, halfway to Logan, is the *Best Western Sherwood Hills Resort* (☎ 245-5054, 800-532-5066). Amenities include a good restaurant, three pools, hot tubs, saunas, golf and tennis, and horse, bike, cross-country ski and snowmobile rentals. During the summer, the resort presents outdoor theater and musical revues and hosts murder-mystery dinners. Rooms are $90 and up.

Places to Eat

Main St has a number of inexpensive restaurants. *Peach City Ice Cream* (☎ 723-3923, 306 N Main) is an old-fashioned drive-in; ask for special fruit ice cream in season. Setting a nostalgic mood with a player piano and an authentic soda fountain counter is the family-run *Idle Isle* (☎ 734-2468, 24 S Main St). Since 1921 they've been serving inexpensive meals and homemade desserts, and next door they make their own chocolates; open all day Monday to Saturday; closed Sunday.

The area's best restaurant is in Perry, 2 miles south. Locally renowned for decades, *Maddox Ranch House* (☎ 723-8545, 800-544-5474, 1900 S Hwy 89) serves prized steak ($18-20) that is so tender you can cut it with a spoon. It's open from 11 am to 9:30 pm Tuesday to Saturday; reservations are recommended on weekends.

Getting There & Away

Utah Transit Authority (☎ 734-2901) runs Bus No 630 to Ogden throughout the day except Sunday. Buses stop on most blocks of Main. Bus No 635 services Brigham City itself. Greyhound has a flag stop at 38 E 100 South.

GOLDEN SPIKE NATIONAL HISTORIC SITE

Between the 1830s and early 1860s, more than 30,000 miles of railway tracks were laid in the USA, all east of the Missouri River. In 1863, work began on a transcontinental system. The Union Pacific Railroad was built westward from Omaha, Nebraska, and the Central Pacific Railroad pushed eastward from Sacramento, California. On May 10, 1869, the two railroads met at Promontory Summit and were linked by ceremonial golden spikes – now the nation could be crossed by train, and the face of the American West was changed forever.

The Lucin Cutoff across the Great Salt Lake bypassed the site in 1903, and modern trains take a different route, but the historic site contains almost 2 miles of track laid on the original roadbed. Visitors can watch exact replicas of the original steam engines chugging along the tracks, and various ranger programs include demonstrations of track-laying and descriptions of life in the 1860s. Folks in period costume stage live reenactments on Saturday at 1 and 3 pm. There is a 1½-mile self-guided walk and a 9-mile self-guided auto tour with nice views of the Great Salt Lake.

Information

The visitor center (☎ 435-471-2209) is open 8 am to 4:30 pm (till 6 pm in summer). It has railroad exhibits, shows short films and sells books and gifts (but no food). The site is 32 miles west of Brigham City off Hwy 83.

Steam train demonstrations happen four times a day from late April to mid-October (call for times). There are also demonstrations during the last weekend of the year.

Admission is $7 per car or $3.50 per person, late April till mid-October, $4/2 at other times, and free during special events. National passes are honored. There is no camping.

Special Events

The annual reenactment of the Golden Spike Ceremony every May 10 is very popular. The annual Railroader's Festival takes place on the second Saturday of August and features reenactments and a variety of events ranging from spike-driving contests to buffalo-chip-throwing contests. The last weekend of the year sees the annual Railroader's Film Festival and Winter Steam Demonstration, with classic Hollywood railroading films. Admission during events is free.

AROUND GOLDEN SPIKE

Unfortunately, the 40-mile road to **Promontory Point**, which starts a few miles east of Hwy 83 along the road to Golden Spike, is not recommended. Most of the adjacent land is private, as is the southernmost point, and property owners have earned a less-than-friendly reputation with sightseers.

Adventurous drivers can follow the old **Central Pacific Railroad** bed for about 90 miles west through uninhabited desert. A dirt and gravel road heads west from the Golden Spike to the ghost town of Lucin near the Nevada border (another 4WD-only road connects south to Wendover). High-clearance or 4WD vehicles are required; the section in the best condition is between Golden Spike and the ghost town of Kelton.

Use caution if you decide to travel here. The area is remote and rarely traveled, and flat tires from railroad spikes are common. Drivers must carry emergency food and water, spare tires, fuel etc. The visitor's center and the BLM (☎ 801-977-4300 in Salt Lake City) have more information.

Two miles north of the turnoff to Golden Spike on Hwy 83 is **Thiokol**, a rocket manufacturing plant. Its free outdoor 'rocket garden' exemplifies advanced technology of another century.

LOGAN

☎ 435 • pop 42,670 • elevation 4775 feet

Logan is the largest town in northern Utah. The scenic drive through Logan Canyon, northeast of town, is especially beautiful in fall. Legend has it that the local Shoshone Indians called it 'the house of the Great Spirit' long before the white man recognized the valley's beauty.

Founded by Mormons in 1859, the city remains an important agricultural center; Cache Valley cheeses are sold throughout the West. The magnificent late-19th-century Mormon Temple dominates the city architecturally and culturally.

The tourist industry is also growing; Logan makes a pleasant, comfortable year-round base for enjoying the area's many outdoor activities.

Orientation & Information

Hwy 91 (Main St) is the major street, running north-south. Hwy 89 (400 N) eastbound leads into Logan Canyon.

The chamber of commerce (☎ 752-2161) and the Bridgerland Travel Region office (☎ 800-882-4433), www.bridgerland.com, are both at 160 N Main St, Logan UT 84321; they are open weekdays and on Saturday in summer. The Wasatch-Cache National Forest Logan Ranger Station (☎ 755-3620) is at 1500 E Hwy 89. The local daily newspaper is *The Herald Journal*. Other services include the library (☎ 750-9870); 225 N Main St; post office (☎ 752-7246), 151 N 100 West; hospital (☎ 716-1000), 1400 N 500 East; and police station (☎ 750-9900), 45 W 200 North.

Logan's best bookstore is Chapter Two Books (☎ 752-9089), 130 N 100 East; its redwood porch is nice on a sunny day.

Historic Main Street

Many notable, turn-of-the-19th-century buildings are on or just off the three blocks of Main between 200 North and 100 South, including the Mormon **Tabernacle**, which was completed in 1891 and recently renovated. The chamber of commerce has a self-guided walking tour brochure; in the same building is the local **DUP Museum** (☎ 752-5139), which is open on summer afternoons, Tuesday to Friday.

Mormon Temple

Built between 1877 and 1884, the temple is Utah's third oldest, and the massive, 170-foot tall, twin-towered building, at 175 N 300 East, is visible from many parts of Logan. Although it is open only to Mormons on church business, you are welcome to walk the grounds.

Utah State University

Founded in 1888, this agricultural school's 21,500 students and 2800 staff enliven Logan's cultural scene. The campus is famous for **Old Main**, the late-19th-century center of university life. The Taggart Student Center has an information desk (☎ 797-1710) and restaurants serving the

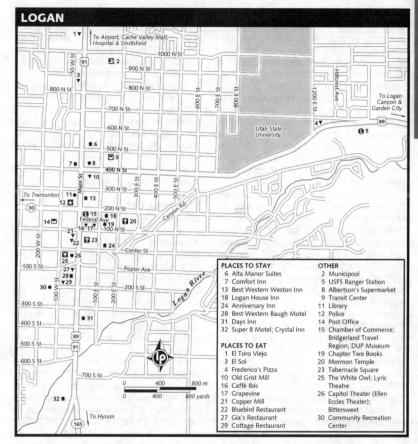

LOGAN

To Airport, Cache Valley Mall, Hospital & Smithfield

To Logan Canyon & Garden City

To Tremonton

To Hyrum

PLACES TO STAY	OTHER
6 Alta Manor Suites	2 Municipool
7 Comfort Inn	5 USFS Ranger Station
13 Best Western Weston Inn	8 Albertson's Supermarket
18 Logan House Inn	9 Transit Center
24 Anniversary Inn	11 Library
28 Best Western Baugh Motel	12 Police
31 Days Inn	14 Post Office
32 Super 8 Motel; Crystal Inn	15 Chamber of Commerce; Bridgerland Travel Region; DUP Museum
PLACES TO EAT	19 Chapter Two Books
1 El Toro Viejo	20 Mormon Temple
3 El Sol	23 Tabernacle Square
4 Frederico's Pizza	25 The White Owl; Lyric Theatre
10 Old Grist Mill	
16 Caffè Ibis	26 Capitol Theater (Ellen Eccles Theater); Bittersweet
17 Grapevine	
21 Copper Mill	
22 Bluebird Restaurant	30 Community Recreation Center
27 Gia's Restaurant	
29 Cottage Restaurant	

locally popular student-made Aggie Ice Cream. The **Nora Eccles Harrison Museum of Art** (☎ 797-0163) has both permanent exhibits and changing shows in various media. It's open daily; admission is free.

The university hosts many concerts, festivals and sports events; call ☎ 797-0305/40 for date and ticket information.

Activities

You can go **golfing** at the 18-hole Logan River Golf Course (☎ 750-0123), 1 mile south on Hwy 89/91. The Community Recreation Center (☎ 716-9250), 195 S 100

West, has tennis, racquetball, a gym and a sauna. There's **swimming** at the Municipool (☎ 750-9890) at 114 E 1000 North.

See Around Logan, below, for descriptions of the many **outdoor activities** in the area. The USU Outdoor Recreation Center (☎ 797-3264), 1050 N 950 East, is the most complete rental center, with camping gear, various watercraft, and every kind of winter sports gear except downhill skis. Bittersweet (☎ 752-8152), 51 S Main, has a climbing gym. Both the chamber of commerce and the USFS Ranger Station have details of other rental places and trails.

Special Events

The **Festival of the American West** is the premiere annual event; it lasts for eight days beginning the last Friday in July. Held at the American West Heritage Center in Wellsville (later in this chapter), the 30-year-old festival includes a panoply of events: from the nightly historical pageant reenacting Western settlement to a cowboy poetry gathering, art and quilt shows, a cowboy concert and a Dutch-oven cook off. Every day (except Sunday) there is also a fair with all kinds of Western entertainment. Advance tickets are sold at the university ticket office (☎ 245-6050, 800-225-3378).

Other noteworthy events include the Summerfest Art Fair every June and the Opera Festival (see Entertainment below) from July through August. The Saturday closest to the Fourth of July features 'Cruise-In,' a vintage car and hot-rod rally and parade that attracts over 60,000 folks. Since 1892, the Cache County Fair & Rodeo has been held in Logan; it's usually the second week of August.

Places to Stay

There's camping at **Riverside RV Park** (☎ 245-4469, 445 W 1700 South), east of Hwy 89/91, which has showers and coin laundry and charges $10/16.50 for tents/RVs. (See also Hardware Ranch Rd and Logan Canyon later in this chapter.)

Logan has few budget choices, none of them recommended. The Zanavoo Lodge (see Places to Eat, below) has a few rustic rooms (no TVs or telephones). Your best bet is one of the mid-range **chain motels**, such as Days Inn, Super 8, Comfort Inn or Best Western, which have doubles from $58 to $69.

The **Crystal Inn** (☎ 752-0707, 800-280-0707, 853 S Main St) offers comfortable rooms for $65 to $90.

Popular with business travelers, **Alta Manor Suites** (☎ 752-0808, 42 E 500 North) has eight nonsmoking, somewhat elegantly furnished one- and two-bedroom suites, each with full kitchen. Rates are $95 to $105.

In a comfortable, 100-year-old mansion, **Logan House Inn** (☎ 752-7727, 800-478-7459, 168 N 100 East) makes a wonderful romantic getaway in the heart of town. All six nonsmoking rooms are tastefully decorated with antiques and modern art and include a homemade breakfast. The smallest room is $99, but most are $150.

The Anniversary Inn (☎ 752-3443, 800-574-7605, 169 E Center St) has 21 memorable suites, each decorated as if it were its own theme park; see the listing of its sister inn in Salt Lake City for a complete description. Midweek rates range from $99 to $189, $20 more on weekends.

See also the Best Western Sherwood Hills Resort, near Brigham City.

Places to Eat

Logan has a nice range of restaurants. A local favorite is the 1920s-style **Bluebird Restaurant** (☎ 752-3155, 19 N Main St). Dining in the 1914 building transports you to an almost-lost small town Americana – the back room has a wraparound mural of Logan's history, various antiques are displayed, the service is attentive and the inexpensive menu doesn't stray from traditional American comfort food. It's open for lunch and dinner every day except Sunday; no alcohol is served.

Hip and popular with the university crowd, **Caffé Ibis** (☎ 753-4777, 52 Federal Ave) serves gourmet organic coffees, loose teas, fruit smoothies, pastries and fancy deli sandwiches. It's open daily and has an attached health food store. The **Old Grist Mill** (☎ 753-6463, 100 E 400 North) bakes homemade bread Monday to Saturday, slicing it for sandwiches if you wish.

Cache Valley is known for cheese, and a good place to sample and buy it is at the source, **Gossner Foods** (☎ 752-9365, 1000 W 1000 North).

For quick meals, **Fredrico's Pizza** (☎ 752-0130, 1349 E 700 North) is convenient to the university and recommended. For Mexican food, both **El Toro Viejo** (☎ 753-4084, 1079 N Main St) and **El Sol** (☎ 752-5743, 871 N Main St) have their local boosters. All are open daily.

The homey **Cottage Restaurant** (☎ 752-5260, 51 W 200 South) serves good American food daily (till 2 pm on Sunday), ranging from sandwiches to steak and seafood ($6-20). The more upscale *Copper Mill (☎ 752-0647, 55 N Main St)*, top of the Emporium Building, specializes in prime beef and seafood ($14-20) and serves alcohol. It's open for lunch and dinner Monday to Saturday. The best choice for Italian food is *Gia's Restaurant (☎ 752-8384, 119 S Main St)*, open daily for lunch and dinner; alcohol is served.

The *Zanavoo Lodge (☎ 752-0085)*, 2½ miles out of town in Logan Canyon, serves satisfying American dinners in a casual, rustic setting ($10-18). Hours are 5 to 10 pm Monday to Saturday. The seafood and prime rib (on weekends) are recommended.

Logan is home to what is regarded as the best restaurant in northern Utah, *Grapevine (☎ 752-1977, 129 N 100 East)*. The spare dining room and attractive outdoor patio make a fine setting for the excellent, inventive preparations of squab, roast duck and 'seafood hash' ($19-24). It's open for dinner only Wednesday to Saturday; reservations are recommended.

Entertainment

The major arts event here is the Utah Festival Opera Company performing at the historic Capitol Theater, which has been renovated and renamed the *Ellen Eccles Theatre (☎ 752-0026, 43 S Main St)*. Three or four operas are offered from mid-July to mid-August. During the rest of the year, the Capitol Arts Alliance produces a series of concerts, musicals and plays here. The Old Lyric Repertory Company produces four plays during its June-July season at the 1913 *Lyric Theatre (☎ 752-1500, 797-0305, 28 W Center St)*.

Logan has several movie houses, including the *Cache Valley 3 (☎ 753-3112, 1300 N Main St)* in the Cache Valley Mall.

For other events, see Utah State University earlier.

The White Owl (☎ 753-9165, 36 W Center St) is Logan's watering hole for non-Mormons. The large place encompasses a pool hall, high-ceilinged main bar and an outdoor deck with its own grill, which is lively on warm evenings.

Getting There & Around

Logan Cache Airport (☎ 752-5955), 2500 N 900 West, can arrange charters or rentals; there are no commercial flights.

Greyhound (☎ 752-4921), at the airport, has a daily evening bus to Salt Lake City (1½ hours) and a couple of buses a day up to Idaho.

The Logan Transit District (LTD; ☎ 752-2877) runs free buses around town every day but Sunday. All seven routes leave every half hour from the Transit Center, 150 E 500 North.

AROUND LOGAN
American West Heritage Center

This excellent new center (☎ 245-6050, 800-225-3378,), 6 miles southwest of Logan on S Hwy 89/91 in Wellsville, is made up of several re-created historical 'villages,' including the Jensen Living Historical Farm (for years run by university students), a frontier town and a pioneer village. Over the next few years a Shoshone village, a mountain man area, a military encampment and a museum will be added – all exemplifying frontier life from 1820 to 1920 and staffed by guides in period clothing. A wide array of hands-on demonstrations and activities are offered; these change often but include harness making, a kids rodeo, butter churning, sheep shearing and cowboy storytelling. There are always baby animals to pet and wagon rides.

The site is open 10 am to 5 pm Monday to Saturday, Memorial Day through Labor Day, and for other special events throughout the year; Saturdays have the largest slate of activities. The visitor center is open year-round, and the center hosts the Festival of the American West in late July (see Special Events in Logan). Adult admission is $5; $4 for seniors and students, and $3 for kids under 13. Family tickets are $15.
website: www.americanwestcenter.org

Wellsville Mountains

This is reputedly the highest range in the world rising from such a narrow base, so there are no roads and only a few steep trails up the almost-vertical sides. Call the Logan

Ranger Station for information and trail maps. Hikers must carry water and know what they are doing. There are no campsites, and wilderness camping is permitted but not recommended, due to the scarcity of flat areas and water, and the high elevation. Access is from the small town of Mendon, 10 miles west of Logan, and trails along the ridge (8100 feet) have excellent views; one leads to a vista point where Hawk Watch International sets up their annual observatory – this is one of Utah's best hawk-watching spots during fall migration.

Hardware Ranch Road

This road, which leaves east from Hyrum as Hwy 101, is a designated 'Scenic Backway.' After a few miles it enters pretty Blacksmith Canyon, which has hiking trails, trout fishing, 4WD roads, primitive camping and one summer-only USFS campground ($9) with water and toilets.

In winter, the canyon and surrounding countryside is crisscrossed with an extensive and extremely popular network of trails for **snowmobiling**. The paved road is plowed for the 18 miles between Hyrum and **Hardware Ranch**, which is also a game management area. With the arrival of snow, 500 to 700 head of elk (Utah's state animal) are fed at the ranch, and there are sleigh rides – a local highlight – to view the animals from December to March. A visitor center (☎ 753-6206) has information, exhibits and a café in winter (☎ 753-6168). In spring, the elk move off into the forest, though a few are sometimes kept behind.
website: www.hardwareranch.com

LOGAN CANYON

Northeast of Logan is Logan Canyon (Hwy 89), one of Utah's best-known scenic areas: Native Americans, mountain men, fur trappers and Mormon pioneers all noted its beauty. Today, countless drivers take Hwy 89 to visit Bear Lake and/or continue to Yellowstone and Grand Teton National Parks in Wyoming. Travelers in fall drive the canyon just to admire the autumn colors

splashing the steep limestone walls. In winter, this road is a jumping-off point for a popular network of **snowmobile trails**, or you can go **downhill skiing** at Beaver Mountain Ski Resort. In summer, many come for **rock climbing**, and the Logan ranger can advise you on routes (some areas are restricted; Tim Monsell's *Logan Canyon Climbs* is a good guide). In addition, many **hiking and biking** trails, dirt roads, historical markers, fishing spots, campgrounds and picnic areas line the 40-mile drive through Logan Canyon to Bear Lake.

The drive begins as Hwy 89 crosses the Logan River at the east end of town. The visitor center gives out a good guide describing all the stops in the canyon, and the Logan Ranger Station, at the mouth of the canyon, has an informative outdoor kiosk, as well as great views of Cache Valley.

The small, 464-acre **Beaver Mountain Ski Resort** (☎ 435-753-0921) is 27 miles from Logan in Logan Canyon (or 13 miles from Garden City). A day lodge has food, ski rentals and instruction. Three lifts service 26 runs between 7200 and 8840 feet elevation. A full-day lift pass is $24. There are no accommodations in winter; in summer, camping is available for tents/RVs ($6/15).
website: www.skithebeav.com

Places to Stay

Logan Canyon has several USFS campgrounds. Most open in May and close in September/October; actual dates depend on weather conditions. Most campgrounds ($10 -12) have pit or flush toilets and drinking water. The majority of sites are first-come, first-served (they fill up on summer weekends), but some can be reserved (☎ 877-444-6777). Most of the campgrounds have only 10 or 12 sites, except for *Guinavah-Malibu* (40 sites), *Tony Grove* (37 sites) and *Sunrise* (27 sites).

Half a mile beyond the turnoff for Beaver Mountain Ski Resort is *Beaver Creek Lodge* (☎ *753-1076, 800-946-4485),* which has 10 rooms for $79 midweek, $99 weekends. They are open year-round but are busiest in winter, when they rent snowmobiles. In summer, they have guided horseback rides.

GARDEN CITY & BEAR LAKE
☎ 435 • pop 357 • elevation 5918 feet
Garden City, a village on the west shore of Bear Lake, is busiest in summer, when it's inundated with lake visitors; winter is snowmobile season (rentals are available). Bear Lake extends into Idaho, covers 112 sq miles and supports four endemic fish species, which are sought after by anglers. The lake's striking deep-blue color is caused by limestone particles suspended in the water.

Bear Lake Visitors Bureau (☎ 208-945-2072, 800-448-2377,) is a few miles north in Idaho. There is a summer-only tourist information center in Garden City on Hwy 89 (next to Canyon Cove Inn) just before Hwy 30.

website: www.bearlake.org

Bear Lake State Park
Three areas on the west, south and east sides of the lake are all administered by the park (☎ 946-3343, 800-322-2770 for camping reservations), PO Box 184, Garden City, UT 84028. In addition, there are a few more facilities on the Idaho end (☎ 208-945-2790).

During summer, boating, fishing and even scuba diving are popular activities, and watercraft rentals are available. Day use is $5 per vehicle, or $3 for cyclists and walkins. Camping reservations are recommended on weekends.

The ever-busy **Bear Lake Marina**, 1 mile north of Garden City, is the main park headquarters. Open all year, it has a visitor center, picnic area, swimming, watercraft rental (☎ 946-2717), launch ramps and a 13-site campground ($15) with showers.

Rendezvous Beach, on the south side, has the only sandy beach; four nice, large campgrounds (with showers) are $15 to $19 (with hookups). The **Eastside** area has picnic areas and several primitive, first-come, first-served campsites ($7).

Special Events
Bear Lake is known far and wide for raspberries, and the popular Raspberry Days festival is held the first Thursday to Saturday in August. In mid-September, the Mountain Man Rendezvous is held at Rendezvous Beach (campsite reservations are suggested).

Places to Stay & Eat
Camping is plentiful at Bear Lake State Park (above). A large *KOA* (☎ *946-3454, 800-562-3442)* just north of Garden City is open April through October; sites are $20 to $29 (with hookups).

In Garden City, the simple *Bear Lake Motor Lodge* (☎ *946-3271, 50 S Bear Lake Blvd)* charges $50 to $80, and the newer *Canyon Cove Inn* (☎ *946-3565, 877-232-7525, 315 W Hwy 89)* has 32 chain-quality rooms for $70 to $80.

Three resorts hug the west side of the lake. Open year-round, *Harbor Village Resort* (☎ *946-3448, 800-324-6840, 900 N Bear Lake Blvd)* has one- and two-bedroom units for $119 and $200. *Blue Water Beach Resort* (☎ *946-3333, 800-756-6795, 2126 S Bear Lake Blvd)* and *Ideal Beach Resort* (☎ *946-3364, 800-634-1018, 2176 S Bear Lake Blvd)* specialize in furnished condos. In summer, they are $170 to $260 a night and $900 to $1,500 a week. Call for complete details.

Aside from a few hotel restaurants, places to eat in Garden City consist mainly of pizza parlors and burger joints. You'll have to decide for yourself who makes the best raspberry milkshake – the debate is renewed annually.

Northeastern Utah

High wilderness terrain dominates northeastern Utah. The few small towns are all a mile above sea level, and the highest mountains in the state, the rugged Uintas, rise a further 8000 feet above the towns. These mountains are relatively undeveloped – self-sufficient camping, backpacking, fishing and hiking are prime activities. East of the Uintas, the Flaming Gorge National Recreation Area offers record-breaking fishing and the Green River is known for good river running.

Near the Colorado border lies Vernal, the region's largest town, and Dinosaur National Monument, one of the largest dinosaur fossil quarries in the West. Though tourist brochures dub the entire northeast 'Dinosaurland,' the national monument is the primary dinosaur site.

This chapter begins its description of northeastern Utah at the western edge of the wild Uinta Mountains, continues through the Uintas to the area around Vernal and then heads north to spectacular Flaming Gorge. It ends to the east at Dinosaur National Monument.

MIRROR LAKE HIGHWAY (HWY 150)

The highway begins in the small community of **Kamas**, 16 miles southeast of exit 156 on I-80. Kamas is the western gateway to the Uinta Mountains, and the road cuts through gorgeous high-altitude terrain – in early summer, electric green aspens mingle with dusty olive pines. Mountain passes and trails (including extended backpacking trips into the High Uintas Wilderness Area) lead to spacious views, and the route passes scores of lakes for fishing. For complete information, call or visit the Wasatch-Cache National Forest Kamas Ranger Station (☎ 435-783-4338), 50 E Center, open Monday through Saturday.

The alpine route covers 55 miles to the Wyoming border, climbing from Kamas (6400 feet) over Bald Mountain Pass (10,620 feet) and continuing at elevations of over 8000 feet into Wyoming. Evanston, Wyoming, is 23 miles north of the border and has hotels; a further 65 miles north brings you to Garden City (see the Northern Utah chapter). In winter, snowplows clear the first 15 miles from Kamas for cross-country skiing and snowmobiling access, but the road over Bald Mountain Pass is open only Memorial Day through October, depending on weather conditions.

The USFS operates more than two dozen campgrounds along the highway within the national forest. Most campgrounds cost $10 to $12 and provide outhouses and water; none have RV hookups. The few that don't provide drinking water are free. Campgrounds can fill up on summer weekends – either arrive early or make a reservation (☎ 877-444-6777). While it's free to drive Hwy 150, a recreation fee is charged to visit the national forest; a day pass is $3, weekly $6, and it can be purchased at the ranger station or at most businesses in Kamas.

MAP INDEX

Wyoming

Flaming Gorge
National Recreation
Area page 189

Vernal ●
page 185

Colorado

Northeastern Utah page 181

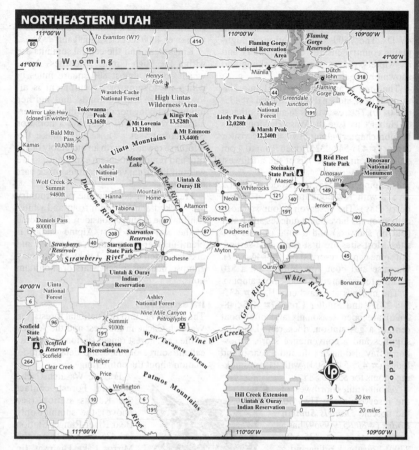

NORTHEASTERN UTAH

WOLF CREEK PASS (HWY 35)

This very pretty route leaves Hwy 32 at Francis (just south of Kamas), leads over Wolf Creek Summit (9480 feet) and ends about 65 miles later at Duchesne. Now completely paved, it makes a great route to/from the northeast, especially in fall. On Hwy 35, the Heber Ranger District operates two campgrounds, *Mill Hollow* and *Wolf Creek* ($12). Near Hanna, USFS Rd 144 leads north into Ashley National Forest and ends at a popular access points for the High Uintas Wilderness (see below). The Duchesne Ranger District maintains three

campgrounds along this road – *Aspen Groves*, *Hades* and *Iron Mine* ($10). All these USFS campgrounds are open May 15 to October and have drinking water and pit toilets. Just past Hades is *Defa's Dude Ranch* (☎ 435-848-5590), which offers inexpensive, rustic cabins and horseback trips; it is open May to October.

STRAWBERRY RESERVOIR AREA

This large reservoir is a pleasant spot with the expected lakeside attractions – summer boating and year-round fishing. During September and October, many come to watch the kokanee salmon spawning. In addition, backcountry roads lure motor bikers and 4WDs. The 7600-foot elevation in high-plains country ensures cool summers and icy winters, when cross-country skiing and snowmobiling are popular.

The area is managed by the Uinta National Forest, Heber Ranger Station (☎ 435-654-0470). The reservoir is 26 miles southeast of Heber City (see the Wasatch Mountains Region chapter) along Hwy 40. The visitor center (☎ 435-548-2321), open 9 am to 4 pm daily (later in summer), is at the northwest end of the reservoir.

Camping from May to October costs $12, or $22 with RV hookups (only at Strawberry Bay). The reservoir's four spacious campgrounds have boat launches and water (but no showers) and a total of over 550 sites. Most sites are first-come, first-served, but some can be reserved (☎ 877-444-6777). Day use and boat launching is $4; a $10 parking fee is charged to those not camping.

The marinas at Strawberry Bay (☎ 435-548-2261) and Soldier Creek (☎ 435-548-2696) are open seasonally and offer boat rentals, a gas station, dock rental, fishing supplies and a convenience store. Strawberry Bay also has a café and a year-round lodge (☎ 435-548-2500), with 21 nonsmoking rooms for $55 to $85.

About 6 miles northwest of the reservoir along Hwy 40, the upscale *Daniels Summit Lodge* (☎ 800-519-9969) has a general store (☎ 435-548-2300), horseback riding and a recommended restaurant. Its 48 comfortable, nonsmoking rooms are $110 to $140 for two people.

UINTA MOUNTAINS

These mountains are unusual in that they run east-west; all other major mountain ranges in the lower 48 states run north-south. Several peaks rise to more than 13,000 feet, including Kings Peak (13,528), which is the highest point in the Southwest. However, this is not one of those

peaks that can be reached by car! The shortest route requires a 32-mile roundtrip hike with over 4000 feet elevation gain.

Kings Peak and the central summits are within the High Uintas Wilderness Area, which covers almost 800 square miles in which no logging or development is allowed. There are no roads, and neither mountain biking nor off-road driving is permitted. You have to hike, ride a horse or cross-country ski. Those who make the effort are rewarded with an incredibly beautiful and remote mountain experience – one without the usual visitor centers, snack bars or lodges.

Hundreds of lakes in the high country are stocked annually with trout and whitefish, and the fishing is considered to be some of the best in the West. Alpine wildlife is plentiful: deer are common, and moose and elk are often spotted. Lucky hikers may glimpse martens, black bears or mountain lions.

Information

The Uintas fall into two national forests: the Wasatch-Cache in the west and the Ashley in the east. Forest ranger stations are an excellent source of maps and detailed information about the entire range.

Mountain lion

For the Wasatch-Cache National Forest, contact the Kamas station (see above); the summer-only Bear River Ranger Station (☎ 435-642-6662) on the Mirror Lake Highway (in the northwestern corner); the Evanston Ranger Station (☎ 307-789-3194), PO Box 1880, Evanston, WY 82931; or from the northern side (which also offers the shortest access to Kings Peak), the Mountain View Ranger Station (☎ 307-782-6555), PO Box 129, Mountain View, WY 82939.

The Ashley National Forest Ranger Stations in Roosevelt and Duchesne (see below) are also good places for information on the

High Uintas, while the Vernal and Manila stations mainly cover the national forest.

Hiking

The best hiking and backpacking guide to the area is *High Uinta Trails* by Mel Davis and John Vernath.

The hiking season here is about June to October in the lower elevations, July to September in the upper elevations, and just July and August for the highest peaks. Even in midsummer, be prepared for cold, drenching rain, even snow; you need warm and waterproof gear. Definitely bring insect repellent (July is murder). While canyon trails at wilderness access points are well marked and fine for beginners, high-country trails are very remote and strenuous; hiker, know thyself. Always carry an emergency kit.

Hikes of all lengths are possible, from a few hours to many days, and about 20 trailheads give access to all sides of the Uintas. Many trailheads have 'hosts' in summer who provide advice and trail condition updates.

Those wishing to climb **Kings Peak** will find the shortest access is from Henrys Fork trailhead on the north side (a 16-mile trek, though you can reach the summit via other longer trails). Those who scramble to the final rocky summit get the pleasure of signing the logbook. The 100-mile **Highline Trail** is the main east-west trail, extending from Mirror Lake Highway to East Park Reservoir in the Ashley National Forest (near Hwy 191). One of the busiest hikes is the 5 miles from Grandview trailhead to **Grand-daddy Basin**; this large natural lake is a popular place to fish.

Fishing

Serious anglers should read *Lakes of the High Uintas*, a series of booklets listing all necessary access and permit information. The booklets are published by the Utah Wildlife Resources Division (☎ 801-538-4700), 1594 W North Temple, Salt Lake City, UT 84114, and are also available in the Vernal office (☎ 435-789-3103), 152 E 100 North. Many backpackers supplement their rations with fresh fish.

Places to Stay

In the Uintas Wilderness, backcountry camping is free and no permits are required. Ranger stations can suggest areas in which to camp. In the surrounding Ashley National Forest, drive-in campgrounds are positioned on all sides of the range; most provide drinking water, toilets and fire pits as well as access to trailheads. Most cost $8 to $10; a few without water are $5 (sometimes free). Due to snow, most drive-in campgrounds operate from about May to October.

On the southern border are a growing number of seasonal **lodges**; most provide guided horseback and fishing trips into the wilderness. *Rock Creek B&B* (☎ 435-454-3853), in Mountain Home, has a store, coin laundry and seven clean, nonsmoking rooms for $40 to $95, including breakfast. Another 22 miles north, at the edge of the wilderness, is *Rock Creek Guest Ranch* (☎ 435-454-3332, 888-753-6603), which has both rustic and modern cabins (from $39 to $150) and a restaurant.

Also north of Mountain Home is *Moon Lake Resort* (☎ 435-454-3142, 970-731-9906 *in winter*), which rents a variety of cabins for $40 to $85 in high season.

About 20 miles north of Neola off Hwy 121 is *U-Bar Ranch* (☎ 435-645-7256, 800-303-7256), which has six log cabins ($69 for two) and a cabin sleeping 10 (about $40 per person). Bathrooms are shared and three meals a day are included. Overnight pack trips are available.

DUCHESNE
☎ 435 • pop 1408 • elevation 5515 feet

Pronounced 'doo-SHANE' (rhymes with 'blue train'), this small town is a southern gateway to the Uintas.

The city hall (☎ 738-2464), 165 S Center, provides basic visitor information. A new Welcome Center (☎ 722-4598) on Main should open in 2002. The Ashley National Forest Duchesne Ranger Station (☎ 738-2482), 85 W Main, Duchesne, UT 84021, is open weekdays year-round and on Saturday in summer and fall. The town has a few small motels and cafés, and the Greyhound bus stops at the Chevron gas station (☎ 738-5961), 432 W Main.

Four miles northwest of Duchesne, **Starvation State Park** (☎ 738-2326), PO Box 584, Duchesne, UT 84021, includes a 3500-acre reservoir and two campgrounds ($12, with showers but no hookups) with about 60 sites. Day use is $5.

ROOSEVELT
☎ 435 • pop 4299 • elevation 5282 feet
Founded in 1905, Roosevelt is the center of the region's cattle and oil industries. South of Roosevelt, near Myton, a partly paved road leads about 33 miles south to **Nine Mile Canyon**; see Price (in the Central Utah chapter) for information on this fascinating drive lined with petroglyphs.

For area information, go to the chamber of commerce (☎ 722-4598), 50 E 200 South, and the Ashley National Forest Roosevelt Ranger Station (☎ 722-5018), 244 W Hwy 40, PO Box 338, Roosevelt, UT 84066. The Greyhound bus office (☎ 722-3342) is at Jiffy Enterprises, 296 E 200 North (though the location often moves).

Roosevelt has a few rough-and-ready budget motels. A better night's sleep can be had at the *Frontier Motel (☎ 722-2201, 800-248-1014, 75 S 200 East)*, with 54 plain but clean rooms in the $40s or the *Best Western Inn (☎ 722-4644, 800-528-1234)*, 1 mile east of town on Hwy 40, with doubles for $69 to $79. Fast-food joints and simple family restaurants constitute dining options.

UINTAH & OURAY INDIAN RESERVATION
Much of the land around Roosevelt belongs to the Ute tribe. At one time, Roosevelt and many other areas were part of the reservation, but in the late 19th and early 20th centuries the reservation was cut in size, and homesteaders and oil prospectors moved in. Today, a little over 19,000 Utes live on the reservation.

The reservation runs a plaza on Hwy 40 that has seen better days. The hotel has closed, but the restaurant and tribal museum may remain open. Call the tribal offices (see below) to find out. The main

public Indian event in northeastern Utah is the annual Northern Ute Powwow and Rodeo held for several days around the Fourth of July. Other events, held throughout the year, are more tribal in nature, and no photography or other recording devices are allowed.

The Ute Tribal Offices (☎ 435-722-5141) are in Fort Duchesne, PO Box 190, UT 84026, about a mile south of Hwy 40 and 8 miles east of Roosevelt. The Ute Public Relations Department (☎ 435-722-3736), PO Box 400, also has information. Offices are open Monday to Thursday. Non-Utes can freely travel the reservation by road. Tribal permits (obtainable in Fort Duchesne or in sporting or fishing stores) are required for fishing, hunting, camping, boating or backcountry use.

VERNAL
☎ 435 • pop 7714 • elevation 5331 feet
Vernal was settled in 1878. In the late 1800s, outlaws used to hide out in the area because it was remote and inaccessible; since then, northeastern Utah's mineral wealth (oil, natural gas, Gilsonite and other deposits) as well as stock grazing have made Vernal an important industrial and agricultural center. Today, Vernal is the cultural and commercial center of 'Dinosaurland,' and it is the area's best base for supplies, restaurants and motels.

Greyhound (☎ 789-0404), in Frontier Travel at 72 S 100 West, has two buses a day to Salt Lake City ($32, five hours).

Information
The Northeastern Utah Visitors Center (☎ 789-7894) is open daily, till 9 pm in summer. Currently located in the state park at 235 E Main, it will move to a new site during 2002-3 while a new building is constructed. Thirteen miles east on Hwy 40 in Jensen is a brand-new Utah Welcome Center (☎ 789-4002), which is open daily and has statewide information. Also contact the Dinosaurland Travel Board (☎ 789-6932, 800-477-5558) or www.dinoland.com.

For public lands information, go to the Ashley National Forest Vernal Ranger

VERNAL

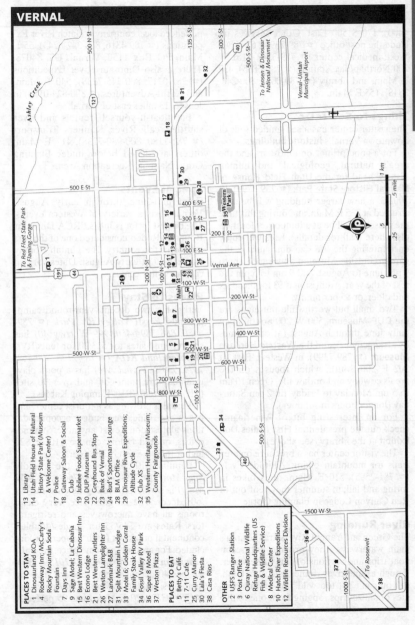

Ashley Creek

To Red Fleet State Park
& Flaming Gorge

To Jensen & Dinosaur
National Monument

Vernal-Uintah
Municipal Airport

Western
Park

Vernal Ave

To Roosevelt

1 km
1 mile
.25   .5

PLACES TO STAY
1 Dinosaurland KOA
4 Rodeway Inn; McCarty's
   Rocky Mountain Soda
   Fountain
7 Days Inn
9 Sage Motel; La Cabaña
15 Best Western Dinosaur Inn
16 Econo Lodge
21 Best Western Antlers
26 Weston Lamplighter Inn
27 Landmark B&B
31 Split Mountain Lodge
33 Motel 6; Golden Corral
   Family Steak House
34 Fossil Valley RV Park
36 Super 8 Motel
37 Weston Plaza

PLACES TO EAT
5 Betty's Café
11 7-11 Cafe
25 Curry Manor
30 Lala's Fiesta
38 Casa Rios

OTHER
2 USFS Ranger Station
3 Post Office
6 Ouray National Wildlife
   Refuge Headquarters (US
   Fish & Wildlife Service)
8 Medical Center
10 Hatch River Expeditions
12 Wildlife Resources Division

13 Library
14 Utah Field House of Natural
   History State Park (Museum
   & Welcome Center)
17 Police
18 Gateway Saloon & Social
   Club
19 Jubilee Foods Supermarket
20 DUP Museum
22 Greyhound Bus Stop
23 Bank of Vernal
24 Bud's Sportsman's Lounge
28 BLM Office
29 Dinosaur River Expeditions;
   Altitude Cycle
32 Club XS
35 Western Heritage Museum;
   County Fairgrounds

Station (☎ 789-1181), 355 N Vernal Ave, Vernal, UT 84078, and the BLM (☎ 781-4400), 170 S 500 East. Other services include the post office (☎ 789-2393), 67 N 800 West; medical center (☎ 789-3342), 151 W 200 North; police station (☎ 789-5835), 437 E Main; and library (☎ 789-0091, 800-246-3848), 155 E Main.

Things to See & Do

The visitor center has a self-guided tour of downtown Vernal's **historic buildings**.

For a good primer on dinosaurs and the area's natural, geological and human history, head for the **Utah Field House of Natural History State Park** (☎ 789-3799). In 2002-3, a new, larger building will be constructed at 235 E Main, and during this time the museum will be at a temporary location elsewhere (call for details). Kids will enjoy encountering the life-size dinosaurs in the gardens outside. Museum hours are 8 am to 9 pm June to August, and 9 am to 5 pm the rest of the year. Admission is $3 for those six and older, or $5 per family.

Two small but worthwhile museums are the **DUP Museum**, 500 W 200 South, open daily June through August (at other times by arrangement), and the **Western Heritage Museum** (☎ 789-7399), in Western Park at 302 E 200 South, which focuses on the area's cowboy and outlaw life. Open 10 am to 5 pm Monday to Friday, till 2 pm Saturday (longer hours in summer).

For an interesting bit of Americana, check out the presidential **First Ladies Doll Exhibit** at the library (see above).

The visitor center has a brochure on area trails for **mountain biking**. Altitude Cycle (☎ 781-2595), 510 E Main, rents bikes in spring and fall; in summer they rent out of Red Canyon Lodge in Flaming Gorge.

River Running

The Green and Yampa Rivers are the area's main waterways. They provide both calm float trips and sections of fun white water, though as one river runner said, 'It's Utah, so you can't get too wild.' Several companies organize trips ranging from one to five

days for about $65 to $700. The season is May to mid-September. A friendly and experienced local company is Hatch River Expeditions (☎ 789-4316, 800-342-8243), 55 E Main, PO Box 1150, Vernal, UT 84078. There is also Dinosaur River Expeditions (☎ 781-0717, 800-345-7238), 540 E Main, and Adrift Adventures (☎ 800-824-0150) in Jensen, 13 miles east of Vernal.

For float-it-yourself rentals and river shuttles, call River Runners Transport (☎ 781-1180, 800-930-7238), 417 E Main; others are listed below under Flaming Gorge National Recreation Area.

Special Events

From mid-June through early August, Vernal hosts a variety of Western events. The biggest by far is July's PRCA Dinosaur Roundup Rodeo, considered one of the best rodeos in the country. The Uintah County Fair is held in early August. Dates vary, so call the visitor center.

Places to Stay

Vernal has two decent, year-round campgrounds. *Fossil Valley RV Park* (☎ 789-6450, 888-789-6450, 999 W Hwy 40) has showers and sites for $13/20 for tents/RVs. *Dinosaurland KOA* (☎ 789-2148, 800-562-7574, 930 N Vernal Ave) has a pool, playground, store, mini-golf and over 90 sites ($17/22/34 tents/RVs/Kamping Kabins).

Vernal is growing as a tourist center, and prices are rising; true budget accommodations almost don't exist anymore. Summer prices, quoted below, can be $10 or $20 higher than the rest of the year.

Popular with Europeans, the friendly *Sage Motel* (☎ 789-1442, 800-760-1442, 54 W Main) is slowly renovating its once-far out '60s décor. The 26 good-size, very clean rooms all have microwaves and refrigerators. Rates are $45/55 for singles/doubles, continental breakfast (with 'proper tea') included. For around the same price, the *Split Mountain Lodge* (☎ 789-9020, 1015 E Hwy 40) has 40 decent rooms that are showing their ages, and the *Weston Lamplighter Inn* (☎ 789-0312, 120 E Main) has 95 perfectly clean but uninspired accommodations; the Lamplighter also has a pool and restaurant.

For $50 to $60 a night (less when it's slow), try any of the *chain motels* in town: Rodeway Inn, Days Inn, Super 8 and Motel 6. For $60 to $85, there's an Econo Lodge and two Best Westerns.

For rooms in the $60s, *Weston Plaza* (☎ 789-9550, 1684 W Hwy 40) has an indoor pool and hot tub, coin laundry, restaurant and bar (with occasional music and dancing).

Landmark B&B (☎ 781-1800, 888-738-1800, 288 E 100 South) has eight rooms ($65 to $75) with private bath and three suites ($135-175) with fireplaces and double-sized spa tubs. There is no smoking, and an extended continental breakfast is included.

Places to Eat

Several coffeehouses line Main St near Vernal Ave, and the town has grocery stores and a full range of fast food. Get your ice cream fix at *McCarty's Rocky Mountain Soda Fountain* (☎ 789-7825, 590 W Main). For a typical diner breakfast, the locals gather at *Betty's Café* (☎ 781-2728, 416 W Main).

Most restaurants are simple affairs. Try the inexpensive *7-11 Cafe* (☎ 789-1170, 77 E Main). Filling American dinner specials for $6 to $9 are a good value. For steaks, the *Golden Corral Family Steak House* (☎ 789-7268, 1046 W Hwy 40) is not bad.

For Mexican food, try *Casa Rios* (☎ 789-0103, 2015 W Hwy 40), *La Cabaña* (☎ 789-3151, 56 W Main) and *Lala's Fiesta* (☎ 789-2966, 550 E Main).

The most upscale meal is served at *Curry Manor* (☎ 789-2289, 189 S Vernal Ave); steaks, seafood and pasta are prepared for lunch weekdays and dinner Monday to Saturday.

Entertainment

The only dance club in town is the cavernous *Club XS* (☎ 781-0122, 1089 E Hwy 40), a private club with mostly DJs. For a beer and pub grub, there's the *Gateway Saloon & Social Club* (☎ 789-9842, 773 E Main) and *Bud's Sportsman's Lounge* (☎ 789-9963, 65 S Vernal Ave).

AROUND VERNAL
State Parks

Six miles north of Vernal, **Steinaker State Park** (☎ 789-4432) is a popular fishing, boating and water-skiing area during the summer. There is a sandy beach (good for swimming), picnic area and a pleasant campground ($10) with water, but no showers. The water is shut off in winter. Day use is $4.

Twelve miles north of Vernal, the scenic **Red Fleet State Park** (same phone) has nearly the same attractions, facilities and prices as Steinaker, though no real beach. A 1½-mile hike (roundtrip) passes fossilized dinosaur tracks.

Driving Tours

The visitor center in Vernal has brochures detailing about a dozen driving tours. The easiest and most popular is the **Drive Through the Ages**, which is the name given to 30 miles of Hwy 191 between Vernal and Flaming Gorge. This route has beautiful views (especially coming south) and passes some 20 geological strata with signs and pull-offs.

For those with more time, the extremely scenic 74-mile **Red Cloud Loop** is a highlight; it includes a portion of Hwy 191 and a tour of the **Dry Fork Canyon Petroglyphs**, which can be driven separately. The petroglyphs are part of the privately owned McConkie Ranch, which charges a small admission to see the site, but it's worth it: hundreds of Indian petroglyphs are spread over a mile-long canyon wall. The Red Cloud Loop has sections of dirt road that are passable to cars in good weather, but can be impassable or very rough after wet weather; the Vernal ranger has updated road conditions, as well as information about hiking and camping along the route.

The **Ouray National Wildlife Refuge** includes marshlands along the Green River that form an oasis for hundreds of species of migrating waterfowl. October and April are the busiest months. About 30 miles from Vernal, the refuge includes a self-guided 9-mile auto tour. Get information at the

Vernal visitor center or refuge headquarters (☎ 789-0351), 266 W 100 North in Vernal.

FLAMING GORGE NATIONAL RECREATION AREA

A striking red-rock canyon, Flaming Gorge was named by John Wesley Powell, who explored the area in 1869 during his historic first descent of the Green and Colorado Rivers. Between 1957 and 1964, the Bureau of Reclamation built the Flaming Gorge Dam across the Green River, which backed up for more than 90 miles to form the present reservoir. The reservoir straddles the Utah-Wyoming state line, but the visitor center and most of the best scenery, campsites and other facilities are on the Utah side.

As with many of the artificial lakes of the Southwest, fishing and boating are prime attractions. The lake is stocked with half a million fish annually and the fishing is some of the best in the Southwest, especially for giant lake trout and kokanee salmon. Various fishing records have been set here and the season is year-round.

In addition, Flaming Gorge provides plenty of hiking, camping, picnicking and backpacking opportunities in the summer. In winter, cross-country skiing, snowshoeing and snow camping are all possible. Wildlife such as moose, elk, pronghorn antelope and mule deer are common, and you may also see bighorn sheep, black bears and mountain lions.

The lake's 6040-foot elevation ensures pleasantly warm but not desperately hot summers – daytime highs average about 80°F. The main season is May to October. At other times, most services are shut down, though there are still places to stay and eat, and the main roads are kept open with snowplows in winter.

Orientation

Greendale Junction, at the entrance of the recreation area, is 35 miles north of Vernal on Hwy 191. From here, Hwy 191 continues 6 miles northeast past the Flaming Gorge Dam and the Visitor Center, then a further 3 miles through the small community of Dutch John and on up into Wyoming. Heading west from Greendale Junction, Hwy 44 passes the turnoff for the Red Canyon Visitor Center (after 3 miles) and goes north to the small town of Manila (about 28 miles), continuing up the west side of the lake into Wyoming. All these roads are paved.

Information

The Flaming Gorge Dam and Reservoir are managed by the BLM and the surrounding area is part of the Ashley National Forest. Information is available from the USFS or BLM in Vernal or at the USFS Flaming Gorge Headquarters (☎ 435-784-3445), PO Box 278, Manila, UT 84046. The Manila office is open weekdays year-round, plus weekends in summer.

The Flaming Gorge Dam Visitor Center (☎ 435-885-3135) is open from 8 am to 8 pm, Thursday to Saturday, till 7 pm Sunday to Wednesday in the summer; 9 am to 5 pm the rest of the year. The Red Canyon Visitor Center (☎ 435-889-3713) is open from 10 am to 5 pm daily from mid-May to late September. The views at Red Canyon are some of the most impressive. Both visitor centers have exhibits, audio-visual displays, bookstores and ranger programs and talks.

It is free to drive any of the roads and to visit the dam and nearby sites. The USFS requires a recreational pass ($2 per day, $5 for 16 days, $20 per year) for people wishing to hike, fish, hunt, ski, boat or do similar recreational activities.

Flaming Gorge Dam

Free guided, one-hour tours leave from the visitor center between 9 am and 4 pm during the summer. An elevator within the dam drops you to the base of the structure, which rises 502 feet above bedrock.

Swett Ranch National Historic Site

On Hwy 191 northeast of Greendale Junction, a signed road leads to Swett Ranch, which dates to the early 1900s and provides a glimpse of what life was like before roads opened up the area. Hours are 10 am to

UTAH

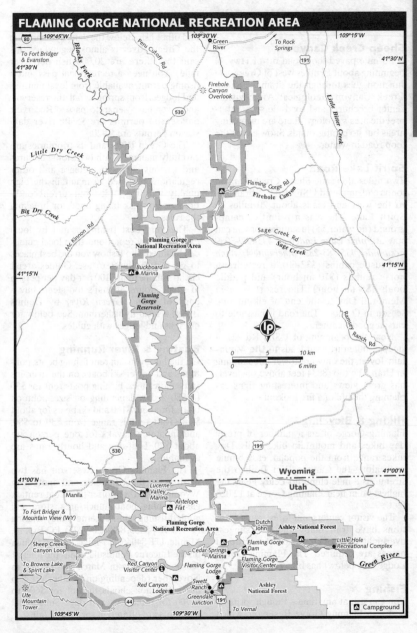

FLAMING GORGE NATIONAL RECREATION AREA

To Fort Bridger
& Evanston

Peru Cutoff Rd

Green
River

To Rock
Springs

Blacks Fork

Firehole
Canyon
Overlook

Little Bitter Creek

Little Dry Creek

Flaming Gorge Rd

Firehole Canyon

Big Dry Creek

McKinnon Rd

Sage Creek Rd

Sage Creek

Flaming Gorge
National Recreation Area

Buckboard
Marina

Flaming
Gorge
Reservoir

Ramsey Ranch Rd

0   5   10 km
0   3   6 miles

Wyoming

Utah

Lucerne
Valley
Marina

Antelope
Flat

To Fort Bridger &
Mountain View (WY)

Manila

Flaming Gorge
National Recreation Area

Dutch
John

Ashley National Forest

Sheep Creek
Canyon Loop

To Browne Lake
& Spirit Lake

Cedar Springs
Marina

Flaming Gorge
Dam

Little Hole
Recreational Complex

Green River

Red Canyon
Visitor Center

Flaming Gorge
Visitor Center

Ute
Mountain
Tower

Red Canyon
Lodge

Flaming Gorge
Lodge

Swett
Ranch

Greendale
Junction

Ashley
National Forest

To Vernal

Campground

5 pm Thursday to Monday, Memorial Day to Labor Day.

Sheep Creek Canyon

A 13-mile paved loop road off of Hwy 44 beginning about 15 miles west of Greendale Junction goes through the dramatic Sheep Creek Canyon Geological Area; visitor center brochures and roadside signs interpret the area's geology. There are picnicking areas but no campgrounds. Snow closes the loop road in winter.

Spirit Lake Road

Two miles along the Sheep Creek Canyon loop road, unpaved USFS Rd 221 branches to the west and leads about 20 miles to Spirit Lake. There is a primitive campground (no water, $5) in summer, or you can stay at *Spirit Lake Lodge* (☎ 435-880-3089 *in summer, 435-783-2339 other times),* which has rustic cabins ($32-60), a restaurant, horse rentals ($10 an hour) and paddle boats ($5 an hour). The resort is open Memorial Day to the end of elk-hunting season in October. The road is passable to cars in good weather.

Near the beginning of USFS Rd 221, a steep, 2-mile dirt road leads to **Ute Mountain Tower**, the only fire tower left standing in Utah. The top (8834 feet above sea level) has great views and interesting signs explaining the life of a fire lookout.

Hiking & Bicycling

Flaming Gorge offers a number of pretty day hikes and mountain bike trails. Day hikes range from the popular, easy 5-mile walk along the Canyon Rim Trail to the strenuous 8-mile climb up Leidy Peak, the highest point near Flaming Gorge at 12,028 feet.

The visitor centers and forest-ranger stations have trail maps and can suggest overnight backpacking trips. Recreational passes are required. The Flaming Gorge Lodge (see below) has bike rentals.

Fishing

You can fish at any time – though spring is best – in Flaming Gorge Reservoir, which has produced record-breaking lake trout (current record: 51 lbs 8 oz), salmon, bass and other fish. Below the dam, fly-fishing on the Green River is almost legendary (it's said that there are 20,000 fish per river mile). You need a recreational pass and a fishing permit, available from local marinas and lodges; from spring to fall, the reservoir and river have separate passes. Reservoir day/season permits are $5/40; river day/season permits are $2/20.

The Green River and its tributaries are carefully managed with occasional closures and various catch-and-release and other regulations designed to maintain the high quality of fishing – ask about current conditions or you risk being fined for breaking the rules.

The very best fishing is had by local experts. If you're not one, then local guides can be hired who'll show you the best places to go and the lures to use. Guides aren't cheap – more than $100 per day per person in small groups. If that's too steep, buy a copy of *Utah's Green River* by Dennis Breer, a local fly fisherman. See below for marinas and lodges with guides.

Boating & River Running

On the lake, you can rent fishing boats, pontoons and power/ski boats; on the river, it's rafts and canoes. Fishing boats rent for $30 to $80 a day, depending on size, pontoon boats for about $160 and ski boats for about $250. Raft rentals range from $30 to $80, and inflatable kayaks for one person are about $20. Half-day and hourly rates are available.

The Flaming Gorge Reservoir has two marinas on the Utah side and another in Wyoming. All three offer lake boat rentals, gas, camping, boat launch area, store and guided fishing trips. **Lucerne Valley Marina** (☎ 435-784-3483, 888-820-9225), PO Box 10, Manila, UT 84046, is 7 miles east of Manila on the Lucerne Peninsula. It has the longest season, beginning in March and ending in November (depending on weather). It also has a few houseboats to rent for $600 to $1700 for three to seven days. Substantial discounts are offered in spring and fall.

Cedar Springs Marina (☎ 435-889-3795), PO Box 337, Dutch John, UT 84023, a little over a mile west of Flaming Gorge Dam, is open from about April to October. The third marina, **Buckboard Marina** (☎ 307-875-6927), is 23 miles northeast of Manila in Wyoming. In addition to the marinas, there are several other boat launch areas for privately owned boats.

River rafts and kayaks can be rented from Flaming Gorge Lodge (see Places to Stay & Eat below); **Green River Outfitters** (☎ 435-885-3338), PO Box 200, Dutch John, UT 84023; and **Flaming Gorge Recreational Services** (☎ 435-885-3191), PO Box 326, Dutch John, UT 84023. All three provide fishing guides as well as shuttle vehicles. There are raft launch areas for privately owned boats on the Green River, a short way below the dam. Life jackets must be worn by all boaters and recreational passes are required.

For rafting, the most popular section is the first 7 miles from the dam spillway to the pull out at Little Hole; there are several minor (Class I and II) rapids. Depending on river flow (which varies each day), the trip can take from one to three hours. A shuttle bus (up to eight passengers) will meet you and bring you and your raft back for about $30, if arranged in advance. The next section, from Little Hole to Browns Park, has bigger rapids and camping is allowed; near John Jarvie Historic Site, two campsites ($5) have water and toilets (no showers), and the rest of the river has a number of free dispersed campsites (no facilities, portable toilets required). Summer weekends are amusement-park busy – be sure to reserve a raft rental in advance or make your trip midweek.

Winter Activities

Cross-country skiers will find marked trails following the Canyon Rim Trail and around Swett Ranch and several other areas. Snowmobilers use the forest roads to the east; the Dowd Springs picnic area just south of the Sheep Creek Canyon loop road is the base for snowmobiling. There are restrooms but no other facilities.

Places to Stay & Eat

Camping The Ashley National Forest operates about two dozen campgrounds in the Flaming Gorge area and just outside it. Most campgrounds are open May to October. Reservations (☎ 877-444-6777) for some of the more popular campsites are suggested.

Primitive campgrounds (bring your own water) are $5 and $6; some can be reached only by boat. In addition, more than a dozen campgrounds scattered around the south end of the reservoir provide drinking water and toilets but no showers or hookups ($13). Lakeside campgrounds have boat launch ramps. A few more developed campgrounds have showers (which are open to non-campers for $2) and cost $13 or $15 per person. A favorite campground is *Lucerne Valley*, near the marina, with more than 150 sites ($13 per person). *Antelope Flat*, 10 miles west of Dutch John, is another large, popular campground ($13 per site), as is *Firefighters Memorial* ($13 per site), conveniently located between Greendale Junction and the dam.

In Manila, the *Flaming Gorge KOA* (☎ 435-784-3184, 800-562-3254), a quarter mile east on Hwy 43 from Hwy 44, is open from about April to October. Nice facilities are geared to families. Sites are $17/24 for tents/hookups; six Kamping Kabins are $33.

Cabins & Motels The *Red Canyon Lodge* (☎ 435-889-3759,) near the Red Canyon Visitor Center, provides simple rustic cabins with shared bathrooms for $40 to $50. Cabins with private bathrooms are $15 more. Luxury cabins, with a kitchenette, rent for $115 to $125. The lodge has a restaurant and tackle store. The lodge is open from April to October and by arrangement on weekends in other months; check availability at www.redcanyonlodge.com.

The year-round *Flaming Gorge Lodge* (☎ 435-889-3773) is just off Hwy 191 between Greendale Junction and the dam. Motel rooms for one to four people are $63 to $81 and condominiums with kitchens run $111 to $129. November through February rates are lower. Facilities include a store,

restaurant and café; rafts, snowmobiles and cross-country skis can be rented.
website: www.fglodge.com

Manila, just outside the west end of Flaming Gorge, is a tiny crossroads that attracts the hunting and fishing crowd. The *Flaming Gorge Bunkhouse (☎ 435-784-3131/268)* here has very simple, older rooms in the $40s in summer (less in winter) and a café serving home-cooked meals. Better bets are a few miles west along Hwy 43: *Rainbow Inn (☎ 435-784-3117)* has 10 decent rooms for around $60 and a restaurant. *Vacation Inn (☎ 435-784-3259, 800-662-4327)* has 22 rooms with kitchenettes for $66, less for longer stays. It closes in winter.

DINOSAUR NATIONAL MONUMENT

No creature to walk the earth has captured the human imagination as much as the dinosaur. They were the undisputed dominant species tens of millions of years ago, but in only a few places have the right geological and climatic conditions combined to preserve these extraordinary beasts as fossils. One of the largest dinosaur fossil beds in North America was discovered here, about 20 miles east of Vernal, in 1909 and the site was protected as a national monument in 1915.

The highlight is the enclosed, main dinosaur quarry, which is one of the few places where dinosaur bones can be seen in the earth exactly as they were found. While the monument contains other fossil excavations, they are not open to the public. The national monument also contains gorgeous, starkly eroded canyons that are a joy to experience, whether driving, hiking, camping, backpacking, or river running.

Orientation & Information

Dinosaur National Monument straddles the Utah-Colorado state line and is best reached from Hwy 40. The park headquarters and most of the land are within Colorado, but the dinosaur quarry is in Utah. Reach the quarry by driving north from Jensen (13 miles east of Vernal) on a 7-mile paved road. The headquarters are just off Hwy 40, 25 miles east of Jensen and about 4 miles into Colorado.

Information is available from Dinosaur National Monument Headquarters (☎ 970-374-3000), 4545 Hwy 40, Dinosaur, CO 81610. The small visitor center here has exhibits, ranger programs in summer and a bookstore (but no fossils). It is open daily in summer, weekdays only in winter. Entrance to this visitor center is free; entrance to all other parts of the monument (including the dinosaur quarry) is $10 per vehicle or $5 per cyclist; national passes are accepted.

Summer daytime temperatures average in the mid to upper 80°s F. Snow during the winter may close some of the areas described below, though the road to the quarry is usually open.

Dinosaur Quarry

This educational spot (☎ 435-781-7700) is open daily 8 am to 7 pm from Memorial Day to Labor Day, and 8 am to 4:30 pm the rest of the year. The Jurassic rock layer that holds the fossils is an amazing sight – it gives an idea of how hard paleontologists work to transform the solid rock into, on the one hand, the beautiful skeletons seen in museums and, on the other hand, the scientifically accurate interpretation of what life was like for the dinosaurs.

Rangers, brochures and exhibits help explain the jumble of bones. Rangers also lead events in summer, and the quarry has a gift and bookstore.

During the busy summer, park your car and either walk about a half-mile to the quarry or take the frequent and free shuttle bus. Disabled visitors can drive all the way to the small parking lot at the quarry, as can the general public during off-peak periods.

Park Drives & Hiking Trails

You shouldn't leave without taking one of the scenic drives, which lead to overlooks, short nature trails and backcountry roads and hikes.

The mostly paved **Cub Creek Rd** goes east of the dinosaur quarry for 11 miles, ending at mountain woman Josie Morris' cabin. It passes three **nature trails** (1¼ to 2

Extreme skiing, Alta, UT

Calling it a day in Park City, UT

Not exactly the Olympics, Liberty Park, SLC

Always ready for action, Park City, UT

Paragliding at Delicate Arch, Arches National Park, UT

Towering spires and other rock formations of the Needles, Canyonlands National Park, UT

miles long each), Indian petroglyphs, picnic areas and two campgrounds.

One of the park's highlights is the paved **Harpers Corner Rd**, which leaves Hwy 40 at the park headquarters and heads north for 31 miles into the heart of the backcountry. This scenic and popular drive has several pullouts, picnic areas and trailheads but no campgrounds. Two trails, **Ruple Point Trail** and **Harpers Corner Trail**, lead to dramatic views of Green River canyons, the latter being especially recommended and memorable at sunset.

The unpaved 13-mile **Echo Park Rd** leaves the Harpers Corner Rd 25 miles north of the headquarters and drops steeply down to Echo Park at the confluence of the Yampa and Green Rivers. High-clearance vehicles are recommended, but cars can drive it in dry weather. In wet weather, the clay surface becomes very slick and is impassable, even for 4WD, and it should never be attempted with motor homes or trailers. There is a simple campground in a splendid setting at Echo Park. People with trucks or 4WDs can also explore the rough 38-mile **Yampa Bench Rd**, which leaves Echo Park Rd about 8 miles from Harpers Corner Rd and comes out on Hwy 40 at Elk Springs, Colorado. Again, this road becomes impassable after heavy rains.

The paved but narrow **Jones Hole Rd** leaves from 4 miles south of the dinosaur quarry and goes 48 miles around the west and north sides of the monument to Jones Hole National Fish Hatchery (☎ 435-789-4481). The hatchery is open to the public daily 7 am to 3:30 pm. From here, the recommended **Jones Hole Trail** descends 4 miles to the Green River, passing Indian petroglyphs. Backcountry camping (with a permit) is allowed.

A few other roads cross the monument and lead to more campsites. Note that all vehicles (including bicycles) must travel on designated roads; off-road vehicle travel is prohibited.

Backpacking
Most hikers take one of the trails described above. There are designated backcountry

campsites only on the Jones Hole Trail. Otherwise, wilderness camping is allowed anywhere that is at least a quarter mile from an established road or trail. Backpackers must register with a ranger at any of the visitor centers or ranger stations, where they receive free permits.

River Running
The Yampa River is the only major tributary of the Colorado River that has not had its flow severely impounded by major dams. Both the Yampa and Green Rivers offer excellent river-running opportunities, with plenty of exciting rapids and white water amidst splendid scenery. Trips range from one to five days and normally go from mid-May to early September. Several companies are listed under Vernal and about 10 others are authorized by the National Park Service to do tours – call the monument for a current list.

Experienced rafters wishing to go without a guide need a permit obtainable from the River Ranger Office (☎ 970-374-2468) between 8 am and noon weekdays. However, since permits are both limited and extremely popular, pretty much all are given out by lottery months ahead. Call or check the website at www.nps.gov/dino/river by November of the preceding year to enter the following year's lottery.

Places to Stay
The monument has no lodges or restaurants, so camping is your only option. The main campground is the summer-only **Green River**, 5 miles east of the dinosaur quarry along Cub Creek Rd. It has 88 sites ($12) with modern bathrooms and drinking water but no showers or hookups. Camping is first-come, first-served, and it can fill up on summer weekends. During the winter the water is turned off at all campgrounds and camping is free.

Free camping is permitted at *Rainbow Park* (two sites) and *Deerlodge Park* (eight sites), neither of which have drinking water. *Gates of Lodore* (17 sites) and *Echo Park* (21 sites) have drinking water and cost $6 in summer. You must carry your garbage out.

Central Utah

This chapter covers a wide territory, from Utah's Great Basin in the west to the rugged desert of the San Rafael Swell in the east. In between are the San Pitch Mountains and Pahvant Range (southern extensions of the Wasatch Mountains), through which run Utah's primary north-south arteries, I-15 and Hwy 89. This chapter also extends from south of Provo (see the Wasatch Mountains Region chapter) to the towns along I-70 (for Green River, see the Southeastern Utah chapter).

Those wanting to experience Utah's desolate western desert can either drive the historic Pony Express Trail or take Hwy 6, which skirts the desert to the town of Delta and then cuts straight across to Great Basin National Park in Nevada.

Running along the mountains, I-15 and Hwy 89 trace routes established in the 1850s by Mormon pioneers, who founded a string of settlements along them. This incursion led to several minor 'wars' between the Mormon pioneers and the Ute Indians as well as between Mormons and 'Gentiles' (non-Mormon whites). Today, especially along Hwy 89, many of these towns retain a definite early Mormon feel, with their turn-of-the-20th-century Main St architecture, magnificent temples and traditional, clean-living, friendly inhabitants. In addition, the mountains surrounding these towns offer splendid scenery and lots of opportunities for outdoor recreation.

East of the Wasatch Plateau, Hwys 6 and 10 lead through Carbon County and Castle Valley, respectively. Price and Helper are coal mining towns with interesting museums, and the dry, eroded country east and south of them have more opportunities for adventure.

The Western Desert

The grim names on local maps describe western Utah: Snake Valley, Black Rock Desert, Skull Valley, Little Sahara, Blood Mountain, Disappointment Hills, Confusion Range. This harsh desert country has had few settlements, except for those of the hardiest miners and ranchers. As a result, no one put up much protest when the US military fenced off large portions of the Great Salt Lake Desert for nuclear and chemical weapons testing, training and proving grounds (and today, the destruction of banned chemical weapons). In recent years, Tooele County residents, many of whom feel they have suffered physically from living 'downwind' of these tests, have been fighting for the military to better protect and clean up the environment.

PONY EXPRESS TRAIL

Over 130 miles of the original Pony Express Trail can be followed on a backcountry byway operated by the BLM (☎ 801-977-4300 in Salt Lake City). Today, stone markers and interpretive signs indicate rider stations along the route, and it is easy to imagine

---

MAP INDEX

OTHER MAPS
Pony Express Trail pages 196-197

Wyoming

Central Utah page 195

Price page 207 ●

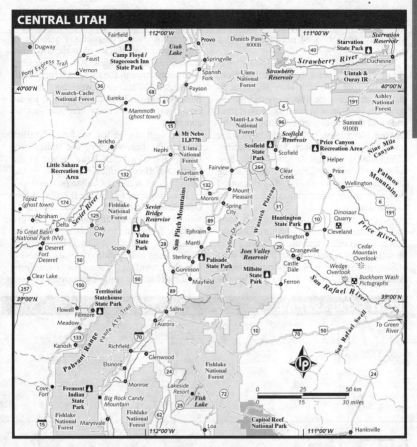

CENTRAL UTAH

Pony Express riders galloping urgently across the lonely expanse (see the boxed text 'Delivering Mail by Trusty Steed'). Indeed, following this trail is the best way to experience Utah's 'other' desert: the oft-unloved grass-covered plains and low ranges of the Great Basin, once an ancient sea bottom.

Most of the road is maintained gravel or dirt and is passable to ordinary cars in good weather. In winter, snow may close the route, and in summer, heavy rains may bog down vehicles. Spring and fall are best. There are no services, and drivers should carry plenty of food, water and gas; check

your tires and spare before departing. Depending on stops, the one-way drive takes five to seven hours.

The trail begins at **Camp Floyd/Stagecoach Inn State Park** (☎ 385-768-8932, 801-254-9036 in winter) in Fairfield about 25 miles southwest of I-15 along Hwy 73. Camp Floyd was established in 1858 when President Buchanan stationed 3500 troops here to quash what the government believed was an imminent Mormon rebellion (none occurred). Today, the park contains the restored Stagecoach Inn (no accommodations), a small museum and a pretty

UTAH

picnic area. It's open 9 am to 5 pm daily from Easter to September; closed Sunday in winter. Admission is $4 per car, or $2 for cyclists.

From Fairfield on Hwy 73, follow signs about 16 miles west to **Faust Junction**, where the trail intersects Hwy 36, about 30 miles south of Tooele; this is another access point. On Hwy 36 at Vernon, the paved road ends, and the gravel road continues past the Onaqui Mountains, where wild horses are sometimes seen. **Simpson Springs Station**, 25 miles west of Faust Junction, is the best restored of the Pony Express stations along the route. It has a 14-site BLM campground ($3) with water (purification advised) and vault toilets.

West of Simpson Springs are two good rockhounding areas: the northern Dugway Range (for geodes) and the southern Topaz Mountain (for topaz). About 37 miles west of Simpson Springs is **Fish Springs National Wildlife Refuge** (☎ 435-831-5353). This un-expected desert oasis – a sea-like marsh filled with birdsong – is a vital migratory habitat for over 250 species. Especially in spring and fall, flocks of waterfowl and shorebirds can be seen. An 11-mile loop road leads through the refuge. Refuge headquarters is staffed most weekdays and has information, a 24-hour restroom, picnic areas, water and a soda machine, but no camping.

The next 14 miles to **Boyd Station** provide the best views of the white, awesomely flat Great Salt Lake Desert to the north. Another 9 miles brings you to the ranching community of **Callao** (no services).

Towering over Callao are the 12,000-foot **Deep Creek Mountains** – a remote and rarely visited wilderness. Climbing and hiking are possible from June to October; to reach the mountains, take Trout Creek Rd south of Callao, then follow side roads leading west into the mountains. *Hiking the Great Basin* by John Hart has trail descriptions.

PONY EXPRESS TRAIL

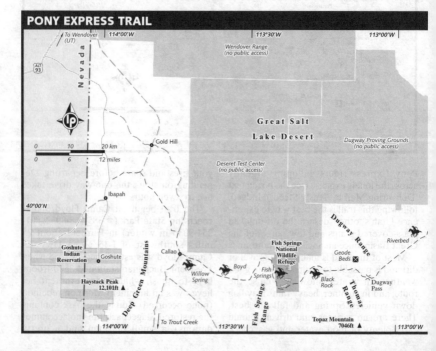

About 6 miles northwest of Callao is a crossroads; west follows the Pony Express Trail another 23 miles to **Ibapah**, where the trail ends (and there is sometimes a gas station). North leads 18 miles to **Gold Hill**, a mostly abandoned gold mining town with some interesting buildings. The road then continues past Gold Hill another 14 miles back to Ibapah. From here, a paved road leads north into Nevada and emerges at Wendover, 60 miles away. South of Ibapah is the **Goshute Indian Reservation** (☎ 435-234-1138), most of which requires a permit to visit.

DELTA

☎ 435 • pop 3209 • elevation 4650 feet

This town is an agricultural center for the farms irrigated by the Sevier River. Delta's main importance for travelers is as the 'Gateway to Great Basin National Park,' which lies almost 100 miles west. Its selection of hotels and services, though small, is still the best west of I-15 in Utah. The chamber of commerce (☎ 864-4316), 76 N 200 West, has area information and is open from 8:30 am to 3 pm weekdays.

Kitten Klean Trailer Park (☎ *864-2614, 200 E Main*) has tent/RV sites for $6/12, and ***Antelope Valley RV Park*** (☎ *864-1813, 776 W Main*) has 96 sites for $10/18.

The town's motels are nothing fancy, but all are acceptable. The following have basic singles/doubles for around $27/32: ***Rancher Motel & Cafe*** (☎ *864-2741, 171 W Main*), ***Diamond D Motor Lodge*** (☎ *864-2041, 234 W Main*) and ***Delta Inn Motel*** (☎ *864-5318, 347 E Main*). ***Budget Motel*** (☎ *864-4533, 75 S 350 East*) is a noticeable step up in quality. It has 29 clean, attractive rooms for $31/36. The best and largest place is the ***Best Western Motor Inn*** (☎ *864-3882, 800-354-9378, 527 E Topaz Blvd*); 82 rooms are $45/65.

Delta's restaurant choices are mainly cafés and steakhouses, but prices are reasonable and the food good. ***Rancher Cafe***,

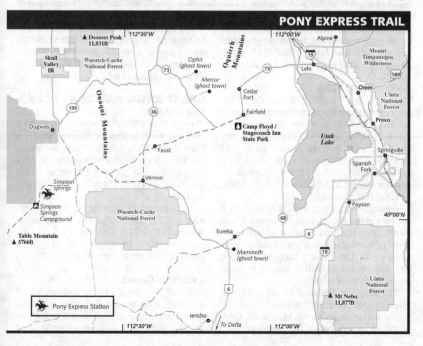

PONY EXPRESS TRAIL

112°30'W

112°00'W

▲ Deseret Peak 11,031ft

Skull Valley IR

Wasatch-Cache National Forest

Ophir (ghost town)

73

Oquirrh Mountains

73

Alpine

15

Lehi

Mount Timpanogos Wilderness

189

Onaqui Mountains

199

Mercur (ghost town)

Cedar Fort

Orem

Uinta National Forest

Dugway

36

Fairfield

Provo

Faust

Camp Floyd / Stagecoach Inn State Park

Utah Lake

Springville

Simpson Springs

Vernon

Spanish Fork

Simpson Springs Campground

Wasatch-Cache National Forest

Payson

68

40°00'N

Table Mountain ▲ 5766ft

Eureka

6

Mammoth (ghost town)

15

Uinta National Forest

6

▲ Mt Nebo 11,877ft

🐎 Pony Express Station

Jericho

To Delta

112°30'W

112°00'W

Delivering Mail by Trusty Steed

Those who complain that mail delivery is too slow would not have been happy in the mid-1800s, when a letter took two months to reach California from the East Coast of the USA. Delivery was by boat to Caribbean Panama, by mule to the Pacific Coast, and by boat again up to San Francisco, California.

The Pony Express was founded in 1860 to speed mail across the country. Expert horsemen who weighed under 120 lb were hired to ride the almost 1900 miles from St Joseph, Missouri, to Sacramento, California; they were equipped only with a leather pouch and a Colt revolver. At home stations, roughly 60 miles apart, riders were changed, and at swing stations, about 12 miles apart, horses were changed. Speeds averaged 190 miles per day, though 'Buffalo Bill' (William F Cody) rode a record 322 miles in less than 22 hours, using 21 different horses. It took approximately 10 days to complete the route, which was credited with keeping California in the Union at the outbreak of the Civil War. Incredibly, only one pouch was ever lost. The Pony Express service lasted only 19 months. Although it never made money, it was the completion of a transcontinental telegraph system in 1861 that did it in.

at the motel, has Mexican food; upstairs the more expensive *Gold Room* serves steak and seafood. *The Loft* (☎ 864-4223, 411 E Main) is another recommended steakhouse.

AROUND DELTA

Thirty-five miles north of Delta is the BLM-run **Little Sahara Recreation Area**, so named for its almost 40 sq miles of sand dunes. OHVs (off-highway vehicles) swarm the place like ants; best advice is to bring your own machine. Day-use, which includes a sandy campground, is $6. For information, contact the BLM in Fillmore or Richfield (later in this chapter).

About 50 miles north of Delta off Hwy 6 are two **ghost towns**, Silver City and Mammoth, plus the tiny, atmospheric mining town of **Eureka**, which is approaching ghost town status. The Tintic Mining Museum, in city hall (☎ 435-433-6915), should be open on summer weekends.

The **Fishlake National Forest**, about 15 miles east of Delta, has camping, fishing and hiking in the small Canyon Mountains. Contact the Fillmore ranger for information.

Along Hwy 6/50 east of Delta, about halfway to Nevada, are the **House Range** mountains, with several gravel or dirt roads leading to rockhounding sites. The Fillmore BLM has information.

GREAT BASIN NATIONAL PARK (NEVADA)

This park is 100 miles west of Delta, just over the Nevada state line, along what has been dubbed 'the loneliest road in America.' In addition to relative solitude, the park has two main attractions – Lehman Caves and Wheeler Peak. There are also interesting hiking trails.

Get information from the Superintendent (☎ 775-234-7331), Great Basin NP, Baker, NV 89311. Entrance is free. The visitor center is open daily 7 am to 6 pm in summer, 8:30 am to 5 pm in winter.

Lehman Caves

Most visitors come for these caves, which are thick with beautiful geological formations. Entrance is only allowed if you go on a ranger-led tour, which lasts either 30, 60 or

90 minutes. Passages are narrow and the caves are a constant 50°F – bring a sweater. Numerous tours are offered daily year-round; the most departures are on summer weekends. Ninety-minute tours cost $6 for adults (12 and up) and $3 for everyone else; shorter tours are cheaper. Buy tickets at the visitor center or reserve by phone up to a month ahead.

Wheeler Peak
At 13,063 feet, Wheeler Peak is Nevada's second-highest mountain and the only one that boasts a (small) year-round ice field. A scenic road climbs 12 miles to Wheeler Peak Campground at about 10,000 feet. From here a strenuous 5-mile (one-way) trail climbs to the summit, passing a grove of bristlecone pines. The entire road is open from about June to September; in winter, cross-country skiing is possible.

Places to Stay & Eat
The park has four first-come, first-served campgrounds ($7); three are summer only. There are toilets and water but no showers. Free backcountry camping is permitted – check in with the rangers first. The visitor center has a summer-only café.

The little town of Baker, Nevada, just outside the park, has a couple of cafés and *Silver Jack Motel* (☎ 702-234-7323) and *Whispering Elms Motel and Campground* (☎ 702-234-7343); simple rooms are in the $40s.

Central I-15 Corridor

Most folks speed along I-15 heading north or south, but the mountains to the east have several opportunities for scenic detours.

NEPHI & AROUND
☎ 435 • pop 4733 • elevation 5119 feet
Nephi, named after a Mormon prophet, was established in 1851. Though only 40 miles south of Provo, it makes a convenient stop for travelers. A big annual event is the Ute Stampede (☎ 623-4407), held in July and featuring a rodeo, parades, carnivals and concerts.

There is limited tourist information at the Juab County Center (☎ 623-2411), 160 N Main, and at the chamber of commerce (☎ 623-5203), 4 S Main, in the DUP Museum (☎ 623-5202). The Uinta National Forest Nephi Ranger Station (☎ 623-2735), 635 N Main, Nephi, UT 84648, has information about the Nebo Loop.

Greyhound (☎ 623-0823) stops at 563 N Main on its daily runs up and down I-15.

Nebo Loop Scenic Byway
This beautiful road climbs from Payson at 4500 feet to more than 9000 feet before dropping to 5100 feet at Nephi, about 37 miles away. The paved road is open from June to October and provides lovely views of 11,877-foot Mount Nebo. Elk and bighorn sheep roam the area and fishing is good. In winter, the roads are open part of the way and give access for snowshoers, cross-country skiers and snowmobilers. Reach the loop by driving east of Nephi on Hwy 132, or take 600 East southbound in Payson (look for signs). Allow one to two hours.

There are many good hiking trails. Separate, strenuous 5-mile climbs reach **Loafer Peak** (10,687 feet) and **Mount Nebo**, which has fantastic views from the summit. A much easier walk is the quarter-mile trail to the eroded red sandstone formations at **Devil's Kitchen**. See Dave Hall's *The Hiker's Guide to Utah* for a full description of these and other hikes.

Places to Stay & Eat
KOA (☎ 623-0811), 6 miles east of town along Hwy 132, is open from mid-May through September; it has nice facilities and tent/RV sites for $17/23. Kamping Kabins are $30. *Yuba State Park* (☎ 758-2611), 25 miles south of Nephi on I-15, has a year-round campground ($8) with showers. Along the Nebo Loop are five summer-only USFS campgrounds ($12) with water and toilets; call ☎ 800-280-2267 for reservations.

In town, *Safari Motel* (☎ 623-1071, 413 S Main) is a decent budget choice; ask for a renovated room. Singles/doubles are $28/38

A Different Kind of Gamble

Indian reservation casinos are scattered across the Southwest. They have become one well-known way that reservations have used their partial sovereignty from state and federal laws to generate much-needed income (despite continuing debates over their legality). In the same way and for the same reason, the Skull Valley band of Goshute Indians is attempting to skirt Utah law and build, with the help of a consortium of power companies, a temporary nuclear waste dump for spent nuclear fuel on its reservation about 45 miles southwest of Salt Lake City.

Two centuries ago, around 20,000 Goshutes lived in the Great Basin of Utah and Nevada, but disease and conquest reduced their numbers, and in 1863 they signed a treaty that allowed them to live on a postage-stamp-size parcel of worthless desert. Today, only 30 of the 120 remaining Goshute Indians live on the reservation, and each tribal member stands to gain up to $2 million if the nuclear waste dump is ever built.

Utah's current governor is doing everything he can to stop it (including passing a law that bans spent nuclear fuel in the state), and the tiny Goshute tribe is bitterly divided against itself over the issue. The nuclear power industry, meanwhile, says that it can't continue to operate at current levels if storage facilities aren't built somewhere – and nuclear power generates about 20% of the nation's electricity. The $43-billion industry has put its full weight behind the Skull Valley waste dump (which would last for 40 years) as well as the proposed permanent spent fuel repository beneath Yucca Mountain in Nevada.

This tangle of issues will ultimately be decided in US courts over the next several years. But it is unlikely to resolve any of the underlying issues: those of Native American poverty and adequate restitution for historical injustices, the Southwest's (and the nation's) overconsumption of its resources, and the ever-increasing pressure to turn the 'unscenic' Great Basin Desert into, as some opponents have called it, an 'environmental sacrifice zone.'

---

in summer. Across the street is a recommended Mexican restaurant. At exit 222 off I-15, there's **Super 8** (☎ 623-0888), **Motel 6** (☎ 623-0666) and **Roberta's Cove Motor Inn** (☎ 623-2629, 800-456-6460). All have standard rooms in the $40s to mid-$50s.

FILLMORE & AROUND
☎ 435 • pop 2253 • elevation 5200 feet

Fillmore became Utah's territorial capital in 1851, even before the town was settled. A statehouse was built, but Fillmore's capital status lasted only till 1856. Today, Fillmore is a quiet rural town offering a few accommodations for travelers. It is also a start point for the **Paiute ATV Trail** (for all-terrain vehicles); see Richfield, later, for a description of the trail. In late June, it hosts the National ATV Jamboree, the year's biggest event.

A tourist information booth in North Park, 500 N Main, operates from late spring to early fall. The Fishlake National Forest Fillmore Ranger Station (☎ 743-5721) is at 390 S Main, Fillmore, UT 84631. The BLM (☎ 743-3100), 35 E 500 North, provides information about BLM areas west of Fillmore. Greyhound (☎ 743-6876) stops by Caleb's Country Grill, 590 N Main.

Territorial Statehouse State Park

This park (☎ 743-5316), 50 W Capitol Ave, contains Utah's oldest government building, which is now furnished with period pieces and pioneer memorabilia. Open daily in summer, Monday to Saturday in winter. Admission is $3 per person or $5 for a group of up to eight.

Cove Fort

Thirty miles south of Fillmore is Cove Fort, built in 1867 and today the only restored fort along this historic corridor of Mormon settlement. Surrounded by black locust trees and a reconstructed pioneer cabin, the fort's 12 rooms are furnished with antiques. Mormon guides tell interesting stories of the fort's history, and there are programs for kids in summer. It's open daily 8 am till dusk; admission is free. The site is reached from exit 135 on I-15 or exit 1 on I-70.

I-15 south of here is described in the Southwestern Utah chapter. East of here, I-70 leads to Fremont Indian State Park (15 miles) and intersects with Hwy 89 (23 miles), both described below.

Places to Stay & Eat
KOA (☎ 743-4420, 800-562-1516, 410 W 900 South), near I-15 exit 163, has tent/RV sites for $16/21; Kamping Kabins are $29 to $34. They are open March to mid-December. Contact the Fillmore ranger for information on several basic USFS campgrounds in Fishlake National Forest.

In town are a couple of simple motels with rooms in the $40s in summer. The friendly *Suite Dreams B&B* (☎ 743-6860/2, 172 N Main) has two large, nonsmoking rooms with private hot tubs for $90, breakfast included. Otherwise, you'll find a *Best Western* and *Best Inn & Suites* at the I-15 exits; rooms are in the $50s in summer.

Simple restaurants are at the freeway exits, and there's a pizzeria on Main St in town.

Central Hwy 89 Corridor

Scenic Hwy 89 is a much more enjoyable, only slightly slower alternative to I-15, especially if you want to experience some of Utah's pleasant, traditional Mormon towns.

SKYLINE DRIVE
This gravel and dirt road parallels Hwy 89 and traverses 90 miles of the Wasatch Plateau from Hwy 6 in the north to I-70 in the south. The very scenic but difficult drive reaches 10,900 feet and is passable only in summer and fall, when many people come

to look at wildflowers and fall colors. You'll need a 4WD vehicle to complete the drive, but several sections are passable to cars, such as the first 27 miles between Hwy 6 and Hwy 31, as well as the access roads from towns along Hwys 89 and 10. Most of the drive is within the Manti-La Sal National Forest, and you can get information from ranger stations in Price, Ephraim and Ferron.

The drive begins near the Tucker Rest Area, 30 miles east of Spanish Fork along Hwy 6. It follows USFS Rd 150 for most of its length except the final few miles along USFS Rds 001 and 009 in the Fishlake National Forest. There are campgrounds at *Gooseberry*, near the Hwy 31 junction, and at *Ferron Reservoir* and *Twelvemile Flat*, near the junction to Ferron. These have drinking water, toilets and fire pits and are open from June to September. Fees are about $7. Free primitive camping is allowed, hiking trails are plentiful and much mountain wildlife, especially mule deer and elk, can be seen. During the winter, cross-country skiers and snowmobilers traverse the area.

FAIRVIEW
☎ 435 • pop 1160 • elevation 6000 feet
Settled by Mormons in 1859, Fairview is a minor agricultural center for the surrounding sheep and turkey farms. Hwy 31 east of town is the Huntington and Eccles Canyon Scenic Byway (see Carbon County & Castle Valley later in this chapter), which leads to an important access point for Skyline Drive. The city hall (☎ 427-3858), 85 S State, has visitor information. The Sanpete Shuttle (☎ 283-4580) now runs six times a day from Fairview to Manti, with stops in Mt Pleasant, Moroni, Spring City and Ephraim. Fare is $1.

Fairview Museum of History & Arts
This splendid small-town museum (☎ 427-9216), 85 N 100 East, is well worth seeing. Its eclectic collection, housed in two buildings, reflects the love and caring of the museum's dedicated volunteers.

The modern Horizon Building was built in 1995 specifically to house a life-size replica of the 12,000-year-old Columbian mammoth unearthed under Huntington Reservoir dam in 1988. Also here are paintings and sculptures mainly by regional artists (including the largest collection of noted Mormon sculpture Avard Fairbanks), a collection of Indian and pioneer memorabilia and a gift shop.

Next door, the old Heritage Building, originally a 1900 schoolhouse, contains the work of Fairview's Lyndon Graham, a sculptor and wood carver, as well as the 'National Shrine to Love and Devotion' – a sculpture of a Fairview couple, Peter and Celestia Peterson, who were married for 82 years, setting a world record. You can also see arts and crafts exhibits and pioneer memorabilia here.

The museum is open year-round 10 am to 5 pm Monday to Saturday, and 2 to 5 pm on Sunday. In summer, it closes at 6 pm. Admission is free; donations are welcome.

Places to Stay & Eat

The small *Skyline Motel* (☎ 427-3312, 236 N State) has ten rooms for $49 to $59. The *Tomato Garden* (☎ 435-427-9500, 44 S State) serves Italian dishes for lunch and dinner daily.

Five miles south in Mt Pleasant is the area's largest hotel, the *Horseshoe Mountain Lodge* (☎ 800-462-9330, 850 S Hwy 89). It has a restaurant (☎ 462-9533) and large, standard rooms for $60 to $85.

SPRING CITY

☎ 435 • pop 956 • elevation 5800 feet

The entirety of Spring City, settled in 1852 and about 6 miles south of Mt Pleasant, is on the National Register; it's a model of Mormon town planning and has an abundance of well-preserved historic buildings. The **city hall** (☎ 462-2244), 150 E Center, dispenses information and sells a detailed booklet ($5) describing the town and the history of Mormon settlement; you can also ask at the nearby post office. On the Saturday before Memorial Day there is a tour of old homes.

EPHRAIM

☎ 435 • pop 4505 • elevation 5500 feet

Ephraim, settled in 1854, is a major turkey-farming center. Several restored historic buildings line Main St, one of which now houses a small art gallery. Another noteworthy building is the Homestead B&B (see below).

There is no tourist office. The Manti-La Sal National Forest Ephraim Ranger Station (☎ 283-4151) is at 540 N Main, PO Box 692, Ephraim, UT 84627.

Main St contains two small, bottom-end motels (charging in the $30s) as well as some simple restaurants. *Willow Creek Inn* (☎ 283-4566, 450 S Main) has 58 chain-quality rooms from $89 to $125 in summer.

For a truly special experience, call *Ephraim Homestead B&B* (☎ 283-6367, 135 W 100 North), which may be the only place in Utah where you can spend the night in an authentic, restored Mormon homestead. Called 'The Granary,' the 1860s two-story log cabin is furnished with museum-quality period pieces (spinning wheel, wood stove, fireplace, antique beds and claw-footed tub). It rents for $95 a couple. Another, modern building, 'The Barn,' was built in 1981 using old materials and is furnished in a 19th-century style. Two rooms sharing a bath rent for $55 and $65. Breakfast is served in the 1880s Victorian house where the owners live. No smoking or liquor is allowed, but children are welcome and the owners are friendly. Units can accommodate families.

MANTI

☎ 435 • pop 3040 • elevation 5500 feet

This is one of Utah's earliest towns, settled in 1849. It is overlooked and dominated by a magnificent temple dedicated by Brigham Young in 1877 and completed in 1888. Manti is locally renowned for its annual Mormon pageant – a major highlight that attracts more than 100,000 visitors. The town also has several nice motels and B&Bs.

The History House Visitors Center (☎ 835-8411), 402 N Main, provides information during the summer. Sanpete County tourist information is available at ☎ 800-281-4346, or visit www.sanpete.com. The Sanpete Shuttle (☎ 283-4580) makes six daily runs between Manti and Fairview, stopping at all the towns in between. The fare is $1.

Special Events
The **Mormon Miracle Pageant** (☎ 835-3000, 888-255-8860) is a major Mormon Church event held annually since 1967. Several hundred performers tell the story of Mormon beginnings and migration to Utah, and the festival lasts almost two weeks in mid-June. The pageant takes place on the grassy hill below the Manti Temple (which is open only to Mormons on church business). The many visitors somewhat overwhelm the small town, and hotels are booked for miles around. For information, there's an unofficial website at www.mormonmiracle.com.

The **Sanpete County Fair**, featuring a rodeo, square dance, parade and other activities, is held in late August.

Places to Stay & Eat
Temple Hill Resort (☎ 835-2267, 296 E 900 N), on Hwy 89, is actually a very comfortable campground with showers and laundry. Tent/RV sites are $15/22, and tent cabins are $30.

The pleasant *Palisade State Park* (☎ 835-7275) has a campground ($13) with hot showers (open April to October), plus swimming and canoeing and an 18-hole golf course. Campsites often fill on summer weekends; call ☎ 800-322-3770 for reservations. The park is 5 miles south of Manti near Sterling.

Both recently renovated, *Manti Motel* (☎ 835-8533, 445 N Main) and *Temple View Lodge* (☎ 835-6663, 888-505-7566, 260 E 400 North) each have 12 very nice rooms in the $30s to mid-$40s. *Manti Country Village Motel* (☎ 835-9300, 800-452-0787, 145 N Main) is a comfortable, 23-room motel; rates are about $50.

In a historic building with some quaint touches, *Manti House Inn* (☎ 835-0161, 401 N Main) has six rooms and suites for $70 to

$120. For honeymoon-quality lodgings, *Yardley B&B* (☎ 835-1861, 800-858-6634, 190 W 200 South) is in a 100-year-old home with two rooms and three enormous, sumptuous suites ($100 to $150), including full breakfast. Plans are underway to add a holistic health spa with solarium, sauna and various natural treatments.

Manti has few restaurants. *Don's Gallery Café* (☎ 835-3663, 115 N Main) serves average American fare daily.

SALINA
☎ 435 • pop 2393 • elevation 5147 feet
Salina is a crossroads town, especially for truckers getting on and off I-70, which is 1½ miles south. Salina feels less quaint and historic than the towns north on Hwy 89, but it can be a good place to stock up on groceries or spend the night.

Greyhound buses (☎ 529-3781) stop at 1525 S State St, the only stop in Sevier County. No tickets are sold here.

The year-round *Butch Cassidy Campground* (☎ 529-7400, 800-551-6842, 1100 S State) is a very nice and well-kept place; tents sites are $6 per person and full hookups are $22.

If you're watching every penny, W Main St has a couple of down-at-the-heels motels. Better places are the only slightly frayed *Ranch Motel* (☎ 529-7789, 80 N State), with doubles for $39 to $46 in summer, and *Henry's Hideaway* (☎ 529-7467, 800-354-6468, 60 N State), which has a laundry and decent rooms for $46 to $55. Near I-70, exit 54, you'll find a *Super 8* and *Best Western*.

For a meal, try *Mom's Cafe* (☎ 529-3921, 10 E Main), which has been serving home cooking in Salina since 1929.

RICHFIELD
☎ 435 • pop 6847 • elevation 5482 feet
Richfield, settled in 1864, is an important agricultural center as well as the largest town for 100 road miles in any direction. It is the most comfortable town from which to explore central Utah.

In summer, you can get tourist information Monday to Saturday from a booth (☎ 896-1789) in the city park, 400 N Main; it has a self-guided walking tour of the town's historic buildings. Or, check with the chamber of commerce (☎ 896-4241) or the County Travel Council (☎ 896-8898, 800-662-8898), both in the county courthouse, 250 N Main. The Fishlake National Forest Richfield Ranger Station (☎ 896-9233) and the BLM (☎ 896-8221) are both at 115 E 900 North, Richfield, UT 84701.

Other services include the post office (☎ 896-6231), 93 N Main; library (☎ 896-5169), 83 E Center; hospital (☎ 896-8271), 1100 N Main; and police (☎ 896-8484), 75 E Center.

Paiute ATV Trail

The unpaved Paiute ATV Trail (for all-terrain vehicles) follows a 230-mile loop across three mountain ranges, mostly in USFS and BLM lands. The trail can be accessed at Richfield and Marysvale off Hwy 89, at Fillmore and Kanosh off I-15, and at other places. Information and maps are available at the Fillmore and Richfield USFS ranger stations. This extremely popular trail leads into some very remote wilderness areas, and yet it's easy to do portions of the trail as day trips. Fall is the best time to ride, as valley portions of the trail are extremely hot in summer. The trail's elevation ranges from 5000 to 11,500 feet, which means that camping is cold at night year-round.

In Richfield, you can rent ATVs from Five Star Rental (☎ 896-7368), 25 E 900 North. Richfield also hosts a large weeklong ATV Jamboree (☎ 800-639-0528) every September (see Fillmore earlier for more ATV activities).

Places to Stay

If you're camping, your only choice in town is *Richfield KOA* (☎ 896-6674, 888-562-4703, 600 W 600 South), which has complete facilities and tent/RV sites for $17/24. Kamping Kabins are $31.

S Main Street has several low-end budget motels that have seen better days; rates are in the $30s. The best of the lot is *Topsfield Lodge & Steak House* (☎ 896-5437, 1200 S

Main). Richfield has a nicer selection of mid-range accommodations; most are *chain motels*, such as Super 8, Travelodge, Days Inn, Quality Inn and Best Western. Doubles at these run $55 to $75 in summer, and rates drop by $10 to $20 in the off-season.

The attractive and friendly *Romanico Inn* (☎ 896-8471, 800-948-0001, 1170 S Main) has pleasant rooms for $44. Chain-quality rooms can be had at *Luxury Inn* (☎ 893-0100, 1355 N Main) and *Budget Host Night's Inn* (☎ 896-8228, 69 S Main), which offers doubles for $55 to $65.

Places to Eat

Little Wonder Cafe (☎ 896-8960, 101 N Main) is a quintessential country diner that has even had the occasional celebrity occupying a booth. Breakfasts are inexpensive and satisfying. Open Monday to Saturday till 8 pm, Sunday till 4 pm. A block away, *Parson's Bakery* (☎ 896-1844, 60 W 100 North) serves up fresh doughnuts, pies, and breads and makes very cheap sandwiches.

Pepperbelly's (☎ 896-2097, 680 S Main) serves Mexican food in nostalgic 1950s gas station surroundings; open Monday through Saturday till 9:30 pm. There's also *El Mexicano* (☎ 529-2132, 499 S Main), with a full menu of reasonably priced Mexican entrées.

Two reasonable hotel restaurants are *Someplace Else* (☎ 896-5501, 89 S Main), next to the Budget Host Night's Inn, and the more upscale *Garden Grill* in the Days Inn (☎ 896-6476, 333 N Main). Both serve American meals daily. The well-regarded *Topsfield Lodge Steak House* (☎ 896-5437, 1200 S Main) has been closed recently, but plans to reopen soon. The fireplace makes this a homey restaurant, with good steaks and seafood ($10-18).

MONROE

☎ 435 • pop 1845 • elevation 5395 feet

Settled in 1864, Monroe is a quiet, conservative Mormon farming community with several historic buildings. However, the main draw for travelers is the very unconservative **Mystic Hot Springs** (☎ 527-3286), 475 E 100 North, east of town at the edge of the Fishlake National Forest. This labor of love is an almost nostalgic hippie oasis; it has a network of natural-soaking pools and tubs, a summer-only swimming pool and an art studio. Year-round they host concerts by well-known musicians (many associated with the Grateful Dead). You can put up a tent ($10 per person), park your RV (add $3 for hookups) or stay in a rustic 19th-century cabin ($25); rates include use of the springs. Day use is $5. No drugs or alcohol, no nudity and no smoking are allowed.

FREMONT INDIAN STATE PARK

This state park contains over 500 panels of Fremont Indian rock art, one of the largest such collections in the state, as well as a partially excavated Fremont village. The Fremont Indians lived throughout much of Utah from approximately AD 500 to 1300. They were contemporaries with but distinct from the Ancestral Puebloans, who lived to the south. Though we still have much to learn about the Fremont culture and the meanings of their evocative petroglyphs and pictographs, this state park provides one of the best overviews.

The visitor center (☎ 527-4631) has excellent exhibits and trail guides describing the area's Indians and rock art. Two very short trails (wheelchair accessible) pass petroglyphs on nearby cliffs, and longer nature trails lead to the Fremont village, more rock art panels and other historic sites. Rangers and volunteers lead interpretive walks and give talks in summer; or call ahead to make arrangements any time of year. The center is open 9 am to 5 pm daily (to 6 pm in summer). Admission is $5 per car or $2 for walkers and bikers. Rangers know of good local mountain-biking routes, and an entrance to the Paiute ATV Trail is nearby.

The park is near I-70 exit 17. The 31-site *Castle Rock Campground*, 3 miles from the visitor center in the Fishlake National Forest (☎ 800-322-3770 for reservations) has toilets and drinking water; it is open from May to October. Sites are $10 and include park admission.

MARYSVALE
☎ 435 • pop 381 • elevation 5850 feet
This rural town is an access point for the Paiute ATV Trail (see Richfield, above). Local businesses rent out ATVs, horses and rafts for the Sevier River. The town is 11 miles south of I-70 on Hwy 89.

Moore's Old Pine Inn (☎ 326-4565, 888-887-4565), on Hwy 89 in town, is an old historic hotel with seven country-style rooms and suites ($85 to $100) and two cabins ($55); all include breakfast. Smaller rooms with shared bath are $50. It makes a nice country experience.

Five miles north on Hwy 89 is the *Big Rock Candy Mountain Resort* (☎ 326-2000, 888-560-7625). The mineral-stained mountain is a riot of color and was made famous in a song by Burl Ives. The resort (which closes in winter) has nine large modern motel rooms ($59) and seven cabins right on the river ($39 to $89). All are nonsmoking and have TVs and telephones. There is a restaurant and grocery store.

Carbon County & Castle Valley

This section begins with the coal-mining towns of Carbon County on Hwy 6 and continues southeast along Hwy 10 through the towns of the Castle Valley. This colorful, dry region, with numerous imposing buttes, was settled in the 1870s and 1880s, after pioneers had settled the moister valleys west of the Wasatch Plateau. The discovery of one of the world's largest coal fields and the arrival of the railroad in 1883 attracted many immigrants from diverse backgrounds, and the Mormon heritage that predominates in the valleys west of here is diluted. Price is the most important town in the area.

HELPER
☎ 435 • pop 2025 • elevation 5840 feet
Named after the 'helper' locomotives that once pulled coal-laden trains over the steep Soldier Summit nearby, Helper was a major

railroad and coal-mining center. Today, it's fallen on hard times, and many of its historic, turn-of-the-20th-century buildings along Main are boarded up or for sale. Nevertheless, people still live here, the train stops every day (call Amtrak at ☎ 800-872-7245) and a good museum is worth visiting. Price, 6 miles to the southeast, has information and other visitor services.

Helper is known for its colorful Christmas light displays, which culminate in an electric light parade in mid-December.

Western Mining & Railroad Museum

This museum (☎ 472-3009), 296 S Main, has excellent exhibits on its subjects – mining and trains – as well as on the everyday life of workers, from their schools to their baseball teams. Exhibits and a video describe the 1900 Scofield mining disaster, which killed 228 people and was the largest mine explosion up to that time. Ask them to run the extensive model train display. The museum is open 10 am to 6 pm Tuesday to Saturday, from May to September, and 11 am to 4 pm October to April. A $2 donation is suggested.

Price Canyon Recreation Area

This recreation area, 8 miles north of Helper off Hwy 6, is notable for the strenuous, mile-long **Bristlecone Ridge Hiking Trail**, which reaches an area of bristlecone pines – the oldest living things on earth. An expansive overlook and cooler summer temperatures make this a nice stop. The 15-site campground ($8) is run by the BLM (☎ 636-3600) in Price. It's open from May to October and has water and pit toilets.

PRICE

☎ 435 • pop 8402 • elevation 5600 feet

Founded as an agricultural center in 1879 and named after William Price, an early Mormon bishop, Price quickly became a coal-mining and railroad center. Coal mining continues to be important, and uranium and natural gas are also mined. Price is the best base for exploring the area and stocking up on supplies. The turnoff for

Nine Mile Canyon (see below) is 2 miles southeast of Wellington.

Hwy 6/191 continues almost 60 miles southeast till it intersects with I-70. Green River, 4 miles east of this intersection, is described in the Southeastern Utah chapter.

Information

The Castle Country Travel Office (☎ 637-3009, 800-842-0789) and the Carbon County chamber of commerce (☎ 637-2788) are both at 90 N 100 East and online at www .castlecountry.com and www.carboncounty chamber.com respectively. For public lands information, visit the Manti-La Sal National Forest Price Ranger Station (☎ 637-2817), 599 W Price River Drive and the BLM (☎ 636-3600), 125 S 600 West.

Other services include the post office (☎ 637-1638), 95 S Carbon Ave; library (☎ 636-3188), 159 E Main; hospital (☎ 637-4800), 300 N Hospital Drive; and police (☎ 636-3190), 81 N 200 East.

College of Eastern Utah Prehistoric Museum

The collection at this non-profit museum (☎ 637-5060, 800-817-9949), 155 E Main, is a fine surprise. Several well-displayed dinosaur skeletons and woolly mammoths, plenty of superb Indian artifacts, a kids' area, local art, a good gift shop and knowledgeable staff combine to make this a recommended stop. It's free but deserves a donation ($2 per adult is suggested). Hours are 9 am to 6 pm daily from April to September; 9 am to 5 pm Monday to Saturday the rest of the year.

Historic Buildings

The Castle Country Travel Office has a brochure detailing Price's historic early-20th-century buildings. The Price Municipal Building, at 185 E Main St, is especially noteworthy for its WPA mural in the lobby, which was painted by local artist Lynn Fausett.

Special Events

The Black Diamond PRCA Rodeo is held in mid- to late June. Greek Days on the

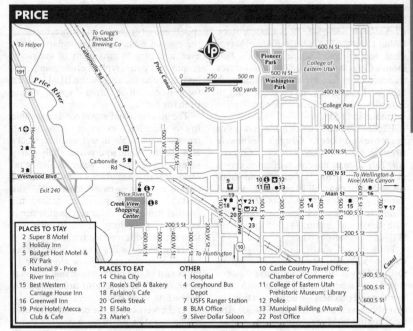

PRICE

PLACES TO STAY
2 Super 8 Motel
3 Holiday Inn
5 Budget Host Motel &
  RV Park
6 National 9 - Price
  River Inn
15 Best Western
  Carriage House Inn
16 Greenwell Inn
19 Price Hotel; Mecca
  Club & Cafe

PLACES TO EAT
14 China City
17 Rosie's Deli & Bakery
18 Farlaino's Cafe
20 Greek Streak
21 El Salto
23 Marie's

OTHER
1 Hospital
4 Greyhound Bus
  Depot
7 USFS Ranger Station
8 BLM Office
9 Silver Dollar Saloon
10 Castle Country Travel Office;
  Chamber of Commerce
11 College of Eastern Utah
  Prehistoric Museum; Library
12 Police
13 Municipal Building (Mural)
22 Post Office

second weekend in July includes tours of Utah's oldest Greek Orthodox Church. International Days and the Carbon County Fair are held concurrently in the first week in August. They celebrate the county's diverse, multicultural background.

Places to Stay

Prices only drop slightly in winter (and they go up during special events).

If you're uncrumpling your last dollars and aren't picky, *Price Hotel* (☎ 637-9852, *41 W Main*) is an acceptable dive. The teeny-tiny rooms are just clean enough, as are the shared bathrooms. Rooms are $15 without bath, $20 to $25 with.

Price's best budget choice is *Budget Host Motel & RV Park* (☎ 637-2424, 800-283-4678, 145 N Carbonville Rd). It has a pool, coin laundry and RV hookups ($18). Neat and clean rooms, some recently renovated, are $39/55 for singles/doubles in summer. Rooms with kitchenettes are $10 more.

National 9 – Price River Inn (☎ 637-7000, *641 W Price River Drive*) has 94 plain but clean rooms for $37/47.

Greenwell Inn (☎ 637-3520, 800-666-3520, 655 E Main) has 125 plain but spacious rooms, an indoor pool, exercise rooms and a restaurant. Year-round rates are $43 to $63. *Chain motels* make up the rest of the mid-range options, including Super 8, Best Western and Holiday Inn.

Places to Eat

The Creek View Shopping Center, 700 W Price River Dr, has a large grocery store. Head to *Rosie's Deli & Bakery* (☎ 637-6743, 61 S 700 East) for fresh pastries and good deli sandwiches.

Price offers more international dining choices than most small towns in Utah. A little hole-in-the-wall, *Greek Streak* (☎ 637-1930, 84 S Carbon Ave) serves some of the best Greek food in Utah. Everything is made fresh; they even crush their own spices. It is open 11 am to 9 pm, Monday to Saturday. For inexpensive Mexican food, try *El Salto* (☎ 637-6545, 19 S Carbon Ave). *China City* (☎ 637-8211, 350 E Main) serves steak, seafood and Chinese fare daily. *Far-laino's Cafe* (☎ 637-9217, 87 W Main) serves standard diner fare for breakfast and lunch Monday to Saturday, and on Wednesday to Saturday nights offers a decent Italian menu for $8 to $15.

Recommended as much for its food as its microbrewed beer, *Grogg's Pinnacle Brewing Co* (☎ 637-2914, 1653 N Carbonville Rd), 2 miles northwest of town, serves pizzas, steaks ($10-15), burgers and sandwiches ($6-8) daily, till 10 pm on Friday and Saturday. *Marie's* (☎ 637-5500, 86 E 100 South) is as fancy as Price restaurants get, with steaks and seafood ($12-15), prime rib ($10-16) and various pastas.

Four miles south in Wellington is *Cowboy's Kitchen* (☎ 637-4223, 31 E Main), just off Hwy 6/191. This authentic Western steakhouse and lounge fills up with area farmers and ranchers – who know a thing or two about well-cooked meat ($10-30). The local lamb is highly recommended.

Entertainment

For a beer, try *Mecca Club & Cafe* (☎ 637-9958, 75 W Main), which is in the 1913 Mahleres-Siampenos Building. Across the street, the *Silver Dollar Saloon* (☎ 637-9446, 36 W Main) has pool tables. There are several other bars within a block; all are fun and draw a young crowd, and most serve food.

Getting There & Away

The Greyhound bus (☎ 637-7153) stops at the Phillips 66 Service Station, 277 N Carbonville Rd, with one or two daily buses to Green River ($14, 1½ hours) and Denver, Colorado or to Salt Lake City ($23, 2½ hours).

NINE MILE CANYON

This National Backcountry Byway is billed as the 'longest art gallery in the world' for its abundance of Fremont Indian rock art; only Fremont Indian State Park (earlier in this chapter) can claim to have as high a concentration in Utah. In addition, you can spot Fremont granaries and structures along the canyon walls (bring binoculars). However, it is easy to miss many of the pictographs and petroglyphs; before going, pick up a guide to the sites at the BLM in Price (or in Roosevelt or Vernal, if you're coming from the north).

The good dirt and gravel road is passable to cars, though it is extremely dusty and can become impassable in wet weather; trucks also use the route, so drive carefully. Carry plenty of gas, food and water, as almost no services are available. From Price, the turnoff is 7½ miles east off Hwy 6/191; the first 12 miles are paved, and then it's another 9 miles to the canyon itself, which is actually 40 miles long. About 30 miles into the canyon, a dirt road leads north to Myton on Hwy 40 (33 miles away). Some of the best sites in the canyon are along the 10 miles east of this intersection; side canyons, some for 4WD only, also hold surprises. Allow four to six hours.

At the west end of the canyon is the only public rest stop, which has a covered picnic area and vault toilets. Otherwise, almost all of the land on either side of the road is private and off-limits for picnicking or camping, with one exception. About 23 miles from Hwy 6/191 is the simple *Nine Mile Ranch* (☎ 435-613-9794, 435-637-2572), which has spacious grounds and rustic pioneer cabins ($30-50), campsites ($10) and showers ($2). 'Bunk and breakfast' is $50 to $65. It's run by a 'retired' ranching couple who are the nicest folks you'd ever want to meet; they can arrange horse tours and hay rides and will cook Dutch-oven dinners on request ($13).

HUNTINGTON & AROUND

☎ 435 • pop 2131 • elevation 5680 feet

This mining town, settled in 1878, is about 20 miles south of Price on Hwy 10. It has few services for travelers. However, **Huntington State Park** (☎ 687-2491), 2 miles north of town, has a pretty lake offering fishing, boating, water-skiing and swimming. The tree-shaded, 22-site campground

($12) has showers (turned off in winter). Day use is $4.

Cleveland-Lloyd Dinosaur Quarry

This National Natural Landmark is operated by the BLM (☎ 636-3600 in Price). Over a dozen species of dinosaur were buried here 150 million years ago, making this one of the largest sites for dinosaur bones in the world. Excavations are intermittent but ongoing, and getting a peek at the exposed bones is the main attraction; there are no reconstructed dinosaurs. The stark high desert scenery also makes this worth a visit. A small visitor center has information and a gift shop; behind this are two large sheds protecting the quarry itself. Northwest of the quarry is the **Desert Lake State Waterfowl Reserve** (☎ 653-2900), an unusual desert marsh and lake where waterfowl and shorebirds migrate in spring and summer.

The quarry and visitor center are open daily from 10 am to 5 pm, Memorial Day to Labor Day, and on weekends only in spring and fall, but phone the BLM to confirm. Admission is $2; children under six are free. The remote site is well signed and the dirt roads are passable to cars (in dry weather). From Hwy 10, eight miles north of Huntington, Hwy 155 leads 17 miles to the quarry.

Cedar Mountain Overlook

Six miles west of the quarry, a good gravel road heads south for 20 miles (about 40 minutes), climbing 2000 feet through forest to the stunning overlook. There are toilets and picnic areas and dispersed camping is possible. The road is passable to cars only when dry. The BLM in Price has maps and information.

HUNTINGTON & ECCLES CANYONS SCENIC BYWAY

Hwys 31 and 264 west of Huntington are now a National Scenic Byway. This gorgeous drive – 86 miles in all – on the Wasatch Plateau parallels Huntington Creek, passes several mountain lakes (with fishing and boating) and contains numerous informa-

tion kiosks, picnicking spots and hiking trails. It connects with Skyline Drive (cars can drive from here north to Hwy 6), Fairview (44 miles to the end of Hwy 31) and **Scofield State Park** (☎ 435-448-9449), which surrounds a reservoir and has two summer-only campgrounds ($10). Along the byway, three summer-only USFS campgrounds ($8) have water and toilets but no showers. The ranger station and visitor centers in Price have complete details and maps.

CASTLE DALE
☎ 435 • pop 1657 • elevation 5771 feet
Settled in 1875, the mining town of Castle Dale is 9 miles south of Huntington. Its small **Museum of the San Rafael** (☎ 381-5252), 96 N 100 East, has tourist information and well-done natural history exhibits, along with a few standing dinosaurs and Indian artifacts (including the famous Sitterud Bundle). In city hall a half block away, the **County Pioneer Museum** (☎ 381-5154) features warmly displayed pioneer artifacts, many of them donated by residents. Both are open 10 am to 4 pm Monday to Friday, noon to 4 pm Saturday, year-round. Admission is by donation.

In late July or early August, the **Castle Valley Pageant** is a reenactment of the valley's pioneer history.

If you need a motel, *Village Inn Motel* (☎ 381-2309, 375 E Main) has two dozen that are clean and well-kept; rates are in the $30s.

JOES VALLEY RESERVOIR
From Hwy 10, 2 miles north of Castle Dale, paved Hwy 29 heads west 22 miles to the popular Joes Valley Reservoir. A small marina rents boats in summer, the fishing is great, and a store and restaurant are open May to early November. Cross-country skiing is popular in winter. The 49-site campground ($8) has water but no showers and is open from late May to mid-October. Other USFS campgrounds are nearby; the ranger stations in Price and Ferron have more information.

West of the reservoir, a dirt road climbs about 15 miles to Skyline Drive.

SAN RAFAEL RIVER & SWELL

This remote and ruggedly scenic area east of Hwy 10 used to be the hideout of outlaws. The BLM in Price has maps and information. You can explore by car and 4WD and camp in designated sites only, but be prepared in case you break down – you may see few other people.

The best road, and well worth the two- to three-hour commitment, is a graded gravel one that leaves Hwy 10 two miles north of Castle Dale and finishes about 43 miles later at I-70, 30 miles west of Green River. After 12½ miles, a spur road (look for a well; a sign follows) leads 6 miles south to **Wedge Overlook**, which offers spectacular views of the San Rafael River, 1200 feet below, as it cuts the 'Little Grand Canyon.' There is primitive camping here. Returning from the overlook, the road continues southeast for another 8 miles to the famous **Buckhorn Wash Pictographs**, a 100-foot-long panel of ghostly Barrier Canyon-style rock paintings. Four miles farther, the road crosses the San Rafael River and passes a historic suspension bridge (foot traffic only); a campground here has toilets but no drinking water. You reach I-70 after another 19 miles. The road is passable in ordinary cars except after heavy snow or rain. Numerous other 4WD trails lead off of it.

The San Rafael Swell continues south of I-70 – see the Southeastern Utah chapter.

FERRON

☎ 435 • pop 1623 • elevation 5996 feet

Settled in 1877, Ferron is 11 miles south of Castle Dale. The Manti-La Sal National Forest Ferron Ranger Station (☎ 384-2372, 384-2505), 115 W Canyon, PO Box 310, Ferron, UT 84523, has information on camping and boating at **Ferron Reservoir**, 28 miles west of town. Four miles west of town, **Millsite State Park** (☎ 687-2491) has golfing, trout fishing and a campground ($11) with showers. Day use is $4.

In town, *Gilly's Inn & Convenience Store* (☎ 384-3333, 15 N State) has nine surprisingly clean and comfortable nonsmoking rooms ($40-46).

Southwestern Utah

Locals call this part of the state 'Color Country,' but the prosaic label doesn't do it justice. The scenery in this part of Utah is so spectacular it has warranted the creation of three national parks – Zion, Bryce Canyon and Capitol Reef – as well as of the vast Grand Staircase-Escalante National Monument. The region is a veritable kaleidoscope of geological layers, and every day, every season, the shifting sunlight transforms each vista anew. After a few days, it is easy to understand why so many Utahns talk of becoming 'addicted' to the red rock.

Relatively little is known of the Indians who lived in this part of Utah. Ancestral Puebloans inhabited the area beginning about 1400 years ago, and their rock art can still be seen, but little remains here in the way of buildings. The Spanish Domínguez-Escalante missionaries passed quickly through the area in 1776, but it was not until the Mormons arrived in 1851 that permanent white settlement occurred in southwestern Utah.

This chapter is organized along the two main routes of Mormon settlement: the I-15 and Hwy 89 corridors. And it ends with the lovely drive along Hwy 12, from Bryce Canyon to Capitol Reef National Park.

I-15 Corridor & Zion National Park

East of I-15, the mountains start high in the 12,000-foot Tushars east of Beaver, drop to 11,000 in the Markagunt Plateau east of Cedar City, and drop farther to about 7000 feet in Zion National Park east of St George.

BEAVER
☎ 435 • pop 2454 • elevation 6000 feet

Settled by Mormons in 1856, Beaver soon became the gateway of a mining boom to the west, which led to tense confrontations between the rough, tough miners and the Mormon farmers. The outlaw Butch Cassidy was born here in 1866.

Today Beaver is an agricultural center and a crossroads town on I-15. Hwy 153 leads east into the Tushar Mountains, and Hwy 21 heads west into the desert. The Beaver County Travel Council (☎ 438-5438) has an office in the log cabin behind the library. The Fishlake National Forest Beaver Ranger Station (☎ 438-2436) is at 575 S Main, Beaver, UT 84713.

The Greyhound bus (☎ 438-2229) stops at the El Bambi Cafe, 935 N Main, on its I-15 run.

The best place to camp is the large *Beaver Canyon Campground (☎ 438-5654, 1419 E 200 North).* Open from May to October, it has tent/RV sites for $10/12, plus (surprise!) a decent Mexican restaurant (dinner only). *Beaver KOA (☎ 438-2924, 1428 N Manderfield Rd),* open February to November, has sites for $15.50/20. On the shore of a reservoir, *Minersville State Park*

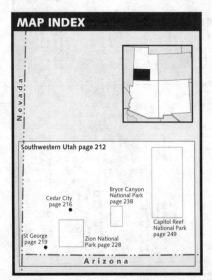

MAP INDEX

Nevada

Arizona

211

UTAH

SOUTHWESTERN UTAH

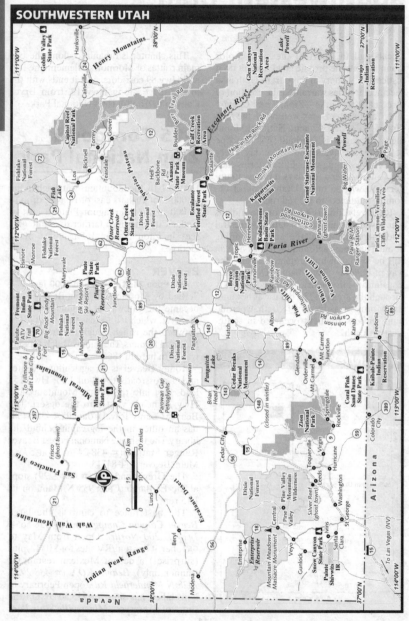

When Silver Was King

Today, all that remains of the silver mining town of Frisco, situated in the midst of lonely sagebrush plains, are the broken stone walls and foundations of a dozen buildings, five beehive kilns (on the National Historic Register), rusted and tumbled machinery and a cemetery.

The fenceless landscape looked much the same in 1875, when a vein of nearly pure silver was discovered in the nearby San Francisco Mountains. In a matter of weeks, a town sprung up, one that was as wild and rough as any in the West. By one count, it had 21 saloons, attracting all manner of gamblers, outlaws, prostitutes and miners eager for quick riches. Gunfights were a nightly occurrence, and soon Frisco had the largest cemetery in the state. A Nevada sheriff brought in to restore order killed six men his first night, just to make it clear that one building Frisco wouldn't need was a jail.

By 1885, Frisco had a railroad station and population of 6000. The main concern, the Silver Horn Mine, had already pulled out $50 million in silver when the unconventional open-pit mine collapsed between shift changes, miraculously killing no one but burying the vein beneath shattered timbers and thousands of tons of rock. Like tumbleweeds, people vanished, though over the next 35 years a few stayed on, dug a new shaft and slowly extracted another $20 million, making this one of the richest silver lodes in the world.

To reach the ghost town, take Hwy 21 off I-15 and look for a historical marker about 15 miles past Milford. Dirt roads crisscross the area (avoid in wet weather) and lead through the ruins. Those leading into the mountains are 4WD only.

(☎ 438-5472), 12 miles west of Beaver on Hwy 21, has a 29-site campground (closed in winter) with hookups and showers; camping is $14, day use $4.

A few rundown motels line S Main (rooms in the $30s). A noticeable step up, with rooms in the low $40s, are the attractive **Sleepy Lagoon Motel** (☎ 438-5681, 882 S Main); **Super 8** (☎ 438-3888), at exit 112; and **Country Inn** (☎ 438-2484), also at exit 112. Next door to a decent restaurant, the good-looking **Best Western Butch Cassidy Inn** (☎ 438-2438, 161 S Main) has 35 renovated rooms for $55 to $65.

EAST OF BEAVER

Hwy 153 heads east into Fishlake National Forest and the Tushar Mountains, emerging at Junction, 40 miles away. The east end of the road is gravel but passable to cars (closed by snow in winter). Contact the Beaver ranger for information on hiking and camping.

Eighteen miles east of Beaver, the **Elk Meadows Ski & Summer Resort** (☎ 888-881-7669) has recently expanded to 420 skiable acres. Still Utah's smallest alpine ski resort, it is a popular family destination. However, note that it has had some unusual closures; call ahead for seasonal dates or check online at www.elkmeadows.com.

In winter, six lifts service 36 runs between 900 and 10,400 feet in elevation. Adult lift tickets are $25, children are $15 and those over 65 ski free. There are ski rentals and lessons, a grocery store, places to eat and condos for rent.

During summer, the resort is a good base for fishing in the area. Hiking, picnicking and mountain biking are also popular – a mountain-bike shop offers rentals and guided trips.

PAROWAN

☎ 435 • pop 2565 • elevation 5990 feet

Founded in 1851, this small town 35 miles south of Beaver on I-15 offers mainly cheaper lodgings than Brian Head Ski Resort (see below). The city office (☎ 477-3331) and the summer-only visitor center

(☎ 477-8190, 888-727-6926) are both at 73 N Main.

The **Parowan Gap Petroglyphs**, an extensive array of rock art chiseled over a thousand-year period (now marred by modern graffiti), line a gravel road 11 miles west of Parowan along 400 North. Contact the Cedar City BLM for information.

For a night's sleep, try *Crimson Hills Motel (☎ 477-8662, 400 S Hwy 91),* with basic rooms in the mid-$30s; *Days Inn (☎ 477-3326, 888-530-3138, 625 W 200 South);* or *Swiss Village Inn (☎ 477-3391, 800-793-7401, 580 N Main),* the nicest place around with rooms for $60 to $64. Parowan's few restaurants are all closed Sunday.

BRIAN HEAD
☎ 435 • pop 118 • elevation 9700 feet

Brian Head is Utah's highest town and home to Brian Head Ski Resort. The chamber of commerce (☎ 677-2810, 888-677-2810), PO Box 190325, Brian Head, UT 84719, has information by mail or at www.brianheadutah.com. Note that altitude sickness can be a problem; a hasty descent usually provides relief (see Health in the Facts for the Visitor chapter).

Brian Head Ski Resort

This laid-back, increasingly popular resort (☎ 677-2035) is southern Utah's largest, offering great downhill skiing from Thanksgiving to early April. Six lifts service 53 runs between 9600 and 10,920 feet elevation. Adult day passes are $38; children under 12 and seniors over 60 pay $25. Snowboards are allowed. Brian Head bills itself as a family resort, and it has a snow tube park, childcare, a kids camp and ski instruction.

Cross-country skiing and snowmobiling are also popular, and groomed tracks lead to Cedar Breaks National Monument. Rentals are available.

Summers are deliciously cool (daytime highs in the 70°s F). There's plenty of great hiking and lift-served mountain biking. From July to October, the unpaved road up to 11,307-foot Brian Head Summit is open – great views!
website: www.brianhead.com

Places to Stay & Eat

There are no bottom-end lodgings. Reservations are unnecessary in summer (when discounts are offered) but suggested in winter. New lodgings are opening annually. Most are within walking distance of the slopes.

The Lodge at Brian Head (☎ 677-3222, 800-386-5634) has rooms starting in the $70s in winter. If you want a condominium, **Brian Head Reservation Center** *(☎ 677-2042, 800-845-9718, PO Box 190055, Brian Head, UT 84719)* and **Brian Head Condo Reservations** *(☎ 677-2045, 800-722-4742, PO Box 190217, Brian Head, UT 84719)* represent hundreds of choices, from $85 to $450.

The hotels and lodges have restaurants, and the Brian Head Mall has cheaper choices. The *Edge Restaurant (☎ 677-3343)* serves good steaks and seafood.

CEDAR BREAKS NATIONAL MONUMENT

This small national monument, about 10,400 feet above sea level atop the Markagunt Plateau, contains a massive natural amphitheater. Inside, a cascade of eroded spires and columns forms a neon-colored tapestry: fantastical layers of yellows, oranges, reds, purples and browns (the result of iron and manganese in the soil). Because of the high elevation, cars can reach Cedar Breaks only late May to October; during winter, it is the province of snowmobilers and cross-country skiers.

Most visitors simply stop at the four scenic overlooks, but two forested hiking trails lead a couple of miles along the rim. In addition, a 30-site summer-only campground ($9) has water and toilets. However, come prepared for near-freezing nighttime temperatures.

Cedar Breaks is on Hwy 148 between Hwys 143 and 14. The visitor center, near the south entrance, is open 8 am to 6 pm Memorial Day to Labor Day and 8 am to 5 pm to early October. There are exhibits, a bookshop and restrooms. Park rangers provide information and lead walks and other programs. Admission is free out of season or if you're just driving through. Otherwise, day use is $3 per person; national passes are accepted.

Further information is available from Cedar Breaks National Monument (☎ 435-586-9451), 2390 W Highway 56, Suite 11, Cedar City, UT 84720.

CEDAR CITY
☎ 435 • pop 20,527 • elevation 5800 feet

Mormon settlers founded Cedar City in November 1851. They found no cedars here, but they thought the abundant junipers smelled like them, and thus the town's name.

Today, Cedar City is southern Utah's second-largest town, and it is a natural stopping place for travelers headed to Zion, Cedar Breaks or Brian Head. In addition, its nationally recognized Utah Shakespearean Festival draws around 150,000 theatergoers annually from across the country.

Information
The chamber of commerce (☎ 586-4484), online at www.chambercedarcity.org, and the Iron County Tourism Bureau (☎ 586-5124, 800-354-4849), at www.scenicsouthern utah.com, are both at 581 N Main. They are open weekdays year-round, also on Saturday in summer.

For public lands information, contact the Dixie National Forest Cedar City Ranger Station (☎ 865-3200, 865-3799 for a recorded message), 82 N 100 East, PO Box 627, Cedar City, UT 84720; and the BLM (☎ 586-2401), 176 E DL Sargent Drive, which manages most of the land west of I-15.

Other services include the library (☎ 586-6661), 136 W Center; post office (☎ 586-6701), 333 N Main; medical center (☎ 586-6587), 595 S 75 East; and police (☎ 586-2956), 110 N Main.

Things to See & Do
Founded in 1897, Southern Utah University (☎ 586-7700), 351 W Center, has more than 7000 students. The campus is home to two early Mormon pioneer buildings, an attractive library (☎ 586-7933) and the intimate Braithwaite Fine Arts Gallery (☎ 586-5432),

which is open Monday to Saturday (admission is free).

The Mormon Tabernacle, popularly called the Rock Church, 75 E Center, was built in 1930 from locally quarried red rock; free tours are given Monday to Saturday in summer. Exhibits at Iron Mission State Park (☎ 586-9290), 635 N Main, describe the Mormons' early mining attempts. More interesting are the scores of horse-drawn 19th-century vehicles (stagecoaches, buggies, hearses, farm implements). Hours are 9 am to 5 pm (to 6 pm in summer); admission is $3 per person or $5 per car.

Special Events
Cedar City's main event, held annually at SUU since 1962, is the Utah Shakespearean Festival, which won the 2000 Tony Award for Outstanding Regional Theatre. The festival's summer season (late June to September) presents three of the Bard's plays plus three classics of the stage. In the expanded fall season (mid-September to mid-October), they present two more theatrical chestnuts. The productions are top quality, but it's the many extras that really draw the crowds and keep the town buzzing. During the summer, there are free seminars discussing the plays, free 'Greenshows' with minstrels in Elizabethan dress, Renaissance feasts with more entertainment, backstage visits, a range of classes for credit, child care during performances and more. The fall season has fewer extras.

Shakespeare's plays are performed in the roofless Adams Memorial Theater, which is an excellent reproduction of London's original Globe Theater. The other plays are performed in nearby Randall Jones Theater, and all stages are on the SUU campus. Reservations are recommended (☎ 586-7878, 800-752-9849) at least a week or two in advance. If you just show up, ask about returned tickets at the Courtesy Booth (☎ 586-7790), near the Adams Theater. A few last-row gallery tickets ($14, but still good seats) go on sale at the booth the day of the performance; come early. Tickets range from $20 to $42.

website: www.bard.org

UTAH

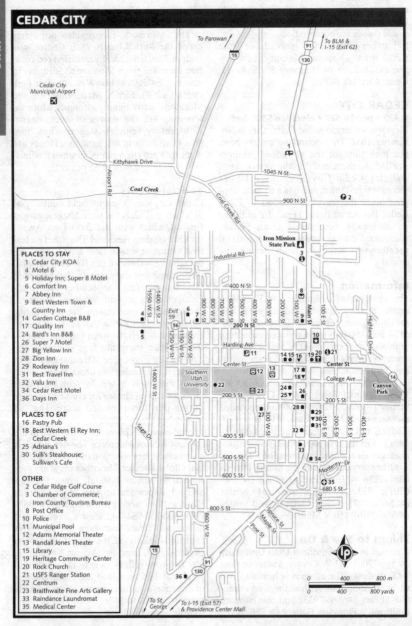

CEDAR CITY

To Parowan

Cedar City
Municipal Airport

Kittyhawk Drive

Coal Creek

1045 N St

900 N St

Airport Rd

Coal Creek Rd

To BLM &
I-15 (Exit 62)

Iron Mission
State Park

Industrial Rd

400 N St

200 N St

Harding Ave

Center St

Southern
Utah
University

200 S St

Center St

College Ave

Canyon
Park

Highland Drive

Sage Dr

400 S St

500 S St

600 S St

800 S St

Monterey Dr

680 S St

Spruce St

Maple St

Pine St

To St
George

To I-15 (Exit 57)
& Providence Center Mall

PLACES TO STAY
1 Cedar City KOA
4 Motel 6
5 Holiday Inn; Super 8 Motel
6 Comfort Inn
7 Abbey Inn
9 Best Western Town &
  Country Inn
14 Garden Cottage B&B
17 Quality Inn
24 Bard's Inn B&B
26 Super 7 Motel
27 Big Yellow Inn
28 Zion Inn
29 Rodeway Inn
31 Best Travel Inn
32 Valu Inn
34 Cedar Rest Motel
36 Days Inn

PLACES TO EAT
16 Pastry Pub
18 Best Western El Rey Inn;
  Cedar Creek
29 Adriana's
30 Sulli's Steakhouse;
  Sullivan's Cafe

OTHER
2 Cedar Ridge Golf Course
3 Chamber of Commerce;
  Iron County Tourism Bureau
8 Post Office
10 Police
11 Municipal Pool
12 Adams Memorial Theater
13 Randall Jones Theater
15 Library
19 Heritage Community Center
20 Rock Church
21 USFS Ranger Station
22 Centrum
23 Braithwaite Fine Arts Gallery
33 Raindance Laundromat
35 Medical Center

0   400   800 m
0   400   800 yards

Other special events can be combined with the Shakespearean Festival. The Utah Summer Games (☎ 865-8421) in mid- to late June are styled as a mini-Olympics and attract over 7600 amateur athletes competing in almost 40 events. The Midsummer Renaissance Fair (☎ 586-3711), in early July, is free and features more Renaissance entertainment. The American Folk Ballet (☎ 586-7872) has performances in mid-July in the new Heritage Community Center, at Main and Center. For a full list of annual events, contact the tourism bureau.

Places to Stay

Camping *Cedar City KOA* (☎ 586-9872, 1121 N Main) has showers, a pool, a playground, a grocery store and coin laundry. Sites range from $20 to $24; seven Kamping Kabins are $34. Also see Hwy 14 East of Cedar City (later in this chapter).

Budget & Mid-Range During the Shakespearean Festival (especially weekends) rates can be 50% higher than at other times. The following budget choices are no more than ports in a storm; all charge in the $40s to $50s in summer, in the $30s otherwise: *Valu Inn* (☎ 586-9114, 344 S Main); *Zion Inn* (☎ 586-9487, 222 S Main); *Cedar Rest Motel* (☎ 586-9471, 479 S Main); and *Best Travel Inn* (☎ 586-6557, 323 S Main). Your best bet in town is the newly renovated *Super 7 Motel* (☎ 586-6566, 190 S Main). Near I-15, exit 59, you'll find a *Motel 6* and *Super 8*.

Most of Cedar City's mid-range options are *chain hotels*; each has a swimming pool and nicely kept rooms. In summer, doubles run $60 to $100. Try Rodeway Inn, Comfort Inn, Days Inn, Quality Inn, Best Western (two locations) or Holiday Inn. The *Best Western Town & Country Inn* (☎ 586-9900, 800-493-4089, 200 N Main), is the biggest place in town, with 157 rooms. It's well run, has excellent facilities (including two pools and two hot tubs) and rents double rooms for $75 to $95.

The attractive non-chain *Abbey Inn* (☎ 586-9966, 800-325-5411, 940 W 200 North) has doubles for $80 to $85; ask about skier specials in winter.

B&Bs B&Bs are quite popular in Cedar City; below is just a sample. Call the tourism bureau for a full list, and make reservations far in advance for the Shakespearean Festival. All are nonsmoking.

The *Garden Cottage B&B* (☎ 586-4919, 16 N 200 West) has four charming rooms that run $85 to $95; see them at www.the gardencottagebnb.com. The *Bard's Inn B&B* (☎ 586-6612, 150 S 100 West) has seven rooms from $75 to $90.

The *Big Yellow Inn* (☎ 586-0960, 234 S 300 West) is a beautiful Georgian Revival home with 11 sumptuously eclectic rooms; rates are $85 to $180 and include full breakfast; the website is www.bigyellowinn.com. Even more luxurious is *Baker House B&B* (☎ 867-5695, 888-611-8181, 1800 Royal Hunte Dr), west of I-15. Its five rooms have king-size beds, spas and fireplaces, and run $109 to $159, including full breakfast.

Places to Eat

Fine dining is not Cedar City's strong suit, but with 30 or 40 places in town, you certainly won't go hungry.

For a morning or evening espresso, head to the friendly *Pastry Pub* (☎ 867-1400, 86 W Center), which serves baked goods and sandwiches all day.

Downtown, the place to go for reasonably priced American-style meals is *Sullivan's Cafe* (☎ 586-6761, 301 S Main). It adjoins the more upmarket *Sulli's Steakhouse*, which is open for dinner only; you can order a cocktail along with steaks, seafood and Italian entrées ($12-18). Serving breakfast all day, along with a wide-ranging sandwich and dinner menu, is *Cedar Creek Restaurant* (☎ 586-6311, 80 S Main) in the Best Western El Rey Inn.

East of town along Hwy 14 are two good Western steakhouses. *Rusty's Ranch House* (☎ 586-3839) is two miles east, and *Milt's Stage Stop* (☎ 586-9344) is five miles east. Both serve dinner only; make reservations.

Adriana's (☎ 865-1234, 164 S 100 West), with an Olde Worlde ambience, is famous among festival-goers. Decent American food is served at reasonable prices – under $10 for lunch and $10 to $20 for dinner.

Other easy-on-the-wallet choices line Main St; you can also try the Providence Center, a new mall south of town at Cross Hollow Rd and Royal Hunte Dr.

Entertainment

The new *Heritage Community Center*, at Center and Main, is meant to be the focus of community events, concerts, theater and dance. Call the visitors center for schedule information.

For 24-hour movie information, call ☎ 867-6261.

Getting There & Around

Skywest Airlines (☎ 586-3033, 800-453-9417) flies to and from Salt Lake City three times a day. The airport is 2 miles northwest of downtown Cedar City.

Greyhound (☎ 586-9465), 1744 Royal Hunte Dr (in a Chevron station at I-15, exit 57), runs four buses a day to Las Vegas, Nevada, ($31; 3½ hours) and two buses a day to Salt Lake City ($40; five hours). Another three go to Denver, Colorado ($85; 13 hours).

National Car Rental is at the airport (☎ 586-4004) and at the Best Western Town & Country Inn (☎ 586-9900). Speedy Rental (☎ 586-7368), 650 N Main, is another choice.

HWY 14 EAST OF CEDAR CITY

This paved scenic route leads 40 miles over the Markagunt Plateau, ending in Long Valley Junction at Hwy 89. The road crests at 10,000 feet with splendid views of Zion National Park to the south. There are campgrounds, hiking trails, fishing lakes and lodges; the Cedar City USFS Ranger Station has maps and information. Hwy 14 is kept open all year by snowplows, but snow tires or chains are required November to March. (Distances below are east of Cedar City.)

At 9200 feet **Navajo Lake** (25 miles) has a small marina with boat rentals, a lodge, a store, a small restaurant and three campgrounds ($10) with water. These facilities are open Memorial Day to October.

The **Duck Creek Area** (30 miles) has a summer-only National Forest visitor center

and *Duck Creek Campground* ($10). Tiny Duck Creek Village has several simple restaurants, equipment rental places and comfortable lodges, which fill up on many weekends year-round. Right on Hwy 14 are *Duck Creek Village Inn* (☎ 435-682-2565) and *Meadow View Lodge & Cabins* (☎ 435-682-2495, 977-384-0361). Rates range from $50 to $90.

A couple of miles east of Duck Creek Village, a signed dirt road (passable late May to October) to the south leads about 10 miles to **Strawberry Point**, with superb vistas. Near this intersection, a scenic alternate route north is paved Mammoth Creek Road, which leads to Hwy 143 and Panguitch Lake (later in this chapter).

ST GEORGE

☎ 435 • pop 49,663 • elevation 2880 feet

Less than an hour southwest of Cedar City along I-15, and 3000 feet lower in elevation, St George has a noticeably different climate. Summers are hot, with frequent highs over 100°F, and winters are exceedingly mild. As a result, the city is extremely popular with retirees and snowbirds, who relish the 300 days of sunshine a year and have made it Utah's fastest growing city outside of the Salt Lake metropolitan area. Its population nearly doubled from 1990 to 2000.

Tourism is St George's economic mainstay, and it has three main attractions: the state's best golfing, proximity to Zion National Park and an abundance of affordable lodgings. In addition, the Pine Valley Mountains west of town make for a cool summer retreat, and there are several well preserved Mormon buildings here, including the impressive Temple and Tabernacle.

Information

The chamber of commerce (☎ 628-1658), 97 E St George Blvd, is open weekdays and until 1 pm on Saturday. Online, try www.st georgechamber.com. The new Interagency Information Center (☎ 688-3246), 345 E Riverside Drive, has information on USFS and BLM lands, state parks and other recreation. It has maps and guides for sale and is open Monday to Saturday.

UTAH

ST GEORGE

PLACES TO STAY
1 Seven Wives Inn
2 An Olde Penny Farthing Inn
5 Western Safari Motel
9 Ancestor Inn
12 Best Western Coral Hills
13 Dixie Palm Motel
14 Desert Edge
15 Sands Motel
16 Comfort Inn
17 Motel 6
18 Travelodge
19 Days Inn
22 Ramada Inn
25 Greene Gate Village B&B; Judd's Store; Bentley House
27 Singletree Inn
28 Best Western Travel Inn
29 Sun Time Inn
30 Econo Lodge
31 Chalet Motel
32 Sunbird Inn
37 Settlers RV Park
39 Sullivan's Rococo Inn; Sullivan's Rococo Steak House
41 Holiday Inn
42 Super 8 Motel
44 Ranch Inn
45 McArthur's Temple View RV Park
46 Best Western Abbey Inn; Quality Inn
47 Claridge Inn
49 Budget Inn
50 Comfort Suites
51 Budget 8 Motel
52 Four Points Hotel-Sheraton
53 Ambassador Inn

PLACES TO EAT
10 Ancestor Square
21 Chuck-A-Rama
24 Bear Paw Coffee Company
43 Pancho & Lefty's

OTHER
3 Center for the Arts
4 Police; City Offices
6 Brigham Young Winter Home
7 Post Office
8 DUP Museum
11 Chamber of Commerce
20 Zion Factory Stores
23 Smith's Supermarket
26 Main St Theater & Ballroom
33 Mormon Tabernacle
34 Library
35 Federal Building
36 Red Rock Bicycle Company
38 Mormon Temple
40 Medical Center
48 Greyhound Bus Stop
54 Interagency Information Center

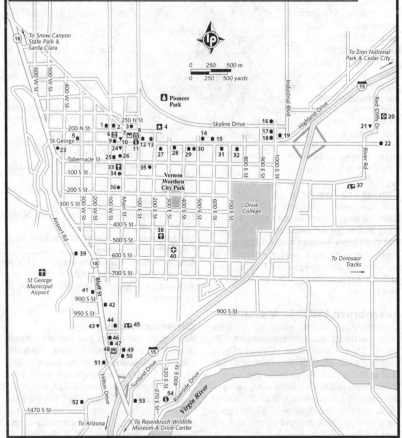

Other services include the library (☎ 634-5737), 50 S Main; post office (☎ 673-3312), 180 N Main; medical center (☎ 634-4000), 544 S 400 East; and police (☎ 634-5001), in the city offices, 175 E 200 North.

Historic Buildings
Tourist information offices have walking-tour brochures. Also Historic St George Live! (☎ 634-5942) runs guided tours ($2) June through August. Among the highlights are the 1877 **Mormon Temple**, Utah's first, which has a visitor center (☎ 673-5181), 250 E 400 South, that is open daily. The pretty **Mormon Tabernacle**, on Tabernacle and Main Sts, offers guided tours (☎ 628-4072) and hosts free music programs. The **Brigham Young Winter Home** (☎ 673-2517), 89 W 200 North, has free guided tours, and St George has a good **DUP Museum** (☎ 628-7274), 135 N 100 East.

Center for the Arts
This collection of historic buildings at 47 East 200 North contains the small yet satisfying **St George Art Museum** (☎ 634-5942) and the **Opera House** (☎ 634-5859), which hosts concerts and performances. The museum is open 6 to 8 pm on Monday, noon to 5 pm Tuesday through Saturday; admission is free.

Rosenbruch Wildlife Museum
Containing around 200 animal species from every continent, this new museum (☎ 656-0033), 1835 Convention Center Drive (south of Bluff St), is the fourth largest of its kind in the world. The animals are meticulously displayed in simulated outdoor environments. Adult admission is $5.50, seniors $4.50, and children three to 12 $2.50. Hours are 5 to 9 pm Monday and 10 am to 6 pm Tuesday through Saturday.

Dinosaur Tracks
In 2000, a St George resident unearthed what has turned out to be a spectacular collection of dinosaur footprints. Now covered and fenced, the dozens of tracks lie bare on the ground where they were made. Open 9 am to 5 pm Monday to Saturday, the site is free, but donations are encouraged. To get there, take 700 South to Riverside Drive.

Golf
The following courses are open to the public. Fees vary, but run from about $12 for nine holes to $25 for 18 holes in summer, and from $16 to $45 in winter, when tee times are best reserved in advance. The following courses in St George and nearby towns are in roughly ascending order of cost.

Twin Lakes (☎ 673-4441) 660 N Twin Lakes Drive, nine holes/par 27

Dixie Red Hills (☎ 634-5852) 1000 N 700 West nine holes/par 34

Southgate (☎ 628-0000) 1975 S Tonaquint Drive, 18 holes/par 70

St George Golf Club (☎ 634-5854) 2190 S 1400 East, 18 holes/par 73

Green Spring (☎ 673-7888) 588 N Green Spring Drive, Washington, 18 holes/par 71

Sky Mountain (☎ 635-7888) 1030 N 2600 West, Hurricane, 18 holes/par 72

Entrada at Snow Canyon (☎ 674-7500) 2511 W Entrada Trail, 18 holes/par 72

Sunbrook (☎ 634-5866) 2240 Sunbrook Drive, 18 holes/par 72

Other Activities
After your golf round, you can play **tennis** at the Vernon Worthen City Park, 200 S 400 East. Or go **swimming** at the indoor Sand Hollow Aquatics Center (☎ 634-5938), 1144 N Lava Flow Dr in Santa Clara, which includes a fun-filled 'leisure pool' for the kids.

The area has a number of trails for **mountain biking**, and the uncrowded and scenic Gooseberry Mesa off of Hwy 59 near

Hurricane (see the Zion National Park map) has some challenging slickrock trails. The Interagency Information Center has details and directions, as does Red Rock Bicycle Company (☎ 674-3185), 190 S Main, which rents bikes.

Special Events

St George is the spring break capital of Utah. For several weekends around Easter, students convene en masse and cruise St George Boulevard, which is closed to traffic. The St George Arts Festival elbows its way onto Main Street during Easter weekend itself. The Dixie Round-up, a PRCA rodeo, takes place in mid-September. October sees the St George Marathon and the World Senior Games; both are increasingly popular.

Places to Stay

St George has the biggest selection of accommodations in southern Utah. National chains are predominant, and most are clustered along St George Boulevard and on Bluff St near I-15. Rates remain fairly constant year-round, except for special events and conventions, when the town can become almost entirely booked. If the town is quiet, expect deep discounts.

Camping Snowbirds in RVs flock to St George in the winter, and a number of campgrounds cater to them; tenters are not as well cared for. All the following have toilets, showers, coin laundry, pools and play areas; rates range from $12 to $16 for tents and from $18 to $24 for full hookups. Try *McArthur's Temple View RV Park* (☎ 673-6400, 800-776-6410, 975 S Main); *Redlands RV Park* (☎ 673-9700, 800-553-8269, 650 W Telegraph), in Washington; *Settlers RV Park* (☎ 628-1624, 800-628-1624, 1333 E 100 South); or *St George Campground & RV Park* (☎ 673-2970, 2100 E Middleton Drive).

There's also camping in Snow Canyon State Park and Pine Valley later in this chapter.

Budget Many of the inexpensive motels offer weekly rates, and most have pools. At the bottom of the budgets is *Western Safari Motel* (☎ 673-5238, 310 W St George Blvd), which has 16 worn rooms in the mid-$20s. A step up, with plain but acceptably clean rooms in the low to mid $30s, are *Sands Motel* (☎ 673-3501, 581 E St George Blvd); *Ancestor Inn* (☎ 673-4666, 800-864-6882, 60 W St George Blvd); and *Desert Edge* (☎ 673-6137, 525 E St George Blvd), which specializes in weekly rentals.

The renovated rooms at *Chalet Motel* (☎ 628-6272, 664 E St George Blvd) are the same price and a better deal, as is the *Dixie Palm Motel* (☎ 673-3531, 185 E St George Blvd).

One of the best budget choices is the *Sun Time Inn* (☎ 673-6181, 800-237-6253, 420 E St George Blvd), which has pleasant non-smoking rooms for $33/39 single/double midweek, and $6 more on weekends.

Mid-Range At *Sullivan's Rococo Inn* (☎ 628-3671, 888-628-3671, 511 S Airport Rd), it's the location – on the bluff overlooking St George and the distant red cliffs – that makes this a recommended choice. Though it's next to the airport, there's very little noise, and the standard rooms (in the $40s) are perfectly clean; all have balconies. There is also a good steak house (see Places to Eat).

Also pleasant is the Southwestern-themed *Sunbird Inn* (☎ 628-9000, 888-628-9081, 750 E St George Blvd), which has newly renovated and spacious rooms for $35/45 single/double midweek ($10 more on weekends) and a particularly nice pool area.

Chain hotels make up most of the rest of the mid-range offerings; all have pools and rates that range from the $40s to the mid-$50s, with higher prices for suites. They include Motel 6, Super 8, Budget Inn, Quality Inn, Claridge Inn, Days Inn, Comfort Inn, Travelodge and Econo Lodge. Three nicer Best Western properties and a Ramada Inn are $10 to $15 more. Chain-equivalent independent hotels include *Ambassador Inn* (☎ 673-7900, 877-373-7900, 1481 S Sunland Drive); *Budget 8 Motel* (☎ 628-5234, 800-275-3494, 1230 S Bluff); *Ranch Inn* (☎ 628-8000, 800-332-0040, 1040

S Main); and *Singletree Inn* (☎ 673-6161, 800-528-8890, 260 E St George Blvd).

Top End There are 122 mini-suites at the *Comfort Suites* (☎ 673-7000, 800-245-8602, 1239 S Main) in the $70s and $80s. Two large full-service hotels with convention facilities, health spas and restaurants are *Four Points Hotel – Sheraton* (☎ 628-0463, 800-662-2525, 1450 S Hilton Drive), and *Holiday Inn* (☎ 628-4235, 800-465-4329, 850 S Bluff). Doubles are $80 to $100 and up.

B&Bs Nine different historic buildings, some dating from the 1870s, make up the *Greene Gate Village B&B* (☎ 628-6999, 800-350-6999, 76 W Tabernacle), a pleasant, relaxing complex of about 18 rooms and suites. Though they vary, each room is furnished with authentic, lovely antiques and has a modern private bathroom. Individual rooms and suites are $80 to $130 (most under $100) from Sunday to Thursday and $10 more on weekends; full breakfast is included. Entire houses can be rented. Large grounds include a pool, hot tub, picnic and barbecue areas and a library. Smoking is not permitted.
website: www.greenegate.com

The *Seven Wives Inn* (☎ 628-3737, 800-600-3737, 217 N 100 West) is made up of two historic homes with 12 rooms between them; each has a private bath with a claw-foot tub. The antique furnishings are sometimes playfully unique. Rates are $75 to $150, including full breakfast. There is a pool, and no smoking is allowed.
website: www.sevenwivesinn.com

Nearby is *An Olde Penny Farthing Inn* (☎ 673-7755, 800-943-2920, 278 N 100 West), a restored pioneer house with five non-smoking rooms with private bath. Rates are $60 to $120.

Places to Eat
As with its hotels, St George has more than its share of middle-of-the-road chain restaurants lining the main thoroughfares, but there are a few surprises worth searching out.

Bear Paw Coffee Company (☎ 634-0126, 75 N Main) specializes in Belgian waffles, country breakfasts, espresso coffees and fruit smoothies. Open daily till 3 pm (till 2 pm on Sunday).

The northwest corner of Main and St George Blvd is called **Ancestor Square**, and has several restaurants of varying quality. *Pizza Factory* (☎ 628-1234) and *Pasta Factory* (☎ 674-3753) are as good as their names; *JJ Hunan* (☎ 628-7219) serves sushi and Chinese. The new *Painted Pony* (☎ 634-1700) aims higher. It has a nice ambience and modestly inventive Southwestern cuisine. Dinner entrees run $15 to $18; open daily for lunch and dinner.

For decent Mexican food, there's the family-friendly *Paula's Cazuela* (☎ 673-6568, 745 W Ridge View Drive) a little northwest of downtown, and *Pancho & Lefty's* (☎ 628-4772, 1050 S Bluff).

Among the Zion Factory Stores along Red Cliffs Drive are a number of chain restaurants, but the best value is at *Chuck-A-Rama* (☎ 673-4464, 127 N Red Cliffs Drive), with a variety of good all-you-can-eat buffets.

The premiere place in town for steak or seafood is *Sullivan's Rococo Steak House* (☎ 673-3305) at the Rococo Inn. The cliff-side dining room boasts wonderful city views, and the succulent prime rib couldn't be thicker. Hours are 11 am to 3 pm Monday to Saturday and 5 to 10 pm nightly.

The *Seven Wives Inn* (☎ 628-3737) serves dinners by reservation only in the house's atmospheric dining room (see B&Bs, above). The chef prepares a special five-course set menu most nights for around $30 per person. A similar romantic experience can be had at the *Bentley House* (☎ 628-6999) in the Greene Gate Village B&B, which also prepares an elegant five-course meal, by reservation only, on Thursday, Friday and Saturday nights. Also part of Greene Gate Village is the old-fashioned *Judd's Store* (☎ 628-2596, 62 W Tabernacle), which serves sandwiches and delicious shakes.

Entertainment
From October to May, Dixie College (☎ 652-7994) hosts a Celebrity Concert Series as well as plays and musicals at the

Fine Arts Center Theater (☎ 628-3121, 225 S
700 East). During the summer, the Community Arts Program (☎ 634-5942) hosts
outdoor concerts and festivals. Also call the
Dixie Center (☎ 628-7003) for other cultural entertainment.

Once renovations are complete, the
Main St Theater and Ballroom, 35 N Main,
will produce a variety of concerts, shows
and dances; for more information, contact
the Roland Lee Guitar Gallery (☎ 688-9500,
877-679-9500), in the same location.

The outdoor *Tuacahn Amphitheater*
(☎ 652-3200, 800-746-9882), 10 miles northwest of town in Ivins, has a summer season
of two or three classic Broadway musicals,
and hosts a variety of concerts and performances the rest of the year. In summer,
performances are Monday to Saturday, and
dinner is served before the show. Tickets
range from $20 to $29 for adults, $14 to $20
for six- to 12-year-olds; dinner is about $10
extra. For details see www.tuacahn.org.

Movies (☎ 673-1994) are shown at six
cinema complexes around town.

Getting There & Away
The airport (☎ 673-3451) is on a bluff overlooking downtown. Skywest Airlines
(☎ 800-453-9417) has six daily flights to and
from Salt Lake City, with connections to
other cities.

Greyhound (☎ 673-2933) leaves from the
McDonald's at 1235 S Bluff, with four buses
to Salt Lake City ($44, six hours) and Las
Vegas ($25, two hours).

St George Shuttle (☎ 628-8320, 800-933-
8320) has nine vans a day direct to Las
Vegas Airport ($25). Another daily van goes
to and from Salt Lake ($55), making stops
at all the major towns on I-15.

Getting Around
Dixie Area Rapid Transit (☎ 652-0640) runs
a citywide bus service. Cost is $1, and buses
run every half hour.

For a car rental, National (☎ 673-5098),
Avis (☎ 634-3940) and Hertz (☎ 652-9941)
are at the airport. Also try Budget (☎ 673-
6825), 176 W St George Blvd; Dollar
(☎ 628-6549), 150 E 1160 South; Enterprise

(☎ 634-1556), 652 E St George Blvd; and
Thrifty (☎ 656-3247), 1405 S Sunland Dr.

AROUND ST GEORGE
Snow Canyon State Park
Snow? Ha! Not in this hot desert country.
But the striking, beautiful canyon is well
worth visiting: Cinder cones and jumbled
black lava flows are juxtaposed against red
and white sandstone cliffs. Relatively short,
one- to three-mile hikes lead to unusual formations, including lava caves. Summers are
searingly hot, so bring plenty of water and
sun protection. Some areas may be closed in
spring to protect nesting raptors and breeding desert tortoises.

The scenic campground has showers and
costs $13/15 for tents/RVs; reservations
(☎ 800-322-3770) are recommended during
spring and fall weekends.

On Hwy 18, 1½ miles north of St George,
take Snow Canyon Parkway and follow
signs through the towns of Santa Clara and
Ivins to the main entrance; the park road
returns to Hwy 18, and this 17-mile loop is a
popular drive or bike ride. Day use is $5 per
vehicle. For further information, contact the
park (☎ 435-628-2255).

Veyo Pool
This recreation area (☎ 574-2300) is on the
Santa Clara River near the tiny village of
Veyo, 19 miles north of St George on Hwy
18. The main attraction is a swimming pool
filled by naturally warmed spring water
(about 80°F), but there's also a café, picnicking area, sun deck and rock climbing
areas. It is open from May to Labor Day
from noon to 8 pm (or later). Swims are
about $4, picnicking $6, climbing (18 or
older) $4, and two large campsites are $20.

Mountain Meadows
Massacre Monument
About 10 miles north of Veyo on Hwy 18 is
this somber monument to one of the darkest
incidents in the Mormon settlement of Utah.
In 1857, for reasons that remain unclear,
Mormons and local Indians killed about 120
non-Mormon pioneers – including women
and children – who were migrating through

the area. You can visit the gravesite and get a scenic panorama of the valley where the incident occurred.

Pine Valley Mountain Wilderness

At 70 sq miles, this is Utah's second largest wilderness area, after the High Uintas, and it offers gorgeous, temperate hiking in July and August when the rest of southwest Utah is hotter than a cast-iron skillet. To get there, exit Hwy 18 at Central and head east to the bucolic village of Pine Valley (32 miles from St George); the wilderness area, within the Dixie National Forest, begins a few miles farther. The mountains rise sharply from the desert floor. The highest point, Signal Peak (10,365 feet), still has snow in July. Pine Valley, at 6529 feet, is usually 10 to 15 degrees cooler than St George.

Many hikes begin as strenuous climbs. The 5-mile Mill Canyon Trail is the 'easiest' to hook up with the 35-mile Summit Trail; it has a few stream crossings and reaches a pretty meadow. *Loving the Laccolith* by Bridget McColville is a good hiking guide.

Three miles beyond Pine Valley is a cluster of popular campgrounds (open late May through October, weather depending); all have water but no showers and cost $8 to $11. Day use is $2. Reservations (☎ 877-444-6777) are recommended on weekends; bring mosquito repellent. The ranger station in St George can provide maps and useful trail information.

The town of Pine Valley has only one place to stay, the newly renovated *Pine Valley Lodge* (☎ 574-2544, 888-750-7800, 960 E Main). Four simple, clean lodge rooms are $75, and six rustic cabins (shared bath) are $50. There's a café and various rentals.

Silver Reef Ghost Town

Near Leeds, off I-15 exit 22, 13 miles northeast of St George, is this abandoned, 19th-century silver-mining town. Today, the cemetery and a few dilapidated ruins remain. The Wells Fargo building has been restored. It houses a small museum and art gallery (☎ 879-2254). An adjacent information center has accurate dioramas of the old town and mine, providing a good feel for what it was like.

HURRICANE

☎ 435 • pop 8250 • elevation 3266 feet

As with St George, retirees have flocked to this town, doubling its population in the past decade. And as with St George, the main draw is affordable accommodations close to Zion National Park (25 miles east). The small chamber of commerce (☎ 635-3402) is at Main and 100 South.

Pah Tempe Hot Springs

A mile north of town, these pleasant hot springs (☎ 635-2879, 888-726-8367), 825 N 800 East, make a healthy, relaxing oasis. They include a swimming pool and a series of dip pools that empty into the Virgin River, plus there are massage therapists, yoga programs and other treatments. The hot springs are smoke-free, alcohol-free, and require bathing suits, and you can camp or stay in B&B rooms (see below). Day-use fees are $10 for adults, $5 for two- to 12-year-olds; it's open daily, and reservations are recommended on weekends.

Places to Stay & Eat

Fast-food places make up the bulk of dining options. *Jerry's Café* (☎ 635-1005, 270 W State St), serves cheap diner food daily.

Eschew Hurricane's dusty RV parks and drive 10 miles east on Hwy 9 to *Zion River Resort* (☎ 635-8594, 800-838-8594). Open year-round, it has 70 pristine – almost sparkling – sites and a slew of amenities: pool, cable TV, showers, laundromat, convenience store and much more. Tents/RVs are $20/$30-33; simple cabins are $35 to $40.

Hurricane boasts the excellent, well-run HI *Dixie Hostel* (☎ 635-8202/9000, 73 S Main), at the junction of Hwys 9 and 59, which charges $15 per person in dorms and has a few private doubles. Kitchen, laundry and linen are provided and reservations are suggested; a health food store is next door.

Otherwise, the rest of the choices in town are *chain motels*, with summer rates from the $50s to the $70s; choices include Motel 6, Best Western, Super 8, Days Inn and Comfort Inn.

Just outside of town, the *Pah Tempe Hot Springs B&B* (see above) is not posh, but the six spacious rooms, some of which share a bath, run $70 to $80; rates include full breakfast and use of the springs. It also has tent sites ($30 for two).

SPRINGDALE
☎ 435 • pop 457 • elevation 3800 feet
Perfectly positioned in an attractive red rock canyon at the entrance to Zion National Park, Springdale offers park visitors a relative abundance of interesting lodgings and good restaurants. Despite generally higher prices than St George and Hurricane, it makes the area's most comfortable base. Most businesses are along Zion Park Blvd (lower address numbers are closest to the park entrance).

Tourist information is available in summer; look for a sign. Year-round, you can contact the Zion Canyon Chamber of Commerce (☎ 722-3757), PO Box 331, Springdale, UT 84767-0331 or www.zionpark.com. Emergency medical care is available May through October at Zion Medical Clinic (☎ 772-3226), 120 Lion Blvd.

Things to See & Do
Overshadowed by magnificent cliffs, the **OC Tanner Amphitheater** (☎ 652-7994) hosts a variety of musical, theatrical and multimedia events – happenings occur nightly throughout the summer. The **Southern Utah Folklife Festival** is held here in September.

In summer, the **Zion Canyon Cinemax Theater** (☎ 772-2400), in a retail complex at the entrance to Zion National Park, has hourly showings of the giant-screen movie *Zion Canyon – Treasures of the Gods*. At night, they screen 35mm Hollywood blockbusters like *Star Wars*. Admission is $7.50 for adults and $4.50 for children.

Bicycles, kayaks and inner tubes (for tubing down the Virgin River) are available for rent – just look for signs. Zion Adventure Company (☎ 772-1001), 36 Lion Blvd, leads canyoneering and rock climbing trips;

come here to rent gear and to get maps and advice if you're planning to hike The Narrows (in Zion National Park), or consult www.zionadventures.com.

In nearby Rockville, **Grafton ghost town** contains a restored 1886 meeting house, a crumbling general store and several log homes (on private property) – all standing empty and mute save for the wind ghosting through them. The bicycle scene in *Butch Cassidy and the Sundance Kid* was filmed here. From Hwy 9, turn south on 200 East (also called Bridge Lane), then follow signs to the right and, after the second cattle guard, bear right at the fork. It's about 3 miles.

Springdale has numerous **gift stores**, ranging from roadside Western stands to galleries with expensive Southwestern art.

Places to Stay
Camping *Zion Canyon Campground* (☎ 772-3237, 479 Zion Park Blvd) has almost 200 sites, a restaurant, store, playground and coin laundry – not to mention a gorgeous riverside location. Tents/RVs are $16/20, and several camping cabins are about $40; reservations are essential. Showers are available for walk-ins ($3). The national park also has campgrounds.

Motels Roughly April to October is the high season; Memorial Day to Labor Day is particularly busy and hotels charge much more. In winter, you can expect discounts of around $20 on the prices quoted below. Lodgings in Springdale are almost uniformly good, and most have at least a few rooms with marvelous views. Reservations are recommended, especially on weekends.

The always friendly *El Rio Lodge* (☎ 772-3205, 888-772-3205, 995 Zion Park Blvd) has 11 clean rooms for $47/52 with one/two beds in summer. The rustic-looking and popular *Pioneer Lodge* (☎ 772-3233, 800-772-3233, 838 Zion Park Blvd) has 41 rooms ($60 to $70) and two sizeable apartments ($130 and $160). *Terrace Brook Lodge* (☎ 772-3932, 800-342-6779, 990 Zion Park Blvd) has 26 rooms for about $50/65 for singles/doubles.

Zion Park Motel (☎ 772-3251, 855 Zion Park Blvd) has a pool, playground and coin laundry. Doubles are $69, and two apartments are $110. The pleasant *Bumbleberry Inn* (☎ 772-3224, 800-828-1534, 897 Zion Park Blvd) has a popular restaurant, a pool and indoor racquetball court. Forty-seven sizable clean rooms, each with a private deck, are $65 to $80; see www.bumble berry.com.

Canyon Ranch Motel (☎ 772-3357, 668 Zion Park Blvd) is a little different: rooms are in homey, spacious cottages around a shaded lawn. Summer rates are $58 to $88; kitchenettes are $10 more. The *Best Western Zion Park Inn* (☎ 772-3200, 800-934-7275, 1215 Zion Park Blvd) has 120 nice but surprise-free rooms ($95).

You may get the most for your upscale dollar at *Flanigan's Inn* (☎ 772-3244, 800-765-7787, 428 Zion Park Blvd), not far from the park entrance. A pool, hot tub and wood-framed buildings are set in attractively landscaped grounds. Most of the cozy, artfully rustic rooms have porches with good views. Doubles are $80 to $100, and four suites are $150 to $190. It also has a top-notch restaurant.

Cliffrose Lodge (☎ 772-3234, 800-243-8824, 281 Zion Park Blvd) is set in five wooded acres so close to the park you can walk. All rooms are large and have great views, but the location will cost you: namely, $119 to $145.
website: www.cliffroselodge.com

It's hard to find fault in the artfully modern, romantic *Desert Pearl Inn* (☎ 772-8888, 888-828-0898, 707 Zion Park Blvd). Everything reflects the exceedingly good taste and jet-setting lifestyle of the owners: pressed tin headboards, earthen jugs, vaulted ceilings, historic railroad trestle beams, bidets, hardwood floors and all the expected upscale conveniences. Rates are $98 to $118; the most secluded hideaways are in the riverside building. The pool and hot tub are fabulous.
website: www.desertpearl.com

B&Bs As you might expect, Springdale has a growing number of very nice B&Bs;

unless otherwise noted, all are nonsmoking and include full breakfast. To write to them, add Springdale, UT 84767 to the address.

Quaint *O'Toole's B&B* (☎ 772-3457, 980 Zion Park Blvd) has four antique-filled rooms ($69 to $79) and a larger suite ($125). Next door is *Red Rock Inn B&B* (☎ 772-3139, 998 Zion Park Blvd) or online at www.redrockinn.com. The four spacious rooms ($82) and one suite ($135) have jetted tubs and breakfast baskets delivered in the morning.

Harvest House (☎ 772-3880, 29 Canyon View Drive) is a modern house with four spacious and light bedrooms, each with private bath. Rates range from $90 to $110 a double.

The tiny town of Rockville, a few miles west of Springdale, contains a few more modest but very friendly B&Bs. Add Rockville, UT 84763 to addresses. Rates range from $55 to $90 in summer. The *Blue House* (☎ 772-3912, 125 E Main), *Hummingbird Inn* (☎ 772-3632, 800-964-2473, 37 W Main) and *Dream Catcher Inn* (☎ 772-3600, 225 E Main) each have four rooms. The plain, two-room *Serenity House* (☎ 772-3393, 800-266-3393, 149 E Main) has a fruit orchard and serves organic meals.

Places to Eat

In season, the *Springdale Market*, on Hwy 9 just outside town, sells local organic fruits and vegetables, plus sandwiches and breads. The *Zion Park Market*, 855 Zion Park Blvd, is a small grocery.

The most popular place in town is the *Bit & Spur Restaurant & Saloon* (☎ 772-3498, 1212 Zion Park Blvd), which serves dinner from 5 to 9:30 pm; the saloon stays open till midnight. You'll find tasty, upscale Mexican and Southwestern cuisine (entrées $9 to $16), plus live music on weekends. Open daily, the *Pioneer Restaurant* (☎ 772-3009, 828 Zion Park Blvd), next to the Pioneer Lodge, is the local choice for a home-style breakfast; lunch and dinner are good, too.

Zion Pizza & Noodle Company (☎ 772-3815, 868 Zion Park Blvd) is another favorite, with inventive pizzas ($13), good pastas ($10) and a beer garden with a wide selection of microbrews. Half a dozen delis make it easy to put together an interesting park lunch, or there's ***Oscar's Café (☎ 772-3232, 948 Zion Park Blvd)***, which has a wider menu, including breakfast, and a great attitude.

The ***Bumbleberry Restaurant (☎ 772-3611)***, in the Bumbleberry Inn, serves decent American food, but the real draw is the yummy bumbleberry pies and pancakes. What are bumbleberries? They'll be happy to show you. The more upmarket ***Switchback Grille (☎ 772-3700)***, at the Best Western Zion Park Inn, features wood-fired pizza and grilled steaks ($13 to $25). The ***Spotted Dog Café (☎ 772-3244)***, at Flanigan's Inn, is one of the fanciest places in this casual town. It's open for breakfast and dinner only. In the evening, you can count on gourmet, Western-style cooking – though the menu changes frequently with the season and the whims of the chef.

ZION NATIONAL PARK
☎ 435

The white, pink and red rocks of Zion are so huge, overpowering and magnificent that they are at once a photographer's dream and despair. Few photos can do justice to the unparalleled scenery found in this, the first national park established in Utah (in 1919).

But heaven knows, people try. In fact, 2.5 million people arrive annually, about half of them from June to September, everyone wanting to drive the narrow, paved scenic road through Zion Canyon, a half-mile-deep slash formed by the humble Virgin River. Traffic had gotten so bad – with 5000 cars a day trying to fit into 450 parking spaces – that in 2000 the National Park Service (NPS) implemented a shuttle bus service (for details, see 'The Zion Park Shuttle' boxed text). Now, from spring to fall, Zion Canyon is closed to private automobiles, and this has resulted in some immediate and salutary changes: the park is much quieter, people seem calmer and more respectful, and you can see more wildlife than ever before.

And, ironically enough, more people can get into the park, and they are staying longer. It is relatively easy to escape the tourist hordes, however: simply hike, or take a guided horseback-riding trip, into the spectacularly wild country beyond the scenic pullouts.

Orientation
Three roads enter the park. Hiking trails depart from all three roads, leading you further into the splendor.

At the southern end, the paved Zion-Mt Carmel Hwy (Hwy 9 between Mt Carmel Junction and Springdale) is the most popular route and leads past the entrance of Zion Canyon. This road has fine views, but it is also steep, twisting and narrow. A tunnel on the east side of Zion Canyon is so narrow that escorts must accompany vehicles over 7 feet, 10 inches (2.4m) wide or 11 feet, 4 inches (3.46m) tall (in summer, the tunnel is staffed; in the off season, call ☎ 772-3256 in advance to arrange an escort; the fee is $10). Bicycles are prohibited in the tunnel unless they are transported on a vehicle. The Zion Canyon Rd itself is an off-shoot of Hwy 9, dead-ending about 7 miles up the canyon. The main visitor center, museum and two campgrounds lie at the mouth of Zion Canyon, and Zion Lodge is partway along Zion Canyon Rd. The elevation in Zion Canyon is about 4000 feet, increasing to 5700 feet at the east entrance.

For the middle of the park, paved **Kolob Terrace Rd** leaves Hwy 9 at the village of Virgin (elevation 3550 feet) and climbs north for about 11 miles to Lava Point (elevation 7890 feet), where there is a ranger station and primitive campground. This road is closed by snow from about November to May. The road continues out of the park past Kolob Reservoir to Hwy 14 and Cedar City as a dirt road (impassable after rain). Another dirt road branches off to I-15. This is the least used park road, and vehicles over 20 feet long are not recommended.

At the north end, the paved **Kolob Canyons Rd** leaves I-15 at exit 40 and extends 5 miles into the park. There is a small visitor center, but no camping. The

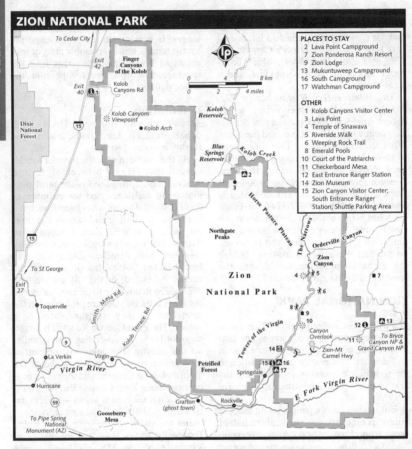

ZION NATIONAL PARK

PLACES TO STAY
2   Lava Point Campground
7   Zion Ponderosa Ranch Resort
9   Zion Lodge
13 Mukuntuweep Campground
16 South Campground
17 Watchman Campground

OTHER
1   Kolob Canyons Visitor Center
3   Lava Point
4   Temple of Sinawava
5   Riverside Walk
6   Weeping Rock Trail
8   Emerald Pools
10 Court of the Patriarchs
11 Checkerboard Mesa
12 East Entrance Ranger Station
14 Zion Museum
15 Zion Canyon Visitor Center;
    South Entrance Ranger
    Station; Shuttle Parking Area

road (more than 5000 feet above sea level)
is open all year.

There is so much to see in Zion that
entire books have been written about it. The
descriptions below are necessarily brief, but
remember that free maps and information
are available from the entrance stations and
visitor centers, and hiking guidebooks can
be useful.

Information

In 2000, a new, expanded visitor center
(☎ 772-3256) opened on Hwy 9 near the
park entrance. The building itself is a model

of energy-efficient building techniques, and
outdoor displays help orient you to the
park. Inside is an excellent bookstore and
other interesting exhibits.

Park rangers answer questions and present a variety of programs, including Junior
Ranger Programs for six- to 12-year-olds.
These run from Memorial Day to Labor
Day, last 2½ hours, and are offered twice a
day Tuesday to Saturday ($2). Other free
programs (discussions, demonstrations,
hikes etc) run March to November. Visitor
center hours are 8 am to 5 pm daily, till 7 pm
in summer.

Zion Museum, a half-mile north of the visitor center, is slated to open in 2002. This cultural museum will focus on the human history of Zion Canyon.

The smaller Kolob Canyons Visitor Center (☎ 586-9548), at the beginning of Kolob Canyons Rd, is open 8 am to 4:30 pm and also has park exhibits, information, books and maps.

Park entrance fees vary depending on which road you use to enter the park. At the southern, Hwy 9, entrance, it's $10 per person (on foot, bicycle or motorcycle) or $20 per private vehicle. At Kolob Canyons Rd, it's $10 per vehicle; entrance along Kolob Terrace Rd is free. Tickets are valid for entrance for seven days, and national passes are accepted.

In an emergency, call the visitor centers, or ☎ 911 or ☎ 772-3322, 24 hours a day.

Further information is available from the Superintendent, Zion National Park, Springdale, UT 84767.

Climate & When to Go The park's 'high season' extends from April to November, but the largest crush of visitors is from Memorial Day to Labor Day; if you're camping, arrive early in the morning to be assured a spot. Only about 7% of the annual visitors come in the December to February period.

Summer weather is hot (well over 100°F is common), so be prepared with plenty of water and sun protection. Temperatures drop into the 60°s F at night, even in midsummer. The summers are generally dry with the exception of about six weeks from late July to early September, when the so-called 'monsoons' – short but heavy rainstorms – occur, transforming dry canyon walls into waterfalls.

Fall is a great season at Zion. The foliage is beautiful, and by October, daytime weather is pleasantly hot and nights are in the 40°s and 50°s F. Winter brings snow, but the main roads are plowed. While it may freeze at night, daytime temperatures usually rise to about 50°F.

Spring weather is hard to predict – rainstorms and hot sunny spells are both likely.

May is the peak of the wildflower blooms. Spring and early summer is also the peak of the bug season – bring insect repellent.

Books & Maps Many books and maps are available at the visitor centers and from good bookstores or libraries. They can also be ordered in advance from Zion Natural History Association (ZNHA), Springdale, UT 84767 (☎ 772-3264, 800-635-3959 for credit card orders).
website: www.zionpark.org

Average hikers on the main trails will not need a hiking guide, but backpackers and more adventurous day hikers may want to obtain a copy of *Exploring the Backcountry of Zion National Park – Off Trail Routes* by T Brereton and J Dunaway, or *Zion: The Trails* by B Lineback – both inexpensive and published by the ZNHA.

Topographic maps with scales of one inch:one half-mile are also available.

Zion Canyon

From spring to fall, the shuttle bus stops at all the major trailheads along the 7-mile road through Zion Canyon. If you're driving in the low season, these shuttle stops, and a few other scenic pullouts, are the only places you can park along the road.

In order of increasing difficulty, the best trails accessible from Zion Canyon Rd are mentioned below. Which have the best views? All of them! There are signs at the trailheads. (All distances listed below are one-way.)

The paved **Pa'rus Trail** parallels the road for almost 2 miles from the Watchman Campground to the main park junction. This is the only trail that allows bicycles and dogs. The best and most popular of the easy trails is the paved, mile-long **Riverside Walk**, which begins at the end of the road, at the Temple of Sinawava. From the trail's end, you can continue along (and in) the Virgin River for several miles; this is the final portion of The Narrows – a difficult backpacking trip (see below). The quarter-mile-long **Weeping Rock Trail** climbs 100 feet to a lovely area of moist hanging gardens. **Emerald Pools** is another favorite; a paved

The Zion Park Shuttle

The conga line of cars is gone.

In an effort to save Zion from being loved to death, the National Park Service now closes the road through Zion Canyon to private automobiles from early April through late October and ferries people in using a free shuttle bus. The system is simple and convenient; it's also new (2000 was its first full year), so some details may change.

There are actually two shuttles: one loops through Springdale, making six stops; the other loops through Zion, making nine stops. The transfer point between the two is the Zion Visitor Center. The shuttles begin at 6:30 am, and the last shuttle sweeps through the park at 11 pm. At peak times they run every six to eight minutes, while early and late they run every half-hour. A roundtrip on the park shuttle would take 90 minutes, but you can get on and off as often as you want. The buses can carry two bikes each, and no pets are allowed.

It's still possible to drive into Zion and park at the Visitor Center (and Hwy 9 through the park remains open at all times). However, the lot is usually full by 10 am; unless you drive into the park very early, it's actually easier to use one of the designated parking lots in Springdale and ride the shuttle from town. Cost to enter the park is the same: $10 for individuals, or $20 for groups who would have arrived by car.

Of course, the system isn't perfect. At peak times, the buses can be SRO and waits can grow long; the NPS is working to improve this. But so far, traffic in Springdale hasn't gotten bad, and riding the bus seems to have created a more congenial atmosphere among visitors.

Has the shuttle solved the problem of human impact on Zion? Not by a long shot. For instance, now that parking lots are no longer a limiting factor, more people are getting in, using the trails and exploring the backcountry. So the NPS will continue to set limits on use, trying to maintain a semblance of balance between its twin mandates: providing access for people and preserving the park in all its natural glory.

---

half-mile-long trail leads to the lower pool and waterfall, while a mile-long unpaved trail leads to the upper pool (swimming is not allowed).

Hidden Canyon Trail has a few long drop-offs and climbs 850 feet in just over a mile to a very narrow and shady canyon. More strenuous, but leading to great views, are the 2½-mile **Angels Landing Trail** and the 4-mile **Observation Point Trail**. Other day hikes and extended overnight backpacking trips are possible (see Backpacking below).

Note that all these trails can be slippery with snow or ice in winter, or after heavy rain; ask park rangers for advice on trail conditions.

Zion-Mt Carmel Hwy

It's 10 miles from Zion Canyon to the east exit of the park. The road east of the mile-long Zion-Mount Carmel Tunnel (see Ori-

entation for vehicle restrictions) leads quickly into quite different terrain – a landscape of carved and etched slickrock, of which the mountainous Checkerboard Mesa is an especially memorable example. The only marked trail is just east of the tunnel – the half-mile-long **Canyon Overlook Trail**, which gives fine views into Zion Canyon, 1000 feet below.

Kolob Canyons Road

This 5-mile-long road, which penetrates the Finger Canyons area at the north end of the park, sees about one-tenth the visitors that the south entrance does, but the scenery and hiking are just as stupendous. The entrance is at I-15, exit 40; it's about 40 miles from the main visitor center on Hwy 9.

The road includes several parking areas and a picnic site. At the end, from the picnic area, the easiest trail is the half-mile **Timber**

Creek Overlook Trail, which climbs to a small peak with great views. The main day hike is the 2.7-mile-long Taylor Creek Trail, which crosses the creek many times. The hike to Kolob Arch is also interesting; the arch vies with Landscape Arch in Arches National Park in southeastern Utah for the title of 'biggest arch in the world.' Fit hikers can do the 14.4-mile roundtrip to the arch in a day.

Kolob Terrace Road

This 11-mile road reaches Lava Point (7890 feet), a cool relief from the Zion Canyon summer heat. Though not as crowded as the main park roads, it's still busy in the high season and is as scenically rewarding. Three trails leave the road. The Hop Valley Trail is an alternate way of reaching Kolob Arch; it's about 7 miles and an 1100-foot elevation drop. The 6-mile Wildcat Canyon Trail goes between Kolob Terrace Rd and Lava Point. Also from Lava Point, the West Rim Trail goes about 14 miles to Zion Canyon.

Backpacking

Zion has around 100 miles of backcountry trails that allow wilderness camping. The entirety of Zion can be hiked north to south (a traverse of 50 miles or more), and park rangers can suggest numerous shorter options (see also Adkison's *Utah's National Parks*). Despite summer crowds elsewhere, the backcountry offers solitude and quiet enough to hear the woosh of ravens wings soaring overhead.

The most famous backpacking trip is through The Narrows – a 16-mile journey through narrow canyons along the North Fork of the Virgin River. The easiest and busiest of the backcountry hikes, it is an unforgettable experience – so long as you don't mind getting wet. About 50% of the hike is in the river, mostly wading but sometimes swimming. The trip takes about 12 hours and camping for a night is recommended (if not, you must finish the hike in time to catch the last park shuttle out). So that you move with the current, you must begin at Chamberlain's Ranch (outside the park); the trail ends at the Riverside Walk

Trail at the north end of Zion Canyon. This hike is limited to June to October and may be closed from late July to early September because of flash flood danger. Since day hikers are allowed to wade up the river as far as Big Springs, the final few miles can sometimes get as crowded as free swim at the community pool.

All backpackers for all routes need to obtain a permit from either visitor center. Permits cost $5 per person per night. Permits are issued the day before or the morning of the trip – the only route that fills up is The Narrows, but waits are no more than a day or two. Camping is allowed in the backcountry, but certain areas are restricted (notably Kolob Canyon and The Narrows). Rangers will warn you about restrictions and also give you current information about the availability of water. Unlike many desert parks, Zion has a number of springs and rivers flowing year-round; all water must be boiled or treated. Maximum group size is 12 people, but most backcountry sites take only four to six people.

Neither animals nor campfires are allowed. Sun protection is essential, and insect repellent is needed in spring and early summer. Backpacking supplies are limited in Springdale – stock up in St George. Hikers attempting The Narrows can get outfitted at Zion Adventure Company (see Springdale earlier in this chapter).

Permits aren't required for day hikes, except for people attempting The Narrows in one day.

If you need a shuttle at the start or end of your backpacking trip, check with the main visitor center in Zion Canyon, which has a 'Ride Board' where you can connect with other backpackers. Or call Zion Canyon Transportation (☎ 635-5993) for van service to/from trailheads.

Horseback Riding & Bicycling

Three-hour guided rides from the Zion Lodge up the Sandbench Trail are offered daily from mid-March to mid-October by Bryce-Zion Trail Rides (☎ 679-8665, or call the lodge) for about $45 a person. Riders must be eight or older and weigh less than

220lbs. One-hour trail rides (minimum age seven) are $20.

Bicycles are prohibited in the Zion-Mt Carmel Tunnel and on all park trails except the Pa'rus Trail. Biking on park roads is allowed but not very easy because of the steep grades, narrow roads and heavy traffic.

Other Activities

Zion's precipitous walls make for awesome **rock climbing**, but it's not a place for beginners. The visitor center has informal route books and information on restrictions. Spring and fall are the best times, as summer is too hot. **Fishing** is very poor but permitted with a Utah fishing license.

Places to Stay & Eat

Near the south entrance are two Park Service campgrounds, *Watchman* with 170 sites and *South* with 141 sites. Both offer water, barbecue grills, picnic tables and toilets but no showers; sites are $14. Watchman is open year-round, has a few RV hookups ($16) and a few reservable sites (☎ 800-365-2267). South is open from March to October and is entirely first-come, first-served. Campgrounds usually fill up in the afternoon, so arrive early.

The summer-only *Lava Point* has a free six-site campground (no water). Just outside the east entrance, *Mukuntuweep* (☎ 648-2154) has a store, restaurant, laundry, showers and 110 tent sites ($15) and 34 RV sites ($19); eight camping cabins and several camping teepees are $25.

Zion Lodge (☎ 772-3213, reservations at 303-297-2757) is beautifully set in the middle of Zion Canyon. It offers about 80 comfortable motel rooms and 40 cabins – most have excellent views and private porches. Reservations should be made four to six months in advance for the peak season. Motel rooms sleep up to five and start at $97. A few suites are $127 for two. The cabins are $107 for two. It's $10 for each additional person; winter rates are $20 to $30 less. No pets are allowed; children 16 and under are free.
website: www.zionlodge.com

The *Zion Lodge Restaurant* is open for breakfast and dinner year-round, and also for lunch from mid-March to November – dinner reservations are requested. The newly expanded **Castle Dome Café** is open daily most of the year and serves burgers, sandwiches and pizzas. Otherwise, stay and eat in Springdale.

Outside the east entrance, a few small B&Bs have opened up, and there is an all-inclusive resort: *Zion Ponderosa Ranch Resort* (☎ 648-2700, 800-293-5444), about 5 miles north from Hwy 9 on North Fork County Rd. The resort's all-inclusive packages include all meals (in their restaurant) and an overwhelming array of activities: horseback riding, mountain biking, ATV tours, tennis, basketball, archery, a rock climbing wall, evening entertainment and much more. Snowmobiling, downhill skiing, fishing and boating have extra charges. Tent sites are $65 per person; cowboy cabins, which share a large bath facility, cost $75 per person for six people (fewer people cost progressively more per person); and modern log cabins with private bath are $115 per person for six people. These are peak rates from late May through early September; spring and fall have fewer activities and cheaper rates. Lodging only is available in January and February.
website: www.zionponderosa.com

Southern Hwy 89 Corridor

In southwestern Utah, Hwy 89 follows the Sevier River Valley and retraces the route of Mormon pioneers. South of the Sevier River, Hwy 89 has a junction with Hwy 9 (for Zion) and continues south to Kanab and on to Arizona and the North Rim of Grand Canyon National Park.

This makes a very pleasant alternative to I-15; with the exception of Panguitch and Kanab, the small towns along Hwy 89 offer only a handful of simple places to stay and eat. Circleville is where Butch Cassidy grew up. His (unrestored and dilapidated) childhood home is on the west side of Hwy 89, just over 2 miles south of town.

PANGUITCH
☎ 435 • pop 1623 • elevation 6666 feet

Founded in 1864, Panguitch is a center for the local ranching and lumbering communities. It is also a popular stopping place for travelers, as it has pleasant summer weather and is surrounded by Scenic Byways – Hwy 89 itself, Hwy 143 to the west and Hwy 12 to the east. The town has long been the gateway for Bryce Canyon National Park (24 miles east). If you're here for Pioneer Day (July 24), there's a rodeo. The Garfield County Fair takes place in August.

Orientation & Information

Hwy 89 is the main drag through town and comes in along Main from the north, then turns east at Center. Main south of Center becomes Hwy 143 leading to Panguitch Lake.

The Garfield County Travel Council (☎ 800-444-6689) has regional travel information year-round. There is also an information booth (☎ 676-8131), 800 N Main, open May to October, and information online at www.infowest.com/panguitch. The Dixie National Forest Powell Ranger Station (☎ 676-8815), PO Box 80, Panguitch, UT 84759, is at 225 E Center.

Other services include the library (☎ 676-2431), 25 S 200 East; post office (☎ 676-8853), 65 N 100 West; hospital (☎ 676-8811), 224 N 400 East; and police (☎ 676-8807), 45 S Main.

Things to See & Do

The **Paunsagaunt Wildlife Museum** (☎ 676-2500), 250 E Center, has a fine display of more than 400 professionally mounted animals from the West and around the world. A butterfly and giant bug room was added in 2001. Hours are 9 am to 8 pm daily May through October. Admission is $4; $2.50 for six- to 12-year-olds.

The information booth has a self-guided tour of some of the historic buildings and red-brick houses in town.

Ten miles east of town on Hwy 12 is **Red Canyon** in the Dixie National Forest, an un-crowded and beautiful place to hike. A national forest visitor center is open in summer only. The mile-long Buckhorn Trail, from the campground, leads to wonderful views.

Places to Stay

Camping Most private campgrounds close in winter. The *Big Fish KOA* (☎ 676-2225, 555 S Main) has complete facilities and tent/RV sites for $19/23; five Kamping Kabins are $44. Both *Hitch-n-Post* (☎ 676-2436, 420 N Main) and *Paradise Campground* (☎ 676-8348, 2153 N Hwy 89), 2 miles north, have tent/RV sites for $16/18.

Near the Hwy 89/12 junction, the private *Red Canyon* (☎ 676-2690) has showers and a convenience store. Sites range from $10 to $18; camping cabins are $28 to $45. East on Hwy 12 is the USFS *Red Canyon Campground*; pretty shaded sites (with water and showers) are $9. Contact the USFS for other sites in the area.

Motels & Hotels Panguitch and the nearby junction of Hwys 89 and 12 (7 miles south) contain a good selection of budget and mid-range accommodations, which are uniformly clean and well kept – though prices creep up in summer. May to October rates are quoted below; these can drop by $10 and more when things are slow and in the off-season.

Two of the cheapest places, with doubles in the low $40s, are *Tod's Travel Center* (☎ 676-8863, 445 E Center) and *Nelson Motel* (☎ 676-8441, 308 N Main), which don't look like much but are fine. Friendly, well-run and showing pride of ownership, with doubles in the high $40s, are *Blue Pine Motel* (☎ 676-8197, 800-299-6115, 130 N Main) and *Horizon Motel* (☎ 676-2651, 800-776-2651, 730 N Main). Spotless and attractive, *Canyon Lodge* (☎ 676-8292, 800-440-8292, 210 N Main) has 10 nonsmoking rooms for $45 to $55.

The following have doubles for around $65 in summer, and all are recommended: *Bryce Way Motel* (☎ 676-2400, 800-225-6534, 429 N Main); *Hiett Lamplighter Inn* (☎ 676-8362, 800-322-6966, 581 N Main); *Purple Sage Motel* (☎ 676-2659, 800-241-6889,

132 E Center); and *Marianna Inn* (☎ 676-8844, 800-331-7407, 699 N Main). Panguitch also has a *Best Western*, which is $10 to $20 more.

At the Hwy 89/12 intersection, *Harold's Place* (☎ 676-2350) has 20 cozy, modern log cabins and a restaurant and is open mid-March to mid-November. Rates peak at $70 for two. Also here, *Western Town Resort* (☎ 676-8770, 888-687-4339) has 80 chain-quality rooms ($82) behind faux-Wild West shop fronts. There's a restaurant, bar with entertainment and various rentals; see details at www.westerntownresort.com.

Places to Eat

Panguitch's selection of restaurants, unlike that of its hotels, is neither wide nor notable. *Foy's Country Corner Cafe* (☎ 676-8851, 80 N Main) and *Flying M Restaurant* (☎ 676-8008, 580 Main) are both fairly bland, family restaurants. *Cowboy's Smokehouse BBQ* (☎ 676-8030, 95 N Main) serves Western-style cookin', and *Grandma Tina's* (☎ 676-2377, 523 N Main) serves authentic Italian and vegetarian meals from 7 am daily. With a retro, Route 66-inspired décor, *Buffalo Java* (☎ 676-8900, 47 N Main) stands out as a modestly hip coffeehouse.

PANGUITCH LAKE

The highly scenic Hwy 143 goes south then west from Panguitch into the Dixie National Forest, passing Panguitch Lake (15 miles) and Cedar Breaks National Monument (30 miles), where there is a fantastic overlook. The upper portion of the road may be closed in winter.

Locals proclaim Panguitch Lake to be one of the 10 best trout-fishing lakes in the USA. Native boosterism is a common trait among Utah anglers; join them in summer to see if their boast has merit. Winter gives way to ice fishing, snowmobiling, cross-country skiing and snowshoeing, though there are few rental places.

The Dixie National Forest (☎ 865-3200 in Cedar City) runs three campgrounds ($8-10) on Hwy 143 north and south of the lake. All have water but no showers or RV hookups and are open from May to October, depending on weather. Near the lake is a convenience store with fishing supplies.

Ringing the lake are several low-key, pleasant lodges. The following all have boat rentals, convenience stores and restaurants and offer discounts in winter. Open mid-April through mid-October, *Bear Paw Lakeview Resort* (☎ 435-676-2650, 888-555-8439) is on Hwy 143 on the east shore; it has RV sites ($19) and 10 cabins ($63 to $68). On North Shore Rd and open year-round are *Aspen Cove Resort* (☎ 435-676-8988, 866-497-5581), with 10 rooms ($95 to $125), and *Rustic Lodge* (☎ 435-676-2627, 800-427-8345), with tent/RV sites ($12/18) and 11 cabins ($62 to $85).

GLENDALE & AROUND

☎ 435 • pop 355 • elevation 5500 feet

Glendale is the center of an apple-growing region, and it's notable to travelers only for having one of the route's best campgrounds and its most pleasant B&B.

Situated beneath scenic cliffs, the *Glendale KOA* (☎ 648-2490), 5 miles north on Hwy 89, has a complete range of facilities, including bike and horse rentals and a restaurant (serving lunch and dinner) specializing in game (such as buffalo burgers and wild boar). It is open from May to October and charges from $18 to $22. Three Kamping Kabins are $32.

The friendly *Historic Smith Hotel* (☎ 648-2156, 800-528-3558, 295 N Main), on Hwy 89, offers a taste of relaxed country living far removed from the tourist hubbub. The restored 1927 boardinghouse includes a breezy porch, hot tub, sitting room with fireplace and spacious tree-filled yard and gardens. The seven nonsmoking rooms are homey but not overly fancy; each has a private bath and includes breakfast. Rates are $44 to $80; it is open year-round.

CORAL PINK SAND DUNES STATE PARK

Over half of this 3700-acre park is covered with shifting pink sand dunes, a unique and surprising sight in this desert of eroded rocks. On weekends, the park becomes a sandbox for OHVs (off-highway vehicles), though interesting hiking trails, a short nature trail and a visitor center draw hikers. Day use is $4 (OHV day use $6). A 22-site *campground* with showers and picnic areas is $13 (no water in winter), but the same winds that bring the sand can make camping unpleasant. Ranger programs on summer weekends include a popular nighttime 'scorpion hike.' The park is reached via a 12-mile paved road heading southwest from Hwy 89. The signed turnoff is 6 miles southeast of Mt Carmel Junction or 13 miles north of Kanab. Dirt roads provide alternate access routes. More information is available from ☎ 874-2408, PO Box 95, Kanab, UT 84741.

KANAB

☎ 435 • pop 3564 • elevation 4925 feet

The remote town of Kanab was permanently settled by Mormons in 1874; surrounded by unyielding desert on all sides, it remained one of Utah's most inaccessible towns until the advent of roads.

Ranching has been the traditional economic mainstay, but tourism has continued to increase in importance, as paved roads now lead quickly to some of the Southwest's most wonderful terrain: Grand Staircase-Escalante National Monument (20 miles), Zion (40 miles), Bryce Canyon (80 miles), North Rim of the Grand Canyon (80 miles) and Glen Canyon National Recreation Area (74 miles).

Kanab was 'discovered' in the 1930s by the film industry and almost 100 movies have been filmed here, most in the 1940s and 1970s, including Westerns by John Wayne, Clint Eastwood and many others.

Orientation & Information

Hwy 89 snakes through town and most motels and businesses lie along it. From the north, the highway enters along 300 West and turns to become Center. Hwy 89 then turns south along 100 East, and finally turns east on 300 South, leading to Page, Arizona, 64 miles away. From the 300 South intersection, Alt Hwy 89 leads south to Arizona (3 miles) and the Grand Canyon's North Rim. All these routes are well signed.

The More the Merrier

Polygamy has not been condoned by the Mormon Church for more than a century, but small communities quietly continue the practice of what they call 'original Mormonism' in remote areas along the Utah-Arizona and Utah-Nevada borders. There are an estimated 30,000 polygamists in Utah today. Rarely have practitioners ever been jailed for their views, though in a highly publicized trial in 2001, polygamist Tom Green became the first since the 1940s.

The outspoken Green has five wives and 30 children (and counting), and rather than live quietly, he appeared on national TV talk shows, openly discussing and advocating his way of life. These appearances led him to be singled out by Utah prosecutors and ultimately convicted by a jury on four counts of bigamy. He is now serving a five-year sentence.

However, most Utah polygamists are not worried about further prosecutions – on the one hand, evidence against polygamists is hard to gather (without videotaped self-incrimination), and on the other, most Mormons, and as a consequence, most Utahns, are deeply ambivalent about the issue. Independence and freedom of religion are prized highly in general, but more to the point, most Mormons come from practicing polygamists. Indeed, both the prosecuting attorney and the judge in the Green case acknowledged they had polygamist forebears, and by the time he died in 1877, church founder Brigham Young had married a total of 56 women and sired an untold number of progeny.

The county Travel Information Center (☎ 644-5033, 800-733-5263), 78 S 100 East, is open weekdays, till 4 pm on Saturday, and in summer till 1 pm on Sunday. The website is www.kaneutah.com. The BLM (☎ 644-2672) is at 180 W 300 North. Other services include the library (☎ 644-2394), 374 N Main; post office (☎ 644-2760), 39 S Main;

hospital (☎ 644-5811), 355 N Main; and police (☎ 644-5854), 140 E 100 South.

Things to See & Do

Stop by the visitor center for a self-guided walking tour of **historic houses**. The best known is Heritage House (☎ 644-3506), 100 South at Main; it's open Monday to Saturday in summer.

The **Frontier Movie Town** (☎ 644-5337, 800-551-1714), 297 W Center, is hokey fun: during summer, 'gunfights' are staged among buildings from old Western movies, plus they have Dutch-oven dinners and other entertainment. It's free to visit the town and movie museum, but activities and meals have various charges; open year-round, call for hours.

The idiosyncratic **Moqui Cave** (☎ 644-2987), 5 miles north of town on Hwy 89, is notable for its collection of fluorescent minerals. It's open Monday to Saturday year-round. Admission is $4, $3.50 for seniors, $2.50 for teenagers and $2 for children.

Thirty-five miles east of Kanab on Hwy 89, and 6 miles north on a passable dirt road, is **Pahreah**, which is both a ghost town and a re-created Old West movie set. There are interpretive displays and a picnic area. Contact the BLM for information.

For **hiking** try the popular well-marked, 1-mile Squaw Trail, which leaves from the north end of 100 East and leads 400 feet up to the Vermilion Cliffs.

Backcountry Drives

There are many unpaved roads leading into the Vermilion Cliffs and White Cliffs areas. Some roads are passable to ordinary cars, others require 4WD and most are impassable after heavy rain. The BLM has good maps and information.

A popular drive is the **Johnson Canyon/ Alton Amphitheater Backway**, which leaves Hwy 89 nine miles east of Kanab and heads north for 30 or 40 miles, emerging at either Glendale or Alton. The road is paved to the Alton/Glendale junction, and the remainder is gravel in fair condition. The road passes a Western movie set (on private land about 6 miles north of Hwy 89). For a few

miles, the road enters the Grand Staircase-Escalante National Monument (described later in this chapter).

Special Events

The Western Legends Round-Up, over three days in September, celebrates cowboys, both in life and in the movies. The May Greyhound Gathering, for folks who've adopted the racing dog, is a hoot. Fourth of July events are also a local highlight.

Places to Stay

In Kanab, high season begins when the North Rim of the Grand Canyon opens – around mid-May – and lasts till October. However, rates fluctuate year-round with demand and drop by nearly half in winter. Call ahead during busy periods.

The small, friendly *Hitch'n Post RV Park* (☎ 644-2142, 800-458-3516, 196 E 300 South) offers 18 tent ($14) and RV sites ($16). Loosen up a bit at *Crazy Horse Campark* (☎ 644-2782, 625 E 300 South), which offers impromptu piano singalongs and fresh hens' eggs every morning in addition to 80 nice sites ($13.50 to $15) and good facilities.

The privately run *Canyonlands International Hostel* (☎ 644-5554, 143 E 100 South) has four worn dorm rooms with 25 beds ($10). Despite appearances, it still fills up with international budget travelers. There are lockers, a kitchen, travel information, coin laundry and TV lounge.

A good bargain is *Bob-Bon Inn Motel* (☎ 644-5094, 236 N 300 West), which has small, clean doubles in the high $30s. Plain, simple but acceptable rooms in the high $40s can be found at *National 9 Aiken's Lodge* (☎ 644-2625, 800-524-9999, 79 W Center); *Brandon Motel* (☎ 644-2631, 800-839-2631, 223 W Center); *Sun-n-Sand Motel* (☎ 644-5050, 800-654-1868, 347 S 100 East); *Kanab Mission Inn* (☎ 644-5373, 386 E 300 South); and *Quail Park Lodge* (☎ 644-2651, 125 N 300 West). The *Treasure Trail Motel* (☎ 644-2687, 800-603-2687, 150 W Center) has somewhat nicer, more spacious rooms in the high $50s. All the above, except for Kanab Mission Inn, have a pool. Some places may close in winter.

In the mid-range category, the *Parry Lodge* (☎ 644-2601, 800-748-4104, 89 E Center) has long been *the* place to stay in Kanab. Many of the actors who made films here stayed at Parry's, and there is plenty of movie memorabilia, as well as a coin laundry, a pool, and a restaurant and bar. The place has some character, but its 89 rooms, though nicely kept up, are not particularly special. High-season rates are $58 for a double, with kitchenettes for $77.

Mid-range *chain hotels* include Super 8, Holiday Inn Express and Best Western. *Shilo Inn* (☎ 644-2562, 296 W 100 North) is the biggest hotel in town, with 118 mini-suites. Summer rates are $70 to $90.

Places to Eat

For espresso and a good book, head to *Willow Creek* (☎ 644-8884, 263 S 100 East). The surprisingly hip *Vermillion Café* (☎ 644-3886, 4 E Center) serves espresso coffees and light meals, and has Internet access. Next door, *Wildflower Health Food* (☎ 644-3200, 18 E Center) serves sandwiches and a range of healthy foods.

There are three locally recommended Mexican restaurants in town: *Nedra's Too* (☎ 435-644-2030, 310 S 100 East), *Escobar's* (☎ 644-3739, 373 E 300 South) and *Fernando's Hideaway* (☎ 644-3222, 332 W 300 North).

Chef's Palace (☎ 435-644-5052), 153 W Center, is a slightly more upmarket family restaurant that is open daily. *Rocking V Café* (☎ 644-8001, 97 W Center) attempts to be more interesting than you'd expect with Southwestern-inspired dishes ($10 to $19); open for lunch on weekdays and dinner nightly.

The waitresses wear six-shooters at *Houston's Trail's End Restaurant* (☎ 644-2488, 32 E Center). This fun Kanab institution specializes in Western cooking: steaks, barbecue ($9 to $19) and country breakfasts with biscuits and gravy. It's open all day. *Parry Lodge Restaurant* (in the hotel) is the closest to upscale that Kanab has, with good American breakfasts and dinner in a setting celebrating the famous film stars who have dined here.

Hwy 12: Bryce Canyon to Capitol Reef

Hwy 12 leaves Hwy 89 and heads east past Bryce Canyon and several small towns, terminating at Torrey on Hwy 24, about 4 miles from Capitol Reef National Park. The 122-mile-long Hwy 12 could be the most scenic road in Utah; east of Escalante, the scenery matches any of the national parks for jaw-dropping splendor.

BRYCE CANYON NATIONAL PARK
☎ 435

The Grand Staircase, a series of step-like uplifted rock layers stretching north from the Grand Canyon, culminates in the Pink Cliffs formation at Bryce Canyon National Park. These cliffs were deposited as a 2000-foot-deep sediment in a huge prehistoric lake some 50 to 60 million years ago; slowly lifted up to between 7000 and more than 9000 feet above sea level; and then eroded into wondrous ranks of pinnacles and points, steeples and spires, cliffs and crevices, and the strangely named formations called *hoodoos*. The 'canyon' is actually a series of amphitheaters eroded from the cliffs by the weather, rather than a real canyon formed by a river.

There is something magical about the formations, standing crowded like platoons of soldiers or melting like sandcastles, all painted in endless shades of coral and magenta, ochre and white, and set against a pine forest. A shaft of sunlight suddenly breaking through clouds can transform the view from merely magnificent to almost other-worldly.

Orientation

Scenic Hwy 12, the main paved road to the park, cuts across the northern portion (no fee). From Hwy 12 (14 miles east of Hwy 89), Hwy 63 heads south to the official park entrance about 3 miles away. From here, the 18-mile Rim Rd climbs slowly past turnoffs to the visitor center (at 8000 feet), the lodge,

UTAH

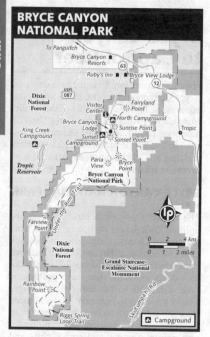

BRYCE CANYON NATIONAL PARK

two campgrounds, scenic viewpoints and some trailheads, ending at Rainbow Point, 9115 feet above sea level. Trailers are allowed only as far as Sunset Campground, about 3 miles south of the entrance. Vehicles over 25 feet in length have access restrictions to Paria View in summer. See below for information on the new, voluntary shuttle bus system.

Information

The visitor center (☎ 834-5322) is the first main building along Hwy 63 after you officially enter the park. It is open daily 8 am to 4:30 pm in winter, till 6 pm in spring and fall, and till 8 pm in summer. The center is being expanded and remodeled (to be finished in 2002) to include an auditorium and a larger museum in addition to its audiovisual programs and bookstore; rangers answer questions and (mainly during the summer) lead discussions, hikes etc. Free Junior Ranger

Programs are offered for six- to 12-year-olds.

The entrance fee to the park is $10 per person (bicycle, motorcycle, foot and non-commercial bus passengers) or $20 per private vehicle; cars that park outside and use the shuttle are charged $15. Tickets are valid for seven days, and passes are accepted. The entrance station and the visitor center provide free park maps and informative brochures.

Further information is available from the Superintendent, Bryce Canyon National Park, Bryce Canyon, UT 84717.

Climate & When to Go The park is open year-round, with the five months of May through September seeing about 75% of the approximately 1.7 million annual visitors. Summer high temperatures at the 8000- to 9000-foot elevation of the rim may reach the 80°s F, but it's hotter below the rim. Summer nights can be chilly, with temperatures in the 40°s F. June is relatively dry, but in July and August the torrential late-summer storms descend – these are usually short-lived, afternoon showers.

Snows blanket the ground from about November to April, but most of the park's roads are kept open. A few remain unplowed and are designated for cross-country skiing or snowshoeing.

Flora & Fauna Mule deer are frequently seen, especially early and late in the day. Drive carefully to avoid hitting them. Although other medium-to-large mammals are present, they are rarely seen, but smaller critters abound. At least 164 bird species have been recorded in the park. The visitor center has complete lists. Under *no* circumstances should you feed wildlife, even friendly squirrels. This is a particular problem at Bryce, where it is in fact illegal; more importantly, it draws animals away from their natural habitats and may lead them to lose their ability to find food in winter.

Shuttle Service You can drive your own car into the park, as described below, or use the voluntary, free shuttle system. First implemented in 2000, the service offers an alternative to driving from mid-May to mid-September. The shuttle parking lot is just past the junction of Hwys 12 and 63 outside the park; the shuttle operates from approximately 7:30 am to 9 pm and runs every 10 minutes or so. There are three shuttle lines: the blue line takes you into the park to the visitor center (and also stops at Ruby's Inn); the red line goes from the visitor center to Bryce Point and all the major amphitheater lookouts; and the green line goes to the south end of the park (a trip of two hours; reservations required).

Even with only 15% of visitors using the shuttle system in 2000, changes were seen. In years past, every summer weekend found the parking lots full and cars incessantly circling for spaces, while in 2000 that only happened twice. If ridership continues to grow, the shuttle will most likely remain voluntary.

Rim Road

Every visitor wants to drive (or bike) the Rim Rd, going at least as far as the Bryce Amphitheater overlooks (a few miles past the visitor center), which provide Bryce's postcard views. Past the amphitheater, the road continues another 14 miles, passing half a dozen small parking areas and viewpoints and ending at Rainbow Point.

Hiking

The views from the rim are superb, but the best way to experience the canyons and get close to the eroded hoodoos is to hike below the rim. Descents and ascents can be long and sometimes steep, and the altitude of more than 8000 feet can make them strenuous, so allow enough time, wear good boots and carry extra water. Also, most trails skirt exposed drop-offs until you reach the canyon floor.

The easiest hike is along the **Rim Trail**, which is 5½ miles long (one way) and skirts the Bryce Amphitheater between Fairyland Point and Bryce Point. Several sections are paved and accessible to wheelchairs and strollers; the most level section is the half

mile between Sunrise and Sunset Points. The one-mile **Bristlecone Loop** is another easy, rewarding walk offering fantastic vistas from Rainbow Point.

Many trails descend below the rim. One of the most popular is **Queen's Garden**, which drops 320 feet from Sunrise Point. Many people combine this with the **Navajo Trail**, which descends 521 feet from Sunset Point and passes through the famous narrow canyon 'Wall Street.' This moderate, 2.4-mile combined hike sees a lot of traffic in summer and is among the few trails that may remain open in winter.

Two of the most popular longer loop trails are the 8-mile **Fairyland Trail**, which leaves from Fairyland Point north of the visitor center, and the 7-mile-long **Peekaboo Trail**, which leaves from Bryce Point. Both have superb scenery and involve 800-foot elevation changes, plus much additional up and down – allow half a day. Peekaboo Trail is also used by horses.

The backcountry, multiday Under-the-Rim Trail, south of Bryce Amphitheater, can be broken up into several athletic day hikes. The 11-mile stretch between Bryce Point and Swamp Canyon trailheads, which includes the 'Hat Shop,' is one of the hardest and best sections.

Backpacking

Few visitors camp in the backcountry below the rim, making this the best strategy for escaping the crowds. There are 10 designated campsites that can accommodate up to six backpackers (two sites will take 15).

All backpackers must register and get permits ($5) at the visitor center. Park rangers will discuss your route and show you where camping is permitted and where water may be found. Campgrounds are primitive and you must be completely self-sufficient: all water below the rim must be purified; no fires are allowed (but camp-stoves are); and you must bury your waste and carry out *all* your trash, including toilet paper.

When snow falls from November to April, backcountry camping is difficult but still possible. One or two campsites should be accessible – the rangers will know.

Note that, while beautiful, backcountry trails are primarily forested. The 23-mile **Under-the-Rim Trail** is the longest in the park, from Bryce Point to Rainbow Point, and it can be combined with the 9-mile **Riggs Spring Loop Trail** at Rainbow Point for a one-way trip of more than 30 miles. All backcountry campsites are along these two trails. Numerous connecting trails make a variety of shorter lengths possible.

Stargazing

Bryce Canyon is remote and skies are clear. Visibility is usually more than 100 miles year-round, and it can exceed 150 miles in the crisp, clear winters. The stargazing is superb, and park rangers host new moon and full moon astronomy evenings during the summer.

Winter Activities

The 1-mile road to Fairyland Point is not plowed in winter and access is by snowshoe or cross-country skis. The Rim Trail and other areas may be reached this way too. The visitor center lends snowshoes for free. Snowmobiles are prohibited.

Organized Tours

Canyon Trail Rides (☎ 679-8665), PO Box 128, Tropic, UT 84776, operates horse and mule tours into the backcountry. Two-hour rides to the canyon floor are $30 (no riders under seven years old) and half-day loop tours are $45 (no riders under eight). There is a 220-pound weight limit. The Bryce Canyon Lodge (see Places to Stay & Eat below) also has information – the tours start there. Comparably priced trail rides are offered by lodges outside the park.

Places to Stay & Eat

Inside the Park The Park Service operates *North Campground*, open year-round, near the visitor center and *Sunset Campground*, closed in winter, more than a mile south. There are toilets, drinking water, picnic tables and barbecue grills. Sites are $10 a night. During summer, all of the more than 200 sites are often full by noon or early afternoon. Between the two campgrounds, a grocery store offers basic food, camping supplies and coin-operated showers and laundry April through October. (See Outside the Park, below, for places to shower in winter.)

The *Bryce Canyon Lodge* (☎ 834-5361), near the visitor center, is open from April through October. The attractive Western building dates from 1924 and has 114 units. A restaurant (open from 6:30 am to 9:30 pm; dinner reservations required) has occasional entertainment. Lodge reservations (☎ 303-297-2757) are essential; in summer, the lodge can be fully booked six months in advance. Check online at www.bryce canyonlodge.com.

Motel rooms with two queen-size beds, bath and private porch are $92 (plus 10% tax) for two to five people. Four lodge suites are $122 a double. Cabins with two double beds, bath, fireplace and porch are $102 for two to four people.

Outside the Park The *Best Western Ruby's Inn & Campground* (☎ 834-5341) is a huge, popular and unrelentingly 'Western' complex on Hwy 63, just over a mile north of the park entrance. It has everything you could want: a campground, hotel, two restaurants, store (with groceries, camping supplies, books and souvenirs), foreign currency exchange and a whole Western town of gift shops. Facilities include a pool, hot tub, post office, coin laundry and showers (open year-round). Scenic flights plus horse, bike, ATV and ski rentals are available. In summer, they offer 'chuck wagon' dinners and a nightly rodeo (except Sunday). The complex has become so overwhelming they now have a free train to cart guests from point to point.

The campground has 200 sites ranging from $16 (tents) to $25 (hookups) open April through October. The well-run motel has 369 good-size, high-end chain-quality rooms. Rates are $95 to $120 in summer (make reservations as far in advance as possible) and about half that from January through March. A few family suites are $135. For details, see www.rubysinn.com.

Right across the highway, Ruby's also runs **Bryce View Lodge** (☎ 834-5180, 888-279-2304), which is aimed at budget travelers. Its 130 plain, merely adequate rooms rent for $60 to $66 in summer, $44 to $48 in winter.

Near the Hwy 12/63 junction, **Bryce Canyon Resorts** (☎ 834-5351, 800-834-0043) has 54 renovated, clean rooms for $65/85 single/double in summer; eight smaller, older rooms are $69 a double. Rates are high for what you get; you are paying for location. Facilities are much more modest than Ruby's Inn.

On Hwy 12 near the turnoff to King Creek Campground (see below) are two more overpriced motels, a private campground and a grocery store. Travelers willing to drive a few more minutes will do better in Panguitch or Tropic.

The Dixie National Forest borders much of Bryce Canyon National Park. The 38-site **King Creek Campground** ($8) is open June to September and has water but no showers. It's 7 miles south of Hwy 12 on USFS Rd 087, 3 miles west of Hwy 63. The similar 30-site **Pine Lake** National Forest campground is about 17 miles north of the junction of Hwys 12 and 63 on USFS Rd 16. The ranger stations in Panguitch and Escalante have maps and information.

TROPIC
☎ 435 • pop 508 • elevation 6200 feet
This small town is not much more than a waypoint catering to visitors to Bryce (10 miles west) and Grand Staircase-Escalante National Monument (14 miles east). A small information center is open at the east end of town during the summer; for area information, or to make hotel reservations, call ☎ 877-733-2792.

website: www.brycevalley-tropic.com

All the motels in Tropic are on Main St. Summer prices (listed below) are high; winter prices can drop by half. **Bryce Pioneer Village** (☎ 679-8546, 800-222-0381) has 37 ambience-free rooms ($65 to $75) and 18 cabins ($55), some with kitchenettes ($85). Fifteen RV sites are $10 to $15. **Doug's Place Country Inn** (☎ 679-8600, 800-993-6847) has 28 equally plain rooms

($55 to $65) and a restaurant and grocery store. The nicer **Bryce Valley Inn** (☎ 679-8811, 800-442-1890) has 65 clean, spacious rooms ($60 to $85) and a restaurant serving Western meals. **Bryce Canyon Inn & Pizza** (☎ 679-8502, 800-592-1468) has eight motel rooms ($55) and 10 cabins ($68), plus a pizzeria. Maybe the nicest accommodations are the homey **Bryce Country Cabins** (☎ 679-8643, 888-679-8643), which go for $65.

Tropic also has quite a few small B&Bs; call the toll-free reservations number above or ask at the information center for a complete list.

About 5 miles east on Hwy 12 (at Redrock Road) is the **Cannonville KOA** (☎ 679-8988, 888-562-4710), which has tent and RV sites ($18 to $26) and Kamping Kabins ($44).

KODACHROME BASIN STATE PARK
Dozens of red, pink and white sandstone chimneys, and many other formations, make this, indeed, a very colorful state park. Most of the sights are along hiking and mountain-biking trails or dirt roads. Horses can be rented in summer from Scenic Safaris (☎ 679-8536/8787) at its Trailhead Station in the park. It also sells basic groceries and camping supplies, has area information and offers stagecoach rides.

Park information is available by calling (☎ 679-8562, 800-322-3770) or writing to PO Box 238, Cannonville, UT 84718. The park's 27-site campground ($13) has hot showers and is open all year. Day use is $4. In Cannonville, on Hwy 12 five miles south of Tropic, a sign points the way to the park, which is 9 miles farther. South of the park is the Grand Staircase-Escalante National Monument (see below).

ESCALANTE & AROUND
☎ 435 • pop 818 • elevation 5600 feet
Escalante, the largest town on Hwy 12, lies halfway between Bryce Canyon and Capitol Reef National Parks. Many people speed through en route to one of the parks, but now it is becoming a base for visitors to the Grand Staircase-Escalante National Monument.

The Escalante Interagency Office (☎ 826-5499), PO Box 246, Escalante, UT 84726, 755 W Main (Hwy 12), is open daily April to October and weekdays otherwise. The BLM, Dixie National Forest and National Park Service are all represented at this information center, which will be expanding soon. Information, permits, brochures, maps and guidebooks are available. There is also a city information booth near Main and Center, which has brochures detailing local historic buildings; however it is open in summer only.

Escalante Petrified Forest State Park

This park is about 2 miles northwest of town along Hwy 12. In addition to a small 'forest' of petrified wood, there's a modest lake and a 22-site, year-round campground with hot showers ($13). Day use is $4. Information is available from PO Box 350, Escalante, UT 84726 (☎ 826-4466, 800-322-3770 for camping reservations).

Backcountry Drives North of Escalante

The national monument south of town is described below, but the Dixie National Forest north of town also has several interesting, adventurous dirt and gravel roads with opportunities to fish, hike and camp. Before driving, get maps and road condition updates in Escalante; snow closes the roads from fall to spring, rain does so at any time, and high-clearance 2WD is recommended for all, though roads are sometimes passable to passenger cars.

Posy Lake Rd goes north from Escalante. After 13 miles, a right fork, USFS Rd 153, becomes Hell's Backbone Rd and the left fork, USFS Rd 154, goes 2 miles to the summer-only *Posy Lake Campground* ($8), which has water. The small lake is popular for fishing and boating. Beyond Posy Lake, the road climbs over the Aquarius Plateau at about 10,000 feet and emerges at Bicknell on Hwy 24, 25 miles away. Herds of pronghorn antelope roam the plateau.

After 5 miles, **Hell's Backbone Rd** passes the six-site, summer-only *Blue Spruce*

Campground ($6), which has water. The incredibly scenic road continues east and south for another 20 miles, emerging on Hwy 12 near Boulder. The road crosses the narrow, death-defying Hell's Backbone Bridge and skirts the completely undeveloped **Box-Death Hollow Wilderness** – which has no campgrounds or roads and only rudimentary hiking routes.

Places to Stay & Eat

Budget travelers head over to *Escalante Outfitters* (☎ 826-4266, 310 W Main), which has seven real log cabins ($30) that are small, clean, cozy and heated. All share an immaculate bathhouse. Their *Esca-latte* coffee shop and store sells topographical maps, guidebooks, liquor, camping supplies and clothes.

Late summer and fall are Escalante's high season. The best motel deal in town is the entirely refurbished *Circle D Motel* (☎ 826-4297, 475 W Main); its 25 spiffed-up rooms range from $60 for a nice, large double to $35-45 for other, smaller rooms. Several other adequate motels have high-season doubles in the $60s.

The newer *Escalante's Grand Staircase B&B Inn* (☎ 866-826-4890, 280 W Main) has five Southwestern-style rooms with log-frame beds. Doubles are $85, including a homecooked breakfast. Bike rentals and a shuttle service are available.

Escalante has a few modest family restaurants, plus the *Trailhead Café* (☎ 826-4714, 800-839-7567, 125 E Main), which serves breakfast and good deli sandwiches on its outdoor patio.

GRAND STAIRCASE-ESCALANTE NATIONAL MONUMENT
☎ 435

This 1.9-million-acre monument, established in 1996 by President Bill Clinton, is the largest park in the Southwest. It links the area between Bryce Canyon and Capitol Reef National Parks (in the west and east, respectively) and Glen Canyon National Recreation Area in the southeast. The name refers to the 'grand staircase' geological strata (see Bryce Canyon National Park, earlier in the chapter) and the Escalante River canyons.

The monument, which protects what was the last region in the continental USA to be mapped, was created over the objections of some local residents and legislators, who had hoped to develop the area's mining potential. There continue to be calls to revise the monument's management plan to allow for more use of its resources. Whether and when this might be done remains to be seen. The monument currently receives just under a million visitors a year, and residents are trying to harness the potential of tourism as an alternative to mining.

The monument is somewhat unique for a BLM-managed area. While it allows some uses that would be restricted if this were a national park (such as hunting and grazing with proper permits), it allows fewer uses than other BLM lands in order to maintain its 'remote frontier' quality. To this end, development of a tourist infrastructure is minimal and restricted to the park's edges, leaving a vast desert area suitable for scientific research and adventurous exploration.

Travelers who have the time and necessary outdoor equipment will find the area has some of the least visited and most spectacular scenery in the country. Note that water sources must be chemically treated or boiled; campfires are permitted only in certain areas (use a stove instead); and biting insects are a problem in spring and early summer.

Orientation

Scenic Hwy 12 crosses some of the northern parts of the monument between the towns of Tropic, Escalante and Boulder. Hwy 89 crosses parts of the southern reaches of the monument east of Kanab. Three unpaved roads cross the monument roughly north to south between Hwys 12 and Hwy 89, and a fourth unpaved road crosses the monument from Hwy 12, dead-ending at the Glen Canyon National Recreation Area. These four roads, described below, provide the main access into the monument. (In addition, the partly paved Burr Trail from Boulder to Lake Powell crosses the north-

eastern corner of the monument – see Boulder, below.)

Always check with a ranger about weather and road conditions before driving or hiking; in good weather, most roads are passable to cars, but they are dusty, rough and remote – and intended to be. After heavy rain or snow, the roads may be impassable even with 4WD and should not be attempted if a storm is approaching. After light rains, the clay surface can become dangerously slippery. Always carry extra water and food in case of breakdown, foul weather or other emergency; help may be hard to find in case of an accident.

Information

Information is available in advance from the BLM Grand Staircase-Escalante National Monument (☎ 826-5499), PO Box 225, Escalante, UT 84726. If you are already in the region, the BLM has, or is adding, offices with maps and information at each of the major entrance roads: in the north are the Escalante Interagency Office (☎ 826-5400) and a new Cannonville office (☎ 679-8981), on the road to Kodachrome Basin State Park off Hwy 12. In the south are the headquarters in Kanab (☎ 644-2672), the Paria office (no phone), and a future office in Big Water on Hwy 89.

To access many places in the Escalante area you'll need a good USGS or BLM map. Recommended reading is *Hiking the Escalante* by Rudi Lambrechtse (1999 revised edition), with background information and many hikes.

Skutumpah & Johnson Canyon Roads

This is the most westerly route through the monument, and 4WD or high-clearance 2WD is advised. The unpaved Skutumpah Rd heads southwest a few miles west of Kodachrome State Park and goes past the Bull Valley Gorge and around the southern end of Bryce Canyon's pink cliffs. After 35 miles, Skutumpah Rd intersects with the 16-mile, paved Johnson Canyon Rd, which goes past the White Cliffs and Vermilion Cliffs areas on the way to Hwy 89 and Kanab.

Cottonwood Canyon Road

This scenic backway goes 46 miles east and then south of Kodachrome Basin State Park, emerging at Hwy 89 near Paria Canyon (see the 'Paria Canyon-Vermilion Cliffs Wilderness Area' boxed text). This dirt road, which is rough but passable to cars, cuts about 50 miles off the drive between Bryce Canyon and Lake Powell and therefore sees the most traffic (allow two to three hours). A good destination for a short trip is **Grosvenor Arch**, an unusual double arch. It's about 11 miles southeast of Kodachrome State Park.

The road then continues south along the west side of the Cockscomb, a distinctive long and narrow ridge caused by a flexure, or monocline, in the earth's crust. The Cockscomb divides the Grand Staircase from the Kaiparowits Plateau to the east; there are superb views in all directions.

Farther south, the road follows the Paria River valley, where there are numerous hiking possibilities.

Smoky Mountain Road

This 78-mile, dirt-and-gravel road is little traveled. It crosses the rugged Kaiparowits Plateau between Escalante on Hwy 12 and Big Water on Hwy 89 (near the western end of Glen Canyon National Recreation Area); 4WD is recommended. The southern section has good views of Lake Powell.

Hole-in-the-Rock Road

Both the scenery and the history are wild along this scenic backway, which stretches about 60 miles southeast of Escalante and dead-ends at Lake Powell (allow at least five hours one-way).

Pioneering Mormons followed this route in 1879–1880 on their way to settle new

---

Paria Canyon-Vermilion Cliffs Wilderness Area

This remote, extremely rugged area crosses the Utah-Arizona state line south of the Grand Staircase-Escalante National Monument. Experienced canyoneers enjoy the Paria Canyon because of the amazing Buckskin Gulch arm – miles of slot canyons so deep and narrow that the sun almost never shines directly into them. Hiking Buckskin Gulch-Paria Canyon to the exit point near Lees Ferry, Arizona, requires four to six days, and involves long stretches of ankle- and knee-deep muddy water. Trailheads are along dirt roads off Hwy 89 in Utah, which start near the Paria BLM Ranger Station (no phone) about midway between Kanab and Page. The station is open March 15 to November 15, and it posts weather information and flash flood warnings when closed; the nearby *White House Campground* is $5. The area is managed by the BLM in Kanab.

The best time to do this adventurous hike is spring or fall. Winter is too cold and summer downpours create deadly flash floods. The hike must be done in the direction of river flow (north to south). The Arizona Strip Interpretive Association has published a water-resistant *Paria Hikers Guide*, available from BLM offices for $8. Also read Annerino's *Adventuring in Arizona*. As there are no maintained trails or campgrounds in the canyon, maps and guides are useful. A hiking permit costs $5 per person per night. Shuttles can be arranged by Marble Canyon Lodge or Cliff Dwellers Lodge (see Marble Canyon & Lees Ferry Area in the Grand Canyon & Lake Powell chapter).

The area also contains Coyote Buttes on the Paria Plateau and the 3-mile, half-day hike to the famous geological formation called 'The Wave.' This hike leaves from the Wire Pass trailhead, 8 miles south of Hwy 89 along a dirt road. Hiking permits are $5; no overnight camping is allowed.

Despite the area's remoteness, these hikes are extremely popular and permits are limited; you can make reservations on the Internet at http://paria.az.blm.gov up to seven months in advance, which is a good idea.

lands in southeastern Utah. Little did they know that the precipitous walls of Glen Canyon of the Colorado River blocked their mission. More than 200 pioneers literally blasted and hammered their way through the cliff, creating a route wide enough to lower their 80 wagons – a feat that is remembered and honored today by markers along the road. The final part of the descent cannot be seen – the Glen Canyon Dam flooded it under Lake Powell along with countless other historical sites.

The dirt and gravel road leaves Hwy 12 about 5 miles east of Escalante and is passable to ordinary cars when dry – except for the last 7 miles, which require 4WD. Two popular stops are Devil's Garden (12 miles along), with hiking trails among giant rocks, and Dry Fork (26 miles), which has the most easily accessible slot canyon day hikes. There are no campgrounds or other facilities, although dispersed camping is possible; a free backcountry permit is required. The main road stops short of the hole in the rock, but hikers can continue down to Lake Powell, a scrambling descent that can be done in less than an hour. There are no taxis for the climb back up.

Hiking the Escalante Canyon

Escalante is near the headwaters of the Escalante River, which flows southeast to Lake Powell, nearly 90 miles away. You can hike the entire length, but you'll get wet – the 'trail' frequently crosses the river. Some canyoneers carry an inflatable air mattress to float gear across in the deepest sections. There are no campgrounds. The first third is monument land, the rest is within Glen Canyon National Recreation Area.

Road access is from Escalante (at a trailhead near the cemetery) or from the Hwy 12 bridge midway between Escalante and Boulder, near Calf Creek Recreation Area. Hiking access is from several routes heading east from Hole-in-the-Rock Rd, so you can do a day hike or a backpacking trip for as many nights as you want. (For details, read Lambrechtse's book.) The canyon scenery is marvelous, with sheer cliffs and soaring arches, waterfalls and pools, and

many side canyons where the chances of seeing anyone are slim indeed. You may, however, encounter Indian artifacts – it is illegal to disturb or collect these.

The best seasons are spring and fall – summer sees high temperatures and flash flood danger. In addition, rattlesnakes and scorpions call this area home; use caution and watch where you put your hands and feet. It bears repeating that you must be completely self-sufficient in the monument. Before hiking, get local information about current conditions, maps and overnight permits from any of the BLM offices mentioned above.

Calf Creek Recreation Area

This BLM-managed area is 15 miles east of Escalante on Hwy 12. It has a small but scenic campground and a recommended 3-mile hike to Lower Calf Creek Falls, a simply beautiful spot. Other more difficult hikes are also possible. Day use is $2. Call ☎ 826-5499 for information.

Places to Stay

The *Calf Creek Campground* has 13 sites ($7) and water but no showers. The *Deer Creek Campground* is about 10 miles east of Boulder on Burr Trail Rd (part of the paved portion of the Burr Trail) and has seven sites ($4) but no water. Both are open year-round. Apart from these two simple campgrounds, there are no developed camping facilities within the monument.

In the past, the BLM has allowed dispersed wilderness camping, but it is currently establishing designated backcountry sites. All overnight use requires a permit, currently free although a fee is under consideration. Check with the BLM for details.

BOULDER

☎ 435 • pop 180 • elevation 6593 feet

The 25 miles on Hwy 12 from Escalante to this tiny village are memorable, to put it mildly. At one point the road traverses the 'Hogsback,' a knife-edge ridge with stunning views all around – drivers will have a hard time keeping their eyes on the road! If that's not enough excitement, Hell's

Backbone Rd also leaves from Boulder (see Escalante earlier).

On the north side of Boulder is **Anasazi State Park Museum** (☎ 335-7308), which includes an archaeological site that dates from AD 1130 to 1175. The museum includes a re-created six-room pueblo, an art gallery and good exhibits about the Anasazi (or Ancestral Puebloan) peoples. In addition, the BLM staffs a desk here (☎ 335-7382) with information, permits and road updates. Hours are 8 am to 6 pm in summer, 9 am to 5 pm at other times. Admission is $3 per person, or $5 per carload.

A popular scenic backway, the **Burr Trail** heads east from Boulder as a paved road, crosses the northeastern corner of the Grand Staircase-Escalante National Monument and after 30 miles reaches the Waterpocket Fold area of Capitol Reef National Park, providing unbelievable vistas. From here, a series of unpaved, dramatic switchbacks descend into the park, and the road continues unpaved until it turns south, becoming paved again as it continues toward Bullfrog Marina on Lake Powell, about 70 miles from Boulder. In good weather, the dirt portion of the road is passable to cars, though low-slung vehicles may have trouble on the switchbacks. Rain or snow can close the road.

If you're looking for a **guided hiking** trip in the adjacent national monument, Escalante Canyon Outfitters (☎ 335-7311, 888-326-4453) offers several and has a good reputation.

Places to Stay & Eat
Boulder is notably upscale for such a small community; fall is the busiest season. *Pole's Place* (☎ 335-7422, 800-730-7422), near the state park, has a café, gift shop and 12 nice motel rooms in the $50s. Nearby, the simple *Circle Cliff Motel* (☎ 355-7333) has three renovated rooms, one with a kitchen, for $40 to $50.

Boulder Mountain Lodge (☎ 335-7460, 800-556-3446), at the junction of Hwy 12 and Burr Trail, is a laid-back resort-type place. Comfortably large doubles are $85, suites $135. An organic restaurant serves fancified Western cuisine for breakfast and dinner.

At the same intersection are *Boulder Mesa Restaurant* (☎ 335-7447), open all day, and *Burr Trail Trading Post & Grill* (☎ 335-7500), which is everything you could want in a country diner. *Hall's Store* (☎ 335-7304), a grocery at the west end of Boulder, is the only place to buy beer in this dry town.

TORREY & AROUND
☎ 435 • pop 171 • elevation 6843 feet
Hwy 12 terminates at Hwy 24 at the village of Torrey, about 40 miles northeast of Boulder; fluttering stands of aspen make this a gorgeous drive in fall. Located 11 miles west of the Capitol Reef National Park visitor center, Torrey, with nearby Teasdale, provides the closest hotels to the park. More than that, though, Torrey provides a rare experience for Utah: it is a quiet, uncommercial, but comfortable rural town with a whiff of countercultural sophistication. If you're here during the third weekend in July, don't miss the Bicknell International Film Festival (BIFF). This wacky spoof on the Sundance Film Festival includes films, parties and the 'fastest parade in America.'

Information
Wayne County Travel Council (☎ 425-3365, 800-858-7951) runs an information booth in Torrey, on the north side of Hwy 24 at Hwy 12; it's open noon to 7 pm April through October. You can write to the council at PO Box 7, Teasdale, UT 84773 or go online to www.capitolreef.org.

Also in Teasdale, 3 miles west of Torrey, is the Dixie National Forest Teasdale Ranger Station (☎ 425-3702), PO Box 90, UT 84773, at 138 E Main.

Outfitters
Hondoo Rivers & Trails (☎ 425-3519, 800-332-2696,), 90 E Main, runs various hiking, horse and jeep expeditions; review options at www.hondoo.com. Wild Hare Expeditions (☎ 425-3999, 888-304-4273), 116 W Main, arranges shuttles and guided driving

and hiking tours. Capitol Reef Riding Stables (☎ 425-3761), 2600 E Hwy 24, offers guided horseback rides as well as bike and 4WD rentals.

Places to Stay

Camping Area campgrounds, both public and private, are open generally April to October. *Thousand Lakes RV Park* (☎ 425-3500, 800-355-8995), a mile west of Torrey on Hwy 24, has good facilities and tent/RV sites for $13/19; three camping cabins are $29. Nearby, the friendly *Sandcreek RV Park, Campground & Hostel* (☎ 425-3577, 877-425-3578) has tent/RV sites for $10/15 and camping cabins for $28. There are showers ($3 for the public), a coin laundry, gift store and espresso bar.

The Fishlake National Forest *Sunglow Campground* ($10) is 6 miles west of Torrey amid red-rock cliffs. About 17 to 22 miles south of Torrey along Hwy 12, the Dixie National Forest runs the small *Oak Creek*, *Pleasant Creek* (both $9) and *Singletree* campgrounds ($10). All USFS campgrounds have water but no showers.

Budget Reservations are a good idea during the busy summer season. In winter, prices plummet and some places close. *Sandcreek* (see Camping above) has an exceptionally nice, one-room, eight-bed hostel ($10 to $12 a bed).

The unpretentious and appealing *Capitol Reef Inn & Cafe* (☎ 425-3271, 360 W Main) has 10 comfortable, clean rooms, most with two beds. Rates are $40 for one person, and $4 for each additional person. Its gift shop specializes in local maps, guidebooks and books about the Southwest, and the café is recommended (see Places to Eat below).

Chuckwagon Lodge & General Store (☎ 425-3335, 800-863-3288, 12 W Main) has a slew of attractive sleeping options: 15 modern motel rooms are $59, five older but clean rooms are $45, three new cabins with kitchens are $100, and a three-bedroom apartment is $100. All have satellite TV, and there's a pool, hot tub, coin laundry and showers open to the public ($4).

The *Boulder View Inn* (☎ 425-3800, 800-444-3980, 385 W Main) has 11 spotless rooms for $45/48 single/double.

Two miles southeast of Teasdale, the *Cactus Hill Guest Ranch* (☎ 425-3578, 800-507-2624, 830 S 1000 East) is a working farm with four clean motel rooms for $48 and a two-bedroom cabin for $65.

Bicknell, 9 miles west of Torrey, has a couple of budget motels to try if the places in Torrey are full.

Mid-Range The junction of Hwys 24 and 12 has several mid-range options. The *Wonderland Inn & Restaurant* (☎ 425-3775, 800-458-0216) is on a little hill with pleasant views. The inn has an indoor pool, hot tub, restaurant and nearby campground ($12-15). Fifty chain-quality rooms are about $60/65 for singles/doubles in summer. Also here is a *Days Inn* and *Super 8*.

On Hwy 24 about 2 to 3 miles west of the Capitol Reef National Park boundary are three good hotels with great views. The 19 nicely renovated rooms at *Rim Rock Inn* (☎ 425-3398) are a relative bargain at $60 for two in summer. There's also a restaurant (☎ 425-3388) serving Western fare. The *Best Western Capitol Reef Resort* (☎ 425-3761, 888-610-9600) has expanded to 100 units and offers the most complete facilities; rooms are $100. Not quite as perfectly situated is *Holiday Inn Express* (☎ 425-3866). The 39 well-decorated rooms go for $90, but insist on a park view.

B&Bs This is a great area to splurge on a B&B. *Skyridge B&B* (☎ 425-3222, 950 E Hwy 24), at the Hwy 12 junction, has six stylish rooms decorated with modern Southwest art and antique and contemporary furniture, some designed by the owner. Gorgeous quilts, full breakfast, happy hour, perfect views, a hot tub: it adds up to a wonderful, romantic experience. Rates are $107 to $158. Call for availability in winter.

Tucked beneath a cliff-face in nearby Teasdale, *Muley Twist Inn* (☎ 425-3640, 800-530-1038, 125 South), has five very comfortable, if not splashy, rooms. All have private bath and include full breakfast; rates are $80 to $100. The owners have hiked or biked much of southwest Utah and are happy to share their knowledge.

On Hwy 12 west of Torrey, the *Lodge at Red River Ranch* (☎ 425-3322, 800-205-6343) is an upscale lodge with an exclusive air. The 15 rooms and suites live up to the opulant Western décor of the public areas and rent for $95/120. Amenities are many and include a restaurant and expansive grounds with access to river fishing. The lodge may close in winter.

For more B&Bs and cabins, check with the information booth in Torrey.

Places to Eat

The Chuckwagon Lodge has a great bakery open early every morning, and *Robber's Roost* (☎ 425-3265, 185 W Main) serves espresso coffees and other hot drinks in addition to being a sophisticated bookstore. The hotel restaurants are generally good, but the Capitol Reef Cafe is especially noteworthy. They serve excellent fresh and smoked local trout ($12), but they have been known for years for their tasty vegetarian dishes ($9-14). Breakfast here is also delicious.

Torrey also boasts a first-class Southwestern restaurant, *Café Diablo* (☎ 425-3070, 599 W Main). Its combination of inventive cuisine, head-turning presentation and mountain setting almost can't be beat. The wild mushroom salad ($7) comes wrapped in a branded tortilla, and glazed pork ribs ($20) arrive like a medieval castle. It is open for lunch and dinner daily in summer; call for hours or to make reservations, and to check about winter closings.

Entertainment

Wayne Theater (☎ 425-3123, 11 E Main), in Bicknell, shows movies on weekends and hosts BIFF in July.

Robber's Roost (see Places to Eat) is the home of the Entrada Institute (☎ 425-3791), a nonprofit arts and education organization that presents a series of lectures and workshops on local ecology and history as well as author readings and music.

AROUND TORREY
Fish Lake

About 20 miles northwest of the small town of Loa, Fish Lake is an attractive natural lake that is considered one of the state's best fishing spots for large Mackinaw and rainbow trout. The elevation of 8800 feet makes it a cool summer destination with pretty hiking and biking trails. The USFS operates several campgrounds here, all with water, one with showers and none with hookups; fees are $8 to $10. These are open from May to October (call ☎ 877-444-6777 for reservations). For information contact the Loa Ranger Station (☎ 836-2811), 138 S Main, Loa, UT 84747.

Several resorts around the lake offer a variety of rustic and modern cabins, ranging from $30 to $300 depending on amenities and the number of people. There are also marinas with boat rentals, stores, RV hookups and showers. Try the summer-only *Bowery Haven Resort* (☎ 638-1040) and the year-round *Fish Lake Resort* (☎ 638-1000).

CAPITOL REEF NATIONAL PARK
☎ 435

Utah's second-largest national park (at 375 sq miles) is also its second-least-crowded – with only 700,000 annual visitors. Yet it is just as scenic as Utah's other national parks, with great drives and hikes, petroglyphs, fruit orchards and Mormon pioneer buildings.

Capitol Reef is a textbook example of geology at work. For hundreds of millions of years, layer after layer of rock was deposited. Then, some 65 million years ago, the earth's surface buckled up and folded, and it has since been eroding to form what is today the 100-mile-long Waterpocket Fold, most of which lies within the park and is almost painterly in its intensity of color. Gray-greens, magentas, yellows and oranges – but most evocatively the deep chocolate of the Moenkopi sandstone – are layered like neopolitan ice cream.

Orientation & Information

Hwy 24 cuts through the northern section of this long, thin park – the Waterpocket Fold stretches north to south. Unpaved roads that are partly outside the park itself lead north and south of the highway.

The visitor center (☎ 425-3791) is on Hwy 24 at the junction with the paved scenic drive. It's free to drive through on Hwy 24, but visitors taking the scenic drive pay $4 per vehicle or $2 per person; national passes are accepted. Entrance is valid for a week.

The visitor center is open 8 am to 7 pm Memorial Day to Labor Day and 8 am to 4:30 pm otherwise. Various ranger-led programs and activities are scheduled during the summer. The center has books and maps for sale and exhibits. For further information, contact the Superintendent, Capitol Reef National Park, HCR 70, Box 15, Torrey, UT 84775.

The park is open year-round. Rainfall and humidity are low, although occasional summer thunderstorms introduce flash flood dangers. At the visitor center (5400 feet), summer temperatures occasionally reach more than 100°F, though Capitol Reef is traditionally cooler than Zion, Canyonlands or Arches. Evenings usually drop into the 60°s F. Biting insects are the worst from mid-May to late June. Spring and fall are more pleasant months for hiking. The dry winter months see average highs in the 40°s F and lows around 20°F, although temperatures below 0°F are possible. Snowfall is light but may close some roads briefly.

CAPITOL REEF NATIONAL PARK

Fruita

At the junction of the Fremont River and Sulphur Creek, Fruita was a settlement established by Mormon pioneers in 1880. Today, the park's visitor center is here and nearby are several picturesque, turn-of-the-19th-century buildings as well as a nice campground and grassy picnic areas.

The well-tended Fruita orchards produce apricots, cherries, peaches, apples and pears. From early March to the end of April the orchards are a mass of flowers. The fruit is harvested from mid-June to mid-October and can be picked and eaten at no charge inside any unlocked orchard. During designated harvest days, fruit can be picked in quantity for a fee.

Visitors can view Fremont Indian petroglyphs on a cliff just over a mile east of the visitor center along Hwy 24. Park rangers can suggest other places where Indian artifacts can be seen.

Main Park Drives

The visitor center has a brochure describing **Scenic Drive**, a curving, narrow, mostly paved road passable to all vehicles. This 25-mile roundtrip runs along the western side of the Waterpocket Fold and includes dirt side roads and access to trailheads.

Notom-Bullfrog Road is a dirt and gravel road that follows the east side of the Waterpocket Fold. It is accessible to ordinary vehicles in dry weather but may be impassable after heavy rains (get current road conditions from the ranger before driving). The road heads south from Hwy 24 just outside the eastern park boundary and remains outside the park for the first 20 miles, then enters the park for about 17 miles. About 34 miles south of Hwy 24, it intersects the Burr Trail Rd (see Boulder, earlier, for a description), which heads west over the Waterpocket Fold (the only road to do so) and east to Lake Powell, almost 40 miles away. The road gives access to many trailheads.

Two roads leave Hwy 24 a few miles east of the park boundary and head northwest to the **Cathedral Valley** area – a scenic desert landscape of peaks and pinnacles – at the north end of the park. **River Ford Rd** is just over 3 miles east of the park and **Caineville Wash Rd** is almost 11 miles east of the park; they can be combined to make an 80-mile roundtrip. However, River Ford Rd involves fording the Fremont River, which often requires 4WD. Even in good weather, both roads require high-clearance vehicles.

Hiking

Capital Reef has a number of rewarding, easy hikes. Just over 2 miles west of the visitor center on Hwy 24, a short unpaved road reaches Panorama Point. From here, two short walks – **Goosenecks Trail** and **Sunset Point Trail** – provide as much view as it's possible to get for so little effort.

Along Scenic Drive, a good dirt road leads to **Grand Wash Trail**, a flat, 2¼-mile hike through a canyon wash. The walls become impressively towering and narrow near the end at Hwy 24. The 1.8-mile **Cassidy Arch Trail** climbs steeply, switchbacking to the top of cliffs looking down upon the arch. The 1-mile **Hickman Bridge Trail** is a moderate, varied hike leading to this dramatic bridge; pretty wildflowers adorn the trail in spring.

At the end of Scenic Drive, a good unpaved road dead-ends in the Capitol Gorge. From here, the easy, 1-mile **Capitol Gorge Trail** leads east past petroglyphs, while the 2-mile **Golden Throne Trail** climbs steeply west to the cliff tops, with fine views of its namesake landmark.

Backpacking

You can hike and camp almost at will in this desert wilderness as long as you have a free permit, available from the visitor center (or from the Anasazi State Park Museum in Boulder).

Backcountry trails are often poorly marked, and route-finding skills are helpful; frequently you must look for cairns (piles of stones) to find your way. You can camp almost anywhere as long as it's more than 100 feet away from water (all sources must be treated) and a half-mile away from and out of sight of the main roads. Backpacking at Capitol Reef is a desert wilderness adventure – get advice and maps from park rangers before leaving. Beginners should start with an easy trip. Adkison's *Utah's National Parks* suggests several good choices.

This dry desert environment does not recover quickly from human impact – the normal rules of no fires, no garbage and no cutting of vegetation are even more important here. Leave campsites as you found them. Don't bury garbage, as it decomposes very slowly and desert critters try to dig it up.

Places to Stay

The *Fruita Campground* ($10) has 71 sites (with water but no showers) and is open all year on a first-come, first-served basis. In the summer high season, sites fill up by early afternoon.

Free primitive camping is possible year-round at *Cathedral Valley Campground* at the end of the River Ford Rd and at *Cedar Mesa Campground*, about 23 miles south along the Notom-Bullfrog Rd. Each has five sites, grills and pit toilets but no water.

There are no lodges. The closest motels are those described earlier in Torrey, which is 11 miles west. About 15 to 20 miles east along Hwy 24, in the settlement of Caineville, are a couple of other options. The *Sleepy Hollow Campground* (☎ 456-9130) has showers and tent/RV sites for \$12/15. The surprisingly decent *Caineville Cove Inn* (☎ 456-9133), has 16 clean rooms

for \$55. It is open April to October. *Luna Mesa Oasis* (☎ 456-9142, 800-629-9141) beckons laid-back budget travelers with tent (\$8) and RV (\$12) sites, four camping teepees (\$25), and three motel rooms (\$35). A Mexican/American café serves food all day, and 4WD tours are offered.

Southeastern Utah

UTAH

'Canyonlands' – as Utahns call the southeastern corner of their state – contains some of the most inhospitable and beautiful terrain in the world. Over millennia the Colorado River and its tributaries, most notably the Green and San Juan Rivers, have carved a landscape of such sheer-walled majesty and otherworldly desolation that it can challenge one's capacity for wonder. Utah's largest and wildest national park, appropriately enough named Canyonlands, is found here, along with the exquisite Arches National Park and numerous other protected areas.

Native Indian rock art and buildings, some dating as far back as 5000 BC, are abundant throughout the area. The exact meanings of the sometimes haunting petroglyphs and pictographs are elusive, but most mark sacred sites. Representations of shamanism are clear, and some abstract forms may be the products of trance states.

The canyons have been formidable barriers to travel. Even the hardy Mormon pioneers settled this corner of the state last. Towns were tiny and distances were great until the discovery of uranium and the consequent 1950s, post-WWII mining boom. Miners searched for radioactive pay dirt, populations swelled and word slowly spread about the area's spectacular but unforgiving landscape.

It is ironic that the greatest canyon of them all has been destroyed. The Glen Canyon of the Colorado River was flooded by the Glen Canyon Dam (just across the state line in Arizona) and is now the artificial Lake Powell. The dam's flooding of Glen Canyon in the 1960s caused a great uproar, and still today some call for the lake to be drained, though it's unlikely this will ever happen.

Author Edward Abbey, one of the strongest protestors against the flooding of Glen Canyon, wrote not so much for the preservation of the desert Southwest itself, but rather for its incalculable quality of untouched remoteness. It is another irony that in so unerringly evoking the stark beauty of life in the canyonlands in his books, he inadvertently helped attract to the Southwest hundreds of thousands of people seeking that very remoteness.

For the past two decades, southeastern Utah has been experiencing a tourist boom, which has been both wonderful and damaging. The canyonlands are one of the most splendid areas in the Americas, and that splendor needs to be cared for. Travel lightly, thoughtfully, respectfully. Millions of footsteps are taking their toll on this deceptively fragile environment.

This chapter is organized in a 'clockwise' fashion: it begins at Green River on I-15 and then follows Hwy 191 south, Hwy 163 west, and finally Hwys 261 and 95 north, ending at the San Rafael Swell just south of I-15.

MAP INDEX

Colorado

Southeastern Utah page 253

Arches National Park page 257

Moab page 267

Canyonlands National Park page 261

Arizona

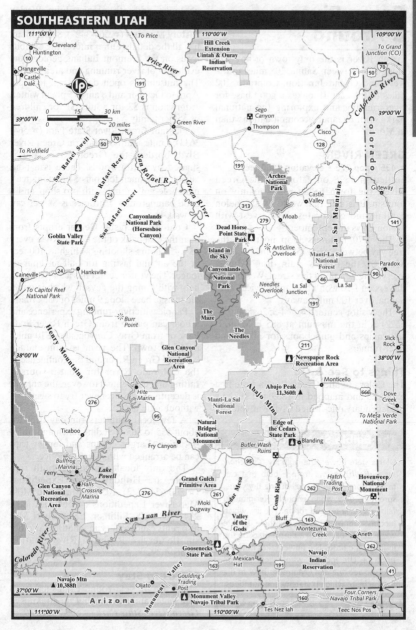

Green River & Around

Green River is the only town of any size along I-70 between Salina, 108 miles to the west, and Grand Junction, Colorado, 102 miles to the east. It makes a good base for river running and exploring the national parks, with cheaper accommodations than in Moab.

GREEN RIVER
☎ 435 • pop 973 • elevation 4100 feet

Settled in 1878 on a ford of the Green River, the town today relies mainly on tourism. It is also the 'world's watermelon capital' and celebrates the harvest with Melon Days in September.

The I-70 business loop north of the freeway between exits 158 and 162 becomes Main St, the town's main drag. Almost everything lies along this street. Westbound drivers on I-70 won't find any services until Salina, over 100 miles away.

The visitor center (☎ 564-3526, 800-635-6622) is in the museum at 885 E Main. It sells maps and guidebooks for hikers and river runners.

Things to See & Do

The Colorado and Green Rivers were first explored and mapped in 1869 and 1871 by the legendary one-armed Civil War veteran, geologist and ethnologist John Wesley Powell. The fine **John Wesley Powell River History Museum** (☎ 564-3427), 885 E Main, has all the details. Other interesting exhibits focus on the Fremont Indians, geology, the evolution of river running and area history. The museum is open daily 8 am to 8 pm April to October and 8 am to 5 pm in winter. Admission is $2 for adults, $1 for children or $5 per family.

Pleasant **Green River State Park** (☎ 564-3633), a mile south of Main on Green River Blvd, borders the Green River and is shaded by cottonwoods. There is a boat launch ($4 launch fee, plus $4 parking fee), nine-hole golf course with pro shop, and a good campground. Entrance is $4 per car, $2 walk-in.

Cold-water **Crystal Geyser** erupts from near the east bank of the Green River every 13 to 17 hours, shooting as high as 100 feet in the air and lasting for half an hour or longer. The visitor center has a map and can help with timing the geyser, which is on an old missile base along 9 miles of back roads.

People with **river-running** experience and a boat can put in from Green River State Park or from Gray Canyon, about 10 miles north of town. The river is calm enough between Green River and the confluence of the Colorado River for float-it-yourself rafting and canoeing. However, the current is deceptively strong; never try to swim in it without a life jacket.

A few local outfitters run day trips for about $55 to $65 including lunch and transportation. Larger groups and longer trips can be arranged with advance notice.

The only local companies, both reputable, are Holiday River Expeditions (☎ 800-624-6323), 1055 E Main, and Moki Mac River Expeditions (☎ 564-3361, 800-284-7280), 100 Silliman Lane. Moki Mac also rents canoes and runs shuttles. Another shuttle service is Green River Shuttles (☎ 564-8292).

Places to Stay

There are 42 year-round campsites ($12) with water and showers but no hookups at **Green River State Park** (☎ 800-322-3770 for

---

The Edible State Flower

Utah's state flower, the sego lily (*Calochortus nuttallii*), grows from a bulb that can remain dormant in the soil during dry years, sprouting only when enough precipitation falls in the winter and spring. The lily, which blooms from May to July, has three delicate white petals, each with a purple mark on the inside at the base. The flower takes its name from the Ute Indians, who called it 'sago' and showed the early Mormons how to dig for the bulb, which is starchy and nutritious.

reservations). All of the following *camp-grounds* have showers, coin laundries, play areas and small convenience stores; tents/RVs are around $16/22. There's *Green River KOA (☎ 564-3651, 550 S Green River Blvd)*, open April to October; *United Campground (☎ 564-8195, 910 E Main)*; and *Shady Acres RV Park (☎ 564-8290, 800-537-8674, 350 E Main)*, which lives up to its name.

Summer rates (listed here) are substantially higher than the rest of the year, but competition is stiff, so it pays to shop around. The cheapest places have small, frayed, sometimes musty rooms – but they're acceptable *budget motels*; rates are $35 to $45 in summer. Try the friendly *Mancos Rose Motel (☎ 564-9660, 20 W Main)*, *Oasis Motel (☎ 564-8272, 118 W Main)*, *Budget Inn (☎ 564-3441, 60 E Main)* or *Robbers Roost Motel (☎ 564-3452, 225 W Main)*.

Several good *chain motels* provide reliable lodgings. From the cheapest ($50) to the most expensive ($80 to $100) are Motel 6, Rodeway Inn, Super 8, Comfort Inn and Best Western. *Bookcliff Lodge (☎ 564-3406, 800-493-4699, 395 E Main)* has 100 average but spacious rooms for $40 to $45, and *Green River Inn (☎ 564-8237, 800-474-3304, 456 W Main)* ranges from $40 to $60.

Places to Eat

Melon Vine Food Store (☎ 564-3228, 76 S Broadway) is a small grocery.

Westwinds Restaurant (☎ 564-8240, 525 E Main), in the Rodeway Inn, is a 24-hour truck stop. *Ben's Cafe (☎ 564-3352, 115 W Main)* is an inexpensive diner with Mexican dinners. The *River Club (☎ 564-3674, 118 W Main)* is Green River's only private club, a smoky locals' bar that serves steaks and sandwiches 'til 11 pm daily. Far and away the best place in town is *Ray's Tavern (☎ 564-3511, 25 S Broadway)*, which has long been popular with river rafters. It serves burgers worth stopping for, plus excellent steaks ($11-20) and pizza. Microbrews, a pool table and occasional live music keep everyone entertained.

With river views and somewhat more formal, *Tamarisk Restaurant (☎ 564-8109, 870 E Main)* serves typical American fare.

Getting There & Away

Greyhound (☎ 564-3421), in the Rodeway Inn, 525 E Main, runs several buses daily to Grand Junction, Colorado; Salt Lake City ($32; four hours); and Las Vegas ($58; 7½ hours). Bighorn Express (☎ 888-655-7433) also stops here in summer on its daily Blanding to Salt Lake City run.

The Amtrak station (☎ 872-7245) is at 250 S Broadway (at Green River Ave). The *California Zephyr* stops here on its daily runs between Salt Lake City ($48; five hours) and Denver, Colorado ($59; 11 hours). It's the only Amtrak stop in southeastern Utah.

THOMPSON & SEGO CANYONS

Thompson, a tiny village on I-70 about 25 miles east of Green River, is very nearly a ghost town itself. Due north of town, Thompson and Sego Canyons contain notable prehistoric rock art and an actual ghost town.

After 4 miles, the paved road leads to rock art panels that represent four distinct periods; most impressive are the elongated, shamanistic Barrier Canyon–style figures. A mile farther, turn right on a good dirt road (avoid after rain), which leads to a cemetery and the ghost town of Sego. You can't miss the general store and dilapidated saloon of this former coal-mining town, which was finally abandoned around 1950. The canyons are within the Book Cliffs – a 250-mile-long escarpment stretching from Price, Utah, to Grand Junction, Colorado.

Arches, Canyonlands & Moab

Approximately 20 miles east of Green River, Hwy 191 branches off of I-70 and heads southeast, leading first to Arches and Canyonlands National Parks and then to the town of Moab. Be aware that Horseshoe Canyon and the Maze (both in Canyonlands National Park) are not accessible

UTAH

from Hwy 191 – see those sections, later, for further information.

ARCHES NATIONAL PARK
☎ 435

Arches National Park boasts the greatest concentration of arches in the world. The park itself covers a relatively small area, only 116 sq miles, and paved roads and short hiking trails make many of the most spectacular arches accessible to everyone.

To qualify as an arch, a formation must be at least 3 feet across; over 2000 have been found in the national park, including the spectacularly elongated Landscape Arch, which is over 100 feet high and 300 feet across and may be the largest arch in the world. In recent years it has been heard 'groaning' occasionally, meaning that it might soon collapse in the near geological future. The trail running directly beneath it has been closed indefinitely, but don't spend too much time watching for it to fall. In geological terms, 'soon' might be another few thousand years.

What's the difference between an arch and a bridge? In the Southwest all are formed by the erosion of sandstone – an arch is carved by erosion from weather and rock fall, while a bridge begins by erosion from a river. After centuries have passed, it can sometimes be difficult to tell which is which after a river has dried up or shifted. (A good place to see bridges is Natural Bridges National Monument, discussed later in this chapter.)

The park has 22 miles of paved roads, but with annual visitation at nearly a million people, crowds are an unavoidable fact of life at Arches. Parking areas are often overflowing in summer, and the park may institute a shuttle system if visitation increases. For now, to keep people from parking in dangerous or damaging areas, the park has stepped up ticketing. The best strategy is to arrive at the park early, by 9 am, but at any time if you can't find a designated parking spot at one place, keep going to the next parking area. Also, drive carefully – accidents most often occur when drivers forget the road for the scenery.

Orientation & Information

The park, along Hwy 191, is 20 miles southeast of I-70 and 5 miles northwest of Moab. The entrance station and visitor center are just off the highway; the paved park road continues 9 miles to a 'Y' near Balanced Rock. From here, a 2½-mile road leads to the Windows Section and a 10-mile road goes to Devils Garden. All these roads have numerous scenic pullouts and trailheads. In addition, a few dirt roads are suitable for high-clearance or 4WD vehicles and mountain bikes.

The pleasant visitor center (☎ 719-2299) is open 7:30 am to 6:30 pm from mid-April through September and 8 am to 4:30 pm at other times. It has information, exhibits, and book and map sales. In summer, rangers lead programs.

Park entrance, valid for seven days, is $10 per private vehicle or $5 per person; national passes are accepted. Note that dogs are not allowed on any trails, though they are allowed on the roads and in parking lots and campgrounds on a leash.

Climate & When to Go The summer is the busiest period, though July highs *average* 100°F. Spring and fall are more pleasant and less crowded. Snowfall is not very heavy at the 4000- to 5500-foot elevation of most of the park's roads and trails, and winter can be the most enchanting time to visit. Winter nighttime temperatures are often in the 20°s F; daytime temperatures are above freezing. Rainfall is very low. There is little water in the park – carry at least a gallon per person per day in summer.

Books & Maps In the 1950s, Arches was a smaller national monument and only a few hundred hardy souls visited each year. That's when Edward Abbey got a job here as a park ranger. He described his experiences in *Desert Solitaire – A Season in the Wilderness,* which has become a classic and is highly recommended. Also see the Books section in the Facts for the Visitor chapter.

The visitor center has free park maps and brochures describing all roads, trails and major features.

Driving Tour & Backcountry Routes

The park has 22 miles of paved roads leading right up to many of the most impressive sites, but with annual visitation at nearly a million people, crowds are an unavoidable fact of life at Arches. Parking areas are often overflowing in summer, and the park may institute a shuttle system if visitation increases. For now, to keep people from parking in dangerous or damaging areas, the park has stepped up ticketing. The best strategy is to arrive at the park early, by 9 am, but at any time if you can't find a designated parking spot at one place, keep going to the next parking area. Also, drive carefully – accidents most often occur when drivers forget the road for the scenery. See Hiking & Backpacking below for a list of highlights.

The park also has three unpaved roads. **Salt Valley Rd** is suitable for cars most of the time (inclement weather may close the road). It leaves the main road just over a mile before the end and heads 9 miles west to the very scenic **Klondike Bluffs**. You'll get away from the densest crowds – but don't expect to be alone! From here, a moderately difficult 3.4-mile roundtrip hike leads to **Tower Arch**.

From Klondike Bluffs, an unnamed 10-mile, 4WD-only dirt road leads back to the main park road at Balanced Rock. This is best done from north to south (going the other way involves a steep and sandy climb that may be impassable). This road also goes near Tower Arch.

From Balanced Rock, the Willow Flats Rd goes west. This used to be the main road into the park (back in Abbey's day), and it requires high clearance or 4WD to reach Hwy 191, about 8 miles away. There are no important arches here, just distant views and solitude. Before you go, check with the rangers about road conditions.

Hiking & Backpacking

Along the main park road are a number of short to moderate hikes – all are very rewarding. Just over 2 miles from the entrance is **Park Ave**, a mile-long trail through

ARCHES NATIONAL PARK

impressive sandstone cliffs that emerges farther along the road. The gravity-defying **Balanced Rock** (9 miles from the entrance) can be reached by a 0.3-mile-loop trail; you get different, equally impressive, perspectives from the roadside and the trail. The **Windows Section** (2½ miles along a spur road) has several scenic arches. The three-quarter-mile Double Arch Trail and the 1-mile Windows Trail are easy hikes that get you up close to the most impressive ones.

Sand Dune Arch and **Broken Arch** (8½ miles after Balanced Rock on the main road) are reached from the same trailhead – which also leads to a sand dune that's popular with kids. A short way beyond is **Skyline Arch**, which almost doubled in size with a 1940 rock fall – a quarter-mile trail takes you underneath it.

Many visitors' favorite is the **Delicate Arch Trail**. About 2½ miles beyond Balanced Rock, a good road leads almost 2 miles to **Wolfe Ranch**, which has a well-preserved,

1908 pioneer cabin. Just east of the ranch, a footbridge crosses Salt Wash (passing near some Ute Indian rock art) and marks the beginning of the moderately difficult arch trail. The trail crosses slickrock, passes fine vistas and culminates in a wall-hugging narrow ledge to the oft-photographed Delicate Arch itself – one of the most beautiful in the park and well worth the 3-mile roundtrip hike.

Nineteen miles from the visitor center at the end of the paved road is **Devils Garden**. A variety of trails here, from 2 to 7 miles roundtrip, pass nearly a dozen arches. The 2-mile roundtrip to Landscape Arch is quite easy and busy; beyond, the trail gets less crowded but is rougher and rockier. It offers spectacular views of the La Sal Mountains.

About 5 miles north of Balanced Rock is **Fiery Furnace**, a maze of spectacularly narrow canyons and cracks without proper trails. Because of the disorienting nature of the furnace and the damage done by so many people (particularly to the cryptobiotic crust), the park urges you to go with a ranger-led group. Space for the popular tours fills up fast and there could be a two-day waiting period. Register at the visitor center up to a week in advance. The three-hour hike leaves at 10 am and 4 pm from March to October and costs $6 for those over 12 and $3 for seven- to 12-year-olds. If you insist on going on your own, you still must get a permit. Other ranger-led hikes are sometimes offered.

Other Activities

Mountain bikes are welcomed on paved and unpaved roads maintained for vehicles, but there are no bike trails. Biking is not allowed on any foot trails.

Arches is not a popular place for backpacking, mainly because most of the park and all the named arches are easily reached on day trips. Then, of course, there's the heat and scarcity of water. But also, there are no designated backcountry campsites, and very little of the park is open to dispersed camping. However, it's possible to backpack with a permit from the visitor center. Talk to the rangers for the best suggestions – and be

prepared. Carry at least a gallon of water per day, bring a stove (fires are prohibited) and refrain from trampling the cryptobiotic crust.

Rock-climbing sites marked on USGS maps are off limits (ie, most of the famous arches), but rock climbing is permitted in much of the park. Climbers should ask at the visitor center for advice and a free permit.

Places to Stay

The scenic **Devils Garden** campground, at the end of the main park road, has 52 well-placed sites ($10), picnic tables, grills, water and toilets, but no showers. All campers must register at the visitor center on a first-come, first-served basis. Registration begins at 7:30 am, and in summer it can fill up in half an hour, so arrive early.

There are also two group campsites near Devils Garden for tent campers only. Fees are $3 per person per night (11 people minimum) plus a $15 reservation fee per group. Make reservations (at least two weeks in advance) through the NPS Reservations Office (☎ 259-4351, fax 435-259-4285), 2282 S West Resource Blvd, Moab, UT 84532.

DEAD HORSE POINT STATE PARK

This tiny state park packs a wallop: drop-dead gorgeous views of the serpentine Colorado River, Canyonlands National Park and the distant La Sal Mountains tucked in a blanket of clouds. Even if you've seen enough of epic landscapes, you won't regret a side trip here on your way to or from Canyonlands – it's only 4 miles from the turnoff along paved Hwy 313 (and just over 30 miles northwest of Moab). The lovely drive's most exciting section is near the end – the road crosses a narrow neck of land only 30 yards wide. A rough footpath follows the edge of the point, allowing views in all directions, and other short hikes rim the mesa. The best times are early morning and sunset.

The visitor center (☎ 259-2614) is open 8 am to 6 pm in summer and 9 am to 5 pm in winter, and it has slide shows (nightly in summer), exhibits, information, books and a gift shop. Rangers occasionally lead walks and give talks in summer.

The park's 21-site *Kayenta Campground* ($13) has limited water but no showers. For RVs, there are electrical hookups and a sewer dump. Reservations can be made (☎ 800-322-3770) or just show up early. Even in summer, the campground doesn't fill up until midday. Day use is $6.

CANYONLANDS NATIONAL PARK

Covering 527 sq miles, this is Utah's largest national park and its most rugged – indeed, few places on the planet possess such inhospitable terrain. But what majesty! Inconceivably vast canyons tipped with white cliffs tumble down to the Colorado River, 2000 feet below. Scattered everywhere are arches, bridges, needles, spires, craters, mesas, buttes – Canyonlands is a crumbling beauty, a vision of ancient earth.

But if you want to accomplish more than a casual day trip to the main overlooks, be prepared to be self-sufficient. Discounting the inaccessible rivers, most areas are completely waterless – even visitor centers (which sell only bottled water) and campgrounds (only one of which has water in summer). Dirt roads are difficult, distances are long, many trails are steep and the summer heat can be brutal. Taken together, it's not hard to understand why, despite its beauty, this is the least visited of all the major Southwestern national parks.

Orientation

The canyons of the Colorado and Green Rivers divide the park into *three completely separate* and very different areas (called 'districts' by the NPS). The canyons form a 'Y' – the long northeast-southwest arm of the Y is the Colorado River and the northwest arm is the Green River. The most developed district is 'Island in the Sky' – the area enclosed by the two rivers at the top of the Y. This is easily reached by paved Hwy 313, about a 30-mile drive from Moab. To the southeast of the Colorado is 'The

The Desert's Delicate Skin

Travelers to deserts of the Southwest are often told to avoid stepping on the **cryptobiotic crust** – but what is this odd-sounding stuff? The crust is a unique combination of living organisms such as lichen, cyanobacteria, fungi and algae that forms a dark, powdery coating on the high deserts of the Colorado Plateau. It acts both as a protective covering and as a binding agent for tiny soil particles, retarding erosion, absorbing moisture and providing nutrients (especially nitrogen) for desert plants and the animals that rely on them. The cryptobiotic crust may not look like much, but it is the delicate and fragile basis of life in the desert.

In some ways, the crust is tough stuff – it survives the scorching summer sun, freezing winters, irregular downpours and windstorms. But it's not built to withstand a hiking boot: The force of a footprint crushes and kills the crust. Millions of visitors, billions of footprints – the crust can suffer irreversible damage. Worse damage is caused by bicycle or vehicle tires; the crust breaks down in a continuous strip that makes the desert especially vulnerable to erosion. That's why it's vitally important to stay on established roads and trails, and to step on rock or in sandy washes when traveling off the trail.

Needles' – about a 75-mile drive from Moab via paved Hwys 191 and 211. To the west of the two rivers is the 'Maze' – about 130 miles from Moab and accessible by dirt roads. In addition, 'Horseshoe Canyon,' an unconnected unit northwest of the Maze, is also reached by dirt roads. Because of the river canyons, the districts are inaccessible to one another from within the park, so each district is described separately below.

Island in the Sky and The Needles have visitor centers, developed campgrounds and paved roads leading to scenic overlooks and picnic areas. They also have dirt roads and hiking trails. The Maze and Horseshoe Canyon have only dirt roads (most accessible only to 4WD), hiking trails and primitive campgrounds – these areas have much fewer visitors.

Information

Maps, guidebooks and information for all park areas are available from the Moab Information Center (see Moab). For information only, call or visit the NPS headquarters in Moab (☎ 259-7164), 2282 S W Resource Blvd, Moab, UT 84532, open 8 am to 4:30 pm Monday to Friday. Also see the separate park districts below.

Entrance to the park is $10 per vehicle or $5 per person, valid for seven days and for all three districts; national passes are accepted. In winter and in the remote Maze district, fees aren't collected.

Pets are not allowed on hiking or backcountry 4WD trails, even inside a vehicle. ATVs are not allowed anywhere. There are no lodges in the park.

Climate & When to Go The weather in Canyonlands is very similar to Arches. Summer has average temperatures in the 90°s F (often over 100°F) and short but heavy thunderstorms in July and August. Biting insects are worst in late May and June. Spring and fall are the most pleasant seasons (particularly April and October). January, the coldest month, has average highs around 40°F and lows in the teens. Winter snows aren't very heavy but can close some roads. Summer months are busy

with driving visitors while spring and fall are busy with backcountry users.

Backcountry Permits & Reservations
Permits are required for all backcountry camping, backpacking, mountain biking, 4WD trips and river trips. They are in addition to the park entrance fee. Backpackers pay $15 per group (call for group size maximums). Mountain-bike or 4WD groups pay $30 for up to three vehicles. River trips are $30 per group in Cataract Canyon and $20 per group in flatwater areas. Permits are valid for up to 14 consecutive days. In addition, certain backcountry sections of The Needles are open for day use by horses, bikes and 4WD vehicles and cost $5 per day per vehicle or per group of up to seven bikes or horses.

Reservations must be made at least two weeks in advance with the NPS Reservations Office (☎ 259-4351, fax 435-259-4285), 2282 S West Resource Blvd, Moab UT 84532. They answer questions from 8 am to 12:30 pm Monday to Friday (phones are often busy, just keep trying). For backpacking, mountain-biking and 4WD trips, reservations can be made no earlier than the second Monday in July for the following calendar year. Reservations are especially recommended for spring and fall. For raft trips and day use, reservations are taken at the beginning of January for the same year.

If you don't have a reservation, permits can be obtained on a space-available basis the day before or the day of your trip from the visitor center at which your trip begins. While you can call the visitor center to find out if permits are available, reservations by phone are not accepted.

Books Dedicated Canyonlands travelers will find the following useful: *Canyon Country Hiking* by FA Barnes; *Hiking, Biking and Exploring Canyonlands National Park and Vicinity* and *River Guide to Canyonlands National Park,* both by MR Kelsey; and *Mountain Biking Moab* by D Crowell. Note that books are guides only; hiking times can vary considerably. Always check unfamiliar routes with a ranger for up-to-date information.

UTAH

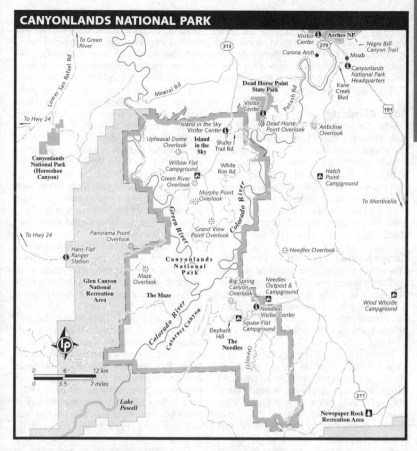

CANYONLANDS NATIONAL PARK

To Green
River

Mineral Rd

Lower San Rafael Rd

To Hwy 24

Canyonlands
National Park
(Horseshoe
Canyon)

Island in the Sky
Visitor Center

Upheaval Dome
Overlook

Willow Flat
Campground

Green River
Overlook

Murphy Point
Overlook

Island
in the
Sky

Shafer
Trail Rd

White
Rim Rd

Grand View
Point Overlook

To Hwy 24

Panorama Point
Overlook

Hans Flat
Ranger
Station

Glen Canyon
National
Recreation
Area

Maze
Overlook

The Maze

Colorado River

Cataract Canyon

Green River

Canyonlands
National
Park

Big Spring
Canyon
Overlook

Needles
Outpost &
Campground

Needles
Visitor Center

Squaw Flat
Campground

Elephant
Hill

The
Needles

(closed)

Lake
Powell

Visitor
Center

Arches NP

279

Corona Arch

Negro Bill
Canyon Trail

Moab

Canyonlands
National Park
Headquarters

Kane
Creek
Blvd

313

191

Dead Horse Point
State Park

Visitor
Center

Island in the Sky
Visitor Center

Dead Horse
Point Overlook

Anticline
Overlook

Potash Rd

Hatch
Point
Campground

To Monticello

Needles Overlook

Wind Whistle
Campground

211

Newspaper Rock
Recreation Area

0   6   12 km
0   3.5   7 miles

Exploring the Backcountry

Hiking, biking and 4WD are used to explore the backcountry. These activities are described below under the three Canyonlands districts. Mountain bikers and all vehicles must use roads (both paved and unpaved) and cannot bike or drive on hiking trails or off roads. Everyone should use high-scale topographic maps because signs are few and trails not always clear. Outfitters in Moab and other places can arrange guided backcountry trips (visitor centers have a list of NPS authorized outfitters), or you can do it yourself.

River Running

Guided river trips are available from the town of Green River for the Green River and from Moab for the Colorado River. A limited number of permits (see below) are available to members of the public who have the appropriate skills, experience and boating equipment; you must apply far in advance.

The trip from Green River down to the confluence with the Colorado is scenic and relatively easy; the same is true of the Colorado above the confluence. These are the best stretches for do-it-yourselfers. Almost immediately below the confluence, however, the Colorado goes through the wild white water of Cataract Canyon – navigable by experienced or guided boaters only. Beyond this canyon, the river eases off as it approaches Lake Powell in the Glen Canyon National Recreation Area.

Rock Climbing

Climbing is permitted in most parts of the park. However, there is no climbing in the Horseshoe Canyon unit, on any archaeological site or cultural resource, or on any arch or natural bridge marked on USGS maps, with the exception of Washerwoman Arch. All climbing must be free or clean-aid climbing. The soft rock in The Needles is unsuitable for climbing. Climbers should check with a ranger prior to a climb.

Canyonlands – Island in the Sky

This is the most easily reached and popular district – it sees about 260,000 visitors a year. The heart is a 6000-foot-high mesa (the 'Island in the Sky') surrounded by a sandstone bench called the White Rim, 1200 feet below. From this rim, cliffs drop another 1000 feet to the rivers.

The small Island in the Sky Visitor Center (☎ 259-4712) is on the mesa top about 2 miles after the park boundary (and entrance station). From the visitor center, the road goes 12 miles south to Grand View Point; about halfway along the drive, another paved road forks to the northwest and leads 5 miles to Upheaval Dome. A number of overlooks and mesa-top trails line these roads – all are well worth a stop (see Hiking & Backpacking below).

The visitor center is open 8 am to 4:30 pm daily, extended to 5 or 6 pm from spring to fall. Interpretive activities are offered mainly on weekends.

Hiking & Backpacking The visitor center is on the mesa top about 2 miles after the park boundary (and entrance station). From the visitor center, the road goes 12 miles south to Grand View Point; about halfway along the drive, another paved road forks to the northwest and leads 5 miles to Up-

heaval Dome. A number of overlooks and mesa-top trails line these roads – all are well worth a stop. The best are described below. Note that many trails, even the easiest, cross slickrock and are marked by cairns, or come close to cliff edges, so keep your eyes open.

If you want a lot of view for little effort, try any of the following: the **Mesa Arch Nature Trail**, 6 miles south of the visitor center is an easy half-mile loop trail that passes Mesa Arch, dramatically set on the very edge of the rim. Almost a mile before Grand View Point, the **White Rim Overlook Trail** is an easy, almost 2-mile roundtrip. Another easy 2-mile walk is the **Grand View Trail** at the road's end. These two trails provide some of the best views in the park; if nothing else, a stop at **Grand View Point Overlook** is a must.

Six miles south of the visitor center, a paved road leads to the **Upheaval Dome Trail**. This easy half-mile spur leads to an overlook with fine views of a crater thought to have been the result of a meteor crashing into the planet.

There are plenty of possibilities for half-day, all-day or overnight trips. These are strenuous because they involve the steep and often slippery descent down to the White Rim and then back out. About seven foot trails descend from the mesa top, forming the basis of longer hikes. The trails have little or no shade or water; the lack of water limits most backpacking trips to what you can carry. Permits are required for overnight trips.

Perhaps the most varied and satisfying full-day hike is the 8-mile **Syncline Loop**, which rings Upheaval Dome; at the midpoint, a 1½-mile spur leads into the crater, and another 3½-mile trail leads to the Green River.

White Rim Loop Built partially by uranium prospectors after WWII, this 4WD track goes all the way around the Island in the Sky. About 100 miles long, it is reached from the visitor center by the steep Shafer Trail Rd and is a great favorite for 4WD trips, mountain-bike trips and, to some extent, backpacking trips; it generally takes two days to complete in a 4WD. To maintain the area's wilderness quality, the Park Service limits the number of vehicles. If you arrive without an overnight permit, call the Park Service about possible cancellations or no-shows.

Park rangers regularly patrol the route to assist people whose vehicles break down or who have other problems. They also check for permits.

A recommended book is *A Naturalist's Guide to the White Rim Trail* by David Williams and Damian Fagon.

Places to Stay Six miles from the visitor center, the year-round *Willow Flat Campground* has 12 sites ($5) and pit toilets but no water – you must haul it in from Moab. Camping is on a first-come, first-served basis.

Near the Upheaval Dome Trail is the *Syncline Campsite* for backpackers only. Backpackers can also camp at large in many designated areas. Along the White Rim Rd are 10 primitive campgrounds, each with two campsites – except for *White Crack*, which has only one site but the best views. There are no facilities or reliable water supplies and permits are required (see Backcountry Permits & Reservations, above).

Canyonlands – The Needles

The Needles is named after the mind-boggling landscape of striped white and orange spires, which really has to be seen to be believed. Despite paved access roads, this district sees less than half the visitors that Island in the Sky does, perhaps because there are few overlooks. The otherworldly terrain, which contains plenty of arches as well as Ancestral Puebloan sites and petroglyphs, is accessible mostly by hiking and 4WD trails.

The Needles Visitor Center (☎ 259-4711) is 2½ miles beyond the park boundary (where you pay your entrance fee). From the visitor center, the paved road continues for almost 7 miles to **Big Spring Canyon Overlook** and is lined with various trails and side roads. Almost 3 miles beyond the visitor center, a side road goes to a pump

house with water year-round. A little farther is Squaw Flat Campground.

The visitor center also provides water and is open 8 am to 4:30 pm daily, extended to 5 or 6 pm from spring to fall. From spring to fall, especially on weekends, interpretive activities are offered.

Hiking & Backpacking The visitor center is 2½ miles beyond the park boundary (where you pay your entrance fee). From the visitor center, the paved road continues for almost 7 miles to **Big Spring Canyon Overlook** and is lined with various trails and side roads. Some of the best are described here:

Almost a mile beyond the visitor center, a side road leads 1½ miles to **Cave Spring Trail**. This easy, 0.6-mile loop is fun and diverse: it crosses slickrock, descends two ladders and passes Fremont Indian artwork and the remains of an old cowboy camp.

About 5 miles from the visitor center is the 0.6-mile loop **Pothole Point Trail** – one of the easiest in the park, with nice views. Just before the road ends, the interesting **Slickrock Trail** is a scenic, fairly easy 2.4-mile loop.

The Needles is the park's best backpacking area because a network of hiking trails allows you to reach some primitive campgrounds (overnight permits required) without long stretches on 4WD roads. In addition, the trails criss-cross enough so that many can be done as moderate to challenging day hikes. Unlike the Island in the Sky district, trails here don't have major elevation changes, but they can be very uneven, involve scrambling and cross slickrock sections – keep your eyes peeled for rock cairn markers or you can get lost. Good boots are recommended. There is little shade and rarely any water (which, if found, must always be purified). Carry a gallon of water per person per day in the hottest months.

From Squaw Flat Campground, climb up a short way along the **Squaw Canyon Trail** for fine views of The Needles. You can make this a moderate day hike by returning via the **Big Spring Canyon Trail** (roundtrip of 7½ miles) or the less used and more difficult

Lost Canyon Trail (roundtrip 9 miles). These trails provide a good cross-section of slickrock, canyons, seasonal streams and distant views.

A longer day hike is the 5½-mile each way **Confluence Overlook Trail**, which leads from Big Spring Canyon Overlook to a point above the confluence of the Green and Colorado Rivers – watching the gray-green Colorado flowing next to and then mixing with the reddish Green is a memorable sight.

A special area with incredible views is **Chesler Park**; this is usually done as an overnight backpack, or 4WDs can reach it by a 9-mile drive from Squaw Flat Campground. Here is the unforgettable **Joint Trail**, which at one point goes through a slot canyon only 3 feet wide. Fit hikers can do this as an all-day hike.

4WD Roads The Needles is famous for its challenging 4WD roads, particularly the notorious **Elephant Hill**, a couple of miles west of Squaw Flat. Before descending, review the road, your skills and your vehicle, remembering that you must come back up on your return (and the cost of rescue is over $1000!). Wide vehicles or those with long wheelbases are likely to have difficulty on some of the tight, steep switchbacks – scrapes and vehicle damage are a high possibility. After Elephant Hill, the roads get easier (though they remain tough but passable for mountain bikes) and lead to backcountry campsites and various hiking trails. A few other 4WD roads require day-use permits.

It is possible to enter (or exit) the park along equally rugged 4WD roads; the shortest route is 46 miles and would take at least two days. Ask the rangers for details.

Places to Stay The 26-site, year-round *Squaw Flat Campground* ($10), 3 miles beyond the visitor center, is available on a first-come, first-served basis. Spring (from March to May) is the busiest time. There is drinking water. In addition, three group campsites nearby must be reserved at least two weeks ahead (but call far in advance). Group reservations cost $15 plus $3 per person.

Primitive waterless campgrounds are available in the backcountry for backpackers, mountain bikers and those using 4WD; sites are limited. In some areas there is dispersed camping. See Backcountry Permits & Reservations, above, for permit and fee information.

Just outside the park boundary, and signed from Hwy 211, *Needles Outpost* (cell ☎ 979-4007) is a true, off-the-grid outpost. Open March to November, it has gas, a store, a small café, information and maps. The 20-site campground is $15; showers are $3 ($5 for the public). Ask if they have their 'home domes' set up (fiberglass sleep-in observatories), and call ahead for bike and telescope rentals, star parties and scenic flights.

Canyonlands – Horseshoe Canyon & The Maze

The only access to these two remote western sectors of Canyonlands National Park is via dirt roads. There is no drinking water anywhere (though seasonal water exists and must be purified), so this area is for experienced and prepared desert rats.

The Hans Flat Ranger Station (☎ 259-2652) is open 8 am to 4:30 pm daily year-round, and has information about both sectors.

You can reach both Horseshoe Canyon and The Maze directly from Green River via a long dirt road (47 miles to Horseshoe Canyon, 40 additional miles to The Maze). An easier way is via the dirt road that heads southeast from Hwy 24 just south of the turnoff to Goblin Valley State Park. Follow this road 30 miles to Horseshoe Canyon, or after 25 miles, turn onto the road for The Maze. This latter road is suitable for cars only as far as the Hans Flat Ranger Station (20 miles; total trip is about 2½ hours); after that you need 4WD.

Horseshoe Canyon Among several panels of rock art, the most important is the Great Gallery, which contains superb Barrier

Canyon–style pictographs that are between 2000 and 7000 years old. The heroic, supernatural figures are magnificent. Please don't disturb them in any way – even touching them with fingers deposits body oils that damage the paintings. (Damaging the art is also a criminal offense.)

The Great Gallery can be reached by a 7-mile roundtrip hike from the 'main' dirt road, though you can get closer with 4WD. Rangers may lead hikes here in the spring to fall season. The access is downhill to the site.

The Maze The only access to this remote jumble of colorful canyons is via 4WD tracks or hiking trails east of the Hans Flat Ranger Station. This is a rare preserve of true wilderness. The few roads are very poor and can be closed by rain or snow; short-wheelbase, high-clearance 4WDs are the best choice. Hiking trails cut miles from the vehicle routes. Contact the ranger before beginning any trip; plan for stays of at least three days.

Places to Stay Overnight camping, as elsewhere in the park, is by permit only. Those driving or mountain biking must use designated camping areas in The Maze and in areas west of The Maze, which are administered by the Glen Canyon National Recreation Area. None have any facilities and campers must provide their own washable, reusable toilet systems. Hikers have more camping flexibility, but trails are often technical and may require a rope to raise and lower backpacks.

No camping is allowed in Horseshoe Canyon, but you can camp on the rim on BLM land. Carry water.

MOAB
☎ 435 • pop 4779 • elevation 4000 feet
Moab was originally founded by Mormon ranchers and farmers in the late 1870s after repeated attempts by Indians to get rid of them finally failed. Nothing much changed from then until the 1950s, when valuable uranium ores were discovered and the population tripled in three years. In the search

for radioactive gold, miners wove a network of 4WD roads in the area, which now are used by tourists. They also left scars on the landscape, such as radioactive tailings ponds. (Tailings are the waste product of mineral extraction processes.) Mining of salt and potash continues.

As word spread of the grand scenery in southeastern Utah, the movie industry arrived and has since shot hundreds of Westerns here, most from the 1950s to 1970s. But neither the mining boom (which didn't last long) nor Hollywood has had as much influence on the character of Moab today as has the humble mountain biker. In the mid-1980s, an influx of bikers 'discovered' the challenging and scenic slickrock desert and triggered a massive surge in tourism that continues unabated to the present day.

Moab, now the largest town in southeastern Utah, has almost lost its small-town rural roots beneath an ever-growing wave of upscale hotels, chic restaurants and art galleries and over 50 companies offering biking, river-running, backpacking and 4WD tours and rentals. Recreationalists swamp the place from spring to fall, and the impact of all those feet, bikes and 4WDs on the fragile desert is a vital concern. However, the bigger issue for the town itself is how it will shape the next wave of development. Several proposals are currently under review for building exclusive, gated, all-inclusive resorts that, if approved, might turn touristy but still quaint Moab into a desert version of Vail, an upscale Colorado ski town.

Orientation & Information
Hwy 191 becomes Main St, the main drag through town.

The comprehensive, multi-agency Moab Information Center, at the corner of Main and Center, is open for walk-in visitors 8 am to 8 pm. The staff can answer almost any question about the area's national parks, national forests, BLM areas, state parks and the county and city. They have weather and river updates, as well as current availability for the national and state park campgrounds. For information ahead of time, contact the Grand County Travel Council (☎ 259-8825, 800-635-6622), PO Box 550, Moab, UT 84532; visit the council online at www.discovermoab.com.

The following agencies are not open to walk-in visitors, but you can call for information: Canyonlands National Park Headquarters (☎ 259-7164), Manti–La Sal National Forest Moab Ranger Station (☎ 259-7155), and the BLM (☎ 259-6111).

Other services include the post office (☎ 259-7427), 50 E 100 North; library (☎ 259-5421), 25 S 100 East (Internet access is $20 for nonresidents); County Recycling Center (☎ 259-8640), 1000 E Sand Flats Rd; hospital (☎ 259-7191), 719 W 400 North; and police (☎ 259-8938), 115 W 200 South.

Free newspapers include *Moab Happenings,* strongly geared to visitors, and the iconoclastic *Canyon Country Zephyr,* which is recommended reading.

Dan O'Laurie Museum

The diverse collection at this museum (☎ 259-7985), 118 E Center, includes attractive exhibits on everything from local archaeology to uranium to art. They also give out a free, self-guided walking tour brochure of Moab's historic buildings. Hours are 1 to 8 pm Monday to Saturday April to October; 3 to 7 pm (from 1 pm Friday and Saturday) in winter. Admission is free.

Scenic & Backcountry Routes

Around Moab, almost every road, paved or unpaved, is scenic, and the information center has free trip brochures. However, if you travel any of the many hundreds of miles of dirt and 4WD roads (of all levels of difficulty), please stay on them. Driving off established roads causes considerable damage to the land and is usually illegal. The drives below are the cream of the crop.

The paved **Colorado River Byway** (Hwy 128) follows the Colorado River northeast of Moab to Cisco, 44 miles away just off I-70. Highlights are the prominent Fisher Towers and Castle Rock, the 1916 Dewey Bridge (one of the first to cross the Colo-

rado), and sights of rafts running the Colorado River.

About 15 miles along Hwy 128, **La Sal Rd** heads south into the Manti–La Sal National Forest, ascending switchbacks (large RVs not recommended) into the forest and giving fantastic views of canyon country below. The road emerges on Hwy 191, 8 miles south of Moab. This 67-mile loop from Moab (allow three to four hours) is mostly paved and closed in winter.

The 15-mile, paved **Potash Rd** (Hwy 279) goes south from Hwy 191 about 3 miles north of Moab. It is named for the potash extraction plant at the end of it; near the beginning, you pass a radioactive tailings pond – and in the middle, natural beauty abounds. Such are the contradictions of Utah's desert. Highlights are 'Wall St' (a favorite of climbers), Indian petroglyphs and dinosaur tracks, a 1½-mile hiking trail to Corona Arch, and near the end, Jug Handle Arch, which is only 3 feet wide, but 15 times as high. Just past the potash plant, the road continues as a rough 4WD track into the Island in the Sky district of Canyonlands.

The BLM **Canyon Rims Recreation Area** lies east of Canyonlands National Park. The area is reached by turning right off Hwy 191 32 miles south of Moab. The paved Needles Overlook Rd goes about 22 miles to a great view of the national park. About two-thirds of the way along this road, the gravel Anticline Overlook Rd stretches 16 miles north to a promontory with awesome views of the Colorado River. The road is passable to cars. The two roads combined make a good day trip (allow four hours).

The Canyon Rims Recreation Area can also be reached via **Kane Creek Blvd**, a paved road heading west from Moab. It passes petroglyphs and a rock-climbing area, after 4 miles becoming a gravel road as it enters Kane Springs Canyon. After 10 miles you must ford the creek, which, depending on the weather, may be impassable. After 14 miles you reach Hurrah Pass, after which only 4WD vehicles can get through. From here, the road is much more difficult and sometimes confusing, eventually ending about 50 miles later at Hwy 211, east of the

MOAB

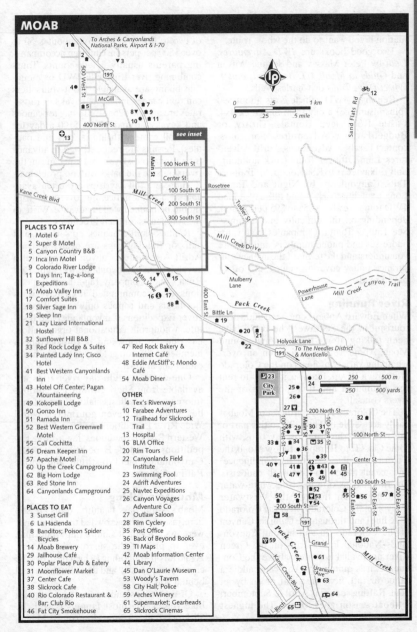

To Arches & Canyonlands
National Parks, Airport & I-70

McGill

500 West St

400 North St

Kane Creek Blvd

Main St

100 North St
Center St
100 South St   Rosetree
200 South St
300 South St

Mill Creek

Tucker St

see inset

Mill Creek Drive

0   .5   1 km
0   .25   .5 mile

Mulberry
Lane

Mill Creek Canyon Trail

Powerhouse
Lane

Mtn View Dr

Pack Creek

Bittle Ln

Holyoak Lane
To The Needles District
& Monticello

Sand Flats Rd

City
Park

200 North St

100 North St

Center St

100 South St

200 South St

300 South St

Grand

Uranium
Ave

Pack Creek

Kane Creek Blvd

Mill Creek

0   250   500 m
0   250   500 yards

PLACES TO STAY
1 Motel 6
2 Super 8 Motel
5 Canyon Country B&B
7 Inca Inn Motel
9 Colorado River Lodge
11 Days Inn; Tag-a-long
   Expeditions
15 Moab Valley Inn
17 Comfort Suites
18 Silver Sage Inn
19 Sleep Inn
21 Lazy Lizard International
   Hostel
32 Sunflower Hill B&B
33 Red Rock Lodge & Suites
34 Painted Lady Inn; Cisco
   Hotel
41 Best Western Canyonlands
   Inn
43 Hotel Off Center; Pagan
   Mountaineering
49 Kokopelli Lodge
50 Gonzo Inn
51 Ramada Inn
52 Best Western Greenwell
   Motel
55 Cali Cochitta
56 Dream Keeper Inn
57 Apache Motel
60 Up the Creek Campground
62 Big Horn Lodge
63 Red Stone Inn
64 Canyonlands Campground

PLACES TO EAT
3 Sunset Grill
6 La Hacienda
8 Banditos; Poison Spider
   Bicycles
14 Moab Brewery
29 Jailhouse Café
30 Poplar Place Pub & Eatery
31 Moonflower Market
37 Center Cafe
38 Slickrock Cafe
40 Rio Colorado Restaurant &
   Bar; Club Rio
46 Fat City Smokehouse

47 Red Rock Bakery &
   Internet Café
48 Eddie McStiff's; Mondo
   Café
54 Moab Diner

OTHER
4 Tex's Riverways
10 Farabee Adventures
12 Trailhead for Slickrock
   Trail
13 Hospital
16 BLM Office
20 Rim Tours
22 Canyonlands Field
   Institute
23 Swimming Pool
24 Adrift Adventures
25 Navtec Expeditions
26 Canyon Voyages
   Adventure Co
27 Outlaw Saloon
28 Rim Cyclery
35 Post Office
36 Back of Beyond Books
39 TI Maps
42 Moab Information Center
44 Library
45 Dan O'Laurie Museum
53 Woody's Tavern
58 City Hall; Police
59 Arches Winery
61 Supermarket; Gearheads
65 Slickrock Cinemas

Needles area of Canyonlands National Park. Contact the BLM for maps and information if you want to do the whole route.

Two good books are *4WD Adventures: Utah* by Peter Massey and Jeanne Wilson and *Guide to Moab, UT, Backroads and 4-Wheel Drive Trails* by Charles Wells.

Renting a 4WD vehicle costs about $90 (plus insurance) a day from Slickrock 4x4, Castle Rock Jeep Rentals, Thrifty, or Budget/Farabee Adventures. For tours, contact Farabee Adventures, Adrift Adventures, Linn Ottinger Tours (rock hounding only), Navtec, OARS, Kokopelli Trails & Tails, Canyonlands by Night and Tag-a-Long Expeditions. Half- and full-day guided 4WD tours are about $55 to $95 per person, depending on the difficulty and distance. See Tour & Rental Companies, below, for addresses and phone numbers, and be sure you understand the terms of the agency's insurance policy covering vehicle use off of paved roads.

River Running

When Edward Abbey bemoaned 'industrial tourism' in the Southwest, he could have been talking about river rafting around Moab. About 18 companies run an overwhelming variety of floats on the Colorado and Green Rivers, but also, it's easy to rent the equipment and float portions of the rivers yourself.

The Colorado River northeast of Moab is easily accessible by Hwy 128, so this part of the river is a favorite for day trips, with some Class II to III rapids. Below Moab, the Colorado is placid (until the Confluence) and excellent for do-it-yourself canoeists. Overnight trips offering true white-water excitement run through the Westwater Canyon of the Colorado (near the Colorado state line) and through the Cataract Canyon of the Colorado (in and beyond Canyonlands National Park). Trips on the Green River are available as well; above the Confluence, it is quite calm. You can paddle a canoe or raft, float on a raft or go by jet boat. Rafting season is April to September; jet-boat season goes longer. The highest water is usually in May and June.

Most rafting tours cost $35 to $45 for a day; jet boats cost up to $70. Overnight tours of two to five days run from about $350 to over $800 per person. Children accompanying parents usually get discounts. Tours combining river trips with 4WD or mountain biking are available. Do-it-yourselfers can rent canoes, inflatable kayaks or rafts – rates are around $25 to $40 a day for canoes and kayaks; around $65 to $100 a day for rafts (all come with life jackets and paddles). Permits are required well in advance for national park rivers, but you can run the rivers outside the parks with no problems.

Half- and full-day trips are often available at a day's notice, but overnight trips should be booked well in advance. Write to the companies for their brochures.

Rentals, shuttle or pick-up services, and half- or full-day trips are available from Adrift Adventures, Canyon Voyages (also kayak lessons), Canyonlands by Night, Red River Canoe Company, Tag-a-Long Expeditions, the recommended Tex's Riverways (jet boats and canoes only) and Western River Expeditions. Canyonlands Field Institute, a nonprofit educational organization, has one-day trips, and if you become a member ($20), you get access to the cheapest rentals in town.

One-day and multi-day river trips are available from Sheri Griffith Expeditions (more upscale, with specialty trips for families, women and even gourmets), World Wide River Expeditions, Adrift Adventures, Western River Expeditions, Tag-a-Long Expeditions, Navtec Expeditions, OARS, Canyonlands Field Institute and Moab Rafting Company.

Mountain Biking

Moab's world-class, beautiful trails are still here, just a *lot* more crowded than they once were. As a result, it's more important than ever to protect the surrounding desert. Avoid all off-trail riding (which destroys the cryptobiotic crusts), and don't litter the trail behind you.

Of the dozens and dozens of mountain-bike routes, the most famous is still the **Slickrock Trail**, a 9.6-mile loop on BLM land beginning from the end of Sand Flats Rd about 3 miles east of town. This challenging trip can take half a day; novices can practice on a 2-mile loop near the start. The trail is the only one with a fee ($5 for three days).

The BLM and Travel Council have brochures describing other routes. The 'bible' of biking is the comprehensive *Above and Beyond Slickrock* by Todd Campbell. A fun read by a serious biker is *Rider Mel's Mountain Bike Guide to Moab,* which is small enough to ride with.

The busiest biking seasons are spring and fall when thousands of riders visit the area. Summer is too hot and snow can cover trails in winter.

The original Rim Cyclery, the oldest rental place, has a 'museum' of mountain bike technology. For rentals and tours, also try Kaibab Outfitters & Moab Cyclery, Poison Spider Bicycles & Nichols Expeditions, the venerable Rim Tours, Western Spirit Cycling and others. Full suspension bikes start around $30, and day tours with rentals are around $95.

Rock Climbing

In addition to the national parks, other recommended spots are Fisher Towers, top roping at Wall St on Potash Road (a good place to meet other climbers) and Indian Creek off Hwy 211 on the way to the Needles district of Canyonlands National Park.

Buy all the equipment you need at Gearheads and Pagan Mountaineering, which runs custom guided trips. Moab Desert Adventures offers guided trips, and Moab Adventure Outfitters has lessons.

Hiking

No roof rack, trailer or 4WD? Don't worry. They aren't really requirements in Moab, it just seems that way. Hikers will of course head first for the national parks, but don't miss the following local spots.

Three miles along Hwy 128 (from Hwy 191) is the **Negro Bill Canyon Trail**, which follows a pretty stream for 2 miles to the expansive Morning Glory Natural Bridge. Twenty-one miles along Hwy 128 (from Hwy 191) is the 2.2-mile **Fisher Towers Trail;**

you'll recognize the stunning towers from TV and the movies. Follow Hwy 279 for 10 miles to reach the trailhead to **Corona Arch**, which even local rangers rave about. Many locals prefer the uncrowded **Mill Creek Canyon**, which also follows a stream and leads to a natural bridge; to reach the trailhead, go to the end of Powerhouse Lane off of Mill Creek Dr. The visitor center also has a hiking brochure.

For guided hikes, Canyonlands Field Institute offers interesting half- and full-day hikes (and longer trips) led by knowledgeable guides. The hiking and rock art tours run by Canyon Voyages Adventure Co also come recommended.

Other Activities

Those interested in **horseback riding** can enjoy two-hour trail rides for around $30 and full-day rides for $85. Call Cowboy Adventures or the Pack Creek Ranch for information. **Golf** at the 18-hole/par 72 Moab Golf Course (☎ 259-6488), 2705 S E Bench Rd. **Butch Cassidy's King World Waterpark** (☎ 259-2837), 1500 N Hwy 191, just north of town, provides cool relief May to September; all-day passes are $11 for adults and $9 for children three to 12.

Tour & Rental Companies

Rim Cyclery rents backpacking, skiing and camping gear. Others renting camping gear include Canyonlands Field Institute, Tag-a-Long Expeditions, Western River Expeditions, Gearheads and Pagan Mountaineering.

Scenic flights are available at the airport. Many local people and visitors and most NPS officials disapprove of them because the noise from the low-flying airplanes (and helicopters) ruins the quiet and scenic outdoor experience.

The companies mentioned above (and listed below) come variously recommended; many have been around for years, if not decades, and new companies open every year. The information center lists over 50 tour and rental companies. Some of these offices may be closed in winter. To send mail to any of the companies listed here, add Moab, UT 84532 to the address.

Adrift Adventures (☎ 259-8594, 800-874-4483)
378 N Main; PO Box 577
website: www.adrift.net

Canyon Voyages (☎ 259-4121, 800-733-6007)
211 N Main; PO Box 416
website: www.canyonvoyages.com

Canyonlands by Night (☎ 259-5261, 800-394-9978)
PO Box 328

Canyonlands Field Institute (☎ 259-7750,
800-860-5262) 1320 S Hwy 191; PO Box 68
website: www.canyonlandsfieldinst.org

Castle Rock Jeep Rentals (☎ 259-5432)
481 S Main; PO Box 939

Cowboy Adventures (☎ 259-7410)
2231 S Hwy 191; PO Box 104

Farabee Adventures (☎ 259-7494, 888-806-5337)
401 N Main; PO Box 664

Gearheads (☎ 259-4327, 888-740-4327) 471 S Main

Kaibab Outfitters & Moab Cyclery (☎ 259-7423,
800-451-1133) 391 S Main
website: www.moabcyclery.com

Kokopelli Trails & Tails (☎ 259-5498, 800-206-
3669) 2182 Buena Vista; PO Box 1462

Lin Ottinger Tours (☎ 259-7312) 600 N Main

Moab Adventure Outfitters (☎ 259-2725)
550 N Main

Moab Desert Adventures (☎ 260-2404, 259-3586)
801 E Oak
website: www.moabdesertadventures.com

Moab Rafting (☎ 259-7238, 800-746-6622)
PO Box 801
website: www.moab-rafting.com

Navtec Expeditions (☎ 259-7983, 800-833-1278)
321 N Main; PO Box 1267
website: www.navtec.com

Nichols Expeditions (☎ 259-3999, 800-648-8488)
497 N Main
website: www.nicholsexpeditions.com

OARS (☎ 259-5865, 800-346-6277) 543 N Main
website: www.oarsutah.com

Pack Creek Ranch (☎ 259-5505) PO Box 1270
website: www.packcreekranch.com

Pagan Mountaineering (☎ 259-1117) 88 E Center

Poison Spider Bicycles (☎ 259-7882, 800-635-1792)
497 N Main
website: www.poisonspiderbicycles.com

Red River Canoe Company (☎ 259-7722, 800-753-
8216) PO Box 3116, Castle Valley, UT 84532
website: www.redrivercanoe.com

Rim Cyclery (☎ 259-5333) 94 W 100 North
website: www.rimcyclery.com

Rim Tours (☎ 259-5223, 800-626-7335)
1233 S Hwy 191
website: www.rimtours.com

Sheri Griffith Expeditions (☎ 259-8229, 800-332-
2439) 2231 S Hwy 191; PO Box 1324
website: www.griffithexp.com

Slickrock 4x4 (☎ 259-5678, 888-238-5337)
284 N Main

Tag-a-Long Expeditions (☎ 259-8946, 800-453-
3292) 452 N Main
website: www.tagalong.com

Tex's Riverways (☎ 259-5101) 691 N 500 West;
PO Box 67
website: www.texsriverways.com

Thrifty (☎ 259-7317) 711 S Main

Western River Expeditions (☎ 259-7019, 888-622-
4097) 1371 N Hwy 191
website: www.westernriver.com

Western Spirit Cycling (☎ 259-8732, 800-845-2453)
478 Mill Creek Dr
website: www.westernspirit.com

World Wide River Expeditions (☎ 259-7515, 800-
231-2769) 625 N Riversands
website: www.worldwideriver.com

Special Events

Moab loves to celebrate the outdoor activities for which it is famous. Dates vary each year – call the Travel Council (☎ 259-8825, 800-635-6622). Kicking off the season is a half marathon in late March. Over 2000 Jeeps arrive for the year's biggest event, the Jeep Safari, the week before Easter. The Arts Festival in late May keeps growing. In June there's a rodeo, and in early August, the Grand County Fair. October sees the Moab Gem & Mineral Show and the Fat Tire Bike Festival – one of the biggest biking events in Utah and the last fling of the season. The festival has tours, workshops, lessons, competitions and plenty of musical entertainment. Afterward, Moab gets very quiet; it's a good time to be here if the weather holds.

Places to Stay

Moab has a wide variety of good accommodations, suiting all budgets and tastes, with more hotels being built all the time. Moab Central Reservations (☎ 259-5125, 800-748-4386), 50 E Center, Moab, UT 84532, makes reservations for hotels and tours; visit www.moabutahlodging.com. Another agency is Moab Realty Property Management (☎ 259-6050, 800-897-7325).

The Moab high season is a long one – from mid-March to late October. Reservations are always recommended. High-season rates are given below, but rates during holiday weekends or special events may be higher. After the October Fat Tire Bike Festival, rates can drop 50% overnight.

Camping The bucolic, well-located *Up the Creek Campground* (☎ 259-2213, 210 E 300 South) is the backpackers' choice. It has nice showers ($5 for nonguests) and 20 tent-only walk-in sites ($10) open March through October. Also near downtown, the year-round *Canyonlands Campground* (☎ 259-6848, 800-522-6848, 555 S Main) has 130 dusty sites; tents/RVs are $16/22.

Five private campgrounds line Hwy 191 north of town; all have showers and laundry. The closest is *Portal RV Park* (☎ 259-6108, 800-574-2028, 1261 N Hwy 191). Grassy sites are $17/25 for tents/RVs. Seven camping cabins are $35 to $42. Nearby is *Slickrock Campground* (☎ 259-7660, 800-448-8873, 1301½ N Hwy 191), with over 200 pretty tree-shaded sites ($16-22); camping cabins are $27. Facilities include a pool, hot tub and groceries.

The two closest campgrounds to Arches are *Moab Valley RV & Campark* (☎ 259-4469, 1773 N Hwy 191) and *Riverside Oasis* (☎ 259-3424, 877-285-7757, 1861 N Hwy 191). Both have pleasant sites for $16 to $24; camping cabins are $40.

Archview Campground (☎ 259-7854, 800-813-6622) is 9 miles north of Moab on Hwy 191 at Hwy 313 (the turnoff for Canyonlands). Its 85 sites are $16.50 to $20; cabins are $28. It may close in winter. Complete facilities include a pool, gas station and grocery store.

Heading south of Moab, you'll find *Moab Rim Campark* (☎ 259-5002, 888-599-6622, 1900 S Hwy 191). Grassy and scenic sites run $15 to $20. Also pretty, *Spanish Trail RV Park* (☎ 259-2411, 800-787-2751, 2980 S

Hwy 191) has sites for $17 to $24. About 4 miles south of town, *Moab KOA* (☎ 259-6682, 3225 S Hwy 191) is packed with amenities. Open from early March through October, its 130 sites are $20 to $27. Kamping Kabins are $40 to $48.

In the La Sal Mountains off La Sal Rd, east of Moab, are two summer-only Manti–La Sal National Forest campgrounds. The free *Oowah Lake Campground* has six sites but no water. The 20-site *Warner Lake Campground* ($5) has water (no showers).

The BLM (☎ 259-2100) operates a number of year-round campgrounds in the area. Along Hwy 128 are nine campgrounds ($5-10); all have vault toilets, none have water, and some have picnic tables and grills. In the Canyon Rims Recreation Area, *Wind Whistle Campground* on the Needles Overlook Rd, and *Hatch Point Campground* on Anticline Overlook Rd, both have water, pit toilets and charge $10 from April to October. On Kane Creek Rd are four primitive campsites (pit toilets but no water) for $5. The *Sand Flats Recreation Area*, at the Slickrock Trail, has almost 150 sites ($6) with pit toilets but no water.

A dozen places in town allow public use of their **showers** for $3 to $5. The information center has a list.

Budget The friendly *Lazy Lizard International Hostel* (☎ 259-6057, 1213 S Hwy 191) has four dorms with 23 beds ($8 per person), and a few basic rooms ($20-22). Eight newer log cabins ($25-44) are pleasant. Facilities include a hot tub, coin laundry, guest kitchen, a TV/video room, Internet access ($1/10 minutes) and showers ($2 for nonguests).

Otherwise, the cheapest motels are $40/50 for singles/doubles in the high season. *Inca Inn Motel* (☎ 259-7261, 570 N Main) has small but perfectly tidy rooms (no phones); doubles are only $45, and rates are the same all week. *Silver Sage Inn* (☎ 259-4420, 840 S Main) has remodeled but still basic motel rooms (with phones) and is run by the Lutheran Church; profits go to charity. The charming *Hotel Off Center*

(☎ 259-4244, 96 E Center) reflects the wry personality of its owner, a sometime prop- and set-maker for films. The eight rooms lack phones but are otherwise homespun works of art. Exceedingly clean bathrooms are down the hall, the communal kitchen is a joy, and a five-bed dorm room is $12 per person.

Mid-Range Moab has a slew of independent motels, from run-of-the-mill to very nice, renting doubles for $65 to $90 in high season, plus a few *chain motels* like Motel 6, Super 8 and Days Inn. Below are the non-chain highlights.

Closed in winter, the *Colorado River Lodge* (☎ 259-6122, 512 N Main) has 22 plain but clean motel rooms; single/doubles are $55/65. One of the best values in town is the charming *Kokopelli Lodge* (☎ 259-7615, 888-530-3134, 72 S 100 East). A quiet block from the hub of Moab, its eight small rooms ($56-67) have access to a shaded garden and hot tub. Another good deal is the rustic-looking *Red Stone Inn* (☎ 259-3500, 535 S Main), which has 50 small, wood-paneled rooms (doubles $55 to $65), all with microwave and refrigerator.

The *Red Rock Lodge & Suites* (☎ 259-5431, 877-207-9708, 51 N 100 West) has 23 comfortable, clean motel rooms for $60 to $70 and suites with full kitchens for $125. It also runs two nearby properties; for both, call the Red Rock Lodge. The historic *Cisco Hotel*, across the street, has nine attractive rooms with kitchenettes ($75-95), and the *Painted Lady Inn*, (41 W 100 North) has a pool and 52 completely remodeled cottages of various sizes, some with kitchens ($60-95).

For $80 a night, the *Apache Motel* (☎ 259-5727, 800-228-6882, 166 S 400 East) has nice rooms a bit far from the main drag. If you're a fan, John Wayne's Suite, where the actor stayed whenever he was filming, might be worth the splurge ($120). The *Big Horn Lodge* (☎ 259-6171, 800-325-6171, 550 S Main) has been remodeled in the 'log pine gothic' style, but is very comfortable.

The reservation services listed at the beginning of this section will find you condo and house rentals from $60 to $200 a night,

or you can call the information center (☎ 259-8825, 800-635-6622) for a list. Most condo complexes have about six units or less and require advance reservations.

Top End Top-end *chain motels* include Comfort Suites, Ramada Inn and Best Western. The latter has two properties in the heart of town and charges $90 to $130 in high season. With doubles from $85 to $110, the large *Moab Valley Inn* (☎ 259-4419, 800-831-6622, 711 S Main) has smaller standard rooms, some with kitchenettes.

Equivalent to Best Western is *Aarchway Inn* (☎ 259-2599, 800-341-9359, 1551 N Hwy 191), just north of town, with 97 rooms for $90 to $95; suites run $120 to $150.

With more style than any other top-end hotel, the *Gonzo Inn* (☎ 259-2515, 800-791-4044, 100 W 200 South) appeals to the upscale mountain biker with areas for storage, wash and repair. The hip modern décor emphasizes brushed metal, earth tones and funky light fixtures. All 43 rooms ($120) and suites ($155 to $185) are quite large and have balconies, while suites also have a wet bar, kitchenette, fireplace and jetted tub. There's a pool and hot tub. Just look for the giant gecko.

A special place that's worth the trek is *Pack Creek Ranch* (☎ 259-5505). To get there, take Hwy 191 south of Moab about 9 miles and turn east on La Sal Mountain Loop Rd; almost immediately, take a right at the T Junction and drive about 6 miles to the 300-acre ranch, scenically located at over 6000 feet in the La Sal Mountains. It has 11 historic, fully equipped, comfortable cabins sleeping between two and 12 guests. All exude Western authenticity, though the Ranch House and M-4 Cabin are particularly memorable. Edward Abbey, who was a friend of the owner's, wrote *Fool's Progress* in the Road House. Facilities include a seasonal pool, hot tub, sauna and large lawn with picnic areas. Summer rates range from $175 to $300 (with weekly discounts) and include full breakfast. The restaurant (open to guests only) also does pack lunches and 'cook-your-own-meat' dinners. Winter rates, when the restaurant is closed, are $120 to

$230. There are hiking trails (cross-country skiing in winter) and guided horseback trips into the mountains.

website: www.packcreekranch.com

New B&Bs crop up every year in Moab; the information center has a full list. Almost all have no-smoking policies.

One of the best is actually in Castle Valley, 20 miles northeast of Moab. The *Castle Valley Inn* (☎ 259-6012, 888-466-6012, 424 Amber Lane) has five rooms and three cottages, with excellent views of the mountains. All rooms have private baths, and the cottages have kitchenettes. The owners are well traveled and friendly. Amenities include a hot tub, pleasant gardens and a living room with fireplace. Good lunches and dinners are available with advance notice. It may close in winter. Rates are $95 to $140 for double rooms, $160 for cottages.

website: www.castlevalleyinn.com

Much more modest, the *Canyon Country B&B* (☎ 259-5262, 888-350-5262, 590 N 500 West) is in a quiet residential home with five rooms (no phones), two with shared bath, for $65 to $110.

website: www.canyoncountrybb.com

The following three have rates from $90 to $150, include full breakfast and are lovely and romantic. The *Sunflower Hill B&B* (☎ 259-2974, 800-662-2786, 185 N 300 East) has 11 rooms in a restored historic home; visit www.sunflowerhill.com. At *Cali Cochitta* (☎ 259-4961, 888-429-8112, 110 S 200 East), the owners love to cook and do gourmet dinners on request; its website is www.moabdreaminn.com. The *Dream Keeper Inn* (☎ 259-5998, 888-230-3247, 191 S 200 East) has relaxing grounds, a pool and hot tub, and bike storage and workbench; visit www.dreamkeeperinn.com.

Places to Eat

With so many tourists passing through, it's hardly surprising that Moab has a good selection of restaurants.

In the historic 1885 courthouse, the *Jailhouse Café* (☎ 259-3900, 101 N Main) serves delicious breakfasts ($7-10) until noon daily, 'til 1 pm on weekends. Get a morning latte and Belgian waffle at the tiny, crowded

Mondo Café (☎ 259-5551), in the plaza at Center and Main, or opt for a fresh-baked pastry at *Red Rock Bakery & Internet Café* (☎ 259-5941, 74 S Main), which also makes fat sandwiches on homemade bread (Internet access is $1/5 minutes). *Moab Diner* (☎ 259-4006, 189 S Main) dishes up classic, reasonably priced diner fare all day.

Though it's a private club, the popular *Rio Colorado Restaurant & Bar* (☎ 259-6666, 2 S 100 West) allows children in its restaurant section. Its Southwestern-inspired, dinner-only menu has entrees for $9 to $15; open from 4 pm daily (from 11 am Sunday). Everyone packs into *La Hacienda* (☎ 259-6319, 574 N Main) for its excellent Mexican meals ($7-14), served from 11 am daily.

Local bikers claim you get the most burrito for your buck at *Banditos* (☎ 259-3894, 467 N Main). For unpretentious, smoky-good barbecue, pedal over to *Fat City Smokehouse* (☎ 259-4302, 36 S 100 West). Ribs, steaks, tuna and sandwiches range from $6 to $17. It opens daily at 4:30 pm.

Buck's Grill House (☎ 259-5201, 1393 N Hwy 191), is a premium steakhouse and local favorite, open nightly at 5:30 pm. In addition to steaks ($15-20), it serves Southwestern cuisine and other meats, such as venison, buffalo and game hen. Serving American food that's vaguely Southwestern, *Slickrock Cafe* (☎ 259-8004, 5 N Main) is relaxed and very Moab, but it's so popular with the biking and outdoor crowd that service can suffer when it's busy.

You can't beat the views at the *Sunset Grill* (☎ 259-7146, 900 N Hwy 191), which serves the old standbys of prime rib, filet mignon and shrimp scampi ($14-21). The restaurant is up a steep, ill-maintained road and opens nightly at 5 pm. The critically acclaimed *Center Cafe* (☎ 259-4295, 60 N 100 West) consistently tops the lists of best restaurants in southern Utah. Its seasonally changing menu never fails to be inventive and satisfying, is paired with a good wine list, and served by a professional waitstaff who are appropriately casual and friendly. The gourmet food isn't cheap – appetizers run $9 to $12 and entrees $20 to $27 – but you won't regret a penny while lapping up the last of your delectably fresh fruit sorbet. Open nightly from 5:30 pm; reservations recommended.

The boisterous and busy *Eddie McStiff's* (☎ 259-2337, 57 S Main) runs a microbrewery (not on the premises) and a restaurant with a complete menu; the pizzas here are great. The bar side offers pool, shuffleboard and foosball tables, as well as a big-screen sports TV.

Poplar Place Pub & Eatery (☎ 259-6018, 11 E 100 North) remains a 'popular' watering hole; it has microbrews on tap and good pub grub. A quieter place is *Moab Brewery* (☎ 259-6333, 686 S Main), which brews its own on the premises, serves lunch and dinner, and has pool tables and other games.

Or, round off your day with a Western cookout at the *Bar M Chuckwagon* (☎ 259-2276, 800-214-2085), 7 miles north of Moab on Hwy 191. It's unapologetic tourist fun: get there by 7 pm to catch the gunfight in the faux Western town, which is followed by a meaty cowboy dinner and a Western music show. Everything is included for $20; reservations are suggested. Open daily except Sunday from April to September.

Moab also has *Moonflower Market* (☎ 259-5712, 39 E 100 North), a nonprofit, organic produce store with bulk spices and grains, plus a lending library, art gallery and general good vibes.

Entertainment

In addition to the pubs mentioned above, you can get a drink and listen to live music (mainly rock and blues on the weekends) at the following private clubs: *Woody's Tavern* (☎ 259-9323, 165 S Main), *Outlaw Saloon* (☎ 259-2654, 44 W 200 North) and *Club Rio* in the Rio Colorado Restaurant. The *Sportsman's Lounge* (☎ 259-9972, 1991 S Hwy 191) has country & western bands and dancing.

Canyonlands by Night (☎ 259-5261) runs a two-hour guided boat trip on the Colorado at sunset (including a light show on the cliffs), with a barbecue dinner beforehand. A boat trip is $25/15 for adults/children six to 12; a trip and dinner is $38/22. Trips

depart from 1861 N Hwy 191 (by the river bridge) at sunset nightly during the summer.

See movies at *Slickrock Cinemas* (☎ 259-4441, 580 Kane Creek Blvd).

Shopping

Southeast Utah's premiere independent bookstore is Back of Beyond Books (☎ 259-5154), 83 N Main. It has a comprehensive selection of regional guides, histories, fiction and magazines – and a very knowledgeable staff. TI Maps (☎ 259-5525), 29 E Center, has all the maps and guides you'll need, and the visitor information center also has a good selection. To purchase a book in advance, get a mail-order catalog from Canyonlands Natural History Association (☎ 259-6003, 800-840-8978), 3031 S Hwy 191, Moab, UT 84532; order online at www.cnha.org.

The Moab Rock Shop (☎ 259-7312), 600 N Main, is a rock hound's paradise. And you can't throw a spoke without hitting a gift shop or art gallery on Main St – some are actually quite good.

For good wine without all the extras, go for a tasting at *Arches Winery* (☎ 259-5397, 420 Kane Creek Blvd); it's open noon to 8 pm Monday to Saturday.

Getting There & Away

For information on train and Greyhound bus service, see Green River, earlier. Bighorn Express (☎ 888-655-7433) has a daily van between Moab and the Salt Lake City Airport ($49, 4½ hours). Taxis and bike shuttles are available from Coyote Shuttle (☎ 259-8656), Roadrunner Shuttle (☎ 259-9402) and Acme Bike Shuttle (☎ 259-2534).

NEWSPAPER ROCK RECREATION AREA

This tiny, free recreation area showcases a single large sandstone rock packed with over 300 petroglyphs chipped out by different Indian groups over a 3000-year period. The site, about 12 miles along Hwy 211 from Hwy 191, is usually visited as a short stop on the way to the Needles section of Canyonlands National Park.

Trail of the Ancients

The tourist office moniker 'Trail of the Ancients' refers generally to all of the splendid natural and historic sites in the Four Corners area (where Utah, Arizona, Colorado and New Mexico meet). In Utah, it describes a route that, starting at Monticello, makes a rough, clockwise circle in the sparsely populated southeast corner of the state. This section follows that same path, though other routes are possible. You will find that the crowds thin out considerably south of Moab.

MONTICELLO
☎ 435 • pop 1958 • elevation 7069 feet

Pronounced 'Montisello,' this ranching and mining town in the Abajo Mountains foothills is greener and cooler than others in the region. The seat of San Juan County, which covers the entire southeast corner of Utah, Monticello is the best place to stop for area information before heading farther south.

The Abajo Mountains, rising to 11,360 feet in the Manti–La Sal National Forest, have plenty of camping, hiking, cross-country skiing and snowmobiling opportunities. The paved Harts Draw Road, closed by snow in winter, goes 17 scenic miles through the mountains to Newspaper Rock Recreation Area on Hwy 211.

Orientation & Information
Hwy 191 (Main St) is the main drag through town. Central St becomes Hwy 666, heading east into Colorado.

The multi-agency San Juan Visitor Center (☎ 587-3235, 800-574-4386), 117 S Main, PO Box 490, Monticello, UT 84535, is open from 9 am to 5 pm weekdays in winter. From mid-March to October it is also open 10 am to 5 pm on weekends and may have longer weekday hours. The center has a bookstore and extensive area information, including the national parks, national forests, BLM and state areas of southeastern Utah. Its website is www

.southeastutah.com. The USFS Manti–La Sal Forest Ranger Station (☎ 587-2041), 496 E Central, and the BLM (☎ 587-2141), 435 N Main, are open to walk-in visitors.

Places to Stay & Eat
In town are a few modest RV parks (tents/RVs are $17/20 or less). West of town are two Manti–La Sal National Forest campgrounds ($7) with water and pit toilets. All are open mid-May to October.

The very clean and tidy *Triangle H Motel* (☎ 587-2274, 800-657-6622, 164 E Central) has singles/doubles in the $30s/40s in summer. The larger *Canyonlands Motor Inn* (☎ 587-2266, 800-952-6212, 197 N Main) is only slightly more expensive. *Chain motels*, with doubles in the $60s and $70s, include Super 8, Days Inn and Best Western.

For a meal, *Los Tachos* (☎ 587-2959, 280 E Central) serves authentic Mexican food, and *Grandma's Kitchen* (☎ 587-3017, 133 E Central) is the real deal: Grandma whips up filling country dinners ($6-8) and an all-you-can-eat buffet ($10). For good steaks and burgers ($7-18) in a Western setting there's *MD Ranch Cookhouse* (☎ 587-3299, 380 S Main).

BLANDING
☎ 435 • pop 3162 • elevation 6000 feet

Settled relatively late, in 1905, Blanding is now an agricultural center. Until the new visitor center is completed at Main and Center Sts, get information at the museum (see below).

Edge of the Cedars State Park
Well worth a stop, this park (☎ 678-2238), 660 W 400 North, has a short self-guided trail through partially excavated Puebloan ceremonial and living quarters built on this site between AD 750 and 1220. The adjoining museum has an extensive collection of Ancestral Puebloan pottery and other good exhibits. Programs occur year-round. Hours are 9 am to 5 pm (8 am to 8 pm mid-May to mid-September); admission is $3 per person, $5 per carload.

Places to Stay & Eat

The year-round *Kampark* (☎ 678-2770, 861 S Main) has tent/RV sites for $10/14. Off Hwy 191 north of town are two summer-only USFS campgrounds ($6-10) with water and pit toilets.

For decent rooms in the $30s in summer, try *Blanding Sunset Inn* (☎ 678-3323, 88 W Center) or *Cliff Palace Motel* (☎ 678-2264, 800-553-8093, 132 S Main). *Prospector Motor Lodge* (☎ 678-3231, 591 S Main) has better rooms in the $40s. *Four Corners Inn* (☎ 678-3257, 800-574-3150, 131 E Center) has large, well-kept rooms for $50/62 a single/double. The 19th-century *Rogers House B&B* (☎ 678-3932, 800-355-3932, 412 S Main) has five lovely rooms that are a great deal for $55 to $65, including full breakfast.

Blanding is a dry town, so no alcohol is sold anywhere. This may or may not explain its dearth of good places to eat. A few mediocre restaurants are on Main and Center Sts.

HOVENWEEP NATIONAL MONUMENT

Hovenweep, meaning 'deserted valley' in the Ute language, is a remote place straddling the Utah–Colorado state line. Six sets of prehistoric Puebloan Indian sites are found here – this was once home to a large population before droughts forced them out in the late 1200s.

Established in 1923, Hovenweep has long had the reputation for being in the middle of nowhere. While nowhere is still close by, well-signed paved roads now lead travelers unerringly to the ranger station and main site, the Square Tower area. Those who make the drive are rewarded with a quiet experience of ancient ruins that remain virtually untouched – neither excavated, restored nor reconstructed.

Information

The ranger station (☎ 970-560-4282) stays open 8 am to 4:30 pm daily, a little later in summer. Rangers give out information and water and sell maps and books. A new visitor center is due to be completed in 2002. However, travelers should be self-sufficient when coming here; there is no food or con-

cessions. Gnats, more than mosquitos, can be a problem in late spring, when there are also strong winds. Entrance fee is $6 per car. Further information is available from Hovenweep National Monument, McElmo Route, Cortez, CO 81321.

A nice 31-site *campground* ($10) with water and toilets is about a mile from the ranger station. It is open year-round on a first-come, first-served basis; it almost never fills up.

The best route to get here is on paved Hwy 262, east of Hwy 191, via Hatch Trading Post (itself an atmospheric stop). Use extreme caution traveling any of the unpaved roads in this region; all become treacherous in wet weather and it is easy to get lost.

Hiking

Two loop hiking trails (the longest is 1½ miles) leave from near the ranger station and pass a number of buildings in the Square Tower area. The trails take you right up to the sites – please don't touch or climb on the buildings; they are fragile and easily damaged. It is illegal to move or disturb anything within the monument.

The Square Tower area is the largest and best-preserved site. The five other groupings are isolated and more difficult to reach, involving several miles of very rough driving or hiking. Ask the rangers for directions and advice.

BLUFF

☎ 435 • pop 320 • elevation 4380 feet

The 'Hole-in-the-Rock' pioneers (see Grand Staircase–Escalante National Monument, in the Southwestern Utah chapter) finished their arduous journey here and established San Juan County's first non-Indian settlement in 1880. A number of interesting early pioneer homes are still in use.

This pleasant town, surrounded by red-rock scenery, makes a great, laid-back base for exploring the surrounding countryside. West of town are a number of spectacular drives, and Bluff is an ideal starting point for running the San Juan River. Across the river is the **Navajo Indian Reservation**, and several trading posts in town sell high-quality Navajo crafts, rugs, jewelry and pottery. In late August, Bluff hosts a major Navajo Fair.

Orientation & Information

Almost all businesses are along Hwy 163/191, which is Main St in town. North of Main is the historic town center.

Informal visitor information (including a self-guided tour of historic buildings and local rock art sites) is available from most Bluff businesses; townsfolk are almost uniformly friendly and helpful. There is a post office on Main St, but no bank. The Sinclair gas station has an ATM.

Backcountry Drives

This corner of Utah is ripe for adventurous exploration. Two dirt roads straddling Comb Ridge stand out; both run for about 20 miles between Hwys 163 and 95 (parallel to Hwy 191). The first, CR262/230, runs in Butler Wash, above the ridge, and ends at the Butler Wash Ruins near Hwy 95. The second, CR235, runs in Comb Wash, below the ridge; views are fantastic, and the ridge contains numerous ancient cliff dwellings (bring binoculars). High-clearance vehicles are preferred; in wet weather, these roads are impassable. Check the Monticello BLM (☎ 587-2141) for information and road conditions; primitive camping in established sites is free. To find the roads, head west on Hwy 163 and look for small county road signs on either side of mile marker 37.

River Running

Most trips begin at the Sand Island Recreation Area (see Places to Stay, below). Boaters must obtain permits from the BLM (see Monticello, earlier; ☎ 587-2141) as far ahead as possible. A good guidebook is *San Juan Canyons: A River Runner's Guide* by D Baars & G Stevenson. The main season is March through October.

Wild Rivers Expeditions (☎ 672-2244, 800-422-7654) has been leading fun, educational river trips for over four decades; guides are knowledgeable about area geology, archaeology and history. White water

is minimal to moderate. Tours range from one-day trips ($120) to seven-day adventures ($1095). A four-person minimum usually applies.
website: www.riversandruins.com

Organized Tours

The hip folks at Far Out Expeditions (☎ 672-2294), 7th East and Mulberry Ave, arrange off-the-beaten-track day trips; the one to Monument Valley includes lunch with a Navajo family and a weaving demonstration ($100 per person). Or just tell them what you want to see: customized half- and full-day tours are $65/125 per person (four-person minimums apply). Ask about their cookouts (for small groups) and their bunkhouse (see Places to Stay, below).
website: www.faroutexpeditions.com

The Pioneer House Inn (see Places to Stay) also arranges guided trips.

Places to Stay

Bluff has a great selection of lodgings; reservations are recommended in summer. Unless otherwise noted, all businesses are on Main St.

The BLM's *Sand Island Recreation Area*, on the San Juan River west of town off Hwy 163, has water, pit toilets and five camping sites ($6).

Cottonwood RV Park (☎ 672-2287), off Main St behind the Cottonwood Steakhouse, has showers and tent/RV sites for $10/16. *Cadillac Ranch RV Park* (☎ 672-2262, 800-538-6195) has showers and sites for $16.

The very attractive *Far Out Bunkouse* run by Far Out Expeditions (see above) has a fabulous kitchen and two cozy rooms, each with six bunks and a private bath. Rates range from $65 to $85 per room depending on the number of people.

The *Dairy Café* (☎ 672-2287) has seven clean, take-them-as-they-are cabins (no phones) for $40; they close in winter. The friendly *Mokee Motel* (☎ 672-2242) has six small, nicely renovated rooms ($45 for two), and *Kokopelli Inn* (☎ 672-2322, 800-541-8854) has 26 clean, standard motel rooms ($50).

Recapture Lodge (☎ 672-2281) has been the center of hospitality in Bluff since 1959. Its 28 wood-paneled rooms have balconies or porches ($44 to $56 for two people). Facilities include a pool, hot tub, coin laundry, picnic areas and hiking trails to the San Juan River. Every night in summer local naturalists present free slide shows.

The nicest digs in town are at the timbered *Desert Rose Inn* (☎ 672-2303, 888-475-7673), whose 30 rooms and six cabins are plushly rustic, with lovely quilts, satellite TVs and data ports. Rooms are $70 to $80 in high season; cabins are $15 more.

The lively 1898 *Pioneer House Inn* (☎ 672-2446, 888-637-2582), at 3rd East and Mulberry Ave, has three enormous suites with kitchens that are full of character ($70 for two people). Two smaller rooms ($56) are less appealing. All rooms have private bath, and a hearty breakfast is included. website: www.pioneerhouseinn.com

Bluff has several other attractive B&Bs, including *Calf Canyon B&B* (☎ 672-2470, 888-922-2470), at 7th East and Black Locust Ave; its three Southwestern-decorated rooms are $70 to $90.

Places to Eat

The prominent *Twin Rocks Café* (☎ 672-2341, 800-526-3448) serves delicious Mexican and country cooking daily; this is a good place to try a Navajo taco. *Turquoise Restaurant* (☎ 672-2279) serves a small menu of Navajo and American food daily.

Cottonwood Steakhouse (☎ 672-2282) serves steak or barbecued chicken dinners both inside and outside (under an old cottonwood tree) from 6 pm March through November. The delightful owner at *Cow Canyon Trading Post & Restaurant* (☎ 672-2208) cooks homemade gourmet meals in summer from 6 to 9 pm Thursday to Monday. The trading post, open daily, includes a bookstore with a sophisticated selection of regional histories.

VALLEY OF THE GODS

In most other states, this uncrowded, intimate, butte-filled valley would be a state park, if not a national park, but such are the riches of Utah that here it is merely a BLM-administered area (get information in Monticello). Locals call it a 'mini–Monument Valley,' and the 17-mile drive (between Hwys 163 and 261) on a good graded dirt road provides wonderful views of the Cedar Mesa cliffs. There are no facilities; free primitive camping is possible in a few established spots.

Or, spend a romantic night in the *Valley of the Gods B&B* (☎ 970-749-1164), a half-mile from Hwy 261. The 1930s ranch house has four attractive rooms with private bath for $100, including full breakfast.

MEXICAN HAT

☎ 435 • pop 88 • elevation 4244 feet

The tiny settlement of Mexican Hat is named after a sombrero-shaped rock about 3 miles northeast on Hwy 163. A stopping point for travelers, the town lies on the north banks of the San Juan River; the south bank is the northern edge of the Navajo Indian Reservation.

Mexican Hat has a handful of rustic and simple lodgings (from $45 to $70) and places to eat. Try *Burches Indian Trading Company* (☎ 683-2221), which has a motel and campsites ($10-15); *Mexican Hat Lodge* (☎ 683-2222), which also operates an outdoor steakhouse in summer; and *San Juan Inn & Trading Post* (☎ 683-2220, 800-447-2022), which is the nicest place.

MONUMENT VALLEY

Southwest of Mexican Hat, Hwy 163 enters the Navajo Indian Reservation and Monument Valley. The scenery has appeared in hundreds of TV commercials and Hollywood Westerns, but that doesn't decrease the awe of seeing, for the first time, the fantastically sheer red buttes and colossal mesas silhouetted against a painfully clear blue sky. To get up close and personal, you must visit the Monument Valley Navajo Tribal Park just across the border in Arizona (see the Northeastern Arizona chapter for details).

Just inside the Utah border, about 25 miles southwest of Mexican Hat, a full-service outpost, **Goulding's Lodge & Trading**

Post, contains the only hotel near the tribal park. The original 1924 trading post remains, now converted into an interesting museum of Indian artifacts and movie memorabilia. There is also a theater (with a multimedia show), a gift shop selling Indian crafts, a campground, a mediocre restaurant, and a convenience store and gas station.

Goulding's offers its own half- and full-day Monument Valley tours ($30-60), or book a guided horseback ride with Ed Black's Monument Valley Trail Rides (☎ 739-4285); these run $30 to $134 for one to five hours. If you wish to buy Navajo crafts direct from the Navajos, stop by the roadside stands on the road to the tribal park or visit the small Oljato Trading Post (☎ 727-3210) in nearby **Oljato**, which is 10 miles from Goulding's. Ask for directions at the museum or the gas station.

The comfortable *Goulding's Lodge* (☎ 727-3231) has a seasonal pool and coin laundry. Each of the 62 standard motel rooms has a balcony with the same jaw-dropping valley view. Rates are equally mind-blowing: doubles are $155 from June to mid-October, dropping to a low of $62 from January to mid-March (to which a 17% tax is added). A mile beyond the lodge, in a canyon with only partial views, is *Goulding's Campground* (same phone) with showers, coin laundry and a convenience store. About 100 sites are $15/25 for tents/RVs. It is open mid-March through October.

website: www.gouldings.com

HWY 261:
THE MOKI DUGWAY BACKWAY

Magnificently scenic Hwy 261 leaves Hwy 163 and heads north to Hwy 95, about 34 miles away.

Goosenecks State Park

At the southern end of Hwy 261, a 4-mile paved road leads to this state park, which is little more than an overlook. Once you reach it, you'll understand why: 1100 feet below, the San Juan River carves the desert in a series of massive, meandering curves. There are pit toilets, picnic tables and you

can camp for free, but the frequent winds discourage it.

Moki Dugway

Forget Lombard St in San Francisco. The Moki Dugway is the most memorable curved road you'll ever drive. The dugway is a (still unpaved) 3-mile section of hairpin turns descending 1100 feet from Cedar Mesa (you ascend coming from the south). From the top, the views of southern Utah and northern Arizona are among the best in the country, and from here an unpaved side road leads west about 5 miles to the **Muley Point Overlook**, which gives equally stunning – some say better – views.

Cedar Mesa & Grand Gulch
Primitive Area

The 650,000-acre Cedar Mesa area contains a network of rugged canyons that extend south of Hwy 95 from Hwy 276 to Comb Wash in the east. Grand Gulch Primitive Area is the most well known; this wild canyon twists all the way to the San Juan River. The entire area is quite popular with adventurers seeking remote and beautiful wilderness, but note that this is difficult country with primitive trails and no developed camping. Spring and fall are the best times to visit; summer is too hot and snow may close the area in winter.

The canyons of Cedar Mesa also contain hundreds of Ancestral Puebloan sites, many of which have been vandalized by pot hunters. It bears repeating that all prehistoric Indian sites are protected by law, and authorities crack down severely on offenders. Remember, not only are these sites and early dwellings important for archeological and cultural reasons, but Native Americans believe they are still of intrinsic religious significance. Backcountry travelers should respect the spiritual and historical value of these places. Please report damage of archaeological sites to a ranger.

You must have a permit to hike into any of the canyons in Cedar Mesa. Four miles south of Hwy 95 is the Kane Gulch Ranger Station (no phone), open from March to November. Rangers are here daily 8 am to noon; afternoon hours are irregular. This BLM station issues same-day walk-in permits only, sells books and has limited maps. For topo and illustrated trail maps, contact the Canyonlands Natural History Association (☎ 800-840-8978); it's online at www.cnha.org. The Monticello BLM (☎ 587-2141) also sells permits and has information.

A day-use, self-pay hiking permit is $2; overnight permits for backcountry camping are $8 per trip in high season, and all back-packers must register at Kane Gulch. Over-night permits are extremely limited; call or write to reserve in advance: Cedar Mesa BLM (☎ 587-1532), Permit Reservation Office, PO Box 7, Monticello, UT 84535. Other-wise, take a chance on a same-day permit at the Kane Gulch Station.

NATURAL BRIDGES NATIONAL MONUMENT

This compact area, near the junction of Hwys 261 and 95 (40 miles west of Blanding), became a national monu-ment in 1908 – the first NPS land in Utah. In the middle of a 'pygmy' forest of juniper and pine, three natural bridges are found in a dramatic white sand-stone canyon. All the bridges are visible from a ring road and approachable by short hikes. They represent a natural aging process: One is young, one middle-aged and one old. The oldest – the beautifully delicate Owachomo Bridge – spans 180 feet and rises over 100 feet above ground but is only 9 feet thick. The Sipapu and Kachina natural bridges are the second and third largest known anywhere.

Orientation & Information

Hwy 275 branches off Hwy 95 and leads 6 miles to the visitor center, open 8 am to 6 pm in summer, to 5 pm in spring and fall, to 4:30 pm in winter. The center has nice in-terpretive exhibits, information, books, toilets and water (but no food). Rangers lead programs in summer.

Beyond the visitor center, the paved one-way **Bridge View Drive** is a scenic 9-mile loop passing all three bridges (open daily dawn to dusk). Trailers are prohibited (leave them at the visitor center). Mountain biking is allowed only on this drive.

Entrance is $6 per car or $3 per hiker or biker (valid for seven days). National passes are accepted.

Information is available from the Super-intendent, Natural Bridges National Monu-ment (☎ 692-1234), PO Box 1, Lake Powell, UT 84533.

Hiking

The foot trails to the bridges all leave from Bridge View Drive and all are very reward-ing. Distances are short; the longest is just over half a mile one-way. However, descents can be steep, and at Sipapu Bridge it involves stairs and ladders. Enthusias-tic hikers can take unmain-tained loop trails that join any two or all three of the bridges (a total of over 8 miles). Pick up a map at the visitor center.

The elevation here is 6500 feet and trails are open all year, but the steeper sections may be closed after heavy rains or snow. Carry lots of water in summer; there is no water or toilets along the drive itself.

Golden eagle

Places to Stay

A small 13-site *campground* ($10), almost half a mile past the visitor center, is open year-round. There are pit toilets and grills; water is available only at the visitor center. The campground fills on summer after-noons, after which you are allowed to camp in the pullouts along Hwy 275 leading to the park. There is no backcountry camping.

GLEN CANYON NATIONAL RECREATION AREA

The massive Glen Canyon Dam flooded Glen Canyon in the 1960s, forming Lake Powell, most of which lies in Utah. The lake is GCNRA's foremost attraction, with four marinas in Utah. However, Glen Canyon Dam itself, the main GCNRA visitor center, the largest and most developed marina

(Wahweap), the biggest town on the lake (Page) and the main boating concession are all in Arizona. The entire GCNRA is described in the Grand Canyon & Lake Powell chapter, including the **Lake Powell Car Ferry** between the Halls Crossing and Bullfrog Marinas on Hwy 276 in Utah, the turnoff for which is just past Natural Bridges National Monument. (See the 'Lake Powell Ferry' boxed text in that chapter.)

Hwy 95 to the San Rafael Reef

This route is described south to north, but it can easily be reversed. San Rafael Reef and Goblin Valley are reasonable day trips from Green River.

HWY 95: FRY CANYON TO HANKSVILLE

Hwy 95 isn't bookended by national parks, so it sees little traffic. However, it's one of the most scenic routes in the state. At times, the eroded, cracked, stained, ever-changing layers of rock pass by like the worn pages of a book incessantly thumbed by the wind.

Just north of Natural Bridges National Monument is the forested Fry Canyon, which was a uranium-mining center in the 1950s and 1960s. Today, it is home to the upscale *Fry Canyon Lodge* (☎ 259-5334), which has a store, a cozy '50s-style café and 11 small but attractive rooms for $68 to $89. The restaurant serves good country breakfasts and dinners; get details at www .frycanyon.com.

Continuing northwest, a bridge crosses Lake Powell; the Hite overlook is a worthy place to contemplate the otherworldly scenery. Past Hite, Hwy 276 heads southwest to Bullfrog, which has a car ferry across the lake to Halls Crossing. All these places are described in the Grand Canyon & Lake Powell chapter.

Farther north, a BLM sign (between mile markers 15 and 16) indicates the **Burr Point Trail**. This 10-mile dirt road (passable to cars in dry weather only) leads into the Robbers

Roost area – famous as a hiding place for outlaws – and dead ends at a panoramic overlook of the Dirty Devil River Canyon.

About 16 miles past this turnoff, Hwy 95 ends at Hanksville. From here, Hwy 24 heads west about 30 miles to Capitol Reef National Park and heads north some 44 miles to I-70.

HENRY MOUNTAINS

This 11,000-foot-high range was the last to be named and explored in the lower 48 states. Extremely remote and scenic, it boasts one of the country's last wild bison herds, with some 400 head freely roaming the range. Pronghorn antelopes, mule deer and bighorn sheep are also seen.

There are two main access roads. From Hanksville, follow 100 east south, which becomes Sawmill Basin Rd; from Hwy 95, about 20 miles south of Hanksville, follow the Bull Mountain Scenic Backway west. Both are very rough and rocky dirt roads; flat tires are common. 4WD vehicles are highly recommended. The BLM in Hanksville (see below) has complete information and updated road conditions.

The BLM operates three small *campgrounds* ($4) in the mountains. All have pit toilets and water but no showers or RV hookups; they are open April to October or November.

HANKSVILLE

☎ 435 • pop 240 • elevation 4300 feet

This village is a convenient stopping place at the junction of Hwys 24 and 95.

Open weekdays, the BLM (☎ 542-3461), 406 S 100 West, has maps and information about the lands surrounding Hanksville, especially the Henry Mountains (see above).

Red Rock Campground & Restaurant (☎ 542-3235, 226 E 100 North) has 60 sites ($10-16) and is open from mid-March through October. The cheaper, dustier *Jurassic Park* (☎ 542-3433, 100 S Center) is open year-round.

Desert Inn (☎ 542-3241, 197 E Hwy 24), fronted by a whimsical metal dinosaur fence, and nearby *Best Value Inn* (☎ 542-3471) have frayed but adequate rooms ($35-45).

Friendly ***Fern's Place*** *(☎ 542-3251, 99 E 100 North)* gets a thumbs up from readers; eight comfortable rooms, some with kitchenettes, are $30 to $55. Best in town is ***Whispering Sands Motel*** *(☎ 542-3238, 132 S Hwy 95)*, with 23 clean singles/doubles for $50/$60.

The ***Red Rock Restaurant***, a simple diner and a fast-food burger joint, constitute your dining options.

GOBLIN VALLEY STATE PARK

This small, 3654-acre park is just plain fun. Melted rock formations – looking like a Salvador Dali fantasy – fill a stadium-like valley where visitors are free to wander up to, among and through them. Kids have a blast. The park was used for a scene in the 2000 film *Galaxy Quest,* and the evocative 'goblins' do make you feel like you are on another planet – one inhabited by lots of other gawking humans, of course. A few trails lead out of the valley, and a year-round, 21-site ***campground*** *(☎ 800-322-3770)* has water and showers ($12); it books up on most weekends. Day use is $5.

The park is about 46 miles southwest of Green River (slightly closer to Hanksville); from Hwy 24, a signed, paved road leads 12 miles to the entrance. There is no visitor center (headquarters are officially at Green River State Park), but the rangers at the fee booth have area information.

SAN RAFAEL SWELL, DESERT & REEF

The San Rafael Swell (see also the Central Utah chapter) extends below I-70 and is separated from the easterly San Rafael Desert by a 2000-foot natural barrier called the San Rafael Reef. I-70 west of Green River goes through the north end of the San Rafael Desert before climbing up past the reef and into the swell – a very scenic freeway drive through remote and almost uninhabited territory.

The rugged, starkly beautiful terrain below I-70 contains numerous dirt roads (many 4WD-only), scenic hikes, panoramic views and places for dispersed primitive camping (no facilities). Carry at least a gallon of water per person per day. The main route for visiting the San Rafael Desert (east of Hwy 24) is a 100-mile loop road from Green River (over half of which is unpaved but passable to ordinary vehicles in dry weather), which leaves town along Airport Rd and eventually reaches Hwy 24 just south of the entrance road to Goblin Valley State Park. The drive connects with other 4WD and hiking trails and provides the only access to the remote **Horseshoe Canyon** and **Maze** sections of Canyonlands National Park (see that section, earlier, for further details).

In the San Rafael Swell (west of Hwy 24), popular destinations are Temple Mountain, Hondoo Arch and Swasey's Cabin. Before heading into the swell, make sure to get maps and road condition updates, as it is easy to get lost and stuck. Twelve miles from Hwy 24, at the turnoff to Goblin Valley State Park, the new Temple Mountain Ranger Station has information on the swell; it is staffed 24 hours a day, though the rangers may be in the field. It has no phone, but the BLM in Price (☎ 636-3600) can contact the rangers. The Green River Visitor Center, Goblin Valley State Park and the Hanksville BLM also have road updates, maps and information.

Las Vegas

NEIL SETCHFIELD

☎ 702 • pop 483,448 • elevation 2025 feet

Fabulous Las Vegas has grown in 90 years from nothing to a city of nearly a half-million people. If you've come for the gambling and glitter, you'll love it. At least for a few days, until your money disappears and sunshine seems unnatural.

A few years back, Vegas was known as a place filled with tour buses, elderly vacationers and high-rolling mafiosos. Recently, with help from such movies as *Swingers* and *Fear & Loathing in Las Vegas*, it has become a hip playland for 20- and 30-somethings looking for a weekend of excess and faux glamour. Also, unlike the rest of the US, there is no 'last call' and you can drink and smoke pretty much everywhere 24 hours a day.

Even if you can't stand lounge singers, the incessant 'ding-ding-ding' of the slot machines and the haggard countenance of down-and-out gamblers, Vegas is a place like no other and a great stop between California and points east.

History

A small spring north of downtown was used by Paiute Indians and later by emigrants en route to California. Mormons established a small mission, but in 1902 most of the land was sold to a railroad company and Las Vegas became a railroad town with ice works, hotels and saloons. There were gambling houses, too, but local Mormon conservatism did not encourage gaming even after it was legalized. The first casinos were built by Los Angeles developers and Mafia associates. In 1946, Bugsy Siegel's Fabulous Flamingo pioneered the new style of casinos – big and flashy, with lavish entertainment to draw in the gamblers.

Orientation & Information

Downtown Las Vegas is the original town center; its main artery, Fremont St, is now a covered pedestrian mall lined with low-key casinos and hotels. Las Vegas Blvd goes through downtown and continues south for about 10 miles. A 3-mile stretch of this boulevard, known as 'The Strip,' has most of the really big new and noteworthy hotels and casinos.

The Las Vegas Visitor Center (☎ 892-7575) is in the Convention Center at 3150 Paradise Rd.

website: www.lasvegas24hours.com

The Gay & Lesbian Community Center (☎ 733-9800), 912 E Sahara Ave, gives referrals for gay-friendly hotels, clubs and the like. Like most of Nevada, Las Vegas is not particularly gay friendly.

Most of the tourist areas are safe, but Las Vegas Blvd between downtown and The Strip can feel a bit threatening.

Casinos

Most casinos entice gamblers with free booze (don't forget to tip the waitresses!), cheap food and glitzy entertainment. Inside, casinos are hideously gaudy, noisy and deliberately disorienting, with no clocks or windows. The Strip's new mega-casinos also feature gimmicky themes, attention-grabbing architecture and some nongambling amusements.

The casinos listed below (from north to south) are worth visiting as attractions in themselves.

Stratosphere (☎ 800-998-6937) – This casino's landmark is its 1149-foot tower with a restaurant and two rides up top – the world's highest roller coaster ($5) and the free-fall Big Shot ($8).

Las Vegas Hilton (☎ 800-732-7117) – Popular with trekkies, this casino has a flashy sci-fi theme, plus the infamous 'Star Trek: The Experience' ride ($15).

Circus Circus (☎ 794-3939) – One of the original casino-cum-theme-parks, this place has free circus acts and the small amusement park, Adventuredome (day pass $19).

Treasure Island (☎ 800-944-7444) – The pirate ship and man o' war in the lagoon out front stage a sea battle every hour and a half from 4:30 pm to midnight.

Mirage (☎ 800-627-6667) – A fake volcano erupts out front every half hour. Inside the casino are a re-created tropical rain forest, a dolphin tank and the white tigers used in the Siegfried & Roy stage show.

Venetian (☎ 888-283-6423) – Take a gondola ride ($10) on the indoor canal that runs through the corridors of the upscale shopping center.

Caesar's Palace (☎ 800-634-6001) – You enter stylish Caesar's along a moving footpath, past classic columns and 'ancient' talking statues. Inside, the Forum is an imitation Roman street, with a painted sky that changes from dawn to dusk every three hours.

Bellagio (☎ 888-987-6667) – The lake in front of this glamorous palace comes alive each night with more than 1000 fountains dancing to Frank Sinatra tunes. Inside are amazing shops, 16 restaurants and the top-notch Bellagio Gallery of Fine Art ($12).

Paris (☎ 888-266-5687) – Before you even walk inside, this hotel is impressive with its Eiffel Tower (half the size of the original), Arc de Triomphe, Opera House, fountains and sidewalk restaurants. Inside, it's always dawn and there are boutiques and eight restaurants, including one on top of the Eiffel Tower.

Hard Rock Hotel & Casino (☎ 800-693-7625) – A place to see and be seen, this hotel and casino is for the young and hip. The pool has two sand beaches, a swim-up blackjack table and a waterslide. All sorts of memorabilia is on display – from Britney Spears' schoolgirl outfit to Eric Clapton's guitar.

MGM Grand (☎ 800-929-1111) – With over 5000 rooms, this is the world's largest hotel. MGM Grand Adventure is a 33-acre theme park behind the main casino, with water rides, top-notch roller coasters and restaurants; a day pass is $13.

New York, New York (☎ 800-693-6763) – The hotel's facade re-creates many Manhattan landmarks, with replicas of the Statue of Liberty, Brooklyn Bridge and more. Try the Manhattan Express roller coaster ($10) for a major thrill ride.

Luxor (☎ 888-777-0188) – A 10-mile-high beam of light blazes straight into the sky each night and the casino is a remarkable glass-covered pyramid with a huge sphinx outside.

Mandalay Bay (☎ 877-632-7000) – Floors 35 through 39 are owned by the Four Seasons while the rest of the hotel is still an upscale place to stay. The complex includes a House of Blues and an 11-acre garden complete with a manmade beach.

Other Attractions

There are many things to do apart from gambling, and discount coupons are available for most of them. The **Wet 'n' Wild** water park (☎ 734-0088), 2601 Las Vegas Blvd S, looks mighty tempting on a hot day ($26). The **Imperial Palace Auto Museum** (☎ 731-3311), at the Imperial Palace casino, has an excellent collection of vehicles once owned by the rich and famous, from Hitler to Howard Hughes ($7).

A Vegas favorite is the campy **Liberace Museum** (☎ 798-5595), 1775 E Tropicana, sequined capes, rhinestone jewelry, flashy cars and fabulous candelabra ($7). If you've ever had a fondness for Elvis, check out **Elvis-A-Rama** (☎ 309-7200), 3401 Industrial Rd, to view $3,500,000 worth of Elvis memorabilia ($10).

Places to Stay

The best room deals are midweek at the big casinos, when doubles are as low as $35. On a busy Friday or Saturday or during a convention, the same room might be $100 or more. Try free discount booking services

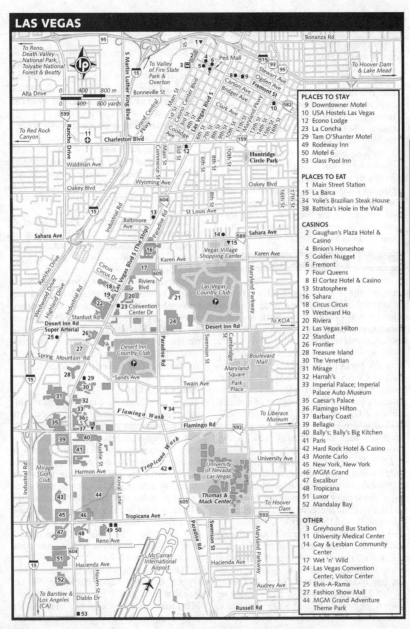

LAS VEGAS

PLACES TO STAY
9 Downtowner Motel
10 USA Hostels Las Vegas
12 Econo Lodge
23 La Concha
29 Tam O'Shanter Motel
49 Rodeway Inn
50 Motel 6
53 Glass Pool Inn

PLACES TO EAT
1 Main Street Station
15 La Barca
34 Yolie's Brazilian Steak House
38 Battista's Hole in the Wall

CASINOS
2 Gaughan's Plaza Hotel & Casino
4 Binion's Horseshoe
5 Golden Nugget
6 Fremont
7 Four Queens
8 El Cortez Hotel & Casino
13 Stratosphere
16 Sahara
18 Circus Circus
19 Westward Ho
20 Riviera
21 Las Vegas Hilton
22 Stardust
26 Frontier
28 Treasure Island
30 The Venetian
31 Mirage
32 Harrah's
33 Imperial Palace; Imperial Palace Auto Museum
35 Caesar's Palace
36 Flamingo Hilton
37 Barbary Coast
39 Bellagio
40 Bally's; Bally's Big Kitchen
41 Paris
42 Hard Rock Hotel & Casino
43 Monte Carlo
45 New York, New York
46 MGM Grand
47 Excalibur
48 Tropicana
51 Luxor
52 Mandalay Bay

OTHER
3 Greyhound Bus Station
11 University Medical Center
14 Gay & Lesbian Community Center
17 Wet 'n' Wild
24 Las Vegas Convention Center; Visitor Center
25 Elvis-A-Rama
27 Fashion Show Mall
44 MGM Grand Adventure Theme Park

Marriage & Divorce

You can get hitched quickly in Nevada if you're over 18 years old and have proof of identity. If either party has been married before, the divorce must be final and the date and location of the decree is required. Then get a marriage license from the nearest county courthouse ($50 cash), and find the Commissioner of Civil Marriages or a wedding chapel.

For a divorce, both parties must reside in Nevada for at least six weeks; then they can go to a lawyer or paralegal service and complete the papers. An uncontested divorce will take another one to four weeks, depending on how quickly the lawyer can obtain any necessary documents from other states. The cost can be as low as $250.

such as the Las Vegas Tourist Bureau (☎ 800-522-9555) and City-Wide Reservations (☎ 800-733-6644) or check online at www.travelworm.com or www.discountlas-vegas-hotel.com.

Some of the hotel/casinos on The Strip have RV parks for around $15 per night, including *Circus Circus* and *Stardust*. These parking lots are not pleasant for tent campers, but they do include use of hotel facilities. *KOA* (☎ 451-5527, 800-562-7782, 4315 Boulder Hwy), a few miles south of town, has tent and RV sites ($24 for two people) and a swimming pool.

USA Hostels Las Vegas (☎ 385-1150, 1322 Fremont St) is on the not-so-nice outskirts of downtown, but the facilities, including a pool, jacuzzi and bar, are top-notch and the staff are incredibly accommodating. Dorm beds are $15, singles $35, doubles $45. Call for free pick-up from the Greyhound station. *Downtowner Motel* (☎ 384-1441, 129 N 8th St) is not very appealing but has cheap singles/doubles for $39/49. The pleasant but older *El Cortez Hotel & Casino* (☎ 385-5200, 800-634-6703, 600 E Fremont St) has singles/doubles at $20/35 midweek. Among the most budget-friendly casinos

are *Circus Circus* (☎ 800-634-3450), the *Stardust* (☎ 800-824-6033) and *Riviera* (☎ 800-634-6753).

Steps away from the south end of the Strip, *Rodeway Inn* (☎ (795-3311) and *Motel 6* (☎ 798-0728), both on E Tropicana Ave, are good options with clean rooms at $33/48. Also on the south end is the *Glass Pool Inn* (☎ 739-6636, 4613 Las Vegas Blvd S) with consistently low-priced rooms ($48/59) and of course, the infamous 'glass' pool.

Mid-strip, *La Concha* (☎ 800-331-2431, 2955 Las Vegas Blvd S) is convenient with rooms at $38 midweek and $68 on weekends. *Tam O'Shanter Motel* (☎ 735-7331, 3317 Las Vegas Blvd S) is popular with budget travelers with doubles for around $45.

Downtown, *Gaughan's Plaza Hotel & Casino* (☎ 386-2110, 1 Main St) is right on top of the bus station and has above-average rooms from $40 midweek and $65 on weekends.

Even the 'nice' casinos in town have packages – rooms plus dinner shows and discounted meals – so call around. Standard rates are $70 to $95 midweek, $125 and up on the weekends. For the money, the nicest spot on The Strip is *Caesar's Palace* (☎ 800-634-6001), followed by the *Luxor* (☎ 800-288-1000) and *MGM Grand* (☎ 800-929-1111).

Places to Eat
The larger casinos have multiple restaurants ranging from moderately priced cafés to top-end gourmet restaurants. The all-you-can-eat buffet, a Las Vegas institution, is where gluttonous gamblers pile plates with wide and heavy loads, only to return later for dessert. The best buffet in town is a subject of debate, but those commonly mentioned include the *Main Street Station* for a $14 dinner, *Bally's Big Kitchen* for $16, and the Palatium Buffet at *Caesar's Palace* for $20. Cheapest is the buffet at *Circus Circus*, only $6/7/8 for breakfast/lunch/dinner; you get what you pay for.

When you need a break from casino life, try *La Barca* (☎ 657-9700, 953 E Sahara Ave), where you'll be served authentic Mexican seafood dishes for around $10 in a festive atmosphere. You'll have a ball at

Battista's Hole in the Wall (☎ 732-1424, *4041 Audrie St*), behind the Flamingo Hilton. For a set price of $17 to $30 depending on entrée, you get minestrone or salad, pasta side, an entrée, cappuccino and all the house wine you can drink. *Yolie's Brazilian Steak House* (*3900 Paradise Rd*) cooks outstanding grilled meats for $9-$15.

Entertainment
An incredible amount of entertainment is offered every night; for listings, get a copy of *What's On,* online at www.ilovevegas.com, or *Showbiz.* 'Big-room' casino shows can be either concerts by famous musicians, Broadway musicals or flashy song-and-dance shows.

The hottest show in town is Cirque du Soleil's aquatic show, *O;* performed at the Bellagio in and around a 1½-million-gallon pool. Tickets are pricey at $90/$110 but since the show is sold out weeks in advance, it gives you time to save up. Also recom-

mended is Cirque du Soleil's *Mystère,* held at Treasure Island ($70 and up), and *Siegfried & Roy* at the Mirage ($100). For the more budget-conscious, try the Riviera's *Evening at La Cage,* with a cast of over-the-top female impersonators ($22), and the Stratosphere's daytime classic *Viva Las Vegas* ($12, $14 including buffet).

Getting There & Around
McCarran International Airport (☎ 261-5743) has direct flights from most US cities, and a few from Canada and Europe. Bell Trans (☎ 739-7990) and Gray Line (☎ 384-1234) both provide airport shuttle service ($3.50 to $5 per person).

Greyhound (☎ 384-9561), downtown on Main St, has regular buses to/from Los Angeles ($35) and San Diego ($42), plus connections to San Francisco via Reno.

Amtrak does not run trains to Las Vegas, although it does offer bus service from Los Angeles ($35).

NEVADA

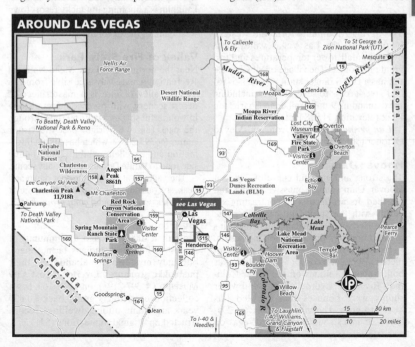

AROUND LAS VEGAS

Local bus service is provided by Citizens Area Transport (CAT; ☎ 228-7433); bus No 301 runs up and down The Strip 24 hours a day, all the way to downtown ($1.50).

The Strip Trolley (☎ 382-1404) does a loop from Mandalay Bay to the Stratosphere and out to the Las Vegas Hilton every 25 minutes until 2 am ($1.50).

Dozens of agencies along The Strip rent cars for $25 to $45 per day. Try Budget (☎ 736-1212) or Thrifty (☎ 896-7600).

AROUND LAS VEGAS
Red Rock Canyon

Only 20 miles west of Vegas, this dramatic valley is noted for the steep Red Rock escarpment, rising 3000 feet on its western edge. A 13-mile, one-way scenic loop starts at the BLM visitor center (☎ 363-1921) near Hwy 159. It's especially impressive at sunset and sunrise. Day use is $5. Camping at the *Oak Creek* campground is available year-round on a first-come, first-served basis.

Toiyabe National Forest

The Spring Mountains form the western boundary of the Las Vegas valley, with higher rainfall, lower temperatures and fragrant pine forests. The village of Mt Charleston has a USFS ranger station (☎ 872-5486) and gives access to several hikes, including the demanding 9-mile trail up to Charleston Peak (elevation 11,918 feet).

Campgrounds are open from mid-May to October ($6).

Hoover Dam

The strong and graceful curve of 726-foot Hoover Dam spans a massive ravine and riverbed, its art-deco style contrasting superbly with the stark landscape. To some people, Hoover is only a dam, but to many it's the best nongambling attraction in Nevada.

Hoover Dam, a New Deal project completed in 1935 at a cost of $175 million, was built to control floods on the lower Colorado River. The hydroelectricity and water supply were bonuses that enabled Las Vegas to grow. The visitor center (☎ 294-3517), 35 miles southeast of Las Vegas on

Hwy 93, has interesting exhibits as well as a great rooftop view of the dam. Tickets cost $4, or you can take one of two highly recommended tours – a 35-minute introductory tour ($10) and an hour-long hard-hat tour ($25). Both are offered daily year-round. A walk across the dam not only gives great perspectives but also allows you to cross the Nevada–Arizona border as well as the Pacific/Mountain time zone.

Lake Mead National Recreation Area

With 500 miles of shoreline, Lake Mead is popular for fishing, boating, swimming, water skiing and even scuba diving. The Lake Mead visitor center (☎ 293-8906) is on Hwy 93 about 4 miles northeast of Boulder City. From there, the scenic **North Shore Rd** winds around the lake, passing several campgrounds.

Just to the south of Hoover Dam, close to the California-Arizona-Nevada border, **Laughlin** is a booming but tacky resort town with a dozen large casinos/hotels along the west bank of the Colorado River.

Valley of Fire State Park

Near the north end of Lake Mead National Recreation Area, easily accessible from Las Vegas, Valley of Fire is a masterpiece of desert scenery, with psychedelic sandstone in wonderful shapes. Hwy 169 runs through the park (entry $5), right past the visitor center (☎ 397-2088), which has hiking information and excellent exhibits. The winding side road to **White Domes** is especially scenic.

The valley is at its most fiery at dawn and dusk, so consider staying overnight in one of the park's two year-round *campgrounds* ($7).

Overton

More than 1000 years ago, a community of Ancestral Puebloan Indians farmed here, but they mysteriously abandoned their pueblolike structures. Overton's **Lost City Museum** (☎ 397-2193), on Hwy 169, has a collection of artifacts going back 10,000 years and some adobe dwellings reconstructed on original foundations ($2).

Native American art and artifacts at a street stall

Hopi pottery

Hand-painted bowls in an Indian art gallery

Unique patterns on a Navajo blanket

Simpson hedgehog cacti, Kolob Canyon, Zion National Park, UT   A succulent cholla cactus

The saguaro is even more impressive underground, with roots up to 65 feet long.

Barrel cactus in Saguaro National Park, AZ   Claret cup cactus in southeastern New Mexico

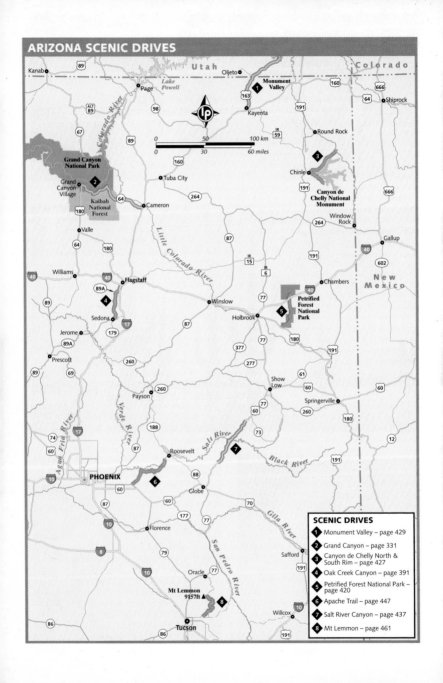

ARIZONA SCENIC DRIVES

SCENIC DRIVES
1. Monument Valley – page 429
2. Grand Canyon – page 331
3. Canyon de Chelly North & South Rim – page 427
4. Oak Creek Canyon – page 391
5. Petrified Forest National Park – page 420
6. Apache Trail – page 447
7. Salt River Canyon – page 437
8. Mt Lemmon – page 461

Facts about Arizona

It's called the Grand Canyon State, and certainly the Grand Canyon is the one thing that schoolchildren from Nova Scotia to New Zealand will mention if quizzed about Arizona. But there's much more than canyons in this state, as visitors quickly discover. Deserts, mountains, forests and rivers provide a range of scenic attractions and outdoor activities. This variety is particularly enjoyed by Arizonans themselves, most of whom live in the hot desert metropolises centered on Phoenix and Tucson and in summer enjoy the cool mountains, forests and artificial lakes. Out-of-state visitors, on the other hand, are attracted more to the essentially Southwestern elements of the region, such as the spectacular canyons and mesas, the fascinating deserts and, of course, the Native American heritage.

Arizona has the third largest Native American population of the 50 states (after California and Oklahoma) and the two largest Indian reservations in the country (the Navajo and the Tohono O'odham). About 26% of the state is reservation land. Many tribes have retained much of their cultures, languages and traditions, all of which differ from tribe to tribe. Some of their ancient dances and ceremonies are open to the public, but many are not. However, all visitors can experience the Indian cultures in the villages, trading posts and crafts stores that dot the reservations, and in the Indian fairs, powwows and rodeos held regularly throughout the state.

Oraibi village, on the Hopi Reservation, was built in the 12th century and is one of only two places in the country that have been continuously occupied for more than 800 years. Visitors can learn about the ancestors of today's tribes through the fascinating ancient pueblos that have been preserved throughout the state, and in several excellent museums.

The southern reaches of the state have particularly close ties to Mexico. Architec-

Highlights

- It's not called 'Grand Canyon State' for nothing – the canyon is definitely Arizona's major attraction.

- Many thousands of five-story high, multi-armed cacti in Saguaro National Park are guaranteed to catch your attention.

- Dejá vu at stunning Monument Valley – you've seen it in dozens of Western movies.

- Canyon de Chelly's interior can be visited only on Navajo-led tours, but driving the rim to scenic overlooks is free to anyone.

- Southeastern Arizona is the bird-watching mecca of the entire country.

Scenic Drives

The map opposite this page is a sampling of favorite routes through Arizona. Some are designated 'Scenic Byways' and some are quiet dirt trails; some are alternative highways and some are rewarding detours. The text includes many more recommended roads for exploring this scenic country.

ture, cuisine and language in Arizona are a mix of Mexican, native and Spanish cultures. The Spanish heritage can be discovered in the centuries-old missions of southern Arizona established by Padre Kino and in the historic barrios of Tucson, where Spanish is as commonly heard as English. Tucson has a wonderful selection of Mexican restaurants that are as good as those in Mexico itself.

Visitors interested in natural history can spot numerous species in Arizona found nowhere else in the USA. Southeastern Arizona is the undisputed hummingbird capital of the country, and many other rarities fly in from Mexico, including two species of tropical trogons. The tall, majestic

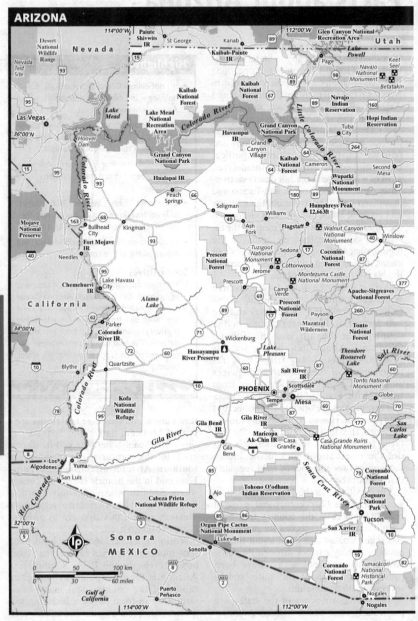

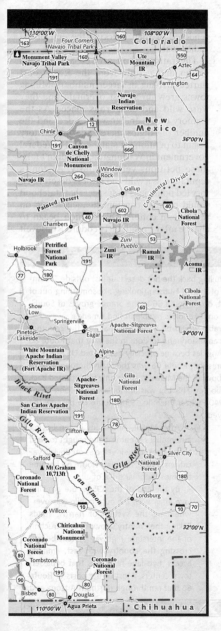

saguaro and organ-pipe cacti are found only in parts of southern Arizona and in Mexico. These cacti provide nests and shelter for many desert birds and animals.

Arizona is one of three states where the wild pigs (javelinas) and the raccoonlike coatis are regularly glimpsed in the wild. The country's only poisonous lizard, the gila monster, lives here too.

Recent History

At the end of the Mexican War in 1848, the land north of the Gila River was claimed by the USA and incorporated into the New Mexico Territory, which then included Arizona. The USA soon realized that the best route from the Mississippi River to the burgeoning territory of California lay south of the Gila River, passing through the Mexican town of Tucson. US diplomat James Gadsden arranged for the USA to purchase the land between the present international border and the Gila River from Mexico. In 1854, the USA annexed the territory and Americans began to cross the area en route to California. Some travelers noted the potential mineral and agricultural wealth of the region and stopped to make the area their home. These settlers began the copper-mining and cattle-ranching industries that became mainstays of Arizona's economy.

Many of the settlers were from southern states and when the American Civil War broke out in 1861, Arizona declared itself a Confederate state. This resulted in the westernmost battle of the Civil War, when a small Confederate force was defeated by Union troops at Picacho Peak in 1862. The Confederate forces killed three Union soldiers before retreating to Tucson and dispersing, aware that they would soon be greatly outnumbered.

When Arizona was designated as a separate territory the following year, Tucson was the largest town, but Prescott was chosen as the territorial capital because Tucson was perceived as a bastion of Confederate loyalty. From 1867 to 1877, however, Tucson held the position of territorial capital, after which it was returned to

ARIZONA

Prescott and finally moved to the Anglo-founded town of Phoenix in 1889, where it has remained. Historians, Hispanic and non-Hispanic alike, attribute this to the anti-Hispanic sentiment then prevalent in US politics.

Meanwhile, the US Army was fighting the Indian wars, protecting settlers and wresting the land from the Indians, who had little use for European concepts of land ownership. In 1864 the Navajos were forced to march from their land to the high plains of eastern New Mexico in the infamous 'Long Walk'; countless of them died. Over the next two decades a small number of Apache warriors under the leadership of Cochise and Geronimo fought far greater numbers of US settlers and soldiers using guerrilla tactics. Finally, the ever-growing

numbers of Anglo settlers overwhelmed the dwindling Indian forces, and Geronimo surrendered in 1886, marking the end of the Indian wars.

The railroad had arrived a few years earlier and people from the East Coast started arriving in larger numbers. Mining towns grew up almost overnight and they were wild and dangerous places. As the memory of the Indian wars faded and the number of Anglos increased, the territory began to petition for statehood. The federal government in Washington, DC, didn't take these petitions very seriously; Arizona's reputation as a wild and lawless desert territory led politicians to suspect that statehood would prove a constant financial drain on the federal coffers. This opinion began to change after President Theodore Roosevelt

Kickin' Down Route 66

Fenders! Huge, unwieldy, voluptuous fenders, pulling back the hot desert air just outside Tucumcari, New Mexico. It's 1949, and the occupants of this fat Hudson (looking like something out of a sci-fi serial from the '40s) have pointed it west, down Route 66 to the orange groves of Southern California. Maybe it's Kerouac's Sal Paradise on his endless ramble to find America.

That's the quintessential image that innumerable would-be bohemians have of the country's possibilities. Few highways have entered American history and folklore in the way that Route 66 has. In 1926 the road linking Chicago with Los Angeles became officially designated US Route 66 for its entire 2448-mile length. During the Depression, Route 66 was the main thoroughfare to California for migrant families escaping the dust bowl of the Midwest, some only to be turned back by state immigration at the California-Arizona border. This trip was immortalized in John Steinbeck's *The Grapes of Wrath*, which won the 1940 Pulitzer Prize. In 1938, Route 66 became the first cross-country highway to be completely paved.

After WWII, Americans began buying automobiles in earnest and sought to weld themselves to their vehicles on driving vacations. Along the way, Route 66 became the most popular drive of all.

By the end of the 1950s, the growing love affair with the automobile was overwhelming the system of narrow roads linking the country's towns. Construction of the interstate highway system began, crossing the country with fast, limited-access, two-lane highways that bypassed town centers. Most of the parts of Route 66 that ran through northern Arizona and

visited Arizona in 1903 and supported the damming of the territory's rivers. The first dam, the Theodore Roosevelt Dam on the Salt River, was finished in 1911, providing year-round water for irrigation and drinking. This finally paved the way to statehood, and Arizona became the 48th state on February 14, 1912.

Over the next few decades, more dams were built and copper mining flourished. Some mines prospered, while others went bust and their accompanying towns dwindled to ghost towns. Irrigation increased crop yields, and cotton and cattle were important products. Tourists also started arriving, especially in the winter, and resorts and guest ranches for the wealthy began to appear in the Phoenix area in the '20s and '30s. Growth was steady but slow until WWII, when the

population swelled with an influx of military personnel training for war in the deserts of Africa and other hot regions.

After the war, air conditioning became increasingly available and many veterans who had trained in Arizona decided to return and settle in what appeared to be a land of new opportunity. Growth was phenomenal and the small towns of Phoenix and Tucson quickly grew into the important cities they are today, with all the accompanying big-city problems of air pollution, urban crime and sprawling suburban growth. The warm climate has also attracted large numbers of retirees, some of whom spend winters in Arizona and summers in their northern home states. These 'snowbirds' are an important part of the socioeconomic fabric of the state.

Kickin' Down Route 66

New Mexico were replaced by I-40. By 1984, the modern, efficient, soulless I-40 finally supplanted the last bit of Route 66, and the USA suddenly became a whole lot wider and the possibilities no longer so infinite. Williams was the last town on Route 66 to be bypassed by the freeway.

Many sections of old Route 66 fell into disuse and disrepair, but some sections, for example, Bill Williams Ave and Santa Fe Ave in Flagstaff, have been revived for nostalgic and historic reasons. The longest remaining sections of Route 66 are in western Arizona between Seligman and Kingman and between Kingman and Topock.

Today, Route 66 inspires a strange blend of patriotism, nostalgia and melancholy in most Americans. Emblematic of the enduring restless nature of the country, it has become America's Silk Road – exotic.

So exotic, in fact, that the road was the basis for the 1960s *Route 66* TV series and has appeared in many films, including *Bagdad Café*, released in 1988. (Bagdad is in California, near Siberia.) In 1946, a song by Bobby Troup reached the airwaves and by the 1990s more than 20 musicians had recorded '(Get Your Kicks on) Route 66,' including Perry Como, Bob Dylan, Buckwheat Zydeco, Asleep at the Wheel, Depeche Mode, the Rolling Stones, and – the most famous of all – Nat King Cole.

ARIZONA

Problems related to the scarce water resources remain among the foremost issues in Arizona. Dam after dam has been built, and every drop of water has a designated use, but there is not enough for the still-growing state. The simple solution, of course, would be to stop further building and development, but governmentally imposed limitations on growth are unlikely at best. And so growth continues, and the state desperately searches for water for its burgeoning desert cities.

The most recent water effort is the Central Arizona Project (CAP), which channels water hundreds of miles from the Colorado River to the Phoenix and Tucson areas. When CAP water arrived in Tucson households in 1994, residents shunned it, complaining that it looked bad and tasted worse and that the mineral content of the water was ruining their plumbing. In 1995, use of CAP water was temporarily put on hold, and legal steps commenced to reduce wasteful water use by residents. In 1997, another attempt to legalize CAP water for household use was electorally defeated, although the water was still used for irrigation. In 2001, small amounts of CAP water were mixed into drinking water with no immediate problems. Paradoxically, the state has the world's highest water fountain and hundreds of golf courses sucking up moisture. The debate over water allocation and use will be among the most important issues the state faces as it moves into the future.

Economy

Similarly to other Southwestern states, much of Arizona's economy has been directly linked to the scarcity of water and projects to divert water to agricultural areas and population centers. Where farmers and ranchers can tap water reserves, crops such as cotton, citrus fruits, grains, lettuce and broccoli thrive, and cattle and dairy products are major farm products. In the less arid central and northern areas, extensive forests, owned primarily by the US government, produce large lumber yields.

Nicknamed the Copper State, Arizona has benefited heavily from huge copper reserves first noted by miners passing through the area on their way to the 1849 Gold Rush in California. The state has been the USA's largest producer of the mineral since 1907. In addition, growing high-tech industries such as electronics and aerospace employ thousands of workers. Tourism is an important economic factor, with national parks luring millions of visitors each year.

Historically, Arizona's economy is based on the 'Four Cs' – copper, cattle, cotton and citrus. For many years, copper mining was the most important industry. Copper was the main product of the $2.5 billion 1999 nonfuel mineral production in Arizona.

Citrus and cotton in the midst of the Southwestern desert is more of a surprise – irrigation from the Gila River has provided the necessary moisture. Cotton continues to be the most important crop, but citrus appears to have been replaced by several other 'C' crops – carrots, cauliflower, corn and celery – as well as other vegetables. The 1999 value of all farm marketings was $2.18 billion, of which about 55% was crops and 45% livestock and related products.

Today, all these have been surpassed by manufacturing, construction and tourism. Major products include aircraft and missiles (Hughes Missile System Co employs many thousands in Tucson), electronics, metals, foods, clothes and the printing and publishing industry. Tourism now brings in about $9 billion annually. This growth has led to an expanded construction industry in the major metropolitan areas, and the value of construction in 1997 was $10 billion.

For Arizonans, more than 70% of jobs are in the service, trade and government sectors. Unemployment was 4.4% in 1999. Per capita income in 1999 was about $25,300 per year.

Information

Statewide travel information is available through the Arizona Office of Tourism (☎ 602-230-7733, 800-842-8257, 888-520-3433), 2702 N 3rd, Suite 4015, Phoenix, AZ 85004.

website: www.arizonaguide.com

Telephone The Phoenix metropolitan area and surrounding Maricopa County use the ☎ 602, 480 and 623 area codes. Most of southeastern Arizona (including Tucson) uses the ☎ 520 area code, while the rest of the state uses the new ☎ 928 area code, introduced in 2001 and mandatory as of early 2002.

Internet Resources For general state information, visit the state's official website, www.az.gov. Road closures and other transportation details can be found online at www.dot.state.az.us. Information on the state parks is at www.pr.state.az.us. You can search the state yellow pages at www.access arizona.com. The Game & Fish Dept's website is www.gf.state.az.us and the state Bureau of Land Management (BLM)'s website is www.az.blm.gov.

Time Arizona is on Mountain Standard Time (seven hours behind GMT). However, it is the only Western state that does not observe daylight saving time. From late spring to early fall, therefore, Arizona is eight hours behind GMT. The exception is the Navajo Reservation, which, in keeping with those parts of the reservation in Utah and New Mexico, observes daylight saving time.

Driving Laws You must be at least 18 years old (16 with parental consent) to obtain a driver's license. Drivers and front-seat passengers are required to wear safety belts. Children under age five must use child restraints. You must be over 16 to obtain a motorcycle license. Motorcycle helmets are required for the rider and the passenger if under 18. The blood-alcohol concentration over which you are legally considered drunk while driving is 0.08%. You are considered guilty of a more serious drunk driving offense if your blood-alcohol concentration is over 0.15%.

Drinking Laws You must be 21 to buy a drink in a store, bar or restaurant. Beer, wine and spirits are sold in grocery stores from 6 am to midnight except Sunday, when sales begin at 10 am. Restaurants must have licenses to serve alcohol; some licenses are limited to beer and wine. Bars close at 2 am and the sale of alcohol in them stops at 1 am. Alcohol is prohibited on most Indian reservations.

Gambling The gambling laws in the state of Arizona are complicated. Casino gambling is illegal, but you can buy lottery tickets, bet on horse and dog races, and take part in bingo games organized by local church groups. Indian reservations have their own laws, and increasing numbers of tribes have been opening casinos in the past few years. Arizona state leaders are not happy with this and threaten to take the tribes to federal court if necessary. The Feds, however, seem to be leaning in favor of allowing the Indians to do what they want on the reservations, as long as they keep within federal laws. To avoid lawsuits, the tribes and the state recently agreed to permit casinos under a 10-year 'compact' in which gamblers could compete with machines or each other, but not against a dealer. Hence, games like blackjack (21) are not allowed, but poker, video keno, bingo and slot machines are. Profits are used to improve the reservations by investing in education and health programs and the like, though detractors say that associated problems such as alcoholism and prostitution make the picture less rosy than it might sound.

About 20 casinos operate on reservations throughout the state, attracting good-sized crowds of locals who don't have the time or money to make it to Las Vegas. Only the two Apache casinos serve alcohol. Generally, Arizona casinos' slot machines have lower payoff rates than the ones in Las Vegas, and they tend to be smokier. Most patrons are Arizonans; visitors to the Southwest are more likely to head for glitzy, glamorous and altogether more over-the-top exciting Las Vegas.

ARIZONA

Phoenix & Around

☎ 602, 480, 623 • pop 1,321,045;
metro area 3,251,876 • elevation 1200 feet

Phoenix, easily the largest city in the Southwest and the sixth largest in the country, was surrounded by other towns before WWII, but rapid growth in the latter half of the 20th century has linked these into one huge, still-growing metropolitan area. Major towns adjoining Phoenix include Tempe (pronounced 'TEM-pee,' with 158,625 inhabitants), Scottsdale (population 202,705), Mesa (population 396,375), and over a dozen other communities. Together, they cover almost 2000 sq miles, an area that is locally called 'the Valley of the Sun' or just 'the valley.' Sunny it certainly is; with more than 300 days of sunshine a year, it's searingly hot in summer but delightful in winter.

The climate attracts winter visitors (locally called 'snowbirds') who leave their colder northern states to spend several months soaking up the rays. Fall, winter and spring are the main cultural and tourist seasons, when places charge the highest prices. Visitors arriving during summer vacation periods will find the lowest prices in the hotels and resorts, but also daytime high temperatures above 100°F for weeks on end, commonly reaching well over 110°F in midsummer. Clothing is appropriately casual – you can wear shorts almost anywhere in summer.

Phoenix is the Southwest's most important gateway, with nonstop international flights to Europe, as well as all over the country. Major museums, superlative shopping (especially in Scottsdale, which vies with Santa Fe as an arts center), relaxing resorts, delectable dining, warm winters, spectator sports and golfing greens (where do they get that water?) are the main reasons why visitors spend some time here before moving on to the rest of the Southwest. Relaxed sophistication is a hallmark of Phoenix, where a cowboy hat and jeans are rarely out of place and where ties are seldom required.

Phoenix rising

HISTORY

Hohokam people lived here 2300 years ago (see the section on Pueblo Grande Museum, later) and small groups of Pima and Maricopa Indians eked out an existence along the Gila and Salt Rivers. In the mid-1860s, the US Army built Fort McDowell northeast of Phoenix. This prompted Jack Swilling to reopen Hohokam canals to produce crops for the garrison and led to the establishment of a town in 1870. Darrel Duppa, a British settler, suggested that the town had risen from the ashes of the Hohokam culture like the fabled phoenix, and the name stuck.

Phoenix established itself as an agricultural and transportation center. The railway arrived from the Pacific in 1887 and when Phoenix became the territorial capital in 1889, it had 3000 inhabitants. Settlers built Victorian houses that today stand as Phoenix's oldest historical buildings. In 1886 the Arizona Normal School, later to become Arizona State University (ASU), was established in Tempe. Other villages appeared; Mesa was founded by Mormon settlers in

1878, and Scottsdale followed a decade later, named after army chaplain Winfield Scott.

The lack of water was a major stumbling block to further growth until 1911, when the Roosevelt Dam on the Salt River was finished, the first of many large dams to be built in the state. The stage was set for growth, and grow Phoenix did.

In 1926, Phoenix's railway link became transcontinental, enabling people from the East to pour into the state in increasing numbers. Many came for recreation – to play cowboy in dude ranches, or to relax at the luxurious Arizona Biltmore resort, opened in 1929 and still one of the finest in the West. Others came for their health; the dry desert air was said to cure various respiratory ailments. Many visitors stayed, including Dwight and Maie Heard, who arrived in 1895 to cure Dwight's lung complaints. They founded Phoenix's most interesting museum, the Heard. The combination of recreation and culture has been the valley's main attraction ever since.

ORIENTATION

The greater Phoenix area is ringed by mountains that range from 2500 feet in elevation to more than 7000 feet. Because metro Phoenix grew to engulf many small towns, there are several historical centers, of which Phoenix, Scottsdale and Tempe and Mesa are the most interesting. Most of this chapter is devoted to these towns.

Phoenix is the largest town and houses the state capitol, the oldest buildings, several important museums and professional sport facilities. Southeast of Phoenix lies Tempe, home of ASU and an active student population. East of Tempe, Mesa is the second largest town in the valley and is home to several museums and Arizona's main Mormon temple. Scottsdale, northeast of Phoenix and Tempe, is known for both its Western downtown area, now full of fine galleries, boutiques and crafts stores, and its many upscale resorts and restaurants.

Other towns, including Chandler to the southeast and Glendale and Peoria to the northwest, are thriving residential and manufacturing communities off the travelers'

normal circuit, unless you're into antiques, in which case Glendale's downtown has dozens of antique stores. Sun City and Sun City West, in the northwest of the valley, are among the largest retirement communities in the country, with little industry or tourism but numerous quiet streets and golf courses for the dynamic older residents. Paradise Valley, nestled between the arms of Phoenix and Scottsdale, is the valley's most exclusive residential neighborhood, and Apache Junction, at the far east end of metropolitan Phoenix, is the gateway to the wild Superstition Mountains and the Apache Trail leading into east-central Arizona.

Because the valley's roads run north-south or east-west, to get from one point to another you often have to take two sides of a triangle; this, combined with large distances and slow traffic, can make getting around time-consuming.

Central Ave, running north-south in Phoenix, divides west addresses from east addresses; west of Central Ave, *avenues* are north-south bound, while east of Central Ave *streets* run north-south. Washington St, running west-east in Phoenix, divides north addresses from south addresses; thus 4100 N 16th St would be 16 blocks east of Central Ave and 41 blocks north of Washington (this is only an approximation – blocks don't always correspond exactly to 100-address increments). This numbering system continues into Scottsdale and Glendale.

Tempe and Mesa each have their own numbering systems, which means you can drive from Phoenix's 4800 E Southern Ave to Tempe's 2800 W Southern Ave just by crossing the city limits. In Tempe, Mill Ave, running north-south, divides west addresses from east addresses, while the east-west flowing Salt River divides north from south addresses. In Mesa, north-south Center St divides west from east, and west-east Main St divides north from south. Other valley towns have similar systems.

Major freeways include I-17 North (Black Canyon Hwy; this has many motels along it), I-10 West (the Papago Freeway), I-10 South (the Maricopa Freeway) and Hwy 60 East (the Superstition Freeway).

INFORMATION

The Greater Phoenix Convention and Visitors Bureau (CVB – Map 3; ☎ 602-254-6500, 877-225-5749), 50 N 2nd St, is open Monday to Friday 8 am to 5 pm. This is the valley's most complete source of tourist information; visit it at www.phoenixcvb.com. Another office (☎ 602-955-1963) is at the Biltmore Fashion Park Shopping Mall, Center Lawn, 2404 E Camelback Rd, open during mall hours daily. A useful website is www.phoenix.gov with hundreds of searchable links.

Individual towns each offer their own services. The Scottsdale CVB (☎ 480-945-8481, 800-877-1117), 7343 Scottsdale Mall, is open Monday to Friday 8:30 am to 6 pm, Saturday 10 am to 4 pm and Sunday 11 am to 4 pm (closed summer Sundays); its website is www.scottsdalecvb.com. The Tempe CVB (☎ 480-894-8158, 800-283-6734), 51 W 3rd, Suite 105, has a website at www.tempecvb.com; it and the Mesa CVB (☎ 480-827-4700, 800-283-6372), 120 N Center, and the Glendale Tourist Office (☎ 623-930-2957, 623-930-2957), 5850 W Glendale Ave, are all open Monday to Friday 8 am to 5 pm.

The Arizona Public Lands Information Center (Map 3; ☎ 602-417-9300), 222 N Central Ave, provides information about USFS, NPS, BLM and state lands and parks from 7:30 am to 4:30 pm Monday to Friday; look at www.publiclands.org.

Foreign exchange is available at the airport and some banks; call Bank of America (☎ 800-944-0404) or Bank One (☎ 800-366-2265) for addresses and hours of the nearest branch. The main post office is at 4949 E Van Buren (Map 2), and the main downtown post office is at 522 N Central Ave (Map 3).

The Phoenix area has three telephone area codes. These are considered local numbers when dialing from one to another, as from a hotel room, but the different area codes must be dialed.

The huge main library (Map 3; ☎ 602-262-4636) is at 1221 N Central Ave and there are many others throughout the city. The local daily is the *Arizona Republic*. The area's bookstore scene is now dominated by huge chain stores. If you're after used books, Bookman's (☎ 480-835-0505), 1056 S Country Club Dr, Mesa, is among the largest. One of the best selections of periodicals and magazines is at The Book Store (Map 2; ☎ 602-279-3910), 4230 N 7th Ave. Wide World of Maps (Map 2; ☎ 602-279-2323), 2626 W Indian School Rd, has a fine selection of maps and guidebooks.

Banner Health Arizona (☎ 602-230-2273) operates several valley hospitals and provides 24-hour doctor referral; there are also many other hospitals and clinics. For 24-hour dentist referral, call the Arizona Dental Association (☎ 602-957-4777).

The Phoenix police (Map 3; ☎ 602-262-6151) are at 620 W Washington.

CENTRAL PHOENIX

All museums are closed on at least some major holidays.

Heard Museum

The museum (Map 3; ☎ 602-252-8840, 252-8848), 2301 N Central Ave, emphasizes quality rather than quantity and is one of America's best museums in which to learn Southwest Indian tribes' history, life, arts and culture. Certainly, there are thousands of exhibits, but these are well displayed in a relatively small space, making a visit here much more relaxing than the torturous slog of many major museums. The kachina-doll room is outstanding, as are the audio-visual displays, occasional live demonstrations and the superb gift shop. If you are at all interested in Native American history and culture, this museum should be at the top of your list. Combined with a visit to the nearby Phoenix Art Museum, it makes a great cultural day.

The museum is open daily from 9:30 am to 5 pm. Admission is $7 for adults; $6 for seniors; $3 for four- to 12-year-olds; free for Native Americans. You can take a free guided tour (noon, 1:30 and 3 pm) or rent a 45-minute audiotape tour for $3.
website: www.heard.org

Phoenix Art Museum

Galleries show works from around the world produced between the 14th and 20th

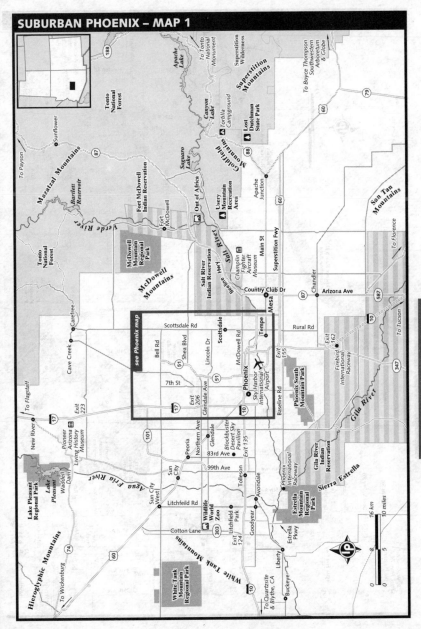

SUBURBAN PHOENIX – MAP 1

ARIZONA

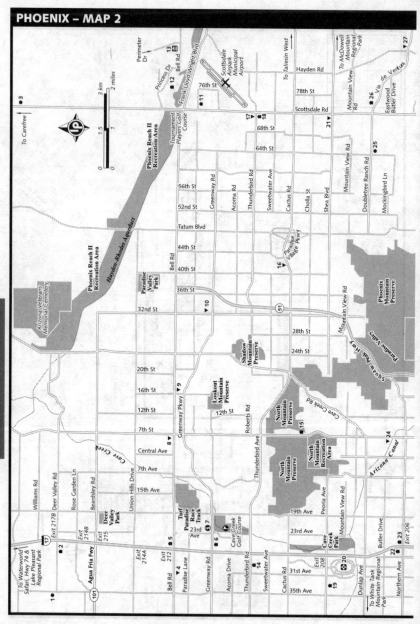

PHOENIX – MAP 2

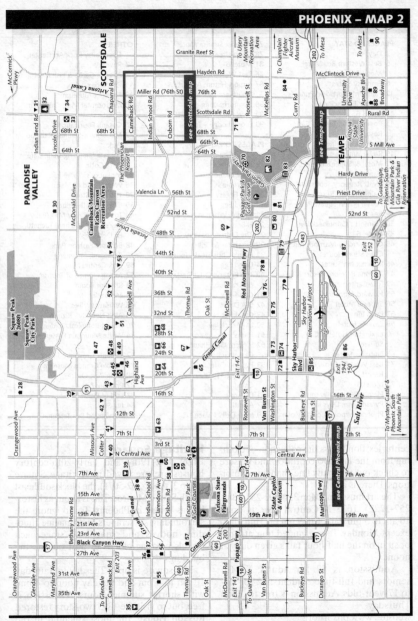

PHOENIX – MAP 2

SCOTTSDALE

PARADISE VALLEY

TEMPE

ARIZONA

PHOENIX – MAP 2

PLACES TO STAY
2 Days Inn
5 Best Western Bell Motel; Motel 6; Fairfield Inn
6 Embassy Suites
12 Fairmont Scottsdale Princess Resort; La Hacienda
14 Motel 6
15 Pointe Hilton Tapatio Cliffs Resort
18 Scottsdale Fairfield Inn
19 Royal Suites
22 Motel 6; Super 8 Motel
23 Hampton Inn
26 Hyatt Regency Scottsdale at Gainey Ranch Resort
28 Pointe Hilton Squaw Peak Resort
30 Marriott's Camelback Inn
37 Motel 6
45 Courtyard by Marriott; Ruth's Chris Steak House
46 Phoenix Inn Suites
47 Arizona Biltmore Resort & Spa
49 Ritz-Carlton
55 Howard Johnson
56 Super 8 Motel
57 Days Inn
58 Quality Hotel
60 Lexington Hotel at City Square
65 Embassy Suites
71 Best Western Papago Inn & Resort
72 Motel 6
73 Flamingo Airporter Inn
75 Pyramid Inn; Days Inn; Phoenix Airport Super 8 Motel

76 Phoenix Sunrise Motel
78 Doubletree Suites
81 Motel 6
86 Best Western Airport Inn
87 Airport Hilton; Airport Courtyard by Marriott
88 Comfort Suites
89 Days Inn - Tempe/ASU
90 Econo Lodge - Tempe

PLACES TO EAT
4 Good Egg
8 India Palace
1 Taste of India
10 Chompie's
16 The Eggery
17 Good Egg
21 Maria's When in Naples
24 El Bravo
27 The Coffee Roastery
29 Texaz Bar & Grill
31 Ruth's Chris Steak House
34 Good Egg
40 The Eggery; Orbit Restaurant & Jazz Club
41 Good Egg
42 5 & Diner
43 Greekfest
50 La Madeleine
51 Harris'
52 Vincent Guerithault on Camelback
53 Havana Cafe
54 The Eggery; The News Café
61 Durant's
67 Avanti
69 India Delhi Palace

OTHER
1 Deer Valley Rock Art Center
3 Rawhide
7 Arizona Game & Fish Dept
11 Crackerjax
13 Fleischer Museum
20 Metrocenter Mall; Castles 'n Coasters
25 Cosanti Foundation
32 McCormick-Stillman Railroad Park
33 Borgata Shopping Mall; Café Terra Cotta
35 Mr Lucky's
36 Wide World of Maps
38 The Book Store
39 Char's Has the Blues
44 Town & Country Mall (Baby Kay's Cajun Kitchen, Tuchetti, Ed Debevic's)
48 Biltmore Fashion Park (RoxSand, Steamers)
59 Park Central Mall
62 Arizona Office of Tourism
63 Rhythm Room
64 Mason Jar
66 Warsaw Wallies
68 Ain't Nobody's Bizness
70 Desert Botanical Garden
74 White Mountain Passenger Lines
77 Phoenix Greyhound Park
79 Pueblo Grande Museum
80 Main Post Office
82 Phoenix Zoo
83 Hall of Flame
84 Big Surf
85 Greyhound Bus Terminal

centuries; don't miss the collection of clothing from the last two centuries, and be sure to check out the many fine changing exhibitions. There is a café.

The art museum (Map 3; ☎ 602-257-1880, 257-1222), 1625 N Central Ave, is open 10 am to 5 pm daily ('til 9 pm on Thursday) except Monday. Take a guided tour at 2 pm or sit in on the half-hour talks given daily at noon.

Admission is $7 for adults; $5 for seniors and full-time students; $2 for six-to 17-year-olds. Admission is free to all on Thursday.
website: www.phxart.org

Heritage Square

Eight late-19th- and early-20th-century houses are preserved in Heritage Square (Map 3; ☎ 602-262-5071), the block southeast of 6th St and Monroe. This is about as historical as it gets in Phoenix. Try to ignore the surrounding skyscrapers and imagine thudding hooves and squeaking stagecoach wheels creating clouds of dust outside the buildings.

The square is open Tuesday to Saturday 10 am to 4 pm and Sunday noon to 4 pm, with shorter summer hours. Admission is free, but to visit the 1895 two-story restored **Rosson House**, the most splendid in the

CENTRAL PHOENIX – MAP 3

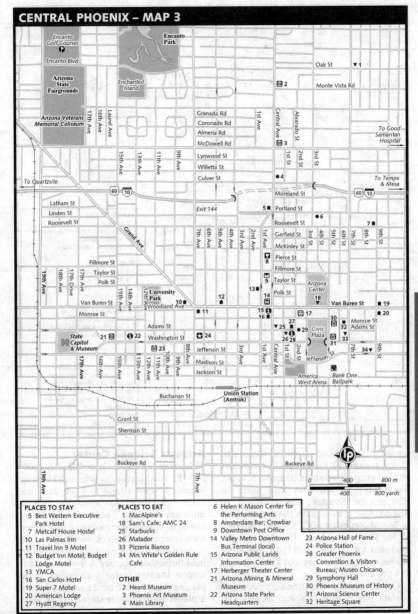

Encanto Golf Courses
Encanto Blvd
Encanto Park
Oak St ▼1
Arizona State Fairgrounds
Enchanted Island
🏛2   Monte Vista Rd
Arizona Veterans Memorial Coliseum
Granada Rd
Coronado Rd
Almeria Rd
McDowell Rd
🏛3
To Good Samaritan Hospital
17th Ave
16th Ave
Laurel Ave
15th Ave
13th Ave
11th Ave
9th Ave
Central Ave
Alvarado St
1st Ave
1st St
2nd St
3rd St
Lynwood St
Willetta St
Culver St
●4
To Quartzsite
60 10
Moreland St
60 10
To Tempe & Mesa
Latham St
Linden St
Roosevelt St
Exit 144
5🛏 Portland St
●6
7🛏
Grand Ave
7th Ave
6th Ave
5th Ave
4th Ave
3rd Ave
2nd Ave
1st Ave
Garfield St
McKinley St
Pierce St
Fillmore St
Taylor St
Polk St
3rd St
4th St
5th St
6th St
7th St
8th St
9th St
19th Ave
18th Ave
17th Drive
17th Ave
Fillmore St
Taylor St
Polk St
🅿8
🅿9
Arizona Center
18
Van Buren St
15th Ave
14th Ave
12th Ave
University Park
Woodland Ave
Van Buren St
10🛏
12
🏛
13🛏
14
15🛈
16🛏
🏛17
●19
Monroe St
🛏11
30 🏛
32
●20
State Capitol & Museum
21 🏛
🛈22
Adams St
Washington St
27
25▼
26 28
🏛24
●29 Civic Plaza
31
33
Monroe St
Adams St
34▼
17th Ave
16th Ave
15th Ave
13th Ave
12th Ave
10th Ave
9th Ave
🏛23
8th Ave
Jefferson St
Madison St
Jackson St
3rd St
1st St
Central Ave
1st Ave
Jefferson St
7th St
9th St
America West Arena
🅿
Bank One Ballpark
Buchanan St
Union Station (Amtrak)
Grant St
Sherman St
19th Ave
Buckeye Rd
7th Ave
Buckeye Rd
℗
0   400   800 m
0   400   800 yards

PLACES TO STAY
5 Best Western Executive Park Hotel
7 Metcalf House Hostel
10 Las Palmas Inn
11 Travel Inn 9 Motel
12 Budget Inn Motel; Budget Lodge Motel
13 YMCA
16 San Carlos Hotel
19 Super 7 Motel
20 American Lodge
27 Hyatt Regency

PLACES TO EAT
1 MacAlpine's
18 Sam's Cafe; AMC 24
25 Starbucks
26 Matador
33 Pizzeria Bianco
34 Mrs White's Golden Rule Cafe

OTHER
2 Heard Museum
3 Phoenix Art Museum
4 Main Library
6 Helen K Mason Center for the Performing Arts
8 Amsterdam Bar; Crowbar
9 Downtown Post Office
14 Valley Metro Downtown Bus Terminal (local)
15 Arizona Public Lands Information Center
17 Herberger Theater Center
21 Arizona Mining & Mineral Museum
22 Arizona State Parks Headquarters
23 Arizona Hall of Fame
24 Police Station
28 Greater Phoenix Convention & Visitors Bureau; Museo Chicano
29 Symphony Hall
30 Phoenix Museum of History
31 Arizona Science Center
32 Heritage Square

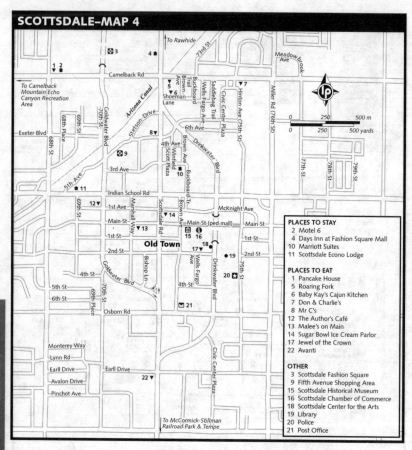

SCOTTSDALE–MAP 4

To Rawhide
To Camelback Mountain Echo Canyon Recreation Area
Camelback Rd
Arizona Canal
Stetson Drive
Shoeman Lane
Exeter Blvd
68th St
69th St
70th St
Goldwater Blvd
68th Place
5th Ave
3rd Ave
4th Ave
Winfield Scott Plaza
Buckboard Tr
Brown Ave
6th Ave
Indian School Rd
1st Ave
Main St
1st St
2nd St
Scottsdale Rd
Marshall Way
Main St (ped mall)
Old Town
4th St
5th St
6th St
Osborn Rd
Goldwater Blvd
69th Place
70th St
Bishop Ln
Monterey Way
Lynn Rd
Earll Drive
Avalon Drive
Pinchot Ave
To Camelback Mountain Echo Canyon Recreation Area
73rd St
Saddlebag Trail
Wells Fargo Ave
Buckboard Ave
Civic Center Plaza
Hinton Ave
75th St
Miller Rd (76th St)
Meadow brook Ave
McKnight Ave
Main St
1st St
2nd St
Drinkwater Blvd
Wells Fargo Ave
75th St
Civic Center Plaza
To McCormick-Stillman Railroad Park & Tempe
77th St
78th St
79th St
0   250   500 m
0   250   500 yards

PLACES TO STAY
2 Motel 6
4 Days Inn at Fashion Square Mall
10 Marriott Suites
11 Scottsdale Econo Lodge

PLACES TO EAT
1 Pancake House
5 Roaring Fork
6 Baby Kay's Cajun Kitchen
7 Don & Charlie's
8 Mr C's
12 The Author's Café
13 Malee's on Main
14 Sugar Bowl Ice Cream Parlor
17 Jewel of the Crown
22 Avanti

OTHER
3 Scottsdale Fashion Square
9 Fifth Avenue Shopping Area
15 Scottsdale Historical Museum
16 Scottsdale Chamber of Commerce
18 Scottsdale Center for the Arts
19 Library
20 Police
21 Post Office

ARIZONA

square, you must join a tour ($3 for adults; $2 for seniors; $1 for six- to 13-year-olds) offered every 30 minutes 10 am to 3:30 pm Wednesday to Saturday and noon to 3:30 pm on Sunday; shorter hours in August. Also in the square, the **Arizona Doll & Toy Museum** (☎ 602-253-9337) charges $2.50, $1 for children. The **African Art Museum** (☎ 602-307-0893) in the Silva House is open Thursday and Friday 10 am to 4 pm and is free.

Other buildings offer free admission and contain places to eat as well as arts and crafts shops.

Arizona Science Center

This complex (Map 3; ☎ 602-716-2000), 600 E Washington, adjoining Heritage Square, is open 10 am to 5 pm daily, and stays open later for special events. A **museum** with 350 hands-on exhibits encourages visitors to explore and experiment with computers, bubbles, weather, physics, biology and more. Live demonstrations are held throughout the day. A five-story **giant-screen theater** features changing shows playing every hour from 11 am to 4 pm and a **planetarium** has star shows two or three times a day.

TEMPE – MAP 5

PLACES TO STAY
4 Tempe Mission Palms
12 Super 8 Motel of Tempe
13 Holiday Inn
14 Tempe-University
   Travelodge
15 Motel 6
16 Fiesta Inn
17 Motel 6

PLACES TO EAT
6 Coffee Plantation
7 House of Tricks
9 India Palace

OTHER
1 Tempe Convention and
   Visitors Bureau
2 Bash on Ash
3 Hayden Square
5 Valley Art Theater
8 ASU Geology Museum;
   Planetarium
10 ASU Art Museum (Nelson
   Fine Arts Center)
11 Gammage Auditorium

Museum admission is $8 for adults; $6 for seniors and three- to 12-year-olds. Tickets for the theater or planetarium are an extra $3 each per person.
website: www.azscience.org

Phoenix Museum of History

Displays at this modern and attractive museum range from 2000-year-old archaeological artifacts to an exhibit about the sinking of the USS *Arizona* at Pearl Harbor in 1941. The museum (Map 3; ☎ 602-253-2734), 105 N 5th St, adjoining Heritage Square, is open from 10 am to 5 pm Monday

to Saturday, and noon to 5 pm on Sunday. Admission is $5 for adults; $3.50 for seniors; $2.50 for seven- to 12-year olds.

Other Central Museums

The old state capitol building (Map 3; ☎ 602-542-4675), 1700 W Washington, built in 1900, is now the **Arizona State Capitol Museum** displaying documents and exhibits from late-territorial and early-state days. The **Arizona Hall of Fame** (Map 3; ☎ 602-255-2110), housed in the 1908 Carnegie Library building at 1101 W Washington, presents changing exhibits on people who

ARIZONA

have contributed to Arizona's history in memorable and not-so-memorable ways. Both museums are free and open from 8 am to 5 pm Monday to Friday.

The **Arizona Mining & Mineral Museum** (Map 3; ☎ 602-255-3791), 1502 W Washington, also has a Rose Mofford room displaying memorabilia of Arizona's first woman governor. Hours are Monday to Friday 8 am to 5 pm, Saturday 11 am to 4 pm; free.

The **Museo Chicano** (☎ 602-257-5536), 147 E Adams, exhibits mainly artwork by local and national Hispanic artists. Hours are 10 am to 4 pm Tuesday to Saturday; admission is $2, seniors and students $1.

OUTER PHOENIX
Desert Botanical Garden

This recommended, 145-acre garden in Papago Park (Map 2) exhibits thousands of species of arid-land plants from Arizona and around the world. The flowering season of March to May is the busiest and most colorful time to visit, but any month provides insight into how plants survive in the desert. The garden (☎ 480-941-1225), 1201 N Galvin Parkway, has a gift shop and café and offers occasional tours and events; it is open daily 8 am to 8 pm (from 7 am May through September). Admission is $7.50 adults; $6.50 for seniors; $1.50 for five- to 12-year-olds.

The surrounding **Papago Park** has picnic areas, jogging, biking and equestrian trails, a city golf course and a children's fishing pond; it also houses the Phoenix Zoo.

Phoenix Zoo

The zoo (Map 2; ☎ 602-273-1341), 455 N Galvin Parkway, houses a wide variety of animals, including some rare ones, in several distinct and natural-looking environments. There is a children's petting zoo, walk-in aviary, demonstrations and food facilities. The zoo is open 9 am to 5 pm September through June. Admission is $10; $9 for seniors; $5 for three- to 12-year-olds. Narrated safari train tours cost $2 and last 30 minutes. Call for shorter summer hours and discounted admissions.

Hall of Flame

Opposite Papago Park, the Hall of Flame (Map 2; ☎ 602-275-3473), 6101 E Van Buren, exhibits more than 90 fully restored fire-fighting machines and related paraphernalia from 1725 onward. The hall is open 9 am to 5 pm Monday to Saturday, and noon to 4 pm on Sunday. Admission is $5; $4 for seniors; $3 for six-to 17-year-olds.

Pueblo Grande Museum

As early as 300 BC, the dry desert soil yielded crops for the Hohokam people, who spent centuries developing a complex system of irrigation canals only to mysteriously abandon them around AD 1450. Pueblo Grande is a Hohokam village that has been partially excavated and then reburied for its protection. Parts of the excavation remain exposed for the visitor, and a nice little on-site museum (Map 2; ☎ 602-495-0901), 4619 E Washington, explains all that is known of the canal-building Hohokam culture. Admission is $2; $1.50 for seniors; $1 for six- to 18-year-olds; free on Sunday. Hours are 9 am to 4:45 pm Monday to Saturday, and 1 to 4:45 pm on Sunday. website: www.pueblogrande.com

Mystery Castle

This 18-room fantasy was built between 1927 and 1945 by the reclusive Boyce Luther Gulley for his daughter, Mary Lou, who now gives tours of the oddly furnished property. Mystery Castle (☎ 602-268-1581), 800 E Mineral Rd (on the north border of Phoenix South Mountain Park), is open October to June, Thursday to Sunday 11 am to 4 pm; admission is $5; $4 for seniors; $2 for five- to 15-year-olds.

Deer Valley Rock Art Center

A small museum (Map 2; ☎ 602-582-8007), 3711 W Deer Valley Rd (west of I-17 exit 215A), interprets the significance and techniques involved in making the approximately 1500 prehistoric petroglyphs chipped into boulders along a quarter-mile trail outside. Hours are 9 am to 5 pm Tuesday to Saturday, and noon to 5 pm on Sunday; call about shorter summer hours.

Admission is $3; $2 for students and seniors; $1 for six- to 12-year-olds.

SCOTTSDALE
Old Town

Half a dozen blocks near the chamber of commerce constitute 'Old Town,' with some early-20th-century buildings and some more recent buildings styled to look like those of the Old West. One of the oldest is the 'Little Red School House,' built in 1909 and now housing the **Scottsdale Historical Museum** (Map 4; ☎ 480-945-4499), 7333 Scottsdale Mall. Hours are 10 am to 5 pm Wednesday to Saturday, and noon to 4 pm Sunday; the museum is closed on holidays and throughout July and August. Admission is free.

Nearby, the **Scottsdale Center for the Arts** (Map 4; ☎ 480-994-2787), 7374 E 2nd St, includes the **Museum of Contemporary Art** and hosts various performing arts. The museum is open Tuesday and Wednesday 10 am to 5 pm, Thursday to Saturday 10 am to 8 pm, and Sunday noon to 5 pm; admission is $7 and $5 for students. The whole mall area is beautifully and restfully landscaped with green areas, shade trees and fountains. Several good ethnic restaurants are near the center for the arts. West of the Scottsdale Mall, centered around Brown Ave and Main, old Western-style buildings house art galleries, restaurants and souvenir shops. The chamber of commerce offers brochures describing this popular area.

Fleischer Museum

Few art museums have as specific a focus as the Fleischer, dedicated to American Impressionism of the California School. The Fleischer Museum (Map 2; ☎ 480-585-3108), 17207 N Perimeter Dr, is open 10 am to 4 pm daily except holidays; free.

Rawhide

About 14 miles north of downtown Scottsdale, Rawhide (Map 2; ☎ 480-502-5600), 23023 N Scottsdale Rd, is a re-created late-1800s Western town with saloons, showdowns, stagecoaches and all that stuff. Popular with tourists and fun for kids, it's

The Desert as Muse

Frank Lloyd Wright (1867–1959), America's most iconoclastic well-known architect, lived, designed and taught in Scottsdale at **Taliesin West** (☎ 480-860-2700, 480-860-8810), 12621 Frank Lloyd Wright Blvd (Cactus Rd at 104th St). Set on 600 acres of desert, Taliesin West is an example of his organic architecture, which uses natural forms to shape most structures. Wright moved here in 1927 and set up a tent camp. He began building a decade later and wasn't finished until 20 years after that. Today, the natural rock, wood and canvas structures continue to be both living quarters and a teaching establishment.

Visits are limited to guided tours. One-hour tours are given daily on the hour, October to May from 10 am to 4 pm (call about summer hours), and cost $12 (discounted to $9 for students and seniors, and to $3 for four- to 12-year-olds). Ninety-minute tours are offered at 9 am Monday to Saturday, and cost $16/14. Ninety-minute desert walks on the grounds are given at 11:15 am and 1:15 pm Monday to Saturday; $14 for all. Three-hour 'behind the scenes' tours at 9 am Tuesday and Thursday are $25; call for reservations.

Paolo Soleri was a student of Frank Lloyd Wright who went on to develop his own form of organic architecture, which he termed 'arcology' (the combined form of architecture and ecology). Soleri's headquarters are at **Cosanti Foundation** (Map 1; ☎ 480-948-6145), 6433 Doubletree Ranch Rd, where you can see a scale model of his futuristic Arcosanti (see Around Camp Verde in the Central Arizona chapter) and various other structures, and can pick up a souvenir at the gift shop. Hours are 9 am to 5 pm daily, and a $1 donation is suggested.

ARIZONA

open 5 to 10 pm daily year-round; October to May hours are extended to 3 to 10 pm Monday to Thursday, and 11 am to 10 pm on weekends. Admission is $5, $2 for four- to 11-year olds, and free on some weekdays;

call for details. Attractions, such as the stage-coach, burro or train rides, the Indian village (with dance performances) and the children's petting zoo, charge an extra $2 to $4. A steak house is open from 5 pm daily, plus 11:30 am to 3 pm during winter weekends, and admission costs are refunded to diners. website: www.rawhide.com

TEMPE
Arizona State University
With some 45,000 students, this is the largest college in the Southwest. General information (☎ 480-965-9011) and a 24-hour recorded calendar of campus events during the academic year (☎ 480-965-2278) will help orient you.

The **ASU Art Museum** (Map 5; ☎ 480-965-2787), headquartered in the architecturally acclaimed Nelson Fine Arts Center at 10th St and Mill Ave, showcases a varied collection of European and American art along with changing exhibits; hours are Wednesday to Saturday 10 am to 5 pm, Sunday 1 to 5 pm and Tuesday 10 am to 9 pm. For an experimental gallery exhibiting the work of emerging artists, visit the Matthews Center branch of the museum, about a quarter-mile northeast of the Nelson Center. Hours are 10 am to 5 pm Tuesday to Saturday. Admission is free to both.

The interesting and free **ASU Geology Museum** (Map 5; ☎ 480-965-7065), 250 yards west of McAllister and University Dr, exhibiting dinosaur bones, rocks, minerals and gems, is open Monday to Friday 9 am to noon. The **Planetarium** (Map 5; ☎ 480-727-6234), next to the Geology Museum, has star shows from October to May for $2; call for hours. The **Gammage Auditorium** at Mill Ave and Apache Blvd (Map 5) was Frank Lloyd Wright's last major building; tour the inside between October and May, Monday to Friday 1 to 4 pm.

Tempe Historical Museum
Permanent and changing displays as well as interactive exhibits showcase Tempe's prehistory and modern history at this small museum. The museum (☎ 480-350-5100), 809 E Southern Ave, is open Monday to Thurs-day and Saturday 10 am to 5 pm, Sunday 1 to 5 pm and is closed on Friday and major holidays. Admission is by donation.

MESA
There are quite a few museums in Mesa, including the **Arizona Museum for Youth** (see the 'Especially for Kids' boxed text).

Mesa Southwest Museum
Animated dinosaurs, dioramas of ancient Indians, an eight-cell territorial jail, gold panning near the Dutchman's Mine and changing art shows are just a few of the many displays and interactive exhibits at this museum with a Southwestern theme.

The museum (☎ 480-644-2230), 53 N MacDonald, is open 10 am to 5 pm Tuesday to Saturday, 1 to 5 pm on Sunday, and closed Monday and holidays. Admission is $6 for adults; $5 for seniors and students; $3 for three- to 12-year-olds.

Mesa Historical Society Museum
Mesa's pioneer history is remembered through more than 4000 artifacts displayed at this museum (☎ 480-835-7358), 2345 N Horne. Hours are 10 am to 4 pm Tuesday to Saturday, and 9 am to 1 pm in summer. Admission is free.

Champlin Fighter Aircraft Museum
The museum (Map 1; ☎ 480-830-4540), in Falcon Field Airport at 4800 E McKellips Rd, has one of the largest collections of fighter aircraft in the world. Thirty-three flyable airplanes from WWI to the Vietnam War are on display and are explained in extensive supporting exhibits. The museum is open daily 8:30 am to 3:30 pm in summer and 10 am to 5 pm the rest of the year. Admission is $6.50 for adults; $3 for five- to 12-year-olds. Guided tours (call to reserve a spot) are given at 10:30 am, 1:30 and 3 pm.

SUBURBAN PHOENIX
Pioneer Arizona Living History Museum
About 25 authentic territorial buildings (brought here from elsewhere) and farm

animals (which can be petted) form a complete village inhabited by guides/interpreters in period dress. Daily performances in a turn-of-the-19th-century opera house and various other re-enactments present a historically accurate depiction of pioneering life. The museum (Map 1; ☎ 623-465-1052), 3901 W Pioneer Rd, is at I-17 exit 225. It's open Wednesday to Sunday 9 am to 5 pm, and 9 am to 3 pm June to September. Admission is $6 for adults; $4 for four- to 12-year-olds.

Wildlife World Zoo

This zoo specializes in rare and exotic species ranging from white tigers to black jaguars. The attractions include a walk-in aviary filled with tropical birds, a parrot feeding area, a petting zoo and an aquarium with seahorses, piranhas and electric eels. The zoo (Map 1; ☎ 623-935-9453), 16501 W Northern Ave, is open 9 am to 5 pm daily. Admission is $12 for adults; $5 for three- to 12-year-olds.

Out of Africa

See big cats from Africa and other continents, pet a lion cub or watch keepers swim with big cats at this wildlife park. The park presents a variety of continuous shows. Out of Africa (☎ 480-837-7779, 480-837-7677),

---

Especially for Kids

Places like the zoo, the wildlife park, the Arizona Science Center, the Hall of Flame and Rawhide will interest the whole family, but the following are especially for kids.

Art exhibits and hands-on art workshops are aimed at elementary school children at the **Arizona Museum for Youth** (☎ 480-644-2467), 35 N Robson St, Mesa. Exhibitions and workshops change every few months, so call ahead for details. Hours are 9 am to 5 pm Tuesday to Saturday. Admission is $2.50 for ages three and up. Preregistration for workshops is suggested. The 30-acre **McCormick-Stillman Railroad Park** (Map 1; ☎ 480-312-2312), 7301 E Indian Bend Rd, Scottsdale, has a miniature railroad at 5/12 scale. Rides, open from 10 am to about 6 pm, cost $1. Other attractions are model railroads, a traditional carousel and a railroad museum ($1).

Cool off in summer at **Waterworld Safari** (☎ 623-581-1947), 4243 W Pinnacle Peak Rd (2 miles west of I-17 exit 217), with a six-story-high water slide; **Big Surf Waterpark** (☎ 480-947-7873), 1500 N McClintock Dr, Tempe; and **Golfland/Sunsplash** (☎ 480-834-8319), 155 W Hampton Ave, Mesa. All offer acres of swimming pools, water slides and wave-making machines; Golfland also has tube floats, bumper boats, miniature golf and go-carts. It is open daily from Memorial Day to Labor Day, and admission is about $17 ($14 for four- to 11-year-olds).

Castles 'n Coasters (Map 1; ☎ 602-997-7575), 9445 E Metro Pkwy (by the Metrocenter Mall) is the area's largest amusement park, with the 2000-foot-long Desert Storm roller coaster, complete with two 360° loops, providing fun for kids of all ages with strong stomachs. Smaller coasters are suitable for younger riders and there are a dozen other attractions, including four miniature golf courses, video arcades, go-carts and carousels. Desert Storm and major rides are $4.50; smaller rides are $2 and miniature golf is $6.50. All-day unlimited rides are $18; $23 with unlimited miniature golf. The park is open daily. Near downtown, **Enchanted Island** (Map 2; ☎ 602-254-2020), 1202 W Encanto Blvd, has 12 rides aimed at younger kids for 75¢ each; $9 for unlimited day use. It's open Wednesday to Sunday year-round, and some Mondays and Tuesdays.

Local 'Family Fun Parks' offering miniature golf, video games, batting cages, bumper boats, go-carts, volleyball and other activities year-round include the **Crackerjax** (Map 1; ☎ 480-998-2800), 16001 N Scottsdale Rd, and **Fiddlesticks** (☎ 480-961-0800), 1155 W Elliot Rd in Tempe (a mile east of I-10 exit 157), and in Scottsdale (☎ 480-951-6060), 8800 E Indian Bend Rd. They are open daily (hours vary seasonally) and you pay for the activities you want. Multiple-activity passes may be available.

ARIZONA

2 S Fort McDowell Rd (off Hwy 87 near the Fort McDowell Indian Reservation), is open 9:30 am to 5 pm Tuesday to Sunday from October through May. In summer, hours are 4 to 9 pm Wednesday and Thursday, 9:30 am to 9 pm Friday and Saturday, and 5 to 9 pm on Sunday. Some Monday holidays are open. Admission is $15 for adults; $13 for seniors; $6 for three- to 12-year-olds.

SUBURBAN PARKS

Several large parks in the mountains ringing the valley provide residents with many hiking, cycling, horseback riding and picnicking areas. Some are very popular and of course get crowded; nevertheless, these parks are as wild as you can get near a major city. Outdoors, people must beware of dehydration and sunburn in summer; be sure to carry water and sun protection.

The following are some of the most important parks, going from south to north. Unless noted under Places to Stay, later, camping is not allowed.

Phoenix South Mountain Park

Covering 25 sq miles, this is the largest city park in the USA and is part of the Phoenix Mountain Preserve system (☎ 602-495-0222). The park provides over 40 miles of multi-use trails open from dawn until dusk. There are good views and dozens of Indian petroglyph sites to admire. The park is topped by South Mountain (2690 feet) and is at 10919 S Central Ave (Map 1). Rangers can help plan your visit (8 am to 5 pm), and maps are available. Rangers emphasize: 'Don't leave valuables in your car'.

Estrella Mountain Regional Park

On the southwestern outskirts of town, this 31-sq-mile county park (Map 1; ☎ 623-932-3811) is at the north end of the extremely rugged Sierra Estrella, providing 34 miles of multi-use trails, a golf course, rodeo arena and picnicking areas, mainly in the northwest corner of the park.

The park is on the Gila River Indian Reservation; reach it by driving 5 miles south of I-10 along Estrella Parkway in Goodyear. Hours are 6 am to 8 pm (10 pm on Friday and Saturday); admission is $3 per vehicle.

Squaw Peak City Park

The 2608-foot summit of Squaw Peak affords one of Phoenix's most popular hikes (no bikes or horses are allowed), and parking is very hard to find on weekends outside of summer; get there early in the morning. The park opens at 5:30 am and the parking areas along Squaw Peak Dr, northeast of Lincoln Dr between 22nd and 24th Sts, may be full by 7:30 am on winter weekends. For information, call ☎ 602-262-7901.

McDowell Mountain Regional Park

Hiking, biking, horseback riding and camping are all permitted in this 33-sq-mile county park (☎ 480-471-0173). Access is along Fountain Hills Blvd from Shea Blvd east of Scottsdale. Hours are dawn 'til dusk and admission is $3 per vehicle.

White Tank Mountain Regional Park

This 41-sq-mile park (Map 1; ☎ 623-935-2505) offers hiking, mountain biking, horseback riding and camping. Of the many trails, one leads to the 4018-foot summit of White Tank Mountain and another goes to a waterfall (which is sometimes dry). Park hours are dawn 'til dusk and admission is $3 per vehicle. To reach the park from Phoenix, drive 10 miles northwest on Grand Ave (Hwy 60), then 15 miles west on Olive Ave (the western extension of Dunlap Ave).

ACTIVITIES

In addition to the activities listed below, look in the yellow pages for skating rinks (both ice and roller), skydiving, gliding, bicycle rentals and other activities offered in the valley.

Golf, Tennis & Swimming

Serious golf players probably already know that the valley, despite its desert location, is a major golfing center with almost 200 greens ranging from 'pitch and putt' to

PGA championship courses. Many resorts offer fine courses and package golfing or tennis vacations (see Places to Stay). American Golf Reservations (☎ 480-962-4653, 602-953-1127), 443 N Central Ave, Suite 819, Phoenix, 85032, makes local tee-time reservations up to 60 days in advance.

Phoenix Parks and Recreation (☎ 602-262) runs dozens of city parks with several golf courses, many tennis courts, swimming pools and other recreational programs. City courses generally offer the cheapest golfing, often at a quarter the price of the fancier places. Search www.phoenix.gov for sports listings or check with the tourist office.

The city operates 27 swimming pools (call ☎ 602-534-7946 for general pool information). Also see the 'Especially for Kids' boxed text.

Horseback Riding

As if to emphasize the valley's Western roots, over 30 horse rental and riding outfits are listed in the Phoenix yellow pages. Short rides, often combined with a country breakfast or barbecue cookout, are popular activities, and overnight packing trips can be arranged. Rates are about $20 for an hour, reservations are suggested from late fall through spring, and it's too darn hot to do much riding in the summer, pardner.

Some better-known outfits include Ponderosa Stables (☎ 602-268-1261), 10215 S Central Ave, which leads rides into South Mountain Park. For both short and overnight trips into the mountains east of Phoenix, contact Don Donnelly Stables (☎ 480-982-7822, 800-346- 4403), 6010 S Kings Ranch Rd, Apache Junction. In Scottsdale, there's MacDonald's Ranch (☎ 480-585-0239), 26540 N Scottsdale Rd.

Tubing

Floating down the Salt River in an inner tube is a great way to relax and cool down in summer. From 6800 E Main, Mesa, head north on Power Rd, which becomes Bush Hwy and intersects with the Salt River. Follow Bush Hwy east along the river; the road reaches Saguaro Lake after about 10 miles.

Along the Bush Hwy, Salt River Recreation (☎ 480-984-3305, 480-984-1857) gives information, rents tubes and provides van shuttles to good starting places for short or all-day floats. Costs are $10 per person for shuttle and tube; rent an extra tube for your cooler full of cold drinks (don't bring glass). Bring sunblock and shoes suitable to protect your feet from the river bottom. Tubing season is mid-April through September, and weekends draw crowds of people bent on cooling off and partying on.

Hot-Air Ballooning

Some experienced outfits include A Aerozona Adventures (☎ 480-991-4260, 888-991-9260) and Unicorn Balloon Company (☎ 480-991-3666, 800-468-2478), but many others are just as good. Also see the Outdoor Activities chapter.

Shooting & Archery

The Ben Avery Shooting Range (☎ 623-582-8313), northwest of I-17 on Hwy 74, is the largest public recreational shooting area in the USA, providing practice facilities and competitions for a variety of firearms as well as archery.

ORGANIZED TOURS

Several companies offer tours in and around Phoenix. Gray Line (☎ 602-495-9100, 800-732-0327) has a website at www .greylinearizona.com. Vaughan's Southwest (☎ 602-971-1381, 800-513-1381) offers 4½-hour tours for a few dollars more; they're online at www.southwest tours.com. Both these and other companies do longer tours, such as a 14-hour tour to the Grand Canyon for $100 (for people with really limited time!); children under 12 get discounts.

Many companies offer 4WD tours into the surrounding desert that last anywhere from four hours to all day and stress various themes: ghost towns, cookouts, Indian petroglyphs and ruins, natural history, sunset tours and target shooting. Costs start around $60 a person. Some reputable companies include Arizona Desert Mountain Jeep Tours (☎ 480-860-1777) in Scottsdale (go to

ARIZONA

www.azdesertmountain.com); Arrowhead Desert Tours (☎ 602-942-3361), 841 E Paradise Lane, Phoenix; and Wild West Jeep Tours (☎ 480-922-0144), 7127 E Becker Lane in Scottsdale.

SPECIAL EVENTS

Something is happening just about all the time from October to May in Phoenix, but few events occur during the searing summer. The chambers of commerce are knowledgeable about all the scheduled events and provide free calendars. Some of the most important follow.

One of the Southwest's biggest parades precedes the Fiesta Bowl college football game on New Year's Day at the ASU Sun Devil Stadium. Late January and early February see Western events in Scottsdale, such as a horse-drawn parade, a rodeo, Pony Express re-enactments and an All-Arabian Horse Show. Performers dress in Renaissance garb, joust and host many other medieval events on weekends from late February through early April during the Renaissance Festival, held on Hwy 60, 9 miles southeast of Apache Junction. Admission is $16 for adults; $8 for four- to 12-year-olds.

The Heard Museum hosts the Guild Indian Fair and Market during the first weekend in March, which has been held annually since 1958. View Indian dancers, eat Native American food, and browse and buy top-quality arts and crafts.

In mid-March, watch the Phoenix Rodeo of Rodeos, held at the Veterans Memorial Coliseum, 1826 W McDowell Rd. The costumed Yaqui Indian Easter Ceremonies (☎ 480-883-2838) are held Friday afternoon during Lent and from Wednesday to Easter Sunday of Holy Week. The events occur in the main plaza of the village of Guadalupe at the south end of Tempe.

The Arizona State Fair takes place in the last two weeks of October. Simultaneously and continuing into mid-November, the Cowboy Artists of America exhibition is on display at the Phoenix Art Museum. The Thunderbird Hot-Air Balloon Classic lifts off in early November, and dance, song and arts and crafts are featured at Pueblo Grande's Annual Indian Market during the second weekend in December.

PLACES TO STAY

From very basic motels to ritzy resorts, the valley's hundreds of accommodations have one thing in common – prices plummet in summer. January-to-April rates can be two or even three times more expensive than summer rates in the top-end places, although at the cheapest ones, the seasonal price difference is not so vast. The price drop presents bargains for summer vacationers. Winter rates are overpriced because that is when hotels make enough money to offset the low rates in the stiflingly hot summers. Always ask for discounts – AAA, senior, student, military, business, whatever you can think of. Note that special events, such as the Fiesta Bowl, command very high prices. Also, when travelers might least expect it, a major rock concert at the Sun Devil Stadium drawing tens of thousands of fans from all over Arizona can suddenly fill rooms.

Chain motels outnumber everything else in town. Many chains are represented by a dozen or more properties scattered around the valley, so if you have a favorite, check their websites for a suitable choice. Travelers watching their budget will find cheaper motels strung out along several of the main drags in and around Phoenix. Most every hotel will boast at least a swimming pool. At the other end of the scale, expensive spas and resorts are destinations in themselves. Swanky and stylish Scottsdale tends to the upper end.

One area in which the valley appears to be lacking, though, is B&Bs. Agencies are helpful in booking the upper mid-range and top end hotels and resorts.

Camping

You can camp at several of the suburban parks and recreation areas: **McDowell Mountain Regional Park** has about 70 campsites with water and electrical hookups for $15, as well as showers. The year-round campground at **White Tank Mountain Regional Park** offers 40 sites for $8, and provides showers but no hookups. *Estrella Mountain Regional Park* has both developed and undeveloped sites for $15/8.

Mesa/Apache Junction KOA (☎ 480-982-4015, 1540 S Tomahawk Rd, Apache Junction) is the closest KOA to the center of things. It has a pool and hot tub and charges $18 for tents and $22 to $27 for RV sites. Check www.koa.com for others in the Phoenix area.

For those 55 or older, huge adult-only RV parks (they should call them RV cities) are found in Mesa. All have extensive recreation facilities and are popular with long-term visitors (who get substantial discounts) so reservations are suggested. *Trailer Village* (☎ 480-832-1770, 3020 E Main) has almost 1700 sites priced at about $20. The *Mesa Regal RV Resort* (☎ 480-830-2821, 800-845-4752, 4700 E Main) has about 1800 sites priced at $30. There are many others.

About 100 more RV parks, many for adults only, are listed in the Phoenix yellow pages.

Check with the US Forest Service for information about campgrounds in the Tonto National Forest, north and east of the Phoenix area. Also see the Apache Trail in the East-Central Arizona chapter.

Budget

Central Phoenix has the region's best selection of cheap places to stay. Many young budget travelers head over to the friendly *Metcalf House Hostel* (Map 3; ☎ 602-254-9803, 1026 N 9th St). This hostel will not take telephone reservations but nearly always has space in the dorms, priced at $15 per person ($12 for HI-AYH members). Just show up. Kitchen and laundry facilities are available.

The *YMCA* (Map 3; ☎ 602-253-6181, 350 N 1st Ave) rents single rooms with shared showers for $28 a night or $110 to US$140 a week, and doubles for not much more. It is usually full and does not take reservations – show up around 9 am for the best chance at a room. The guests are primarily men, but women are welcome to stay in rooms on the women's floor and use the gym and other fitness facilities.

Most of the area's cheapest motels are along Van Buren. The downtown area is OK, but as you head east of 10th St, the neighborhood deteriorates into blocks of boarded-up buildings, used-car lots and streetwalkers' turf (police patrols periodically scout the area). The neighborhood from around 24th to about 36th Sts, north of the airport, improves and is where more cheap hotels are located, some of which are acceptable though the area remains seedy. Many places will give weekly discounts.

For decent, clean lodging for $30 to $45, try the following (all on Map 4):

Budget Lodge Motel (☎ 602-254-7247) 402 W Van Buren

Budget Inn Motel (☎ 602-257-8331) 424 W Van Buren

Travel Inn 9 Motel (☎ 602-254-6521) 201 N 7th Ave

Las Palmas Inn (☎ 602-256-9161) 765 NW Grand Ave

American Lodge (☎ 602-252-6823) 965 E Van Buren

Super 7 Motel (☎ 602-258-5540) 938 E Van Buren

The *Flamingo Airporter Inn* (Map 2; ☎ 602-275-6211, 2501 E Van Buren) charges about $40 for one or two people and is the closest cheapie to the airport. Not much farther is the *Pyramid Inn* (Map 2; ☎ 602-275-3691, 3307 E Van Buren), also cheap, and the *Phoenix Sunrise Motel* (Map 2; ☎ 602-275-7661, 800-432-6483, 3644 E Van Buren).

In Tempe, Apache Blvd has a couple of nondescript cheap motels, as well as chains. Apache Blvd becomes Main St in Mesa, and continues for about 20 miles into and through Apache Junction. This long strip of ugly, modern Americana has a number of budget motels scattered along it – if you don't need to stay near the center, drive and see.

Motel 6 is represented by 17(!) motels in the greater Phoenix area. Most charge in the $40s in summer and the $50s or $60s in winter for a double. The most expensive Motel 6 is in classy Scottsdale, where winter rooms in the $70s are the cheapest choice in that town.

Mid-Range

Many of the major *chain motels and hotels* have properties close to the airport and provide a free shuttle. Other properties are scattered along most of the exits of I-17 and I-10. See the Accommodations section in the Facts for the Visitor chapter for toll-free reservation numbers and websites.

Right in downtown Phoenix, the *San Carlos Hotel* (Map 3; ☎ 602-253-4121, 800-528-5446, 202 N Central Ave) has all the character you'll want if chains aren't your thing. Built in 1927, it was downtown's swankiest hotel for decades, and although recently refurbished and comfortable, the hotel retains many of its early fixtures and atmosphere. The 130 rooms ($100 to $150 a double) are small, but there are six suites (up to $210) if you need to spread out, and facilities include an exercise room, café, restaurant and bar (the latter two being re-modeled at presstime).
website: www.hotelsancarlos.com

North of downtown Phoenix, the *Lexington Hotel at City Square* (Map 2; ☎ 602-279-9811, 100 W Clarendon Ave) charges $80 to $130 for 180 standard hotel rooms. The rates include access to 35,000 sq feet of sports club amenities that include large locker rooms, aerobics and well-equipped machine workout rooms with trainers, a dozen racquetball courts, a basketball court, spa, sauna and steam room. There's also a restaurant open 6:30 am to 10 pm, a busy sports bar and nightclub, and free airport transportation.
website: www.phxihc.com

The *Phoenix Inn Suites* (Map 2; ☎ 602-956-5221, 800-956-5221, 2310 E Highland Ave) has 120 spacious rooms, all with refrigerators, coffee-makers and microwaves, for $130 to $170 including continental breakfast. Some larger suites go up to $240. A pool, Jacuzzi, exercise room and airport transportation are offered; visit www.phoenixinn.com. Farther north, the *Royal Suites* (Map 2; ☎ 602-942-1000, 800-647-5786, 10421 N 33rd Ave) offers 80 clean and modern mini-suites with kitchenettes. It charges $110 to $150 in winter, with discounts for longer stays.

South of Tempe, the *InnSuites* (☎ 480-897-7900, 800-842-4242, 1651 W Baseline Rd), near I-10 exit 155, has pleasant rooms of various sizes for $110 to $150; all rooms include kitchenettes, and some have sitting rooms or full kitchens. Continental breakfast, evening cocktail hour and airport transportation are included. With two tennis courts and an exercise room, you can get a workout while the kids are on the playground, or you can relax in the spa.

The *Scottsdale Econo Lodge* (Map 4; ☎ 480-994-9461, 800-528-7396, 6935 5th Ave) has comfortable motel rooms priced at $70 to $110 in winter, and fashionable shopping is within walking distance.

Top End

The 24-story *Hyatt Regency* (Map 3; ☎ 602-252-1234, 800-233-1234, 122 N 2nd) is a huge downtown convention center/hotel with the expected amenities such as a health club, restaurants, room service, a concierge and shopping. More than 700 rooms, many with balconies, go for $220 to $280 a double in winter; some suites go for more than $1000 on peak nights. This is the city's biggest hotel, and the revolving rooftop restaurant (The Compass) has great views and excellent Southwestern food.
website: www.phoenix.hyatt.com

The ritziest hotel in Phoenix is, of course, the elegant *Ritz-Carlton* (Map 2; ☎ 602-468-0700, 800-241-3333, 2401 E Camelback Rd), offering attractive rooms and suites from $300 to over $400 in winter. Amenities include expensive but excellent restaurants, 24-hour room service, a bar with light entertainment, a fitness center with trainers and massage therapists, a spa, sauna, tennis court and golf privileges, including transportation to the courses. Traditionally elegant, The Grill is one of the best American grills in Arizona.

The nearest 1st-class hotel to ASU is the Southwestern-styled *Tempe Mission Palms* (Map 5; ☎ 480-894-1400, 800-547-8705, 60 E 5th St) with 300 rooms and suites, and in-room coffeemakers, tennis courts, golf privileges, a sauna and exercise room. Its restaurant has pool-side and room service, and there is a popular sports bar here. The Southwestern decor tends toward wood and stone which is a pleasant change from the relentlessly bright chain hotels, but may be a bit dark for some tastes. Rates are in the high $200s in winter; visit www.mission-palms.com. Fairly similar facilities at substantially lower rates are offered at the 270-room *Fiesta Inn (Map 5; ☎ 480-967-1441, 800-501-7590, 2100 S Priest Dr)* also in Tempe; visit www.fiestainnresort.com.

The most elegant and expensive places to stay are the resorts, of which Phoenix has more than its share. These aren't just places to stay – they are destinations to spend an entire vacation. Summer visitors can get a room for well under $200. Expect attractively landscaped grounds suitable for strolling or jogging, spacious rooms or suites (including presidential suites priced well over $1000 a night), extensive indoor and outdoor public areas, helpful and attentive staff, a variety of dining possibilities and room service, bars and entertainment, as well as several swimming pools, whirlpools, saunas, a fully equipped exercise/health center with instructors and trainers, and (at extra cost) massage, beauty treatments, tennis, racquetball and golf. Most can provide babysitting and some have children's clubs (again, at extra cost). Gift and sundries shops should be on the premises along with a hairdresser, and various other attractions may include anything from bicycle rental to basketball courts, video rental to volleyball and horseback riding to hot-air ballooning. Some of the major resorts and their main claims to fame are listed below, and you can expect them to have most of the features mentioned above. If you plan on vacationing in a valley resort, we suggest you contact the establishment for complete details or talk to a travel agent.

Much of the design for the city's first luxury resort, the *Arizona Biltmore Resort & Spa (Map 2; ☎ 602-955-6600, 800-950-0086)*, at 24th St and E Missouri Ave, was influenced by Frank Lloyd Wright. This beautiful and historically interesting resort (opened in 1929) underwent various renovations and additions throughout the 1990s,

and now boasts over 700 units, many with private balconies and some suites. Its modern facilities include two golf courses, several swimming pools (one with a long water slide) and tennis courts, an athletic club, a health spa, a children's program and two very good restaurants. Room rates are $350 to $530 in the high season and suites start at $680.
website: www.arizonabiltmore.com

The Hilton chain runs three Phoenix resorts (☎ 800-876-4683) which have less luxurious rooms and more reasonable prices than most of the area's resorts; www.pointehilton.com has information about all three. The *Pointe Hilton Squaw Peak Resort (Map 2; ☎ 602-997-2626, 7677 N 16th St)* offers nine acres of pools, including water slides and a 'river' tubing area, as well as a popular kids' program, making this a good family choice. The *Pointe Hilton Tapatio Cliffs Resort (Map 2; ☎ 602-866-7500, 11111 N 7th St)* and the *Pointe Hilton South Mountain Resort (☎ 602-438-9000, 7777 S Pointe Parkway)* both have full resort facilities, including excellent (but expensive) golf courses. Rooms are around $250 in the high season. The South Mountain location has a children's program as well as horseback riding; it's at the northeastern corner of Phoenix South Mountain Park. All three include a complimentary evening beverage service and have good restaurants, but the chain's best is the spectacularly located Different Pointe of View, serving continental food atop Tapatio Cliffs.

The 120-acre *Marriott's Camelback Inn (Map 2; ☎ 480-948-1700, 800-242-2635, 5402 E Lincoln Dr)* opened in 1936 and, with many dedicated customers, is considered a world-class resort. Highlights are 36 holes of excellent golf, a full-service spa and health club, several pools and tennis courts, and the highly rated Chaparral restaurant, serving pricey continental food. Rates are in the $400s for rooms with microwaves, refrigerators and coffeemakers; suites start in the $600s.
website: www.camelbackinn.com

Yet another world-class option is the *Fairmont Scottsdale Princess Resort (Map*

ARIZONA

2; ☎ 480-585-4848, 7575 E Princess Dr), the home of the annual PGA Phoenix Open. With 450 beautifully landscaped acres, this is one of the valley's largest full-scale resorts. The resort's La Hacienda restaurant serves the valley's most sophisticated and pricey Mexican food, and the Marquesa is simply the best Spanish (Catalan) restaurant in Arizona. Rooms start at $470, and casitas and suites are around $600; look at www.fairmont.com. At close to these prices, an even larger property, the **Hyatt Regency Scottsdale at Gainey Ranch Resort** (Map 2; ☎ 480-991-3388, 800-233-1234, 7500 E Doubletree Ranch Rd) is popular with families. Enjoy the dozens of fountains and waterfalls, 11 pools, artificial beach, huge water slide, or playground while the kids take part in a program just for them. The resort's well-reviewed Golden Swan restaurant serves varied Southwestern fare; visit.www.hyatt.com.

Probably the most expensive is the almost overpoweringly opulent and modern **Phoenician** (☎ 480-941-8200, 800-888-8234, 6000 E Camelback Rd), a world-class, super-deluxe resort with the usual amenities as well as some less usual activities such as archery, badminton and croquet. The resort's top-rated Mary Elaine's restaurant serves contemporary French cuisine and is one of the Southwest's most expensive and formal restaurants; there are several more casual eating choices as well.
website: www.thephoenician.com

PLACES TO EAT

Phoenix has the biggest selection of restaurants in the Southwest. From fast-food to ultra fancy, it's all here. Serious foodies will find several kitchens that will lighten their wallets, if nothing else. A useful little book is 100 Best Restaurants in Arizona by the serendipitously named Harry and Trudy Plate. This book is updated every year or two and, despite its name, squeezes about 150 restaurants into its covers; the reviews are fun. About two-thirds of these places are in the valley, and some of the very best are in the resorts (see the top end listings in Places to Stay, above, for excellent restaurants at resorts). You don't have to stay at the resorts to eat at the restaurants. Many of these resorts serve classy Sunday brunches that require reservations. In fact, reservations are recommended at all the fancier eateries.

Several free publications available from the chambers of commerce, visitors bureau and newsstands around the valley have extensive restaurant listings, though they lean toward the top end. The selection below is just some of the best, including good lower-priced places. All addresses are in Phoenix, unless otherwise indicated.

Breakfast

While the diners and coffeehouses are often good choices, die-hard egg fans can have their breakfast omeleted, creped, Benedicted, scrambled, spiced or otherwise smashed at any **Eggery** or the similar **Good Egg**; see Map 4 for locations. The Good Egg also is in the Park Central Mall (3110 N Central Ave) and in Scottsdale (☎ 480-483-1090, 14046 N Scottsdale Rd) and (☎ 480-991-5416, 6149 N Scottsdale Rd). All are open daily from 6:30 am to 2:30 pm and serve other brunch items in a bright and cheerful environment. Most breakfasts are $5 to $7.50.

Some folks prefer pancakes for breakfast; the best choice is the **Pancake House** (Map 4; ☎ 480-946-4902, 6840 E Camelback Rd) in Scottsdale. These come with a European twist – German, Dutch and apple pancakes are worth trying. Hours are 7 am to 2 pm.

Open wide at **Chompie's** (Map 2; ☎ 602-971-8010, 3202 E Greenway Rd) and (☎ 480-860-0475, 9301 E Shea Blvd) in Scottsdale, as well as (☎ 480-557-0700, 1160 E University Dr) in Tempe. These are genuine New York kosher delis with a wide variety of fresh bagels, giant blintzes, huge puffy omelets, bialys, knishes, the kind of sandwiches you can't get your mouth around, sweet pastries and mouth-watering treats, all made on the premises. Hours are about 6 am to 9 pm. There's always a line for takeout and it's always noisily busy.

On a Sunday, you can defer breakfast into a leisurely brunch, which most of the valley's resorts serve from late morning through early afternoon. Prices are mainly in the $20s (though the *Phoenician* really goes to town with a $45 brunch) and though these are all-you-can-eat food fests, the many varied choices are carefully prepared and delicious, and champagne and incredible desserts are included. Call any of the resorts for details.

Coffeehouses

Dozens of coffeehouses dot the valley, many providing entertainment in the evenings. Tempe's *Coffee Plantation (Map 5; ☎ 480-829-7878, 680 S Mill Ave)* is an espresso and cappuccino place popular with ASU students. It also serves light meals and a selection of tasty pastries, and stays open 'til around midnight. About 10 other Coffee Plantations have opened in the Greater Phoenix area. In downtown Phoenix, *Starbucks (Map 3; ☎ 602-340-0455, 100 N 1st St)* is one of about two dozen Starbucks in the valley.

The News Café (Map 2; ☎ 602-852-0982, 5053 N 44th St) features a newsstand with arty publications you can read along with your java. In Scottsdale, a popular place is *The Author's Café (Map 4; ☎ 480-481-3998, 4014 N Goldwater Blvd)*, open from 7 am to 10 pm Monday to Saturday. Also in Scottsdale, *The Coffee Roastery (Map 2; ☎ 480-905-0881, 8120 N Hayden)* is open on Sunday and has a wide selection of beans from all over the world.

Steak Houses

Ruth's Chris Steak House (Map 2; ☎ 602-957-9600, 2201 E Camelback Rd) and *(Map 2; ☎ 480-991-5988, 7001 N Scottsdale Rd)*, both part of a nationwide chain known for superb steak, serve up huge steaks priced around $25 and slathered with melted butter but nothing else; if you want vegetables or potatoes, you'll have to pay $4 or $5 more. (Perhaps they could make another buck by renting you a steak knife.) Seafood and the other meat dishes are also very good. Hours are 5 to 10 pm daily.

Tough to say which is the best steak house in central Phoenix, but a definite contender is *Harris' (Map 2; ☎ 602-508-8888,* *3101 E Camelback Rd)*, which also does a fine salmon dinner. Closer to downtown, the traditional place is *Durant's (Map 2; ☎ 602-264-5967, 2611 N Central Ave)*, which has been serving steaks for over half a century and retains its conservative atmosphere by banning cell phones in the dining room! Both places are expensive.

Phoenix is a major baseball spring-training center, drawing the sports fans who crowd into *Don & Charlie's (Map 4; ☎ 480-990-0900, 7501 E Camelback Rd)* in Scottsdale. Here, baseball memorabilia and photos of sports personalities cover the walls and the food is meaty, with barbecue priced in the teens and steaks heading into the $20s. Hours are 5 to 10 pm daily.

Texaz Bar & Grill (Map 2; ☎ 602-248-7827, 6003 N 16th St) is not exactly a steak house but has huge, meaty meals – they don't skimp on potatoes and gravy. You can get a bowl of chili for $2 or an 18oz T-bone steak for $15; burgers and chicken-fried steaks are also popular. This fun, down-home place has every available space filled with Texan 'stuff' and is popular with locals and visitors. It's open for lunch and dinner daily, except Sunday when hours are 4 to 10 pm.

Getting into the outskirts, *Rawhide Steakhouse (☎ 480-502-1880)* in the Rawhide tourist attraction (see the Scottsdale section, earlier) is fun, kid-friendly, and serves decent cowboy steaks – perhaps not the best in town but a good value. Also good for cowboy steaks, the *T-Bone Steakhouse (☎ 602-276-0945, 10037 S 19th Ave)*, way south on the north side of Phoenix South Mountain Park, has good city views. This hospitably Western steak house has a rustic setting and is locally popular for its mesquite-grilled steaks, which run into the lower $20s. It opens for dinner only. Another similar choice is *Pinnacle Peak Patio (☎ 480-585-1599, 10426 E Jomax Rd)* in northern Scottsdale, which features country music and dance lessons every evening to help shake down that steak.

Soul Food & Southern

Mrs White's Golden Rule Cafe (Map 3; ☎ 602-262-9256, 808 E Jefferson) is a hole in the wall with hanging, hand-lettered menus, but a greasy spoon it ain't. The food is home-style, well prepared and tasty, though you won't find any low-calorie plates here. The Golden Rule is to remember what you ate when you pay at the register at the end of your meal, which typically runs around $8. It's open for lunch but not dinner Monday to Friday.

For Cajun catfish and crawfish, try *Baby Kay's Cajun Kitchen (Map 2; ☎ 602-955-0011, 2119 E Camelback Rd)* in the Town & Country Mall, or in Scottsdale *(Map 4; ☎ 480-990-9080, 7216 E Shoeman Lane)*. Both are locally famed for delicious 'dirty rice,' a mixture of rice with sausage, onions, peppers and seasonings, and a whole bunch of other Southern specials. Dinner entrées are in the $8 to $16 range, and lunches are cheaper.

Southwestern

After enjoying great success as a Tucson favorite, the owners of *Café Terra Cotta (Map 2; ☎ 480-948-8100, 6166 N Scottsdale Rd)* opened a second location in Scottsdale at the Borgata Mall. The menu has steadily become pricier, with most entrées now in the teens and low $20s, but it remains innovative, even wild-sounding at times, with a few fairly straightforward choices for the less adventurous. Be sure to leave room for one of the heavenly desserts. Also in Scottsdale, the similarly priced *Roaring Fork (Map 4; ☎ 480-947-0795, 7243 E Camelback Rd)* is among the valley's trendiest Southwestern eateries, and deservedly so.

The classiest Southwestern restaurant is *Vincent Guerithault on Camelback (Map 2; ☎ 602-224-0225, 3930 E Camelback Rd)*, serving food with the famous chef's French touch. With dinner entrées priced in the $20s, the restaurant is not outrageously expensive, considering the haute cuisine. The restaurant is open for weekday lunches and dinner daily except Sunday.

For somewhat cheaper but still classy Southwestern fare, visit *Sam's Cafe (Map 3; ☎ 602-252-3545, 455 N 3rd St, No 114)* downtown in the Arizona Center. Sam's is open daily from 11 am to 10 pm, staying open to midnight on Friday and Saturday.

There are other Sam's at the Biltmore Fashion Park *(☎ 602-954-7100)* and at 10100 N Scottsdale Rd *(☎ 480-368-2800)*.

Other American Cuisine

The *5 & Diner (Map 2; ☎ 602-264-5220, 5220 N 16th St)* is a lot of fun, with inexpensive, 24-hour food and friendly service in a '50s setting. The menu is the predictable pre–nouvelle American cuisine – burgers, fries, tuna melts, shakes, etc. The diner's success has led to the opening of eight others in the valley, but they aren't all open 24 hours. If you like this kind of atmosphere, you'll enjoy the ever-popular *Ed Debevic's (☎ 602-956-2760, 2102 E Highland Ave),* which calls itself 'Short Orders Deluxe'; it makes great burgers and shakes, and also has a salad bar. Bring change for Elvis on the jukebox. The diner is open 11 am to 9 pm daily, 'til 10 pm on weekends. The oldest diner in Phoenix and perhaps Arizona is *MacAlpine's (Map 3; ☎ 602-252-3039, 2303 N 7th St),* which features an authentic soda fountain serving up genuine sundaes and other icy delights. It opens daily for huge breakfasts and lunches.

One of Mesa's best restaurants, the *Landmark (☎ 480-962-4652, 809 W Main St)* has been serving good American food for about 25 years. Built as a Mormon church in the early 1900s, the restaurant is decorated with antiques and photos and has a huge salad bar. The home-style, traditional American dinner entrées priced in the range of $10 to $20 (including salad bar) draw crowds of knowing locals. It is open daily for lunch and dinner.

Scottsdale shoppers like to stop at the pink and white *Sugar Bowl Ice Cream Parlor (Map 4; ☎ 480-946-0051, 4005 N Scottsdale Rd),* which serves light meals but specializes in the cold stuff; it is open from 11 am to 11 pm daily. For good and inexpensive New Mexican fare, *Carlsbad Tavern (480-970-8164, 3313 N Hayden Rd)* in Scottsdale is popular with a younger adult crowd who enjoy outdoor dining, even in summer, when a pond and mist sprinkler system keeps temperatures bearable. Inside, a mischievous menu ('the Carlsbad Daily Guano') plays up to the batty cavernous interior.

If you're a jazz fan, *Orbit Restaurant & Jazz Club (Map 2;* ☎ *602-265-2354)*, in the Uptown Plaza at Camelback Rd and Central Ave, provides dinner and live jazz every night.

For seafood lovers, the fanciest fresh fins are found at *Oceana (*☎ *480-515-2277, 9800 E Pinnacle Peak Rd)* in Scottsdale's La Mirada shopping center. Many dinner entrées approach $30. For the adventurous, sea urchins, scallops and sushi are on the menu. The selection is also wide at *Steamers (Map 2;* ☎ *602-956-3631, 2576 E Camelback Rd)* in Biltmore Fashion Park, where entrées are in the $18 to $25 range.

In Tempe, the *House of Tricks (Map 5;* ☎ *480-968-1114, 114 E 7th St)* has a shady patio that is often full with enthusiastic diners enjoying reasonably priced innovative meat, chicken and fish plates. Behind the patio, two early-20th-century cottages form a charming indoor section. Dinner entrées are in the teens – a good deal.

French

The closest thing to French fast food is *La Madeleine*, serving French pastries, baguette sandwiches and light meals for breakfast, lunch and dinner every day. Dinner entrées are mostly under $10. La Madeleine has three locations: *(Map 2;* ☎ *602-952-0349, 3102 E Camelback Rd)*; *(*☎ *480-483-0730, 10625 N Tatum Blvd)*; and *(Map 4;* ☎ *480-945-1663, 7014 E Camelback Rd)* in Scottsdale Fashion Square.

Way at the other end of the credit card scale is *Mary Elaine's (*☎ *480-423-2530)* in the posh Phoenician resort. The only Southwestern restaurant to get five stars from the folks at Mobil, it's elegant, pricey, requests reservations and expects men to wear jackets.

Italian

The valley probably has more noteworthy Italian restaurants than any other 'non-American' cuisine. The following is just a short selection.

For top-notch food in a sophisticated setting, dine at *Avanti (Map 2;* ☎ *602-956-0900, 2728 E Thomas Rd)* and *(Map 4;*

☎ *480-949-8333, 3102 N Scottsdale Rd)*. Most entrées are in the $20s, though simple pasta dishes are around $15. Dinner is served daily and, in Phoenix only, lunch Monday to Friday.

Homemade pasta (you can watch it being made in the open kitchen) is the highlight at *Maria's When in Naples (Map 2;* ☎ *480-991-6887, 7000 E Shea Blvd)* in Scottsdale. Prices for pasta dishes are in the teens, and there are other more expensive entrées. Lunch is served Monday to Friday, and dinner 5 to 10 pm daily.

Families with small children enjoy the kids' menu and the wide selection of pizza and pasta dishes (many around $10) at *Tuchetti (*☎ *602-957-0222, 2135 E Camelback Rd)* close to the Town & Country Mall. The decor is Italy à la Disney; dinner is served daily and lunch Monday to Saturday.

After a hard day of sight-seeing, visitors to Phoenix's Heritage Square can enjoy excellent wood-oven baked pizza and healthful salads at *Pizzeria Bianco (Map 3;* ☎ *602-258-8300, 623 E Adams St)*. Unfortunately, they aren't open at lunch, so you'll have to wait 'til 5 pm, Tuesday to Sunday.

Mexican

El Bravo (Map 2; ☎ *602-943-9753, 8338 N 7th St)* serves good combination plates for just $5 and offers a choice of inexpensive à la carte Sonoran dishes as well as Navajo tacos. This simple and genuine family restaurant has received great reviews but remains uncrowded because of its noncentral location. It is open Monday to Thursday 10 am to 8 pm (until 9 pm Friday and Saturday).

A downtown favorite, the large, modern *Matador (Map 3;* ☎ *602-254-7563, 125 E Adams)* is open 7 am to 11 pm, so you can get a Mexican breakfast and a hangover-curing menudo as well as lunch and dinner mainly in the $6 to $10 range. Choices include a few non-Mexican items as well, and lines are often out the door with office workers grabbing breakfast or lunch, but these usually move quickly.

If you want great south-of-the-border food, try *Los Dos Molinos (*☎ *602-243-9113, 8646 S Central Ave)* or *(*☎ *602-835-5356,*

260 S Alma School Rd) in Mesa. The food is New Mexican influenced, so it's hotter than Sonoran cuisine and delicious if you like chiles. These friendly, family-run restaurants (their slogan is 'some like it hot!') have family members working the stove and tables; ask them to hold the hot sauce if you're not a hot-chile fan. The restaurants are open Tuesday to Saturday 11 am to 9 pm. The Mesa location doesn't take credit cards, though with dinners around $7 or $12, you hardly need them.

Mexican dining is normally inexpensive, though an exception is the very fine *La Hacienda (Map 2; ☎ 480-585-4848)* in the upscale Fairmont Scottsdale Princess Resort. You'll find beautiful surroundings, strolling mariachis and superb food and service for dinner daily. Most entrées are in the high $20s.

Asian

Most Indian restaurants offer all-you-can-eat lunch buffets for about $5. À-la-carte dinners, while somewhat pricier ($7 to $20), are freshly prepared and are also a good value.

Among the best is the recommended *Jewel of the Crown (Map 4; ☎ 602-840-2412, 7373 E Scottsdale Mall)*, one of several ethnic restaurants in Scottsdale Mall. Some other locally popular places are *Taste of India (☎ 602-788-3190, 1609 E Bell Rd)*; *India Delhi Palace (Map 2; ☎ 602-244-8181, 5050 E McDowell Rd)*; and two locations of *India Palace (Map 2; ☎ 602-942-4224, 16842 N 7th St)* and in Tempe *(Map 5; ☎ 480-921-2200, 933 E University Dr)*.

There are scores of Chinese restaurants. If you want opulent surroundings with your Peking duck, *Mr C's (Map 4; ☎ 480-941-4460, 4302 N Scottsdale Rd)* will take care of you. The food is classic and slightly pricey Cantonese; many say it's the best in town. Mr C's is open daily for lunch and dinner.

Out in Chandler is *C-Fu Gourmet (☎ 480-899-3888, 2051 W Warner Rd)*. C-Fu? That's 'sea food' and it is super fresh – you can see it swimming before it's cooked. A meal here is about $15 to $20 and selections vary from day to day depending on what's floating

around; fish, crab, shrimp and other shellfish are available. This restaurant also has a recommended dim sum selection for lunch.

In Scottsdale, *Malee's on Main (Map 4; ☎ 602-947-6042, 7131 E Main)* is open for lunch and dinner daily, and is perhaps the best of the many Thai restaurants in the valley. Most entrées are around $12.

Other Eateries

Set back from the road and with only a small sign, *Greekfest (Map 2; ☎ 602-265-2990, 1940 E Camelback Rd)* is an excellent bet for Greek food. Both food and ambiance are delightful, and the entrée prices, mainly in the teens and some low $20s, are reasonable. It is open for lunch and dinner daily except Sunday.

For recommended Cuban food, visit the *Havana Cafe (Map 2; ☎ 602-952-1991, 4225 E Camelback Rd)*. The food is excellent and most dinner entrées are priced in the teens. The café is open for lunch daily except Sunday, and dinner daily, though it may close on summer Sundays.

Eclectic, adventurous, risky, creative, international and transcontinental have all been used to describe fashionable *RoxSand (Map 2; ☎ 602-381-0444, 2594 E Camelback Rd)* in the Biltmore Fashion Park. The changing menu has roamed from Jamaican jerked rabbit to African pheasant to Japanese scallops (these entrées are in the $20s) as well as some cheaper and less adventurous options (such as pizza). This is a good place to eat a complete meal or just drop in for a super dessert. They are open daily for lunch and dinner.

ENTERTAINMENT

For what's going on, read the free alternative weekly *New Times,* published every Thursday and available at numerous boxes and other outlets around the city. On the same day, the Arizona Republic's *The Rep* also has exhaustive entertainment listings, with an emphasis on popular music and nightlife.

Cinemas

There are dozens of cinema multiplexes throughout the valley showing the year's

The spectacular Phoenician resort's golf course, Scottsdale, AZ

Old Mission Church, Scottsdale, AZ

Arizona State University, Tempe, AZ

Museum of Contemporary Art, Scottsdale, AZ

Wright's influence at the Biltmore, Phoenix

The Grand Canyon – 10 miles wide and a mile deep

On the road from Monument Valley Navajo Tribal Park, AZ

Ancestral Puebloan sites at Montezuma Castle and Canyon de Chelly National Monuments, AZ

best and worst movies, including the huge *AMC 24 (☎ 602-244-2262)* in the Arizona Center with armrests that fold up so you can cuddle with your date, and steep seating so you don't have to peer around people's heads at the screen. There are some alternatives, including the *Valley Art Theater (Map 5; ☎ 602-222-4275 ext 027, 509 S Mill Ave)* in Tempe, with a variety of foreign and alternative flicks. The *Imax Theatre (☎ 480-897-1453)* in the Arizona Mills Mall at Priest and Baseline, shows several docu-movies on their eight-times-larger-than-normal screen.

Nightlife

Many of the following spots are very busy on Friday and Saturday nights, but usually provide entertainment five to seven nights a week at varying cover charges.

The entertainment scene in Tempe, home of ASU, is aimed at students. Mill Ave between 3rd and 7th Sts is the off-campus nightlife center with several bars and clubs. There are plenty of cops hanging around at closing time, and their attitude is generally friendly. Places come and go, check the **Hayden Square** area (Map 5) for what sounds good.

In downtown Phoenix, the *Arizona Center* provides a number of options aimed at the younger post-work crowd, and it gets quiet early, except on Friday and Saturday when there are several bars, some with dancing, open late. To make a night of it, there are a few places to eat in the center.

Go west for the best in country & western. *Mr Lucky's (Map 2; ☎ 602-246-0686, 3660 NW Grand Ave)* has live country & western and dancing, and a corral outside with bull-riding competitions on weekends (with real bulls, not the mechanical kind; there's a $5 cover). Almost every patron is dressed in Western wear. More upscale country & western places are found in some of the resorts, including *Rustlers Rooste (☎ 602-431-6474)* at the Pointe Hilton on South Mountain. Popular places in Scottsdale include the *Handlebar-J (☎ 480-424-7100, 7116 E Becker St)*, which has live bands and free dance lessons some nights. The Rawhide and Pinnacle Peak Patio

steak houses (see Places to Eat, earlier) also have country music.

Jazz lovers can listen to KJZZ FM (91.5) on the radio or call the jazz hotline (☎ 602-254-4545) for a schedule of top performances. Also see The Orbit Restaurant & Jazz Club under Places to Eat.

For good blues, stop by the popular and crowded *Char's Has the Blues (Map 2; ☎ 602-230-0205, 4631 N 7th Ave)*, with some excellent acts most nights. *Warsaw Wallies (Map 2; ☎ 602-955-0881, 2547 E Indian School Rd)* is a small funky place but often has exceptional blues bands with low or no cover. Watch for the local band The Rocket 88s with an outstanding harpist. Good blues is also the staple of the *Rhythm Room (Map 2; ☎ 602-265-4842, 1019 E Indian School Rd)*. For more blues information, contact the Phoenix Blues Society (☎ 602-252-0599), online at www.phoenixblues.org.

For a variety of alternative rock aimed at young people, the *Mason Jar (Map 2; ☎ 602-956-6271, 2303 E Indian School Rd)* is a good choice. They have a no-alcohol area for people under 21. In Tempe, the *Bash on Ash (Map 5; ☎ 480-966-8200, 230 W 5th St)* has good live rock bands and an 'all-ages area.'

Ain't Nobody's Bizness (Map 2; ☎ 224-9977, 3031 E Indian School Rd) is a friendly lesbian bar. Gay men dance at *Crowbar (Map 3; 702 N Central Ave)* and *Amsterdam Bar (Map 3; 718 N Central Ave)*.

Performing Arts

The following are the most highly acclaimed places to hear and see performing arts, but not much goes on here during the summer. For sold-out events, the ticket companies listed in 'Buying Tickets' can often help.

The *Herberger Theater Center (Map 3; ☎ 602-252-8497, 222 E Monroe)* has two stages that host productions put together by the Arizona Theater Company (☎ 602-256-6995), Ballet Arizona (☎ 602-381-0184); the Actors Theater of Phoenix (☎ 602-253-6701) and occasionally others.

The *Helen K Mason Center for the Performing Arts (Map 3; ☎ 602-258-8128, 333 E Portland)* is the home of the Black Theater

ARIZONA

Buying Tickets

Ticketmaster (☎ 480-784-4444) sells tickets for most big sporting and cultural events. Call or buy online at www.ticketmaster.com as far in advance as possible or, if nothing is available, look in the yellow pages under Ticket Sales or in newspaper classifieds for tickets (they're often overpriced). Scalpers hang out near event venues; scalping is legal as long as it is off the actual event property. Also try Ticket City (☎ 480-507-5757, www.ticketcity .com), the Ticket Company (☎ 602-842-5387), Ticket Connection (☎ 480-777-1111), Tickets Unlimited (☎ 602-840-2340, 800-289-8497, www.ticketsunlimitedinc.com) or Western States Ticket Service (☎ 602-254-3300, www.wstickets.com).

Troupe and also hosts other African American performers.

Symphony Hall (Map 3; ☎ 602-262-7272, 225 E Adams) is the home of the Arizona Opera (☎ 602-266-7464) as well as the Phoenix Symphony Orchestra (☎ 602-495-1999, 495-1117).

The *Gammage Auditorium (☎ 480-965-3434)*, on the ASU Campus at Mill Ave and Apache Blvd, is the university's main center for performing arts.

The *Blockbuster Desert Sky Pavilion (Map 1; ☎ 602-254-7200)*, north of I-10 exit 135 at 83rd Ave, is a huge outdoor amphitheater hosting big-name rock bands.

SPECTATOR SPORTS

Phoenix has some of the nation's top professional teams, but getting tickets for the best games is not always easy, as they sell out early; see the boxed text 'Buying Tickets.'

The NBA's Phoenix Suns (☎ 602-379-7800), www.suns.com, play professional basketball at the *America West Arena (Map 3; ☎ 602-379-7867, 201 E Jefferson)* from December to April. The (women's) WNBA's Phoenix Mercury (☎ 602-252-9622) also play here in summer months. From May through August, the arena is home of the Arizona Rattlers (☎ 602-514-8383) arena football team, who were the 1994 world champions. The NHL's Phoenix Coyotes (☎ 480-473-5600) play ice hockey here from December to March. The West Coast Hockey League's Phoenix Mustangs (☎ 602-340-0001) play ice hockey at the *Arizona Veterans Memorial Coliseum (Map 3; 1826 W McDowell Rd)* in the State Fairgrounds.

The NFL's Arizona Cardinals (☎ 602-379-0102) play professional football (fall to spring) at ASU *Sun Devil Stadium* in Tempe (Map 5), the site of the 1996 Super Bowl, the nation's most prestigious football game. ASU student teams (☎ 602-965-2381), such as the Sun Devils, also use the stadium.

The Arizona Diamondbacks major-league baseball team played their first season in 1998 in the specially constructed *Bank One Ballpark (Map 3; ☎ 602-462-6500)*, southwest of E Jefferson and S 7th Sts.

Professional golfers compete for a seven-figure purse at the PGA Phoenix Open, held every January at the *Tournament Players Golf Course (☎ 480-585-3600, 480-585-4334, 17020 N Hayden Rd)* in Scottsdale.

You can watch horseracing at *Turf Paradise (☎ 602-942-1101)*, at 19th Ave and Bell, from October to May, and see greyhounds race year-round at *Phoenix Greyhound Park (Map 2; ☎ 602-273-7181, 3801 E Washington)*. NASCAR car racing takes place at *Phoenix International Raceway (Map 1; ☎ 602-254-4622, 7602 S 115th Ave)* at Baseline Rd, Avondale. Drag racing is presented at *Firebird International Raceway (Map 1; ☎ 602-323-2000, 520-796-1010)*, off I-10 exit 162, Chandler.

SHOPPING

The question is not so much what to buy (you can buy just about anything) but where to go. Scottsdale is the **art gallery** capital of Arizona. The **Heard Museum** has the best bookshop about Native Americans and the most reliable, excellent and expensive selection of Native American arts and crafts.

The valley has several notable shopping malls. You may not be a fan of malls, but the air conditioning does give them a certain allure when the mercury climbs in the summer. **Shopping malls** include the Metrocenter at I-17 exit 208 and Peoria Ave (Map 2), the largest enclosed mall in Arizona; it has four department stores, standard shopping and many attractions for kids. The Park Central Mall, at Central Ave and Osborn Rd (Map 2), is the city's oldest (but still reasonably fashionable) shopping center.

For more upscale shopping, visit the Scottsdale Fashion Square at Camelback and Scottsdale Rds in Scottsdale (Map 4), or the more exclusive Biltmore Fashion Park at Camelback Rd and 24th St in Phoenix (Map 2). Both provide a good selection of cheap to expensive restaurants, and the Biltmore is home to some of the valley's best eateries. Near the Biltmore, the Town & Country Mall also has several decent restaurants.

Perhaps the fanciest selection of **boutiques and galleries** is at the Borgata, 6166 N Scottsdale Rd in Scottsdale (Map 2), a mall designed to look like a medieval town. Also very trendy is the Fifth Avenue Shopping Area (Map 4) east of Scottsdale Rd, where you'll find many galleries, boutiques and tourist-oriented shops. The Legacy Gallery, at the corner of Main west of Scottsdale Rd, is like a museum of bronze masterpieces. It anchors a couple of blocks with about 20 galleries of all kinds and of a generally high quality, with many items priced in the five figures. Look for the life-size metal horseman sculptures keeping watch on the streets. Many galleries are open from 7 to 9 pm on Thursday evening 'Art Walks.'

The outdoor **Arizona Center** is revitalizing downtown at 3rd St and Van Buren, with several popular bars, restaurants and a small selection of interesting shops.

If you need **camping or outdoor gear**, REI (☎ 480-967-5494), 1405 W Southern Ave in Tempe, has one of the largest selections in the Southwest and does mail order as well.

GETTING THERE & AWAY
Air
Phoenix's Sky Harbor International Airport (Map 2; ☎ 602-273-3300 main switchboard,

☎ 602-392-0126, 602-392-0310 airport information) is 3 miles southeast of downtown. By far the largest airport in the Southwest, its three terminals (illogically called Terminals 2, 3 and 4) contain all the standard features of any major airport. There are economy long-term parking lots ($5 or $8 a day) within a short walk or shuttle-bus ride of the terminals and pricier short-term lots ($20 a day) next to the terminals. See the Getting There & Away chapter for more information about airlines.

Bus
Greyhound Bus Terminal (Map 2; ☎ 602-389-4200) is at 2115 E Buckeye but they can drop you at several stops throughout the Greater Phoenix area. Phoenix is at the center of a fairly extensive bus network throughout and beyond the state. White Mountain Passenger Lines (Map 2; ☎ 602-275-4245), 319 S 24th St, has a 1 pm bus to Show Low ($40), and the Arizona Shuttle Service (☎ 800-888-2749) has many vans a day linking Phoenix Airport with Tucson. Other local bus companies linking Phoenix Airport with Arizona towns beyond the valley are listed in Getting There & Away sections for those towns.

GETTING AROUND
To/From the Airport
Valley Metro (see below) operates its Red Line every 15 to 30 minutes Monday to Friday from about 4 am to 10 pm, driving to Tempe and Mesa along Apache Blvd and Main, or west into downtown and then into north Phoenix. Weekend buses are less frequent.

SuperShuttle (☎ 602-244-9000) has vans providing airport-to-your-door service at any time. Fares are lower than those of taxis, which add a $1 airport surcharge in addition to their metered rates. Traveler information desks provide more details.

Bus
Valley Metro (☎ 602-253-5000) operates buses all over the valley. Phones are answered 4 am to 10 pm Monday to Friday and 7 am to 7 pm weekends; other times

there's a recording. Some routes are limited-stop Express Services. Most routes operate from about 4 am to 10 pm. Fares are $1.25 (including one transfer) or $3.60 for an all-day pass. The latter can be bought at only a few locations such as the Valley Metro Downtown Bus Terminal at Central Ave and Van Buren (Map 3); call Valley Metro for other locations. A few Express Services cost $1.75. People over 65 or between six and 18 years old with a picture ID ride for half-fare. Exact fare is required. Riders can pay with Visa or MasterCard.

websites: www.valleymetro.maricopa.gov, www.bus.maricopa.gov

Valley Metro also runs free DASH buses around downtown Phoenix every six minutes 6:30 am to 11 pm Monday to Friday. From 11 am to 2 pm, DASH goes out to the State Capitol. Valley Metro's FLASH buses offer free rides every 10 minutes around the ASU area from 7 am to 6 pm on weekdays. FLASHLite goes from Tempe to the zoo and botanical gardens on weekends.

Car & Motorcycle

All the main car-rental companies have airport offices and many have offices in other parts of the valley or will deliver your car. Reserve a car in advance for the best rates.

Western States Motorcycle Tours (☎ 602-943-9030), 9401 N 7th Ave, rents big bikes to riders aged 21, at least 5 feet 5 inches tall, with a motorcycle license and with two years recent riding experience. Daily rates range from $75 for an 800 cc Suzuki Intruder to $175 for an Electra-Glide Classic Harley. Weekly rates are available.

Taxi

There are several 24-hour cab services, but with a $3 drop fee and fares of well over $1 per mile, you can rack up a pricey ride fairly rapidly in the large valley area. Renting a car is better for most longer drives. Some of the main cab companies are Ace Taxi (☎ 602-254-1999), Checker Cab (☎ 602-257-1818) and Yellow Cab (☎ 602-252-5252).

Bicycle

The following are a few of several bike-rental shops:

Adventure Bicycle Co (☎ 480-649-3394) 1110 W Southern Ave, Mesa

Airpark Bicycle Center (☎ 480-596-6633) 8666 E Shea Blvd, Scottsdale

Tempe Bicycles (☎ 480-966-6896) 330 W University Dr, Tempe

Wheels 'n Gear (☎ 480-945-2881) 7607 E McDowell Rd, Scottsdale

Grand Canyon & Lake Powell

The slogan on the Arizona license plate says it all: 'Grand Canyon State.' The Grand Canyon of the Colorado River is Arizona's most famous sight – indeed, it is arguably the best known natural attraction in the entire country. This grandest of all canyons has been declared a UN World Heritage Site to be protected for all people.

At 277 miles long, roughly 10 miles wide and a mile deep, the canyon sounds big. But its sheer size is not all that makes the sight so tremendous. The incredible spectacle of differently colored rock strata, the many buttes and peaks within the canyon itself, and the meandering rims give access to fantastic views that amaze the visitor. Staring from the many rim overlooks gives you a great impression of the grandeur, but walking down into the canyon on a short hike or a multi-day backpacking trip gives you a better sense of the variety in the landscape, wildlife and climate.

Although the rims are only 10 miles apart as the crow flies, it is a 215-mile, five-hour drive on narrow roads from the visitor center on the South Rim to the visitor center on the North Rim. Thus the Grand Canyon National Park is essentially two separate areas that are treated separately in this chapter. The South Rim is described first, continuing with the areas south of the park. Then comes the remote northern area known as the Arizona Strip, containing the North Rim of Grand Canyon National Park. Finally comes Page and the Glen Canyon Dam area, which is on the Colorado River just outside the northeastern corner of the park.

Scattered throughout the Grand Canyon are signs of ancient Native American inhabitants. The oldest artifacts are little twig figures of animals made by hunters and gatherers about 4000 years ago – a few of these can be seen in the Tusayan Museum, east of the Grand Canyon Village. Within the canyon are stone buildings left by Native Americans before their unexplained departure during the 12th century.

Cerbat people began living at the western end of the canyon around AD 1300 and were the ancestors of contemporary Hualapai and Havasupai tribes. Despite attempts by Europeans to dislodge them, these two tribes continue living in reservations on the southwestern rim of the canyon. These reservations (described further in this chapter) abut the Grand Canyon National Park but can't be entered from the park.

The canyon's earliest European visitors were Spaniards who gazed into the depths in 1540. The canyon was difficult to reach and involved crossing large areas with little water. Because there didn't appear to be any mineral wealth and the area was generally considered magnificent but valueless, European visits were infrequent for over three centuries.

The first serious European exploration was in 1869, when John Wesley Powell, a one-armed Civil War veteran, led an expedition along the Colorado River. Using wooden boats, they ran the entire length

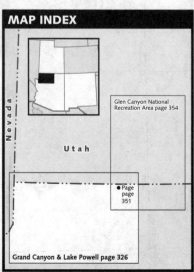

MAP INDEX

Nevada

Utah

Glen Canyon National Recreation Area page 354

● Page page 351

Grand Canyon & Lake Powell page 326

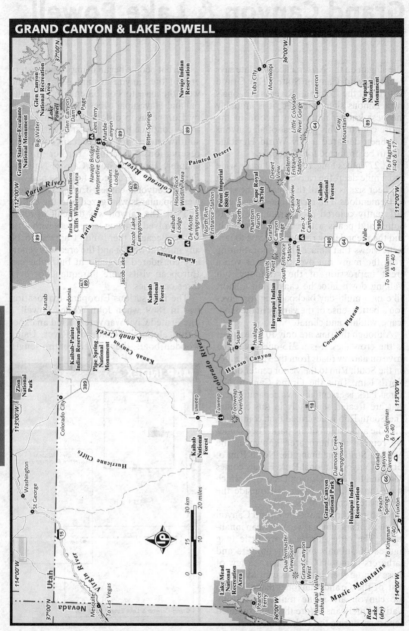

of the Grand and other canyons – a remarkable achievement. Powell led a similar expedition in 1871–72, which resulted in detailed scientific observations and writings.

During the late 19th century, Mormons began settling the remote Arizona Strip, and prospectors and miners ventured into the canyon in search of mineral wealth but found little. One miner, John Hance, arrived in 1883 and decided that catering to tourists would be more profitable than mining. He became one of the most colorful and well-known guides into the canyon, famous for his tall tales. Some simple lodges were built for the few tourists who made it to the South Rim by stagecoach or horseback.

In 1901, the railroad arrived and tourism became big business. President Theodore Roosevelt visited the canyon in 1903, said 'You cannot improve on it' and protected the canyon, first as a national monument in 1908 and later as a park in 1919. The park has expanded since and its current size is 1892 sq miles.

South of the Colorado River

The Colorado River has always been a major barrier for travelers in this region. If state boundaries had been made on purely geographical divisions, the river would have divided Arizona and Utah. This didn't happen.

GRAND CANYON NATIONAL PARK – SOUTH RIM
☎ 928

The South Rim, just over 7000 feet in elevation, is lower than the North Rim and accessible year-round. Ninety percent of park visitors go to the South Rim.

The foremost attraction is the rim itself, paralleled by a 33-mile scenic drive with numerous parking areas, scenic views and trailheads. Most visitors make part of this drive or walk some of the 9 miles of trails along the rim. However, this drive can become overcrowded, so timing your visit early in the day is suggested.

Another attraction is Grand Canyon Village, with historic early-20th-century hotels and most modern amenities. Numerous hiking trails into the canyon are described below. To really get away from the traffic at the top, hike down to the canyon bottom and stay at Phantom Ranch or at one of several campgrounds, which require reservations well in advance. Other activities include mule rides, river running and backcountry backpacking, but all require advance planning.

Information
Climate & When to Go On average, temperatures are 20°F cooler on the South Rim than at the bottom of the Grand Canyon. This means you could wake up on the rim to frost on the ground in April and be basking in the 80°s F by afternoon if you hike down into the inner gorge. The peak season ranges from about April to November, and the park is busiest from Memorial Day to Labor Day.

At the South Rim in summer, expect highs in the 80°s F and lows around 50°F. June is the driest month, but summer thunderstorms make July and August the wettest months. Weather is cooler and changeable in the fall, and snow and freezing overnight temperatures are likely by November. January has average overnight lows in the teens and daytime highs around 40°F. Winter weather can be beautifully clear, but be prepared for occasional storms that can cause havoc.

The inner canyon is much drier with about eight inches of rain annually, about half that of the South Rim. During the summer, temperatures inside the canyon go above 100°F almost every day and often exceed 110°F in midsummer, which can be potentially lethal for unprepared hikers. Strong hot winds often blow in summer. Even in midwinter, freezing overnight temperatures are rare in the inner canyon, with average lows in the upper 30°s F and highs in the upper 50°s F.

ARIZONA

Geology of the Grand Canyon

Approximately two billion years of geologic history are exposed in the Grand Canyon – a huge amount of time considering the earth is just 4.6 billion years old. The oldest rock in the canyon, exposed just above the Colorado River, is the **Vishnu Schist**. Deposited in the Precambrian Era as sands, silts and muds interlayered with volcanic ash, these sediments were metamorphosed (hardened by heat and pressure) about 1.7 billion years ago by a collision of tectonic plates that baked and squeezed the entire region and uplifted the Mazatzal Mountains (which have since eroded). This metamorphism continued when **Zoroaster Granite** intruded into the Vishnu as molten magma. Between 1.2 billion and 800 million years ago, the area was covered by an ocean that rose and fell more than 18 times, depositing a thick series of marine sediments and volcanic flows; these were later metamorphosed into a rock unit named the **Grand Canyon Supergroup**.

The layers making up most of the canyon walls were laid during the Paleozoic (ancient life) and Mesozoic (middle life) Eras between 570 and 65 million years ago, which is why there are so many fossils in the Grand Canyon today. During much of this time, the entire Grand Canyon region was submerged under a tropical ocean, which rose and fell repeatedly. When sea levels were high, fine-grained clays and deep-sea oozes settled to the ocean floor – sediments that would later become thinly layered shales and limestones. When sea levels fell, the area became sandy beachfront property, complete with dunes, deltas and swamps, eventually forming silt-stones and sandstones. Well-known examples include the **Redwall** and **Kaibab** limestones, the **Hermit** and **Bright Angel** shales, and the **Coconino** and **Tapeats** sandstones. Around 65 million years ago, tectonic forces once again uplifted the region and the sea retreated permanently. The final rocks to be deposited in the Grand Canyon were volcanic flows that erupted into the canyon about one million years ago.

The tremendous depth and the unusually steep sides of the Grand Canyon are closely tied to the evolution of the Colorado River. The Grand Canyon lies within the **Colorado Plateau** geologic province, an area composed largely of flat-lying sedimentary and volcanic rocks. Both the Colorado Plateau and the Colorado River's source area in the Rocky Mountains has been rapidly uplifted several times since the end of which is why there are so many fossils in the Grand Canyon today. During much of this time, the entire Grand Canyon region was submerged under a tropical ocean, which rose and fell repeatedly. When sea levels were high, fine-grained clays and deep-sea oozes settled to the ocean floor – sediments that would later become thinly layered shales and lime-stones. When sea levels fell, the area became sandy beachfront property, complete with dunes, deltas and swamps, eventually forming siltstones and sandstones. Well-known examples include the **Redwall** and **Kaibab** limestones, the **Hermit** and **Bright Angel** shales, and the **Coconino** and **Tapeats** sandstones. Around 65 million years ago, tectonic forces once again uplifted the region and the sea retreated permanently. The final rocks to be deposited in the Grand Canyon were vol-canic flows that erupted into the canyon about one million years ago.

The tremendous depth and the unusually steep sides of the Grand Canyon are closely tied to the evolution of the Colorado River. The Grand Canyon lies within the **Colorado Plateau** geologic province, an area composed largely of flat-lying sedimentary and volcanic rocks. Both the Colorado Plateau and the Colorado River's source area in the Rocky Mountains has been rapidly uplifted several times since the end of debris. The lower section of the canyon, called the Inner Gorge, is narrow and V-shaped. Composed largely of metamorphic rocks of similar hardness, each layer is eroded at about the same rate as its neighbors so none stand out farther than the others.

– **Rhawn Denniston, geologist**

Tourist Offices & Services Canyon View Information Plaza, at the northeast end of Grand Canyon Village, 6 miles north of the South Entrance Station, is open daily 8 am to 6 pm. It is reached on foot (about a quarter-mile walk) or by frequent shuttle buses – there is no parking at the information plaza. There is a small museum, an excellent bookstore, and large bulletin boards with information about lodging, weather, tours, talks and a host of other things. If you can't find the information you need on the bulletin boards, rangers are available to assist you; they are often swamped by visitors, so check the posted information first.

A smaller visitor center at Desert View, near the east entrance of the park, is open daily in summer and closed in winter (depending on staff availability).

Visitors can receive assistance at ranger stations near the Grand Canyon Railway depot, Indian Garden below the South Rim, the River ranger station and Phantom Ranch at the canyon bottom, and Cottonwood Campground below the North Rim.

Telephoning the park (☎ 928-638-7888) gives you an automated system with recorded information on everything from weather conditions to applying for a river-running permit. You can leave your address to receive written information or you can speak with a ranger during business hours. All park numbers are in the 928 area code; the park's website is www.nps.gov/grca.

A park map and a seasonal newspaper, *The Guide,* are available at no charge to all visitors. *The Guide* is the best up-to-date source of park information available upon arrival. French, German and Spanish versions are available. Also very useful is the free *Grand Canyon Trip Planner.* You can receive information in advance from the Superintendent, Grand Canyon National Park, PO Box 129, Grand Canyon, AZ 86023.

Grand Canyon Village has most visitor services. However, prices here are substantially higher and the lines are longer than in Flagstaff, so think ahead.

Services available include hotels, restaurants, campgrounds, coin-operated laundry and showers, gift shops, pet kennels, churches and transportation services. Car towing and mechanics (☎ 638-2631) are available from 8 am to 5 pm and for 24-hour emergency service. A gas station is open daily; hours vary from 6 am to 9:30 pm in summer and 8 am to 6 pm in midwinter. A medical clinic (☎ 638-2551, pharmacy ☎ 638-2460) is open 9 am to 6 pm, Monday to Friday, and 9 am to 1 pm on Saturday.

Mather Shopping Center contains the following: A bank (☎ 638-2437) with foreign exchange is open 10 am to 3 pm, Monday to Friday, and till 5 pm on Friday. A 24-hour ATM accepts major credit/debit cards. A post office (☎ 638-2512) is open 9 am to 4:30 pm, Monday to Friday, and 11 am to 3 pm on Saturday. Stamp machines in the lobby are accessible from 5 am to 10 pm daily.

Canyon Village Marketplace (☎ 638-2262) sells food, clothing and camping supplies (rentals are possible) from 8 am to 7 pm daily.

Recycling bins are found where there are trash containers. Visitors are urged to place recyclables in the designated bins.

Near the east entrance, the Desert View Service Center has a visitor center, general store, gas station (closed in winter), campground (closed in winter), cafeteria and the Watchtower, which is the highest point on the South Rim.

Books & Maps The Grand Canyon Association (GCA) (☎ 638-2481), PO Box 399, AZ 86023, sells over 350 books, maps, trail guides and videos about the Grand Canyon. Stores are in the visitor centers, or the GCA will send you a mail-order catalog. Profits benefit the national park.
website: www.grandcanyon.org

Fees & Permits Entrance to the park is $20 per private vehicle or $10 for bicyclists and pedestrians. The entrance ticket is valid for seven days and can be used at any entrance point, including the North Rim. All passes are honored. Bus and train passengers either pay a lesser fee or may have the fee included in the tour.

ARIZONA

For backcountry camping, permits are required from the Backcountry Office (see Hiking & Backpacking, below).

Pets Pets are allowed (when leashed) on developed sections of the rim but nowhere below the rim (except guide/service dogs). Kennels are available, but leaving pets at home is encouraged.

Dangers & Annoyances Each year, a few people fall to their deaths in the Grand Canyon. When visiting the rim, stay inside guardrails and on trails. When hiking below the rim, use hiking shoes or boots rather than tennis shoes or sandals. Only a few trails below the rim are maintained; use extra caution when hiking on unmaintained trails.

Some 250 hikers a year on the most popular below-the-rim trails require ranger assistance to get out safely. The main problems are too much sun and too little water. Wear a hat and sunblock, and carry at least a gallon of water per person per day in summer. Hikers can (and do) run out of water and die. Even if it turns out you don't need it, carrying extra water may save someone else's life. Before attempting long hikes, speak with backcountry rangers about where you can replenish your water bottles. (See Hiking & Backpacking, below, and the 'Water Woes' boxed text.)

Feeding wildlife is detrimental to the animals and illegal. It is also dangerous – observe them from a distance. Every year visitors are injured by wild animals. Animals that are fed by visitors become used to human food and seek it out. Frequently, rangers have the sad task of shooting deer to spare them the pain of starving to death: their stomachs are so clogged with several pounds of indigestible food wrappers and plastic bags, they cannot feed anymore.

Other annoyances come from outside the park. Air pollution has seriously reduced visibility in the canyon in recent years. Smog from as far west as Los Angeles and sulfur emissions from the Navajo Generating Station near Glen Canyon Dam in the east are blown in. Sometimes, the far rim of the canyon is just a distant blur. Winter usually offers the clearest visibility.

The flow and characteristics of the Colorado River have changed and continue to change because of the Glen Canyon Dam. Half the species of fish in the river before the dam was built are now extinct. Anglers and river runners have had to adapt to these problems.

Hikers descending into the canyon to get away from the crowded rims hear aircraft noise from the many tourist flights over the national park.

These annoyances are being recognized and corrected to some extent, but the political ramifications are very complex.

With so many visitors, crime is also a growing problem. Lock cars and hotel rooms. Do not leave valuable objects such as cameras in view inside your car.

Museums & Historic Buildings

In addition to the exhibits at the visitor centers, check out the following.

Yavapai Observation Station At Yavapai Point, at the northeast end of Grand Canyon Village, this station has a geology museum and spectacular views all the way down to Phantom Ranch at the canyon bottom. There is a bookstore and ranger-led

---

Water Woes

It's easy to forget that much of the Grand Canyon is essentially a desert. Visitors require water for drinking, cooking and washing, but the only available water must be piped in from a spring on the north wall of the canyon. A quick look over the rim will convince you that this was not the easiest pipe-laying project! Try to conserve water by taking short showers and not letting water run unnecessarily. When a storm broke the pipe in 1995, all water had to be trucked in. It's always a good idea to carry a few gallons of water in your car – you never know when you might need it in the Southwest.

activities. Winter hours are 8 am to 5 pm, extended to 6, 7 or 8 pm in other seasons.

Kolb Studio In Grand Canyon Village, this was a photography studio opened in 1904 and run by Emery Kolb until his death in 1976. Throughout the year, a variety of changing exhibits display photographs or other items related to the canyon. Hours are the same as the Yavapai museum's, and there is a bookstore. Several other nearby historic buildings date from the same period, including the El Tovar Hotel and the gift shops of Hopi House and Verkamps Curios.

Tusayan Museum Located off of East Rim Drive, 23 miles east of Grand Canyon Village, this little museum has exhibits about Ancestral Puebloan life, including ancient twig figures of animals. You can visit the small Tusayan Ruin nearby; guided walks are offered several times a day in summer and less frequently in the off-peak season. Hours are 9 am to 5 pm in summer, with shorter winter hours. Admission is free.

Watchtower At Desert View near the east entrance, you can climb the stairs of the Watchtower (☎ 638-2736), built in 1932 and the highest point on the South Rim. Inside, the walls are decorated with reproductions of ancient petroglyphs as well as contemporary Native American artwork. There is a 25¢ admission to the tower and coin-operated telescopes are available. Hours are 8 am to 7:30 pm in summer, 9 am to 4:30 pm in winter.

Ranger-Led Activities
Call the park's information service (☎ 638-7888) or ask at a visitor center about free ranger-led activities. These occur year-round, though with much greater frequency in summer. Programs include talks (including slide shows) and walks (some wheelchair accessible) throughout the day and into the evening. Guided walks range from a few hundred flat yards (40 minutes) to 3 miles below the rim (three to four hours). During the summer there are Junior Ranger activities for four- to 12-year-olds.

Volunteers can join the **Habitat Restoration Team**. Projects include planting native plants or removing non-native ones, helping restore historic miners' cabins, collecting litter or doing maintenance work. A regular two-hour plant removal and restoration effort occurs at 8:30 am several mornings a week (depending on season) and families are encouraged to help and learn (minimum age is five). Information about this project and longer volunteer projects is available at the main visitor center.

The **Grand Canyon Field Institute** (☎ 638-2485, fax 638-2484), PO Box 399, Grand Canyon, AZ 86023, is the educational arm of the GCA (see Books & Maps, above). It offers in-depth classes of one to eight days from mid-March to mid-November. Some topics include geology, biology, ecology, Native American cultures and photography. Classes are held both in classrooms and in the field, including hiking and multi-night backpacking trips. Contact the Field Institute for a course catalog.

Scenic Drives
Driving 51 miles north from Flagstaff on Hwy 89 to the tiny community of Cameron, and heading west on Hwy 64, entering the park from the east after driving through the Kaibab National Forest and Navajo Indian Reservation gives easier access to the Rim Drive pullouts, mostly on the north side of the road. Early morning, with the sun behind you, is suggested. It's 53 miles from Cameron to Grand Canyon Village.

Hwy 64 north from Williams, through the South Entrance Station, reaches Grand Canyon Village (about 60 miles). Here, Hwy 64 turns east and becomes the Rim Drive. After exiting the national park, Hwy 64 continues east to Cameron. This way, sunlight is best in the afternoon.

Rim Trail
The paved Rim Trail is accessible to wheelchairs and extends for over 3 miles along the rim from **Yavapai Point** to **Maricopa Point**. It extends unpaved almost 7 miles farther west past several viewpoints to Hermits Rest (see the next section). The

Rim Trail is the park's most popular walk and visitors can hike as far as they are comfortable. The rewards are beautiful views with many interpretive signs. Only foot and wheelchair traffic is allowed – no bicycles. During winter, snow or ice may temporarily cover the trail.

Hermits Rest Route

The west rim is accessible by this road for 8 miles west of Grand Canyon Village (and by the Rim Trail described above). At the end of the drive and trail is Hermits Rest, where there is a snack bar and the Hermit trailhead down into the canyon; if you don't descend, you have to return the way you came.

Year-round you can hike the western Rim Trail or cycle along the road. Cars are not allowed along this road, but free shuttle buses operate (see Getting Around, later in the chapter). Narrated bus tours are also available (see Organized Tours, below).

Desert View Drive

The east rim drive is longer and a little less crowded than the west rim but offers equally spectacular views. Free shuttle buses along the Kaibab Trail Route (the first section of the Desert View Drive) leave every 15 minutes as far as Yaki Point. You can also drive, bike or take a narrated bus tour.

Tusayan, the most accessible of the park's approximately 2000 Ancestral Puebloan sites, is along the Desert View Drive which ends at **Desert View**, about 25 miles east of Grand Canyon Village and the highest point on the South Rim. The road then leaves the national park through the Navajo Indian Reservation to Cameron. There are a couple of viewpoints into the smaller Little Colorado River canyon along the way. The Grand Canyon itself turns north at Desert View.

Hiking & Backpacking

For backpacking, the Backcountry Office (☎ 638-7875, 1 to 5 pm Monday to Friday), PO Box 129, Grand Canyon, AZ 86023, has all relevant information. The office in the Maswik Transportation Center is open 8 am to noon and 1 to 5 pm daily.

The easiest walks are along the Rim Trail, described above. Hikes below the rim into the canyon are strenuous and some visitors prefer to use mules (see Organized Tours, below). Hikers meeting a mule train should stand quietly on the upper side of the trail until the animals have passed. Mule riders have the right of way.

Two important things to bear in mind when attempting any hike into the canyon: First, it's easy to stride down the trail for a few hours, but the steep uphill return during the heat of the day when you are tired is much more demanding. Allow two hours to return uphill for every hour of hiking downhill. Second, the temperatures inside the gorge are much hotter than at the rim and water is scarcely available. Carry plenty of water and protection from the sun. In summer, temperatures can exceed 110°F in the inner gorge.

The two most popular below-the-rim trails are the Bright Angel Trail and the South Kaibab Trail. These are the best-maintained trails and are both used by mule riders. Both are suitable for either day hikes or, with a permit and advance reservation, overnight backpacking trips. No permit is necessary for a day trip. Both trails are steep and strenuous. Nevertheless, they are considered the easiest rim-to-river trails in the canyon and even a short descent along part of these trails will completely alter your perspective. Day hikers should not expect to reach the river and return in one day.

Bright Angel Trail The trail leaves from the Rim Trail a few yards west of Bright Angel Lodge in Grand Canyon Village. From the trailhead at about 6900 feet, the trail drops to Indian Garden 4.6 miles away at about 3800 feet. Here, there is a ranger station, campground, restrooms and water. From Indian Garden, an almost flat trail goes 1½ miles to Plateau Point, with exceptional views into the inner gorge. The 12.2 miles roundtrip from the rim to Plateau Point is a strenuous all-day hike. Shorter hikes are of course possible – just walk down from the rim as far as you want. There are resthouses after 1½ miles (1130-foot elevation drop) and 3 miles (2110-foot elevation drop). The 1½-mile resthouse has restrooms; both have water in summer only.

From Indian Garden, the Bright Angel Trail continues down to the Colorado River (2450 feet elevation), which is crossed by a suspension bridge – the only bridge within the park. The Bright Angel Campground is a short way north of the bridge and 9½ miles from the South Rim. A few hundred yards beyond is Phantom Ranch. Water, food, accommodations and a ranger station are all here.

South Kaibab Trail This trail leaves the South Rim from near Yaki Point, about 4½ miles east of Grand Canyon Village. From the trailhead at 7262 feet, it's more than 4800 feet down to the river and Bright Angel Campground, but the distance is only 6.7 miles. Clearly, South Kaibab is a much steeper trail than Bright Angel. It follows a ridge with glorious views. The first 1½ miles drop 1300 feet to Cedar Ridge and this makes a good short half-day hike.

From the Bright Angel Campground on the north side of the river, the **North Kaibab Trail** climbs to the North Rim at 8200 feet in 14 miles (see the Grand Canyon National Park – North Rim section, later in this chapter). You can cross the canyon rim to rim. Although extremely fit hikers can descend from the South Rim to the river and return or make a rim-to-rim crossing in one long day (the record for running rim to rim is now under four hours), the NPS strongly discourages such endeavors. Certainly, during the summer the extreme temperatures make such attempts very dangerous for inexperienced hikers.

Other Trails Although other trails receive little or no maintenance, several are not beyond the limits of any hiker with some experience. The least difficult are the **Hermit Trail**, which leaves from Hermits Rest at the end of the West Rim Drive, and the **Grandview Trail**, which leaves from Grandview Point of the East Rim Drive, 12 miles east of Grand Canyon Village. Both of these are steep and strenuous but offer popular

day hikes as well as backcountry camping possibilities.

Details of the many unmaintained trails and backcountry campgrounds in the canyon are beyond the scope of this book – read a backpacking guidebook and contact the Backcountry Office for further information.

Backpacking Itineraries Most overnight backpacking trips go from the South Rim to the river and return because rim-to-rim trips involve a five-hour car shuttle. Typically, three days and two nights are spent below the rim, with a choice of spending two nights at either Bright Angel or Indian Garden Campground, or one night at each (normally Bright Angel on the first night). If you arrange a shuttle, you could add a night at Cottonwood Campground on the way up to the North Rim. If your time is limited, a two-day/one-night trip is also rewarding. Because the Kaibab Trail is steep, this is the usual descent route, with the longer but less steep Bright Angel Trail used for climbing out. These two trails are called the 'corridor trails' and are recommended for first-time visitors.

If you want to hike but prefer a bed to a sleeping bag, you can stay at the canyon-bottom Phantom Ranch Lodge (see Places to Stay, below).

Backcountry Permits Permits cost $10 plus $5 per person per night. Applications can be mailed or faxed to the Backcountry Office (fax 928-638-2125), PO Box 129, Grand Canyon, AZ 86023. Alternatively, use the website or deliver applications in person. Applications are accepted for the current month and the next four months *only*. In 1999 the park received 30,000 permit applications and was able to issue 14,000 permits, so your chances are pretty good if you apply early and provide alternative hiking itineraries.

If you arrive without a backcountry permit, don't despair! Immediately head over to the Backcountry Office (☎ 638-7875, 1 to 5 pm Monday to Friday), by the Maswik Lodge, and get on the waiting list for cancellations, and you'll likely get a permit within one to six days depending on season and itinerary. You have a better chance of getting a permit on short notice if you are prepared to hike unmaintained trails to less developed campgrounds (ask the ranger for advice) or if you avoid the peak season.

Although it may be tempting to try backpacking without a permit, remember that backcountry rangers patrol the trails and check permits on a regular and frequent basis, so you are quite likely to get caught and fined. Backpacking without a permit is considered a serious offense by the NPS.

River Running

You can run the Colorado River with a tour or arrange your own private trip. But before you throw a rubber raft into the back of a pickup and head up to the Colorado River, make sure you have serious river-running experience and a permit.

Obtaining a permit is straightforward but time consuming. Call or write the national park for an application, mail it and wait about 12 years. Then throw your raft into your pickup....

Currently, well over 20,000 visitors a year run the river, almost all with commercial trips. These can be most simply divided into motorized and nonmotorized. The motorized trips are usually in huge inflatable boats that go twice as fast as the oar boats, but you have to put up with the roar of the engine. Nonmotorized trips are slow, but the only roar you'll hear is the roar of the rapids, mingled with gurgled screams. Whichever way you go, expect to get very wet during the day and spend nights camping on riverside beaches. This is not as primitive as it sounds – professional river guides are legendary for their combination of white-water abilities, gastronomy and information.

Most trips run the river from Lees Ferry to Diamond Creek (in the Hualapai Indian Reservation), dropping more than 2000 feet in almost 300 miles and running scores of rapids. Passengers have the option of getting on or off at Phantom Ranch on the main rim-to-rim trail (the South and North Kaibab Trails) almost halfway into the

entire river trip. Combining these options, you can take anything from a three- or four-day motorized trip of part of the canyon to a three-week nonmotorized trip of the entire canyon.

Nonmotorized trips are varied. Many are oar trips, where the captain controls the boat with large oars and the passengers hang on. Some are paddle trips, where the passengers paddle in response to the captain's commands. All these are generally in inflatable rafts, but a couple of companies do paddle trips in wooden dories, reminiscent of those used by John Wesley Powell in 1869. In addition, experienced kayakers can join commercial trips – the gear goes in the rafts.

Commercial trips aren't cheap – expect to pay about $200 per person per day. Family discounts can be arranged, but small children are not allowed – minimum-age requirements vary from trip to trip. Sixteen companies are authorized to run the Colorado River through the national park; contact the park through phone, mail or its website for an up-to-date list. These trips fill up several months (even a year) in advance, so contact the companies early for information.

Occasionally, a cancellation will enable you to run the river on short notice, but this is unreliable. If you want to run the river on short notice, see Hualapai River Runners in the Hualapai Indian Reservation, below, for one-day whitewater trips. Also see Organized Tours, below, for one-day, smoothwater raft trips.

Bicycling

Bicycles are allowed only on roads. Mountain biking on trails is not permitted – you need to go outside the park in the Kaibab National Forest for that. In fact, no wheeled vehicles of any kind are permitted on the trails (except for wheelchairs and baby strollers on the paved Rim Trail).

The story is told of a river runner who pushed a dolly loaded with 10 cases of beer down the Bright Angel Trail to his rafting group. He received a ticket for using a wheeled vehicle on the trail and also had to push the loaded dolly all the way back to the South Rim. Bummer!

Fishing

There is good trout fishing in the Colorado River and several of its tributaries. Licenses and tackle can be purchased at the general store in Grand Canyon Village.

Licenses are not available for purchase on the national park's North Rim – the nearest area to get a permit is Marble Canyon, where there are also guides.

Cross-Country Skiing

The higher North Rim area offers more snow for better cross-country skiing than the South Rim area (see also the Jacob Lake Area section, later in the chapter). However, you can ski in the South Rim area in the Kaibab National Forest at the Grandview Ski Area when snow conditions permit. There are 18 miles of easy- to medium-difficulty, groomed and signed skiing trails near the east entrance of the park. The plowed parking area and access to the trails is on East Rim Drive, 10.1 miles north of the junction of Hwys 64 and 180, 2 miles east of Grandview Point.

About a half-mile into the access trail is an information kiosk that describes routes and distances; the longest trail is 7½ miles. One trail has a canyon-view overlook, but all trails stay in the national forest and do not go to the South Rim of the national park.

Skiers are free to tour the national forest regardless of trails and there are no restrictions on camping unless you enter the park.

Organized Tours

Once you are inside the park, most tours are run by Amfac (☎ 303-297-2757). Amfac has a transportation desk (☎ 638-2631) at the Bright Angel Lodge and information desks at the visitor center and Maswik and Yavapai Lodges.
website: www.amfac.com

See Williams, in the Central Arizona chapter, for information about train tours to the Grand Canyon.

Bus Narrated bus tours with several photo stops leave from lodges in the Grand Canyon Village. These include a two-hour Hermits Rest Route tour, a 3¾-hour

Kaibab Trail Route tour or a combination of both. Both leave twice daily year-round and cost about $16 and $28, or $33 for combining both. Sunset and sunrise tours are $11. Children under 16 are free with an adult.

Some buses are wheelchair accessible by prior arrangement. Reservations are advised in summer but even then there are usually enough buses that you can get on a tour the next day by reserving at the transportation desk. Tax (6%) and guide tips are not included in these prices.

Mule A one-day trip to Plateau Point inside the canyon is offered daily. It takes about seven hours roundtrip, of which six hours are spent in the saddle. The cost is $119 plus tax and tips, including lunch.

Overnight trips to Phantom Ranch at the canyon bottom are offered daily. These take

5½ hours down and 4½ hours back up and cost about $335 for one or $600 for two persons, including meals and dormitory accommodations. During winter only, three-day/two-night trips to Phantom Ranch cost $450 or $770 for two. Rates don't include tax and tips.

Reservations are suggested, although you can get on a waiting list if you don't have one. During winter, trips can often be arranged with a day's notice; during the summer the waiting list is much longer and a wait of several days or even weeks may be necessary.

These trips are strenuous – they are supposedly easier than walking, but riders must be in good physical shape and be able to mount and dismount without assistance, weigh under 200lb (including clothing and camera), be at least 4' 7" in height, be fluent in English (so they can understand instructions) and cannot be pregnant.

Horse and mule rides are also available from the town of Tusayan (see below).

You can ride your own horse into the park, but a permit is required from the Backcountry Office (see Hiking & Backpacking, earlier). Permit procedures and costs are the same as for backpackers, with an additional fee of $5 per horse per night; there is a limit of 12 horses per group of up to six people, or five pack animals for a single mounted rider. Horse trips are allowed only on the corridor routes and only Bright Angel and Cottonwood Campgrounds have overnight horse facilities. Feed must be carried.

Special Events

The Grand Canyon Chamber Music Festival (☎ 638-9215), PO Box 1332, Grand Canyon, AZ 86023, has been presented at the Shrine of the Ages at Grand Canyon Village in September for more than a decade. Typically, about eight concerts are performed during a two-week period in mid-September. Tickets are $18; $6 for children and students.

Places to Stay

Reservations for all the places listed below are essential in summer and a good idea in winter. Cancellations provide a lucky few with last-minute rooms; call to check. If you can't find accommodations in the national park, see the sections on Tusayan (6 miles south of Grand Canyon Village outside the South Entrance Station), Valle (31 miles south) and Cameron (53 miles east), later in this chapter. Also see Williams (about 60 miles away) and Flagstaff (about 80 miles) in the Central Arizona chapter.

Camping Be prepared for freezing winter nights. In Grand Canyon Village, *Mather Campground* (☎ 301-722-1257, 800-365-2267 has 320 sites (no hookups) for $10 to $15 depending on season. Make reservations up to five months in advance. Otherwise it's first-come, first-served. Even in summer, a few sites may be available in the mornings. Coin showers and laundry are available near the campground entrance. Nearby, the Amfac *Trailer Village* has 80 RV sites with hookups for $24 year-round.

The *Desert View Campground* near the east entrance has 75 campsites on a first-come, first-served basis from April to October. They are often full by early morning so arrive early. There is water but no showers or RV hookups and fees are $10.

Lodges About 1000 rooms are available on the South Rim in a variety of lodges all run by Amfac Grand Canyon National Park Lodges (☎ 638-2631 for same-day information, ☎ 303-297-2757), whose website for advance reservations is www.amfac.com. In Grand Canyon Village, there are four lodges on the canyon rim – canyon-view rooms command higher prices. Two lodges, Maswik and Yavapai, are away from the rim, while Phantom Ranch is at the bottom of the canyon near the Colorado River. Approximate prices given below are the same for single or double occupancy; add tax (about 6%) and $7 to $14 per extra person. Prices vary by room, not by season.

On the rim, the most famous and expensive is the 1905 *El Tovar Hotel*, a rustic lodge with high standards of comfort and the best dining in the area. It was renovated in 1998 but still retains its historic flavor.

There are 78 small to midsized rooms from $116 to $174. About 12 mini-suites are $200 to $284 and three have private balconies with canyon views.

Budget travelers use the rustic 1935 **Bright Angel Lodge & Cabins** with more than 30 simple lodge rooms, many with shared bath, from $48 to $66. There are 42 cabins, all with bath, mostly for $73 to $121 and very popular. Some have fireplaces and canyon views. A suite with fireplace and canyon views is $220.

Between these two places are the modern **Kachina Lodge** with 49 rooms and **Thunderbird Lodge** with 55 rooms, all comfortable motel-style units with private bath, some with canyon views. Rates are about $114 to $124.

A short walk away from the rim, the **Maswik Lodge** has almost 300 rooms with private baths. Most are motel-style units, some with balconies, for $73 to $118; there are a few slightly cheaper rustic cabins with baths. Near the park headquarters, the **Yavapai Lodge** has about 360 reasonably sized motel rooms, all with private baths and some with forest views. Rates are $88 to $102. The Yavapai Lodge and the Maswik cabins may close in winter.

Phantom Ranch has basic cabins sleeping four to 10 people and segregated dorms sleeping 10 people in bunk beds. Most cabins are reserved for the overnight mule tours, but hikers may make reservations (from $64 double) if space is available. There are separate shower facilities. Dorm rates are $22 per person, and bedding, soap and towels are provided. Meals are available in the dining hall by advance reservation only. Breakfast is $14.50; box lunch is $7.50; and dinner varies from $17.75 (stew) to $27.75 (steak). Meals are not fancy but are enough to feed hungry hikers. If you lack a reservation, try showing up at the Bright Angel Lodge transportation desk at 6 am to snag a canceled bunk (some folks show up earlier and wait). Snacks, limited supplies, beer and wine are also sold. Postcards bought and mailed here are stamped 'Mailed by Mule from the bottom of the Canyon.'

Places to Eat

By far the best place for quality food in an elegant setting is the historic **El Tovar Dining Room** where dinner reservations are recommended, especially in summer when they are often booked weeks ahead. Hours are 6:30 am to 2 pm and 5 to 10 pm. Continental dinner entrées are in the $15 to $25 range and smoking is not permitted. The El Tovar has a piano bar.

More moderate prices and an American menu are available at the **Bright Angel Restaurant**, which is open 6:30 am to 10 pm; an adjoining lounge is open 11 am to 11 pm and may have live entertainment Wednesday to Saturday. Next door to the Bright Angel Lodge, the **Arizona Steakhouse** serves steaks and seafood 4:30 to 10 pm March through December. Some tables have canyon views and lines can be long – reservations are not accepted.

Self-service dining is available at the **Maswik Cafeteria** 6 am to 10 pm. The Maswik Lodge has a sports bar open 5 pm to midnight. The **Yavapai Cafeteria and Grill**, in the market plaza, is open 6 am to 9 pm. There's also a **delicatessen** in the market plaza, open 8 am to 6 pm.

Canyonside snacks and sandwiches are sold from 8 am to 4 pm at the **Bright Angel Fountain** near the Bright Angel trailhead, but it closes in bad weather and in winter. **Hermits Rest Snack Bar**, at the end of the West Rim Drive, and **Desert View Fountain** near the east entrance, are both open daily for snacks and fast food; hours vary by season.

Getting There & Away

The majority of people drive or arrive on bus tours. The nearest airport is in Tusayan (see below).

See Flagstaff, in the Central Arizona chapter, for the Nava-Hopi bus company, which is the only regularly scheduled bus service into the park. See Williams, in the Central Arizona chapter, for train service offered by the Grand Canyon Railway.

Canyon Airport Shuttle (☎ 638-0821) leaves the airport in Tusayan every hour on the half-hour with several stops in Tusayan en

ARIZONA

route to the Grand Canyon Village. One-way fare is $5; park entrance fees are not included.

Getting Around

Free shuttles operate along three routes: around the Grand Canyon Village, west along Hermits Rest Route and east along Kaibab Trail Route. Buses run every 15 minutes during the day and every 30 minutes from one hour before sunrise 'til daylight and from dusk 'til one hour after sunset. Bus stops are clearly marked and free maps are available. Park your car and ride – it's easier.

Shuttles from rim to rim are available from May to October (when the North Rim is open), leave at 1:30 pm, take five hours and cost $60 one-way or $100 roundtrip. Call Trans-Canyon Shuttle (☎ 638-2820). Other services are available on request.

TUSAYAN

Seven miles south of Grand Canyon Village and a couple of miles south of the south entrance, the sprawling community of Tusayan offers several motels, restaurants, souvenir shops and the Grand Canyon Airport, all strung along Hwy 64.

The chamber of commerce (☎ 638-2901) has a visitor information booth in the IMAX Theater lobby. The Kaibab National Forest Tusayan Ranger Station (☎ 638-2443) is at the north end of town and is open 8 am to 5 pm Monday to Friday. The post office is opposite the IMAX Theater and an ATM is inside the theater.

IMAX Theater

Using a film format three times larger than normal 70mm movie frames, a screen up to eight times the size of conventional cinema screens and a 14-speaker stereo surround system, the IMAX Theater presents *Grand Canyon – The Hidden Secrets*. This 34-minute movie plunges you into the history and geology of the canyon through the eyes of ancient Indians, John Wesley Powell and a soaring eagle. The effects are quite splendid and are a cheaper, safer and quieter way of getting an aerial perspective than taking a flight. The IMAX Theater (☎ 638-2468) is

on Hwy 64, a few miles south of the park entrance. Shows are at 30 minutes past the hour from 8:30 am to 8:30 pm March through October and from 10:30 am to 6:30 pm the rest of the year. Admission is $9.50; $6.50 for three- to 11-year-olds. Credit cards are not accepted.

Horseback Riding

Apache Stables (☎ 638-2891, 638-2424) at the Moqui Lodge, a half-mile south of the park entrance, has a variety of horseback rides available in both the national forest and national park from about March to November. Rides are $25 to $65 for one to four hours. Children as young as six can ride on the shorter trips.

Other Activities

The Kaibab National Forest provides many opportunities for outdoor fun. Mountain biking on dirt roads and trails (not allowed in the Grand Canyon) is permitted throughout the national forest. About 13 miles of groomed cross-country skiing trails are found on forest lands south of the national park; these trails are accessed from a national park parking area near Grandview Point. You can enjoy hiking, backpacking and camping without the crowds and without a backcountry permit from the NPS Backcountry Office. Of course, you don't get the canyon views either.

Places to Stay

Visit www.gcanyon.com for information on accommodations in the Grand Canyon area, as well as activities and information for your stay.

Camping In the Kaibab National Forest, free dispersed camping is allowed at least a quarter of a mile from paved highways. USFS roads provide access, but many are closed in winter. USFS Rd 686 heading west from Hwy 64, almost a mile south of the Ten-X turnoff, is often open year-round.

The USFS operates the *Ten-X Campground* about 3 miles south of Tusayan. It is open from May through September and has

70 sites for $10 on a first-come, first-served basis. There is water but no showers or RV hookups.

Grand Canyon Camper Village (☎ 638-2887) is at the north end of Tusayan, 1½ miles south of the park entrance. About 300 sites are available year-round, ranging from $15 for tents to $23 for full hookups. There are showers, a playground and mini-golf. This place often has a tent site when everywhere else is full.

Hotels As with the Grand Canyon, reservations are recommended, especially in summer. Summer rates are pricey for what are basically motel rooms, but if you can't get a room on the South Rim and want to stay close to the canyon, this is what you're stuck with. Winter rates (November to March) are $30 to $50 lower. All motels are along Hwy 64.

The cheapest motel is **Seven Mile Lodge** (☎ 638-2291), with 20 basic rooms for about $72 single or double. They don't take reservations – just show up. **Moqui Lodge**, which is the closest to the park entrance and operated by Amfac (see Lodges in the Grand Canyon National Park – South Rim section, above), has 140 rooms at $100, including breakfast. Rooms vary somewhat in quality though not in price. It is closed November through March. There is a tour desk and a decent restaurant and bar with inexpensive Mexican and American food. Both these hotels advertise horseback riding.

The **Rodeway Inn – Red Feather Lodge** (☎ 638-2414, 800-228-2000) has about 100 older motel rooms plus 130 newer hotel rooms. Consequently, prices vary from about $85 to $130 in summer, $60 to $90 in winter. There is a seasonal pool as well as a spa, exercise room, game room and restaurant. This is the only hotel allowing pets. website: www.redfeatherlodge.com

The **Holiday Inn Express** (☎ 638-3000, 888-473-2269) has almost 200 rooms for about $130 in summer, including continental breakfast. Rooms are new, modern and comfortable, but the hotel lacks a restaurant and swimming pool. Some attractive suites are $160.

The **Quality Inn** (☎ 638-2673) has over 200 pleasant rooms and mini-suites for $125 to about $200 in summer. The mini-suites, of which there are about 50, each have a microwave, refrigerator and separate sitting area. Most have balconies. There is a pool, spa, restaurant and bar.
website: www.grandcanyonqualityinn.com

The **Best Western Grand Canyon Squire Inn** (☎ 638-2681, 800-622-6966) has 250 spacious rooms at $110 to $190 and a few suites for $210 to $240. There is a seasonal pool as well as a spa, sauna, tennis court, exercise room, coin laundry, gift shop and (at extra charge) a fun center with bowling, billiards and other games. A good restaurant, an inexpensive coffee shop and a bar are on the premises.

The **Grand Hotel** (☎ 638-3333, 888-634-7263) is the area's newest hotel with an indoor pool and spa, Tusayan's best restaurant and 'Native American Experience' which ranges from Indian-led workshops to dance performances. The bar also features cowboy and country singers. The 120 spacious rooms range from $120 to $150 in summer.

Places to Eat

Apart from the hotel restaurants, there is a steakhouse opposite the IMAX theater, a pizza restaurant, some cafés and several fast-food places.

Getting There & Away

The Grand Canyon Airport is at the south end of Tusayan. Flights to and from Las Vegas, Nevada, operate several times a day with Grand Canyon Airlines (☎ 638-2407); visit www.grandcanyonairlines.com. Scenic Airlines (☎ 702-739-1900, 638-2436, 800-634-6801), Air Vegas (☎ 800-255-7474) and others also fly here.

Many of these flights include an overflight of the Grand Canyon. In addition, tours in airplanes and helicopters starting from and returning to the Grand Canyon Airport are available from about $50 for the shortest flights. Everybody will try and sell you one. (See the 'Grand Canyon Overflights' boxed text.)

Grand Canyon Overflights

The idea of flying over the Grand Canyon at low altitude appeals to some people. However, passengers may want to consider that there have been many complaints about aircraft noise in the park and concerns about flight safety.

It is very difficult to get away from aircraft noise anywhere in the park for more than a few minutes. The NPS has estimated that visitors have to tolerate aircraft noise during 75% of daylight hours. The natural quiet of the Grand Canyon is part of its magnificence and the current levels of aircraft noise are not acceptable in a national park.

While recent efforts to limit air pollution have met with some success, eliminating noise pollution has been a losing battle. Regulations to keep aircraft above 14,500 feet in 44% of the park and above the rim in the remaining area were a step toward limiting future increases in noise, but these regulations have not always been adhered to and the number of flights has increased. Although air-tour companies are using quieter aircraft, many visitors still find aircraft noise to be annoying.

Safety is another concern. Almost every year one or more tour aircraft crash in or near the canyon. Since the growth of air-tourism in the 1980s, more national park visitors have died in these accidents than in river-running, backpacking, hiking, mule-riding, train and car accidents combined.

There are shuttles from the airport to Grand Canyon Village (see Getting There & Away in the South Rim section, above).

VALLE

Located about 25 miles south of the Grand Canyon National Park south entrance, Valle is the intersection of Hwy 64 to Williams and Hwy 180 to Flagstaff. There is no town here, just a couple of places to stay and eat, a gas station and an airport near the intersection. The **Planes of Fame** (☎ 635-1000) is an air-craft museum with several classic military and civilian aircraft in flying condition, as well as models and memorabilia. It opens daily except Thanksgiving and Christmas; admission is $5; $2 for five- to 12-year-olds. The museum is in the airport, which may offer some flight services to the Grand Canyon.

Flintstones Bedrock City (☎ 635-2600) has 60 sites ($12.70 for tents and $17 for hookups). There are coin showers and laundry, a snack bar (Bronto Burgers and Dino Dogs) and a Flintstones recreation area complete with concretosaurs. The campground is open mid-March through November.

The *Grand Canyon Inn* (☎ 635-9203) has several sections with standard motel rooms around $80 in summer. There is a restaurant, gift shop, spa and seasonal pool. The gas station and grocery store are next-door.

HUALAPAI INDIAN RESERVATION

This reservation borders many miles of the south side of the Colorado River northeast of Kingman. It contains the only road to the river within the Grand Canyon area. Back in the 1800s, when the area was being invaded by miners, the Hualapai fought hard to retain control of their lands. Today, most of the tribe works in ranching, logging or tourism. The reservation offers visitors a good opportunity to see some of the Grand Canyon area (outside the national park and away from the crowds) accompanied by guides from a tribe that originally inhabited the region.

Orientation & Information

The tribal headquarters (☎ 769-2216), PO Box 179, Peach Springs, AZ 86434, are in a small community about 50 miles northeast of Kingman or almost 40 miles northwest of Seligman on Route 66. Hualapai Central Reservations (☎ 769-2419, 888-255-9550) has information about the tribally operated lodge, campground, river-running trips and bus tours; online you'll find them at www.hualapaitours.com.

Entrance into the reservation for sightseeing, picnicking and hiking is $10 per day per person (free for children under seven). No firearms are allowed on the reservation. Camping is available for $10.25 per person per night. Fishing costs $10 per day with a catch limit of eight fish. Permits can be bought in Peach Springs at the river-running office or lodge, both easy to find as you drive through on Route 66. (There is no charge for driving through on Route 66.)

Apart from 66, there are three roads of interest through the reservation. One is the paved road to the Havasupai Reservation (see the next section). The other two are unpaved.

From Peach Springs, 22-mile, unpaved **Diamond Creek Rd** heads north to the Colorado River. With the appropriate permit, you can drive to the Colorado River – 2WD cars with good clearance can usually make it except after heavy rains when you'll need a high-clearance 4WD. This is the only place within the canyon that the river can be reached by road.

Three miles west of Peach Springs on Route 66 is unpaved Buck and Doe Rd, which leads about 50 miles to Grand Canyon West (see Things to See & Do, below). This road is entirely within the reservation. Grand Canyon West can also be reached from Kingman by heading northwest on Hwy 93 for about 26 miles, then northeast along the paved Pearce Ferry Rd (heading toward Lake Mead) for about 30 miles, and then 21 miles east along the dirt Diamond Bar Rd. (This route is 20 miles shorter than driving from Kingman to Peach Springs.)

Things to See & Do
There's little to do in Peach Springs itself apart from seeing the **tribal powwow** held in late August. The lodge has a small cultural center.

The **Grand Canyon West** area has an airstrip and tribal office where permits, bathroom facilities and soft drinks are available. A tribally operated guided bus tour goes out to the canyon rim for $32.50 ($22 for three- to 11-year-olds) and includes a barbecue lunch on the rim and plenty of local lore and information as presented by the Hualapai guide – an interesting trip. The tour goes year-round.

A $10 permit (small children are free) allows you to drive 3 miles to the **Quartermaster Viewpoint**, which has a parking area and good views of the lower Grand Canyon but no facilities. A five-minute hike on a rough trail brings you to a small bluff with better views. You won't see many people – it's a far cry from the masses thronging the (admittedly more spectacular) South Rim of the national park.

Hualapai River Running (see Hualapai Central Reservations in the Orientation & Information section, above) offers one-day **river running** trips along the lower reaches of the Colorado River from May through October for $250 per person. Day trips run Monday to Friday; two-day trips run on weekends and include riverside camping. This company uses motorized rafts guided by Hualapai Indians. Both white-water and floating is involved. Packages are also offered with rooms at the Hualapai Lodge before and after your trip. Children must be at least eight years old to participate.

Places to Stay & Eat
In Peach Springs, the tribe-operated *Huala-pai Lodge* (☎ 769-2419, 888-255-9550) has 60 motel rooms for $75 to $85 double in summer, and a *restaurant* open 6 am to 9 pm. It provides shuttles to the Grand Canyon West. Otherwise there are no hotels on the Hualapai Reservation.

The Hualapai tribe operates a basic *campground* near the end of Diamond Creek Rd by the Colorado River. The elevation here is 1900 feet, which makes it extremely hot in summer. There are restrooms and picnic tables but no drinking water; bring everything you'll need.

HAVASUPAI INDIAN RESERVATION
Centered on Havasu Canyon, carved by Havasu Creek, a southern tributary of the Colorado River, this is the traditional home of the peaceful and energetic Havasupai Indians, who now offer Grand Canyon visitors a unique look at the canyon and river.

Tribal headquarters are in Supai, which has been there for centuries – the only village within the Grand Canyon. The first European visitor was the Spanish priest Francisco Garcés in 1776. Just as in the old days, Supai can be accessed only by a steep 8-mile-long trail from the canyon rim. Below Supai, the trail leads past some of the prettiest waterfalls within the Grand Canyon.

Word has gotten out about this beautiful area. Although no roads directly connect Grand Canyon National Park's South Rim with the reservation, there are hundreds of daily visitors during the peak summer months. Nevertheless, it is much more tranquil than the South Rim.

Information
Information is available from the Havasupai Tourist Enterprise (☎ 448-2141, 800-448-2121), Supai, AZ 86435. All visitors pay an entry fee of $20; $15 in winter (November to March). The fee is valid for the length of your visit. The Supai Post Office distributes its mail by pack animals – postcards mailed from here have a special postmark to prove it. There is a small emergency clinic. Alcohol, firearms and pets aren't allowed.

Some visitors have expressed surprise that the village looks shabby, littered and unattractive. This is partly because the village is periodically flooded and partly because tribe members have a different concept of what is and isn't attractive. Come for the scenic and natural beauty and leave your urban planning ideas at home.

Things to See & Do
The 8-mile hike down to Supai is attractive, as it follows Havasu Creek and is lined with trees, but the most memorable sections are along the 4 or 5 miles of trail below the village. Here, there are four major **waterfalls** and many minor ones.

Just over a mile beyond Supai is Navajo Falls, the first of the four big falls. Next comes the 100-foot-high Havasu Falls, with a sparkling blue pool that is popular for swimming. Beyond is the campground, and the trail then passes 200-foot-high Mooney Falls, the largest in the canyon. The falls

were named after a miner who died in a terrifying climbing accident in 1880: although Mooney was roped, he was unable to extricate himself and hung there for many hours until the rope finally broke and he was killed. A very steep trail (chains provide welcome handholds) leads to the pool at the bottom, another popular swimming spot. Finally, 2½ miles farther is Beaver Falls. From there, it is a farther 4½ miles down to the Colorado River (about 8 miles below the campground).

Special Events
Tribal dances are held around Memorial Day and a Peach Festival is in August. Call Havasupai Tourist Enterprise (see Information, above) for exact dates.

Places to Stay & Eat
In Supai, the **Havasupai Lodge** (☎ 448-2111) has 24 modern rooms, all with canyon views, two double beds, air conditioning and private showers. There are no TVs or telephones – a plus for travelers wishing to get away from that stuff! Reservations are essential and should be made well in advance in the summer. Rates range from $75 to $96 for one to four people ($30 less in winter). Nearby, a small cultural center has tribal exhibits. Meals and snacks are served from 7 am to 6 pm daily at the **Village Cafe** (☎ 448-2981) near the lodge, and a general store sells food and camping fuel. Prices are high (though not prohibitive) because everything comes in by horse or helicopter.

Two miles below Supai, the **Havasupai Campground** has 400 tent sites stretching along the river between Havasu and Mooney Falls. The campground suffered disastrous flooding in 1997 and tourists were evacuated, though it was reopened soon after. There are latrines but no showers. You can swim in the river or pools, and there is a spring for drinking water, though it should be purified. Fires are not permitted, so bring a camp stove to cook. Camping fees are $10 per person ($9 in winter) and reservations (with Havasupai Tourist Enterprise) should be made because after hiking more than 10 miles in, you don't want to be turned back! The campground fills on holiday weekends and most days in summer. Don't leave gear unattended at the campground or anywhere else – thefts have occurred. There is no camping allowed elsewhere in the area.

Note that the entrance fees are in addition to the lodge or campground fees. During summer, campers outnumber villagers so don't expect much in the way of cultural interaction. To enjoy the scenery and beautiful waterfalls, a two-night trip is suggested.

Shopping
The Havasupai are noted for basketmaking and beadwork. Their crafts are sold in the lodge's souvenir shop.

Getting There & Away
Seven miles east of Peach Springs on Route 66, a signed turnoff indicates a 62-mile paved road to Hualapai Hilltop on the Havasu Canyon rim in the Havasupai Reservation. There are no services.

Hualapai Hilltop has an unguarded parking area – lock in the trunk what you aren't taking to Supai. Don't leave your valuables. From the hilltop, a trail drops steeply and then flattens out, reaching Supai after about 8 miles and a 2000-foot elevation drop. The trail continues over a half mile through the village, then a farther 2 miles to the campground.

Havasupai Tourist Enterprise can arrange horses or mules by advance reservation (call a few weeks ahead). Fees per animal are $70 from hilltop to Supai, one-way. If you want to hike down and hire a mule for the climb out, you can often arrange it when you get to Supai if you are flexible with your departure time. You can bring your own horse for a $20 trail fee – you supply feed. Mountain bikes are not allowed. Most visitors walk.

A helicopter service flies from the hilltop to Supai – this is mainly for tribal use.

CAMERON & AROUND
Cameron, a tiny community 31 miles east of the national park's eastern entrance, is on the western end of the Navajo Indian Reservation (see the Northeastern Arizona chapter). It is included here because it is on the main route from the South Rim to the North Rim of the Grand Canyon.

The historic **Cameron Trading Post**, opened in 1916 and still operating, sells museum-quality Navajo rugs and other crafts, some of which date from the turn of the 19th century and sell for many thousands of dollars. Even if you're not in the market for the finest-quality rugs, it's worth stopping in just to see the attractive building and the beautifully displayed pieces, including some pre-European pots and items from several other tribes. The trading post sits scenically on the south side of the Little Colorado River. Next-door is a motel, restaurant, RV park, grocery store, post office and a gift shop selling a huge variety of crafts and souvenirs at affordable prices.

About 10 miles west of Cameron on the way to the Grand Canyon is the **Little Colorado River Gorge Navajo Tribal Park** with a scenic overlook – it's worth a stop. Along the road are numerous stalls set up by Navajo families selling arts and crafts.

Right at the corner of Hwys 64 and 89 is the **Cameron Visitor Center**, open daily in summer and open erratically out of season. It has information about Navajo land as well as the Grand Canyon.

Places to Stay & Eat
The **Cameron Trading Post & Motel** (☎ 679-2231, 800-338-7385) has more than 60 pleasant Southwestern-style rooms, many with balconies, for about $80 and a handful of suites with separate living quarters for $145 to $175. In summer it's difficult to get a room without a reservation and they don't take credit cards, so book ahead and mail them a check. Ask about discounts in winter. There are also **RV sites** with hookups for $16, but no tent sites or public showers. A **restaurant and café** serves decent meals and snacks but no alcohol (reservation land, remember?).

Eight miles south along Hwy 89 is the even smaller community of **Gray Mountain** where you'll find a gas station, small store and the **Anasazi Inn** (☎ 679-2214), with a restaurant and several dozen motel rooms around $70 in summer.

The Arizona Strip

Traditionally and geographically, this area north of the Grand Canyon has closer ties with Mormon Utah than with Arizona. The Arizona Strip is wild, large, poorly roaded, a long way from Salt Lake City and remains one of the last holdouts of the 19th-century practice of polygamy. The places described below are on the few routes from the South Rim of the Grand Canyon to the North Rim and beyond into Utah.

MARBLE CANYON & LEES FERRY AREA

Hwy 89 splits a few miles before crossing the Colorado River, with Hwy 89 heading northeast to Page and then swinging west to Kanab, Utah, and Hwy 89A taking a shorter route to Kanab through the Arizona Strip. Hwy 89A crosses the Navajo Bridge over the Colorado at Marble Canyon. This is the only road bridge into the Arizona Strip from the south and the only one on the Colorado River between Glen Canyon Dam and Hoover Dam in Nevada. Motorists use a new bridge; the original bridge was opened in 1929 and is now closed to vehicles, though you can park your car and walk across the old bridge, staring down onto the river almost 500 feet below. The bridge marks the southwestern end of the Glen Canyon National Recreation Area (GCNRA), described later in this chapter. At the west end is the Navajo Bridge Interpretive Center, run by the GCNRA and open April through October. Almost immediately after the bridge, a side road to the right leads 6 miles to Lees Ferry, historically the only crossing point of the river for many miles and today the major put-in spot for river runners making the exciting descent through the Grand Canyon.

Lees Ferry is named after John D Lee, who established the Lonely Dell Ranch and primitive raft ferry here in 1872. Later, Lee was executed for his part in the Mountain Meadows Massacre (see Around St George in the Southwestern Utah chapter). The ferry operated until the Navajo Bridge was opened in 1929. Some of the historic ranch buildings near Lees Ferry can still be seen. The GCNRA has a ranger station (☎ 355-2234) here, and a booklet and map describing the ranch, ferry and area's history is available. Less than a mile southwest of Lees Ferry is the mouth of the spectacular Paria River Canyon (see the boxed text, 'Paria Canyon–Vermilion Cliffs Wilderness Area' in the Southwestern Utah chapter).

In the smooth waters of the Colorado, below the Glen Canyon Dam, the ecosystem has changed from the tumultuous rapids of pre-dam years. The result has been favorable for fly-fishers, and the waters provide some of the country's most reliable and sought-after year-round fly fishing serviced by several nearby fishing lodges. Approximate rates for a full guided day of fly-fishing range from about $200 (one angler, walking and wading) to $400 (three anglers, river boat). March and April are the busiest months.

Places to Stay & Eat
The GCNRA runs the **Lees Ferry Campground** at Lees Ferry, with 54 sites for $10. There is drinking water, toilets and a nearby boat ramp but no showers or RV hookups. Public coin showers ($2.50) are at the Marble Canyon Lodge.

Marble Canyon Lodge (☎ 355-2225, 800-726-1789), on Hwy 89A a half-mile west of Navajo Bridge, has 45 rooms for $58/68 single/double (one bed) or $74 (two beds). Eight apartments sleeping eight are $145. A restaurant is open 6 am to 9 pm, and there is a coin laundry, store, bar and fly shop. Guide service information (☎ 355-2245, 800-533-7339) is at www.mcg-leesferry.com.

Lees Ferry Lodge (☎ 355-2231, 355-2230), on Hwy 89A 3 miles west of Navajo Bridge, has 12 rooms at $54 a double. There is a restaurant and bar (with 135 types of beer!), and a fishing tackle shop. Visit www.ambassadorguides.com for guide service (☎ 800-256-7596) details.

Cliff Dwellers Lodge (☎ 355-2228, 800-433-2543) is under the Vermilion Cliffs, 8½ miles west of the Navajo Bridge. Twenty motel rooms (no TV or phone) rent for about $70 a double in summer. There is a restaurant, bar, store and gas. For nearby angling services (☎ 355-2261, 800-962-9755) go to www.leesferry.com.

JACOB LAKE AREA
Orientation & Information

Hwy 89A intersects with Hwy 67 at the small community of Jacob Lake, 41 miles west of Marble Canyon. Hwy 67 heads south to the North Rim of Grand Canyon National Park, 44 miles away, but is closed December 1 to May 15. If a major snowstorm comes early, the road closes in November or even late October. Jacob Lake's high elevation (7921 feet) explains the long snow season. Hwy 89A remains open year-round, but winter travelers should carry chains or have 4WD.

A USFS visitor center (☎ 643-7298) in Jacob Lake, on Alt Hwy 89 near the intersection, has information, displays and interpretive programs on the Kaibab National Forest. The district headquarters are in Fredonia.

House Rock Wildlife Area

About 17 miles east of Jacob Lake along Hwy 89A, a signed turnoff to the south indicates unpaved USFS Rd 8910, which goes another 17 miles to this wildlife area on Kaibab National Forest land. House Rock Wildlife Area is known for a wild herd of buffalo, which you may be able to see with any luck. Remember, however, the wildlife area covers more than 100 sq miles so your sightings are likely to be distant. Continuing past the ranch about another 10 miles will bring you to a couple of remote viewpoints overlooking the Marble Canyon area of the Grand Canyon National Park. Condors have been sighted here. (See the boxed text 'Condors at Vermilion Cliffs.') This road is closed by snow during the long winter.

Condors at Vermilion Cliffs

The spectacular Vermilion Cliffs, which stretch along the north side of Hwy 89A for most of the way from Marble Canyon to Jacob Lake, were chosen as one of the first release sites for California condors, members of the vulture family. These endangered birds are magnificent – with a wingspan of 10 feet and weighing as much as 24lb, they are the largest land birds in North America. Before the arrival of Europeans, condors ranged throughout much of North America, but by the early 19th century they were found only west of the Rockies. The last confirmed sighting in Arizona was in 1924. By the 1980s, condors were extinct in the wild, but a small breeding population in the Los Angeles Zoo gave ornithologists hope that the birds could be reintroduced into the wild.

The first reintroduction was in Southern California, but this was not very successful because the release sites, though remote, were still too close to major metropolises. Condors require areas that are hundreds of miles from large cities and that provide mountain ridges or cliffs from which they can launch themselves for soaring flights. (The birds can fly as fast as 50mph under the right conditions.) The birds' preferred nesting areas are caves in inaccessible cliffs or mountains. The Vermilion Cliffs seem to meet these requirements, and six condors were initially released here in December 1996, with more releases in 1997 swelling the number to about 20. A few more have been released since then. Inevitably, some condors have not survived; one was reportedly killed by a golden eagle and another died in a clash with power lines. Others, however, appear to be thriving and there have been recent sightings from both the Grand Canyon and Lake Powell. Keep your eyes open!

Exciting news came in 2001 when a pair nested and an egg was laid in the wild. Unfortunately, the egg was damaged and the chick did not hatch, but it is an encouraging step toward the return of the condor.

ARIZONA

Places to Stay & Eat

Free dispersed *camping* in the Kaibab National Forest is permitted as long as you are more than a quarter-mile from the paved highway – several unpaved forest roads give access.

Jacob Lake Campground (☎ 643-7395) is near the USFS visitor center on Hwy 89A. More than 50 sites are $10 on a first-come, first-served basis, with limited free camping in winter. There is water but no showers or hookups. *De Motte Campground* is about 25 miles south on Hwy 67 and has 22 similar $10 sites, open mid-May through October. Both are USFS campgrounds.

Kaibab Lodge Camper Village (☎ 643-7804), off Hwy 67 a mile south of Hwy 89A, has more than 100 sites from $12 (tents) to $23 (hookups) open mid-May through October. There is water but no showers.

Jacob Lake Inn (☎ 643-7232) has about 50 simple motel rooms and cabins for about $75 to $98 double ($125 for family units sleeping six) in summer. At the junction of Hwy 89A and Hwy 67, it has a restaurant and store; visit www.jacoblake.com. The *Kaibab Lodge (☎ 638-2389 in season, ☎ 526-0924, 800-525-0924 year-round),* on Hwy 67, 25 miles south of Jacob Lake, is open when the road is open. Rooms with private bath in duplex cabins rent from $80 for a double to $120 for rooms that sleep five. A restaurant serves breakfast and dinner.

GRAND CANYON NATIONAL PARK – NORTH RIM

The differences between the North and South Rims of the Grand Canyon are elevation and accessibility. The North Rim exceeds 8000 feet above sea level with some points reaching over 8800 feet. Winters are colder, the climate is wetter and the spruce-fir forest above the rim is much thicker than the forests of the South Rim. There is only one road in, so visitors must backtrack more than 60 miles after their visit. Winter snows close the road to car traffic from December 1 (earlier in snowy years) until mid-May.

Because it's such a long drive from any major city or airport, only 10% of Grand Canyon visitors come to the North Rim. But the views here are spectacular. North Rim visitors are drawn by the lack of huge crowds and the desire for a more peaceful, if more spartan, experience of the canyon's majesty.

Orientation & Information

Forty-four miles from Jacob Lake is **Bright Angel Point**, which has the main visitors' services at the North Rim. Almost 30 miles of paved roads lead to various other overlooks. The park headquarters are at the South Rim. See the South Rim section for general information, entrance fees and backcountry permits. The park's automated telephone system (☎ 638-7888) has both South and North Rim information.

The North Rim Visitor Center (☎ 638-7864) is in the Grand Canyon Lodge (the North Rim's only hotel) and is open 8 am to 8 pm May 15 through October 15. The usual NPS activities and information are available. The Backcountry Office (for backpackers) is in the ranger station near the campground, 1½ miles north of the visitor center/lodge. Other services available at the North Rim (in season) are a restaurant, gas station, post office, bookstore, general store, coin laundry and showers, medical clinic and tours. After October 15, all services are closed except the campground, which remains open weather permitting. After December 1, everything is closed.

Summer temperatures are about 10°F lower than on the South Rim. Winter snowfall is heaviest from late December to early March, when overnight temperatures normally fall into the teens and sometimes below 10°F, though very few people visit then.

During winter, you can ski in and, with a backcountry camping permit, camp. It takes about three days to ski in from where the road is closed, so this journey is for adventurous and highly experienced winter campers/skiers. Call the Backcountry Office for details.

North Rim Drives

The drive on Hwy 67 through the Kaibab Plateau to Bright Angel Point takes you through thick forest. There are excellent canyon views from the point, but to reach other overlooks you need to drive north for almost 3 miles and take the signed turn east to **Point Imperial** and **Cape Royal**. It is 9 miles to Point Imperial, which is, at a lofty 8803 feet, the highest overlook in the entire park and has stunning views.

Backtrack about 4 miles from Point Imperial and then drive 15 miles south to Cape Royal where there are more great views and some short hiking trails.

With 4WD and high clearance, you can take unpaved roads to several other outlooks along the North Rim. These roads may be closed by bad weather or other factors – information is available from any ranger or the park information line. Many of these roads require leaving the park, driving through USFS or BLM lands, then re-entering the park.

One of the most spectacular of these remote overlooks is the **Toroweap Overlook** at **Tuweep**, far to the west of the main park facilities. An unpaved road, usually passable to cars, leaves Hwy 389 from 9 miles west of Fredonia and heads 55 miles to the Tuweep Ranger Station, which is staffed year-round. An alternative route is a 90-mile dirt road from St George, Utah. It is five more miles from Tuweep to the Toroweap Overlook, where there is *primitive camping* but no water or other facilities – you must be totally self-sufficient.

Hiking & Backpacking

The most popular quick hike is the paved half-mile trail from the Grand Canyon Lodge south to the extreme tip of **Bright Angel Point**, which offers great views at sunset. The 1½-mile **Transept Trail** goes north from the lodge through forest to the North Rim Campground, where there are also rim views. Other trails in the area are rugged and relatively poorly maintained. Before embarking on them, consult with a North Rim ranger.

The **North Kaibab Trail** plunges down to Phantom Ranch at the Colorado River, 5750 feet below and 14 miles away. This is the only maintained rim-to-river trail from

the North Rim and it connects with trails to the South Rim. The first 4.7 miles are the steepest, dropping well over 3000 feet to **Roaring Springs** – a popular all-day hike and mule-ride destination. Drinking water is available at Roaring Springs from May to September only. If you prefer a shorter day hike below the rim, you can walk just three-quarters of a mile down to **Coconino Overlook** or a mile to the **Supai Tunnel**, 1400 feet below the rim, to get a flavor of steep inner-canyon hiking.

Hikers wishing to continue to the river will normally camp. **Cottonwood Campground** is 7 miles and 4200 feet below the rim and is the only campground between the North Rim and the river. Here, there are 14 backcountry campsites (available by permit only), drinking water from May through September and a ranger station. About 1½ miles below the campground a short side trail leads to pretty **Ribbon Falls**, a popular bathing spot but with no camping. Phantom Ranch Lodge and the Bright Angel Campground are 7 and 7½ miles below Cottonwood (see the South Rim section).

Because it is about twice as far from the North Rim to the river as from the South Rim, rangers suggest three nights as a minimum to enjoy a rim-to-river and return hike, staying at Cottonwood on the first and third nights and Bright Angel on the second. Fit and experienced hikers could enjoy a two-night trip, staying at Cottonwood both nights and hiking down to the river and back to Cottonwood on the second day. Faster trips, while technically feasible, would be an endurance slog and not much fun.

Hiking from North to South Rim requires a shuttle to get you back (see Getting Around in the South Rim section for details).

Backcountry Permits In the winter, the trails of the North Rim are regarded as backcountry-use areas, and snow can accumulate to five feet at the rim. Though the North Rim Campground (see Places to Stay, below) is closed in winter, it is available for backcountry use. However, there are only two ways to get to the campground in winter – either hike from the South Rim up to the North Rim via the North Kaibab Trail or cross-country ski 52 miles from Jacob Lake, a route that takes three days.

Permits for all backcountry campgrounds must be applied for as far in advance as possible from the Backcountry Office (☎ 638-7875, 1 to 5 pm Monday to Friday), PO Box 129, Grand Canyon, AZ 86023, (see the South Rim section for details). If you don't have a permit, get on the waiting list at the Backcountry Office (open 8 am to noon and 1 to 5 pm daily in season) in the North Rim ranger station near the campground as soon as you arrive. Your chances of getting a Cottonwood or Bright Angel Campground permit for the next day are slim; however, if you can wait two to four days, you'll probably get one. The ranger station can advise you of other, much more remote, backcountry campgrounds, most of which require a long drive on dirt roads followed by a hike.

A hikers' shuttle from the lodge to the Bright Angel trailhead is $5 for the first hiker and $2 for each additional hiker in your group. Ask at the lodge for tickets. Shuttles are available from 6 am to 8 pm.

Bicycling
Mountain bikes are allowed on all paved roads and some unpaved roads on the North Rim. No wheeled vehicles are allowed on hiking trails.

Organized Tours
In season, daily three-hour narrated tours to Point Imperial and Cape Royal leave from the lodge and cost $24 ($12 for four- to 12-year-olds). A schedule is posted in the lobby.

Trail Rides (☎ 638-9875 in season, ☎ 435-679-8665 otherwise) offers rides for $15 for an hour (minimum age is six), $40 for a half-day (minimum age is eight) and $95 for an all-day tour into the Grand Canyon, including lunch (minimum age is 12). Advance reservations are recommended, or stop by their desk (open 7 am to 7 pm) in the Grand Lodge to see what is available. Mule rides

are not available to the Colorado River except from the South Rim.

Places to Stay & Eat
Backcountry camping requires a permit (see Hiking & Backpacking, above).

The only other place to camp is *North Rim Campground*, 1½ miles north of the Grand Canyon Lodge, with 82 sites for $14 each. There is water, a store, snack bar and coin-operated showers and laundry, but no hookups. Make reservations (☎ 301-722-1257, 800-365-2267) up to five months in advance. Without a reservation, show up before 10 am and hope for the best.

The historic *Grand Canyon Lodge* (Amfac; ☎ 303-297-2757 for reservations) is usually full and reservations should be made as far in advance as possible. There are about 200 units: both motel rooms and a variety of rustic and modern cabins sleeping up to five people. All have private bath; only a few cabins have canyon views. Rates range from $80 to $113 double.

The lodge has a *snack bar and restaurant* open for all meals, but dinner reservations are required and breakfast reservations are advised in the attractive restaurant.

A *general store* by the campground sells food and camping supplies.

Getting There & Away
There is no public transport. A North to South Rim shuttle (☎ 638-2820) leaves daily at 7 am for $60 one-way or $100 roundtrip and takes five hours.

FREDONIA
☎ 928 • pop 1036 • elevation 4671 feet
From Jacob Lake, Hwy 89A drops 3250 feet in 30 miles to Fredonia, which is much warmer. Founded by Mormons in 1885, Fredonia is the main town in the Arizona Strip. The larger Kanab, 7 miles north in Utah, has much better developed tourist facilities, but Fredonia has information about the Kaibab National Forest.

Information
The town offices and chamber of commerce (☎ 643-7241) are at 130 N Main

(Hwy 89). Other services include the Kaibab National Forest District Headquarters (☎ 643-7395), 430 S Main; post office (☎ 643-7122), 85 N Main; and the police (☎ 643-7108), 116 N Main.

Places to Stay & Eat
A few small places with basic rooms in the $30s include *Blue Sage Motel (☎ 643-7125, 330 S Main)*, and *Ship Rock Motel (☎ 643-7355, 337 S Main)*.

The *Grand Canyon Motel (☎ 643-7646, 175 S Main)* has stone cabins with kitchenettes in some units. The *Crazy Jug Motel (☎ 643-7752, 465 S Main)* charges about $50 and has a restaurant.

Nedra's Cafe (☎ 643-7591, 165 N Main) serves Mexican and American food, Navajo tacos and breakfast from Monday to Saturday; closed some days in winter.

Two miles north of town, *Travelers Inn Restaurant & Lounge (☎ 643-7402, 2631 N Hwy 89A)* serves American dinner Monday to Saturday in summer and Friday and Saturday the rest of the year.

AROUND FREDONIA
Pipe Spring National Monument
Ancient Indians and Mormon pioneers knew about this permanent spring in the arid Arizona Strip. Ranching began here in 1863 and a fort named **Winsor Castle** was built in 1870 to protect the ranchers from Indian attacks. In 1923, the 40-acre ranch was bought by the NPS as a historical monument documenting pioneer and Indian life and interactions on the Western frontier.

Today, visitors can learn about frontier life by touring the well-preserved ranch buildings and fort, examining historic exhibits and attending cultural demonstrations (summer only) by rangers and volunteers. Tours of Winsor Castle are offered every half-hour (last tour at 4 pm) and a short video is shown on request at the visitor center.

A visitor center (☎ 643-7105) with a bookstore is open 8 am to 5 pm daily except New Year's Day, Thanksgiving and Christmas. Admission is $3 for adults, or by pass.

The monument is 14 miles west of Fredonia on Hwy 389. Further information is available from the superintendent, HC65, Box 5, Fredonia, AZ 86022.

Kaibab-Paiute Indian Reservation
Fewer than 200 Paiutes live in this reservation, which completely surrounds the Pipe Spring National Monument. The tribally operated *campground (☎ 643-7245)* is a half-mile east of Pipe Spring. The remote campground offers showers, RV hookups for $10 and tent sites for $5.

Kanab Canyon
Marked on most maps as Kanab Creek, this is actually the largest canyon leading to the Colorado River's north side. In places, Kanab Canyon is 3500 feet deep and it effectively splits the relatively developed eastern part of the Arizona Strip from the remote western part.

From Fredonia, Kanab Canyon goes south for 60 miles to the Grand Canyon. Adventurous canyoneers enjoy hiking this route, which is described in John Annerino's useful *Adventuring in Arizona*. Permits are required in some stretches. Drivers of high-clearance vehicles can drive through the Kaibab National Forest to Hack Canyon and Jumpup Canyon, both of which are popular entry points into the lower part of Kanab Canyon.

The Northwest Corner
This is the most remote part of the state. Much of it is BLM land managed by offices in Kanab and St George, Utah. A few ranches and mines are surrounded by wilderness areas with absolutely no development, reachable by a network of dirt roads. To explore this area, a reliable high-clearance vehicle and plenty of water and food are essential. If you break down, you might not see another car for days. Consult with the BLM before you go.

The 'best' unpaved roads are the ones heading to Tuweep Ranger Station and Toroweap Overlook Campground (see North Rim Drives, above).

ARIZONA

Lake Powell Area

The next major canyon system on the Colorado River northeast of the Grand Canyon is (was) Glen Canyon. Called 'The Canyon That No One Knew,' in the 1950s it was the heart of the largest roadless area in the continental USA. A few old-time river runners and canyoneers tell of a canyon that rivaled the Grand Canyon for scenic grandeur and was full of ancestral Indian sites, but most people hadn't even heard of this remote wilderness area when work began on the Glen Canyon Dam in 1956.

Conservationists fought hard against the construction of the dam, realizing not only that the beautiful canyon would be destroyed, but also that the character of the Southwest would change dramatically. Seven years later, the dam was finished, and Glen Canyon slowly began filling up to become the second largest artificial reservoir in the country, helping fuel the uncurbed population growth of the desert. The reservoir is Lake Powell.

PAGE

☎ 928 • pop 6809 • elevation 4300 feet

Dam construction in the late 1950s gave birth to this new town in the high desert. Once a drab construction town, Page is now the largest Arizonan town in the huge area north of I-40 and is a regional center for southeastern Utah as well. Tourists value Page not only as a convenient stopping place between the two states but also for the recreation opportunities afforded by Lake Powell (7 miles from the town center). The tourism industry is experiencing a boom and hotel rooms are over-priced and booked up in summer.

Information

The chamber of commerce (☎ 645-2741, 888-261-7243), 644 N Navajo Dr, is open from 8:30 am to 5 pm Monday to Friday, with extended hours and weekend openings in spring, summer and fall; visit www.pagelakepowellchamber.org. The Powell Museum (see below) has visitor information and will make motel and tour reservations. Numerous kiosks around town are stocked with useful brochures. A useful website is www.powellguide.com.

Services include the library (☎ 645-5800), 4795 Lake Powell Blvd; post office (☎ 645-2571), 44 6th Ave; hospital (☎ 645-2424), at Vista Ave and N Navajo Dr; and the police (☎ 645-2463), 547 Vista Ave.

Things to See & Do

The small **Powell Museum** (☎ 645-9496, 888-5873), 6 N Lake Powell Blvd, has exhibits pertaining to Colorado River explorer John Wesley Powell, changing local art shows from April to October as well as regional information. Hours (subject to change) are 8:30 am to 5:30 pm Monday through Saturday; closed mid-December through mid-February. Admission is $1 or 50¢ for children five to 14.
website: www.powellmuseum.org

Navajo Village: A Living Museum (☎ 660-0304), 531 Haul Rd, is a collection of Navajo hogans and other buildings featuring demonstrations of the Navajo way of life – cooking, weaving, dancing, jewelry work, singing and storytelling. Guided tours of a Navajo home are offered 9 am to 3 pm Monday to Saturday; admission is $10, $5 for six- to 13-year olds, and $25 for a family. The Navajo Village also arranges a four-hour 'Evening with the Navajo' featuring detailed presentations of many facets of their lives, including a Navajo dinner. Rates are $50, $35 for children or $135 for families. Shorter, cheaper presentations are also offered. Tickets and reservations are available at the chamber of commerce or Powell Museum.

Several **trading posts** offer first-class Native American art, craft and jewelry. An excellent place for seeing both new and old Navajo crafts, including some exceptional old pawn jewelry and fabulous new kachina dolls for serious collectors, is Blair's Dinnebito Trading Post (☎ 645-3008), 626 N Navajo Dr. Family patriarch, Elijah Blair, has been trading on the reservation for over half a century and he and his family know all there is to know about traditional reservation crafts. Ask to see their private family

PAGE

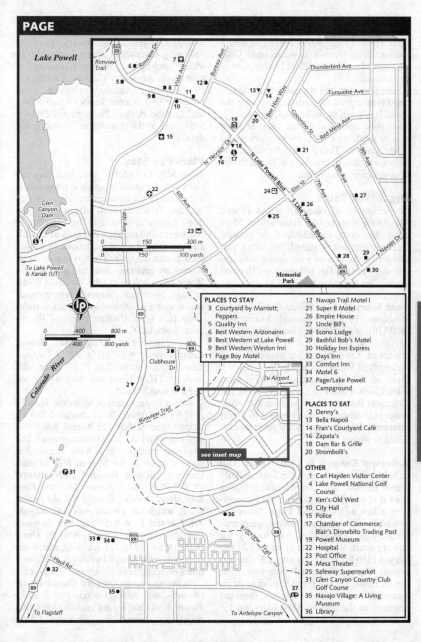

Lake Powell

Rimview Trail

Glen Canyon Dam

To Lake Powell & Kanab (UT)

Colorado River

Clubhouse Dr

To Airport

Rimview Trail

To Flagstaff

Haul Rd

To Antelope Canyon

Memorial Park

see inset map

PLACES TO STAY
3 Courtyard by Marriott;
   Peppers
5 Quality Inn
6 Best Western Arizonainn
8 Best Western at Lake Powell
9 Best Western Weston Inn
11 Page Boy Motel
12 Navajo Trail Motel I
21 Super 8 Motel
26 Empire House
27 Uncle Bill's
28 Econo Lodge
29 Bashful Bob's Motel
30 Holiday Inn Express
32 Days Inn
33 Comfort Inn
34 Motel 6
37 Page/Lake Powell
   Campground

PLACES TO EAT
2 Denny's
13 Bella Napoli
14 Fran's Courtyard Café
16 Zapata's
18 Dam Bar & Grille
20 Strombolli's

OTHER
1 Carl Hayden Visitor Center
4 Lake Powell National Golf
   Course
7 Ken's Old West
10 City Hall
15 Police
17 Chamber of Commerce;
   Blair's Dinnebito Trading Post
19 Powell Museum
22 Hospital
23 Post Office
24 Mesa Theater
25 Safeway Supermarket
31 Glen Canyon Country Club
   Golf Course
35 Navajo Village: A Living
   Museum
36 Library

ARIZONA

collection; get information at www
.blairstradingpost.com. Also stop by the Big
Lake Trading Post (☎ 645-2404), just over a
mile south on Hwy 89, to see its small Diné
Bikeyah Museum of ancient Native American artifacts.

The **Rimview Trail** is a municipally developed 8-mile trail that circumnavigates the
town. It is open to walkers, joggers and cyclists (who must stay on the trail) and is a
mix of sand, slick rock, rocky washes and
other terrain. There are several access
points – pick up a brochure at the chamber
of commerce or museum.

Organized Tours

The chamber of commerce and Powell
Museum will make tour reservations. Most
offer discounts for children or groups.
Reservations are required, but often you
can get on the tour of your choice with just
one day's notice. The following are the best
known, but there are others.

Boat Tours Half- or full-day boat tours to
Rainbow Bridge National Monument
($80/110), cruises on Wahweap Bay for 1½
or more hours ($25 to $75) and other
cruises on Lake Powell are available from
Aramark at Wahweap Marina (see below).
Half- or full-day float trips ($59/79) from
Glen Canyon Dam to Lees Ferry along the
Colorado River are also offered. No white
water is involved. Children ages 3 to 12 get
discounts. Tour schedules are severely curtailed in winter.

Antelope Canyon & Land Tours Also
called Corkscrew Canyon, this spectacularly
scenic narrow 'slot' canyon (much higher
than it is wide) is on the Navajo Reservation a few miles east of Page. Tours are
available into the upper canyon, accompanied by Navajo guides. Ask locally for
current tours, which start at about $20 per
person ($10 for children) plus a $5 Navajo
permit. Cheaper tours will drop you off at
the entrance, but not provide guiding or information service. It is over a mile from the
entrance to the canyon. Most tours last 1½
hours.

Various other canyons and scenic areas
can be visited. Some tours are specifically
designed for photographers. Try any of the
following: Overland Canyon Tours (☎ 680-
4072), online at www.overlandcanyon
tours.com; Antelope Canyon Adventures
(☎ 645-5501); Antelope Canyon Tours
(☎ 645-8579); Scenic Tours (☎ 645-5594);
and Jackson Bridges Photography (☎ 645-
5451). Ask at the chamber of commerce for
details.

Places to Stay

From May to October, very high summer
rates apply, demand is high and reservations
are strongly recommended, especially in
August. Arrive by early afternoon if you
don't have a reservation. The chamber of
commerce and museum can help with B&B
and last-minute accommodations. In winter,
some hotels charge half or less or may close.
Rooms are generally clean and modern – no
Route 66 motels or creaky Victorian hotels
in Page. Note that there are campgrounds
and a motel at Wahweap Marina, 5 miles
away (see Glen Canyon National Recreation Area, later).

For camping, the ***Page/Lake Powell
Campground*** (☎ 645-3374, 849 S Copper-
mine Rd) has more than 70 RV sites, with
hookups ($22). There are showers, a pool,
spa and coin laundry.

As for budget choices, when the ***Motel 6***
(637 S Lake Powell Blvd) charges $76 for a
double room in July and August, you know
you won't find any bargains in summer. The
cheapest motels, which have simple but
clean doubles in the $50s or $60s in midsummer, include ***Bashful Bob's Motel***
(☎ 645-3919, 750 S Navajo Dr), the ***Page
Boy Motel*** (☎ 645-2416, 150 N Lake Powell
Blvd), which has a small pool, and ***Navajo
Trail Motel I*** (☎ 645-9508, 800 Bureau).
Call ahead for all of these! Also try ***Uncle
Bill's*** (☎ 645-1224, 115 8th Ave), which has
12 rooms with shared bathroom facilities –
other budget places are also on this block.

In the mid-range category, ***Empire House***
(☎ 645-2406, 800-551-9005, 100 S Lake
Powell Blvd) has a pool and 70 nice motel
rooms for about $75 – fair value. ***Chain***

La Casa Cordova (1848), at the Tucson Museum of Art, is believed to be Tucson's oldest house.

Sculpture at the public library, Tucson

Baptistery of the Mission San Xavier del Bac

Gold King mining ghost town near Jerome, AZ

OK Corral, Tombstone, AZ

'Standin' on the corner in Winslow, Arizona…'

motels with rooms under $100 include the Econo Lodge and Super 8.

All the top end places are comfortable *chain motels* – not luxurious but not under $100 either. These include three Best Westerns, a Quality Inn and a Comfort Inn, a Days Inn, a Holiday Inn Express and a Courtyard by Marriott, considered the town's best hotel and with a golf course. All boast pools, and most have restaurants or at least breakfast areas. Some have balconies – the Best Western Arizonainn and the Quality Inn even have distant lake views.

Places to Eat
For an early breakfast, try the hotel restaurants, which serve mainly American food. *Peppers* in the Marriott is especially good and also features Southwestern food.

Fran's Courtyard Café (☎ 645-6906, 809 N Navajo Dr) features baked goods, cappuccinos and coffees, and freshly made sandwiches and salads. It opens at 6 am and may stay open for dinner in summer.

Strombolli's (☎ 645-2605, 711 N Navajo Drive), serves pizza and other Italian specialties and is popular because of its large outdoor deck and cheap dinners, which are advertised as 'under $10.' More upscale Italian dining in a more intimate atmosphere is found at *Bella Napoli* (☎ 645-2706, 810 N Navajo Dr) with dinners only in the $8 to $18 range.

Page's 'Wild West' steak house is *Ken's Old West* (☎ 645-5160, 718 Vista Ave), open for meaty dinners priced from $10 to $20. The *Dam Bar & Grille* (☎ 645-2161, 644 N Navajo Dr) serves good steaks and Italian food in dam modern surroundings that remind you why Page is here. Lunch and dinners are served and it has sports TV and live music on weekends. *Zapata's* (☎ 645-9006, 615 N Navajo Dr) does decent Mexican meals.

Entertainment
Movies are shown at the *Mesa Theater* (☎ 645-9565, 42 S Lake Powell Blvd).

Ken's Old West features both live and recorded country & western music and dancing every night except Sunday in the summer and a few times a week during other seasons.

Getting There & Around
Air services to Page Airport may be available in summer but not year-round. Great Lakes Aviation has flown to Phoenix, Denver and Moab in the past. There are no regular bus services, though van shuttles to Flagstaff may run in summer. Contact the chamber of commerce for details.

Avis (☎ 645-2024) rents cars at the Page Airport. Rates are expensive and you can save money by renting in Flagstaff or Phoenix.

GLEN CANYON NATIONAL RECREATION AREA
When the Glen Canyon Dam was finished in 1963, the Colorado River and its tributaries (especially the San Juan River) began backing up for 186 miles. It took until 1980 to fill the artificial Lake Powell, flooding the canyon to a depth of 560 feet at the dam and creating almost 2000 miles of shoreline. The 1933-sq-mile Glen Canyon National Recreation Area (GCNRA) was established in 1972, primarily emphasizing activities on the lake, which accounts for 13% of the total area. The remainder is many square miles of remote backcountry, which can be explored on foot or by a few roads north of the confluence of the Colorado and San Juan Rivers.

Information
The Carl Hayden Visitor Center (☎ 608-6404) is at the dam, 2 miles north of Page (the only town close to the GCNRA). Hours are 8 am to 7 pm May through September and 8 am to 5 pm at other times. Most of the GCNRA is in Utah, but it is treated as a whole here. Entrance to the area costs $10 per vehicle or $3 per individual and is valid for up to seven days. Boats are $10 for up to seven days or $20 a year. All passes are accepted. Up-to-date information is available in the free newspaper *Reflections*, available on arrival.

Five miles north of the visitor center is Wahweap Marina, the largest marina on Lake Powell. It offers complete visitors'

ARIZONA

GLEN CANYON NATIONAL RECREATION AREA

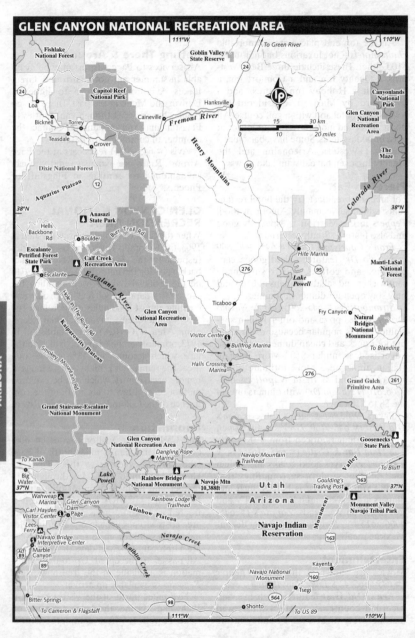

services. Four more marinas are scattered along the shores of Lake Powell in Utah. All marinas have an NPS ranger station and there's a smaller visitor center at Bullfrog Marina. Details of services available in each marina are described under individual marina headings below. Aramark (☎ 602-331-5200, 800-528-6154) is the concessionaire for houseboats, tours and lodges at the lake; visit www.visitlakepowell.com.

The GCNRA also operates a ranger station at Lees Ferry and an interpretive center at Navajo Bridge on Hwy 89A (see Marble Canyon & Lees Ferry Area, earlier in this chapter).

Further information is available from the Superintendent (☎ 608-6200), GCNRA, PO Box 1507, Page, AZ 86040.

Climate & When to Go The area is open year-round. The water-level elevation of 3700 feet makes the GCNRA cooler than Lake Mead and other downstream recreation areas, but summer temperatures can still rise to more than 100°F on some days. Combined with reflections off the water and canyon walls, the heat can be quite stultifying until you get acclimatized. Average summer maximum temperatures are in the 90°s F, with water temperatures ranging from 70°F to 80°F from June to September. Overnight temperatures drop into the 70°s F, making sleeping comfortable. The humidity is low year-round and there is little rainfall.

Summer is the most popular season with the highest rates for boat rentals and motel rooms. The areas around the marinas are a noisy zoo of boat engines, yahoos on jet skis and inexperienced sailors, all bent on getting their money's worth after paying $200 or $300 for a day of fast boat rental. It'll take a few hours to navigate beyond this, but it makes a huge difference.

Spring can be very windy, and cold water temperatures preclude swimming or water-skiing without a wet suit – in May the water averages a brisk 64°F. Fall water temperatures average 69°F in October; the lowest average is 46°F in February.

Hikers and backpackers will find April to June and September to October the most

pleasant months. In winter, overnight temperatures often fall into the 20°s F but rise into the 40°s F during the day in December and January, the coldest months.

Water levels fluctuate depending on season and water use. The highest levels are in late spring and early summer, when you can boat just a little farther into some of the side canyons.

Books & Maps The *Boater's Guide to Lake Powell,* by Michael R Kelsey, is for boaters interested in taking side hikes from the shore, including information about shore camping for people using small boats. *Lake Powell and Its 96 Canyons: Boating and Exploring Map* by Stan Jones is an annotated map with plenty of other useful information.

Camping Regulations Rising and falling water levels have caused buried human waste to contaminate the lake and make some areas unsafe for swimming. These areas are closed and marked with yellow buoys and signs. Anyone camping within a quarter-mile of the lake must use a portable toilet. Rangers can tell you which beaches have toilets. If you camp on a beach without a toilet, you can rent portable ones from the marinas. Human waste must be disposed of in designated dump stations; sewage dumping is illegal. There are eight floating toilets on the lake.

Dangers & Annoyances Several people drown every year in boating, swimming or diving accidents, many of which are alcohol related. Lake Powell has no lifeguards, but the lake is patrolled by park rangers. Children under 12 are required by law to wear life jackets when on a boat, while everyone in a boat, regardless of age, is required to have a preserver immediately accessible (not stowed). Use common sense.

In recent years, several deaths have been attributed to carbon monoxide emitted by boat engines and gathering under the platforms overhanging the water from most boats. This gas is odorless and can result in swift unconsciousness of swimmers near the boat. Check with park authorities or rental agencies for information about this potentially lethal hazard.

Glen Canyon Dam

Right next to the Carl Hayden Visitor Center, the dam can be visited on self-guided tours year-round. From April through October, free guided tours lasting 60 to 90 minutes leave hourly on the half-hour until 90 minutes before the center closes. Tours take you along the top and then deep inside the dam in elevators that drop to near the bottom. The dam is 710 feet high and required over 5 million cubic yards of concrete to build.

Wahweap Marina

Only 7 miles from Page, Wahweap Marina & Lodge (run by Aramark; ☎ 645-2433, 800-528-6154) offers complete services – boat tours and rentals (see Water Sports and Houseboating, below); boat and car service and fuel; laundry; showers; and a supply store. Call the marina directly for information and reservations less than seven days in advance. Otherwise, call Aramark for reservations, which are strongly recommended in summer; its website is www .visitlakepowell.com.

Wahweap Campground has about 180 sites without hookups on a first-come, first-served basis open April through October. Sites are $15. Next door *Wahweap RV Park* has 123 year-round sites with hookups for $26, or $17 November through March (when tenting is permitted). There are showers and a playground.

Wahweap Lodge has 350 comfortable rooms with coffeemakers, refrigerators, balconies or patios, for about $155 to $165 in summer, dropping to $116 in winter. Suites are $225 in summer. About half the rooms have lake views, and there are two pools and a whirlpool. The lodge has room service, a moderately priced coffee shop and a good restaurant.

Aramark offers several boat tours ranging from a one-hour ride on a steam-powered paddlewheel riverboat ($14) to a seven-hour tour to Rainbow Bridge ($106). There are discounts for three- to 11-year-olds. All tours leave from Wahweap Marina. Rainbow Bridge tours also leave from Bullfrog and Halls Crossing Marinas.

Bullfrog Marina

Bullfrog Resort & Marina (☎ 435-684-3000) is 96 miles upstream from the dam and is the lake's second largest marina. It is located on Lake Powell's north shore and the nearest town is tiny Hanksville, Utah, 72 miles north.

There is a GCNRA visitor center (open 8 am to 5 pm daily April to October, intermittently in November, and closed in winter); a medical clinic (summer only); post office; ranger station; laundry; showers; boat rentals (see Water Sports and Houseboating, below); fuel and services; auto fuel and services; and an expensive supply store. Reservations (which should be made well in advance) for houseboats, the campground and Defiance House Lodge are provided by Aramark (see Information, above).

Bullfrog RV Park and Campground is open year-round with about 100 tent sites ($10) and 24 RV sites ($22). Ask at the ranger station about free primitive camping (no water) at several places along the shore. Note the new camping regulations (see Information, above).

Defiance House Lodge has about 60 comfortable rooms with TV, refrigerator and coffeemaker for $110 to $120 in summer, less in winter. A few housekeeping trailers, with two or three bedrooms, two bathrooms, fully equipped kitchen and electricity range from $120 a double to $160 for six people in summer, less in winter. The lodge has a restaurant open for breakfast, lunch and dinner year-round and a fast-food place open during the summer.

A ferry connects Bullfrog Marina with Halls Crossing Marina. (See the 'Lake Powell Ferry' boxed text.)

Halls Crossing Marina

Halls Crossing Marina (☎ 435-684-7000) is on the south shore of the lake, opposite Bullfrog. The nearest town is Blanding, Utah, 75 miles to the east. Services include a

Lake Powell Ferry

The 150-foot-long *John Atlantic Burr* or the identical sister-ship *Charles Hall* provide a link between Bullfrog and Halls Crossing Marinas year-round. Each holds 150 passengers, 14 cars and 2 buses. The 3.2-mile crossing takes 27 minutes and can save as many as 130 miles of driving. The ferries may be delayed or canceled by bad weather. Phone Halls Crossing (☎ 435-684-7000) or Bullfrog Marina (☎ 435-684-3000) for more information.

Fares

Foot Passengers

12 to 64 years	$2
5 to 11 years	$1
Other ages	free

Vehicles
(including driver and passengers)

Bicycle	$2
Motorcycle	$3
Vehicles under 20 feet	$9
Vehicles 20 to 70 feet	$12 to $38
Vehicles over 70 feet	$50

Schedule

Departs Halls Crossing	*Departs Bullfrog*
8 am	9 am
10 am	11 am
Noon	1 pm
2 pm	3 pm*

Additional Service
Mid-April through October

4 pm	5 pm

Additional Service
Mid-May through September

6 pm	7 pm

*The 3 pm crossing may be delayed until 3:30 pm when school is in session.

ranger station; boat rentals, fuel and service; auto fuel and service; laundry; showers; a supply store; and an air strip. Services are provided by Aramark.

Halls Crossing RV Park and Campground has about 60 tent sites ($10) and 20 RV sites ($22). The ranger can suggest free campsites along the shore.

Hite Marina

Hite Marina (☎ 435-684-2278) is 139 miles upriver from the dam and is the most northerly marina. Hanksville, Utah, is 45 miles northwest and is the nearest small town. Services at Hite include a ranger station; boat rentals, fuel and service; auto fuel and service; and a supply shop. Aramark provides reservations.

The marina has a free primitive **campground** (no water). Water is available from the boat ramp.

Dangling Rope Marina

This marina is about 40 miles upriver from the dam and can be reached only by boat. This is the closest marina to Rainbow Bridge National Monument (see below). Services include a ranger station, boat fuel and services, and a supply store.

Fishing

You can fish year-round. Spring and fall are considered the best times, although summer isn't bad. Bass, crappie and walleye are the main catches on the lake. Licenses are required and are available from any marina; you'll need Arizona and/or Utah licenses depending on where you fish.

Water Sports

The public can launch boats from NPS launch ramps at the marinas. Boats ranging from 16-foot runabouts to 59-foot houseboats sleeping 12 are available for rental from Aramark. Water skis and jet skis can also be rented, but the marinas aren't geared to renting kayaks or dinghies.

Water-skiing, scuba diving, sailing and swimming are summer activities. Average water temperatures of 62°F in November and 64°F in May are too chilly except for the most dedicated enthusiasts with wet or dry suits.

Aramark rents boats: A 16-foot skiff seating six with a 25-hp motor is $75 a day in summer. Use skiffs for slow exploring and

ARIZONA

fishing. Larger boats with larger engines for towing water-skiers or getting around more quickly cost three or four times as much. Kayaks are $47 a day. Water 'toys' include jet skis for about $260 a day and water skis and other equipment packages for $25. Note that there are federal plans to limit jet-ski use in national parks as of 2002. Weekly rates usually give one free day.

All marinas except Dangling Rope rent boats.

Houseboating

Houseboating is popular – hundreds of houseboats are available for rent and there are more every year. Despite the number of boats, the large size of the lake still allows houseboaters to get away from others. Houseboats can sleep from eight to 12 people, but accommodations are tight so make sure you are good friends with your fellow shipmates, or rent a boat with flexibility in sleeping arrangements. The larger boats are quite luxurious; the smaller boats are very utilitarian.

Houseboats on Lake Powell are provided by Aramark (see Information, above), which also provides small boats, tours and lodging in marinas – these can be combined into a variety of packages. Houseboats can be rented from any marina except Dangling Rope and advance reservations are required.

Summer rates range from about $1100 to $3100 for three days to $1900 to $6100 for a week in boats ranging from 36 to 59 feet in length. Four-, five- and six-day rentals are available and two-day rentals are available outside of summer. From about October to April (dates vary with boats and marinas), discounts of about 40% are offered.

Small houseboats have tiny to midsize refrigerators, simple cooking facilities, a toilet and shower, a gas barbecue grill and 150-quart ice chests.

Larger boats may have some of the following: electric generator (allowing air conditioning, microwave, toaster, coffeemaker, TV, VCR and radio), canopies, swim slides and ladders. Luxury boats have all these features upgraded and with extra space. Boats are booked up well in advance in summer.

RAINBOW BRIDGE NATIONAL MONUMENT

On the south shore of Lake Powell, Rainbow Bridge is the largest natural bridge in the world and a site of religious importance to the Navajo. No camping or climbing on the bridge is permitted, but visitors can come by boat, horse or on foot. Primitive camping is allowed outside the monument, less than a mile from the bridge. Almost all visitors come by boat tour and then hike a short trail. Serious photographers will find that the overhead light does not lend itself to good shots; arranging dawn and dusk visits is difficult and potentially expensive.

Very few people arrive on foot. However, hikers leave from the Rainbow Lodge trailhead in Arizona (the lodge is abandoned) or Navajo Mountain trailhead (technically in Utah but approachable only from Arizona) and walk about 14 miles to the monument. The trailheads are reached by dirt roads and the trails themselves are not maintained. This hike is for experienced backpackers only; you should carry water and be self-sufficient. Both trailheads are on the Navajo Reservation and a tribal permit should be obtained from the Navajo Parks & Recreation Dept (☎ 871-6647, fax 871-6637) in Window Rock (see the Northeastern Arizona chapter). The monument is administered by the GCNRA.

Western Arizona

Western Arizona is not only the hottest part of the state, it is often the hottest area in the nation. The low-lying towns along the Colorado River (Bullhead City, Lake Havasu City and Yuma) boast average maximum daily temperatures of more than 100°F from June to September, and temperatures exceeding 110°F are not unusual. Balmy weather during the rest of the year attracts thousands of winter visitors, many of whom end up staying – western Arizonan cities have some of the fastest growing populations in the USA.

After the Colorado River leaves the Grand Canyon, it turns south and forms the western boundary of Arizona, referred to as Arizona's 'west coast.' Several dams along it form huge artificial lakes that attract those vacationers escaping the intense summer heat – water-skiing and jet-skiing, sailing and boating, fishing, scuba diving and plain old swimming are popular activities. In addition, travelers enjoy the wild scenery, visit dams, explore wildlife refuges and ghost towns, gamble in casinos and see perhaps the most incongruous of sights in the desert Southwest, London Bridge.

KINGMAN
☎ 928 • pop 20,069; metro area 38,000
• elevation 3345 feet

This area was virtually unknown to Europeans until 1857, when Edward Beale, using camel caravans, surveyed a wagon route across northern Arizona near what is now Kingman. Lewis Kingman surveyed a railway route through northern Arizona in 1880; the railroad was completed in 1883. Kingman is the most historic of the area's larger towns and several turn-of-the-19th-century buildings survive. Although attracting fewer visitors than the nearby resorts of Bullhead City and Lake Havasu City, Kingman provides an excellent base for exploring the northwestern corner of the state and offers plenty of inexpensive and mid-priced accommodations.

Orientation & Information

Exits 48 and 53 from I-40 freeway span Kingman's main street, Andy Devine Ave. Named after a Hollywood actor who was raised here, Andy Devine Ave also forms part of historic Route 66 and most of the accommodations and services you will need are found along it.

The visitor center (☎ 753-6106) is open daily at 120 W Andy Devine Ave. Its website is at www.arizonaguide.com/visit kingman.

Other services in Kingman include the BLM (☎ 692-4400), 2475 Beverly Ave, library (☎ 692-2665), 3269 N Burbank, post office (☎ 753-2480), 1901 Johnson Ave, Medical Center (☎ 757-2101), 3269 Stockton Hill Rd, and police (☎ 753-2191), 2730 E Andy Devine Ave.

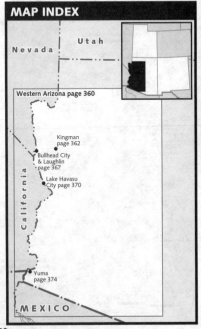

MAP INDEX

Nevada

Utah

Western Arizona page 360

Kingman page 362

Bullhead City & Laughlin page 367

Lake Havasu City page 370

California

Yuma page 374

MEXICO

ARIZONA

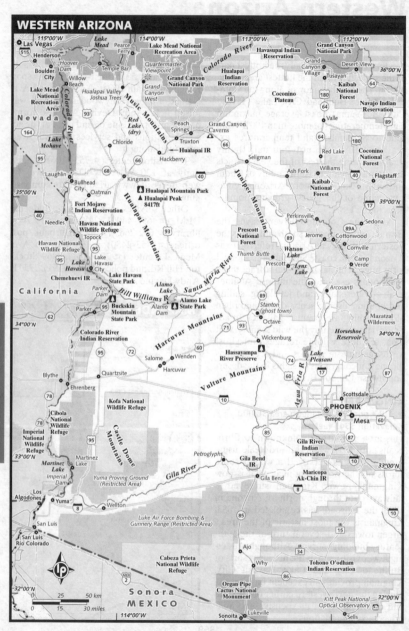

WESTERN ARIZONA

Things to See & Do
The visitor center is inside the old Power-house, built in 1907 and now also housing a Route 66 gift shop and diner, an art display and the **Route 66 Museum** which follows the history of the route and has the best collection of Route 66 memorabilia west of Oklahoma. Admission is $3. The visitor center has a map detailing late-19th-century buildings that can be visited on a **Historic Walking Tour** that covers nearby streets.

The **Mohave Museum of History & Arts** (☎ 753-3195), 400 W Beale, highlights local history and homeboy Andy Devine. Hours are 9 am to 5 pm on weekdays and 1 to 5 pm on weekends except major holidays. Admission is $3; free for children under 13. The **Bonelli House** (☎ 753-1413), N 5th and Spring, was built in 1894 by pioneers, rebuilt in 1915 after a fire and is now municipally owned and is open as an example of early Anglo architecture in Arizona. Its hours are 1 to 4 pm Thursday to Monday, except major holidays. Admission is by donation.

Hualapai Mountain Park (☎ 757-3859) surrounds 8417-foot Hualapai Peak and offers a popular summer getaway for local residents. Fourteen miles southeast of Kingman (take Hualapai Mountain Rd from Andy Devine Ave), it features picnicking, camping, rooms and cabins, wildlife observation, and miles of maintained and undeveloped trails.

Special Events
Route 66 Fun Run (753-5001), a vintage car rally along Route 66 between Seligman and Topock, runs over the last weekend in April or first weekend in May. Kingman has a car show followed by dancing in the evening. There are also events in the small towns along the route.
website: www.azrt66.com

The Arts Festival during Mother's Day weekend in May includes metal workers and woodcarvers as well as the more usual types of artists. The Mohave County Fair is held in mid-September and Andy Devine Days, with a parade, rodeo and other events, happens during late September.

Places to Stay
Camping At *Hualapai Mountain Park*, 70 campsites are available on a first-come first-served basis for $6, most with picnic tables and grills. Eleven RV sites with hookups are $12. Water and toilets are available.

The **KOA** (☎ 757-4397, 800-562-3991, *3820 N Roosevelt)* has mainly RV sites ($23-$28) and a small area for tents ($17), plus a swimming pool, game room, coin laundry, and convenience store. The **Quality Stars RV Park** (☎ 753-2277, *3131 MacDonald Ave)*, offers sites from $13 to $20 depending on whether you use the hookups. There is a coin laundry and small pool.

Motels & Hotels Cheap hotels are found along old Route 66. The cheapest places have basic double rooms in the $20s, including the *Arcadia Lodge* (☎ 753-1925, *909 E Andy Devine Ave)* with 48 rooms, the small *Lido Motel* (☎ 753-4515, *3133 E Andy Devine Ave)*, the friendly *High Desert Inn* (☎ 753-2935, *2803 E Andy Devine Ave)* and the 29-room *Hilltop Motel* (☎ 753-2198, *1901 E Andy Devine Ave)* which has a small pool. There are a dozen others with rooms in the $20s and $30s.

Plenty of *chain motels* are to be found. I-40 exit 53 is a good place to look for most of them (see map).

The most memorable accommodations are at the *Hotel Brunswick* (☎ 718-1800, *888-559-1800, 315 E Andy Devine Ave)*, established in 1909 and recently renovated. Twelve old-fashioned cowboy/girl rooms with single beds share four bathrooms; rates are $25. Thirteen more rooms have private baths and TVs; rates range from $50 to $75. A restaurant and bar are on the premises and a breakfast is included.
website: www.hotel-brunswick.com

Near Hualapai Mountain Park is the *Hualapai Mountain Lodge Resort* (☎ 757-3545)*, with rooms from $75 to $110 and a restaurant.

Places to Eat
The popular and cheap *Silver Spoon Family Restaurant* (☎ 753-4030, *2011 E Andy Devine Ave)* is open from 5 am to 10 pm.

KINGMAN

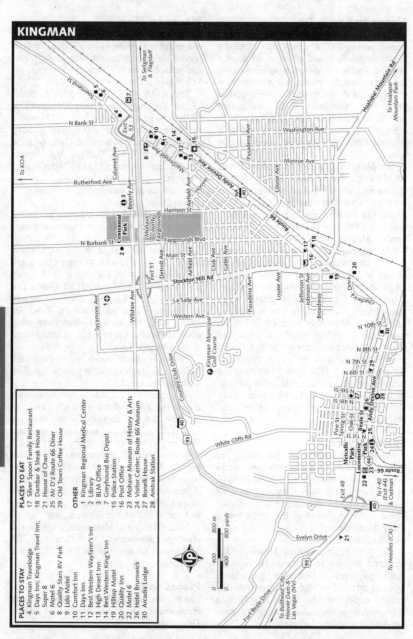

PLACES TO STAY
4   Kingman Travelodge
5   Days Inn; Kingman Travel Inn;
    Super 8
6   Motel 6
8   Quality Stars RV Park
10 Lido Motel
11 Comfort Inn
12 Days Inn
13 Best Western Wayfarer's Inn
14 High Desert Inn
19 Best Western King's Inn
20 Hilltop Motel
22 Quality Inn
26 Motel 6
27 Hotel Brunswick
30 Arcadia Lodge

PLACES TO EAT
17 Silver Spoon Family Restaurant
18 Dambar & Steak House
21 House of Chan
25 Mr D'z Route 66 Diner
29 Old Town Coffee House

OTHER
1   Kingman Regional Medical Center
2   Library
3   BLM Office
7   Greyhound Bus Depot
15 Police Station
16 Post Office
23 Mohave Museum of History & Arts
24 Visitor Center; Route 66 Museum
27 Bonelli House
28 Amtrak Station

The well-recommended *House of Chan* (☎ 753-3232, 960 W Beale), is open from 11 am to 9:30 pm and is closed on Sundays. The service is good and prime rib, steak and seafood are featured in addition to Chinese food. Dinners are in the $7 to $20 range.

The popular *Dambar & Steak House* (☎ 753-3523, 1960 E Andy Devine Ave) specializes in large steaks ($10 to $20) for dinner. Grab a burger or blue plate special at the '50s style *Mr D'z Route 66 Diner* (☎ 718-0066, 105 E Andy Devine Ave). Light snacks and international coffees are served at the *Old Town Coffee House* (☎ 753-2244, 616 E Beale).

Getting There & Away

Kingman Airport (☎ 757-2134) is 6 miles northeast of town off Route 66. America West flies between Kingman and Phoenix, stopping at Prescott, three times a day on weekdays.

The Greyhound Bus Depot (☎ 757-8400), 3264 E Andy Devine Ave, is behind McDonald's. Buses go to Phoenix, Tucson, Las Vegas, Salt Lake City, Flagstaff, Los Angeles and other cities.

ROUTE 66

Historic Route 66, once the main highway from Chicago to Los Angeles, has been largely forgotten in favor of the interstate freeway system (see the 'Kickin' Down Route 66' boxed text in the Facts about Arizona chapter). Several cities have vestiges of the old route but the longest remaining stretch of what was once called 'The Main Street of America' stretches 160 miles from Seligman to Topock on the Arizona-California border. Other than Kingman, Route 66 winds through mostly empty and lesser-traveled northwestern Arizonan countryside. Every year, this desolate stretch is transformed into its bustling former self with the annual Route 66 Fun Run (see Special Events in Kingman). All places below are ☎ 928.

Seligman has half a dozen basic motels including the popular *Historic Route 66 Motel* (☎ 422-3204), with rooms in the $50s, and several cheaper places like the *Romney*

Motel (☎ 422-3700) or the *Supai Motel* (☎ 422-3663). For a traditional '50s-style malt or milkshake, stop by *Delgadillo's Snow Cap* (☎ 422-3291).

Grand Canyon Caverns, 23 miles west of Seligman, are 210 feet underground. Early tourists were lowered on a rope and the caverns became a popular roadside attraction during Route 66's heyday. Today, an elevator takes people below ground, where a three-quarter-mile trail winds by geological formations, including stalagmites and stalactites. Entrance, including a 45-minute guided tour, costs $9.50 for adults and $6.75 for four- to 12-year-olds. Hours are 8 am to 6 pm in summer and 10 am to 5 pm in winter. The *Grand Canyon Caverns Motel* (☎ 422-3223/4) has a restaurant and charges about $45 to $65 for one to five people in summer and substantially less in winter. The caverns are a mile behind the motel.

Peach Springs, 12 miles west of the Grand Canyon Caverns, contains the Hualapai Indian Reservation tribal offices and tourist lodge (see the Grand Canyon & Lake Powell chapter). During the Route 66 Fun Run, the tribe prepares a barbecue for passing motorists. Nine miles farther west, the blink-and-you'll-miss-it town of **Truxton**, has the basic and inexpensive (though prices rise dramatically during the Route 66 Fun Run) *Frontier Motel & Café* (☎ 769-2238) and an RV park. There is entertainment here during the Fun Run. Tiny **Hackberry**, 15 miles west and 25 miles from Kingman, features the eccentric **Old Route 66 Visitor Center** (☎ 769-2605), built in 1934 as the Hackberry General Store and now run by a Route 66 memorialist, Robert Waldmire.

The gold-mining town of **Oatman** in the rugged Black Mountains about 25 miles southwest of Kingman was founded in 1906. Two million ounces of gold were extracted before the last mine closed in 1942 and the population of thousands plummeted to hundreds. Today, 500,000 visitors annually come through this self-styled 'ghost town' to see the old buildings, browse the gift shops, enjoy the weekend shenanigans (gunfights at high noon and Western dancing at night) and feed the wild burros. The **Oatman Hotel** (☎ 768-4408) is on the National Register of Historic Places and the simple rooms are almost unchanged since Hollywood legends Clark Gable and Carole Lombard honeymooned here in the 1930s. Rooms with shared bathroom are a $35 'donation'. Nonguests can go upstairs to see the Gable-Lombard room, or grab a bite alongside the grizzled miners in the **Saloon & Restaurant** downstairs (the bar is wallpapered with $1 bills).

This stretch of Route 66 ends in tiny **Topock**, where travelers continue on I-40. **Golden Shores Trailer Park** (☎ 768-1193) has spaces for RVs.

CHLORIDE

☎ 928 • pop 250 • elevation 4200 feet

Founded in 1862 by silver miners, Chloride is the oldest mining town in Arizona and home to the oldest continuously operating post office in the state (since 1871). The semi-ghost town, 20 miles northwest of Kingman, is quieter and more low-key than crowded Oatman and Jerome mining towns. There are antique and art stores, old buildings, the original jail with two tiny, grimly barred cells flanking the woodstove-heated guard's room, a visitor center (☎ 565-2204) and occasional melodramas, usually held on the first and third Saturdays of summer months. A signed dirt road goes 1.3 miles to a rocky hillside with huge murals painted by artist Roy Purcell. For more about the town, see www.chloridearizona.com.

On Old Miners Day, the last Saturday in June, locals dress in turn-of-the-19th-century garb and there's a parade and old-time music and dancing. Watch out for gunfights and showdowns!

There is a small **RV park** (☎ 565-4492). **Sheps Miners Inn B&B** (☎ 565-4251, 877-565-4251) rents 12 rooms for $35 to $65. There are three homey cafés and a couple of Western saloons.

LAKE MEAD NATIONAL RECREATION AREA

Hoover Dam (at the time the world's largest) was built between 1931 and 1936 in this hot, arid and desolate area. It backed up the Colorado River, flooding canyons, archaeological sites, wilderness areas and communities and producing Lake Mead, one of the world's largest artificial lakes. In 1953, the smaller Davis Dam was completed, forming Lake Mohave. The dams were built for flood control, irrigation, hydroelectricity and as a water supply to the burgeoning population of the Southwest and southern California.

When the dams were built, people decried the flooding as a destructive waste of archaeological, historical, natural and scenic resources. Today the two lakes, surrounded by wild desert scenery, attract millions of annual visitors, ranging from curious day-trippers looking at the dams to vacationing families spending a week boating on the lakes. Barely an hour's drive from Las Vegas, the area certainly doesn't suffer from a shortage of visitors.

The 2337-sq-mile recreation area encompasses two major lakes with over 280 sq surface miles of water, almost 1000 miles of shoreline, and many square miles of desert in both Arizona and Nevada. Motels, developed campgrounds, restaurants, marinas, grocery stores and gas stations are available in lakeside areas in Arizona and Nevada. There are also several undeveloped backcountry campgrounds and boat-launch areas.

Orientation & Information

Hwy 93 (between Kingman and Las Vegas) crosses the Hoover Dam and passes the main visitor center and park headquarters. Hwy 68 (between Kingman and Bullhead City) goes near the Davis Dam. Both dams straddle the Arizona/Nevada state line, as does most of the recreation area. Minor roads provide access to marinas and other areas.

The Alan Bible Visitor Center (☎ 702-293-8990) in Nevada, 5 miles west of Hoover Dam, is open from 8:30 am to 4:30 pm (Pacific time) daily except Thanksgiving, Christmas and New Year's Day. The center has maps, books, information, exhibits, films and a small desert botanical garden. The smaller Katherine Landing

Visitor Center (☎ 928-754-3272) in Arizona, 3 miles north of Davis Dam, is open 8 am to 4 pm. There are also ranger stations throughout the area. Get advance information from the Superintendent, Lake Mead NRA, 601 Nevada Hwy, Boulder City, NV 89005 (☎ 702-293-8906/7).

Every year, people die here in boating, swimming or diving accidents, many of which are alcohol related. In an emergency, contact a ranger or call the 24-hour emergency number (☎ 702-293-8932, 800-680-5851).

Summer temperatures rise over 100°F most days (best for water activities), but winter highs are in the 50°s and 60°s (best for hiking and backpacking). Long hikes are not recommended in summer, when heat exhaustion is a real problem.

Admission is $5 per vehicle, $3 each for bikers and hikers and $10 for a boat. Admission is valid for five days. All passes are honored. Driving through on the main highways is free.

Hoover Dam

At 726 feet high, Hoover Dam remains one of the tallest dams in the world and is an impressive feat of engineering and architecture. There is an exhibit center, and guided tours leave from here at frequent intervals throughout the day between 8:30 am and 5:45 pm.

The standard tours leave every 10 minutes and take up to 80 people. These tours descend into the dam by elevator, last 40 minutes, and are followed by a 25-minute video presentation. The cost is $8 ($7 for those over 62; $2 for six- to 16-year-olds). One-hour 'behind the scenes' hardhat tours are limited to 20 people paying $25 each; minimum age is seven. No bags, including camera bags, are allowed on tours, which leave several times a day.

Parking on the Arizona side is limited to several lots along Hwy 93; free shuttle buses take visitors to the dam. On the Nevada side, there is a parking area ($2) just past the exhibit center.

Hwy 93 crosses the Colorado River as a two-lane road over the dam. The narrow, steep and winding road down to the dam

gets backed up for miles on busy days, so prepare for delays.

Fishing

The lakes are said to have some of the best sport fishing in the country. Striped bass (up to 50lb!) are one attraction; rainbow trout, largemouth bass, channel catfish, black crappie and bluegill are also likely catches. November to February is the best time for trout and crappie; March to May is OK for trout, catfish, crappie and bass; June to August is best for catfish, bass and bluegill; September to mid-October continues to be OK for bass and, as the water cools, for crappie. Check with a visitor center or ranger station for current fishing tips.

You can fish year-round with a license, available at the boating marinas (which also have fishing supplies and charters).

Boating

Because of the many powerboats and the huge area of the lakes, small vessels such as canoes and rafts are not encouraged, except at parts of Boulder Beach (near Hoover Dam and Lake Mead Marina). Larger boats can be rented from the marinas.

Boat Tours Lake Mead Cruises (☎ 702-293-6180) has several narrated cruises a day from Lake Mead Marina to Hoover Dam (1½ hours roundtrip). The boat is an air-conditioned, three-decked, Mississippi-style paddle wheeler. Fares are $19/9 for adults/children two to 12. Also available are two-hour weekend breakfast buffet cruises ($29/15), dinner cruises from Sunday to Thursday ($40/21) and dinner/dance cruises on Friday and Saturday ($45, adults only). Departure times vary with season, and reservations for meal cruises are recommended. website: www.lakemeadcruises.com

The more adventurous can do a raft float (no whitewater) from below the Hoover Dam, down the Black Canyon of the Colorado River to Willow Beach Resort. The motorized rafts hold 40 passengers and the tour is $70 for adults, $40 for children under 12, and free for children under five. Lunch is included and a bus returns you to your

ARIZONA

starting point at Black Canyon River Raft Tours (☎ 702-293-3776, 800-696-7238) in Boulder City near Hoover Dam. Tours are from February to November and the roundtrip takes 5½ hours (three hours of boating). During the summer months, you may see desert bighorn sheep, especially in the early hours of the day.

website: www.rafts.com

Boat Rentals Fishing, ski, patio and house-boats are available as well as jet skis (though these may be banned in the future). Two NPS-authorized concessionaires provide most of the boats available, ranging from small fishing boats at $70 a day to lux-urious houseboats sleeping 10 for $5000 a week. Houseboat rentals for three or four nights are also possible, and rates drop outside of the summer high season. The cheaper, less crowded shoulder-seasons are recommended. Houseboats are very popular and reservations should be made months in advance for the high season. Seven Crown Resorts (☎ 800-752-9669) op-erates from several marinas on both lakes and has houseboat rentals sleeping four, six, eight, 10 and 14 people, as well as small boats. Forever Resorts (☎/fax 602-968-5449, 800-255-5561) has more luxurious and ex-pensive houseboats sleeping up to 10. In ad-dition to boat rentals, these concessionaires provide motel rooms and restaurants,

grocery stores, gas stations, and fishing bait, tackle and license facilities. You can browse options from the two agencies online at www.sevencrown.com and www.forever resorts.com.

Two things to consider when renting a boat: bring binoculars (they help to read buoy numbers) and make sure you are good friends with your shipmates – a boat sleep-ing 10 will be very cramped for 10 adults.

Places to Stay & Eat

The *National Park Service* operates eight campgrounds for tents and RVs (no hookups) for $10. These are mainly on the Nevada side. Several of the marinas have RV campgrounds for $20 a night with hookups.

Seven Crown Resorts and Forever Resorts (see Boat Rentals, earlier) operate motels and restaurants at several marinas. The *Temple Bar Resort (☎ 928-767-3211)* is 47 miles by paved road east of the Hoover Dam. Rates range from $43 to $99 for fishing cabins, double rooms and kitchen suites sleeping four. Rooms are comfortable enough and this is one of the more remote spots on Lake Mead, which makes it fun. The *Lake Mohave Resort* (☎ 928-754-3245) at Katherine Landing near Bullhead City charges $70 to $120 for doubles, some with kitchenettes. Both of these have nearby RV sites, restaurant, groceries and small boat rentals.

Seven Crown Resorts (☎ 800-752-9669) also has similarly priced motels at *Lake Mead Resort* and *Echo Bay Resort*. Forever Resorts' *Cottonwood Cove Motel* (☎ 702-297-1464) on the Nevada shore charges $90 for doubles from May to October and holi-days, and $60 the rest of the year.

BULLHEAD CITY & LAUGHLIN
☎ 928 • pop 33,769 • elevation 540 feet

Bullhead City, or 'Bull' as some locals call it, is just south of the south end of Lake Mohave and was established in the 1940s for the builders of Davis Dam. It's a popular destination for Arizonans, who visit Lake Mohave or cross the bridge over the Colo-rado River to Laughlin, Nevada, which has

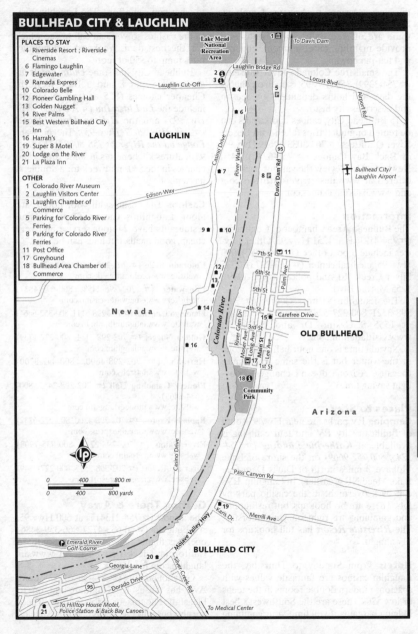

BULLHEAD CITY & LAUGHLIN

PLACES TO STAY
4 Riverside Resort ; Riverside Cinemas
6 Flamingo Laughlin
8 Edgewater
9 Ramada Express
10 Colorado Belle
12 Pioneer Gambling Hall
13 Golden Nugget
14 River Palms
15 Best Western Bullhead City Inn
16 Harrah's
19 Super 8 Motel
20 Lodge on the River
21 La Plaza Inn

OTHER
1 Colorado River Museum
2 Laughlin Visitors Center
3 Laughlin Chamber of Commerce
5 Parking for Colorado River Ferries
8 Parking for Colorado River Ferries
11 Post Office
17 Greyhound
18 Bullhead Area Chamber of Commerce

ARIZONA

ARIZONA

the closest casinos to Arizona. Gambling here is the main attraction, though river tours are offered daily. The casinos also provide nightlife, entertainment, cinemas and ten-pin bowling.

The small free **Colorado River Museum** (☎ 754-3399), 355 Hwy 95, is open on changing days and hours dependent on season and describes city history.

In Bullhead City, canoes and kayaks can be rented or guided trips taken with Desert River Outfitters (☎ 763-3033), 9649 Hwy 95, or Back Bay Canoes (☎ 758-6242), 1450 Newberry Dr. Review the various packages offered at www.desertriveroutfitters.com and www.backbaycanoes.com

Information

The Bullhead Area Chamber of Commerce (☎ 754-4121) is at 1251 Hwy 95. Other services include a post office (☎ 754-3717), 990 Hwy 95, medical center (☎ 763-2273), 2735 Silver Creek Rd, and police (☎ 763-1999), 1255 Marina Blvd.

The Laughlin Visitors Center (☎ 702-298-3321, 800-227-5245) is open weekdays at 1555 S Casino Dr and online at www.visitlaughlin.com.

Nevada time is one hour behind Arizona in the winter but is the same in summer (because Arizona doesn't change to daylight saving time).

Places to Stay

Camping RV parks are near Hwy 95 south of Bullhead City. RV and tent camping is available at *Katherine Landing* (☎ 754-3245, 800-752-9669) on the shore of Lake Mohave, 3 miles north of Davis Dam (see Lake Mead NRA earlier). In Laughlin, RVs can park overnight in the casino parking lots. There are no hookups, but restaurants and gambling are right on your doorstep. The *Riverside Resort* has full hookups for $17 a night.

Hotels From Sunday to Thursday, the Laughlin casinos are fantastic values with spacious modern double rooms in the teens or low $20s. These are the Southwest's best lodging bargains, if you limit your gambling

to what you can afford. The Laughlin Visitors Center has a free phone that connects to the casinos so you can call to see which has the best deal. Weekend and holiday rates jump to $50 or more.

Bullhead City has some *chain hotels* including a Super 8 and a Best Western. Cheaper choices ($25 and up midweek) include the *La Plaza Inn* (☎ 763-8080, 1978 Hwy 95) and the *Hilltop House Motel* (☎ 753-2198, 2037 Hwy 95). The pleasant *Lodge on the River* (☎ 758-8080, 1717 Hwy 95) features kitchenettes in some rooms and charges in the $30s midweek for a double. It has a pool.

Casinos The casinos, all with hotels, are along Laughlin's Casino Drive. Casino restaurants have 24-hour service and very cheap, good meals, but lines can be long.

Colorado Belle (☎ 702-298-4000, 800-477-4837)
website: www.coloradobelle.com

Edgewater (☎ 702-298-2453, 800-677-4837)
website: www.edgewater-casino.com

Flamingo Laughlin (☎ 702-298-5111, 800-352-6464)
website: www.laughlinflamingo.com

Golden Nugget (☎ 702-298-7111, 800-237-1739)
website: www.gnlaughlin.com

Harrah's (☎ 702-298-4600, 800-447-8700)
website: www.harrahs.com

Pioneer Gambling Hall (☎ 702-298-2442, 800-634-3469)
website: www.pioneerlaughlin.com

Ramada Express (☎ 702-298-4200, 800-272-6232)
website: www.ramadaexpress.com

River Palms (☎ 702-298-2242, 800-835-7903)
website: www.rvrpalm.com

Riverside Resort (☎ 702-298-2535, 800-227-3849)
website: www.riversideresort.com

Getting There & Away

The airport (☎ 754-2134) is at 600 Hwy 95. Air Laughlin (☎ 60-633-4727, 866-359-3486) operates flights to Phoenix and Southern California; check its website at www.air laughlin.com for details.

Greyhound Bus (☎ 754-5586), 125 Long Ave, has buses to Kingman and on to Flagstaff, Phoenix or Albuquerque. There are also buses to Las Vegas and Los Angeles.

Tri-State Super Shuttle (☎ 704-9000, 800-801-8687) has buses between Bullhead City and the Las Vegas airport. It picks up at major hotels.

HAVASU NATIONAL WILDLIFE REFUGE

This is one of a string of wildlife refuges and other protected areas along the lower Colorado River. Habitats include marshes, sand dunes, desert and the river itself. Overwintering birds – geese, ducks and cranes – are found here in profusion. After the migrants' departure, herons and egrets nest in large numbers.

The section of the reserve north of I-40 is the Topock Marsh. South of I-40, the Colorado flows through Topock Gorge. The southern boundary of the reserve abuts the northern boundary of Lake Havasu State Park, 3 miles north of London Bridge.

The refuge headquarters (☎ 760-326-3853), 317 Mesquite Ave, Needles, California, has maps, bird lists and information.

The Jerkwater Canoe Company (☎ 768-7753), PO Box 800, Topock, AZ 86436, offers canoe rentals and guided day trips through the gorge as well as a variety of overnight excursions along the river.

LAKE HAVASU CITY

☎ 928 • pop 41,938 • elevation 575 feet

Developer Robert McCulloch planned Lake Havasu City as a center for water sports and light industry/business. The city received a huge infusion of publicity when McCulloch bought London Bridge for $2,460,000, disassembled it into 10,276 granite slabs, and reassembled it here. The bridge, opened in London, England in 1831, was rededicated in 1971 and has become the focus of the city's English Village – a touristy complex of restaurants, hotels and shops built in pseudo-English style. Students flock to town during spring break in March, when hotels get busy and live bands entertain.

Information

The tourism bureau (☎ 453-3444, 800-242-8278), 314 London Bridge Rd, is open Monday to Friday and is online at www.golakehavasu.com. A visitor information center at the English Village is open daily. The English Village parking area costs $3 per day, but ask for a free 30-minute parking pass for the visitor center. Other services include the library (☎ 453-0718), 1770 McCulloch Blvd, post office (☎ 855-2361), 1750 McCulloch Blvd, hospital (☎ 855-8185), 101 Civic Center Blvd, and police (☎ 885-4111), 2360 McCulloch Blvd.

Activities

Once you've walked over London Bridge, you'll find that most of your options are water-related. Plenty of companies provide boat tours and rentals and the visitor center has numerous brochures. One-hour, narrated, day and sunset tours are offered by several boats at English Village and cost about $13 ($7 for four- to 12-year olds). Longer tours (2½ hours) are $25/15 or more, depending on the boat and destination. Just show up and you can usually reserve a tour leaving within an hour or two; many boats are air-conditioned.

Fishing, rowing, water-skiing and sightseeing boats can be rented from Lake Havasu Marina (☎ 855-2159) and Blue Water Rentals (☎ 453-9613) in the English Village. Canoes and kayaks are rented (from $15 a day), sold and guided at Western Arizona Canoe & Kayak Outfitter (WACKO; ☎ 855-6414, 680-9719).

The best months for fishing are April to July and October and November for largemouth bass, May to July for striped bass, June to September for catfish, March to May for crappie and May to September for bluegill. Licenses, gear and information are available from the boat rental places and many other stores.

Outback Off-Road Adventures (☎ 680-6151) has 4WD desert tours for $65 a half day, $130 a full day with lunch. Groups of four or more and children get discounts.

Places to Stay

Camping Two miles north of town on London Bridge Rd is *Windsor Beach Campground* (☎ 855-2784) and 15 miles

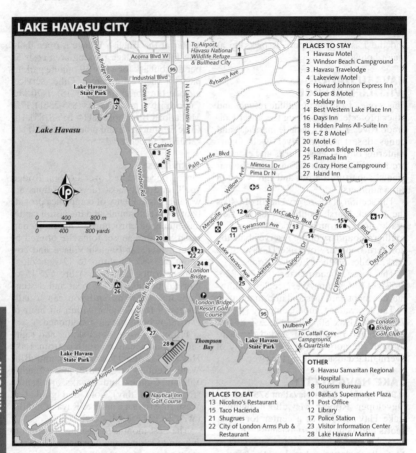

LAKE HAVASU CITY

PLACES TO STAY
1 Havasu Motel
2 Windsor Beach Campground
3 Havasu Travelodge
4 Lakeview Motel
6 Howard Johnson Express Inn
7 Super 8 Motel
9 Holiday Inn
14 Best Western Lake Place Inn
16 Days Inn
18 Hidden Palms All-Suite Inn
19 E-Z 8 Motel
20 Motel 6
24 London Bridge Resort
25 Ramada Inn
26 Crazy Horse Campground
27 Island Inn

PLACES TO EAT
13 Nicolino's Restaurant
15 Taco Hacienda
21 Shugrues
22 City of London Arms Pub & Restaurant

OTHER
5 Havasu Samaritan Regional Hospital
8 Tourism Bureau
10 Basha's Supermarket Plaza
11 Post Office
12 Library
17 Police Station
23 Visitor Information Center
28 Lake Havasu Marina

south on Hwy 95 is *Cattail Cove* (☎ 855-1223); both are state park campgrounds with showers, boat launch and tent/RV camping (no hookups) for $12 per day. Cattail Cove also has 40 RV sites with hookups for $15. Day use is $7 per vehicle. The *Crazy Horse Campground* (☎ 855-4033, 1534 Beachcomber Blvd), has several hundred RV sites with full or partial hookups for $24 and 200 tent sites for $13. Showers, a laundry room and a grocery store are available.

Hotels Rates vary tremendously from summer weekends to winter weekdays. The cheapest places, offering doubles for around $30 in winter but about $50 or more during summer (weekly discounts are often available) include the following: the *E-Z 8 Motel* (☎ 855-4023, 41 Acoma Blvd,) with a pool and whirlpool, the *Havasu Motel* (☎ 855-2311, 2035 Acoma Blvd), and the basic *Lakeview Motel* (☎ 855-3605, 440 London Bridge Rd).

For more upscale lodging, try *Hidden Palms All-Suite Inn* (☎ 855-7144, 2100 Swanson Ave) which has a pool and units with kitchenettes for $60 to $130. The *Island Inn* (☎ 680-0606, 800-243-9955, 1300

McCulloch Blvd) has a pool, spa and many rooms with balconies and lake views for $65 to $120. It also has pricier suites.

The **London Bridge Resort** *(☎ 855-0888, 888-503-9148, 1477 Queens Bay Rd)* has three pools, hot tub, exercise room, golf, tennis, shops and views of London Bridge. Several restaurants, bars and nightclubs offer a range of dining, drinking and dancing options that attracts folks looking for a playful resort rather than restful luxury. Over 120 units feature either one or two bedrooms and come with kitchenette, some with whirlpool bathtubs and dining areas. Rates range from $100 to $300 depending on the room, the date and the time of week (weekends are higher).
website: www.londonbridgeresort.com

Several **chain motels** are represented here, including Motel 6, Days Inn, Super 8, Travelodge, Howard Johnson, Best Western, Ramada Inn and Holiday Inn.

Places to Eat
Several restaurants are on or near the half mile of McCulloch Blvd between Smoketree Ave and Acoma Blvd.

Shugrues *(☎ 453-1400, 1425 McCulloch Blvd),* advertises several dozen entrées featuring fresh seafood, steak, chicken and pastas. Dinner entrées include soup or salad and range from about $10 to over $30, most in the mid-teens. Lunches are cheaper, and many tables have some sort of bridge view. At about half this price, the **City of London Arms Pub & Restaurant** *(☎ 855-8782)* at the English Village has decent pub food and imported British brews.

For Mexican lunches and dinners, head over to **Taco Hacienda** *(☎ 855-8932, 2200 Mesquite Ave).* This locally popular place has been here for two decades (eons by Lake Havasu City standards!). Italian-food lovers can try **Nicolino's Restaurant** *(☎ 855-3484, 86 S Smoketree Ave);* it's closed on Sundays.

Getting There & Away
Lake Havasu City Airport *(☎ 764-3330),* 5600 N Hwy 95, is 7 miles north of town.

America West has several daily flights to and from Phoenix.

Greyhound buses *(☎ 764-4010)* leave from the Busy 'B' Service Station *(☎ 764-2440),* 3201 N Hwy 95, 4 miles north of town.

PARKER
☎ 928 • pop 3140 • elevation 417 feet

Parker, about 30 miles south of Lake Havasu on Hwy 95, thrives on local tourism. The stretch of road between Parker and the Parker Dam, known as the Parker Strip, has many campgrounds, boat-launch areas and marinas. The SCORE 400 in late January is an off-road, 4WD jeep and pickup truck race that covers more than 300 miles and attracts 100,000 visitors. The chamber of commerce lists several other wild events.

Greyhound buses stop at the Hole-in-the-Wall restaurant.

Orientation & Information
Almost all of the town's major businesses are on or near California Ave (Hwy 95/62) or Riverside Drive (Hwy 95), and are easy to find.

The chamber of commerce *(☎ 669-2174)* is at 1217 California Ave and its useful website is at www.coloradoriverinformation.com/parker. Other services include the library *(☎ 669-2622),* 1001 Navajo Ave, post office *(☎ 669-8179),* at Joshua Ave and 14th, hospital *(☎ 669-9201),* 1200 Mohave Rd, and police *(☎ 669-2265),* 1314 11th.

Things to See & Do
Members of four tribes live on the surrounding Colorado River Indian Reservation: Mohave, Chemehuevi, Navajo and Hopi. Their stories are presented in the **Colorado River Indian Tribes Museum** *(☎ 669-9211)* at Mohave Rd and 2nd Ave, southwest of town. Hours are 8 am to noon and 1 to 5 pm Monday to Friday.

Eight miles north of Parker, **La Paz County Park** *(☎ 667-2069)* has a tennis court, horseshoe pits, a playground, beach, boat ramp, swimming, and tent and RV camping. Three miles farther north, **Buckskin Mountain State Park** *(☎ 667-3231)*

ARIZONA

offers tent and RV camping, a boat ramp, beach, swimming, picnicking, a playground, recreation room, laundry, grocery store and ranger-led activities on weekends. A mile north is the River Island Unit (☎ 667-3386), with more camping spaces in a scenic desert setting. Rates are $6 for day use and $12 to $20 for camping.

Parker Dam, 15 miles north of Parker, looks small, but 70% of its structural height is buried beneath the riverbed, making it the world's deepest dam.

Locals go **boating** here and launching areas are located along the Parker Strip. Launching is free or subject to nominal fees. Fishing, water-skiing, jet skiing and inner tubing are also popular. Some rental services are available at the many places along the strip.

Places to Stay & Eat

Apart from the parks listed above, dozens of other places along the Parker Strip and just across the river in California offer both tent and RV camping. These often cost more than the parks, with the exception of BLM campgrounds, several of which can be found on the California side of the river up to 15 miles north of Parker.

The *El Rancho Parker Motel* (☎ 669-2231, 709 California Ave), has a pool, complimentary coffee and rates beginning at $35. The pleasant *Kofa Inn* (☎ 669-2101, 1700 California Ave) has a pool and is adjacent to *Coffee Ern's* (☎ 669-8145), a decent 24-hour family restaurant. Rates start at $40.

The *Stardust Motel* (☎ 669-2278, 800-786-7827, 700 California Ave), has a pool and rooms for similar rates as well as slightly more expensive rooms with kitchenettes. *Chain motels* include a Motel 6 and a Best Western.

The finely named *Hole-in-the-Wall* (☎ 669-9755, 612 California Ave) is good for home-style breakfasts. There are Mexican and fast-food places as well.

In addition, there are several restaurants and motels along the Parker Strip, most with boat docks and launching areas, handy for boaters.

QUARTZSITE
☎ 928 • pop 3354 • elevation 879 feet

Quartzsite's population explodes to hundreds of thousands of people during the early January to mid-February gem and mineral shows. Several thousand dealers and more than a million visitors buy, sell, trade and admire their wares. These folks can't quite squeeze into the town's four tiny motels and so, as the chamber of commerce puts it, the desert around Quartzsite turns into a 'sea of aluminum.' Thousands upon thousands of RVs stretch out as far as the eye can see – a strange sight, indeed.

The chamber of commerce (☎ 927-5600) is on the north side of I-10 exit 17. Hours are 9 am to 4 pm daily in January and February, cutting back to 10 am to 3 pm on Tuesday, Wednesday and Thursday from April to October. Call the chamber for recorded information when it's closed.

During the January/February gem and mineral shows there are stagecoach rides, balloon and helicopter rides, camel and ostrich races, cookouts, dances and other Western events. In the prostrating heat of summer, though, the population dwindles and the town looks like a semi-abandoned junkyard.

Quartzite's most curious and beloved monument is a small stone pyramid topped by a metal camel. The memorial is to Haiji Ali, a Syrian camel driver who arrived in 1856 to help with US army experiments using camels in the desert. After the trials failed, Ali, nicknamed Hi Jolly, became a prospector and died here around 1902. Hi Jolly 'Daze,' with a parade and other festivities, occurs in early January to welcome back winter visitors.

Petroglyphs, ghost towns, ruins, wildlife and desert scenery surround Quartzsite, but visits require long, energetic exploration on poor trails. The chamber of commerce sells a map with over 40 points of interest. Also see below for nearby places that can be visited by car.

The RV camps surrounding town have hookups for RVs and charge up to $20 a night. The farther you park from the center, or the fewer facilities you need, the less you pay. The BLM (☎ 317-3200 in Yuma) runs the *La Posa Long Term Visitor Area* at the south end of town on Hwy 95. For $100, you can camp here (tent or RV) for as long as you want between September 15 and April 15. Permits for seven days cost $20. Facilities include toilets, water (no showers) and dump stations. South of La Posa at mile marker 99, and north of town at mile marker 112, are areas where you can camp for free anytime (14 day limit) but there are no services.

YUMA
☎ 928 • pop 77,515 • elevation 200 feet

Arizona's sunniest, driest and third-largest metropolitan area, Yuma blazes with sun for 93% of its daylight hours, and receives just three inches of rain annually. Winter temperatures in the 70°s F attract many thousands of visitors, who spend the entire winter in scores of trailer parks around the city.

Local Quechan, Cocopah and Mohave Indians, collectively known as the Yumas, knew this was the easiest place to cross the Colorado River for hundreds of miles. Some 30,000 people crossed the Colorado here during the 1849 California gold rush. Steamships once reached Yuma Crossing from the Gulf of Mexico but dams have changed the site to a shadow of the port it was.

The town was founded in 1854, first named Colorado City, then Arizona City – grandiose names considering that the 'city' population was only 85 in 1860, growing to 1100 by 1870. In 1873, Arizona City was renamed Yuma. Three years later, Arizona's Territorial Prison (now a local attraction) was opened – a notorious hellhole that operated for 33 years until a new prison was built in Florence.

Information
The Convention & Visitors Bureau (☎ 783-0071), 377 S Main St, is open 9 am to 5 pm on weekdays, 9 am to 2 pm on Saturdays, and Sundays in winter from 10 am to 1 pm, or check its website at www.visityuma.com. Other services include the Kofa NWR headquarters (☎ 783-7861), 356 W 1st St;

BLM (☎ 317-3200), 2555 E Gila Ridge Rd; AAA of Arizona (☎ 783-3339), 1045 S 4th Ave; library (☎ 782-1871), 350 3rd St; post office (☎ 783-2124), 2222 4th Ave; Medical Center (☎ 344-2000), 2400 Ave A; police (☎ 783-4421), 1500 1st Ave.

Yuma Territorial Prison State Historic Park
Between 1876 and 1909, the prison housed 3069 prisoners, including 29 women – Arizona's most feared criminals. Some buildings still exist, notably the guard tower and the rock-wall cells fronted by gloomy iron-grille doors, giving an idea of what inmates' lives were like. Despite the grim conditions, this was considered a model prison at the time. The jail is complemented by a small museum of interesting artifacts. The whole place is slightly gruesome, mildly historical, definitely offbeat and suitable for the whole family! The prison (☎ 783-4771) is open 8 am to 5 pm daily except Christmas. Admission is $3 for adults, $2 for seven- to 13-year-olds and free for kids under seven. Guided tours are offered at 11 am, 2 and 3:30 pm in winter.

Yuma Crossing State Historic Park
US Army supply buildings predate the prison by a decade or more and parts of them still exist here. Other buildings have been restored, and there is a museum and guided tours of what was once the hub of southwestern Arizona. The depot (☎ 783-4771), 180 1st St, is open from 10 am to 5 pm, closed Christmas and Tuesday and Wednesday from May to October. Admission is the same price as the prison (above).

Century House Museum
Sponsored by the Arizona Historical Society, this museum (☎ 782-1841), 240 S Madison Ave, is in one of the oldest houses (built 1891) in Arizona's southwestern corner. There are exhibits of local historical interest and a garden full of exotic plants and birds. Hours are 10 am to 4 pm Tuesday to Saturday. Admission is free (donations encouraged).

YUMA

PLACES TO STAY
4   Best Western Coronado Motor Hotel
11 Regalodge
18 Motel 6
19 Super 8 Motel
20 Comfort Inn
21 Best Western Innsuites Hotel
22 Shilo Inn
24 Motel 6
25 La Fuente Inn & Suites; Days Inn
26 Fairfield Inn
30 Fourth Ave Travelodge
31 Yuma Cabaña
33 El Rancho Motel
37 Radisson Suites Inn
40 Holiday Inn Express
42 Best Western Chilton Inn
45 Airport Travelodge

PLACES TO EAT
6   Garden Café
8   Lutes Casino; Red's Bird Cage Saloon
13 Chretin's Restaurant
23 Denny's
35 Hunter Steakhouse
38 The Crossing
44 Mandarin Palace

OTHER
1   Quechan Museum at Fort Yuma
2   Kofa NWR Headquarters
3   Yuma Territorial Prison State Historic Park
5   Century House Museum
7   Yuma Theater
9   Convention & Visitors Bureau; Chamber of Commerce
10 Amtrak Train Depot
12 Library
14 AAA of Arizona
15 Plaza Theaters
16 Colorado King River Cruises
17 Police Station
27 Greyhound Bus Terminal
28 Yuma River Tours
29 Yuma Recycling Center
32 Post Office
34 Fry's Supermarket
36 Yuma Regional Medical Center
39 South Gate Shopping Mall
41 Albertson's Supermarket
43 Mandarin Cinemas

Quechan Museum at Fort Yuma

Across the river in California on Indian Hill Rd (off Picacho Rd), Fort Yuma was built in the 1850s. The building now houses a small museum (☎ 760-572-0661) of photographs and historical artifacts operated by the Quechan tribe. Tribal offices are nearby. Museum hours are 8 am to noon and 1 to 5 pm Monday to Friday. Admission is $1 for those over 12. Get there by taking the first California exit on I-8 and heading north.

Agricultural Attractions

During winter (about October through March) several farms offer tours (call for reservations) and sell products. **Saihati Camel Farm** (☎ 627-2553), 15672 S Ave 1E, breeds camels, Asian water buffalo, desert foxes, Arabian horses, Watusi cattle and desert antelopes. **The Peanut Patch** (☎ 726-6292), 4322 E County 13th St, gives tours of the shelling plant during the October-to-December harvest. **The Farm** (☎ 627-3631), Ave A1/2 and County 17 near Somerton, allows you to pick citrus and other fruits. **Imperial Date Gardens** (☎ 760-572-0277), 1517 York Rd, is across the state line in Bard. The free **McElhaney Cattle Company Museum** (☎ 785-3384), 36 miles east of Yuma, displays 19th-century wagons and antique cars. Take I-8 exit 30, head east on old Hwy 80 and follow museum signs. Hours are 8 am to 4 pm Monday to Friday, to noon on Saturday.

Organized Tours

Yuma River Tours (☎ 783-4400), 1920 Arizona Ave, has jet-boat tours to Imperial NWR, Imperial Dam and historic sites (petroglyphs, mining camps etc). Tour guides provide chatty explanations of local history and Indian lore. Five-hour tours are $52 ($25 for children three to 12) and include lunch. Sunset cruises and custom charters are available. Departures are from Fisher's Landing (see Imperial NWR later in this chapter) and run almost daily in winter, less frequently in the hot months.
website: www.yumarivertours.com

The Yuma Railway (☎ 783-3456) leaves from the west end of 8th St, 6 miles west of

downtown. The vintage train makes two-hour runs along the Arizona-Sonora border. Departures are at 1 pm on Saturday and Sunday from November to March, Sunday only in October, April and May. Fares are $13 for adults, $12 for those over 55 and $7 for those four to 16. Call ahead for hours and prices for family picnic runs and steak dinner runs.

The *Colorado King I* is a small, two-deck paddleboat offering narrated, three-hour Colorado River cruises from Fisher's Landing (see Imperial NWR). Departure times vary seasonally; contact the Colorado King River Cruises office (☎ 782-2412, 1636 S 4th Ave) for information. Costs are about $30 with discounts for children 12 and under.

Special Events

The annual Silver Spur Rodeo in early February has been held for more than half a century and features Yuma's biggest parade, arts and crafts shows and various other events along with the rodeo. The Yuma County Fair is held at the beginning of April. Several times a year there are Main Street Block Parties with free street entertainment.

Places to Stay

Winter rates (usually January to April) can be up to $30 higher than summer rates, especially on weekends. In addition, hotels are booked in advance and charge their highest prices during the opening days of dove-hunting season (Labor Day weekend). Rates vary substantially according to demand and those given below are only approximate.

Camping There are over 70 campgrounds, mainly geared to RVs on a long-term basis during the winter. Most have age restrictions (no children, sometimes only for people over 50) and prohibit tents. People planning a long RV stay should contact the visitor's bureau for lists.

Budget All Yuma motels listed have swimming pools (some very small). Many budget hotels charge mid-range prices in winter and the opening of dove-hunting season.

ARIZONA

They include the simple **El Rancho Motel** (☎ 783-4481, 2201 4th Ave), with doubles for $28 in summer and $38 in winter; this is among the cheapest of them. The well recommended and well maintained **Yuma Cabaña** (☎ 783-8311, 800-874-0811, fax 783-1126, 2151 4th Ave) has a large pool and good rooms with interior entrances. A few rooms have kitchenettes. Rates run from about $40 to $70, depending on rooms and season. Continental breakfast is included. Many other budget places are found in this area of 4th Ave. The **Regalodge** (☎ 782-4571, 344 S 4th Ave), is one of the better cheap motels near downtown and has rooms with refrigerators and some kitchenettes. Summer rates are in the $30s, going up to the $40s in winter and more in dove season.

Mid-Range & Top End Most **chain motels** are found near I-8, exit 2. They include two Motel 6s, a good Super 8, a Days Inn, a well-appointed Comfort Inn and an upscale Fairfield Inn with interior corridors. Two Travelodges, a Holiday Inn Express and a Radisson Suites are found away from the freeway.

Of the three Best Westerns, the nicest is the **Best Western Coronado Motor Hotel** (☎ 783-4453, 233 4th Ave), the most attractive hotel close to downtown. It features two pools, a whirlpool, gift shop, continental breakfast and a decent mid-priced adjoining restaurant. Rooms have refrigerators; some have a microwave and/or spa. Some units have two bedrooms, and there are several suites. Summer rates start in the $50s, winter rates in the $70s, with larger units going up to $100.

The **La Fuente Inn & Suites** (☎ 329-1814, 800-841-1814, fax 343-2671, 1513 E 16th St), is a modern, Spanish-colonial-style building surrounding a landscaped garden and pool. There is a hot tub and exercise room for guest use. Rooms are mainly one- or two-room suites, many including microwaves and refrigerators. Rates, which include continental breakfast and evening cocktail hour, are $80 in summer and $100 and up in winter.

The **Shilo Inn** (☎ 782-9511, 800-222-2244, fax 783-1538, 1550 Castle Dome Ave), is the fanciest place in town. Amenities include an exercise room, spa, sauna and steam bath, and the pool is said to be the town's largest. There is a good restaurant and lounge, room service and an airport shuttle. Some rooms have kitchenettes; others feature a balcony or open onto the courtyard. All have refrigerators and interior corridors. Rates range from $100 to $160; the kitchenette suites can go to $225.

Places to Eat

Restaurants can be fairly dead midweek in summer but bustling during the busy winter season. **Lutes Casino** (☎ 782-2192, 221 Main St), is a locally popular hamburger joint. Eclectically decorated and with a bar, pool tables, dominoes and arcade games, it claims to be Arizona's oldest pool hall. Read about its history on the souvenir menu. Kids are welcome.

For more elegant breakfasts and lunches, the **Garden Café** (☎ 783-1491, 250 Madison Ave), is locally popular. It serves good breakfasts, coffees, sandwiches, salads and desserts in a pleasant outdoor patio; there's also an indoor dining room. Hours are 9 am to 2:30 pm, closed Monday. For lunches and dinners, **The Crossing** (☎ 726-5551, 2690 4th Ave), specializes in prime rib, catfish and ribs and also has Italian dishes. Dinner entrées are in the $7 to $17 range.

Yuma has many Mexican restaurants. **Chretin's** (☎ 782-1291, 485 15th Ave) is a locally popular place tucked away inconspicuously on a residential street. It is closed Sunday. For Chinese food, the **Mandarin Palace** (☎ 344-2805, 350 E 32nd St) is both elegant and excellent. The **Hunter Steakhouse** (☎ 782-3637, 2355 4th Ave) open Monday to Friday for lunch and daily for dinner, does good steaks and prime rib.

By far the fanciest place in Yuma is **Julieanna's Patio Cafe** (☎ 317-1961, 1951 W 5th) (call for directions) which features excellent beef, seafood and veal entrées averaging $20. Open for lunch on weekdays, but a better bet is dinner (Monday to Saturday) when the place glows romantically.

Entertainment

Professional baseball teams do their spring training in sunny Yuma at the 7000-seat *Desert Sun Stadium* (☎ 317-3394), south of town off Avenue A. Call for a schedule (most games are in February).

Yuma Theater (☎ 783-4566, 800-386-5477, 254 Main) presents musical reviews most evenings from November to March. The visitor's bureau can provide dates of occasional performances by the local chamber orchestra, community theater and both classical and Mexican folkloric ballet companies.

Choose movies from the multiscreened *Plaza Theaters* (☎ 782-9292, 1560 4th Ave), or *Mandarin Cinemas* (☎ 782-7409, 3142 S Arizona Ave).

For pool, dominoes and other games during the day, see Lutes Casino under Places to Eat. Next door is *Red's Bird Cage Saloon* (☎ 783-1050, 231 Main St), for pool, darts and drinking after Lutes closes. It sometimes has live entertainment.

Getting There & Away

The airport (south of 32nd St) is served by Skywest Airlines, America West Express and United Express. Many flights serve Phoenix, and some go to Los Angeles. Avis, Budget, Hertz and Enterprise rent cars at the airport.

The Greyhound Bus Terminal (☎ 783-4403, 170 E 17 Place, has buses to Phoenix; Tucson; Lordsburg, New Mexico; El Paso, Texas; and San Diego, California.

San Luis-Yuma Transit (☎ 627-1130), at the Greyhound terminal, has several daily departures to San Luis on the Mexican border. American Shuttle Express (☎ 726-0906, 888-749-9862) has vans from Yuma to Phoenix Airport ($48).

WILDLIFE REFUGES NEAR YUMA
Imperial National Wildlife Refuge

Thousands of overwintering waterfowl make mid-December through February the best time to visit this refuge, 36 miles north of Yuma, for birding. The small **Martinez Lake** has some water-skiing and boating ac-

tivity in summer. Refuge headquarters (☎ 783-3371), on Martinez Lake, is open 7:30 am to 4 pm Monday to Friday. An observation tower nearby gives views, and a dirt road reaches several observation points and a 1-mile interpretive trail. There is no camping.

Martinez Lake Resort (☎ 783-0253, 783-9589, 800-876-7004) and the smaller *Fisher's Landing* (☎ 783-6513, 783-5357) both offer boating, RV camping, a grocery store and lounge. Martinez Lake Resort also has boat rental, motel and restaurant; Fisher's Landing has tent camping. These places are reserved weeks in advance for national holidays in summer.

Cibola National Wildlife Refuge

This is an important overwintering site for Canada geese (up to 25,000 in midwinter), about 1000 greater sandhill cranes and many other waterfowl – a good place to watch for migrants from mid-November to late February. Some 237 species have been recorded, including the endangered Yuma clapper rail. Information is available from Cibola NWR (☎ 857-3253). There is no camping.

Hours are from 8 am to 4:30 pm Monday to Friday. From the headquarters, the Canada Geese Drive auto tour road is open daily during daylight hours.

Kofa National Wildlife Refuge

Three rugged mountain ranges, the Kofa, the Castle Dome and the Tank Mountains, meet together in a splendidly wild tangle. The refuge covers just over 1000 sq miles, most of which is designated wilderness with vehicular access limited to a few dirt roads. Off-road driving is prohibited. Other visitor facilities are nonexistent. Bighorn sheep roam the area, but are hard to spot.

Most visitors drive into the refuge from the west on Hwy 95 to the entrance to Palm Canyon, about 29 miles south of Quartzsite, or 51 miles northeast of Yuma. A passable 7.2-mile dirt road leads to a parking area from where a steep, rocky, half-mile trail climbs to views of Palm Canyon: a sheer-walled crack to the north within which a stand of California palms *(Washingtonia filifera)* can be seen – the only place in Arizona where they grow naturally. Best views are around midday; at other times the palms are in shadow. There are several other access points and poor

dirt roads through the refuge. Obtain information from Kofa NWR (☎ 783-7861), 356 W 1st St, Yuma. Camping is allowed anytime, anywhere (except within a quarter mile of water holes), with a 14-day limit.

Central Arizona

North of Phoenix there is nowhere to go but up. In summer, droves of southern Arizonans head north to camp, fish, sightsee, shop and find cool relief. During the winter, many of the same folks make the trip in search of snow and skiing. But central Arizona isn't just the province of canny locals; this area, with the important town of Flagstaff, is the gateway to the Grand Canyon.

Apart from the outdoor activities visitors will find several national monuments sprinkled throughout the area, some protecting Indian sites. Old mining towns either lie forgotten or flourish with a new lease on life as artists' communities. Prescott, the first territorial capital, preserves architecture from its Wild West days. Sedona, a modern town amid splendid red-rock scenery, draws tourists seeking relaxation as well as New Agers looking for spiritual and psychic insights at the area's many vortexes. And Flagstaff provides museums, cultural events, nightlife and a laid-back atmosphere fueled by students, skiers and international visitors.

From Phoenix to Flagstaff takes under three hours along I-17, or you can spend a few days wandering through the intriguing small towns that dot the countryside along and around Hwys 89 and 89A, the route described in this chapter.

WICKENBURG
☎ 928 • pop 5082 • elevation 2093 feet
In the 1860s Wickenburg was a thriving community surrounded by gold mines. Today Wickenburg, just an hour northwest of Phoenix, has several ranches offering cowboy-style vacations in fall, winter and spring. Casual visitors stop to see the Western buildings constructed between the 1860s and the 1920s (ask the chamber of commerce for a walking map). The 1863 **Trinidad House** is said to be Arizona's oldest home. Locals like to point out the 19th-century 'jail' – a tree to which outlaws were chained.

There is no bus service. Hwy 93 to Kingman is dubbed Joshua Tree Parkway for the many stands of those plants lining the highway.

Information
The chamber of commerce (☎ 684-5479, 800-942-5242), 216 N Frontier, is open daily and offers information at www.wickenburg chamber.com. Other services include the library (☎ 684-2665), 160 N Valentine, post office (☎ 684-2138), 2030 W Wickenburg Way, hospital (☎ 684-5421), 520 Rose Lane, and police (☎ 684-5411), 155 N Tegner.

Things to See & Do
The **Desert Caballeros Western Museum** (☎ 684-2272), 21 N Frontier, features a fine collection of canvases and bronzes by

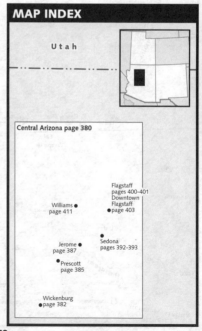

MAP INDEX

Utah

Central Arizona page 380

Flagstaff
pages 400-401
Downtown
Flagstaff
page 403

Williams
page 411

Jerome
page 387

Sedona
pages 392-393

Prescott
page 385

Wickenburg
page 382

ARIZONA

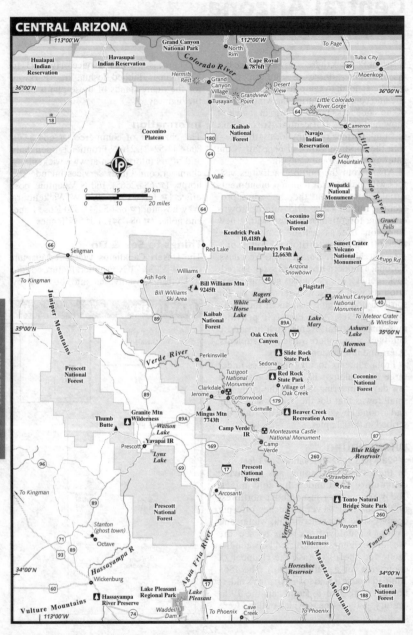

CENTRAL ARIZONA

famous Western artists such as Frederic Remington and Indian arts. There are changing shows and a gift shop. Hours are 10 am to 5 pm daily except noon to 4 pm on Sundays, and closed on major holidays. Admission is $5 for adults, $4 for seniors and $1 for six- to 18-year-olds.

website: www.westernmuseum.org

The **Hassayampa River Preserve**, on the west side of Hwy 60, 3 miles south of town, is operated by The Nature Conservancy and protects one of the few riparian habitats remaining in Arizona. A visitor center (☎ 684-2772) provides information about 2 miles of trails. Hours are 8 am to 5 pm, Friday to Sunday in summer and Wednesday to Sunday the rest of the year. A $5 donation to The Nature Conservancy is suggested.

The **Vulture Mine** (☎ 859-2743), where Henry Wickenburg found gold nuggets lying on the ground in 1863, can be visited for $5; $4 for six- to 12-year-olds. Rent a gold pan for another $4 – you just might strike it rich! Hours are 8 am to 4 pm daily from fall to spring. The mine is 12 miles south along Vulture Mine Rd, which is 3 miles west of downtown.

Robson's Mining World (☎ 685-2609), about 30 miles west of town on Hwy 71, has two dozen restored buildings, a huge collection of early mining equipment, a restaurant (offering lunch daily and dinner by reservation) and a B&B. Hiking trails lead to Indian pictographs. Hours are 10 am to 4 pm on weekdays and 8 am to 6 pm weekends, from October through April. Admission is $5; free for B&B guests and children ages 10 and under.

Cowboy-Up Hummer Tours (☎ 684-4970), 295 E Wickenburg Way, and BC Jeep Tours (☎ 684-7901) drive you into the backcountry. Rincon Ranch Lodge (☎ 684-2328, rideaz@primenet.com) offers horse rides from $45 (two hours) to $100 (all day).

Wickenburg celebrates its Western heritage during Gold Rush Days, held the second Friday to Sunday in February since the 1940s. Rodeo action, parades, gold panning and shootouts headline the events. The chamber of commerce lists numerous other events throughout the year.

Places to Stay

Camping *Horspitality RV Park* (☎ 684-2519), 2 miles southeast on Hwy 60, has hookups, showers and horse stables. Rates are $16 per vehicle, and winter reservations are suggested. Similar facilities, plus a pool, are found at the adult-only *Desert Cypress Trailer Ranch* (☎ 684-2153, 610 Jack Burden Rd).

Hotels Rates drop during the hot summer months and rise during winter weekends or special events. Basic cheapies include the *Capri Motel* (☎ 684-7232, 521-A W Wickenburg Way) and *Circle JR Motel* (☎ 684-2661, 741 W Wickenburg Way), with simple rooms around $40. The well-run *Americinn* (☎/fax 684-5461, 800-634-3444, 850 E Wickenburg Way) has a pool, whirlpool and restaurant serving breakfast, lunch and dinner. Some rooms have balconies. Rates range from $50 to $80. Spacious rooms with patios or balconies are featured at *Los Viajeros* (☎ 684-7099, 1000 N Tegner), with a pool and whirlpool. Rates are $80/110, single/double. The *Best Western Rancho Grande* (☎ 684-544, 5293 E Wickenburg Way) has a pool and tennis court and some rooms with kitchenettes at rates from $70 to $100. Both this and the cheaper *Super 8* (☎ 684-0808, 925 N Tegner) have attractive Western motifs.

Guest Ranches Ranches usually close in summer. During the cooler months, they offer all-inclusive packages including horseback riding, meals and other activities such as shuffleboard, mountain biking, tennis, golf etc. Daily rates range from $100 to over $300 depending on dates, rooms and activities chosen. Contact the following to compare what's offered (all addresses are in Wickenburg): *Flying E Ranch* (☎ 684-2690/2173, 2801 W Wickenburg Way, AZ 85390-1087), www.flyingeranch.com; *Kay El Bar Ranch* (☎ 684-7593, 800-684-7583, PO Box 2480, AZ 85358), www.KAYELBAR.com; *Rancho de los Caballeros* (☎ 684-5484, 1551 S Vulture Mine Rd, AZ 85390), www.SunC.com; and *Rancho Casitas* (☎ 684-2628, 56550 Rancho Casitas Rd, AZ 85390).

ARIZONA

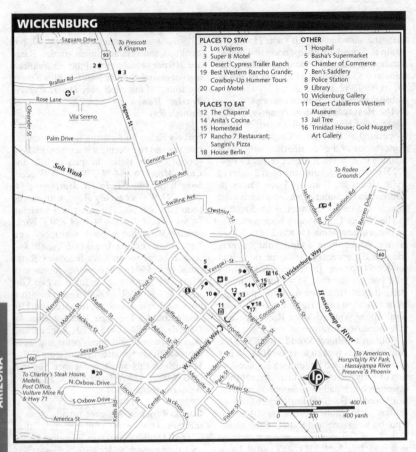

WICKENBURG

PLACES TO STAY
2 Los Viajeros
3 Super 8 Motel
4 Desert Cypress Trailer Ranch
19 Best Western Rancho Grande;
   Cowboy-Up Hummer Tours
20 Capri Motel

PLACES TO EAT
12 The Chaparral
14 Anita's Cocina
15 Homestead
17 Rancho 7 Restaurant;
   Sangini's Pizza
18 House Berlin

OTHER
1 Hospital
5 Basha's Supermarket
6 Chamber of Commerce
7 Ben's Saddlery
8 Police Station
9 Library
10 Wickenburg Gallery
11 Desert Caballeros Western
   Museum
13 Jail Tree
16 Trinidad House; Gold Nugget
   Art Gallery

Places to Eat

Easily found by referring to the map, the
Homestead (☎ 684-2858) is open from 6 am
to 10 pm daily and has a lounge with 1890s-
style flowered wallpaper. American meals
here are moderately priced and good.
Rancho 7 Restaurant (☎ 684-2492), locally
popular for decades, features home-style
American and Mexican cooking from
11 am to 9 pm daily. Play darts, pool and
shuffleboard in the adjoining bar. *Charley's
Steak House* (☎ 684-2413, 1181 W Wickenburg Way), the town's best steak house, is
open from 5 to 9 pm Tuesday to Saturday.

The *House Berlin* (☎ 684-5004) offers
haute German cuisine for lunch and dinner
daily except Monday. Dinner entrées are
$10 to $14.

Sangini's Pizza (☎ 684-7828) serves
lunch and dinner daily. They deliver. Try
Anita's Cocina (☎ 684-5777) for Mexican
lunch and dinners. *The Chaparral* (☎ 684-
3252) serves homemade ice cream, pastries
and snacks.

Shopping

The chamber of commerce can give you a list
of art galleries and antique shops downtown.

The Gold Nugget Art Gallery (☎ 684-5849), in the historic Trinidad House, and the Wickenburg Gallery (☎ 684-7047), 10 W Apache, are among the best. For a real whiff of the Old West, mosey into Ben's Saddlery (☎ 684-2683), 184 N Tegner; even if you aren't in the market for a saddle, the leathery smell makes it the most memorable shop in town.

PRESCOTT
☎ 928 • pop 33,938 • elevation 5346 feet
Founded in 1864 by gold prospectors, Prescott, 60 miles north of Wickenburg, became Arizona's first territorial capital. President Abraham Lincoln preferred the progressive mining town over conservative Tucson, considered to have Confederate leanings. Vestiges of early territorial life remain in Prescott's many early buildings, including the first governor's mansion. Prescott's historic character, outdoor recreation in surrounding national forest, the adjacent Yavapai Indian Reservation with legal gambling, two colleges, a small artists' community and galleries give the town a bohemian air.

Frontier Days, held around the Fourth of July, features the world's oldest rodeo. Hotels are booked well in advance and rates rise.

Information
The chamber of commerce (☎ 445-2000, 800-266-7534), 117 W Goodwin, is open from 9 am to 5 pm, Monday to Friday, 9 am to 3 pm on Saturday, and 10 am to 2 pm on Sunday. Call them for a list of the many special events held in summer.
website: www.prescott.org

Other services include Prescott National Forest Supervisor's Office (☎ 771-4700), 344 S Cortez; the library (☎ 445-8110), 215 E Goodwin; main post office (☎ 778-1890), 442 Miller Valley Rd; the downtown branch at Goodwin and Cortez; medical center (☎ 445-2700), 1003 Willow Creek Rd; and police (☎ 778-1444), 222 S Marina.

Historic Buildings
Montezuma St west of Courthouse Plaza was once the infamous 'Whiskey Row,' with 40 drinking establishments serving cowboys and miners who attempted to have a drink in each. A devastating 1900 fire destroyed 25 saloons, five hotels and the red-light district, but many early buildings remain so you can still have a drink on colorful Whiskey Row. The County Courthouse in the center of the shady and relaxing plaza dates from 1918.

Buildings east and south of the plaza escaped the 1900 fire and date from the late 19th century. Some were built by East Coast settlers who built wooden Victorian houses in New England style, markedly different from adobe Southwestern buildings.

Museums
The **Sharlot Hall Museum** (☎ 445-3122), 415 W Gurley, covering two city blocks, is Prescott's most important museum. You can stroll by the two-story log building that was the first governor's mansion and view many other buildings from the 1860s and '70s surrounded by flowery gardens. The Museum Center displays historical artifacts and old photographs. Hours are 10 am to 5 pm Monday to Saturday (till 4 pm in winter) and 1 to 5 pm on Sunday. Admission is a suggested $4 donation per adult or $5 per family.
website: www.sharlot.org

Six miles north of town, the **Phippen Museum of Western Art** (☎ 778-1385), 4701 N Hwy 89, named after cowboy artist George Phippen and displaying some of his works, has a good collection of Western paintings, bronzes and photographs, as well as changing exhibits. Hours are 10 am to 4 pm daily except Sunday (1 to 4 pm) and Tuesday (closed). Admission is $3 for adults, $2 for seniors and children 12 and over.
website: www.phippenmuseum.org

Built like an Indian pueblo, the **Smoki Museum** (☎ 445-1230), 147 N Arizona, displays Southwestern Indian artifacts dating from prehistoric times to the present. Hours from April 15 through October are 10 am to 4 pm, 1 to 4 pm Sunday. Admission is a $2 donation for adults.
website: www.smoki.com

Sharlot Hall

Twelve-year-old Sharlot Mabrith Hall arrived in Prescott in February 1882 after an arduous horseback trip from Kansas with her family. During the journey, she was thrown by her horse, causing a back injury that plagued her for the rest of her life.

While helping run her family's ranch, she became fascinated with life on the frontier. Largely self-schooled, she began describing the gold miners, Indians and ranchers around her in a series of stories and poems that soon gained local admiration. In 1909 she was appointed Territorial Historian, the first woman to hold a political office in Arizona.

In 1924 she traveled to Washington, DC, to represent Arizona in the Electoral College. She caused a stir in the capital with her outfit that included a copper mesh coat provided by a local mine. There was no mistaking that Arizona was 'The Copper State.' During her visit to the east, she toured several museums; these inspired her to found a museum of Arizona history.

On her return to Prescott, Hall leased the first territorial capitol building and restored the governor's mansion. In 1928, she moved her extensive personal collection of historical artifacts into the mansion and opened it as a museum. She lived on the property, expanding and adding to the collection until her death in 1943. The museum bearing her name has continued to flourish since then. In 1981, Sharlot Hall was elected to the Arizona Women's Hall of Fame.

Activities

The Prescott National Forest office can suggest hikes, climbs, picnic areas, campgrounds and fishing holes. Local lakes are stocked with trout, bluegill, bass and catfish. Popular nearby areas are Thumb Butte, Lynx Lake and the Granite Mountain Wilderness.

Looming over the west side of town, **Thumb Butte** is reached by driving 3 miles along Gurley and Thumb Butte Rd. A 1.2-mile trail makes it almost to the summit, 1000 feet above town. The last 200 feet are the province of rock climbers.

To reach **Lynx Lake**, drive 4 miles east on Hwy 69, then 3 miles south on Walker Rd. Here you'll find fishing, hiking, camping, a store, a small-boat rental (summer only), a small Indian site and bird watching.

The **Granite Mountain Wilderness** has a fishing lake, campgrounds and hiking trails, and is popular with rock climbers. Head north on Grove Ave from downtown, which becomes Miller Valley Rd, bear left on Iron Springs Rd, and about 4 miles from Prescott, turn right on unpaved USFS Rd 347 and continue for another 4 miles.

Try picnicking, fishing and camping at **Watson Lake**, about 4 miles north on Hwy 89. Just beyond are the **Granite Dells**, a landscape of 100-foot-high, rounded red-rock outcrops that you can hike through or climb.

Buy or rent camping and climbing equipment at Mountain Sports (☎ 445-8310), 142 N Cortez, or Granite Mountain Outfitters (☎ 776-4949), 320 W Gurley. Rent mountain bikes from Ironclad Bicycles (☎ 776-1755), 710 White Spar Rd. For horseback riding, try Granite Mountain Stables (☎ 771-9551), about 10 miles northwest of town. Mile High Adventures (☎ 776-9115) does guided hikes, bike and jeep rides.

Places to Stay

Summer weekend rates are often much higher than weekdays. Prescott Valley, 8 miles east along Hwy 69, has several other motels (mainly chains).

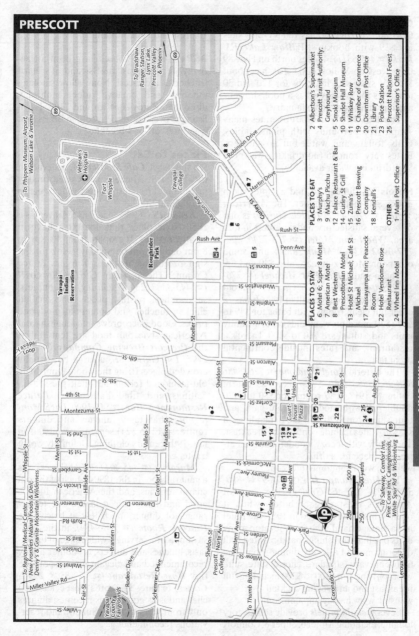

PRESCOTT

PLACES TO STAY
6 Motel 6; Super 8 Motel
7 American Motel
8 Best Western
   Prescottonian Motel
13 Hotel St Michael; Café St
   Michael
17 Hassayampa Inn; Peacock
   Room
22 Hotel Vendome; Rose
   Restaurant
24 Wheel Inn Motel

PLACES TO EAT
3 Murphy's
9 Machu Picchu
12 Palace Restaurant & Bar
14 Gurley St Grill
15 Zuma's
16 Prescott Brewing
   Company
18 Kendall's

OTHER
1 Main Post Office
2 Albertson's Supermarket
4 Prescott Transit Authority;
   Greyhound
5 Smoki Museum
10 Sharlot Hall Museum
11 Whiskey Row
19 Chamber of Commerce
20 Downtown Post Office
21 Library
23 Police Station
25 Prescott National Forest
   Supervisor's Office

ARIZONA

Camping *Point of Rocks RV Park* (☎ 445-9018, 3025 N Hwy 89) has 100 RV-only sites for $19 with hookups. *Willow Lake RV Park* (☎ 445-6311), 4 miles north on Hwy 89 then west on Willow Lake Rd, has about 170 RV sites with hookups for $20 and 30 tent sites for $14 as well as a pool, showers, a playground and a coin laundry.

The USFS (☎ 771-4700) operates many simple campgrounds with picnic tables, grills, toilets, and water but no showers. Rates vary from $6 (no drinking water) to $10 (drinking water available).

Hotels It's difficult to find a motel room under $40 in the summer. The *American Motel* (☎ 778- 4322, 1211 E Gurley) is one of several satisfactory budget hotels in that area. *Wheel Inn Motel* (☎ 778-7346, 800-717-0902, 333 S Montezuma) and some others on Montezuma are also $40 and up.

The popular *Hotel St Michael* (☎ 776-1999, 800-678-3757, 205 W Gurley) is an old Whiskey Row hotel rebuilt in 1900. It has 72 older but clean rooms with baths for $49 to $59 ($20 more on weekends); a few family units and 'suites' are $80 to $100. There's a restaurant, and rates include continental breakfast.

The historic *Hotel Vendome* (☎ 776-0900, 888-463-3583, 230 S Cortez) has charm dating to 1917 in 17 rooms for $80 to $120 double, all with modern private bath, and four suites for $120 and up, depending on season. Rates include continental breakfast. The lobby with a cozy wooden bar is an attractive place for a drink.
website: www.vendomehotel.com

The *Hassayampa Inn* (☎ 778-9434, 800-322-1927, 122 E Gurley) was one of Arizona's most elegant hotels when it opened in 1927. Restored in 1985, the hotel has a vintage hand-operated elevator, many of its original furnishings, hand-painted wall decorations and a lovely dining room. The 68 rooms vary (standard, choice, suite, suite with spa) and run $100 to $200 including full breakfast and an evening cocktail.
website: www.hassayampainn.com

Several *chain motels* provide satisfactory lodging, including Motel 6, Super 8, Comfort Inn, Days Inn, Best Western, Holiday Inn Express and Hampton Inn.

B&Bs Some old houses have been attractively restored as B&Bs, and it's hard to choose the nicest. None allow smoking indoors and many offer multi-day discounts. Rates start around $100. For a listing of over a dozen Prescottian B&Bs, visit www.prescott-bed-breakfast.org.

Places to Eat
On the plaza, *Café St Michael*, underneath the Hotel St Michael, serves reasonably priced breakfasts, espressos and light meals throughout the day.

Kendall's (☎ 778-3658, 113 S Cortez) is a 1950s-style place that doesn't believe in small portions. It's open from 11 am to 8 pm daily (6 pm on Sunday); look for the sign promising 'Famous Burgers & Ice Cream.' The popular *Gurley St Grill* (☎ 445-3388, 230 W Gurley) has burgers, sandwiches, pastas, pizzas and grilled chicken lunches and dinners at moderate prices. Good microbrews and English- and American-style pub food are featured at the *Prescott Brewing Company* (☎ 771-2795, 130 Gurley St), a large but usually crowded place. Bring the whole family. The old-fashioned (check out their pressed-tin ceilings and tiled bathrooms) *Palace Restaurant & Bar* (☎ 541-1996, 120 S Montezuma) has tasty lunches and dinners (entrees $12 to $24) served by waitstaff in late-19th-century clothing. Definitely worth a bite.

Murphy's (☎ 445-4044, 201 N Cortez) was a general store in the 1890s. Much of the old charm remains, and the American food is good and fairly priced in the $12 to $19 range for dinner, much less at lunch. The *Peacock Room* (☎ 778-9434), in the Hassayampa Inn, serving a wide range of breakfasts, lunches and dinners, is another highly recommended and elegant dining spot. The tiny *Rose Restaurant* (☎ 777-8308, 235 S Cortez) features Prescott's most celebrated chef and is as gourmet as it comes; dinners only from Wednesday to Sunday and reservations recommended.

Zuma's (☎ 541-1400, 124 N Montezuma) has wood-fired pizzas, decent Italian food (entrées up to $18), an above-average selection of libations and a slightly alternative atmosphere. *Machu Picchu* (☎ 717-8241, 111 Grove Ave) has a Peruvian chef and serves authentic ceviches and all things Peruvian for lunch and dinner daily except Sunday. Prices are around $10.

The *Pine Cone Inn* (☎ 445-2970, 1245 White Spar Rd) opens at 7 am for breakfast and serves good American lunches and dinners; Prescottians drive out from town for a change of pace and to enjoy the frequent live music and dancing.

Getting There & Away

America West Express flies daily to Phoenix from Prescott Airport, 9 miles north on Hwy 89.

Prescott Transit Authority/Greyhound (☎ 445-5470, 800-445-7978), 820 E Sheldon, has 13 buses a day to Phoenix ($24). Shuttle U (☎ 800-304-6114), or www.shuttleu.com, runs several vans a day to Phoenix Airport. Coconino/Yavapai Shuttle (☎ 775-8929) has two buses a day to Flagstaff ($22).

JEROME

☎ 928 • pop 329 • elevation 5400 feet

Rich in copper, gold and silver, this area was mined by Indians before the arrival of Europeans. Jerome had 15,000 inhabitants in the 1920s, but the 1929 stock market crash shut down many of the mines. The last closed in 1953 and Jerome looked as if it would become another ghost town.

In the late 1960s, Jerome's spectacular location and empty houses were discovered by hippies, artists and retirees, and slowly Jerome became what it is today, a collection of late-19th- and early-20th-century buildings housing art galleries, souvenir shops, restaurants, saloons and a few B&Bs, all precariously perched on a steep hillside. Hwy 89A slowly wends through town 34 miles northeast of Prescott (not recommended for large trailers, allow 90 minutes), and the 15 mph speed limit makes this a tourist trap in more ways than one. However, many of the antique shops and art galleries feature high quality pieces – the shopping can be definitely upscale.

The **Mine Museum** (☎ 634-5477), 200 Main, displays old photos, documents, tools and other memorabilia explaining Jerome's history. Hours are 9 am to 4:30 pm and admission is $1 for people 13 and over. A mile north of town, the **Gold King Mine Museum** (☎ 634-0053) is a miniature ghost town with demonstrations of antique mining equipment, a walk-in mine, a gift shop and a few animals for children to pet. Hours are 9 am to 5 pm daily; admission is $4, $3 for seniors and $2 for six- to 12-year-olds.

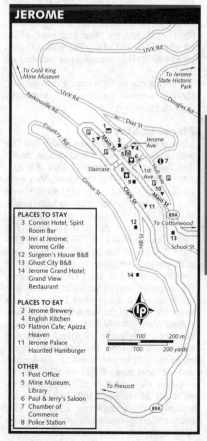

JEROME

PLACES TO STAY
3 Connor Hotel; Spirit Room Bar
9 Inn at Jerome; Jerome Grille
12 Surgeon's House B&B
13 Ghost City B&B
14 Jerome Grand Hotel; Grand View Restaurant

PLACES TO EAT
2 Jerome Brewery
4 English Kitchen
10 Flatiron Cafe; Apizza Heaven
11 Jerome Palace Haunted Hamburger

OTHER
1 Post Office
5 Mine Museum; Library
6 Paul & Jerry's Saloon
7 Chamber of Commerce
8 Police Station

ARIZONA

The **Jerome State Historic Park** (☎ 634-5381), 2 miles beyond Jerome en route to Cottonwood, surrounds the 1916 mansion of colorful mining mogul 'Rawhide' Jimmy Douglas and gives a thorough understanding of the town's mining history. View models, exhibits, a video presentation inside the mansion and old mining equipment outside. Admission is $2.50; $1 for seven- to 13-year-olds. Hours are 8 am to 5 pm daily except Christmas.

Information

The chamber of commerce (☎ 634-2900), on Hull Ave, is open 10 am to 4 pm in summer and is online at www.Jeromechamber.com. Other services include the library (☎ 639-0574), 111 Jerome Ave and post office (☎ 634-8241), 120 Main. The police station (☎ 634-8992) is in the town hall building on Main St.

Parking can be tight during the summer, though several parking lots generally provide enough space.

Places to Stay

Most accommodations are pricey but fun with antique flourishes and quaint decor. The **Inn at Jerome** (☎ 634-5094, 800-634-5094, 309 Main) has six clean Victorian rooms with shared baths ($55 to $75) and two with a private bath ($75 to $85) including breakfast. All rooms have sinks and TVs, and a guest parlor is available. The 1898 **Connor Hotel** (☎ 634-5006, 800-523-3554, 164 Main) has 10 restored bedrooms with period furniture and private baths ranging from $75 to $125. The hotel is over the popular Spirit Room Bar with live music on weekends; rooms 1 to 4 get the worst (or best) of the bar noise. The **Jerome Grand Hotel** (☎ 634-8200, 200 Hill St) was built as a hospital in 1926 and renovated into a hotel in 1996. Perched above town, many of its 30 simple rooms have balconies and excellent views. Rates are $70 to $110.

Ghost City B&B (☎ 634-4678, 888-634-4678, 541 Main), in an 1898 building, has a verandah with great views, a hot tub, four rooms sharing two bathrooms for $80 a double, and two with private baths for $100,

including breakfast and afternoon tea. The **Surgeon's House B&B** (☎ 639-1452, 800-639-1452, 101 Hill St), built in 1917 at the top of the town, has three suites with great views (one has a huge picture window) at $100 to $150, including full breakfast. Check the chamber of commerce for details of these and several other small B&Bs.

Places to Eat & Drink

The **English Kitchen** (☎ 634-2132, 119 Jerome Ave), serving meals since 1899, claims to be Arizona's oldest restaurant. Eat standard inexpensive breakfasts and lunches inside or on the outside deck from Tuesday to Sunday. It's often busy with day-trippers.

The **Flatiron Cafe** (☎ 634-2733, 416 Main) has a great selection of coffee and baked goods and also serves trendy light meals. Next door, **Apizza Heaven** (☎ 649-1834)does good pizzas daily except Tuesday. **Jerome Brewery** (☎ 634-8477, 111 Main) has the best sandwiches in town and serves microbrews. The **Jerome Palace Haunted Hamburger** (☎ 634-0554, 410 Clark) features a tasty selection of burgers, steaks, salads and pasta; they have a full-service bar.

The **Jerome Grille**, in the Inn at Jerome, serves reasonably priced American and Southwestern breakfast, lunch and dinner daily. The **Grand View Restaurant**, in the Jerome Grand Hotel, has varied but mainly American cuisine.

A good place to get drinks is **Paul & Jerry's Saloon** (☎ 634-2603, 206 Main), originally called the Senate Saloon when it first opened in 1899. The **Spirit Room Bar**, under the Hotel Connor, is the town's liveliest bar; both places feature live music on weekends.

COTTONWOOD
☎ 928 • pop 9179 • elevation 3320 feet

Named after the trees growing along the Verde River, Cottonwood was first settled in the 1870s but is essentially a modern town and a good base for exploring the area. Main St north of the police station is 'Old Town.' The **Clemenceau Heritage Museum** (☎ 634-2868), 1 N Willard, illustrates local history and has a superb and realistic model railroad exhibit of the area. Hours are 9 am to noon on Wednesday and 11 am to 3 pm Friday to Sunday; admission is by donation. The **Old Town Palace** (☎ 634-7167), 914 N Main, claims to be America's oldest running single-screen cinema.

The Sedona-Phoenix Shuttle (☎ 282-2066) stops in Cottonwood.

Information

The chamber of commerce (☎ 634-7593), 1010 S Main, open from 9 am to 5 pm, has limited information; see http://chamber .verdevalley.com. Other services include the library (☎ 634-7559),100 S 6th; post office (☎ 634-9526), 700 E Mingus Ave; medical center (☎ 634-2251), 269 S Candy Lane; and police (☎ 634-4246), 816 N Main.

Tuzigoot National Monument

Tuzigoot (☎ 634-5564) features a two-story Sinaguan pueblo (1125 to 1425 AD) that once housed 200 people; the remnants can be visited on a short, steep trail (no wheelchairs) and are memorable for their ridgetop location affording fine views of the Verde River Valley. Don't miss the visitor center's exhibit of Sinaguan artifacts. Hours are 8 am to 7 pm from Memorial Day to Labor Day and 8 am to 5 pm the rest of the year. Admission is $2 for adults; all passes are honored. Tuzigoot is 2 miles north of Cottonwood – follow signs from Hwy 89A.

Verde Canyon Railroad

Vintage FP7 engines pull coaches on four-hour guided roundtrips into splendid countryside north of Cottonwood Pass, traveling through roadless areas with views of red rock cliffs, riparian areas, Indian sites, wildlife and, from December to April, bald eagles. The mid-point is Perkinsville, a remote ranch where parts of *How the West Was Won* were filmed; the train returns the way it came, over bridges and trestles. Views far surpass that of the Grand Canyon Railway. Year-round departures from Clarkdale (2½ miles north of Cottonwood) leave every Wednesday and Sunday at 1 pm. Most months feature additional departures

on several other days and some 9 am or 2:30 pm runs. Moonlight rides leave at 5:30 pm on full-moon nights in summer. First-class carriages feature plush seating, complimentary hors d'oeuvres and cash bar service; coach class is comfortable but more crowded and has a cash snack bar. All first-class tickets cost $55. Coach-class tickets are $36; seniors pay $33 and kids under 12 pay $21. Reservations are required. Carriages are climate controlled and all passengers have access to open-air viewing cars. The Clarkdale depot has a café and small museum. For schedule and reservations call ☎ 639-0010 or 800-293-7245.

website: www.verdecanyonrr.com

Places to Stay

For camping, the **Dead Horse Ranch State Park** (☎ 634-5283), on the north side of Cottonwood, has showers and 45 basic sites for $10, as well as some with hookups for $15. The park also offers picnicking, fishing, nature trails and a playground ($4 for day-use).

Rio Verde RV Park (☎ 634-5990, 3420 Hwy 89A) has showers and a coin laundry and charges $11 for tents or $21 with hookups. The **Turquoise Triangle RV Park** (☎ 634-5294, 2501 E Hwy 89A) is RV-only for $22.

The funky older **Sundial Motel** (☎ 634-8031, 1034 N Main) charges $40 a double. The **View Motel** (☎ 634-7581, 818 S Main) has a pool, whirlpool and hilltop location. Rates start at $36 and go over $50 with kitchenettes. The **Willow Tree Inn** (☎ 634-3678, 1089 S Hwy 260) lacks a pool but is clean and about $45 to $60.

Cottonwood's three **chain motels**, the Super 8, Quality Inn and Best Western, all with pools, whirlpools and free continental breakfasts, provide rooms for $60 to $90.

Places to Eat

Rosalie's Bluewater Inn (☎ 634-8702, 517 N 12th) features good and inexpensive home-style breakfast, lunch and dinner. A handful of hole-in-the-wall eateries in Old Town yield surprisingly good cheap food, especially **Old Town Café** (☎ 634-5980, 1025 N Main) for sandwiches and salads, and *Gas Works Mexican Restaurant* (☎ *634-7426, 1033 N Main*). More upscale dining featuring Southwestern cuisine is the focus of the *Main Street Café* (☎ *639-4443, 315 S Main*).

Blazin' M Ranch (☎ *634-0334, 800-937-8643, oldwest@blazinm.com*), next to Dead Horse Ranch State Park, has filling chuck-wagon suppers with rootin' tootin' cowboy entertainment for $20 ($10 for kids 10 and under). Call for dates and reservations.

AROUND CAMP VERDE

On I-17, 85 miles north of Phoenix, Camp Verde (elevation 3133 feet) is on the way to Jerome, Sedona and Flagstaff for travelers taking the quicker freeway rather than the long trip through Wickenburg and Prescott. Several places along the interstate north and south of Camp Verde are worth a look. Near exit 287, stay at the *Microtel Inn* (☎ *567-3700, 888-567-8483*) for $50 to $80, or at the *Super 8 Motel* or *Comfort Inn*.

Fort Verde State Historic Park

Four original fort buildings have been restored, which together with the original parade grounds and some foundations, give the visitor an idea of what life was like here in the 1880s. Visit the museum (☎ 567-3275) for self-guided tour brochures describing the area. Volunteers in period costumes give interpretive demonstrations periodically. Fort Verde Day, on the second Saturday of October, has several historical reenactments. Hours are 8 am to 4:30 pm daily except Christmas. Admission is $2 for adults; $1 for seven- to 14-year-olds.

Montezuma Castle National Monument

Like nearby Tuzigoot, Montezuma Castle is an Ancestral Puebloan site built and occupied between the 12th and 14th centuries. The name refers to the splendid castle-like location high on a cliff; early explorers thought the five-story-high pueblo was Aztec and hence dubbed it Montezuma. A museum (☎ 567-3322) interprets the archaeology of this well-preserved site, visible from a self-guiding, wheelchair-accessible

trail. Entrance into the 'castle' itself is prohibited. Access the monument from I-17 exit 289, then follow signs for 2 miles.

Montezuma Well, 10 miles northeast of the castle, is also part of the monument. It's a natural limestone sinkhole, 470 feet across and surrounded by remnants of Sinaguan and Hohokam dwellings. Water from the sinkhole was used for irrigation by the Indians as it is today. Access is from exit 293.

Both areas have picnic sites and are open from 8 am to 5 pm, to 7 pm from Memorial Day to Labor Day. Admission to the castle is $3 for adults, the well is free; all passes are honored.

Arcosanti

Two miles east of I-17 exit 262, a short unpaved road leads to this architectural experiment in urban living. Designed by architect Paolo Soleri, Arcosanti will be home to 6000 people who want to live in a futuristic, aesthetic, relaxing and environmentally sound development. The space-age project has been under construction for decades, and rivals the Biosphere and London Bridge as one of Arizona's most unexpected tourist attractions. Tours leave hourly from 10 am to 4 pm and cost $6. A gift shop sells the famous ceramic and cast bronze Soleri windbells and a café is on site. Overnight accommodations, week- and month-long seminars and other events are offered. For information contact Arcosanti (☎ 632-7135), HC 74, PO Box 4136, Mayer, AZ 86333.

website: www.arcosanti.org

SEDONA

☎ 928 • pop 10,195; metro area 16,500
• elevation 4500 feet

Sedona, seated among splendid crimson sandstone formations at the south end of lovely Oak Creek Canyon, is one of the prettiest locations in Arizona. For decades, Sedona was a quiet farming community but in the 1940s and '50s, Hollywood began using Sedona as a movie location. In the 1960s and '70s the beauty of the surroundings started attracting retirees, artists and tourists in large numbers and the town experienced much growth. Around 1980, New Agers began finding vortexes (see the boxed text 'In Search of the New Age').

Rapid, poorly controlled growth took the area somewhat by surprise and the strip malls look out of place among the red-rock scenery, although the town is making efforts to blend in with its surroundings. (The Sedona McDonald's lacks the famous golden arches; instead, pastel green arcs are painted on a pink stuccoed wall.) Tourist development has tended toward the high-end curiously blended with the psychic. The town is home to several fine resorts, some of Arizona's best restaurants, fine art galleries and boutiques, and numerous New Age businesses, but no cheap motels.

Despite the bustle of four million annual visitors, it's possible to get away from the crowds and enjoy the beautiful scenery on a 4WD tour, bike ride or hike. It's the environs that make Sedona an attractive, if pricey, destination. It is about 110 miles north of Phoenix, if you are driving directly from there, 20 miles northeast of Cottonwood, if you're coming up Hwy 89A, or 25 miles south of Flagstaff (later in this chapter).

Information
The chamber of commerce (☎ 282-7722, 800-288-7336,), Forest Rd at Hwy 89A, has oodles of information from 8:30 am to 5 pm daily (till 3 pm on Sunday) and also at www.VisitSedona.com. Other services include USFS Ranger Station (☎ 282-4119), 250 Brewer Rd, AZ 86339; the library (☎ 282-7714), 3250 White Bear Rd; post office (☎ 282-3511) on Hwy 89A at Hwy 179; medical center (☎ 204-3000), 3700 W Hwy 89A; police (☎ 282-3100), 100 Road Runner Dr. Note that the intersection of Hwy 89A with Hwy 179 is called 'the Y.'

Much of the surrounding land is National Forest and a Red Rock Pass parking pass is required ($5 per day, $15 per week, $20 per year). Buy it at the chamber of commerce or various local businesses.

Chapel of the Holy Cross
Spectacularly located between red-rock towers 3 miles south of town, this non-denominational chapel (☎ 282-4069) is open daily from 9 am to 5 pm. Head south on Hwy 179 and turn left on Chapel Rd.

Sedona Arts Center
The center (☎ 282-3809, 888-954-4442), at the corner of Hwy 89A and Art Barn Rd, has changing exhibits, a gift shop, classes in performing and visual arts, and a variety of cultural events during the September to May season. Hours are 10 am to 4:30 pm. website: www.sedonaartscenter.com

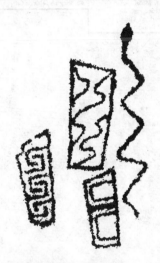

Red Rock State Park
This park has an environmental education center, visitor center (☎ 282-6907), picnic areas and six short hiking trails in a riparian habitat amid gorgeous scenery. Ranger-led activities include nature walks, bird walks and full-moon hikes during the warmer months. Hours are 8 am to 5 pm, to 6 pm in summer. Admission is $5 per vehicle (four passengers) and $1 for extra passengers or pedestrians/cyclists. The park is 5½ miles west of the Y along Hwy 89A, then 3 miles left on Lower Red Rock Loop Rd.

Oak Creek Canyon
The section of Oak Creek northeast of Sedona along Hwy 89A is where the canyon

ARIZONA

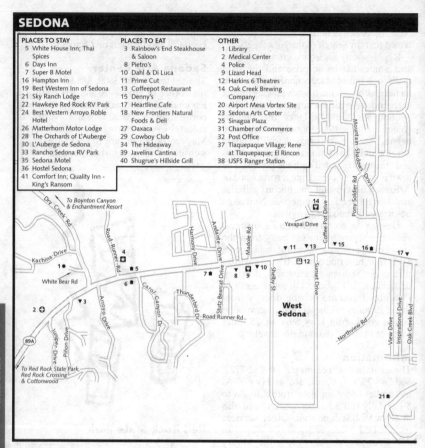

SEDONA

PLACES TO STAY
5 White House Inn; Thai Spices
6 Days Inn
7 Super 8 Motel
16 Hampton Inn
19 Best Western Inn of Sedona
21 Sky Ranch Lodge
22 Hawkeye Red Rock RV Park
24 Best Western Arroyo Roble Hotel
26 Matterhorn Motor Lodge
28 The Orchards of L'Auberge
30 L'Auberge de Sedona
33 Rancho Sedona RV Park
35 Sedona Motel
36 Hostel Sedona
41 Comfort Inn; Quality Inn - King's Ransom

PLACES TO EAT
3 Rainbow's End Steakhouse & Saloon
8 Pietro's
10 Dahl & Di Luca
11 Prime Cut
13 Coffeepot Restaurant
15 Denny's
17 Heartline Cafe
18 New Frontiers Natural Foods & Deli
27 Oaxaca
29 Cowboy Club
34 The Hideaway
39 Javelina Cantina
40 Shugrue's Hillside Grill

OTHER
1 Library
2 Medical Center
4 Police
9 Lizard Head
14 Harkins 6 Theatres
14 Oak Creek Brewing Company
20 Airport Mesa Vortex Site
23 Sedona Arts Center
25 Sinagua Plaza
31 Chamber of Commerce
32 Post Office
37 Tlaquepaque Village; Rene at Tlaquepaque; El Rincon
38 USFS Ranger Station

is at its narrowest, and the red, orange and white cliffs are the most dramatic. Forests of pine and juniper clothe the canyon, providing a scenic backdrop for trout fishing in the creek.

The USFS maintains six campgrounds in the canyon as well as picnic areas. It also maintains the **Oak Creek Scenic Viewpoint**, 16 miles north of Sedona at the top of a particularly steep and winding section of N Hwy 89A.

Seven miles northeast of Sedona along N Hwy 89A, **Slide Rock State Park** (☎ 282-3034) is a very popular spot for swimming,

picnicking and bird watching. Oak Creek sweeps swimmers (especially kids) through the natural rock chute from which the park derives its name. Hours are 8 am to 6 pm (5 pm in winter) and admission is $5 per car or $1 for pedestrians/cyclists. Another popular swimming hole is **Grasshopper Point**, just over 2 miles north of town on the right side of N Hwy 89A.

Southwest of Sedona is **Red Rock Crossing**, best reached via Upper Red Rock Loop Rd, off Hwy 89A. The area is managed by the USFS, which provides picnicking areas and parking on either side of

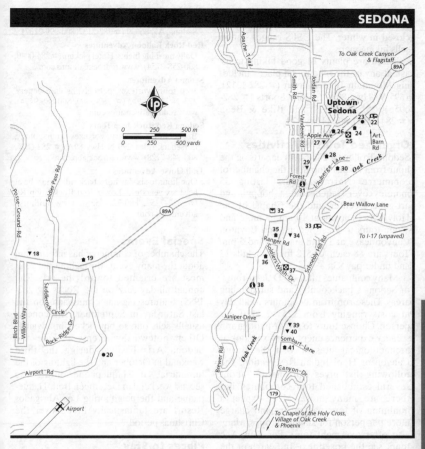

SEDONA

this section of Oak Creek. The creek can be waded (usually with little difficulty), but there is no bridge. The highlights are the splendid views of Cathedral Rock above a pretty stretch of Oak Creek.

Note that Village of Oak Creek, 7 miles south on Hwy 179, has places to stay and eat, but is not part of the canyon.

Backcountry Drives
Aside from the scenic drives around Oak Creek Canyon and the Chapel of the Holy Cross (see above), the following offer good views. The short drive up paved **Airport Rd** is

one good option, especially at sunset. **Dry Creek Rd**, at the west end of town, leads to scenic Boynton Canyon, where you can hike as well. View the photogenic Cathedral Rock along the roads of Lower and Upper **Red Rock Loop** (which you can take without entering the park). A rough unpaved road is the scenic 12-mile **Schnebly Hill Rd**, which turns off Hwy 179 near Oak Creek and ends up at I-17 exit 320. This road is closed in winter.

Hiking & Mountain Biking
There are easy scenic trails in Red Rock State Park and more difficult ones in the

National Forest. Hiking is possible year-round, though some higher trails may be closed in winter. The USFS ranger station sells hiking maps.

There are plenty of good biking trails; ask at any of the bike rental places, including Mountain Bike Heaven (☎ 282-1312), 1695 W Hwy 89A; Sedona Sports (☎ 282-6956), 251 Hwy 179; and Bike & Bean (☎ 284-0210), 6020 Hwy 179.

Organized Tours & Activities

Sedona Trolley (☎ 282-5400) departs on the hour from its bus stop near the chamber of commerce. Narrated tours lasting 55 minutes cover Tlaquepaque, a shopping and art-gallery center, and the Chapel of the Holy Cross leaving at 10 am, noon, 2 and 4 pm; tours to West Sedona and Boynton Canyon leave at 11 am and 1, 3 and 5 pm. Tours are $8 each, or $12 for both; kids 12 and under pay $3.

Many companies offer 4WD 'Jeep Tours' of Sedona's backcountry and surrounding areas. These run from two hours to all day at costs ranging from $25 to $130 per person. Choose tours to see or photograph scenery, experience energy vortexes, look at archaeological sites or visit the Grand Canyon or Hopi Indian Reservation. The following list gives information about several established tour companies, but there are many more. Most expect a minimum of four passengers and charge more per person for smaller groups. Many also offer overnight tours. For New Age tours, see the boxed text 'In Search of the New Age.'

Crossing Worlds
Hopi, Navajo and other Indian cultures, Sedona vortexes. (☎ 649-3060, 800-350-2693, crossing@sedona.net)

Earth Wisdom Tours
Vortexes, Indian lore. 293 N Hwy 89A (☎ 282-4714, 800-482-4714)

Northern Light Balloon Expeditions
Daily sunrise flights. Hotel pickup. (☎ 282-2274, 800-230-6222), www.sedona.net/fun/balloon

Pink Jeep Tours
Backcountry scenery. 204 N Hwy 89A (☎ 282-5000, 800-873-3662), www.pinkjeep.com

Pink Jeep Tours-Ancient Expeditions
Indian sites. 276 N Hwy 89A, PO Box 1447, Sedona, AZ 86339 (☎ 282-2137, 800-999-2137)

Red Rock Balloon Adventures
Daily morning flights. Hotel pickup. (☎ 284-0040, 800-258-3754), www.redrockballoons.com

Sedona Adventures
Jeep tours, vortexes, petroglyphs and scenery. 273 N Hwy 89A (☎ 282-3500, 800-888-9494), www.sedonaadventures.com

Sedona Red Rock Jeep Tours
Backcountry scenery, vortexes, archaeology, horseback rides. 270 N Hwy 89A (☎ 282-6826, 800-848-7728), www.redrockjeep.com

Trail Horse Adventures
One-hour to six-day horseback rides; must be at least six years old. Lower Red Rock Loop Rd (☎ 282-7252, 800-723-3538), www.trailhorseadventures.com

Special Events

The chamber of commerce has information about the many events throughout the year; most are oriented toward the arts. The annual all-day Jazz on the Rocks (☎ 282-1985) features big-name musicians on the last Saturday in September. The concert usually sells out, so buy tickets in advance. Other noteworthy events include the Sedona Arts Festival during the third weekend in October and the lighting of the luminarias at Tlaquepaque during the second weekend in December. Both Tlaquepaque and the neighboring Los Abrigados Resort are fantastically lit up over the Christmas period.

Places to Stay

Camping The USFS (☎ 282-4119) runs the following campgrounds, none with hookups or showers, in Oak Creek Canyon along N Hwy 89A: *Manzanita*, 6 miles north of town, 19 sites; *Banjo Bill*, 8 miles, eight sites; *Bootlegger*, 8½ miles, 10 sites; *Cave Springs*, 11½ miles, 78 sites; and *Pine Flat*, 12½ miles; 58 sites. Sites cost $12. The season is May through September, but some campgrounds may open longer. Be sure to arrive early: Sites are on a first-come, first-served basis, and campgrounds are often full on Friday morning for the weekend.

Rancho Sedona RV Park (☎ 282-7255, 888-641-4261, 135 Bear Wallow Lane) has a laundry, showers and 30 RV sites, most with full hookups, for $20 to $40. *Hawkeye Red Rock RV Park* (☎ 282-2222, 40 Art Barn Rd) offers coin showers that are available to the public and has both tent and RV sites for $17 to $28.

Hostels *Hostel Sedona* (☎ 282-2772, 5 Soldiers Wash Drive) offers basic accommodations in two small, single-gender dormitories, each with eight bunks and a bathroom. Rates are $15 to $18 per person. There are two rooms for couples ($30 and $40). Free tea, coffee and simple kitchen facilities are provided.

In Search of the New Age

Sedona is the foremost New Age center in the Southwest and one of the most important anywhere. The term 'New Age' loosely refers to a trend toward seeking alternative explanations or interpretations of what constitutes health, religion, the psyche and enlightenment. Drawing upon new and old factual and mystical traditions from around the world, 'New Agers' often seek to transform themselves psychologically and spiritually in the hope that such personal efforts will eventually transform the world at large.

You can't miss the New Age stores in town – many of them have the word 'crystal' in their names. They sell books, crystals and various New Age paraphernalia, distribute free maps showing vortex sites, provide information, and may arrange various spiritual or healing events. The Center for the New Age (☎ 520-282-2085), 341 Hwy 179, is open daily and is a good place to start or visit online at www.SedonaNewAge.com. Sedona's offerings include mainstream services such as massages, nutrition counseling, acupressure, meditation, and yoga and tai chi classes, all the way through increasingly esoteric practices such as herbology, psychic channeling, aura photography, astrology, palmistry, tarot card and runes reading, aromatherapy, past-life regressions, crystal healing, shamanism, drumming workshops, reflexology, hypnotherapy and more…

The four best known vortexes, or high-energy sites where the earth's power is said to be strongly felt, are in the Sedona's local red rock mountains. These include Bell Rock near Village of Oak Creek east of Hwy 179, Cathedral Rock near Red Rock Crossing, Airport Mesa along the Airport Rd, and Boynton Canyon. Local maps show these four main sites, though some individuals claim that others exist.

Several people lead guided tours of vortexes and other important New Age sites. These tours differ from many of the standard vortex tours in that the guides believe in what they tell you, as opposed to simply showing you the place. Try the following (there are others):

Sedona Nature Excursions/Mystic Tours by Rahelio
1405 W Hwy 89A, PO Box 1171, Sedona, AZ 86339 (☎ 520-282-6735)

Spirit Steps Tours
PO Box 3151, West Sedona, AZ 86340 (☎ 520-282-4562, 800-728-4562)

Vortex Tours/Medicine Wheel Journeys
PO Box 535, Sedona, AZ 86339 (☎ 520-282-2733, 800-943-3266)

'New Agers' (for want of a better term) are generally gentle folk, but some have been criticized for performing rituals, such as chantings or offerings, in scenic areas. Chanting in a public scenic area can be as irritating as a loud radio, revving motorcycle or droning aircraft, and leaving offerings of crystals or food is tantamount to littering. If you want to participate in such public rituals, please keep your vocal interactions with the planet to a peacefully personal level, pick up your offerings when you're through, and leave nothing but your love, energy and blessings.

ARIZONA

Hotels – Budget & Mid-Range The following are $50 to $80 for a double, which is considered budget during Sedona's lengthy (mid-February to mid-November!) high season. Most also have rooms sleeping up to four or five.

The *White House Inn* (☎ 282-6680, 2986 W Hwy 89A) has 22 motel rooms, some with kitchenettes. The *Sedona Motel* (☎ 282-7187), on Hwy 179 near 89A, has 16 pleasant rooms with refrigerators and is often full. Down in Village of Oak Creek, the *Village Lodge* (☎ 284-3626, 800-890-0521, 78 Bell Rock Blvd) has rooms with refrigerators, some with fireplaces (see www.sedonalodge.com).

In the $80 to $130 range, the *Sky Ranch Lodge* (☎ 282-6400, 888-708-6400) on Airport Rd is a good value by Sedona standards; its 94 rooms, pool and hot tub are in a nicely landscaped setting above town. Some pricier and larger units have kitchenettes, fireplaces and good views; see them at www.skyranchlodge.com. The 23 rooms at the *Matterhorn Motor Lodge* (☎ 282-7176, fax 282-0727, 230 Apple Ave), all have balconies or patios overlooking uptown Sedona and Oak Creek. Amenities include in-room coffeemakers and refrigerators, a pool and a whirlpool. There are several *chain motels* including a Super 8, Days Inn, two Best Westerns, Comfort Inn, Quality Inn, Hampton Inn and, down in Village of Oak Creek, a Holiday Inn Express. Most have interior corridors, swimming pool and continental breakfast.

Hotels – Top End The *Briar Patch Inn* (☎ 282-2342, 888-809-3030, 3190 N Hwy 89A), 3 miles north of town, has 17 rustic traditional cottages (frequently renovated), some with kitchenettes and/or fireplaces, attractively located on eight wooded acres right next to Oak Creek, making it convenient for swimming and fishing. Most cabins are for two; a few hold four people. Rates are $155 to $295 for a double. There are no TVs, but classical music performances may accompany breakfast, and occasional workshops and seminars keeps guests entertained. website: www.briarpatchinn.com

The *Junipine Resort* (☎ 282-3375, 800-742-7463, 8351 N Hwy 89A), in woodland 8 miles north of Sedona, provides easy access to hiking, swimming and fishing in Oak Creek. The 50 one- and two-bedroom townhouses (called 'creek houses'), all with kitchens, living/dining rooms, fireplaces and decks and some with lofts, range from $180 to $280. Try the excellent restaurant if you're not in the mood to cook. website: www.junipine.com

L'Auberge de Sedona (☎ 282-1661, 800-272-6777, 301 L'Auberge Lane) is a 'Country French Inn' next to Oak Creek in uptown Sedona. Although there is a pool and whirlpool, the emphasis is on romantic relaxation and eating fancy French food (this is one of the few places in Arizona where a jacket is required for men). The highlight is the 34 romantic one- and two-bedroom cottages scattered in the gardens and along the creek. With fireplaces and no TVs, these run about $300 to $450 in the high season, while spacious rooms in the attractive lodge overlooking the cottages are $210 to $300. *The Orchards of L'Auberge*, under the same management but up the hill on Hwy 89A, overlooks the L'Auberge complex and affords the best views. The two are linked by a short aerial tram. Rooms here are more American style and run $170 to $250; most have private balconies and some have fireplaces. website: www.lauberge.com

Of several resorts, the full-service, world-class *Enchantment Resort* (☎ 282-2900, 800-826-4180, 525 Boynton Canyon Rd) is the most spectacularly located, tucked in a canyon northwest of Sedona. Over 200 rooms, casitas and suites have private balconies and great views; trails take you high above or far into the canyon. You'll also get plenty of on-site exercise with several pools and whirlpools, seven tennis courts (lessons are available), saunas, a croquet field and a fitness center, and can recover with one of 10 kinds of massages or dozens of other treatments in their Mii amo spa. A children's program provides activities for four- to 12-year-olds. Their fine innovative restaurant and bar has Sedona's best dining views. High-season rates are from about $350 for a spacious, amenities-filled room to over $1000 for the largest two-bedroom, three-bathroom casita suite with kitchen, living room, fireplace, deck with grill and several balconies.

website: www.enchantmentresort.com

B&Bs With over two dozen B&Bs, Sedona may be the B&B capital of Arizona. Most strive for a rural elegance to accompany the beauty of the surroundings, usually require advance reservations, and tend to the $125 to $250 range, with a few exceptions. Rooms with lovely views, fireplaces and spas are often featured, and fancy breakfasts are de rigeur. Often, the owners live on-site and provide a personal touch. Many B&Bs don't accept young children and most are non-smoking. A good place to start looking is the Sedona Bed & Breakfast Guild, which features 19 B&Bs on its site at www.bbsedona.net.

Places to Eat

Sedona has plenty of upscale restaurants but also a good selection of budget places serving decent food. Even the pricier places are often a reasonable value, providing high-quality, innovative dishes and agreeable surroundings, especially if you take advantage of early bird specials. In fact, some visitors consider the cuisine to be as much of an attraction as the scenery. Reputable chefs are drawn to the town, rewarded both by the lovely setting and by an appreciative and (sometimes) discerning audience of food-loving travelers. Reservations are a good idea.

If you prefer to fix your own healthy meal, stop by *New Frontiers Natural Foods & Deli* (☎ 282-6311, 1420 W Hwy 89A), open from 8 am to 8 pm daily. They also serve sandwiches to eat in or take out.

For breakfast and lunch, the *Coffeepot Restaurant* (☎ 282-6626, 2050 W Hwy 89A) has been the place to go for decades. It's always busy and service can be slow, but meals are inexpensive and the selection is huge – it offers more types of omelets than

most restaurants have menu items (it claims 101).

Oaxaca (☎ 282-4179, 321 N Hwy 89A) serves authentic Mexican fare from 8 am to 9 pm daily; dinners range from $10 to $15 but daily specials for about $7.50 are recommended as well. Their outdoor deck provides quiet creek views. The bustling and popular *Javelina Cantina* (☎ 203-9514, 671 Hwy 179) does a slightly more Americanized version of Mexican food for lunch and dinner. Make dinner reservations or prepare for an hour's wait. *El Rincon* (☎ 282-4648) in Tlaquepaque serves very good Sonoran Mexican lunches and dinners; closed on Mondays. Prices are somewhat higher than most Mexican places but still moderate. Out in Village of Oak Creek, the *Wild Toucan Restaurant and Cantina* (☎ 284-1604, 6376 Hwy 179) serves large portions of Mexican and American food inside or out on the patio and has a kids' menu. Dinner entrées start at around $9.

For Italian dining, the *Hideaway* (☎ 282-4204, 251 Hwy 179) serves tasty, good-value lunches and dinners (about $10) on a patio overlooking the steep and wooded walls of Oak Creek. The more expensive *Pietro's* (☎ 282-2525, 2445 W Hwy 89A) vies with *Dahl & Di Luca* (☎ 282-5219, 2321 W Hwy 89A) for the title of the best Italian food in the region. Pietro's is busier and more fun; Dahl & Di Luca is slightly quieter and more romantic. Reservations are suggested for both.

Thai Spices (☎ 282-0599, 2986 W Hwy 89A), despite its unpretentious exterior, serves good, spicy and inexpensive Thai food, including a wonderful coconut soup and some macrobiotic dishes. There's dinner daily and lunch on weekdays. For authentic Japanese food prepared by a chef from Tokyo (via Chicago and New York, no less) *Sasaki* (284-1757), on Hwy 179 in Village of Oak Creek at Bell Rock Blvd, is definitely recommended. Dinners run $15 to $25 served in a modern, elegant restaurant with a sushi bar and tatami room.

The *Heartline Cafe* (☎ 282-0785, 1610 W Hwy 89A) serves imaginative and tasty continental cuisine with a Southwestern twist. (The restaurant's name refers to a Zuni Indian symbol for good health and long life rather than low-cal cooking.) It's a pretty place filled with flowers and has a patio for summer dining. Dinners, priced in the teens and $20s, are a fair value, and lunches, most under $10, are also very good. If you prefer a good old-fashioned steak, head over to *Prime Cut* (☎ 282-2943, 2250 W Hwy 89A) where top-notch cuts are in the $20s.

The *Cowboy Club* (☎ 282-4200, 241 Hwy 89A) looks like a saloon from the outside but is a large and determinedly Southwestern restaurant. The Grille Room has a good and interesting selection of snacks (rattlesnake if you must try a bite!) and meals at moderate to high prices. Pricier fine dining is offered in the Silver Saddle Room. The *Rainbow's End Steakhouse & Saloon* (☎ 282-1593, 3235 W Hwy 89A) serves excellent burgers and steaks in its restaurant, and has country & western bands and dancing on weekends.

Shugrue's Hillside Grill (☎ 282-5300, 671 Hwy 179) affords memorably panoramic red-rock views and both indoor and outdoor lunch and dinner, as well as jazz entertainment on weekends. The specialty is seafood, but the beef and lamb menu is just as good, though prices are at the high end. Reservations are recommended.

Rene at Tlaquepaque (☎ 282-9225), long considered one of Sedona's best, is a non-smoking restaurant with upscale continental cuisine (lamb is a specialty) and some unusual meats (pronghorn antelope, ostrich) and plenty of art on the walls. Though food, service and surroundings are top notch, diners dress neatly but casually for lunch and dinner. Entrées at dinner are in the high teens and $20s. Reservations are recommended.

All Sedona's resorts have good restaurants. The most famous is *L'Auberge de Sedona* (☎ 282-1667). It's beautiful, elegant, romantic and very French. The high prices, small portions and formal dining are irresistible to many visitors; reservations and dinner jackets are required. The best value

is the prix-fixe dinner menu, which changes daily and runs at about $60 for six courses. Otherwise, dinner entrées are around $30 and include French delicacies such as frog legs, pheasant, veal and escargot. The Enchantment Resort's *Yavapai Dining Room* (☎ 282-2900) serves superb food in a jaw-dropping setting (make a reservation). The Southwestern cuisine has all sorts of interesting twists and the menu changes regularly. Seafood, meat and pasta dinner entrées range from $15 to $25, a fair value for the food and a bargain considering the location. The restaurant also puts together a good champagne Sunday brunch ($28.50).

Entertainment

Read the monthly *Red Rock Review* for local events. Nightlife is fairly quiet, with mainly lounge entertainment at the resorts. Exceptions include the *Oak Creek Brewing Company* (☎ 204-1300, 2050 Yavapai Drive), which serves hand-crafted beers and has an outdoor patio and live music (rock, blues, reggae) on most evenings. Dance to live and recorded music at the *Lizard Head* (282-1808, 2375 W Hwy 89A) every night. The *Rainbow's End* (see Places to Eat) also has music and dancing.

The *Sedona Cultural Park* (☎ 282-0747, 800-780-2787), at the far west end of town, opened for its first full season in 2001. From Shakespeare to the symphony, film festivals to jazz; this is where highbrow events happen amid great scenery. For details see www.sedonaculturalpark.org. Also check the *Sedona Arts Center* (see earlier in this chapter) for cultural events.

The *Harkins 6 Theatres* (☎ 282-0222, 2081 W Hwy 89A) shows movies.

Shopping

Sedona is a prime shopping destination. The uptown area along Hwy 89A is the place to get souvenirs. The Book Loft (☎ 282-5173), 175 Hwy 179, has new and used books.

Tlaquepaque Village (☎ 282-4838) has dozens of high-quality art galleries that are also high priced, but they are a good place to start for comparison shopping. Almost opposite is the Crystal Castle (☎ 282-5910), one of several stores selling New Age books and gifts. Continuing south, Garland's Navajo Rugs (☎ 282-4070), 411 Hwy 179, has the area's best selection of rugs as well as other Indian crafts. Village of Oak Creek has Oak Creek Factory Outlets (☎ 284-2150), 6601 Hwy 179, with about 30 outlets providing name brands at discounted prices.

Getting There & Away

The Sedona-Phoenix Shuttle (☎ 282-2066, 800-448-7988) leaves Phoenix Airport seven times a day for $35 one-way or $60 roundtrip.

FLAGSTAFF

☎ 928 • pop 52,894; metro area 61,000
• elevation 6900 feet

Flagstaff was first settled in early 1876 by sheepherder Thomas Forsyth McMillan. On the Fourth of July of that year, a pine tree was stripped of its branches and a US flag hung from it to celebrate the country's centennial, hence the town's name. The arrival of the railroad in 1882 really put Flagstaff on the map. Cattle and sheep ranching became economic mainstays, and the surrounding forests formed the basis of a small logging industry. The Lowell Observatory was founded in 1894, the still-functioning Hotel Weatherford was built in 1897, and the school that later became Northern Arizona University (NAU) was established in 1899. In the early 1900s, the Riordan Mansion and several other historic buildings were erected.

Today, tourism is Flagstaff's major industry. The cool summer temperatures attract Arizonans; it's 141 freeway miles north of Phoenix, 25 slow rural highway miles north of Sedona. From Flagstaff it's under a two-hour drive to the Grand Canyon, with the Navajo and Hopi Indian Reservations longer day trips. In winter, there's Alpine and cross-country skiing.

Although 'Flag,' as locals dub it, is a great base for travel, it is also a destination in its own right, with museums, a historical downtown, cultural attractions and northern Arizona's best nightlife. Flagstaff is Arizona's fourth largest urban area, and the largest between Phoenix and Salt Lake City.

Information

The visitor center (☎ 774-9541, 800-842-7293), 1 E Route 66 (also called Santa Fe Ave), is in the historic Amtrak railway station. The center is open daily; the station is open from 6:15 am to 11:25 pm daily, when free maps and brochures are available. Two blocks north and east from the visitor center, many late-19th- and early-20th-century buildings comprise 'historic downtown.'
website: www.flagstaff.az.us

Other services include the Coconino National Forest Supervisor's Office (☎ 527-3600), 2323 Greenlaw Ln; USFS Peaks Ranger Station (☎ 526-0866), 5075 N Hwy 89; Mormon Lake Ranger Station (☎ 774-1147), 4373 S Lake Mary Rd; Arizona Game & Fish (☎ 774-5045), 3500 S Lake Mary Rd; the library (☎ 774-4000); 300 W Aspen Ave; main post office (☎ 527-2440), 2400 Postal Blvd and the downtown branch (☎ 527-2440), 104 N Agassiz; medical center (☎ 779-3366), 1200 N Beaver; police (☎ 556-2316, 774-1414), southeast corner of Butler and Lone Tree.

Museum of Northern Arizona

In an attractive stone building set in a pine grove, this small but thorough museum (☎ 774-5211), 3001 N Fort Valley Rd, is Flagstaff's most important and worth visiting. Galleries feature exhibits on local Indian archaeology, history and customs as well as geology, biology and the arts. Call for information about its excellent changing exhibits. The museum sponsors workshops and tours, ranging from half-day to multiday trips exploring the surrounding country. For a program call the museum's education department (☎ 774-5213).

You can also browse the gift and bookstore, examine the exhibits and sales of Navajo, Hopi and Zuni art, and stretch your legs on the short nature trail. Museum hours are 9 am to 5 pm daily except major holidays. Admission is $5, seniors $4, students $3 and children aged 7 to 17 $2.
website: www.musnaz.org

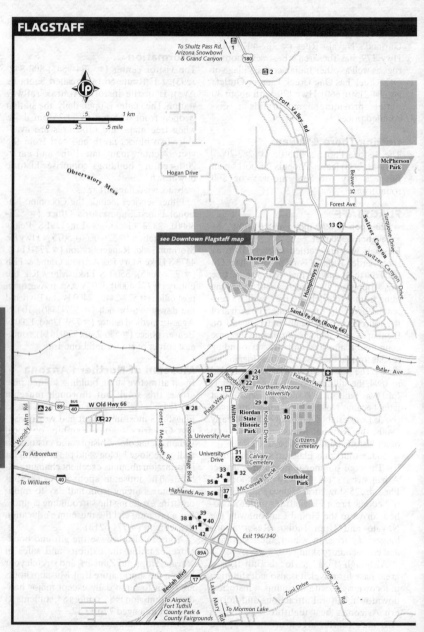

FLAGSTAFF

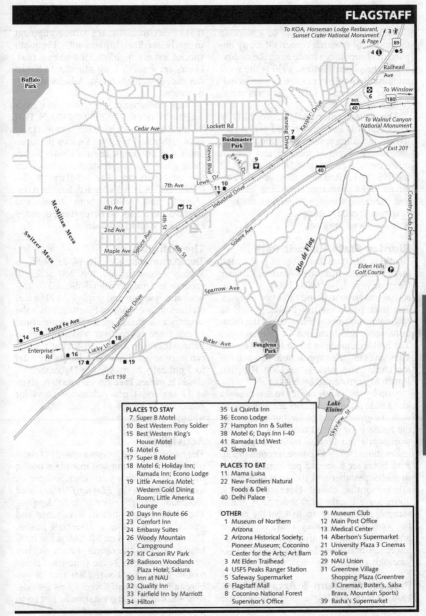

FLAGSTAFF

PLACES TO STAY
7 Super 8 Motel
10 Best Western Pony Soldier
15 Best Western King's
      House Motel
16 Motel 6
17 Super 8 Motel
18 Motel 6; Holiday Inn;
      Ramada Inn; Econo Lodge
19 Little America Motel;
      Western Gold Dining
      Room; Little America
      Lounge
20 Days Inn Route 66
23 Comfort Inn
24 Embassy Suites
26 Woody Mountain
      Campground
27 Kit Carson RV Park
28 Radisson Woodlands
      Plaza Hotel; Sakura
30 Inn at NAU
32 Quality Inn
33 Fairfield Inn by Marriott
34 Hilton

35 La Quinta Inn
36 Econo Lodge
37 Hampton Inn & Suites
38 Motel 6; Days Inn I-40
41 Ramada Ltd West
42 Sleep Inn

PLACES TO EAT
11 Mama Luisa
22 New Frontiers Natural
      Foods & Deli
40 Delhi Palace

OTHER
1 Museum of Northern
      Arizona
2 Arizona Historical Society;
      Pioneer Museum; Coconino
      Center for the Arts; Art Barn
3 Mt Elden Trailhead
4 USFS Peaks Ranger Station
5 Safeway Supermarket
6 Flagstaff Mall
8 Coconino National Forest
      Supervisor's Office

9 Museum Club
12 Main Post Office
13 Medical Center
14 Albertson's Supermarket
21 University Plaza 3 Cinemas
25 Police
29 NAU Union
31 Greentree Village
      Shopping Plaza (Greentree
      3 Cinemas, Buster's, Salsa
      Brava, Mountain Sports)
39 Basha's Supermarket

ARIZONA

Lowell Observatory

Named after its founder, Percival Lowell, this observatory continues to be a working astronomical research center. Of many important observations made here, the discovery of the planet Pluto in 1930 is the most famous. Eight telescopes are in use, including the historic 24-inch Clark refractor (which visitors can try).

The visitor center (☎ 774-2096, 1400 W Mars Hill Rd) has exhibits and various activities, including several daily tours. Hours are 9 am to 5 pm in summer and vary at other times. Admission is $4 for adults; $2 for five- to 17- and over 65-year-olds. Frequent night programs, including lectures and stargazing through telescopes, are held year-round; call for hours.

website: www.lowell.edu

Riordan State Historic Park

Brothers Michael and Timothy Riordan made a fortune from their Arizona Lumber Company and, in 1904, built a 13,000-sq-foot mansion to house their two families. The park preserves this building with its original furnishings, which were of the then-fashionable and luxurious Craftsman style. The building, made of stone fronted by log slabs, gives the false appearance of a palatial log cabin. The park is at 1300 Riordan Ranch St, surrounded by NAU.

Stop by the visitor center to see exhibits and a slide program. Visitors are welcome to walk the grounds and picnic, but entrance to the house is by guided tour only. Tours are worthwhile but limited to 20 people and reservations (☎ 779-4395) are recommended. Park hours are 8 am to 5 pm from mid-May to mid-September and 10:30 am to 5 pm in other months; closed December 24-25. Tours leave hourly from 9 am to 4 pm in summer and from 11 am to 4 pm the rest of the year. For a spooky tour, reserve in advance for an evening preceding Halloween. Admission is $4; $2.50 for 12- to 17-year-olds.

Pioneer Museum & Arts Centers

Housed in the old 1908 county hospital, the Pioneer Museum (☎ 774-6272), 2340 N Fort Valley Rd, preserves Flagstaff's early history in photographs and memorabilia that ranges from vintage farm equipment to early medical instruments. Frequent special events highlight the area's past. Hours are 9 am to 5 pm Monday to Saturday except major holidays. Admission is by donation.

Near the museum, the Coconino Center for the Arts (☎ 779-2300), 2300 N Fort Valley Rd, exhibits a wide scope of works by local artists and presents various performances and programs. There's always something going on. A gift shop features local fine art. Hours vary. The Art Barn (☎ 774-0822), 2320 N Fort Valley Rd, has been displaying and selling both local and Reservation artists' work for three decades. Hours are 9 am to 5 pm daily.

The Arboretum

The Arboretum (☎ 774-1442), 4001 S Woody Mountain Rd, has 200 acres of grounds and greenhouses dedicated to horticultural research and display. At 7150 feet on the southwest side of Flagstaff, this is the country's highest research arboretum. Locals come to discover what to grow in their backyards, and plant-loving visitors can learn about alpine flora. Hours are 9 am to 5 pm daily from April to December 15; closed in winter. Free guided tours are given at 11 am and 1 pm. Admission is $4 for adults and $1 for six- to 12-year-olds.

website: www.thearb.org

Activities

The mountains and forests around Flagstaff offer scores of **hiking** and **mountain biking** trails – far too many to describe here. A useful resource is *Flagstaff Hikes and Mountain Bike Rides* by R & S Mangum. The USFS ranger stations have maps and advice, and bookstores have trail guides. The closest hiking is on Mt Elden; the trailhead is just past the ranger station on Hwy 89, and it's a steep 3-mile (one-way) climb to the Elden Lookout, 2300 feet above Flagstaff. Shorter and longer loops are possible – ask at the ranger station or just go to the trailhead; it's well signed.

DOWNTOWN FLAGSTAFF

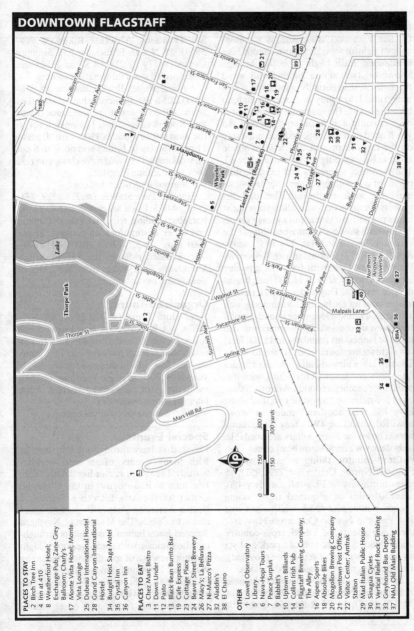

ARIZONA

PLACES TO STAY
2 Birch Tree Inn
4 Inn at 410
8 Weatherford Hotel;
   Exchange Pub; Zane Grey
   Ballroom; Charly's
17 Monte Vista Hotel; Monte
   Vista Lounge
25 Dubeau International Hostel
28 Grand Canyon International
   Hostel
34 Budget Host Saga Motel
35 Crystal Inn
36 Canyon Inn

PLACES TO EAT
3 Chez Marc Bistro
11 Down Under
12 Pasto
13 Black Bean Burrito Bar
19 Cafe Express
23 Cottage Place
24 Beaver Street Brewery
26 Macy's; La Bellavia
27 Ni-Marco's Pizza
32 Aladdin's
38 El Charro

OTHER
1 Lowell Observatory
5 Library
6 Nava-Hopi Tours
7 Peace Surplus
9 Babbitt's
10 Uptown Billiards
14 Collins Irish Pub
15 Flagstaff Brewing Company;
   The Alley
16 Aspen Sports
18 Absolute Bikes
20 Mogollon Brewing Company
21 Downtown Post Office
22 Visitor Center; Amtrak
   Station
29 Mad Italian Public House
30 Sinagua Cycles
31 Vertical Relief Rock Climbing
33 Greyhound Bus Depot
37 NAU Old Main Building

Arizona's highest mountain, the 12,663-foot Humphreys Peak north of Flagstaff in the San Francisco Mountains, is a reasonably straightforward though strenuous hike in summer. Trails begin from the Arizona Snowbowl (see skiing, below) and wend through forest, eventually coming out above timberline. It is windy and cold up high, so hike prepared. The last mile of the trail is over crumbly and loose volcanic rock, so you'll need decent boots, and you must stay on the trails to protect the delicate alpine tundra. No camping or fires are allowed. The elevation, steepness and loose footing make for a breathless ascent, but the views make the work worthwhile. The total distance is 4½ miles one-way; allow six to eight hours roundtrip if you are in average shape.

Downhill skiing and **snowboarding** at the Arizona Snowbowl (☎ 779-1951, snow report 779-4577) is popular with Arizonans. It's small but high, with four lifts servicing 30 runs between 9200 to 11,500 feet; beginners to experts. Day lodges offer rentals, lessons and meals, but no accommodations. The season is mid-December to mid-April if the snowfall is good. In summer, you can take the longest lift (climbing to 11,500 feet) for **sightseeing** tours from 10 am to 4 pm. The trip takes almost half an hour, provides fine views and costs $9 for adults, with discounts for seniors and kids. Arizona Snowbowl is 7 miles northwest of Flagstaff along Hwy 180, then another 7 miles on Snowbowl Rd; chains or 4WD may be required but ski buses for a few dollars are available. website: www.arizonasnowbowl.com

Cross-country skiing is good at the Flagstaff Nordic Center (☎ 779-1951), 15 miles northwest of Flagstaff on Hwy 180, with 30 miles of groomed trails, skiing lessons, rentals and food. Trail passes cost $10. Past the Nordic Center on Hwy 180, there are plenty of USFS cross-country skiing pullouts where you can park and ski for free (no facilities or rentals are provided). The season is short, so call for conditions.

Sports stores that have maps, books, gear or rental equipment include Peace Surplus (☎ 779-4521), 14 W Route 66; Babbitt's (☎ 774-4775), 12 E Aspen Ave; Mountain Sports (☎ 779-5156, 800-286-5156), 1800 S Milton Rd; Aspen Sports (☎ 779-1935), 15 N San Francisco; Absolute Bikes (☎ 779-5969), 18 N San Francisco; and Sinagua Cycles (☎ 779-1092), 113 S San Francisco. These are all good information sources.

Vertical Relief Rock Climbing (☎ 556-9909), 205 S San Francisco, has 6000 sq ft of artificial indoor walls to practice **rock climbing**. Routes range from beginner level to the most difficult grades. Hours are 10 am to 11 pm Monday to Friday and noon to 8 pm on weekends. They also have classes on real rock surrounding Flagstaff.
website: www.verticalrelief.com

Hitchin' Post Stables (☎ 774-1719, 774-7131), 448 S Lake Mary Rd, has day-long **horseback riding** trips to Walnut Canyon and other destinations on request; Flying Hart Barn (☎ 526-2788), 8400 N Hwy 89, offers guided rides in the San Francisco Mountains. Both places offer horse-drawn sleigh rides in winter.

Organized Tours

Nava-Hopi Tours (☎ 774-5003, 800-892-8687), 114 W Route 66, has narrated bus tours of the Grand Canyon and Indian reservations. Tours last seven to 11½ hours and cost $40 to $80; half price for five- to 15-year-olds. National park admission and meals are extra; see Getting There & Away later for its other services.
website: www.navahopitours.com

Special Events

Flagstaff is busy throughout the summer with many events, often held simultaneously. The visitor center has details. From late June to mid-August, in the Coconino Center for the Arts, there is a Festival of Native American Arts with performances and art exhibits. The Museum of Northern Arizona hosts Indian arts exhibits throughout the summer with some weekends highlighting the work of specific tribes, including the Zuni, Hopi and Navajo. The Flagstaff Winter Festival throughout February is also a big highlight, with sled dog races, skiing excursions and races, and other snowy events.

Grand Falls of the Little Colorado

The Grand Falls give an insight into Southwestern hydrography. The Little Colorado River is a minor tributary of the Colorado, and like many Arizonan rivers, it is nearly dry for much of the year. During spring runoff, however, the river swells and the Grand Falls come into being. The 185-foot drop is impressive, with muddy-brown spray giving the falls their local nickname of 'Chocolate Falls.' The best time for viewing is March and April, although earlier in the year can be good if there has been enough winter precipitation. Occasional summer storms will also fill the falls.

The falls are on the Navajo Reservation. Drive 14 miles east of Flagstaff along I-40 to the Winona exit, then backtrack northwest about 2 miles to Leupp Rd. Head northeast on Leupp Rd for 13 miles to the signed turn for Grand Falls. An unpaved road, passable by car, leads 10 miles to the river and a quarter-mile trail goes to a falls overlook. The Navajo tribe allows free access to the falls, where there are basic picnic facilities.

Places to Stay

Flagstaff provides the best cheap and moderate lodging in this region for most of the year. Summer is the high season and hotel prices rise accordingly – a room that costs $20 in April can be $50 on an August weekend. Avoid summer weekends if possible.

Flagstaff Central Reservations (☎ 527-8333, 800-527-8388) makes reservations for the better motels and B&Bs in northern Arizona; call or go online to www.flagstaff rooms.com.

Camping Campgrounds can fill in summer, so make reservations where possible. *Fort Tuthill County Park* (☎ 774-3464), near I-17 exit 337, has 100 tent sites for $9 and 14 sites with hookups for $13. There are no showers. The campground is open from May to September. *Woody Mountain Campground* (☎ 774-7727, 2727 W Route 66), offers 146 sites for tents and RVs for $16 to $22, as well as a pool, playground and coin laundry. It is open from April through October. Nearby, the *Kit Carson RV Park* (☎ 774-6993, 2101 W Route 66) has 265 RV sites amid ponderosa pines available all year, with full hookups for $27. *Flagstaff KOA* (☎ 526-9926, 800-562-3524, 5803 N Hwy 89) has over 200 year-round sites, many with full RV hookups, ranging in price from $20 (tents) to $27 (full hookups).

Budget Cheap and basic motels line Route 66, especially the 3-mile stretch east of downtown and near NAU southwest of downtown. Route 66 parallels the railway and the cheap places don't have soundproof rooms. Almost anytime from September to May you can cruise along here and find 15 motels advertising rooms for about $20, or even less; prices rise dramatically during busy summer weekends. Check the room before you pay, though – some are worse than others. They are perfectly satisfactory if you are paying $20 off-season, not if you are paying more.

Flagstaff attracts international budget travelers, many of whom stay downtown in two independent youth hostels (☎ 888-442-2696), both owned by the same folks. Look for the huge neon 'Downtowner' sign to find them. The *Grand Canyon International Hostel* (☎ 779-9421, 19 S San Francisco) sleeps 62 people and *Dubeau International Hostel* (☎ 774-6731, 19 W Phoenix Ave) handles another 58. They each charge $14 to $16 per person in dorm rooms (four people maximum) and have some private doubles (shared bathroom) for $28 to $35. Breakfast is included and guests have use of a kitchen, BBQ area, laundry and TV/video room. The hostels offer pickup from the Greyhound station and arrange reasonably priced tours to the Grand Canyon and other local attractions. website: www.grandcanyonhostel.com

The **Weatherford Hotel** (☎ 779-1919, weathtel@infomagic.com, 23 N Leroux) dates back to 1898 and was then northern Arizona's finest hotel and is now Flagstaff's most historic. Eight rooms with a turn-of-the-19th-century feel (no TV or telephone) rent for $50 to $60. The popular Charly's (restaurant and pub) is downstairs and the Zane Grey ballroom is an attractive and authentic-looking old-fashioned place for a drink. The entertainment might mean some noise in the rooms on weekends.

There are dozens of **chain motels** including four Motel 6s, all of which have pools (in summer) and singles ranging from the high $20s to $50s depending on season. Most other chains are represented, often with two or more hotels (see map). A good area to look for the cheaper ones is I-40, exit 198. The clean **Budget Host Saga Motel** (☎ 779-3631, 820 W Route 66) has a pool and charges $50 to $60 in summer.

Mid-Range Scenes of the movie *Casablanca* were filmed at the 1927 **Monte Vista Hotel** (☎ 779-6971, 800-545-3068, 100 N San Francisco), where many of the 50 rooms and suites are named after the film stars who slept in them. Rooms are comfortable and old-fashioned but not luxurious (John Wayne and Humphrey Bogart handled it just fine) though TV and telephone are included. Rates are $60 to $120 in summer. The popular basement bar is deep enough not to disturb the peace.
website: www.hotelmontevista.com

Many of the standard **chain motels** are priced in the high middle range, especially in summer. A good place to look for the better ones, most with interior corridors, pools, whirlpools and continental breakfasts, and some with in-room coffee-makers and other facilities, is north of I-40 exit 196 where it intersects with I-17 exit 340 (see map).

Crystal Inn (☎ 774-4581, 800-654-4667, 602 W Route 66) has spacious rooms, a pool, spa and exercise room. Summer rates vary from $60 to $100; in winter you can find a room in the $30s. Also in this price range, but lacking a pool, is the **Canyon Inn**

(☎ 774-7301, 888-822-6966, 500 S Milton). These rates are similar to the chains.

The **Inn at NAU** (☎ 523-1616), on the east side of the campus, is used as a training facility for NAU's School of Hotel & Restaurant Management. The inn's 19 nonsmoking rooms are spacious and well maintained, and the student staff is well-trained and eager to please. Rates range from $60 in winter to $100 in summer, including a satisfying continental breakfast, and are a a good value. A restaurant and lounge serves lunch and dinner on some days.
website: www.nau.edu/~hrm

Top End Of several hotels charging over $100 for a double in summer, the **Little America Motel** (☎ 779-7900, 800-865-1401, 2515 E Butler Ave) is one of the better ones, set amid acres of lawns and pine trees. The 250 spacious rooms have balconies, refrigerators and large TVs with Nintendo, and there is a pool, spa, and exercise room as well as a 24-hour coffee shop, a good restaurant and a lounge providing occasional entertainment. Rates are a a good value at about $110 to $120; a few suites with fireplaces or saunas go up to about $200.
website: www.littleamerica.com

The **Radisson Woodlands Plaza Hotel** (☎ 773-8888, 1175 W Route 66) is the best chain hotel near downtown. The ambiance is trans-Pacific, with a Japanese restaurant and Southwestern coffee shop, severely square chandeliers and tightly clipped plants in the lobby, and contemporary desert colors in the guest rooms. Facilities include a pool, spa, sauna, steamroom and exercise equipment. Almost 200 large and attractive rooms are priced at $100 to $170 in summer; there are a few pricier suites. Room service is available and the restaurants are both very good.

Comfi Cottages (☎ 774-0731, 888-774-0731) offers six quaint 'cottages,' each with a kitchen stocked with your choice of breakfast items – cook your own whenever you feel like it. Cottages range from one bedroom/one bathroom at $110 a night to four bedrooms/two bathrooms at $250 a night. All are less than a mile from downtown, and have

yards or gardens with barbecue grills and bicycles available for use. Some have fireplaces.
website: www.comficcottages.com

If you prefer a B&B, the *Birch Tree Inn* (☎ 774-1042, 888-774-1042, 824 W Birch Ave) is a 1917 house with a wraparound verandah, a game room with billiards and an outdoor hot tub. Two rooms with shared bath are $69 and three more with private bath are $99 to $119, including a big breakfast and afternoon tea and snacks.
website: www.birchtreeinn.com

The *Inn at 410* (☎ 774-0088, 800-774-2008, 410 N Leroux), an elegant and fully renovated 1907 house, offers nine spacious and unique bedrooms, each with private bath, coffeemaker and refrigerator, and most with a fireplace or whirlpool bath. This popular place charges $135 to $190 a double, including full gourmet breakfast and afternoon snacks. Two units have adjoining rooms suitable for two children.
website: www.inn410.com

Places to Eat

Local laws prohibit smoking in all city restaurants (but not restaurant/bars).

Breakfast & Coffee A long-time favorite coffee shop, *Macy's* (☎ 774-2243, 14 S Beaver) also serves good pastries and eclectic light meals. Students, outdoorsy types and coffee lovers crowd this place, which is open all day from 6 am daily. Neighboring *La Bellavia* (☎ 774-8301, 18 S Beaver) is equally casual, has just as much caffeine in its espressos and cappuccinos and serves breakfast and lunch.

In the heart of downtown, *Cafe Express* (☎ 774-0541, 16 N San Francisco) has something for almost everyone except dedicated carnivores, including various coffees, vegetarian and natural-food meals and salads, juices, beer, wine, and pastries, which you can consume on the outdoor deck. Daily hours are 7 am to 10 pm.

American For one of Flag's best fresh seafood selections, including an oyster bar, try *Buster's* (☎ 774-5155, 1800 S Milton Rd), which also offers steaks and prime rib.

While most dinner entrées are in the teens, you can eat cheaper 'sunset dinners' between 6:30 and 7:30 pm. Inexpensive lunches include good salads, sandwiches and burgers. The bar selection is excellent and Buster's is popular (and often noisy) with locals and tourists.

The *Western Gold Dining Room* (☎ 779-2741), in the Little America Hotel, has a lunchtime buffet and one of the best American dinner menus in town.

For big old-fashioned steaks, *Horseman Lodge Restaurant* (☎ 526-2655, 8500 N Hwy 89) is a fine choice and is locally popular. It also has a wide selection of other American food.

New Frontiers Natural Foods & Deli (☎ 774-5747, 1000 S Milton Rd) has natural-food sandwiches, salads, soups, juices etc to go, or you can eat in the inexpensive deli.

Mexican Of the dozen or so Mexican restaurants in town, *Salsa Brava* (☎ 774-1083, 1800 S Milton Rd) with Guadalajaran rather than Sonoran food, is a good popular choice. For cheaper Mexican food, *El Charro* (☎ 779-0552, 409 S San Francisco) is good and may have mariachis playing on weekends. The cheap *Black Bean Burrito Bar* (☎ 779-9905, 12 E Route 66), in a little alley/plaza, is a simple diner with big burritos and a great variety of fillings. You can eat in (no comfort here, but there's a good people-watching window) or take out.

Italian Flag's best Italian restaurant is traditionally *Mama Luisa* (☎ 526-6809, 2710 E N Steves Blvd). Open for dinner only, Mama Luisa serves a wide range of Italian food for $9 to $18 in an appropriately cozy, red-checked-tablecloth setting. Popular *Pasto* (☎ 779-1937, 19 E Aspen) has a courtyard and vies with Mama Luisa for 'best Italian' honors. Again, dinner only. *Ni-Marco's Pizza* (☎ 779-2691, 101 S Beaver) is open for lunch and dinner and is popular with the student crowd.

Asian The recommended Japanese *Sakura* (☎ 773-9118), in the Woodlands Plaza Hotel, has fresh seafood served either as sushi or grilled right in front of you. Steak and other food is also available sliced, diced and flamed tableside. Most entrées are in the teens. At the other end of both the price range and the Asian continent is *Aladdin's* (☎ 213-0033, 211 S San Francisco), which serves inexpensive Middle Eastern and Greek food to dine in, outside or take-away. For Indian food, try the *Delhi Palace* (☎ 556-0019, 2700 S Woodlands Village Blvd), offering all-you-can-eat lunch buffets ($5.95) as well as à la carte dinners.

New Zealand Imported lamb ranks high on the menu of the *Down Under* (☎ 774-6677, 6 E Aspen). New Zealand wines, beers, venison, kangaroo, sea bass and mussels are among some of the imported foods available at this popular restaurant. Lunches ($3 to $9) include sausage rolls, meat pies and vegetarian frittata (a crustless quiche). Dinner entrées range from $10 to $25.

Continental The *Cottage Place* (☎ 774-8431, 126 W Cottage Ave) has several intimate and pretty rooms in an early-20th-century house. The varied continental menu has entrées (including several vegetarian plates) ranging in price from $16 to $26. The inviting and delicious appetizers pose a minor dilemma in that the entrées already include both soup and salad; it's best to come hungry and with a reservation. Dinners are served daily except Monday. Beer and wine are the only alcoholic beverages served.

The *Chez Marc Bistro* (☎ 774-1343, 503 N Humphreys) is classic French, complete with a French-born chef and a romantic, country-French atmosphere in a lace-curtained 1911 house. Dinner entrées are $16 to $30 and range from vegetarian to excellent seafood and meats. The extensive bar list includes French wines and single-malt scotches. It's a small, intimate place with fireplaces blazing inside in winter and an outdoor patio open in summer. Reservations recommended.

Pub Grub *Beaver Street Brewery* (☎ 779-0079, 11 S Beaver) is very popular for its microbrewery (five handmade ales are usually on tap) and well-prepared gourmet pizzas as well as other food. It opens at 11:30 am and has a beer garden in the summer. *Charly's* (☎ 779-1919, 23 N Leroux), on the ground floor of the historic Weatherford Hotel, offers soups, salads and sandwiches for $4 to $8 as well as a small selection of steak, chicken and pasta dinners in the $11 to $16 range.

Entertainment

During the summer there are many cultural performances (see Special Events, earlier in this chapter) and skiers, students and passers-through seem to fuel a lively nightlife year-round. Read the Sundial (the Friday entertainment supplement to Flag's *Arizona Daily Sun* and the free *Flagstaff Live* (published on the first and third Thursday of the month) to find out what's happening.

Several cinemas and multiplexes scattered around town show movies.

Flagstaff has plenty of bars, especially downtown, where you can relax to live music (usually for a small cover charge on weekends but often free otherwise). Wander around a few blocks and make your choice. The *Exchange Pub* in the Weatherford Hotel has varied live music, ranging from bluegrass to blues, folk to fusion, jazz to jive. On the hotel's top floor, the fancy *Zane Grey Ballroom* is worth checking out for... who knows? Jazz? Tango? Poetry? The *Monte Vista Lounge* (☎ 774-2403), in the Monte Vista Hotel, has alternative music. The *Flagstaff Brewing Co* (☎ 773-1442, 16 E Route 66) and nearby *The Alley* (☎ 774-7929, 22 E Hwy 89) both have hand-crafted beers and a variety of live music as does the *Mogollon Brewing Company* (☎ 773-8950, 15 N Agassiz). *Collins Irish Pub*, Leroux at Route 66, is somewhat more upscale.

More sedate live music can be heard on weekends at the *Little America Lounge* (☎ 779-2741) in the Little America Hotel. For a livelier tune, try the far-from-sedate country & western music, both live and recorded, at the *Museum Club* (☎ 526-9434, 3404 E Route 66). This popular barn-like place dates from the 1920s and '30s, and used to house a taxidermy museum, which may account for its local nickname, 'The Zoo.' For pure spectacle, The Zoo, with its open and friendly cowboy spirit and spacious dance floor (which the locals unsuccessfully try to hide with their huge Stetsons) is not to be missed. Check out the entrance, which is made from a single, forked trunk of a large ponderosa pine. The Zoo provides free roundtrip taxi service (☎ 774-2934) if you're planning on making a hard-drinkin' night of it.

Uptown Billiards (☎ 773-0551, 114 N Leroux) has plenty of pool tables and a good beer selection in a nonsmoking environment. The *Mad Italian Public House (☎ 779-1820, 101 S San Francisco)* is a decent pub with pool tables.

Getting There & Away
Pulliam Airport is 3 miles south of town on I-17. America West Express has several flights a day to and from Phoenix.

Greyhound (☎ 774-4573), 399 S Malpais Lane, sends buses between Flagstaff and Albuquerque along I-40; to Las Vegas (via Kingman and Bullhead City); to Los Angeles (via Kingman); and to Phoenix.

Nava-Hopi Tours (☎ 774-5003, 800-892-8687), 114 W Route 66, has buses one to three times a day (depending on season) to the Grand Canyon for $14 one way, plus the national park entrance fee. Nava-Hopi also has buses to Phoenix.

There are no buses north to Page. Ask the hostels about shuttles.

Getting Around
Pine Country Transit (☎ 779-6624) has three local bus routes running Monday to Saturday during the daytime. There is no service on Sunday.

Flagstaff Airport has offices of the following car-rental agencies: Avis, Budget, Enterprise, Hertz, National and Sears.

A Friendly Cab (☎ 774-4444), Sun Taxi (☎ 774-7400, 800-483-4488), Alternative Taxi (☎ 213-1111) and Arizona Taxi & Tours (☎ 779-1111) provide local and long-distance taxi service.

AROUND FLAGSTAFF
The places described here are within an hour's drive of Flagstaff.

Sunset Crater Volcano National Monument
Sunset Crater (elevation 8029 feet) was formed in AD 1064-65 by volcanic eruptions that covered large areas with lava and ash. Minor eruptions continued for over 200 years, but none are currently predicted. Today, Loop Rd goes through the Bonito Lava Flow and skirts the Kana-a Lava Flow. Overlooks and a mile-long interpretive trail enable visitors to get a good look at volcanic features, although walking on the unstable cinders of the crater itself is prohibited.

The visitor center (☎ 526-0502), 2 miles from Hwy 89, houses a seismograph and other exhibits pertaining to volcanology and the region. Rangers give interpretive programs in summer. Hours are 8 am to 6 pm in summer; 9 am to 5 pm in winter. Admission is $3 for those over 16 (all passes honored) and includes the Wupatki National Monument (see below). The 1-mile interpretive Lava Flow Nature Trail, with a quarter-mile wheelchair accessible, is a mile beyond the center.

Combine your trip to Sunset Crater with a side trip to neighboring Wupatki National Monument for an excellent day-long excursion from Flagstaff, covering 80 miles roundtrip.

Wupatki National Monument
This monument is off Hwy 89 about 30 miles north of Flagstaff, or can be reached by continuing along the Loop Rd from Sunset Crater. Wupatki has Ancestral Puebloan sites that differ from most others because they are freestanding rather than built into a cliff or cave. They have a distinct southern influence, indicating trading links with people from the south. The pueblos date mainly from the 1100s and early 1200s, and some of today's Hopi Indians are descended from the ancient inhabitants of Wupatki; the Hopi call their ancestors the Hisatsinom.

Information The narrow Loop Rd passes the visitor center and continues on past pullouts or short side roads that lead to the pueblos. Five pueblos are easily visited, and Crack-In-Rock requires an overnight backpacking trip. A brochure describing them in detail is available upon admission. Other pullouts along Loop Rd offer scenic views.

At the visitor center (☎ 679-2365), 18 miles beyond Sunset Crater, there is a museum, gift and book shop, and vending machines. In summer, rangers may give talks or lead walks. Hours are 8 am to 5 pm (to 6 pm in summer, open at 9 am in winter) daily except Christmas. See Sunset Crater for admission information.

Crack-In-Rock Pueblo can be visited only on a ranger-led, 16-mile roundtrip, weekend backpacking tour offered during weekends in April and October; call for fees. You must supply all equipment, food and water. Each trip is limited to 15 participants and these are chosen by lottery; apply two months in advance. For further information, call the visitor center or write to Wupatki National Monument, Attention CIR Reservations, HC33, Box 444A, NO.14, Flagstaff, AZ 86004.

Walnut Canyon National Monument

The Sinagua buildings at Walnut Canyon are not as immediately impressive as those at other nearby sites, but their spectacular setting makes this a worthwhile visit. The buildings are set in shallow caves in the near-vertical walls of a small limestone butte set like an island in the middle of the heavily pine-forested canyon.

The mile-long **Island Trail** steeply descends 185 feet (with more than 200 stairs) and then encircles the 'island,' passing 25 cliff-dwelling rooms; many more can be seen in the distance. A shorter, wheelchair-accessible **Rim Trail** affords several views of the rooms from a distance.

A visitor center (☎ 526-3367) is near the beginning of both trails and has a museum, bookstore and overlook. Rangers may give talks during the summer; the museum is open from 8 am to 5 pm (until 6 pm in

summer, from 9 am in winter) daily except Christmas. The Island Trail closes one hour before the visitor center. Admission is $3 per person over 16; all passes are honored. No food or overnight facilities are available.

Meteor Crater

A huge meteor crashing into our planet almost 50,000 years ago produced this crater, 570 feet deep and almost a mile across. It was used as a training ground for some of the Apollo astronauts; the on-site museum has exhibits about meteors and space missions. Descending into the crater isn't allowed, but you can walk the 3½-mile Rim Trail. However, apart from a big hole in the ground, there's not much to see and several readers suggest that it is an overpriced attraction.

The crater (☎ 289-2362, 800-289-5898) is privately owned and operated, and national park passes aren't accepted. Hours are 6 am to 6 pm mid-May to mid-September and from 8 am to 5 pm the rest of the year. Admission is $10, $5 for six- to 17-year-olds.

Meteor Crater RV Park *(☎ 289-4002)* has 80 RV sites with hookups for $20 and a few tent sites for $15. Showers, coin laundry, a playground, coffeeshop and groceries are available.

WILLIAMS

☎ 928 • pop 2842 • elevation 6762 feet

Mountain man Bill Williams passed through here several times before he died in 1849, and settlers in 1874 named the town after him. In 1901, the railway to the Grand Canyon opened, making Williams a tourist center. Easy road and car access closed the railway in 1969, only to return in 1989 as a popular historic steam train. The visitor center has a Route 66 display which relates that Williams had the last traffic light on that famous highway. The town is the closest to the Grand Canyon with moderately priced accommodations.

Information

The visitor's center (☎ 635-4061, 800-863-0546, williams@thegrandcanyon.com), 200 W Railroad Ave, is open from 8 am to 5 pm daily (till 6:30 in summer) and is operated

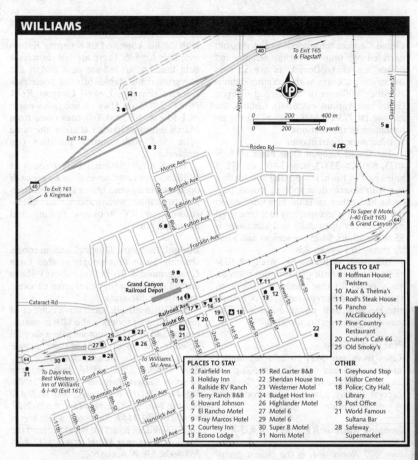

WILLIAMS

To Exit 165
& Flagstaff

Airport Rd

Quarter Horse St

To Exit 163

1

2

3

Exit 163

To Exit 161
& Kingman

Morse Ave
Burbank Ave
Edison Ave
Fulton Ave
Franklin Ave

Grand Canyon Blvd

Rodeo Rd

5

4

To Super 8 Motel,
I-40 (Exit 165)
& Grand Canyon

6

Grand Canyon
Railroad Depot

Cataract Rd

Railroad Ave
Route 66

9
10
14
17 16
19 18
20
21
15

11
13 12

8
7

Pine St
Lewis St
Slagel St
Taber St

22

25
27 23 24
26
28 29
30
31

64

To Days Inn,
Best Western
Inn of Williams
& I-40 (Exit 161)

Grant Ave
Sherman Ave
Sheridan Ave
Hancock Ave
Mead Ave

7th St
6th St
5th St
4th St
2nd St
1st St
9th St
11th St
10th St

To Williams
Ski Area

PLACES TO EAT
8 Hoffman House;
 Twisters
10 Max & Thelma's
11 Rod's Steak House
16 Pancho
 McGillicuddy's
17 Pine Country
 Restaurant
20 Cruiser's Café 66
25 Old Smoky's

PLACES TO STAY
2 Fairfield Inn
3 Holiday Inn
4 Railside RV Ranch
5 Terry Ranch B&B
6 Howard Johnson
7 El Rancho Motel
9 Fray Marcos Hotel
12 Courtesy Inn
13 Econo Lodge

15 Red Garter B&B
22 Sheridan House Inn
23 Westerner Motel
24 Budget Host Inn
26 Highlander Motel
27 Motel 6
29 Motel 6
30 Super 8 Motel
31 Norris Motel

OTHER
1 Greyhound Stop
14 Visitor Center
18 Police; City Hall;
 Library
19 Post Office
21 World Famous
 Sultana Bar
28 Safeway
 Supermarket

ARIZONA

by both the chamber of commerce and the USFS. Pick up a walking tour brochure here if the turn-of-the-19th-century buildings downtown spark your interest. Other services include the library (☎ 635-2263), 113 S 1st; post office (☎ 635-4572) 120 S 1st; police (☎ 635-4461), 113 S 1st.

Things to See & Do
The **Grand Canyon Railway** uses turn-of-the-19th-century steam locomotives from late May through September and 1950s diesels the rest of the year. The trip is 2¼ hours to the Grand Canyon, with characters

in period costume offering historical and regional narration, or strolling around playing a banjo and answering questions. Often, the train is held up by train robbers, but the sheriff usually takes care of them. Roundtrips allow about 3 hours at the canyon. Trains leave at 10 am daily except December 24-25, returning to Williams by 5:45 pm.

The fare was $3.95 when the railway opened in 1901. Today, passengers travel coach class ($55 roundtrip, $25 for two- to 16-year-olds) in a 1923 car, or in four other classes (up to $140/110). Tax is an extra

8.8% and national park admission is $6 extra for adults. It's a short walk from the Grand Canyon train depot to the rim, but narrated bus tours of various lengths and prices are also offered, as are various overnight packages with accommodations at either Williams or the Grand Canyon (hotel reservations essential). Contact the railway (☎ 773-1976, 800-843-8724) for information or reservations.

website: www.thetrain.com

The **Grand Canyon Deer Farm** (☎ 635-4073, 800-926-3337), near I-40 exit 171, 8 miles east of town, is a petting and feeding zoo with several deer species, llamas, peacocks and other animals. Fawning season (May to July) is an especially nice time to go with kids. It's open daily and admission is $5.50 for adults, $4.25 for seniors and $3.50 for three- to 13-year-olds.

The small **Williams Ski Area** (☎ 635-9330), 4 miles south of town along 4th St, has a poma lift that climbs from 7500 to 8150 feet and serves runs for beginner, intermediate and advanced skiers. The season depends on the snowfall.

Places to Stay

Rates from mid-May to mid-September (given below) can halve in winter, or rise during special events and holidays. Summer reservations are advised unless you arrive by early afternoon.

Camping *Railside RV Ranch* (☎ 635-4077, 888-635-4077, railside@thegrandcanyon .com, 877 Rodeo Rd) is the closest campground to the center, with 100 RV sites with hookups for $20; four sites allow tents. There are showers, a game room and laundry.

Red Lake Campground & Hostel (☎ 635-5321, 800-581-4753, redlake@azaccess .com), on Hwy 64 eight miles north of I-40 exit 165, has 14 RV and eight year-round sites. Tenting costs $12, RVs with hookups cost $18, and there are coin showers, laundry and a grocery store. Summer reservations are recommended.

The *Circle Pines KOA* (☎ 635-4545, 800-732-0537), half a mile north of I-40 exit

167, has about 150 year-round sites ranging in price from $18 for tents to $27 for RVs with full hookups, and six Kamping Kabins available for $35. There are hot showers, a coin laundry, an indoor pool and spa, a playground and stables offering horseback rides in summer. *Grand Canyon KOA* (☎ 635-2307), on Hwy 64 five miles north of I-40 exit 165, has 100 sites open from March through October at about the same price and with similar facilities (no stables).

The Kaibab National Forest south of Williams operates several *campgrounds* open on a first-come, first-served basis from May to October, with drinking water but no showers or RV hookups. Fishing and boating is possible.

Budget There are 32 hostel beds in rooms sleeping up to four people at *Red Lake Campground & Hostel* (see above). Rates are $11 per person (more for private rooms) with winter discounts.

In Williams itself, you'll see a number of motels offering rooms in the $20s in winter, but for $40 to $55 in summer when they fill up early. The most reliable of these include the 12-room *Highlander Motel* (☎ 635-2541, 800-800-8288, 533 W Route 66); the 26-room *Budget Host Inn* (☎ 635-4415, 800-745-4415, xz003ns@aol.com, 620 W Route 66); the 24-room *Courtesy Inn* (☎ 635-2619, 800-235-7029, 344 E Route 66), which serves coffee and doughnuts for breakfast; and the 24-room *Westerner Motel* (☎ 635-4312, 800-385-8608, 530 W Route 66).

Mid-Range Among the *chain motels* in town are two Motel 6s, two Super 8s and an Econo Lodge. Shortly north of town at I-40, exit 163, are a Holiday Inn and Fairfield Inn, a bit closer is a Howard Johnson, and west of town near exit 161 you'll find a Days Inn and Best Western.

The pleasant *El Rancho Motel* (☎ 635-2552, 800-228-2370, ranchol@frontiernet .com, 617 E Route 66), has 25 rooms with coffeemakers (some with microwaves and refrigerators) and a pool in summer.

Summer rates are in the $60s. The **Norris Motel** (☎ 635-2202, 888-315-2378, norrismotel@thegrandcanyon.com, 1001 W Route 66) has a pool and whirlpool, and refrigerators in its 33 rooms which are in the $60s in summer. A few suites are about $100. The owners advertise 'British hospitality' (though they don't serve kippers and warm beer at odd hours of the day!).

Top End The **Fray Marcos Hotel** (☎ 635-4010, 235 N Grand Canyon Blvd), next to the Williams Grand Canyon Railway depot, is managed by the railway, which uses the hotel for its overnight packages. Although new, the hotel was built in the style of the original railroad hotel, part of which now forms a museum. About 200 spacious modern rooms rent for $120 a double in summer, $80 in winter with discounts if you buy a railway package. The hotel features interior corridors, indoor pool and whirlpool, and an exercise room.

Downtown, the **Red Garter B&B** (☎ 635-1484, 800-328-1484, 137 W Railroad Ave) has four rooms with private baths in a restored 1890s bordello. Rates of $75 to $110 include a continental breakfast in the downstairs bakery.
website: www.redgarter.com

The smoke- and alcohol-free **Terry Ranch B&B** (☎ 635-4171, 800-210-5908, 701 Quarter Horse Rd), has four rooms with turn-of-the-19th-century furnishings, some with fireplaces, one with a TV/VCR, and one with a two-person jetted tub. A wrap-around verandah makes a nice place to relax. Rates are $115 to $155 with a full breakfast; see the website at www.bbonline.com/az/terryranch.

The ten-room **Sheridan House Inn** (☎ 635-9441, 888-635-9345, 460 E Sheridan) is owned by a chef who prepares great breakfasts and provides generous hors d'oeuvres and free drinks in the inn bar every evening. The smoke-free inn features a fitness room, whirlpool, entertainment room, a video and CD library (and all the rooms have TV/VCRs and CD players). Summer rates range from $135 to

$235; check www.thegrandcanyon.com/sheridan.

Places to Eat
Note that restaurant hours may be shortened in winter.

For home-style breakfasts, try **Old Smoky's** (☎ 635-2091, 624 W Route 66), which advertises 14 kinds of homemade breads as well as pancakes and cinnamon rolls.

If you're looking for simple family restaurants serving reasonably priced standard American food all day, try the **Hoffman House** (☎ 635-9955, 425 E Route 66) and **Pine Country Restaurant** (☎ 635-9718, 107 N Grand Canyon Blvd).

Twisters (☎ 635-0266, 417 E Route 66) is a '50s-style 'Route 66' soda fountain with ice cream treats, hot dogs, burgers etc. Route 66 fans will also want to check the memorabilia in **Cruiser's Café 66** (☎ 635-2445, 233 W Route 66) with a widely varied menu in the $6 to $15 range.

For a more upscale eatery there is **Max & Thelma's** (☎ 635-4010) at the Grand Canyon Railroad complex, named after the railroad owners. Breakfast, lunch and dinner buffets are inexpensive and crowded, but dinner in the dining room is a more sedate and pricey affair, with entrées in the teens and $20s.

Pancho McGillicuddy's (☎ 635-4150, 141 W Railroad Ave) is a 'Mexican cantina' popular with tourists; it also serves gringo food and has a patio outside. The restaurant is housed in one of the town's oldest buildings – constructed of stone in 1895, the building survived several fires that burned down other buildings in this block. This was once known as 'Saloon Row' with many bars, brothels and opium dens along here. If only walls could talk... Since they don't, you'll have to wet your whistle with a brew at the quirky **World Famous Sultana Bar** (301 W Route 66).

Rod's Steak House (☎ 635-2671, 301 E Route 66) has been here half a century and is among the best in town. Apart from good steaks priced in the teens and $20s, there are cheaper chicken and fish dinners and a kids' menu.

Getting There & Away

Greyhound (☎ 635-0870) stops at Williams Chevron gas station at 1050 N Grand Canyon Blvd. Nava-Hopi Tours (see Organized Tours in the Flagstaff section) stop at the Grand Canyon Railway depot on the way to and from the Grand Canyon.

Amtrak stops on the outskirts of town, not at the Grand Canyon Railway depot.

Northeastern Arizona

Some of Arizona's most beautiful and photogenic landscapes lie in the northeastern corner of the state. Between the fabulous buttes of Monument Valley on the Utah state border and the fossilized logs of the Petrified Forest National Park at the southern edge of the area lie lands that are locked into ancient history. Here is the Navajo National Monument, with ancient, deserted pueblos, and Canyon de Chelly, with equally ancient pueblos adjacent to contemporary farms. Here are mesas topped by some of the oldest continuously inhabited villages on the continent. Traditional and modernized Navajo hogans dot the landscape and Hopi kivas nestle into it. Native Americans have inhabited this land for centuries; it is known today as the Navajo and Hopi Indian Reservations.

Tribal laws take precedence over state laws, although both tribes accept federal laws and are fiercely proud and patriotic citizens. The Navajo Indian Reservation is the country's biggest and spills over into the neighboring states of Utah, Colorado and New Mexico. It completely surrounds the Hopi Indian Reservation. It's the biggest reservation partly because its harsh landscape didn't seem to offer much when reservations were doled out.

The Navajo and Hopi are recent neighbors. The Hopi are the descendants of people who left more westerly pueblos in the 12th and early 13th centuries while the Navajos are descendants of Athapaskan Indians who arrived from the north between the 14th and 16th centuries. The two peoples speak different languages and have different religions and customs. Today, they live side by side in an uneasy alliance, disagreeing, often bitterly, on their reservation borders, a dispute exacerbated by tribal population growth.

I-40 Corridor

The southern boundary of the Navajo Reservation is roughly paralleled by I-40.

WINSLOW
☎ 928 • pop 9520 • elevation 4880 feet

Established as a railroad town in 1882, Winslow soon became a ranching center and remains an important shipping center. Some 60 miles south of the Hopi mesas, Winslow provides the closest off-reservation accommodations. The high school at Oak and Berry is shaped like a hogan.

Greyhound (☎ 289-2171) stops at the Circle K, 4th and Williamson.

Information
The chamber of commerce (☎ 289-2434) is by I-40 exit 253, next to one of Peter Toth's famous wooden Indian carvings. Its website is www.winslowarizona.org. The library (☎ 289-4982), 420 W Gilmore, has Internet access. Other services for travelers include the post office (☎ 289-2131), 223 Williamson; hospital (☎ 289-4691), 1501 Williamson and police (☎ 289-2431), 115 E 2nd.

MAP INDEX

ARIZONA

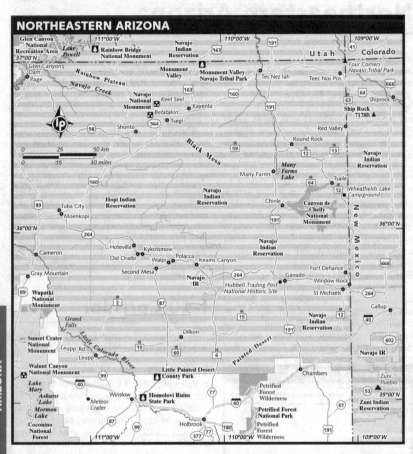

Things to See & Do

The memorable lyrics 'I'm standing on the corner in Winslow, Arizona, such a fine sight to see' from the '70s song *Take It Easy* by the Eagles, have given rise to a small plaza on Route 66 at Kinsley Ave and 2nd, in the heart of old downtown. A life-sized bronze statue of a hitchhiker backed by a trompe l'oeil wall mural of the girl in a flatbed Ford always attracts a posse of photographers.

Winslow's past is not forgotten in the **Old Trails Museum** (☎ 289-5861), 212 Kinsley Ave. It's open 1 to 5 pm Tuesday to Saturday from April to October and Tuesday,

Thursday and Saturday during other months; free admission. More history is found at La Posada Hotel (see Places to Stay) and at the **Lorenzo Hubbell Trading Post**, 523 W 2nd, where the Arizona Indian Arts Cooperative (☎ 289-3986) demonstrates silversmithing and has a small display of contemporary Indian crafts. Ask them to show you around the trading post. Hours are 9 am to 5 pm weekdays and some Saturdays. Also check out **Moore's Saw and Pawn**, 1020 W 3rd, which repairs chainsaws; sells saddles, guns and old and new Navajo jewelry; and is a step back in time.

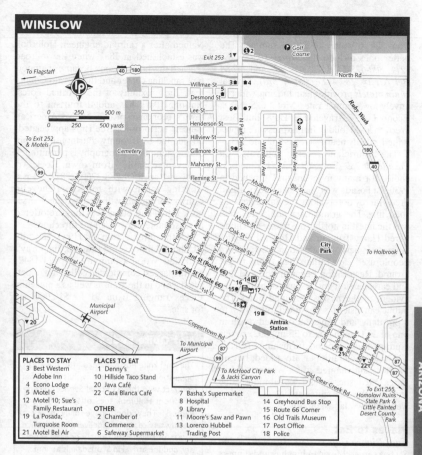

WINSLOW

To Flagstaff

Exit 253

Golf Course

North Rd

Willmae St
Desmond St
Lee St
Henderson St
Hillview St
Gillmore St
Mahoney St
Fleming St

N Park Drive

Winslow Ave
Warren Ave
Kinsley Ave

Ruby Wash

To Exit 252 & Motels

Cemetery

0   250   500 m
0   250   500 yards

To Exit 252
& Motels

Gorman Ave
Francis Ave
Edwin Ave
Dent Ave
Charlton Ave
Berton Ave
Alfred Ave
Davis Ave
Douglas Ave
Prairie Ave
Cantebel Ave
Hicks Ave
Berry Ave
4th St
Aspinwall Ave
Williamson Ave
Apache Ave
Colorado Ave
Snider Ave
Donnelly Ave
Pope Ave
Cottonwood Ave
Taylor Ave
Leonard Ave
Parker Ave
Alder Ave

Mulberry St
Cherry St
Elm St
Maple St
Oak St

3rd St (Route 66)
2nd St (Route 66)
1st St

Front St
Central St
Short St

Municipal
Airport

Coppertown Rd

Amtrak
Station

To Municipal
Airport

To McHood City Park
& Jacks Canyon

Old Clear Creek Rd

City
Park

To Holbrook

To Exit 255,
Homolovi Ruins
State Park &
Little Painted
Desert County
Park

ARIZONA

PLACES TO STAY	PLACES TO EAT	OTHER
3 Best Western Adobe Inn	1 Denny's	2 Chamber of Commerce
4 Econo Lodge	10 Hillside Taco Stand	6 Safeway Supermarket
5 Motel 6	20 Java Café	7 Basha's Supermarket
12 Motel 10; Sue's Family Restaurant	22 Casa Blanca Café	8 Hospital
19 La Posada; Turquoise Room		9 Library
21 Motel Bel Air		11 Moore's Saw and Pawn
		13 Lorenzo Hubbell Trading Post

14 Greyhound Bus Stop	15 Route 66 Corner
16 Old Trails Museum	17 Post Office
18 Police	

Homolovi Ruins State Park (☎ 289-4106), a mile north from exit 257 off Hwy 87, features petroglyphs, hundreds of small dwellings and four larger Pueblo sites, most eroded and under investigation. A visitor center is open daily. Day use is $4 per vehicle. **Little Painted Desert County Park** (☎ 524-4251) 13 miles north from exit 257 on Hwy 87, offers picnic facilities, walking trails and colorful views.

Locally popular **McHood City Park** (☎ 289-1300), 4 miles along Hwy 99, offers fishing, boating, swimming, picnicking and camping. Day use is $3 per vehicle.

International rock climbers head 30 miles south along Hwy 87 to **Jacks Canyon**, where there is free camping and over 200 routes on French limestone ranging from 5.5 to 5.13 in difficulty.

Places to Stay

Homolovi Ruins State Park has 52 sites at $10 for tents and $15 with hookups (including park entrance fee). There are showers. Another camping option is *McHood City Park*, with a few inexpensive sites open April through October on a first-come, first-served basis.

About a dozen old motels, some run-down, are found along Route 66. Rates range from $20 in winter to $40 in summer. The better ones include the *Motel 10* (☎ 289-3211, 800-675-7478, 725 W 3rd) and *Motel Bel Air* (☎ 289-4727, 400 W 3rd). Several *chain motels* provide clean lodging, with relatively low summer rates. Motel 6, Super 8, Econo Lodge, Travelodge, Days Inn, Best Western and Holiday Inn Express are represented, mainly near I-40 exits 252 and 253.

The historic and recently renovated *La Posada* (☎ 289-4366, 303 E 2nd) is the best choice for many miles around. Opened in 1930, La Posada was one of a chain of grand Fred Harvey hotels along the Santa Fe Railroad line. The grand hacienda-style hotel was the finest in northern Arizona and numbered Harry Truman and Howard Hughes among its guests, but closed in 1959 as more people used cars rather than trains to get around. Restoration began in the mid '90s and care, passion and a sense of history are evident in the newly reopened hotel. The public can visit on self-guided tours 8 am to 8 pm daily, and travelers can bed down in one of 20 (expanding to 35 in 2002) rooms equipped with period furnishings (OK, a TV and air-conditioner are added, but no phones) and named after Western dignitaries and desperadoes. It's a fabulous value at $79, with a few suites at $99.
website: www.laposada.org

Places to Eat

Casa Blanca Café (☎ 289-4191, 1201 E 2nd St) has served Mexican lunches and dinners for half a century, or stop by the *Hillside Taco Stand* in a bright yellow hut at the west end of 2nd St for authentic tacos in no-frills surroundings. *Sue's Family Restaurant* (☎ 289-1234, 723 W 3rd) is your basic diner where the locals go for home cooking. The *Java Café* (☎ 289-0850, 703 Airport Rd) is worth a drive a couple of miles out to the airport terminal. Lunches and dinners daily, except Monday, are surprisingly good. Best in town is the *Turquoise Room* in La Posada, with an eclectic menu reflecting the hotel's historical and geographical heritage. It's closed on Monday.

HOLBROOK

☎ 928 • pop 4917 • elevation 5080 feet

Named after a railroad engineer, Holbrook was established in 1881 when the railroad reached this point. It soon became an important ranching center and the Navajo County seat. The proximity of the Petrified Forest National Park has added tourism to the town's economic profile. Native American dancers perform for free (tips appreciated) outside the 1898 county courthouse at 7 pm during summer. Photography is permitted.

Seventeen miles from town, Rock Art Canyon Ranch (☎ 288-3260, 288-3527) is a working ranch with tours of Chevelin Canyon, brimming with petroglyphs. Horseback riding and other activities are offered at reasonable prices. Call for directions.

At the intersection of Hwys 180 and 77, about 2 miles south of town, Jim Gray's Petrified Wood Company (☎ 524-1842) has the largest commercial collection of petrified wood in the area, as well as a museum. Pieces ranging from $1 to $10,000 are for sale.

Not Quite FedEx

The Hashknife Posse, named after the area's biggest early cattle company, has an official contract with the US Postal Service to carry mail from Holbrook to Scottsdale via pony express. They don't have daily or even weekly service. In fact, delivery is only once a year, usually in late January or early February, and the arrival in Scottsdale is an important part of that city's Western Week. The ride takes three days. Letters with normal postage marked 'Via Pony Express' in the lower left will receive special postmarks and be delivered by the Hashknife Posse if left at the Holbrook post office during the first two weeks in January. Or put your stamped and marked letter in another envelope and send it to the Postmaster, Pony Express Ride, Holbrook, AZ 86025. After letters reach Scottsdale, they continue via normal mail. This tradition dates back to 1959.

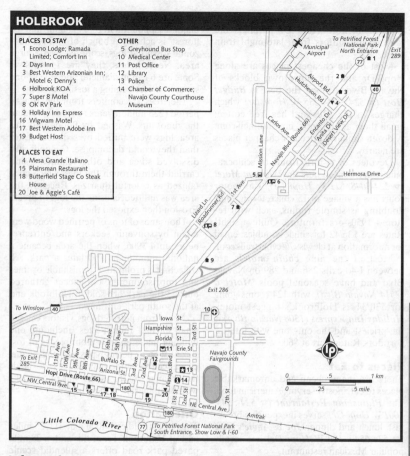

HOLBROOK

PLACES TO STAY
1 Econo Lodge; Ramada Limited; Comfort Inn
2 Days Inn
3 Best Western Arizonian Inn; Motel 6; Denny's
6 Holbrook KOA
7 Super 8 Motel
8 OK RV Park
9 Holiday Inn Express
16 Wigwam Motel
17 Best Western Adobe Inn
19 Budget Host

PLACES TO EAT
4 Mesa Grande Italiano
15 Plainsman Restaurant
18 Butterfield Stage Co Steak House
20 Joe & Aggie's Café

OTHER
5 Greyhound Bus Stop
10 Medical Center
11 Post Office
12 Library
13 Police
14 Chamber of Commerce; Navajo County Courthouse Museum

Information

The chamber of commerce (☎ 524-6558, 800-524-2459) is in the county courthouse at 100 E Arizona. The courthouse retains the old city jail and records the area's history, which was wild and bloodthirsty in the 19th century. The library (☎ 524-3732), 451 1st Ave, has Internet access. Other services in town include the post office (☎ 524-3311), 100 W Erie; a medical center (☎ 524-3913), 500 E Iowa; and police (☎ 524-3991), 100 E Buffalo.

Greyhound (☎ 524-3832) stops at the Circle K, 101 Mission Lane.

Places to Stay

The **Holbrook KOA** (☎ 524-6689), northwest of I-40 between exits 286 and 289, has over 100 tent and RV sites, showers, a pool, recreation room, playground and coin laundry. Rates are $20 to $25, and Kamping Kabins are $31. Summer reservations are suggested. The **OK RV Park** (☎ 524-3226, 1576 Roadrunner Rd) has showers and more than 100 tent and RV sites from $20.

Most motels and hotels line Hopi Dr (east of I-40, exit 285) or Navajo Blvd, north of Hopi Dr intersecting with I-40, exits 286 and 289. Holbrook has a surplus of hotels, so finding reasonably priced rooms is rarely a problem; note Hopi Dr parallels the railway and suffers from late-night train noise.

Most of the cheapest places are along Hopi Dr and the downtown blocks of Navajo Blvd. Among the best is *Budget Host* (☎ 524-3809, 235 W Hopi Dr) which charges in the $20s and has free coffee; email them at holbrook_inn@hotmail.com. A dozen similarly priced or cheaper places are nearby.

Devotees of historic Route 66 schlockabilia won't want to miss the *Wigwam Motel* (☎ 524-3048, 811 W Hopi Dr). This motor court has a village of 15 concrete wigwams doubling as simple rooms, each with restored 1950s-era furniture. Quite a sight! Rates are $36/42 for singles/doubles; email for information at clewis97@cybertrails.com.

Most of the nine *chain motels* are between I-40 exits 286 and 289 on Navajo Blvd and have seasonal pools. *Motel 6 (2514 Navajo Blvd)*, with 124 rooms going for $30/34, is Holbrook's biggest motel. *Holiday Inn Express (1308 Navajo Blvd)* is the priciest and the only one with interior corridors. Rates start at $60.

Places to Eat

There are many cheap and unremarkable places to eat, mostly serving American food. The *Plainsman Restaurant* (☎ 524-3345, 1001 W Hopi Dr) serves inexpensive breakfast, lunch and dinner. *Joe & Aggie's Café* (☎ 524-6540, 120 W Hopi Dr) is a locally popular Mexican restaurant.

The *Butterfield Stage Co Steak House* (☎ 524-3447, 609 W Hopi Drive) is open for lunch and dinner in summer, dinner only in winter. Full of western memorabilia, this place delivers the region's best steaks at reasonable prices. Also recommended is *Mesa Grande Italiano* (☎ 524-6696, 2318 Navajo Blvd), with the best Italian food for miles around.

PETRIFIED FOREST NATIONAL PARK

Children may have the naive impression that trees here are still standing in little glades,

eerily frozen in time. Parents might avoid major disappointment by explaining that the 'forest' is actually a bunch of broken, horizontal fossilized logs, scattered over a large area. Nevertheless, they are impressive: Some are 6 feet in diameter and at least one spans a ravine, forming a fossilized bridge.

The trees are conifers from the Triassic period (225 million years ago) and pre-date the dinosaurs. Washed by floods into this area, logs were buried by sediment faster than they could decompose. Groundwater dissolved silica and other elements, and carried them through the logs, which crystallized as colorful quartzes. Recently, the area was uplifted, causing the logs to break. Erosion then exposed the logs.

Thousands of tons of petrified wood were taken by souvenir seekers and entrepreneurs until 1906, when the area became a national monument and later a park. All collecting is prohibited (punishable by fines and imprisonment), but pieces gathered outside the park are sold in Holbrook and at the south park entrance.

Apart from petrified logs, visitors can see small ancient Indian sites (including one building made entirely from blocks of fossilized wood), petroglyphs and the picturesque scenery of the Painted Desert – lands that change colors as the sun plays tricks with the minerals in the earth.

Orientation

The park straddles I-40 at exit 311, 25 miles east of Holbrook. From this exit, a 28-mile paved park road offers a splendid **scenic drive**, going briefly north and then heading south, over the freeway, to emerge at Hwy 180, 19 miles southeast of Holbrook. Unless making the complete loop from Holbrook, it is more convenient to begin at the north end if you are driving west and the south end if you are driving east.

Information

The Painted Desert Visitor Center near the north entrance, and the Rainbow Forest Museum near the south entrance, have bookstores, park exhibits, and rangers on duty. At Painted Desert Visitor Center, a

20-minute film describes how the logs were fossilized, and at Rainbow Forest there are giant reptile skeletons. Between the two, the park road passes over 20 pullouts with interpretive signs and some short trails.

Hours are 8 am to 5 pm; from Memorial Day to Labor Day, hours are 7 am to 7 pm if staff is available; closed on December 25. Entrance is $10 per vehicle; $5 per bus passenger or bike rider. The usual passes are accepted. Visitors receive a (free) park map showing pullouts along the road. Further information is available from the superintendent (☎ 524-6228), Petrified Forest National Park, AZ 86028.

Hiking & Backpacking

Apart from short trails at some of the pullouts, there are no trails into the park. Hikers can walk cross-country, but should speak with a ranger first to discuss their plans as there are no maintained trails, campsites or water sources; all water must be carried. Backpackers can camp in the backcountry after obtaining a free permit from a ranger; camps must be at least a mile from paved roads and no fires, firearms, pets or collecting are allowed. Some areas are closed to camping.

Places to Stay & Eat

The park has no accommodations. Snacks can be purchased by the Rainbow Forest

Museum and meals by the Painted Desert Visitor Center. There are two picnic areas. In **Chambers**, 22 miles east of the park on I-40, the ***Best Western Chieftain Inn*** has rooms ($60) and a restaurant. Otherwise, stay in Holbrook (listed earlier).

Navajo Indian Reservation

The Navajo Indian Reservation, or the Navajo Nation as the Navajos themselves call it, covers 27,000 sq miles; it's the largest reservation in the USA. It is mainly in northeastern Arizona, but also includes parts of neighboring Utah and New Mexico. About 75% is high desert and the remainder is high forest. The scenery is, in places, some of the most spectacular in North America, particularly in Monument Valley. Equally impressive are the beautiful (but uninhabited) ancient pueblos amid splendid settings in the Canyon de Chelly and Navajo National Monuments.

History

Anthropological research indicates that in the 14th and 15th centuries, bands of Athabaskan-speaking people migrated from Canada into the Southwest. By 1500 these people had established themselves and they became the ancestors of both the Navajo and the Apache Indians. In those days, they were a hunting and gathering people, occasionally raiding neighboring tribes. Influenced by the more sedentary and agricultural Pueblo tribes, the Navajos eventually began farming and making arts and crafts, but never built large stone villages such as the Pueblo Indians did.

The Navajo call themselves the *Diné* (the People) and explain their arrival in the Southwest quite differently. According to their oral legends, the Diné passed through three different worlds in various human, animal, spiritual, and natural forms before finally emerging into the fourth world, called the Glittering World. Today's Diné maintain close links with their past worlds,

ARIZONA

and believe that their lives should be in harmony with all the elements of the present and the earlier worlds. Dozens of ceremonies and rituals, learned with painstaking care from tribal elders and medicine men, are done for various reasons to enable the people to live in harmony with the rest of the universe.

Contact with the Spaniards in the 16th, 17th and 18th centuries was surprisingly limited, considering the Spaniards' involvement with the Pueblo and Hopi peoples. The best-documented Navajo-Spanish interaction was the massacre of more than 100 Indians at Canyon de Chelly in 1805 in response to years of Navajo raids.

When the Anglos arrived in the 19th century, they tended to follow the better-known routes in New Mexico and southern Arizona. By the middle of the 1800s, the US Army was defeating tribes, including the Navajo, along the Western frontier and 'buying' the land from the Indians in exchange for peace. (This may have made sense to the Anglos, but it didn't to the Indians, who didn't value the European concept of land ownership.) Once their land had been purchased, the surviving tribes were often 'relocated' onto distant reservations.

During the winter of 1863–64, US Cavalry troops led by Colonel Kit Carson destroyed fields and property, killed anyone they found and drove the Indians up into Canyon de Chelly until starvation forced their surrender. Thousands of Indians were rounded up and forced to march to Fort Sumner in the plains of eastern New Mexico (see Fort Sumner in the Southeast New Mexico chapter) in an episode remembered in tribal history as 'The Long Walk.'

Hundreds of Navajos died on the march or on the inhospitable new reservation. Despite this, the Navajo were one of the luckier tribes. A treaty in 1868 gave them a reservation of about 5500 sq miles in the heart of their ancient lands, and 8000 inhabitants of Fort Sumner along with about another 8000 scattered Navajos were allowed to settle on this new reservation. This grew over the years to its present size, and today over half of the approximately

The Navajo Language

Navajo belongs to the Athapaskan language family, a group of languages that also includes Apache. Other tribes speaking Athapaskan languages live in Alaska, northwestern Canada, and coastal Oregon and California. The distribution of these tribes is considered evidence of migration patterns across the continent.

Some Navajo, especially the elders, speak only the Navajo language, but most speak both Navajo and English. All members of the tribe have a deep respect for the Navajo language whether they are fluent or not.

Navajo and English have very different sentence structures and Navajo is not an easy language for outsiders to learn. During WWII, the Navajo Code Talkers spoke a code based on Navajo for US military radio transmissions. The code was never broken. The Code Talkers are now famous for their wartime contribution and the remaining members of this unit are frequently honored at tribal functions.

175,000 members of the Navajo Nation live on the reservation. About one in seven Native Americans in the USA is a Navajo, making it the country's largest tribe.

Information

The best information about the reservation is found at Window Rock. Other good information sources are the *Navajo Times* newspaper (www.navajotimes.com) and KTNN AM 660/KWRK 96.1 FM radio station. This broadcasts out of Window Rock with mainly Navajo-language programming in the morning and English in the afternoon and evening. The music varies between country & western and traditional and recent Navajo music, much of which involves drums and singing or flutes.

Banking facilities on the reservation are available at banks in Window Rock, Tuba City, Chinle and Kayenta. The Navajo Reservation, unlike Arizona, does observe

Mountain daylight saving time. Thus during the summer, the reservation is *one hour ahead* of Arizona; on the same time as Utah and New Mexico.

Photography is permitted almost anywhere. Taking photographs of people, however, is not appropriate unless you ask for and receive permission from the individual involved. A tip is expected. Alcohol and drugs are strictly prohibited. The few hotels and restaurants in Navajoland provide clean accommodations and tasty food, but no alcohol. It is a violation of federal, state and Navajo tribal laws to disturb, destroy, injure, deface or remove any natural feature or prehistoric object.

Beware of farm animals on the roads because most of the land is not fenced. Hitting one can do as much damage to you as to the animal. Be careful of the occasional drunk driver. Despite the ban on alcohol, there are problems with drunk driving.

The reservation's phone system occasionally goes dead for short or sometimes long periods, particularly in remote locations and during severe weather.

Special Events

The world's biggest Indian event is the Annual Navajo Nation Fair, held for several days soon after Labor Day in Window Rock. The fair has been taking place since 1946. Most visitors stay in Gallup, New Mexico, and travel to Window Rock for the intertribal powwow, Indian rodeo, traditional song and dance displays and competitions, a barbecue with Navajo food and many other events.

See Farmington in the Northwestern New Mexico chapter for information on the oldest and most traditional fair, held in Shiprock in late September or early October. The Navajo Tourism Office (see Window Rock, later) has the exact dates of smaller rodeos and powwows that are held in many smaller towns on the reservation.

Places to Stay

Some tribally operated campgrounds are found at or near Monument Valley, the Navajo National Monument, Chinle, Tsaile and Window Rock. RV facilities are very limited.

The few motels on the reservation are found at Window Rock, Chinle, Kayenta, Tuba City, Cameron (see Cameron & Around in the Grand Canyon & Lake Powell chapter), Goulding's Trading Post (see Monument Valley in the Southeastern Utah chapter), and Teec Nos Pos. These are often full in summer; reservations are a good idea.

Navajo guides can arrange stays with local families or in a traditional hogan (a sleeping bag is a good idea) with primitive bathroom facilities (most hogans lack plumbing). Rates are about $90 including a Navajo breakfast; add $10 per extra person. Hiking and backpacking tours can be arranged. The Navajo Tourism Office can supply a list of approved guides.

Shopping

The Anglo towns on the perimeter of the reservation have galleries and pawn shops where Navajo rugs, silverwork, jewelry and other arts can be purchased. On the reservation itself, you can buy from trading posts, gift shops, museums, and roadside stands.

Buying items at 'official' stores is no guarantee of their quality; high- and low-quality wares appear on the trading-post shelves just as they do at roadside stalls. When you buy direct, you may find that you pay less and have more luck negotiating the price down; the sellers may still make more from the transaction than if they had sold their wares to a trading post. In addition, you may be able to talk directly to the artisan.

Getting There & Away

The Navajo Transit System (☎ 729-4002, 729-4110) provides the only public transportation on the reservation using modern buses. Call for times.

From Gallup, New Mexico, the Navajo Transit System has buses to Window Rock and Fort Defiance four times a day on weekdays and three times on Saturday. The ride takes an hour. There is no Sunday service. Several daily buses connect Window Rock and Fort Defiance on weekdays; three do so on Saturday.

On weekdays, there is one daily bus linking Window Rock with Tuba City along Hwy 264 via the Hopi Reservation. Another bus leaves on weekdays from Fort Defiance (a few miles north of Window Rock) for Kayenta via Tsaile, Chinle and other small villages. A third goes to Shiprock, New Mexico.

WINDOW ROCK
☎ 928 • pop 3500 • elevation 6900 feet
The tribal capital is at Window Rock, at the intersection of Hwys 264 and 12. The town is named after a natural arch at the north end of town more than a mile north of the intersection.

Orientation & Information
Information about the whole reservation is available from Navajo Tourism Office (☎ 871-6436, 871-7371, fax 871-7381), PO Box 663, Window Rock, AZ 86515. The tribal website is www.navajo.org.

The main area of tourist interest is at the east end of town on Hwy 264 just east of Hwy 12. Here you'll find the FedMart shopping plaza (where the Navajo Transit System bus leaves from and where there is a

Navajo Weaving

The Navajo are the best-known rug-weavers of the Native American tribes. A Navajo rug requires many months of labor and can involve several family members. Children tend the sheep, and various people participate in shearing, washing, carding, spinning and dyeing the wool before it even touches the loom. All is done by hand. The loom is a simple upright wooden frame, and the designs and colors are passed down from generation to generation, usually to the women. Legend has it that Spider Woman taught the women how to weave. You can watch weavers at work at some museums and trading posts; the Hubbell Trading Post near Ganado is a good place for this.

Navajo weavings were originally heavy blankets used in winter. When Anglos became interested in the work as a folk craft, they found that the origin of the rug could be recognized by the various designs and colors used in the rug. For instance, a Ganado Red was a rug with a red background coming from the settlement of Ganado. Rugs with geometrical designs in earth colors bordered by black were from the Two Grey Hills region from the eastern part of Navajo lands. And the Shiprock area was known for Yei rugs, depicting supernatural beings revered by the Navajo. Several other regional styles can easily be detected with a little experience.

Today, weavers from any part of the reservation can produce designs that were once specific to a particular area. While traditionally the designs have been geometric, some weavers currently use figurative designs. Such rugs are technically as valuable as the traditional ones.

Tips on Buying a Rug Whether used as a floor covering or displayed on a wall, a good quality rug can last a lifetime. Given the cost of purchasing a good quality rug, buying one is not for the average souvenir-seeker. It can take months of research, or can be bought on a whim if you see one you really love. If you're a more cautious shopper, visit museums, trading posts and crafts stores in Indian country. Talk to weavers, exhibitors and traders to learn about the various designs. Don't just look at the rugs – feel them. A good rug will be tightly woven and even in width. Prices of rugs vary from the low hundreds to thousands of dollars. This reflects the size of the rug, the weeks of work involved, the skill of the weaver and whether the yarn is store-bought or hand-spun.

Be aware that cheap imitation rugs are available. These may look nice, but they aren't hand-made by Navajos. Some are mass-produced in Mexico using Navajo designs. The staff at a reputable store can show you the difference.

cinema), bank, arts and crafts stores, the Navajo Nation Inn, the museum, post office and parks office all within a few hundred yards of one another.

Backpacking and other backcountry use anywhere on the reservation requires a permit from the Navajo Parks & Recreation Dept (☎ 871-6647, fax 871-6637). The office is next to the Zoo & Botanical Park on the east side of Window Rock. (Note that the campgrounds mentioned in this chapter are not considered 'backcountry' and don't require a tribal permit beyond the camping fee.) Hunting (very limited), fishing, and boating require tribal (not state) licenses obtainable from Navajo Fish & Wildlife (☎ 871-6451/2); details are given at www.navajofishandwildlife.org.

Navajo Nation Museum & Library

This museum (☎ 871-7941) features permanent collections, changing shows and the tribal library. A gift shop has an excellent selection of books about the Navajo and other tribes as well as other items. Hours are 8 am to 5 pm Monday to Saturday, to 8 pm on Wednesday; admission free.

In keeping with the traditional Navajo hogan, the museum's door faces east and is not immediately obvious from the highway. It's on Hwy 264 at Post Office Loop Rd at the east end of Window Rock. Next door is the Zoo & Botanical Park.

Navajo Nation Council Chambers

The chambers (☎ 871-6417) are below the Window Rock Arch north of town. During tribal council sessions, you can hear the 88 elected council delegates representing the 110 Navajo chapters (communities) discussing issues in the Navajo language. Full council sessions are held at least four times a year, usually on the third Monday of January, April, July and October. At other times visitors can tour the chambers' colorful murals.

Nearby is the Window Rock Tribal Park with picnic areas and the Navajo Veterans Memorial. Camping is not allowed. The arch is important in Navajo ceremonies and is off-limits during some ceremonies.

St Michael's Mission Museum

Housed in an 1898 Franciscan mission, 3 miles west of Window Rock just off Hwy 264, this museum (☎ 871-4171) describes the missionary work of the Franciscans in Navajoland. Hours are 9 am to 5 pm Monday to Friday from Memorial Day to Labor Day. Call for an appointment at other times.

Places to Stay & Eat

There are no developed campgrounds though you can park your RV next to the Zoo & Botanical Park. A $2 per person fee may be charged.

The *Navajo Nation Inn* (☎ *871-4108, 800-662-6189*) is on Hwy 264 east of Hwy 12. There are 56 aging rooms with Southwestern motifs. Rates range from $65 to $75 for a single and $5 for each extra person. A reasonably priced restaurant serves Navajo and American breakfast, lunch and dinner. There are several fast-food restaurants.

Half a mile west of St Michael's Mission on Hwy 264 is a *Days Inn* (☎ *871-5690*) with indoor pool, sauna and exercise room.

Shopping

Window Rock is the headquarters of the Navajo Arts and Crafts Enterprise (NACE), which runs a jewelry and crafts store (☎ 871-4090) next to the Navajo Nation Inn. The NACE was established in 1941 and is wholly Navajo operated. It guarantees the authenticity and quality of its products.

HUBBELL TRADING POST NATIONAL HISTORIC SITE

John Lorenzo Hubbell established this trading post at **Ganado** (30 miles west of Window Rock) in 1878 and worked here until his death in 1930. He was widely respected by Indians and non-Indians alike for his honesty and passion for excellence. Today, his trading post is operated by the NPS and looks much as it would have a century ago. Indian artists still trade here.

Next to the trading post is a visitor center where respected Navajo women often give weaving demonstrations and men might demonstrate silversmithing.

ARIZONA

Helpful interpretive signs explain what is being woven, and rangers can help with questions.

Tours of Hubbell's house (with a superb collection of early Navajo rugs and period furniture) are given several times a day. The trading post continues to sell local crafts, specializing in top-quality Navajo weavings worth thousands of dollars. If you can't quite scrape the money together, buy a postcard or a candy bar instead!

Hours are 8 am to 6 pm May through September, 8 am to 5 pm otherwise, and it's closed major holidays. Admission is free. There's a picnic area but nowhere to stay. Further information is available from the superintendent (☎ 755-3475), PO Box 150, Ganado, AZ 86505.

CANYON DE CHELLY NATIONAL MONUMENT

Pronounced 'd-SHAY,' this many-fingered canyon contains several beautiful Ancestral Puebloan sites that are important in Navajo history. Ancient Basketmaker people inhabited the canyon almost 2000 years ago and left some pit dwellings dated to AD 350. These inhabitants evolved into the Pueblo people who built large cliff dwellings in the canyon walls between AD 1100 and 1300. Droughts and other unknown conditions forced them to leave the canyon after 1300 and it is supposed that they were the ancestors of some of today's Pueblo or Hopi Indians.

The Navajo began farming the canyon bottom around 1700 and used the canyon as a stronghold and retreat for their raids on other nearby Indian groups and Spanish settlers. In 1805, the Spaniards retaliated and killed over 100 Navajos in what is now called Massacre Cave in the Canyon del Muerto. The Spaniards claimed that the dead were almost all warriors but the Navajo say that it was mostly women and children. In 1864, the US Army drove thousands of Navajos into the canyon and starved them until they surrendered over the winter, then relocated them in eastern New Mexico after 'The Long Walk.' Four years later, the Navajos were allowed to

return. Today, many families have hogans and farms on the canyon bottom. Most families live on the canyon rims in winter, and move to the canyon bottom in the spring and summer. The whole canyon is private Navajo property administered by the NPS. Please don't enter hogans unless with a guide and don't photograph people without their permission!

The canyon begins at its west end near the village of **Chinle**. Here, the canyon walls are only a few feet high but soon become higher until they top out at about 1000 feet in the depths of the canyon. Two main arms divide early on in the canyon and several side canyons connect with them. A paved road follows the southernmost and northernmost rims of the canyon complex, affording excellent views into the splendid scenery of the canyon and distant views of uninhabited pueblos in the canyon walls; this is a worthy **scenic drive**. Most of the bottom of the canyon is off-limits to visitors unless they enter with a guide. The exception is a trail to the White House.

Information

The visitor center, just east of Chinle, features exhibits about the canyon, a bookstore, information about guides and tours and a free newspaper guide. Inexpensive booklets with descriptions of the sights on South and North Rim Drives are available. Outside is a traditional Navajo hogan that you can enter (it's empty). Hours are 8 am to 5 pm daily, extended to 6 pm May through September. Admission is free as long as you stick to the visitor center, paved rim roads and White House Trail. Further information is available from the superintendent (☎ 674-5500), PO Box 588, Chinle, AZ 86503.

For information not sponsored by the NPS, take a look at the Unofficial Canyon de Chelly and Navajo website at www.navajocentral.org.

White House Trail

The trailhead is about 6 miles east of the visitor center on South Rim Drive, and the steep trail is about 1¼ miles one-way; carry water. The pueblo dates to about AD 1040 to 1284 and is one of the largest in the monument.

Rim Drives

Both drives afford several scenic overlooks into the canyon. Lock your car and don't leave valuables in sight when taking the short walks at each scenic point.

South Rim Drive is 16 miles long and passes six viewpoints before ending at the spectacular Spider Rock Overlook, with views down onto the 800-foot-high sheer-walled tower atop of which lives Spider Woman. The Navajos say that she carries off children who don't listen to their parents! This is a dead-end drive so return the way you came.

North Rim Drive has four overlooks and ends at the Massacre Cave overlook, 15 miles from the visitor center. The paved road continues to Tsaile, 13 miles further east, from which Hwy 12 heads to Window Rock or into the northern reaches of the reservation.

The lighting for photography on the north rim is best in early morning and on the south rim in late afternoon.

Organized Tours

Ask at the visitor center about all tours. Guides belong to the Canyon de Chelly Guide Association, and are usually local Navajos who know the area well and liven up tours with witty commentary.

Hiking & Backpacking The Guide Association offers guided hikes into the canyon. A four-hour, 4½-mile hike is offered twice daily May to September for $15 per person (five to 15 people). Other hikes may be available. Definitely bring insect repellent in spring and summer.

For more difficult hikes or to visit more remote areas, guides charge $15 an hour (three hours minimum, 15 people per guide maximum). Overnight hikes with camping in the canyon can be arranged at the visitor center (allow at least a day to organize).

During the summer, park rangers may lead free hikes. Inquire and register in advance at the visitor center.

Horseback Riding Justin Tso's Horseback Tours (☎ 674-5678), near the visitor center, has horses available year-round for $10 per person per hour plus $10 an hour for the guide. Tohtsonii Ranch (☎ 755-6209), at the end of South Rim Drive, charges similar prices. The ranch offers four-hour roundtrip rides to Spider Rock. Overnight trips can be arranged.

4WD Only rough tracks enter the canyon, so you need 4WD. With your own vehicle you can hire a guide for $15 an hour (one guide can accompany up to five vehicles; three-hour minimum). Heavy rain may make the roads impassable.

Navajo-owned Unimog Tours (☎ 674-1044, 674-5433) leave from the Holiday Inn for three-hour tours at 9 am and 1 pm. Rates are $40 ($25 for children under 13). They rent 4WD vehicles for $125 for three hours plus $30 for each additional hour. Thunderbird Tours (☎ 674-5841), at the Thunderbird Lodge, use heavy-duty, army-style 6WD vehicles that can cross through streams that would stop a 4WD. Some Navajos refer to these as the 'shake-n-bake' tours. Half-day trips leave at 9 am and 2 pm and cost $42 ($32 for children). Seasonal full-day tours are $67 for everyone and include a picnic lunch.

Places to Stay & Eat

Cottonwood Campground, near the visitor center, has 96 sites on a first-come, first-served basis. There is water but no hookups or showers. Camping is free and popular, so in summer get there early. During the summer, rangers may give talks. Group campgrounds are available by reservation. From November to March, water may be shut off. The remote, Navajo-run *Spider Rock Campground (☎ 674-8261)*, 10 miles east of the visitor center along South Rim Drive, is surrounded by piñon and juniper trees and gets away from the activity of the visitor center. Sites cost $10. There is no water or electricity, but the owner has bottled water and lanterns available.

The attractive *Thunderbird Lodge (☎ 674-5841/2, 800-679-2473)*, half a mile

from the visitor center, is the only lodge with the monument. Over 70 comfortable rooms vary in size; some are in the old lodge (which dates from the late 1800s) but all have private baths, air-conditioning, TVs and telephones. Rates are $100 to $150 a double; there are discounts mid-November through March. An inexpensive cafeteria offers tasty American and Navajo food from 6:30 am to 9 pm, with shorter winter hours.
website: www.tbirdlodge.com.

A half-mile west of the visitor center is the *Holiday Inn* (☎ 674-5000). They have an outdoor pool and the area's most upscale restaurant (though still not very fancy), open from 6:30 am to 10 pm. Parts of the public areas incorporate an old trading post, but the 108 rooms are modern and have coffee makers. Rates range from $100 to $120 in summer; email them at holidayinncdc@cybertrails.com.

In Chinle, just east of Hwy 191 and 3 miles west of the visitor center, is the *Best Western Canyon de Chelly Inn* (☎ 674-5875), with 100 pleasant motel rooms, all with coffee makers, for $100 to $140 from May to October dropping to $60 to $80 in winter. They have an indoor pool and an inexpensive dining room open from 6:30 am to 9 pm (10 pm in summer).
website: www.canyondechelly.com

Seventeen miles north of Chinle, near the intersection of Hwys 191 and 59, the high school at Many Farms operates the *Many Farms Inn* (☎ 781-6362/6226) where Navajo students train in hotel management. Rooms have two single beds and bathrooms are shared. There is a TV room and a game room. Rates are $30 per person.

Apart from the hotel restaurants, there are some fast-food restaurants and Chinle's *Basha's*, the only supermarket for at least 50 miles. Alcohol is not available (reservation law).

Shopping
The Navajo Arts & Crafts Enterprise (see Window Rock, earlier in this chapter) has a store in Chinle (☎ 674-5338) at the intersection of Hwys 191 and 7. The Thunderbird Lodge gift shop also sells a good range of crafts and T-shirts. The Thunderbird cafeteria walls are hung with high-quality Navajo rugs and paintings, which are for sale.

TSAILE
A small town at the northeast end of Canyon de Chelly, Tsaile (pronounced 'say-LEE') is the home of Diné College (☎ 724-6600), a Navajo-owned community college. On campus, the modern six-story glass **Ned A Hatathli Center** (☎ 724-6650) has its entrance facing east, just like a traditional hogan. The center features a museum with exhibits about Indian history, culture and arts and crafts, a variety of which are offered for sale in the gift shop. Hours are 8:30 am to 4:30 pm Monday to Friday; admission is by donation. The college bookstore has a superb selection of books about the Navajo.

South of the college and 2 miles off of Hwy 12 is the small *Tsaile Lake Campground* accessible by dirt road. RVs aren't recommended and there is no drinking water or facilities. Ten miles south of Tsaile on Hwy 12 is the larger and more attractive *Wheatfields Lake Campground* (☎ 871-6645, 871-7307) with nice lake views. There are pit toilets but no water. RV and tent sites are inexpensive. A nearby store sells food and fishing permits. Both lakes are stocked with rainbow and cutthroat trout and offer some of Navajoland's best fishing.

Will B Tsosie of *Coyote Pass Hospitality* (☎ 724-3383, 787-2295) can arrange local tours and overnight stays in hogans; visit www.navajocentral.org/cppage.htm.

FOUR CORNERS NAVAJO TRIBAL PARK
Make a fool of yourself as you put a foot into Arizona, another into New Mexico, a hand into Utah and another into Colorado. Wiggle your butt for the camera. Everyone does! The site is marked with a slab and state flags, and is surrounded by booths selling Indian souvenirs, crafts and food. This is the only place in the USA where four states come together at one point. Hours are 7 am to 8 pm May to August, and 8 am to 5 pm at other times. Admission is a

steep $2.50 per person (though it might not be collected in winter). Seniors pay $1 and children under eight are free.

KAYENTA & AROUND
☎ 928 • pop 4500 • elevation 5641 feet

Established in 1908 as a trading post, Kayenta has in recent decades developed strong (if controversial) uranium- and coal-mining industries. It provides lodging for Monument Valley, 24 miles away.

The visitor center (☎ 697-3572) provides information, has a small museum, and sells local crafts and books. Vehicle tours to Monument Valley are provided by Roland's Navajoland Tours (☎ 697-3524, fax 697-2382) and Crawley's Tours (☎ 697-3463, 697-3734); email crawley@crawleytours.com.

Halfway between Four Corners and Kayenta, the village of Teec Nos Pos has the small *Navajo Trails Motel* (☎ 674-3618) with basic double rooms for $49 in summer – the cheapest motel in Navajoland.

Pricey chain motels are your main choice. The Navajo-operated *Best Western Wetherill Inn* (☎ 697-3231) is 1½ miles north of Hwy 160 on Hwy 163. It has an indoor pool and 54 standard motel rooms with coffeemakers at almost $100 May to October, about $50 to $70 otherwise. The *Hampton Inn* (☎ 697-3170) features an outdoor pool and complimentary continental breakfast. Summer rates for the 73 spacious, modern rooms are in the low $100s.

The *Holiday Inn* (☎ 697-3221), at the junction of Hwys 160 and 163, is the reservation's largest hotel, with 160 rooms and a few suites. Rates are about $150 for a double July to October, dropping to about $80 in midwinter. There is an outdoor pool, a kids' pool, and a decent restaurant open all day.

The *Golden Sands Cafe* (☎ 697-3684) serves American and Navajo food near the Wetherill Inn, and the *Amigo Cafe* (☎ 697-8448), on Hwy 163 a short way north of Hwy 160, serves Mexican food. Both are open for breakfast, lunch and dinner. The *Burger King* has an interesting exhibit on the Navajo Code Talkers, which makes it the Southwest's most unique chain fast-

The High Cost of Coal

In satellite photos taken from 567 miles above the Navajo and Hopi Indian Reservations, the Peabody Coal Company's mine to the west of Kayenta looks like a blackhead. The fact that it appears at all is testimony to its size and to the size of the controversies surrounding the mine at Black Mesa. One of the main issues that arises is the use of groundwater. Coal mines use exorbitant amounts of water to transport the coal to smelters, depleting a vast supply of rainwater that has accumulated over the centuries.

Take into account that this land is desert and water is a precious resource for the Navajo and Hopi. Without the water, their ability to raise livestock and grow crops – the basis of their lifestyle – is threatened. Historically, treaties about tribal land have only defined the land, not the water under the surface. Bureaucracy takes over and the Indians find themselves fighting not only the federal bureaucracy, but also each other over disputed borders and use of land and resources. The issue is further complicated by the fact that Peabody is one of the primary employers on the reservation.

food place. There's also a *Basha's* supermarket for picnic shopping.

About 10 miles west on Hwy 160 at the village of Tsegi is the *Anasazi Inn* (☎ 697-3793), with 60 simple motel rooms (many with good views) for about $80 in summer, less in winter; email tsegi@redmesa.com for information. It has a 24-hour *restaurant*.

MONUMENT VALLEY NAVAJO TRIBAL PARK

Some people have a feeling of déjà vu here: This is the landscape seen in famous Westerns like the classic 1939 production of *Stagecoach*, directed by John Ford, or *How the West Was Won* (1962). The landscape is stupendous.

Great views of Monument Valley are had from the **scenic drive** along Hwy 163, but to really get up close you need to visit the

ARIZONA

Monument Valley Navajo Tribal Park (☎ 435-727-3287, 727-3353). Most of the park is in Arizona, the area code is for Utah. A 4-mile paved road leads to a visitor center with information, exhibits, restaurant and tour companies.

From the visitor center, a rough unpaved loop road covers 17 miles of stunning valley views. You can drive it in your own vehicle (ordinary cars can just get by) or take a tour. Self-driven visitors pay $3 ($1 for seniors, free for kids under eight). Tour companies at the visitor center offer 2½-hour trips for about $30 a person (two minimum). Horseback rides are around $30. Note that tours enter areas that cannot be visited by private vehicle. Tours leave frequently in summer but are infrequent in winter. Outfitters in Kayenta and at Goulding's in Utah also offer tours. The road is open 7 am to 7 pm May through September, and 8 am to 4:30 pm the rest of the year, except Christmas. Bad weather may close the road.

The tribally operated *Mitten View Campground* has some coin-operated hot showers but no RV hookups. About 100 sites are $10 each on a first-come, first-served basis and may fill in summer. The showers are closed in winter, when the sites cost $5 and can be cold, windy and snowy.

See the Southeastern Utah chapter for camping and motel facilities in nearby Goulding's Trading Post.

NAVAJO NATIONAL MONUMENT

This monument protects three Ancestral Puebloan sites, of which Betatakin and Keet Seel pueblos are exceptionally well preserved, extensive and impressive, and are open to the public. Well worth a visit, they are difficult to reach so part of their charm comes from your sense of achievement getting there. Visits are only in summer.

The visitor center (☎ 672-2700), 9 miles north of Hwy 160 along Hwy 564, offers audio-visual shows, a small museum and a

well-stocked gift shop. Information, ranger-led programs, camping and picnicking are available.

Betatakin

This pueblo is distantly visible from the Sandal Trail, open year-round and an easy 1-mile loop from the visitor center.

From mid-May through September, rangers lead 5-mile, five-hour (roundtrip) hikes to Betatakin at 9 am daily. Hikers must obtain *their own* free tickets for the hike at the visitor center. The hike is limited to 25 persons and, occasionally, 25 people are waiting in line before the visitor center opens! The elevation (7300 feet at the visitor center, 6600 at Betatakin) means the return hike can be strenuous, so carry plenty of water and sun protection. Unguided hikes aren't allowed.

Keet Seel

This is one of the largest and best-preserved ancient pueblos in the Southwest and can be reached by foot only. Keet Seel is 8½ miles (one-way) from the visitor center, but the destination is worth the challenging hike involving a steep 1000-foot descent and then a 400-foot gentle climb. The trail is loose and sandy and may necessitate wading through a shallow streambed.

Although the 17-mile roundtrip can be done in a day, most visitors backpack in and stay at the primitive campsite below Keet Seel. There's no drinking water, so carry your own. Camping is limited to one night. At the site, visitors must register at a small ranger station. The pueblo may be visited only with the ranger and visitation is limited to 20 people a day and five people at a time, so you may need to wait. The last visit is at 3:30 pm. Entrance requires using a very long ladder, so it's not for people afraid of heights.

Keet Seel is open daily from Memorial Day to Labor Day. The 20 daily permits are free and often taken early, so call ahead to reserve one. No fires are allowed so bring a stove or cold food.

Places to Stay

The *campground* at the visitor center is open May through September and has 31 sites with water, but no showers or RV hookups. Camping is free on a first-come, first-served basis. Two large group sites are available by reservation. During other months, the campground remains open but the water is turned off.

TUBA CITY

☎ 928 • pop 7300 • elevation 4936 feet

Originally settled by Mormons in 1875 and named after a Hopi leader, Tuba City, a mile north of the intersection of Hwys 160 and 264, is the major town in the western half of the Navajo Reservation.

The **Tuba Trading Post** (☎ 283-4545) dates back to the 1880s and sells authentic Indian arts and crafts as well as food. A motel and restaurant are next door. The trading post has information about upcoming public dances and events on the Hopi and Navajo Reservations. **Dinosaur tracks** are seen 5 miles west along Hwy 160 on the north side of the road. Look for a small sign and a few Navajo crafts stalls at the turnoff. Children will guide you for $2.

The *Grey Hills Inn* (☎ 283-6271, ext 2) is in the Grey Hills High School, a half-mile east along Hwy 160 from the intersection with Hwy 264. Students operate a simple motel with private rooms with shared baths at $42 to $58 for one to four people from May to October, less in winter.

Navajo-run *Diné Inn Motel* (☎ 283-6107), on Hwy 160 at Peshlakai Ave, has 15 clean, modern rooms with TV and telephone in the $70s in summer, $50s the rest of the year. More rooms are planned.

The 80-room *Quality Inn* (☎ 283-4545, 800-644-8383) is part of the Tuba Trading Post complex. Rooms are $70 to $130 for a double. The *Hogan Restaurant* (☎ 283-5260) is on the premises, open daily 6 am to 9 pm.

See the Navajo Indian Reservation section, earlier in this chapter, for details on getting to and from Tuba City by bus.

Hopi Indian Reservation

The Hopi are the oldest and most traditional tribe in Arizona, if not the entire continent. Their earliest villages were contemporary with the ancestral cliff dwellings seen in several of the Southwest's national parks. Unlike the residents of those dwellings, however, who abandoned them about AD 1300, the Hopi have continuously inhabited three mesas in the high deserts of northeastern Arizona for centuries. Old Oraibi, for example, has been continuously inhabited since the early AD 1100s and vies with Acoma Pueblo in New Mexico for the title of oldest continuously inhabited town in North America. It is thought that the ancestors of some of today's Hopi were also the people who migrated from other cliff dwellings 700 years ago.

The Hopi are a deeply religious and agricultural people. They are also private people and would just as soon be left alone to celebrate their cycle of life on the mesa tops. Because of their isolated location, they have received less outside influence than most other tribes and they have limited facilities for tourism.

When the Spaniards arrived, they stuck mainly to the Rio Grande valley and rarely struck out into the high deserts where the Hopi lived. Spanish explorers Pedro de Tovar and García López de Cárdenas, members of Coronado's expedition, were the first Europeans to visit the Hopi mesas in 1540, and Hopi guides led Cárdenas to see the Grand Canyon. In 1592, a Spanish mission was established at Awatovi and the zealous friars attempted to close down kivas and stop the religious dance cycle that is an integral part of the Hopi way of life. Because of this, the Hopi joined the Pueblo Revolt of 1680, drove out Spanish missionaries and destroyed the church. When the Spaniards returned to New Mexico in 1692, their attempts at reviving this mission failed. Although unsuccessful in establishing their religion among the Hopi, the Europeans were, unfortunately, successful importers of disease: Smallpox wiped out 70% of the tribe in the 1800s.

Meanwhile, the Hopi were forced to deal with raids by Navajo and other groups. When the Navajo were rounded up for 'The Long Walk,' the Hopi, perceived as peaceful and less of a threat to US expansion, were left on their mesa tops. After the Navajo were allowed to return from their forced exile, they came back to the lands surrounding the Hopi mesas. Historically, the Hopi have distrusted the Navajo, and it is ironic, therefore, that the Hopi Reservation is completely surrounded by the Navajo Reservation.

Today, about 11,000 Hopi live on the 2410-sq-mile reservation, of which more than 1400 square miles are partitioned lands used by the Navajo. A US Senate bill officially resolved a complicated century-old legal conflict between the two tribes about the boundaries of the reservations in 1996, but there are still disagreements between the two tribes.

Orientation

The reservation is crossed by Hwy 264, which passes the three mesas that form the heart of the reservation. These are pragmatically named, from east to west, First Mesa, Second Mesa and Third Mesa. In addition, paved Hwys 87, 77 and 2 enter the reservation from the south, giving access from the I-40 corridor. Travel on paved highways is freely allowed but you can't drive or hike off the main highways without a permit.

Information

A tribal government coordinates activities among the 12 main Hopi villages and between the tribe and the outside world. Information is available from the tribe's Office of Public Relations (☎ 734-3283), PO Box 123, Kykotsmovi, AZ 86039. Tribal office hours are 8 am to 5 pm Monday to Friday. Each village has its own leader, who often plays an important role in the religious practices of the village. Rules about visiting villages vary from place to place and you should contact each village (telephone numbers given below) to learn about their

particular rules. These rules can change at any time. The village with the best tourism infrastructure is Walpi on First Mesa.

Outside each village and in prominent places on the highways are signs informing visitors about the villages' individual policies. All villages strictly prohibit any form of recording, be it camera, video- or audiotape or sketching. Students of anthropology and related disciplines require tribal permits, not easily obtained because the Hopi are not interested in having their culture dissected by outsiders. Alcohol and drug use is prohibited throughout the reservation. Visitors are allowed to attend some ceremonial dances but most are closed to the public.

As with the rest of Arizona (and different from the surrounding Navajo Reservation) the Hopi Reservation does not observe daylight saving time in summer.

There are no banks, although ATMs are found in the Circle M Store in Polacca, the Secakuku Store at the junction of Hwy 264 and 87 and at the Hopi Cultural Center. Cash is preferred for most transactions. An ambulatory health care center can be reached at 738-0911 in emergencies. For other emergencies, call the BIA police (☎ 738-2233).

Special Events

Most of the many annual ceremonial dances were closed in 1992 to the non-Indian public. This was because the religious nature of the Hopi dances was being threatened by visitors, and also because their remote mesa-top locations did not have the infrastructure (bathrooms, water, food, emergency services and space) to deal with scores of visitors.

Each individual village determines the attendance of non-Indian visitors at dances. The Kachina Dances, held frequently from January to July, are mostly closed to the non-Indian public, as are the famous Snake or Flute Dances held in August. Social Dances and Butterfly Dances, held late August through November, are often open to public viewing. All dances are very important to the Hopi people, who attend them in large numbers.

The dances are part of the Hopi ceremonial cycle and are performed in order to create harmony with nature. A particularly important aspect of this is ensuring rainfall for the benefit of all living things. The dances are expressions of prayer that require a traditional and responsible performance. The precise dates are not known until a few weeks in advance. Village officials can tell you about dance dates close to when they will happen and advise you whether they will be open to the public.

The best bet for tourists is to try and see a Social Dance or Butterfly Dance in the fall. These normally occur on weekends and go intermittently from dawn to dusk. See the boxed text 'Visitors' Etiquette in Pueblos & on Reservations' in the Facts for the Visitor chapter for information on visiting pueblos.

Shopping

Apart from kachina dolls, the Hopi are known for fine pottery, basketware and, more recently, jewelry and paintings. These can be purchased from individuals or from stores on the reservation at prices below what you'd pay elsewhere. Hopi religious paraphernalia, however, is not offered for sale. Some reputable stores are mentioned under individual villages.

FIRST MESA

At the bottom of the mesa, **Polacca** is a non-traditional village. A steep road climbs to the mesa top but large RVs will not make it; leave them in Polacca. The first village on the mesa is **Hano**, inhabited by Tewa-speaking Pueblo Indians who arrived in 1696 after fleeing from the Spaniards. They have been integrated into the Hopi tribe. Hano merges into the Hopi village of **Sichomovi** (you can't tell the difference), which is an 'overflow' of Walpi. The mesa is closed to visitors during Kachina Dances.

At the end of First Mesa is the tiny village of **Walpi**, built around AD 1200 in a spectacular setting on a finger-mesa jutting out into space. It is the most dramatic of the Hopi villages. The mesa is so narrow at this point that you can't drive in; cars must be

Kachinas

Kachinas are several hundred sacred spirits that live in the San Francisco Mountains north of Flagstaff. At prescribed intervals during the year they come to the Hopi Reservation and dance in a precise and ritualized fashion. These dances maintain harmony among all living things and are especially important for rainfall and fertility.

Some Hopi who carefully and respectfully perform these dances prepare for the events over many days. They are important figures in the religion of the tribe, and it can be said that the dancers are the kachinas that they represent. This is why the dances have such a sacred significance to the Hopi and why the tribe is reluctant to trivialize their importance by turning a religious ceremony into a tourist spectacle. The masks and costumes used by each kachina are often spectacular.

One of the biggest Kachina Dances is the Powamuya, or 'Bean Dance,' held in February. During this time, young Hopi girls are presented with kachina dolls that incorporate the girls into the religious cycle of the tribe. The dolls are traditionally carved from the dried root of a cottonwood tree, a tree that is an indicator of moisture. Over time, these dolls have become popular collectors' items and Hopi craftsmen produce them for the general public as an art form. Not all kachinas are carved for the tourist trade: some are considered too sacred. Other tribes, notably the Navajo, have copied kachina dolls from the Hopi.

In March 1992, Marvel Comics, the well-known comic-book publisher, issued an *NHL Superpro* comic book in which there was a story about kachinas trying to violently capture a Hopi ice-skating champion who was not living a traditional lifestyle. The Hopi people considered this an inaccurate and blasphemous portrayal of the sacred nature of the kachina's role in Hopi life. It was also the last straw in many years of inappropriate actions regarding Hopi religious practices, and most Kachina Dances are now closed to tourists.

ARIZONA

left in a parking area near the entrance to the village. There is no water or electricity, so the handful of year-round residents has to walk into Sichomovi to get water.

A tourist office (☎ 737-2262, 737-2670) at the parking area has Hopi guides for a 45-minute Walpi walking tour (9:30 am to 4 pm). Fees are $8 for adults; $5 for five- to 17-year-olds; free for those under five. The guides speak excellent English and the tour is a highlight of a visit to Hopiland.

Artisans living on First Mesa sell pots, kachina dolls and other crafts at fair prices. There are always several in front of the tourist office and they'll give you detailed verbal explanations of the work they sell. Cameras and recorders are not allowed on the tours. Leave them locked in your car.

SECOND MESA
Called 'the center of the universe' by the tribe, Second Mesa is 10 miles west of First Mesa. The **Hopi Cultural Center** (☎ 734-2401) is here, with a small but informative museum – no photography or note-taking allowed. Admission is $3 ($1 for children 12 and under) and hours are 8 am to 5 pm Monday to Friday; shorter hours on summer weekends. It may close on major holidays.

Next door is the *Hopi Cultural Center Restaurant & Inn* (☎ 734-2401, fax 734-6651), with 33 modern nonsmoking rooms for $90/95 in summer, less in winter. It is often fully booked in summer so call as far ahead as possible. The restaurant is open 6 am to 9 pm in summer, 7 am to 8 pm in winter and serves American meals and a few Hopi foods. Nearby is a free *RV area* with no facilities.

Crafts are sold in the Cultural Center complex; in the nearby Hopi Arts and Crafts Guild (☎ 734-2463), which has good silverwork, and at Takurshovi, 1½ miles east of the Cultural Center, which has both high-quality arts (including baskets) and cheap 'Don't Worry, Be Hopi' souvenirs.

Also on Second Mesa are three Hopi villages that often have dances, a few of which may be open to public viewing. Call between 8 am and 5 pm Monday to Friday for information or ask at the Hopi Cultural Center. **Shungopavi** (☎ 734-7135) is the oldest village on the mesa and is famous for its Snake Dances, where dancers carry live rattlesnakes in their mouths. These are religious events, not circus acts, and tourists have been banned since 1984. Kachina Dances held here are off-limits too, but Social and Butterfly Dances may be open to public viewing. The other villages are **Mishongnovi** (☎ 737-2520) and **Sipaulovi** (☎ 737-2570), both of which may have some dances open to the public.

THIRD MESA
Ten miles west of Second Mesa, this area includes both villages on the mesa and others to the west of it. The first is **Kykotsmovi** (☎ 734-2474), founded in the late 1800s and now the tribal capital.

On top of the mesa is **Old Oraibi**, which Hopis say has been continuously inhabited since the early 12th century. Oraibi is a couple of miles west of Kykotsmovi. The roads are unpaved and dusty so park next to crafts shops near the village entrance and visit on foot, to avoid stirring up clouds of dust.

Many residents left in 1906, after a disagreement over educational philosophies led to a 'pushing contest.' One faction wanted US-funded schools for their children while the other preferred a more traditional approach. The traditionalists lost and left to establish the new town of **Hotevilla** (☎ 734-2420) and, soon after, **Bacavi** (☎ 734-9360) where inhabitants remain very traditional.

There are picnic areas off Hwy 264 just east of Oraibi and just east of Kykotsmovi on Oraibi Wash. On the highway leading to Oraibi is the Monongya Gallery (☎ 734-2344) and in Oraibi itself is Old Oraibi Crafts, both with good crafts selections.

East-Central Arizona

This region features forests lining the Mogollon Rim, a 1000- to 2000-foot-high geological break between the high desert of northeastern Arizona and the low desert of southeastern Arizona. The forested lands belong mainly to the USFS and the Fort Apache, San Carlos and Tonto Apache Indian Reservations. These highland forests offer cool respite for the citizens of Phoenix who dominate tourism in the area.

PAYSON & AROUND
☎ 928 • pop 13,620 • elevation 5000 feet
Founded by gold miners in 1882, the town became a ranching and logging center, but is now mainly a tourism and retirement center for Phoenix citizens, although ranching remains important in surrounding areas. The main drags are a curious but unappealing mix of strip malls and many **antique shops**. Check with the Forest Ranger Station about fishing and camping, which is the best reason to be here.

Learn more about the region's history at the **Rim Country Museum** (☎ 474-3483) on Main at Green Valley Pkwy, a mile west of the chamber of commerce. Hours are noon to 4 pm Wednesday through Sunday; admission is $3.

If you are a fan of novelist Zane Grey, you will want to stop at the little **Zane Grey Museum** (☎ 474-6243), 503 W Main, open 11 am to 4 pm Thursday through Monday. The town of Strawberry, 20 miles north of Payson, has Arizona's **oldest schoolhouse** built in 1885.

Horseback riders can get information and rent horses from OK Corral (☎ 476-4303) in Pine.

Information
Hwy 87 is known as Beeline Hwy through Payson. The chamber of commerce (☎ 474-4515, 800-672-9766), 100 W Main at Hwy 87, is open weekdays 8 am to 5 pm, and weekends 10 am to 2 pm.

Other services include the Tonto National Forest Payson Ranger Station (☎ 474-7900), 1009 E Hwy 260; library (☎ 474-5242), 510 W Main; post office (☎ 474-2972), 100 W Frontier; hospital (☎ 474-3222), 807 S Ponderosa and police (☎ 474-5177), 303 N Beeline Hwy.

Tonto Natural Bridge State Park
Spanning a 150-foot-wide canyon and measuring over 400 feet wide itself, the Tonto Natural Bridge was formed from calcium carbonate deposited over the years by mineral-laden spring waters. This is the largest travertine bridge in the world. You can go under it, walk over it or see it from several viewpoints along the short but steep trail. A guest lodge was built here in the early 1900s (everything had to be lowered into the canyon). It's been renovated and tours are available on weekends, but the lodge is currently not in operation.

The park (☎ 476-4202) is 11 miles north of Payson on Hwy 87, then 3 miles west on

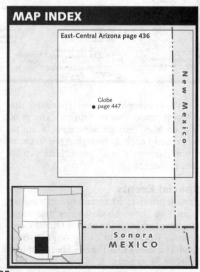

MAP INDEX

East-Central Arizona page 436

New Mexico

Globe
• page 447

Sonora
MEXICO

EAST-CENTRAL ARIZONA

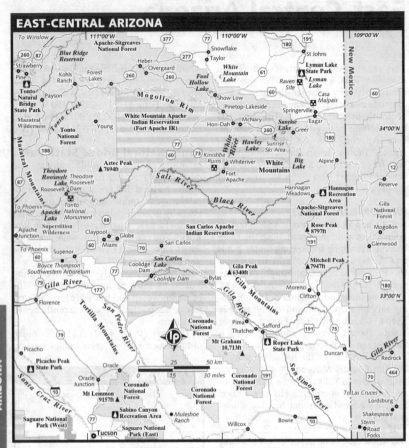

a 14%-grade paved road (perhaps the steepest paved road in Arizona). The park is open May through September 8 am to 6 pm, and October through April 9 am to 5 pm. Admission is $5 per vehicle (up to four passengers).

Special Events

Payson has over 50 annual events ranging from dog shows to doll sales, the most famous of which is the annual Oldest Continuous Rodeo, held every August since 1884. The state's Old Time Fiddlers Contest is in late September.

Places to Stay

Camping Free camping is allowed in the national forest, as long as you are a quarter-mile from a paved road.

Several developed USFS campsites sit along Hwy 260 east of Payson. They have drinking water but no showers. *Tonto Creek* ($8) is 17 miles east on Hwy 260, then a short drive north on USFS Rd 289. *Ponderosa*, 15 miles east, and *Christopher Creek*, 21 miles east and a short way south on USFS Rd 159, both charge $12. Other primitive campgrounds are scattered along dirt roads in the forest.

The USFS operates **Houston Mesa Campground**, a mile north of town along Hwy 87, with sites for tents, RVs and horses from $12 and up. There are showers. **Oxbow Estates RV Park** (☎ 474-2042), about 4 miles south of Payson off Hwy 87, offers tent and RV sites with hookups year-round and has showers, a coin laundry and a recreation room. Sites are $18.75 and summer reservations are recommended.

Motels & Hotels Rates vary depending on demand; double rooms start in the $60s during summer weekends, in the $80s during holiday weekends. However, midweek in winter, the same room could be $40. There are no budget-priced places.

Some of the cheaper places include the basic **Trails End Motel** (☎ 474-2283, 800-474-2283, 811 S Beeline Hwy) and the nicer **Rim Country Inn** (☎ 474-4526, 101 W Phoenix) at the south end of town.

Nicer places in town charging $80 to $130 in summer include the **Majestic Mountain Inn** (☎ 474-0185, 800-408-2442, 602 E Hwy 260), set in landscaped pines and lawns with a seasonal pool, 50 rooms, all with refrigerators and coffeemakers, and many larger units with wet bars and patios, fireplaces or whirlpool baths.
website: www.majesticmountaininn.com

All the 99 rooms at the **Inn of Payson** (☎ 474-3241, 800-247-9477, 801 N Beeline Hwy) have balconies or patios, coffeemakers and refrigerators; three have fireplaces. The hotel has a pool and whirlpool, and includes continental breakfast; visit www.innof payson.com. **Chain motels** include a Days Inn, Holiday Inn Express and Best Western.

Places to Eat
The town's best Italian food is served at **Mario's** (☎ 474-5429, 600 E Hwy 260). Rates are a reasonable $7 to $14. For Mexican food, dine at **El Rancho** (☎ 474-3111, 200 S Beeline Hwy).

Entertainment
Sawmill Theatres (☎ 468-7535, 201 W Main) has six screens. **Mazatzal Casino**, run by the

Tonto Apaches at the south end of town, is open 24 hours.

SHOW LOW
☎ 928 • pop 7695 • elevation 6331 feet
Named after the 1876 card game in which the winner won a ranch by showing the lowest card (it was the deuce of clubs, the name of the main street), Show Low is the gateway to the White Mountains, a region of forests and mountains popular with Arizonans. Along with neighboring Pinetop-Lakeside, it's a center for outdoor activities, including winter skiing. Though popular with lowland Arizonans escaping the heat, out-of-state visitors find it less interesting than more northerly and central parts of Arizona.

White Mountain Passenger Lines (☎ 537-4539) has a bus to Phoenix airport daily except Sunday.

Orientation & Information
Most businesses are along Hwy 60/77, Deuce of Clubs. Services include the chamber of commerce (☎ 537-2326), 951 W Deuce of Clubs, which you can email at slrcofc@showlow.com; library (☎ 537-2447), 20 N 6th; post office (☎ 537-4588), 191 W Deuce of Clubs; hospital (☎ 537-4375) on Hwy 260 between Show Low and Pinetop-Lakeside and the police (☎ 537-5091), 150 N 6th.

Things to See & Do
A small **historical museum** (☎ 532-7115), 542 E Deuce of Clubs, is open 1 to 5 pm Tuesday to Friday, and 10 am to 2 pm Saturday from May through October. **Thunder Raceway** (☎ 537-1111), at the northeast end of town, has stock car, motocross and other races from March to November.

Three miles northwest of town, the **Fool Hollow Lake Recreation Area** (☎ 537-3680) has boat ramps, fishing, showers and a campground, and **Show Low Lake**, 4 miles south on Hwy 260 and a mile east on Show Low Lake Rd, has boat rentals (☎ 537-4126), fishing and camping.

The **scenic drive** along Hwy 60 to Globe goes through the Salt River Canyon and is one of the area's most spectacular drives.

ARIZONA

Places to Stay & Eat

Undeveloped free dispersed camping is available in the Apache-Sitgreaves National Forest surrounding town. (The ranger station is in Pinetop-Lakeside.) The USFS campground at *Fool Hollow Lake* offers showers, tent sites for $10 and RV sites with electric hookups for $15, while the one at *Show Low Lake* charges $8/16.

A dozen hotels line Deuce of Clubs. The cheapest, for about $30 to $50, include *Downtown 9 Motel* (☎ 537-4334, 1457 E Deuce of Clubs) and *Thunderbird Motel* (☎ 537-4391, 1131 E Deuce of Clubs). Nicer rooms with refrigerators and coffeemakers are $50 to $80 at the *KC Motel* (☎ 537-4433, 800-531-7152, 60 W Deuce of Clubs) which offers a whirlpool and continental breakfast.

Five *chain motels* include the Motel 6, Best Western, Days Inn, Sleep Inn and Holiday Inn Express, all with rooms under $100. The last three have indoor pools.

Food in Show Low definitely leans toward standard American, with numerous eateries lining Deuce of Clubs.

PINETOP-LAKESIDE

☎ 928 • pop 3582 • elevation 7000 feet

Southeast of Show Low, Hwy 260 (White Mountain Blvd) wends its way past three public lakes and passes numerous motels, cabins and stores.

The Pinetop-Lakeside Chamber of Commerce (☎ 367-4290, 800-573-4031), 674 E White Mountain Blvd, is open 9 am to 5 pm ('til 4 pm in winter) Monday to Friday, plus 9 am to 3 pm on summer weekends. Its website is www.whitemtns.com. Other services include the USFS Apache-Sitgreaves Lakeside Ranger Station (☎ 368-5111), 2022 W White Mountain Blvd; the Arizona Dept of Fish & Game (☎ 367-4281, 367-4342), 2878 E White Mountain Blvd; library (☎ 368-6688), 1595 W Johnson Lane; post office (☎ 367-4756), 712 E White Mountain Blvd; police (☎ 368-8802), 1360 Niels Hansen Lane. The hospital is in Show Low.

Activities

The chamber of commerce has brochures describing scores of White Mountain lakes and streams suitable for **fishing**, and the USFS ranger station and Dept of Fish & Game are also excellent sources of information. Right in town, Rainbow Lake, Woodland Lake and Scotts Reservoir all offer fishing and **boating**, and Rainbow Lake has boat rentals.

Pinetop-Lakeside is a base for **cross-country skiing** and **hiking** as well as other activities in the White Mountains. Thirty miles east of town on Hwy 260, the Sunrise Ski Area (see White Mountain Apache Indian Reservation, later in this chapter) has **downhill skiing**. There are numerous **mountain-biking** trails. Several stores in town sell or rent camping gear, skis or bikes. For **horseback riding**, Porter Mountain Stables (☎ 368-5306) charges from $20 an hour to $75 all day for all levels of experience (minimum age six).

The White Mountains Trail System (☎ 368-6700) is a 180-mile series of loop trails designed for hiking, biking, horseback riding and cross-country skiing.

Places to Stay

Accommodations are set in the forest and are more rural than in Show Low. The location brings higher prices and two-day minimum stays may apply during summer.

Pick up a USFS map to find several roads heading northeast into the forest where free dispersed camping is allowed. Opposite the ranger station, the USFS *Lakeside Campground* (☎ 368-6841) offers more than 80 sites for $10 each, and provides drinking water but no showers or hookups. The *Rainbow Forest RV Park* (☎ 368-5286, 3720 Rainbow Lake Dr), offers a few tent sites for $10 and 44 RV sites with hookups for $15.

Basic motel rooms are priced in the $50s and $60s in summer, more on weekends and holidays, less off-season. The *Nine Pines Motel* (☎ 367-2999, 888-597-4637, 2089 E White Mountain Blvd) has 23 standard rooms; visit www.9pines.com. The *Bonanza Motel* (☎ 367-4440, 888-577-4440, 850 E White Mountain Blvd) has simple rooms and a few more-expensive units with kitchenettes; email for more information at bonanzamotel@cybertrails.com.

ARIZONA

The *Mountain Hacienda Lodge* (☎ 367-4146, 888-567-4148, 1023 E White Mountain Blvd) has 24 standard motel rooms with coffeemakers; its website is www.mountainhacienda.com. The nearby *Timber Lodge Motel* (☎ 367-4463, 1078 E White Mountain Blvd), has 31 rooms, most with microwave and refrigerator; visit www.timberlodge.com.

Chain motels include a Super 8 with a swimming pool, and a Best Western, Comfort Inn and Holiday Inn Express with whirlpools.

The following charge $60 to $120 a double. The small *Lazy Oaks Resort* (☎ 368-6203, 1075 Larson Rd), on a quiet street along Rainbow Lake, offers boat rentals and 15 one- and two-bedroom cabins with kitchens and fireplaces. Each sleeps from two to 10 people; its website is www.lazyoaks.com. The 11 cabins at *Hidden Rest Resort* (☎ 368-6336, 800-260-7378, 3448 Hwy 260) have fireplaces, kitchens and porches, and some have hot tubs; visit www.hiddenrest.com. The *Rainbow's End Resort* (☎ 368-9004, 267 Trout Rd) has eight lakeside cabins, all with kitchenettes and some with fireplaces. Boats can be rented; take a look at www.rainbowsendresort.com.

The *Coldstream B&B* (☎ 369-0115), at the southeast end of Pinetop (call for directions or look at www.wmonline.com/coldstream), rents six rooms with private bath for $95 to $160 double, and provides a hot tub, pool table, bicycles and afternoon tea as well as full breakfast. Several less expensive B&Bs belong to the White Mountain B&B Association – check out www.wmbba.com.

Lake of the Woods (☎ 368-5353) has two dozen cabins and chalets sleeping two to eight people for $100 to $190. A playground, game room and whirlpool are available, and boat rental is nearby; visit www.privatelake.com. The *Northwoods Resort* (☎ 367-2966, 800-813-2966, 165 E White Mountain Blvd) has 15 pleasant one- to three-bedroom cabins, each with fireplace and kitchen, ranging from $100 to $300 a double in summer; its website is www.northwoodsaz.com.

The area's most upscale accommodations are at *Sierra Springs Ranch* (☎ 369-3900, 800-492-4059, Sierra Springs Dr). Eight fully furnished cabins, including fireplace and kitchen, start at $175 double and go up to $525 for a cabin sleeping 13. The grounds feature fishing ponds, a tennis court, game room, playground and exercise room.
website: www.sierraspringsranch.com

Places to Eat
As in Show Low, the best places serve American food. The following serve good dinners in the $13 to $25 range. *Charlie Clark's* (☎ 367-4900, 1701 E White Mountain Blvd) has been a favorite steak house for decades. The *Christmas Tree Restaurant* (☎ 367-3107, 455 Woodland Rd) has an oddly rustic Christmassy décor; the varied menu is not limited to steak and seafood, offering chicken 'n dumplings as the house specialty. Dine outside in summer. The *Chalet Restaurant & Lounge* (☎ 367-1514, 348 E White Mountain Blvd) offers steak and seafood and has the biggest salad bar in town; closed on Sunday and Monday except summer.

WHITE MOUNTAIN APACHE INDIAN RESERVATION
Lying north of the Salt River, this reservation is separate from the San Carlos Apache Indian Reservation, described later in this chapter.

Like the Navajo, with whom they share linguistic similarities, the Apache were relatively late arrivals in the Southwest, arriving in the 14th century from the north. A hunting people, they lived in temporary shelters and moved often, frequently raiding other tribes and, later, Europeans. The White Mountain Apache were willing to accommodate US expansion more than most, and many of the US Army's Apache scouts were secured from this group.

The White Mountain Apache were fairly isolated until the 1950s, when tribal leaders began long-term development to take advantage of modern lifestyles. Building roads and dams, they created some of the Southwest's best outdoor recreation. Over 2500 sq miles of forest offer beautiful hiking, cross-country and downhill skiing, fishing, camping and boating. State licenses for fishing, boating or hunting aren't needed, but you do need tribal permits for these activities, as well as for all outdoor activities. Permits are available from stores on the reservation or from surrounding towns.

Whiteriver (population 3800) is the tribal capital, with the tribal offices, a supermarket, bank, post office, restaurant and basic motel ($55).

Fort Apache, 4 miles south of Whiteriver, was a US Army post in 1870. It remains in much better condition than most structures from that period. Two dozen remaining buildings give visitors a sense of army life on the Western frontier. Closed in 1922, the fort became an Indian boarding school, which contributed to its preservation. Stop by the Apache Cultural Center (☎ 338-4625), open Monday to Friday 8 am to 5 pm (with extended summer hours) to learn about the history of the fort and the soldiers and scouts stationed there. The center also has informative exhibits about the tribe's cultural heritage and an excellent display of basketry. Admission is $3 for 15- to 62-year-olds, $2 for seniors and children over five.

Activities
Sunrise Park Resort has good skiing, excellent summer fishing and a comfortable, if characterless, hotel. The Sunrise Ski Area (☎ 735-7669, 735-7600, 800-772-7669 for a snow report, ☎ 735-7518 for the ski school) is the state's largest ski area with 60 runs serviced by seven chair and four tow lifts. Snowboarders are welcome. Two miles from the alpine ski area, the Sunrise Sports Center (☎ 735-7335) has 6 miles of groomed cross-country trails. At 9100 feet, Sunrise Lake has some of the best trout fishing in the area and boat rental is available. Other lakes are close by.

Hon-Dah Casino & Resort (☎ 369-0299, 800-929-8744), 2 miles south of Pinetop-Lakeside at the junction of Hwys 260 and 73, has slot machines and live poker. Hawley Lake is one of the two most developed fishing areas on the reservation. Rent

canoes, rowboats and electric motorboats from the marina (☎ 335-7511) from mid-May to mid-October.

Places to Stay
The Hon-Dah Casino complex includes the **Hon-Dah Resort** (see above), with 128 comfortable rooms and a restaurant and lounge with entertainment. Weekend rates are $99; $20 less midweek. **Hon-Dah RV Park** (☎ 369-7400) has 120 sites at $17.

Hawley Lake Resort (☎ 335-7871, 369-1753) has about 30 motel rooms and cabins, all with kitchenettes, for $110 to $150; they sleep from four to ten people. Campsites are also available.

The **Sunrise Park Hotel** (☎ 735-7669, 800-554-6835) is by Sunrise Lake and a couple of miles from the ski area. Free shuttle buses run frequently in winter, and the restaurant, swimming pool, whirlpool, sauna and bar – with winter weekend entertainment – keep guests relaxed and happy. During the high season (winter weekends, holidays and mid-December through the first week in January) room prices jump to between $95 and $125, and suites to $300. At other times, rates start around $60. The hotel offers a variety of special packages to tie in with resort activities; call for details. Near the hotel are inexpensive *camping sites*.

GREER
☎ 928 • pop 100 • elevation 8500 feet
In summer, tiny Greer provides a cool getaway with convenient fishing and shady hikes. Get information about its offerings at www.greeraz.com. In winter the town is a base for skiing, with the Sunrise Park Resort 15 miles away and cross-country skiing, if conditions permit, outside your door. Lee Valley Stables (☎ 735-7454) leads horseback-riding trips in summer, and the Greer Lodge arranges romantic horse-drawn sleigh rides when winter conditions permit. The small Circle B Market (☎ 735-7540) has food, fishing information, maps and cross-country ski rentals. There is no public transportation.

The USFS has two *campgrounds* on Hwy 373. Benny Creek offers 30 sites for $8 with no drinking water. Rolfe C Hoyer offers 100 sites for $14 and has drinking water, electric hookups, lake access and a boat ramp. Both are open mid-May to mid-September.

Most places are pretty rustic, and two-night minimum stays are often required. For basic *motel rooms* from $50, call the Circle B Market. The *Molly Butler Lodge* (☎ 735-7226) opened in 1910, claims to be the oldest lodge in Arizona; it offers simple rooms for $35 to $50 a double and has a good *restaurant*.

The *Greer Lodge* (☎ 735-7216, 888-475-6343) offers nine lodge rooms for $120 a double and ten cabins with full kitchens. Most cabins are $120 a double, but sleep up to six. Two smaller ones are $75 and $95 a double and two larger ones are $35 per person with a six- or eight-person minimum. The lodge has private fishing on the premises and a fly-fishing school; horseback riding, ice-skating and cross-country skiing are also offered.
website: www.greerlodge.com

Surrounded by forest and with a deck overlooking the town of Greer, the *Peaks at Greer* (☎ 735-7777, 800-556-9997) is the fanciest hotel in town. Rooms with two queen-size beds cost about $100 double, the honeymoon suite costs $150, as do larger suites sleeping four to eight people. A few older cabins with kitchenettes are $120 double. All the suites and cabins have fireplaces. The resort does not allow smoking, has an indoor hot tub, a game room and a recommended *restaurant* open for breakfast, lunch and dinner.
website: www.peaksresort.com

The *Snowy Mountain Inn* (☎ 735-7576, 888-766-9971), set back off Hwy 373 amid the trees, has seven log cabins with fireplaces, kitchens, TV/VCRs and hot tubs. Two one-bedroom cabins are $150 and five two- and three-bedroom cabins are $165. It also has five homes with three beds and two baths sleeping six to 12 people for $255 to $350.
website: www.snowymountaininn.com

At the far south end of Greer, the attractive award-winning *Red Setter Inn B&B* (☎ 735-7441, 888-994-7337) is a three-story hand-hewn log building. Nine individually decorated rooms with private baths and some with a fireplace, Jacuzzi, deck or patio are $120 to $160 a double, including full breakfast. Smoking and children under 16 are not allowed.
website: www.redsetterinn.com

The *White Mountain Lodge B&B* (☎ 735-7568, 888-493-7568) is in an 1892 farmhouse. Seven rooms with private baths, some with fireplace or whirlpool tub, cost from $85 to $155 a double including full breakfast; six cabins with kitchens and fireplaces range from $85 to $155 double, not including breakfast.
website: www.wmlodge.com

SPRINGERVILLE & EAGAR
☎ 928 • pop 1972; pop 4033 • elevation 7000 feet

These adjoining towns are important ranching centers and the cool climate attracts tourists, anglers and hunters. The area has the added attraction of being close to two archaeological sites currently under excavation. West of town, notice over 400 volcanic vents in a 1200-sq-mile volcanic field, the continent's third largest. The chamber of commerce has information about this as well as about the private Renee Cushman collection of European art from the Renaissance to the early 20th century, in the Springerville Church, which can be viewed on request.

The area has several good fishing and boating lakes, as well as trails for hiking, mountain biking and horseback riding. The USFS and chamber of commerce have information. Fishing permits, supplies and information are available from the Sport Shack (☎ 333-2222), 329 E Main, Springerville, or Western Drug (☎ 333-4321), 105 E Main, Springerville. You can rent skis, snowboards and mountain bikes at the Sweat Shop (☎ 333-2950), 74 N Main, Eagar.

Information
The Round Valley Chamber of Commerce (☎ 333-2123,), 318 E Main, Springerville, is open daily from 9 am to 4 pm; visit www .az-tourist.com. Other services include the Springerville USFS Ranger Station

(☎ 333-4372), Mountain Ave at Airport Rd;
library (☎ 333-4694), 367 N Main, Eagar;
Springerville Post Office (☎ 333-4962), 5
Main; hospital (☎ 333-4368), 118 S Mountain Ave, Springerville; and police (☎ 333-
4000), 418 E Main, Springerville.

Archaeological Sites

At the **Casa Malpais** site, a kiva, burial
chambers, plaza, buildings, two stairways and
many rock art panels were created by the
Mogollon people in the mid-13th century
and abandoned in the late 14th century. The
site, 2 miles northeast of Springerville, can be
visited only on guided tours from the Casa
Malpais Archaeology Center (☎ 333-5375)
in the chamber of commerce building. The
center has a tiny museum, a short video
about the site, and a bookstore. Hours are
9 am to 4 pm daily. In summer, tours are
offered at 9 and 11 am and 2 pm, with fewer
departures in winter. Tours are weather dependent, last about 90 minutes, and involve a
half-mile walk with some climbing. Fees are
$5; $3 for those over 55 or between 12 and 18
years old. Call about the center's participatory archaeological research program.
website: www.casamalpais.com

The **Raven Site** is a Mogollon pueblo built
and occupied between AD 1100 and 1450.
Over 600 rooms have been identified at this
site, about 12 miles north of Springerville.
The adjacent White Mountain Archaeological Center (☎ 333-5857) has a museum and
gift shop. Guided tours of the site leave
several times a day. Tours cost $4; $3 for those
ages 12 to 17 and over 60. Self-guided tours
are available at the same price. The center is
open daily from May through mid-October
10 am to 5 pm, and is closed in the other
months. During summer, longer guided hikes
from a half to a full day are offered for $18 to
$40. Summer archaeological programs from
one day to several days, with lectures and
hands-on fieldwork, are offered.
website: www.ravensite.com

Places to Stay

The USFS office can tell you about campgrounds in the Apache-Sitgreaves National
Forest (some of the closest are at Greer,

Archaeology in Action

The Mogollon people left fewer sites than
did some other cultures living in the early
part of the second millennium, but two that
did survive are currently being excavated in
the Springerville area. Ever wondered what
archaeologists do for a living? You can watch
them work at Casa Malpais or Raven Site.

If you really want to get involved, ask
about the participatory research programs,
but be aware that research procedures are
deliberate and painstaking. The archaeolo-
gist uses brushes and hand trowels to slowly
and gingerly loosen centuries of debris from
the sites. Each object found, be it an entire
pot or just a tiny shard or scrap of wood,
must be carefully labeled and recorded. Archaeologists must know exactly where one
piece was found in relation to the next in
order to build up an accurate record of the
history of the site. A helper who removes an
artifact and says 'Look what I found!' is no
help at all; archaeologists must know exactly
where the item was found and what was
underneath, over and next to it. The work
requires care and attention but can be very
rewarding.

---

above, and at Big Lake). *Casa Malpais
Campground & RV Park* (☎ 333-4632), 1½
miles northwest of Springerville on Hwy 60,
offers showers and RV sites with hookups for
$16 and a few tent sites for $10. *Bear Paw RV
Park* (*☎ 333-4650, 425 E Central, Eagar*)
offers RV hookups for $13, but lacks showers.

The *White Mountain Motel* (*☎ 333-5482,
333 E Main, Springerville*) has basic rooms
in the $20s and $30s, some with kitchenettes.
Friendly *Reed's Lodge* (*☎ 333-4323, 800-
814-6451, 514 E Main, Springerville*) has an
outdoor spa, a game room, gift shop,
morning coffee, and a few bicycles to loan.
It's a pleasant old Western inn, and John
Wayne (who owned a ranch nearby) used to
hang out here. Clean and comfortable older
rooms are $30/38 single/double, and newer
'deluxe' rooms are $10 more. Chains
include the *Super 8* and *Best Western*.

Four rooms in the 1910 *Paisley Corner B&B* (☎ *333-4665, 287 N Main, Eagar)* are furnished with antiques, have private baths, and are priced from $75 to $95. Its mailing address is PO Box 458, AZ 85938.

Places to Eat
In Springerville, *Booga Reds Restaurant & Cantina* (☎ *333-5036, 521 E Main)* serves inexpensive Mexican and American food from 5:30 am to 9 pm daily. *Los Dos Molinos* (☎ *333-4846, 900 E Main)* prides itself on its hot homemade salsa, and is open for Mexican lunch and dinner Tuesday to Saturday. The *Safire Restaurant & Lounge* (☎ *333-4512, 411 E Main)* opens at 6 am daily and serves a good variety of reasonably priced American food, with some Italian and Mexican plates and nightly dinner specials.

LYMAN LAKE STATE PARK
Lyman Lake was formed when settlers dammed the Little Colorado River in 1915, bringing fine fishing, boating and water sports to an area where, even at 6000 feet, summer temperatures are often over 90°F. A small marina has boat rentals, supplies and a boat ramp. Rangers offer special programs in summer, including tours of nearby petroglyphs and sites. A small herd of buffalo lives in the park. Day use costs $4.

The park (☎ 337-4441), off Hwy 191 about 12 miles south of St Johns, offers tent

camping for $10, partial RV hookups for $15, and provides showers.

CORONADO TRAIL SCENIC ROAD
In 1540 Francisco Vásquez de Coronado (see Coronado National Memorial in the Southeastern Arizona chapter) headed northeast in search of riches and the legendary Seven Cities of Cibola. Hwys 180 and 191 between Springerville and Clifton roughly parallel this historic route. Although it is only 120 miles, it takes four hours to drive. The road climbs to 9000 feet before dropping to 3500 feet at Clifton, and many hairpin bends in the descent slow you down to 10mph. Scenic views provide occasional pullouts, but trailers over 20 feet long are not recommended. Fall colors, peaking in September and October, are among the most spectacular in the state, especially on aspen-covered Escudilla Mountain near Alpine. Many unpaved side roads lead into pristine forest for hiking, camping, fishing, hunting and cross-country skiing, but winter snows can sometimes close the road south of Alpine for days. There are several USFS campgrounds along the main road, and others on unpaved side roads. The Apache-Sitgreaves Ranger Stations in Clifton, Alpine and Springerville have information. Remember that there are no gas stations along the 90 miles between Alpine and Morenci.

Alpine
☎ 928 • pop 650 • elevation 8050 feet
One of Arizona's highest towns, Alpine is an excellent base for outdoor activities in the surrounding Apache-Sitgreaves National Forest. The village is loosely scattered around the junction of Hwy 180 and Hwy 191; visit its chamber of commerce at www.alpine-az.com. The Apache-Sitgreaves Alpine Ranger Station (☎ 339-4384) is at the junction.

Hannagan Recreation Area At over 9000 feet and 22 miles south of Alpine along Hwy 191, the Hannagan Recreation Area is the highest part of the Coronado Trail, and offers summertime mountain biking and hiking, as well as some of the best cross-country skiing and snowmobiling in the state. You can fish in a nearby lake and camp in one of the many campgrounds near the area. Stop at the ranger station to pick up more information. The Hannagan Meadow Lodge is open year-round.

Places to Stay & Eat On Hwy 180 near the junction, *Alpine Village RV Park* (☎ 339-1841) has showers ($4) and tent and RV sites with hookups for $5/15. *Meadow View RV Park* (☎ 339-1850), on Hwy 191 south of the junction, has RV sites for $20. Free dispersed camping is allowed throughout much of the forest, and there are many developed USFS campgrounds. The closest ones are *Alpine Divide*, 4 miles north of town on Hwy 180, offering 12 sites for $8 mid-May to mid-September, and *Luna Lake*, 6 miles east on Hwy 180, with sites for $10. Fishing and boat rental are nearby.

Four basic motels or cabin complexes are near the Hwy 191/180 junction. They charge $35 to $55. A couple of simple diners are nearby. The *Tal-Wi-Wi Lodge* (☎ 339-4319), 4 miles north on Hwy 180, offers 20 rooms ranging from standard motel rooms to rooms with hot tubs and fireplaces for $65 to $95. *Hannagan Meadow Lodge* (☎ 339-4370, 800-547-1416), 20 miles south along Hwy 191, provides 16 attractively rustic rooms and cabins from $70 to $100. Its restaurant is open in summer and winter.

Clifton

☎ 928 • pop 2596 • elevation 3500 feet
Although Clifton is the Greenlee County seat, it is one of the most decrepit towns in Arizona and most of the once-splendid buildings lining historic Chase Street (off Hwy 191 in the center) are boarded up; it's still worth a stroll. The neighboring town, Morenci, was swallowed up by a huge open-pit mine and rebuilt in the 1960s at its present site. Six miles above Morenci, an overlook from Hwy 191 gives dizzying views of the country's biggest producer of copper. As you look down on this open-pit mine 2 miles in length, 200-ton trucks with tires 9 feet in diameter crawl like insects at

the bottom. Free mine tours are by Phelps Dodge (☎ 865-1180, 800-882-1291); call for tour times and an appointment. The tours last three hours and children under nine are not permitted.

Standard motel rooms are available in the $40s at the *Rode Inn* (☎ 865-4536, *186 S Coronado Blvd*), on Hwy 191 at the south end of Clifton, and in the $70s at the *Morenci Motel* (☎ 865-4111) on the main street in Morenci.

SAFFORD

☎ 928 • pop 9232 • elevation 2920 feet
Safford's motels make this the most convenient gateway for the Coronado Trail to the northeast, the San Carlos Apache Indian Reservation to the northwest and the Swift Trail up lofty Mt Graham to the southwest.

Greyhound (☎ 428-2150) stops at 404 5th en route to Phoenix and Lordsburg, New Mexico.

Orientation & Information

Safford is mostly spread out along east-west Hwy 70, also called Thatcher Blvd and 5th St in the town center.

The chamber of commerce (☎ 428-2511, 888-837-1841), 1111 W Thatcher Blvd, is open weekdays 8 am to 5 pm, and 9 am to 3 pm on weekends: look at www.graham-chamber .com. It has a display on local industries as well as tourist information. Other services include the Coronado National Forest Ranger Station (☎ 428-4150) in the post office building; BLM (☎ 348-4400), 711 14th Ave; library (☎ 348-3202), 808 7th Ave; post office (☎ 428-0220), 504 5th Ave; hospital (☎ 348-4000), 1600 20th Ave; police (☎ 348-3190, 428-3141), 525 10th Ave.

Things to See & Do

Discovery Park (☎ 428-6260, 888-837-1841), 2 miles south along 20th Ave, has trails, nature exhibits and a short narrow-gauge railway. The highlight is the **Gov Aker Observatory**, with a 20-inch reflecting astronomical telescope, a space-flight simulator and astronomy exhibits. The park is open 1 to 10 pm, Tuesday through Saturday. Admission is $4; $3 for

ARIZONA

children; $6 for the space-flight simulator and $1 for a train ride. This observatory will arrange tours of the observatory at Mt Graham (see the boxed text, 'Development on Mt Graham'). Tours cost $15 and leave at 10 am Monday to Saturday from June to November, weather permitting.
website: www.discoverypark.com

Several natural mineral **hot springs** are six miles south of town. Two commercial spas charge $5 to use their hot tubs and offer massage and reflexology treatments for $25 and up. Call Essence of Tranquility (☎ 428-9312, 877-895-6810) or Kachina Mineral Springs (☎ 428-7212) for rates and directions.

Roper Lake State Park (☎ 428-6760), on the east side of Hwy 191, 6 miles south of Safford, offers camping, boating, fishing, swimming and a hot springs. Day use costs $4 per vehicle.

Hwy 366, popularly called the **Swift Trail Scenic Drive** is a paved road up the Pinaleno Mountains almost to the top of 10,713-foot **Mt Graham**. The road begins from Hwy 191 almost 8 miles south of Safford and climbs 34 miles to the summit, all within the Coronado National Forest. The Columbine Visitor Station, more than 20 miles along the Swift Trail, offers maps and information and is open daily 9 am to 6 pm Memorial Day to Labor Day.

Places to Stay & Eat
Several *USFS campgrounds* (☎ 428-4150) along the Swift Trail cost $8 to $12 and have water but no showers or hookups. *Roper Lake State Park* charges $10 for tents and $15 for RVs with hookups; the campgrounds have showers. *Essence of Tranquility Hot Springs* (see above) allows camping for $10 and has teepees for rent. The teepees come with beds and communal baths and start at $20/30 for a single/double bed. Reservations are required.

For rooms around $30, try the *Motel Western* (☎ 428-7850, 1215 W Thatcher Blvd), which has a small pool. Otherwise, it's mainly *chain motels* including Econolodge, Days Inn, Best Western, Comfort Inn and Ramada Inn.

Development on Mt Graham

Mt Graham is one of the 'sky islands' of southeastern Arizona, separated from other summits in the area by lowlands. Because plants and animals living near the top of the mountain have been isolated from similar species living on other nearby ranges, some have evolved into different species or subspecies; this makes these high peaks a living natural laboratory for the study of evolution.

However, because Mt Graham is the highest mountain in the area and a long way from city lights and other sky pollutants, it has been chosen as the site of a major telescope observatory. Currently under construction, the project threatens the habitat of the Mt Graham red squirrel, among other 'sky island' species, and is therefore embroiled in controversy. Mt Graham is also a sacred site for some Apache Indians, an additional conflict. A small exhibit in the Safford Chamber of Commerce describes the astronomy project in glowing terms as a source of more employment and tourism for the area.

Olney House B&B (☎ 428-5118, 800-814-5118, 1104 Central Ave) has a hot tub and charges $80 per couple in three rooms with shared bath or in two cottages with kitchenettes. Email the B&B at olney@zekes.com.

Casa Mañana (☎ 428-3170, 502 1st Ave) has been here for half a century and serves tasty Mexican lunches and dinners daily. Standard American fare is offered at restaurants next to all the chain motels.

SAN CARLOS APACHE INDIAN RESERVATION

About 2900 sq miles of lakes, rivers, forests and desert belong to the San Carlos Apache Tribe. Over 8000 people live here, of whom 3000 live in the tribal capital of San Carlos just off Hwy 70. Cattle ranching is the primary business.

Most tourists come for outdoor recreation or the tribal casino. A maze of unpaved roads penetrates the reservation, leading to

ARIZONA

scores of little lakes and river fishing areas as well as primitive camping areas. The best known is **San Carlos Lake**, formed by the Coolidge Dam on the Gila River. When full, it covers 30 sq miles and has excellent fishing, including state record–winning catfish, largemouth bass and crappie. Near Coolidge Dam are a marina, convenience store and campground (no phone) with RV hookups, water and tent spaces, but no showers. Fees are $5 a person. Trout fishing on the Black River is good, and big-game hunting is permitted in season; local guides can be hired.

To camp, hike, fish, hunt and drive off the main highways, you'll need a permit from the San Carlos Recreation and Wildlife Dept (☎ 475-2343, 888-475-2344), PO Box 97, San Carlos, AZ 85550. The tribal offices (☎ 475-2361) have other information.

The small but informative **San Carlos Apache Cultural Center** (☎ 475-2894) tells of the history and culture of the tribe. The center is near mileage marker 272 on Hwy 70, about 20 miles east of Globe. Hours are 9 am to 5 pm but days change so call ahead. Admission is $3; $1.50 for seniors; $1 for students and children.

Sunrise Ceremonies, held in the summer, feature traditional dances in honor of young girls' coming of age. Some ceremonies may be open to the public; call the tribal office for details. The tribal **rodeo and fair**, held in San Carlos over Veterans Day weekend (closest weekend to November 11) also features traditional dancing.

The only motel is the **Best Western Apache Gold Hotel** (☎ 402-5600, 800-272-2438) near the tribal casino (☎ 425-8000), 5 miles east of Globe. It features a pool, sauna, whirlpool, restaurant and lounge, and 146 rooms in the $50 to $100 range. There is an RV park here as well, and a campground near Coolidge Dam (see above).

GLOBE
☎ 928 • pop 7486 • elevation 3544 feet
The discovery of a globe-shaped boulder formed of almost pure silver sparked a short-lived silver boom here in the 1870s, followed by the development of a long-

lasting copper mining industry. Globe offers the best accommodations in the area, and its various attractions provide a pleasant rural alternative to Phoenix (80 miles west).

Greyhound (☎ 425-2301), 1660 E Ash, has three buses a day to Phoenix and three to Safford and beyond.

Information
The Globe-Miami Chamber of Commerce (☎ 425-4495, 800-804-5623), 1360 N Broad, is open Monday to Friday 8 am to 5 pm. Other services include the Tonto National Forest USFS Ranger Station (☎ 402-6200) on Six Shooter Canyon Rd at the south end of town; library (☎ 425-6111), 339 S Broad; post office (☎ 425-2381), 101 S Hill; hospital (☎ 425-3261), between Globe and Miami south of the Hwy 60/88 intersection, and the police (☎ 425-5752), 175 N Pine.

Things to See & Do
Behind the chamber of commerce, the Gila County Historical Museum (☎ 425-7385) displays much about Globe's history; hours are 10 am to 4 pm Monday to Friday; free. Ask at the chamber about the many turn-of-the-19th-century buildings lining Broad St south of Hackney Ave – a pleasant stroll with few tourists.

Globe's highlight is the Besh-Ba-Gowah Archaeological Park (☎ 425-0320), 150 N Pine (follow signs south of town). The centerpiece is a small pueblo built by the Salado people in the 1200s and abandoned by the early 1400s. The park also has a museum with a fine collection of Salado pottery and an ethnobotanical garden. Admission is $3 for those over 12 years old.

Far Flung Adventures (☎ 425-7272, 800-359-2627) offers one- to five-day Salt River rafting trips. High water is February to April.

Places to Stay & Eat
Several inexpensive mom 'n pop motels are found along Hwy 60. The **El Rey Motel** (☎ 425-4427, 1201 E Ash) is an old-fashioned motor court surrounding a lawn and barbecue area; this glimpse of Americana has basic but clean rooms for $22/32

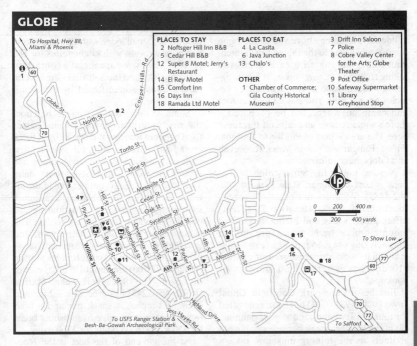

GLOBE

To Hospital, Hwy 88,
Miami & Phoenix

PLACES TO STAY
2 Noftsger Hill Inn B&B
5 Cedar Hill B&B
12 Super 8 Motel; Jerry's Restaurant
14 El Rey Motel
15 Comfort Inn
16 Days Inn
18 Ramada Ltd Motel

PLACES TO EAT
4 La Casita
6 Java Junction
13 Chalo's

OTHER
1 Chamber of Commerce; Gila County Historical Museum

3 Drift Inn Saloon
7 Police
8 Cobre Valley Center for the Arts; Globe Theater
9 Post Office
10 Safeway Supermarket
11 Library
17 Greyhound Stop

To Show Low
To Safford
To USFS Ranger Station & Besh-Ba-Gowah Archaeological Park

with one or two beds. *Chain motels* along Hwy 60 include a Days Inn, Comfort Inn, Super 8, Ramada Limited and Holiday Inn Express.

Housed in a renovated school dating from 1907, the *Noftsger Hill Inn B&B* (☎ 425-2260, 425 North) has rooms with shared bath or with private bath and king-size beds; prices range from $45 to $75. *Cedar Hill B&B* (☎ 425-7530, 175 E Cedar) charges $55.

In the old-town center of town, *La Casita* (☎ 425-8462, 470 N Broad) serves good Mexican lunches and dinners. Another good Mexican-food choice is *Chalo's* (☎ 425-0515, 902 E Ash). The best coffee in town is at *Java Junction* (☎ 402-8926) at the corner of Broad and Cedar. *Jerry's Restaurant* (☎ 425-5282, 699 E Ash) serves standard American fare 24 hours a day.

Wet your whistle at one of the old bars, such as the *Drift Inn Saloon* (☎ 425-9573, 636 N Broad).

BOYCE THOMPSON SOUTHWESTERN ARBORETUM

About 28 miles west of Globe on Hwy 60, this arboretum (☎ 520-689-2811) is the Southwest's oldest and is a great place for a quiet garden walk. The visitor center has information about the trails winding through these 35 acres of arid-land plants. It's open daily except Christmas; admission is $5; $2 for five- to 12-year-olds.
website: http://arboretum.ag.arizona.edu

THE APACHE TRAIL

The Apache Trail (Hwy 88) heads northwest of Apache Junction (west of Phoenix) ending at Globe 75 miles later and is one of the more spectacular drives in the area. A 20-mile section west of the Roosevelt Dam is steep, winding, narrow and unpaved; not recommended for trailers or large RVs. Once you reach Globe, return via the much faster paved Hwy 60. Stop at the arboretum for a good roundtrip from Phoenix.

Almost immediately after leaving Apache Junction, you'll see the **Superstition Wilderness** looming above you to the right. Supposedly home to the fabled Lost Dutchman Mine, this rugged area is filled with hiking trails and mining stories. It is a designated wilderness, so no development or vehicles are allowed. You can hike in on foot and camp anywhere, but be prepared – there's some remote and difficult terrain in here. The area is part of the Tonto National Forest. Ranger stations in Mesa, Roosevelt and Globe have information.

Nestled under the Superstition Mountains is **Lost Dutchman State Park** (☎ 480-982-4485), 5½ miles northeast of Apache Junction. The park (elevation 2000 feet) offers picnic areas and hiking, horse and mountain-bike trails, which are hot in summer. Day use is $5 per vehicle or $1 per individual. A 35-site *campground* charges $10 and has water but no showers or hookups.

Just before the park **Goldfield Ghost Town** (☎ 480-983-0333) has been renovated for tourism. Try your hand at gold panning, eat at the Western steak house, examine old artifacts in the mining museum, take a horse ride or jump aboard the steam-train circling the town. Admission is free, though the attractions charge a few dollars each. A dry *campground* charges $10. A few miles beyond, the 20-mile unpaved section begins.

Fifteen miles from Apache Junction, **Canyon Lake** (☎ 602-944-6504) offers boat rentals, a *restaurant* and *bar*, and *camping* ($10 for tents and $25 for RV hookups). Ninety-minute cruises (☎ 480-827-9144) are $14, $8 for five- to 12-year olds. Given its proximity to Phoenix, it's a busy lake. Two miles beyond, you hit the Wild West at **Tortilla Flat**, once a stagecoach stop and now a touristy but popular stop for drivers on the trail. You can eat lunch in the saloon (10 am to 4 pm), or spend the night in the *campground* opposite, which offers sites without drinking water for $10. Soon after, the road begins the unpaved section.

Long, narrow **Apache Lake** features the *Apache Lake Resort* (☎ 928-467-2511) where a marina offers a boat ramp and rentals, tent and RV camping with hookups ($20), and a small lodge with standard motel rooms and rooms with kitchenettes for $60 to $90; visit www.apachelake.com. Also along the lake and the Salt River are several *campgrounds* administered by the Tonto National Forest.

Some 45 miles out of Apache Junction, the road returns to pavement and passes the **Theodore Roosevelt Dam**. Built of brick on the Salt River in 1911, this was the first large dam to flood the Southwest and, at 280 feet, is the world's highest masonry dam. The Roosevelt Lake behind the dam attracts water-sport enthusiasts year-round; swimming, water-skiing and boating are popular activities from spring to fall. The fishing is great throughout the year, and bass and crappie are favored catches. A marina and the Tonto Basin Ranger Station (☎ 928-467-3200) are about 1½ miles east of the dam. The **Roosevelt Lake Marina** (☎ 928-467-2245) has groceries, fishing and camping supplies, a snack bar and a boat ramp; boat rentals range from fishing boats for $50 a day to ski boats for $260 a day.

At the far end of the lake is the *Roosevelt Lake Resort* (☎ 928-467-2888), where a motel has rooms for $45 or rooms with kitchenettes for $65 to $75; RV sites are $20. website: www.rooseveltlake.com

TONTO NATIONAL MONUMENT

About 28 miles northwest of Globe off paved Hwy 88, the monument protects a highlight of the area: a two-story Salado pueblo built in a cave. Like most other pueblos, it was mysteriously abandoned in the early 1400s.

From the visitor center (☎ 928-467-2241), a paved half-mile footpath climbs gently to the site, with good views of the saguaro cactus–studded hillsides in the foreground and Roosevelt Lake in the distance. The visitor center has a museum and water but no food or camping facilities.

The monument is open 8 am to 5 pm daily except Christmas, but the trail closes an hour earlier. Admission is $3 per person over 16 and all passes are honored.

Tucson & Southern Arizona

When isolated groups of Spanish explorers straggled through in the 1530s, this region of desert, mountain ranges and grasslands was inhabited by the Tohono O'odham (called Papago until 1986) and the closely related Pima Indians, who were perhaps the descendants of the Hohokam people, whose culture disappeared around AD 1400. The Apache Indians, who arrived later on, lived in the far southeast of present-day Arizona.

The first big Spanish expedition was in 1540, led by Francisco Vásquez de Coronado, who entered the area near present-day Sierra Vista on his way north in search of the 'Seven Cities of Cibola.' His descriptions are the earliest we have of the region, which was largely ignored by the Spanish for well over a century until the Jesuit priest Padre Eusebio Francisco Kino arrived in the late 1600s and spent two decades establishing missions primarily among the Pima people. One of the churches he founded, Mission San Xavier del Bac, south of Tucson, is still used today. It is the finest example of Spanish colonial architecture in Arizona, rivaling the missions of New Mexico for architectural beauty and historical interest. Kino was also responsible for introducing cattle into the area.

With the missions came immigrants: Spanish settlers from the Mexican colonies. They lived in an uneasy truce with the Indians until 1751, when the Pimas rebelled against the unwanted newcomers and killed or forced out many settlers and missionaries. The Spanish authorities sent in soldiers to control the Indians and protect the settlers, building several walled forts, or *presidios,* one of which became the city of Tucson. After Mexico won its independence from Spain in 1821, Tucson became a Mexican town. Thus southeastern Arizona, more than other parts of the state, had both a traditional Indian culture and a rich Hispanic heritage that predated the arrival of the Anglos.

The Gadsden Purchase of 1853 turned southeastern Arizona, on paper at least, from Mexican into US territory. Anglos began to arrive, homesteading the grasslands in the southeastern corner and finding that it made good ranching country. But they failed to realize that the Apaches, who inhabited the desert grasslands and mountains of the far southeastern corner of Arizona, didn't much care about the Gadsden Purchase – after all, from their point of view, it was Apache country and not Mexican in the first place. Tensions arising from this difference erupted in conflicts between Indians and Americans. Although such conflicts marked the US expansion from the east through most of the 1800s, the ones in Apache territory were especially fierce. Led by legendary warrior-chiefs Cochise and Geronimo, Apaches were the last holdouts in the so-called Indian Wars, which lasted until the 1886 surrender of Geronimo.

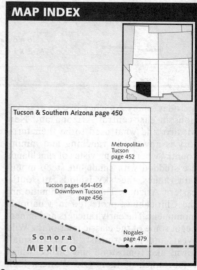

MAP INDEX

Tucson & Southern Arizona page 450

Metropolitan Tucson page 452

Tucson pages 454-455
Downtown Tucson page 456

Nogales page 479

Sonora
MEXICO

ARIZONA

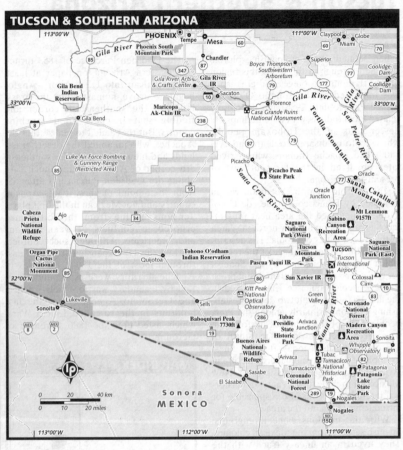

TUCSON & SOUTHERN ARIZONA

Today, many Apaches live on reservations in east-central Arizona and New Mexico, and what used to be their territory is now cattle ranching and mining country, where rolling vistas of ranchlands are studded with small but steep mountain ranges, the 'sky islands' of southeastern Arizona. The most dramatic are the Chiricahuas, protected in a national monument. The early ranchers and miners begot some of the classic tales of the Wild West, and now tourists flock to small towns like Tombstone and Bisbee, which retain much of their Old Western look

(see the Southeastern Arizona chapter for more on these sights).

West of these ranchlands lies the Arizona-Sonora desert, home of the majestic saguaro cacti, which are a symbol of this region. The Sonoran desert is also home to the Tohono O'odham Indians, who live west of Tucson on Arizona's second largest Indian reservation. And in between is Tucson itself, a major tourist destination both for travelers throughout the year and for the retired 'snowbirds' who enjoy spending several months each winter in the Tucson area, escaping the snows of their northern homes.

Tucson

☎ 520 • pop 486,699; metro area 843,746
• elevation 2500 feet

Tucson is attractively set in a flat valley surrounded on all sides by close mountain ranges, some of which top 9000 feet. The elevation gives Tucson a slightly milder climate than that of Tucson's northern neighbor, Phoenix. Summers are still hot, however, with frequent days exceeding 100°F. But an hour's drive can take you up to the cooler mountains that are high and accessible enough to afford relief from summer heat. In winter, you can ski on Mt Lemmon, which is the southernmost ski resort in the country. After a day on the slopes, you can drop down to the city where pleasant winter daytime temperatures in the 70°s F are not unusual. The surrounding Sonoran desert is more accessible from Tucson than it is from Phoenix.

Tucson is Arizona's second largest city. Well over 20% of Tucson's inhabitants are Hispanic, and this is reflected both in the language and the food. Spanish is frequently spoken and Mexican restaurants abound.

Tucson is also the home of the University of Arizona (U of A), which has about 35,000 students and plays an important role in Tucson's economy. Also important to the city's economy are tourism and high-tech industries such as Hughes Missile Systems Company and IBM Corporation, which employ thousands of Tucsonans. The Davis-Monthan Air Force Base also contributes to the economy. It is one of the largest aircraft storage bases in the country and if you drive along Kolb Rd on the east side of town, you'll witness the eerie sight of almost 5000 mothballed aircraft lined up as far as the eye can see.

HISTORY

Visitors to downtown Tucson see 'A Mountain' looming over the city to the southwest. Its proper name is Sentinel Peak, but its nickname comes from the giant 'A' whitewashed onto the mountain by students from the U of A in 1915 and now repainted by freshmen as an annual tradition. But the peak's history goes back much farther than 1915. When the Spaniards arrived, the village below A Mountain was known as 'Stjukshon,' meaning 'at the foot of the dark mountain' in the Indian language. The Spaniards pronounced it 'Took Son' and later the Anglos dropped the 'k' sound, giving the city's name its current pronunciation of 'TOO-sahn.'

The first permanent Spanish settlement in Tucson was in 1775, when a large walled presidio was built here to house a garrison that protected settlers from the Indians. The Presidio District is now the most historic in Tucson, though almost nothing remains of the original buildings. Most of the oldest buildings date back to the mid-1800s, when arriving Anglos nicknamed the Hispanic fort 'the Old Pueblo.' The name has stuck and is often heard today as a nickname for Tucson.

Anglos began to arrive in greater numbers after the Butterfield Stage Company started passing through Tucson in 1857. War with the Apaches prompted the construction of Fort Lowell in 1866. The town was a wild place in those days, and soldiers on drinking sprees added to the general mayhem. In 1873, in an attempt to minimize carousing by the army, Fort Lowell was moved to its present location 7 miles northeast of town. It was abandoned in 1891 and there is a museum and a small historic district on the site today. In 1880 the railroad arrived and the university opened in 1891 – an air of sophistication and coming-of-age descended on the wild city.

Tucson grew slowly until WWII brought an influx of young men to train at the Davis-Monthan Air Force Base. After WWII, many of these trainees came back to Tucson and this, along with the widespread development of air conditioning, ensured Tucson's rapid growth in the latter half of the 20th century.

ORIENTATION

Tucson lies mainly to the north and east of I-10 at its intersection with I-19, which goes to the Mexican border at Nogales. Downtown Tucson and the main historic districts are east of I-10 exit 258 at Congress St/Broadway Blvd.

Congress/Broadway Blvd is a major west-east thoroughfare. Most west-east thoroughfares are called streets, while most north-south thoroughfares are called avenues (although there is a sprinkling of Rds, Blvds etc). Stone Ave, at its intersection with Congress, forms the zero point for Tucson addresses. Streets are designated west and east and avenues north and south from this point.

Downtown Tucson is quite compact and is best visited on foot, although you have to battle the heat from May to September.

Away from downtown, major thoroughfares are at 1-mile intervals, with minor streets and avenues (mainly residential) filling in a checkerboard arrangement.

About a mile northeast of downtown is the U of A campus, with some worthwhile museums, and just over a mile south of downtown is the square mile of South Tucson. This is a separate town inhabited mainly by a traditional Hispanic population with few tourist sites, but it does have some cheap and funky restaurants with tasty Mexican food. The rest of the city is mainly an urban sprawl of shopping malls and residential areas interspersed

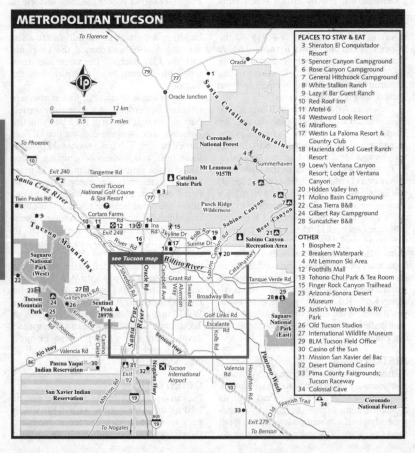

METROPOLITAN TUCSON

PLACES TO STAY & EAT
3 Sheraton El Conquistador Resort
5 Spencer Canyon Campground
6 Rose Canyon Campground
7 General Hitchcock Campground
8 White Stallion Ranch
9 Lazy K Bar Guest Ranch
10 Red Roof Inn
11 Motel 6
14 Westward Look Resort
16 Miraflores
17 Westin La Paloma Resort & Country Club
18 Hacienda del Sol Guest Ranch Resort
19 Loew's Ventana Canyon Resort; Lodge at Ventana Canyon
20 Hidden Valley Inn
21 Molino Basin Campground
22 Casa Tierra B&B
24 Gilbert Ray Campground
28 Suncatcher B&B

OTHER
1 Biosphere 2
2 Breakers Waterpark
4 Mt Lemmon Ski Area
12 Foothills Mall
13 Tohono Chul Park & Tea Room
15 Finger Rock Canyon Trailhead
23 Arizona-Sonora Desert Museum
25 Justin's Water World & RV Park
26 Old Tucson Studios
27 International Wildlife Museum
29 BLM Tucson Field Office
30 Casino of the Sun
31 Mission San Xavier del Bac
32 Desert Diamond Casino
33 Pima County Fairgrounds; Tucson Raceway
34 Colossal Cave

with golf courses and parks. The main section of the city, between Campbell Ave and Kolb Rd, is known as midtown.

The south end of town is the industrial area with Tucson International Airport, the Davis-Monthan Air Force Base and industrial parks. You'll go past this to visit Mission San Xavier del Bac, Arizona's most impressive Spanish colonial site.

The north end of town is the Catalina Foothills, bounded by the steep and rugged Santa Catalina Mountains and home to the pricier residential districts, resorts and country clubs. Northwest of town, the city oozes around the western edge of the Catalinas into the I-10 corridor to Phoenix. This is where most of the current development is taking place.

East and west of town are wilderness areas, parts of which are protected by the east and west units of Saguaro National Park.

INFORMATION

The Convention & Visitors Bureau (☎ 624-1817, 800-638-8350), 110 S Church, Suite 7199, is open daily except on major holidays. Ask for its free *Official Visitors Guide*. website: www.visittucson.org

The Coronado National Forest Supervisor's Office (☎ 670-4552), inside the Federal Building at 300 W Congress, is open weekdays. Also, the Santa Catalina Ranger Station (☎ 749-8700), 5700 N Sabino Canyon Rd, at the entrance to Sabino Canyon, is open daily.

The BLM Tucson Field Office (☎ 722-4289) is at 12661 E Broadway Blvd, just before Saguaro National Park (East) and the Arizona Game & Fish Dept (☎ 628-5376) is at 555 N Greasewood Rd.

Foreign exchange is available at most banks; a $5 fee is charged if you don't have an account. The Tucson airport does not offer currency exchange.

The main post office (☎ 800-275-8777) is at 1501 S Cherrybell. The downtown branch is at 141 S 6th Ave and there are numerous other branches.

The main library (☎ 791-4393) is open daily at 101 N Stone Ave. There are many other branch libraries. The U of A libraries

(☎ 621-6441) have excellent and extensive collections, including a superb map room open to the general public.

Independent bookstores include Antigone Books (☎ 792-3715), 411 N 4th Ave, specializing in books for, about and by women. Readers Oasis (☎ 319-7887), 3400 E Speedway, No 14, often has readings on weekends.

The local newspapers are the morning *Arizona Daily Star,* the afternoon *Tucson Citizen* and the free *Tucson Weekly,* published on Thursdays. The *Citizen* leans to the right and the *Star* is more liberal.

Tucson's community radio station, KXCI, at 91.3 FM, is funded by listeners and has an eclectic and excellent range of programs from all over the musical spectrum (with the notable exceptions of classical music and top 40 stuff).

Pima County Medical Society (☎ 795-7985) gives doctor referrals during business hours. There are 10 hospitals and many smaller health care facilities in Tucson. The police (☎ 791-4444, or 911 in emergencies) are at 270 S Stone Ave.

DOWNTOWN TUCSON
Historic Buildings

The Convention & Visitors Bureau has a brochure detailing a downtown walking tour with more than 40 sites. Some of the more noteworthy ones are mentioned here.

Many of the most interesting and colorful historic buildings are in the **Presidio Historic District**, especially in the few blocks between Franklin and Alameda and Main and Court Aves. This district merits a leisurely stroll. **La Casa Cordova**, at 175 N Meyer Ave, at the northern end of the Tucson Museum of Art (see below) is believed to be the oldest house, dating from 1848, and can be visited during museum hours. Just north of La Casa Cordova is the 1868 **Romero House**, now part of the Tucson Museum of Art School. Behind the museum, buildings dating from 1862 to 1875 feature saguaro-rib ceilings and now house La Cocina Restaurant and six interconnected, good-quality arts and crafts

TUCSON

Christopher Columbus Park

To Phoenix

Silverbell Golf Course

Santa Cruz River

Silverbell Rd

Ironwood Hill Drive

Exit 254

Exit 255

Exit 256

Northwest District Park

El Rio Golf Course

Greasewood Park

Pima Community College

Anklam Rd

Speedway Blvd

Exit 257

Exit 257A

Santa Cruz River Park

St Marys Rd

University of Arizona Range Experimental Station

Starr Pass Golf Course

Sentinel Peak 2897ft

Sentinel Peak Park

Starr Pass Blvd

San Juan Park

San Juan Trail

Mission Rd

Greasewood Rd

Shannon Rd

Tucson Mountain Park

JFK Park

Ajo Hwy

36th St

Exit 260

Exit 261

Exit 99

Ajo Way

Michigan St

Exit 98

Irvington Rd

Valley Rd

Drexel Rd

San Xavier Indian Reservation

Westover Rd

Manor Mission Park

Bilby Rd

To Nogales

Exit 95

Valencia Rd

To Tucson International Airport & Airport Hotels

Wetmore Rd

Romero Rd

Flowing Wells Rd

Fairview Ave

Roger Rd

Prince Rd

Jacobs Park

Miracle Mile

Glenn St

Oracle Rd

Stone Ave

4th Ave

Park Ave

Mountain Ave

Main Ave

6th Ave

Euclid Ave

1st Ave

Fort Lowell Rd

Grant Rd

Elm St

Drachman St

Speedway Blvd

University Blvd

University of Arizona

see Downtown Tucson map

see University of Arizona inset

Congress St

Grande Ave

10th Ave

Santa Rita Park

22nd St

Cherrybell Strav

Silverlake Rd

SOUTH TUCSON

36th St

6th Ave

12th Ave

Rodeo Park

Campbell Ave

Tucson Blvd

Country Club Rd

River Rd

Catalina Foothills

Hacienda del Sol Rd

Rillito River

Palo Verde Blvd

Dodge Blvd

Alvernon Way

Alvina Himmel Park

3rd St

6th St

Broadway Blvd

Randolph Park Municipal Golf Course

Reid Park

Fairland Strav

Benson Hwy

Sam Lena Park

Julian Wash

Alvernon Way

Nogales Hwy

Park Ave

Campbell Ave

Tucson Blvd

Country Club Rd

Palo Verde Rd

King Parkway

Exit 257A
Exit 258
Exit 259
Exit 262
Exit 263
Exit 264

0   1   2 km
0   .5   1 mile

ARIZONA

TUCSON

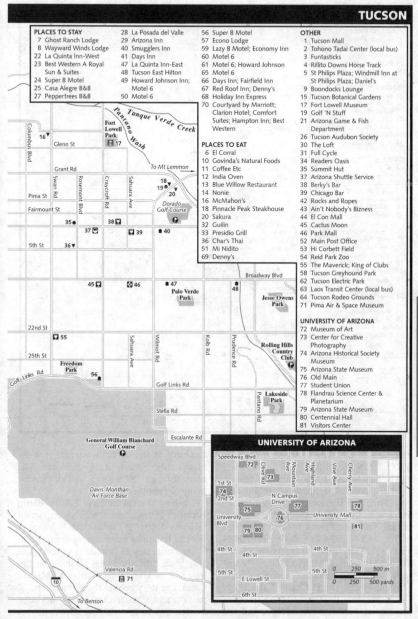

PLACES TO STAY
- 7 Ghost Ranch Lodge
- 8 Wayward Winds Lodge
- 22 La Quinta Inn-West
- 23 Best Western A Royal Sun & Suites
- 24 Super 8 Motel
- 25 Casa Alegre B&B
- 27 Peppertrees B&B
- 28 La Posada del Valle
- 29 Arizona Inn
- 40 Smugglers Inn
- 41 Days Inn
- 47 La Quinta Inn-East
- 48 Tucson East Hilton
- 49 Howard Johnson Inn; Motel 6
- 50 Motel 6
- 56 Super 8 Motel
- 57 Econo Lodge
- 59 Lazy 8 Motel; Economy Inn
- 60 Motel 6
- 61 Motel 6; Howard Johnson
- 65 Motel 6
- 66 Days Inn; Fairfield Inn
- 67 Red Roof Inn; Denny's
- 68 Holiday Inn Express
- 70 Courtyard by Marriott; Clarion Hotel; Comfort Suites; Hampton Inn; Best Western

PLACES TO EAT
- 6 El Corral
- 10 Govinda's Natural Foods
- 11 Coffee Etc
- 12 India Oven
- 13 Blue Willow Restaurant
- 14 Nonie
- 16 McMahon's
- 18 Pinnacle Peak Steakhouse
- 20 Sakura
- 32 Guilin
- 33 Presidio Grill
- 36 Char's Thai
- 51 Mi Nidito
- 69 Denny's

OTHER
- 1 Tucson Mall
- 2 Tohono Tadai Center (local bus)
- 3 Funtasticks
- 4 Rillito Downs Horse Track
- 5 St Philips Plaza; Windmill Inn at St Philips Plaza; Daniel's
- 9 Boondocks Lounge
- 15 Tucson Botanical Gardens
- 17 Fort Lowell Museum
- 19 Golf 'N Stuff
- 21 Arizona Game & Fish Department
- 26 Tucson Audubon Society
- 30 The Loft
- 31 Full Cycle
- 34 Readers Oasis
- 35 Summit Hut
- 37 Arizona Shuttle Service
- 38 Berky's Bar
- 39 Chicago Bar
- 42 Rocks and Ropes
- 43 Ain't Nobody's Bizness
- 44 El Con Mall
- 45 Cactus Moon
- 46 Park Mall
- 52 Main Post Office
- 53 Hi Corbett Field
- 54 Reid Park Zoo
- 55 The Maverick; King of Clubs
- 58 Tucson Greyhound Park
- 62 Tucson Electric Park
- 63 Laos Transit Center (local bus)
- 64 Tucson Rodeo Grounds
- 71 Pima Air & Space Museum

UNIVERSITY OF ARIZONA
- 72 Museum of Art
- 73 Center for Creative Photography
- 74 Arizona Historical Society Museum
- 75 Arizona State Museum
- 76 Old Main
- 77 Student Union
- 78 Flandrau Science Center & Planetarium
- 79 Arizona State Museum
- 80 Centennial Hall
- 81 Visitors Center

ARIZONA

UNIVERSITY OF ARIZONA

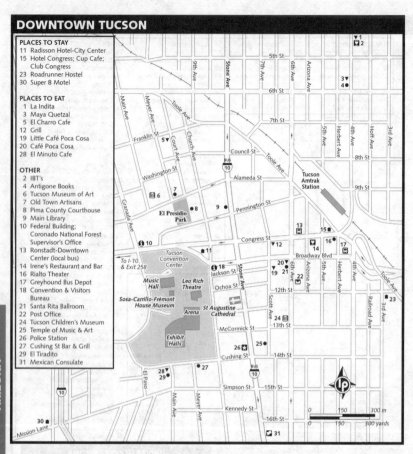

DOWNTOWN TUCSON

PLACES TO STAY
11 Radisson Hotel-City Center
15 Hotel Congress; Cup Cafe;
   Club Congress
23 Roadrunner Hostel
30 Super 8 Motel

PLACES TO EAT
1 La Indita
3 Maya Quetzal
5 El Charro Cafe
12 Grill
19 Little Café Poca Cosa
20 Café Poca Cosa
28 El Minuto Cafe

OTHER
2 IBT's
4 Antigone Books
6 Tucson Museum of Art
7 Old Town Artisans
8 Pima County Courthouse
9 Main Library
10 Federal Building;
   Coronado National Forest
   Supervisor's Office
13 Ronstadt-Downtown
   Center (local bus)
14 Irene's Restaurant and Bar
16 Rialto Theater
17 Greyhound Bus Depot
18 Convention & Visitors
   Bureau
21 Santa Rita Ballroom
22 Post Office
24 Tucson Children's Museum
25 Temple of Music & Art
26 Police Station
27 Cushing St Bar & Grill
29 El Tiradito
31 Mexican Consulate

galleries of **Old Town Artisans** (☎ 623-6024), 186 N Meyer Ave.

The **Fish House**, 120 N Main Ave, built in 1868 for political representative Edward Nye Fish, and the roughly contemporary **Stevens House**, 150 N Main Ave, home of Hiram Sanford Stevens, formed the heart of Tucson's social scene during the 1870s and '80s. They now house parts of the Tucson Museum of Art. Restaurants in historic buildings include Tucson's oldest Mexican restaurant, **El Charro Cafe**, 311 N Court Ave, in a 1900 stone house (most of the earlier houses were adobe), and the

Cushing St Bar & Grill, several lengthy blocks to the south at 343 S Meyer Ave, housed in an 1880s store and displaying many old photographs.

Cushing St is the north end of the **Barrio Historico** district, which was an important business district in the late 1800s. Many of the old buildings around here continue to house businesses. **El Tiradito** is a quirky and crumbling little shrine on Cushing on the west side of Main Ave (south of El Minuto Café). The story behind the shrine is one of passion and murder. Apparently a young herder was caught making love with his mother-in-law and was shot dead by his father-in-law at this spot, where he was buried. Pious locals burned candles here because it was unconsecrated ground. The practice continues today, with candle-burners praying for their own wishes to be granted. If a candle burns throughout the night, your wish will be granted!

Between the Presidio and Barrio Historico districts is the modern Tucson Convention Center (TCC) complex. Only one house survived the construction of the TCC. At the northwest end is hidden the **Sosa-Carrillo-Frémont House Museum** (☎ 622-0956), at 151 S Granada Ave. Built in the 1850s by the Sosa family, it was then bought by the Carrillo family and rented briefly by John C Frémont, Arizona's fifth governor. The restored house is now an 1880s period museum open 10 am to 4 pm Wednesday to Saturday; admission is free. It is operated by the Arizona Historical Society, which offers guided walking tours (☎ 622-0956 to register) of historic Tucson at 10 am on Saturday from October through March ($4).

The downtown area also has several notable newer buildings from the early 20th century. The **Pima County Courthouse**, at 115 N Church Ave, is a colorful blend of Spanish and Southwestern architecture with an impressive mosaic-tile dome. **El Presidio Park**, on the west side of the courthouse, covers what was the southern half of the original presidio and also houses a Vietnam Veterans Memorial. A few blocks south is the elegant, whitewashed St Augustine Cathedral, 192 S Stone Ave, begun in 1896. Stained-glass windows and a Mexican-style sandstone facade were added in the 1920s. Two blocks to the southeast is the **Temple of Music & Art**, 330 S Scott Ave, built in 1927 and gloriously restored as the home of the Arizona Theater Company. A block northeast of it is the **Tucson Children's Museum** (see below), 200 S 6th Ave, housed in a 1901 library designed by the noted Southwestern architect Henry Trost, who also designed several other turn-of-the-19th-century buildings in Tucson. Two still standing are the **Steinfeld House**, 300 N Main Ave, and the **Owl's Club Mansion**, 378 N Main Ave.

Tucson Museum of Art

The museum (☎ 624-2333), 140 N Main Ave, houses a small collection of pre-Columbian artifacts from Latin America, varied exhibits of 20th-century Western art, a decent little multimedia collection, changing shows and a gift shop with local art. Hours are 10 am to 4 pm daily except Sunday, when it opens at noon. It is closed on Monday from the last Monday in May to the first Monday in October. Admission is $5, $4 for seniors, $3 for students, and free to children under 12 and to everyone on Sunday.

Tucson Children's Museum

Hands-on activities for kids and permanent exhibits are featured at this museum (☎ 884-7511), 200 S 6th Ave. Special programs occur frequently. Hours are 10 am to 5 pm, Tuesday to Saturday and noon to 5 pm on Sunday. Admission is $5.50 for adults, $4.50 for seniors and $3.50 for two- to 16-year-olds. On Sundays, a $14 family pass will admit four family members.

UNIVERSITY OF ARIZONA

This fine campus houses some excellent museums and several notable outdoor sculptures. This is not just a place for students; it's a worthwhile stop for everyone. Note that hours can change during school holidays; call ahead.

A visitor center (☎ 621-5130), at the southeast corner of University Blvd and Cherry Ave, is open weekdays. Campus tours are offered during the school year. **Old Main** on University Blvd near the middle of the campus is the original university. The **Student Union**, just northeast of Old Main, has an information desk (☎ 621-7755) as well as various restaurants, art displays, a campus bookstore and the Gallagher movie theater. Note that University Blvd, east of Old Main, becomes a grassy pedestrian walkway called the University Mall.

Parking can be problematic when school is in session, especially if the U of A Wildcats are playing a home game. Large parking garages at the northeast corner of Park Ave and E Speedway Blvd and at Cherry Ave and E 4th charge a few dollars but fill during games. Call the U of A Parking & Transportation Dept (☎ 621-3550) for details.

Other useful campus numbers are the general operator (☎ 621-2211), athletic events ticket information (☎ 621-2287), Centennial Hall cultural events ticket office (☎ 621-3341) and the fine arts box office (☎ 621-1162).

Center for Creative Photography

This has one of the world's best collections of works by American photographers, as well as some European and other artists. The small public gallery displays images by famous photographers and changing exhibits throughout the year. Most of Ansel Adams's and Edward Weston's work, as well as images by many other photographers, are stored in the archives. Serious photography buffs can call for an appointment to view the works of one or two particular photographers; this is a remarkable opportunity rarely offered elsewhere. The center (☎ 621-7968), 1030 N Olive Ave, is open from 9 am to 5 pm, Monday to Friday, and from noon to 5 pm on weekends. Admission is free.

website: www.creativephotography.org

University of Arizona Museum of Art

Opposite the photography center, this museum (☎ 621-7567) displays changing shows of mainly student works. These exhibits range widely in quality but are always intriguing. There are also fine permanent collections of European art and a variety of sculptures. Hours are 9 am to 5 pm Monday to Friday and noon to 4 pm on Sunday during the school year; summer weekday hours are 10 am to 3:30 pm. Admission is free.

Arizona State Museum

This anthropological museum (☎ 621-6302) focuses on the region's Indians. One of the permanent exhibits entitled 'Paths of Life: American Indians of the Southwest' is a state-of-the-art representation of the past and present lives of several tribes; well worth seeing. The museum is in two buildings on the north and south sides of University Blvd, east of the campus entrance at Park Ave. 'Paths of Life' is in the north hall; admission is free. Hours are 10 am to 5 pm Monday to Saturday and noon to 5 pm on Sunday.

Arizona Historical Society Museum

This is the society's flagship museum; it also manages the Sosa-Carrillo-Frémont House Museum (see Historic Buildings, above) and the Fort Lowell Museum (see Beyond Downtown, below). The museum's collection (☎ 628-5774), 949 E 2nd, is a comprehensive trip through Tucson's history as a Spanish colonial, Mexican, territorial and state city. Anything from colonial silverware to vintage automobiles is shown in this wide-ranging selection of historical artifacts. Changing exhibits keep bringing locals back, too. Hours are 10 am to 4 pm daily except Sunday (noon to 4 pm); closed major holidays. It's free, but donations are appreciated.

Flandrau Science Center, Planetarium & Mineral Museum

At the northeast corner of Cherry Ave and University Mall, the Flandrau (☎ 621-7827) has a permanent collection and many changing shows. Permanent exhibits include a 'walk-in' meteor and a variety of hands-on science displays. The Mineral Museum is in the basement of the Science Center. Minerals, meteorites and gemstones from all over the world are exhibited, with an emphasis on local stones. Varying planetarium shows are shown throughout the day; call for times and titles. Laser rock shows are occasionally featured.

Admission to the science center is $3, and $2 for three- to 12-year-olds. Admission to planetarium shows (including exhibits admission) is $5 for adults; $4 for children. Those under three are not permitted in the shows. The science center is open from 9 am to 5 pm Monday to Saturday, 7 to 9 pm Wednesday to Saturday, 1 to 5 pm on Sunday. The mineral museum is open the same daytime hours, but not in the evenings. Various astronomical events are scheduled throughout the year.

website: www.flandrau.org

Campus Sculptures

Beginning with *The Flute Player*, commissioned in 1979 and now standing in front of the main library, the U of A has steadily acquired an eclectic collection of about a dozen sculptures scattered throughout the campus. The most controversial? The huge *Curving Arcades (Homage to Bernini)* at the main eastern entrance at University Mall and N Campbell Ave. Visitors' favorite? The whimsical *25 Scientists* in front of the new chemistry and biology building on University Mall, just west of the main library. Ask at the visitor center or the Museum of Art about the others.

BEYOND DOWNTOWN
Tucson Botanical Gardens

These quiet and pleasant gardens (☎ 326-9255/686), 2150 N Alvernon Way, cover 5½ acres and focus on native dry-land plants. There is also a small tropical greenhouse, an herb garden and other plant attractions forming a quiet midtown oasis. All paths are wheelchair accessible. Various workshops and events are offered throughout the year, including garden tours (not in summer). There is a gift shop. Hours are 8:30 am to 4:30 pm daily. Admission is $5, $4 for seniors and $1 for those six to 11.
website: www.tucsonbotanical.org

Reid Park Zoo

This small but excellent zoo (☎ 791-4022), in Reid Park north of 22nd St, provides a good look at animals from all over the world, including some unusual ones such as giant anteaters and pygmy hippos. All the standard favorites are here, as well as some well-themed exhibits (especially the South American area). The zoo's compact size makes it a great excursion for children because they don't get overwhelmed and tired out. A gift shop and a fast-food restaurant are here. Hours are 9 am to 4 pm daily. Admission is $4, $3 for seniors and 75¢ for five- to 14-year-olds accompanied by an adult.

Outside the zoo, the surrounding Reid Park provides picnic areas, playgrounds and a duck pond with paddleboat rentals in summer.

Kids' Stuff

The Tucson Children's Museum, open year-round, appeals to younger kids, while the Flandrau Science Center shows are aimed at older kids and teenagers. The Reid Park Zoo and the Arizona-Sonora Desert Museum are good for the entire family, as is the Pima Air & Space Museum, especially if your kids are plane nuts.

Two places that offer miniature golf, go-carts, bumper boats, batting cages and other fun stuff are Funtasticks (☎ 888-4653), 221 E Wetmore, and Golf 'N Stuff (☎ 885-3569), 6503 E Tanque Verde Rd.

During the summer, water parks offer something a little more exciting than swimming laps. Breakers (☎ 682-2530), 8555 W Tangerine Rd (1½ miles east of I-10 exit 242, 16 miles north of downtown), has a huge wave pool for surfing, as well as water slides and nonwave pools. Hours are 9 am to dusk; admission is $14 for adults, $9 for kids under 48 inches tall and free for children under three. Children under 13 must be accompanied by an adult. Justin's Water World & RV Park (☎ 883-8340), at 3551 S San Joaquin Rd (8 miles west of I-19 exit 99 along Ajo Way, then 2 miles north) has swimming pools, toddlers' paddling pools, water slides galore, a tubing area and an 'Atlantis – The Lost Continent' attraction. Hours are 10 am to 5 pm Friday to Sunday and holidays. Admission is $11 with one child under six free with each paid admission.

Fort Lowell Museum

After Geronimo surrendered, Fort Lowell's important role in the Indian Wars faded, and the army closed it in 1891. Only weathered ruins remain today, with a museum (☎ 885-3832) housed in reconstructed officers' quarters with furnishings and exhibits of the fort's heyday. Hours are 10 am to 4 pm, Wednesday to Saturday; admission is free. Fort Lowell Park is off the 2900 block of N Craycroft Rd and also features playgrounds, duck pond and picnic areas. Across Craycroft Rd, a short way north of the fort, Fort Lowell Rd heads west past several early houses in the small Fort Lowell historical district.

Pima Air & Space Museum

With over 250 aircraft representing a history of aviation, this museum (☎ 574-0462) 6000 E Valencia Rd, is a must-see for aircraft buffs. The museum also operates the Titan Missile Museum (see Green Valley later in this chapter). Hours are 9 am to 5 pm daily except Thanksgiving and Christmas. Admission is $9.75 for adults, $6 for children. From 10 am to 3 pm, there are wheelchair-accessible tram tours for another $2.
website: www.pimaair.org

Nearby, note the approximately 5000 mothballed aircraft at Davis-Monthan Air Force Base (see them driving north on Kolb Rd and then west on Escalante Rd). Bus tours of the aircraft 'graveyard' are given several times a day weekdays except holidays, beginning at 9:30 am. Reservations (☎ 618-4806) are required well in advance. Tours cost $6, or $3 for those under 13. Discounts are given for combined visits with the Air & Space or Titan Missile museums (see South of Tucson).

Tohono Chul Park

This small desert oasis, surrounded by encroaching development north of town, is a good place to see desert flora and fauna in a natural setting. There are demonstrations and ethnobotanical gardens, an exhibit room with changing shows, gift shops, plant sales and a tea room. A variety of docent-led tours are offered. The park (☎ 575-8468, 742-6455), 7366 N Paseo del Norte, is open 7 am to dusk daily; the other attractions have shorter hours. Admission is free, but a $2 donation is suggested.
website: www.tohonochulpark.org

SANTA CATALINA MOUNTAINS

The Santa Catalina Mountains, within the Coronado National Forest and topped by 9157-foot Mt Lemmon, form Tucson's northern boundary and are the best loved and most visited of Tucson's many mountain ranges.

Sabino Canyon

This area is the most popular and accessible part of the Santa Catalinas. A visitor center includes a USFS ranger station (☎ 749-8700), open weekdays from 8 am to 4:30 pm and on weekends from 8:30 am to 4:30 pm. Maps, hiking guides and information are available here, and there is a short nature trail nearby. The visitor center is at the entrance of the canyon at 5900 N Sabino Canyon Rd, where there is a large parking lot. Admission is $5 per vehicle, valid also on Mt Lemmon.

Roads continue beyond the visitor center into the canyon, but only shuttle buses (☎ 749-2861 for recorded information) are allowed to drive on these. The Sabino Canyon Rd goes a scenic 3.8 miles up the canyon, crossing the river several times. Narrated shuttle bus tours spend 45 minutes doing the roundtrip and stop at nine points along the way. Tours leave every half hour from 9 am to 4:30 pm, and ticket holders can get on and off at any point whenever they feel like it. There are several riverside spots and picnic places on the way. At the top is a trailhead for hikers wanting to go high into the Santa Catalinas. Fares are $6; $2.50 for three- to 12-year-olds. Full-moon shuttle tours are given by reservation on the nights around a full moon from September to June. Call ☎ 749-2327 for information.

Another road from the visitor center goes 2½ miles to the Bear Canyon trailhead. A shuttle bus (no narration or stops) takes hikers there every hour from 9 am to 4 pm. The fare is $3; $1 for children. From the trailhead a 2.3-mile (one-way) hike leads to Seven Falls, a scenic and popular spot for picnics and swimming, with no facilities (allow 3½ hours roundtrip). From the falls, the trail continues up as high as you want to go.

Bicycles are allowed on the roads only before 9 am and after 5 pm and not at all on Wednesday and Sunday. Hikers can walk along the roads at any time from dawn to dusk. You don't have to take a shuttle to get to a trailhead; starting from the visitor center, there are plenty of hiking possibilities. The Phoneline Trail, skirting Sabino

Canyon high on its southeastern side, is an alternative to taking the road.

Several picnic areas with grills, tables and bathrooms are in the area. Camping is not allowed within those areas. Backpackers can hike into the Santa Catalinas and wilderness camp almost anywhere that is more than a quarter-mile away from a road or trailhead.

Catalina State Park

This park is in the western foothills of the Santa Catalinas and is popular for hiking, picnicking, bird watching and camping. You'll find both short nature trails and trailheads for long-distance hiking and backpacking. Horseback riding is permitted and one trail is specifically developed for horses. The Equestrian Center has boarding for horses. Natural swimming holes occur along some of the trails and make good day-hike destinations. Ask the ranger for directions. For more information call Catalina State Park (☎ 628-5798). The park is about 15 miles north of Tucson along Oracle Rd (Hwy 77). Day use is $5 per vehicle or $1 for cyclists.

Mt Lemmon

Spend a couple of days hiking up to Mt Lemmon's summit along the many trails in the Santa Catalinas, or head east on Tanque Verde Rd, pick up the Catalina Hwy and enjoy the hour-long **scenic drive** to the top. This is a favorite getaway for Tucsonans wishing to escape the summer heat. Along the way are four USFS campgrounds and several pullouts with great views. The road is narrow and winding, however, and requires some concentration, as well as a $5 per vehicle toll. Several hiking trails intersect with the highway. Near the top of the drive is the Palisades Ranger Station (no ☎) with useful information about the area, or call the Sabino Canyon Ranger Station (☎ 749-8700).

At the top is the small village of **Summerhaven** where there are cabins to rent, some restaurants, a picnic area and a ski area (see Skiing, below). During the summer you can take scenic rides on the chair lift from 10:30 am to 5 pm for $8 ($4 for three- to 12-

year-olds). Families pay $21 for two adults and up to four children. Gas up in Tucson; there's no gas on Mt Lemmon.

ACTIVITIES

The Convention & Visitors Bureau can provide lists of golf courses, tennis courts and other local attractions. The Summit Hut (☎ 325-1554), 5045 E Speedway, is an excellent source of outdoor gear, including guidebooks (Lonely Planet titles are sold), maps and equipment; you can shop online at www.summithut.com.

Hiking & Backpacking

Tucson is ringed by mountains. The Rincons to the east and the Tucson Mountains to the west are easily explored from Saguaro National Park. The Santa Ritas, topped by 9453-foot Mt Wrightson, are visible in the distance, to the south (see Green Valley).

The Santa Catalina Mountains can be accessed from several trailheads, including the Finger Rock Canyon (Mt Kimball) trailhead at the far north end of Alvernon Way, which leads steeply up past Finger Rock – an obvious point on the northern skyline from many parts of Tucson. (Note that Alvernon stops in midtown Tucson at Fort Lowell Rd. Take Campbell Ave north to Skyline and then go east to pick up Alvernon again.) Other trailheads are found in Sabino Canyon and Catalina State Park (see earlier).

Take extra precautions hiking around Tucson in summer, when dehydration can be a potentially lethal problem. You should carry water at all times and drink a gallon of water per day. Sunburn can be debilitating, so protect yourself. Also, watch out for those spiny plants. It's worth carrying tweezers and a comb – they help remove cactus spines from your skin.

Backpackers should contact a USFS ranger station about suitable places to camp and where to leave their cars.

Rock Climbing

Mt Lemmon has good rock climbing – route books are available from the Summit Hut. Rocks and Ropes (☎ 882-5294), 330 S Toole Ave (hard to find; call for directions), is an indoor rock-climbing facility with equipment rental.

Bird Watching

Bird watchers come here from all over the USA to see birds found nowhere else in the country. While the months between April to September see the most species of hummingbirds, there are always a few around. In addition, common desert birds such as roadrunners, gila woodpeckers, elf owls and cactus wrens attract out-of-state birders wanting to add to their life lists.

The best resource for bird watchers is the Tucson Audubon Society (☎ 629-0510), 300 E University Blvd. It has an excellent nature shop with a fine selection of bird guides and related materials. Hours are 10 am to 4 pm, Monday to Saturday, and to 6 pm on Thursday. A research library is also available. Ask here about monthly meetings and slide shows held from September to May, as well as field trips, many of them free. An essential handbook for birders is *Finding Birds in Southeastern Arizona* by William A Davis and Stephen M Russell. A bird-sightings and information hotline (☎ 798-1005) is updated weekly. website: www.tucsonaudubon.org

Skiing

Mt Lemmon Ski Area (☎ 576-1400/1321) is the most southerly ski area in the USA and is mainly for intermediate and experienced skiers. Rentals, lessons and food are available. Depending on the weather, the slopes are open from mid-December to late March. Lift tickets are $32.

Hot-Air Ballooning

Several companies offer hot-air-balloon flights which usually take place in the calm morning air, last about an hour and finish with a traditional champagne breakfast. Costs are about $150 to $200 per person. Flights may be canceled in windy or very hot weather. Most companies can arrange flights on a day's notice. Experienced companies include Balloon America (☎ 299-7744), or online at www.Balloon RidesUSA.com, and A Southern Arizona

Balloon Excursion (☎ 624-3599, 800-524-3599).

Horseback Riding

Several stables offer excursions by the hour, half day or longer. Summer trips tend to be short breakfast or sunset rides because of the heat. Desert cookouts can be arranged. One of the most reputable companies is Pusch Ridge Stables (☎ 825-1664), 13700 N Oracle Rd, which also offers overnight pack trips. Nearby, Walking Winds Stables (☎ 742-4422), 10811 N Oracle, specializes in Catalina State Park rides. At the other end of town is Pantano Stables (☎ 298-8980), 4450 S Houghton Rd. Several others advertise locally. Rates start around $20 for the first hour, but are much lower for subsequent hours.

ORGANIZED TOURS

Gray Line (☎ 622-8811) offers standard coach and van tours of the city and its surroundings as well as excursions all over the state. Tours of Tucson and southeastern Arizona are offered by Off the Beaten Path Tours (☎ 529-6090). Trail Dust Jeep Tours (☎ 747-0323) takes you into the desert in open jeeps. Old Pueblo Tours (☎ 795-7448) specializes in historical tours of Tucson. Note that some tours don't operate in the summer heat.

PLACES TO STAY

December through April is the high season and May to September is the low. During the Gem and Mineral Show in early February, prices rise way above their already high winter rates, so budget travelers should avoid Tucson then unless they're attending that show. A $99 room in January can be $49 in July and $139 during the Gem and Mineral Show. Prices given below tend towards the winter rates but can only be used as an approximation.

Camping

The USFS (☎ 749-8700) operates four basic campgrounds on the Catalina Hwy going up to Mt Lemmon. The campground at *Catalina State Park* (☎ 628-5798), about 15 miles north of downtown along Oracle Rd (Hwy 77), has tent/RV sites for $10/15. *Gilbert Ray Campground* (☎ 883-4200), on Kinney Rd a couple of miles east of the Arizona-Sonora Desert Museum (see Around Tucson later), has 152 sites open year-round, some with electrical hookups. There's water but no showers. Site rates are $8 or $12.50 with hookups. Check the Yellow Pages for long-term RV parks.

Budget

The friendly *Roadrunner Hostel* (☎ 628-4709, 346 E 12th St), offers dorm rooms ($16 per person, four nights for $32 in summer) and doubles ($35). Free Internet access, kitchen privileges, TV/video room and coin laundry are included; bicycles can be rented ($7). Check the website for more information: www.roadrunnerhostel.com. Also downtown, the very popular *Hotel Congress* (☎ 622-8848, 800-722-8848, 311 E Congress), with a hip music club, a café and bar (with Internet access) downstairs, dates back to the 1920s and has dorm beds ($17 for IYHA members with passport) and singles/doubles for $33/38 in summer. Rates are $68/72 in winter, when reservations are suggested. Rooms can be loud because of the club.

The *Lazy 8 Motel* (622-3336, 314 E Benson Hwy), with a pool and continental breakfast, is the best of several independent cheap motels ($25 to $50) near I-10 exit 261, though this is not the best of neighborhoods. Nearby, an *Econo Lodge* is in this price range. Other cheap but very basic places are southeast along the Benson Hwy.

Rooms are $40 to $65 in Tucson's six *Motels 6s*.

Mid-Range

Hotels The 1940s *Ghost Ranch Lodge* (☎ 791-7565, 800-456-7565, 801 W Miracle Mile) sits in eight acres of cactus-filled desert gardens surrounded by rooms. Some have private patios or kitchenettes. A pool, whirlpool and restaurant are on the premises. Rates are an excellent value at $50 to $100, perhaps because the surrounding neighborhood is run-down. Once you enter the lodge, you can forget about that.

Nearby, the slightly cheaper *Wayward Winds Lodge* (☎ 791-7526, 628-2010, 707 W Miracle Mile) has 40 good-sized rooms, and a swimming pool on pleasant grounds.

Many *chain motels* offer satisfactory lodging in the $60 to $175 range for a double in winter (except during the Gem and Mineral Show). Most have a pool and whirlpool; many include continental breakfast. Many of the ones listed in the Facts for the Visitor chapter have at least one, and often three or four, properties in Tucson. See the maps for a selection.

The *Smugglers Inn* (☎ 296-3292, 800-525-8852, 6350 E Speedway Blvd), has attractive gardens and spacious rooms with balconies or patios. Facilities include a pool, spa, putting green, restaurant and bar with room service. Rates are $70 to $125.
website: www.smugglersinn.com

The *Windmill Inn at St Philips Plaza* (☎ 577-0007, 800-547-4747, 4250 N Campbell Ave) is in one of the more upscale shopping plazas. The 120 attractive two-room suites are decorated in Southwestern style and many have microwaves, wet bars and refrigerators. Winter rates are $100 to $150, with newspapers, coffee and pastries delivered to your room every morning. There is a pool, a spa and a lending library of paperback bestsellers as well as bicycles for guest use.
website: www.windmillinns.com

B&Bs Tucson has dozens of B&Bs; many are listed at www.bbonline.com/az or get a listing from the visitors bureau.

Casa Alegre (☎ 628-1800, 800-628-5654, 316 E Speedway Blvd) is a peaceful 1915 house that is convenient to U of A and downtown and is decorated with historical memorabilia. Seven rooms with baths range from $70 to $125, and there is a pool and spa. *Peppertrees B&B* (☎/fax 622-7167, 800-348-5763, 724 E University Blvd), is a quick walk away from U of A. Four large guest rooms in the 1905 house cost $110, and two guesthouses, equipped with TVs, phones, laundry facilities, full kitchen and two bedrooms, are $180 – about 30% less in summer. Gourmet breakfasts and an afternoon tea are included in the price. *La Posada del Valle* (☎/fax 795-3840, 888-404-7113,1640 N Campbell Rd), is also close to U of A and has a beautiful courtyard. It features five rooms with private entrances and bathrooms; rates are $100 to $140.

Take Broadway all the way east to the Saguaro National Park and look for signs before the fork in the road to find the luxurious and remote *Suncatcher B&B* (☎/fax 885-0883, 877-775-8355, 105 N Avenida Javelina). This B&B has four rooms all individually decorated to resemble some of the world's most exclusive hotels. It also has a pool and spa. Rates are $80 to $145.

Top End

The grand dame of Tucson hotels is the sedate and beautiful *Arizona Inn* (☎ 325-1541, 800-933-1093, 2200 E Elm), built in 1929. The 14-acre grounds are attractively landscaped and the public areas are elegant and traditional. Swimming, tennis and croquet are available. The rooms, decorated in Southwestern style, are spacious though the bathrooms are not very large (people spent less time in them in 1929, perhaps). There are 70 rooms and 16 suites with patios or fireplaces. The restaurant is good enough to attract the local citizenry, and you can order room service. The service is friendly and unpretentious, yet professional. Expect to pay $200 to $300 in the winter.
website: www.arizonainn.com

Casa Tierra B&B (☎ 578-3058, 11155 W Calle Pima) is just west of the western section of Saguaro National Park. It's a modern-day adobe surrounded by desert, with a hot tub for relaxing. Four rooms, each with private bathrooms, patios, microwaves and refrigerators are between $145 and $175, and a two-bedroom suite is $200. This B&B closes from June through September.

Tucson's ranches and resorts, often destinations in themselves, rival those in the Valley of the Sun for beauty, comfort and diversity of facilities. Rates are in the $200 to $400 a double range, including meals and activities; note that 8% tax and 15% gratuities may be added to ranch rates. Minimum stays

are usually required and weekly discounts offered. Ranches may close in summer.

Lazy K Bar Guest Ranch (☎ 744-3050, 800-321-7018, 8401 N Scenic Drive) offers horseback riding twice a day on desert and mountain trails. Tennis, mountain biking and hayrides are some of the other activities. The style is very much family-oriented with plenty of activities for children and large sit-down dinners with all the guests. The ranch has 23 rooms in adobe buildings, all with air conditioning and private baths. website: www.lazykbar.com

White Stallion Ranch (☎ 297-0252, 888-977-2624, 9251 W Twin Peaks Rd) is a quiet, peaceful, family-style ranch where you can groom your own horse before a ride, let the children roam free in a petting zoo, relax on a patio and listen to the birds or take a challenging hike throughout the desert mountain wilderness. This 3000-acre ranch has 32 rooms.
website: www.wsranch.com

Fifteen miles east of Tucson, *Tanque Verde Guest Ranch* (☎ 296-6275, 800-234-3833, 14301 E Speedway Blvd) sits in the Rincon Mountains, offering plenty of opportunities for hiking, riding and nature walks. For more 'resort-style' activities, there are two pools, five tennis courts, a spa, sauna, exercise room and basketball courts. But 100 head of horses remind you what Tucson ranches are about. This is one of the more famous and comfortable ranches in the area, with 74 well-decorated 'casitas,' attentive service, great food and beautiful surroundings.
website: www.tanqueverderanch.com

Several big resorts center around a top-notch golf course (or two!), along with tennis courts, pools and fitness and relaxation activities galore. All have good, if pricey, restaurants. Winter rates start around $250 for large and comfortable rooms (plus about $100 for greens fees), and go up from there for deluxe rooms and suites. Prices drop in summer. The following golf resorts are highly recommended:

Lodge at Ventana Canyon (☎ 577-1400, 800-828-5701) 6200 N Clubhouse Lane
website: www.wyndham.com

Loew's Ventana Canyon Resort (☎ 299-2020, 800-234-5117) 7000 N Resort Dr
website: www.loewshotels.com

Omni Tucson National Golf Course & Spa Resort (☎ 297-2271, 800-528-4856) 2727 W Club Dr
website: www.tucsonnational.com

Sheraton El Conquistador Resort & Country Club (☎ 544-5000, 800-325-7832) 10000 N Oracle Rd
website: www.sheratonelconquistador.com

Westin La Paloma Resort (☎ 742-6000, 800-937-8461) 3800 E Sunrise Dr
website: www.westin.com/lapaloma

If you're not looking for on-site golf but do want extensive resort facilities, a good bet is the *Westward Look Resort* (☎ 297-1151, 800-722-2500, 245 E Ina Rd); visit it online at www.westwardlook.com. Another good top-end choice is *Hacienda del Sol Guest Ranch Resort* (☎ 299-1501, 800-728-6514, 5601 N Hacienda del Sol Rd), which allows guests to relax in an authentic Southwest setting with lovely views but without all the golf and tennis hoopla. The resort dates from 1929 and they say that Clark Gable, Spencer Tracy and other stars stayed here. It does offer tennis, croquet, horseshoes, a whirlpool and a small swimming pool, but with only 33 units, everything is much lower key than other resorts. The Hacienda's website is www.haciendadelsol.com.

Finally, if you want to pamper yourself in a dedicated spa and can afford rates starting at $500 a day, including healthy gourmet meals and some treatments, a top choice is the *Canyon Ranch* (☎ 749-9000, 800-742-9000, 8600 E Rockcliff Rd). Guests normally stay for several days and indulge in numerous spa and health services provided by health, beauty, well-being and fitness professionals. No alcohol is served; for details, see www.canyonranch.com. Another option, with alternative treatments/lectures such as equine therapy, ayurveda and the intriguingly named 'Zen Bootcamp' accompanying the usual spa activities are offered at the highly recommended *Miraval* (☎ 825-4000, 800-824-4000, 500 E Via Estancia) about 20 miles north of Tucson. Alcohol is served; see the resort online at www.miravalresort.com.

PLACES TO EAT

Tucson has a well-deserved reputation for Mexican food and if you like it, you'll never be at a loss for a place to eat. If you don't like Mexican food, you'll still find an extensive and varied selection of excellent American and international restaurants, as well as Southwestern cuisine. Note that smoking is not allowed inside Tucson's restaurants.

The popular and busy *Coffee Etc* (☎ 881-8070, 2830 N Campbell Ave) serves breakfast 24 hours a day, as well as burgers, sandwiches, soups, salads, light meals and, of course, a variety of coffees. There is another branch (☎ 544-8588) at 6091 N Oracle. Downtown, the *Cup Cafe* (☎ 798-1618), in the Hotel Congress, has good breakfasts, light meals and, especially, desserts from 7 am to 11 pm daily. Also good and locally popular is *Grill* (☎ 623-7621, 100 E Congress), which is open 24 hours.

The *Blue Willow Restaurant* (☎ 795-8736, 2616 N Campbell Ave) serves many vegetarian dishes, has excellent breakfasts, and its soups, salads and sandwiches are both good and an excellent value ($5 to $8). It has an attractive patio with a shade roof and mist-makers to keep you cool. Beer and wine are served. *Govinda's Natural Foods* (☎ 792-0630, 711 E Blacklidge Drive) has Indian-influenced vegetarian food served buffet-style. The atmosphere is meditative and vegan food is also available. Hours are from 11:30 am to 2:30 pm Wednesday to Saturday, and 5 to 9 pm Tuesday to Saturday. *Guilin* (☎ 320-7768, 3250 Speedway) has Tucson's best Chinese dining and numerous vegetarian options ($7 to $14).

For Mexican dining, there are half a dozen good places along S 4th Ave between 22nd and I-10, any one of which provides satisfactory food (most entrées are $6 to $10). *Mi Nidito* (☎ 622-5081, 1813 S 4th Ave) frequently gets the best reviews and there's often a wait; they don't take reservations. Bill Clinton ate here when he was president. Downtown, *La Indita* (☎ 792-0523, 622 N 4th Ave) serves inexpensive and excellent Mexican food, as well as some Michoacan Tarascan Indian dishes.

Mexican food in more upscale environments costs a few dollars more but has some innovative twists and is still an excellent value. Recommended downtown places include the excellent *Café Poca Cosa* (☎ 622-6400, 88 E Broadway Blvd), in the Clarion Hotel, with beautifully presented, freshly prepared, innovative meals and a full bar. The menu changes often and reservations are requested. It closes on Sunday. Around the corner is *Little Café Poca Cosa* (no ☎, 20 S Scott), open from 7:30 am to 2:30 pm, Monday to Friday; alcohol is not served.

El Minuto Cafe (☎ 882-4145, 354 S Main Ave), has been in business for six decades and is famous for its chiles rellenos, among other dishes. A branch (☎ 290-9591, 8 N Kolb Rd) serves similar food. The oldest place in town is *El Charro Cafe* (☎ 622-1922, 311 N Court Ave), which they say has been in the same family since 1922 and is very popular with tourists and locals alike. Its carne seca used to be dried on the roof in the old days. There are two branches, at 6310 E Broadway (☎ 745-1922), and at the airport, for your last (or first) Mexican meal.

Maya Quetzal (☎ 622-8207, 429 N 4th Ave) is a small, friendly place that serves delicious Guatemalan dishes at pequeño prices; closed Sunday. *Miraflores* (☎ 888-4880, 5845 N Oracle Rd) serves authentic Peruvian cuisine daily except Monday ($8 to $14).

The *Tohono Chul Tea Room* (☎ 797-1222, 7366 N Paseo del Norte) has a pleasant patio open from 8 am to 5 pm daily. The menu features both Mexican and American food, and they serve an English-style high tea from 2:30 to 5 pm.

Sakura (☎ 298-7777, 6534 E Tanque Verde Rd) serves a varied Japanese menu including sushi and *teppan* (fun table-side chopping and pyrotechnics) with prices ($7 to $18) as varied as the menu. *India Oven* (☎ 326-8635, 2727 N Campbell), serves great Punjab food and has an inexpensive lunch buffet. It's very popular; service can be slow. *Char's Thai* (☎ 795-1715, 5039 E 5th St) has super-spicy plates (though mild dishes are also available) and is open weekdays for lunch and daily for dinner.

Italian-food lovers will like elegant *Daniel's* (☎ 742-3200, 4340 N Campbell Ave) in St Philips Plaza, which specializes in Tuscan-style meals. Many dinner entrées are in the $20s, except for some pasta selections. Hours are 5 to 9 pm daily. Recommended, less-expensive Italian choices include *Gavi* with three locations in town.

Cafe Terra Cotta (☎ 577-8100, 3500 E Sunrise) (east of 1st Ave), is the best Southwestern restaurant in Tucson. The menu is innovative, even wild sounding at times, but there are also a few fairly straightforward choices. The appetizers sound so appetizing that many people order two of them and forgo an entrée, supposedly to leave room for one of the divine desserts. Prices are in the teens for most entrees and a good value. Another moderately priced restaurant with a delicious and eclectic Southwestern menu but a decidedly un-Southwestern ambiance is the *Presidio Grill* (☎ 327-4667, 3352 E Speedway Blvd). Reservations are recommended.

Nonie (☎ 319-1965, 2526 E Grant Rd) is a New Orleans bistro serving authentic French Creole and Cajun cuisine. If crawfish, jambalaya, alligator and fried pickles are your idea of good food, the cooks know how to prepare them here. They also have the world's hottest hot sauce – available on special request only. Prices are reasonable; $6 for a set lunch and $8 to $20 for dinner.

There are plenty of steak houses. For those on a budget, *El Corral* (☎ 299-6092, 2201 E River Rd) is a good choice. Service is a little amateurish but aims to please. Prime rib is the specialty of the house and a great deal at about $10. Hours are 5 to 10 pm daily; reservations aren't taken and there's always a line outside. The same owners run the *Pinnacle Peak Steakhouse* (☎ 296-0911, 6541E Tanque Verde Rd), where the atmosphere is Wild Western and fun, if slightly touristy. Wooden sidewalks pass dance halls and saloons as you swagger into the dining room. The sign outside warns 'Stop! No Ties Allowed'; if you've got one on, you can donate it to the rafter decorations. The food is inexpensive and good; dinner only.

The **Hidden Valley Inn** (☎ 299-4941, 4825 N Sabino Canyon Rd) has that Old Wild West look to bring in the crowds as well as reasonable prices ($6 for hamburgers to $17 for big steaks). It's a great family place with hundreds of animated models of the Old West around the walls – kids can wander around and look at them while waiting for a meal. Open daily for lunch and dinner. The most upscale steak house is **McMahon's** (☎ 327-7463, 2959 N Swan Rd), which has an excellent seafood selection as well.

All the resorts listed under Places to Stay have top-class restaurants.

ENTERTAINMENT

The free alternative *Tucson Weekly,* published every Thursday, has the most detailed club and bar listings. Also read the Friday 'Starlight' section of the *Arizona Daily Star* and the Thursday 'Calendar' section of the *Tucson Citizen.* Performances are fewer in summer.

Cinemas

Tucson has many cinema multiplexes showing the year's best and worst movies. **The Loft** (☎ 795-7777, 3233 E Speedway Blvd) is the best bet for alternative or foreign flicks.

Nightlife

The Maverick, King of Clubs (☎ 748-0456, 4702 E 22nd) is a friendly place with live country & western music most nights. The **Cactus Moon** (☎ 748-0049, 5470 E Broadway Blvd), is loud, brash and the place to see and be seen if you're into two-stepping to recorded music. Come dressed in the latest Western wear. Call these places if you are interested in dance lessons.

Downtown, 4th Ave near 6th St is a good spot to bar hop. **Club Congress** (622-8848) in the Hotel Congress, has alternative dance music (recorded and occasionally live). For Latin music, try **Irene's Restaurant and Bar** (☎ 206-9385, 254 E Congress). **IBT's** (☎ 882-3053, 616 N 4th Ave) is Tucson's best gay dance club, while **Ain't Nobody's Bizness**

(318-4838, 2900 E Broadway) (in a shopping plaza) attracts lesbians.

Students head to **Chicago Bar,** (☎ 748-8169, 5954 E Speedway Blvd) for blues and rock. **Berky's Bar** (☎ 296-1981, 5769 E Speedway Blvd) attracts an older crowd and often has decent live bands (mainly blues) and dancing; **Boondocks Lounge** (☎ 690-0991, 3360 N 1st Ave) is a pretty good blues venue.

Some older theaters now function as performance venues for musicians playing anything from a cappella through punk to zydeco, and where dancing is sometimes allowed. These include the **Rialto Theater** (☎ 740-0126, 318 E Congress) and the **Santa Rita Ballroom** at 6th Ave and Broadway Blvd.

Performing Arts

The renovated 1920s **Temple of Music & Art** (☎ 884-4875, 622-2823, 330 S Scott Ave) is the home of the Arizona Theater Company, which produces shows from October to May. The **Tucson Convention Center** (☎ 791-4101, 791-4266, 260 S Church), has a Music Hall, the Leo Rich Theatre and a convention area that plays host to many events, including performances by the Arizona Opera Company (☎ 293-4336) from October to March; the Tucson Symphony Orchestra (☎ 882-8585) November to March; and sporting and theatrical events. The U of A **Centennial Hall** (☎ 621-3364/41, 1020 E University Blvd) hosts excellent international acts throughout the academic year and presents Ballet Arizona (☎ 602-381-1096, 888-322-5538) from December to May. Several local theater companies present alternative and avant-garde productions.

Downtown Saturday Night is held along Congress St and Broadway Blvd between Stone and 4th Aves the first and third Saturday of every month from about 7 pm to 10 pm. Galleries stay open late and there are plenty of free street performances. This event is sponsored by the Tucson Arts District (☎ 624-9977).

SHOPPING

Southwestern arts and crafts are of the most interest to travelers. Small but exquisite pieces of jewelry can easily be carried and bulky items can be shipped.

Some of the best stores are in the Presidio Historic District (see Downtown Tucson, earlier in this chapter). Another good place for quality arts and crafts is St Philips Plaza at the southeast corner of River Rd and Campbell Ave. Prices are high, but so is the quality. Particularly good stores here are the Obsidian Gallery (☎ 577-3598) for art and jewelry, Bahti Indian Arts (☎ 577-0290) for varied Native Americana and the Turquoise Door (☎ 299-7787) for stunning jewelry.

For fun shopping and browsing, you can't beat 4th Ave between University Blvd and Congress St. Here you'll find books and beads, antiques and African art, jewelry and junk, clothes and collectibles, and all sorts of treasures. Then head west along Congress for the Arts District.

GETTING THERE & AWAY
Air
Tucson International Airport (☎ 573-8000) is 9 miles south of downtown. It has a few direct flights into Mexico, but international airport facilities are limited to immigration and customs. Many major US carriers have direct flights between Tucson and many large US cities.

The local bus agency, Sun Tran (☎ 792-9222), has buses (No 25) during the day to the Laos Transit Center at Irvington and Liberty Ave, halfway between the airport and downtown. From here you have to connect to another bus. The fare is $1 and a transfer is free. Bus No 11 from the airport goes north through town along Alvernon Way, connecting with many east-west routes. There's information at the airport.

A more convenient option is using Arizona Stagecoach (☎ 889-1000,), which has door-to-door, 24-hour van service to anywhere in the metropolitan Tucson area. The fare ranges from $10 to more than $20 – roughly half of a cab fare.
website: www.arizonastagecoach.com

Bus
The Greyhound terminal (☎ 792-3475) is at 2 S 4th Ave. Several buses a day run east along I-10 to New Mexico, and northwest along I-10 to Phoenix, connecting to the rest of Arizona and California. Greyhound also connects with vans to Nogales every hour from 7 am to 7 pm for $6.50 and with Golden State (☎ 623-1675) buses for Douglas ($20), via Sierra Vista and Bisbee, leaving five times a day.

Arizona Shuttle Service (☎ 320-3881, 800-888-2749), 5350 E Speedway Blvd, has hourly vans from three Tucson locations to Phoenix Airport from 4 am to 11 pm. The fare is $24 with discounts for roundtrips, children and groups.
www.arizonashuttle.com

GETTING AROUND
Bus & Trolley
Sun Tran (☎ 792-9222 6 am to 7 pm on weekdays and 8 am to 5 pm weekends and holidays) has buses all over the metro Tucson area from early morning into the evening every day, but no night buses. Fares are $1 with a free transfer. Passes and timetables are available at many locations; call Sun Tran for the nearest one. There are many park-and-ride lots around town and some buses have bike racks. Major transit centers are the Laos Transit Center near Irvington and Liberty Ave to the south; the Ronstadt-Downtown Center at Congress and 6th Ave; and the Tohono Tadai Center at Stone Ave and Wetmore Rd to the north.

Sun Tran Trolley is an old-fashioned-looking trolley (fit with air conditioning) linking U of A (it leaves from Old Main) with the 4th Ave shopping area, Congress and the Arts District, historical downtown, and the Ronstadt-Downtown Center. Trolleys run two or three times an hour from about 10 am to 6:30 pm weekdays and less frequently on Saturday (no Sunday service). Trolleys run until 11 pm on the nights of Downtown Saturday Night and when the U of A has a home game. Trolley fare is 25¢.

Car
All the main companies have offices in the airport and many have offices in other parts of the valley or will deliver your car.

Taxi

The fare from the airport to downtown is around $15. Companies include Yellow Cab (☎ 624-6611), Allstate Cab (☎ 798-1111) and Checker Cab (☎ 623-1133). Apart from the cab rack at the airport, you need to phone to get a cab – they don't cruise the streets.

Bicycle

Tucson takes pride in being bike-friendly, with bike lanes on many major roads. Public libraries have free maps of the bike-lane system. Tucson's bike shops can provide you with information, rentals (about $20 a day) and details of mountain biking off the main roads. Check out Bargain Basement Bikes (☎ 624-9673), 428 N Fremont Ave or Full Cycle (☎ 327-3232), at 3232 E Speedway Blvd. Helmets are required for cyclists under 18.

AROUND TUCSON
Mission San Xavier del Bac

Founded by Padre Kino in 1700, this is Arizona's oldest European building still in use. Mostly destroyed in the Pima Indian uprising of 1751, it was rebuilt in the late 1700s and today looks much like it did 200 years ago. The building has been restored, and work continues on the frescoes inside. A visit to San Xavier is a highlight of many people's trip to Tucson.

Nicknamed 'the white dove of the desert,' its dazzling white walls are a splendid sight as you drive south on I-19 (take exit 92). The mission is on the San Xavier Indian Reservation (part of the Tohono O'odham tribe), and the plaza by the mission parking lot has stores selling Indian jewelry, arts and crafts, and snacks.

Catholic masses are held daily. The church itself (☎ 294-2624) is open daily 7 am to 5 pm, and the church museum and gift shop is open 9 am to 5 pm. Admission is by donation. Photography is permitted when religious ceremonies are not taking place.

Colorful religious ceremonies are held on the Friday after Easter, the Fiesta of San Xavier in early December, and Christmas. Call the mission for details.

Arizona-Sonora Desert Museum

The ASDM (☎ 883-2702), 2021 N Kinney Rd, is a living museum representing the flora and fauna of the Arizona-Sonora Desert and, as such, is more like a zoo than a museum. It is one of the best of its kind in the country and well worth a visit. Almost all local desert animals are displayed, often in quite natural-looking settings. The grounds are thick with desert plants too, many of which are labeled. You'll see scorpions and saguaros, coatis and coyotes, bighorn sheep and rattlesnakes, golden eagles and tiny hummingbirds, javelinas and agaves. It's all here.

Docents are on hand to answer questions about the live animals and to show other exhibits throughout the day – you might get a chance to pet a snake! There are two walk-through aviaries, one dedicated solely to hummingbirds; a geological exhibit featuring an underground cave (kids love that one); an underground exhibit with windows into ponds containing beavers, otters and ducks (found along the riparian corridors of the desert); and much more.

Allow at least two hours (half a day is better) and come prepared for outdoor walking. Strollers and wheelchairs are available, as are a gift shop, art gallery, restaurant and café.

The drive out to the ASDM is about 14 miles west along Speedway Blvd, which crosses over the very scenic Gates Pass and turns into Gates Pass Rd. The narrow and winding Gates Pass Rd is impassable for trailers and RVs, which must take the longer route west along Ajo Hwy. The visit can be combined with Old Tucson Studios, the International Wildlife Museum or Saguaro National Park (West) to make a full-day outing.

The ASDM is open 8:30 am to 5 pm daily, and from 7:30 am from March to September. (On summer Saturdays, it's open until 10 pm.) Admission is $9.95 ($8.95 from May to October), and $1.75 for six- to 12-year-olds.

website: www.desertmuseum.org

Old Tucson Studios

This film set was used in hundreds of Western movie productions from 1939 onward. Unfortunately, 65% of it burned down in 1995, but it has been rebuilt and expanded as a Western theme park, and movies are still shot here. Visitors are treated to shootouts, stagecoach rides, saloons, sheriffs and Wild West events galore; it is one of Tucson's most popular tourist spots. Old Tucson (☎ 883-0100) is on Kinney Rd a few miles southeast of the ASDM. Hours are 10 am to 6 pm daily, and admission is $14.95 ($9.45 for four- to 11-year-olds) plus tax. website: www.oldtucson.com

International Wildlife Museum

Housed in an odd castle-like building at 4800 W Gates Pass Rd (between Speedway Blvd and Gates Pass), this museum (☎ 617-1439) is a taxidermist's delight. Hundreds of animals from all over the world have been killed and expertly mounted. There are various hands-on exhibits and hourly movies about wildlife but no live animals. Hours are 9 am to 5 pm daily; admission is $7 for adults, $5.50 for students and seniors and $2.50 for six- to 12-year-olds.

Biosphere 2

This unique 3.15-acre glassed dome was built to be completely sealed off from Biosphere 1 (our planet). Inside, different micro-habitats, ranging from tropical forest to ocean environment, were designed to be completely self-sustaining. In 1991, eight bionauts entered Biosphere 2 for a two-year tour of duty during which they were physically cut off from the outside world. The experiment was criticized because the dome leaked gases and it was opened to allow a bionaut to emerge for medical treatment and to bring in supplies. The facility is now operated by Columbia University and the public can tour the site and enter parts of the biosphere.

Biosphere 2 (☎ 800-828-2462, 825-1289, 896-6200) is 5 miles northeast of the junction of Hwy 77 and Hwy 79, 30 miles north of Tucson. Hours are 8:30 am to 5 pm and guided tours are offered all day. Admission is $12.95, $8.95 for 13- to 17-year-olds and $6 for six- to 12-year-olds. Those over 10 can actually enter Biosphere 2 for an additional $10; reservations are required as tours entering the biosphere are limited to 20 people. There is a restaurant, gift shop and the ***Biosphere 2 Hotel*** with 27 rooms, all with coffeemakers, mini-fridge bars and balconies, for $149/169 ($79 in summer). website: www.bio2.edu

Colossal Cave

This dry limestone cave, six stories under the ground, was a legendary outlaw hideout. It's a 'dry' cave with no dripping water: formations are no longer growing. A half-mile trail takes visitors through several different chambers with many geological formations. The temperature inside is a pleasant 72°F year-round.

Colossal Cave (☎ 647-7275) is open every day for tours 9 am to 5 pm mid-September to mid-March and 8 am to 6 pm the rest of the year. It stays open one hour later on Sundays and holidays. Admission is $3 per vehicle. Cave entrance includes a 45-minute guided tour for $7.50; $4 for six- to 12-year-olds. The cave is 8 miles north of I-10 exit 279, about 25 miles southeast of Tucson. Alternatively, head southeast on Old Spanish Trail and follow the signs.

SAGUARO NATIONAL PARK

This park has two sections, Saguaro East and Saguaro West, about 30 miles apart and separated by Tucson. There are no drive-in campgrounds or lodges and only Saguaro East allows overnight backpacking, but the park is a fine day trip. As its name implies, it preserves large stands of the giant saguaro cactus and associated habitat.

Flora & Fauna

Saguaro seedlings are vulnerable to intense sun and frost, so they often grow in the shade of palo verde or mesquite trees, which

Gila monster

act as 'nurse trees.' Saguaros grow slowly, taking about 15 years to reach a foot in height, 50 years to reach 7 feet and almost a century before they begin to take on their typical many-armed appearance.

Saguaros are only part of the landscape. Many birds nest in holes in these giant cacti. Gila woodpeckers and flickers excavate the holes, which form hard scar tissue on the inside of the plant, protecting the nest and the cactus. In subsequent years, owls, cactus wrens, kestrels and other birds may use these nests, which are often 20°F cooler than the outside. On the ground, many other kinds of cacti and a variety of vegetation is home to javelinas, desert tortoises, gila monsters, jackrabbits, coyotes, kangaroo rats, rattlesnakes, roadrunners, tarantulas and many other animals.

Late April is a good time to visit the park, when the saguaros begin blossoming with lovely white flowers – Arizona's state flower. By June and July, the flowers give way to ripe red fruit that has been traditionally picked by desert Indians; they use them both for food (as fruit and jam) and to make saguaro wine.

Saguaro East

Also called the Rincon Mountain District, this larger and older section of the park encompasses both the desert and mountain country of the Rincon Mountains and their western slopes. The saguaro grows up to about 4000 feet and then the scenery gives way first to oak woodland, then pine and finally, at elevations of more than 7000 feet, to mixed conifer forest.

Information The park is open daily from 7 am to sunset. The visitor center (☎ 733-5153) at the park entrance is open from 8:30 am to 5 pm daily except Christmas and is the only place with drinking water. It has a bookstore, information, an audio-visual display and exhibits. Ranger-led programs are offered, especially in the cooler months. The park is 15 miles east of downtown along Old Spanish Trail. Admission is $6 per private vehicle or $3 for walkers, cyclists or bus passengers; all passes are honored.

Cactus Forest Drive This paved, one-way, 8-mile loop road gives access to picnic areas (no water), nature trails of varying lengths and views of the saguaro forest. The road is accessible to all vehicles, including bicycles. A 2½-mile trail off the drive is suitable for mountain bikes only.

Hiking & Backpacking Of almost 130 miles of trails in Saguaro East, the easiest is the quarter-mile, wheelchair-accessible Desert Ecology Nature Trail, which leaves from the north end of Cactus Forest Drive. Progressively longer trails strike off into the park, including the Tanque Verde Ridge Trail, which climbs steeply from the south end of Cactus Forest Drive up into the Rincon Mountains, where the highest elevation is Mica Mountain at 8666 feet. There are six designated backcountry camping areas, most of which lack water. Campers must have permits, which are available at the visitor center at no charge up to two months ahead of your chosen date. Permits must be picked up by noon on the day you start hiking to allow time to reach the first camping area. Horses are also permitted on trails.

Saguaro West

Also called the Tucson Mountain District, this is just north of the Arizona-Sonora Desert Museum, and a drive through the area can be combined with a visit to the ASDM. Saguaro West is much lower than Saguaro East, with the highest point being 4687-foot Wasson Peak.

Information The visitor center (☎ 733-5158) on Kinney Rd, 2 miles northwest of the ASDM, is open 8:30 am to 5 pm daily except Christmas, with similar facilities to Saguaro East. The two paved roads through the park (Kinney Rd and Picture Rocks Rd) are open 24 hours a day. Unpaved loop roads and hiking trailheads close at sunset, however. Admission is free but plans are to adopt Saguaro East's fee structure.

Bajada Loop Drive The unpaved, 6-mile Bajada Loop Dr begins 1½ miles west of the visitor center and can normally be negotiated by ordinary vehicles. Apart from fine views of cactus forests, there are several picnic areas as well as trailheads.

Hiking Short, paved nature trails are near the visitor center. Longer trails climb several miles into the Tucson Mountains and give access to Indian petroglyphs as well as admirable views. The King Canyon trailhead, just outside the park boundary almost opposite the ASDM, is open until 10 pm. Although night hiking is permitted, camping is not. The nearest campground is the Gilbert Ray Campground about 4 miles southeast of the park (see Places to Stay – Camping, earlier in the chapter).

Tucson to Phoenix

Most people barrel through from city to city along I-10 in a couple of hours. It's not a particularly attractive ride except for the view of Picacho Peak. There are several worthwhile side trips, however, for travelers with a little time.

PICACHO PEAK STATE PARK
Picacho Peak (3374 feet) is an obvious landmark on the west side of I-10 exit 219, 40 miles northwest of Tucson. The westernmost 'battle' of the American Civil War was fought here, with the Confederate forces killing two or three Union soldiers. The Confederates then retreated to Tucson and dispersed, knowing their forces would soon be greatly outnumbered.

The state park (☎ 466-3183) provides camping, picnicking and two steep hiking trails to the summit. Fixed ropes and ladders are used to aid hikers, but no technical climbing is involved. It's about 2 miles and 1500 feet up to the top. Day use is $5 per vehicle (up to four passengers).

The *campground* has 95 sites open year-round on a first-come, first-served basis. Rates are $10 for tents, $15 for hookups. Drinking water and showers are available. The campground's 1800-foot elevation makes this a hot stop in summer.

CASA GRANDE & AROUND
The modern town of Casa Grande is a few miles northwest of the I-10 interchange with I-8, on Hwy 238. The archaeological site of Casa Grande (described below) is about 30 miles away.

Indian dances and a powwow are held annually during **O'odham Tash** (☎ 836-4723, fax 426-1731), an annual celebration in mid-February.

Some cheap motels and chains line Florence Blvd, west of exit 194.

Casa Grande Ruins National Monument
Once a major Hohokam Indian village covering about 1 sq mile, this site was abandoned around AD 1350 and little remains today except for one building, the Casa Grande (big house).

The Casa Grande is quite imposing. About 30 or 40 feet high, it is built of mud walls several feet thick. The mud was made from caliche, the rock-hard soil of the area that is the bane of the modern gardener. A huge amount of work went into constructing the building, which is the most unusual Hohokam structure standing today. Rain and human intrusion have caused some damage, but the general structure of the building remains clear. To prevent further erosion, Casa Grande has been capped by a large metal awning built in the 1930s, an effective, if incongruous, preservation tool. You cannot enter the building itself, though the outside is quite impressive.

The site, about 20 miles north of I-10 exit 212 or 14 miles east of I-10 exit 185, has a visitor center (☎ 723-3172) with a good small museum explaining the general history of the Hohokam and this ruin in particular. There are picnic tables, drinking water and a bookstore, but no overnight facilities. The monument is open daily except Christmas, from 8 am to 5 pm. Admission is $3 per person and passes are honored.

Florence
☎ 520 • pop 17,054 • elevation 1493 feet
Founded in 1866, this is one of Arizona's earliest Anglo towns and is the home of the

Arizona State Prison, which replaced Yuma's notorious prison in 1909. The visitor center (☎ 868-4331), 330 Butte, is open weekdays 9 am to 3 pm, and has a brochure describing some of the historic buildings. The most interesting is the 1878 adobe brick courthouse (with assorted later additions) in McFarland Historical State Park (☎ 868-5216), Main at Ruggles Ave, which offers exhibits about Florence's past. Hours are 8 am to 5 pm, Thursday to Monday; admission is $2; $1 for 12- to 17-year-olds.

Gila River Arts & Crafts Center

This is named for the Gila River Indian Reservation, Arizona's earliest reservation, established in 1859 for the Pima and Maricopa Indian tribes. Near I-10 exit 175, the center has a museum (☎ 315-3411) about the Pima and Maricopa tribes and a gift shop selling arts and crafts from several Southwestern tribes. Hours are 8 am to 5 pm. A simple restaurant serves up mainly American food along with a few Indian items.

West of Tucson

Hwy 86 heads west of Tucson toward some of the driest parts of the Sonora Desert. Much of the land is part of the Tohono O'odham Indian Reservation, the second largest in the country, though the reservation itself has little of tourist interest. Highlights of a trip out west are the Kitt Peak Observatory and the Organ Pipe Cactus National Monument.

BUENOS AIRES NATIONAL WILDLIFE REFUGE LOOP

From Robles Junction, on Hwy 86 about 20 miles west of Tucson, Hwy 286 goes south to the 175-sq-mile Buenos Aires National Wildlife Refuge, good for grassland birding with an ongoing project to reintroduce the masked bobwhite, which became extinct in Arizona about a century ago. The refuge is open daily during the daylight hours, and guided tours are occasionally offered. Backpacking and overnight camping are permitted at about 100 sites,

none of which have facilities. Information is available from Buenos Aires NWR Visitor Center (☎ 823-4251) open 7 am to 4 pm daily.

A few miles east of the refuge is the little village of **Arivaca** with several buildings dating from the 1880s. There is a café but no motel. From Arivaca, you can return to Tucson via the paved road to Arivaca Junction and then I-19, the quickest way, or take the unpaved **Ruby Road** (Hwy 289) to Nogales. This is a scenic route with plenty of border history. The road is passable to ordinary cars in dry weather but should be avoided in rain; it passes through the Coronado National Forest (see Nogales later) where you can camp almost anywhere. There are some small lakes along the way that attract wildlife.

The Buenos Aires NWR and Ruby Road make an interesting trip, which few people make, so you'll get away from the crowds.

TOHONO O'ODHAM INDIAN RESERVATION

This large desert and mountain reservation of almost 4500 sq miles is home to the Tohono O'odham, traditionally an agricultural people who still practice farming and, since the Spaniards introduced cattle, ranching as well. Maize, beans and cotton are important crops and naturally growing saguaro fruit is harvested for jams and a kind of wine. Mesquite beans and other naturally occurring plants are also harvested. There are small branches of the reservation around Mission San Xavier del Bac (see Around Tucson, earlier in this chapter) and just north of Gila Bend, but the majority of the land is in the deserts beginning about 25 miles west of Tucson.

Heading west out of Tucson, you'll see humpbacked Baboquivari Peak (7730 feet), the highest in this area and sacred to the tribe. To its north is Kitt Peak (6875 feet), home of the observatory described below. The tribal capital, Sells, 60 miles west of Tucson on Hwy 86, has a couple of places to eat and some stores but no accommodations.

The Tohono O'odham have little interest in tourism except for casinos near Tucson. They are known for their fine basket work, which can be purchased from the gift shop at Kitt Peak and the Gu-Achi Trading Post at Quijotoa, on Hwy 86, 23 miles west of Sells.

The main event is the annual Tohono O'odham All-Indian Tribal Fair & Rodeo, which has been held for over 60 years, attracts Indians from many tribes and is open to the general public. The rodeo is the main attraction, but there are also dances, concerts, Indian food stands and basket work for sale. This is usually held in February. For information, call the Tucson Visitor Center or the Tribal Office (☎ 383-2221). Other events are held at the San Xavier Mission and the O'odham Tash Indian Celebration in Casa Grande in February.

KITT PEAK NATIONAL OBSERVATORY

From Tucson you can make out the white telescope domes on top of Kitt Peak, even though it is 40 miles as the crow flies.

This is the largest optical observatory in the world and includes 22 telescopes, one of which is a solar telescope used for studying the sun via a series of mirrors. The largest telescope has a diameter of 4 meters and is housed in a 19-story-high dome.

A visitor center (☎ 318-8726) with a museum, audio-visual presentations, gift shop, but no food, provides information.

Stargazing under clear desert skies

Guided tours, lasting about an hour and visiting two or three telescopes, leave daily at 10 am, 11:30 am and 1:30 pm. (You don't get to look through the telescopes.) Self-guided tours are available. Hours are 9 am to 3:45 pm daily except major holidays. A $2 donation is suggested. The nearly 6900-foot elevation often means snow in winter, which may close the steep road up the mountain.

Nightly public stargazing, limited to 20 participants, starts with a sunset snack and is followed by three hours of observation. Rates are $35, or $25 for students and seniors. This is very popular and should be booked well in advance. Call for details. website: www.noao.edu/outreach/kpoutreach .html

ORGAN PIPE CACTUS NATIONAL MONUMENT

This giant columnar cactus differs from the saguaro in that it branches from its base – both species are present in the monument, so you can compare them. Organ-pipe cacti are common in Mexico, but this national monument is one of the few places in the USA where they are commonly seen. The third species of columnar cactus found here (and nowhere else in the USA) is the senita, which, like the organ pipe, branches from the bottom but has fewer pleats in its branches, which are topped by the hairy white tufts that give the senita its nickname of 'old man's beard.'

The monument is mainly undisturbed Sonoran Desert habitat. Not only do three types of large columnar cacti grow here, but a profusion of other desert flora and fauna also thrive. In spring, in years that have the right combination of winter rains and temperatures, the monument can be carpeted with wildflowers (mid-February to April is the best time). Cacti flower at different times, particularly from late April to early July, although some species can flower in March or as late as October.

Many animals are present, but the heat and aridity force them to use survival strategies such as hiding out in a hole or burrow during the day. Therefore early morning and evening are the best times to look for wildlife. Walking around the desert by full moon or flashlight is another good way to catch things on the prowl, but wear boots and watch where you step.

The monument offers six hiking trails ranging from a 200-yard paved nature trail to strenuous climbs of over 4 miles. Cross-country hiking is also possible, but have a topographical map and a compass and know how to use them – a mistake out here is deadly if you get lost and run out of water. Two scenic loop drives of 21 and 53 miles start near the visitor center and are steep, winding and unpaved. They are passable to cars except after heavy rain, but RVs and trailers are not recommended. Other roads are passable only to 4WD vehicles. Carry extra water in your car in case of a breakdown. There are several picnic sites along the way, but no water.

Information

A visitor center (☎ 387-6849) on Hwy 85, 22 miles south of Why, is open 8 am to 5 pm daily and has information, drinking water, a bookstore, a small museum and a slide show. Ranger-led programs take place from about October to April. Admission to the monument is $5 per vehicle, or $3 per bike or bus passenger. All passes are honored. There is no charge to drive through the monument on Hwy 85 from Why to Lukeville.

Winter is the most pleasant season to visit. Summer temperatures soar above 100°F most days from June to August, although nights are pleasant, with lows typically 30°F lower than daytime highs. The summer monsoons make July to September the wettest months, although the rains tend to be of the brief, torrential variety and rarely stop anyone for more than an hour or two. Winter temperatures are pleasant, with January, the coolest month, experiencing average highs of 67°F and lows of 38°F.

Places to Stay

Over 200 sites at the campground by the visitor center cost $10 on a first-come, first-served basis and are often full by noon from mid-January through March. There is drinking water but no showers or RV hookups.

Free backcountry camping (no water) is only allowed with a permit obtainable at the visitor center.

AJO
☎ 520 • pop 3000 • elevation 1750 feet

Ajo (pronounced 'AH-ho') was once a major copper mining town; a mile-wide open-pit mine can be seen south of town. Falling copper prices closed the mine in 1985, many miners left and housing costs dropped, attracting retirees who revived the town. The town plaza, built in Spanish-colonial style, has several pleasant restaurants and shops.

The chamber of commerce (☎ 387-7742), near the plaza, is open 9 am to 4 pm from Monday to Friday, with reduced summer hours. The **Ajo Historical Society Museum** (☎ 387-7105), in an attractive church close to the copper mine, south of town, is usually open in the afternoon except in summer.

A few miles west of Ajo is one of the most rugged regions in the country, the **Cabeza Prieta National Wildlife Refuge**. You must have a permit from NWR headquarters (☎ 387-6483), 1611 N 2nd Ave, to visit the area. The refuge was set aside as desert bighorn sheep and pronghorn habitat. This is 135 sq miles of wilderness, with no facilities and only rudimentary dirt roads. The summer heat is, literally, a killer.

Places to Stay

La Siesta RV Resort & Motel (☎ 387-6569, 2561 N Hwy 85) has RV hookups and 11 simple rooms from $35 to $60. The little *Marine Resort Motel & RV Park* (☎ 387-7626, 1966 N Hwy 85) has 20 large, clean motel rooms with refrigerators and coffeemakers for about $50 to $65 in winter, less in summer. RV hookups are available.

The 1925 *Guest House Inn B&B* (☎ 387-6133, 700 Guest House Rd) has four comfortable rooms decorated in a Southwestern motif and with private baths for about $80 a double. The *Mine Manager's House Inn B&B* (☎ 387-6505, 601 Greenway Dr), in one of Ajo's earliest houses (built 1919), is situated on a hill with fine views. The five rooms and suites, all with private bath, run $75 to $110 double. There is a hot tub.

South of Tucson

I-19 due south of Tucson heads to Nogales, on the Mexican border 62 miles away. The distances to freeway exits and speed limits are all in kilometers here. The route follows the Santa Cruz River Valley and has been a historical trading route since pre-Hispanic times.

GREEN VALLEY & AROUND
☎ 520 • pop 26,000 • elevation 2900 feet
Green Valley is a retirement community spread around I-19 exits 69, 65 and 63. The chamber of commerce (☎ 625-7575, 800-858-5872), just west of exit 63, is open year-round 9 am to 5 pm weekdays, and 9 am to noon on Saturdays from September to May. A huge open-pit copper mine can be seen west of the freeway near here.

Asarco Mineral Discovery Center
Asarco, one of the nation's largest producers of non-ferrous metals, operates four copper mines in Arizona, including the Mission Complex open-pit mine between Tucson and Green Valley. The discovery center (☎ 625-7513) is a mining museum opened in 1998. Hours are 9 am to 5 pm Tuesday to Saturday; admission is free. Open-pit mine tours lasting one hour cost $6 for adults, $5 for seniors and $4 for five-to 12-year-olds. The last tour leaves at 3:40 pm. The center is just west of I-19 exit 80, and the mine is 4 miles farther west.

Titan Missile Museum
During the Cold War, the USA had many Intercontinental Ballistic Missiles armed with nuclear warheads and ready to fly within a few seconds of receiving a launch order. Fortunately, that order never came. With the SALT II treaty, all the missiles and their underground launch sites were destroyed except for this one, which has been kept as a national historic landmark. The nuclear warhead was removed, but the rest

remains as it was during the tense 1960s and '70s, when the push of a button could have started a cataclysmic nuclear war.

The public can tour the entire complex. The museum (☎ 574-9658/0462) is west of I-19 exit 69. Guided tours (reservations recommended, ☎ 625-7736 during business hours) leave every half-hour 9 am to 4 pm daily except Thanksgiving and Christmas, November to April. From May to October the museum is closed on Monday and Tuesday. Tours involve stair climbing, but wheelchair-accessible tours can be arranged. Admission is $7.50 for adults, $6.50 for those over 62 or with military ID and $4 for seven-to 12-year-olds. Discount combination admissions with the Pima Air & Space Museum in Tucson are offered.

Madera Canyon Recreation Area
This canyon gives access to hiking trails into the Santa Ritas, including two trails up the biggest peak, Mt Wrightson (9453 feet), in the Coronado National Forest (the ranger station is in Nogales, ☎ 281-2296). These trails are 5.4 and 8.1 miles respectively, and there are numerous others. The riparian habitat in the canyon attracts an unusually large variety and number of birds, and this is one of the most popular places for birding in southeastern Arizona. Parking may be difficult to find, especially on weekends, when an early arrival is essential. Madera Canyon is about 13 miles east of I-19 exit 63. Day use is $5 per vehicle. The elevation is a pleasant pine-shaded 5200 feet.

The USFS runs the 13 campsites at *Bog Springs Campground* on a first-come, first-served basis. There is water but no showers or hookups. The fee is $8. There is also a USFS-run picnic area.

Santa Rita Lodge (☎ 625-8746) has eight rooms and four larger cabins, all with kitchenettes, which are popular with birders and usually booked far in advance from March to May. Rates are $78 for rooms and $93 for cabins. The lodge has hiking information and runs birding tours ($12) and other educational activities.
website: www.santaritalodge.com

Whipple Observatory

A new paved road leads up to the observatory from I-19 exit 56. The multi-mirror telescope atop Mt Hopkins at 8550 feet is one of the world's largest and can be visited only by a bus tour ($7; $2.50 for six- to 12-year-olds) beginning at the visitor center at 9 am on Monday, Wednesday and Friday from mid-March through November. Tours last six hours and are limited to 26 participants by reservation only (☎ 670-5707).

Ten miles below the observatory, a visitor center shows a film and has exhibits about the telescope (admission is free). The visitor center is open 8:30 am to 4:30 pm weekdays. website: http://linmax.sao.arizona.edu/help/FLWO/whipple.html

TUBAC & AROUND

☎ 520 • pop 1200 • elevation 3200 feet

Tubac is one of the main arts and crafts villages in the Southwest and is also among the most historic. If history and/or crafts shopping interest you, Tubac is definitely a worthwhile stop.

There was a Pima Indian village here before Spanish missionaries arrived in the late 17th century, followed by settlers in the 18th century. A Pima revolt in 1751, which the Indians lost, led to the building of Tubac Presidio in 1752, which fell into disuse when the garrison moved to Tucson in 1776. A Spanish/Pima garrison was established a few years later. Tubac became part of Mexico after 1821, but, in 1848, Apache Indians forced the settlers out again. After the Gadsden Purchase of 1853, Americans revived mining operations and Tubac briefly became Arizona's largest town in 1860. Activities ceased during the Civil War, and then afterwards Tubac became a sleepy farming community. After an art school opened in 1948, Tubac began its transformation into a major artists' community.

Information

Tubac is east of I-19 exit 34. It's a small village and is easily visited on foot. The chamber of commerce (☎ 398-2704) answers questions during the week or online at www.tubacaz.com. Most of the approximately 80 galleries, art studios and crafts stores in town have a map showing the location of the shopping district and shops, most of which are open from 10 am to 5 pm daily, year-round.

Tubac Presidio State Historic Park & Museum

The presidio (see above) now lies in ruins, but you can see the 1885 schoolhouse and other historic buildings nearby. The exhibits in the museum (☎ 398-2252) describe the history of Tubac. Hours are 8 am to 5 pm daily except Christmas, and admission is $2; $1 for seven- to 14-year-olds. The park is at the east end of Tubac and has picnicking facilities.

Tumacácori National Historical Park

Three miles south of Tubac at I-19 exit 29 are the well-preserved ruins of the Tumacácori (pronounced 'too-ma-CA-co-ree') Franciscan Church, built in 1800 but never completed. Although abandoned in the late 1800s, the church was protected as a national monument in 1908. It gives the visitor an idea of the Spanish history of the area. A visitor center (☎ 398-2341) features a museum, gift shop and picnic area. Mexican and Indian artists demonstrate their techniques on weekends. Hours are 8 am to 5 pm daily except Thanksgiving and Christmas. Admission is $3 per person over 16, and all passes are honored.

Special Events

The Tubac Arts & Crafts festival is held in early February and lasts several days. Anza Days on the third weekend in October features historical reenactments and cultural events.

A mass is said in the Tumacácori Church on Christmas Eve, and a couple of times a year besides. Call the visitor center for information. An Indian arts and crafts fair is held in Tumacácori in early December.

Places to Stay & Eat

Tubac Country Inn B&B (☎ 398-3178), at Plaza Rd and Burruel in downtown Tubac,

ARIZONA

has four large rooms with private baths (two with kitchenettes) opening onto a porch and garden. Rates are $85. The *Amado Territory Inn* (☎ 398-8684, 888-398-8684,), near I-19 exit 48, has nine non-smoking rooms decorated in territorial (19th-century ranch) style, all with private baths and some with patios or decks. Rates are $95 to $135; see the inn and adjoining restaurant online at www.amado-territory-inn.com. The chamber of commerce has details of several other B&Bs.

Tubac Golf Resort (☎ 398-2211, 800-848-7893) is a mile north of Tubac. Apart from the 18-hole golf course, there is a tennis court, pool, spa, and a good restaurant and bar. The 45 rooms and suites are all spacious and some have fireplaces, living rooms or kitchenettes attached. Winter rates are $140 to $195, depending on the size of the room. Summer rates are $80 to $130.
website: www.tubacgolfresort.com

The restaurants adjoining the Amado Territory Inn and the Tubac Golf Resort are both good. There are several quaint eateries in Tubac.

NOGALES & AROUND
☎ 520 • pop 20,878 • elevation 3865 feet
Nogales (pronounced 'noh-GAH-lez'), Arizona, and Nogales, Sonora, are towns separated only by the USA/Mexico border. You can easily walk from one into the other and many visitors come to shop for Mexican goods. The twin towns are locally called *Ambos Nogales* or 'Both Nogales.' Nogales is Arizona's most important gateway into Mexico and also the major port of entry for the agricultural produce Mexico sells to the USA and Canada.

The Greyhound Terminal (☎ 287-5628), 35 N Terrace Ave, has buses about once an hour during the day and early evening to Tucson ($6.50).

Information
Steep hills, a dividing railroad, one-way streets, a confusing street system and poor local maps make getting around Nogales difficult for visitors. It's not a big town, though, so relax and you'll eventually find where you want to go.

The chamber of commerce (☎ 287-3685), in Kino Park off Grand Ave, is open 8 am to 5 pm weekdays. Other services include the Mexican Consulate (☎ 287-2521), 571 Grand Ave; US Immigration (☎ 287-3609) at the border; Coronado National Forest Ranger Station (☎ 281-2296), near I-19 exit 12; library (☎ 287-3343), 518 Grand Ave; post office (☎ 287-9246), 300 N Morley Ave; hospital (☎ 287-2771), 1171 W Target Range Rd; and police (☎ 287-9111), 777 Grand Ave.

Pimeria Alta Historical Society Museum
This historical museum (☎ 287-4621), in the old town hall (built in 1914) at 136 Grand Ave, gives a good introduction to the area. Hours are 10 am to 4 pm, Thursday to Saturday; admission is free.

Visiting Mexico
Most visitors shop for a few hours and perhaps have a meal in Nogales, Sonora (Mexico). Park on the US side (many lots around Crawford and Terrace Ave charge $4 a day) and walk over into the Mexican shopping district. US dollars and credit cards are accepted and prices are good (though not much cheaper than in Arizona), but the quality varies so shop around. Bargaining is certainly possible. All kinds of Mexican goods are available, such as pottery, stoneware, silver, tin, glass, weavings, leather, basketry and woodcarvings.

From Nogales, buses and trains continue farther into Mexico. Drivers need car insurance, available from Sanborn's (☎ 281-1873), 2921 Grand Ave.

Also see the 'Crossing the Border' boxed text.

Places to Stay
The USFS-operated *Upper/Lower White Rock* campgrounds are on Peña Blanca Lake, 9 miles west of I-19 exit 12, north of Nogales. There are 15 sites with water (but no showers or hookups) available year-round on a first-come, first-served basis. Sites are $8 and there is fishing and boating.

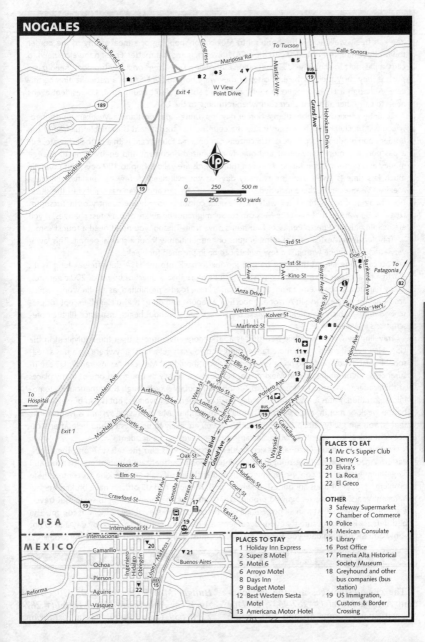

NOGALES

PLACES TO EAT
4 Mr C's Supper Club
11 Denny's
20 Elvira's
21 La Roca
22 El Greco

OTHER
3 Safeway Supermarket
7 Chamber of Commerce
10 Police
14 Mexican Consulate
15 Library
16 Post Office
17 Pimeria Alta Historical
   Society Museum
18 Greyhound and other
   bus companies (bus
   station)
19 US Immigration,
   Customs & Border
   Crossing

PLACES TO STAY
1 Holiday Inn Express
2 Super 8 Motel
5 Motel 6
6 Arroyo Motel
8 Days Inn
9 Budget Motel
12 Best Western Siesta
   Motel
13 Americana Motor Hotel

ARIZONA

Crossing the Border

You can freely walk across the border into Mexico for shopping or a meal at any of the border towns. Returning from Mexico into the USA, however, is another matter. Foreign travelers need to carry a passport to show the US immigration authorities. US citizens on a day trip don't need passports if they carry their birth certificates (if they were born in the USA) or a naturalization certificate. Although a US driver's license will sometimes suffice, don't count on it. US resident aliens need to carry their resident alien card when returning to the USA.

To enter Mexico for more than a border day trip, bring a passport and a Mexican tourist card, which will be checked a few miles inside the country. The tourist card is available for free at the border upon producing a passport. (US citizens can obtain a tourist card with a birth certificate, but a passport is a more convenient and quickly recognized document and enables you to change money and perform other tasks.) Mexican tourist cards are valid for up to 180 days, but normally much less time is given. Ask for as many days as you will need. A few nationalities require a Mexican visa; recently, these included some European, African and Asian nationals, but the situation changes. If in doubt, check with the Mexican consul in your home country or in Tucson or Nogales. Be warned that even the Mexican consul might not be aware of the latest changes. If you are heading just to Puerto Peñasco, four hours drive from Tucson, you don't need a tourist card.

Travelers into Mexico cannot bring in guns or ammunition without a special permit. This law is very strict – someone with just a few bullets can be imprisoned for weeks.

You can bring almost anything bought in Mexico back into the USA duty-free as long as it's worth a total of less than $400 and doesn't include more than a quart of booze or 200 cigarettes. Many handicrafts are exempt from the $400 limit. Fresh food is prohibited, as are fireworks, which are illegal for personal use in Arizona. Importing weapons and drugs is also illegal, except for prescribed drugs, which are cheaper in Mexico – some visitors without health insurance fill their prescriptions in Mexico.

Traveling by Mexican public transport is a little more adventurous than the equivalent in the USA. However, it's also much more far-reaching and you can get almost anywhere on a bus at reasonable cost. If you prefer to bring your own car, you should get Mexican car insurance; US car insurance is not normally valid in Mexico. Car insurance can easily be bought at one of many places at the border (Sanborn's in Nogales and Tucson are reputable) or through the American Automobile Association. Rates are $10 to $15 a day for comprehensive coverage, but if you buy insurance by the week or month, rates drop substantially. Remember: Mexico's legal system is Napoleonic, that is, you are guilty until proven innocent, and you are likely to be arrested and held after a car accident unless you can show Mexican car insurance covering the accident.

Nogales is the main Arizona/Mexico border crossing and is also the safest. Along the southeastern Arizona border, drug smuggling and international car theft are frequent occurrences, and illegal immigration is a concern. Immigration and customs officials are working to control these problems. Not all officials are honest, however; both Mexican and US officers have broken the law in recent years. This is a recognized problem that both countries are working to solve, but travelers should be aware that a small percentage of officials on both sides of the border are corrupt. The best defense is to make sure that your documents are perfectly in order, to travel by day and to not allow officials to intimidate you for any reason. It is most unlikely that you will have any problems.

The cheapest places are the independent **Arroyo Motel** (☎ 287-4637, 20 Doe St), with basic rooms around $30, or the **Budget Motel** (☎ 287-2200, 820 Grand Ave). The **Americana Motor Hotel** (☎ 287-7211, 639 Grand Ave), has a restaurant, pool, and 96 good-sized older double rooms from $50 to $60. Otherwise, you have a choice of *chain motels*, with a Motel 6, Super 8 Motel and Holiday Inn Express near I-19, exit 4, and a Best Western and Days Inn on Grand Ave.

Places to Eat
Mariposa Rd east of I-19 has the usual assortment of fast-food restaurants and a supermarket.

The best restaurant in Nogales is *Mr C's Supper Club* (☎ 281-9000, 282 W View Point Dr). Reserve ahead for a window seat with a view. Guaymas shrimp is the house specialty, and American steak and seafood are served from 11:30 am to 11 pm, Monday to Saturday, with dinner entrées mainly in the teens including a visit to the salad bar.

Several Mexican restaurants are found along Grand Ave. Diners on the Mexican side have a reasonable choice of Mexican restaurants. Good choices are *Elvira's (Calle Obregón 1)*, with meals under $10 and a free margarita thrown in; the similar *El Greco (Calle Obregón 152);* and the slightly pricier *La Roca (Calle Elías 91)*. These clean places have Mexican atmosphere designed with the American visitor in mind.

PATAGONIA & AROUND
☎ 520 • pop 881 • elevation 4050 feet
Patagonia and smaller Sonoita (elevation 4970 feet), 12 miles northeast, are ranching centers and the hub of Arizona's wine country. Both towns were important railway stops, but since the line closed in 1962, tourism and the arts have helped keep them thriving. Nearby grasslands were the surprising setting of the musical *Oklahoma*.

Information
Patagonia has area information at its visitor center (☎ 394-0060, 888-794-0060), 307 McKeown Ave, in the Mariposa Book and gift shop, one block off Hwy 82. In front, the town center is a tree-filled park with the 1900 train depot, now the town hall. There is no hospital; call 911 in emergencies. Many places (including area restaurants) close on Monday and Tuesday.
website: www.patagoniaaz.com

Patagonia Lake State Park
A dam across Sonoita Creek forms this 2½-mile-long lake (elevation 3750 feet), about 7 miles southwest of Patagonia. The park (☎ 287-6965) is open year-round for camping, picnicking, walking, bird-watching, fishing, boating and swimming. A marina provides boat rentals (no motor boats) and supplies. The campground has showers and hookups and 100 plus sites available on a first-come, first-served basis. Rates are $5 for day use, $10 for camping and $15 with hookups.

Patagonia-Sonoita Creek Preserve
Managed by The Nature Conservancy, Sonoita Creek is the home of four endangered species of native fish, and the splendid riparian habitat along the creek attracts almost 300 species of birds, including rarities from Mexico. Birding is good year-round. March to September is the very best time, with peaks of migrants in late April and May, and in late August and September. Beware of insects in spring and summer (chiggers are bad in July and August!) and wear long pants and insect repellent.

Reach the preserve by going northwest on N 4th Ave in Patagonia, then south on Pennsylvania Ave, driving across a small creek. Visitors who aren't members of The Nature Conservancy are asked to donate $5. There is a visitor center (☎ 394-2400) and trails but no camping or picnicking facilities. The preserve is closed on Monday and Tuesday. From April through September hours are 6:30 am to 4 pm, from 7:30 am in other months. Guided tours are given at 9 am on Saturdays.

Wineries
Near tiny Elgin, a few miles east of Sonoita, the Village of Elgin Winery (☎ 455-9309) and Callaghan Vineyards (☎ 455-5322) advertise tours and tastings daily.

Special Events

The Sonoita Quarter Horse Show is the oldest in the country and runs in early June. Sonoita is home of the Santa Cruz County Fair & Rodeo Grounds with a rodeo over Labor Day weekend and county fair over the fourth weekend in September. Call for these and other events (☎ 455-5553). The Fall Festival, second weekend of October, is Patagonia's largest event, with arts, crafts, music and food.

Places to Stay & Eat

Patagonia has a hotel, guest ranch and B&Bs. Sonoita has the best restaurants, with oft-changing hours. Call.

The *Stage Stop Inn* (☎ 394-2211, 800-923-2211, 303 W McKeown) in Patagonia is a modern motel with a Western facade. Over 40 rooms are $70 a double or $80 with a kitchenette, and there is a small pool, restaurant (closed Tuesday in summer) and bar.

The *Circle Z Ranch* (☎ 394-2525, 888-854-2525) is a working cattle ranch a few miles to the southwest of Patagonia. From November to mid-May it offers horseback-riding vacations with a three-night minimum. Accommodations are in rustic but comfortable rooms and cabins, and all meals are provided. Rates are about $800 to $1000 per person for a week, including riding, though families can arrange package discounts.
website: www.circlez.com

The *Duquesne House* (☎ 394-2732, 357 Duquesne St), inside one of Patagonia's first buildings, is the town's longest established B&B. Six old-fashioned units with

private bath are $75 a double. The visitor center can suggest half a dozen other options.

Eat at the *Velvet Elvis* (☎ 394-2102, 292 Hwy 82) in Patagonia, which does include a velvet Elvis among its funky artwork and serves designer pizzas, soups and salads. Outdoor tables are available; they close on Tuesdays.

In Sonoita, the non-smoking *Sonoita Inn* (☎ 455-5935) has 18 rooms from $125 to $140, including continental breakfast. The inn is a celebration of western living, with a decidedly horsey bent; its website is www.sonoitainn.com. Next door, the *Steak-Out* (☎ 455-5205, 3235 Hwy 82), will please carnivores with meals ranging from 1/3 lb burgers for $7 to 2 lb porterhouse steaks for $31. They serve dinner daily and weekend lunches, and feature live entertainment on weekends.

Karen's Wine Country Cafe (☎ 455-5282, 3266 Hwy 82) serves a limited but luscious menu of gourmet meals made with fresh ingredients, many of which they grow themselves. Eat lunch Tuesday to Sunday, dinner Thursday to Saturday. Lunches are about $8, most dinner entrées are in the teens, or opt for the four-course dinner (meat or fish choices), accompanied by three glasses of appropriate wines, for $40. Nearby, *Café Sonoita* (☎ 455-5278, 3280 Hwy 82) is cheaper, popular, and serves dinner Wednesday to Saturday and lunch Friday to Sunday.

Grasslands Natural Food Bakery (☎ 457-4770, 3119 Hwy 83) a half mile south of Sonoita, does great vegetarian options 8 am to 3 pm Wednesday to Sunday.

Southeastern Arizona

This is Cochise County – the land of Indians, cowboys, miners, outlaws, ranchers, gunslingers and Western lore. Today cattle ranches are still here, but mining operations have mainly closed down. The Huachuca Mountains and the Chiricahua Mountains provide scenic and natural beauty.

BENSON

☎ 520 • pop 4711 • elevation 3580 feet

This rural town grew around a railway halt during the 1880s. Today it is a quiet travelers' stop and the nearest to Kartchner Caverns. Book lovers will enjoy the Singing Wind Bookshop (☎ 568-2425), 700 W Singing Wind Rd, 2½ miles north of Benson along Ocotillo Ave and then through a green gate (close it after you). Open 9 am to 5 pm daily, this ranch-house/bookshop has thousands of books mainly with Southwest themes. The small San Pedro Valley Arts & Historical Museum (☎ 586-3070), at 5th and San Pedro St, is open 10 am to 4 pm Tuesday to Friday and 10 am to 2 pm Saturday October to April; 10 am to 2 pm Tuesday to Saturday in May, June, July and September (closed in August). Free admission.

The Greyhound (☎ 586-3141) bus stops at 680 W 4th St on its runs along I-10.

Information

The chamber of commerce (☎ 586-2842), 249 E 4th, is open 10 am to 5 pm Monday to Friday and 1 to 5 pm Saturday; visit www.bensonchamberaz.com. Other services include the library (☎ 586-9535), 300 S Huachuca; post office (☎ 586-3422), 260 S Ocotillo Ave; hospital (☎ 586-2261), 450 S Ocotillo Ave; and the police (☎ 586-2211), 360 S Gila St.

Places to Stay & Eat

Red Barn Campground (☎ 586-2035) and *KOA* (☎ 586-3977) are both just off Ocotillo Rd, north of I-10 exit 304. Red Barn charges $14 for tents and $18 for hookups. KOA charges $19 and up and has a pool, hot tub and mini-golf.

Six basic, old motels along 4th St (Hwy 80) offer rooms in the $30s including the *Benson Motel* (☎ 586-3346, 185 W 4th St), with old-fashioned car-garages and the *Sahara Motel* (☎ 586-3611, 1150 S Hwy 80), with kitchenettes and TVs but no phones. *Chain motels* include a Motel 6 and Holiday Inn Express by I-10, exit 302 (en route to Kartchner Caverns) and Days Inn, Super 8 and Best Western by exit 304.

The *Chute-Out Steakhouse* (☎ 586-7297, 161 S Huachuca) serves steaks and seafood and is locally popular; the steaks aren't great but are relatively cheap and the ribs are pretty tasty. It's open for lunch on weekdays and dinner daily. *Ruiz's* (☎ 586-2707, 687 W 4th St) is a decent little Mexican restaurant. *Galleano's* (☎ 586-3523, 601 W 4th St) is a homey place serving Italian and American breakfast, lunch and dinner.

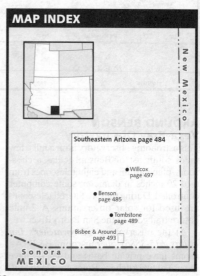

MAP INDEX

Southeastern Arizona page 484

● Willcox
page 497

● Benson
page 485

● Tombstone
page 489

Bisbee & Around
page 493

Sonora
MEXICO

New Mexico

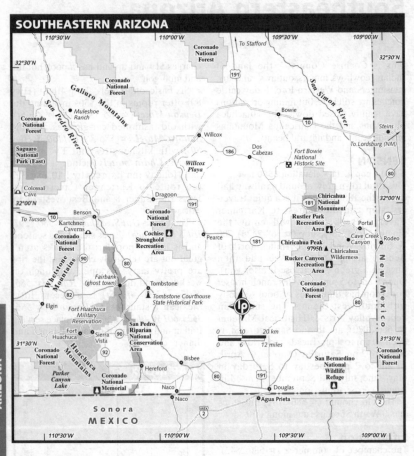

SOUTHEASTERN ARIZONA

AROUND BENSON
Vega-Bray Observatory

This astronomy observatory is on a hill a few miles southeast of Benson. It has a classroom, planetarium and eight telescopes from 6 to 20 inches in diameter, some computer controlled. During the day, filtered telescopes are used for solar observations. A 2-mile nature trail goes to the San Pedro River.

At the observatory is *Skywatcher's Inn* (☎/fax 615-3886), a four-room B&B. All rooms have private baths and guests have the use of two kitchens. Rates are $75 to $110 (one or two people). A four-hour guided introductory astronomy session for up to five people is $85, and other sky-watching packages for beginners to professionals can be arranged. Reservations are necessary.
website: www.communiverse.com/skywatcher

Amerind Foundation

This excellent museum and archaeology research center (☎ 586-3666) is in Dragoon, near I-10 exit 318, 15 miles east of Benson. The exhibits of Native American archaeology, history and culture cover many tribes from Alaska to South America, with a special focus on Southwestern Indians. Don't miss the Western-art gallery in a separate building, featuring a small but superb collection of artists of the past century including some Indian painters whose works have been exhibited internationally. Hours are 10 am to 4 pm daily September to May, closed Monday and Tuesday in summer and major holidays. Admission is $3; $2 for seniors and 12- to 18-year-olds.

Kartchner Caverns State Park

This spectacular limestone cave was almost completely undamaged and unexplored when discovered. The moist cave is 2½ miles long and the geological features within it are still growing. Cavers stumbled across it in 1974, but the location of this spectacular spot was kept secret until 1988, when state park protection could be assured. It opened to the public in 1999. State-of-the-art trail, lighting and misting systems protect this unique and fragile living cave. All equipment and tours have to go through air locks to minimize contaminating the cave, touted as one of the world's 10 best living caves. Thousands of examples of several different kinds of formations are seen, being formed imperceptibly, drop by drop, by water.

A visitor center introduces visitors to the cave with a film and other exhibits. A half-mile wheelchair-accessible trail within the cave can be visited on guided tours only. Twenty-five daily tours (except Christmas) leave between 8:30 am and 4:40 pm, take 75 minutes, and are limited to 20 people. A new tour is in the planning stages. Admission to the park is $10 per vehicle and reserved guided tours cost $14, $6 for seven- to 13-year olds. Reservations (☎ 586-2283) are strongly recommended because the tours sell out months in advance, especially during the busy cooler months and holidays. Each morning, 100 walk-up tickets are available for that day. Cars begin lining up before

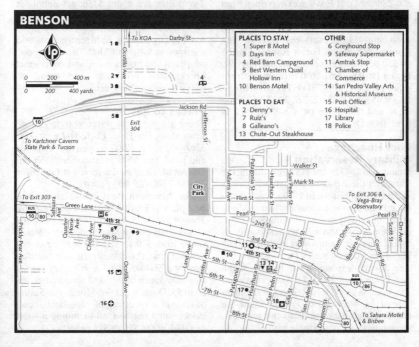

PLACES TO STAY	OTHER
1 Super 8 Motel	6 Greyhound Stop
3 Days Inn	9 Safeway Supermarket
4 Red Barn Campground	11 Amtrak Stop
5 Best Western Quail	12 Chamber of
Hollow Inn	Commerce
10 Benson Motel	14 San Pedro Valley Arts
	& Historical Museum
PLACES TO EAT	15 Post Office
2 Denny's	16 Hospital
7 Ruiz's	17 Library
8 Galleano's	18 Police
13 Chute-Out Steakhouse	

BENSON

To KOA — Darby St

Ocotillo Ave

0   200   400 m
0   200   400 yards

Jackson Rd

Jefferson St

Exit 304

To Kartchner Caverns State Park & Tucson

To Exit 303

Walker St

Mark St

To Exit 306 & Vega-Bray Observatory

City Park

Adams Ave

Patagonia St

Huachuca St

San Pedro St

Flint St

Pearl St

Pearl St

Sahuarita Ave

Green Lane

Quarter Horse Ave

Cholla Ave

4th St

5th St

2nd St

3rd St

4th St

5th St

6th St

7th St

8th St

Land Ave

Central Ave

Patagonia St

Huachuca St

San Pedro St

Gila St

Tawni Drive

Barbara St

Scott St

Orr Ave

County Rd

Dragoon St

San Carlos St

To Sahara Motel & Bisbee

Prickly Pear Ave

ARIZONA

dawn and visitors are often turned away even if they arrive before the park opens. Photography and all food and drinks are not allowed within the cave, which is a comfortable 70°F year-round.

The park (☎ 586-4100) is open from 7:30 am to 6 pm. Outside the visitor center is a wheelchair-accessible hummingbird garden trail, and 2- and 4½-mile hiking trails into the nearby Whetstone Mountains. A campground with showers and RV hookups has 60 sites for $20, including the $10 park entry fee. The park is 9 miles south of I-10, exit 302.

SIERRA VISTA
☎ 505 • pop 37,775 • elevation 4623 feet
Sierra Vista was founded in the 1950s as a service center for Fort Huachuca (see below) and makes a good base from which to visit Cochise County's attractions.

Information
The chamber of commerce (☎ 458-6940, 800-288-3861), 21 E Wilcox Dr, is open 8 am to 5 pm Monday to Friday, and from 9 am to 4 pm on Saturday; visit www.visitsierravista.com. Other services include the Coronado National Forest Ranger Station (☎ 378-0311), 7 miles south at 5990 Hwy 92; library (☎ 458-4225), 2600 E Tacoma St; post office (☎ 458-2540), 2300 E Fry Blvd; hospital (☎ 458-4641, 458-2300), 300 El Camino Real; and the police (☎ 458-3311), 911 N Coronado Dr.

Fort Huachuca Military Reservation
Founded in 1877 by the US Army during the wars with the Apaches, Fort Huachuca has had a colorful history. In 1913 it was a training ground for the famous Buffalo Soldiers, made up entirely of African American fighting men. Today, the military reservation is one of the largest employers in Arizona. The Fort Huachuca Museum (☎ 533-5736) has free displays explaining the history of the fort. Hours are 9 am to 4 pm weekdays and 1 to 4 pm on weekends. Register at the main gate at the west end of Fry Blvd and the guard will give directions to the museum, three miles west of the main gate.

Places to Stay
Several independent motels in the $30s are found along Fry Blvd, including the **Western Motel** (☎ 458-4303, 43 W Fry Blvd), which has a microwave and refrigerator in every room. The **Motel 6** (☎ 459-5035, 1551 E Fry Blvd) has 103 rooms in the $30s. Other **chain motels** in the $45 to $90 range include a Super 8, Best Western and Comfort Inn & Suites.

Sun Canyon Inn (☎ 459-0610, 800-822-6966, 260 N Garden Ave), just off Fry Blvd, has a pool and Jacuzzi; microwaves and refrigerators in every room; continental breakfast; and charges $66 for a double; visit www.suncanyoninn.com. The **Windemere Hotel** (☎ 459-5900, 800-825-4656, 2047 S Hwy 92) has a pool, Jacuzzi, lounge, restaurant with room service and 149 good-size rooms with coffeemakers, microwaves, refrigerators and hairdriers. Rates are about $90, including hot breakfast buffet and complimentary evening cocktails. Two suites are about $150; get details at www.windemere-hotel.com. **Sierra Suites** (☎ 459-4221, 800-852-2430, 391 E Fry Blvd) has 100 large rooms with refrigerators and microwaves for about $100. There is a pool, whirlpool and fitness room, and continental breakfast is provided; send email to sierrasuites@earthlink.net.

Places to Eat
There are plenty of restaurants to choose from along Fry Blvd. **Caffé-O-Le** (☎ 458-6261, 400 E Fry Blvd) is open for breakfast and lunch and has a great coffee selection. Decent Mexican food is served at **La Casita** (☎ 458-2376, 465 E Fry Blvd).

For American steak and seafood, the best place is 7 miles south at **The Mesquite Tree** (☎ 378-2758, 6398 S Hwy 92), open for dinner daily except Sunday. Dinner entrées range from $10 to $18. For a more continental menu, the casually elegant **Outside Inn** (☎ 378-4645, 4907 S Hwy 92) serves weekday lunch salads and sandwiches for $6 to $8. Dinners, served Monday to Saturday, cover a spectrum of veal, lamb, beef, chicken and seafood, all including a soup or salad, in the $10 to $18 range.

Getting There & Around

America West Express flies several times daily between Phoenix and Sierra Vista's Fort Huachuca Airport. Golden State (☎ 458-3471), a Greyhound subsidiary at 28 Fab Ave, has buses on Douglas-Bisbee-Sierra Vista-Tucson-Phoenix runs.

Enterprise and Monty's (☎ 458-2665) rent cars. AA Cab (☎ 378-2100) and ABC Cab (☎ 458-8429) have 24-hour taxi service.

AROUND SIERRA VISTA
Ramsey Canyon Preserve

At 5500-feet elevation in the Huachuca Mountains south of Sierra Vista, this Nature Conservancy–owned preserve is famous throughout the birding world as one of the best places in the USA to see up to 14 species of hummingbirds. The highest numbers are seen from April to September, but there are some year-round. Trogons and other rarities from Mexico are also seen in the wooded riparian habitat in the canyon in summer. Also protected is the Ramsey Canyon leopard frog, found nowhere else in the world. Visitors are quite likely to see deer, and sightings of coatis, ringtails, javelinas, mountain lions and black bears are reported regularly.

Entrance to the preserve (☎ 378-2785, 378-2640) is limited by the 23 spaces of the parking lot, at the end of a very narrow and winding road along which parking is illegal. There's no room for RVs or trailers. Spaces are first-come, first-served.

Preserve hours are 8 am to 5 pm March to October and from 9 am in other months; closed major holidays. A $5 donation is requested from non–Nature Conservancy members, $3 for members. A visitor center features a gift- and bookshop, and hummingbird feeders are hung on the grounds to attract the birds. Two trails lead up into the canyon. The 0.7-mile nature loop is quite easy, and the longer Hamburg Trail climbs high into the Huachucas. Register at the visitor center to use the trails. At 9 am Tuesday, Thursday and Saturday March to October, guided nature walks are offered.
website: www.tncarizona.org

For overnight stays, the *Ramsey Canyon Inn B&B* (☎ 378-3010) has two housekeeping cabins (up to four people, $158) and six B&B rooms (two people, $121 to $145). These are often booked a year ahead for the peak summer season, and reservations are always necessary. Minimum two-night stays are required in the busy season. If the inn is full, Sierra Vista is just 10 miles away. No smoking is allowed in the inn or the preserve.

Coronado National Memorial

This commemorates the first major European expedition into the Southwest when Francisco Vásquez de Coronado, accompanied by hundreds of Spanish soldiers and Mexican Indians, passed through in 1540 on his way from Mexico City, searching for gold in the Seven Cities of Cibola. Coronado is credited with introducing horses to the Indians.

The memorial is at the southern end of the Huachuca Mountains on the Mexican border, 20 miles south of Sierra Vista on Hwy 92. The visitor center (☎ 366-5515), open daily except Thanksgiving and Christmas, features exhibits on Coronado's expedition and the area's wildlife. The memorial itself is open during daylight hours and admission is free.

The road from Sierra Vista to the visitor center is paved. West from the visitor center (at 5230 feet), a graveled road climbs the 6575-foot-high Montezuma Pass, offering great views. A 3.3-mile hiking trail also links these two points. From the pass, a 0.7-mile trail climbs to Coronado Peak (6864 feet) with great views into Mexico. West of the pass, the road continues through the Coronado National Forest emerging at Nogales, about 50 miles away. This road is passable to cars except after rain.

The memorial has no camping, but you can camp for free almost anywhere in the Coronado National Forest to the west. *Lakeview* is a developed USFS campground at **Parker Canyon Lake**, reached by driving west from the memorial or south from Sonoita on Hwy 83. The lake has a marina

ARIZONA

(☎ 455-5847) with boat rentals and fishing supplies. A five-mile hiking trail encircles the lake. There are 65 camping sites with water but no hookups for $10, available on a first-come, first-served basis. Day use is $5.

San Pedro Riparian National Conservation Area

About 95% of Arizona's riparian habitat has disappeared, victim to poor grazing practices, logging for firewood, dropping water tables and development. Loss of this habitat has endangered many species' existence, and about 10% of the more than 500 species on the Endangered Species List are found along the San Pedro River. Clearly, this is valuable habitat. Almost 400 bird species, over 80 mammal species and nearly 50 species of reptiles and amphibians have been recorded along the 40-mile stretch of the San Pedro within the conservation area. This is the healthiest riparian ecosystem in the Southwest and the San Pedro is also the longest remaining undammed river in Arizona.

The conservation area is managed by the BLM (☎ 458-3559) in Sierra Vista. Hwy 82 crosses the river at **Fairbank**, a ghost town with interpretive signs, a picnic area, several hiking trails and a volunteer BLM host. Hwy 90 crosses the river at San Pedro House, a 1930s ranch that now houses an information center (cell 508-4445) and bookshop. It's open daily from 9:30 am to 4:30 pm. Again, hiking trails are nearby.

Further south, there's a parking area where Hereford Rd crosses the river. All hiking trails are ideal for birding. The Southeastern Arizona Bird Observatory (SABO; see Bisbee, later in this chapter) does **birding tours** of the area.

Permits for **backcountry camping** cost $2 per day and are available at self-pay stations at parking areas. You must camp at least a mile away from roads and parking areas. Undocumented migrants pass through the area, so don't leave gear unattended.

The closest accommodations are at *Casa de San Pedro B&B* (☎ 366-1300, 8933 S Yell Lane), near the river off Hereford Rd. It

has 10 comfortable nonsmoking rooms with private bath for $110 to $140 a double (two-night minimum), including full gourmet breakfast. The inn is popular with birders; visit www.naturesinn.com. The rustic *San Pedro River Inn* (☎ 366-5532, 8326 S Hereford Rd) has four nonsmoking housekeeping cottages about 2 miles east of the river. The 20-acre property is also good for birding. Rates (two-night minimum) are $105, including continental breakfast; www.sanpedroriverinn.com.

TOMBSTONE

☎ 520 • pop 1504 • elevation 4539 feet

Despite friends' warnings that all he would find would be his own tombstone, prospector Ed Schieffelin braved the dangers of Apache attack and struck it rich. The year was 1877, and a rip-roaring, brawling, silver-mining town appeared very quickly. In 1881, when the population reached 10,000, 110 saloon licenses were sold, and there were 14 dance halls for the entertainment of the get-rich-quick miners. The famous shootout at the OK Corral also took place in 1881, during which the brothers Earp and Doc Holliday gunned down three members of the Clanton cowboy gang. This was one of dozens of gunfights in Tombstone, but it so caught people's imagination that it now is perhaps the most famous shootout in history.

Tombstone was typical of southwestern mining towns of the period. Saloons, gambling halls and bordellos made up a good portion of the buildings, but there were, as always, a sprinkling of sober citizens running newspapers, businesses and banks. The silver-mining boom was short-lived and declining silver prices and floods in the mines closed down the last operation in the early 1900s. Most other boomtowns became ghost towns, but Tombstone, the 'Town Too Tough to Die,' continued to be a commercial center.

After WWII, Arizona's growing population gave Tombstone a new vitality; the old county courthouse opened as a museum in the 1950s and Tombstone became a National Historic Landmark in 1962. It now

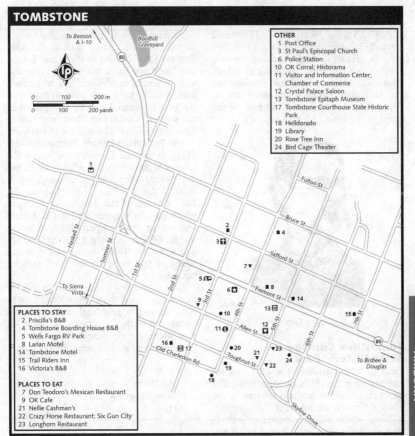

TOMBSTONE

To Benson
& I-10

Boothill
Graveyard

80

0   100   200 m
0   100   200 yards

To Sierra
Vista

OTHER
1 Post Office
3 St Paul's Episcopal Church
6 Police Station
10 OK Corral; Historama
11 Visitor and Information Center;
    Chamber of Commerce
12 Crystal Palace Saloon
13 Tombstone Epitaph Museum
17 Tombstone Courthouse State Historic
    Park
18 Helldorado
19 Library
20 Rose Tree Inn
24 Bird Cage Theater

Fulton St

Bruce St

Safford St

Fremont St

Allen St

Toughnut St

Skyline Drive

Haskell St
Summer St
1st St
2nd St
3rd St
4th St
5th St
6th St
7th St

Old Charleston Rd

To Bisbee &
Douglas

80

PLACES TO STAY
2 Priscilla's B&B
4 Tombstone Boarding House B&B
5 Wells Fargo RV Park
8 Larian Motel
14 Tombstone Motel
15 Trail Riders Inn
16 Victoria's B&B

PLACES TO EAT
7 Don Teodoro's Mexican Restaurant
9 OK Cafe
21 Nellie Cashman's
22 Crazy Horse Restaurant; Six Gun City
23 Longhorn Restaurant

ARIZONA

attracts large crowds of tourists who visit the town's old Western buildings, many of which are now gift shops. Reenactments of gunfights and other late 1800s events provide entertainment.

There are no bus services to Tombstone. Visitors either come in their own vehicle or on a guided tour.

Information

The visitor and information center (☎ 457-3929, 800-457-3423) at the corner of 4th and Allen Sts, is open 9 am to 4 pm, and 10 am to 4 pm on Sunday. Other services include the library (☎ 457-3612), at 4th St and Toughnut; post office (☎ 457-3479), 100 Haskell St; and the police (☎ 457-2244), 313 E Fremont St.

The OK Corral

Site of the famous gunfight, the OK Corral (☎ 457-3456), on Allen St between 3rd and 4th Sts, is the heart of both historic and touristic Tombstone, as well as the first stop for many visitors. It's open 9 am to 5 pm daily; admission is $2.50 (free for children under six) and it has models of the gunfighters and numerous other Western exhibits;

email for details at okcorral@ok-corral.com. The most interesting is CS Fly's early photography studio. Next-door is **Historama** with 26-minute presentations of Tombstone's history using animated figures, movies and narration (by Vincent Price). This is an additional $2.50, and showings are on the hour between 9 am and 4 pm. At 2 pm daily there is a re-enactment of the gunfight ($1.50).

Wyatt Earp

Tombstone Courthouse State Historic Park

Built in 1882, abandoned in 1931, and rehabilitated in the 1950s, the courthouse displays thousands of artifacts relating to the town's history, including a 19th-century gallows, which will (for better or worse) pique children's interest. Staffed by knowledgeable state-park rangers, this museum deserves a visit. The courthouse (☎ 457-3311) at 3rd St and Toughnut is open daily 8 am to 5 pm. Admission is $2.50, or $1 for seven- to 13-year-olds.

Other Attractions

The **Bird Cage Theater** (☎ 457-3421, 800-457-3423), 517 E Allen St, got its name from the 14 bed-sized, draped cages suspended from the ceiling, used by prostitutes to entertain their clients. A bordello, gambling den, dance hall and saloon during the 1880s, this was the wildest place in the West, and you can see it for $4.50, $3

for six- to 18-year olds. Hours are 8 am to 6 pm daily.

Antique 1880s furniture and the world's largest rosebush can be seen at the **Rose Tree Inn** (☎ 457-3326) at 4th St and Toughnut. The White Banksia rosebush arrived as a shoot sent from Scotland to a young emigrant wife in 1885; now over 8600 sq feet, the bush is especially pretty in April when the white flowers bloom. Hours are 9 am to 5 pm; admission is $2 for those 14 and over.

The **Tombstone Epitaph Museum** (☎ 457-2211), at 5th and Fremont Sts, houses the presses of the town's first newspaper. Hours are 9:30 am to 5 pm daily; free admission. It costs $1 for a replica of the October 27, 1881, edition of the *Tombstone Epitaph*, which reports the gunfight at OK Corral and contains various period ads, including one for **GF Spangenberg**, a gun dealer at 4th and Allen Sts. This business still operates today, selling both modern and antique weapons.

One of the few places you can see for free in this tourist town (though you have to enter through a gift shop!) is the **Boothill Graveyard** with the graves of many of Tombstone's early desperadoes. Some of the headstones make interesting reading:

> Here lies
> Lester Moore
> Four slugs from a .44
> No Les
> No more.

The graveyard is off Hwy 80 just north of town and is open to visitors from 7:30 am to late afternoon.

St Paul's Episcopal Church at Safford and 3rd, is Arizona's oldest non-Catholic church, dating from 1882.

Staged Shootouts

A prime tourist attraction, the shootouts are re-enacted by various acting troupes in town. Most charge about $4 for the show ($1 for six- to 12-year-olds) though this varies. Apart from the daily 2 pm show at the OK Corral (which sells out early on busy days), there are shows at Helldorado daily at 11:30 am, 1 and 3 pm. At Six Gun City, you can eat an outdoor lunch at the Crazy Horse Restaurant while enjoying shoot-outs several times a day. Shootouts, some at no charge, occur spontaneously at other times, especially during special events.

Organized Tours

Ride a stagecoach around town while listening to narration by local guides, many of whom trace their ancestors back to the Old West. Old Tombstone Tours (☎ 457-3018) leave frequently from Allen between 4th and 5th Sts. Tours last 20 minutes and cost $5, $4 for seniors and $3 for three- to 12-year olds. Ask about horseback-riding tours.

Special Events

Tombstone's events revolve around weekends of Western fun with shootouts (of course!), stagecoach rides, chili cook-offs, fiddling contests, 'vigilette' fashion shows, mock hangings and melodramas. The biggest event is Helldorado Days over the third weekend in October. Other events are Territorial Days (variable dates in March), Wyatt Earp Days (Memorial Day weekend), Vigilante Days (second weekend in August) and Rendezvous of the Gunfighters (Labor Day weekend).

Places to Stay

One and a half miles north on Hwy 80, *Tombstone Hills* (☎ 457-3829) has a pool, showers, laundry and over 80 tent and RV sites from $22 to $28. *Wells Fargo RV Park* (☎ 457-3966), near 3rd and Fremont Sts, allows tents and has about 60 sites with hookups at $22.

Motels raise their rates during special events, when reservations are recommended. Summer rates are the lowest.

The friendly *Larian Motel* (☎/fax 457-2272, 410 E Fremont St) has 14 very clean rooms with coffeemakers, most with two beds and many with mini-fridge and microwave, for $40 to $59 a double; go to www.tombstonemotels.com. The *Trail Riders Inn* (☎ 457-3573, 800-574-0417, 13 N 7th St) has 14 plain but reasonably sized rooms with two beds for $45 to $60 for two

to four people in winter, $5 less in summer. The *Tombstone Motel* (☎ 457-3478, 888-455-4578, 502 E Fremont St) has 12 decent rooms at $45 to $55 single and $50 to $70 double in winter, $10 less in summer; visit www.tombstonemotel.com.

Priscilla's B&B (☎ 457-3844, 101 N 3rd St), a lacy-curtained, two-story Victorian clapboard house dating from 1904, has three rooms, each with a sink and shared bathroom for $39/59 for single/double occupancy. One two-room suite with TV and private bath is $69 double.
website: www.tombstone1880.com/priscilla

The most comfortable motel is the *Best Western Lookout Lodge* (☎ 457-2223), on Hwy 80 a mile north of town, which has a pool, nice views and 40 good-size rooms for $65 to $90, including continental breakfast.

The visitor center can point out about eight B&Bs. *Tombstone Boarding House B&B* (☎ 457-3716, 108 N 4th St) is in two restored 1880s adobe homes. Eight bedrooms with private baths and entrances are furnished with period pieces and rent for $65 to $80 double. Its breakfast is reputedly the best in town – it includes champagne – and dinner is sometimes available on request; email for information at tombstonebandb@theriver.com.

Victoria's B&B (☎ 457-3677, 800-952-8216, 211 Toughnut), dates from 1880 and has a checkered past featuring gamblers, judges and ghosts. Nowadays, it has a private wedding chapel (!) and the owner will arrange for a minister if you bring a partner and the wedding license. Three rooms with private bath rent for $65 to $75 double.
website: www.tombstone1880.com/vsbb

Places to Eat

Nellie Cashman's (☎ 457-2212), near 5th St and Toughnut, dates from 1882. Nellie was a tough Irishwoman who stood no nonsense but helped out many a miner down on his luck. This no-alcohol establishment serves home-style meals 7 am to 9 pm daily in the quietly charming dining room. Huge hamburger plates are around $6 and varied dinner entrées are in the $9 to $19 range. For something a little wilder, cross the street to the ***Crazy Horse Restaurant*** (☎ 457-3827), which serves good, reasonably priced Western food outside during daily shootouts, and quieter dinners.

The popular ***Longhorn Restaurant*** (☎ 457-3405), near 5th St and Allen, serves American and Mexican breakfast, lunch and dinner. Tourists line up outside the door at lunchtime. ***Don Teodoro's Mexican Restaurant*** (☎ 457-3647, 15 N 4th St), has inexpensive lunches and dinners, the latter accompanied by a flamenco guitarist most nights. For buffalo, ostrich and emu burgers and other American delights, the ***OK Cafe*** (☎ 457-3980, 220 E Allen St) is open 7 am to 2 pm daily.

Entertainment

Several bars along Allen St have old Wild West ambiance. The best kept of these is the ***Crystal Palace Saloon*** (☎ 457-3611), near 5th and Allen Sts, dating from 1879. Nearby, ***Big Nose Kate's*** (☎ 457-3107) often has dancing. There's little to do in the evening but go on a pub crawl – or make that a saloon stagger.

BISBEE & AROUND
☎ 520 • pop 6090 • elevation 5300 feet

Bisbee, 24 miles south of Tombstone, shares a similarly wild early mining history. The difference was that Tombstone had silver, which fizzled out in the 1890s, while Bisbee had copper, which became Arizona's most important industry. By 1910 Bisbee had 25,000 inhabitants, making it the biggest city between El Paso, Texas, and San Francisco, California. Residents built elegant Victorian brick buildings, reminiscent of the East Coast and reasonably suited to the cooler elevation. Built in a narrow canyon, the town soon had no room for further construction. Today, Bisbee has more of a Victorian feel to it than any other town in Arizona. Copper mining declined after WWII and the mine closed in 1975, when production became unprofitable.

Bisbee's pleasant climate and old-fashioned ambiance attracted artists and the artistically inclined, and now the town is

an intriguing mix of aging miners and gallery owners, ex-hippies and artists. It has more of an upscale air than Tombstone. Whereas Tombstone thrives on gunfight re-enactments, Bisbee offers mine tours.

One World Travel (☎ 432-5359), 7 OK St, sells tickets for buses between Douglas and Tucson (via Sierra Vista).

Orientation & Information

The steep canyon walls make Old Bisbee's layout rather contorted; Bisbee wasn't set up on the typical Western grid-like formation. East of Old Bisbee is the Lavender Pit Copper Mine, over a mile wide (a pullout on Hwy 80 has good views) followed by the traffic circle at Lowell (a useful landmark) and the suburb of Warren, 3 miles southeast of Bisbee. Warren has many Victorian homes and the local hospital. The modern district of San Jose, about 3 miles southwest of Warren, has the golf course.

At the chamber of commerce (☎ 432-5421, 866-224-7233), 31 Subway St, staff can reserve space and sell tickets for a mine tour, and they keep track of available lodging; visit www.bisbeearizona.com. Other services include the library (☎ 432-4232) and post office (☎ 432-2052), both at 6 Main St; hospital (☎ 432-5383), on Bisbee Rd at Cole Ave, Warren; and the police (☎ 432-2261).

Bisbee Mining & Historical Museum

Housed in the 1897 office building of the Phelps Dodge Copper Mining Co, the museum (☎ 432-7071), at Copper Queen Plaza, has a fine display depicting the first 40 years of Bisbee's history, along with exhibits about mining. It also has a history and mining research library and is associated with the Smithsonian Institute. Hours are 10 am to 4 pm daily except January 1 and December 25; admission is $4, free for kids under 16.

Organized Tours

The **Queen Mine** (☎ 432-2071) can be visited in underground mine cars. Reservations are suggested. Tours, given by retired

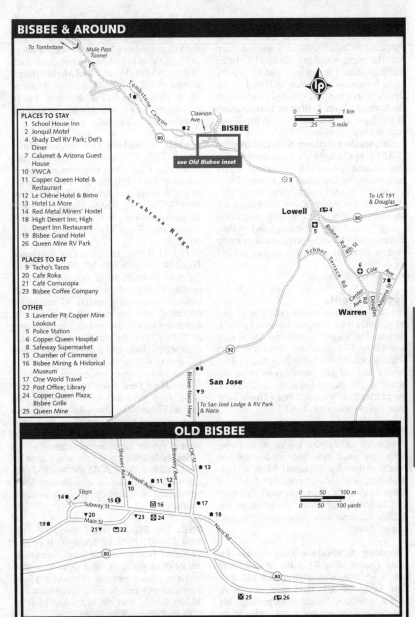

BISBEE & AROUND

To Tombstone
Mule Pass Tunnel

Tombstone Canyon

1

2

Clawson Ave

BISBEE

80

see Old Bisbee inset

Escabrosa Ridge

3

To US 191 & Douglas

Lowell

4

80

5

Bisbee Rd 4th St

School Terrace Rd

6 Cole

7

Center Ave

Douglas Ave

Arizona St

Warren

92

Bisbee-Naco Hwy

8

9

San Jose

To San José Lodge & RV Park & Naco

0   .5   1 km
0   .25   .5 mile

PLACES TO STAY
1   School House Inn
2   Jonquil Motel
4   Shady Dell RV Park; Dot's Diner
7   Calumet & Arizona Guest House
10 YWCA
11 Copper Queen Hotel & Restaurant
12 Le Chêne Hotel & Bistro
13 Hotel La More
15 Red Metal Miners' Hostel
18 High Desert Inn; High Desert Inn Restaurant
19 Bisbee Grand Hotel
26 Queen Mine RV Park

PLACES TO EAT
9   Tacho's Tacos
20 Cafe Roka
21 Café Cornucopia
23 Bisbee Coffee Company

OTHER
3   Lavender Pit Copper Mine Lookout
5   Police Station
6   Copper Queen Hospital
8   Safeway Supermarket
14 Chamber of Commerce
16 Bisbee Mining & Historical Museum
17 One World Travel
22 Post Office; Library
24 Copper Queen Plaza; Bisbee Grille
25 Queen Mine

OLD BISBEE

Shearer Ave

Howell Ave

Brewery Ave

OK St

13

Steps

14

15 Subway St

10

11 12

16

17

18

20

19

Main St

21   22

23 24

Naco Rd

80

80

25   26

0   50   100 m
0   50   100 yards

ARIZONA

miners, last about an hour and leave at 9 and 10:30 am, noon, 2 and 3:30 pm daily. Participants wear hard hats and go deep into the mine, which is a chilly 47°F; bring warm clothes. The price is $10 for adults, $3.50 for seven- to 15-year-olds and $2 for three- to six-year-olds. Guided van tours of the **Surface Mines & Historic District** leave at 10:30 am, noon, 2 and 3:30 pm for $7 per person over age two.

Southeastern Arizona Bird Observatory (SABO; ☎ 432-1388), a conservation, research and education program, offers various birding tours and workshops. There are weekly guided walks (three hours, $12) along the San Pedro River and Huachuca Mountains during the spring migration (April and May). Evening owl walks, hummingbird-banding programs and other birding tours are offered – contact SABO for details.

website: www.sabo.org

Special Events

Art fairs and other events take place regularly; dates and programs are subject to change. The biggest events are the Spring Arts Festival on the second Sunday in May; Underground Film Festival at the end of June; Fourth of July parade (said to be the oldest in the state); Brewery Gulch Daze over Labor Day weekend; and a Home Tour over Thanksgiving weekend.

Places to Stay

Most beds are full on weekends and you definitely need reservations for special events or holiday weekends. Most accommodations are historic hotels or B&Bs in older houses; there are no modern chain motels. Call the chamber of commerce for details of numerous other places in and around town.

Camping & Hostels Near the Queen Mine, *Queen Mine RV Park* (☎ 432-5006) has 25 RV sites with hookups for $16. *San Jose Lodge & RV Park* (see Motels & Hotels) has 50 RV spaces with hookups for $14. Several others are a few miles from Bisbee.

The *YWCA* (☎ 432-3542, 26 Howell Ave) has 12-person women's and men's dorms for $10 per person. You must bring a sleeping bag; there is no kitchen and doors lock at 9 pm. The funky, arty *Red Metal Miners' Hostel* (☎ 432-6671, 59-N Subway St) sleeps up to 12 folks at $18 in dorms or $40 in private rooms, has Internet access, kitchen, laundry and bike rental.

Motels & Hotels The *Jonquil Motel* (☎ 432-7371, 317 Tombstone Canyon) has seven older but clean nonsmoking budget rooms at $40 to $70. Budget rooms are also available at the *San Jose Lodge & RV Park* (☎ 432-5761, 1002 Bisbee-Naco Hwy), with 45 modern rooms, a seasonal pool and a restaurant. Rates are $70 to $90 for a double.

In Old Bisbee, the 1902 *Copper Queen Hotel* (☎ 432-2216, 800-247-5829, 11 Howell St) was Bisbee's most famous hotel. It retains its turn-of-the-century feel, especially in the public areas. The 47 rooms are furnished with antiques but have modern amenities, vary in size and comfort, and rent at $70 to $136. An outdoor pool, an old-fashioned saloon and a good dining room provide all you need.

website: www.copperqueen.com

The *High Desert Inn* (☎ 432-1442, 800-281-0510, 8 Naco Rd) has five comfortable rooms ($70 to $100) in contemporary European style with modern amenities, housed in what was the county jail back in 1901. Its website is www.highdesertinn.com.

Similarly modern rooms are found in the *Le Chêne Hotel & Bistro* (☎ 432-1832, 1 Howell Ave), also in a renovated 1901 building; see it online at www.lechene bistro.com.

B&Bs The *Bisbee Grand Hotel* (☎ 432-5900, 800-421-1909, 61 Main St) is of the Victorian red-velvet and stuffed-peacock school of elegance. A billiards room and a Western saloon provide relaxation. Eight rooms, all with private baths, range from $55 to $90 double, and six suites are $100 to $150, including full breakfast.

website: www.bisbeegrandhotel.com

The *Hotel La More* (☎ 432-5131, 888-432-5131, 45 OK St) is a 20-room hotel built in 1916, when rates were $2 a night. Renovated in 1996, the antique-filled hotel now charges $60 to $80 a double for 16 rooms with private bath, or $55 for four rooms with shared bath, and $120 to $165 for three suites. The delicious breakfast is all-you-can-eat.

The *School House Inn* (☎ 432-2996, 800-537-4333, 818 Tombstone Canyon), built in 1918 as a school, now has nine attractive guest rooms following themes such as the Principal's Office and the Writing Room. Rates are $60 to $90 a double with full breakfast. All rooms have private baths.

In the historical suburb of Warren is the *Calumet & Arizona Guest House* (☎ 432-4815, 608 Powell), a grand house built in 1906. Now it features six spacious, old-fashioned but comfortable rooms, two with private bath and four sharing two baths, for $60 to $70 double with a full breakfast. A whirlpool, library and fireplace add cozy touches; send email to timbersj@juno.com.

Places to Eat
The attractive *Bisbee Grille* (☎ 432-6788), in Copper Queen Plaza, serves moderately priced breakfasts, lunches and dinners daily with a changing menu. Near this plaza, *Bisbee Coffee Company* (☎ 432-7879) serves mainly coffees and some sandwiches from 7 am to 7 pm daily, 'til 9 pm on Friday and Saturday. For excellent soup, salad and sandwich lunches daily except Sunday, stop by *Café Cornucopia* (☎ 432-4820, 14 Main St).

For Mexican food, the best is *Tacho's Tacos* (☎ 432-7811, 115 Bisbee-Naco Hwy). *Cafe Roka* (☎ 432-5153, 35 Main St) serves excellent and innovative dinners Wednesday to Saturday. The changing menu is a limited gourmet American selection in the $13 to $20 range, including soup and salad. Jazz is played on Friday and Saturday.

The *Copper Queen Hotel* serves good meals all day. Also check out the *High Desert Inn Restaurant* with fine and highly acclaimed dinners served Thursday to Sunday, and *Le Chêne Bistro*, with genuine and fresh French country dinners served daily in the $15 to $30 range.

Vintage Vacation
One of the most unusual places to stay in Bisbee is the *Shady Dell RV Park* (☎ 432-3567, 1 Douglas Rd) at the Lowell traffic circle, which rents seven antique aluminum camping trailers. Among the lineup are a 1949 Airstream, a 1951 Spartan Royal Mansion and others from the 1940s and 1950s. They have been restored and fitted with refrigerators and propane stoves; dishes and bedding are provided. Most of them do not have their own showers and bathrooms. Trailers will sleep from one to four people and rent for $35 to $75. If you have your own rig, a few RV hookups are available and tent camping is possible.

Also on the premises is *Dot's Diner* (☎ 432-2046), an authentic 1957 Valentine 10-stool dining trailer where you can have a burger or milkshake – it's not fast food. Hours are 7 am to 8 pm daily.

Shopping
Galleries in Old Bisbee exhibit and sell local artists' work. The quality is mixed, but a discerning eye may discover an as-yet-undiscovered artist here.

DOUGLAS & AROUND
☎ 520 • pop 14,312 • elevation 4000 feet
Once a copper town, Douglas, along with its much larger sister city of Agua Prieta (pop 100,000) in Mexico, has become a ranching and manufacturing center. The downtown area looks pre-WWII without the hoopla of Bisbee or Tombstone.

Golden State (☎ 364-2233), on 2nd at S 4th Ave, has buses to Tucson and Phoenix; they connect with Greyhound. Douglas Shuttle (☎ 364-9442) has eight vans a day to the Tucson and Phoenix airports.

Information
The chamber of commerce (☎ 364-2477), 1125 Pan American Ave, is open 9 am to 5 pm Monday to Friday; visit www.ci.douglas.az.us. Other services include the

Coronado National Forest Ranger Station
(☎ 364-3468, 364-3231), on Leslie Canyon
Rd; library (☎ 364-3851), at 560 10th St; post
office (☎ 364-3631), 601 10th St; hospital
(☎ 364-7931), 4 miles west of Douglas; and
the police (☎ 364-8422), 300 14th St.

Things to See & Do
Established in 1907, the **Gadsden Hotel** (see
Places to Stay) is on the National Register of
Historic Places. The lobby is one of the most
opulent early-20th-century public areas in
Arizona. A white Italian marble staircase
and marble pillars with gold-leaf decorations, a superb 42-foot Tiffany stained-glass
Southwestern mural, and vaulted stained-
glass skylights combine for an elegant surprise. It's well worth a visit even if you aren't
staying here.

The **John Slaughter Ranch** (☎ 558-2474)
was one of the largest and most successful
ranches of the late 1800s. The buildings have
been restored and the ranch is on the National Register of Historic Places. Photo exhibits and a video show what life was like on
the property a century ago. The ranch is 16
miles east of Douglas (leave town via 15th
St) along a gravel road paralleling the
border. Hours are 10 am to 3 pm Wednesday to Sunday, and admission is $3 for those
over 14. The ranchlands are now a wildlife
refuge (☎ 364-2104).

Agua Prieta can be entered on foot. In daylight, the atmosphere is much more leisurely
and relaxed than in Nogales and you'll find a
selection of gift shops (no bargaining) and
restaurants. From the international border,
walk south six blocks to Calle 6 and turn left
for two blocks to the church and plaza, which
are pleasant. At night, this area becomes a
major illegal crossing place for undocu-
mented aliens; expect to see border patrols
and to be asked for identification.

Special events celebrating the town's
Mexican ties are Cinco de Mayo, celebrated
on or near May 5th, and Douglas Fiestas in
mid-September.

Places to Stay & Eat
The rooms are nowhere near as fancy as the
lobby in the *Gadsden Hotel* (☎ 364-4481,

1046 G Ave), but they are comfortable
enough and the price is right. There are 160
rooms and suites ranging from $40 to $85;
most are under $60. The rooms contain an
eclectic grouping of styles and amenities,
but just sitting in the lobby makes this a
great value.
website: www.theriver.com/gadsdenhotel

Otherwise, there are a few basic mom 'n'
pop places and a *Motel 6 (☎ 364-2457, 111
16th St)* with a pool and rooms around $40.

The restaurants in the Gadsden Hotel
are good, or you can eat Mexican and
American food across the street in the
Grand Cafe (☎ 364-2344, 1119 G Ave).

WILLCOX
☎ 520 • pop 3733 • elevation 4167 feet
Settled in 1880 as a railroad camp, Willcox
quickly became a major shipping center for
southeastern Arizona's cattle ranches.
Today Willcox is also famous as a fruit-
growing center, and people drive from all
over southeastern Arizona for the apple
harvest. Willcox is the boyhood home of
cowboy singer and movie actor Rex Allen
(1920–99). Nearby is a playa – a lake that
dries in summer – which is the wintering
ground of thousands of sandhill cranes, a
spectacular sight for bird watchers.

Greyhound (☎ 384-2183) buses stop at the
Lifestyle RV Resort (622 N Haskell Ave)
several times a day on their runs along I-10.

Information
The chamber of commerce (☎ 384-2272,
800-200-2272), by I-10 exit 340, is open 8 am
to 5 pm Monday to Saturday, and 10 am to
2 pm on Sunday. Other services include the
library (☎ 384-4271), 207 W Maley St; post
office (☎ 384-2689), 200 S Curtis Ave; hospital (☎ 384-3541), 901 W Rex Allen Dr; and
the police (☎ 384-4673), 151 W Maley St.

Things to See & Do
The **Rex Allen Arizona Cowboy Museum**
(☎ 384-4583), 155 N Railroad Ave, is in an
1890s adobe building in the Willcox Historic
District. Exhibits interpret the lives of pioneers as well as Rex Allen. Hours are 10 am
to 4 pm daily except some Sundays and

major holidays; admission is $2 per person, $3 for a couple and $5 for a family. Nearby, the Willcox Commercial Store dates to 1881 and is the oldest continuously operating store in Arizona. Other old buildings can be visited.

South of town, the huge **Willcox Playa** is the winter home of approximately 10,000 sandhill cranes. Drive southeast on Hwy 186 a few miles and then take the left fork for Kansas Settlement. At dawn, the birds fly out of the playa and land in the corn stubble around Kansas Settlement, where they feed during the day, flying back to the playa at sunset.

On the third weekend in January, Wings Over Willcox Sandhill Cranes Celebration has guided tours to good viewing sites near Willcox Playa and offers related birding activities. In late summer and fall, there are pick-your-own apple orchards, roadside fruit and vegetable stands, and often an apple harvest festival in December. Rex

Allen Days, with rodeo and other events, is the first week in October.

Places to Stay & Eat

Magic Circle RV Park (☎ 384-3212), at I-10 exit 340, has 80 RV sites with hookups at $20; *Lifestyle RV Resort* (☎ 384-3303, 622 N Haskell Ave) has 60 RV sites with hookups for $22. *Grande Vista* (☎ 384-4002, 711 N Prescott Ave) charges $15.50 for 50 RV sites with hookups.

The cheapest places are small mom-and-pop establishments along Haskell Ave charging in the $20s and $30s. Otherwise, choose from a *chain motel* at I-10 exit 340. These all have pools and include a Motel 6, Days Inn, and Super 8, with rooms in the $40 to $60 range. Also at exit 340 is Willcox's most comfortable hotel: the *Best Western Plaza Inn* (☎ 384-3556), with a pool, whirlpool, lounge and restaurant with room service. Rooms feature coffeemakers and some refrigerators; six have whirlpool baths

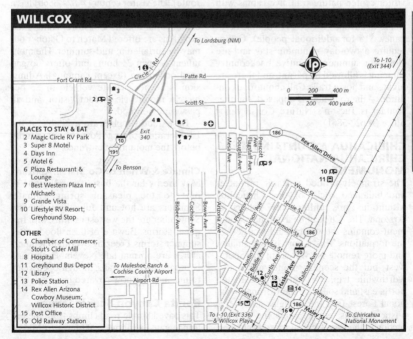

WILLCOX

To Lordsburg (NM)

To I-10 (Exit 344)

Fort Grant Rd

Patte Rd

Scott St

0   200   400 m
0   200   400 yards

Exit 340

To Benson

Rex Allen Drive

Wood St

Jesse St

Fremont St

Delos St

Grant St

Maley St

To Muleshoe Ranch & Cochise County Airport

Airport Rd

To I-10 (Exit 336) & Willcox Playa

To Chiricahua National Monument

Stewart St

PLACES TO STAY & EAT
2 Magic Circle RV Park
3 Super 8 Motel
4 Days Inn
5 Motel 6
6 Plaza Restaurant & Lounge
7 Best Western Plaza Inn; Michaels
9 Grande Vista
10 Lifestyle RV Resort; Greyhound Stop

OTHER
1 Chamber of Commerce; Stout's Cider Mill
8 Hospital
11 Greyhound Bus Depot
12 Library
13 Police Station
14 Rex Allen Arizona Cowboy Museum; Willcox Historic District
15 Post Office
16 Old Railway Station

ARIZONA

as well. Rates are $60 to $90 a double, and include full breakfast.

The best restaurant is *Michaels* in the Best Western, open 6 am to 9 pm daily and serving moderately priced American and Mexican food, ranging from $5 to $17. Otherwise, there's the *Plaza Restaurant & Lounge* (☎ 384-3819) next door, open 24 hours, and a slew of fast-food places. By the chamber of commerce, *Stout's Cider Mill* (☎ 384-3696) sells every imaginable apple concoction.

MULESHOE RANCH

Cooperatively managed by the Nature Conservancy, BLM and USFS, the ranch is a good place for birding and wildlife observation. It's about 30 miles northwest of Willcox (leave town via Airport Rd) in the foothills of the rugged Galiuro Mountains, which are the watershed of seven permanently flowing streams – an important ecosystem.

At ranch headquarters (☎ 586-7072) is a visitor center, nature trail, five cabins with kitchens for rent by reservation (at least two weeks in advance, $85 to $125 double occupancy, $15 for additional people). Cabins require a two-day minimum stay and are closed in summer. Primitive backcountry camping is allowed by permit, and there are hiking and horse trails. Call about road conditions – the road here is unpaved. Another contact is Tucson's Nature Conservancy office (☎ 622-3861).

CHIRICAHUA MOUNTAINS & CHIRICAHUA NATIONAL MONUMENT

The strangely eroded volcanic pinnacles and balanced rocks of the Chiricahua Mountains are unlike any others in Arizona. The Chiricahua National Monument contains the wildest and weirdest of the formations. This is one of the smaller and more remote NPS areas in the Southwest, but the scenery alone makes it a worthwhile trip. It is surrounded to the north, east and south by the Coronado National Forest (see the Douglas and Sierra Vista sections, earlier, and the Safford section in the East-Central Arizona chapter,

for the nearest USFS offices), which also has interesting rock formations as well as camping.

The remoteness of the area makes it attractive to wildlife – a jaguar was recently recorded near here! There is a good chance of seeing deer, coatis and javelinas. Mountain lions, bobcats and bears are sighted many times a year on the hiking trails within the monument. The Chiricahuas are the nearest high mountains to the Mexican mountain ranges, and several Mexican bird species are found here. The highest peak is 9795-foot Chiricahua Peak, just south of the monument in the national forest.

History and architecture can be found at Faraway Ranch, built in the early part of the 20th century. Tours of the now-restored ranch are led by monument rangers.

Orientation & Information

The monument is almost 40 miles southeast of Willcox by paved road (no gas along this route). The visitor center (☎ 824-3560) has a slide show about the Chiricahuas, a small exhibit area and a bookstore. Ranger-led programs are offered March to October but may be curtailed in mid-summer. The monument is open 24 hours but offers no gas, food or lodging (except camping). Admission is $6 per private vehicle or $3 per bicycle, motorcycle or foot visitor, and all passes are honored.

Basic food supplies are available at the El Dorado Trading Post, about a mile before the monument entrance.

Climate & When to Go March, April and May are by far the busiest months, due in part to the pleasant spring climate. Summers are hot and July through early September are the wettest months, with frequent storms. Beware of flash floods after summer storms. Freezing overnight temperatures are normal late November through February, and the trails, though open year-round, may be snow-covered in winter.

Bonita Canyon Scenic Drive

This paved 8-mile road climbs from the entrance gate (at about 5000 feet) to Massai

Point at 6870 feet. The visitor center is 2 miles along this road from the entrance station. There are several scenic pullouts and trailheads and views from Massai Point are spectacular.

Faraway Ranch
Originally a pioneer's cattle ranch begun in 1888, it became one of Arizona's earliest guest ranches in the 1920s. The ranch is near the monument entrance. To enter, you must go on a ranger-led tour ($2; free for those under 12) offered several times a day during the busy season, less often in other months.

Hiking
Seventeen miles of hiking trails range from easy, flat loops of 0.2 miles to strenuous 7-mile climbs. The short, flat trails west of the visitor center and campground are the easiest and are good for birding and wildlife observation.

The trails east of the visitor center lead into rugged mountain country with the most spectacular geology. A hikers' shuttle bus leaves daily from the visitor center at 8:30 am, going up to Massai Point for $2. Hikers return by hiking downhill.

Places to Stay
The *Bonita Campground*, with 24 sites just north of the visitor center, has water but no hookups or showers. During the busy months, the campground is often full by noon. Sites cost $8 on a first-come, first-served basis. No wilderness camping is permitted.

If the campground is full, there are numerous campgrounds in the Coronado National Forest south of the monument. Rangers will give you a map (there's one outside the visitor center if the center is closed) showing where the campgrounds are. These usually have space available.

Southwestern Colorado

CAROL POLICH

The southwest section of this region is also known as the 'Four Corners' area, in reference to the point where the borders of Colorado, New Mexico, Arizona and Utah meet. Here the mountains and mesas give way to desert, a stark contrast with the rest of Colorado.

The prime attractions in this area are the many sites of the pre-Columbian peoples known formally as the Ancestral Puebloans. Together the Mesa Verde National Park and Ute Mountain Tribal Park protect the archaeological remains at hundreds of these prehistoric communities, while providing access to a few of the most spectacular sites.

Nearby towns such as Cortez and Mancos offer places to stay and further information about the Ancestral Puebloans and their legacy. A bit farther north is the sleepy Dolores River Canyon, which offers unrestrained access to desert backcountry hiking, biking and river rafting. Travelers wanting to visit more of Colorado should check out Lonely Planet's *Rocky Mountains*.

CORTEZ
☎ 970 • pop 8900 • elevation 6200 feet

For visitors to Mesa Verde National Park and other nearby Ancestral Puebloan sites, Cortez is the main lodging spot. Those seeking a more relaxed environment can try Mancos, 17 miles east, or Dolores, 11 miles north.

The Colorado Welcome Center (☎ 565-4048), 928 E Main St, is housed in an adobe-style building at the City Park. It has maps, brochures and some excellent pamphlets and maps on local activities such as fishing and mountain biking. Hours are 8 am to 5 pm (6 pm in summer) daily.

Other services include the post office, 35 S Beech St, and Southwest Memorial Hospital (☎ 565-6666), 1311 N Mildred Rd.

Quality Book Store (☎ 565-9125), 34 W Main St, sells travel books and maps and offers a good selection on local history and Native American cultures.

A laundry is at the corner of E Main St and Mildred Rd opposite the City Park and Colorado Welcome Center. M&M Truckstop (☎ 565-6511), south of town at 7006 US 160/666, offers showers for $5.

Colorado University Center Museum

Throughout the year this museum (☎ 565-1151), 25 N Market St, hosts exhibits on the Ancestral Puebloans as well as visiting art displays in its gallery.

The **Cultural Park** is an outdoor space where Ute, Navajo and Hopi tribe members share their cultures with visitors through dance and crafts demonstrations. Weaving demonstrations and Ute Mountain art also are displayed, and visitors can check out a Navajo hogan.

Summer evening programs feature Native American dances six nights a week at 7:30 pm, followed at 8:30 pm by cultural programs such as Native American storytellers.

The Center Museum is open 10 am to 9 pm Monday to Saturday in summer, 10 am to 5 pm in winter.

Places to Stay

Sadly, the only campground in town not right next to a highway or dedicated to RVs is the ***Cortez-Mesa Verde KOA*** (☎ 565-9301, 27432 E Hwy 160) at the east end of town. Tent sites for parties of two are a pricey $21, full RV hookups are $28, with $3 per extra person. It's open April through mid-October.

Summer or winter the basic but clean ***Ute Mountain Motel*** (☎ 565-8507, 531 S Broadway) offers singles/doubles for $30 to $45 in summer, and $23 to $40 in winter. Another economy choice is the ***Aneth Lodge*** (☎ 565-3453, 645 E Main St), where high-season rates for fairly large, comfortable rooms are $36/53.

Taking a slight step upward in quality, the ***Budget Host Bel Rau Inn*** (☎ 565-3738, 2040 E Main St) has a pool, hot tub and spacious, spotless rooms for $78 in summer; singles/doubles are as low as $30/43 in winter. On the western side of town, the ***Sand Canyon Inn*** (☎ 565-8562, 800-257-3699) is another pleasant spot with a pool, sundeck and laundry. Peak summer rates are $39/48.

Still farther west, ***The Tomahawk Lodge*** (☎ 565-8521, 800-643-7705, 728 S Broadway) has a pool, 24-hour coffee and tea and rooms from $47/57 (summer rates). The friendly owners of the ***Travel Lodge*** (☎ 565-7778, 800-578-7878, 440 S Broadway) offer clean rooms for $56/79 in summer. Facilities include a pool, hot tub and laundry.

The ***Anasazi Motor Inn*** (☎ 565-3773, 640 S Broadway) is not bad, but rooms are overpriced at $57/71; even winter rates are fairly steep.

Fifteen miles west of Cortez, ***Kelly Place*** (☎ 565-3125, 14663 Montezuma County Rd G), in McElmo Canyon, is a unique

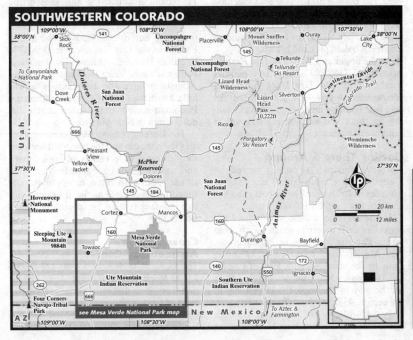

SOUTHWESTERN COLORADO

COLORADO

adobe-style guest lodge on a 100-acre archaeological and horticultural preserve founded by the late George Kelly, botanist and author of many outstanding guides to Rocky Mountains plants. Tastefully appointed rooms cost $65/75 and include private bath and breakfast. Cabins with kitchenettes start at $95. Horseback rides, cultural tours and archaeological programs also are offered.

Places to Eat

You can start the day with an espresso and light breakfast at the Quality Book Store's *Earth Song Haven (☎ 565-9125, 34 W Main St)*, which also serves tasty lunches featuring fresh ingredients.

The *Main Street Brewery & Restaurant (☎ 544-9112, 21 E Main St)* serves a mix of Southwestern, Mexican and Italian dishes. Its house-brewed beer is excellent, reason enough in itself to stop by.

Locals nominate *Francisca's (☎ 565-4093, 125 E Main St)* the best Mexican food in town. For standard American family fare there's *Homesteaders (☎ 565-6253, 45 E Main St)*, open all day for barbecue dinners and fresh-baked pies and breads.

At the upper end, *Nero's Italian Restaurant (☎ 565-7366, 303 W Main St)* is another local favorite. The *Dry Dock Lounge & Restaurant (☎ 564-9404, 220 W Main St)* also occupies the higher-end bracket, dishing up steak and seafood platters with a Southwestern flair.

Getting There & Around

Cortez Municipal Airport is served by United Express, which offers daily turboprop flights to Denver. The airport is 2 miles south of town off US 160/666.

In the extreme southwest corner of the state, Cortez is easier to reach by car from either Phoenix, Arizona, or Albuquerque, New Mexico, than from Denver, 379 miles away by the shortest route. East of Cortez, US 160 passes Mesa Verde National Park on the way to Durango, the largest city in the region, 45 miles away. To the northeast, Hwy 145 follows the beautiful Dolores River through the San Juan Mountains on an old Rio Grande Southern narrow-gauge route over Lizard Head Pass (10,222 feet) to Telluride, 77 miles distant.

Budget and U-Save Auto Rental (☎ 565-9168) operate out of the Cortez airport.

AROUND CORTEZ
Anasazi Heritage Center

One of the largest archaeological projects in the Four Corners region was undertaken along the Dolores River between 1978 and 1981, prior to the filling of the McPhee Reservoir. The Anasazi Heritage Center (☎ 882-4811), 27501 Hwy 184, 10 miles north of Cortez or 3 miles west of Dolores, offers modern displays of Ancestral Puebloan artifacts found during this project and other archaeological work in the area.

Hands-on exhibits include weaving, corn-grinding, tree-ring analysis and an introduction to the way in which archaeologists examine potsherds.

Between AD 1 and 1300, Ancestral Puebloans inhabited the hilly sites of the Escalante and Domínguez Pueblos overlooking the Montezuma Valley. A short interpretive nature trail leads to the hilltop Escalante site that was discovered in 1776 by Father Francisco Atanasio Escalante and Father Silvestre Vélez Domínguez. Archaeologists believe the Escalante site was linked with the Chaco Culture, an Ancestral Puebloan society that existed nearly 200 miles south in New Mexico.

The Bureau of Land Management operates the museum and the nonprofit museum shop offers a wide variety of books, maps and nature guides ranging from professional reports to introductory materials suited to the general public. It's open 9 am to 5 pm daily (until 4 pm in winter); admission is $3.

Crow Canyon
Archaeology Center

The center (☎ 565-8975, 800-422-8975), 23390 Road K, offers a day-long educational program that visits an excavation site west of Cortez. Programs teach the significance of found artifacts and are offered Wednesday and Thursday from June to

mid-September. This is an excellent way to learn about Ancestral Puebloan culture first-hand. The fee is $50/25 adults/children under 18.
website: www.crowcanyon.org

An adult research program costs $900 and includes Southwestern meals and log cabin lodging for a week. Classroom time culminates with visits to the dig site and active participation in excavation. Reservations are required for both programs.

Fishing
The 11-mile stretch of the lower Dolores River, below McPhee Dam to the Bradfield Bridge, is a state-designated quality water stream where a catch-and-release program is in effect. To reach the area, turn east off US 666 onto Montezuma County Rd DD a mile north of Pleasant View. Follow the signs for 6 miles to the Bradfield Bridge and USFS campground; from the bridge, the Lone Dome Rd follows the east bank of the river to the dam.

If trolling is your preference, McPhee Reservoir offers both warm- and cold-water species in the recently flooded Dolores River Canyon. Perhaps to make amends for drowning Ancestral Puebloan sites, burial grounds and untold artifacts, the reservoir is kept well stocked with fish for the visiting angler.

Pick up the *Guide to Fishing in Mesa Verde Country* at the Colorado Welcome Center for additional information.

Bicycling
The Four Corners area offers some outstanding mountain bike trails among piñon-juniper woodland and over 'slickrock' mesa trails. The dispersed sites at Hovenweep National Monument are ideal riding destinations. In fact, the roads are often better suited for bikes than cars.

A good ride begins at the Sand Canyon archaeological site west of Cortez and follows a downhill trail west for 18 miles to Cannonball Mesa near the state line. If you're looking for a shorter ride, at the 8-mile mark the Burro Point overlook of Yellow Jacket and Burro Canyons is a good place

to turn back. Mountain-bike enthusiasts should be sure to take the 26-mile trail from Dove Creek to Slick Rock along the Dolores River.

Pick up a copy of *Mountain and Road Bike Routes* for the Cortez-Dolores-Mancos area, available at the Colorado Welcome Center in Cortez and at local chambers of commerce. It provides maps and profiles for several road and mountain-bike routes. The booklet *Bicycle Routes on Public Lands of Southwest Colorado* also describes area rides in good detail. It's available for $7 from the USFS Dolores Ranger Station (☎ 882-7296), 100 N 6th St in Dolores. You can contact the Colorado Plateau Mountain Bike Trail Association (☎ 241-9561) for even more route recommendations and information.

In Cortez, Kokopelli Bike & Board (☎ 565-4408), 30 W Main St, rents mountain bikes for $20 per day, including helmet, air pump, water bottle and tools. They also can provide information about trails in the area.

Places to Stay
A few walk-in tent sites are available for $8 at the USFS **McPhee Campground** (☎ 970-882-9905, 800-280-2267), but most of the 70 reservable campsites are set up for RVs and cost $12. The sites look out over the Montezuma Valley and are convenient to McPhee Recreation Area and reservoir fishing 14 miles north of Cortez on Hwy 184.

Below McPhee Dam to the reservoir, the USFS operates three campgrounds on a first-come, first-served basis: **Bradfield**, **Cabin Canyon** and **Ferris Canyon**. Tent sites are $8. To reach them from US 666, travel 1 mile north of Pleasant View (20 miles north of Cortez), turn east on Montezuma County Rd DD and follow the signs for 6 miles to the bridge. The Bradfield site is a half-mile downstream from the bridge; the other two are within 6 miles to your right (south) on USFS Rd 504. For more camping locations in the San Juan National Forest contact the USFS Dolores Ranger Station (☎ 882-7296).
website: www.fs.fed.us/r2/sanjuan

COLORADO

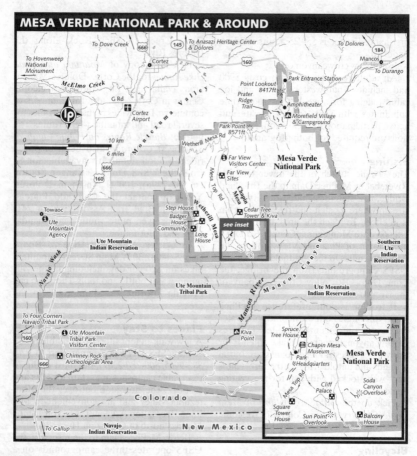

MESA VERDE NATIONAL PARK & AROUND

MESA VERDE NATIONAL PARK

Among national parks, Mesa Verde is unique for its focus on preserving cultural relics so future generations may continue to interpret the puzzling settlement, and subsequent abandonment, of the area by its early inhabitants.

Ancestral Puebloan sites are found throughout the canyons and mesas of Mesa Verde, a high plateau south of Cortez and Mancos. If you have time for only a short visit, check out the Chapin Mesa Museum and try a walk through the Spruce Tree House, where you can climb down a wooden ladder into the cool chamber of a kiva.

Mesa Verde rewards travelers who set aside a day or more to take the ranger-led tours of Cliff Palace and Balcony House, explore Wetherill Mesa, simply linger in the museum or participate in one of the campfire programs.

Preserving the Ancestral Puebloan sites while accommodating ever-increasing numbers of visitors continues to challenge the National Park Service (NPS). The NPS strictly enforces the Antiquities Act, which prohibits removal or destruction of any such items and also prohibits public access to many of the approximately 4000 known Ancestral Puebloan sites.

History

A US army lieutenant recorded the spectacular cliff dwellings in the canyons of Mesa Verde in 1849–50. The large number of sites on Ute tribal land, and their relative inaccessibility, protected the majority of these antiquities from pothunters.

The first scientific investigation of the sites in 1874 failed to identify Cliff Palace, the largest cliff dwelling in North America. Discovery of the 'magnificent city' occurred only when local cowboys Richard Wetherill and Charlie Mason were searching for stray cattle after a December 1888 snowfall. The cowboys exploited their 'discovery' for the next 18 years by guiding both amateur and trained archaeologists to the site, particularly to collect the distinctive black-on-white pottery.

The shipping of artifacts overseas motivated Virginia McClurg of Colorado Springs to embark on a long campaign to preserve the site and its contents. McClurg's efforts led Congress to protect artifacts on federal land with passage of the Antiquities Act and to establish Mesa Verde National Park in 1906.

Orientation

The North Rim summit at Park Point (8571 feet) towers more than 2000 feet above the Montezuma Valley. From Park Point the mesa gently slopes southward to 6000-foot elevation above the Mancos River in the Ute Mountain Tribal Park. The mesa-top is dissected by parallel canyons, typically 500 feet below the rim, which carry the drainage southward. Mesa Verde National Park occupies 81 sq miles of the northernmost portion of the mesa and contains the largest and most frequented cliff dwellings and surface sites.

The park entrance is off US 160 midway between Cortez and Mancos. From the entrance it's about 21 miles to park headquarters, Chapin Mesa Museum and Spruce Tree House. Along the way are Morefield Camp-

Square Tower House

ground (4 miles), the panoramic viewpoint at Park Point (8 miles) and the Far View Visitors Center opposite the Far View Lodge and Restaurant (about 11 miles). Towed vehicles are not allowed beyond Morefield Campground.

Chapin Mesa contains the largest concentration of sites in the area. South from park headquarters, Mesa Top Rd consists of two one-way circuits. Turn left about one-quarter mile from the start of Mesa Top Rd to visit Cliff Palace and Balcony House on the east loop. Take the west loop by continuing straight to mesa-top sites and many fine cliff-dwelling vantages. Taking the west loop first allows you to roughly follow the Ancestral Puebloan chronology in proper sequence.

At Wetherill Mesa, the second-largest concentration of sites, visitors may enter stabilized surface dwellings and two cliff dwellings. From the junction with the main road at Far View Visitors Center, the 12-mile mountainous Wetherill Mesa Rd snakes along the North Rim, acting as a natural barrier to tourbuses and indifferent

Ancestral Puebloan Settlement

Why the Ancestral Puebloans entered Mesa Verde is a subject for speculation. Habitations in Mesa Verde evolved greatly between 450, when the earliest simple structures were constructed, and 1300, when the great cities were mysteriously left behind.

The earliest period of settlement, the so-called Modified Basket Maker phase that extended to about 750, found the Ancestral Puebloans dispersed across the mesatops in small clusters of permanent pithouse dwellings – semi-subterranean structures with posts supporting low-profile roofs.

During the Developmental Pueblo Period, up to 1100, Ancestral Puebloans built surface houses with simple shared walls – like row-house apartments – forming small hamlets surrounded by fields of maize, beans and squash.

The following Classic Pueblo phase, to 1300, saw the Mesa Verde Ancestral Puebloans elaborate on the earlier structures using masonry building materials. Their efforts housed a peak population of perhaps several thousand in pueblo villages, the precursors to cities. Greater clusters of people created opportunities for united accomplishments and perhaps a rudimentary division of labor, social organization, political control and even organized raids on neighboring villages. During this period the Ancestral Puebloans developed subsurface roundrooms, or kivas – for decades believed by archaeologists to be only for ceremonial use, but more recently seen to have more basic functions as well. At this time the Ancestral Puebloans also developed hydraulic schemes to irrigate crops and provide water for villages.

There is mounting evidence of regular communication between Mesa Verdeans and Chaco Canyon peoples in northwestern New Mexico during this period. Some researchers suggest that the political, economic and social influences extended from even farther afield in Mesoamerica (present-day Mexico and Central America).

The Puebloans suddenly moved to the alcoves of the cliff faces around 1200. Community size depended on available cliff space, so while small cavities may have contained only a few compartments, there were many larger communities with more than 200 compartments, including elaborate blocks or rooms, cantilevered balconies, sunken round rooms and even tower structures – many connected with internal passageways.

Ancestral Puebloans inhabited the cliff dwellings for less than a century before disappearing in accord with a regional demographic collapse that is the greatest unexplained event of the era. Death, disease, invasion, internal warfare, resource depletion and climatic change are among the hardships that these peoples faced. Tree-ring chronologies offer proof of a widespread drought from 1276 to 1299, yet this explanation fails to account for the earlier population decline at Chaco Canyon or Mesa Verde's survival of earlier droughts. Population movements did occur and it is probable that many Ancestral Puebloans migrated south to the Pueblos of present-day New Mexico and Arizona.

Period	Chronology
I Basketmaker	AD 1–550
II Modified Basketmaker	550–750
III Developmental Pueblo	750–1100
IV Classic Pueblo	1100–1300

travelers. The road is open only from Memorial Day in late May to Labor Day in early September.

Information

Far View Visitors Center (☎ 970-529-5036) is open 8 am to 5 pm, late spring through early autumn. More comprehensive information is available at the Chapin Mesa Museum, but visitors must first stop at Far View to obtain the required tickets ($2) for tours of Cliff Palace, Long House or Balcony House.

Park headquarters (☎ 970-529-4461) is open weekdays during park hours. For additional information write Mesa Verde National Park, CO 81330. The Chapin Mesa Museum (☎ 970-529-4475) is open 8 am to 5 pm daily (to 6:30 pm in summer) and provides information on weekends when park headquarters is closed.

The park entry fee is $10 per vehicle, $5 for bicyclists, hikers and motorcyclists, and is valid for seven days. The combined brochure and map handed to each visitor also is available in French, Spanish and German. Park roads are open 8 am to sunset, except Wetherill Mesa Rd, which closes at 4:30 pm. Winter vehicle travel on Mesa Top Rd is subject to weather conditions. You may snowshoe or cross-country ski on the roadway when conditions permit.

The post office is at park headquarters in Chapin Mesa. The Mesa Verde Museum Association (☎ 970-529-4445), located in the Chapin Mesa Museum, has an excellent selection of materials on the Ancestral Puebloan and modern tribes in the American Southwest.

From May to mid-October, Morefield Village, near the Morefield Campground turnoff, has 10¢ showers and $1 per load washers. It's open 24 hours.

Chapin Mesa

There is no other place where so many remnants of Ancestral Puebloan settlement are clustered together, providing an opportunity to see and compare examples of all phases of construction – from pithouses to pueblo villages to the elaborate multiroom cities tucked into cliff recesses. Pamphlets describing most excavated sites are available at either Far View Visitors Center or Chapin Mesa Museum.

On the upper portion of Chapin Mesa are the **Far View Sites**, perhaps the most densely settled area in Mesa Verde after 1100. The large walled pueblo sites at Far View House enclose a central kiva and planned room layout that originally was two stories high. To the north is a small row of rooms and attached circular tower that likely extended just above the adjacent 'pygmy forest' of piñon pine and juniper trees. This tower is one of 57 found throughout Mesa Verde that the Ancestral Puebloans may have built as watchtowers, religious structures or astronomical observatories for agricultural schedules. They also built a system to divert streamwater to fields and into nearby Mummy Lake Reservoir – a masonry ditch that leads toward Spruce Tree House.

Near park headquarters, an easy walk without ladders or steps leads to **Spruce Tree House**. This sheltered alcove, more than 200 feet wide and almost 90 feet deep, contains about 114 rooms and eight kivas and once housed about 100 people. One kiva has a reconstructed roof and ladder for entry. During the winter when many portions of the park are closed, access to this site is by ranger-led tours only. Spruce Tree House is open 9 am to 5 pm daily.

South from park headquarters, the 6-mile Mesa Top Rd circuit connects 10 excavated mesa-top sites, three accessible cliff dwellings and many vantages of inaccessible cliff dwellings from the mesa rim. It's open 8 am to sunset.

Perhaps the most photographed site in the park is the secluded four-story **Square Tower House** on the west loop of Mesa Top Rd. Among the excellent late afternoon views of many cliff dwellings from **Sun Point** is the vista of Cliff Palace, sighted by Richard Wetherill in 1888. The mesa-top sites on the west loop of Mesa Top Rd also feature the astronomically aligned **Sun Temple**.

On the east loop of Mesa Top Rd, you must have a ticket to take part in the one-hour guided tours of either **Cliff Palace** or **Balcony House**, open 9 am to 5 pm daily (closed in winter).

Foot access to Cliff Palace, the largest site in the park, resembles the approach taken by the Ancestral Puebloans – visitors must climb a stone stairway and four 10-foot ladders. This grand representative of engineering achievement, with 217 rooms and 23 kivas, provided shelter for as many as 250 people. However, the inhabitants were without running water – springs across the canyon, below Sun Temple, were the most likely water sources. Use of small 'chinking' stones between the large blocks is strikingly similar to Ancestral Puebloan construction employed at distant Chaco Canyon.

The residents of Balcony House had outstanding views of Soda Canyon, 600 feet below the sandstone overhang that served as the ceiling for 35 to 40 rooms. Panoramic views, however, were apparently secondary either to concerns for security (entry was via a narrow tunnel) or to the attraction of two reliable springs. Today, visitors enter the obviously stabilized sites by a 32-foot ladder to see the cantilevered balcony and enjoy clambering throughout the tunnel and dwelling.

Wetherill Mesa

The less frequented western portion of the park offers a comprehensive display of Ancestral Puebloan relics. From Memorial to Labor Day, the winding Wetherill Mesa Rd is open 8 am to 4:30 pm daily. The **Badger House Community** consists of a short trail between four excavated surface sites depicting various phases of Ancestral Puebloan development. For a complete chronological circuit, continue on the trail to **Long House**, the second largest cliff dwelling in Mesa Verde (for this you'll first need a $2 ticket purchased at the Far View Visitors Center). The nearby **Step House**, initially occupied by Modified Basketmaker peoples residing in pithouses, later became the site of a Classic Pueblo period masonry complex of rooms and kivas. Stairways and indentations in the rocks provided access to the partially irrigated crops in the terraces on the mesa top.

Park Point

The fire lookout at Park Point (8571 feet) is the highest elevation in the park and accordingly offers panoramic views. To the north are the 14,000-foot peaks of the San Juan Mountains; in the northeast can be seen the 12,000-foot crests of the La Plata Mountains; to the southwest, beyond the southward sloping Mesa Verde plateau, is the distant volcanic plug of Shiprock; and to the west is the prone humanlike profile of Sleeping Ute Mountain.

Hiking

Backcountry access is specifically forbidden within Mesa Verde National Park. However, there are several marked trails open to hikers.

From park headquarters and adjacent Chapin Mesa Museum, two trail loops, each less than 3 miles in length, are accessed from the short path to Spruce Tree House. All hikers must first register at park headquarters. While you're there, pick up pamphlets for the **Petroglyph Point Trail** and the self-guided tour of Spruce Tree House.

From the museum overlook of Spruce Tree House, follow the path to the canyon floor. Return via Petroglyph Point Trail to view the petroglyphs etched into the naturally varnished rock surface and interpret the uses of native plants. After climbing about 300 feet back to the rim, either return directly to park headquarters or continue to the left on another loop, the **Spruce Canyon Trail**.

From the amphitheater parking area near Morefield Campground, a spur trail climbs to **Point Lookout** (8417 feet) about 2 miles away, where you may witness a fabulous sunset over Sleeping Ute Mountain (9884 feet). The 8-mile **Prater Ridge Trail** loop starts at the Hopi group area in Morefield Campground. Neither trail requires a permit.

Bicycling

Finding convenient parking at the many stops along Mesa Top Rd is not a problem

Carvings dance on the rocks at Petroglyph Point.

MARK PARKES

for those on bikes. Only the hardiest cyclists, however, will want to enter the park by bike and immediately face the grueling 4-mile ascent to Morefield Campground, followed by a narrow tunnel, to reach the North Rim. An easier option is to unlimber your muscles and mount up at Morefield, Far View Visitors Center or park headquarters.

If you choose to cycle, note that the NPS prohibits bicyclists from Wetherill Mesa Rd, and throughout the park secure bicycle parking is rare. Ride *only* on paved roadways.

Organized Tours

The park concessionaire, ARAMARK Mesa Verde (☎ 970-529-4421), PO Box 277, Mancos, CO 81328, offers guided tours to excavated pit homes, views of cliff dwellings and the Spruce Tree House daily from May to mid-October.

Introductory three-hour tours ($32/21 adults/children) depart from Morefield Campground at 8:30 am and from Far View

Lodge at 9 am. Afternoon tours ($34/23) include the Balcony House and depart the Far View Lodge *only* at 1 pm.

A full-day tour ($53/41 adults/children) leaving at 9:30 am from the Far View Lodge, includes the morning tour sites and goes on to examine later architecture and social developments, also taking in the Cliff Palace and providing lunch along the way.

Places to Stay & Eat

Nearby Cortez and Mancos have plenty of mid-range places to stay; Farmington, New Mexico, also has plenty of accommodations and is only 1½ hours away. Within the national park, visitors must choose between two extremes: camping or staying at a high-end lodge. An overnight stay in the park allows convenient access to the many sites during the best viewing hours, participation in evening programs and the sheer pleasure of watching the sun set over Ute Mountain from the quiet of the mesa top.

With 445 campsites only 4 miles from the park entrance, *Morefield Campground*

COLORADO

(☎ 970-529-4421), open from May to mid-October, has plenty of capacity for the peak season. Grassy tent sites at Navajo Loop are conveniently located near Morefield Village (which offers a general store, gas station, restaurant, showers and laundry) and cost $18. Full hookups are available for $25. Free evening campfire programs take place nightly from Memorial Day to Labor Day at the Morefield Campground Amphitheater; for information contact the NPS (☎ 970-529-4631).

The nonsmoking *Far View Lodge* (☎ 970-529-4421), 15 miles from the park entrance perched on the mesa top, has rooms with Southwestern furnishings, private balconies and outstanding views. Rooms are available mid-April through October 26th; the rates are $92–101 in October and $100–110 during the rest of the season. Compared to top-end lodging in Cortez, the Far View Lodge is a good value and offers a memorable visit (and there are no TVs or phones to disturb guests).

The self-service *Far View Terrace*, immediately south of the visitor center, serves reasonably priced meals 7 am to 8 pm (closed winter). Near the Chapin Mesa Museum, the *Spruce Tree Terrace* serves sandwiches, salads and the like 10 am to 5 pm daily.

The *Metate Room* (☎ 970-529-4421), at the Far View Lodge, is the nearest restaurant to Dove Creek serving gourmet Anasazi beans (a variegated pinto bean). Open 5 to 9:30 pm nightly, the Metate Room also serves steak, seafood, game specialties and good Mexican dishes.

MANCOS
☎ 970 • pop 900 • elevation 7000 feet

The historic homes and landmark buildings in tiny Mancos, between Cortez and Durango, make for a worthwhile stop and a pleasant place to stay while visiting Mesa Verde National Park, only 7 miles west.

Historic displays and a walking tour map are available at the visitor center (☎ 533-7434), at the corner of Main St and Railroad Ave (US 160). It also has information on outdoor activities in the area and local ranches that offer horseback rides and Western-style overnight trips.
website: www.mancos.org

Places to Stay

At the east end of Grand Ave, the Mancos River runs beside the town's wooded *Boyle Park*. Tent campsites and restrooms are free; a small donation goes to help fund park upkeep. Please register with the park host in the trailer at the park entrance.

The best bet in town is *Old Mancos Inn* (☎ 533-9019, fax 970-533-7138, 200 W Grand Ave). The hotel's friendly owners, Dean and Greg, have worked hard to renovate the place and provide unique, pleasant rooms for reasonable prices. Twelve rooms with shared bath cost $30/35 singles/doubles; three rooms with private bath are $45/50. The outside deck adds yet more value. This is also one of the few truly gay-friendly hotels in Colorado. Greg is the town mayor, one of only five openly gay mayors in the United States.

A nice nearby B&B is the historic *Bauer House* (☎ 533-9707, 800-733-9707, 100 Bauer Ave), an 1880s brick Victorian mansion that has two rooms starting at $95, and two suites (one complete with kitchen and bar) for $125.

Comfortable rooms cost $45/55 ($35/45 in winter) at *Enchanted Mesa Motel* (☎ 533-7729, 862 W Grand Ave). The *Mesa Verde Motel* (☎ 533-7741, 191 Railroad Ave) isn't as cozy but does have a hot tub. Rooms are around $49/59 during high season.

How about spending the night in a former fire lookout tower? Standing 55 feet above a meadow 14 miles north of Mancos at 9800 feet elevation, the *Jersey Jim Lookout* (☎ 533-7060) is on the National Historic Lookout Register and is complete with its Osborne fire-finder and topographic map. The tower accommodates up to four adults (bring your own bedding) and must be reserved long in advance: The reservation office opens on the first workday of March (1 to 5 pm) and the entire season (usually late May to mid-October) is typically booked within days. The nightly fee is $40, with a two-night maximum.

Places to Eat

The congenial owners of the *Absolute Baking Co* (☎ 533-1200, 110 S Main St) are justified in advertising 'sublime breads…food with integrity.' They bake fresh bread and pastries using only organic flours and grains, and prepare excellent light meals from scrumptious sandwiches ($4) to quiche and quesadillas. The cafe also doubles as a used bookstore and is open daily for breakfast and lunch, except Wednesday.

For dinner, the *Dusty Rose Cafe* (☎ 533-9042, 200 W Grand Ave) offers tasty dishes like fresh seafood and veal, all made from fresh ingredients. Try the homemade desserts and don't miss the champagne brunch on Saturday and Sunday (8 am to 2 pm).

A popular steak and seafood dinner joint is *Millwood Junction* (☎ 533-7338), at the corner of Main St and Railroad Ave. Folks from miles around come to Mancos on Friday night for the $14 seafood buffet.

DOLORES

☎ 970 • pop 1100 • elevation 7000 feet

In the narrow Dolores River Canyon, Dolores enjoys a scenic location 11 miles north of Cortez on Hwy 145 (also called Railroad Ave). Housed in a replica of the town's old railroad depot, the Dolores Visitor Center (☎ 882-4018, 800-807-4712), 421 Railroad Ave, has information on lodging and outdoor activities in the area. It's open 9 am to 5 pm Monday to Saturday (10 am to 4 pm Sunday) from May to October, and 8 am to noon Monday to Friday in winter.

Adjacent to the visitor center is the **Galloping Goose Museum**, which has displays and one example of the rather odd-looking gasoline-powered vehicles used by the Rio Grande Southern Railroad to continue rail service into the San Juan Mountains during the economic troubles of the 1930s.

You can find out about nearby camping and hiking opportunities in the San Juan National Forest at the USFS Dolores Ranger Station (☎ 882-7296) at the corner of 6th St and Central Ave. It's open 8 am to 5 pm weekdays year-round. To get cleaned up after your outings, the Dolores Laundry & Public Showers, 302 Railroad Ave, offers a shower and towel for about $3.

The *Dolores River RV Park* (☎ 882-7761, 18680 Railroad Ave), located about 1½ miles east of town, has pleasantly located tent sites for $12. RV hookups are $20. At the east end of town, the *Outpost Motel* (☎ 882-7271, 800-382-4892, 1800 Central Ave) has small but clean singles/doubles for $43/49, as well as cabins for $95. Some of the motel rooms have kitchenettes and the courtyard features a pleasant little wooden deck overlooking the Dolores River.

Dolores Mountain Inn (☎ 882-7203, 800-842-8113, 701 Railroad Ave) has immaculate modern rooms from around $60 to $120. The motel's genial owner also offers bike rentals, shuttle service and guided tours.

Near the visitor center and listed on the National Register of Historic Places, the three-story *Rio Grande Southern Hotel* (☎ 882-7527, 101 S 1st St) dates from 1893 and has B&B rooms with shared bath for $39/65; rooms with private bath are $50/75.

The *German Stone Oven Restaurant* (☎ 882-7033, 811 Railroad Ave) dishes up platters of bratwurst for lunch ($8.50 with two homemade side dishes) and wienerschnitzel ($14.95) for dinner.

New Mexico

Mural on an adobe building near Taos, NM

San Francisco de Asis Church near Taos, NM

Taos Pueblo, continuously inhabited since 1450

Rancho de Taos church

LOU JACOBS JR

The Rio Grande, NM

VITOR VIEIRA

JOHN HAY

The Old West, alive and kicking in New Mexico

ROB RACHOWIECKI

Socorro, New Mexico's biggest town during the 1880s

ROB RACHOWIECKI

Adobe building in Santa Fe

JOHN HAY

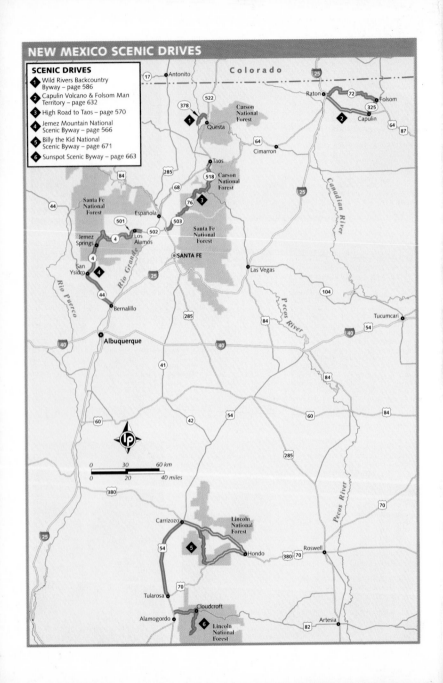

NEW MEXICO SCENIC DRIVES

Colorado

Antonito

Raton
Folsom
Capulin

Carson National Forest

Questa

Taos
Cimarron

Española
Santa Fe National Forest

Los Alamos
Jemez Springs

SANTA FE
Las Vegas

San Ysidro
Bernalillo

Rio Grande
Rio Puerco
Canadian River
Pecos River

Albuquerque

Tucumcari

0   30   60 km
0   20   40 miles

Carrizozo
Lincoln National Forest

Roswell
Hondo

Tularosa

Cloudcroft
Alamogordo
Lincoln National Forest
Artesia

Facts about New Mexico

New Mexico, with its strong Indian, Hispanic and Anglo heritages and influences, is as much a cultural experience as a place to visit. The USA prides itself on its multicultural diversity, so what's the big deal about New Mexico? The state's triculturalism is simply older and can appear to be seamless; many visitors glide almost effortlessly from one culture to another.

Some of the country's most inspiring ancient Indian sites are found in the northwestern corner of the state, among them a favorite, the Chaco Culture National Historical Park. It is more than just a ruin: It has a sense of timelessness and spirituality that is palpable. Not far away are more than a dozen centuries-old pueblos (Indian villages constructed permanently in adobe or stone), the most famous of which is the living mesa-top town of Acoma Pueblo, which has been continuously inhabited for about eight centuries. These pueblos provide insight into life here before the continent received the name of America.

Thousands of years before advanced Indian cultures built these massive stone buildings and towns, nomadic hunters and gatherers wandered through the area tracking woolly mammoths and giant sloths and were themselves tracked by saber-toothed tigers. The continent's oldest known Indian sites have been discovered in eastern New Mexico: in Folsom, where the remains of the Folsom man, dating back 10,800 years, were uncovered, and near Clovis, where items from Clovis culture date back 11,000 years.

New Mexico's European history, by comparison, is very recent. Nevertheless, the late-16th- and early-17th-century Spanish buildings are the oldest non-Indian structures in the country, predating the arrival of the Pilgrims in New England. Santa Fe's old center is as historic a place as any in the country, and it attracts and charms throngs of visitors every year.

The natural beauty of the state comprises many unique features, not the least of which

Highlights

- Santa Fe – explore the SoHo of the Southwest, ringed by mountains and desert.
- White Sands National Monument – romp, hike and drive through miles of pure-white gypsum dunes.
- Acoma Pueblo – an ancient pueblo perches on a mesa.
- Gila Cliff Dwellings National Monument – visit a quiet Indian site in the mountains.
- Taos – wander through this pleasant small town, a mecca for skiers and artists.
- El Morro National Monument – this sandstone outcrop offers graffiti, from ancient petroglyphs to pioneer signatures, as history.

Scenic Drives

The map opposite this page is a sampling of favorite routes through New Mexico. Some are designated 'Scenic Byways' and some are quiet dirt trails; some are alternative highways and some are rewarding detours. The text includes many more recommended roads for exploring this scenic country.

is the luminescent quality of the light. The play between the landscape and the light has attracted artists and writers since the early 20th century, including DH Lawrence, Georgia O'Keeffe and Ernest Blumenschein. Today, Santa Fe and Taos are vibrant artists' communities. The southern part of New Mexico draws attention with the huge and empty dunes of the White Sands National Monument as well as with one of the most impressive and accessible natural cave systems in the world at Carlsbad Caverns National Park.

One way to explore New Mexico is to travel some of the 24 state-designated scenic byways, which are dedicated to preserving

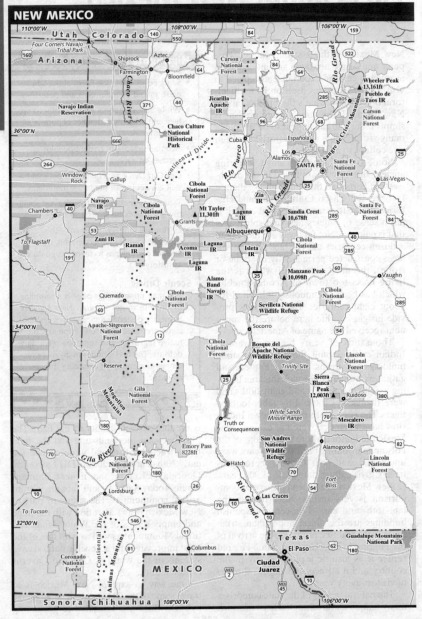

and promoting historic, cultural or natural assets located on or near them. Four have been selected as National Scenic Byways: the Santa Fe Trail, the Jemez Mountain Trail, Billy the Kid, and El Camino Real.

Unlike any other state license plate in the country, the New Mexico plate says 'USA,' a reminder that despite its quirky nature, New Mexico is indeed a part of the contiguous 48. With its distinct combination of history, peoples, light and landscape, it's no wonder that the license plate also reads 'land of enchantment.'

Recent History

The territory of New Mexico included Arizona and some of Colorado when the USA annexed the land from Mexico in 1848. When the territories of Colorado and Arizona were proclaimed in 1861 and 1863, respectively, New Mexico's present borders were defined.

During the American Civil War, the Confederate forces tried to control New Mexico in an effort to keep access to the ports of California, but they were defeated by the Union in the second of two major battles in 1862. After the Civil War came the Indian Wars, particularly against the Navajos and Apaches in western New Mexico and eastern Arizona. Despite the wars with the Indians, settlers in the form of cowboys and miners began to arrive in large numbers in the 1870s. Cattle drives from Texas up the Pecos River Valley into the high plains of eastern New Mexico were some of the largest ever known, with tens of thousands of head of cattle moving across the land. The miners ventured even farther west, especially into the mountains around Silver City.

The arrival of the railroads in the late 1870s opened the state to a period of economic boom, with settlers arriving and cattle and ores being shipped east, where there was a ready market for them. Fortunes were made and lives lost in the lawless days of the Wild West. Most famous among the many violent incidents was the Lincoln County War, which pitted rival ranch factions against one another from

1878 to 1881. A major player in this incident was Billy the Kid, perhaps the West's most famous outlaw even though he was gunned down at the early age of 21. The violence and lawlessness was one factor that dissuaded the federal government from granting statehood to the territory of New Mexico. A second factor was an unfounded distrust of the Hispanic population by the Anglo powers in Washington, DC.

This distrust was partially dispelled by the Hispanic New Mexican soldiers who fought with distinction in the Spanish-American war of 1898. The lawlessness of the late 19th century was brought under control, and by the early 20th century, New Mexico was ready for statehood. After a drawn-out process, New Mexico became the 47th state on January 6, 1912.

As with most of the Southwest, the lack of water greatly limited the state's growth. The construction of the Elephant Butte Dam on the Rio Grande in 1916 began to relieve this. The 1920s were an important decade for New Mexicans. Pueblo Indians gained legal control over their lands after white squatters tried to take them over, and all Indians won US citizenship (although it

Breaking Stereotypes of Pueblo Indians

People of European heritage have always found the towns of the Pueblo Indians familiar, at least upon first impression. Seeing the organized streets and permanent, multistory buildings, they have inferred that Pueblo cultures parallel European cultures more so than do other Indian cultures. In fact, Spanish conquistadors believed the pueblos were the fabled 'Seven Cities of Gold' and set about pillaging them. However, such inferences are misguided and one-sided, and have had harsh consequences for the Pueblo Indians.

The Pueblo villages have survived physically and culturally throughout the centuries despite barrages of intrusions. Inhabitants have not been forced onto reservations distant and disparate from their original homes, and their leadership remains traditionally theocratic: The religious leaders choose tribal officers rather than acquiescing to the representative system of government that has been forced onto other tribes.

But intrusions have forced Pueblo peoples to forgo some customs for the sake of preserving others. The Hopi, for example, have traditionally placed a high value on the virtue of hospitality, which led them to open many ceremonies to the public. But in the early 1990s, excessive tourism threatened to turn the ceremonies into spectacles. The Hopi could have profited from the tourist interest in their ceremonies, but they opted to preserve their religious integrity by closing most of their ceremonial dances to the general public.

The ceremonies that are open to the public have many restrictions that arise from their spiritual nature. Tribal members participate in ceremonial dances on a prescribed basis – dancers are carefully chosen, and the observers support them and watch with understanding and appreciation.

When non-Indian visitors are allowed to enter pueblos and attend ceremonies, they are often surprised to find that the pueblos and Pueblo culture are unique and distinct from Anglo culture. The pueblos have few or none of the modern trappings of other US towns, such as cars, phones and neon signs. Many areas are off-limits, for no obvious reason. Pueblo Indians rarely offer a hearty handshake or direct eye contact when welcoming visitors, because eye contact is considered disrespectful. Their conversation can seem muted or limited, but quiet listening is valued, and incessant interjections in conversations such as 'Uh huh' and 'Oh, really?' are considered rude.

Another assumption visitors make about the Pueblo Indians is that only one Pueblo culture exists. The Pueblo groups are united in architecture and theocracy, but in language and dialect, religion and ritual, they differ widely. For instance, the Hopi and Taos Pueblo Indians are both Pueblo tribes

was not until 1947 that they were allowed to vote). The 1920s also saw the arrival of many artists to the fledgling artist colonies in the Santa Fe and Taos areas.

The Great Depression of the 1930s hit New Mexico hard, although various WPA projects served to alleviate the misery somewhat. WWII revived the state's economy and initiated perhaps the most important project of the war. The Manhattan Project at Los Alamos saw the secret development and testing of the nuclear bomb, which was deployed against Japan in 1945 and quickly led to the end of the war. Los

Alamos remains an important military research and development center, as does the White Sands Missile Range.

The second half of the 20th century saw great population growth in New Mexico and throughout the Southwest. This has created pressure on the oldest inhabitants of the state, the Indians and the Hispanic inhabitants who have farmed the land for generations. In 1970, the Taos Pueblo Indians contested the United States Forest Service's use of their sacred Blue Lake and the surrounding region in the Carson National Forest, and Congress set aside the

Breaking Stereotypes of Pueblo Indians

living in ancient towns, but their languages and customs are very different. The same differences apply to the many pueblos in the Four Corners area, where several languages and dialects are spoken and customs are distinct. These disparities arose not only from the distances between the pueblos but also from the assimilation of various tribes into many of them, sometimes centuries ago.

Being prepared to encounter and respect these differences will help non-Indian visitors focus on each pueblo's unique traditions. It's also important to remember that each pueblo has its own rules pertaining to acceptable behavior, particularly in the realm of photography, sketching and other forms of recording sights and sounds.

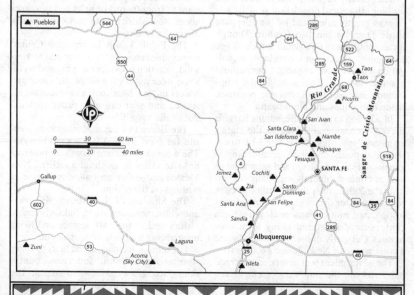

contested area for sole use of the tribe. Disagreements over the land and resource rights continue today, usually taking the form of lengthy legal wranglings.

Economy

Although the Spanish established missions and haciendas during their first two centuries in New Mexico, agricultural growth was not extensive due to the aridity of the region and Indian opposition to being forced to work Spanish farms. In the 18th century, however, the development of farming, mining and ranching expanded. Not long after Mexico won its independence from Spain, the Santa Fe Trail opened trade with the USA to the east. Despite opposition from Indian tribes, ranchers and farmers slowly took over the state's extensive grasslands, and in 1879 the Santa Fe Railroad arrived, fueling the growth of the cattle industry during the next decade. Ranching continues to be important to the state's economy today despite extensive overgrazing.

The scarcity of water that had impeded farming efforts and population growth early on was greatly alleviated by the Elephant Butte Dam on the Rio Grande. Though water continues to be a significant challenge to farming and economic development, irrigation efforts have improved agricultural potential and today the state's major crops include hay, sorghum, onions, potatoes, piñon nuts, chiles and pinto beans.

In addition to agriculture, mining has also played a considerable role in the state's economy. New Mexico has tapped into extensive deposits of potash, uranium, manganese and salt, petroleum and natural gas as well as nonfuel minerals, especially copper.

In the 20th century the US military began to acquire extensive land tracts for weapons testing, and military and nuclear research centers have bolstered many local economies. Currently military-related jobs are a cornerstone of New Mexico's economy.

The government sector, service and trade industries are the state's major employers. Unemployment is 5.6%. Per capita income is $21,836 per year, the third lowest of the 50 states. The US Census Bureau estimates that over 20.8% of the population lives in poverty (highest in the nation), and 27.5% of New Mexican children live in poverty (the national average is 19.9%).

Information

To obtain visitor information, write to the New Mexico Tourism Bureau (☎ 800-646-2040) at 491 Old Santa Fe Trail, Santa Fe NM 87503.

Telephone Most of New Mexico uses the ☎ 505 area code. Though the area code in Santa Fe, Albuquerque, Los Alamos and the surrounding area (Bernalillo and Santa Fe, counties) is scheduled to change to ☎ 575 in May 2002, opposition from local individuals and businesses may delay the changeover. Calls made to the 505 area code after the proposed change will connect to a recorded message announcing the new area code.

Internet Resources For statewide information, go online to www.newmexico.org; you can link to pretty much anything you want to from there. For links and resources about New Mexico state parks, go to www.nmparks.com.

The Public Lands Information Center, www.publiclands.org, is a convenient consolidation that provides camping and recreation information for all public lands and waters in New Mexico. It's an excellent resource and you can also order regional books and maps there.

The Bureau of Land Management website for New Mexico is www.nm.blm.gov. The website www.zianet.com/snm provides links to cities throughout southern New Mexico and offers an online magazine of writings on the region. The Museum of New Mexico site, www.museumofnewmexico.org, links visitors to history and culture, art, science and living museums as well as state monuments.

For more information and links to other sites about downhill and cross-country skiing, access www.skinewmexico.com. The comprehensive website www.psych.nmsu.edu/~linda/chilepg.htm offers links to every

New Mexican Food

The heart and soul of New Mexican food, and indeed a symbol of the state as evidenced by the red *ristras* that hang on adobe walls everywhere, is the chile pepper. New Mexico harvests more than 30,000 acres of chile annually, predominantly in the southwestern town of Hatch, and just about every restaurant (including McDonalds) offers it. When you see it on a menu, it refers either to chopped-up fresh-roasted chile (served, for example, on a hamburger) or chile sauce, usually with ground pork or beef (vegetarian options are usually just plain chile sauce) and most commonly drenching burritos, enchiladas and tamales. Unlike Tex-Mex or Mexican sauce, made predominantly with tomatoes and meat, chile (pureéd or chopped) is the foundation of the sauce. The unpretentious bowl of chile, which is basically a bowl of chopped chile and pinto beans served with a flour tortilla, is perhaps the quintessential New Mexican meal (decidedly different from the Midwestern and Texan 'chili,' which is essentially the reverse; beans and/or meat with diced or powdered chile only as a spice).

When ordering chile you will be asked 'red or green?' The green chile, though distinctly different in flavor from the red, is simply an unripened red chile. Because the heat of the chile varies from crop to crop, variety to variety, ask which is hotter and, if you want to try both, ask for 'Christmas.' Pueblo Indians and Spaniards found the heat of the chile (capsaicin), high in vitamin C, to be a natural medicine, curing everything from ulcers to acne. Whatever its medical benefits, any New Mexican will tell you that the stuff is addictive. Everyone seems to have an opinion as to where to find the best chile or the perfect green-chile cheeseburger and you'll soon discover the subtle and not-so-subtle differences among chiles.

Beyond the chile pepper, New Mexican food is characterized by its use of *pozole, sopaipillas* and blue corn. The sopaipilla, often served as a dessert elsewhere, is served along with the main course in New Mexico. It is deep-fried flour dough, soft and hollow in the center, eaten warm with honey between bites of hot chile. You will also find them stuffed with beans or meat and served as a main dish (covered, of course, with chile). Pozole, the Spanish name for hominy, is dried or frozen kernels of corn that have been processed in a lime solution to remove the hulls. It is generally served plain, along with pinto beans, as a side dish. Blue corn, served primarily in the form of blue corn tortillas, have a heartier flavor than the more common yellow corn tortillas. Finally, pinto beans, while not unique to New Mexican food and indeed a key element of Mexican and Tex-Mex fare as well, is a basic element of most New Mexican dishes. Pinto beans are served either whole or refried.

Throughout the state, from cafés to diners to trailers along the road, travelers will find cheap, delicious New Mexican food. In the fall, farmers markets and fruit stands sell fresh-roasted chiles, and friends and family gather to roast and peel chiles, a rather messy and slimy affair.

If you can, take some chiles home with you; after a few weeks without them, you just may find yourself craving a 'bowl of green.'

---

imaginable thing you'd want to know about New Mexico, from outdoor recreation to where to buy chile products.

Time The state is on Mountain Time, which is one hour later than the West Coast, two hours earlier than the East Coast, and seven hours behind Greenwich Mean Time (GMT).

Driving Laws You must be 16 years old, or at least 15 with parental consent, to obtain a driver's license. Drivers and front-seat passengers are required to wear a safety belt. Children under age 11 must use child restraints. You must be over 16 to obtain a motorcycle license. Motorcycle helmets are required for rider and passenger if under 18.

The blood alcohol concentration over which you are legally considered drunk while driving is 0.08, but you can be arrested for driving with a blood alcohol level of 0.05. It is illegal to have an open container of alcohol in your car while driving.

Drinking Laws You must be 21 to buy a drink in a store, bar or restaurant. Beer, wine and spirits are sold in grocery stores and liquor stores from 6 am to midnight, except Sunday, when sales begin at noon. Restaurants must have licenses to serve alcohol; some licenses are limited to beer and wine. Sales of alcohol stop at 1 am and bars close at 2 am except on Sunday, when bars are open from noon until midnight. Alcohol is prohibited on Indian reservations.

Albuquerque Area

☎ 505 • pop 678,820 • elevation 5000 feet

The largest and most populous city in New Mexico has long been just a dot on the map of Route 66, the road that snaked its way from Chicago to Los Angeles in the prehistory of the interstate system. But Albuquerque, positioned in the valley between the impressive Sandia Mountains to the east and the Rio Grande to the west, offers inexpensive accommodations and a convenient base for exploring nearby deserts, mountains and Indian sites. Plus, you won't find the tourist schlock or the tourist prices of nearby Santa Fe and Taos.

HISTORY

The Ancestral Puebloans were the area's first permanent occupants, probably arriving in the 6th century. They planted corn, beans and squash, and constructed dwellings of adobe and brick along the banks of the Rio Grande. The Ancestral Puebloans ultimately abandoned the region around AD 1300.

In 1540 the Spanish explorer Francisco Vásquez de Coronado arrived in search of riches in the legendary Seven Cities of Cíbola (which he never found). His forces wintered at Kuaua pueblo on the west bank of the Rio Grande, 20 miles north of present-day Albuquerque. Juan de Oñate's expedition brought settlers in 1598. Farms and ranches sprung up, and a trading center was established at Bernalillo (a few miles north of Albuquerque). This was abandoned during the Pueblo Revolt of 1680.

In 1706, provisional governor Don Francisco Cuervo y Valdez established a *villa* (settlement) south of Bernalillo and named it after the Duke of Alburquerque, viceroy of New Spain. The first 'r' was dropped in the late 19th century, but Albuquerque is still called the 'Duke City.' During the 18th and much of the 19th centuries, the villa was a dusty trading center along the trail linking Mexico with Santa Fe. Close-knit families of Spanish descent accounted for most of the population. They lived around the central plaza that is today called Old Town.

Albuquerque changed with the arrival of the railroad in 1880. By the time it was incorporated as a town in 1885, Albuquerque had become predominantly Anglo. Growth continued in the 20th century. Route 66, the easiest way to travel east to west through New Mexico, brought a steady stream of traffic through the town. During the 1930s, motels, restaurants and shops arose along Central Ave to service those motorists.

ORIENTATION

Two interstate highways, I-25 (north-south) and I-40 (east-west), intersect in Albuquerque. An approximate grid surrounds that intersection, the major boundaries of which are Paseo del Norte Dr to the north, Central Ave (old Route 66) to the south, Rio Grande Blvd to the west and Tramway Blvd to the east. Central Ave is the main street, passing through Old Town, downtown, the university, Nob Hill and state fairground areas.

Street addresses often conclude with a directional designation, such as Wyoming NE. The center point is where Central crosses the railroad tracks, just east of downtown (see Downtown Albuquerque map). Locations north of Central and east of the tracks would have a NE designation. Any place south of Central and west of the tracks is called SW, and so on.

INFORMATION

The Albuquerque Convention & Visitors Bureau (☎ 842-9918, 800-284-2282, 800-733-9918), 20 First Plaza, in the Galeria, provides information on Albuquerque and New Mexico. It's open 8 am to 5 pm Monday to Friday. Write PO Box 26866, Albuquerque, NM 87125; website: www .abqcvb.org. The Old Town Information Center (☎ 243-3215), 303 Romero St NW, is open 9:30 am to 4:30 pm daily. For information on Albuquerque's gay community,

NEW MEXICO

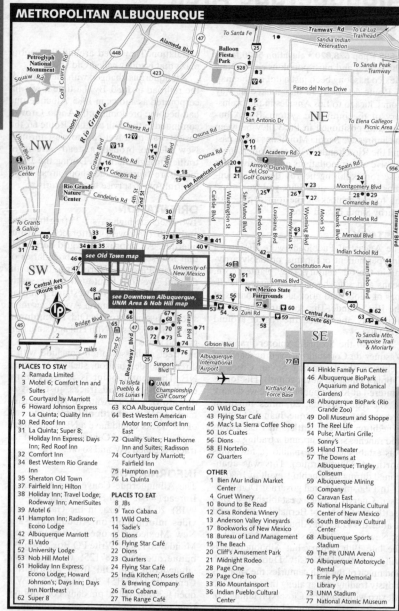

METROPOLITAN ALBUQUERQUE

To Santa Fe
To La Luz Trailhead
Tramway Rd
Sandia Indian Reservation
Alameda Blvd
Balloon Fiesta Park
To Santa Peak Tramway
Petroglyph National Monument
Squaw Rd
Paseo del Norte Drive
Chavez Rd
San Antonio Dr
NE
To Elena Gallegos Picnic Area
Osuna Rd
Montaño Rd
Osuna Rd
Academy Rd
Griegos Rd
Pan American Fwy
Arroyo del Oso Golf Course
Osuna Rd
Spain Rd
NW
Rio Grande Nature Center
Candelaria Rd
Montgomery Blvd
Comanche Rd
Candelaria Rd
Menaul Blvd
Visitor Center
To Grants & Gallup
University of New Mexico
Indian School Rd
SW
see Old Town map
Constitution Ave
Central Ave (Route 66)
see Downtown Albuquerque, UNM Area & Nob Hill map
Lomas Blvd
New Mexico State Fairgrounds
Central Ave (Route 66)
SE
To Sandia Mtn, Turquoise Trail & Moriarty
Bridge Blvd
Zuni Rd
Gibson Blvd
Sunport Blvd
Albuquerque International Airport
To Isleta Pueblo & Los Lunas
UNM Championship Golf Course
Kirtland Air Force Base

PLACES TO STAY

2 Ramada Limited
3 Motel 6; Comfort Inn and Suites
5 Courtyard by Marriott
6 Howard Johnson Express
7 La Quinta; Quality Inn
30 Red Roof Inn
31 La Quinta; Super 8; Holiday Inn Express; Days Inn; Red Roof Inn
32 Comfort Inn
34 Best Western Rio Grande Inn
35 Sheraton Old Town
37 Fairfield Inn; Hilton
38 Holiday Inn; Travel Lodge; Rodeway Inn; AmeriSuites
39 Motel 6
41 Hampton Inn; Radisson; Econo Lodge
42 Albuquerque Marriott
47 El Vado
52 University Lodge
53 Nob Hill Motel
61 Holiday Inn Express; Econo Lodge; Howard Johnson's; Days Inn; Days Inn Northeast
62 Super 8

63 KOA Albuquerque Central
64 Best Western American Motor Inn; Comfort Inn East
72 Quality Suites; Hawthorne Inn and Suites; Radisson
74 Courtyard by Marriott; Fairfield Inn
75 Hampton Inn
76 La Quinta

PLACES TO EAT

8 JBs
9 Taco Cabana
11 Wild Oats
14 Sadie's
15 Dions
16 Flying Star Café
22 Dions
23 Quarters
25 Flying Star Café
25 India Kitchen; Assets Grille & Brewing Company
26 Taco Cabana
27 The Range Café

40 Wild Oats
43 Flying Star Café
45 Mac's La Sierra Coffee Shop
50 Los Cuates
56 Dions
58 El Norteño
67 Quarters

OTHER

1 Bien Mur Indian Market Center
4 Gruet Winery
10 Bound to Be Read
12 Casa Rondena Winery
13 Anderson Valley Vineyards
17 Bookworks of New Mexico
18 Bureau of Land Management
19 The Beach
20 Cliff's Amusement Park
21 Midnight Rodeo
28 Page One
29 Page One Too
33 Rio Mountainsport
36 Indian Pueblo Cultural Center

44 Hinkle Family Fun Center
46 Albuquerque BioPark (Aquarium and Botanical Gardens)
48 Albuquerque BioPark (Rio Grande Zoo)
49 Doll Museum and Shoppe
51 The Reel Life
54 Pulse; Martini Grille; Sonny's
55 Hiland Theater
57 The Downs at Albuquerque; Tingley Coliseum
59 Albuquerque Mining Company
60 Caravan East
65 National Hispanic Cultural Center of New Mexico
66 South Broadway Cultural Center
68 Albuquerque Sports Stadium
69 The Pit (UNM Arena)
70 Albuquerque Motorcycle Rental
71 Ernie Pyle Memorial Library
73 UNM Stadium
77 National Atomic Museum

call the Albuquerque Lesbian and Gay Chamber of Commerce Information Line (☎ 243-6767).

The Cibola National Forest office (☎ 842-3292) is on the 5th floor of the Federal Building, 517 Gold Ave SW; it's open 8 am to 4:30 pm Monday to Friday. The Bureau of Land Management (☎ 761-8700) is at 435 Montaño Rd NW.

Page One (☎ 294-2026), 11018 Montgomery Blvd NE, is a huge and comprehensive bookstore. Across the street, Page One Too (☎ 294-5623), 11200 Montgomery Blvd NE, sells used books. Also try Bound to Be Read (☎ 828-3500), 6300 San Mateo NE, the University of New Mexico Bookstore (☎ 277-5451), on the south side of campus on Central at Cornell and Bookworks NM (☎ 344-8139), 4022 Rio Grande Blvd NW.

Other services include the library (☎ 768-5140), 501 Copper Ave NW; the downtown post office (☎ 245-9614), 201 5th SW; the main post office (☎ 245-9624), 1135 Broadway Ave NE; Presbyterian Hospital (☎ 841-1234 or 841-1111 for emergencies), 1100 Central SE; and the police (☎ 768-2020), 400 Roma Ave NW. For free answers to healthcare questions, call ☎ 224-7737.

OLD TOWN

From its founding in 1706 until the arrival of the railroad in 1880, Old Town Plaza was the hub of Albuquerque. With many original buildings, and museums and galleries within walking distance, this is the city's most popular tourist area (I-40 exit 157A).

During April to November, the Albuquerque Museum (see below) offers informative and free guided **walking tours** of Old Town at 11 am Tuesday to Sunday. The Old Town Information Center on Romero has a pamphlet called *Old Town: A Walking Tour of History and Architecture* that guides you to 17 of the area's historically significant structures.

San Felipe de Neri Church

Built in 1706 (though renovated several times since), this adobe church is Old Town's most famous sight. Hours are 7 am to 7 pm daily. A Spanish mass is held at 8:15 am. Call ☎ 243-4628 to confirm times and ask about other masses.

Albuquerque Museum

This museum (☎ 242-4600), 2000 Mountain Rd NW, explores the city's Indian, Hispanic

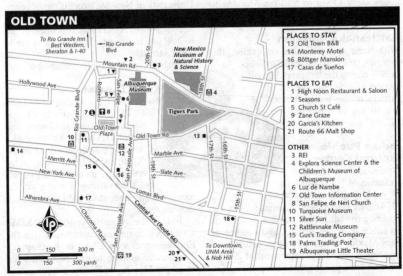

OLD TOWN

To Rio Grande Inn
Best Western,
Sheraton & I-40

Rio Grande Blvd

New Mexico Museum of Natural History & Science

Mountain Rd

Albuquerque Museum

Hollywood Ave

Romero

San Felipe

Tiguex Park

Old Town Plaza

Old Town Rd

Merritt Ave

New York Ave

Marble Ave

Slate Ave

Alhambra Ave

Lomas Blvd

Central Ave (Route 66)

Chacoma Place

San Pasquale Ave

To Downtown,
UNM Area
& Nob Hill

0   150   300 m
0   150   300 yards

PLACES TO STAY
13 Old Town B&B
14 Monterey Motel
16 Böttger Mansion
17 Casas de Sueños

PLACES TO EAT
1   High Noon Restaurant & Saloon
2   Seasons
5   Church St Café
9   Zane Graze
20 Garcia's Kitchen
21 Route 66 Malt Shop

OTHER
3   REI
4   Explora Science Center & the Children's Museum of Albuquerque
6   Luz de Nambe
7   Old Town Information Center
8   San Felipe de Neri Church
10 Turquoise Museum
11 Silver Sun
12 Rattlesnake Museum
15 Gus's Trading Company
17 Palms Trading Post
19 Albuquerque Little Theater

and Anglo history. A gallery exhibits changing shows of New Mexican artists. The museum is open 9 am to 5 pm Tuesday to Sunday (free).

New Mexico Museum of Natural History & Science

This kid-friendly museum (☎ 841-2800), 1801 Mountain Rd NW, features the Evolator (evolution elevator), which transports visitors through 38 million years of New Mexico's geologic and evolutionary history through the use of video technology. Hours are 9 am to 5 pm daily. Admission is $5 for adults, $4 for seniors and students and $2 for kids under 11. The huge-screen **Dynamax Theater** within the museum costs $5.20/4.20 for adults/students and $2.10 for seniors and children.

Turquoise Museum

Less than 10% of the state's multibillion-dollar turquoise businesses create products using natural turquoise. This private museum (☎ 247-8650), 2107 Central NW, helps you to recognize the real stuff with specimens from all over the world. It's a small place, but well worth a visit. The museum's hours are 9:30 am to 5:30 pm Monday to Saturday ($2).

Rattlesnake Museum

With some 45 live snakes on exhibit, this museum (☎ 242-6569), 202 San Felipe St NW, claims the largest public collection of different species of rattlers in the world. Hours are 10 am to 5 pm daily ($2.50).

Indian Pueblo Cultural Center

Owned and run by an association of New Mexico's 19 pueblos, this center (☎ 843-7270), 2401 12th St NW, is a must for anyone planning to visit Indian pueblos or who has an interest in the history and culture of New Mexico's Pueblo Indians. A historical museum traces the development of Pueblo cultures from prehistory to the present. Exhibits allow for comparison of cultures through examination of languages, customs and crafts. There is also an art gallery with exhibits that change monthly and a restaurant serving Pueblo fare. It's open 9 am to 5:30 pm daily ($4/2 for adults/children).

DOWNTOWN

This area lies southeast of Old Town and west of the university area. In recent years Albuquerque's downtown has experienced rejuvenation, and trendy restaurants, galleries and clubs are replacing the 1950s department stores and sleepy diners.

New Mexico Holocaust & Intolerance Museum and Study Center

The premise of this small museum (☎ 247-0606), 415 Central NW, is that discrimination and intolerance inevitably precede holocausts, and education can work to combat discrimination based on race, color, religion, sex, national origin, ancestry and sexual orientation. The permanent collection includes photographs of Nazi concentration camps that were found stuffed in a box and abandoned in an alley behind the University of New Mexico. Still in development are exhibits on the cultural genocide against Native Americans. It is open 11 am to 3:30 pm Tuesday to Friday, and 11 am to 4 pm Saturday.

website: www.nmholocaustmuseum.org

KiMo Theater

Built in 1927, the KiMo (☎ 848-1370, 764-1700 for tickets), 423 Central NW, is a historic landmark. The architect, Carl Boller, created a kind of pueblo art deco in the KiMo using impressions gathered on visits to Indian pueblos and reservations: Unique adornments include steer-skull light fixtures with glowing eyes.

Today, the recently renovated KiMo serves as a community arts center (see the Entertainment section later in this chapter). The theater may be toured between 9 am and 3 pm Monday to Friday.

Kids' Stuff

Albuquerque has a number of attractions that are great for kids. Although many of the attractions listed below are suitable for adults too, they are primarily aimed at kids.

The **Explora Science Center & the Children's Museum of Albuquerque** (☎ 842-1537), next to the Museum of Natural History & Science in Old Town, has programs and exhibits designed to give free reign to creativity and imagination. With demonstrations involving light, electricity, sound, motion, anatomy and more, the Explora Science Center is an interactive museum geared toward teaching kids scientific principles. Admission is $4 per person over 13 years old, $2 for those two to 12 and free for children under two.

Use **Cliff's Amusement Park** (☎ 881-9373), 4800 Osuna NE, on San Mateo Blvd just south of the Osuna exit on I-25, to reward your kids for being so patient and cooperative in the back seat. The park has about 25 rides, including a roller coaster, the Water Monkey, a play area and other traditional favorites. An unlimited-ride pass costs $16; individual ride tickets cost $1.50. The park is open May to October (weekends only in May) and is closed Monday and Tuesday.

Adults might enjoy **The Beach** (☎ 345-6066), 3 Desert Surf Circle, just as much as the kids do. There are seven water slides and a giant pool that creates 5-foot swells for body surfers. If you're timid, tired or just a toddler, float down the Lazy River or in one of the kiddie pools. From May to Labor Day you can splash all day for $15, or from 4:30 to 6:30 pm closing for $7 (kids under three are free). Call to confirm ever-changing times and prices.

Celebrating 40 years in 2002, the **Albuquerque Children's Theater** (☎ 242-4750), 224 San Pasquale NW, performs two or three shows a year at the Albuquerque Little Theater.

With bumper cars, laser tag, mini-golf and a huge 'jungle play area' where kids can crawl and climb and slide around, **Hinkle Family Fun Center** (☎ 299-3100), 12931 Indian School Rd NE, will keep little ones of all ages amused. It's a great place to run off some energy, especially if it's too hot or cold or wet to play outside.

Telephone Pioneer Museum of New Mexico

This museum (☎ 842-2937), 110 4th St NW, has hundreds of telephones and phone memorabilia from the days of Alexander Graham Bell to the present. Museum hours are 10 am to 2 pm Monday to Friday (free).

UNIVERSITY OF NEW MEXICO AREA

With about 18,000 full-time students in some 125 fields, UNM is New Mexico's leading university. Several museums and many cultural events are of interest to the visitor. Tours are available through Recruitment Services (☎ 277-2260) at 9 am and 2 pm Monday to Friday. Contact Public Affairs (☎ 277-5813) or the Visitors Center (☎ 277-1989), on Las Lomas Rd at the northwestern corner of campus, for further information. Redondo Dr loops around the campus; campus maps are available at the University of New Mexico Bookstore on Central Ave.

Maxwell Museum of Anthropology

This UNM museum (☎ 277-4404), just off University Blvd near the visitor center, has a permanent 'People of the Southwest' exhibit depicting 11,000 years of the region's cultural history. A fabricated dig, complete with tools, demonstrates the painstaking methods of archaeology. Hours are 9 am to 4 pm Tuesday to Friday, with varying weekend hours; closed Monday.

University Art Museum

This collection (☎ 277-4001), renowned for its photographs, is in the Center for the Arts building at Redondo and Cornell Drs on the south side of campus. The smallish space is crammed with paintings, prints and sculptures from a permanent collection of 24,000 pieces, many of which highlight New Mexico's rich Hispanic tradition. Hours are 9 am to 4 pm Tuesday to Friday, 5 to 8 pm Tuesday and 1 to 4 pm Sunday.

The affiliated **Jonson Gallery** (☎ 277-4967), 1909 Las Lomas Rd, is in the former home and studio of painter and longtime UNM professor Raymond Jonson; it's open 9 am to 4 pm Tuesday to Friday and 5 to 8 pm Tuesday.

Tamarind Institute

Highly regarded by lithographers, the Tamarind Institute (☎ 277-3901), 110 Cornell Dr SE, features modern lithographs, most of which are for sale. It's open 9 am to 5 pm weekdays (free).

METROPOLITAN ALBUQUERQUE
Rio Grande Nature Center

The center (☎ 344-7240), 2901 Candelaria Rd NE, is a 270-acre reserve on the Rio Grande, with gentle hiking and biking trails winding through meadows and groves of trees. About 260 bird species have been ob-

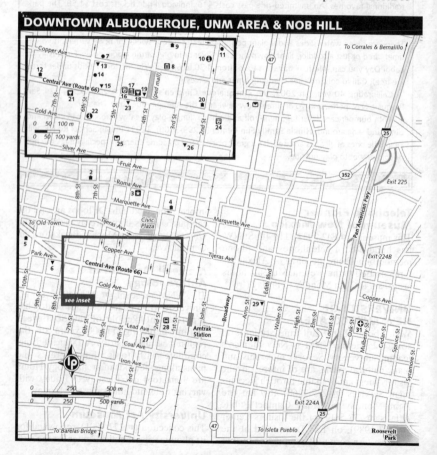

DOWNTOWN ALBUQUERQUE, UNM AREA & NOB HILL

served here. Admission is $1. Hours are 8 am to 5 pm daily (until 8:30 pm on Friday from June to August), though the visitor center doesn't open until 10 am.

Petroglyph National Monument

At this monument (☎ 899-0205) three trails of varying degree of difficulty lead visitors around 15,000 rock etchings dated from AD 1300. To get here, head west on I-40 across the Rio Grande and take exit 154 north. Admission is $1 per car on weekdays, $2 on weekends.

website: www.nps.gov/petr

Sandia Peak Tramway

Albuquerque boasts one of the world's longest tramways (☎ 856-7325). The 2.7-mile ride starts in the desert realm of cholla cactus and soars to the pines of the 10,300-foot Sandia Peak in 18 minutes ($14/10 roundtrip for adults/children; children under five are free). Riders can enjoy an observation deck, restaurant (☎ 243-9742) and trails for hiking, cross-country skiing and biking.

From May to August, the tram runs from 9 am to 10 pm; during the rest of the year it runs from 9 am to 8 pm. On Wednesday

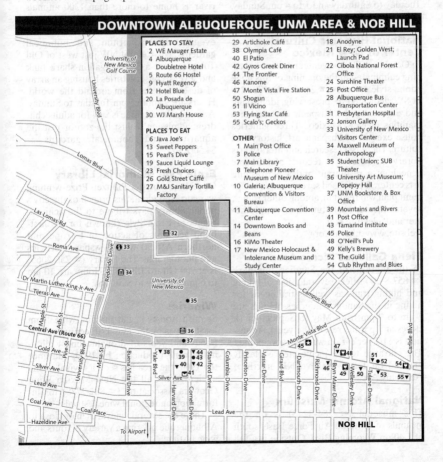

DOWNTOWN ALBUQUERQUE, UNM AREA & NOB HILL

PLACES TO STAY
2 WE Mauger Estate
4 Albuquerque Doubletree Hotel
5 Route 66 Hostel
9 Hyatt Regency
12 Hotel Blue
20 La Posada de Albuquerque
30 WJ Marsh House

PLACES TO EAT
6 Java Joe's
13 Sweet Peppers
15 Pearl's Dive
19 Sauce Liquid Lounge
23 Fresh Choices
26 Gold Street Caffé
27 M&J Sanitary Tortilla Factory

29 Artichoke Café
38 Olympia Café
40 El Patio
42 Gyros Greek Diner
44 The Frontier
46 Kanome
47 Monte Vista Fire Station
50 Shogun
51 Il Vicino
53 Flying Star Café
55 Scalo's; Geckos

OTHER
1 Main Post Office
3 Police
7 Main Library
8 Telephone Pioneer Museum of New Mexico
10 Galeria; Albuquerque Convention & Visitors Bureau
11 Albuquerque Convention Center
14 Downtown Books and Beans
16 KiMo Theater
17 New Mexico Holocaust & Intolerance Museum and Study Center

18 Anodyne
21 El Rey; Golden West; Launch Pad
22 Cibola National Forest Office
24 Sunshine Theater
25 Post Office
28 Albuquerque Bus Transportation Center
31 Presbyterian Hospital
32 Jonson Gallery
33 University of New Mexico Visitors Center
34 Maxwell Museum of Anthropology
35 Student Union; SUB Theater
36 University Art Museum; Popejoy Hall
37 UNM Bookstore & Box Office
39 Mountains and Rivers
41 Post Office
43 Tamarind Institute
45 Police
48 O'Neill's Pub
49 Kelly's Brewery
52 The Guild
54 Club Rhythm and Blues

year-round it opens at 5 pm. To reach the tram, take Tramway Blvd north on the east side of town, or take I-25 exit 234 and head east on Hwy 556.

Doll Museum & Shoppe

This small and quirky museum (☎ 255-8555), 5201 Constitution Ave NE, houses a wonderful collection of Barbie dolls and Barbie paraphernalia dating back to 1959, including the fur trimmed 'Furry Go Round Francie.' You'll also find cases of dolls (from 1880 to the present) displayed in creative ways. The museum is open 10 am to 4 pm Tuesday to Saturday and 1 to 4 pm Sunday. Admission is $5 for one year of visits.

National Hispanic Cultural Center of New Mexico

In October of 2000, seventeen years of planning culminated in the opening of this huge adobe-style complex (☎ 246-2261), 1701 4th St SW, dedicated to 'preserving, identifying and enhancing the Hispanic arts and humanities in New Mexico.' Three galleries house exhibits of Hispanic art, history and culture. There is a research and literary arts library with access to records of Hispanic genealogy, a restaurant and a performing arts center. A proposed seven-year development plan will result in, among other things, several theaters, art studios, an amphitheater and a lecture hall.
website: www.nhccnm.org

Elena Gallegos Picnic Area

In the foothills of the Sandias, this park (☎ 857-8334) offers several miles of biking and hiking trails as well as trailheads for hiking in the Sandia Wilderness. Hours are 7 am to 9 pm from May to September (it closes at 7 pm the rest of the year). Admission is $1/2 per car on weekdays/weekends. The entrance to the picnic area is clearly marked on Tramway Blvd NE, north of Academy Ave.

National Atomic Museum

This museum (☎ 284-3243) is on the grounds of Kirtland Air Force Base, south of I-40 on Wyoming Blvd. Outside is a full range of atomic weaponry, including replicas of the innocuously named 'Little Boy' and 'Fat Man' – the bombs that destroyed Hiroshima and Nagasaki. Inside, a theater shows *Ten Seconds That Shook the World*, an hour-long film about the development of the atomic bomb. Hours are 9 am to 5 pm daily (except major holidays); $3.

Albuquerque BioPark

This biological park (☎ 843-7413) includes the Rio Grande Zoo, the aquarium and the botanical gardens in two locations. The zoo, 903 10th St SW, on 60 shady acres along the river, is home to more than 1300 animals from around the world. Weekly in summer, the zoo hosts outdoor music events in the evening. The aquarium and botanical gardens, 2601 Central NW just west of Old Town, feature a 285,000-gallon shark tank and several conservatories housing an array of desert species from around the world. Hours are 9 am to 5 pm Tuesday to Sunday. Admission to all three is $8/4 for adults/children; admission to just the zoo or just the aquarium and botanical gardens is $4.50/2.50.

Ernie Pyle Memorial Library

Once home of the Pulitzer Prize-winning war correspondent, this branch of the city's public library pays tribute to the achievements of Ernie Pyle (known for his first-hand accounts of action in Europe and northern Africa) with newspaper articles and photographs. The library (☎ 256-2065) is at 900 Girard Blvd SE. Hours are 10 am to 6 pm Tuesday to Saturday.

Wineries

Spanish priests began making wine from local grapes by the mid-17th century. Flash floods and years of drought almost eliminated wine production by 1900, but since the 1960s the area has seen a revival of the ancient art. Call the New Mexico Wine Growers Association (☎ 881-7778) for information on regional wine festivals.

There are several vineyards in or close to Albuquerque offering a variety of tours and wine tasting:

Anasazi Fields (☎ 867-3062) Camino de los Pueblitos Rd

Anderson Valley Vineyards (☎ 344-7266) 4920 Rio Grande Blvd NW

Casa Rondena (☎ 344-5911) 733 Chavez Rd NW

Gruet Winery (☎ 821-0055) 8400 Pan American Fwy NE

Sandia Crest National Scenic Byway

This scenic drive (Hwy 536) passes several trailheads ($3 parking fee) as it winds up the eastern slope of the Sandias to Sandia Peak. From Albuquerque, take I-40 east to exit 175, and drive about 6 miles north on Hwy 14 to Hwy 536. An alternative route is to go north on I-25 to exit 242 and take Hwy 165 east past Placitas; this bumpy dirt road through Las Huertas Canyon connects with Hwy 536 just north of the ski base and a few miles south of the peak. Along the way, stop at **Sandia Man Cave**, a prehistoric dwelling site. It's a beautiful drive, though it may be closed due to snow. Call the helpful Sandia Ranger Station (☎ 281-3304), 11776 Hwy 337, about a mile south of I-40 exit 175, for maps and information on the Sandia Wilderness Area. It is open every day.

ACTIVITIES

The omnipresent Sandia Mountains offer many opportunities for hiking, skiing, picnicking, biking and camping.

Skiing

The 200-acre Sandia Peak Ski Area (☎ 242-9133) is less than an hour from downtown. Ride the tram from the western base of the Sandias to the top of the ski area, or drive up the eastern side (I-40 east to Hwy 14 north) and park at the bottom of the slopes. You can rent downhill skis at the ski base ($15), but be warned that there is no ski rental at the top of the ski area where the tram drops you off, so if you want to rent skis at the mountain you have to drive. Full/half-day lift tickets are $34/25 for adults, and $25/18 for kids and seniors.

Cross-country trails atop the mountain are maintained by the Cibola National Forest. In town, Rio Mountainsport (☎ 766-9970), 1210 Rio Grande Blvd NW, rents cross-country skis and snowshoes for about $15 a day. REI (☎ 247-1191), 1905 Mountain Rd NW in Old Town, and Mountains and Rivers (☎ 268-4876), 2320 Central SE, across from UNM, also rent equipment.

Bicycling

There are extensive mountain-biking trails in the Sandia Mountains, as well as in the Rio Grande Bosque. From late May through mid-October, the Sandia Peak Ski Area operates one summer chairlift from 10 am to 4 pm Friday to Sunday. You can rent bikes at the top of the lift (accessed by the tram) or at the ski base for $35 a day, including unlimited lift rides. Bikes are not allowed on the tram. The lift costs $7 roundtrip or $12 for unlimited rides all day.

Hiking

Albuquerque's most attractive day hike is perhaps the beautiful 8-mile **La Luz Trail** to the top of the Sandias. The trail goes from high desert, past a small waterfall and into the pine forests of the peak. You can hike up and take the tram down, but then you'll need to hike 2 miles north from the tram base, along the foothills of the Sandia Mountains on the **Tramway Trail**, to return to your car at La Luz trailhead. To reach the trailhead, take I-25 north to the Tramway exit and head east. The first road on the left, USFS Rd 444, heads toward the Sandias, and La Luz starts at the end of the road.

The **Crest Trail** is a 27-mile trail along the top of the Sandias. There are three access points, including one in the center at Sandia Peak. From Simms Park, you can take the 5.3-mile **Pino Trail** to the top of the Sandias; it becomes difficult near the end. There are many shorter hikes throughout the Sandias, including several easily accessed by the tram. Call the Sandia Ranger Station (☎ 281-3304) for information. (Also see the Tent Rocks National Monument section later in this chapter).

Other Activities

Call the Albuquerque Tennis Complex (☎ 843-1382) for information on the city's many **tennis** courts and ☎ 768-3520 for information on municipal **swimming** pools.

Albuquerque is famous for its **hot-air ballooning**, and several companies offer rides over the city and the Rio Grande. Try the World Balloon Corporation (☎ 293-6800, 800-351-9588) or Enchanted Winds (☎ 293-0000, 888-246-6359). Your $140 will get you the ride, hotel pickup and the traditional champagne breakfast upon landing.

The Reel Life (☎ 268-1693), 1100 San Mateo NE, rents **fly-fishing** equipment and arranges guides. Bob Gerding at Outdoor Adventures (☎ 299-5204) also offers fishing trips.

ORGANIZED TOURS

Numerous companies tour Albuquerque and outlying areas of interest. Gray Line (☎ 242-3880) has, among other things, narrated bus tours of the city ($23), Acoma pueblo ($39) and Santa Fe ($39). Taxi Tours (☎ 250-8683, 459-5652) offers personalized tours for one to four people.

New Mexico native Christy Rojas runs Aventura Artistica (☎ 800-808-7352), offering both day and overnight tours of the Albuquerque–Santa Fe area.

For a complete listing of the more than 30 organized tour companies, including those offering specialty tours like pueblo art and adventure trips, contact the visitors bureau.

SPECIAL EVENTS

The Friday *Albuquerque Journal* includes a venue section with an exhaustive listing of festivals and activities. Also contact the visitor center. The following are some of the most notable.

International Balloon Fiesta

This spectacular festival (☎ 821-1000, 800-422-7277) attracts almost a million spectators during nine days between the first and second weekends in October. Hundreds of hot-air balloon pilots show their skills in a variety of events and competitions; daily morning mass ascensions lure photographers. Parking and accommodations are a big problem, with most hotels booked

months in advance. Last-minute visitors will likely have difficulty finding accommodations even in Santa Fe or beyond.

Other Special Events

The **Gathering of Nations Powwow** (☎ 836-2810), held for two days in late April in The Pit (☎ 925-5626), features dance competitions, displays of Native American arts and crafts and the 'Miss Indian World' contest. In late June, the fairgrounds host the three-day **New Mexico Arts & Crafts Fair**.

During summer, the city runs **Summerfest** in downtown Albuquerque, featuring a kind of food and entertainment each Saturday evening. Enjoy New Mexican wine and live music at the **Bernalillo Wine Festival** (☎ 867-3311), staged in the village of Bernalillo about 15 minutes north of Albuquerque on Labor Day weekend ($10).

For 16 days in September, Albuquerque hosts the **New Mexico State Fair** featuring rodeos and live music. Call ☎ 265-1791 or check the website, www.nmstatefair.com, for a schedule of events.

PLACES TO STAY
Camping

At I-40 exit 166 (Juan Tabo Blvd), *KOA Albuquerque Central* (☎ 296-2729, 800-562-7781) has RV sites ($24 to $31), tent sites ($22) and Kamping Kabins ($37 to $47).

There is free primitive camping in the Sandia Mountains; only two-person tents are allowed, and you have to camp 50 feet from a picnic area and 300 feet from a trailhead. There is a $3 day charge to park at any of the designated areas. Call the Sandia Ranger Station (☎ 281-3304) for specific information on camping in the Sandias. The nearest national forest campsites with facilities are in the east side of the Manzanos, south of I-40 (see the Manzano Mountains section later in this chapter).

Hostels

The *Route 66 Hostel* (☎ 247-1813, 1012 Central SW) offers dormitory bunk beds for $13/14 for HI-AYH members/nonmembers and is conveniently located between downtown and Old Town. Private rooms with shared bath cost $18/24 for singles/doubles; rooms with private bath are $28.

The independent, rural **Sandia Mountain Hostel** (☎ 281-4117, 12234 Hwy 14), 20 miles east of the city on the opposite side of the Sandias, gives you easy access to the Manzano and Sandia Mountains ($12/30 dormitory/private).

Motels & Hotels

Albuquerque offers an abundance of motel and hotel lodging. Rates fluctuate tremendously according to season and sometimes for seemingly no reason at all. High season (May to September) rates are given below. During the balloon fiesta in October, rooms are hard to find and can cost 30% more than high season.

Also see Corrales, later, for places to stay outside of the city.

Budget The least expensive places, with rooms in the $20 range, are along Central. This urban thoroughfare passes Old Town, downtown, the UNM campus, trendy Nob Hill, the state fairgrounds, fine restaurants, sleazy dives and porno stores. While some areas can be rather dangerous and seedy, others have been spruced up in recent years as part of a national effort to preserve and restore historic Route 66. At I-25 exit 224B (the UNM exit), you'll find several inexpensive and somewhat run-down motels in both directions. Below are some places that are clean and pleasant with convenient and safe locations.

Near Old Town there are two old Route 66 motels, **El Vado** (☎ 243-4594, 2500 Central SW) and the **Monterey Motel** (☎ 243-3554, 2402 Central SW). El Vado, built with adobe bricks in 1936, claims to be the purest surviving Route 66 motel in Albuquerque, and it certainly has that Route 66 feel. Clean, simple rooms, many with individual carports, cost $32 for one queen- or king-size bed. The rooms at the Monterey are about $48.

On the eastern edge of the trendy Nob Hill district, with many restaurants, bars and an art theater within blocks, are the **Nob Hill Motel** (☎ 255-3172, 3712 Central SE) and the **University Lodge** (☎ 266-7663, 3711 Central NE). The University Lodge is a cut above the competition, offering free coffee and donuts, a pool and a tidy appearance. Rates at both Nob Hill spots start at about $30. There are many other cheapies east of Carlisle, though the neighborhood becomes more questionable as you head that direction.

Mid-Range The best bets for mid-range accommodations are the endless **chain motels** that hug I-25 and I-40. I-25 exit 227A and I-40 exit 155 are good options, as is the airport area. An alternative to expensive Santa Fe accommodations is to stay at one of the chains, including Super 8 and Days Inn, off of I-25 at exit 242. It's about a 40-minute drive to Santa Fe from there and 15 minutes to downtown Albuquerque.

The **Best Western Rio Grande Inn** (☎ 843-9500, 800-959-4726, 1015 Rio Grande Blvd NW), south of I-40 and convenient to Old Town, has a pool and pleasant singles/doubles for $99/109. Downtown, the six-story **Hotel Blue** (☎ 924-2400, 717 Central NW) offers basic doubles for $59 to $119.

Top End The **Sheraton Inn** (☎ 843-6300, 800-237-2133, 800 Rio Grande Blvd NW), just a stroll away from Old Town, offers Southwestern-style rooms from $120 to $170. Two modern, luxury downtown hotels, the **Hyatt Regency** (☎ 842-1234, 800-233-1234, 330 Tijeras Ave NW) and the **Albuquerque Doubletree Hotel** (☎ 247-3344, 800-222-8733, 201 Marquette Ave NW) are full-service establishments, featuring all the amenities. Rates at both vary, with an incredible range of $89 to $315, depending on occupancy.

La Posada de Albuquerque (☎ 242-9090, 800-777-5732, 125 2nd St NW) was built in 1939 by Conrad Hilton, a Socorro-area native, and is registered with Historic Hotels of America. The lobby's relaxed bar, with weekend jazz, tiled fountain, white stucco walls rising to a dark-wooded mezzanine and gaslight-style chandeliers all give La Posada the look of an Old World hacienda. The spacious Southwestern rooms with handmade furniture are in the $80 to $160 range.

See the Bernalillo section, later in this chapter, for information on the new Hyatt Tamaya, which is the most luxurious hotel in Albuquerque.

B&Bs

Built in 1912, the friendly *Böttger Mansion* (☎ 243-3639, 800-758-3639, 110 San Felipe St NW) retains its original early Anglo style – no Old West or Southwestern feel here! A full breakfast and evening wine and hors d'oeuvres are included in the $120 to $160 rate.

Old Town B&B (☎ 764-9144, 888-900-9144, 707 17th St NW), two blocks from Old Town, is a simple place in a private home with a pleasant garden courtyard and two rooms for $75 and $90.

Also convenient to Old Town, across the street from the country club golf course is the lovely *Casas de Sueños* (☎ 247-4560, 310 Rio Grande Blvd SW, Albuquerque, NM 87104), with 1½ acres of luscious gardens and a pool enclosed within a grassy courtyard. The 22 adobe *casitas* (small cottages) feature handcrafted furniture and original artwork by the many artists who have used the peaceful spot as a studio over the years. All casitas have private bath and some have a kitchenette, fireplace and/or private hot tub (a couple of casitas have them outside in a private garden). Rates range from $95 to $245 and include a full breakfast. It is currently for sale, so call to confirm information and rates.

website: www.casasdesuenos.com

Near downtown, the *WJ Marsh House* (☎ 247-1001, 301 Edith Blvd SE) is an 1895 brick Queen Anne Victorian. Rates range from $60 to $120 for the six rooms with shared bath and the separate Snyder Cottage, which sleeps up to six people and has private bath and kitchen. Renovations are scheduled, however, so call for updated information. *WE Mauger Estate* (☎ 242-8755, 800-719-9189, 701 Roma Ave NW), built in 1897, is another restored Victorian convenient to both Old Town and downtown. Rooms and suites range from $100 to $180.

PLACES TO EAT

Most nearby casinos offer all-you-can-eat buffets – see several of the pueblos described in the North of Albuquerque and East & South of Albuquerque sections later in this chapter.

Old Town

Stay away from the tourist traps around the plaza. One exception is *Zone Graze* (☎ 243-4377, 308 San Felipe St NW), where you can sit outside and have a sandwich and coffee. Historic Casa Ruiz, home to one of Albuquerque's founding families for over 250 years, now houses the *Church St Café* (☎ 247-8522, 2111 Church St NW). The cozy café serves New Mexican fare for breakfast and lunch daily (dinner on weekends).

High Noon Restaurant & Saloon (☎ 765-1455, 425 San Felipe St NW) serves up grilled fare and excellent margaritas in a rough-hewn, 18th-century adobe. With bright-yellow walls, high ceilings, fresh flowers and a creative menu, the contemporary *Seasons* (☎ 766-5100, 2031 Mountain Rd NW) is a welcome change from the usual Old Town feel. Eat hearty red-chile-dusted chicken burgers or Baja tacos inside or on the rooftop cantina (limited menu, open from 4 pm).

Down the street from the Route 66 hostel is the nostalgic *Route 66 Malt Shop* (☎ 242-7866, 1720 Central SW), with only a tiny counter with four stools, one table and one booth. This friendly place serves great green-chile cheeseburgers, hot pastrami and other sandwiches for under $5. A small store sells Route 66 paraphernalia, and there's delivery to Old Town and downtown. *Garcia's Kitchen* (☎ 842-0273, 1736 Central SW) is a family restaurant that draws crowds of locals with its homemade specialties, *carne adobada* (pork marinated in red chile and spices), fajitas and chile stew. Dinners range from $4 to $9. It's open 6:30 am to 10 pm, but stays open until midnight on Friday and Saturday.

Downtown

The brick-walled *Fresh Choices* (☎ 242-6447, 402 Central SW) has a soup, salad, pizza and pasta bar for $7. A cozy and relaxed Italian option is *Sweet Peppers* (☎ 842-1273, *521 Central NW*). *M&J Sanitary Tortilla Factory* (☎ 242-4890, *403 2nd St SW*) serves very good New Mexican fare, and you can buy a stack of fresh tortillas to go. It's open 9 am to 4 pm Monday to Saturday.

For coffee and huge portions of very good eggs, pancakes and sandwiches, try the contemporary *Gold Street Café* (☎ 765-1633, *218 Gold St SW*). It's open 7 am to 2 pm Monday to Friday, 8 am to 2 pm weekends. The low-key *Java Joe's* (☎ 765-1514, *906 Park Ave SW*) caters to the young earthy crowd, with scrambled tofu as well as the usual breakfast burrito and pastries. It's open 7 am to 3:30 pm daily. *Sauce Liquid Lounge* (☎ 242-5839, *405 Central NW*), a popular, trendy spot, serves primarily gourmet pizza – very tasty! The funky lounge in the back is a busy spot to hang out for a late-night drink. Nearby is *Pearl's Dive* (☎ 244-9405, *509 Central NW*), an airy place with green-chile turkey burgers and vegetarian options.

The unpretentious service at the *Artichoke Café* (☎ 243-0200, *424 Central SE*) belies the fact that the place has been voted an Albuquerque favorite many times. Dinners from their creative menu can reach $20, but it's certainly possible to dine for much less. The outdoor patio in the back offers relief from Central Ave traffic.

UNM Area & Nob Hill

You can place an order and take a number 24 hours a day at *The Frontier*, an Albuquerque tradition for delicious but inexpensive meals – the green chile is outstanding but be forewarned it's hot! The restaurant is on Central, across from the university. The *Flying Star Café* (☎ 255-6633, *3416 Central SE*) is the place to go for homemade soups, muffins, breads, desserts and ice cream. It also serves a variety of hot dishes, including innovative daily specials, and beer and wine. There are three other locations, one at 4501 Juan Tabo Blvd NE (☎ 275-8311), another at 4026 Rio Grande Blvd NW (☎ 344-6714) and a third at 8001 Menaul Blvd NE (☎ 293-6911). Hours are 6:30 am to 11 pm daily

(until midnight on Friday and Saturday). UNM students favor *El Patio* (☎ 268-4245, *142 Harvard Dr SE*) for its tasty New Mexican dishes ($4 to $8), relaxed atmosphere and patio dining.

Across from the university, *Gyros Greek Diner* (☎ 255-4401, *106 Cornell Dr SE*) and the recommended *Olympia Café\'* (☎ 266-5222, *2210 Central SE*) specialize in generously portioned and tasty Greek dishes for around $5.

Il Vicino (☎ 266-7855, *3403 Central NE*), a trendy bistro with sidewalk tables and microbrewed beer, has wood-burning-oven pizza with toppings like spinach, feta and fresh herbs. Across the street, *Scalo's* (☎ 255-8781, *3500 Central SE*), one of the best restaurants in town, mixes excellent Northern Italian cuisine with casual elegance. There's a candle-lit outdoor patio and a bustling upscale bar. Most entrées are in the $10 to $18 range. The bar, open until 11 pm or midnight daily (until 9 pm Sunday) serves a full menu.

For Japanese fare, including sushi, try the small and airy *Shogun* (☎ 265-9166, *3310 Central SE*). Down the street, *Kanome* (☎ 265-7773, *3128 Central SE*) has a spectrum of creative Asian dishes in a bright and modern space. It's open for dinner only; expect to pay at least $35 for two.

A relaxed hangout for good food and patio people-watching is *Geckos* (☎ 262-1848, *3500 Central SE*). Locals go to the *Monte Vista Fire Station* (☎ 255-2424, *3201 Central NE*) for crab-cake appetizers and tasty, ambitious dishes with hints of Southwestern and European influences. Entrées range from $14 to $20. The pueblo-revival building was home to Fire Engine Company Three for nearly 40 years and still has the brass pole. Upstairs, the popular bar spills onto a balcony overlooking the nighttime scene.

Metropolitan Albuquerque

On Lomas Blvd at Monroe St, *Los Cuates* (☎ 255-5079) serves up huge plates of Southwestern specialties for under $8; this place is not for tender palates, as the salsa and chile are full-strength, but the food is excellent and the locals keep coming! If the tiny place is packed, try the restaurant directly across the street – same name, same owners. *Sadie's* (☎ 345-5339, 6230 4th St NW), a massive place with a barnlike atmosphere (and a big-screen TV in the bar), is a local institution and a favorite with many. Giant New Mexican dinners run from $5 to $13.

Leo and Martha Nuñez (both from Mexico) and their children run *El Norteño* (☎ 256-1431, 6416 Zuni Rd SE), two blocks east of San Pedro Blvd. This family restaurant focuses on fresh ingredients and traditional Mexican recipes. The *pollo norteño* is fantastic, as is the carne adobada, the chicken mole and the *cabrito al horno* (oven-roasted goat). *India Kitchen* (☎ 884-2333, 6910 Montgomery Blvd NE), open for dinner only and closed on Monday, is locally favored for its spicy East Indian cuisine. Tandooris, curries, seafood and vegetarian dishes are custom-made to suit anyone's heat tolerance ($7 to $12).

The best place for barbecue is *Quarters* (☎ 843-7505, 801 Yale Blvd SE). It's a dark little place that doesn't look like much from the outside, but the food is excellent. Eat in or get it to go. Another more airy Quarters is at 4516 Wyoming NE (☎ 299-9864). *Assets Grille and Brewing Company* (☎ 889-6400, 6910 Montgomery Blvd NE) serves fresh-brewed beer, as well as a broad menu. The bar, often filled with young professionals, is open until 11 pm Monday to Saturday. Unfortunately located in a strip mall and without the views and feel of the original in Bernalillo (see that section later in this chapter), *The Range Café* (☎ 293-2633, 4200 Wyoming Blvd NE) still serves excellent food. The varied and creative menu has something for everyone, and the portions are generous.

Mac's La Sierra Coffee Shop (☎ 836-1212, 6217 Central NW), across the Rio Grande and three blocks east of Coors Blvd, has been catering to local families for 40 years. Mac's is open 5:30 am to midnight Monday to Saturday, 6 am to 10 pm Sunday. *Taco Cabana* (6500 San Mateo Blvd NE), with another branch on Montgomery Blvd

at Wyoming Blvd, serves pretty good drive-through and sit-down Mexican and New Mexican food, as well as beer and margaritas (open 24 hours). Though it's a chain, the privately owned *JBs* (☎ 345-5087, 6621 4th St NW) offers all-you-can-eat chicken-fried steak for $7 and a salad bar that includes tacos and barbecue for under $6. With several drive-through locations in town, *Dion's* is a great choice for fast and delicious pizza, salads and subs.

For a meal with a view, try *High Finance* (☎ 243-9742), at the top of Sandia Peak; take the tramway there or drive up the eastern side of the Sandias and walk about a half mile along the crest to the restaurant. While lunch here is affordable, dinners can range from $14 for the basics to about $30 for more elaborate creations. The bar opens for early birds at 9 am (noon on Sunday).

Wild Oats is an organic grocery store with a large selection of ready-made dishes, great sandwiches and a large salad bar. There's one on Carlisle Blvd just south of I-40 and another on San Mateo Blvd at Academy St.

ENTERTAINMENT

For a comprehensive list of Albuquerque's diverse nightspots and a detailed calendar of upcoming events in arts and entertainment, get the *Alibi*, a free weekly. It's published every Tuesday and available where newspapers are sold and at many restaurants and bars. The entertainment sections of Thursday evening's *Albuquerque Tribune* and the Friday and Sunday *Albuquerque Journal* are helpful, too. Call before heading out to ask about cover charges.

Cinemas

A complete listing of what's showing in Albuquerque's many cinemas can be found in the entertainment section of the daily newspapers.

The Guild (☎ 255-1848, 3405 Central NE), about a mile east of the university, screens foreign films and the Hollywood fringe. On the UNM campus, the *Southwest Film Center* (☎ 277-5608) runs several series concurrently, though it is closed from

May to August. Films are shown in the basement of the Student Union Building in the SUB Theater.

Nightlife

Several live-music clubs and bars are concentrated downtown. The *El Rey* (☎ 764-2624, 624 Central SW) attracts national rock, blues, jazz and country acts, as well as local favorites. The cavernous former movie theater has two large dance floors, three bars, a Friday blues happy hour and a lively crowd. Next door the *Golden West* (☎ 764-2624) has an Old West feel, with a dance floor and a couple of pool tables.

The retro-modern *Launch Pad* (☎ 764-8887, 618 Central SW) focuses on alternative sounds, mostly punk (both local and national bands), and serves a full menu at the contemporary diner in the front. *Sauce Liquid Lounge* (☎ 242-5839, 405 Central NW) is a hip little place with a bit of a New York-lounge feel. The front part is an open and airy restaurant (see Places to Eat) while the back is a rather dark bar with plush chairs. A DJ plays house music on the weekend, but it's not so loud that you can't just hang and talk.

An excellent spot for a game of pool is *Anodyne* (☎ 244-1820, 409 Central NW), open from 4:30 pm daily. A huge space with book-lined walls, wood ceilings, plenty of overstuffed chairs, more than a hundred bottled beers and a long window to sit and watch Central, this comfortable pool hall and bar has a relaxed feel. Come just to hang out, or pay $6 an hour for pool. The genteel hotel lobby of the historic *La Posada* (☎ 242-9090, 125 2nd St NW) – see Places to Stay – features a happy hour 5 to 7 pm Thursday and Friday, with finger foods and a piano bar. There's a jazz combo every Friday and Saturday night.

A second concentration of nightspots, including a couple in classic Route 66 buildings, is in the Nob Hill area. The piano bar at *Martini Grille* (☎ 255-4111, 4200 Central SE), open from 4 pm, attracts all ages; next door is *Sonny's* (☎ 255-5932), a low-key bar with a mixed crowd and live rock bands on weekends. Housed in the 1946 Johnston Standard Motor Company building, the popular *Club Rhythm and Blues* (☎ 256-0849, 3523 Central NE) showcases local and national blues bands Tuesday to Saturday. Down the street, the 1939 Jones Motor Company building is now *Kelly's Brewery* (☎ 362-2739, 3226 Central SE), open daily with dancing and live bands on the weekend. Another spot crowded with the post-college urbanites is the smaller *O'Neill's Pub* (☎ 256-0564, 3211 Central NE), also with live music of all sorts.

The Albuquerque Museum (☎ 243-7255; see the Old Town section earlier in this chapter) hosts summer jazz in the courtyard on weekends from May to August. To find out where else to hear big name and local jazz, blues and salsa, call the New Mexico Jazz Workshop (☎ 255-9798). During summer they host the Madrid Blues Festival (see the boxed text 'Turquoise Trail') for one weekend every month.

You can practice your two-step or line dancing to live country & western bands and enjoy a complimentary happy-hour buffet nightly at the *Caravan East* (☎ 265-7877, 7605 Central NE). The *Midnight Rodeo* (☎ 888-0100, 4901 McLeod Rd NE) has live country & western and classic rock bands, pool tables and a race-track dance floor.

Two popular gay and lesbian nightclubs are the *Albuquerque Mining Company* (☎ 255-4022, 7209 Central NE) and *Pulse* (☎ 255-3334, 4100 Central SE).

Performing Arts

The University of New Mexico Box Office (☎ 277-4569), inside the university bookstore on Central at Cornell, sells tickets for *Popejoy Hall*, the primary place in town to see big-name national acts as well as local opera, symphony and theater. *Hiland Theater* (☎ 265-9119, 4804 Central SE), the historic *KiMo* (see the Downtown section earlier in this chapter), the low-key *Sunshine Theater* (☎ 764-0249, 120 Central Ave SW) and the *South Broadway Cultural Center* (☎ 848-1320, 1025 Broadway Ave SE) are the four primary venues for performing arts. *The Pit* (☎ 925-5626) and *Tingley Coliseum*

(☎ 265-1791), in the state fairgrounds, host Albuquerque's major events.

The *Musical Theater Southwest* (☎ 262-9301) stages six Broadway musical productions each year; ticket prices start at $10. The *New Mexico Ballet Company* (☎ 292-4245) performs from October to April, with ticket prices ranging from $5 to $25. For between $15 and $40, you can watch the *New Mexico Symphony Orchestra* (☎ 881-8999) perform at various venues, including three spring performances at the Albuquerque Zoo (ask about other performances at the zoo).

Built in 1936 by the Depression-era Works Progress Administration (WPA), the *Albuquerque Little Theater* (☎ 242-4750, 224 San Pasquale Ave SW), near Old Town, is a long-standing, nonprofit community company that stages about six shows a year from September to May. *La Compañía de Teatro de Albuquerque* (☎ 242-7929), a bilingual Hispanic theater group, performs at the South Broadway Cultural Center and the KiMo.

SPECTATOR SPORTS
The Albuquerque Sports Stadium (☎ 243-1791), on Stadium Blvd at University Ave, is a friendly, intimate baseball park with a sunken playing field and good views – of both the game and the Sandias – from the stands. The triple-A Albuquerque Dukes left in September 2000, and the stadium is currently being renovated for a new triple-A team to begin playing in 2003.

There is no professional football team in Albuquerque, but the UNM Lobos draw huge crowds from throughout the city for college football and basketball games. Call the UNM Box Office (☎ 277-4569) or The Pit (☎ 925-5626) for ticket information.

Though ice hockey and Albuquerque don't seem like natural partners, Albuquerque's Scorpions play October to March at Tingley Coliseum (☎ 265-1791). Also at Tingley Coliseum is the state rodeo, held during the state fair in September. There are plenty of smaller rodeos throughout the year, both in Albuquerque and the surrounding area. For information on rodeo

events, call the New Mexico Rodeo Association (☎ 873-7770).

The Downs at Albuquerque (☎ 266-5555), on the state fairgrounds, has live and simulcast horse races from early March through June.

SHOPPING
Though nearby Santa Fe and Taos are more popular (and more expensive) for shopping, Albuquerque has a few areas worth visiting. Galleries and trading posts, popular with visitors looking for 'southwestern art' and souvenirs, cluster around the Old Town Plaza. In addition, Indian vendors spread out jewelry and crafts along the sidewalks.

For a wide selection of Native American crafts and informed salespeople, stop by the Palms Trading Post (☎ 247-8504), 1504 Lomas Blvd NW, or Gus's Trading Company (☎ 843-6381), 2026 Central SW. Luz de Nambe (☎ 242-5699), 328 San Felipe St NW, sells discounted Nambeware (see Shopping in the Santa Fe section of the Santa Fe & Taos chapter). Silver Sun (☎ 242-8265), 2042 South Plaza NW, is a reputable spot for turquoise.

Another good spot to stroll, without the touristy feel of Old Town, is around the university and in Nob Hill. If you walk east from the university down and around Central, there are CD stores and an eclectic mix of shops (from a tattoo parlor to an herbal medicine shop to a toy store) until you reach the Nob Hill Shopping Center at Carlisle.

GETTING THERE & AWAY
Though the Albuquerque International Airport is New Mexico's biggest, it is still relatively small. Southwest Airlines, American Airlines and America West often have the most reasonable rates to Albuquerque. Mesa Airlines (☎ 842-4218, 800-637-2247) provides service to cities within New Mexico, to Colorado Springs, Colorado, and to Dallas, Texas. Rio Grande Air (☎ 764-3041, 877-435-9742) services Albuquerque, Farmington, Taos and Durango, Colorado.

The Albuquerque Bus Transportation Center, 300 2nd St SW, is home to Grey-

Turquoise Trail

East of Albuquerque, Hwy 14 parallels I-25 heading north, offering a scenic alternative for reaching Santa Fe. This 'trail' passes through three mining towns where silver, gold, turquoise and coal were once excavated. Today, many artists and craftspeople live in the former 'ghost towns,' bringing new life to the historic sites.

The highway begins at Tijeras, at I-40 exit 175. Take a detour, a few miles on Hwy 536 toward Sandia Crest, to visit the quirky **Tinkertown Museum** (☎ 281-5233). Here you'll see over 20,000 hand-carved wooden miniatures of all kinds, including a full circus, surrounded by a wall made of over 40,000 bottles (open April to November). Return to Hwy 14. After 23 miles, the winding, narrow but paved highway passes through **Golden**, where gold was discovered in 1825 and, later, silver. The town's heyday was in the 1890s, when the population reached about 1500. Today, it's nearly a ghost town with a general store and an old adobe church that provides a great photo opportunity.

About 12 miles farther north is **Madrid**, a thriving coal-mining town from the late 1800s to the mid-1950s. Madrid went bust with the development of alternative energy sources. In 1974 the town was purchased lot by lot in just two weeks and has been experiencing a resurgence ever since. Artists and craftspeople now make up the bulk of the population, opening their studios to the public during the town's 'Christmas in Madrid' celebration in December. Galleries and boutiques, housed in the old storefronts along the main street lure tourists. On weekends from June to August, there's a series of classical, jazz and bluegrass concerts held outdoors at the old ballpark.

Remnants of the town's boom years are now part of the attraction. The **Old Coal Mine Museum** (☎ 438-3780) is more of a junk yard than a museum ($3/1 for adults/kids). Within the museum is the Engine House Theater, with Saturday and Sunday melodrama performances from May to mid-October.

In front of the museum, the **Mine Shaft Tavern** (☎ 473-0743) proudly features the longest stand-up bar in New Mexico. You'll see why it's needed when the tour buses drop off a hundred thirsty tourists for lunch. At other times it's kind of quiet in the 50-year-old bar. The restaurant serves generously portioned lunches and dinners until 8 pm on weekends ($5 to $10). There's live local music on Sunday afternoon. The Tavern opens at noon daily.

Another boom-to-bust town, **Cerrillos**, is 3 miles farther north. Built by the Santa Fe Railroad after gold was discovered in 1879, Cerrillos had 21 saloons, four hotels and a population of about 2500 miners at its peak. Today, the shell of the old town is home to a couple of gift shops. The **Casa Grande** (☎ 438-3008), is something of a mining museum, with local turquoise, lots of rocks and relics from the turn-of-the-19th-century ($2), as well as a petting zoo, gift shop and information outlet. See Activities in the Santa Fe chapter for horseback, mountain biking and hiking trips.

For more information on the area traversed by the Turquoise Trail, visit http://turquoisetrail.org.

---

hound (☎ 243-4435, 800-231-2222). Greyhound has four buses a day to Santa Fe ($11.50, 90 minutes), Carlsbad ($44, 5½ hours), Roswell ($35, four hours), Farmington ($32.50, 3½ hours) and throughout New Mexico.

Several shuttles depart from the airport; call for reservations. Sandia Shuttle (☎ 243-3244) runs 10 shuttles daily to several Santa Fe hotels, from 8 am to 5 pm ($20). Fausts

Transportation (☎ 758-3410, 888-830-3410) leaves at 1 pm daily and Twin Hearts (☎ 751-1201, 800-654-9456) leaves four times daily for Santa Fe, Taos, Red River and Angel Fire.

Amtrak's *Southwest Chief* stops daily at Albuquerque's train station (☎ 842-9650), 214 1st St SW, heading east to Kansas City ($144, 17 hours) and Chicago ($160, 25 hours) at 12:55 pm, and west to Flagstaff,

Arizona ($85, five hours) and Los Angeles ($95, 16 hours) at 5:32 pm. Service to Santa Fe ($32) is via the 12:55 pm train to Lamy, connecting with a bus to arrive in Santa Fe by 3:40 pm.

GETTING AROUND

The airport, about 4 miles south of downtown, is served by the No 50 SunTran bus weekdays from 7 am to 6 pm and Saturday from 8 am to 4 pm. A taxi downtown takes 10 minutes and charges about $8, and most hotels and motels offer free shuttles.

SunTran (☎ 843-9200), Albuquerque's bus company, stops running around 9 pm, and only 12 lines run on Sunday (75¢, free transfers). Schedules are available at the visitor centers, the airport, city shopping malls and at most big hotels. Three open-sided red trolleys run along and around Central Ave: The No 24 services Old Town to the Zoo, stopping at museums; the No 23 goes from Nob Hill to downtown along Central Ave; and the No 40 circulates through the downtown area. The downtown trolley runs from 7 am to 7 pm, and the others run from 10 am to 6 pm.

Most major agencies are at the airport. If the desert air has you hankering to hit the road on a motorcycle, try Albuquerque Motorcycle Rentals (☎ 830-9500), 1001 Yale Blvd SE. You will need a motorcycle license. Wheelchair Getaways (☎ 247-2626, 800-642-2042) rents wheelchair-accessible vans.

Cabbies patrol the airport, train and bus stations and the major hotels, but are rarely roaming the streets to be hailed down. Yellow Cab (☎ 247-8888, 800-657-6232) has 24-hour service.

Rio Mountainsport (☎ 766-9970), 1210 Rio Grande NW just north of I-40, rents mountain bikes ($14 to $25 for a half day and $20 to $35 for a full day, including lock and helmet) and inline skates ($14 a day). Bike racks for cars are available, as are maps and local information.

NORTH OF ALBUQUERQUE
Sandia Pueblo
This Indian pueblo, 13 miles north of Albuquerque, was established around AD 1300,

but is perhaps best known for its modern offerings, including a casino (☎ 897-2173) and the **Bien Mur Indian Market Center** (☎ 821-5400), which has a nice selection of arts and crafts from pueblos around the state.

The **Sandia Lakes Recreation Area** (☎ 897-3971) has three lakes well-stocked with trout, catfish and bass. Fishing costs $9 for a full day. You can rent poles for $4, but they only have three. Nearby, **Sandia Trails** (☎ 898-6970), 10601 4th St NW, offers horseback rides along the river and through the bosque for $15 an hour. To get to the pueblo take exit 234 west off of I-25 to Hwy 313 and head north.

Saint Anthony's Day (June 13) is celebrated with ceremonial dancing open to the public. Photography and sketching are prohibited. Other dances are held on January 6 and Christmas. Further information is available from the governor's office (☎ 867-3317), PO Box 6008, Bernalillo, NM 87004.

Corrales
Squished between ever-expanding Albuquerque, the developing west mesa and the suburban sprawl of Rio Rancho is the rural village of Corrales (☎ 897-0502 for town information), about 20 minutes from downtown Albuquerque along the Rio Grande. The village was Spanish speaking from the time of the 1710 land grant until the late 1800s, when Europeans began moving here. Now horses, llamas, sheep and other animals live side by side with million-dollar homes and traditional working farms. The main thoroughfare is Corrales Rd (Hwy 448), a New Mexico Scenic Byway, and most others are dirt. Corrales offers easy access to the Rio Grande and walks along the bosque.

Off of Corrales Rd is **Old San Ysidro Church** (follow the sign). Built in 1776–78, it is a beautiful example of Spanish-colonial architecture. Today it is used as a venue for concerts. The Albuquerque Museum owns **Casa San Ysidro** (☎ 898-3915), a restored 1740s home across the street from the church. Tours are available by reservation only, Wednesday to Friday ($4). It is closed December and January.

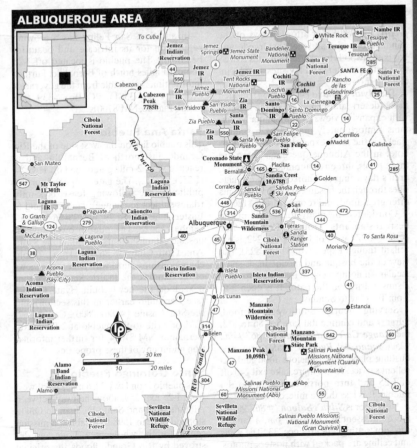

ALBUQUERQUE AREA

There are several pleasant places to eat on Corrales Rd. Enjoy a drink and summer jazz on the patio or a winter fire in the cozy adobe bar at *Casa Vieja* (☎ 898-7847). You can eat here as well, but the food is expensive and not very good. Excellent pizza is served at *Village Pizza* (☎ 898-0045) – for real New Mexico pizza, order your pie with green chile. *Essencia* (☎ 792-4210), a brightly colored café with great food, is open limited hours for lunch and dinner.

If you plan to spend the night, try the warm and friendly *Nora Dixon Place* (☎ 898-3662, 888-667-2349, 312 Dixon Rd).

Three rooms look out on a peaceful courtyard with spectacular views of the Sandias, and the Rio Grande bosque is a five-minute walk. Rates start at $75.
website: www.noradixon.com

Bernalillo

On the west bank of the Rio Grande, just north of Corrales in the town of Bernalillo, is the **Coronado State Monument** (☎ 867-5351). This multitiered Kuaua pueblo (circa 1300) served as the explorer Coronado's winter dwelling in 1540 and features a restored *kiva* (a circular, underground ceremonial chamber) and 15 original kiva paintings ($3/ free adults/children). The adjacent *campground* (☎ 980-8256) affords views of the Sandia Mountains and the Rio Grande, and has cottonwoods for shade. Tent sites cost $8 ($11 with a shelter) and RV sites are $11, including showers.

The *Hyatt Tamaya* (☎ 867-1234), hidden in the desert landscape next to the bosque, with expansive views of the Sandia Mountains (unfortunately marred by a smokestack), is the most expensive and luxurious hotel in the Albuquerque area. There are three pools, three restaurants, a spa, a children's day camp and horse-drawn carriage rides through the bosque. Several restaurants offer great food, and rooms start at $180.

Considered by many to be one of the best restaurants around, *Prairie Star* (☎ 867-3327), west of I-25 at exit 242, is excellent though expensive ($14 to $25). The view of the bosque and mountains is spectacular – if nothing else, it is an ideal spot for a sunset drink on the patio. It is open 5 to 9 pm Tuesday to Sunday.

Serving hearty Southwestern food, burgers and continental fare for $6 to $13, the *Range Cafe and Bakery* (☎ 867-1700, 925 Camino del Pueblo) is an open, airy, bustling place with delicious food and excellent service. To get there, take exit 240 off of I-25 and turn north onto Camino del Pueblo. It is less than a mile, on your left.

Next door is *Silva's Saloon* (☎ 867-9976), the quintessential Old West bar, a family-run spot 'setting 'em up since '33.' The walls and ceiling are packed with posters, photos, dollar bills, memorabilia and whatever else someone happens to donate, hence its claim to be a 'historical museum.' Stop by for a classic margarita and great conversation – you may have to knock, since it's sometimes locked to keep out ruffians!

San Felipe Pueblo

This conservative Keresan pueblo is best known for the ceremonial Green Corn Dance performed on May 1. Feast day, on February 2, features the Buffalo Dance. Photography, recording and sketching are strictly prohibited. The pueblo runs the Casino Hollywood (☎ 867-6700).

In addition, San Felipe has a growing reputation for its intricate and beautiful beadwork. The pueblo is located off I-25 about 10 miles north of Bernalillo. Further information is available from the governor's office (☎ 867-3381), PO Box 4339, San Felipe Pueblo, NM 87001.

Santa Ana Pueblo

This pueblo lies on the west side of the Rio Grande, just north of Bernalillo, and is reached via a 2-mile gated road off Hwy 44 (I-25, exit 242). The gate is opened for the public on the following feast days only (dates subject to change): January 1 and 6, Easter, June 24 and 29, July 25–26 and December 25–28. The pueblo owns several upscale establishments, including the Santa Ana Golf Club (☎ 867-9464), a 27-hole championship course with panoramic views of the Sandias, the Prairie Star Restaurant next door, the newly built Hyatt Tamaya (see Bernalillo earlier in this section) and the Star Casino (☎ 867-0000). Call ☎ 867-3301 or write to the pueblo at 2 Dove Rd, Bernalillo, NM 87004, for further information about any of these properties.

Santo Domingo Pueblo

This pueblo is on Hwy 22, 6 miles northwest from I-25 exit 259, about halfway between Albuquerque and Santa Fe. Juan de Oñate stopped here in 1598 to establish a mission center for the whole area. Long ago destroyed by Rio Grande floods, the original mission was replaced in 1886 by the current church, which contains paintings and frescoes by local artists.

The church and plaza are the center of the pueblo, and some small shops sell both crafts and food. The pueblo is known for its jewelry, especially the delicate *heishi* beads that are carved from shells and turquoise, and for its traditional pottery. Near the I-25 exit is a small museum with historical artifacts, photographs, crafts and a gift shop.

The impressive annual Feast and Corn Dance, which is usually held on August 4, but may be held the first weekend in August, involves hundreds of dancers and is open to public viewing. There is also a Corn Dance as part of the Easter and Christmas celebrations. Santo Domingo is open to the public from about 8 am to an hour before sunset every day. No photography, sketching or any other kind of recording is allowed. Further information is available from the governor's office (☎ 465-2214), Santo Domingo Pueblo, NM 87052.

Cochiti Pueblo

This pueblo is due north of Santo Domingo. Either continue north on Hwy 22 for about 10 miles or take I-25 exit 264 and head northwest on Hwy 16. The Cochiti pueblo mission dates from 1628, and parts of the original building are still visible. There are no shops or trading posts in the pueblo, but local artisans may post signs on their houses advertising work for sale.

Cochiti is the main center for making the bass drums used in ceremonials. They are usually constructed of hollow sections of aspen log covered with leather and then painted. Also noteworthy are the storyteller ceramic figurines first made famous in the 1960s by Cochiti potter Helen Cordero.

Photography, sketching and other recording are prohibited. The annual feast day is on July 14 and is open to the public. Further information is available from the governor's office (☎ 465-2244), Cochiti Pueblo, NM 87072.

Cochiti Lake

This artificial lake, formed by a dam across the Rio Grande and surrounded by desert, provides water recreation on land leased by the federal government from Cochiti pueblo. Though locals recommend it for a swim, it's often shallow and mucky. You can camp at *Cochiti Lake Campground* and *Tetilla Campground* (☎ 465-0307 for both), on opposite sides of the lake. While Cochiti is open year-round, Tetilla is open only from April to October. RV/tent sites cost $12/8. Reach them via a signed road off Hwy 16, about 4 miles from I-25.

Tent Rocks National Monument

If you're driving I-25 between Albuquerque and Santa Fe, try to make the time to detour to Tent Rocks. Here, volcanic ash that erupted from the nearby Jemez Mountain volcanoes has been sculpted into teepee-like formations and steep sided, narrow canyons. Visitors can hike up a dry riverbed through the piñon-covered desert to the formations, where sandy paths weave through the rocks and canyons. You'll need a couple hours to drive the dirt road through the desert to get here and to hike around a bit, but it's well worth it. Take I-25 exit 264; follow Hwy 16 west to Hwy 22, where there are signs.

EAST & SOUTH OF ALBUQUERQUE
Moriarty

☎ 505 • pop 1500 • elevation 6325 feet

Thirty-five miles east of Albuquerque along I-40, this small town is a bean-growing center and hosts an annual bean festival in August. Most of the town is along Central Ave, paralleling I-40 to the south. Except for a few motels, there isn't much reason to stop here. The pleasant *Luxury Inn* (☎ 832-4457, 1316 Central Ave) offers rooms for about $50. Cheaper basic accommodations along the strip include the *Sands Motel* (☎ 832-4445) and the *Ponderosa Motel* (☎ 832-4403). There's Mexican food at *El Comedor* (☎ 832-4442).

Isleta Pueblo

This pueblo is 16 miles south of Albuquerque at I-25 exit 215. It is best known for its church, the **San Augustine Mission** (☎ 869-3398), which was built in 1613 and has been in constant use since 1692. Call to find out when it is open for visits and services. A few shops on the plaza sell local pottery, and there is gambling at the Isleta Casino and Resort (☎ 869-2614). On September 4 (Saint Augustine's Day) and on August 28, ceremonial dancing is open to the public. Confirm dates with the governor's office (☎ 869-3111), PO Box 1270, Isleta Pueblo, NM 87022, before planning a visit.

Los Lunas

☎ 505 • pop 10,600 • elevation 4800 feet
There is little of interest here apart from a
Comfort Inn and *Days Inn* and a historic
restaurant. Just east of I-25 is *Luna Mansion
Restaurant* (☎ 865-7333), housed in a restored 1881 adobe mansion and open for
dinner only Tuesday to Saturday. Though
the à-la-carte menu can run up to $20,
there's also a daily home-style deal: ribs,
green-chile chicken pot pie and other
family-style meals for about $8.

Belen

☎ 505 • pop 8000 • elevation 4800 feet
This small town is not exactly a tourist destination, but there are a couple quirky
museums worth a visit. The **Harvey House**
(☎ 861-0581), along the tracks at 104 N 1st
St, is a small railroad museum originally
built in 1910 as an eating house for tourists
traveling along the Santa Fe Railroad. It's
open 12:30 to 3:30 pm Tuesday to Saturday;
donations accepted.

The **P&M Farm Museum** (☎ 864-8354)
displays the eclectic personal collection of
Pablo and Manuela Chavez, which includes
everything from frontier furniture and
silver to about 25 beautifully restored, original covered wagons, buggies and antique
cars ($5/3 for adults/children). To get here,
cross the railroad tracks in Belen and drive
2.7 miles south at the first light (Reinken
Ave) toward Jarales. As Manuela explained
her hours, they are open daily 'unless we
have to go to the doctor in Clovis.'

You can camp ($10 for tent sites and RV
hookups) at the *Willie Chavez Educational
Center* (☎ 864-3915), next to the Rio Grande
2 miles east of town. The *Super 8* (☎ 864-
8188, 428 S Main St) has rooms for about
$50; there's a family restaurant next door,
and a Mexican restaurant across the street.

Manzano Mountains

Often overlooked in favor of the Sandias,
the Manzano Mountains are easily accessible from Albuquerque and have plenty of
opportunities for camping, hiking (including
the breathtaking 22-mile crest trail with
several access trails), biking and cross-

country skiing. Tiny Mountainair is the
central town for the Manzano region. The
Cibola National Forest Mountainair Ranger
District (☎ 847-2990), on the west end of
Beal St, sells wilderness maps of the Man-
zanos for $7.

Nestled in the foothills 12 miles north of
Mountainair, **Manzano Mountains State
Park** (☎ 847-2820) affords spectacular views
of the distant mountains to the east. Trails
head into the mountains ($3 day-use fee)
and six tent/RV *campsites* cost $7/11; there
is water but no showers. The park is open
April to December. From April to October
or November, you can also camp at *Red
Canyon Campground* (off of Forest Rd 253;
follow signs in Manzano) or *Fourth of July
Campground* (look for signs on Hwy 55 in
Tajique).

In Mountainair, *Tillies* (☎ 847-0248) has
tent/hookup sites for $9/16, doubles for $36
and rooms with kitchenettes for up to four
people for $45. *El Rancho Motel* (☎ 847-
2577) offers basic accommodations for $28
a double. There are two basic restaurants,
and a good pizza place in town.

To get to the Manzanos from Albuquerque, drive east on I-40 to Tijeras
Canyon/Cedar Crest (exit 175) and drive
south on Hwy 337, which becomes Hwy 55
after 30 miles. From Belen, take Hwy 47
southeast to Hwy 60, go east till you reach
Hwy 55 at Mountainair, and then go north.

Salinas Pueblo Missions National Monument

This relatively tourist-free monument, well
worth a visit, consists of three separate
pueblos and their accompanying 17th-
century Spanish missions, which were each
abandoned in the late 17th century. The
small museum at the monument headquarters in Mountainair (☎ 847-2585), PO Box
496, Mountainair, NM 87036, gives a good
overview of the monument, and each site
has a small visitor center. The sites are open
9 am to 5 pm daily (free).
website: www.nps.gov/sapu

The biggest of the three sites is **Gran
Quivira** (☎ 847-2770), 25 miles south of
Mountainair along Hwy 55. Around 300

rooms and several kivas have been excavated. The ruins of two churches, dating from 1630 and 1659, can also be visited. Eight miles north of Mountainair on Hwy 55 is **Quarai** (☎ 847-2290). The 40-foot-high remains of a 1630 church are the highlight

here. The remains of the Tiwa-speaking Indian pueblo have not been excavated. Featuring a ruined 1620 church, one of the oldest in the country, and the remains of a large Tompiro pueblo, **Abo** (☎ 847-2400) is 9 miles west of Mountainair along Hwy 60.

Santa Fe & Taos

The last 30 years have brought extraordinary changes to the land and cultures of Santa Fe and Taos. In the 1970s most roads in Santa Fe were unpaved, and Taos was a dusty mecca primarily for artists and hippies. But land development and an influx of tourism have drastically altered the region's landscape and character. And while tourism has prompted interest in preserving what is unique to the area, savvy marketing has trivialized the very term 'Southwestern.'

Today, Santa Fe and Taos rank among the top tourist destinations in the USA. Santa Fe, especially, offers cosmopolitan conveniences and culinary delights. Movie stars and other wealthy Americans have built adobe mansions in the piñon- and cedar-spotted hills. Hispanic families who have lived in the river valleys for generations and Native Americans who have called the area home for even longer find themselves confronting wave after wave of newcomers and tourists. The ensuing sociopolitical problems are complex.

Nevertheless, the national forests and deserts surrounding Santa Fe and Taos are stunning. The phenomenon of desert light, in part a factor of the high altitude, can be appreciated only through experience. The Chama and Rio Grande Rivers cut through dry hills and form oases of green valleys, whose cottonwood trees turn brilliant yellow in the fall. The incredibly varied landscapes of red rocks, tubular rock formations, desert and high mountain lakes, and ponderosa-pine forests assure a spectacular drive no matter where you go. Take the time to explore beyond the cities. Wander into small Hispanic villages, and follow your nose down dirt roads and through canyons.

In addition to simply wandering, you can hike the forests, ski at the world-renowned Taos Ski Valley, cross-country ski, camp, white-water raft, fly fish, rock climb, mountain bike and swim within minutes of either Santa Fe or Taos, and numerous companies are eager to arrange guided tours or rent you equipment. The surrounding Indian pueblos offer tours, and their feast days and festivals provide a window into the history and spirituality of Native American cultures. The history of all the area's peoples – Indians, Hispanic settlers, traders and mountain men – cannot be separated from the landscape. Any visit to Santa Fe and Taos can shed light on this primal relationship, especially if you combine visits to museums, pueblos and ancient dwellings with some outdoor activities.

Today, dining – ranging from cheap dives with green-chile cheeseburgers to world-renowned restaurants – and shopping are integral parts of Santa Fe and Taos. In recent decades, the abundance of artists has supported numerous galleries showcasing contemporary works that rank among the

MAP INDEX

OTHER MAPS
Santa Fe Trail page 546

Colorado

Santa Fe & Taos page 545

Taos Area
page 573

Taos
page 575

Santa Fe page 547
Downtown Santa Fe
pages 548-549

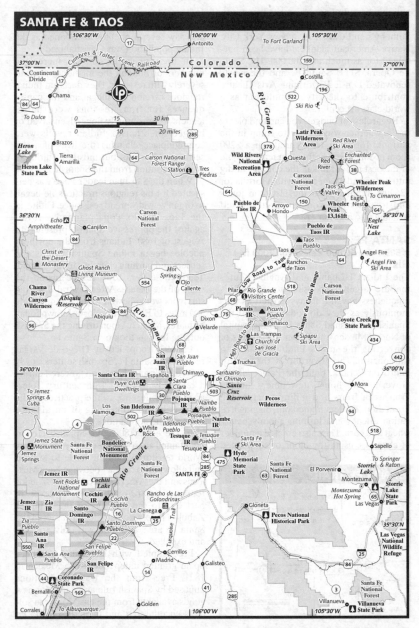

SANTA FE & TAOS

Colorado
New Mexico

To Fort Garland

Antonito

Cumbres & Toltec Scenic Railroad

37°00'N

106°30'W
106°00'W
105°30'W

159

Continental
Divide

17

Costilla

Chama

522

196

Ski Rio

84 64

To Dulce

0   15   30 km
0   10   20 miles

285

Brazos

Tierra
Amarilla

Latir Peak
Wilderness
Area

Red River
Ski Area

378

Enchanted
Forest

Heron
Lake

Heron Lake
State Park

64

Carson National
Forest Ranger
Station

Tres
Piedras

Wild Rivers
National
Recreation
Area

Questa

Red
River

38

Carson
National
Forest

Taos Ski
Valley

Wheeler Peak
Wilderness

To Cimarron

36°30'N

Echo
Amphitheater

Canjilon

64

150

Arroyo
Hondo

Eagle
Nest

64

36°30'N

Christ in
the Desert
Monastery

84

Pueblo de
Taos IR

Wheeler
Peak
13,161ft

Eagle
Nest
Lake

Ghost Ranch
Living Museum

Hot
Springs

554

Pueblo de
Taos IR

Taos
Pueblo

Angel Fire

Chama River
Canyon
Wilderness

Abiquiu
Reservoir

Camping

Ojo
Caliente

Taos

Angel Fire
Ski Area

Ranchos
de Taos

64

96

Abiquiu

84

285

Pilar

68

Rio Grande
Visitors Center

518

Carson
National
Forest

Dixon

75

Picuris
IR

Picuris
Pueblo

Coyote Creek
State Park

Velarde

Peñasco

434

San Juan
Pueblo

San Juan
IR

Las Trampas

Church of
San José
de Gracia

Sipapu
Ski Area

442

518

36°00'N

68

Santa Clara IR

Española

Chimayo

Santuario
de Chimayo

Truchas

36°00'N

To Jemez
Springs &
Cuba

Puye Cliff
Dwellings

30

Santa
Clara
Pueblo

Pojoaque
IR

503

Santa
Cruz
Reservoir

Mora

Pecos
Wilderness

94

Los
Alamos

502

San
Ildefonso
Pueblo

San Ildefonso
IR

Nambe
Pueblo

Nambe
IR

Pojoaque
Pueblo

518

4

Jemez State
Monument

White
Rock

Tesuque
IR

Tesuque
Pueblo

Santa Fe
Ski Area

Sapello

Jemez
Springs

Bandelier
National
Monument

Tesuque

84

285

Hyde
Memorial
State Park

63

Santa Fe
National
Forest

To Springer
& Raton

Jemez IR

Santa Fe
National
Forest

SANTA FE

475

El Porvenir

Storrie
Lake

Montezuma

Storrie
Lake
State Park

Tent Rocks
National
Monument

Cochiti
Lake

Rancho de Las
Golondrinas

Glorieta

Montezuma
Hot Spring

65

Las Vegas

Jemez
IR

Zia
IR

Santo
Domingo
IR

Cochiti
IR

Cochiti
Pueblo

La Cienega

16

25

Pecos National
Historical Park

Las Vegas
National
Wildlife
Refuge

Zia
Pueblo

Santo Domingo
Pueblo

22

35°30'N

550

Santa
Ana
IR

Santa Ana
Pueblo

San Felipe
Pueblo

San Felipe
IR

Cerrillos

14

Madrid

Galisteo

25

84

Santa Fe
National
Forest

44

Coronado
State Park

Bernalillo

165

41

285

3

Villanueva

Santa Fe
National
Forest

Corrales

To Albuquerque

Golden

106°00'W

Villanueva
State Park

105°30'W

Rio Grande

Rio Chama

Rio Grande

Low Road to Taos

High Road to Taos

Sangre de Cristo Range

Turquoise Trail

nation's best. Indian art and cultural artifacts have become popular collectibles – at Sotheby's and Christie's in New York City, Native American blankets have been auctioned for as much as $500,000. The Santa Fe Opera, SITE Santa Fe and the newly renovated Lensic Performing Arts Theatre contribute to the city's reputation as a world-class art center.

Regardless of budget, you can find plenty to do, whether you choose to camp in the national forest or to luxuriate in a $290 room in Santa Fe, whether you feast at some of the best restaurants in the country or dig into beans and green chile with a tortilla for $2. Just minutes from the fast-food joints and tourist traps, you can find yourself strolling into another era.

SANTA FE
☎ 505 • pop 60,000 • elevation 7000 feet
History
The Indian, Hispanic and Anglo cultures that are largely responsible for Santa Fe's uniqueness haven't always existed as harmoniously as they do today. In 1610 the Spanish established Santa Fe as the capital of Nuevo Mexico and began the process of converting the area's Pueblo Indians to Catholicism. The governor of the colony, Pedro de Peralta, built the Palace of the Governors to house newcomers, mostly Franciscan friars and military personnel. From there, settlers fanned out, digging irrigation ditches and farming mainly beans, wheat and corn. They also erected a number of churches, using the labor of subjugated

Indians. More than 50 churches were built in a space of 10 years, a period of time that also saw several pueblos abandoned as the Indian population was Christianized.

In their drive to convert increasing numbers of Indians, the missionaries dealt severely with resistors. They declared Indian religious ceremonies illegal and the consequences for transgressions were harsh; leaders were routinely flogged, enslaved or hanged for offenses. Indian revolts were commonplace, claiming the lives of a few settlers and priests, but mostly resulting in swift retribution from the Spanish.

When the San Juan leader Popé was persecuted for his religious practices, he began to organize widespread resistance. Hiding in the Taos Pueblo, Popé planned a revolt against the oppressive Spanish presence. In August of 1680, Indians from the northern pueblos began killing Spanish priests and settlers and burning churches to the ground. Terrified settlers took refuge inside the walls of the palace. After several days, the survivors were allowed to depart, marching 300 miles to El Paso del Norte, known today as Juárez, Mexico. Upon driving the Spanish out, the Indians took over Santa Fe.

In 1692, troops led by Diego de Vargas recaptured Santa Fe. Spanish settlers slowly moved back, and the region flowered during a relatively peaceful 18th century. Tolerance or indifference to the practices of the Indians led to something of an alliance between the populations.

In the early 1800s, the Spanish crown maintained an isolationist policy for its New World territories, limiting trade to Mexico and allowing no contact between New Mexicans and the Americans to the east. Anglos remained aware of the area, however, in part due to the writings of the explorer Zebulon Pike, who had illegally entered the Santa Fe area, and then was duly arrested and expelled.

Preoccupied with European conflicts, Spain granted independence to Mexico in 1821. Free from the trade restrictions imposed by Spanish rule and eager for new goods available from the east, Mexican soldiers encountered and invited to Santa Fe

SANTA FE TRAIL

Nebraska

Colorado   Kansas   Independence   Missouri

La Junta

Oklahoma

Santa Fe

New Mexico   Texas

0   150   300 km
0   90   180 miles

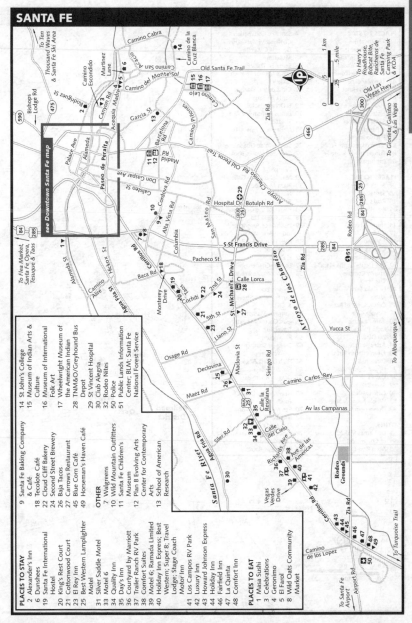

SANTA FE

see Downtown Santa Fe map

1 km

.5 mile

PLACES TO STAY
2 Alexander's Inn
6 Dunshees
19 Santa Fe International Hostel
20 King's Rest Court
21 Cottonwood Court
23 El Rey Inn
25 Best Western Lamplighter Motel
31 Silver Saddle Motel
33 Motel 6
35 Quality Inn
35 Day's Inn
36 Courtyard by Marriott
37 Trailer Ranch RV Park
38 Comfort Suites
39 Motel 6; Ramada Limited
40 Holiday Inn Express; Best Western; Super 8; Travel Lodge; Stage Coach Motor Inn
41 Los Campos RV Park
42 Luxury Inn
44 Howard Johnson Express
46 Holiday Inn
46 Fairfield Inn
47 La Quinta
48 Comfort Inn

PLACES TO EAT
1 Masa Sushi
3 Celebrations
4 Geronimo
5 El Farol
8 Wild Oats Community Market

9 Santa Fe Baking Company & Café
18 Tecolote Café
22 Cloud Cliff Bakery
24 Second Street Brewery
26 Baja Tacos
27 Carrows Restaurant
45 Blue Corn Café
49 Horseman's Haven Café

OTHER
7 Walgreens
10 Wild Mountain Outfitters
11 Santa Fe Children's Museum
12 Plan B Evolving Arts Center for Contemporary Arts
13 School of American Research

14 St John's College
15 Museum of Indian Arts & Culture
16 Museum of International Folk Art
17 Wheelwright Museum of the American Indian
28 TNM&O/Greyhound Bus Depot
29 St Vincent Hospital
30 Club Alegria
32 Rodeo Nites
50 Police
51 Public Lands Information Center; BLM; Santa Fe National Forest Service

NEW MEXICO

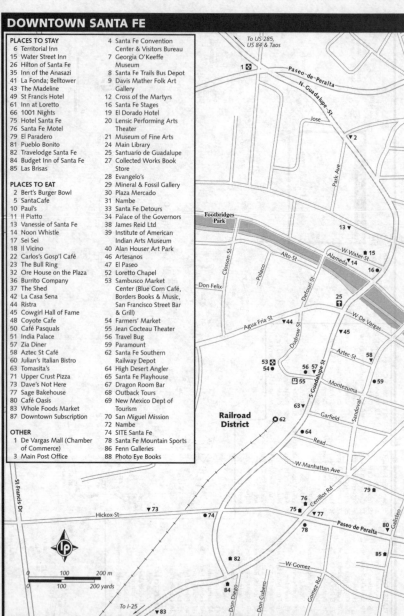

DOWNTOWN SANTA FE

PLACES TO STAY
6 Territorial Inn
15 Water Street Inn
26 Hilton of Santa Fe
35 Inn of the Anasazi
41 La Fonda; Belltower
43 The Madeline
49 St Francis Hotel
61 Inn at Loretto
66 1001 Nights
75 Hotel Santa Fe
76 Santa Fe Motel
79 El Paradero
81 Pueblo Bonito
82 Travelodge Santa Fe
84 Budget Inn of Santa Fe
85 Las Brisas

PLACES TO EAT
2 Bert's Burger Bowl
5 SantaCafe
10 Paul's
11 Il Piatto
13 Vanessie of Santa Fe
14 Noon Whistle
17 Sei Sei
18 Il Vicino
22 Carlos's Gosp'l Café
23 The Bull Ring
30 Ore House on the Plaza
36 Burrito Company
37 The Shed
42 La Casa Sena
44 Ristra
45 Cowgirl Hall of Fame
48 Coyote Cafe
50 Café Pasquals
51 India Palace
57 Zia Diner
58 Aztec St Café
60 Julian's Italian Bistro
63 Tomasita's
71 Upper Crust Pizza
73 Dave's Not Here
77 Sage Bakehouse
80 Café Oasis
83 Whole Foods Market
87 Downtown Subscription

OTHER
1 De Vargas Mall (Chamber
   of Commerce)
3 Main Post Office

4 Santa Fe Convention
   Center & Visitors Bureau
7 Georgia O'Keeffe
   Museum
8 Santa Fe Trails Bus Depot
9 Davis Mather Folk Art
   Gallery
12 Cross of the Martyrs
16 Santa Fe Stages
19 El Dorado Hotel
20 Lensic Performing Arts
   Theater
21 Museum of Fine Arts
24 Main Library
25 Santuario de Guadalupe
27 Collected Works Book
   Store
28 Evangelo's
29 Mineral & Fossil Gallery
30 Plaza Mercado
31 Nambe
33 Santa Fe Detours
34 Palace of the Governors
38 James Reid Ltd
39 Institute of American
   Indian Arts Museum
40 Alan Houser Art Park
46 Artesanos
47 El Paseo
52 Loretto Chapel
53 Sambusco Market
   Center (Blue Corn Café,
   Borders Books & Music,
   San Francisco Street Bar
   & Grill)
54 Farmers' Market
55 Jean Cocteau Theater
56 Travel Bug
59 Paramount
62 Santa Fe Southern
   Railway Depot
64 High Desert Angler
65 Santa Fe Playhouse
67 Dragon Room Bar
68 Outback Tours
69 New Mexico Dept of
   Tourism
70 San Miguel Mission
72 Nambe
74 SITE Santa Fe
78 Santa Fe Mountain Sports
86 Fenn Galleries
88 Photo Eye Books

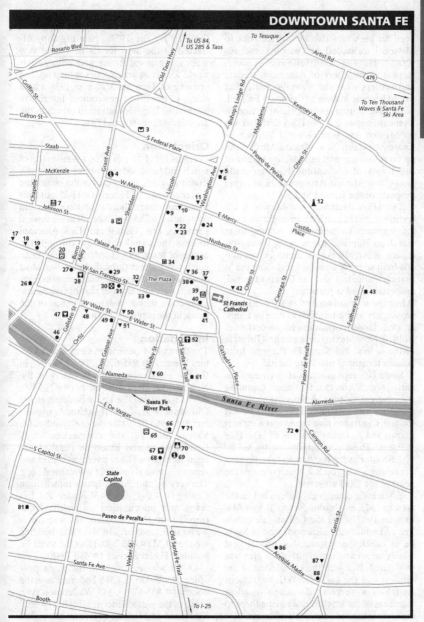

DOWNTOWN SANTA FE

one William Becknell, a trapper and trader. Becknell found the citizens of Santa Fe so keen for his wares that he hurried back to Missouri, reloaded his wagons and returned. He was soon followed by ever-increasing numbers of American traders and settlers over the 800-mile route that would become known as the Santa Fe Trail.

In 1846, during an imperialist period of westward expansion, the USA declared war on Mexico and sent General Stephen W Kearny to claim New Mexico. Mexico put up no resistance, and in 1848, the signing of the Treaty of Guadalupe Hidalgo made Texas, New Mexico, Arizona and California property of the United States.

The USA declared New Mexico a US territory in 1851, which brought in even more settlers from the east. Among them was Jean Baptiste Lamy, who, during his tenure as Archbishop of Santa Fe, eventually built some 40 churches, including the St Francis Cathedral and the Loretto Chapel, and established a parochial school system. When the railroad arrived in 1879, bringing passengers to the terminal in nearby Lamy, an even larger population boom occurred. In 1912, New Mexico became the 47th state in the union, and Santa Fe changed from being a territorial to a state capital.

Santa Fe's reputation as an art mecca has early roots. Painters intent upon capturing the ethereal essence of the area arrived in the 1920s and established the Santa Fe Art Colony. Central to that group was a quintet known as Los Cinco Pintores, or 'The Five Painters.' These post-impressionists, led by Will Shuster, were the first to take up residence along Canyon Rd, which remains the heart of the local art scene.

A scientific community descended on the area in 1943, establishing a lab at Los Alamos for developing the first atomic bomb. The community, 35 miles northwest of Santa Fe in the Jemez Mountains, was at first wholly secret and travel out of the area was prohibited. But with the completion of the mission and the end of WWII, restrictions on travel were relaxed enough to allow members of the intelligentsia living there to take advantage of Santa Fe's offerings.

The birth and subsequent rise of the tourist industry has had a great impact on the city. By the 1950s, painters, long attracted to the area for its land- and sky-scapes, began exhibiting and selling their works locally as art galleries sprang up. The opening of Taos Ski Valley in 1956 added skiers to the list of newcomers. Interest in alternative lifestyles attracted others to the area during the '60s and '70s.

Orientation

Cerrillos Rd (I-25 exit 278), a 6-mile strip of hotels and fast-food restaurants, enters town from the south; Paseo de Peralta circles the center of town; St Francis Dr (I-25 exit 282) forms the western border of downtown and turns into US 285, which heads north toward Española, Los Alamos and Taos. Alameda follows the canal east-west through the center of town, and Guadalupe is the main north-south street through downtown. Most downtown restaurants, galleries, museums and sites are either on or east of Guadalupe St and are within walking distance of the plaza, in the center of town.

Information

The Santa Fe Convention Center and Visitors Bureau (☎ 955-6200, 800-777-2489), in the Sweeny Center at 201 W Marcy St; the New Mexico Dept of Tourism (☎ 827-7400, 800-545-2040), in the Lamy Building at 491 Old Santa Fe Trail; and the chamber of commerce (☎ 988-3279), at the north end of De Vargas Mall (at the intersection of N Guadalupe St and Paseo de Peralta), are open weekdays. The convention center and visitors bureau is online at www.santafe.org. The very helpful Public Lands Information Center (☎ 438-7542), 1474 Rodeo Rd, has maps and information on public lands throughout New Mexico; its website is www.publiclands.org. In the same building are the BLM (☎ 438-7400) and the Santa Fe National Forest Service (☎ 438-7840).

Other services include the main post office (☎ 988-6351), 120 S Federal Place; the library (☎ 955-6789), 145 Washington Ave, north of the plaza; Vincent Hospital (☎ 983-3361), 455 St Michael's Dr; and the police

(☎ 955-5000), 2515 Camino Entrada. Walgreens (☎ 982-4643), 1096 S St Francis Dr, has a 24-hour pharmacy.

If you need travel books or maps, those are the specialties at Travel Bug (☎ 992-0418), just off of Guadalupe St by the Sambusco Market Center. Though small, the privately owned Collected Works (☎ 988-2226), across from the Lensic on W San Francisco St, is recommended for its selection of regional, travel and other books. The chain retailer, Borders Books & Music (☎ 954-4707), is in Sambusco Market Center.

The Plaza

The plaza dates back to the city's beginning in 1610, and from 1821 to 1880 it was the end of the Santa Fe Trail. Traders from as far away as Missouri drove here in their wagons laden with goods. Today, Native Americans sell their jewelry and pottery along the wall of the Palace of the Governors, kids skateboard and play hacky-sack and tourists weighed down with cameras and purchases flock the square.

Museum of New Mexico

The Museum of New Mexico administers four museums in Santa Fe open 10 am to 5 pm Tuesday to Sunday. All museums cost $5 for one visit/one museum and $10 for four days of unlimited visits to all four. Admission for children under 16 is free. Friday evening at the Museum of Fine Arts and Palace of the Governors is free.

The **Palace of the Governors** (☎ 476-5100), 100 Palace Ave on the plaza, is one of the oldest public buildings in the country. Built in 1610 by Spanish officials, it housed thousands of villagers when the Indians revolted in 1680 and was home to the territorial governors after 1846. Since 1909 the building has been a museum, with more than 17,000 historical objects reflecting Santa Fe's Indian, Spanish, Mexican and American heritage.

The **Museum of Fine Arts** (☎ 476-5072), 107 Palace Ave, features works by regional artists and sponsors regular gallery talks and slide lectures. Built in 1918, the architecture is an excellent example of the original Santa Fe–style adobe.

The state opened the **Museum of Indian Arts & Culture** (☎ 476-1250), 710 Camino Lejo, in 1987 to display artifacts that have been unearthed by the Laboratory of Anthropology, which must confirm that any proposed building site in New Mexico is not historically significant. Since 1931 it has collected over 50,000 artifacts. Rotating exhibits explore the historical and contemporary lives of the Pueblo, Navajo and Apache cultures.

The recommended **Museum of International Folk Art** (☎ 476-1200), 706 Camino Lejo, houses more than a 100,000 objects from more than 100 countries and is arguably the best museum in Santa Fe. The exhibits aren't simplistically arranged behind glass cases; the historical and cultural information is concise and thorough; and a festive feel permeates the rooms. The Hispanic Wing displays religious art, tin work, jewelry and textiles from northern New Mexico and throughout the Spanish Colonial Empire, dating from the 1600s to the present.
website: www.museumofnewmexico.org

Georgia O'Keeffe Museum

The artist Georgia O'Keeffe first visited New Mexico in 1917 and lived in Abiquiu, a village 45 minutes northwest of Santa Fe, from 1949 until her death in 1986 (see the boxed text 'Georgia O'Keeffe'). This museum (☎ 946-1000), 217 Johnson St, which opened in 1997, is the largest exhibit of her work. Housed in a former Spanish Baptist church, its adobe walls have been renovated to form 10 skylighted galleries. Hours are 10 am to 5 pm Tuesday to Sunday (until 8 pm on Friday). Admission is $5/free for adults and children. Tours of her home in Abiquiu require advance notice (see Abiquiu in the Northwest New Mexico chapter).

Institute of American Indian Arts Museum

The National Collection of Contemporary Indian Art, with more than 8000 pieces of basketry, paintings, pottery, sculpture,

Georgia O'Keeffe

One of the 20th century's most admired American artists and certainly the Southwest's most internationally famous painter, Georgia O'Keeffe (1887–1986) was born and raised on a Wisconsin farm before moving to Chicago and later New York to study art. She taught art in several southern states and in Texas from 1912 to 1916. Then her work was shown to photographer and gallery owner Alfred Steiglitz, whose 291 was New York's foremost avant-garde gallery of the time (where Europeans such as Rodin, Cézanne and Picasso had their works introduced to America). Steiglitz called O'Keeffe's drawings 'the purest, most sincere work that has entered 291 in a long while.'

So began a long and often complicated relationship between O'Keeffe and Steiglitz, who was 23 years her senior. In 1918 she moved in with him, causing a scandal because Steiglitz was married. Over the next two decades, she posed for his camera hundreds of times, forming one of the most remarkable series of photographic portraits ever made. They married in 1924, but their relationship remained enigmatic with both partners having affairs with other men and women.

O'Keeffe often left Steiglitz and New York City to seek inspiration elsewhere – upstate New York and Maine were favorite places. During this period she painted pictures of city skyscrapers and began painting the sensual enlargements of flowers (such as *Black Iris,* 1926) for which she is especially remembered. But she frequently hankered after the wide-open spaces of the West, recalling her teaching experiences in Texas and a 1917 vacation in New Mexico. Her opportunity came in 1929, when she was invited to Santa Fe and Taos by Mabel Dodge Luhan, New Mexico's leading patron of the arts.

New Mexico enchanted and influenced the artist. She began collecting bleached bones from the desert and incorporating them into her landscapes or painting them as close-ups; bones are

---

textiles and beadwork, is on permanent display (☎ 983-8900), 108 Cathedral Place. This is an excellent place to not only see beautiful art but also to understand its role in Native American culture. Hours are 10 am to 5 pm Monday through Saturday and noon to 5 pm Sunday. Admission is $4.

SITE Santa Fe
Housed in the old Coors Brewery, this 8000-sq-foot space (☎ 989-1199), 1606 Paseo de Peralta, presents work by contemporary international, national and regional visual artists. It doesn't have a permanent collection, and thus officially cannot be called a museum, but it does feature changing exhibitions, performances and a lecture series. Hours are 10 am to 5 pm Wednesday to Sunday. Admission is $5/2.50 for adults/seniors and students, and Sunday is free.

St Francis Cathedral
Jean Baptiste Lamy was sent to Santa Fe by the Pope with orders to tame the wild western outpost town through culture and religion. Convinced that the town needed a focal point for religious life, he began construction of this cathedral in 1869. Lamy's story has been immortalized in Willa Cather's *Death Comes for the Archbishop.* Inside the cathedral (☎ 982-5619), 131 Cathedral Place, is a small chapel, Capilla de Nuestra Señora la Conquistadora, Reina de la Paz, where the oldest Madonna statue in North America is housed. The statue was carved in Mexico and brought to Santa Fe in 1625, but when the Indians revolted in 1680, the villagers took it into exile with them. When Don Diego de Vargas retook the city in 1692, he brought the statue back, and legend has it that its extraordinary powers are responsible for the reconquest of the city. The cathedral is open daily, with services on Sunday.

Loretto Chapel
This gothic structure (☎ 982-0092), 207 Old Santa Fe Trail, is modeled on St Chapelle in

Georgia O'Keeffe

another of her most recognizable trademarks. Her works were imbued by her own mixed emotions, lending the paintings abstractly suggestive and subtly symbolic qualities that made them uniquely her own. Although she returned to New York after several months in New Mexico, she continued to visit year after year until Steiglitz's death in 1946. After settling her husband's affairs, she moved permanently back to New Mexico in 1949, where she had renovated an adobe home in the tiny village of Abiquiu.

By this time she had completed her most famous works, but continued to paint until she lost her sight in the 1980s. Some of the best-known work of her later life was inspired by world travel, especially the airplane flights that provided her with vistas of clouds, which led to the painting of a 24-foot-wide mural, *Sky Above the Clouds* (1965). Throughout her life she was an intensely private person, but she did write an autobiography, published in 1976. Failing health caused her to move to Santa Fe, where she died in 1986 at the age of 98, one of the Southwest's best known artists.

Today, O'Keeffe's work is exhibited in major museums throughout the world, and she is considered one of the best painters of the 20th century. Her home in Abiquiu can now be visited by advance appointment (see Abiquiu in the Northwestern New Mexico chapter), but for most visitors the best opportunity to come into contact with her iconic work is at the Georgia O'Keeffe Museum in Santa Fe.

Paris, and it was built from 1873 to 1878 for the Sisters of Loretto, the first nuns to come to New Mexico. St Chapelle has a circular stone staircase, but when the Loretto Chapel was being constructed, no local stone masons were skilled enough to build one and the young architect didn't know how to build one of wood. The nuns prayed for help and a mysterious traveling carpenter, whom the nuns believed afterward to be St Joseph, arrived. He built what is known as the Miraculous Staircase, a wooden spiral staircase with two complete 360° turns and no central or visible support. He left without charging for his labors and his identity remains unknown. The chapel is open 9 am to 6 pm daily, until 5 pm from September to April (on Sunday it opens after services at 10:30 am). There is a $1 fee.

San Miguel Mission

Original construction of this church (☎ 983-3974), 401 Old Santa Fe Trail, was started in 1625, and it served as a mission church for the Spanish settlers' Tlaxcalan Indian servants, who had been brought from Mexico. Though considered the oldest church in the United States, much of the original building was destroyed during the Pueblo Revolt of 1680, and it was rebuilt in 1710, with new walls added to what remained. The current square tower was added in 1887, and the interior was restored in 1955. From May to August, the chapel and gift shop are open 9 am to 5 pm Monday through Saturday and 1:30 to 4 pm Sunday. On Sunday there is a 5 pm mass. Call for hours during the rest of the year.

Cross of the Martyrs

At the northeastern end of downtown, on Paseo de Peralta, a short walk takes you to a cross at the top of a hill. Along the way, a series of plaques recount the city's history. It is an easy walk and there are views of the city and three mountain ranges – the Sangre de Cristos to the northeast, the Jemez to the west and the Sandias to the south. The cross at the top is a memorial to over 20 Franciscan priests who were killed during the Pueblo Revolt of 1680.

Canyon Road

At one time Canyon Rd, on the east side of downtown, was a dusty street lined with artists' homes and studios, but today most of the artists have fled to cheaper digs and the private homes have been replaced with a flock of upscale galleries. There are about a hundred galleries and a few restaurants on this small, adobe-lined street, and despite the commercialism and packs of tourists, it's worth a stroll. Come on foot, though – the one-way street provides very little parking.

Alan Houser Art Park

This small sculpture garden, across from the upscale hotel La Fonda, features huge, fluidly designed bronzes by one of New Mexico's most celebrated sculptors, Alan Houser.

State Capitol

The Roundhouse, as it is locally known, on Old Santa Fe Trail at Paseo de Peralta, is the center of New Mexico's government and where the governor and legislators have their offices. It is designed after the state symbol, the Zia sign. Call (☎ 986-4589) to arrange a tour.

Santuario de Guadalupe

This adobe church (☎ 988-2027), 100 S Guadalupe St, is the oldest extant shrine to Our Lady of Guadalupe, the patroness of the poor in Mexico. It was constructed between 1776 and 1796 near the end of the Camino Real, a 1500-mile trading route from Mexico that ended in Santa Fe. There have been several additions and renovations since. The oil-on-canvas Spanish baroque retablo (altar painting) inside the chapel was painted in Mexico in 1783 by José de Alzíbar. For the trip to Santa Fe, the painting had to be taken apart and transported up the Camino Real in pieces on muleback. Look closely to see the seams where the painting was put back together. Hours are 9 am to 4 pm Monday to Saturday (closed Saturday from November to April), and there is one mass a month.

Santa Fe Southern Railway

The old Santa Fe Southern Railway train (☎ 989-8600), 410 S Guadalupe St, runs to Lamy, 18 miles through the desert to the south and back, several times a week ($30). Call for hours. Bring a picnic lunch or eat at the Legal Tender restaurant in Lamy. On Friday night there is a cocktail trip for $30, and on Saturday there is a barbecue train, including a buffet (eat on your lap), a campfire in Lamy and live music (old railroad songs) for $45.

Santa Fe Children's Museum

This museum (☎ 989-8359), 1050 Old Pecos Trail, features hands-on exhibits on science, art and so on for children ages two to nine, but adults will enjoy it as well. Admission is $4/3 for adults/children under 12. It's open 10 am to 5 pm Thursday to Saturday, noon to 5 pm Sunday. Call for special events.

School of American Research

A center for advanced studies in anthropology and archaeological research since 1907, this school (☎ 954-7205), 660 E Garcia St, has a comprehensive collection of textiles and Indian art in its Indian Arts Research Center. Tours are given Friday at 2 pm. Call for reservations.

Wheelwright Museum of the American Indian

In 1937 Mary Cabot established this museum (☎ 982-4636), 704 Camino Lejo, to showcase Navajo ceremonial art. While its strength continues to be Navajo exhibits, it now includes contemporary Native American art and historical artifacts as well. The gift store offers an extensive selection of books and crafts. It is open 10 am to 5 pm Monday to Saturday, and 1 to 5 pm Sunday (free admission).

Ten Thousand Waves

This delightful and relaxing Japanese health spa (☎ 982-9304), nestled in the quiet hills 3½ miles outside of town, offers private and public hot tubs (outdoors), massages, watsu (massage in water), body treatments and facials. Rates start at $13 for a communal or women-only tub. Spa packages, as well as overnight stays in one of their luxury suites (see Places to Stay, later), are available. It is open daily (evenings only on Tuesday); call for hours. To get here, take Hwy 475 toward the Santa Fe Ski Area.

Santa Fe Opera

Opera fans (as well as those who have never seen or heard an opera in their life) will enjoy seeing a performance at the open-air auditorium in the desert hills north of town. Tickets range from $20 to $128, with weekday seats being the cheapest and standing-room prices going as low as $8. At the end of August two apprentice concerts are $10. Backstage tours ($6) are available at 1 pm Monday to Saturday, July to August. You can enjoy a pre-performance buffet, with a guest speaker, for $36. Many simply bring their own dinner and eat in the parking lot, everything from pizza on the roof of the car to elegant meals with crystal, linens and candles in the beds of pickup trucks. Purchase tickets at the El Dorado Hotel (May to August only) or at the box office (☎ 986-5900, 800-280-4654). The opera grounds are 5 miles north of Santa Fe on Hwy 84/285.

website: www.santafeopera.org

Activities

Several sporting shops in the area give information, sell maps and books, provide guides and rent equipment for outdoor activities. Try Santa Fe Mountain Sports (☎ 988-3337), 607 Cerrillos Rd or Wild Mountain Outfitters (☎ 986-1152), 541 Cordova Rd.

Skiing The **Santa Fe Ski Area** (☎ 982-4429) is a half-hour from the plaza up Hwy 475. From the summit (12,000 feet), you can admire 80,000 sq miles of desert and mountains spread out below. Lift tickets are $28/40 for a half/full day. For a snow report, call ☎ 983-9155. On weekends from June to August and a couple weeks during fall

foliage, the chairlift is open for $4 one-way and $6 roundtrip, and there is an expansive system of hiking trails.

There are numerous cross-country ski trails in the Jemez Mountains and the Santa Fe National Forest. The Public Lands Information Center (☎ 438-7542), 1474 Rodeo Rd, provides a free packet of cross-country ski information. Hyde Memorial State Park (☎ 983-7175), on the road to the ski basin, has trails as well.

River Running Busloads of people head up to the Taos Box for white-water river running, but there are also mellow float trips throughout New Mexico and overnight guided rafting trips. New Wave Rafting Company (☎ 984-1444) is a reputable outfitter to try, but there are many others. For information, call Santa Fe Detours (☎ 983-6565).

Hiking Just walking around Santa Fe can be quite strenuous because of the 7000-foot elevation. Spend a day or two here to acclimatize before rushing off into the mountains of the Santa Fe National Forest, immediately to the east of town. The heart of the national forest is the undeveloped Pecos Wilderness, with trails leading to several peaks over 12,000 feet. Nearly 1000 miles of trails, forming a complex web, are suitable for short hikes and multiday backpacks.

Weather changes rapidly in the mountains and summer storms are frequent, especially in the afternoons, so check weather reports and hike prepared. The trails are usually closed by snow in winter, and the higher trails may be closed through May.

Maps and thorough information on hiking throughout the area are available from the very helpful Public Lands Information Center (☎ 438-7542), 1474 Rodeo Rd and the Pecos/Las Vegas Ranger Station in Pecos (☎ 757-6121). Local bookstores carry New Mexico hiking guides, including the useful *Day Hikes in the Santa Fe Area* by the Sierra Club.

The most immediately accessible trailheads, offering day hikes or entrance into a host of longer hikes, are northeast of Santa

Fe along Hwy 475, within Hyde Memorial State Park (☎ 983-7175) and near the ski base. Short loops are possible – the 5-mile Borrego–Bear Wallow Loop to Tesuque Creek, which starts at the north end of Hyde Memorial State Park, is a good one. These trails connect with the popular Winsor Trail (Trail 254), which gives access to a huge network of trails in the Pecos Wilderness. North of the Pecos National Historical Park in the Santa Fe National Forest, good places to start are the Holy Ghost, Jack's Creek or Iron Gate Campgrounds (see Places to Stay – Camping, later).

Fishing Lake fishing is possible at various pueblo lakes (see individual pueblos) and at Abiquiu Reservoir (75 miles northwest; see the Northwestern New Mexico chapter), as is fly-fishing in streams and rivers throughout northern New Mexico. High Desert Angler (☎ 988-7688), 435 S Guadalupe, rents and sells rods, reels, flies and other fishing gear, gives classes for all levels and provides guide services for the area. Expect to pay $250 for a day of fishing for two people. For regulations and licenses, either ask at High Desert Angler or call the New Mexico Dept of Game and Fish (☎ 827-7911).

Other Activities There is plenty of **mountain biking** in the area. New Mexico Mountain Bike Adventures (☎ 474-0074), guides three hour to five-night mountain biking, hiking and historical tours through the desert and mountains, including one to old turquoise mines (from $50, including bike and helmet; offered all-year). Its website is www.bikefun.com. Bike and Sport (☎ 820-0809), 1829 Cerrillos Rd, rents mountain bikes starting at $22 a day. New Mexico weather is excellent for **horseback riding**; Rancho Encantado (☎ 982-3537, 800-722-9339), in Tesuque just north of Santa Fe, offers trips through the desert. Also try the beautiful – if a bit snooty – Vista Clara Spa (☎ 466-4772) in Galisteo, south of Santa Fe, and Broken Saddle (☎ 470-0074) in Cerrillos.

Call the City Recreation Dept (☎ 438-1485) for information on Santa Fe's three public indoor **swimming pools** and one outdoor pool and its 44 public **tennis courts** (in Abiquiu, 45 minutes northwest, you can swim in the dam; see the Northwestern New Mexico chapter). A popular pastime in northern New Mexico is **hunting** for deer, elk, squirrels, waterfowl, turkey and antelope. For regulations and licenses, call the New Mexico Dept of Game and Fish (☎ 827-7911).

If you develop a love for New Mexican food, as many do, try **cooking lessons** at the Santa Fe School of Cooking (☎ 983-4511). Classes, with 20 options including traditional New Mexican and Southwestern breakfast, are 2½ hours long and range from $40 to $90, including the meal.

Organized Tours

Several companies offer walking and bus tours of Santa Fe and northern New Mexico, and others organize guided trips to the pueblos, as well as air tours and biking, hiking, rafting and horseback riding trips. Ask the visitors bureau for a complete listing. The Gray Line (☎ 983-9491) offers a three-hour lecture tour of the city for $17 per person. Aboot About Santa Fe Walks (☎ 988-2774), a 'destination management company' departs at 9:30 am and 1:30 pm daily from the El Dorado Hotel for a two-hour walking tour of the city ($10); ask about a variety of historical, cultural, outdoor activity and foreign-language tours.

Santa Fe Detours (☎ 983-6565, 800-338-6877), 54½ E San Francisco St, can arrange guided trips for whatever kind of activity you're interested in, and will try to match you to an outfitter that meets your particular needs and style; visit www.sfdetours.com. If you want to try some back roads, Outback Tours (☎ 820-6101, 800-800-5337) focuses on the region's geology, ecology and history on 4WD day, overnight, and evening tours; it's online at www.outbacktours.com. Stefanie Beninato (☎ 988-8022) offers garden, art and ghost tours of Santa Fe ($15) as well as regional day tours; visit www.nmtours.com.

Special Events

The Santa Fe Visitors Bureau website (www.santafe.org) provides an excellent list, with contact information, of special events, musical and theatrical productions and museum shows.

Indian Market On the third weekend in August, more than a thousand Indian artists from around the country show their works in booths on and around the plaza. This is a judged show, and the quality of the work presented here is phenomenal. Collectors arrive in town as early as dawn on Saturday, and often the best items are gone by Saturday afternoon. Downtown hotels as well as the motels on Cerrillos Rd are usually booked months in advance for Indian Market, so plan ahead. The Southwestern Association for Indian Arts (☎ 983-5220) has more information.

Santa Fe Fiesta Every year on the first weekend after Labor Day this fiesta commemorates Don Diego de Vargas' reconquering of the city in 1692. Various religious and historical festivities are scheduled, and food booths are set up on the plaza, where music plays from morning until past midnight. The highlight of the weekend is the **Burning of Zozobra** on Friday night at Fort Marcy Park. Old Man Gloom, a 40-foot-high papier-mâché doll dressed in black and white, is burned to symbolize the end of last year's problems. The whole weekend is characterized by drunken revelry. Call the Santa Fe Fiesta Council (☎ 988-7575) for specific information.

Artist & Craftsman Show Every summer one of eight different pueblos hosts a huge celebration, with all kinds of food, dances and music as well as a comprehensive craft show. Call Eight Northern Indian Pueblos (☎ 800-793-4955) for dates and location.

Other Events Another market, far less crowded than Indian Market, is **Spanish Market** (☎ 983-4038) on the last weekend of July. Traditional and Hispanic crafts are sold at booths set up on and around the plaza. The **Rodeo of Santa Fe** (☎ 471-4300) is a four-day regional rodeo held on the second weekend of July. A rodeo parade marches through the downtown plaza on Wednesday morning, and competitions run through Saturday night. There are two annual New Mexican wine festivals in or near Santa Fe, the **New Mexico Wine and Chile War Festival** on Memorial Day weekend and the **Santa Fe Wine Festival** at El Rancho de las Golondrinas (see Around Santa Fe, later in this chapter) on Fourth of July weekend.

Places to Stay

When choosing from the exhaustive selection of accommodations in Santa Fe, remember that rates seem to vary from week to week, day to day and mood to mood, so always haggle. One traveler arrived in town looking for a place to stay, and the hotel quoted $440 for a double. By the end of a three-minute conversation, the rate had been reduced to $135! Generally, January and February have the lowest rates and September, October, March and April are mid-range; prices listed here are for May to August (high season), but use them only as a rough guide. Rates can be reduced as much as half or more during low season. Cerrillos Rd, the 6-mile strip of **chain motels**, small independent motels and fast-food restaurants southwest of downtown, can be very inconvenient without a car.

Santa Fe Stay (☎ 820-2468, 800-995-2272) specializes in home stays, ranch resorts, casitas and other places beyond hotels and B&Bs. Santa Fe Accommodation (☎ 982-6636, 800-745-9910), a reservation service, is online at www.santafehotels.com. Similar are All Santa Fe Reservations (☎ 474-5557, 877-737-7366) and the Accommodations Hotline (☎ 986-0038, 800-338-6877); all three can help find short-term rooms and condos within your budget. Ask about winter ski packages. Also access the visitors center website and see Española & Around later in this chapter for more options.

Places to Stay – Camping

The Santa Fe National Forest and the Pecos Wilderness have numerous camping sites. Stop by the Public Lands Information Center (☎ 438-7542), 1474 Rodeo Rd, for maps and detailed information. The *New*

NEW MEXICO

Mexico Recreation and Heritage Guide, from the New Mexico Dept of Tourism, is a great map for an overview of camping.

The nearest USFS campgrounds are northeast of Santa Fe along Hwy 475 on the way to the ski basin. They are administered by the Española Ranger Station (☎ 753-7331). None have showers or hookups and most are first-come, first-served, with honesty boxes charging $5 per night. Eight miles from Santa Fe on Hwy 475 is *Black Canyon* (☎ 982-8674), which has 45 tent sites for $8 each. This is one of the few places in which you can reserve ahead of time, but it is open only May to October. *Big Tesuque* and *Aspen Base*, 3 and 4 miles farther on Hwy 475, are open all year; they have primitive toilets and water. Just past Black Canyon, *Hyde Memorial State Park* (☎ 983-7175) has seven sites with hookups ($11) and many more tent sites ($7), some with three-sided wooden shelters. The park has hiking and skiing trails and is open year-round, weather permitting. Day use is $3. If you are desperate to clean up thoroughly, consider a splurge at Ten Thousand Waves, which is along Hwy 475 closer to town (see Ten Thousand Waves, earlier in this chapter).

Just north of Pecos National Historical Park, along Hwy 63, are five campgrounds, open roughly May through October, administered by the Pecos/Las Vegas Ranger District (☎ 757-6121, 438-7699). Showers and hookups are not available. *Jack's Creek* ($10) has water, grills and horse corrals. *Holy Ghost* costs $8 and *Field Tract* is $8. Sixteen miles north of Pecos and a mile on Forest Rd 646 is *Links Track*, with 20 free sites. *Iron Gate*, 23 miles north of Pecos on Forest Rd 223, has 14 sites ($4); however, the last portion of the road to Iron Gate is not publicly maintained and is particularly bad, especially after rain.

RV parks on the outskirts of Santa Fe are more pleasant than the ones on Cerrillos Rd (see the Santa Fe map). Most are closed from November to March; all have hot showers and laundry facilities. Eleven miles northeast of town at I-25 exit 290 is a *KOA* (☎ 466-1419), with RV hookups for $25, tent sites for $20 and cabins for $35. Also at exit

290 is *Rancheros de Santa Fe Camping Park* (☎ 466-3482), with a convenience store and tent/RV sites for $17/23.

Places to Stay – Budget
Santa Fe International Hostel (☎ 988-1153, *1412 Cerrillos Rd*) has dorm rooms for $15. Private rooms with shared/private bath are $25/34 for one person, $10 for each additional person. Doubles, most with kitchenettes, cost about $60 at the friendly and basic '50s *Silver Saddle Motel* (☎ 471-7663, *2810 Cerrillos Rd*). Other good options with doubles starting in the low $50s are *King's Rest Court* (☎ 983-8879, *1452 Cerrillos Rd*), *Cottonwood Court* (☎ 982-5571, *1742 Cerrillos Rd*) and the Route 66–style *Thunderbird Inn* (☎ 983-4397, *1821 Cerrillos Rd*).

Places to Stay – Mid-Range
Hotels & Motels The *Budget Inn of Santa Fe* (☎ 982-5952, 800-288-7600, *725 Cerrillos Rd*), within walking distance of downtown Santa Fe, offers doubles in the $82 to $112 range. Just off Guadalupe, *Santa Fe Motel* (☎ 982-1039, *510 Cerrillos Rd*) offers basic motels rooms ($114), rooms with kitchenettes ($137) and casitas.

An interesting place on the Cerrillos Rd strip is the *El Rey Inn* (☎ 982-1931, 800-521-1349, *1862 Cerrillos Rd*), situated on 3½ grassy acres with a playground, picnic area and pool. Southwest-style rooms and suites, some with fireplace, patio and kitchenette, range from $70 to $155. It's a pleasant spot and is fairly close to downtown Santa Fe. Rooms at the nice looking *Stage Coach Motor Inn* (☎ 471-0707, *3360 Cerrillos Rd*) start at $79.

B&Bs There are so many fantastic B&Bs in Santa Fe that the following can only be a taste. *Dunshees* (☎ 982-0988, *986 Acequia Madre*) offers a spacious and beautifully done suite with a living room, two fireplaces and a refrigerator and a lovely two-bedroom casita with fireplace. Both have private terraces and cost $135 all year; rates include a full hot breakfast at the suite and a stocked refrigerator for breakfast in the casita. This friendly and recommended place, on a dirt road in a residential area, offers a peaceful respite (beautiful gardens in the summer) within walking distance of restaurants and attractions at an excellent price.

Alexander's Inn (☎ 986-1431, 888-321-5123, 529 E Palace Ave) is a turn-of-the-19th-century Victorian house with five doubles and two casitas. Though located in a quiet, tree-lined residential neighborhood with grassy grounds and lilac trees, both Canyon Rd and the plaza are within easy walking distance. There is no attempt at Southwest style here, and no cutesy feel either; visit www.alexanders-inn.com. Built in 1886, the *Madeline* (☎ 982-3465, 106 Faithway St) is a Queen Anne Victorian with a dark wood stair railing and leaded stained-glass windows. Rates at both range from $75 to $175.

The award-winning adobe restoration of the recommended *Water Street Inn* (☎ 984-1193, 800-646-6752, 427 W Water St) features a variety of lovely rooms, some with fireplaces, four-poster beds and patios. New Mexican wine and hot hors d'oeuvres are served nightly. Rates start at $125; online go to www.waterstreetinn.com. Relaxed and friendly, *El Paradero* (☎ 988-1177, 220 W Manhattan Ave) is a mishmash of mission-, territorial- and Victorian-style architecture, some with skylights, fireplaces, tiled floors, woven textiles and folk art. Rooms of varying size range from $80 to $150; visit www.elparadero.com.

You're instantly removed from the bustle and dust of Santa Fe at *1001 Nights* (147 E De Vargas), a cozy adobe with a peaceful grass courtyard. Rooms are richly decorated and have a fireplace, kitchen and living room. Rates are $229/289 for one/two-bedroom suites with kitchens. The *Territorial Inn* (215 Washington Ave), a territorial-style home centrally located 1½ blocks from the plaza, has pretty rooms from $120 to $170. Reservations for both can be made through Santa Fe Accommodations (☎ 800-745-9910), or online at www.santafehotels.com.

All the rooms at the pleasant *Pueblo Bonito* (☎ 984-8001, 800-461-4599, 138 W Manhattan Ave), an adobe complex built around 1900, have kiva fireplaces, and some have kitchenettes. Rates range from $105 to $150 all year and include a cold breakfast buffet and an afternoon tea with margaritas and wine (perhaps 'tea' is a misnomer). website: www.pueblobonitoinn.com

In rural Galisteo, 23 miles southeast of Santa Fe, is the lovely and romantic *Galisteo Inn* (☎ 466-8200, 9 La Vega St), housed in a 250-year-old adobe hacienda set on 8 acres. The inn offers horseback riding ($50 for one hour) and has a grassy courtyard with an outdoor pool and hot tub. Rates for the well-appointed doubles ($120 to $200 all year) and one single ($80) include a full buffet breakfast. A fixed price dinner ($32 to $37) is offered. webiste: www.galisteoinn.com

Condominiums Conveniently located on Galisteo St, *Las Brisas* (☎ 982- 5795), provides fully equipped condos, with pleasant Southwestern-style furnishings, fireplaces and enclosed courtyards. Prices range from $134 for a one-bedroom during low season, to about $207 for a two-bedroom during high season.

Places to Stay – Top End

One block from the plaza and directly across from the St Francis Cathedral is *La Fonda* (☎ 982-5511, 100 E San Francisco St). A hotel has existed on the site since 1610, and the guest list includes Kit Carson, General and Mrs Ulysses S Grant, President and Mrs Rutherford B Hayes, and more recently, Errol Flynn, John Travolta, Shirley MacLaine and Ross Perot. The current hotel, built in 1920, is a huge adobe with a cozy bar/lounge and great local entertainment. Southwest-style rooms, some with fireplaces and balconies, range from $229 for a standard double to $319 for a suite.

The *Inn at Loretto* (☎ 988-5531, 800-727-5531, 211 Old Santa Fe Trail), with architecture inspired by Taos Pueblo, offers pleasant rooms, many with a view of the mountains, from $199. In contrast to the usual Santa Fe style, the *St Francis Hotel* (☎ 983-5700, 800-

529-5700, 210 Don Gaspar Ave) has the feel of a small European hotel with an elegant lobby and afternoon tea. All 82 rooms have a refrigerator; rates range from $122 to $280 for a suite.

Friendly *Hotel Santa Fe* (☎ *982-1200, 800-825-9876, 1501 Paseo de Peralta),* a sprawling adobe in the Guadalupe district, is majority-owned by the Picuris Pueblo. The rooms are spacious and tastefully done, some with a terrace and all with a refrigerator. There is an outdoor pool and hot tub. Rates range from $169 to $259 in the high season, but change seven times during the year and can be as low as $85.

Perhaps the coziest and most elegant place in town is *Inn of the Anasazi* (☎ *988-3030, 800-688-8100, 113 Washington Ave).* It opened in 1991 and achieves an Old World feel with heavy wood, textiles, stone floors and leather furniture. The public rooms – the little bar, restaurant and lounges – are gorgeous, with hand-carved furniture, overstuffed chairs, wood floors and throw rugs, but the bedrooms are rather small. Prices reflect its worldwide reputation for luxury and personal service: Rooms start at $199 in low season, $285 during peak season.

Eight miles north of Santa Fe in the hills around Tesuque is *Rancho Encantado* (☎ *982-3537, 800-722-9339),* a 1932 168-acre ranch offering tennis, horseback riding and swimming. Though this is an expensive place, it is relaxed and casual. Stop by for a drink on the patio to escape the Santa Fe crowds and watch the sun set peacefully over the desert. Rates range from $185 to $395 for doubles and villas.
website: www.puebloencantado.com

At *Ten Thousand Waves* (☎ *982-9304, 988-1047),* a spa on Hwy 475 on the way to the Santa Fe Ski Area (see Ten Thousand Waves, earlier), rooms and luxurious private suites, with fireplaces and some with kitchens, are $185 to $255. Rates include unlimited access to the communal tub.
website: www.tenthousandwaves.com

Places to Eat
With 27 pages of restaurants in the Santa Fe yellow pages, the options are overwhelming

and exhausting to think about. Fortunately, there are very few places that are downright bad, though there are quite a few that are way over-priced. Below is a small selection, from outrageously expensive meals that won't disappoint to excellent places for under $10 (or even cheaper).

The Plaza The number of restaurants within a 3-block radius of the plaza is staggering, and among them you'll find a meal to match any budget and most gastronomic desires. A convenient spot for a quick, cheap meal is the *Burrito Company* (☎ *982-4453, 111 Washington Ave),* where you can get hot dogs and New Mexican fare for under $5. Another inexpensive place for lunch is *Carlos's Gosp'l Café* (☎ *983-1841, 125 Lincoln Ave).* It's a very simple place, serving basically sandwiches and green chile stew, hidden in a courtyard off the main street a block from the plaza. In the Plaza Mercado on San Francisco St just west of the plaza, the *San Francisco Street Bar and Grill* (☎ *982-2044)* serves great burgers, a broiled fish sandwich on a baguette, yummy salads and grilled fare for under $10. The only drawback to this place is that it's in the basement.

Go to *Upper Crust Pizza* (☎ *982-0000, 329 Old Santa Fe Trail)* for unbeatable traditional or whole-wheat crust pizza, Italian sandwiches and calzones. Eat on the front porch or have them deliver. Try *Il Vicino* (☎ *986-8700, 321 W San Francisco St)* for excellent wood-oven pizza with a wide selection of gourmet toppings and courtyard dining.

A favorite, *Café Pasquals* (☎ *983-9340, 121 Don Gaspar Ave)* is deservedly famous for its breakfasts, which are served all day, but lunch and dinner (rather pricey) are excellent as well. The menu incorporates fresh herbs, whole grains and high-quality meats and includes chorizo, salmon (try the salmon burrito), free-range chicken and pancakes with apple-smoked bacon. There is almost always a wait, but it's not long if you're willing to sit at the community table – and it's definitely worth it! Hours are 7 am to 3 pm Monday to Saturday, 8 am to

2 pm Sunday, and 5:30 to 10:30 pm daily. Reservations are accepted for dinner.

Choose from a hundred margaritas and watch the mingling plaza crowds from the 2nd-story balcony of the *Ore House on the Plaza* (☎ 983-8687, 50 Lincoln Ave). Also try the *Blue Corn Café* (☎ 984-1800) in the Plaza Mercado for tasty margaritas and big plates of New Mexican fare. A second location is on the far south end of Cerrillos Rd. Great Indian food, including a $7 lunch buffet and a wide selection of vegetarian dishes, can be found at *India Palace* (☎ 986-5859, 227 Don Gaspar Ave).

Paul's (☎ 982-8738, 72 W Marcy Ave) features imaginative dishes like stuffed pumpkin bread and baked salmon with pecan-herb crust. It's a small, whimsical place, with folk art on the walls and impeccable service; dinner entrées are between $13 and $19. A less expensive option across the street is *Il Piatto* (☎ 984-1091), a casual, unpretentious spot with friendly service and good Italian food in the $8 to $13 range. In the summer, eat at one of the few sidewalk tables and people-watch. It's open daily for dinner and weekdays for lunch. For a quiet, romantic meal, try *Julian's Italian Bistro* (☎ 988-2355, 221 Shelby St), a cozy, adobe restaurant serving excellent duck, pasta and veal in the $12 to $23 range.

SantaCafe (☎ 984-1788, 231 Washington Ave) has enjoyed well-deserved critical acclaim for its eclectic blending of Asian and Southwestern cuisine. Expect to pay between $10 and $25 for an entrée – try the generous grilled filet mignon with roasted garlic/green-chile mashed potatoes. The décor is simple white-walled adobe with white tablecloths (peek down a glass-covered well at the tiny bar), and in warm weather you can eat in the brick courtyard. Another option for a high-end meal is *Anasazi* (☎ 988-3236), inside the Inn of the Anasazi. Though the food can be excellent, it is inconsistent. Come here to enjoy the dramatic and cozy interior of heavy wood and hand-woven textiles. The creative New Mexican and Native American dishes are in the $10 to $25 range, but you can have something less expensive at the bar.

While the main restaurant is overrated, the rooftop cantina at the *Coyote Café* (☎ 983-1615, 132 W Water St) is an excellent spot to watch the street activity and enjoy fresh, delicious Southwestern cooking for half the price of the main restaurant (open from April to October).

La Casa Sena (☎ 988-9232, 125 E Palace Ave) is actually two restaurants; one is a formal, territorial-style adobe home, and the other is a casual cantina, where the waitstaff sings Broadway. Shows run from 6 to 11 pm. Both serve consistently good New Mexican; in the summer, eat in the pleasant courtyard. Less expensive and well-recommended for New Mexican is *The Shed* (☎ 982-9030, 113½ E Palace Ave), housed in an historic adobe with fireplaces and patio dining (from $5).

Though the *The Bull Ring* (☎ 983-3328, 150 Washington Ave) is rather dark and nondescript, they serve excellent steaks (best in Santa Fe, they say), as well as ribs, lamb, chicken and seafood. For sushi and other Japanese dishes, try *Sei Sei* (☎ 983-5353, 321 W San Francisco St), where you can dine in the grassy courtyard or in a private tatami room.

The best spot in town for a sunset drink is the *Belltower*, the rooftop bar at the La Fonda Hotel, where you get far enough above the rooftops to watch the desert sky (open April to October).

Guadalupe Street Area Housed in a former railyard warehouse, *Tomasita's* (☎ 983-5721, 550 S Guadalupe) is popular. It has become a loud and crowded tourist hangout, but the New Mexican food is good (many say it's got the best margaritas in town) and prices are in the $7 to $12 range. A better choice is *Dave's Not Here* (☎ 983-7060), across the railroad tracks several blocks off the far south side of Guadalupe on Hickox St. Its legendary reputation for cheap, delicious New Mexican fare is well deserved; this is one of the best places in town for green chile.

The *Zia Diner* (☎ 988-7008, 326 S Guadalupe) serves reasonably priced, upscale diner food like meatloaf and hot turkey sandwiches, as well as creative Southwestern fare and homemade pies. This popular local hangout, an old standby for many, is always busy, but you're guaranteed a great meal at a great value. Prices range from $6 to $15.

The small and busy *Cowgirl Hall of Fame* (☎ 982-2565, 319 S Guadalupe St) serves hearty Texan specialties with a Cajun twist such as a honey-fried chicken picnic, fried catfish and barbecued chicken. The décor is relaxed Old West – eat inside or on the patio. It's a fun place, open daily for lunch and dinner. Sidle up to the bar's iron saddle seats for live music nightly.

The *Sage Bakehouse* (☎ 820-7243), across from Hotel Santa Fe on Cerrillos Rd, has great bread, hearty sandwiches and breakfast treats. A popular hangout for the black-turtleneck crowd is the *Aztec St Café* (☎ 983-9464, 317 Aztec St), serving coffee drinks, pastries and a light food menu (with a blaring emphasis on 'organic').

Vanessie of Santa Fe (☎ 982-9966, 434 W San Francisco St), a massive place with a high-beamed ceiling, 12-foot adobe doors and big fireplaces, is a popular, fun spot. The menu includes only the basics, like a whole rotisserie chicken for $12 and an 18oz ribeye for $24; everything is à la carte, and everything is huge. The lounge is open 4:30 pm to 2 am, and a piano bar gets going at about 9 pm nightly. Dinner is served from 5:30 to 10:30 pm.

For a quick burger, head to *Bert's Burger Bowl* (☎ 982-0215, 235 N Guadalupe). There are no tables inside, and only a few outside, but don't worry about sitting – just get a green-chile cheeseburger for $3 to go. Just north of the canal, you can escape the tourist crowds and enjoy a good sandwich for under $5 at the *Noon Whistle* (☎ 988-2636, 451 W Alameda).

Recommended for a reasonable upscale meal, the intimate *Ristra* (☎ 982-8608, 548 Aqua Fria) serves excellent French cuisine with a southwestern twist; a three-course set menu is $25.

Canyon Road Housed in an old adobe house, *El Farol* (☎ 983-9912, 808 Canyon Rd) specializes in a delicious variety of Spanish tapas, including grilled cactus, chorizo and mussels. The cozy bar (live music on weekends) is open 2 pm to 1:30 am.

Celebrations (☎ 989-8904, 613 Canyon Rd) offers a pleasant place to relax on its patio or inside by the fire. Hearty breakfasts, big salads, burgers and interesting sandwiches start at $5. It's open 8 am to 2 pm daily and for dinner 5:30 to 9 pm Wednesday through Saturday.

One of the best places in town (and in the state) for an upscale meal is the romantic *Geronimo* (☎ 982-1500, 724 Canyon Rd), housed in a white-walled 1756 adobe home, with a fireplace, plush chairs, and porch dining. Though it is expensive (from $15), the changing menu is creative, the food is outstanding and the service is impeccable (consider stopping in for the less expensive lunch).

Cerrillos Road A great place for a hearty and relatively cheap breakfast or lunch is the unpretentious *Tecolote Café* (☎ 988-1362, 1203 Cerrillos Rd). Try the Atole piñon hotcakes or the carne adovada burrito. Hours are 7 am to 2 pm Tuesday to Sunday. The inexpensive *Horseman's Haven Café* (☎ 471-5420, 6500 Cerrillos Rd) is a little jewel. The tiny space is busy with locals and free of Santa Fe frills (careful not to drive right past!), and it serves up some of the best green chile in town. If there is a quintessential New Mexican diner, this is it. *Baja Tacos* (☎ 471-8762, 2621 Cerrillos Rd) is another popular hangout. It's just a drive-through, and lunch lines can be long, but prices are cheap, and the food is good.

Just off of Cerrillos Rd are two excellent spots. The *Cloud Cliff Bakery* (☎ 983-6254, 1805 2nd St) serves all kinds of breads, scones, muffins and other baked goods as well as hearty breakfasts (including frittatas and blue-corn pancakes) and scrumptious lunch sandwiches daily ($5 to $12). For locally brewed beer and reasonably priced pub fare, far from the Santa Fe tourist crowd, stop by the low-key *Second Street Brewery* (☎ 982-3030, 1814 2nd St). They have live jazz on Wednesday from 5 to 7:30 pm, and reggae, jazz, and acoustic solos on Friday and Saturday nights.

Carrows Restaurant (☎ *471-7856, 1718 St Michael's Dr*) is open 24 hours.

Other Eateries Removed from the tourist bustle of the plaza, *Masa Sushi* (☎ *982-3334, 927 W Alameda*), in Solana Center, is worth finding. The Japanese food is authentic, delicious and fresh, the prices reasonable, the portions generous and the menu varied. It's open for lunch Monday through Friday and for dinner daily.

Café Oasis (☎ *983-9599*), on Paseo del Peralta at Galisteo, is a wonderfully quirky and fun place serving a range of delicious food (from burritos to gyros). You can eat in one of four rooms, each completely different; one has cushions on the floor as chairs and a loft, while another is a cozy pub. On Friday night they have live blues and on Saturday night there is flamenco guitar.

A favorite spot for a casual meal is *Harry's Roadside* (☎ *989-4629*), a mile east of Old Santa Fe Trail on Old Las Vegas Hwy. It's a local favorite, offering hearty portions of New Mexican fare, diner basics and creative options. Just past it a bit is *Bobcat Bite* (*983-5319*), basically just a shack on the side of the road that many swear has the best green-chile burgers in town (open Wednesday to Saturday, May to November).

On Cordova Rd, a half-block east of the Wild Oats market, is the *Santa Fe Baking Company and Café* (☎ *988-4292*), a great spot for a hearty and earthy breakfast. It is open 6 am to 6 pm Monday to Friday, with shortened weekend hours. Avoid the downtown coffeeshops and head to *Downtown Subscription* (☎ *983-3085, 376 Garcia St*), a small but busy local spot with a wide range of newspapers and magazines, pastries and drinks.

Whole Foods Market (☎ *992-1700, 753 Cerrillos Rd*), a huge grocery store, sells all kinds of health foods, including organic produce, free-range chicken and fresh bread. They also have a deli with delicious sandwiches, hot meals, a salad and juice bar,

and pastries. Also try the more expensive *Wild Oats Community Market* (☎ *983-5333*), at St Francis Dr and Cordova Rd.

Several rural restaurants offer an escape from Santa Fe chaos. The *Tesuque Market* (☎ *988-8848*), in the tiny, upscale village of Tesuque (7 miles north of town), has great breakfasts and sandwiches and you can sit outside on the pleasant patio. The bar at *Rancho Encantado* (☎ *982-3537*), nestled in the foothills to the north of town, offers a fantastic view to the west over the Rio Grande Valley (see Places to Stay, earlier). Stop here for a sunset drink. Three other restaurants are worth the drive for the setting alone: *Rancho de Chimayo* (☎ *351-4444*), see Española to Taos, later, for details on Rancho de Chimayo, *Galisteo Inn* (☎ *466-8200*), see Places to Stay, earlier, for more on Galisteo Inn, and the tranquil, upscale *Rancho de San Juan* (☎ *753-6818*), see Española & Around, later.

Entertainment

Check the free weekly *Santa Fe Reporter* for the calendar of weekly events in town. The Pasatiempo section of the Friday edition of the *New Mexican* includes a thorough listing of what's going on in and around Santa Fe as well as reviews of shows, galleries and restaurants.

Cinemas The *Jean Cocteau Theater* (☎ *988-2711, 418 Montezuma St*) and the *Plan B Evolving Arts Center for Contemporary Arts* (☎ *982-1338, 1050 Old Pecos Trail*) play foreign and alternative films.

Nightlife Several restaurants and bars in town offer all kinds of live music; be sure to call first to see who is playing, as most places don't have music every night, and ask if there are cover charges. For nightly blues, jazz, folk, Latin and Dixie music, head to the popular *Cowgirl Hall of Fame* (☎ *982-2565, 319 S Guadalupe*). One of my favorite bars is *El Farol* with flamenco, blues and jazz. For more on these, see Places to Eat.

A great bar with flamenco dancing on some nights is the *Dragon Room Bar* (☎ *983-7712, 406 Old Santa Fe Trail*), a dark, cozy place crowded with locals. The small lounge at *La Fonda* (☎ *982-5511, 100 E San Francisco St)* offers surprisingly good country and folk music; the terrific Bill and Bonnie Hearne, Santa Fe folk musicians of the Nancy Griffith mold, play here. Dance to live music of all sorts at the high-ceilinged *Paramount* (☎ *982-8999, 331 Sandoval St),* or settle into a leopard skin chair in the intimate back bar. *Evangelo's* (☎ *982-9014, 200 W San Francisco St),* a small, unpretentious bar in the center of town, offers over 170 beers, pool and weekend rock and blues bands. Also try *El Paseo* (☎ *992-2848, 208 Galisteo St).*

For live country music and free dance lessons on Monday night, head to *Rodeo Nites* (☎ *473-4138, 2911 Cerrillos Rd).* Covers at *Club Alegria* (☎ *471-2324, Lower Agua Fria)* vary from nothing to $20 for everything from salsa to blues by local musicians to big-name national bands. On Friday night, catch salsa with Pretto (known as the 'salsa priest' because his day job is with the church).

Performing Arts Santa Fe enjoys an incredible variety of music, theater and dance, much of which is recognized internationally. It is not only the quality of the performances but also the variety of venues – cathedrals, chapels and outdoor theaters – that make the scene particularly interesting. Though there are performances of some sort all year, many programs run only from June through August; ask at the visitors bureau, or check its helpful website at www.santafe.org for specific dates and information.

If you can catch a performance at the beautifully renovated 1930 movie house, the *Lensic Performing Arts Theater* (☎ *982-0301, 211 W San Francisco St),* do so. Eight performing groups stage regular performances, and it is open for touring productions as well. Call for information on its weekly classic film series.

The *Santa Fe Symphony* (☎ *983-1414, 800-480-1319)* has eight concerts annually and special event performances. Chamber music performed by the *Ensemble of Santa Fe* (☎ *984-2501)* in the Loretto Chapel and the Santuario de Guadalupe can be heard October through May. The acclaimed *Santa Fe Chamber Music Festival* (☎ *983-2075),* which runs from July through late August, brings internationally renowned classical, folk and jazz musicians to Santa Fe. Another seasonal event is the *Desert Chorale* (☎ *988-7505, 800-244-4011),* with five eclectic programs at various venues from July through mid-August and during the Christmas holidays.

New Mexico's only fully professional theater company, *Santa Fe Stages* (☎ *982-6683, 100 N Guadalupe St)* presents national companies and stages its own productions, including modern dance, musicals, and plays. *Santa Fe Playhouse* (☎ *988-4262),* on E De Vargas, the state's oldest theater company, performs avant-garde and traditional theater and musical comedy year-round.

During July and August, *Shakespeare in the Park* (☎ *982-2910)* takes place every Friday, Saturday and Sunday at St John's College. Tickets range from $10 to $33, or bring your blanket and a picnic and sit on the grass for free. Another outdoor summer program is *Summerscene* (☎ *438-8834),* sponsored by the City of Santa Fe Arts Commission and featuring a series of free noon and evening concerts Tuesday and Thursday on the plaza from June to August.

Poetry readings, dance concerts and other performances are presented at the *Plan B Evolving Arts Center for Contemporary Arts* (☎ *982-1338, 1050 Old Pecos Trail).* The *Maria Benitez Spanish Dance Company* (☎ *982-1237)* performs flamenco and other Spanish dances from June through September. There are numerous other smaller companies performing a variety of shows.

Shopping

You can spend weeks shopping in Santa Fe, and some people do. Native American jewelry, predominantly of silver and turquoise; basket work; pottery; and textiles are for sale at about every other store, as well as along the Palace of the Governors and in the plaza. Quality and prices vary considerably from store to store, and though the choices can be overwhelming, it is worth shopping around before buying (there is, not surprisingly, a lot of junk). Santa Fe is also a mecca for art collectors, and the town is full of galleries. The *Wingspread Collectors Guide* provides specific information and maps for all the galleries in town; you can pick one up at most of the big hotels. Store hours vary according to the season, but generally stores are open from 9 am to 5 pm Monday to Saturday, with many staying open on Sunday.

Coyote Café General Store (☎ 982-2454), 132 W Water St, stocks a variety of Southwestern salsa, hot sauces, chiles, tortilla and sopaipilla mixes and other local food items, as well as cookbooks.

A unique metal alloy that contains no silver, lead or pewter but looks like silver was discovered in 1951 to the north of Santa Fe near Nambe. As durable as iron and able to retain heat and cold for hours, the alloy is ideal for cookware. Nambeware (sold at Nambe) capitalizes on this idea. Each piece is individually sandcast in designs that have won national and international recognition, including being selected for the Museum of Modern Art's exhibition entitled *US Design at Its Best*.

If you're looking for Mexican-style tiles, go to Artesanos (☎ 983-1743), 222 Galisteo St, which has a wide variety of tiles by the piece, as well as tile sinks, doorknobs, bathroom objects and other Mexican folk art. In the fall, you can send *ristras* (wreaths of chile peppers) directly from the store. James Reid Ltd (☎ 988-1147), 114 E Palace Ave, has some beautiful handcrafted silver jewelry and an exceptional collection of belt buckles.

You can buy what has become known as Santa Fe–style folk art, including brightly painted snakes, coyotes and rabbits, at the Davis Mather Folk Art Gallery (☎ 983-1660), 141 Lincoln Ave. For photography books, including 1st editions and out-of-print books, go to Photo Eye Books (☎ 988-4955), 376 Garcia St. The Mineral & Fossil Gallery (☎ 984-1682, 800-762-9777), 127 San Francisco St, has a collection of, of course, minerals and fossils.

Perhaps more a museum than a gallery, Fenn Galleries (☎ 982-4631), 1075 Paseo de Peralta, is one of Santa Fe's best known. The outdoor garden features larger-than-life bronze sculptures, and the low-ceilinged adobe interior is filled with masterpieces. Even if you can't afford to buy anything here, it's worth a stop just to admire the work.

The Farmers Market at Sambusco Market Center features local produce, fresh salsas and chile, and baked goods 7 am to 1 pm Tuesday and Saturday from May to October. Tesuque Pueblo Flea Market, next to the opera north of town, runs 8 am to 4 pm Friday through Sunday from May to October. In a dusty parking lot, hundreds of vendors sell everything from cast-iron pots to Indonesian textiles to old hinges and doorknobs. Though it isn't full of as many great finds as it used to be, it's a fun place to poke around.

Getting There & Away

Great Lakes (☎ 473-4118, 800-241-6522) has eleven flights daily from Denver, Colorado. America West (☎ 800-235-9292) provides daily service from Phoenix, Arizona. Roadrunner Shuttle (☎ 424-3367) provides transportation from the airport to local hotels ($11).

TNM&O/Greyhound (☎ 471-0008), St Michael's Dr at Calle Lorca, has four buses daily to Albuquerque ($12, 80 minutes) and two daily buses to Taos ($17, 1½ hours). Sandia Shuttle (☎ 474-5696, 888-775-5696) runs from the major hotels 10 to 12 times daily to Albuquerque International Airport ($20). Faust (☎ 758-3410) leaves for Taos daily at 2 pm from the Hilton of Santa Fe ($30).

Amtrak's Southwest Chief (☎ 800-872-7245) stops at Lamy; from here, buses continue 17 miles to Santa Fe.

From Albuquerque, there are three routes to Santa Fe. The quickest is straight up I-25, which takes about 50 minutes. You can also drive up the east of the Sandias on the Turquoise Trail (see the 'Turquoise Trail' boxed text in the Albuquerque chapter). Without stopping, this drive takes roughly

1½ hours. Finally, the longest route is through the Jemez Mountains on the **Jemez Mountain National Scenic Byway** into Los Alamos and south on Hwy 84/285 into Santa Fe. This makes a great day trip; leave Albuquerque early to allow time to drive leisurely through the mountains, with stops at Bandelier National Monument and Los Alamos (see the Northwestern New Mexico chapter). From Los Alamos, it is a 40-minute drive to Santa Fe.

Getting Around
Santa Fe Trails (☎ 955-2001) is the country's first natural-gas city bus system. Fares are 50¢, and daily/monthly passes are $1/10. The bus depot is on Sheridan Ave between Palace and Marcy Aves.

Capital City Cab (☎ 438-0000) provides service throughout town.

Most major car-rental agencies have offices either at the airport or on Cerrillos Rd. In town, you can rent a car from Avis (☎ 982-4361) at Garrett's Desert Inn and Enterprise (☎ 989-8859) at the Hilton of Santa Fe.

AROUND SANTA FE
Shidoni Foundry
Located 5 miles north of Santa Fe on Bishop's Lodge Rd in Tesuque, the Shidoni Foundry (☎ 988-8001) is an 8-acre apple orchard devoted to bronze sculptures. Founded in 1971, it has evolved into a world-renowned fine-art casting facility and showplace. A gallery hosts changing exhibits, and there is a year-round outdoor sculpture garden on the lawn. Every Saturday, and periodically throughout the week, you can watch 2000°F molten bronze being poured into ceramic shell molds, one of several steps in the complex lost-wax casting technique. The artists practice mold-making and sand-casting on the premises as well, and will explain the processes and answer questions.

El Rancho de las Golondrinas
In the town of La Cienega, El Rancho de las Golondrinas (☎ 471-2261), a 200-acre ranch with 70 restored and original buildings, is a living-history museum that shows what life was like for Spanish settlers in the 18th and 19th centuries. To get here, take I-25 16 miles southwest to exit 276 and follow the signs. It is closed November to March and costs vary. Call for information on festivals and special events.

Pecos National Historical Park
When the Spanish arrived, Pecos Pueblo, five stories high with almost 700 rooms, was an important center for trade between the Pueblo Indians of the Rio Grande and the Plains Indians to the east. The Spaniards completed a church here in 1625, but it was destroyed in the Pueblo Revolt of the 1680s. The remains of the rebuilt mission, completed in 1717, are the major attraction. The pueblo itself declined, and in 1838 the 17 remaining inhabitants moved to Jemez Pueblo.

The visitor center (☎ 757-6414), PO Drawer 418, Pecos, NM 87552, is open daily 8 am to 5 pm, 'til 6 pm from Memorial Day to Labor Day; its website is www.nps.gov/peco. A museum and short film explain the area's history. A 1¼-mile self-guided trail goes through the site. Admission is $3 for adults, free for children under 16, and passes are honored. Pecos is about 25 miles southeast of Santa Fe. Take I-25 east and follow the signs.

There are no facilities in the park, but you can camp in the Santa Fe National Forest to the north along Hwy 63. (See Places to Stay – Camping, earlier in this chapter.)

SANTA FE TO ESPAÑOLA
Tesuque Pueblo
Nine miles north of Santa Fe along Hwy 285/84 is Tesuque Pueblo, whose members played a major role in the Pueblo Revolt of 1680. Today, the reservation encompasses more than 17,000 acres of spectacular desert landscape, including Aspen Ranch and Vigil Grant, two wooded areas in the Santa Fe National Forest. There is a small plaza with a Catholic church. The pueblo runs the **Camel Rock Casino** (☎ 984-8414), and you can purchase permits to camp or fish at the

local lake or in the mountains nearby. San Diego Feast Day on November 12 features dancing, but no food booths or vendors are allowed. Photography may or may not be allowed. The governor's office (☎ 983-2667, 800-483-1040), Rte 5, Box 360T, Santa Fe, NM 87501, has information. Offices are closed on August 10 to commemorate their first strike against the Spanish.

Pojoaque Pueblo

Although this pueblo's history predates the Spaniards, a smallpox epidemic in the late 19th century killed many inhabitants and forced the survivors to evacuate. No old buildings remain. The few survivors intermarried with other Pueblo people and Hispanics, and their descendants now number about 200. In 1932, a handful of people returned to the pueblo and they have since worked to rebuild their people's traditions, crafts and culture.

The **Poeh Cultural Center and Museum** (☎ 455-3334, 455-1110), on the east side of Hwy 84/285, offers classes in traditional crafts and features exhibits on the history and culture of the Tewa-speaking people. The museum is not completed, but there is a small exhibit. Next door, a large selection of top-quality crafts from the Tewa pueblos is for sale at the visitor center and gift shop (☎ 455-3460).

The pueblo public buildings are 16 miles north of Santa Fe on the east side of Hwy 84/285 just south of Hwy 502. The annual feast day, December 12, is celebrated with ceremonial dancing. Contact the visitor center (☎ 455-3460), 96 Cities of Gold Rd, Santa Fe, NM 87501, for more information.

San Ildefonso Pueblo

Eight miles west of Pojoaque along Hwy 502, the ancient pueblo of San Ildefonso was the home of Maria Martinez, who in 1919, along with her husband, Julian, revived a distinctive traditional black-on-black pottery style. Her work,

now valued at tens of thousands of dollars, has become world famous and is considered by collectors to be some of the best pottery ever produced.

Several exceptional potters (including her direct descendants) work in the pueblo, and many different styles are produced, but black-on-black remains the hallmark of San Ildefonso. Several gift shops and studios, including Sunbeam Indian Arts (☎ 455-7132), sell the pueblo's pottery. The San Ildefonso Pueblo Museum, with exhibits on the pueblo's history and culture and a small store, is next to the visitor center. A fishing lake is stocked during the summer, and visitors can purchase permits on site.

Admission to the pueblo is $3 per car. Camera permits are $10, sketching permits are $25, and videotaping permits are $20. No photography or sketching is allowed during ceremonial dances. Pueblo hours are 8 am to 5 pm daily; shop hours vary. Ceremonial dances take place on the annual January 23 feast day. Other ceremonies include Matachine Dances around Christmas, Easter Dances and Corn Dances in June, August and September. Obtain information from the visitor center (☎ 455-3549) or the governor's office (☎ 455-2273), Rte 5, Box 315 A, Santa Fe, NM 87501.

Nambe Pueblo

Set in the agricultural river valley 18 miles east of Española on Hwy 503 and surrounded by piñon and juniper, Nambe Pueblo encompasses 30 sq miles and is home to some 600 members. Inhabited since around AD 1300, a few precolonial structures still stand. The pueblo has had problems with visitors climbing around in sacred kivas, photographing without permission and meandering into private homes. While they encourage guests to visit public spaces, including the houses of individuals who sell pottery from their homes, ask permission before entering any building or photographing.

In the hills above the pueblo, at **Nambe Falls Recreational Site**, you can hike along the stream through the canyon to the small falls ($5). Nambe Reservoir, a desert lake surrounded by sand and cedar, offers fishing and boating ($10; no gas motors). Camping along the river and at the reservoir costs $20/30 for tent/RV sites. The falls are open March to October.

St Francis of Assisi Feast Day, celebrated on October 4 with evening vespers at sundown October 3, is open to the public, but no photography is allowed. There is a Christmas Eve Buffalo Dance by bonfire, after mass and on January 6 the pueblo celebrates King's Day by honoring elected and appointed officials with Buffalo, Deer and Antelope Dances. An arts and crafts fair is held in July (varying dates) at the falls. All ceremonials are subject to change, so call in advance.

There is a $15 fee to sketch, $20 for use of video cameras and $15 for use of still cameras. Call the ranger station (☎ 455-2304) for information.

Santa Clara Pueblo

The well-marked pueblo entrance is 1.3 miles southwest of Española on Hwy 30. Several galleries and private homes sell intricately carved black pottery. If you call in advance and tell them how many people are in your party, Singing Water Gallery (☎ 753-9663) will serve Indian tacos or a feast dinner, give pottery demonstrations and guide tours of the pueblo.

On the reservation at the entrance to Santa Clara Canyon, 5.7 miles west of Hwy 30 and southwest of Española, are the **Puye Cliff Dwellings**. Ancestors of today's Santa Clara Indians lived here until about 1500. The original carvings were cut into the Puye Cliffs on the Pajarito Plateau, and structures were later added on the mesas and below the cliffs. You can climb around in the 740 apartmentlike rooms on the top and enjoy a spectacular view of the Rio Grande Valley. This small and intimate site, where you are likely to be the only one around, is well worth a visit.

Continuing past the cliff dwellings about 4 miles is the **Santa Clara Canyon Recreation Area**, with camping and four stocked lakes. It is open from April to October. The dwellings and campsites have been closed since 1998 to renovate fire damage, and they open in 2002. Call to be sure. Entrance, camping and fishing fees have not been determined at the time of this writing.

Santa Clara Feast Day (August 12) and St Anthony's Feast Day (June 13) feature the Harvest and Blue Corn Dances and are open to the public. Sketching, photography and videotaping are not allowed. The governor's office (☎ 753-7326), PO Box 580, Española, NM 87532, in the main tribal building just north of the pueblo entrance, is open weekdays.

ESPAÑOLA & AROUND

☎ 505 • pop 12,171; valley 35,000 • elevation 5595 feet

In some ways Española is the gateway to the real New Mexico, separating the tourist-infested wonderland of Santa Fe from the reality of the rural state. The Rio Grande, Rio Chama and Santa Cruz Rivers converge near the city, and the surrounding area is farmland, much of which has been deeded to Hispanic land-grant families since the 17th century. Though the town itself doesn't offer much beyond a strip with fast-food restaurants, a WalMart and a disproportionate number of hair salons, its central location and abundance of good budget restaurants make it a convenient (though not particularly pleasant) place from which to explore northern New Mexico. There has been an increase in violent crime in the area, so be careful walking at night and lock up your valuables.

Orientation & Information

Hwy 84/285 runs through Española and is the main north/south road, splitting north of town into Hwy 84 heading northwest toward Abiquiu and Hwy 285 heading north toward Ojo Caliente. Hwy 30 runs southwest toward Los Alamos. Española is 24 miles north of Santa Fe and 44 miles south of Taos. The chamber of commerce (☎ 753-2831) is in the Big Rock Shopping Center and the Santa Fe National Forest Supervisor's Office (☎ 753-7331) is on the Los Alamos Hwy (Hwy 30). Other services include the police (☎ 753-5555), 408 Paseo de Oñate; and the hospital (☎ 753-7111), 1010 Spruce St.

San Juan Pueblo

Drive a mile north of Española on Hwy 68 and 1 mile west on Hwy 74 to get to San Juan Pueblo (☎ 852-4400), PO Box 1099, which is no more than a bend in the road with a compact main plaza surrounded by cottonwoods. The pueblo was visited in 1598 by Juan de Oñate, who named it San Gabriel and made it the short-lived first capital of New Mexico. The original Catholic mission, dedicated to St John the Baptist, survived until 1913 but was replaced by the adobe, New England–style building that faces the main plaza. Adjacent to the mission is the **Lady of Lourdes Chapel**, built in 1889. The kiva, shrines and some of the original pueblo houses are off-limits to visitors. There is a $5 fee for photography and for video cameras.

The arts and crafts cooperative Oke Oweenge (☎ 852-2372) has a good selection of traditional red pottery, seed jewelry, weavings and drums; it's open 9 am to 4:30 pm Monday to Saturday. The tribe operates the *Ohkay RV Park & San Juan Tribal Lakes* (☎ 753-5067), which has tent/RV sites for $10/21 and is open for fishing at $7 per day. San Juan Feast Day is celebrated June 24 with Buffalo and Comanche Dances from late morning until mid-afternoon, as well as food booths and arts and crafts. Call the pueblo for information on other dances that are not formally scheduled.

Ojo Caliente

Billed as America's oldest health resort, Ojo Caliente (☎ 583-2233, 800-222-9162) draws therapeutic mineral waters from five springs. The waters have traces of arsenic, iron, soda, lithium and sodium, each with unique healing powers. Massages, facials

and herbal wraps cost $35 to $90. Rates at the hotel range from $75/100 for a single/double room to $90/130 for a single/double cottage with a kitchen, including unlimited use of the mud pool, mineral pool and two sweat wraps. Nonguests pay $9.50/12.50 for the mineral pool and $13/17 for a private bath during the week/weekend. From May to August hours are 8 am to 9 pm Sunday to Thursday, until 10 pm Friday and Saturday. Call for hours during the rest of the year. You can hike and ride horses in the surrounding hills, and though this place is nothing fancy, it's relaxing and peaceful. A casual restaurant is open daily, and there is an outdoor pool.
website: www.ojocalientespa.com

Places to Stay

Nambe Pueblo, Santa Clara Pueblo and San Juan Pueblo have camping and RV facilities (see individual pueblos, earlier). Ten miles east of Española outside Chimayo is *Santa Cruz Lake*, which has BLM camping for $7 to $9, with a shelter and a grill. Follow signs down a winding road off Hwy 503 to the desert lake. Due to underwater currents, swimming is not allowed.

As everywhere in New Mexico, hotel rates vary both by the month and according to demand. The simple *Ranchero Motel* (☎ 753-2740), on the Taos Hwy heading north from town, has basic rooms for $33. *Chain motels* including the *Comfort Inn* (☎ 753-2419, 247 S Riverside Dr), the *Days Inn* (☎ 747-1242, 292 S Riverside Dr) and the *Super 8* (☎ 753-5374, 298 S Riverside Dr) all have doubles for $55 to $70.

The nicest place in town is the *Inn at the Delta* (☎ 753-9466, 800-995-8599, 304 Paseo de Oñate). All the rooms are huge, with hot tubs, Mexican tile, a fireplace, high ceilings with vigas and locally carved Southwestern furniture. Rates are $100 to $150 for a double and include a hot buffet breakfast.

Just northwest of town, on the road to Ojo Caliente, is *Rancho de San Juan* (☎ 753-6818, 800-726-7121), a small gem with 1st-class rooms and service and a spectacular setting. The outdoor hot tub lets you

relax in total quiet under the desert stars. Rooms and suites start at $175 (see Places to Eat for more information).
website: www.ranchodesanjuan.com

Places to Eat

Serving some of the best sopaipillas in the area, and delicious beans and green chile, *Angelina's* (☎ 753-8543, 1226 N Railroad Ave) is a great place for simple New Mexican fare (under $8).

At the other extreme is the tranquil *Rancho de San Juan* (☎ 753-6818), a gourmet restaurant nestled into the desert hillside. A set menu (full dinner) starts at $45; reservations (for 6:30 or 8 pm only) are necessary as there are only a handful of tables. Be sure to check out the shrine carved into the sandstone rock (even if you're not eating here, it's worth stopping by and paying the $3 to see it).

There are several other roadside spots serving basic beans, burritos, enchiladas and other regional dishes. You won't find Santa Fe style, but you'll get some great food for little money.

Getting There & Away

TNM&O/Greyhound (☎ 753-8617, 800-231-2222) buses stop at Box Pack Mail (☎ 753-4025), 1227A N Railroad Ave, across from Angelina's (see Places to Eat), and head to Albuquerque ($20, two hours), Santa Fe ($6.50, 45 minutes), Taos ($10.50, one hour) and beyond.

ESPAÑOLA TO TAOS

Taos is northeast of Española. Off Hwy 84/285, you can take either Hwy 68 (known as the Low Road) or Hwy 76 (the High Road). Hwy 76 dead ends at Hwy 75. From there, drive east to Hwy 518 and north to Rancho de Taos, where the Low and High Roads meet just south of Taos.

High Road to Taos

Generally considered the scenic route, the High Road, Hwy 76, winds through river valleys, 100-foot-high sandstone cliffs reminiscent of Roadrunner cartoons, and high mountain pine forests. There are numerous galleries and small villages along the way. Plan on spending at least an afternoon, but if you don't stop at all, you can make it to Taos in 2½ hours.

From Pojoaque, turn east onto Hwy 503 and follow signs for the Nambe Trading Post (☎ 455-2513), where you can find Navajo rugs, painted gourds and other crafts. Surrounded by farmland and woods, it's a welcome change from the hectic pace of Santa Fe. The High Road continues on Hwy 503 to Hwy 76.

Chimayo Originally established by Spanish families with a land grant, Chimayo is famous for its **Santuario de Chimayo**, built in 1816. Legend has it that the dirt from the church has healing powers, and the back room is a shrine to its miracles, with canes, wheelchairs, crutches and other medical aids hanging from the wall. Kneel into a hole in the ground and smear dirt on the parts of your body that are ailing. As many as 30,000 people make an annual pilgrimage to the church every spring on Good Friday.

The Oviedo family has been carving native woods since 1739, and today the Oviedo Gallery (☎ 351-2280), on Hwy 76, is housed in the 270-year-old family farm. Marco Oviedo's carvings have consistently won awards at the Indian Market in Santa Fe. If you're interested in handloomed weaving, you're better off avoiding the tourist-infested Ortegas (☎ 351-4215) and stopping instead at Centinela Traditional Arts (☎ 351-2180). Irvin Trujillo, a seventh-generation Rio Grande weaver, whose carpets are in collections at the Smithsonian in Washington, DC, and the Museum of Fine Arts in Santa Fe, works out of and runs this cooperative gallery of 20 weavers. Naturally dyed blankets, vests and pillows are sold, and you can watch the artists weaving on handlooms in the back.

An old ranch house backing up to the hills on Hwy 520 in Chimayo, *Rancho de Chimayo* (☎ 351-4444) serves New Mexican food in the courtyard or by the fire in the winter; it's a lovely spot for a meal. The ranch (☎ 351-2222) has seven attractive rooms ($70 to $110).

Other accommodations include the unpretentious *La Posada de Chimayo B&B* (☎ 351-4605), at the end of a quiet dirt road ($80), and *Casa Escondida* (☎ 351-4805), with eight rooms and a hot tub ($80 to $140); visit online at www.casaescondida.com.

Quaint-looking Chimayo has developed a reputation for drug and gang problems. Don't be fooled into thinking it's a safe rural village. Be careful walking around after dark, and always lock your car.

Truchas Continue up Hwy 76 to Truchas, originally settled by the Spaniards in the 18th century. Robert Redford's *Milagro Beanfield War* was filmed here, and with the town's dusty New Mexican feel, small farms and spectacular views, it's easy to see why. Twelve galleries, including the Cordovas' Handweaving Workshop (☎ 689-2437), are nestled in the tiny village. Private rooms or casitas for $50 to $90 a night are available at the pleasant *Truchas Farmhouse* (☎ 689-2245). If you drive through town, rather than taking the turn for Taos, you'll find yourself winding into a mountain river valley with fields of daisies in the summer, a creek and the trailhead to Truchas Peak (at 13,101 feet, the second-highest peak in New Mexico) and the Carson Wilderness Area.

Las Trampas Built in 1760, constantly defended against Apache raids and considered one of the finest surviving 18th-century churches, the Church of San José de Gracia is an interesting stop. Original paintings and carvings remain in excellent condition, and bloodstains from the Los Hermanos Penitentes (a 19th-century secretive religious order with a strong following in the northern mountains of New Mexico) are still visible. The church is open 9 am to 5 pm daily in June, July and August. It is open for mass at noon on the first and third Sunday of the month.

Picuris Pueblo Just west of Peñasco village near the junction of Hwys 75 and 76 lies the picturesque Picuris Pueblo. Though the smallest of the pueblos, Picuris played a major role in the Pueblo Revolt of 1680. When the Spanish retook control, the Picuri fled their pueblo. In 1706 they returned, with only about 500 of the original 3000 members, and today that population has fallen to 250.

The pueblo recently received a grant, and is applying for another, to revamp and update their facilities. At the time of this writing, the museum, restaurant and camping facilities were closed. They are looking to find partners to restore the land, perhaps turning 500 acres into an organic farm that could provide fruits and vegetables to Santa Fe's restaurants. Upon completion of renovations, the pueblo plans to open with a new focus on ecofriendly tourism. Until then, Richard Mermejo, the cultural officer for the pueblo, will give you a tour of the pueblo.

The ceremonies celebrating San Lorenzo Feast Day commence on the evening of August 9 with mass at San Lorenzo Mission, native rituals and a procession along the shrine path through the northern part of the village. There are foot races and dances the following day. Photography is allowed at certain times only. Write or call Picuris Pueblo (☎ 587-2519), PO Box 487, Peñasco, NM 87553, for current information.

From Picuris Pueblo, follow Hwy 75 east and go north on Hwy 518 to connect with Hwy 68, the main road to Taos.

Low Road to Taos

Hwy 68 out of Española turns into a winding, two-lane road that follows the Rio Grande 37 miles to Taos. Though the High Road is pushed as the scenic route, the Low Road is beautiful and gets you to Taos more quickly. Much of the road cuts through the river valley, with steep sides of rock to one side and the river on the other. It's crowded with impatient drivers so use caution.

Velarde Fifteen miles north of Española is Black Mesa Winery (☎ 852-2820, 800-852-6372), 1502 Hwy 68, where you can stop and taste the local vintage. The highway then cuts through the apple orchards of Velarde and into the Rio Grande Canyon.

Eight miles farther down the road is **Embudo Station** (☎ 852-4707), a brewery and restaurant that makes a pleasant place to enjoy a freshly brewed beer under the cottonwoods along the Rio Grande. The rather expensive restaurant offers standard New Mexican fare and sandwiches, and specializes in fresh smoked ham and trout. A scenic lunch or dinner float trip along the Rio Grande costs $35; choose from a menu for your meal ($6 to $15). You can rent a large and nicely appointed river-view cabin behind the restaurant for $100 for two, $25 for each additional person, including a refrigerator stocked with breakfast food. The station, closed from December to April, is for sale, so things may change.

You can take a slight detour east on Hwy 75 to the small farming community of **Dixon**. Here there are a couple of galleries as well as the **La Chiripada Winery** (☎ 579-4437), which offers tasting from 10 am to 5 pm Monday to Saturday.

Pilar Seven miles farther north, Pilar is comprised of about four buildings, but it's the regional center for summer white-water rafting. Stop by the visitor center (☎ 751-4899) on Hwy 68 for information on camping, hiking and rafting.

The BLM runs three campgrounds with toilets and drinking water but no hookups at the **Orilla Verde National Recreation Site** (☎ 758-4060). Located right on the Rio Grande, with great fishing and a high desert/river valley landscape, this is a convenient and beautiful place to camp, but it tends to be busy in the summer. There is a $7 charge per vehicle, per night ($3 for day use). To get there, take Hwy 570 west at the Pilar Yacht Club.

The Greyhound bus will drop you off at the **Pilar Yacht Club** (☎ 758-9072). Eva Behrens, the owner, can help arrange rafting trips and horseback riding. Rooms, some with kitchens and private bathrooms, are available for $40/125/300 for a night/week/month.

TAOS
☎ 505 • pop 6213 • town elevation 6950 feet • ski base elevation 9207 feet

History

The first permanent residents of the Taos area were descendants of the Ancestral Puebloans from the Four Corners area. The Taos Pueblo, a spectacular example of Indian architecture dating back to AD 1440, was a thriving community by the time conquistador Hernando de Alvarado came to the area in 1540. By 1598, Padre de Zamora had established the first mission, and in 1617 Fray Pedro de Miranda led the first flock of Spanish colonists to the area we now know as Taos, a Tewa phrase meaning 'place of the red willows.' After 100 years of Spanish rule and shaky tolerance between the Indians and the Spanish colonists, the Pueblo peoples rebelled in the Great Pueblo Revolt of 1680. All the Spaniards in the area were either killed or forced to flee, and many ended up in what is now El Paso, Texas. The next influx of Spanish settlers began in 1692, when Don Diego de Vargas arrived with orders to reconquer the Indians. After four years of violence, colonists came to live in areas around the pueblo and in Rancho de Taos and Taos Plaza.

French trappers came in 1739 to hunt in the rich beaver ponds of the surrounding area, and the second phase of Taos history began. The town soon became a trading center for British and American mountain men and Indians in surrounding pueblos. Its reputation spread, and traders from as far away as Missouri and Mexico came with wagon trains full of goods to the famous Taos trade fairs. Kit Carson, the most prominent name in the westward expansion, first came to Taos in 1826 and continued to visit sporadically between his expeditions. In 1843 he married the 14-year-old daughter of a wealthy Taos family and settled here as a permanent resident.

In 1847 Taos was involved in another uprising after the American victory in the 1846 Mexican War. Hispanics and members of the Taos Pueblo fought against American rule, and Governor Charles Bent died in the massacre that followed. Except for occa-

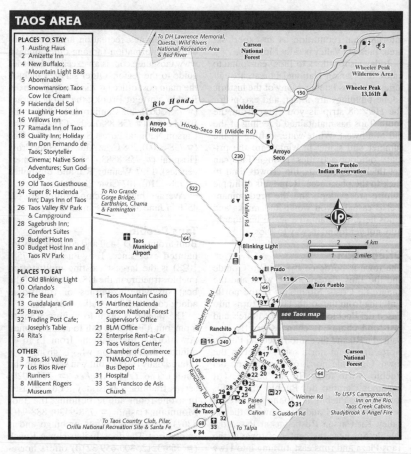

TAOS AREA

PLACES TO STAY
1 Austing Haus
2 Amizette Inn
4 New Buffalo;
  Mountain Light B&B
5 Abominable
  Snowmansion; Taos
  Cow Ice Cream
9 Hacienda del Sol
14 Laughing Horse Inn
16 Willows Inn
17 Ramada Inn of Taos
18 Quality Inn; Holiday
  Inn Don Fernando de
  Taos; Storyteller
  Cinema; Native Sons
  Adventures; Sun God
  Lodge
19 Old Taos Guesthouse
24 Super 8; Hacienda
  Inn; Days Inn of Taos
26 Taos Valley RV Park
  & Campground
28 Sagebrush Inn;
  Comfort Suites
29 Budget Host Inn
30 Budget Host Inn and
  Taos RV Park

PLACES TO EAT
6 Old Blinking Light
10 Orlando's
12 The Bean
13 Guadalajara Grill
25 Bravo
32 Trading Post Cafe;
  Joseph's Table
34 Rita's

11 Taos Mountain Casino
15 Martinez Hacienda
20 Carson National Forest
  Supervisor's Office
21 BLM Office
22 Enterprise Rent-a-Car
23 Taos Visitors Center;
  Chamber of Commerce
27 TNM&O/Greyhound
  Bus Depot
31 Hospital
33 San Francisco de Asis
  Church

OTHER
3 Taos Ski Valley
7 Los Rios River
  Runners
8 Millicent Rogers
  Museum

To DH Lawrence Memorial,
Questa, Wild Rivers
National Recreation Area
& Red River

Carson National Forest

Wheeler Peak Wilderness Area

Wheeler Peak 13,161ft ▲

Rio Honda

Valdez

Arroyo Honda

Hondo-Seco Rd (Middle Rd)

Arroyo Seco

Taos Pueblo Indian Reservation

To Rio Grande
Gorge Bridge,
Earthships, Chama
& Farmington

Taos Municipal Airport

Blinking Light

El Prado

Taos Pueblo

see Taos map

Blueberry Hill Rd

Ranchito

Los Cordovas

Ranchos de Taos

Paseo del Pueblo Sur

Kit Carson Rd

Salazar

Cruz Alta Rd

Lower Ranchitos Rd

Carson National Forest

Weimer Rd

S Gusdorf Rd

Paseo del Cañon

To USFS Campgrounds,
Inn on the Rio,
Taos Creek Cabins,
Shadybrook & Angel Fire

To Taos Country Club, Pilar,
Orilla National Recreation Site & Santa Fe

To Talpa

0   2   4 km
0   1   2 miles

sional disputes during the Civil War and Indian skirmishes, Taos remained a relatively quiet outpost through the rest of the 19th century.

The third phase of Taos' history began with the arrival of Anglo artists and writers at the end of the 19th century. In 1898, the painter Ernest Blumenschein and Bert Phillips were on a sketching expedition that took them 30 miles north of Taos, but a broken wagon wheel forced them to stay for an extended period in town. Blumenschein returned for many summers, and he and his family took up permanent residence in

1919. He was one of six artists to establish the Taos Society of Artists in 1915, and he is recognized as the founding father of Taos' artists' colony. Attracted to the striking landscape and brilliant colors as well as to the Indian history, spirit and lifestyle, Anglo artists thrived in Taos in the early 20th century. Bert Harwood, Nicholai Fechin, Leon Gaspard and later DH Lawrence, Georgia O'Keeffe and Ansel Adams all contributed to Taos' reputation as a center for artists and writers.

In 1957 Ernie Blake transformed the tiny mining village of Twining, north of Taos, into a thriving ski resort. Thus began the fourth phase of Taos history. Despite Taos' current international reputation as an expert ski area, Taos Ski Valley is rather low key.

Today, visitors flock to Taos year-round to enjoy the Carson National Forest, art galleries and Taos Pueblo. Many of the historic adobe buildings are intact, and except for the Hwy 68 strip as you enter from the south, Taos has maintained a feeling of the old Southwest. White-water rafting in the summer and skiing in winter are the primary outdoor activities. Though Taos can get thick with tourists, the crowds tend to stick to the plaza area. Remnants of hippie culture are evident, and the predominant feel is casual – you won't find minks and limos here. The Santa Fe scene has thankfully not yet found its way to Taos.

Orientation

The town is bordered by the Rio Grande and the Taos Plateau to the west, and the Sangre de Cristo Mountains to the north. Entering from the south, Hwy 68 turns into Paseo del Pueblo Sur, a strip of motels and fast-food chains. It changes briefly into Santa Fe Rd and then into Paseo del Pueblo Norte, the main north-south street in the town. One mile north of town, Paseo del Pueblo Norte forks: To the northeast it becomes Camino del Pueblo and heads toward Taos Pueblo, and to the northwest it becomes Hwy 64 and goes toward the ski valley. Kit Carson Rd begins at Paseo del Pueblo Sur near the center of town at the Taos Plaza and runs east, turning into Hwy 64 as it heads toward Angel Fire. The 'blinking light' north of town is a focal point for directions (though it now functions as a regular traffic light); from it, Hwy 64 heads west to the Rio Grande Gorge Bridge, Hwy 522 heads northwest to Arroyo Hondo and Questa, and Hwy 150 heads northeast to Arroyo Seco and the Taos Ski Valley.

Information

The Taos Visitors Center and Chamber of Commerce (☎ 758-3873, 800-732-8267), on Paseo del Pueblo Sur at Paseo del Cañon, is open 9 am to 5 pm daily. Write to them at PO Drawer 1, Taos, NM 87571, or visit www.taoschamber.com. With links to regional websites, recreation and accommodations information (among other things), www.taosguide.com is an excellent Internet guide to the region. Other services include the main post office (☎ 758-2081), Paseo del Pueblo Norte at Brooks; the public library (☎ 758-3063), 402 Camino de la Placita; the BLM office (☎ 758-8851), 226 Cruz Alta; the Carson National Forest Supervisor's Office (☎ 758-6200), 208 Cruz Alta; the Holy Cross Hospital (☎ 758-8883, 751-5895 for emergencies), 1397 Weimer Rd; and the police (☎ 758-2216), 107 Civic Plaza Dr.

Average high/low temperatures are 82/45°F in June and 40/9°F in January.

Taos Pueblo

Built around AD 1450 and continuously inhabited ever since, Taos Pueblo (☎ 758-1028) is the largest existing multistoried pueblo structure in the USA and one of the best surviving examples of traditional adobe construction – well worth a visit.

The pueblo is open to visitors 8 am to 5 pm, but it is best to call to confirm times. An informal tour, ranging from 15 to 40 minutes depending on who is giving it, is offered daily (no fee, but you should tip the guide). The **Tewa Kitchen** (☎ 751-1020) serves traditional feast-day foods. Housed in a one-room adobe building, the Taos Mountain Casino (☎ 758-9430, 888-946-8267) has no big buffets or bingo and is smoke-free. The Taos Indian Horse Ranch (☎ 758-3212, 800-659-3210) offers horseback riding through Indian land, as well as an evening campfire and hayride and a 24-hour rafting/riding/camping trip (from $40).

San Geronimo Day, September 29 and 30, is celebrated with dancing and food. It is one of the largest and most spectacular Indian celebrations in New Mexico. Other special days are the Turtle Dance (January 1), the Deer or Buffalo Dance (January 6), Corn Dances (May 3, June 13 and 24), the powwow (in July), Santiago's Day (July 25) and the Deer Dance or Matachines (Christmas Day). Dances are open to the public, but cannot be photographed. Six kivas (cer-

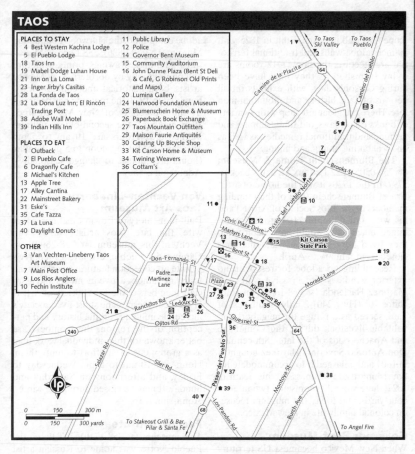

TAOS

PLACES TO STAY
- 4 Best Western Kachina Lodge
- 5 El Pueblo Lodge
- 18 Taos Inn
- 19 Mabel Dodge Luhan House
- 21 Inn on La Loma
- 23 Inger Jirby's Casitas
- 28 La Fonda de Taos
- 32 La Dona Luz Inn; El Rincón Trading Post
- 38 Adobe Wall Motel
- 39 Indian Hills Inn

PLACES TO EAT
- 1 Outback
- 2 El Pueblo Cafe
- 6 Dragonfly Cafe
- 8 Michael's Kitchen
- 13 Apple Tree
- 17 Alley Cantina
- 22 Mainstreet Bakery
- 31 Eske's
- 35 Cafe Tazza
- 37 La Luna
- 40 Daylight Donuts

OTHER
- 3 Van Vechten-Lineberry Taos Art Museum
- 7 Main Post Office
- 9 Los Rios Anglers
- 10 Fechin Institute
- 11 Public Library
- 12 Police
- 14 Governor Bent Museum
- 15 Community Auditorium
- 16 John Dunne Plaza (Bent St Deli & Café, G Robinson Old Prints and Maps)
- 20 Lumina Gallery
- 24 Harwood Foundation Museum
- 25 Blumenschein Home & Museum
- 26 Paperback Book Exchange
- 27 Taos Mountain Outfitters
- 29 Maison Faurie Antiquités
- 30 Gearing Up Bicycle Shop
- 33 Kit Carson Home & Museum
- 34 Twining Weavers
- 36 Cottam's

emonial chambers) are closed to the public. In February, March and August, Taos Pueblo may be closed for sacred ceremonial dances. Visitors are charged $5 for parking, though rates vary. You must pay a fee (ask for current information) to photograph, videotape, sketch or paint the pueblo.

Historic Homes

The historic homes of three influential local figures reflect three distinct elements of Taos history – the mountain man, the artist and the trader. Small and compact, these homes offer a great way to get a feel for Taos history. They are run by the same management (☎ 758-0505), and tickets for one or all can be purchased at any of the three museums – $5 for one museum, $7.50 for two and $10 for all three. There is no expiration limit on the tickets. The homes are open 9 am to 6 pm May to August, with slightly shorter hours the rest of the year.

Kit Carson (1809–68) was the Southwest's most famous mountain man, guide, trapper, soldier and scout, and his home and life serve as an excellent introduction to Taos in the mid-19th century. The **Kit Carson Home & Museum** (☎ 758-4741), located a block from the Plaza on Kit Carson Rd, houses such artifacts as Carson's rifles, telescope and walking cane. Built in 1825 with 30-inch adobe walls and traditional territorial architecture, the home's 12 rooms are today furnished as they may have been during Carson's days, with exhibits on all periods of Taos history and mountain-man lore. There is a great gift shop with a variety of books on outlaws, old-time trapping and farming and traditional remedies, as well as on local biking, skiing and hiking.

The **Blumenschein Home & Museum** (☎ 758-0505), 222 Ledoux St, dates back to 1797. In the 1920s it was the home of artist Ernest Blumenschein (one of the founding members of the Taos Society of Artists) and his wife and daughter. It is today maintained much as it would have been when they lived here. The home is sometimes closed from January to April.

Resembling an adobe fortress with no exterior windows and massive walls, the **Martínez Hacienda** (☎ 758-1000), on Ranchitos Rd (Hwy 240) 2 miles southwest of Taos, served as a refuge for neighbors and valuable livestock during the Comanche and Apache raids of the late 18th century. Don Antonio Severino Martínez bought it in 1804 and enlarged it to accommodate his flourishing trade business. By his death in 1827, there were 21 rooms and two interior courtyards, and today the museum focuses on colonial family life in New Mexico.

Governor Bent Museum

When New Mexico became a US territory after the Mexican War in 1846, Charles Bent was named the first governor. Hispanics and Indians did not appreciate being forced under US rule, and on January 19, 1847, they attacked the governor in his home. Bent's family was allowed to leave, but he was scalped and killed. Today his home is a small museum with memorabilia from his early days as a trader along the Santa Fe Trail and his life as governor. The museum (☎ 758-2376), 117 Bent St, is open 9 am to 5 pm May through August (from 10 am the rest of the year). Admission is $2.

Harwood Foundation Museum

Housed in a historic mid-19th-century adobe compound, the Harwood Foundation Museum (☎ 758-9826), 238 Ledoux St, features paintings, drawings, prints, sculpture and photography by northern New Mexico artists, both historical and contemporary. Founded in 1923, the museum has been run by the University of New Mexico since 1936, making it the second-oldest museum in the state. Hours are 10 am to 5 pm Tuesday to Saturday, noon to 5 pm Sunday (hours are subject to change seasonally). Admission is $5.

Van Vechten–Lineberry Taos Art Museum

Built in memory of Edwin Lineberry's first wife, the late Taos artist Duane Van Vechten, this museum (☎ 758-2690), on Camino del Pueblo, displays Lineberry's private art collection featuring works by the founding fathers, active members and associate members of the Taos Society of Artists (1912 – 26). Despite the short-lived society's incredible influence on the history and perception of the region, the members are better known for their individual work than as a group; this is an effort to unify them. Hours are 10 am to 5 pm Wednesday to Friday, and afternoons on Saturday and Sunday. It may be closed during the winter. Admission is $6.

Fechin Institute

This museum (☎ 758-1710), 227 Paseo del Pueblo Norte, was home to Russian artist Nicolai Fechin, who emigrated to New York City in 1922 at age 42 and moved to Taos in 1926. Today his paintings, drawings and sculptures are in museums and collections worldwide. Between 1927 and 1933, Fechin completely reconstructed the interior of his adobe home, adding his own distinctly Russian woodcarvings. The Fechin House exhibits the artist's private collection, including much Asian art, and hosts occasional chamber music events. It is open 10 am to 2 pm Wednesday to Sunday. Admission is $4 (children free). Five-day wa-

tercolor, sculpture and other arts workshops are offered from May to October at the nearby ranch.
website: www.fechin.com

San Francisco de Asis Church

Four miles south of Taos is the San Francisco de Asis Church (☎ 758-2754), St Francis Plaza in Ranchos de Taos. Built in the mid-18th century and opened in 1815, the church has been memorialized in numerous Georgia O'Keeffe paintings. It's open 9 am to 4 pm daily. Mass is held at 6 pm the first Saturday of the month, and at 7 (in Spanish), 9 and 11:30 am every Sunday (call to confirm times).

Millicent Rogers Museum

This museum (☎ 758-2462), on Millicent Rogers Museum Rd about 4 miles from the plaza, is filled with pottery, jewelry, baskets and textiles from the private collection of Millicent Rogers, a model and oil heiress who moved to Taos in 1947 and acquired one of the best collections of Indian and Spanish colonial art in the USA. Also displayed are contemporary Native American and Hispanic artwork. The hours are 10 am to 5 pm daily, but call to confirm. Admission is $6.

Kit Carson State Park

This 25-acre grassy park (☎ 758-8234) in the center of town has a three-quarter-mile jogging loop, picnic tables and tennis courts.

Rio Grande Gorge Bridge

On Hwy 64 about 12 miles northwest of Taos, this bridge is the second-highest suspension bridge in the USA. Built in 1965, the vertigo-inducing steel bridge spans 500 feet across the gorge and 650 feet above the river below. The views west over the emptiness of the Taos Plateau and down into the jagged walls of the Rio Grande are incredible.

Earthships

Earthships (☎ 751-0462) are the brainchild of architect Michael Reynolds, whose idea was to develop a building method that 'eliminates stress from both the planet and its inhabitants.' The Earthships are constructed of used automobile tires and cans into which earth has been pounded. Buried on three sides by earth, they are designed to heat and cool themselves, make their own electricity and catch their own water. Sewage is decomposed naturally, and dwellers grow their own food. They are open daily for tours ($5) and are available for rental (see Places to Stay, later). The tour office is located 1½ miles past the Rio Grande Gorge Bridge on US 64 West.

Skiing

With a peak elevation of 11,819 feet and a 2612-foot vertical drop, Taos offers some of the most challenging skiing in the USA and yet remains low-key and relaxed. Lift tickets cost $47/28 for adults/children under 12, more at Christmas, less at the start and end of the season. Snowboards are not allowed.

Lodges, tastefully set against the national forest, line the road to the ski base, where there are three ski lodges (about a half-hour drive from downtown Taos). Ski week packages, including seven nights' accommodations with three meals a day, six days of skiing and six ski lessons, average $1400 per person. Summer rates average $70 per night. There is no gas station or grocery store in the valley, and unless meals are included in a ski package, restaurants tend to be pricey. To reach the valley, take Hwy 64 north out of Taos to the blinking light, and veer right on Hwy 150 toward Arroyo Seco. The beautiful winding drive along a mountain stream is about 20 miles.

Contact the Taos Ski Valley (☎ 776-2291, 800-776-1111), PO Box 90, Taos Ski Valley, NM 87525, for details on accommodations, summer activities, ski school and ski packages; they also serve as a reservation agency.
website: www.skitaos.org or www.taosski valley.com

In addition to Taos Ski Valley, less-challenging downhill skiing can be found at Red River, Angel Fire and Ski Rio (see later

NEW MEXICO

in this chapter). See Mora Valley in Northeast New Mexico for the nearby Sipapu Ski Area.

Other Activities

The variety of outdoor activities in the Taos area is exhaustive. Native Sons Adventures (☎ 758-9342, 800-753-7559), 1033-A Paseo del Pueblo Sur, is a good source of information, and they rent equipment and offer various guided trips. Taos Mountain Outfitters (☎ 758-9292), on the plaza, and Cottam's (☎ 758-2822), 207-A Paseo del Pueblo Sur, sell gear, maps and guidebooks. Ask at the visitor center for a complete listing of outfitters.

River Running The major attraction in the summer is white-water rafting in the Taos Box, the steep-sided cliffs that frame the Rio Grande. Busloads of rafters from Santa Fe go up to Pilar, which can become a flurry of sunburned and screaming tourists. Several rafting companies offer day and overnight trips, so it's worth shopping around. Be sure that you raft with a licensed company; there have been deaths due to inexperienced guides.

Some companies to try are Los Rios River Runners (☎ 776-8854, 800-544-1181), a quarter-mile northeast of the blinking light on Ski Valley Rd; the friendly Pilar Yacht Club (☎ 758-9072) in Pilar just south of town; and Big River Raft Trips (☎ 758-9711), also in Pilar. Rafting trips run about $45 for a half day and $70 to $85 for a full day. Los Rios can arrange floating trips where you also stop to participate in a tree-planting conservation program. Also ask about rafting on the Chama and San Juan Rivers. At Embudo Station (see Velarde, earlier in this chapter), you can take leisurely lunch or dinner floats from $35, plus $8 to $15 for a meal from the menu (1½ to 2½ hours).

Hiking There is no shortage of nearby hiking trails, ranging from easy day hikes to overnight backcountry trips, from alpine mountain trails along rivers to awesome hikes along and through the Rio Grande

Gorge. Stop at the Carson National Forest Service, the BLM or an outdoors shop for guides and maps. Several trailheads are along Hwy 150 to Taos Ski Valley and at the northern end of the ski valley parking lot. In summer, lifts at the ski valley run from 10 am to 4 pm Thursday to Sunday and cost $6 roundtrip. No mountain bikes are allowed, but you can take the lift up and hike down or vice versa. If you are coming when the ski slopes are closed, be sure to call in advance to find out what is open, and plan on having a car.

Before setting out on any kind of hike, check weather forecasts, let someone know where you're going and bring rain gear. New Mexico is infamous for its volatile weather patterns, and the northern mountain ranges can be dangerous in sudden rain- or snowstorms.

Fishing There is lots of fly-fishing in the area, and Los Rios Anglers (☎ 758-2798, 800-748-1707), 226 Paseo del Pueblo Norte, provides guided fly-fishing trips. If you're a hardcore angler, know what you're doing and are willing to pay $250/275/300 for a local guide for one/two/three people, this is a fine place, but it's not for beginners.

Horseback Riding Rio Grande Stables (☎ 776-5913), by the ski valley, offers rides through the mountains and in scrub country on Cebolla Mesa, from mid-May to September. Rates start at $30 for one hour. Also see Taos Pueblo, earlier in this chapter.

Organized Tours

Narrated trolley tours (☎ 751-0366) of the town leave from the plaza Tuesday to Saturday at 10:45 am and 2:15 pm (May to October). The trolley stops at the Taos Pueblo for an hour and at the San Francisco de Asis Church ($33/10 for adults/children). Ask about other tours, and be warned that times may change.
website: http://taostrolleytours.com

Special Events

There are numerous athletic and cultural events all year, as well as workshops in the visual arts. For details on seasonal events, call the Taos Visitors Center.

Big annual events include Taos Pueblo dances and celebrations (see Taos Pueblo, earlier in this chapter), as well as the Taos Talking Picture festival in April and the Taos Mountain Balloon Rally over the last full weekend in October. In Taos and Angel Fire, the Summer Chamber Music Festival draws crowds to outdoor concerts.

Places to Stay

Taos offers a wide variety of accommodations, ranging from free camping in national forests to gourmet B&Bs in historic adobes. Along the strip just south of town there are several *chain motels*, including Best Western and Quality Inn. High season for the ski valley is Thanksgiving to Easter (with dips in March and November and peaks during the holidays); from March to October, many lodges are closed and others offer excellent discounts. The village of Taos attracts visitors all year, though December to February and June to August are generally the high seasons.

In typical New Mexico style, prices vary according to how busy an establishment is, the week of the month and the day of week. Call before assuming that the rates below are accurate, and always ask if the place is willing to go lower! Most places offer reduced weekly rates, and many have self-contained suites with a kitchen and hot tub. High-season rates are listed below.

The Taos Ski Valley Visitors Bureau and New Mexico Reservations (☎ 776-2233, 800-776-1111), PO Box 90, Taos Ski Valley, NM 87525, is an excellent general source for booking hotels, B&Bs, condominiums and private homes. They also arrange vacation packages that include car rental and airfare as well as rafting, snowmobiling, horseback riding – whatever you're looking for – for less than you would pay if you worked it out on your own; visit online at www.taosskivalley.com. Other reservation companies include Taos Central Reservations (☎ 758-9767, 800-821-2437) and the Greater Taos Area Information and Reservations Network (☎ 800-732-8267). Access www.taoswebb.com or www.taosguide.com for information on and links to a spectrum of accommodation options.

Also see the Enchanted Circle section, later in this chapter.

Places to Stay – Camping

For a complete and detailed list of camping in the area, stop at the USFS and BLM offices or contact the Public Lands Information Center in Santa Fe (see Places to Stay in Santa Fe). If you are planning on backcountry camping, be prepared and remember that summer storms develop quickly, and winter weather can be treacherous and unpredictable.

Campers can find plenty of basic camping in the *Carson National Forest* from April through October; the closest campgrounds are east of Taos nestled between Hwy 64 and a creek ($8). The *Questa Ranger Station* (☎ 586-0520) maintains five campgrounds along the stream on the road to Taos Ski Valley. Honor box fee sites ($3 to $5) have drinking water, but none have showers.

There are two relatively close places to camp along the Rio Grande Gorge. North of Taos is the beautiful *Wild Rivers National Recreation Area* (see later in this chapter), and south of Taos is the *Orilla Verde National Recreation Site* in Pilar (near river rafting and river access; see Pilar earlier in this chapter).

The *Budget Host Inn and Taos RV Park* (☎ 758-2524, 800-323-6009, 1799 Paseo del Pueblo Sur) has tent/RV sites for $14/22. See below for room rates.

Places to Stay – Budget

Ten minutes north of Taos in the tiny town of Arroyo Seco is the clean and friendly *Abominable Snowmansion* (☎ 776-8298), which provides bunk-style lodging ($16 to $20), private rooms ($34 to $48), single/double teepees ($28/32) and camping ($10 for one, $5 for each additional person). A two-story lodge room with a circular fireplace provides a cozy spot to relax.

Standard doubles at the *Budget Host Inn and Taos RV Park* (see above) cost about

$55. Closer to the center of town, the pleasant *El Pueblo Lodge* (☎ 758-8700, 800-433-9612, 412 Paseo del Pueblo Norte) has singles/doubles for $52/70, and there is a pool and hot tub. Rooms with fireplaces and kitchenettes are available. The recommended *Adobe Wall Motel* (☎ 758-3972, 227 E Kit Carson Rd), open since the early 20th century and within walking distance to town, is an adobe motel with a shady courtyard and 20 standard rooms (some with kiva fireplaces) for $56 to $66.

Also see Pilar, earlier in this chapter.

Places to Stay – Mid-Range

Hotels & Cabins The *Sagebrush Inn* (☎ 758-2254, 800-428-3626, 1508 Paseo del Pueblo Sur) has a great long bar offering nightly live music and two-steppin' on the weekends. It's a huge 1929 mission-style building with giant wooden portals, an outdoor patio and a swimming pool. Rates range from $85 to $140.

With Southwestern-style décor, fireplaces in some rooms and a pleasant hot tub in the back with views of the mountains, the *Sun God Lodge* (☎ 758-3162, 800-821-2437, 909 Paseo del Pueblo Sur) is another good choice ($50 to $90).

One and a half miles east of the plaza on Hwy 64, in a quiet residential setting with a small pool and a peaceful grass area, is *Inn on the Rio* (☎ 758-7199, 800-859-6752). Bright Southwestern rooms at this adobe motel are in the $90 to $140 range, including full breakfast. Close to town, the *Indian Hills Inn* (☎ 758-4293, 800-444-2346, 233 Paseo del Pueblo Sur) has doubles for about $75.

Inger Jirby, an artist from Sweden, owns *Inger Jirby's Casitas* (☎ 758-7333, 207 Ledoux St). Two beautifully appointed homes, with full kitchens, washer and dryer and large living spaces, just a few blocks from the plaza are $150 to $250. The two are quite different, so ask the friendly and enthusiastic Inger to see both.
website: www.jirby.com

Several rural options relatively close to town hug the Carson National Forest along Hwy 64. Six miles east from Taos Plaza,

Taos Creek Cabins (☎ 758-4715) rents five one/two-bedroom cabins with decks overlooking the creek for $90/120. A mile and a half farther down Hwy 64 is *Shadybrook* (☎ 751-1315), where you can rent a casita with a fireplace, microwave and refrigerator for $85 to $121 a night, with the fourth night free. They have a little restaurant where the chef will, with advance notice so he can buy the groceries, cook up most anything you want.

Suncatcher Earthship (☎ 758-8745), a 700-sq-foot Earthship 3½ miles west of Rancho de Taos, can be rented for $70 per night for two people, $10 for each additional person, $5 for a pet (one only). Call ☎ 751-0462 for information on three other Earthships that rent for $130 the first night, $100 each subsequent night. See Earthships, earlier in this chapter, for more information.
website: www.earthship.org

B&Bs There is a plethora of B&B accommodations in Taos and the surrounding area, and the differences among them are significant.

If you're looking for a unique, friendly and relaxed spot with reasonable rates, try the recommended *Laughing Horse Inn* (☎ 758-8350, 800-776-0161, 729 Paseo del Pueblo Norte), a half-mile north of the Taos Pueblo turnoff. In the '20s and '30s it was the home of Spud Johnson, publisher of a local magazine featuring work by DH Lawrence, Gertrude Stein and Georgia O'-Keeffe, who were frequent guests. His quirky home, now more than a hundred years old, has expanded to 10 eclectic rooms of various sizes plus a huge penthouse, most with shared bathrooms and some with a fireplace. The smaller ones have loft beds with the TV/VCR affixed to the ceiling. Singles are $47 to $70, and doubles are $58 to $100. A guest house with kitchen and fireplace is $130 a double, $10 for each additional person. The inn features a free video library, an outdoor hot tub and loaner bikes. The kitchen is open to anyone who needs it, and there is an honor system for beer, wine, juice, snacks and breakfast.
website: www.laughinghorseinn.com

The unpretentious and centrally located *La Dona Luz Inn* (☎ 758-4874, 800-758-9187, 114 Kit Carson Rd) offers rooms ranging from $60 to $125, most with a VCR and fireplace, some with spas and refrigerators. Each one is done in antique furniture and Mexican tile. Breakfast is fruit, muffins and cold cereal – by the fireplace in the winter or in the courtyard in the summer.

Tim and Leslie Reeves, the friendly and helpful owners of the *Old Taos Guesthouse* (☎ 758-5448, 800-758-5448), are experienced outdoors enthusiasts who will gladly share their knowledge of northern New Mexico. The inn is a wonderful and quiet place with a grassy courtyard, well-done and spacious Southwestern rooms, a breakfast 'on the healthy side of continental' and a hot tub with a beautiful view. Prices are $75 to $145 for a double. To get there, drive east on Kit Carson Rd and follow the signs to Geronimo Lodge.
website: www.oldtaos.com

Listed on the National and State Registers of Historic Places, the *Willows Inn* (☎ 758-2558, 800-525-8267, 412 Kit Carson Rd) was once the home and art studio of the late E Martin Hennings, a member of the Taos Society of Artists in the '20s. The large adobe walls enclose a grassy yard, towered over by two willows. Five rooms, all with a fireplace and private entrance, are $95 to $130. It is for sale, but will presumably stay as a B&B.

The *Mabel Dodge Luhan House* (☎ 751-9686, 800-846-2235), PO Box 558, Taos, NM 87571, a National Historic Landmark, was home to Mabel Dodge Luhan, who came to Taos in 1912 and became one of Taos' most celebrated patrons of the arts and writers. Dennis Hopper bought the house in 1970 and continued the tradition of hosting artists at the 12-acre estate. At the end of a dirt road close to the plaza, it is today a quiet spot with beautiful public spaces. Rooms of varying size range from $85 to $160.
website: www.unink.com/mabel

Hacienda del Sol (☎ 758-0287) offers great views of Taos Mountains (particularly nice when soaking in the outdoor hot tub). The grounds are lovely, and the beautiful Southwestern rooms, most with fireplaces, are warm and cozy. Doubles are $85 to $135 and include a full hot breakfast.
website: www.taoshaciendadelsol.com

Inn on La Loma (☎ 758-1717, 800-530-3040, 315 Ranchitos Rd), a beautiful rambling hacienda with several rooms dating back to the early 19th century and huge cottonwoods in the courtyard, offers rooms (all with fireplace) and a studio suite (sleeping six) from $105. It's completely enclosed by an adobe wall and on a bit of a hill, so you feel like you're far from town even though you're only a few blocks from the plaza. The public rooms are spacious, but the bedrooms are rather small. Rates include a full breakfast and snacks, as well as tennis and health club privileges and an outdoor hot tub.
website: www.vacationtaos.com

An inexpensive rural option is *Mountain Light B&B* (☎ 776-8474). The two rooms are small and simple, but the house is perched on top of a hillside near Arroyo Hondo, 12 miles north of Taos, with an incredible 80-mile view over the valley and the Sangre de Cristo Mountain Range from the breakfast porch. Rooms are from $45 to $55 for one person and $65 to $75 for two, including a full breakfast (perhaps blue-corn pancakes) and use of a communal kitchen. It's about one winding mile off the main road in Arroyo Hondo; call for directions.

Also in Arroyo Hondo, the *New Buffalo* (☎ 776-2015, 866-639-2833, 108 Lower Hondo) recently re-opened as a B&B. Once a commune featured in the film *Easy Rider*, this low-key spot is a fun, out-of-the-way place to relax and affords easy access to hot springs. Rates for doubles with shared bathrooms are $55. They are remodeling the property, and private casitas will be offered, though they don't know yet what they will charge. Rates include a 'natural foods breakfast.'

Lodges There are about 20 lodges in and around the ski valley. Condominium rentals are available as well, and the easiest way to book one is through the Taos Valley Resort Association 800-776-1111 (see earlier in this section) or through the ski valley (see

Skiing, earlier in this section). Most places offer weekly rates and ski packages.

Lodges line the drive from the ski valley up to the national forest. The *Amizette Inn* (☎ 776-2451, 800-446-8267), a half-mile from the ski base, offers nightly rates that include a full breakfast, ranging from $95 for two to $200 for six people (in a cabin) from Thanksgiving to Easter (less the rest of the year). Two miles from the slope, the pleasant *Austing Haus* (☎ 776-2649, 800-748-2932) has rooms for $75 to $190 in ski season, and from $45 the rest of the year.

The three ski lodges at the ski base offer ski week packages, which include seven nights, six days of lift tickets, six morning lessons and three meals daily and are about $1400 per person. Accommodations at *Hotel Edelweiss* (☎ 776-2301, 800-458-8754), a small European-style hotel, and *Hotel St Bernard* (☎ 776-2251) are through ski week packages only. The *Inn at Snakedance* (☎ 776-2277, 800-322-9815), the biggest of the three and more like a big hotel than a ski lodge, offers nightly rates. A double in the summer is $75, including a full breakfast; in the ski season they start at $225.

Places to Stay – Top End

Parts of the *Taos Inn* (☎ 758-2233, 800-826-7466, 125 Paseo del Pueblo Norte) date to the 17th century, which is why it's on the National Register of Historic Places. The cozy lobby – with adobe archways, heavy wood furniture and a sunken fireplace – is always busy, and there is live local music, from jazz and pop to classical, several nights a week. The Adobe Bar and the streetside patio in the summer are packed on the weekends with locals and tourists alike. Stop in for a drink or a snack. Doubles range from $85 to $165.

Centrally located right on the Taos Plaza, *La Fonda de Taos* (☎ 758-2211, 800-833-2211, 108 South Plaza) is a late '30s hotel that looks lost in a time warp. The hotel is under renovation, however, and when it's finished the old-world feel will probably be lost. Even if you're not staying here, you might want to pay $3 to see a locked side room containing erotic paintings by DH Lawrence that were banned in England in 1929. Doubles start at $145.

Places to Eat

Eating out in Taos can be pricey, but there are excellent inexpensive options as well. Try any of the open trailers along the road for a cheap, fast burrito or burger. Even the fanciest of places is casual, and restaurants are generally open until 9 or 10 pm.

Coffee Shops For an early cup of coffee and a donut, stop by *Daylight Donuts* (☎ 758-1156, 312 Paseo del Pueblo Sur). It's open 5 am to 11:30 pm Sunday to Friday. *Michael's Kitchen* (☎ 758-4178, 304C Paseo del Pueblo Norte) is a busy breakfast spot for skiers and tourists, despite its claim that this is where the locals hang out. Stop in for the biggest cinnamon roll you'll ever see and other great pastries, or basic American and New Mexican fare.

The outdoor patio and courtyard at *Cafe Tazza* (☎ 758-8706, 122 E Kit Carson Rd) make it a pleasant place to enjoy an espresso and pastry. Menu items include homemade soups and tamales and a wide selection of coffee drinks in a bohemian atmosphere. Live entertainment, including acoustic folk-pop and poetry readings, takes place on most weekend evenings. It's open 8 am to 5:30 pm daily, and until 9:30 pm, when there is entertainment. On the north end of town, *The Bean* (☎ 758-7711, 900 Paseo del Pueblo Norte) is a popular spot for locals to hang out over coffee and pastries, and the little outdoor patio can get pretty crowded.

With 21 sandwiches and salads ranging from hummus and tabouleh to caesar, the *Bent St Deli & Café* (☎ 758-5787), in the John Dunne Plaza, offers something for everyone. Lunches are under $8; dinners range from $10 to $14. Another good spot for sandwiches and burgers, more popular with locals than visitors, is the casual café, store and bar *Bravo* (☎ 758-8100), next door to the Fina station on Paseo del

Pueblo Sur. They also have a wide selection of beer, wine and gourmet snacks to go.

Just west of the plaza but far from the tourist crowds, the *Mainstreet Bakery (☎ 758-9610)*, on Guadalupe Plaza, bakes bread for grocery stores in Santa Fe and Albuquerque. 'All organic – all natural…almost' is the motto in this simple place. It serves such fare as scrambled tofu and oatcakes as well as a huge plate of eggs, beans and potatoes, for about $5. Lunch is a gardenburger or sandwich for $4 to $7 or the special – a bowl of black beans, green chile, red onions, tomatoes and cornbread – for $4. Hours are 7:30 am to 2 pm Monday to Friday, 7:30 am to 1 pm Saturday and Sunday.

Mexican & New Mexican On Hwy 150 toward the ski valley, the friendly and relaxed *Old Blinking Light (☎ 776-8787)*, started by the same Tim of Tim's Stray Dog at the ski base (who was tragically killed in a Taos avalanche in 1996), serves up delicious green chile, huge margaritas and other hearty New Mexican fare, ranging from $5 for nachos to $17 for a cowboy steak. Eat inside the rambling adobe or, weather permitting, enjoy the mountain views from the spacious, open grass and garden courtyard.

Orlando's (☎ 751-1450), just north of Laughing Horse Inn on Paseo del Norte, is recommended for excellent and creative New Mexican fare (wait for your table outside around a fire). *Guadalajara Grill (☎ 737-0816, 822 Paseo del Norte)* is a simple cafeteria-type place with great, inexpensive Mexican food.

The *Alley Cantina (☎ 758-2121, 121 Terracina Lane)* is housed in the oldest building in Taos, which was built in the 16th century by Pueblo Indians and once served as the Taos Pueblo trading post. This cozy place serves mediocre and over-priced food, but, with a pool table in one room, a shuffleboard in another and live blues on Thursday night, it's a good place to hang out for a beer.

One of the few places in town open until 3 am on the weekends is *El Pueblo Café (☎ 758-2053, 625 Paseo del Pueblo Norte)*.

Food at this no-frills café is standard New Mexican fare, including traditional menudo and posole, in the $3 to $9 range. Beer and wine are available. Hours are 6 am to 11:30 pm Sunday to Thursday and 6 am to 3 am Friday and Saturday. Another no-frills option is *Rita's* in El Prado and on the south end of Paseo del Pueblo Sur. This isn't much more than plywood floors, a few tables and a walk-up window with a grill, but the food is great and nothing is more expensive than $6. Hours are sporadic (sometimes it's closed altogether).

Italian One of the best restaurants in town is the *Trading Post Cafe (☎ 758-5089, 4179 Hwy 68)*. Sit at the counter and dip your bread in seasoned olive oil while you wait. Housed in an old trading post, the café has a contemporary and lively décor and it's a favorite with locals. If you're looking for an upscale but relaxed meal, this is one of those places where all the pieces fall together, but you pay for it. The lunch menu runs in the $6 to $12 range, but expect to pay about $33 a person for a dinner with dessert and wine.

The low-key and recommended *Outback (☎ 758-3112, 712 Paseo del Pueblo Norte)*, just north of town behind a secondhand sporting goods store, is a favorite for pizza by the slice or whole. The menu includes calzones and unique pizza toppings like honey-chipotle chile sauce, Thai chicken and, of course, green chile.

La Luna (☎ 751-0023), on Paseo del Pueblo Sur in the Pueblo Alegre Mall, serves traditional Italian specialties, including antipasto, marinated shrimp, fresh mussels and pizzas baked in a wood-burning oven. Prices are in the $9 to $18 range, but the food is fresh and tasty.

Continental Centrally located and busy, with a creative menu and ample servings, the *Apple Tree (☎ 758-1900, 123 Bent St)* is a good bet. Sit in one of the rooms of the large historic adobe or under the stars in the courtyard and enjoy smoked trout, mango chicken enchiladas, lamb, curry and pasta specialties. The food is consistently excellent, though expensive ($11 to $20). Lunch is considerably less. Brunch ($5 to $12) is served from 10 am to 3 pm Sunday.

Probably the best meal in Taos, and maybe one of the best in all of New Mexico, is at *Joseph's Table* (☎ 751-4512) on Paseo de Pueblo Sur in Rancho de Taos. With rough-painted yellow walls, a low beamed ceiling, a huge chalkboard listing specials, about seven tables and a little patio overlooking the Taos Plateau, this is a lovely, quiet spot with delicious food. A second room is equally cozy and romantic. Dinner, including dishes such as dijon-crusted pork, mahi mahi and steak au poivre, runs about $18. If you want an upscale meal and don't want to be disappointed, make reservations for dinner here.

Isolated in the hills 9 miles south of town and offering absolutely incredible views of Taos Valley, *Stakeout Grill & Bar* (☎ 758-2042, 101 Stakeout Dr) is reminiscent of the cowboy West and specializes in steaks, including a New York strip for $17 and a 20oz 'real cowboy steak' for $27. The meat-and-potato meals include excellent quality beef, but stay away from anything that sounds too fancy. If nothing else, it's well worth stopping by for a drink to enjoy the quiet views; it's open nightly from 5 to 9:30 pm. Drive south from the plaza on Hwy 68 for 8 miles, keeping an eye out for the Stakeout sign.

Other Eateries Offering six daily beer specials, each brewed on the premises, *Eske's* (☎ 758-1517), a half-block south of Taos Plaza, is a crowded hangout catering to locals and ski bums alike. A casual, two-room adobe, this is not only an excellent place for a nice cold beer ($3 a pint for such specialties as green-chile beer and Dead Presidents Ale) but for cheap, fresh, hearty pub fare as well. There is often live music, such as banjo, acoustic guitar, jazz or conga drums. Housed in a warm adobe, the *Dragonfly Cafe* (☎ 737-5859, 402 Paseo del Pueblo Norte) offers an eclectic menu ranging from whole-wheat pancakes to pad Thai for brunch and from lamb to Jamaican jerk chicken for dinner. Brunch is about $8, dinner entrées run abo ut $17, and the food is very good.

On the way to Taos Ski Valley in Arroyo Seco, *Taos Cow Ice Cream* (☎ 776-5640) has tasty all-natural ice cream, baked goods, breakfasts and deli sandwiches. At the ski valley, *Tim's Stray Dog Cantina* (☎ 776-2894) serves up some of the best green chile in New Mexico, as well as other pub fare, and is always busy with the ski crowd. Outstanding beans with green chile and a tortilla with a soda will run you $5, and Southwestern basics range from $5 to $10. It's open for breakfast at 7:30 am during ski season, and from 11 am during the rest of the year.

The lodges offer comparable continental gourmet cuisine.

Entertainment

The *Storyteller Cinema* (☎ 758-9715, 110 Old Talpa Canon Rd) is near the Holiday Inn. The *Taos Art Association* (☎ 758-2052) presents dance, community theater and music performances at the Community Auditorium. Several restaurants and bars offer live music (see Places to Eat), and there is weekend country dancing at the Sagebrush Inn and live bands at the Taos Inn (see Places to Stay). Also check with the lodges at the ski base.

Shopping

Taos has historically been a mecca for artists, and the huge number of galleries and studios in and around town are evidence of this. Unfortunately, there is also a lot of junk as well as a bustling tourist industry of T-shirt and coffee-mug shops, which is generally focused around the plaza. You could easily spend an entire day wandering the streets, and a good rule to follow is that the places that look the least inviting – a little dilapidated, with a handwritten sign tacked to the door – often have the most interesting work. The visitor center has a helpful Collectors' Guide with maps and information on galleries.

In order to show work at Lumina Gallery (☎ 758-7282), 239 Morada Lane, artists must have worked in New Mexico for at least 20 years. The gallery is housed in the former home of Victor Higgins, a Taos School artist, and outside is a beautiful sculpture garden with contemporary art. Twining Weavers (☎ 758-9000), on Kit Carson Rd, features handwoven rugs, tapestries and pillows. El Rincón Trading Post (☎ 758-9188), 114 E Kit Carson Rd, dates back to 1909 when German Ralph Meyers, one of the first traders in the area, arrived. Even if you're not looking to buy anything, stop in here just to browse through the dusty museum of artifacts, including Indian crafts, jewelry and Old West memorabilia.

If you're in the market for old medical objects, US military memorabilia or Art Deco lamps, stop in at Maison Faurie Antiquités (☎ 758-8545), 1 McCarthy Plaza. This eclectic mix of antiques – basically anything that catches the eye of owner Robert Faurie – is crammed into cabinets and shelves and makes for a great place to poke around.

The John Donne Plaza, across from the Apple Tree on Bent, has some nice stores. An interesting stop, if for nothing else but to check our original maps of the American West including railroad, geological and army surveys, is G Robinson Old Prints and Maps (☎ 758-2278). It sells antique maps and prints from the 16th to the 19th century. Nambe Mills (☎ 758-8221), 216 Paseo del Pueblo Norte, sells a large selection of Nambeware, both first quality and seconds (see Shopping in the Santa Fe section for a description of Nambeware).

Getting There & Away
Rio Grande Air (☎ 737-9790, 877-435-9742) flies daily to Farmington, Albuquerque and Durango, Colorado.

TNM&O/Greyhound (☎ 758-1144, 800-231-2222), 1238 Gusdorf Rd, has daily bus service to Albuquerque ($24, 2¼ hours) and Santa Fe ($15.75, 1½ hours), with stops at Pilar and Española. Buses leave Taos at 5:45 am and 6:30 pm.

Twin Hearts Express (☎ 751-1201, 800-654-9456) shuttles four times daily to Albuquerque ($40, three hours), Santa Fe ($25, 1½ hours) and Española ($20, 30 minutes). It also offers service to Red River ($25, one hour), Taos Ski Valley ($10, 40 minutes) and southern Colorado – including Antonita, the endpoint for the Cumbres and Toltec Scenic Railroad (see Chama in Northwestern New Mexico). Faust (☎ 758-3410, 888-830-3410) leaves daily at 1 pm from the Albuquerque Airport, with a stop at Santa Fe ($35). The return shuttle leaves Taos for Albuquerque at 7:30 am. Call to confirm times, as they are subject to change.

Beware of crazy drivers on the two routes from Santa Fe (See Española to Taos, earlier), both of which are winding. Also be aware that elevation changes can often result in dramatic differences in weather conditions.

Getting Around
The Chile Line (☎ 751-4459), Taos' local bus service, runs on the half-hour, starting at 7 am southbound from the Taos Pueblo and northbound from the post office in Rancho de Taos. It costs 50¢ per ride or $5 for a seven-day pass.

At the Taos Municipal Airport (☎ 758-4995), on Hwy 64 just west of town, is Dollar Rent A Car (☎ 758-4995). Enterprise (☎ 737-0514) is next to the Chevron Station on Paseo del Pueblo Sur. All of the usual major rental-car agencies are located in Santa Fe and Albuquerque.

Faust (☎ 758-3410, 888-830-3410) runs an on-call taxi service, from 7 am to 9 pm, with costs ranging from $7 for one to two people within the city limits to $200 one-way to Santa Fe.

Mountain bikes, road bikes and bike racks can be rented through Gearing Up Bicycle Shop (☎ 751-0365), 129 Paseo del Pueblo Sur; Cottam's (☎ 758-2822), 207-A Paseo del Pueblo Sur; and Native Sons Adventures (☎ 758-9342, 800-753-7559), 1033-A Paseo del Pueblo Sur. Costs range from $20 to $35 daily, with weekly discounts.

Though hitchhiking is dangerous anywhere, it is common to see people hitching to and from Taos Ski Valley. Use caution hitchhiking; women should not hitchhike alone.

ENCHANTED CIRCLE

This 84-mile loop around Wheeler Peak, New Mexico's highest mountain at 13,161 feet, passes a few small towns, hiking trails, camping sites and two ski basins (though Taos Ski Valley is by far the best skiing). Storms arise quickly in both the summer and winter, and parts of this drive are at 10,000 feet. Be sure to check road conditions before heading out (☎ 800-432-4269).

Begin by taking Hwy 64 north out of downtown Taos to Hwy 522, stopping by the DH Lawrence Memorial (see boxed text), and head to Questa. Take a detour west on Hwy 378 to one of the most spectacular camping and hiking sites in the area, Wild Rivers National Recreation Area.

Retrace your steps back to Questa and continue east on Hwy 38 to Red River, which has both downhill and cross-country skiing. The next stretch is high-mountain terrain to Eagle Nest Lake. In the 19th century, the Moreno Valley boomed with gold seekers, but today Eagle Nest is quiet.

Continue south on Hwy 38 toward Angel Fire, a ski resort plastered on a mountainside. Then take Hwy 64 west through the winding roads of the Carson National Forest, following the stream, back to Taos.

Though it's certainly a lovely drive, 'enchanted' is a bit of a visitors bureau exaggeration.

QUESTA

☎ 505 • pop 2200 • elevation 7670 feet

The USFS Questa Ranger Station (☎ 586-0520), PO Box 110, Questa, NM 87556, a mile east of Questa on Hwy 38, has information about campgrounds in the Carson National Forest (several lie along Hwy 38), which are open mid-May through mid-October. Most are small and available on a first-come, first-served basis. Those with fees, ranging from $6 to $8, have drinking water. Nearby is the 20,000-acre Latir Peak Wilderness Area, which offers scenic camping, picnicking, hiking and fishing. To get to the Latir Peak Wilderness Area from Questa, take Hwy 522 north toward Costilla.

The *Sangre de Cristo Motel* (☎ 586-0300) has standard doubles for about $50. Inside,

the *El Seville Restaurant* (☎ 586-0300) serves New Mexican and American dishes.

WILD RIVERS NATIONAL RECREATION AREA

Awe-inspiring camping and hiking are available year-round at the beautiful and desolate Wild Rivers National Recreation Area, 26 miles north of Taos along Hwy 522 and then west on Hwy 378. The **Wild Rivers Backcountry Byway** (Hwy 378) is a 13-mile scenic drive loop through the area. Flat mesas covered in sagebrush surround the deepest part of the Rio Grande Gorge. Though the area can be relatively busy from May to August, it is easy to get away from the crowds. La Junta and Big Arsenic Springs Trails go about a mile into the gorge at the junction of the Red River and the Rio Grande, where you can fish in designated fly-fishing water. There are other trails for all levels, including one that tracks through an extinct volcano. There is a $5 fee per vehicle for day use.

You can camp and grill at the piñon-studded sites overlooking the Rio Grande Gorge, where there are water and toilets but no showers or hookups ($7). Alternatively, hike down the gorge to backcountry sites by the river ($5). At the time of this writing, the visitor center was closed for renovations, and they don't know when it will reopen; contact the BLM in Taos (☎ 758-8851) for further information.

RED RIVER

☎ 505 • pop 350 • elevation 8750 feet

In the 19th century, gold was discovered in the hills surrounding Red River, and by 1905 there were 3000 people, four hotels, 15 saloons and a thriving red-light district. The town developed a wild reputation, but by 1925 miners had left for golder pastures. Today Red River survives predominantly on tourism. Fortunately, the national forest prevents sprawling development and protects its Old West feel. The buildings look like they're out of a movie set. Small-town family fun and outdoor recreation are the focus here (the website welcomes readers with 'We have the mountains, just bring your boots'). You won't find a wild nightlife or the post-hippie and ski clientele characteristic of Taos.

Red River hosts Mardi Gras in the Mountains, a half-hour north of town, to coincide with New Orleans' street festival. On Memorial Day weekend, 6000 motorcyclists converge on the small town.

Orientation & Information

Three streets run parallel to the river at the base of the ski slope – Rivers, Main and High – and you can walk anywhere within town. The chamber of commerce (☎ 754-2366, 800-348-6444) is in the center of Main St; visit www.redrivernewmex.com. Other services in town include the library (☎ 754-6564), 702 E Main St; the post office (☎ 754-2555), 120 W Main St; and the police (☎ 754-6166), 100 E Main St. A free trolley runs through the town.

Activities

Outdoor recreation is the town's primary draw. The Williams Trading Post (☎ 754-2217) is a local institution and a general source of information on fishing and hiking. New Mexico Adventure Co (☎ 754-2437) rents mountain bikes and jeeps and books guided trips of all kinds. Both are on Main St.

Hiking The area around Red River offers great hiking through the Carson National Forest's mountain meadows, lakes and streams. You can pick up trail maps at the chamber of commerce. Trails of 2 to 16 miles and all levels of difficulty weave through Columbine Canyon, including one to the top of Wheeler Peak. The trailhead for Red River Nature Trail, an easy 2-mile trail along the stream that hugs the town, is at the ski base. Beaver Ponds and Middle Fork Lake Trails start at the end of Upper Valley Rd. You can either take an easy half-day hike to the Beaver Ponds, or park at the Middle Fork Trail lot and hike 2 miles, ascending 2000 vertical feet, to a high mountain lake.

Skiing Though there aren't high-terrain mountain trails at Red River Ski Area

(☎ 754-2223), it's a great place to come if you're just learning or if you find the intensity of Taos intimidating. Lift tickets are $42/32 for a full/half day. Call for package rates, which include lifts and lesson.
website: www.redriverskiarea.com

With 1400 acres and 30 kilometers of groomed trails through national forest and alpine fields, the **Enchanted Forest** (☎ 754-2374) is New Mexico's biggest cross-country ski area. An all-day pass costs $10; ski rentals and snowshoes are $10.50. For the three days before the full moon, they offer Moonlight Ski Tours. Go to Miller's Crossing (☎ 754-2374), 212 Main St, to book trips, rent equipment and arrange drop-offs. The **Just Desserts Eat & Ski Festival** is at the end of February; restaurants in town set up

---

DH Lawrence Memorial

Like many artists in the early 20th century, DH Lawrence found inspiration in the land and lifestyle of northern New Mexico. Three of his books, *The Plumed Serpent, David* and *Mornings in Mexico*, were influenced by his two-year stay at the Kiowa Ranch, just north of Taos. Mabel Dodge Luhan had tried to give the ranch to Lawrence in the 1920s, but he didn't want to be indebted to her. His wife, Frieda, later accepted it in exchange for the original manuscript of *Sons and Lovers*.

When Lawrence died in France in 1930, Frieda brought his ashes back to Kiowa Ranch. She was so afraid that Mabel would try to steal them that, as the story goes, she had them mixed into the cement of a small shrine in the shape of a cabin. Frieda was eventually buried outside the memorial.

Today, the ranch is owned by the University of New Mexico, which uses it for academic research. To get to the DH Lawrence Memorial (☎ 505-776-2245), drive past the farming village of Arroyo Hondo on Hwy 522 and follow signs down a dirt road on the right. There is no museum, but you can come here to pay your respects to the Lawrences. Admission is free.

Tumbleweeds

Huge twiggy balls rolling across the desert seem as much a part of the Southwestern landscape as the cowboy. However, both are recent imports to the Southwestern scene. The tumbleweed, also called the Russian thistle (Salsola kali), arrived in the 19th century with immigrant farmers from Eastern Europe.

The tumbleweed is an annual that grows quickly in disturbed areas and soon becomes a large ball of tough branches attached to the ground by a single stem. Summer winds uproot the dried plants and send them tumbling eerily across the desert.

tables of desserts all along the trail system, and you can eat your way along.

Fishing Due to the 20,000 German brown, cutthroat and rainbow trout that are annually stocked in the river and surrounding lakes, the fishing in Red River is great. A half-day license is $9 to $14, a five-day license is $17 to $22. Talk to staff at Williams Trading Post (☎ 754-2217) or Starr Angler Fly Shop (☎ 754-2320) for information.

Organized Tours

There is no shortage of outdoor adventure organizations in Red River; ask at the chamber of commerce for a complete list. Snowmobiling is popular here; two companies that enjoy a good reputation for tours are Fast Eddies (☎ 754-3103), 619 E Main St, and the Sled Shed (☎ 754-6370), 612 W Main St. For horseback riding, try Timbers (☎ 754-2769).

Places to Stay

Accommodations in Red River generally consist of motel-type lodges in town, condominiums, cabins in the mountains and camping. Bandanna Properties (☎ 754-2949) and Reservations Unlimited (☎ 754-6415, 800-545-6415) can arrange the rental of a private home or any other lodging; visit

online at http://redriverreservations.com. The chamber of commerce has a visitors guide with a complete listing, and offers a reservation service as well. The high seasons are November to February and June to August. Rates vary tremendously and are listed below.

There is plenty of seasonal camping in and around Red River and there are four RV parks. See Questa, earlier, for information about campsites in the national forest along Hwy 38.

The *Lodge at Red River* (☎ 754-6280, 800-915-6343), on Main St, is probably the nicest place in town. This centrally located landmark hotel has a cozy European feel that is lacking in the others. Doubles range from $78 to $106. The *Copper King Lodge* (☎ 754-6210, 800-727-6210, 307 E River St) has doubles and private cabins from $59. The *Riverside* (☎ 754-2252, 800-432-9999) offers cabins with kitchens as well as double rooms for $62 to $85. One of the nicer condominiums is *Valley Condominiums* (☎ 754-2262, 800-333-2393), with condos starting at $109.

Places to Eat

If you wake up starvin', head to *Shotgun Willie's* (☎ 754-6505), across the street from Lifts West, where all-you-can-eat mountain-man breakfasts cost $4. *Sundance Mexican Restaurant* (☎ 754-2971) serves plates of beans and burritos and the like for under $10.

Waits are sometimes four hours long at *Texas Red's Steakhouse* (☎ 754-2964), but you can call the 'hostess hotline' at ☎ 754-2922 to find out. It's a favorite with tourists looking for that taste of the Old West. At the far end of town toward Questa, *Brett's Homestead Steakhouse* (☎ 754-6136) is the locals' alternative to Texas Red's (open Saturday night only November to May). From June to early October, *Timbers* (☎ 754-2769, 402 W Main St) hosts a Cowboy Evening, featuring a horse-drawn carriage ride to a campfire with live music, cowboy poetry and a full steak dinner for $40. Go to the *Black Crow Coffee House* (☎ 754-3150, 500 E Main St) for a strong cup of coffee and pastries, with pasta and live music on the weekends.

For boot-scooting to live country & western music Thursday to Sunday, head to the *Motherlode Saloon* (☎ 754-6280) on Main St in the center of town. Across the street is *Bull o' the Woods* (☎ 754-2593), another popular bar with a happy hour from 3 to 6 pm.

EAGLE NEST
☎ 505 • pop 300 • elevation 8300 feet

This windswept town, set in high plains, is at best a cheap base from which to hike, fish, ski and snowmobile in the surrounding mountains. There are a few restaurants and gift shops along the main road, and several RV parks in the area. *D & D Motel* (☎ 377-2408, 800-913-9548) offers doubles, some with kitchenettes, for about $45. For more information, call the Eagle Nest Chamber of Commerce (☎ 377-2420, 800-494-9117).
website: www.eaglenest.org

ANGEL FIRE
☎ 505 • pop 1600 • elevation 8382 feet

Twenty-two miles east of Taos, the ski resort of Angel Fire has gained a reputation as condominium heaven. This sprawl on the edge of a plateau consists of a few monotonous restaurants and motels and lots of condos.

The chamber of commerce (☎ 377-6661, 800-446-8117), on the right as you drive in, has a list of reservation services; visit www.angelfirechamber.org. Also contact Angel Fire Central Reservations (☎ 800-323-5793), online at www.angelfirenm.com/discover. Roadrunner Tours (☎ 377-6416, 800-377-6416) rents skis and bikes and arranges outdoor trips, including snowmobile tours, sleigh rides and overnight horseback riding trips.

The primary gig in town is the huge *Angel Fire Resort* (☎ 377-6401, 800-633-7463) at the base of the slopes. The 'summer adventure desk' (☎ 377-4282) can arrange all kinds of outdoor activities. Double rooms and condos range from $60 to $110 from April to November and are more expensive during ski season. Eager to attract visitors, the resort often has great ski and golf packages and all kinds of specials.
website: www.angelfireresort.com

The *Inn at Angel Fire* (☎ 377-2504) is an unpretentious and informal ski lodge with motel rooms and a dorm room.

The isolated *Blackfire Flyfishing Guest Ranch* (☎ 377-6870) offers a basic three-bedroom, two-bath guesthouse, with a private fly-fishing lake, for $185 (two-person, three-night minimum). Rates include all meals, lodging and fishing.
website: www.blackfireflyfishing.com

With pool tables and occasional live music, *Zebadiah's* (☎ 377-6358), on Hwy 434, is the best place in town to hang out over a beer. A variety of half-pound burgers cost under $5, and barbecue ranges from $7 to $11.

Northwestern New Mexico

Farmington Area

Northwestern New Mexico showcases some of the Southwest's most fabulous desert landscapes and ancient Indian sites. Much of the land remains in the hands of Native Americans, with the Navajo, Zuni and Acoma pueblos among those of most interest to visitors. People who enjoy the rod and gun find good sport in the Chama area, and railroad buffs revel in a nostalgic steam-engine trip out of Chama on the Cumbres & Toltec Scenic Railroad. South of there is the wide-open, crystal clear, dramatic country made famous by the extraordinary paintings of Georgia O'Keeffe.

Farmington Area

Ancestral Puebloans left some magnificent sites here – foremost among them is Pueblo Bonito in the Chaco Culture National Historical Park, located about two hours' drive south of Farmington. Aztec Ruins National Monument and Salmon Ruin, both worth

MAP INDEX

exploring, can be found a few miles from Farmington.

The area became the home of Navajos and Utes after the departure of the Ancestral Puebloans. Around the beginning of the 19th century, whites found the Animas River Valley to be a profitable beaver-trapping area (the animals were soon hunted into local extinction), but permanent Anglo settlement didn't happen until 1876, when ranchers arrived at the confluence of the Animas, San Juan and La Plata Rivers. Farmingtown (the 'w' was later dropped) developed into an agricultural center.

The population was largely rural until the 1950s, when oil, gas and coal extraction began. Currently, mining, agriculture and tourism all play important parts in Farmington's economy.

FARMINGTON
☎ 505 • pop 40,000 • elevation 5400 feet

Farmington is the largest town in northwestern New Mexico (and the Four Corners area) and serves as a pleasant base for excursions to the various attractions described below.

Average high/low temperatures are 91/60°F in July and 40/18°F in January. Annual rainfall is 7½ inches, and snowfall is 12.3 inches.

Information

The visitors bureau (☎ 326-7602, 800-448-1240) is in the Gateway Museum at 3041 E Main, Farmington, NM 87402. Check the visitors bureau website for more information and links to local businesses.

website: www.farmingtonnm.org

The Bureau of Land Management (☎ 599-8970), 1235 La Plata Hwy (west on Hwy 64, cross La Plata River and head north on La Plata Hwy), is open 9 am to 4 pm Monday to Friday. In nearby Bloomfield, 14 miles east of town on Hwy 64, is the Carson National Forest Ranger Station (☎ 632-2956). Other services include the

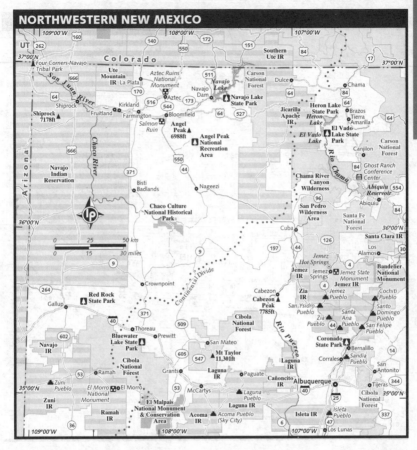

NORTHWESTERN NEW MEXICO

library (☎ 599-1270), 100 W Broadway; the post office (☎ 325-5047), 2301 E 20th St; the hospital (☎ 325-5011), 801 W Maple St; and the police (☎ 325-7547), 10525 W Navajo.

Things to See & Do

The **Children's Museum & Science Center** (☎ 599-1425), 302 N Orchard St, features fun hands-on exhibits on the culture and geology of the region (free admission). National shows, juried regional art shows and a permanent exhibit on the cultures and history of Farmington and the region can be seen at the **Farmington Museum at** **Gateway Park** (☎ 599-1174), 3041 E Main. Hours are 9 am to 5 pm daily, noon to 5 pm Sunday.

The 5 miles of paved and dirt trails at **River Corridor** provide a lovely means of enjoying the Animas River waterfront and surrounding bosque on foot or bike.

Activities

The Animas, La Plata and San Juan Rivers offer **river rafting** and excellent **fishing**; the visitor center has a list of outfitters. Morgan Lake, 15 miles west of Farmington on Hwy 64, is popular for **windsurfing** and **fishing**

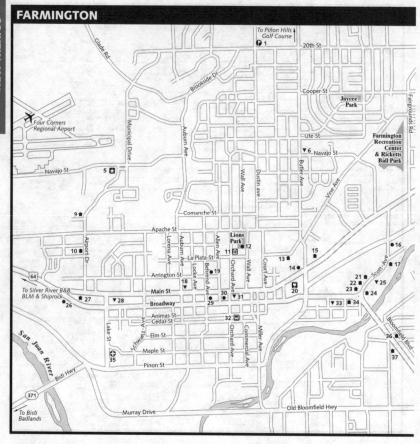

FARMINGTON

(no swimming allowed). One of the few public **golf** courses in the country with a five star rating, Pinon Hills (☎ 326-6066) is a beautiful course (take Butler Ave north to Sunrise Parkway and head west). Locals cross the state line into Colorado to **ski** at Purgatory Ski Area (☎ 970-247-9000), about 80 miles north of Farmington.

The best place in town to rent gear is at the Outdoor Equipment Rental Center at San Juan Community College (☎ 566-3221), 4601 College Blvd (take 30th St east just past Hutton Rd to College Blvd and turn north). Zia's Sporting Goods (☎ 327-6004),

located at 500 E Main, sells skiing, camping and fishing gear.

Special Events

Rodeo events are held all year long at McGee Park (☎ 324-8929), east of town on Hwy 64; the Sheriff Posse Rodeo, held in early June, and the San Juan County Fair Rodeo in mid-August are the two biggest.

Over Memorial Day weekend, Farmington celebrates with the Invitational Balloon Festival and Riverfest. The **Connie Mack World Series Baseball Tournament** in mid-August features top amateur ballplayers

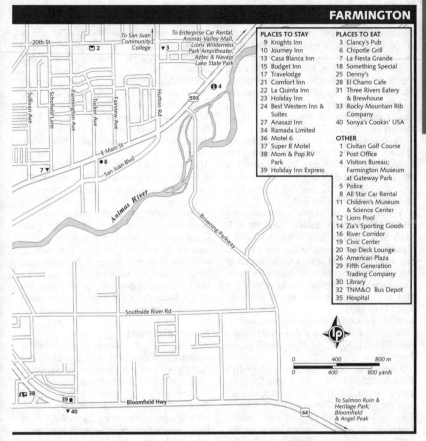

FARMINGTON

PLACES TO STAY
9 Knights Inn
10 Journey Inn
13 Casa Blanca Inn
15 Budget Inn
17 Travelodge
21 Comfort Inn
22 La Quinta Inn
23 Holiday Inn
24 Best Western Inn & Suites
27 Anasazi Inn
34 Ramada Limited
36 Motel 6
37 Super 8 Motel
38 Mom & Pop RV Park
39 Holiday Inn Express

PLACES TO EAT
3 Clancy's Pub
6 Chipotle Grill
7 La Fiesta Grande
18 Something Special
25 Denny's
28 El Charro Cafe
31 Three Rivers Eatery & Brewhouse
33 Rocky Mountain Rib Company
40 Sonya's Cookin' USA

OTHER
1 Civitan Golf Course
2 Post Office
4 Visitors Bureau; Farmington Museum at Gateway Park
5 Police
8 All Star Car Rental
11 Children's Museum & Science Center
12 Lions Pool
14 Zia's Sporting Goods
16 River Corridor
19 Civic Center
20 Top Deck Lounge
26 American Plaza
29 Fifth Generation Trading Company
30 Library
32 TNM&O Bus Depot
35 Hospital

and attracts scouts from college and professional teams. The seven-day event is held at Ricketts Ball Park (☎ 327-9673), 1101 N Fairgrounds Rd. The Totah Festival, held in the Civic Center over Labor Day weekend, has top-quality Native American arts and crafts in juried competition and Navajo rugs for sale by auction. In late September, **Native American Days** is held at the Animas Valley Mall, 4601 E Main.

The Navajo community of Shiprock hosts an annual **Navajo Fair** with a rodeo, powwow and traditional dancing in late September or early October. This is perhaps the most traditional of the large Indian fairs and begins with the Night Way, a complex Navajo healing ceremony, and the *Yei Bei Chei* chant, which lasts for several days.

Places to Stay

High season (Memorial Day to Labor Day) summer rates are given below.

Several campgrounds in town offer RV camping, including *Mom & Pop RV Park* (☎ 800-748-2807, 901 Illinois Ave). However, tent campers in particular would be better off at Navajo Lake State Park (see Navajo Lake State Park later in this chapter) or at Morgan Lake, Bisti Badlands and Angel Peak (see Around Farmington), where there is free primitive camping. Angel Peak has units with fireplaces but no facilities.

The cheapest places have simple but clean rooms at $35 for a double. These include the *Journey Inn* (☎ 325-3548), 317 Airport Dr; the *Knights Inn* (☎ 325-5061, 701 Airport Dr), with large rooms; and the nice looking *Budget Inn* (☎ 326-5521, 652 E Main).

Travelers will find plenty of chain motels in town, including Comfort Inn, Holiday Inn Express and Best Western. The *Anasazi Inn* (☎ 325-4564, 903 W Main), with a restaurant and bar, has good rooms and a few suites with singles/doubles for $40/50.

Though only 3 miles from downtown, the lovely *Silver River Adobe B&B* (☎ 325-8219, 800-382-9251, 3151 W Main St) offers a peaceful respite among the trees on the San Juan River; fall asleep to the sound of the river, wake to organic blueberry juice, and enjoy a morning walk to the prairie dog village. Two handsome rooms and one suite cost $75 to $105.
website: www.cyberport.com/silveradobe

Also try *Casa Blanca Inn* (☎ 327-6503, 800 382-9251, 505 E La Plata), with rooms from $75.

Something truly unique, *Kokopelli's Cave* (☎ 325-7855) is an incredible 1,650-sq-foot cave carved 70 feet below the surface into the sandstone above La Plata River; it takes a 3-mile drive on dirt roads and a short hike to reach it, so you are truly isolated. Equipped with a kitchen stocked for breakfast and lunch, a VCR with videos and a hot tub, this spacious cave dwelling offers magnificent views over the desert and river. It accommodates up to six people (ask about larger parties); rates are $200 for two.
website: www.bbonline.com/nm/kokopelli

Places to Eat
The kid-friendly and trendy-feeling *Three Rivers Eatery & Brewhouse* (☎ 324-2187, 101 E Main), with good food and its own microbrewed beers, bustles with locals for lunch and dinner. A simple place with side-

walk dining, *Chipotle Grill* (☎ 324-1595, 1000 N Butler) is tasty. *Something Special Bakery and Tearoom* (☎ 325-8183, 116 N Auburn Ave), open 7 am to 2 pm Monday to Friday, serves great breakfasts, pastries and desserts.

For Mexican food try *La Fiesta Grande* (☎ 326-6476, 1916 E Main) or the small and homey *El Charro Cafe* (☎ 327-2464, 737 W Main). *Sonya's Cookin' USA* (☎ 327-3526, 2001 Bloomfield Hwy) is a locally popular diner with good inexpensive blue-plate specials and good breakfasts. The *Rocky Mountain Rib Company* (☎ 327-7422, 525 E Broadway Ave) specializes in smoked and barbecued ribs and other meats.

Clancy's Pub (☎ 325-8176, 2703 E 20th St) calls itself an 'Irish cantina,' and it's popular with young adults. They offer a fine selection of imported beers to wash down a variety of hamburgers (one pounders!), Mexican food and pub grub. You can dine inside, where the rock music's loud, or on their patio (overlooking, unfortunately, a strip). *Denny's* (☎ 324-8415, 600 Scott Ave) is open 24 hours.

Entertainment
The big annual entertainment event is *Dreams and Drillbits*, a historical drama ($11) performed Wednesday to Saturday from mid-June to mid-August. For an extra $7, dinner is served before the show. Tickets are available at the door or call ☎ 877-599-3331. It is performed at the Lions Wilderness Park Amphitheater, a natural sandstone outdoor theater 3 miles out of town; the visitors bureau has information on other performances at the theater.

The local Theater Ensemble Arts (☎ 327-0076) presents occasional plays and musicals at the *San Juan College Little Theater*. The *Civic Center* (☎ 877-599-3331, 200 W Arrington Ave) hosts off-Broadway performances by the Civic Center Foundation for the Performing Arts (☎ 599-1145) and city-sponsored theater.

For bar-oriented nightlife Clancy's Pub (see Places to Eat) is popular. Try your country two-step at the busy *Top Deck*

Lounge (☎ 327-7385, 515 E Main). There is a live country-western band and a cover charge on Wednesday, Friday and Saturday.

Shopping
Several trading posts in the Farmington area offer a variety of high-quality Indian crafts – the Navajo rugs (see the 'Navajo Weaving' boxed text in the Northeastern Arizona chapter) are particularly good. Reliable trading posts are found along Hwy 64 west of town and include the Hogback Trading Company (☎ 598-5154), 3221 Hwy 64 (15 miles west of Farmington); the nearby Bob French's Navajo Rugs (☎ 598-5621), 3459 Hwy 64; and Foutz Trading Company (☎ 368-5790), on Hwy 64 in Shiprock. Downtown, Fifth Generation Trading Company (☎ 326-3211), 232 W Broadway, was founded in 1875 and has a big selection.

Getting There & Away
Mesa Airlines (☎ 564-7964, 800-637-2247) flies nine times daily to and from Albuquerque; America West Express (☎ 326-4494, 800-235-9292) offers several flights a day to and from Phoenix; United Express (☎ 800-241-6522) flies to Denver, Colorado; and Rio Grande Air (☎ 877-435-9742) serves Taos and Albuquerque.

TNM&O/Greyhound (☎ 325-1009), 101 E Animas, has one or two daily buses to Albuquerque ($33, four hours), stopping at Cuba and Durango, Colorado ($15, 1¼ hours), some continuing to Salt Lake City, Utah.

Navajo Transit System (☎ 520-729-4111) has a bus to Window Rock (on the Navajo Reservation in Arizona) leaving from the American Plaza on Main St at Broadway at 7 am Monday to Friday.

Getting Around
KB Cab (☎ 325-2999) has 24-hour taxi service in and around Farmington.

Avis, Budget, Hertz and National rent cars at the airport. Car rental is also available from All Star (☎ 325-4313), 2307 E Main, and Enterprise (☎ 327-1356), 4012 E Main.

AROUND FARMINGTON
Mine Tours
Navajo Mine (☎ 598-3396), 25 miles southwest of Farmington on the Navajo Reservation, is the largest open-pit mine in the western USA. Free tours are offered at 10 am on Monday. The San Juan Mine (☎ 598-2000), 15 miles west of Farmington, and La Plata Mine (☎ 598-2800), 20 miles north, also offer tours. Tours are by appointment only. All three mines produce coal used to fire the Four Corners Power Plant (☎ 598-8201) near Morgan Lake on the Navajo Reservation, which can be toured with two weeks' notice.

Shiprock
A landmark for Anglo pioneers and a sacred site to the Navajo, **Shiprock**, a 1700-foot-high volcanic plug, rises eerily over the landscape to the west. You can see Shiprock from Hwy 64, but better views are had from Hwy 666 and Indian Hwy 13, which goes almost to the base of it.

Bisti Badlands
About 35 miles south of Farmington along Hwy 371, the Bisti Badlands, an undeveloped Bureau of Land Management (BLM) wilderness, offers a barren but geologically interesting landscape, with many eroded and colorfully pigmented formations; the best sights are along trails a couple of miles from the roads. Dirt roads lead a few miles east to the even more remote **De-Na-Zin Wilderness**.

Salmon Ruin & Heritage Park
Salmon Ruin is an ancient pueblo similar to the Aztec Ruins: a large village built by the Chaco people in the early 1100s, abandoned, resettled by people from Mesa Verde and again abandoned before 1300. The site is named after George Salmon, an early settler who protected the area.

The adjoining Heritage Park has the remains of the Salmon homestead and a variety of Indian cultural artifacts, including petroglyphs, a Navajo hogan, an early Puebloan pithouse, a teepee (a conical tent used by Plains Indians) and a wickiup (a rough brushwood shelter).

Information is available from Salmon Ruin (☎ 632-2013), PO Box 125, Bloomfield, NM 87413. Hours are 9 am to 5 pm daily. Admission is $3. To get here, take Hwy 64 east toward Bloomfield.

Angel Peak National Recreation Area

Along with Shiprock and Bisti, Angel Peak is another area known for its desolate geological formations. There is a free campground with pit toilets but no water. The turnoff for Angel Peak is 15 miles south of Bloomfield (13 miles east of Farmington), then 7 miles east along an unpaved road.

Bloomfield

There is no reason to come here, though there is a nice looking Super 8, the simple *Bloomfield Motel (☎ 632-3388, 801 W Broadway)* and the Carson National Forest Ranger Station (☎ 632-2956), all on Hwy 64.

AZTEC

☎ 505 • pop 6000 • elevation 5600 feet

Aztec was founded in 1890. The old downtown sector has several interesting turn-of-the-19th-century buildings, many listed in the National Register of Historic Places, and a pleasant tree-lined residential district. The annual Aztec Fiesta Days is held during the first weekend in June, with games, arts and crafts, food booths and a bonfire. The burning of 'Old Man Gloom' celebrates the beginning of summer.

The nearest public transportation is 14 miles southwest, in Farmington.

Orientation & Information

Highway 516 from Farmington (14 miles northeast) becomes Aztez Blvd through town and continues as Hwy 173 toward Navajo Dam State Park. Main St heads west off of Aztec Blvd. The visitor center (☎ 334-9551, 888-838-9551), 110 N Ash, Aztec, NM 87410 (look for signs on Aztec Blvd), is open 8 am to 5 pm Monday to Saturday. Check its website (www.aztecnm.com) for more information.

Other services in town include the library (☎ 334-3658) and the police (☎ 334-6622), which are both behind the visitor center in the Aztec City Offices at 201 W Chaco St, and the post office (☎ 334-6181), 601 S Rio Grande Ave.

Things to See & Do

An alternative to the bigger and more visited sites like Chaco (see Chaco Culture National Historical Park later in this chapter) and Mesa Verde (in Colorado), the 27-acre **Aztec Ruins National Monument** (circa 1100; ☎ 334-6174), PO Box 640, Aztec, NM 87410, features the largest reconstructed kiva in the country, with an internal diameter of almost 50 feet ($4 per person; passes are honored, and children are free). The monument (look for signs off of Aztec Blvd) is open 8 am to 5 pm daily, and stays open until 6 pm June through August. website: www.nps.gov/azru

The small but excellent **Aztec Museum & Pioneer Village** (☎ 334-9829), 125 N Main Ave, features an eclectic collection of historical objects, including telephones, barbershop chairs and a great display of late 19th and early 20th century regional photographs. Outside the museum, a small 'pioneer village' has original or replica early buildings, such as a church, jail and bank. Admission is $2.

On Saturdays from April to September, **Aztec Speedway** (☎ 334-2023) resounds with the roar of automobile engines. The track is a half-mile south of town off Hwy 544.

Organized Tours

Moore Anthropological Research (☎ 334-6675), PO Box 1156, Aztec, NM 87410, on Main St, offers guided half- and full-day tours to all the nearby sites. Half-day rates are $85 for one or two people and $25 for each additional person ($15 for children under 12).

Places to Stay & Eat

Though not recommended for tent campers, *Ruins Rd RV Park (☎ 334-3160, 312 Ruins Rd),* a few minutes' walk from the national monument, has tent/RV sites for $6/15. The

Enchantment Lodge (☎ 334-6143, 1800 W Aztec Blvd), a basic motel with a pleasant pool, offers singles/doubles for $34/44. The historic **Miss Gail's Inn** (☎ 334-3452, 888-534-3452, 300 S Main St), a ramshackle brick structure that was built in 1907 as 'The American Hotel,' is decorated with early photographs and period pieces. Rates are $65/75 with breakfast, but a room for a week, no breakfast, is much less per night. The 40-room, Victorian style **Step Back Inn** (☎ 334-1200, 800-334-1255, 103 W Aztec Blvd), charges $72 for a room.

Inside Miss Gail's Inn, *Giovanni's* is a homey spot serving tasty lunches (quiche, sandwiches, salads and great desserts) from 11 am to 2 pm and dinner on weekends and by reservation only. You can get big portions of reasonably priced Mexican and American fare from 5 am to 9 pm at *Aztec Restaurant* (☎ 334-9586, 107 E Aztec Blvd). For an espresso and a snack, stop by **Hard Backs Books**, a used bookstore on Main St.

NAVAJO DAM & NAVAJO LAKE STATE PARK

Built on the San Juan River, the Navajo Dam created Navajo Lake, which stretches over 30 miles northeast and across into Colorado. At the base of the dam, the San Juan River has trout fishing that the locals call 'world class,' and from the end of June through September, the river is busy with anglers from all over the world.

The state park (☎ 632-2278), 1448 NM 511, No 1, Navajo Dam, NM 87419, is 25 miles east of Aztec via US 550 and Hwy 173; alternatively, take Hwy 64 east from Farmington to Hwy 511 north. Three recreation areas offer boating, hiking, fishing and camping. Day use is $4 per car.

Fishing

The tiny community of Navajo Dam (a few miles west of the park entrance at the intersection of Hwys 173 and 511) has several outfitters that provide fishing equipment and information and guide fishing trips. These include Born-n-Raised on the San Juan River, Inc (☎ 632-2194), Rizuto's Fly Shop (☎ 632-3893, 800-525-1437) and

Soaring Eagle (☎ 632-3721, 800-866-2719). Fishing is year-round, by permit only, and there are catch-and-release and other regulations to protect the high quality of the fishing.

Floating

To float the river, put in at the Texas Hole parking lot at milepost 12 on Hwy 511, where the old Catholic church is, and float 2½ miles to Crusher Hole. Gretchen at the Enchanted Hideaway (see Places to Stay & Eat) rents two drift boats ($125). You can rent boats for the reservoir at the Navajo Lake Marina (☎ 632-3245) at Lake Pine River Campground or at the Sims Mesa Marina (☎ 320-0885) at Sims Mesa Campground (see Places to Stay & Eat).

Places to Stay & Eat

The BLM runs three campgrounds with sites with/without hookups for $14/10. The biggest is **Lake Pine River**, on the west shore of the lake just past the dam on Hwy 511. On the east shore of the lake is the smaller **Sims Mesa**. Both have a visitor center and marina. About 10 miles south of the lake on Hwy 511 is **Cottonwood Campground**, a lovely spot under the cottonwoods on the river. There is drinking water and toilets, but no showers.

Though visitors stay in Farmington, Bloomfield or Aztec, there are a couple of places in and around the town of Navajo Dam that offer more rural accommodation. **Abe's Motel & Fly Shop** (☎ 632-2194), on Hwy 173, has basic double rooms for $58 ($64 with a kitchenette). Next door, try **El Pescador** (☎ 632-5129), which offers standard Mexican and American food daily and a big breakfast buffet for $6.50 Friday to Sunday.

Two miles west of Abe's, the friendly and low-key **Enchanted Hideaway Lodge** (☎ 632-2634) has several pleasant suites and private houses, with kitchens and gas grills, for $55 to $125. The spacious Stone House is particularly nice and sleeps up to six ($15 for each person after two). On the desert property, a walk-up sandwich shop sells great sandwiches and smoothies. Nestled under the cliffs against the river, **Soaring Eagle Lodge** (☎ 632-3721, 800-866-2719) is a beautiful and peaceful spot far from any road. Simple suites with kitchens cost $125; ask for one right on the river. Fishing and lodging packages with meals are available.

CHACO CULTURE NATIONAL HISTORICAL PARK

This park contains massive and spectacular Puebloan buildings, evidence of 5000 years of human occupation, set in a remote high desert environment. The largest building, Pueblo Bonito, towers four stories tall and may have had 600 to 800 rooms and kivas. None of Chaco's sites have been reconstructed or restored.

Chaco was the center of a culture that extended far beyond the immediate area. Aztec and Salmon Ruins (see earlier in this chapter) were linked to the Great Houses of Chaco Canyon by carefully engineered 30-foot-wide roads. Very little of the road system is easily seen today, but about 450 miles have been identified from aerial photos and ground surveys. Clearly, this was a highly organized and integrated culture.

Respecting Ancient Sites

Some sites in Chaco Culture National Historical Park have been severely damaged. One is the 'Sun Dagger,' which consisted of three sandstone slabs arranged so that the sun shone through them to illuminate petroglyphs carved on nearby rocks – researchers found that solstice dates can be determined from the position of the sun on petroglyphs. Unfortunately, researchers and others have caused the slabs to shift, destroying their value as a calendar. The Sun Dagger is now closed to the public (though a film of it can be seen in the visitor center).

Many structures are fragile, and visitors are asked to refrain from climbing on them. Vandals and souvenir hunters are also a problem – leave pottery fragments and stones where they lie.

Orientation & Information

Many visitors arrive from the north (Hwy 44), pass by the campground and arrive at the visitor center (☎ 786-7014), PO Box 220, Nageezi, NM 87037, which is open 8 am to 5 pm daily year-round, and until 6 pm from Memorial Day weekend until Labor Day. website: www.nps.gov/chcu

Note that facilities within the park are minimal – no food, gas or supplies are available. The nearest provisions are along Hwy 44, 21 miles from the visitor center.

The archaeological sites are open from sunrise until sunset. Park admission is $8 per vehicle, or $4 for bikes; passes are honored. Free backcountry hiking permits (no camping) are available at the visitor center. Inquire at the visitor center for night sky programs (June to August).

Places to Stay

The **Gallo Campground** is open year-round on a first-come, first-served basis. Camping is $10 per site (no hookups). Toilets, grills and picnic tables are available. Bring your own wood or charcoal. Water is available at the visitor center parking lot only.

The nearest lodging is at the **Inn at the Post B&B** (☎ 632-3646), at Nageezi Trading Post on Hwy 44. Three rooms are $69/79 with shared/private bath. Kitchen privileges are available. Also see Cuba later in this chapter.

Getting There & Away

All routes to the park involve rough and unpaved dirt roads, which can become impassable after heavy rains or snow. You need a whole day for a trip here.

From the North Three miles south of the Nageezi Trading Post on Hwy 44/550 and about 50 miles west of Cuba, turn south at mile marker 112.5 on CR 7900, which is paved for 5 miles. Continue on the marked unpaved county road for 16 miles to the park entrance. This road is the preferred access route.

From the South Turn off I-40 at Thoreau and go north on Hwy 371 to Crownpoint

(24 miles). Four miles north of Crownpoint, turn right/east on Hwy 9 (also marked 57) and drive 14 miles to Pueblo Pintado. Then turn north and drive 20 miles on unpaved Hwy 57 to the park entrance.

JICARILLA APACHE INDIAN RESERVATION

The Apaches were comparatively late arrivals in the Southwest, migrating from the north in the 14th century. They were a hawkish group, taking advantage of the more peaceful Pueblo peoples who were already living here. Indeed, the Zuni Indian word for 'enemy,' *apachu,* led to the Apaches' present name. Jicarilla (pronounced hic-a-REE-ya) means 'little basket,' reflecting their skill in basket weaving and other crafts.

At the Jicarilla reservation, Apache crafts and outdoor pursuits such as hunting, fishing and skiing all draw visitors. About 3000 Jicarilla Apaches live on the 1360-sq-mile reservation.

Orientation & Information

The tiny town of Dulce, on Hwy 64 in the northern part of the reservation, is the tribal capital. The public relations office at the tribal administration office (☎ 759-3242 ext 218), PO Box 507, Dulce, 87528, and the Best Western Jicarilla Inn (☎ 759-3663) have tourist information. For the tribal police, call ☎ 759-3222.

Unlike at most reservations, alcohol is available at the hotel and in the Apache House of Liquor. No permits or fees are needed to drive through the reservation. Photography is usually permitted.

Things to See & Do

The **Jicarilla Arts & Crafts Museum** (free), on Hwy 64 near the hotel, has exhibits of baskets, beadwork, leather and feather work, though hours are erratic. The reservation's eight lakes and the Navajo River are stocked with trout and provide good **fishing**. From September to December, **hunting** for mule deer and elk is popular. Tribal licenses and information are available at the Jicarilla Game & Fish office

(☎ 759-3442) in Dulce. Trails for **cross-country skiing** are maintained in winter, but the nearest ski rental is in Pegosa, Colorado, about 60 miles north.

Special Events

The **Little Beaver Roundup** features a rodeo and dances on the third weekend in July. On September 14 and 15, the Gojiiya Harvest Festival at Stone Lake (19 miles south of Dulce on Tribal Hwy J8) has a powwow and rodeo. Call the tribal administration office for details on other ceremonials.

Places to Stay & Eat

Most of the fishing lakes have campgrounds. The **Best Western Jicarilla Inn** (☎ 759-3663) has 42 pleasant rooms for $65 to $95. For a meal, try the **Waterhole Café** (☎ 759-3356) or **El Ranchero** (☎ 759-3440) just east of town.

Chama to Española

East of the Jicarilla Apache Indian Reservation, Hwy 64 joins Hwy 84, crosses over the Continental Divide and drops into the small mountain community of Chama. South of Chama, the countryside becomes characteristic of the classic, luminously lit sandstone landscapes favored by artists such as Georgia O'Keeffe, who lived in Abiquiu.

CHAMA

☎ 505 • pop 1250 • elevation 7880 feet

Indians lived and hunted in this area for centuries, and Spanish farmers settled the Chama River Valley in the mid-1700s, but it was the arrival of the Denver & Rio Grande Railroad in 1880 that really put Chama on the map. Eventually, the railroad closed, but the prettiest part later reopened as the Cumbres & Toltec Scenic Railroad, one of the most scenic train trips in the Southwest. Today, Chama attracts visitors with year-round outdoor activities, particularly hunting and fishing, and the scenic railroad. There is no public transportation (apart from the railroad).

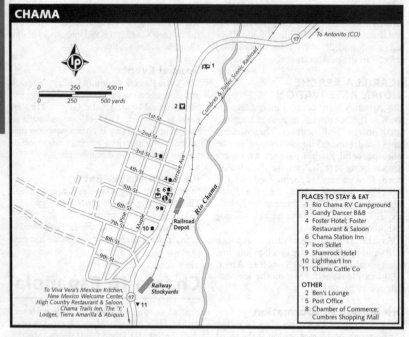

CHAMA

PLACES TO STAY & EAT
1 Rio Chama RV Campground
3 Gandy Dancer B&B
4 Foster Hotel; Foster
   Restaurant & Saloon
6 Chama Station Inn
7 Iron Skillet
9 Shamrock Hotel
10 Lightheart Inn
11 Chama Cattle Co

OTHER
2 Ben's Lounge
5 Post Office
8 Chamber of Commerce;
   Cumbres Shopping Mall

Orientation & Information

Downtown Chama is on Hwy 17, 1½ miles
north of the so-called Y junction of Hwy
84/64 with Hwy 17. The main street is variously called Main, Terrace Ave or Hwy 17;
the intersection, known as the Y, is the main
reference point in town. The New Mexico
Welcome Center (☎ 756-2235) at the Y and
the friendly chamber of commerce (☎ 756-
2306, 800-477-0149), 2291 Main St, are open
weekdays, though their hours may be sporadic. Write to them at PO Box 306, Chama,
NM 87520. The chamber of commerce also
has a website (www.chamavalley.com). The
post office (☎ 756-2240) is at 199 W 5th St.
There is no local police force, but the state
police (☎ 756-2343) are a quarter mile south
of the New Mexico Welcome Center on
Hwy 64/85.

The high elevation makes the climate
cool. July temperatures range from 75°F in
the daytime to 40°F at night. January temperatures are about 32°F in the day, with
overnight lows well below 0°F. Snowfall
usually begins in October.

Cumbres & Toltec Scenic Railroad

This is both the longest (64 miles) and
highest (over the 10,015-foot-high Cumbres
Pass) authentic narrow-gauge steam railroad in the USA. Some carriages are fully
enclosed, but none are heated. It's a beautiful trip, particularly in September and
October during fall foliage, through mountains, canyons and high desert.

The train runs between Chama and Antonito, Colorado, every morning from mid-
May to mid-October. Several options for
riding the train are offered. You can take a
van to Antonito (a 1½ hour drive) and then
ride the train six hours back to Chama
($60/30 for adult/children). Alternatively,
simply take the train to Antonito ($50/25)
and don't return to Chama; or only go to the
midpoint of Osier, Colorado, then return to

your starting point ($40/20, six hours). Ask about other options, as well as occasional Moonlight Train Rides and Winter Weekend Excursions.

For reservations and information, call ☎ 756-2151 or ☎ 888-286-2737, write to PO Box 789, Chama, NM 87520, or check the website at www.cumbresandtoltec.com. Carriages with wheelchair lifts are available with seven-day advance notice. Drinking alcohol and smoking are not allowed on the trains. There is a snack bar and rest room on board, and the train makes a lunch stop in Osier, where you can buy lunch.

It is possible to get off at Osier and be picked up at a later date. This allows the option of backpacking and fishing in the San Juan Mountains. About 13 miles from Osier (on foot) is the HI/AYH *Conejos River Hostel* (☎ 719-376-2518), which is remote and uncrowded, except in July and for holiday weekends. Beds are $12/15 for hostel members/nonmembers, including a full breakfast. If you'd rather not hike so far in, you can get off the train at the sublet water station (between Osier and Antonito) and hike 6 miles downhill to the hostel. The hostel is 10 miles west of Antonito; if arriving by car, call for directions. Reservations are required, and it is likely closed in the winter.

Antonito, Colorado, is smaller than Chama and offers fewer lodging possibilities. Only a short walk into town is the *Narrow Gauge Railroad Inn* (☎ 719-376-5441, 800-323-9469) with singles/doubles for $39/53.

Activities

You can fish in many lakes and streams year-round, and fly-fishing is particularly popular. From September to December, hunting for elk and other large game attracts visitors, while in the summer, horseback riding and boating are favorite activities. During the long winter, cross-country skiing, snowshoeing and snowmobiling are big. Several outfitters in Chama provide guide and rental services. Los Rios River Runners (☎ 776-8854, 800-544-1181), in Taos, runs raft trips on the Chama River.

The following are recommended outfitters.

Chama Ski Service (☎ 756-2492) – snowshoes and cross-country ski rentals

Cumbres Nordic Adventures (☎ 756-2746, 888-660-9878) – backcountry ski tours, yurt rentals website: www.yurtsogood.com

High Country Fishing (☎ 588-7674) – stream and lake fishing

Kayak Kerr (☎ 588-9371) – kayak trips

Ken's Pontoon Express (☎ 756-2900) – Lake Heron boat tours

Reid Hollo (☎ 756-2685) – horseback rides and big game guide

5M Outfitters (☎ 588-7003) – hunting, horse packing

Tricky Dickie's Snowmobile Tours (☎ 588-7657)

Special Events

The Chama Chile Classic Cross-Country Ski Race attracts hundreds of competitors to 5km and 10km races in early or mid-February. The Chama Valley Music Festival features national and international acts every Friday and Saturday in July. Early August sees Chama Days, with a rodeo, firefighters' water fight, chile cook off and several other festivities.

Places to Stay

Rates for high season (May to October) are given below. Most of the lodges and cabins are south of the Y intersection on your way into town from Abiquiu. Also see Tierra Amarilla and Around later in this chapter.

On the Chama River at the north end of town, *Rio Chama RV Campground* (☎ 756-2303) has a view of a railroad bridge, so you can watch (and hear) the steam train. Tent/RV sites go for $11.50/15. It is open from May to mid-October.

Built in 1881, the *Foster Hotel* (☎ 756-2296), opposite the train depot, offers old but clean rooms ($40s). Other simple places with rooms for around $50 include the *Shamrock Hotel* (☎ 756-2416, 800-982-8679, 501 S Terrace Ave) and the *Y Motel* (☎ 756-2166, 2450 S Hwy 84/64), near the Y.

In the mid-range category, the *Chama Trails Inn* (☎ 756-2156, 800-289-1421), 2362 S Hwy 17 by the Y, has 15 rooms ($65 to $85), each with New Mexican decor, a refrigerator and TV. The *Chama Station Inn* (☎ 756-2315, 423 S Terrace Ave), opposite the railroad depot, is one of Chama's earliest lodges. Renovated in 1993, it offers eight attractive rooms for $60 to $75. It's open from May to October only.

The following places are found along the Rio Chama on Hwy 84/64, about a mile south of the Y, and all are within a short walk of good river fishing. Close enough to the river to hear the water, *Spruce Lodge* (☎ 756-2593, 866-695-6343) offers a dozen rustic cabins, some with kitchenettes, for $45 to $95. Nearby, *Little Creel Lodge* (☎ 756-2382, 800-242-6259) has 64 RV sites and 13 cabins starting at around $50. The *Elkhorn Lodge & Café* (☎ 756-2105, 800-532-8874), with rooms for $66/75 single/double and 11 cabins (some accommodate up to ten) in the $70 to $125 range, can arrange outdoor activities. Join 'em for a chuckwagon barbecue dinner on the river.

Housed in an early 1900s house, *Gandy Dancer B&B* (☎ 756-2191, 800-424-6702, 299 Maple Ave) offers seven rooms, an outdoor hot tub and views. The helpful hosts provide local information, reservations and dinners (November to March) or box lunches on request. Rates are $95 to $115, including full breakfast.
website: www.gandydancerbb.com

The two-room *Lightheart Inn* (☎ 756-2908, 631 Terrace Ave) is run by a woman who is a certified masseuse and reiki master. After your massage, relax in the hot tub.

Places to Eat

For inexpensive meals, *Viva Vera's Mexican Kitchen* (☎ 756-2557, 2202 S Hwy 17), 400 yards north of the Y, serves good Mexican food, beer and wine. You can get a decent lunch for about $5 and dinner for $8 to $13 at the *Iron Skillet* (☎ 756-1215), a no-frills café convenient to the railroad depot. The *High Country Restaurant & Saloon* (☎ 756-2384, 2289 S Hwy 17) has a saloon out of the Wild West. The budget-conscious will find burgers and Mexican food; others may opt for steak and seafood, with entrées up to $22. The *Chama Cattle Co* (☎ 756-2808,

1128 S Hwy 17), which has steaks and the 'Blue Duck Microbrewery,' is newer.

Entertainment

Inexpensive and old-fashioned, *Foster Restaurant & Saloon* opens at 6 am. It's a good place to relax with a beer. A pool table, dancing and live music on some weekend nights attract locals to *Ben's Lounge* (☎ 756-2922).

TIERRA AMARILLA & AROUND

Tiny Tierra Amarilla, 15 miles south of Chama on Hwy 84/64, is the Rio Arriba County seat and has several old buildings, but Chama offers many more visitor services. From TA (as it is locally known), scenic Hwy 64 heads east over a 10,000-foot pass in the Tusas Mountains to Taos, 80 miles away. This road is closed in winter.

Just north of TA and slightly west of Hwy 84/64 is the village of Los Ojos. Here, visit **Tierra Wools** (☎ 588-7231 888-709-0979), a weaving cooperative in a rustic, century-old building. On the weekends, watch traditional weavers at work, hand spinning, dying and weaving. All the products are for sale. You can stay at a two bedroom guest house for $65/85 in the winter/summer; ask about weaving class packages that also include accommodations.
website: www.handweavers.com

Three miles north of TA, Hwy 512 heads east of Hwy 84/64 to scenic **Brazos Canyon**, which has spectacular cliffs. Six miles west of TA on Hwy 95, **Heron Lake State Park** (☎ 588-7470), PO Box 31, Rutheron, NM 87563, offers excellent fishing (a record-breaking 36lb lake trout was caught in 1999) and hiking. Motorboats are limited to trolling speed, and sailing, canoeing and windsurfing are popular. Heron Lake Store (☎ 588-7436) has fishing gear, boat rental, a café and a grocery and liquor store. From Heron Lake, a 6-mile trail takes you to **El Vado Lake State Park** (☎ 588-7247), PO Box 29, Tierra Amarilla, NM 87575, which lies 14 miles southwest on Hwy 112. Similar to Heron Lake, this lake allows water-skiing. The Rio Chama can be rafted from the park south to the Abiquiu Dam with a BLM permit. Both parks charge $4 for day use and allow camping (see Places to Stay).

Places to Stay

At *El Vado Lake Campground* 80 developed sites with bathroom and showers cost $10; on the west and south end are primitive sites for $8. The larger *Heron Lake Campground* has 53 sites with partial/full hookups for $15/19 and about 200 sites without hookups for $8. There are bathrooms, showers and drinking water. You can camp at undeveloped sites for $6.

Set on 400 acres on the road to Brazos Canyon, the handsome *Timbers at Chama* (☎ 588-7950) charges from $100 for a double to $200 for two in a private cabin by a fishing hole and a stream ($50 each additional adult). Fishing guides, mountain bikes, horseback riding and snowmobiling are available for an additional charge. website: www.thetimbersatchama.com

CARSON NATIONAL FOREST

Highway 64 between Tierra Amarilla (TA) and Taos crosses this forest. In Tres Piedras, 50 miles east of TA, there is a ranger station (☎ 758-8678). Canjilon, 3 miles east of Hwy 84 on Hwy 115 and about 17 miles south of TA, has another ranger station (☎ 684-2489). The *Canjilon Lakes Campgrounds*, open May to October, are 13 miles northeast of Canjilon along dirt roads at an elevation of 9800 feet. There are 52 sites ($5) with toilets but no drinking water. Some 12 miles south of Canjilon, just off Hwy 84, is the *Echo Amphitheater Campground*, named·after the natural red rock bowl in which it is located. The campground is open all year, and it has drinking water and toilets ($2).

Further information about the Carson National Forest is available from the Supervisor (☎ 758-6200), PO Box 558, Taos, NM 87571.

ABIQUIU

☎ 505 • pop 500 • elevation 6800 feet

The tiny community of Abiquiu is famous as the place where renowned artist Georgia O'Keeffe lived and painted. With the Chama River flowing through farmland and spectacular rock landscape, the area continues to attract artists, and many live and work in Abiquiu. There isn't much of a town here, but a few interesting places make this a worthwhile and relaxing stop.

Things to See & Do

Georgia O'Keeffe died in 1986, aged 98, and her adobe house is open for limited visits. The Georgia O'Keeffe Foundation (☎ 685-4539) offers one-hour **tours of O'Keeffe's home** ($22) four times a day, by reservation only, on Tuesday, Thursday and Friday from April to November. Tours can be booked months in advance, so plan ahead.

The spiritual element of the landscape has lured more than artists: Two religious sanctuaries are perched in the hills. Muslims worship at **Dar Al Islam** (☎ 685-4515), an adobe mosque that welcomes visitors. From Hwy 84, take Hwy 554 (southeast of Abiquiu) towards El Rito, cross the Chama River, take your first left onto County Rd 155 and follow it for 3 miles. The mosque is up a dirt road on the right. Day visitors are welcome to join the monks in prayer at the **Christ in the Desert Monastery** (see Places to Stay & Eat); to get there take Forest Service Rd 151, a dirt road off of Hwy 84 just south of Echo Amphitheater or five miles north of Ghost Ranch, and drive 13 beautiful miles.

At **Ghost Ranch Conference Center** (☎ 685-4333, 877-804-4678), owned by the Presbyterian Church, you can watch scientists painstakingly excavate dinosaur bones from locally quarried rock. This is where *City Slickers* was filmed, and it is a spectacular spot, with adobe buildings, an outdoor pool, and hiking trails nestled in the hills among the red rocks and grassy fields. Ghost ranch hosts a wide assortment of seminars in subjects ranging from photography to natural history. Even if you're not participating in a seminar, you can spend the night (see Places to Stay & Eat). website: www.ghostranch.org

Surrounded by red rock and high-desert terrain, **Abiquiu Dam & Reservoir** (☎ 685-4371) is a beautiful spot for a swim.

Places to Stay & Eat

From mid-April to October, tent/RV sites at Abiquiu Dam are $10/15. The rest of the year they are free.

The Southwestern-style *Abiquiu Inn* (☎ 685-4378, 800-447-5621), on Hwy 84 south of Abiquiu, has 19 units for $60 to $100, double. Ask to see a room, as some are quite nice and others are standard. Two lovely two-bedroom casitas with views onto the bosque are $120 to $140 for up to four people. The adjoining *Café Abiquiu* serves tasty and reasonably priced New Mexican and Middle Eastern dishes. The café and inn are owned by the muslims, and no liquor is served.

Set against the desert hills and surrounded by federal wilderness, the secluded adobe *Christ in the Desert Monastery* (fax 419-831-9113, porter@christdesert.org) is a Benedictine monastery that invites guests to share in their lifestyle through 'charity, prayer, spiritual reading and manual labor.' Incredible hiking trails surround the monastery, and guests are encouraged to retreat into silence. Ten single rooms, 3 double rooms and a suite are available for a minimum of two nights. A $50 reservation charge is required, but beyond that guests are asked to 'pay what they can afford.' They suggest a $50 to $75 donation, depending on the room, per night. Meals, eaten in silence except for prayer or music, are included with the room and are served in the refectory.
website: www.christdesert.org

At *Ghost Ranch* (see Things to See & Do), a double with dorm-style bathroom costs $47, and a double room with shared/private bath is $55/65. All rates are per person and include three meals a day in the cafeteria.

There are a few small and peaceful B&Bs to choose from in this area. *Las Parras de Abiquiu* (☎ 685-4200, 800-817-5955), which translates as 'Grapevines of Abiquiu,' is a lovely spot located on 60 acres across from the elementary school on Hwy 84. Two rooms with private patios and fireplaces overlook the bosque ($110 including a full breakfast), and you can help yourself to organic fruits and vegetables from their garden.

Two rooms at the *Old Abiquiu B&B* (☎ 685-4784), next to the church ruins on the south end of Hwy 84, are nestled in the woods overlooking the river. Also try *Casablanca* (☎ 685-4505). Rates at all both range from $55 to $95.
website: www.oldabiquiu.com

Everyone seems to hang out at *Bodes* (☎ 685-4422), a good deli and small grocery store across from the village plaza. It is open until 8 pm on most days, and on winter nights, this may be the only place in town to eat. In the tiny oasis of El Rito, north of Abiquiu on Hwy 554, is *El Farolito* (☎ 581-9509). This well recommended café serves up good New Mexican fare.

Pajarito Plateau & Jemez Mountains

A series of massive volcanic explosions occurred more than one million years ago and blew an estimated 100 cubic miles (some authorities suggest 450 cubic miles) of ash and pumice into the air. (Compare this to the paltry .25 cubic miles ejected by the famous 1980 eruption of Mt St Helens in Washington State.) Eventually, the volcano collapsed in upon itself, leaving behind a massive caldera surrounded by fingerlike plateaus kicking off into what are now called the Jemez Mountains. Hunter-gatherers lived in the area for thousands of years. The Rio Grande Ancestral Puebloan Indians arrived in about AD 1200 and stayed for almost 400 years, leaving many ancient buildings in the area – 7000 by one account.

With mountain creeks engulfed in wildflowers, red rock and pine forest, this area offers camping, hiking, cross-country skiing, natural hot springs and fishing. Within miles of each other, the Valles Grande Caldera, Bandelier National Monument and Los Alamos evidence the iconographic geological, human and atomic history of the American West.

LOS ALAMOS

☎ 505 • pop 20,000 • elevation 7400 feet

Los Alamos, hugging the national forest and perched on mesas overlooking the desert, offers a fascinating dynamic in which souvenir T-shirts emblazoned with atomic explosions and 'La Bomba' wine are sold next to books on pueblo history and wilderness hiking.

Average high/low temperatures are 80/56°F in July and 40/19°F in January.

Orientation

Built on long thin mesas separated by steep canyons, Los Alamos has a confusing layout that takes some getting used to. The main entrance from the east is Hwy 502, which branches into the east-west streets of Canyon Rd, Central Ave and Trinity Dr – these are the main streets of town. Central Ave and Canyon Rd form an oval enclosing the heart of town. Canyon and Central merge on the west side of town as Canyon Rd and meet back up with Trinity at Hwy 501. The highway veers around past the laboratory towards Bandelier National Monument and turns into Hwy 4.

Information

The chamber of commerce (☎ 662-8105, 800-444-0707), 109 Central Park Sq, Los Alamos, NM 87544, is open 10 am to 2 pm Monday to Friday, longer from June through August. website: www.visit.losalamos.com

The forest service office (☎ 667-5120), on the east side of the pond at 475 20th St, Suite B, 87544, is open 8 am to 4 pm Monday, Wednesday and Friday.

Other services include the hospital (☎ 662-4201), 3917 West Rd; the library (☎ 662-8250), 2400 Central Ave; and the police (☎ 662-8222), 2500 Trinity Dr.

Two good bookstores are R Books (☎ 662-7257), 111 Central Park Sq, which serves coffee drinks, and Otowi Station Museum Shop and Bookstore, which has a

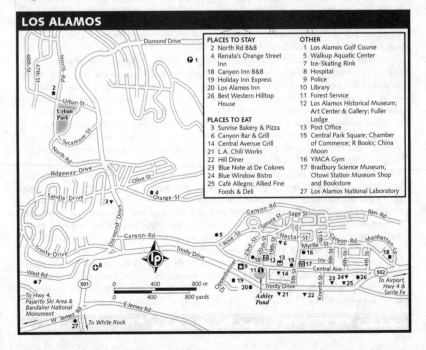

LOS ALAMOS

PLACES TO STAY
2 North Rd B&B
4 Renata's Orange Street Inn
18 Canyon Inn B&B
19 Holiday Inn Express
20 Los Alamos Inn
26 Best Western Hilltop House

PLACES TO EAT
3 Sunrise Bakery & Pizza
6 Canyon Bar & Grill
14 Central Avenue Grill
21 L.A. Chili Works
22 Hill Diner
23 Blue Note at De Colores
24 Blue Window Bistro
25 Café Allegro; Allied Fine Foods & Deli

OTHER
1 Los Alamos Golf Course
5 Walkup Aquatic Center
7 Ice-Skating Rink
8 Hospital
9 Police
10 Library
11 Forest Service
12 Los Alamos Historical Museum; Art Center & Gallery; Fuller Lodge
13 Post Office
15 Central Park Square; Chamber of Commerce; R Books; China Moon
16 YMCA Gym
17 Bradbury Science Museum; Otowi Station Museum Shop and Bookstore
27 Los Alamos National Laboratory

fine selection of science and regional books, next to the science museum.

Things to See & Do

On Central Ave, the well-designed **Bradbury Science Museum** (☎ 667-4444) covers atomic history (free admission). Fuller Lodge, built in 1928 to serve as the dining hall for the boys' school, was purchased by the US government for the Manhattan Project. Inside are two small but good museums. The **Los Alamos Historical Museum** (☎ 662-4493) features atomic age popular culture artifacts and exhibits on the social history of life 'on the hill' during the secret project. Ask for a self-guided downtown **walking-tour** pamphlet. Also in Fuller Lodge is the **Art Center at Fuller Lodge** (☎ 662-9331), with mixed-media shows of local and national artists.

At the Walkup Aquatic Center (☎ 662-8170), you can **swim** in the nation's highest Olympic-size pool. It has been the training ground of several Olympic medal-winning swimmers who claim the elevation helps them build endurance. Pajarito Mountain Ski Area (☎ 662-5725, 888-662-7669), about 7 miles west of downtown, offers challenging **skiing**. It's open Friday, Saturday and Sunday. Lift tickets are $33/22 for adults/children. An outdoor **ice skating** rink (☎ 662-4500), 4475 West Rd, is open from Thanksgiving through February.

From Bandelier National Monument (see Bandelier National Monument later in this chapter), take Hwy 44 west to **Valle Grande**, one of the world's largest calderas. From the edge, it is awe-inspiring to imagine the volcano that produced such an immense crater. Ask at the visitor center about the

---

Atomic City

In 1943, Los Alamos, then a boy's school perched on a 7400-foot mesa, was chosen as the top-secret headquarters of the Manhattan Project (the code name for the research and development of the atomic bomb). The 772-acre site, accessed by two dirt roads, had no gas or oil lines, only one wire service, and it was surrounded by forest.

Isolation and security affected every aspect of life on 'the hill.' Scientists, their wives, men and women of the army who were there to provide security, and local Hispanics and Native Americans who had been recruited as domestic help and manual laborers, lived together in a makeshift community. Surrounded by guards and barbed wire and unknown even to nearby Santa Fe, the residents' postal address was simply 'Box 1663, Santa Fe.' It was indeed the secret city on the hill, a shangri-la.

Before arriving by train in Santa Fe, the scientists, most from large universities, including University of Chicago and Princeton, were told to 'go to 109 E Palace Street, Santa Fe New Mexico. There you will find out how to complete your trip'. Phyliss Fisher, a wife of one of the scientists, remembers her arrival: 'We dutifully followed our little map, found the address alright, and stared at it in amazement. The place was a bakery! Once in, we didn't know what to do. ...Lee finally stated that we were 'told to come here.' Silence reigned. More silence. Believe me, I fully expected the girl to break open a loaf of bread, surreptitiously extract from it a message written in code and slyly slip it to us.'

Not only was the residents' movement restricted and their mail censored, but they were without outside radio or telephone. Perhaps even more unsettling, most of the residents had no idea why they were living in Los Alamos. Knowledge was on a 'need to know' basis, meaning that everyone knew only as much as their job required them to know. Security pamphlets warned residents not to mention topographical details essential to the project. This made things particularly difficult for those residents who did not know what 'the project' was. As a wife of one of the scientists recalls, 'What details, thought I? Were the sunsets essential to the project? Were the mountains? The canyons?'

possibility of camping or hiking in the caldera; it has been private property but is expected to open to the public by 2004.

Organized Tours

Buffalo Tours (☎ 662-3965) offers 1½-hour van tours of the 'Atomic City' from March to November ($10/4.25 adults/children) – call to arrange tours off-season. Tickets and information are available at the Otowi Station Bookstore.

Places to Stay

You can camp for free at the top of the ski mountain from May to October. There are pit toilets and fire pits, but no water.

There is no strip with cheap motels, and the few accommodations in town are fairly standard. The *Los Alamos Inn* (☎ 662-7211, 800-279-9279, 2201 Trinity Dr) and the *Best*

Western Hilltop House (☎ 662-2441, 800-464-0936, 400 Trinity Dr) both have a restaurant and lounge. The new *Holiday Inn Express* (☎ 661-1110) is the nicest hotel. Rooms at all three range from $60 to $140, with more expensive suites available at the Best Western.

Three basic bed & breakfasts offer rooms from $55 to $95: *Renata's Orange Street Inn* (☎ 662-2651, 800-662-3180, 3496 Orange St), *Canyon Inn B&B* (☎ 662-9595, 800-662-2565, 80 Canyon Rd) and *North Road B&B* (☎ 662-3678, 800-279-2898, 2127 North Rd). The Orange St Inn has a website at www.losalamos.com/orangestreetinn, and the Canyon Inn's website is at www.canyoninnbnb.com.

Places to Eat

For a morning espresso jolt, head over to the *Café Allegro* (☎ 662-4040, 800 Trinity Dr),

---

Atomic City

Living conditions, exacerbated by tight and imperfect housing, further contributed to the sense that this life on the hill was neither normal nor permanent. Oppenheimer and other key figures lived in traditional log-style homes on Bathtub Row, called such because they had bathtubs. Other scientists lived in makeshift housing; four-family (and eight-family) dwellings, identical in appearance, painted green. There were no sidewalks; the streets were unpaved; the yards had no lawns, no trees, no flowers. The military lived in barracks, and maintenance staff lived in corrugated metal quonset huts, the poorest housing of all. The downpours of rain, typical of New Mexico, turned the hill into a mud swamp, and it was a daily chore to clean the mud or dust from the houses. Mysterious booms (part of the work of the lab) shook the walls.

On July 16, 1945, the scientists detonated the world's first atomic bomb at the Trinity Site in southern New Mexico, which is now part of the White Sands National Monument. Thirty-five miles west of Carrizozo travelers can visit Trinity Site (see Southeast New Mexico). The test was carried out above ground and resulted in a quarter-mile-wide crater and an 8-mile-high cloud mushrooming above the desert. This desolate area is fittingly called Jornada del Muerto (Journey of Death) and is overlooked by 8638-foot Oscura Peak (Darkness Peak on state maps). Only two public visits are allowed annually – on the first Saturdays in April and October. Call the Alamogordo Chamber of Commerce (☎ 505-437-6120, 800-826-0294) for information (see the Alamogordo section of the Southeast New Mexico chapter).

Upon the US's detonation of the atomic bomb in Japan, the secret city of Los Alamos was exposed to the public and its residents finally understood why they were there. The city continued to be clothed in secrecy, however, until 1957, when restrictions on visiting were lifted. Today, the lab is still the backbone of the town, and a budding tourist industry proudly embraces the town's atomic history with souvenirs like Atomic City T-shirts (emblazoned with a red-and-yellow exploding bomb) and La Bomba wine.

in the Mari-Mac Shopping Center. It has sandwiches, pastries and newspapers 7 am to 5 pm Monday to Friday, 8 am to 2 pm on weekends. Also in the shopping center is **Allied Fine Foods & Deli** (☎ 662-2777), where you can get elk burgers, hot pastrami and other deli delights for about $6. On the north side of the shopping center is the recommended **Blue Window Bistro** (☎ 662-6305, 813 Central Ave). In this brightly colored café, lunches such as gyros and poached salmon are about $7, and dinners of lump crab enchiladas and wild mushroom ragout range from $9 to $17.

The **Blue Note at De Colores** (☎ 662-6285, 820 Trinity Dr) serves good New Mexican fare and has a pool table. **Sunrise Bakery & Pizza** (☎ 661-8000), on Diamond Dr north of Canyon Rd, offers a great selection of breads (including green chile cheddar, potato onion dill, six grain), good lookin' donuts, sandwiches and pizza.

A fine array of American diner fare is served daily at the popular and inexpensive **Hill Diner** (☎ 662-9745, 1315 Trinity Dr). For a more upscale and contemporary setting, with high ceilings and big windows that open onto downtown Los Alamos, try the **Central Avenue Grill** (☎ 662-2005, 1789 Central Ave). The **China Moon** (☎ 662-2883), in Central Park Sq, has a lunch buffet for about $6.

Basically just a shack on the side of the road, my favorite spot is the tiny **L.A. Chili Works** (☎ 662-7591, 1743 Trinity Dr), which serves great chile and is packed with scientists and other locals for breakfast and lunch. It's open 6 am to 1 pm Tuesday to Friday and 7 to 11 am on Saturday. The best place in town for a beer and basic bar fare is the **Canyon Bar & Grill** (☎ 662-3333, 163 Central Park Sq). It's a local hangout with a long bar, pinball, pool and live music and dancing on the weekends – you won't find any glitz or Southwestern affectations here.

Getting There & Around

Public transportation to Los Alamos is limited and liable to change. Rio Grande Air (☎ 877-435-9742) flies daily to Albuquerque for about $70 one way. Call Roadrunner Shuttle (424-3367) for transportation to Santa Fe ($35, advanced reservations required).

Los Alamos Bus (☎ 662-2080) offers local bus service.

BANDELIER NATIONAL MONUMENT

Rio Grande Puebloans lived here until the mid-1500s. Today, several sites (none restored), a convenient location and spectacular landscape make Bandelier an excellent choice for those interested in ancient pueblos. Almost 50 sq miles of canyons, offering backpacking trails and camping, are protected within the monument. The **Ceremonial Cave**, which is 140 feet above the canyon floor and reached by climbing four ladders, is a highlight of a visit to Bandelier. Mesa-top **Tsankawi**, an unexcavated site 13 miles north of the visitor center on Hwy 4, provides good views and a steep 2-mile trail.

The park, 12 miles from Los Alamos, is open 8 am to 5 pm daily and to 6 pm from Memorial Day to Labor Day. Admission is $10 per vehicle; passes are honored. The bookshop (☎ 672-3861) sells trail maps and guidebooks, which can be obtained in advance from Bandelier National Monument, Los Alamos, NM 87544. You can also get information from the website (www.nps.gov/band).

Juniper Campground, set among the pines near the monument entrance, offers about a hundred campsites ($10), drinking water, toilets, picnic tables and fire grates, but no showers or hookups. It may be closed November to March. You can camp in the backcountry with a free permit that must be obtained in person from the visitor center.

JEMEZ SPRINGS

☎ 505 • pop 450 • elevation 6300 feet

The tiny town of Jemez Springs, a pleasant spot squeezed into a narrow river valley flanked by red rock, offers a **bathhouse** (☎ 829-3303) with body treatments, a few monasteries and a Zen Buddhist center. A Santa Fe National Forest Ranger Station (☎ 829-3535), a mile north of town or in the Walatowa Visitor Center (see Jemez Pueblo, later), has information about natural hot spring sites, camping, hiking, fishing, hunting and other activities in the surrounding national forest.

Called Giusewa ('Place of Boiling Waters') by the original inhabitants, the Jemez Pueblo Indians, the **Jemez State Monument** (☎ 829-3530) now houses both Indian sites and the ruins of a Spanish colonial church completed in 1622 ($3).

Just over 2 miles north of the town, look for **Soda Dam** – strange mineral formations across Jemez Creek on the right side of the highway. The natural dam was formed by spring water heavily laden with minerals.

Places to Stay & Eat

The Santa Fe National Forest operates several campgrounds along Hwy 4, open May to October; most charge $8 a site and provide drinking water, toilets and grills but no showers or RV hookups. Free dispersed camping (no facilities) is also possible.

At La Cueva, 9 miles north of Jemez Springs, Hwy 4 intersects with Hwy 126; eight miles west along Hwy 126, *Fenton Lake* (☎ 829-3630) provides year-round camping in 30 sites ($7). Five sites have RV hookups ($11).

In town, the *Laughing Lizard Inn & Café* (☎ 829-3108, 888-532-5290), has four rooms, each decorated differently, for $65 to $75. The café serves good sandwiches, salads, burritos and pizzas in the $6 to $9 range. It is closed Monday in the summer, and open only Thursday to Sunday in the winter.

The lovely *River Dancer* (☎ 829-3262, 16445 Hwy 4), 1 mile south of town, offers six rooms decorated in Southwestern style, with TV, telephone and air-conditioning, for $99 to $109; a three-room casita sleeping four to eight is $129 to $179. Healing arts and massages can be arranged in advance.

The *Desert Willow* (☎ 829-3410) has two pleasant rooms for $110 and a cottage for $135. Both are right on the river, nestled among Cottonwoods under the Jemez Canyon cliffs.

website: www.desertwillowbandb.com

Nine miles north of town, *La Cueva Lodge* (☎ 829-3814) is a basic motel with 15 rooms for $55 and a restaurant next door.

Los Ojos Saloon (☎ 829-3547), an Old West–style saloon with food and pool tables, is open daily.

JEMEZ PUEBLO

The Jemez were among the most active opponents of the Spanish during the Pueblo Revolt of the 1680s and 1690s, and they are the only people who speak the Towa language. Today, their pueblo, 12 miles south of Jemez Springs, is more conservative than most and is generally closed to visitors. Entrance to the pueblo requires a permit, though with advance notice the visitor center can sometimes arrange tours. Contact the Walatowa Visitor Center (☎ 834-7235), PO Box 100, Jemez Pueblo, NM 87024.

website: www.jemezpueblo.org

The scenery around and south of the pueblo is spectacular and intensely red. On weekends between April and October, visitors can buy food and local arts and crafts at Red Rock, three miles north of the pueblo and just south of Jemez Springs on Hwy 4. The small museum at Walatowa Visitor Center, across from Red Rock, describes the pueblo's history and crafts. The pueblo is in the middle of the extensive Jemez Indian Reservation, which the people use for agriculture, hunting and fishing. Two fishing areas open to the public (with a permit from the visitor center) are Holy Ghost Spring and Dragonfly, about 18 and 24 miles north of San Ysidro on Hwy 44.

The Jemez are good potters and make storyteller doll pots and tan background animal ceramics. Some local potters have signs posted along Hwy 4 inviting visitors to stop into their houses. During the first weekend in December and over Memorial Day weekend,

Coyote

the pueblo hosts an arts and crafts show, with traditional food and dance demonstrations. There are several feast days with ceremonial dances that the pueblo does not publicize, to maintain the privacy of the tribe. Contact the visitor center for information about which ones may be open to the general public. Photography, recording and sketching are prohibited.

CUBA
☎ 505 • pop 800 • elevation 6200 feet
Set in the mountains, Cuba is a convenient stop on the way to or from Chaco Culture National Historical Park (see Chaco Culture National Historical Park earlier in this chapter) and may be a good option for a place to stay, since accommodation closer to Chaco is limited (particularly from June to August). It's about another 50 miles to the turnoff to Chaco. The Santa Fe National Forest Ranger Station (☎ 289-3265), PO Box 130, Cuba, NM 87103, is on the south side of Hwy 44 and the visitor center (☎ 289-3808), also found on Hwy 44, is open sporadically.

Highway 126 east of Cuba leads 11 miles to *Clear Creek* and *Rio Las Vacas* campgrounds, operated by the USFS and open May to October ($5). Highway 126 continues 15 miles to Fenton Lake (see Places to Stay & Eat in the Jemez Springs section). Though the dirt road is impassable after bad weather, it's a beautiful drive if you can get through. There are other campgrounds along the way, plus backpacking opportunities.

Set in 360 beautiful acres in the Nacimiento Mountains, the friendly and recommended *Circle A Ranch Hostel* (☎ 289-3350) is a real gem. The lovely old adobe lodge, with exposed beams, beautiful grassy grounds, hiking trails and a classic kitchen, is a peaceful and relaxing place to hang out. Dorms cost $13; private rooms range from $38 to $48 (the pink room is particularly nice, with iron beds and a great view). The hostel is open May 1 to October 15. You can take the TNM&O/Greyhound bus to Cuba (there's no official stop) and call for a pickup.

Of the few cheap motels in the town, the best is the *Frontier Motel* (☎ 289-3474). With a beautiful outdoor patio, a handsome interior and delicious New Mexican food, *El Bruno's Cantina y Restaurante* (☎ 289-9429), on Hwy 44, is one of the best restaurants in northwest New Mexico.

ZIA PUEBLO
Once home to some 6000 people, Zia Pueblo was destroyed during the Pueblo Revolt of the 1680s. Now, less than a thousand people live here. The inhabitants of Zia Pueblo are famous for their pottery. A stylized red sun motif on a yellow background, found on a Zia pot, has been incorporated into the state flag.

The annual ceremonial is on August 15, and the public may attend. The pueblo is about 6 miles southeast of San Ysidro off Hwy 44 (or 17 miles northwest of Bernalillo). Further information is available from the Zia Pueblo Governor's Office (☎ 867-3304), 135 Capital Square Dr, Zia Pueblo, NM 87053-6013.

I-40 Corridor West of Albuquerque

You can zoom along I-40 the 150 miles from Albuquerque to the Arizona border in a little over two hours, but don't. Several pueblos and national monuments are well worth visiting.

LAGUNA PUEBLO
This Indian reservation (about 40 miles west of Albuquerque or 30 miles east of Grants) consists of six small villages. Although it was founded in 1699, it is the youngest of New Mexico's pueblos. The founders were escaping from the Spaniards and came from many different pueblos, so the Laguna people have a very diverse ethnic background. Laguna Pueblo was built on uranium-rich land, and most inhabitants were involved in the local, and very profitable, post-WWII mining boom. Now,

they are involved in a cleanup and reclamation program.

The **San José Mission** (☎ 552-9330) is visible from I-40 and reached from exit 114. The stone and adobe church was completed in 1705 and houses fine examples of early Spanish-influenced religious art. Hours are sporadic.

The main feast days are two St Joseph's (San José's) Days on March 18 and September 19, St John's (San Juan's) Day on June 24, St Laurence's (San Lorenzo's) Day on August 10 and Christmas Eve. Contact Laguna Pueblo (☎ 552-6654), PO Box 194, Laguna, NM 87026, for more information.

ACOMA PUEBLO

Known as 'Sky City' because of its fantastic mesa-top location (7000 feet above sea level and 367 feet above the surrounding plateau), Acoma Pueblo is well worth a visit. People have lived here since the 12th century, making it one of the oldest continuously inhabited settlements in North America. The famous Acoma pottery is sold by individual artists on the mesa; there is a distinction between 'traditional' (made with clay dug on the reservation) and 'ceramic' (made elsewhere with inferior clay and simply painted by the artist), so ask the vendor. To reach Sky City, you must take guided tours ($9/6 for adults/children), which leave from the visitor center at the bottom of the mesa. (☎ 469-1052, 800-747-0181), PO Box 309, Acoma, NM 87034. Tours go daily except for July 10–13 and either the first or second weekend in October, when the pueblo is closed to visitors. Though you must ride the shuttle to the top of the mesa, you can return to the visitor center on your own, walking down the rock path.

Sky City events include a Governor's Feast in February, a Harvest Dance on San Esteban Day (September 2) and festivities at the San Esteban Mission on December 25-28. Photography permits cost $10. No videos or tripods are permitted. For precise dates or information, contact the visitor center. The visitor center is 13 miles south of I-40 exit 96 (15 miles east of Grants) or I-40

exit 108 (50 miles west of Albuquerque). The pueblo-run casino by the highway has a hotel. There is no public transportation.

GRANTS

☎ 505 • pop 10,500 • elevation 6400 feet

Originally an agricultural center and railway stop founded in the 1880s, Grants experienced a major mining boom when uranium was discovered in 1950. Today Grants is basically just a strip, but several motels make it a convenient, if uninteresting, base from which to explore the region.

Greyhound (☎ 285-6268), 1101 W Santa Fe Ave, has several daily buses to Albuquerque ($12.60, 1¼ hours), Flagstaff, Arizona ($48, 5½ hours) and beyond.

Orientation & Information

Santa Fe Ave (business I-40, Hwy 118 or Route 66) is the main drag through town. It runs parallel and north of I-40 between exits 81 and 85.

The chamber of commerce (☎ 287-4802, 800-748-2142,) is at 100 Iron St. Its website is at www.grants.org. The Cibola National Forest Mount Taylor Ranger Station (☎ 287-8833), 1800 Lobo Canyon Rd, Grants, NM 87020, is open from 8 am to noon and 1 pm to 5 pm Monday to Friday. Other services include the library (☎ 287-7927), 525 W High St; the post office (☎ 287-3143), 816 W Santa Fe Ave; the hospital (☎ 287-4446), 1212 Bonita Ave; and the police (☎ 287-4404), on Roosevelt Ave near 1st St.

Things to See & Do

Sharing the chamber of commerce building, the **New Mexico Mining Museum** (☎ 287-4802) is the only uranium-mining museum in the world (they say). Although the mine no longer operates because of decreased demand for this mineral, it remains America's largest uranium reserve. You can go underground by elevator in a miner's cage ($3). Tours are offered daily from May to September, and from 9 am to 3 pm Monday to Friday during the rest of the year. The new **Dinamations Discovery Museum** (☎ 876-6999), just south of I-40 at exit 85, features huge dinosaur replicas and interactive displays.

The 11,301-foot peak of **Mt Taylor** is the highest in the area, and the mountain offers great views and hiking. Head northeast on Lobo Canyon Rd (Hwy 547) for about 13 miles to where it changes into gravel USFS Rd 239. Follow 239 and then USFS Rd 453 for another 3.3 miles to **La Mosca Lookout** at 11,000 feet, about a mile northeast of Mt Taylor's summit.

Special Events

The Mt Taylor Quadrathlon, usually held the second week in February, goes from Grants to Mt Taylor and combines cycling, running, cross-country skiing and snowshoeing. Individuals and teams of two to four athletes compete. In July is the Fire and Ice Route 66 Bike Rally, a two day Harley Davidson festival with motorcycle rodeo events and live music. The Chili Fiesta, on the first Saturday in October, celebrates chile with a chile cook off and other events.

Places to Stay

A surfeit of cheap lodging will delight the budget-conscious. June to August rates given here may drop out of season or rise over holiday weekends. Exit 85 off of I-40 has several newly built *chain motels*, including Days Inn, Super 8 and Holiday Inn Express, all of which look nice and charge anywhere from $45 to $90.

The USFS (☎ 287-8833) operates the *Lobo Canyon Campground*, 8 miles northeast on Lobo Canyon Rd and then 1½ miles east on unpaved USFS Rd 193. There are pit toilets but no water. The pleasantly wooded *Coal Mine Campground*, 10 miles northeast on Lobo Canyon Rd, has a nature trail, drinking water and flush toilets but no showers ($5). Both are open from mid-May to late October. The free, waterless *Ojo Redondo Campground*, about 20 miles west of town along unpaved USFS Rd 49 and USFS Rd 480, is open all year. At I-40 exit 80 is the *Blue Spruce RV Park* (☎ 287-2560), with tent/RV sites for $8/12.

Cheap motels on Santa Fe Ave, including *Leisure Lodge* (☎ 287-2991, 1204 E Santa Fe Ave) and *Western Host Motel* (☎ 287-4418, 1150 E Santa Fe Ave), offer doubles from $20 to $35.

Thirty miles southwest from Grants, the *Cimarron Rose* (☎ 783-4770, 800-856-5776, 689 Oso Ridge Rd), is conveniently located on Hwy 53 between El Morro and El Malpais (see El Malpais National Monument and El Morro National Monument later in this chapter) in the Zuni Mountains. With hiking in the Cibola National Forest just off the 20-acre property, it's a peaceful and pleasant rural alternative to the chain hotel options in Grants or Gallup. Two Southwestern-style suites, with tiles and hardwood floors (one with a kitchen) are $95 to $105. The website (www.cimarron rose.com) provides excellent links to regional and state attractions.

Places to Eat

Across from the Mining Museum is the funky and aptly named *Uranium Café* (☎ 287-7540, 519 W Santa Fe Ave), with an old Chevy parked in the middle of the restaurant and good green chile. It's open for breakfast and lunch only, and is closed Sunday. The busy *Monte Carlo Café* (☎ 287-9250, 721 W Santa Fe Ave) serves reasonably priced and tasty Southwestern food in a traditional setting. For food 24 hours a day, head to *Four B's Restaurant* (☎ 285-6697) on Santa Fe Ave just north of I-40 exit 85.

EL MALPAIS NATIONAL MONUMENT

El Malpais (pronounced el mahl-pie-ees; meaning 'bad land' in Spanish) is almost 200 sq miles of lava flows abutting adjacent sandstone. Five major flows have been identified, with the most recent 2000 to 3000 years old. Local Indian legend tells of 'rivers of fire,' and prehistoric Native Americans may have witnessed the final eruptions. There are cinder cones and spatter cones, smooth *pahoehoe* lava and jagged *aa* lava, ice caves and a 17-mile-long lava tube system.

Information
El Malpais is a hodgepodge of National Park Service (NPS) land, conservation areas and wilderness areas administered by the BLM, and private lands. Each area has different rules and regulations, and these change from year to year. The BLM (☎ 287-7911), PO Box 846, Grants, NM 97020-0846, in Grants and the BLM Ranger Station (☎ 240-0300) on Hwy 117, 9 miles south of I-40 exit 89, have permits and information for the Cibola Wilderness. El Malpais Information Center (☎ 783-4774), 22 miles southwest of Grants on Hwy 53, and the Superintendent, El Malpais National Monument (☎ 285-4641), 123 E Roosevelt Ave, Grants, NM 87020, have permits and information for the lava flows and NPS land. Backcountry camping is allowed, but a free permit is required. Alternatively, camp at the primitive *Narrows Campground* on the east side. The El Malpais Information Center website is at www.nps .gov/elma.

Things to See & Do
Though the terrain can be difficult, there are several opportunities for **hiking** through the monument. An interesting but very rough hike (wear heavy shoes or boots) is the 7½-mile (one way) Zuni-Acoma Trail, which leaves from Hwy 117 about 4 miles farther south of the ranger station. The trail crosses several lava flows and ends at Hwy 53 on the west side of the monument. Just beyond **La Ventana Natural Arch**, visible from Hwy 117 17 miles south of I-40, is the Narrows Trail, which is about 4 miles one way. Thirty miles south of I-40 is Lava Falls, a 1-mile loop.

County Rd 42 leaves Hwy 117 about 34 miles south of I-40 and meanders for 40 miles through the BLM country on the west side of El Malpais. It passes several craters, caves and lava tubes (reached by signed trails) and emerges at Hwy 53 near Bandera Crater. The road is unpaved, and a high-clearance 4WD is recommended. If you go **spelunking**, the park service requires each person to carry two sources of light and to wear a hard hat. Go with a companion – this is an isolated area. Hikers need a gallon of water per person per day.

The privately owned **Bandera Ice Cave** (☎ 783-4303), 25 miles southwest of Grants on Hwy 53, charges $8/4 for adults/children to peer down at a large cave with a chunk of ice in it year-round.

EL MORRO NATIONAL MONUMENT
Well worth a stop, this 200-foot sandstone outcropping, also known as 'Inscription Rock,' has been a travelers' oasis for thousands of years. Thousands of carvings, from petroglyphs in the pueblo at the top (circa 1250) to inscriptions by Spaniard conquistadors and Anglo pioneers, offer, as one Lonely Planet traveler wrote, 'graffiti as history.'

Orientation & Information
El Morro, 43 miles southwest of Grants and 56 miles southeast of Gallup on Hwy 53, is open 9 am to 7 pm daily from Memorial Day to Labor Day and to 5 pm the rest of the year. Admission is $3 for adults, free for children, and passes are honored. Two trails leave the visitor center. The paved, half-mile-loop **Inscription Rock Trail** is wheelchair accessible and the unpaved; 2-mile-loop **Mesa Top Trail** requires a steep climb to the pueblos. Trail access stops one hour before closing.

Further information is available from the Superintendent, El Morro (☎ 783-4226), Route 2, Box 43, Ramah, NM 87321-9603. website: www.nps.gov/elmo

Places to Stay & Eat
An NPS campground, with drinking water and pit toilets, is a mile before the visitor center ($5). It may close from October to April. *El Morro RV Park and Cabins* (☎ 783-4612), on Hwy 53 about 1 mile east of El Morro, offers six tent/RV sites for $7/10 and four cabins ($35 to $60) from mid-March to November. Also see Grants earlier in this chapter.

In the pleasant little town of Ramah, a few miles west of El Morro, the *Stagecoach Café* (☎ 783-4288) is open daily.

ZUNI PUEBLO

Zuni Pueblo, 35 miles south of Gallup, is famous for its jewelry making, and you can buy beautiful jewelry at little stores throughout the town. Most public buildings are stretched along Hwy 53, with side streets curving away into the pueblo. Photography is by permit only. Information is available from the Zuni Tribal Office (☎ 782-4481), PO Box 339, Zuni, NM 87327, or at the museum.

Things to See & Do

Walk past stone houses and beehive-shaped mud ovens to the massive **Our Lady of Guadalupe Mission** (☎ 782-4477), featuring impressive locally painted murals of about 30 life-size kachinas. The church dates from 1629, although it has been rebuilt twice since then. If no one is there when you want to visit, go to St. Anthony's Indian Mission School (☎ 782-2888) one block north of the old church and ask around – it's likely some one will be able to give you a tour.

The **A:shiwi A:wan Museum & Heritage Center** (☎ 782-4403) on Hwy 53 displays early photos and other tribal artifacts. Hours are 9 am to 3:30 pm weekdays and

10 am to 5 pm on Sundays, and admission is by donation. Next door, Pueblo of Zuni Arts & Crafts (☎ 782-5531) sells locally made jewelry, baskets and other crafts.

Special Events

The most famous ceremony is the all-night *Sha:lak'o* ceremonial dance held in late November or early December. In late August, the Zuni Tribal Fair features a powwow, local food, and arts and crafts stalls. Other ceremonials occur on varying dates – ask at the tribal office.

Places to Stay

The only place to stay at the pueblo is the friendly *Inn at Halona* (☎ 782-4547, 800-752-3278, 1 Shalaka Dr) behind Halona Plaza (go south from Hwy 53 at the only four-way stop in town). Be sure to check out each of the pleasant rooms and choose which one fits you, since each is very different and they all cost $85. Full breakfasts are served in the courtyard in the summer, and you can get room service from the grocery store in the back. To find the inn, ask at the grocery store at Halona Plaza.
website: www.halona.com

Information on primitive camping is available from the Zuni Tribal Office.

GALLUP

☎ 505 • pop 22,000 • elevation 6515 feet

Gallup dates back to 1881, when the railroad arrived. Soon thereafter, coal was discovered and Gallup remained an important mining town until the mid-20th century. Today, Gallup serves as the Navajo and Zuni peoples' major trading center, and, in turn, the many trading posts, pawnshops and arts & crafts galleries attract visitors. Though Gallup's economy relies on trade and tourism, in the winter especially, it is a pretty quiet and rather depressing town.

Orientation & Information

The famous old Route 66 (also called Hwy 66 and Historic 66) is the main drag through town and runs east-west, parallel to and south of I-40, the Rio Puerco and the railway line.

ZUNI PUEBLO

Zuni Indian Reservation

To Hwy 602 & Ramah

Zuni Tribal Offices

Post Office

Mustang Store

A:shiwi A:wan Museum & Heritage Center; Pueblo of Zuni Arts & Crafts

To Inn at Halona & Arizona

Malani

Our Lady of Guadalupe Mission

Old Mission Rd

Sunshine

Zuni River

0   100   200 m
0   100   200 yards

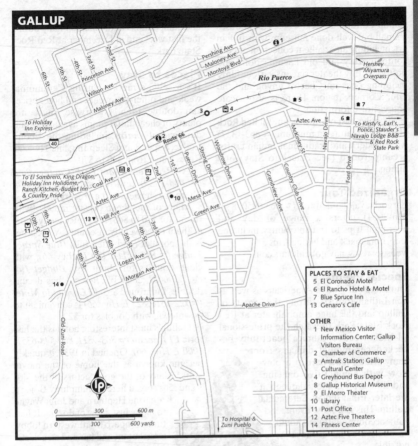

GALLUP

PLACES TO STAY & EAT
5 El Coronado Motel
6 El Rancho Hotel & Motel
7 Blue Spruce Inn
13 Genaro's Cafe

OTHER
1 New Mexico Visitor
  Information Center; Gallup
  Visitors Bureau
2 Chamber of Commerce
3 Amtrak Station; Gallup
  Cultural Center
4 Greyhound Bus Depot
8 Gallup Historical Museum
9 El Morro Theater
10 Library
11 Post Office
12 Aztec Five Theaters
14 Fitness Center

The New Mexico Visitor Information Center (☎ 863-4909) and the Gallup Visitors Bureau (☎ 863-3841, 800-242-4282) are both at 701 Montoya Blvd, Gallup, NM 87301. The visitor bureau's website is at www .gallupnm.org. Local information is also available from the chamber of commerce (☎ 722-2228), 103 E Hwy 66, next to the Gallup Cultural Center. Be sure to check out the permanent exhibit on the Navajo code talkers of WWII. Other services include the post office (☎ 863-3491), 950 W Aztec; the library (☎ 863-1291), 115 W Hill Ave; the hospital (☎ 863-7000),1901 Red

Rock Dr; and the police (☎ 722-2231), 451 State Rd 564.

Things to See & Do
The small **Gallup Historical Museum** (☎ 863-1363), 300 W Route 66, in the renovated turn-of-the-19th-century Rex Hotel, is open daily (closed Sunday). This and 18 other downtown structures of historic and architectural interest, built between 1895 and 1938, are described in a free brochure from the visitor center. Most of these buildings are along 1st, 2nd and 3rd Sts between Hwy 66 and Hill Ave.

Next to the Amtrak building, the new **Gallup Cultural Center** (☎ 863-4131) houses a small but well-done museum with Indian art, including an excellent collection of both contemporary and old kachina dolls and pottery. A tiny theater screens various films, including ones on Chaco Canyon and the Four Corners region. There is also a café and visitor information.

Six miles east of town, beautiful **Red Rock State Park** features a museum (☎ 863-1337) with modern and traditional Indian crafts, a campground (see Places to Stay) and hiking.

Organized Tours

Largo Navajoland Tours (☎ 863-0050, 888-726-9084) offers a range of day and overnight trips to Indian country, including jeep, horseback and hiking trips. website: www.navajolandtours.com

Special Events

Thousands of Native Americans as well as non-Indian tourists throng the streets of Gallup and the huge amphitheater at Red Rock State Park to watch the professional all-Indian rodeo, admire beautifully bedecked ceremonial dancers from many tribes, take part in a powwow with competitive dancing and choose a ceremonial queen at the **Inter-Tribal Indian Ceremonial Gallup**. This is a huge event, and your accommodations should be booked as far ahead as possible.

Apart from the ceremonial, several other annual events attract visitors and fill hotel rooms. Foremost is the **Navajo Nation Fair**, held in nearby Window Rock, Arizona, during the first weekend in September. The **Lions Club Rodeo**, held in the third week in June, is the most professional and prestigious of several rodeos held throughout the year in the Gallup area. Close to two hundred colorful

hot-air balloons take part in demonstrations and competitions at the **Balloon Rally** during the first weekend in December at Red Rock State Park.

Places to Stay

It's a seller's market during Ceremonial week and other big events, and hotel prices can double then. Otherwise, there are plenty of cheap hotel rooms available. Standard *motel chains*, including the Econo Lodge, Super 8 and Sleep Inn, line Hwy 66. Rates range from $40 to $70.

At *Red Rock State Park Campground* (☎ 863-1329) tent/RV sites cost $10/14. There are showers and a grocery store.

Many of the cheap private motels (with rooms for $20 to $40) are pretty seedy; most of them offer weekly discounts. A good bet is the popular (and often full) *Blue Spruce Lodge* (☎ 863-5211, 1119 E Hwy 66), with clean doubles for about $30. *Budget Inn* (☎ 722-6631, 2806 W Hwy 66) has decent doubles for around $35. *El Coronado Motel* (☎ 722-5510, 823 E Hwy 66) is convenient to downtown, with doubles for $22.

Gallup's most interesting hotel is the historic *El Rancho* (☎ 863-9311, 800-543-6351, 1000 E Hwy 66). Opened in 1937, it quickly became known as the 'home of the movie stars.' Many of the great actors of the '40s and '50s stayed here – Humphrey Bogart, Katharine Hepburn and John Wayne to name just a few of dozens. It features a superb Southwestern lobby, a restaurant and bar and an eclectic selection of simple rooms. Rates range from $42/55 for a single/ double to $80 for a suite (sleeping up to six). Next door is a modern 24-room motel under the same ownership with rooms for a few dollars less.

With over 200 rooms, two restaurants and a lounge with entertainment and country & western dancing, the *Holiday Inn Holidome* (☎ 722-2201, 800-432-2211, 722-9616, 2915 W Hwy 66), is the biggest place in town. Most rooms are $65 to $85. Rooms at the newer and comparably priced *Holiday Inn Express* (☎ 726-1000, 1500 W Maloney Ave) include a continental breakfast.

About 20 miles east of town at I-40 exit 55 is *Stauder's Navajo Lodge B&B* (☎ 862-7553). Two one-bedroom cottages, each with kitchen, cost $90 for two. Also see Places to Stay in Zuni and B&Bs in Grants.

Places to Eat

Almost everybody seems to stop by the *Ranch Kitchen* (☎ 722-2537, 3001 W Hwy 66), open 6 am to 9 pm daily. The prices are reasonable, the food is good, and beer and wine are available. Another good and slightly cheaper family restaurant that has been operating for almost half a century is *Earl's Restaurant* (☎ 863-4201, 1400 E Hwy 66), with great green chile and fried chicken, but no alcohol.

Very hungry travelers on a tight budget can try the all-you-can-eat specials offered from 11 am to 2:30 pm every day at the *King Dragon* (☎ 863-6300), north of I-40 on Hwy 66 (just west of downtown).

A small, out-of-the-way place, *Genaro's Café* (☎ 863-6761, 600 W Hill Ave) serves large portions of reasonably priced New Mexican food for lunch and dinner Tuesday to Saturday, but no alcohol. Locals say that Genaro's is the place to go if you like your chile hot. Be warned that the green chile cheeseburger is literally swimming in chile sauce; ask for it on the side if you don't want a soggy bun. Another local favorite for New Mexican is *El Sombrero* (☎ 863-4554), on the southwest corner of Hwy 666 and Hwy 66 just west of downtown, known for its stuffed sopaipillas.

With local art on the walls, overstuffed couches and newspapers, *The Coffee House* (☎ 726-0291, 203 W Coal Ave) has the feel of a college-town coffee shop. It serves soups, salads, sandwiches and desserts, and is open 7 am to 10 pm daily and till midnight on weekends.

Night owls can grab a bite at *Kristy's Coffee Shop* (☎ 863-4742, 1310 E Hwy 66) or at *Country Pride* (☎ 863-6801) in the Truckstops of America Plaza by exit 16 on I-40 west of town. Both are open 24 hours.

Entertainment

Local Native Americans perform social Indian dances at 7 pm nightly from Memorial Day to Labor Day by the Amtrak Station. Admission is free and photography is allowed.

The historic *El Morro Theater* (☎ 722-7469, 207 W Coal Ave), designed by Carl Boller, who also designed Albuquerque's Kimo Theater, was renovated in 1991 and screens Hollywood movies. Also try the modern *Aztec Five* (☎ 863-4651, 911 W Aztec Ave).

Shopping

Gallup has one of the country's biggest selection of stores selling Indian jewelry and other arts and crafts. Check out as many as you can if you are seriously interested in

Rug Auction

The eastern Navajo community of Crownpoint, 25 miles north of Thoreau (exit 53 on I-80), is a great place to seek out Navajo rugs. On the third (occasionally fourth) Friday of the month, a rug auction in the Crownpoint Elementary School attracts several hundred buyers, sellers and visitors. Rug previewing is from 4 to 6pm and bidding is from 7pm to whenever it's over. The auction is standing room only – arrive early.

Admission is free, and the several hundred available rugs sell for anywhere from under $100 to over $3000. Prices are better than in stores – bring cash or checks for purchase. Many Navajos, often traditionally dressed, are in attendance, and other Native Americans sell crafts outside the school.

Information and dates are available from the local Rug Weavers Association (☎ 505-786-5302, 505-786-7386), PO Box 1630, Crownpoint, NM 87313.

There is food and gas in Crownpoint, but nowhere to stay. Gallup and Grants are each about a 75-minute drive away.

getting top-quality goods at fair prices. Many trading posts are found downtown in the Historic District on Hwy 66.

Getting There & Around

America West Express (☎ 800-235-9292) has direct flights to Farmington and Phoenix, Arizona, several times a day from the Gallup Airport at the west end of town.

The Greyhound Bus Station (☎ 863-3761), at the Amtrak building next to the cultural center, has four daily buses to Flagstaff, Arizona ($36, three hours), Albuquerque ($25.20, 2½ hours) and beyond.

The Navajo Transit System (☎ 520-729-4115) has buses every 2½ hours, Monday to Friday, from the Gallup Greyhound Station to Window Rock ($2.60, 30 minutes).

The Amtrak Station, 201 E Hwy 66, has a daily evening train to Flagstaff, Arizona, continuing to Los Angeles, California, and a morning train to Albuquerque continuing on to Chicago, Illinois. Book tickets in advance through Amtrak (☎ 800-872-7245). There is no ticket agent at the Gallup station. Amtrak provides an 'Indian Country Guide' who gives informative narration during the journey between Gallup and Albuquerque.

Budget (☎ 726-1916, 800-748-2540) and Enterprise (☎ 722-5820, 800-325-8007) car rentals are at the airport. Luna's Cab (☎ 722-9777) provides cab service from 6:30 am to midnight Monday to Thursday (until 1:30 am on Friday and Saturday) and from 9 am to 5 pm Sunday.

Northeastern New Mexico

Northeastern New Mexico is high plains country, with grasslands stretching to infinity and fascinating historical and geologic landmarks. Some of the oldest Paleo-Indian artifacts have been found at Folsom, and the Santa Fe Trail, which provided a pioneering and trading route from Missouri to New Mexico, cut through the area (in some places, you can still see the wagon ruts). Hidden in the vastness of the rolling plains, travelers will find volcanoes, dinosaur footprints and hot springs.

I-40 Corridor East of Albuquerque

Santa Rosa, due east of Albuquerque, and Tucumcari, near the Texas state line, were once key stops along old Route 66 (see the boxed text 'Kickin' Down Route 66' in the Facts about Arizona chapter). Today they offer inexpensive accommodations and two museums well worth a stop.

SANTA ROSA

☎ 505 • pop 25,000 • elevation 4600 feet

Settled in the mid-19th century by Spanish farmers, Santa Rosa's modern claim to fame is, oddly enough, as the scuba-diving capital of the Southwest.

There are three freeway exits. From the western exit 273, the main street begins as Coronado St, then becomes Parker Ave through downtown, and then becomes Will Rogers Dr as it passes exits 275 and 277. This main thoroughfare is part of the celebrated Route 66, and most hotels and restaurants lie along it.

The chamber of commerce (☎ 472-3763, 800-450-7084), 486 Parker Ave, Santa Rosa, NM 88435, is open 8 am to 5 pm weekdays; website: www.santarosanm.com. Other services include the library (☎ 472-3101), 208 5th St, the post office (☎ 472-3743), 120 5th St, the hospital (☎ 472-3417), 535 Lake Dr, and the police (☎ 472-3605), by the city hall on 4th St.

Things to See & Do

One of the 10 best spots to dive in the country is, surprisingly, here in Santa Rosa (so they say). The bell-shaped, 81-foot-deep **Blue Hole** is 80 feet in diameter at the surface and 130 feet in diameter below the surface. Platforms for diving are suspended 25 feet down. The sandstone is fed by a natural spring flowing at 3000 gallons a minute, which keeps the water both very clear and pretty cool (about 61°F to 64°F). Divers need a permit from the dive shop (☎ 472-3370) at the hole.

Nine miles south of town the tiny village of **Puerto de Luna**, founded in the 1860s, is one of the oldest settlements in New Mexico. Attractions include the old county courthouse, village church and various weathered adobe buildings. The drive there is pretty, winding through arroyos surrounded by eroded sandstone mesas.

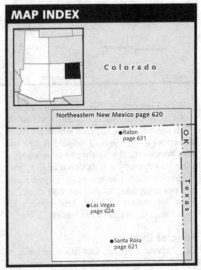

MAP INDEX

Colorado

Northeastern New Mexico page 620

Raton
page 631

O.K.

Texas

Las Vegas
page 624

Santa Rosa
page 621

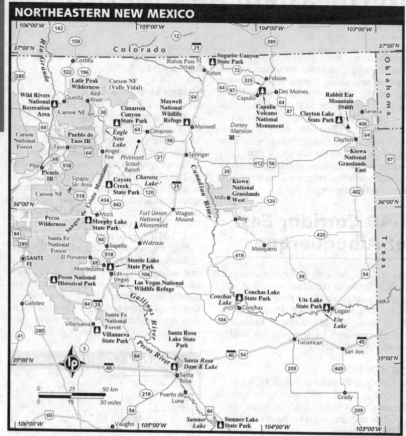

NORTHEASTERN NEW MEXICO

With 33 cars from the 1920s through the 1960s, all in beautiful condition, and lots of 1950s memorabilia, the new **Route 66 Auto Museum** (☎ 472-1966), 2766 Old Route 66, pays homage to the mother of all roads. It's a fun place; enjoy a milkshake at the '50s-style restaurant. The museum is open 8 am to 8 pm daily May to August, and closes at 5 pm September to April. Admission is $5 for adults, free for children under 12.

Special Events

The Annual Custom Car Show is held in August or September and attracts vintage-

and classic-car enthusiasts as well as folks driving strange things on wheels. The third week in August sees the Santa Rosa Fiesta, with a beauty-queen contest and the bizarre, annual Duck Drop, for which contestants buy squares and then wait for a duck suspended over the squares to poop – if the poop lands on your square, you win a cash prize.

Places to Stay & Eat

At **Santa Rosa Lake State Park** (☎ 472-3110), tent/RV sites cost $10/14 (day use is $3 per vehicle). Showers are available. From downtown Santa Rosa, turn north on 2nd St

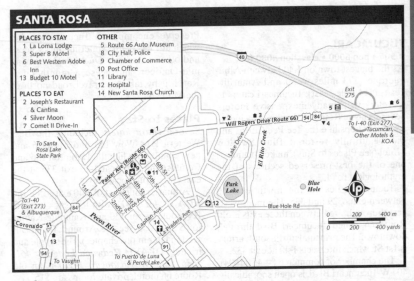

SANTA ROSA

PLACES TO STAY	OTHER
1 La Loma Lodge	5 Route 66 Auto Museum
3 Super 8 Motel	8 City Hall; Police
6 Best Western Adobe Inn	9 Chamber of Commerce
13 Budget 10 Motel	10 Post Office
	11 Library
PLACES TO EAT	12 Hospital
2 Joseph's Restaurant & Cantina	14 New Santa Rosa Church
4 Silver Moon	
7 Comet II Drive-In	

and follow the signs. The **KOA** (☎ 472-3126, *2136 Will Rogers Dr*) has tent sites/hookups/cabins for $18/25/28.

Lots of inexpensive motels, many of which have been around since before the interstate, cater to I-40 traffic. Doubles start in the low $30s at the friendly **Budget 10 Motel** (☎ 472-3454, *120 Hwy 54*), **La Loma Lodge** (☎ 472-4379, *736 Parker Ave*) and the **Sunset Motel** (☎ 472-3762, *929 Will Rogers Dr*). Exits 277 and 275 have **chain motels**, including the Holiday Inn Express, Comfort Inn and Motel 6.

Route 66 nostalgia lines the walls of **Joseph's Restaurant & Cantina** (☎ 472-3361, *865 Will Rogers Dr*), the most popular place for inexpensive Mexican and American food (it's been around since 1956). For drive-in options beyond the usual burgers and fries, like *carne adobada* and green-chile enchiladas, try the classic **Comet II Drive-in** (☎ 472-3663, *239 Parker Ave*). The **Silver Moon** (☎ 472-3162), just west of exit 275 on Will Rogers Dr, has been around for more than 40 years, and the diner food (with a New Mexican twist) is tasty – try the homemade chile rellenos.

Getting There & Away
Greyhound (☎ 472-5720) stops at Mateo's restaurant, 500 Coronado St W; daily buses go west to Albuquerque ($19, two hours), east to Tucumcari ($10.50, one hour) and to Amarillo, Texas ($30, three hours).

VAUGHN
☎ 505 • pop 600 • elevation 4380 feet
This small town, about 40 miles southwest of Santa Rosa near the intersections of Hwys 60, 54 and 285, serves a large rural area. There's not much to do here, but there are half a dozen simple motels, of which the

The drama of the annual Duck Drop

best is the **Bel-Air Motel** (☎ 584-2241), with rooms around $30.

TUCUMCARI

☎ 505 • pop 6000 • elevation 4080 feet

As the biggest town on I-40 between Albuquerque (173 miles west) and Amarillo, Texas (114 miles east), Tucumcari caters to travelers with many inexpensive motels. Several classic Route 66 buildings, including souvenir shops like the Tee Pee Curios and the beautifully restored Blue Swallow Motel (see Places to Stay), make Tucumcari one of the best-preserved sections of the mythological road.

Tucumcari lies to the north of I-40 between exits 329 and 335. The main west-east thoroughfare between these exits is old Route 66, called Tucumcari Blvd through downtown. The principal north-south artery is 1st St, which intersects I-40 at exit 332.

The chamber of commerce (☎ 461-1694), 404 W Tucumcari Blvd, is open sporadically. Other services include the library (☎ 461-0295), 602 S 2nd, the post office (☎ 461-0370), 222 S 1st St, the hospital (☎ 461-0141), 301 Miel de Luna, and the police (☎ 461-2160), 225 E Center St.

Buses to Albuquerque ($30, three hours) and Amarillo, Texas ($27, two hours) depart three or four times daily from the Greyhound Bus Terminal (☎ 461-1350), 2618 S 1st St (behind McDonald's).

Things to See & Do

Several rooms of the **Tucumcari Historical Museum** (☎ 461-4201), 416 S Adams St, are reconstructions of early Western interiors, such as a sheriff's office, a classroom and a hospital room. On display is an eclectic mixture of local memorabilia ranging from Indian artifacts to a barbed-wire collection. Admission is, strangely, $2.11.

Well worth a visit, the new **Mesalands Dinosaur Museum** (☎ 461-3466), 222 E Laughlin St, showcases real dinosaur bones and hands-on exhibits. Casts of dinosaur bones are done in bronze (rather than the usual plaster of paris), which not only shows the finest detail but makes them works of art.

At the east end of town off Tucumcari Blvd, the 770-acre **Ladd S Gordon Wildlife Preserve** encompasses Tucumcari Lake, which attracts many wintering ducks, geese and other waterbirds. Ducks begin arriving mid-October, and geese a month later. Reach it by taking a gravel road north of the Motel 6.

Places to Stay

Several **chain hotels**, including the Best Western Pow Wow Inn and Motel 6 and newly built ones like the Hampton Inn and Comfort Inn, are near I-40 exit 335 at the east end of Tucumcari Blvd.

A quarter mile east of I-40 exit 355 is the **KOA** (☎ 461-1841), with tent sites for $16, RV hookups for $20 and Kamping Kabins for $25. (Also see the Around Tucumcari section later in this chapter.) The simple and friendly HI-AYH **Redwood Lodge** (☎ 461-3635, 1502 W Tucumcari Blvd) is an old Route 66 motel; private rooms are $15.

The neon sign of the **Blue Swallow Motel** (☎ 461-9849, 815 E Tucumcari Blvd) has been featured in many articles about Route 66. Listed on the State and National Registers of Historic Places, this is a classic Route 66 motel with a great lobby and individual garages. Rates are $30/65 for doubles/suites.

The **Americana Motel** (☎ 461-0431, 406 E Tucumcari Blvd) and the **Royal Palacio Motel** (☎ 461-1212, 1620 E Tucumcari Blvd) are both good values and offer rooms from around $20. Decent rooms in the mid- and upper $20s are available at the **Friendship Inn** (☎ 461-0330, 800-537-3893, 629 315 E Tucumcari Blvd), the **Palomino Motel** (☎ 461-3622, 1215 E Tucumcari Blvd) and the clean **Safari Motel** (☎ 461-3642, 722 E Tucumcari Blvd).

Places to Eat & Drink

You'll find all the usual chains lining old Route 66. Among other options, **La Cita** (☎ 461-3930, 812 S 1st St) earns praise for its Mexican food. **Dean's** (☎ 461-3470, 1806 E Tucumcari Blvd) serves country-style dinners for $6, sandwiches, New Mexican fare and homemade pies, and is popular with locals. **Del's Restaurant** (☎ 461-1740, 1202 E Tucumcari Blvd), with a hearty salad bar, is another popular spot. For New Mexican specialties like *chicarones* (fried pork skins), try **Rubees** (☎ 461-1463, 605 W Tucumcari Blvd). **Denny's** (☎ 461-3094, 1102 E Tucumcari Blvd) is open 24 hours.

The renovated old **Odeon Theater** (☎ 461-0100, 123 S 2nd St) shows movies. For a drink and dancing, head to the Best Western Pow Wow Inn. On the weekend, this is the place for two-steppin' to live country & western.

AROUND TUCUMCARI

Twenty-six miles northeast of Tucumcari, **Ute Lake State Park** (☎ 487-2284), PO Box 52, Logan, NM 88426, offers swimming and boating on the 12-sq-mile lake. Walleye fishing is said to be excellent. Three *campgrounds* have tent/RV sites ($10/14) and primitive campgrounds ($8). In Logan (3 miles east of the park), the basic **Yucca Motel** (☎ 487-2272) on the main drag has doubles from $38; there are a couple of restaurants. If you want to rent a boat, Dingy Dicks (☎ 487-2340) in Logan rents pontoon boats for $125 for four hours and $20 each additional hour, with discounts for daily rentals.

Camping and boating are also available at the busier **Conchas Lake State Park** (☎ 868-2270), 32 miles northwest of Tucumcari on Hwy 104. The park is very popular, with fishing competitions drawing hundreds of entrants. On busy summer weekends there may be up to 400 boats on the lake and many thousands of visitors. **Conchas Lodge** (☎ 868-2988) has a restaurant and lounge (with weekend entertainment in summer), groceries and rooms for $45 to $75.

Las Vegas to Colorado

This stretch of I-25 largely traces the route of the Santa Fe Trail. Las Vegas and Raton were important centers of trade in the late 1800s, and both towns retain the flavor of

that era in their many well-preserved buildings. The area is dotted with small lakes and beautiful canyons. If you're looking for a bit of the Old West without a patina of consumer hype, this is the place. Ranching is a mainstay of the economy in the sparsely populated northeast corner of New Mexico. On many stretches of road, you'll see more cattle than people or cars

LAS VEGAS

☎ 505 • pop 16,500 • elevation 6470 feet

Las Vegas is the largest and oldest New Mexican town east of the Sangre de Cristo Mountains. The area was inhabited mainly by Comanches until 15 Hispanic families received a grant from the Mexican government to found Las Vegas in 1835. It became an important Spanish town on the Santa Fe Trail, and in 1846 the US took possession of it.

The building of nearby Fort Union in 1851 and the arrival of the railroad in 1879 spurred progress. During the late 1800s, the wild and booming town of Las Vegas was the most important city in New Mexico, and many buildings were constructed. Historians claim that there are more than 900 19th-century buildings in Las Vegas listed on the National Register of Historic Places. With a small university, a pretty central plaza and an Old West feel (refreshingly free from adobe and howling coyotes), Las Vegas is a pleasant town to spend a lazy afternoon.

Orientation & Information

Las Vegas is on I-25, 65 miles east of Santa Fe and 110 miles south of Raton. The main street is Hwy 85 or Grand Ave, which runs north-south, paralleling the interstate.

The chamber of commerce (☎ 425-8631, 800-832-5947), 513 6th St, and the Tony Martinez Welcome Center (☎ 454-4101), on Hwy 85, are open weekdays. Write to the chamber at PO Box 128, Las Vegas, NM 87701 or see its website at www.lasvegas newmexico.com. The Santa Fe National Forest Ranger Station (☎ 425-3534), 1926 7th St, is open 8 am to 5 pm Monday to Friday. Other services include the Carnegie Public Library (☎ 454-1403), 500 National, the post office (☎ 425-9387), 1001 Douglas

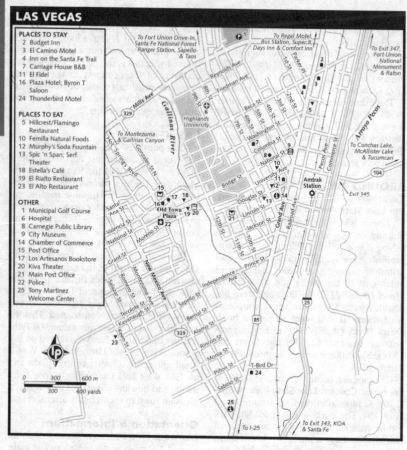

LAS VEGAS

PLACES TO STAY
2 Budget Inn
3 El Camino Motel
4 Inn on the Santa Fe Trail
7 Carriage House B&B
11 El Fidel
16 Plaza Hotel; Byron T Saloon
24 Thunderbird Motel

PLACES TO EAT
5 Hillcrest/Flamingo Restaurant
10 Femilla Natural Foods
12 Murphy's Soda Fountain
13 Spic 'n Span; Serf Theater
18 Estella's Café
19 El Rialto Restaurant
23 El Alto Restaurant

OTHER
1 Municipal Golf Course
6 Hospital
8 Carnegie Public Library
9 City Museum
14 Chamber of Commerce
15 Post Office
17 Los Artesanos Bookstore
20 Kiva Theater
21 Main Post Office
22 Police
25 Tony Martinez Welcome Center

Ave, the hospital (☎ 425-6751), 1235 8th St, and the police (☎ 425-7504), 318 Moreno.

Average high/low temperatures are 46°/18°F in January, 83°/54°F in July.

Historic Buildings

The chamber of commerce has brochures describing walks in various historic districts.

The historic center is the Old Town Plaza. The **Plaza Hotel** (built in 1880) is still in use – see Places to Stay, later. To the right are the **Ilfeld Buildings** (where the Los Artesanos Bookstore is), which were built and improved upon between 1867 and 1921.

Next to the bookstore are the adobe **Dice Apartments**, parts of which predate the annexation by the USA in 1846. The **First National Bank** at the southeast corner of the plaza dates from 1880. Several more historic buildings are on and near the plaza and along Bridge St.

A few blocks east of the plaza on Bridge St is **Highlands University** (☎ 425-7511), established in 1893. Here, the Administration Building houses a huge 1930s New Deal mural by Lloyd Moylan entitled *The Dissemination of Education in New Mexico*. Also on the campus, in the Ilfeld Auditorium, is a series of seven New Deal-era paintings entitled *Music Is the Universal Language of Mankind* by Brooks Willis.

East of the university, Bridge continues as National St. The **Carnegie Library** was built in 1903 and modeled after President Thomas Jefferson's home at Monticello, Virginia. This is the **Library Park** district, and there are many late-19th-century homes in nearby blocks.

City Museum

Apart from the usual local historic artifacts, this museum (☎ 454-1401), 729 Grand Ave, features an exhibit about Teddy Roosevelt's Rough Riders, who fought in the 1898 Spanish-American War. Las Vegas was home to nearly half the Rough Riders. Admission is free.

Special Events

Las Vegas Fourth of July is a colorful mix of Hispanic and Anglo festivities, including Mexican folk music and dancing and mariachi bands. The event lasts up to four days. The San Miguel County Fair is held around the third weekend in August. On the third Saturday in September the town hosts a harvest festival, with music and food.

Places to Stay

If you'd like to camp, rates at the **KOA** (☎ 454-0180), 4 miles south of downtown off I-25 exit 339, start at $20 for tent campers, $25 for RV hookups and $33 for Kamping Kabins. The campground is open from March to mid-November. At **Storrie Lake State Park** (☎ 425-7278), 4 miles north of Las Vegas on Hwy 518, tent/RV sites are $8/12. The 1100-acre lake offers boating and fishing (rainbow trout are stocked). For more camping, see the North and South of Las Vegas sections later.

Rates for the following accommodations are for the high season (May to August). The **Regal Motel** (☎ 454-1456, 1809 Grand Ave), with larger than average rooms, charges about $30 for a double. Several independent motels line Grand Ave. All of the following appear to be reasonably well-kept. Rooms at the **Budget Inn** (☎ 425-9357,

1216 Grand Ave), **El Camino Motel** (☎ 425-5994, 1152 Grand Ave) and the **Thunderbird Motel** (☎ 454-1471), at the south end of Grand Ave near I-25, start at about $40. At I-25 exit 347 travelers will find **chain motels**, with doubles for $50 to $65, including Super 8 and the pleasant Comfort Inn.

The **Inn on the Santa Fe Trail** (☎ 425-6791, 1133 Grand Ave) is set in tree-filled grounds and has attractive rooms with Southwestern decor. Rooms start around $60, and there is a good restaurant.

The **Carriage House B&B** (☎ 454-1784, 925 6th St), in a Victorian home built in 1893, offers five rooms and afternoon tea ($7.50). Rates are $55/75 with shared/private bathroom and include a full breakfast.

Las Vegas' most celebrated lodging is the **Plaza Hotel** (☎ 425-3591, 800-328-1882, 230 Old Town Plaza). Opened in 1882, the elegant building was carefully remodeled a century later and now offers comfortable accommodations in antique-filled rooms (from $90). **El Fidel** (☎ 425-6761, 500 Douglas St) doesn't have the panache or elegance of the Plaza Hotel, but it's a cool old hotel with simple doubles for about $50.

Places to Eat

The best place in town for simple and tasty New Mexican is the crowded **Estella's Café** (☎ 454-0048) on Bridge St. The **Spic 'n Span** (☎ 426-1921, 713 Douglas St) is especially busy at breakfast time, when half the town seems to stop by. Also try the **Hillcrest/Flamingo Restaurant** (☎ 425-7211, 1106 Grand Ave), offering New Mexican and American fare from 6 am daily.

Used as a set in 2000's *All the Pretty Horses*, **Murphy's Soda Fountain** (☎ 425-6811), on Douglas Ave at 6th, serves diner food at a classic soda fountain. Housed in a Victorian building in the historic center, **El Rialto Restaurant** (☎ 454-0037, 141 Bridge St) offers a wide range of meals, but is closed for breakfast.

At the western end of Sapello St is **El Alto Restaurant** (☎ 454-0808). It doesn't look like much, but it is a Las Vegas institution, famous for its steak meals ($12 to $15). Hours are limited, however; it is open 6 to 9 pm Tuesday to Saturday. El Alto also offers cheaper Mexican food, and there is a bar with music on some nights. The Plaza Hotel has the upscale *Landmark Grill (☎ 425-3591),* which serves a reasonably priced breakfast and lunch from 7 am to 2 pm and dinner from 5 to 9 pm daily (though the food is reportedly inconsistent).

There isn't a huge selection of prepared food, but you can find some organic groceries and holistic medicines at *Femilla Natural Foods (☎ 425-8139, 510 University Ave).*

Entertainment

The run-down *Serf Theater (☎ 425-1188, 707 Douglas Ave),* and the historic *Kiva Theater (☎ 454-0152, 109 Bridge St)* show movies nightly. On weekends, the *Byron T Saloon* in the Plaza Hotel has live jazz, blues and country. Cafés and coffee shops on Bridge St may have poetry readings or folk music.

Fort Union Drive-In (425-9934, 3300 7th St), just north of town with views of the surrounding high desert, is one of the few remaining drive-in movie theaters in New Mexico.

Shopping

Los Artesanos Bookstore (☎ 425-8331), 220 Old Town Plaza, has a good selection of used and rare books on Las Vegas and the Southwest. Other bookstores are found along Bridge St, tucked away among funky art galleries and antique stores – it's a fun place to browse and shop.

Getting There & Around

Daily Greyhound and TNM&O buses (☎ 425-8689) leave at 10:55 pm and 3 am for Raton ($27, two hours) and at 2:40 pm for Santa Fe ($12.50, one hour). To get to Taos ($27), you have to take an afternoon bus to Santa Fe and then spend the night in Santa Fe. The bus station, next to Pino's Truck Stop on Grand Ave, shares a building with Classic Travel & Tours (☎ 454-1415), which sells bus, train and plane tickets.

Amtrak (☎ 800-872-7245) runs a daily train to Chicago, Illinois, and to Los Angeles, California.

You can get a taxi at Las Vegas Cab (☎ 454-1864) and rent a car from Highlands Towing & Auto Rental (☎ 425-8769), 3219 N 7th.

SOUTH OF LAS VEGAS
Las Vegas National Wildlife Refuge

Five miles southeast of Las Vegas on Hwys 104 and 67, this 14-sq-mile refuge (☎ 425-3581), Route 1, PO Box 399, Las Vegas, NM 87701, has marshes, woodlands, grasslands and agricultural areas on which 271 bird species have been recorded. The refuge is open daily from dawn to dusk, and visitors can follow a 7-mile drive and walking trails. The ranger station is open 8 am to 4:30 pm Monday to Friday, and admission to the refuge is free.

Villanueva State Park

This pretty park (☎ 421-2957), Villanueva, NM 87583, lies in a red rock canyon on the Pecos River valley. The valley was a main travel route for Indians and, in the 1500s, for the Spanish conquistadors. A small visitor center and self-guided trails explain the history. Trout fishing on the Pecos River is purportedly very good.

The park is 35 miles south of Las Vegas. Take I-25 south for 22 miles to Hwy 3; follow Hwy 3 south for 12 miles to the park entrance. Day use is $4 per car. Tent/RV sites (with showers) cost $10/14.

En route to the park along Hwy 3 are the Spanish colonial villages of **Villanueva** and **San Miguel** (the latter with a fine church built in 1805). All around are the vineyards of **Madison Winery**; the tasting room (☎ 421-8028) is on Hwy 3, 7 miles south of I-25 between Santa Fe and Las Vegas.

NORTH OF LAS VEGAS
Montezuma

This village, 5 miles northwest of Las Vegas on Hwy 65, is famous for the so-called **Montezuma Castle**, built as a luxury hotel near the local hot springs. There were several hotels on the site that were all destroyed by fire; the present building was constructed in 1886. Today it is owned by the Armand

Hammer United World College (☎ 454-4200), and is under renovation. Call for current information on tours.

The nearby natural **hot springs**, just north of the college on Hwy 65, reputedly have curative and therapeutic powers (free).

Gallinas Canyon

Beyond Montezuma, Hwy 65 climbs up to the attractive scenery of Gallinas Canyon in the Santa Fe National Forest. Six miles beyond Montezuma is the village of **El Porvenir**, where *El Rito de San José (☎ 425-7027)* offers 10 rustic and isolated cabins for $55 to $75 from May to October (ask about weekly rentals). Beyond El Porvenir, you can throw up a tent at the *El Porvenir* and *EV Long* United States Forest Service (USFS) campgrounds ($8). The campgrounds, open May to October, have water and nearby hiking and fishing. During winter, the Gallinas River freezes, and there is ice-skating and cross-country skiing.

Sapello

This tiny village, 13 miles north of Las Vegas on Hwy 518, has the *Star Hill Inn (☎ 425-5605,* which calls itself 'an astronomers' retreat in the Rockies.' Various telescopes are available for rent, and astronomy and bird-watching workshops are offered several times a year. Seven comfortable cottages with fireplaces and kitchens rent from $70 to $120, and a two-night minimum is required. The inn, set at 7200 feet, is on 195 acres, with hiking and cross-country skiing trails. There are no stores nearby, so bring food for the kitchens.
website: www.starhillinn.com

Fort Union National Monument

Fort Union was established in 1851 to protect both Santa Fe and the Santa Fe Trail from Indian attack. It was the largest fort in the Southwest and was critical in mounting a defense against Confederate soldiers during the Civil War. It remained very important until the railway arrived in 1879. By 1891, the fort had been abandoned, and today nothing remains except for a surprisingly large area of crumbling walls in the

middle of the grasslands. You can see more wagon ruts from the Santa Fe Trail here than anywhere else. A visitor center provides an informative exhibit and display of area artifacts.

Fort Union National Monument (☎ 425-8025) is 26 miles north of Las Vegas. Take I-25 to Watrous (exit 366) and then Hwy 161 to Fort Union. Admission is $3 for adults, free for children, and passes are honored.
website: www.nps.gov/foun

MORA VALLEY
☎ 505 • pop 4264 • elevation 7180 feet
This pretty rural area in the foothills of the Sangre de Cristo Mountains was once an important wheat-farming region, but is now economically depressed. Driving through the tiny town of Mora, you'll see tumble-down adobe buildings and a variety of farm animals.

On Hwy 518, the main drag through town, there is a bar, a pizza place, a gas station and the recommended *Hatcha's Café (☎ 387-6034),* serving New Mexican food. Two miles north of Mora on Hwy 518 is the **Cleveland Roller Mill** (☎ 387-2645), which was one of the county's major flour mills around 1900. A museum of local history is open 10 am to 5 pm on weekends, Memorial Day to October 31, and by appointment at other times ($2). Tours of **Victory Ranch** (☎ 387-2254), an 1100-acre alpaca ranch, cost $2/1 for adults/children. A gift store sells local crafts, alpaca wool and products, and weaving books; it's open Thursday to Monday.

Six miles southwest of Mora along Hwy 94 is the undeveloped **Morphy Lake State Park** (☎ 387-2328), with a pretty lake set at over 8000 feet in conifer forests. The last 2 miles to the lake is a very narrow, steep and rutted dirt road. Primitive *camping*, with pit toilets but no drinking water, is $6. For developed camping, go to the more crowded **Coyote Creek State Park** (☎ 387-2328), 17 miles north of Mora on Hwy 43. Tent/RV sites cost $7/11. A meandering stream, surrounded by spruce, pine and cottonwoods, is stocked with trout, and there is a short hiking trail.

Twenty-five miles northwest of Mora on Hwy 518 is **Sipapu**, the oldest and one of the smallest and least known of the ski areas in northern New Mexico. Lift rates are $31 for adults, $25 for six- to 12-year-olds and free for those five and under or 70 and older. Half-day rates are $25/21 for adults/children. Rates for the small poma (a small disc that goes between your legs and pulls you up) only are $15. During summer the area is used for hiking, fishing and hunting.

A variety of accommodations are offered year-round, ranging from $8 for a tent site to $90 for a suite. Call the **Sipapu Lodge** (☎ 587-2240, 800-587-2240) for information.

WAGON MOUND

If you're driving along I-25 between Las Vegas and Springer, the homey **Santa Clara Café** (☎ 666-2011, 709 Railroad Ave), with walls adorned with cattle brands of nearby ranches, is a wonderful alternative to fast food and makes this tiny town a good stop. The café serves basic New Mexican and American fare and a large selection of delicious fresh-baked pies.

SPRINGER & AROUND

☎ 505 • pop 1200 • elevation 5000 feet

The quiet town of Springer was founded in 1879 and was the Colfax County seat from 1882 to 1897, when the seat was moved to Raton. Its main importance is as a center for the surrounding ranches, but there is a museum worth visiting. Springer is off I-25, 67 miles north of Las Vegas and 39 miles south of Raton.

Greyhound (☎ 483-2379), 825 4th St, stops around midnight on its way north to Raton ($8.40, 40 minutes) and at 1:30 pm on its way south to Las Vegas ($15.70, one hour) and Albuquerque ($37, 3¼ hours).

Things to See & Do

Housed in the 1882 building that used to be the Colfax County courthouse, the **Santa Fe Trail Museum** (☎ 483-5554) displays the usual historic artifacts plus the only electric chair ever used in New Mexico. Hours are 10 am to 4 pm Tuesday to Saturday, from Memorial Day to Labor Day ($3).

Twenty-four miles east of Springer on Hwy 56, then 12 miles north on a dirt road, is **Dorsey Mansion**. This two-story log-and-stone mansion was built from 1878–86 by cattle rancher and then Arkansas senator Stephen Dorsey. It was the most opulent Southwestern residence of its time, and is still impressive today. After a turbulent history as a home, hospital and hotel (not to mention post office, store and state monument), it is now privately owned – call ahead (☎ 375-2222) if you are interested in touring this grand historic building in the middle of nowhere. Tours are $3/1 for adults/children under 6, with a $5 minimum.

See Around Clayton, later in this chapter, for information on the Kiowa National Grasslands, just south of Springer.

Places to Stay & Eat

There's free camping at **Charette Lake**, southwest of town (take Hwy 569 from I-25), from March through October, with latrines but no drinking water. Free camping is also permitted at **Springer Lake**, 5 miles northwest of Springer off of County Rd 17.

The old-fashioned **Brown Hotel & Café** (☎ 483-2269, 800-570-2269, 302 Maxwell) offers B&B singles/doubles for $43/65. There are 11 rooms decorated in simple late-19th-century style – no TVs or telephones, though a downstairs living room provides these amenities. The homey café serves a small selection of inexpensive Mexican and American meals.

El Taco Café (☎ 483-9924), on Maxwell Ave, serves New Mexican food and is a popular spot to hang out and play pool or enjoy a beer.

CIMARRON

☎ 505 • pop 975 • elevation 6430 feet

The Cimarron area, home of Ute and Apache Indians prior to being settled in the 1840s, became a stop on the Santa Fe Trail as well as being the first Colfax County seat. During the town's wild early decades, it was home to various gunslingers, train robbers, desperadoes, lawmen and other Wild West figures. Kit Carson, Buffalo Bill Cody, Annie Oakley, Wyatt Earp, Jesse James and

Doc Holliday are just a few who passed through here. The old St James Hotel alone saw the deaths of 26 men within its walls.

Today, Cimarron is a quiet village with few street signs; just poke around to find where you're going, or ask the friendly locals. The town is on Hwy 64, 41 miles southwest of Raton and 54 winding miles east of Taos.

The chamber of commerce (☎ 376-2417), PO Box 604, Cimarron, NM 87714, on the main highway, is open 9 am to 6 pm daily May to September, and 9 am to 5 pm (closed Wednesday and Sunday) the rest of the year; they don't, however, adhere strictly to their hours; website: www.cimarronnm.com. Other services include the post office (☎ 376-2548), 120 E 9th St, off of Hwy 64 next to the International Bank, a clinic (☎ 376-2402) and the police (☎ 376-2351), both in Village Hall on 9th St at Washington St.

TNM&O buses run between Denver (via Raton) and Albuquerque (via Taos and Santa Fe) and stop here once a day in each direction.

Things to See & Do

Most of the historic buildings lie south of the Cimarron River on Hwy 21, which heads south from Hwy 64 near the middle of town. The Old Mill Museum is in the Aztec Mill, built in 1864 as a flour mill; it houses historical photographs and local memorabilia. The museum is open on weekends only in May and September, and daily from June through August ($2). Nearby is the historic St James Hotel (see Places to Stay & Eat). Behind the St James is the Santa Fe Trail Inn, built in 1854, the old town plaza and well, and the Dold Trading Post. South of the St James is Schwenk's Gambling Hall, the Wells Fargo Station and the old jail, built in 1872.

About 4 miles south of Cimarron is the 220-sq-mile Philmont Scout Ranch (☎ 376-2281). Waite Phillips, an Oklahoma oilman, donated the ranch to the Boy Scouts of America (BSA), and since 1938 over 500,000 scouts have stayed here – camping, backpacking and learning outdoors skills. The ranch headquarters is in Villa Philmonte, a 1927 Spanish-Mediterranean-style mansion

filled with antiques and Southwestern art. Guided tours ($4) are offered in July and August (by appointment the rest of the year). Nearby, the Seton Memorial Library & Museum features local frontier history and exhibits the works of ET Seton, first Chief Scout of the BSA. Seven miles farther south in the village of Rayado is the Kit Carson Museum (☎ 376-2281), with 1850s-style furnishings and daily guided tours by interpreters in period costumes. It's open June to August (free).

Places to Stay & Eat

There are a couple of RV parks in town, and plenty of camping in the nearby national forest. A mile north of town is the Ponil Campground (☎ 376-2700), with shaded tent/RV sites for $5/14. See the Around Cimarron section, later, for other camping options.

The cheapest motel is the basic Cimarron Inn & RV Park (☎ 376-2268, 800-546-2244), with 12 singles/doubles for $40/62. The friendly Kit Carson Inn (☎ 376-2288, 800-293-7961) has 40 clean motel rooms ($58), a good inexpensive restaurant and a laid-back bar. At Johnson's Cabins (☎ 376-2210), small cabins, each with an equipped kitchenette and queen-size bed, rent for $45. You can fish in the little Cimarron River by the cabins.

The best-known place is the St James Hotel (☎ 376-2664, 800-748-2694). A saloon in 1873, it became a hotel in 1880, and was renovated in 1985. Rates for the 13 simple historical rooms range from $90 to $120. A modern annex has 10 new rooms with TVs and phones for $60 to $100. There is a coffee shop, a decent mid-range restaurant and a cozy bar with a pool table; while waiting for your food, see how many bullet holes you can count in the period pressed-tin ceiling.

For a B&B, try the Casa del Gavilan (☎ 376-2246, 800-428-4526), a 1908 white-adobe house set on 225 acres. Four double rooms, decorated with Southwestern antiques and art, cost $70 to $100. A two-room guesthouse with one bathroom is $130 for up to four people. Rates include a full hot breakfast.
website: www.casadelgavilan.com

From June to August, a couple of trailers along the road sell cheap and delicious New Mexican food. *Heck's Hungry Traveler* (☎ 376-2574) serves inexpensive diner fare. Enjoy an ice cream at the 1937 soda fountain at the *Cimarron Art Gallery* (☎ 376-2614). The gallery sells Southwestern art, souvenirs and fishing licenses.

AROUND CIMARRON
Cimarron Canyon State Park
A scenic steep-walled canyon, this state park (☎ 377-6271), PO Box 185, Eagle Nest, NM 87718, begins 13 miles west of Cimarron and continues for 7 miles along Hwy 64. Several hiking trails leave from three *campgrounds* nestled along the Cimarron River and there's great trout fishing. Campsites with water but no showers cost $10.

Valle Vidal
This mountainous and forested area in the northeastern corner of the Carson National Forest is the nearest national forest to Cimarron. Gravel roads wind through remote countryside, home to elk, bears, mountain lions, deer, turkeys and other wildlife.

Two campgrounds, *McCrystal Creek* (8100 feet) and *Cimarron* (9400 feet), charge $7 and have drinking water but no showers or RV hookups. (Cimarron is closed in winter.) Dispersed and wilderness camping and backpacking are permitted. The nearest ranger stations are in Taos and Questa, where you can get maps of the area.

Go east of Cimarron 7 miles on Hwy 64 and turn northwest on graveled USFS Rd 1950. It is about 20 miles to Valle Vidal, another 20 through the area and a final 20 to Costilla (on Hwy 522, north of Questa). To protect the elk, parts of the area may be closed from January to June.

RATON
☎ 505 • pop 8000 • elevation 6668 feet
One of the most difficult sections of the Santa Fe Trail was the rocky Raton Pass (7834 feet) in the foothills of the Rockies, near what is now the Colorado–New Mexico state line. The arrival of the railroad in 1879 prompted the founding of Raton (at

the town of Willow Springs), which quickly grew into an important railway stop and mining and ranching center. Many turn-of-the-19th-century buildings have been preserved. Though Raton isn't a big tourist destination, it is an interesting town to stroll around; a visit to the museum, an evening at the drive-in (summer only) and a night at the historic hotel makes it a worthwhile stop on your way through.

The elevation gives Raton pleasant summers and cool winters, with average overnight lows of 18°F in January and daytime highs of 82°F in July.

Orientation & Information
Raton lies along I-25, 8 miles south of Raton Pass and the Colorado state line. The main north-south thoroughfare is 2nd St, which runs parallel to and just west of I-25. The main east-west street is Hwy 64/87, called Tiger Dr west of 2nd St and Clayton Rd east of 2nd St.

The visitor center (☎ 445-3689, 800-638-6161), on Clayton Rd, is open daily and has statewide information. Write to it at PO Box 1211, Raton, NM 87740. Other services include the library (☎ 445-9711), 244 Cook Ave, the post office (☎ 445-2681), 245 Park Ave, the hospital (☎ 445-3661), on Hospital Dr at the south end of town, and the police (☎ 445-2704), 224 Savage Ave.

Historic District
The historic district lies along 1st, 2nd and 3rd Sts between Clark and Rio Grande Aves. This small area harbors over two dozen interesting buildings; a detailed brochure is available from the visitor center and the Raton Museum.

The great little **Raton Museum** (☎ 445-8979), 216 S 1st St, well worth a visit, is housed in the 1906 Coors Building. On display are artifacts of Raton's mining and Santa Fe Trail history, as well as lots of great photos. Hours (subject to change) are 9 am to 5 pm Tuesday to Saturday from Labor Day to Memorial Day and Wednesday to Saturday during the rest of the year (free).

From the Raton Museum, head to the **Santa Fe Depot**, which was built in 1903.

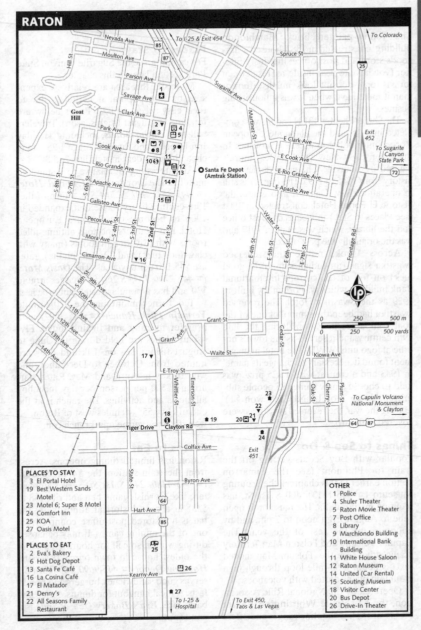

RATON

To I-25 & Exit 454

To Colorado

Nevada Ave

Moulton Ave

Spruce St

Hill St

Parson Ave

Savage Ave

Sugarite Ave

Clark Ave

Goat Hill

Park Ave

E Clark Ave

Cook Ave

Martinez St

E Cook Ave

Exit 452

To Sugarite Canyon State Park

Rio Grande Ave

Santa Fe Depot (Amtrak Station)

E Rio Grande Ave

Apache Ave

E Apache Ave

72

Galisteo Ave

S 8th St · S 7th St · S 6th St · S 3rd St · S 2nd St · S 1st St

Pecos Ave

Mora Ave

Water St

Cimarron Ave

E 4th St · E 5th St · E 6th St · E 7th St

S 9th Ave · S 10th Ave · 11th Ave · 12th Ave · 13th Ave · 14th Ave

0   250   500 m
0   250   500 yards

Grant St

Grant Ave

Cedar St

Waite St

Kiowa Ave

17

To Capulin Volcano National Monument & Clayton

E Troy St

Whittier St · Emerson St

Oak St · Cherry St · Plum St

18 19 20 21 23 22

Clayton Rd

Tiger Drive

24

64 87

Colfax Ave

Exit 451

Byron Ave

State St

64

85

Hart Ave

Kearny Ave

25

26

27

To I-25 & Hospital

To Exit 450, Taos & Las Vegas

PLACES TO STAY
3 El Portal Hotel
19 Best Western Sands Motel
23 Motel 6; Super 8 Motel
24 Comfort Inn
25 KOA
27 Oasis Motel

PLACES TO EAT
2 Eva's Bakery
6 Hot Dog Depot
13 Santa Fe Café
16 La Cosina Café
17 El Matador
21 Denny's
22 All Seasons Family Restaurant

OTHER
1 Police
4 Shuler Theater
5 Raton Movie Theater
7 Post Office
8 Library
9 Marchiondo Building
10 International Bank Building
11 White House Saloon
12 Raton Museum
14 United (Car Rental)
15 Scouting Museum
18 Visitor Center
20 Bus Depot
26 Drive-In Theater

NEW MEXICO

Opposite the railway are several attractive buildings dating from the 1880s and 1890s. The yellow-painted brick **Marchiondo Building**, constructed in 1882, housed a dry-goods store and post office; the dusty interior (you have to peer inside, as it isn't open for visitors) doesn't look much different than it must have when it was a flourishing business.

The **Shuler Theater**, 131 N 2nd St, was completed in 1915, and the elaborate European Rococo interior boasts excellent acoustics. In the foyer, eight New Deal (1930s) murals painted by Manville Chapman depict area history from 1845 to 1895. The theater is still in operation. New Deal art also graces the historic **El Portal Hotel**, constructed in 1904 (see Places to Stay), as well as the **post office** and the **library**, which was built in 1917 and was the originally the post office.

Across Cook, notice the reversed swastika signs (an Indian symbol of good luck) on top of the current **International Bank** building, which was originally built in 1929 as the Swastika Hotel. The reversed swastika had been the symbol of one of the coal companies in Raton during the late 19th century, and it served as the town's unofficial logo until WWII. The hotel management found it 'necessary to change its name' in 1943 and a contest with a $25 prize was held to choose a new name (25 people submitted Yucca Hotel, and each won $1). During the war, the reversed swastikas were covered with tarp.

Things to See & Do

Popular with Boy Scouts getting off the train for Philmont (see the Cimarron section earlier in this chapter), the **Scouting Museum** (☎ 445-1413), 400 S 1st St, has scouting memorabilia. The museum is open June to August from noon to 7 pm, and by appointment the rest of the year. The **Capulin Volcano and Folsom Man Territory scenic drive** (see the 'Folsom Man' boxed text) is about a 50-mile loop through high mountain plains dotted with volcanoes.

Operated by the National Rifle Association, the 52-sq-mile **Whittington Center** (☎ 445-3615) has shooting ranges and offers guided hunts. The center is 7 miles southwest of Raton on Hwy 64.

Places to Stay

For camping, see the Sugarite Canyon State Park section later in this chapter.

Motels in this area are relatively expensive, but are popular nonetheless due to their easy access to I-25. Prices below are for June to August (high season). Travelers will find *chain motels*, including Holiday Inn Express and Super 8, off of I-25. Many cheap independent motels line 2nd St.

An interesting alternative to a standard motel is the wonderful *El Portal Hotel* (☎ 445-3631, 101 N 3rd St), a turn-of-the-19th-century livery stable that expanded in 1904 to become the Seaburg European Hotel. It now offers spacious antique-filled rooms with private bathrooms (many with claw-foot tubs) and TV (no phone); rates are $45/140 per day/week. The *Oasis Motel* (☎ 445-2766, 1445 S 2nd St) charges around $30 and has a popular restaurant attached.

Ted Turner maintains the 920-sq-mile *Vermejo Park Ranch* (☎ 445-3097) as a premier hunting and fishing lodge. Fly-fishing clinics are held during the June to August fishing season. Elk and deer are hunted from October to December, and wild turkey in April and May. Rates start around $300 per person per day, including all meals and activities. The ranch is at the end of Hwy 555, 40 miles west of Raton. website: www.vermejoparkranch.com

Places to Eat

Raton has limited dining options. Across from the train station, the *Santa Fe Café* (☎ 445-4380, 244 S 1st St) serves upscale fare like Cornish game hen and ribs ($8 to $23) in a cozy historical atmosphere; the bar is a restored post-office counter from one of the mining camps. It may be closed during winter, so call for hours. Housed in the oldest house in town (circa 1877), the *Hot Dog Depot* (☎ 445-9090, 100 S 3rd St) serves good sandwiches, burgers and breakfasts. A local hangout for donuts, coffee and basic fare, *Eva's Bakery (134 N 2nd)* is a good spot.

Though neither place serves beer, *La Cosina Café* (☎ 445-9675, 745 S 3rd St) and *El Matador* (☎ 445-9575, 1012 S 2nd St) offer basic New Mexican fare. For early breakfasts, the café at the Oasis Motel and the *All Seasons Family Restaurant* (☎ 445-9889) by I-25 both open at 6 am.

Entertainment

Movies play at the 1940s-era *Raton Movie Theater* (☎ 445-3721), on 2nd St at Park Ave, from August to May. During summer, the theater is closed and films are screened at the drive-in theater on 2nd St at Kearny Ave. The *Shuler Theater* (☎ 445-5520) presents a variety of productions, including dances and plays. The *White House Saloon* (☎ 445-9992, 133 Cook Ave) is the local hangout for a beer.

Getting There & Around

Greyhound (☎ 445-9071) and TNM&O stop behind McDonald's on Clayton Rd. Several buses a day serve the route from Denver, Colorado, to Santa Fe (via both Taos and Las Vegas) and on to Albuquerque ($37). Amtrak (☎ 800-872-7245) stops once a day in each direction: toward Chicago, Illinois, and Los Angeles, California.

United (☎ 445-3644), on 2nd St at Rio Grande Ave, rents cars, though it's expensive ($50 a day). Call Colfax County Transportation (☎ 445-3730) for a taxi (75¢) from 6 am to 6 pm Monday to Friday.

AROUND RATON
Sugarite Canyon State Park

This park (☎ 445-5607), with two lakes stocked with rainbow trout, lies in pretty meadows and forests in the foothills of the Rockies, 10 miles northeast of Raton. In winter, the 7800-foot elevation allows cross-country skiing, skating and ice fishing. There are 15 miles of hiking trails, starting from a half-mile nature trail, and two campgrounds open roughly from May to October offering tent/RV sites for $10/14. The *Lake Alice* campground, cramped by the side of the road across from a lake small enough to throw a rock across, is by reservation only (and there's a $10 fee to make a reservation).

Farther up the road, at the end of a gravel road, is the recommended *Soda Pocket* campground. There are primitive toilets but no water; showers are available several miles away by the visitor center on Hwy 526.

Follow Hwy 72 out of Raton, then turn onto Hwy 526; it's about 10 miles and signposted.

Maxwell National Wildlife Refuge

This refuge (☎ 375-2331), PO Box 276, Maxwell, NM 87728, encompasses 2800 acres of grassland and farmland around three lakes. It is managed for wintering waterfowl and upland game birds, and birding is good from October through the winter. The burrowing owl and many other birds nest here in summer.

The refuge is 28 miles south of Raton along I-25, and 3 miles west of Maxwell along Hwys 445 and 505. A visitor center is open from 7:30 am to 4 pm Monday to Friday. Free camping is permitted (with toilets but no water) from March to October.

CAPULIN VOLCANO NATIONAL MONUMENT

Rising 1300 feet above the surrounding plains, Capulin Volcano is the easiest to visit of several volcanoes in the area. From the visitor center (☎ 278-2201), a 2-mile road winds precariously up the mountain to a parking lot at the crater rim (which is 8182 feet). There, a quarter-mile trail drops into the volcanic crater and a mile-long trail follows the rim. The entrance is 3 miles north of the village of Capulin, which is 30 miles east of Raton on Hwy 87. Admission is $5 per vehicle and passes are honored. website: www.nps.gov/cavo

There is no camping in the monument. In the tiny village of Capulin, the *Capulin Campground* (☎ 278-2921) charges $10 for one person in a tent, and $3 for each additional person. RV sites start at $16. Opposite is a grocery store and the *Capulin Store* (☎ 278-3900), which serves chicken-fried steak and barbecue, among other things. The store is open May through Thanksgiving.

Folsom Man

A few miles north of Capulin Volcano is **Folsom**, the village near which the most important archaeological discovery in America was made. In 1908, George McJunkin, a local African American cowboy, noticed some strange bones in Wild Horse Arroyo. Cowboy that he was, he knew that these were no ordinary cattle bones, and so he kept them, suspecting correctly that they were bones of an extinct form of bison. McJunkin told various people of his find, but it was not until 1926 to 1928 that the site was properly excavated, first by fossil bone expert Jesse Figgins and then by others.

Until that time, scientific dogma stated that humans had inhabited North America for, at most, 4000 years. Suddenly, facts about the continent's ancient inhabitants had to be completely revised. The excavations showed stone arrowheads in association with extinct bison bones dating from 8000 BC, thus proving that people have lived here for at least that long. These Paleo-Indians became known as Folsom Man.

Thus the era of modern American archaeology began in Folsom in the late 1920s. More recent dating techniques have shown these artifacts to be 10,800 years old, among the oldest discovered on the continent, although it is clear that people have lived in the Americas for even longer.

Nine miles east of Capulin in Des Moines, the **Central Motel** (☎ 278-2111) has five clean single/double rooms for $30/35.

CLAYTON

☎ 505 • pop 2500 • elevation 5050 feet

Fifty miles southeast of Capulin is Clayton, a quiet town with a sleepy Western feel. The town lies surrounded by ranch land near the Bravo Dome CO_2 Field, the world's largest natural deposit of carbon dioxide gas. The underground carbon dioxide deposit is injected into nearby oil fields, thus increasing oil production by up to 50%.

The infamous train robber Black Jack Ketchum was caught near Clayton and hanged here in 1901; the gruesome story is documented in the **Herzstein Memorial Museum** (☎ 374-2977), in the Methodist Episcopal Church on 2nd St at Walnut St, open Tuesday to Sunday afternoons.

For the Internet-starved traveler, the library (☎ 374-9423), 17 Chestnut St, offers web access. Though there isn't much reason to spend the night, if you find yourself needing a place to stay, Clayton has a **KOA**, a few **chain motels**, including a Super 8 and Best Western, and some locally owned restaurants. Stop by the **Eklund Dining Room & Saloon** (☎ 374-2551, 15 Main St),

in the historic Eklund Hotel (circa 1890), for a meal in the elegant dining room or a beer in the Old West saloon. For an early breakfast, try the **Rabbit Ear Café** (☎ 374-9912, 1201 S 1 St), open from 6 am, or the **Hi Ho Café** (☎ 374-9515), open from 5 am. Both offer basic New Mexican and American fare.

Greyhound and TNM&O buses stop at the Phillips 66 Truck Stop (☎ 374-9300), on Hwy 87 south of town, on the daily run from Raton to Amarillo, Texas.

AROUND CLAYTON

Over 500 footprints of eight different species of dinosaur can be found at **Clayton Lake State Park** (☎ 374-8808), 12 miles northwest of Clayton on Hwy 370. The pretty lake has swimming and camping. Day use is $3, and tent/RV sites cost $7/11.

Southwest of Clayton in Harding County, the most sparsely populated county in New Mexico, is a section of the **Kiowa National Grasslands**. Farmed throughout the early 20th century, poor agricultural techniques led to the soil becoming useless and blowing away during the dust bowl years of the 1930s. This is high-plains ranch land – open, vast and lonely. The most visited section (though visitors are scarce) is **Mills Canyon**, north of the village of **Roy** (with a gas station and grocery store). About 10 miles northwest of Roy on Hwy 39, a signposted dirt road heads west another 10 miles to the *Mills Camping Area* near the Canadian River, where there is free primitive camping with a pit toilet, but no drinking water. The river forms a small gorge here, and the area is quite scenic. The nearest town of any size is Springer (earlier in this chapter). The Grasslands Headquarters (☎ 374-9652) is in Clayton at 714 Main St.

Southwestern New Mexico

This chapter covers the Rio Grande Valley south of Albuquerque down to the Mexico border, and the area west of there to the Arizona state line. The Rio Grande Valley has always been the main thoroughfare through the area, and I-25 parallels it from Albuquerque south to Las Cruces, the largest city in southwestern New Mexico. At Las Cruces, I-25 joins I-10, which continues south into Texas or heads west into Arizona. Most travelers along these routes cruise through the region quickly, bent on visits to more famous places such as Santa Fe and Taos. Nevertheless, southwestern New Mexico offers much to visitors.

The area's first inhabitants were hunter-gatherers of the Cochise culture, which dates from about 7000 BC. The Cochise gave rise to the Mogollon culture, which ap-peared about 200 BC. The people lived in the mountains and valleys and relied more on hunting and gathering than their Hohokam and Puebloan contemporaries, but eventually the latter strongly influenced the Mogollon culture. This left us with numerous archaeological sites, of which the Gila (pronounced 'HEE-la') Cliff Dwellings north of Silver City are the best known and most spectacular. They also left us with superb Mimbres black-on-white pottery, which can be examined in several museums in the area. The Mogollon culture died out in the early 14th century.

The Pueblo Indians of the northern Rio Grande had a few southern outposts in the area. Late arrivals on the scene, Athapaskan-speaking Indians arrived from the north soon after the disappearance of the Mogollon culture. Among these late arrivals were the Apaches, who came to dominate southwestern New Mexico. The most famous of the Apache leaders was Geronimo.

Spanish explorers appeared in the 16th century. Álvar Cabeza de Vaca went through the Las Cruces area in 1535, and Francisco Vásquez de Coronado marched north along the Rio Grande in 1540. By the 17th century, many of the pueblos had fallen under Spanish control, but the more nomadic Apaches remained free. The arrival of the Anglos in the 19th century changed that forever.

Today, with the exception of Las Cruces and Socorro, most of the towns in southwestern New Mexico are relatively young, dating to the late 19th century. Much of the southernmost part, around I-10, is part of the Chihuahua Desert, where yucca and agave plants dominate the scene. This is ranching country, though the cattle are sparse. North of the desert, the countryside rises to the rugged mountains encompassed by the Gila National Forest. This is wild country where opportunities for adventurous backpacking, fishing and hunting abound. The residents are few, and their

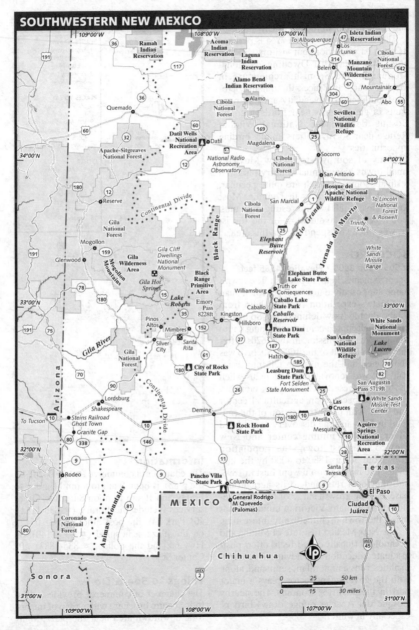

SOUTHWESTERN NEW MEXICO

109°00'W

36 Ramah Indian Reservation

117

108°00'W

Acoma Indian Reservation

Laguna Indian Reservation

Alamo Bend Indian Reservation

107°00'W. To Albuquerque

47 Isleta Indian Reservation

6 Los Lunas

314 Belen

542 Cibola National Forest

47 Manzano Mountain Wilderness

Mountainair

55 Abo

304

60

Sevilleta National Wildlife Refuge

Quemado

60

32

Apache-Sitgreaves National Forest

34°00'N

180

191

12

Reserve

Mogollon

159

Glenwood

Mogollon Mountains

Gila National Forest

78

180

191

75

33°00'N

Gila River

70

Arizona

90

Lordsburg

Shakespeare

Steins Railroad Ghost Town

Granite Gap

80

338

To Tucson

80

Rodeo

Coronado National Forest

Animas Mountains

81

60

Datil Wells National Recreation Area

Datil

12

National Radio Astronomy Observatory

Continental Divide

Gila Cliff Dwellings National Monument

Gila Wilderness Area

Gila Hot Springs

15

Lake Roberts

Black Range Primitive Area

35

Emory Pass 8228ft

Pinos Altos

Mimbres

Silver City

Santa Rita

61

City of Rocks State Park

180

Continental Divide

10

146

9

Deming

Rock Hound State Park

11

9

Pancho Villa State Park

Columbus

MEXICO

General Rodrigo M Quevedo (Palomas)

Chihuahua

Sonora

MEX 2

169

Magdalena

Cibola National Forest

San Marcial

San Antonio

380

Rio Grande

Elephant Butte Reservoir

Williamsburg

Kingston

152

Hillsboro

27

Caballo

Black Range

Cibola National Forest

25

1

Socorro

Bosque del Apache National Wildlife Refuge

To Lincoln National Forest & Roswell

Trinity Site

Jornada del Muerto

White Sands Missile Range

Elephant Butte Lake State Park

Truth or Consequences

Caballo Lake State Park

Caballo Reservoir

Percha Dam State Park

187

Hatch

185

Leasburg Dam State Park

Fort Selden State Monument

26

25

San Andres National Wildlife Refuge

White Sands National Monument

Lake Lucero

70

82

San Agustin Pass 5719ft

White Sands Missile Test Center

Las Cruces

Mesilla

70 180 10

Mesquite

28

Aguirre Springs National Recreation Area

Santa Teresa

9

El Paso

Ciudad Juárez

Texas

10

MEX 2

MEX 45

34°00'N

33°00'N

32°00'N

31°00'N

0   25   50 km
0   15   30 miles

109°00'W

108°00'W

107°00'W

livelihoods tend toward ranching, logging and some mining in the Silver City area.

The very wildness of the area is perhaps its greatest attraction, but visitors will also enjoy the Gila Cliff Dwellings National Monument, the Spanish architecture in Mesilla near Las Cruces, the quaint Victorian buildings in Silver City and the remnants of ghost towns near Lordsburg. The Bosque del Apache National Wildlife Refuge near Socorro offers unique birding opportunities.

Many of southwestern New Mexico's small towns have annual country fairs and festivals, some of which are quite peculiar, such as the duck races in Deming. Most towns have small but interesting museums. You'll certainly avoid most of the tourist crowds when you spend time in this area.

SOCORRO

☎ 505 • pop 8800 • elevation 4585 feet

Socorro means 'help' in Spanish. The town's name supposedly dates to 1598, when Juan de Oñate's expedition received help from Pilabo Pueblo (now defunct). The Spaniards built a small church nearby, expanding it into the San Miguel Mission in the 1620s. After the Pueblo Revolt of the 1680s, Socorro was abandoned and the mission fell into disrepair, but was renovated in the 1820s when the town was resettled by Hispanic pioneers.

Socorro became an agricultural center and later, with the introduction of the railroad in 1880 and the discovery of gold and silver, a major mining center and New Mexico's biggest town; the population grew from 500 in 1880 to 4000 by the late 1880s. The mining boom went bust in 1893, and the town returned to its agricultural base, but the growth surge of the 1880s resulted in the many Victorian buildings that make the town architecturally interesting.

The New Mexico Institute of Mining and Technology (locally called Tech) offers postgraduate education and advanced research facilities, runs a mineral museum and, along with the government sector, plays a major part in the county's economy. The nearby Bosque del Apache refuge draws birders, especially in winter.

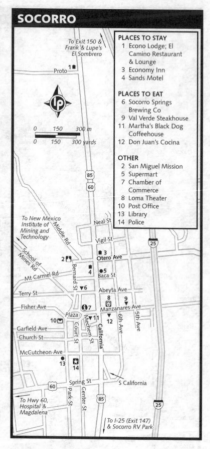

SOCORRO

PLACES TO STAY
1 Econo Lodge; El Camino Restaurant & Lounge
3 Economy Inn
4 Sands Motel

PLACES TO EAT
6 Socorro Springs Brewing Co
9 Val Verde Steakhouse
11 Martha's Black Dog Coffeehouse
12 Don Juan's Cocina

OTHER
2 San Miguel Mission
5 Supermart
7 Chamber of Commerce
8 Loma Theater
10 Post Office
13 Library
14 Police

Information

The chamber of commerce (☎ 835-0424), on the plaza, is open 9 am to 5 pm Monday to Friday and 10 am to noon Saturday. Other services include the library (☎ 835-1114), 401 Park SW; the post office (☎ 835-0542), on the plaza; a hospital (☎ 835-1140), on Hwy 60; and the police (☎ 835-1883), 407 Center St.

Things to See & Do

The chamber of commerce provides a **Historic Socorro** brochure with a map of the historic downtown area near the plaza. Many sites are described, most dating from the late 19th century. The highlight of the walk is the **San Miguel Mission** (☎ 835-1620), three blocks north of the plaza. Although restored and expanded several times, the mission still retains its colonial feel and parts of the walls date back to the original building. The mission is open daily (free).

The **Mineral Museum** (☎ 835-5420), on the Tech campus on the northwestern outskirts of town, displays thousands of minerals from around the world, fossils and other geological exhibits, making this the state's largest mineral collection. Hours are 8 am to 5 pm Monday to Friday and 10 am to 3 pm on weekends; museum admission is free.

Special Events
The Hilton Golf Tournament, held the first week in June, features a unique one-hole event on the last day: The players tee off from the top of a mountain and then golf through a makeshift course in the desert to the hole, about 5 miles away and 3000 feet below. The usual 18-hole tournament games are also held.

The Festival of the Cranes on the third weekend in November features special tours of Bosque del Apache, wildlife workshops and arts and crafts.

Places to Stay
Socorro RV Park (☎ 835-2234), by exit 147 of I-25, has a pool, showers and coin laundry. Rates are $17 without hookups and $20 with.

Budget rooms in the high $20s are available at the *Economy Inn* (☎ 835-4666, 400 California NE), with a small pool, and the *Sands Motel* (☎ 835-1130, 205 California NW), both of which are clean and reasonably well kept. Other *chain motels* include the Motel 6 at I-25 exit 147, the Super 8 and Holiday Inn at exit 150, and the Econo Lodge on California.

Places to Eat
Decent 24-hour dining is available at *El Camino Restaurant & Lounge* (☎ 835-1180, 707 California NW). It serves American and Mexican food.

Of Socorro's several Mexican restaurants, the cheerful, friendly and cheap *Frank & Lupe's El Sombrero* (☎ 835-3945, 210 Mesquite), near I-25 exit 150, is a good bet. Downtown, *Don Juan's Cocina* (☎ 835-9967, 118 Manzanares Ave) is popular for lunch.

Built in 1919, the historic (and now nonoperational) Val Verde Hotel was the center of the area's pre-WWII social life. Today it houses the *Val Verde Steakhouse* (☎ 835-3380, 203 Manzanares Ave). The restaurant is pleasantly old-fashioned and serves good steak and seafood dinner entrées in the $10 to $17 range, more for lobster. It's open noon to 9 pm Sunday, 11 am to 2 pm Monday to Friday for inexpensive lunches, and 5 to 9:30 pm Monday to Saturday.

Martha's Black Dog Coffeehouse (☎ 838-0311, 110 Manzanares Ave) serves quite an interesting and tasty selection of coffee, breakfast, sandwiches and salads. *Socorro Springs Brewing Co* (☎ 838-0650, 115 Abeyta Ave) has a clay oven and serves good pizza and pasta.

Entertainment
The *Loma Theater* (☎ 835-0965, 107 Manzanares Ave) shows Hollywood movies in a remodeled Victorian store.

The *Val Verde Bar* next to the steakhouse is an attractive drinking hole.

Getting There & Away
Greyhound (☎ 835-1767), at the Chevron service station near I-25 exit 147, runs two daily buses to Albuquerque and two to Las Cruces and El Paso, Texas.

Socorro Taxi (☎ 835-4276, 800-991-4276) offers several vans a day between Socorro and the Albuquerque airport for $53 each way.

AROUND SOCORRO
The **Bosque del Apache National Wildlife Refuge** protects almost 90 sq miles of fields and marshes that are a major wintering ground of many migratory birds, notably the very rare and endangered whooping cranes of which about a dozen winter here. Tens of thousands of snow geese, sandhill cranes

and various other waterfowl are also seen, as well as bald eagles. The migration lasts from late October to early April, but December and January are the peak viewing months and offer the best chance of seeing whooping cranes. Year-round, approximately 325 bird species and 135 species of mammal, reptile and amphibian have been recorded here.

The visitor center (☎ 835-1828) is open 7:30 am to 4 pm Monday to Friday, plus weekends in winter. From the center, a 15-mile loop drive goes around the refuge, and hiking trails and viewing platforms are available. The refuge is open from dawn to dusk, and admission is $3 per car. National Park passes are accepted, as are duck stamps (for duck hunters).

Visitors to the refuge often stop by the *Owl Bar Cafe* (☎ 835-9946), half a mile east of Hwy 25 exit 139 at the main intersection in San Antonio. It's the childhood home of Conrad Hilton, founder of the hotel chain. The café's green chile cheeseburger is acclaimed. Hours are 8 am to 9:30 pm Monday to Saturday.

To get to the refuge leave I-25 at San Antonio (10 miles south of Socorro) and drive 8 miles south on Hwy 1, or take the San Marcial exit and drive 10 miles north on Hwy 1.

SOCORRO TO QUEMADO

Hwy 60 west of Socorro goes through forests and high plains on its remote way to the Arizona state line, 140 miles away. **Magdalena**, 26 miles west of and 2000 feet higher than Socorro, was the end of the trail for thousands of range animals herded here to be shipped on the railroad (now defunct). In 1919, a record-breaking 150,000 sheep and more than 20,000 head of cattle were herded along the trail, which saw its last roundup in 1971.

The Cibola National Forest Magdalena Ranger Station (☎ 854-2281) is on the left of Hwy 60 coming from Socorro. They have information about local, waterless camping. Three miles south of the ranger station is the ghost town of Kelly, with a church and some mine-workings still visible. The *Western B&B*

(☎ 854-2417/2, *westernmotel@gilanet.com*) has six pleasant rooms with southwestern motif at $37/49 with continental breakfast or $59/69 with gourmet breakfast. There are several local cafés. *Montosa Ranch Campground* (☎ 854-2235), 14 miles west of Magdalena, has hot showers, tent sites ($7 per person) and RV sites with hookups ($15).

Twenty miles west of Magdalena, the National Radio Astronomy Observatory houses the **Very Large Array** (VLA) Telescope: 27 huge antenna dishes sprouting like giant mushrooms in the high plains. They combine to form an extremely powerful radio telescope used to probe the outer edges of the universe. A sign indicates the visitor center, 4 miles south of the highway, open 8 am to sunset daily (free).

Hwy 60 meets Hwy 12 at **Datil**, once a major stop on the herding trail, now an intersection with a gas station and café. Just beyond is the signed *Datil Well National Recreation Area*, with $5 campsites, water and several miles of nature trails on Bureau of Land Management (BLM) lands. Hwy 60 continues through the tiny settlement of Pie Town (where the *Pie-o-neer Café* sells pies) and then to the ranching town of **Quemado** with an Apache National Forest Ranger Station (☎ 773-4678), three simple motels and some cafés.

TRUTH OR CONSEQUENCES
☎ 505 • pop 7500 • elevation 4260 feet

Originally called Hot Springs and built on the site of natural hot mineral springs in the 1880s, the town voted in 1950 to change its name to that of a famous 1940s radio and TV comedy program as a publicity and fundraising gimmick, and it has been called Truth or Consequences (locally, T or C) since. The chamber of commerce or museum will fill you in on all the details of the name change.

T or C is a resort town for those wishing to use the hot springs or camp and fish in the three lakes/state parks nearby. T or C is also one of New Mexico's funkiest towns, with a lot of character. Wander around the little hole-in-the-wall cafés downtown, and check out the antique, thrift and junk shops.

Greyhound/TNM&O (☎ 894-3649) runs two daily buses north and south along I-25.

Information

The chamber of commerce (☎ 894-3536, 800-831-9487), 201 Foch St, is open 9 am to 5 pm Monday to Friday and 9 am to 1 pm Saturday. Its website is at www.truthor consequencesnm.net. Other services include the Gila National Forest Ranger Station (☎ 894-6677), 1804 N Date St; a library (☎ 894-3027), 325 Library Lane; two post offices (☎ 894-3137), 1507 N Date St, and 300 Main St; a hospital (☎ 894-2111), 800 E 9th St; and the police (☎ 894-7111), 401 McAdoo.

Museums

The extensive **Geronimo Springs Museum** (☎ 894-6600), 325 Main St, has plenty of local historical artifacts ranging from prehistoric Mimbres pots to beautifully worked cowboy saddles. Exhibits clarify the details of the famous 1950 name change. There are also mineral displays and local art. Hours are 9 am to 5 pm Monday to Saturday. Admission is $2 ($5 for a family).

Callahan's Auto Museum (☎ 894-6900), 410 Cedar St, exhibits cars from the 1920s to the 1960s, along with automobile memorabilia. Hours are 10 am to 4:30 pm daily. Admission is $3 ($5 for two people).

Hot Springs

A gazebo outside the Geronimo Springs Museum shelters a natural spring in which Geronimo is said to have bathed. Certainly, Indians have bathed in the area's hot springs for centuries. The mineral-laden waters have therapeutic properties, range in temperature from 98°F to 115°F and have a pH of 7 (neutral). The commercial hot baths in town date from the 1920s and 1930s and look a little the worse for wear from the outside, though they are acceptably clean inside. Most places charge about $3 to $6 per person for a hot bath (private, couple and family tubs available) or $25 and up for a massage or other treatment, which requires advance notice.

Try the following, most of which also offer lodging (see Places to Stay, later): **Charles Motel & Bath House** (☎ 894-7154), 601 Broadway, supposedly with the hottest water in town (open 8 am to 9 pm daily, indoor and outdoor tubs, massage, sauna, reflexology, holistic healing); **Riverbend Hot Springs**

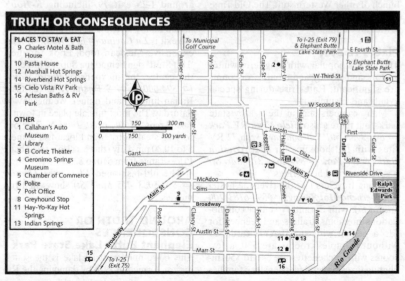

TRUTH OR CONSEQUENCES

PLACES TO STAY & EAT
9 Charles Motel & Bath House
10 Pasta House
12 Marshall Hot Springs
14 Riverbend Hot Springs
15 Cielo Vista RV Park
16 Artesian Baths & RV Park

OTHER
1 Callahan's Auto Museum
2 Library
3 El Cortez Theater
4 Geronimo Springs Museum
5 Chamber of Commerce
6 Police
7 Post Office
8 Greyhound Stop
11 Hay-Yo-Kay Hot Springs
13 Indian Springs

(☎ 894-6183), 100 Austin St, (morning and evening sessions, six outdoor tubs by the river), website: www.riverbendhotsprings.com; **Artesian Baths** (☎ 894-2684), 312 Marr St (eight tubs); **Hay-Yo-Kay Hot Springs** (☎ 894-2228), 300 Austin St, (open 8 am to 7 pm, closed Wednesday, five pools, massage); **Marshall Hot Springs** (☎ 894-9286), 311 Marr St, (five private free-flowing tubs, massage), website: www.marshallhot-springs.com; or **Indian Springs** (☎ 894-2018), 218 Austin St, (one large free-flowing pool).

Special Events
The T or C Fiesta (first weekend in May) celebrates the town's changing its name in 1950; Ralph Edwards, long-retired host of the *Truth or Consequences* radio and TV program, has visited every year since then. There is a rodeo, barbecue, parade and other events.

The Sierra County Fair has livestock and agricultural displays during late August.

Geronimo Days, in the second week of October, features Native American dancers; cowboy poetry; fiddlers contests; gunfights and historical reenactments; cloggers and other dancers; country & western, bluegrass and mariachi music; a procession and a bunch of other Western stuff. The Old Time Fiddlers State Championship is held the following weekend.

Places to Stay
The area is popular with long-term winter visitors, and weekly and monthly discounts are significant. Rates rise during special events and in summer.

Many campers stay in the nearby state parks, but there's also *Cielo Vista RV Park* (☎ 894-3738, 501 S Broadway), with 72 RV sites with full hookups for $21. *Artesian Baths & RV Park* (☎ 894-2684, 312 Marr St) has $10 sites and hot springs.

Young travelers like the riverside hostel at *Riverbend Hot Springs* (☎ 894-6183, 100 Austin St), with dormitory-style accommodations in cabins, trailers and teepees for $15 a person with an HI/AYH card, $17 without. Couples' rooms are $30, a few rooms with kitchenettes are $40 to $50, including taxes. Several teepees sleep families

and small groups. Hot-spring tubs are available morning and evening and are free for guests. The owners are friendly and helpful to budget travelers.

The cheapest motels start in the $20s for a double room; they're basic and worn, although adequate for those on a tight budget. There are seven or eight cheapies along Date St between 6th and 9th Sts.

Better motels in the $30 range include the *Ace Lodge* (☎ 894-2151, 1302 N Date St) and the *Desert View Motel* (☎ 894-3318, 906 N Date St). Several others are nearby. Downtown, you'll find the *Charles Motel & Bath House* (☎ 894-7154, 601 Broadway), which has its own hot springs, as does *Marshall Hot Springs* (☎ 894-9286, 311 Marr St).

For folks looking for reliability, *chain motels*, around I-25 exit 79, include a Super 8, Best Western and Holiday Inn, the latter two with pools. Rates are in the $45 to $80 range. Out by Elephant Butte Lake, the *Quality Inn* (☎ 744-5431) has a pool, tennis court, restaurant and bar, and nice rooms with lake views for about $80.

Places to Eat
Fast food and chain restaurants are found around I-25 exit 79, including *K-Bob's* (☎ 894-2127), which serves reasonably priced family-style meals and steak. Also at the exit is *La Cocina* (☎ 894-6499), with inexpensive Mexican food. Look for their 'Hot Stuff' sign behind the Super 8 motel. In the center, the inexpensive *Pasta House* (☎ 894-0008, 304 S Pershing) serves tasty Italian lunches and dinner Wednesday to Saturday. The most upscale place in town is *Los Arcos* (☎ 894-6200, 1400 N Date St), serving steak, lobster and local-fish dinners 5 to 10:30 pm daily (there's also a salad bar). Prices range from $10 to $23.

The old-fashioned *El Cortez Theater* (☎ 894-5023, 415 Main St) shows first-run movies.

AROUND TRUTH OR CONSEQUENCES
Elephant Butte Lake State Park
This 60-sq-mile artificial lake is the state's largest, formed in 1916 by damming the Rio

Grande. The park is on the west shore of the lake, 5 miles east of town. The lake is very popular for fishing, camping, waterskiing and windsurfing.

A visitor center (☎ 744-5421) has information, a 1½-mile-loop nature trail and a nearby marina with boat rentals. Several campgrounds provide over 100 sites with RV hookups. Hot showers, a playground, and picnic and barbecue areas are available. North along the lake are hundreds of undeveloped sites and other boat launch sites. Day use is $4; undeveloped camping (pit toilets, no water) is $8; developed camping is $10, or $14 with hookups.

At the lake's south end a marina (☎ 894-2041) has tackle, gas, basic groceries and supplies, and boat rentals (fishing, pontoon and skiing) from $40 to $90 for two hours, $110 to $220 per day, plus fuel.

Fishing contests take place regularly at Elephant Butte Lake. Spring and fall are the best seasons, though people fish year-round. Fishing guides charge $200 to $325 a day for one to four anglers. Call Bass Busters (☎ 894-0928), whose website is www.zianet.com/bassbusters; Desert Bass Fishing Services (☎ 744-5314); or Fishing Adventures (☎ 1-800-580-8992), www.stripersnewmexico.com.

Other Parks

Adjacent to another artificial lake resulting from a dam on the Rio Grande, **Caballo Lake State Park** (☎ 743-3942) offers fishing, boating, skiing and windsurfing. A few dozen bald eagles overwinter around the lake and can often be seen between October and February. Fishing is best from mid-March to mid-June. There are boat ramps, a playground, and several campgrounds with hot showers, 60 RV hookups and 250 sites without hookups. The park is a mile northeast of exit 59 on I-25, 17 miles south of T or C.

Three miles south of Caballo Lake State Park and administered by it, **Percha Dam State Park** has a further 80 sites, six with hookups, hot showers and a playground. There is no boat ramp. Fees are $4 per vehicle for day use, $10 for camping and $14 with hookups.

The roadrunner: New Mexico's state bird

HATCH

This village is famed as the center of New Mexico's (and hence the USA's) chile-growing region. You can buy chiles, salsas, *ristras* (decorative strings and wreaths of chiles) and other chile products in one of several stores in this small town.

The chamber of commerce (☎ 267-5050), 112 W Hall (Hwy 187), is open 9 am to 2 pm Monday to Friday. An annual **chile festival** is held over Labor Day weekend. Delicious meals and fresh and prepared chiles of all levels of spiciness are sold, and various country-fair-type events take place. Food lovers could combine this festival with the nearby Hillsboro Apple Festival, held the same weekend.

LAS CRUCES AREA
☎ 505 • pop 78,800 (Las Cruces) • elevation 3890 feet (Las Cruces)

Las Cruces lies in an attractive setting between the Rio Grande Valley and the strangely fluted Organ Mountains rising to the east. In 1535, Spanish explorers heading north from Mexico along the Rio Grande Valley passed through this area, recording that there were Indian villages nearby. In 1787 and again in 1830, Apaches killed bands of travelers camping here, and their graves were marked by a collection of crosses – hence the Spanish name of Las Cruces. There was no permanent settlement here until 1849. Several of the town's early buildings are still standing.

Adjacent to Las Cruces, Mesilla was established in 1850 for Mexican settlers who wished to avoid becoming part of the USA after the Mexican-American War. Their hopes were short-lived, however; in 1853, the USA bought Mesilla with the Gadsden Purchase. Initially, Mesilla was larger and more important than Las Cruces, and Mesilla's plaza and surrounding streets contain many buildings from those early years, including a stagecoach stop for the Butterfield Overland Mail Company.

Las Cruces has boomed in recent decades and is New Mexico's second largest city, while Mesilla has fewer residents than it did in the 19th century. It is an important agricultural, industrial and academic center. Most farms are small and family-owned, and major crops are chiles, pecans, corn and fruit. The nearby White Sands Missile Range provides thousands of jobs. New Mexico State University (NMSU) has some 15,000 students attending undergraduate, graduate and post-graduate programs.

Information

The convention and visitors bureau (☎ 541-2444, 800-343-7827), 211 N Water, Las Cruces, NM 88001, website: www.lascrucescvb.org, and chamber of commerce (☎ 524-1968), 760 W Picacho Ave, Las Cruces, NM 88005, both provide visitor information on weekdays. Other services include the BLM (☎ 525-4300), 1800 Marquess St; a library (☎ 528-4000), 200 E Picacho Ave; the main post office (☎ 524-2841), 201 E Las Cruces Ave; a medical center (☎ 522-8641), 2450 S Telshor Blvd; and the police (☎ 526-0795), 217 E Picacho Ave.

Branigan Cultural Center

In the Downtown Mall, 490-500 N Water St, the center (☎ 541-2155) houses both the **Museum of Fine Art & Culture** and the **Las Cruces Historical Museum**. There are small collections of local art, sculpture, quilts and historic artifacts, and changing art shows. The center also arranges tours of the late 1800s **Log Cabin Museum**, at Lucero Ave

and Main St at the north end of the Downtown Mall. Hours are 9 am to 5 pm Monday to Friday; call for weekend hours. Admission is free.

University Museums

The **NMSU Museum** (☎ 646-3739), in Kent Hall at Solano Dr and University Ave, houses changing exhibits focusing on local art, history and archaeology. It's worth a look. Hours are noon to 4 pm Tuesday to Friday. The **NMSU Art Gallery** (☎ 646-2545), in Williams Hall just east of Kent Hall, has changing exhibits almost every month and a large permanent collection of contemporary art. Hours are 10 am to 5 pm Monday to Saturday. Admission to both is free.

Farm & Ranch Heritage Museum

From pre-historic Indian farming techniques to the life histories of 20th-century ranchers, the exhibits are worth a visit if you are interested in agricultural history. The displays are well laid out and fully signed both in Spanish and English, and children enjoy seeing the livestock up close. Call ahead to find out times for milking and blacksmithing demonstrations. The museum (☎ 522-4100), 4100 Dripping Springs Rd, features a good restaurant as well. Hours are 9 am to 5 pm Tuesday to Saturday, noon to 5 pm Sunday. Admission is $4 for adults, $3 for seniors, $2 for kids six to 17.

Mesilla

For many visitors, a stop in Mesilla is the highlight of their time in Las Cruces. Despite the souvenir shops and tourist-oriented restaurants, the Mesilla Plaza and surrounding blocks are a step back in time. The plaza is the obvious center of things, but wander a few blocks around to get a feeling of an important mid-19th-century Southwestern town of Hispanic heritage.

Formerly a Mexican town, Mesilla became part of the USA after the Gadsden Purchase. For the story, visit the private **Gadsden Museum** (☎ 526-6293), on Boutz Rd just off Hwy 28, a few hundred yards east of the plaza. Hours are 9 to 11 am Monday to

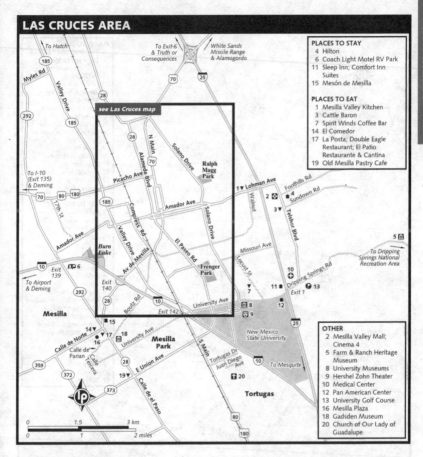

LAS CRUCES AREA

PLACES TO STAY
4 Hilton
6 Coach Light Motel RV Park
11 Sleep Inn; Comfort Inn Suites
15 Mesón de Mesilla

PLACES TO EAT
1 Mesilla Valley Kitchen
3 Cattle Baron
7 Spirit Winds Coffee Bar
14 El Comedor
17 La Posta; Double Eagle Restaurant; El Patio Restaurante & Cantina
19 Old Mesilla Pastry Cafe

OTHER
2 Mesilla Valley Mall; Cinema 4
5 Farm & Ranch Heritage Museum
8 University Museums
9 Hershel Zohn Theater
10 Medical Center
12 Pan American Center
13 University Golf Course
16 Mesilla Plaza
18 Gadsden Museum
20 Church of Our Lady of Guadalupe

Saturday, and 1 to 5 pm daily. Admission is $2 for adults, $1 for kids six to 12.

Dripping Springs National Recreation Area

Once called the Cox Ranch and now jointly managed by the BLM and the Nature Conservancy, this area is a good place for bird-watching in the Organ Mountains. There is a nature trail and picnic area. Head east on University Ave, which becomes unpaved Dripping Springs Rd (it's about 9 miles). Hours are 8 am to sunset; the Cox Visitor Center (☎ 522-

1219) is open 9 am to 5 pm. Admission is $4 per vehicle.

Special Events

The city's best-known event is the Whole Enchilada Fiesta, held the first Friday, Saturday and Sunday in October, featuring live music, food booths, arts and crafts, sporting events, a chile cookoff, carnival rides and a parade, culminating in the cooking of the world's biggest enchilada on Sunday morning. Events are held in the Downtown Mall.

From December 10 to 12, the Fiesta of Our Lady of Guadalupe is held in the

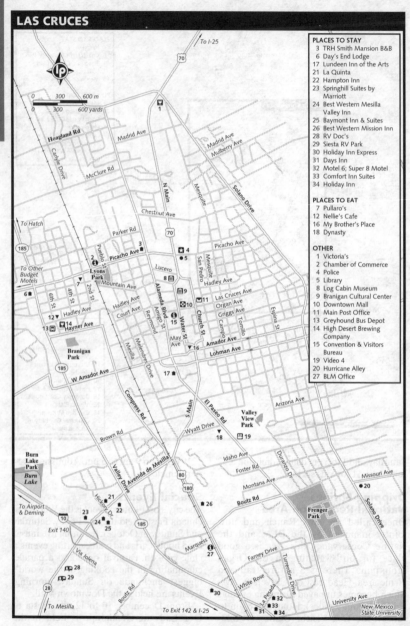

LAS CRUCES

PLACES TO STAY
3 TRH Smith Mansion B&B
6 Day's End Lodge
17 Lundeen Inn of the Arts
21 La Quinta
22 Hampton Inn
23 Springhill Suites by Marriott
24 Best Western Mesilla Valley Inn
25 Baymont Inn & Suites
26 Best Western Mission Inn
28 RV Doc's
29 Siesta RV Park
30 Holiday Inn Express
31 Days Inn
32 Motel 6; Super 8 Motel
33 Comfort Inn Suites
34 Holiday Inn

PLACES TO EAT
7 Pullaro's
12 Nellie's Cafe
16 My Brother's Place
18 Dynasty

OTHER
1 Victoria's
2 Chamber of Commerce
4 Police
5 Library
8 Log Cabin Museum
9 Branigan Cultural Center
10 Downtown Mall
11 Main Post Office
13 Greyhound Bus Depot
14 High Desert Brewing Company
15 Convention & Visitors Bureau
19 Video 4
20 Hurricane Alley
27 BLM Office

Indian village of Tortugas at the south end of Las Cruces. Late into the first night, drummers and masked dancers accompany a statue of Mary in a procession from the church. On the following day, participants climb several miles to 4914-foot Tortugas Mountain for mass; dancing and ceremonies continue in the village into the night. The Church of Our Lady of Guadalupe (☎ 526-8171) has information.

The Mesilla Balloon Rally is held in mid-January. The Southern New Mexico State Fair & Rodeo is held for five days in late September. The Renaissance Arts and Crafts Fair, held the first weekend in November, features performers in 16th-century English garb and is the biggest crafts fair of the year. An International Mariachi Conference, open to the public, is held in mid-November.

Places to Stay

Camping For those interested in camping with amenities, *Siesta RV Park* (☎ 523-6816, 1551 Av de Mesilla) has showers and coin laundry. It charges $19 with full hookups and has a few less expensive tent sites. Nearby, *RV Doc's* (☎ 526-8401, 1475 Av de Mesilla) is cheaper but has no tent spaces. Also try *Coachlight Motel RV Park* (☎ 526-3301, 301 S Motel Blvd), which also has no tent sites, but does offer a budget motel. website: www.zianet.com/coachlight

Motels & Hotels A number of cheap places with doubles in the $20 and $30 ranges are clustered along Picacho Ave east of Hwy 292. The nicest of these is the *Royal Host Motel* (☎ 524-8536, 2146 W Picacho Ave), with a pool, charging $30/34 for singles/doubles. The clean but small *Desert Lodge Motel* (☎ 524-1925, 1900 W Picacho Ave) charges $24/28 as does the 100-room *Economy Inn* (☎ 524-8627, 2160 W Picacho Ave). Half a dozen even cheaper places are nearby.

The pleasant *Day's End Lodge* (☎ 524-7753, fax 523-2127, 755 N Valley Dr), has rooms for about $30/35 including breakfast, but often offers discounts. They have a pool.

Most *chain hotels* are represented, with rates ranging from $40 to $80 for a double

room. Near I-10 exit 142 there's a Motel 6, Super 8, Days Inn, Comfort Inn, Holiday Inn and Holiday Inn Express. North of I-10 exit 140 you have the choice of Best Western Mesilla Valley Inn, Hampton Inn, La Quinta, Baymont Inn & Suites and Springhill Suites by Marriott. Convenient to the university, near I-25 exit 1, are the Sleep Inn and Comfort Inn Suites.

The town's best and biggest hotel is the seven-story *Hilton* (☎ 522-4300, 705 S Telshor Blvd), on the east side of Las Cruces with good city and mountain views. Over 200 spacious rooms, each with a coffeemaker, are in the $80 range, and a few more expensive suites are available.

B&Bs A large, turn-of-the-19th-century adobe house owned by architects, *Lundeen Inn of the Arts* (☎ 526-3326, 888-526-3326, 618 S Alameda Blvd) has 20 guest rooms and an art gallery. Some rooms have kitchenettes and all have private bath and phone. Rates range from $58 to $64 for a single, $75 to $85 for a double and $85 to $105 for suites, including full breakfast. website: www.innofthearts.com

The *TRH Smith Mansion B&B* (☎ 525-2525, 800-526-1914, 909 N Alameda Blvd) is in a historic 1914 mansion. Four guest rooms have phone and bath, but no TV. Two smaller rooms are $60 to $75, and larger rooms, one with a fireplace, are $68 to $95, including a full German-style breakfast. A game room includes a pool table, TV and VCR. Smoking is prohibited in the rooms, and children under 10 are not allowed. website: www.SmithMansion.com

The *Mesón de Mesilla* (☎ 525-9212, 800-732-6025, 1803 Av de Mesilla) is a modern adobe house with 15 guest rooms furnished with antiques and all with private bath and modern amenities. Attractive gardens surround the house, which also has a pool. It's a short walk to the Mesilla Plaza. Rates range from $45 to $92 (rooms vary in size) and a honeymoon suite is $140, including full breakfast in their restaurant (see Places to Eat, below). website: www.mesondemesilla.com

Places to Eat

Las Cruces A good place for breakfast is the *Mesilla Valley Kitchen* (☎ 523-9311, *Arroyo Plaza, Space 102, 2001 E Lohman Ave*), open 6 am to 2:30 pm Monday to Saturday, 7 am to 1:30 pm Sunday. The university crowd hangs out at *Spirit Winds Coffee Bar* (☎ 521-1222, 2260 S Locust), with excellent cappuccino and gourmet coffee and tea, as well as good sandwiches, salads, soups and pastries served all day. There is an eclectic gift and card shop and occasional live entertainment.

Not surprisingly, there are dozens of decent Mexican restaurants. Favorites include *Nellie's Cafe* (☎ 524-9982, 1226 W Hadley Ave), open 8 am to 4 pm Monday to Saturday. Nellie has been around for decades and has a dedicated following, as can be seen by the full tables at noon on any workday. Nellies' slogan is 'Chile with an Attitude' and the food is deliciously spicy and cheap. Alcohol is not served. For that, go to *My Brother's Place* (☎ 523-7681, 334 S Main St), popular for its Mexican lunch specials, which draw downtown workers. It's open for dinner as well. The dining room around a fountain is attractive, and two adjoining bars have pool tables and sports TV.

Good steak, chicken, pasta and seafood are served at the *Cattle Baron* (☎ 522-7533, 790 S Telshor Blvd), open for lunch and dinner daily. Dinner entrées cost $10 to $18, including a salad, and a kids' menu is available. Lunch is much cheaper.

For Chinese food, *Dynasty* (☎ 525-8116, 1210 El Paseo Rd) has been voted best in town by locals. A good choice for Italian food is *Pullaro's* (☎ 523-6801, 901 W Picacho Ave), open 11 am to 2 pm and 5 to 9 pm daily. Also good is the mini-chain *Lorenzo's*, with three locations (check the phone book).

Mesilla Great for breakfast and lunch, *Old Mesilla Pastry Cafe* (☎ 525-2636, 2790 Av de Mesilla) has espresso, cappuccino, pastries, other breakfast fare, vegetarian sandwiches and pizza. Hours are 7:30 am to 2:30 pm Wednesday to Sunday.

For Mexican and New Mexican cuisine, traditional Mesilla provides the appropriate setting. The most famous place is *La Posta* (☎ 524-3524), inside an early-19th-century adobe house (predating the founding of Mesilla) on the east corner of the plaza. A Butterfield stagecoach stop in the 1850s, the restaurant is full of character. The current restaurant, which has been on the premises since the 1930s, serves lunch and dinner Tuesday to Sunday. You can get a good Mexican or steak dinner here for about $7 to $16, depending on your appetite.

Other restaurants on the plaza include *El Patio Restaurante & Cantina* (☎ 524-0982), also housed in an early adobe building and in operation since the 1930s. It has prices a touch lower than La Posta, and the bar attracts local jazz lovers. Hours are 11 am to 2 pm Monday to Friday, and 5:30 to 9 pm Monday to Saturday (the bar stays open late). The *Double Eagle Restaurant* (☎ 523-6700, 523 4999) is Mesilla Plaza's most upscale eatery, offering continental and Southwestern cuisine in an elegant Victorian setting. It is open 11 am to 10 pm Monday to Saturday (call for Sunday hours) and has dinner entrées in the $14 to $30 range. Lunches under $10 are a good value. Visitors are encouraged to stroll around and see the 19th-century architecture in these places, even if you decide not to eat.

A few blocks from the plaza, the recommended *El Comedor* (☎ 524-7002, 2190 Av de Mesilla) is much less expensive and serves good Mexican meals indoors or on a small patio.

The *Mesón de Mesilla* (☎ 525-2380) restaurant (in the B&B) has a small but varied gourmet continental dinner menu with entrées between $20 and $30. Reservations are requested.

Entertainment

The Bulletin is a free weekly appearing on Thursday and has entertainment information.

The area's main cinema complexes (all ☎ 523-6900) are *Cinema 4* in the Mesilla Valley Mall; *Video 4* (1005 El Paseo Rd); and *Telshor 12* (2811 Telshor Blvd). Foreign and art films are screened at the *Fountain*

Theater (☎ 524-8287, 2469 Calle de Guada-lupe), half a block south of the Mesilla Plaza.

The American Southwest Theater Company presents plays at the *Hershel Zohn Theater (☎ 646-4515),* on the NMSU campus. The Las Cruces Symphony (☎ 646-3709) plays at the NMSU *Pan American Center (☎ 646-1420).* Other cultural events take place here; call the special events director (☎ 646-4413) for information. The Las Cruces Community Theatre (☎ 523-1200) performs in the *Downtown Mall* with five shows a year. Their website is at www.zianet.com/lcct.

For the bar scene, check out Mesilla's *El Patio (☎ 526-9943),* next to the restaurant bearing the same name, with jazz acts midweek and rock or blues on weekends. *High Desert Brewing Company (☎ 525-6752, 1201 W Hadley Ave)* is a microbrewery with good beer, food and live music on weekends. *Hurricane Alley (☎ 532-9358, 1490 Missouri Ave),* has live rock or DJs and dancing on weekends. *Victoria's (☎ 523-0440, 2395 N Solano Dr)* features dancing to Latin bands on weekends.

Shopping

The Mesilla Plaza area has about 30 stores selling souvenirs ranging from cheap and kitsch to expensive and excellent. You can pick up jewelry, Navajo rugs, t-shirts, ceramics and artwork of all kinds.

Getting There & Away

Las Cruces airport is 8 miles west of downtown. Mesa Airlines (☎ 526-9743) runs three flights on weekdays, two on weekends, straight to Albuquerque. El Paso International Airport, less than an hour away, has flights to the rest of the US.

Greyhound/TNM&O (☎ 524-8518), 490 N Valley Dr, has buses following the two interstate corridors as well as to Roswell and beyond.

Las Cruces Shuttle Service (☎ 525-1784, 800-288-1784) has 12 vans a day from many Las Cruces stops to the El Paso Airport. The one-way fare is $28 for one person and $10 for each additional person. The service

also runs vans to Deming, Silver City and other destinations on request. Reservations are required.

Getting Around

Roadrunner (☎ 541-2500) operates eight bus routes in Las Cruces (but not to Mesilla or the airport). There is no night or Sunday service. Look in the telephone directory for route maps.

Checker Cab/Yellow Cab (☎ 524-1711) takes reservations and has 24-hour service. If you need to rent a car, Advantage, Enterprise, Hertz and Thrifty are all in Las Cruces.

NORTH OF LAS CRUCES
Fort Selden State Monument

Fort Selden was built in 1865 to protect travelers. Buffalo soldiers (African American army units) were stationed here, and US General Douglas MacArthur spent some of his childhood at the fort. Closed in 1891, Fort Selden is now in ruins, but a small museum presents memorabilia, and an interpretive trail winds through the remains. Park rangers in period dress give demonstrations during summer weekends.

The monument (☎ 526-8911) is 15 miles north of Las Cruces (near I-25 exit 19). Hours are 8:30 am to 5 pm; closed on Tuesday and major holidays. Admission is $3 for those over 16.

website: www.nmculture.org

Leasburg Dam State Park

Adjacent to Fort Selden, this park (☎ 524-4068) offers year-round camping and picnicking in desert scrub scenery. Leasburg Dam impounds a small lake offering limited boating, swimming and fishing, and there is a playground for kids. Water and showers are available. Day use is $4; camping is $8, $10 or $14 with partial hookups. Note that there are different entrances for the campground and the lake.

EAST OF LAS CRUCES
Aguirre Springs
National Recreation Area

About 20 miles east of Las Cruces, this BLM-managed scenic area on the east side of the Organ Mountains offers good bird-watching, strenuous hiking, horse trails and primitive camping. Drive east on Hwy 70, over the scenic **San Agustin Pass** (5719 feet; there is a viewpoint) to the signed Aguirre Springs road 2 miles beyond the pass. It's about 5 miles to the campground along the steep and winding road (trailers over 22 feet not recommended), and the mountain views are worthwhile. Day use is free; the primitive campground costs $5 and has pit toilets and picnic tables but no drinking water.

White Sands Missile Range Museum

The White Sands Missile Test Center, 25 miles east of Las Cruces along Hwy 70, is the heart of the White Sands Missile Range, a major military testing site since 1945 and an alternate landing site for the space shuttle. The museum (☎ 678-2250, 678-8824), near the test center's entrance gate, describes the development of these activities. Hours are 8 am to 4 pm Monday to Friday (free). Outside the museum is Missile Park, with many missiles displayed. At the entrance gate to the test center, tell the guard you are visiting the museum/park; be prepared to show your driver's license and car documents.

DEMING

☎ 505 • pop 16,800 • elevation 4335 feet

On the northern edge of the Chihuahua Desert, Deming was founded in 1881 as a railway junction, and is now an agricultural center and the second largest town in southwestern New Mexico. Water for the farms and ranches comes from the invisible Mimbres River, which disappears underground about 20 miles north of town and emerges in Mexico. A good museum, nearby state parks and the unique duck races attract visitors.

Greyhound (☎ 546-3881), 300 E Spruce St, has three or four daily buses westbound and eastbound along I-10. Las Cruces Shuttle Service (☎ 525-1784, 800-288-1784) runs vans to Silver City, Las Cruces and the El Paso Airport.

Information

The chamber of commerce (☎ 546-2674, 800-848-4955), 800 E Pine St, on the Web at www.demingchamber.com, is open 9 am to 5 pm Monday to Saturday. Other services include the library (☎ 546-9202), 301 S Tin St; the post office (☎ 546-9461), 209 W Spruce St; medical services (☎ 546-2761), 900 W Ash St; and the police (☎ 546-3011), 700 E Pine St.

Deming Luna Mimbres Museum

Run by the Luna County Historical Society (☎ 546-2382), 301 S Silver St, the museum is housed in what was once the National Guard Armory, built in 1916. Exhibits are varied, interesting and well displayed. There's a superb doll collection, many Mimbres pots, several vintage cars, 1200 liquor decanters, beautiful homemade quilts, a Braille edition of *Playboy* and much more. Hours are 9 am to 4 pm Monday to Saturday, 1:30 to 4 pm Sunday; closed major holidays. Admission is free, but contributions are appreciated.

Great American Duck Races

One of the most whimsical and popular festivals in the state, the GADR attracts tens of thousands of visitors the fourth weekend in August. The main events are the duck races themselves, with thousands of dollars in prizes. Anybody can enter for a $10 fee ($5 for kids), which includes 'duck rental.' By strange coincidence, the surname of some of the best duck trainers is Duck. (Robert and Bryce Duck's ducks took first and second place in the 1994 races.) Other events during the GADR include the Tortilla Toss (winners toss tortillas over 170 feet), Outhouse Races, Best Dressed Duck contest and many sporting events. Entertainment ranges from cowboy poets to local musicians, and there's a parade, hot-air balloons and food.

Places to Stay & Eat

Rooms are at a premium and prices rise during the duck races and the southwestern New Mexico state fair (early October), when you need reservations.

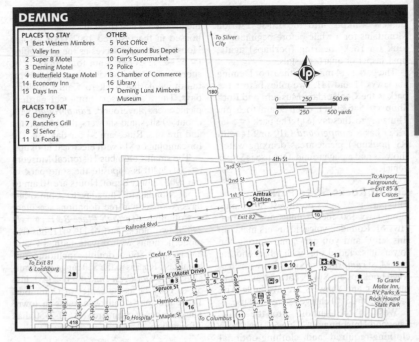

DEMING

PLACES TO STAY
1 Best Western Mimbres Valley Inn
2 Super 8 Motel
3 Deming Motel
4 Butterfield Stage Motel
14 Economy Inn
15 Days Inn

PLACES TO EAT
6 Denny's
7 Ranchers Grill
8 Sí Señor
11 La Fonda

OTHER
5 Post Office
9 Greyhound Bus Depot
10 Furr's Supermarket
12 Police
13 Chamber of Commerce
16 Library
17 Deming Luna Mimbres Museum

RV campgrounds are popular and often full with winter snowbirds, so call ahead. Most charge $10 to $16 and are geared to RVs rather than tents. The best are the **Roadrunner RV Park** (☎ 546-6960, 800-226-9937, 2849 E Pine St), which allows tents, and the **Little Vineyard RV Park** (☎ 546-3560, 2901 E Pine St). Both have an indoor pool, spa, recreation area and coin laundry. Cheaper places are nearby.

About 10 budget motels line Pine St (aka Motel Drive), with rates starting in the $20 range. The **Economy Inn** (☎ 544-2090, 1210 E Pine St) has a small pool and inexpensive restaurant; it looks OK for about $25/30 for singles/doubles. The **Butterfield Stage Motel** (☎ 544-0011, 309 W Pine) is small and tidy with double rooms in the low $30s. The larger **Deming Motel** (☎ 546-2737, 500 W Pine St) has a pool and charges about $30. The **Grand Motor Inn** (☎ 546-2631, 1721 E Pine St) charges in the $40 range, often gives discounts and has 62 nice rooms. The grassy

grounds have both adult and children's pools. Its **restaurant** (☎ 546-2632) is one of Deming's best, with Mexican and American food. Dinner entrées are $7 to $17.

Chain motels include a Motel 6 and Holiday Inn at I-10, exit 85, a Best Western and Super 8 near exit 81, and a Days Inn. All have pools. **Fat Eddies** at the Holiday Inn is a good place to eat a varied menu. It does room service.

Deming has a handful of good Mexican-American restaurants, including **La Fonda** (☎ 546-0465, 601 E Pine St) and the cheaper **Sí Señor** (☎ 546-3938, 200 E Pine St). For steaks, try **Ranchers Grill** (☎ 546-8883, 316 E Cedar St).

AROUND DEMING
Rock Hound State Park
This park is known for the semiprecious or just plain pretty rocks that can be collected here (there's a 15lb limit). You'll need a shovel and some rockhounding experience

to uncover anything special; local experts suggest walking into the Little Florida Mountains for a while before beginning to look for rocks bearing (perhaps) agate, opal, jasper or quartz crystals.

The park is 14 miles southeast of Deming via Hwys 11 and 141. Two miles before the park is the **Geolapidary Museum and Rock Shop** (☎ 546-4021), open 9 am to 5 pm Thursday to Tuesday ($1). The park (☎ 546-6182) has a *campground* ($10 or $14 with RV hookups), picnic areas, drinking water, showers and a playground. Day use is $4 per vehicle.

City of Rocks State Park

This park is 27 miles northwest of Deming along Hwy 180, then 4 miles northeast on Hwy 61. Rounded volcanic towers make up this 'city,' and you can camp among the towers in secluded sites with tables and fire pits. Most *campsites* are $10; a few with electrical hookups are $14. A nature trail, drinking water and showers are available. The park (☎ 536-2800) charges $4 for day use.

West of the turnoff into the park, **Faywood Hotsprings** (☎ 536-9663) has both clothing-required and clothing-optional pools, tent and RV sites, and trailers for rent. website: www.faywood.com

PANCHO VILLA STATE PARK

On March 9, 1916, the Mexican revolutionary and outlaw Pancho Villa, unhappy with the US government's support of his enemies, stormed across the border with several hundred troops. He attacked US Army Camp Furlong and the town of **Columbus** (3 miles north of the Mexican border), killing 18 people and burning several buildings before being pushed back into Mexico, having lost over 100 men. He was chased deep into Mexico by General John 'Black Jack' Pershing, who led US troops using aircraft and motor vehicles – the first time the US used both in warfare. Villa succeeded in eluding capture, however, and the USA hasn't undergone an invasion since.

Camp Furlong is long gone, and once-bustling Columbus is now a village of some 1000 inhabitants, but visitors head there because of its unique history. The story of the invasion is described in a small museum housed in the restored 1902 US Customs House, which also serves as the park office (☎ 531-2711), open 8 am to 5 pm daily. A short film can also be viewed, as can several buildings dating back to Camp Furlong days. There's a desert botanical garden, picnic area, playground, *campground* with about 80 sites and showers, drinking water and fire pits. Rates are $4 for day use, $10 for camping or $14 with electrical hookups.

The small **Columbus Historical Museum** (☎ 531-2620) is opposite the state park in the 1902 railway depot. Hours are 10 am to 1 pm Monday to Thursday, to 4 pm other days. Admission is free; donations accepted.

Columbus' *Martha's Place B&B* (☎ 531-2467), two blocks east of Hwy 11, has five modern rooms with private bath, TV and balcony for $60 a double, including full breakfast. Rooms in the $30 range are available at the *Sun Crest Inn* (☎ 531-2323), just off of Hwy 11 in the center of Columbus. There are four small restaurants in town. The chamber of commerce (☎ 531-2750) has information.

SILVER CITY

☎ 505 • pop 12,300 • elevation 5938 feet

The city's name tells its story: a mining town founded in 1870 after the discovery of silver. Silver prices crashed in 1893, leading to the demise of that industry. But, instead of becoming a ghost town like many others, Silver City tapped another mineral wealth, copper, which is still mined today. Ranching is of some importance, and the city is the part-time home to more than 2000 students at Western New Mexico University.

History is in evidence in the downtown streets, with their Victorian brick buildings and Wild West air. Billy the Kid spent some of his boyhood here, and a few of his haunts can be seen.

North of Silver City, Hwy 15 heads through Pinos Altos and dead-ends at the Gila Cliff Dwellings National Monument, 42 miles away (see that section, later). The road is scenic, mountainous, narrow and winding – allow a couple of hours to drive it.

Silver City is the gateway to outdoor activities in the Gila National Forest. Locals sometimes call the town, simply, Silver.

Information

The chamber of commerce (☎ 538-3785, 800-548-9378), 201 N Hudson St, on the Web at www.silvercity.org, is open 9 am to 5 pm Monday to Saturday. Other services include the Gila National Forest Ranger Station (☎ 538-2771), just north of E Hwy 180 at 32nd St; the library (☎ 538-3672), 515 W College Ave; a post office (☎ 538-2831), 500 N Hudson St; a medical center (☎ 538-4000), 1313 E 32nd; and the police (☎ 538-3723), 1011 N Hudson St.

Many artists work in the area and the chamber of commerce has a map with dozens of the city's galleries.

Historic Downtown

Bullard, Texas, and Arizona Sts between Broadway and 6th St are the heart of Victorian Silver City. The former Main St, one block east of Bullard, was washed out in a series of massive floods, some up to 12 feet deep, beginning in 1895. Caused by runoff from logged and overgrazed areas north of

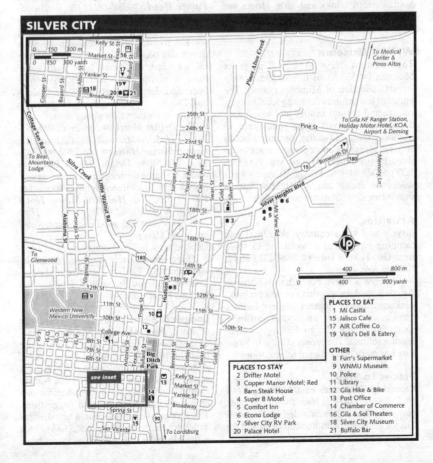

SILVER CITY

PLACES TO EAT
1 Mi Casita
15 Jalisco Cafe
17 AIR Coffee Co
19 Vicki's Deli & Eatery

OTHER
8 Furr's Supermarket
9 WNMU Museum
10 Police
11 Library
12 Gila Hike & Bike
13 Post Office
14 Chamber of Commerce
16 Gila & Sol Theaters
18 Silver City Museum
21 Buffalo Bar

PLACES TO STAY
2 Drifter Motel
3 Copper Manor Motel; Red Barn Steak House
4 Super 8 Motel
5 Comfort Inn
6 Econo Lodge
7 Silver City RV Park
20 Palace Hotel

NEW MEXICO

town, the floods eventually cut 55 feet down below the original height of the street. Consequently, this gouged-out area has been turned into **Big Ditch Park**. Brochures at the chamber of commerce describe self-guided tours of the historic downtown area.

Silver City Museum

This museum (☎ 538-5921), 312 W Broadway, in an elegant 1881 Victorian house, displays Mimbres pottery and mining and household artifacts from Silver City's Victorian heyday. There are also changing exhibits, occasional lectures and a store selling Southwestern books and gifts. Hours are 9 am to 4:30 pm Tuesday to Friday, 10 am to 4 pm weekends (free).

WNMU Museum

The Western New Mexico University Museum (☎ 538-6386) houses the world's largest collection of Mimbres pottery. The museum has exhibits detailing local history, culture and natural history and has changing shows. The gift shop specializes in Mimbres motifs (T-shirts, ceramics, books etc). Lectures and other programs are occasionally presented. Hours are 9 am to 4:30 pm Monday to Friday, 10 am to 4 pm weekends, except major holidays. Admission is free, donations are welcomed.

Activities

Bicycle and **cross-country ski** rental and camping equipment is available in town from Gila Hike & Bike (☎ 388-3222), 103 E College Ave.

The Gila National Forest and Wilderness Area is rugged country that's perfect for backpackers, campers, hunters, anglers, birders, cross-country skiers and other outdoor-sports enthusiasts who are looking for challenging solitude. The ranger station in Silver City has maps and detailed information.

Places to Stay

Camping Five miles east of town, *KOA* (☎ 388-3351, 11824 E Hwy 180) has a pool, playground and coin laundry, and charges $16 for tents, $21 with hookups, and $32 for Kamping Kabins. There are winter discounts,

and reservations are encouraged in summer. Cheaper RV camping is available at *Silver City RV Park* (☎ 538-2239), on Bennett St at 13th St, and at *Continental Divide RV Park* (☎ 388-3005), north in Pinos Altos ($15; see that section, later).

The Gila National Forest (☎ 538-2771) maintains the small *Cherry Creek* and *McMillan* campgrounds, about 12 miles north of town on Hwy 15. Neither have drinking water, but both are free.

Motels & Hotels To experience a little of Silver City's history, stay at the restored *Palace Hotel* (☎ 388-1811, 106 W Broadway), which dates from 1882. The 18 rooms vary from small rooms with a double bed for $33 to two-room suites with king- or queen-size beds for $53, including continental breakfast. All rooms have bath, some have a refrigerator and all have old-fashioned decor, though there are phones and TV.
website: www.zianet.com/palacehotel

The *Drifter Motel* (☎ 538-2916, 800-853-2916, 711 Silver Heights Blvd), faces the *Copper Manor Motel* (☎ 538-5392, 800-853-2916, 710 Silver Heights Blvd). Both are under the same ownership and have a pool, restaurant and lounge. Adequate rooms are $40 to $55. The *Holiday Motor Hotel* (☎ 538-3711, 800-828-8291, 3420 E Hwy 180) has a pool and good restaurant. Rates are in the $50 range.
website: www.holidayhotel.com

Three *chain motels* are clustered on the 1000 block of E Hwy 180: Econo Lodge, Comfort Inn and Super 8. A Holiday Inn Express is east of town.

Lodges & B&Bs About 3 miles northwest of town, *Bear Mountain Lodge* (☎ 538-2538, 877-620-2327) is a large ranch house built in 1928 on 160 acres (leave along Alabama and follow the signs). A B&B since 1959, it is now operated by The Nature Conservancy and the lodge naturalist can help with interpretation and suggestions. Ten rooms and suites, plus a guesthouse with kitchenette, range from $85 to $175 for a double including full breakfast. Other

meals can be arranged and a two-night minimum is requested. No smoking and no children under 10 years.
website: www.bearmountainlodge.com

The Cottages (☎ 388-3000, 800-938-3001, 2037 Cottage San Rd) offers two suites ($89 to $149) and three cottages ($129 to $199); go north on Alabama and follow the signs. All units have stocked kitchens, private verandah or patio, bath, TV, VCR and phone. One suite is the childhood home of Harrison Schmitt, one of the astronauts to have walked on the moon. The Cottages are a quiet getaway surrounded by countryside. website: www.silvercitycottages.com

Places to Eat

AIR Coffee Co (☎ 388-5952, 112 W Yankie St) is good for a gourmet coffee and easy conversation. *Vicki's Deli & Eatery* (☎ 388-5430, 107 W Yankie St), with another location directly opposite, serves good sandwiches and light meals.

The unpretentious but good *Jalisco Cafe* (☎ 388-2060, 100 S Bullard St) is a local Mexican food favorite; it is open 11 am to 8:30 pm Monday to Saturday. (They don't serve alcohol.) Another local favorite is *Mi Casita* (☎ 538-5533, 2340 Bosworth Dr), which serves huge plates for about $5 from 11 am to 7 pm Monday to Friday.

For a good steak, head over to the *Red Barn Steak House* (☎ 538-5666, 708 Silver Heights Blvd). Most steaks are in the $10 to $20 range; the restaurant serves seafood and has a salad bar as well. *Michael's* (☎ 538-3711), in the Holiday Motor Motel, is locally considered to be the best fine-dining experience in town.

Entertainment

You can go to the movies at the *Gila & Sol Theaters* (☎ 538-5732), on Bullard at Kelly, or *Real West Cinema II* (☎ 538-5659, 11585 E Hwy 180).

The *Buffalo Bar* (☎ 538-3201, 201 N Bullard St) has occasional dances with live or recorded music in the adjacent nightclub. Otherwise, it's your basic, not especially salubrious, Western bar.

Getting There & Around

The airport is 11 miles southeast of Silver City off Hwy 180. Mesa Air (☎ 388-4115) has two daily flights to and from Albuquerque from Monday to Friday, and one on weekends.

Las Cruces Shuttle Service (☎ 800-288-1784) has vans leaving Silver City twice daily for El Paso Airport via Deming and Las Cruces. Silver Stage Lines (☎ 800-522-0162) has vans leaving Silver City at 7 am and 2 pm for El Paso Airport. They'll also do charter trips elsewhere.

Grimes Car Rental (☎ 538-2142) is at the Silver City Airport. Taylor Car Rental (☎ 388-1800, 388-4848) is at 808 N Hudson St. Enterprise (☎ 534-0000) is at 145 E Hwy 180.

NORTH OF SILVER CITY
Pinos Altos

Seven miles north of Silver City along Hwy 15 lies Pinos Altos, established in 1859 as a gold-mining town and briefly the county seat. Now it's almost a ghost town with only a few residents, who strive to retain the 19th-century flavor of the place. Along Main St is a log cabin, originally built in 1866 as a school, housing the **museum**. An opera house, restaurant, reconstructed fort and 1870s courthouse are also along Main St. A cemetery, turn-of-the-19th-century church housing local art and historical artifacts, and other buildings are found on back streets.

The *Bear Creek Motel & Cabins* (☎ 388-4501, 888-388-4515), in Pinos Altos, has 15 cabin units, all with fireplaces and wood, some with two bedrooms or kitchenettes and balconies. The managers will lend you a gold pan if you want to try your luck in nearby Bear Creek. Rates are $99 to $149 in summer, $10 more on weekends, $10 less in spring and fall and $20 less in winter. website: www.bearcreekcabins.com

The *Buckhorn Saloon* (☎ 538-9911), on Main St, offers fine dinners Monday to Saturday. Steaks, seafood and more are served amid 1860s Wild West decor, and there is often live country music on Friday and Saturday. Most entrées are in the $10 to $20 range.

NEW MEXICO

Lake Roberts Area

Lake Roberts, 25 miles north of Silver City on Hwy 15 and 4 miles east on Hwy 35, offers boating and fishing facilities. (Hwy 15 from Pinos Altos to Hwy 35 is not recommended for trailers over 22 feet.) Hwy 35 provides an alternate but longer scenic route.

At the Hwy 15 and 35 intersection is *Grey Feathers Lodge* (☎ 536-3206), with 16 nonsmoking rooms with Western decor and private bath (but no TVs) for $40/45. A restaurant serves homemade breakfast and lunch.
website: www.greyfeathers.com

The Gila National Forest (☎ 536-2250) maintains *Mesa* and *Upper End* campgrounds ($8) at the east end of the lake, both with drinking water but no showers.

At the lake's west end, the *Lake Roberts General Store & Cabins* (☎ 536-9929, 800-224-1080) has nine cabins ranging from $50 to $100. Some have TVs, phones or kitchenettes. There are boat rentals, and guided hunting and pack trips are arranged with Gary Webb (☎ 536-9368).
website: www.lakeroberts.com

Gila Hot Springs

Used by Indians since ancient times, the hot springs are 39 miles north of Silver City within the *Gila Hotsprings Vacation Center* (☎ 536-9551). The center has a coin laundry, a snack bar, a gift shop and simple rooms with kitchenettes for $60 double. An RV park with a spa and showers fed by hot springs has sites for $16 with hookups and $12 without. A primitive campground next to hot pools has drinking water and toilets but no showers. Day use is $3 per person; camping is $5 per person age six and over. Horseback rides, guided fishing and wilderness pack trips and other outfitting services can be arranged in advance. Trout fishing for hatchery-raised fish is best in spring on the Middle and West Forks of the Gila River, or year-round for wild fish in the backcountry. The East Fork and main river offer good bass fishing. Guided hunting trips are also available.

The *Wilderness Lodge* (☎ 536-9749) is a rustic B&B in a converted century-old schoolhouse. Five rooms with shared bath are $50 double and a two-bedroom suite with private bath is $65 double, including breakfast. Other meals can be arranged.
website: www.gilanet.com/wildernesslodge

Two free Gila USFS *campgrounds* (no drinking water) are available by the Gila River 2 miles south of the hot springs.

Gila Cliff Dwellings National Monument

The influence of the Ancestral Puebloans on the Mogollon culture can clearly be seen in these cliff dwellings, occupied in the 13th century and reminiscent of ones in the Four Corners area. The site is relatively isolated and therefore not crowded with visitors. A one-mile roundtrip self-guided trail climbs 180 feet to the dwellings, set in cliffs overlooking a lovely forested canyon. Parts of the trail are steep and involve ladders.

The trail begins at the end of Hwy 15, 2 miles past the visitor center (☎ 536-9461), a joint NPS/USFS operation with displays, a gift shop and information about the monument and surrounding forest lands. In summer, the visitor center is open 8 am to 5 pm and the trail 8 am to 6 pm. At other times, the visitor center is open 8 am to 4:30 pm and the trail 9 am to 4 pm. The monument is closed Christmas and New Year's Day. Admission is $3 per person and all passes are honored.

Between the visitor center and trailhead are two small *campgrounds* with drinking water, picnic areas and toilets. They are free on a first-come, first-served basis and may fill on summer weekends. A short trail behind the campground leads to other, older dwellings.

EAST OF SILVER CITY

Hwy 152 takes off from Hwy 180 about 8 miles east of Silver City. The Santa Rita Chino Open Pit Copper Mine has an observation point on Hwy 152 almost 6 miles from Hwy 180. Worked by Indians and Spanish and Anglo settlers, it is the oldest active mine in the Southwest. In 1910 it became an open pit and is now a staggering

1½ miles wide, 1800 feet deep and produces 300 million pounds of copper annually.

Hwy 152 crests the Black Range at 8228-foot Emory Pass, where a lookout gives views of the drier Rio Grande country to the east. This is a scenic but slow road with hairpin bends. A few miles beyond Emory Pass, the almost–ghost town of **Kingston** had 7000 inhabitants in the 1880s, when it was a silver-mining center, but now has only a few dozen full-time residents. The ***Black Range Lodge*** (☎ 895-5652) offers B&B accommodations in seven rooms, all with private bath and balcony access. The rates are $50/60 for singles/doubles, with discounts for multinight stays. A game room and kitchen privileges are available.
website: www.zianet.com/blackrange/lodge

Another late-19th-century mining town, **Hillsboro** was revived by local agriculture after mining went bust. Hillsboro is known for its **Apple Festival** over Labor Day weekend, when fresh-baked apple pies, delicious apple cider, street musicians and arts and crafts stalls attract visitors. Many old buildings are still in use. Have a drink or stay in the ***S Bar X Motel & Saloon*** (☎ 895-5222), which has rooms for about $50. The saloon has been here since 1877 and has live music on some weekends. Food is served in the *café* next door. The more recent ***Enchanted Villa B&B*** (☎ 895-5686) has three rooms and a two-bedroom suite, all with bath. Rates range from $40 to $70 with full breakfast.

SILVER CITY TO RESERVE

Hwy 180 northwest of Silver goes through remote and wild country dotted with a few tiny communities. The Gila National Forest and Mogollon Mountains offer excellent opportunities for remote and primitive backpacking, hiking, camping and fishing.

The village of **Glenwood** has a Gila National Forest Ranger Station (☎ 539-2481) a half mile south of town. Hwy 174 goes east from Glenwood five miles to the **Catwalk** – a trail enclosed by a wire cage hugging the cliff up narrow Whitewater Canyon. It follows water pipes built by miners in 1893.

When the pipes needed repair, the miners walked along them (the 'Catwalk'). It's a short but worthwhile hike with some steep spots. There is a USFS picnic area here.

Mogollon, a semi-ghost town, 4 miles north of Glenwood and then 9 miles east on steep and narrow Hwy 159, was once an important mining town and still has a few people living there, offering 'antiques,' snacks and various services such as licensed massage and hypnotherapy. Many buildings lie deserted and empty – it's a slightly spooky place.

The USFS maintains the ***Bighorn*** campground in Gila National Forest, one mile north of Glenwood, with no drinking water or fee. It is open all year.

In Glenwood, stay at the ***Whitewater Motel*** (☎ 539-2581), the ***Lariat Motel*** (☎ 539-2361) or the ***Crab Apple Cabin Motel*** (☎ 539-2400), all small places charging in the $30 to $60 range.

Founded in the 1870s, **Reserve** now has 600 residents and is the seat of Catron County, which has only some 3000 inhabitants itself – mainly ranchers, cowboys and loggers who particularly loathe federal government interference and environmentalists. Recently, county officials passed a resolution urging every family to own a gun. This is about as close to the old Wild West as you'll get. A Gila National Forest Ranger Station (☎ 533-6231) is south of town.

The decent ***Rode Inn Motel*** (☎ 533-6661) charges $50/55 for singles/doubles. Some rooms have kitchenettes.

LORDSBURG & AROUND
☎ 505 • pop 3200 • elevation 4278 feet
Founded in 1880 as a railroad town, Lordsburg is now a minor ranching center. The main drag through town is Motel Drive, which runs east-west, parallel to and north of I-10.

The chamber of commerce (☎ 542-9864) is at 117 E 2nd St. At I-10 exit 20 at the west end, a New Mexico Welcome Center (☎ 542-8149) gives statewide information 8 am to 5 pm daily except Thanksgiving, Christmas and New Year's Day. Other services include the library (☎ 542-9646),

208 E 3rd St; the post office (☎ 542-9601), 401 Shakespeare St; medical services (☎ 542-8384), 500 Demoss St; and the police (☎ 542-3505), 206 S Main St. Greyhound (☎ 542-3412) is behind McDonald's at exit 22.

Ghost Towns

Dating to 1856, **Shakespeare** (☎ 542-9034), 2½ miles south of Lordsburg, was a boom-and-bust mining town that once housed nearly 3000 inhabitants. The town is now on a private ranch and is open to guided tours about one weekend a year. Call for details.

Steins Railroad Ghost Town (☎ 542-9791), once with 1000 inhabitants, has been owned by Larry and Linda Links since 1988; they have been restoring it since. Guided tours and a gift/snack shop are available. Tours cost $2.50 for those 13 and older. Hours are 9 am to 6 pm daily except Thanksgiving and Christmas.

Places to Stay & Eat

KOA (☎ 542-8003, 1501 Lead St) charges $17 for tent sites and $22 with full hookups. It has a pool and coin laundry.

The **Holiday Motel** (☎ 542-3535, 600 E Motel Dr) charges $23/28 for spacious but spartan singles/doubles. It has a pool, a playground and a restaurant. **Chain motels** near exit 22 include a Super 8, Holiday Inn Express and Best Western. Another Best Western is on Motel Dr. A Days Inn is near exit 20.

El Charro (☎ 542-3400), off Motel Dr, has been here since 1939 and serves inexpensive Mexican and American food, has an adjoining lounge and is open 24 hours. **Kranberry's Family Restaurant** (☎ 542-9400), near exit 22, serves standard American breakfasts, lunches and dinners.

Southeastern New Mexico

This chapter covers the southern portion of New Mexico east of the Rio Grande Valley. While much of this is desert expanse sprinkled with tiny towns, the traveler will find that the region offers a variety of natural and historical attractions. From thousands of years of rock etchings at Three Rivers Petroglyph National Recreation Area to alien sightings in Roswell, from the awesome expanse of gypsum at White Sands National Monument to the 60-mile Lechuguilla Cave at Carlsbad Caverns, from the small mountain village of Cloudcroft to the college town of Portales, southeastern New Mexico epitomizes quirky, diverse, spectacular New Mexico.

WHITE SANDS NATIONAL MONUMENT

A highlight of any trip to New Mexico, White Sands is well worth a visit. Here, gypsum, a chalky mineral used in making plaster of paris, covers 275 sq miles to create a dazzling white sea of sand. From beyond the visitor center (☎ 679-2599), PO Box 1086, Holloman Air Force Base, NM 88330, 15 miles southwest of Alamogordo, a 16-mile scenic drive loop leads into the heart of the park – take the time to get out of the car and climb, romp, slide and roll in the soft dunes. Trails leaving from parking areas include the Alkali Flat (4½ miles roundtrip backcountry trail through the heart of the dunes) and a 1-mile loop nature trail. Admission is $3 for adults, free for children, and passes are honored. The visitor center is open from 8 am to 7 pm June to August and from 8 am to 5 pm the rest of the year. Ask about moonlight bicycle tours and other ranger-led trips.

Backcountry campsites, with no water or toilet facilities, are located a mile from the scenic drive. Backpackers must apply for permits ($3) in person at the visitor center one hour before sunset.

website: www.nps.gov/whsa

ALAMOGORDO
☎ 505 • pop 30,000 • elevation 4350 feet

Alamogordo (Spanish for 'fat cottonwood tree'), 207 miles south of Albuquerque, is not only a ranching and agricultural center, but also the center of one of the most historically important space and atomic research programs in the country.

Orientation & Information

White Sands Blvd (also called Hwy 54, 70 or 82) is the main drag through town and runs north-south. This important thoroughfare is abbreviated to 'WSB' below. Addresses on North WSB correspond to numbered cross-streets (thus 1310 N WSB is just north of 13th); addresses from one block south of 1st are South WSB.

The visitor center (☎ 437-6120, 800-826-0294) is at 1301 N WSB. The Lincoln USFS National Forest Ranger Station (☎ 434-7200) is near the corner of 11th St and New York Ave. Other services include the library (☎ 439-4140), on 10th St at Oregon Ave; the

MAP INDEX

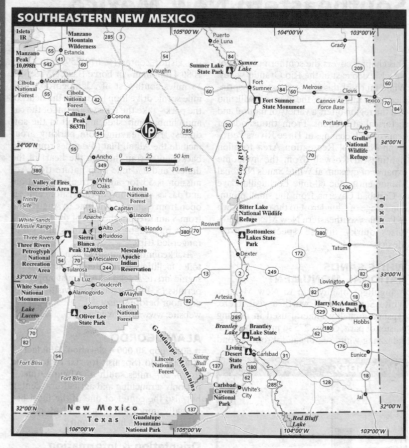

SOUTHEASTERN NEW MEXICO

post office (☎ 437-9390), 30 E 12th St; the hospital (☎ 439-6100), 2669 N Scenic Dr; and the police (☎ 439-4300), 700 Virginia Ave.

New Mexico Museum of Space History

This four-story-high glass museum (☎ 437-2840, 877-333-6589), nicknamed 'the golden cube,' looms over the town and is the town's most important attraction. Inside are exhibits about space research and flight. Excellent films, laser shows and multimedia presentations are presented on a huge wraparound screen in the **Tombaugh IMAX**

Theater and Planetarium. Changing shows feature anything from the Grand Canyon to the dark side of the moon. Ask about the evening shows. Admission for adults/children is $5.50/3.50 for the theater, and $2.50/2 for the museum. The space center is open from 9 am to 5 pm daily.
website: www.zianet.com/space

Alameda Park & Zoo

Established in 1898 as a diversion for railway travelers, this zoo (☎ 439-4290) is the oldest in the state. Small but well run, the zoo features exotics from all over the world, among them the endangered Mexican gray wolf. Hours are 9 am to 5 pm daily; admission is $2.20/1.10 for adults/children.

Toy Train Depot

At the north end of Alameda Park, the Toy Train Depot (☎ 437-2855, 888-207-3564), 1991 N WSB, is an 1898 railway depot that is a must-see for railroad buffs. Take a ride on the 2½-mile narrow-gauge train and wander through five rooms of train memorabilia and toy trains. Hours are noon to 5 pm Wednesday to Sunday. Admission is $2.

Tularosa Basin Historical Society

This small museum (☎ 434-4438), 1301 N WSB, focuses on local history. Hours are from 10 am to 4 pm daily, to 3 pm on Saturday, and closed Sunday. Admission is free.

Historic Buildings

The historical center of town, east of N WSB along and just off 10th St, has many interesting buildings. The attractive USFS building (formerly the federal building) at 11th and New York is home to Peter Hurd's *Sun and Rain* frescoes, painted in the early 1940s as part of the New Deal's WPA art program.

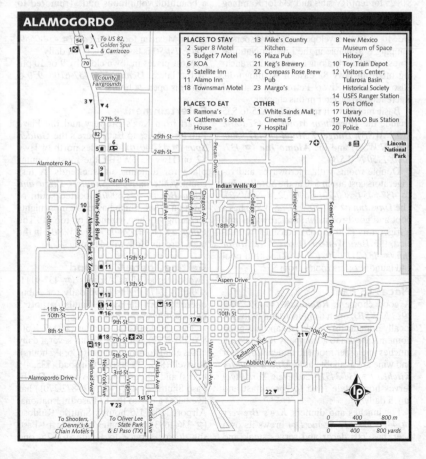

ALAMOGORDO

PLACES TO STAY
2 Super 8 Motel
5 Budget 7 Motel
6 KOA
9 Satellite Inn
11 Alamo Inn
18 Townsman Motel

PLACES TO EAT
3 Ramona's
4 Cattleman's Steak House

13 Mike's Country Kitchen
16 Plaza Pub
21 Keg's Brewery
22 Compass Rose Brew Pub
23 Margo's

OTHER
1 White Sands Mall; Cinema 5
7 Hospital

8 New Mexico Museum of Space History
10 Toy Train Depot
12 Visitors Center; Tularosa Basin Historical Society
14 USFS Ranger Station
15 Post Office
17 Library
19 TNM&O Bus Station
20 Police

Places to Stay

An abundance of motels and *chain hotels*, including Super 8 and Holiday Inn, stretch out along White Sands Blvd for approximately 5 miles. Except for camping, these are your only options for accommodations. Rates are fairly constant year-round. If you're looking for something with a bit more ambiance than a standard motel on a fast-food strip, consider the mountain town of Cloudcroft 19 miles east (see Cloudcroft, later in this chapter). Also see Carrizozo, later in this chapter.

The *KOA* (☎ 437-3003, 412 24th St) charges $18/25 for tent/RV sites and $33 for Kamping Kabins. At *Oliver Lee State Park* (see Around Alamogordo, below) tent/RV sites are $10/14. Both developed and free dispersed camping is available in the Lincoln National Forest, particularly along forest roads branching off from Hwy 82 east of Alamogordo. Also see Three Rivers Petroglyph National Recreation Area, later in this chapter.

Basic motels with rooms from $25 to $35 include the *Townsman Motel* (☎ 437-0210, 710 N WSB), *Budget 7 Motel* (☎ 437-9350, 2404 N WSB) and the *Alamo Inn* (☎ 437-1000, 1450 N WSB).

Double rooms with microwaves and refrigerators cost about $40 at the *Satellite Inn* (☎ 437-8454, 800-221-7690, 2224 N WSB). The *Days Inn* (☎ 437-5090, 907 S WSB) has a pool and good rooms with microwaves and refrigerators ($40 to $65). Recently remodeled, the *Best Western Desert Aire Motor Inn* (☎ 437-2110, 1021 S WSB), with a pool and laundry, offers rooms from $52.

Places to Eat

A good choice is *Ramona's* (☎ 437-7616, 2913 N WSB), open 6 am to 10 pm daily. It's locally popular for breakfasts and has good homemade salsa to accompany the Mexican lunches and diner food (all under $10). Beer and wine are available here. *Mike's Country Kitchen* (☎ 434-3431, 1201 New York Ave) serves home-style food for breakfast and lunch daily.

For lunches and dinners, *Keg's Brewery* (☎ 437-9564, 817 Scenic Dr) brews its own beer, has '60s décor and serves steak and seafood in the $10 to $20 range. The bar has pool tables and weekend dancing with a DJ. If you're tired of green chile and beans, try the slightly yuppyish *Compass Rose Brew Pub* (☎ 434-9633, 2202 E 1st St). Food with a German flair costs about $7. For steaks, the best place to go is the *Cattleman's Steak House* (☎ 434-5252, 2904 N WSB).

Plaza Pub (☎ 437-9495), located on the corner of WSB and 10th St, offers good green chile stew and hamburgers and a wide selection of beers. There are several pool tables and the walls are adorned with stuffed animal heads and a few paintings of a beautiful, voluptuous nude (rumored to have been seen in the bar). On the weekends, there are live bands.

For Mexican food, *Margo's* (☎ 434-0689, 504 E 1st St) is tasty and is open daily.

Most places in town close by 9 or 10 pm at the latest. *Denny's* (☎ 437-6106, 930 S WSB) is open 24 hours.

Entertainment

Apart from Keg's Brewery and the Plaza Pub (see Places to Eat), there's the *Golden Spur* (☎ 437-4010), 4.3 miles north of Hwy 82 on Hwy 55 (WSB), the most popular place for dancing on weekends. A less country alternative is *Shooters Pizza and Patio Bar* (☎ 443-6000), located south of town on WSH, which has music most nights including hip-hop, country, or top 40. The *Cinema 5* (☎ 437-9301, 3199 N WSB), in the mall, screens Hollywood films.

Getting There & Around

Two or three Mesa Airlines (☎ 437-9111, 800-637-2247) flights leave daily for Albuquerque from the White Sands Airport 3 miles southwest of town.

The TNM&O Bus Station (☎ 437-3050, 800-231-2222), 601 N WSB, has several daily buses going to Albuquerque ($36, 4½ hours), Roswell ($25, 2½ hours), Carlsbad ($35, 4½ hours) and El Paso ($21, two hours). The El Paso Shuttle (☎ 437-1472, 800-872-2701) has five buses a day to the El Paso International Airport ($31, 1½ hours); Shuttle Ruidoso (☎ 336-1683) coordinates with the El Paso shuttle for service to Ruidoso ($25, one hour). Shuttles are by reservation and leave from the Best Western, 1020 S WSB.

Avis, Alamo and Enterprise rent cars at the airport. Avis (☎ 437-3140) also has a car-rental office at the Holiday Inn Express.

AROUND ALAMOGORDO

Twelve miles south on Hwy 54 and 4 miles east (follow the signs) is **Oliver Lee State Park** (☎ 437-8284). The visitor center details prehistoric and historic Indian inhabitants of the area, as well as more recent ranchers. Hiking trails provide good views. Park entrance fee is $4 per vehicle.

The oldest village in the area, **La Luz** is 4 miles north of Alamogordo (just east of Hwy 54). It remains unspoiled by tourism and is worth a stroll. Ten miles farther north on Hwy 54 is the attractive village of **Tularosa**, with its St Francis de Paula Church built in 1869 in simple New Mexican style. Tularosa Vineyards (☎ 585-2260), a friendly and picturesque local winery 2 miles north of town on Hwy 54, has daily afternoon tours and tastings.

THREE RIVERS PETROGLYPH NATIONAL RECREATION AREA

This uncrowded site (☎ 525-4300) showcases 20,000 petroglyphs inscribed 1000 years ago by the Jornada Mogollon people. The 1-mile hike through mesquite and cacti offers good views of the Sacramento Mountains to the east and White Sands Monument on the horizon. Nearby is a pithouse in a partially excavated village. Admission is $2 per vehicle, per day. There are six camping shelters with barbecue grills (free), restrooms, water and two hook-ups for RVs ($15). Call the Bureau of Land Management in Las Cruces (☎ 525-4300) for further information.

The site is 17 miles north of Tularosa on Hwy 54, then 5 miles east on a signed road. A dirt road continues for about 10 miles beyond the petroglyph area to the Lincoln National Forest, where there is the *Three Rivers Campground* (☎ 434-7200) and a trailhead.

CLOUDCROFT & AROUND

☎ 505 • pop 750 • elevation 9000 feet

As you drive east of Alamogordo on Hwy 82, a road sign warns drivers to check their brakes and gears because the road climbs 4315 feet in the next 16 miles. The pleasant little town of Cloudcroft, with turn-of-the-19th-century buildings, plenty of outdoor recreation and a low-key feel, provides welcome relief from the heat of the low-lands to the east and is an excellent spot to use as a base for exploring the area.

Orientation & Information

Hwy 82 is the main drag through town, and most places are on this road or within a few blocks of it.

The chamber of commerce (☎ 682-2733), Box 1290, Cloudcroft, NM 88317, is open daily; visit www.cloudcroft.net. The Lincoln National Forest Cloudcroft Ranger Station (☎ 682-2551), Box 288, Cloudcroft, NM 88317, is at the western end of Chipmunk Ave. Other services include the post office (☎ 682-2431), 20 Curlew Place, and the police (☎ 682-2101), 201 Burro Ave. The nearest hospital is in Alamogordo.

Sacramento Mountains Historical Museum

This museum (☎ 682-2932) displays turn-of-the-19th-century buildings, farm equipment, household items and railroad memorabilia. Hours are 10 am to 4 pm Monday, Tuesday, Friday, Saturday and 1 to 4 pm on Sunday. Admission is $2.

National Observatory at Sacramento Peak

One of the world's largest solar observatories is near Sunspot, 20 miles south of Cloudcroft. Take Hwy 130 for 2 miles and then Hwy 6563 to the Sacramento Peak Observatory (☎ 434-7000). Though it's primarily for scientists, guided tours are given at 2 pm on Saturdays from June to August and by appointment at other times. The drive to Sunspot, the **Sunspot Scenic Byway**, is a high and beautiful one, with the mountains to the east and White Sands National Monument visible to the west.

Hiking

Hiking is a popular summer activity, with outings ranging from short hikes close to

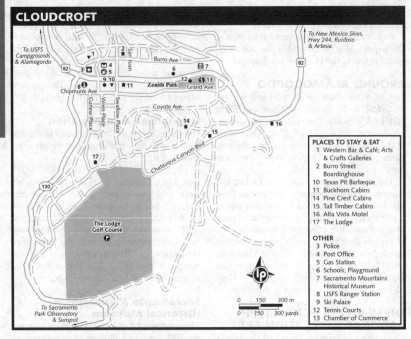

CLOUDCROFT

To New Mexico Skies,
Hwy 244, Ruidoso
& Artesia

To USFS
Campgrounds
& Alamogordo

San Juan

Burro Ave

Zenith Park   Grand Ave

Chipmunk Ave

Coyote Ave

Chatauqua Canyon Blvd

The Lodge
Golf Course

To Sacramento
Park Observatory
& Sunspot

0   150   300 m
0   150   300 yards

PLACES TO STAY & EAT
1 Western Bar & Café; Arts
   & Crafts Galleries
2 Burro Street
   Boardinghouse
10 Texas Pit Barbeque
11 Buckhorn Cabins
14 Pine Crest Cabins
15 Tall Timber Cabins
16 Alta Vista Motel
17 The Lodge

OTHER
3 Police
4 Post Office
5 Gas Station
6 Schools; Playground
7 Sacramento Mountains
   Historical Museum
8 USFS Ranger Station
9 Ski Palace
12 Tennis Courts
13 Chamber of Commerce

town to overnight backpacking trips. Although trails are often fairly flat and easy, the 9000-foot elevation can make hiking strenuous if you are not acclimatized. Trails are open from April to November. The most popular day hike is the 2.6-mile Osha Loop Trail, which leaves Hwy 82 from a small parking area opposite the old railroad trestle, 1 mile west of Cloudcroft. Both the chamber of commerce and the USFS can provide descriptions and maps of this and other hikes.

Golf

The Lodge (see Places to Stay) has a beautiful nine-hole course (☎ 682-2098) that is one of the highest and oldest in the USA. Nine holes of golf are $13/16 for midweek/weekend.

Winter Activities

The newly renovated Snow Canyon Ski Area (☎ 682-2333), about 2 miles east of town on Hwy 8, has 24 runs designed mostly for beginning and intermediate skiers. Lift tickets are $25/16 for adults/children (under 12). Inner-tubing and snowboarding are also possible.

The golf course behind The Lodge (see Places to Stay) becomes a groomed cross-country skiing area in winter. Trail passes are $4 and ski rentals are $12. The Lodge also provides guided snowmobiling and horse-drawn sleigh rides.

Triple M's Snowplay Area (☎ 682-2205), 4.7 miles south of Cloudcroft on the way to Sunspot, has snowmobile tours, horse-drawn sleigh rides and slopes with a lift for inner-tubing (weekends and holidays, $16 per day for lift and tube rental). Just east of town toward the ski valley is Sleepy Grass Campground, good for free, relaxed sledding.

To rent cross-country and downhill skis, inner tubes, snowshoes and sleds, head to Ski Palace (☎ 682-2045).

Other Activities

The miles of trails in the Sacramento Mountains offer great opportunities for **mountain biking**. High Altitude (☎ 682-1229) rents and repairs bikes, sells gear and can tell you where to go. Ask about races along the Rim Trail. For **horseback riding**, contact Chippeway Riding Stables (☎ 682-2565, 800-471-2384), on Hwy 130 six miles out of town. In the fall, **hunting** for elk and other big game is popular. Several outfitters in town offer guided hunting trips.

Special Events

During the first weekend in October, autumn is celebrated with Oktoberfest. In the nearby High Rolls (between Cloudcroft and Alamogordo) you will find lots of cherry orchards, and Cloudcroft celebrates the cherry harvest with an annual Cherry Festival on the third Sunday of June.

Places to Stay

Access the chamber of commerce website (www.cloudcroft.net) for thorough links to cabins, motels and ranches in the area. Rates given below are for high season, which is from June to August and holidays.

Camping The USFS (☎ 682-2551) has several campgrounds that, because of the elevation, are open summer only (May to mid-September), though some may open earlier or later with no services or fees, weather permitting. Fees are $8 to $10, and there are no RV hookups. On Hwy 244, a half-mile north from the intersection with Hwy 82, just east of Cloudcroft, is *The Pines* with water but no showers. About 1.4 miles farther north along Hwy 244 is the turnoff to the USFS' *Silver*, *Saddle* and *Apache* campgrounds (hot showers available). A mile southeast of town on Hwy 130 is the USFS *Deerhead* campground with water but no showers. Ask the ranger for information on free dispersed camping.

Cabins Beyond camping, most accommodations in Cloudcroft are cabins, which vary in size and can accommodate up to eight people. Rates vary depending on the number of guests, time of year, size of cabin and length of stay.

Amateur astronomers will enjoy *New Mexico Skies* (☎ 687-2429, PO Box 559, Cloudcroft, NM 88317). Tucked against the national forest, it allows you to stay in a one-/two-bedroom apartment for $130/160 or a three-bedroom home ($190) and rent high-powered star-gazing equipment (with names you can't even pronounce!).
website: www.nmskies.com

Buckhorn Cabins (☎ 682-2421), close to downtown at the corner of Hwy 82 and Swallow Place, has cabins starting at $45. *Pine Crest Cabins* (☎ 682-2631), at the east end of town away from the main highway, has five units sleeping five or six people, all with kitchens and fireplaces ($70). Nearby is the similar *Tall Timber Cabins* (☎ 682-2301, 800-682-2301).

Hotels & B&Bs At the east end of town, seven spacious rooms at the *Alta Vista Motel* (☎ 682-2221, 1605 James Canyon) are $55. In the historic district, the *Burro Street Boardinghouse* (☎ 682-3601, 608 Burro Ave) offers old-fashioned rooms for $68, including full breakfast.

The Lodge (☎ 682-2566, 800-395-6343, 1 Corona Place) stands out as one of the best historic hotels in the state and, indeed, the entire Southwest. Built in 1899 as the original vacation lodge for railroad employees, it was destroyed by fire and rebuilt in 1911. Rooms are about $100 to $120, and pavilion rooms (a few blocks away in a separate, less attractive building) are $80 to $110. Suites, including four in a mountain home, go for $200 to $300.

Surrounded by the Lincoln National Forest, 28 miles from Cloudcroft, *Raven Wind* (☎ 687-3073, 1234 NM Hwy 24, Weed, NM 88354) offers two basic double rooms (don't expect Southwestern style) for $75, including a full breakfast and afternoon snack.
website: www.ravenwindranch.com

Places to Eat

The *Western Bar & Café* (☎ 682-2445), on Burro Ave, is a popular place that looks like something out of the Wild West. For good

NEW MEXICO

barbecue, head to **Texas Pit Barbeque** (☎ 682-2307, 211 Hwy 82).

By far the best (and most expensive) food is served at the historic **Rebecca's** (☎ 682-3131) in The Lodge. Stop by for the Sunday brunch buffet ($17). Rebecca's offers an outside deck with spectacular views of the mountains and White Sands Monument shimmering in the distance. Dinner entrées run from $12 to $25 (cheaper lunches).

CARRIZOZO
☎ 505 • pop 972 • elevation 5425 feet

Just west of the Sacramento Mountains and 58 miles north of Alamogordo, Carrizozo is surrounded by high desert, with Carrizozo Peak (9650 feet) looming about 9 miles to the east. An old train caboose houses the tiny visitors center (☎ 648-2732), or www.townofcarrizozo.click2site.com, on Hwy 56 at Airport Rd.

North- and southbound TNM&O buses (☎ 648-2964) stop at the Four Winds Restaurant twice daily on the Albuquerque ($25, three hours) to El Paso run ($25, three hours).

Things to See & Do
Four miles west of Carrizozo, the **Valley of Fires Recreation Area** (☎ 648-2241) features the most recent lava flows in the continental USA. Visitors can walk over a lava flow estimated to be 1500 years old, 47 miles long and up to 160 feet thick. Entrance is $5 per vehicle. White Oaks, a gold-mining center in the 1880s, is now a **ghost town** with a small population and some interesting old buildings and historic tombstones. Stop in the **White Oaks Saloon** to cool off and chat with the bartender over a beer. To get there, head 11 miles northeast of Carrizozo on Hwy 349.

For information on visiting nearby **Trinity Site**, the test site of the nuclear bomb, see the 'Atomic City' boxed text in the Northwestern New Mexico chapter.

Places to Stay & Eat
Camping at the Valley of Fires costs $5 to $11 for primitive sites and RV sites with hookups. About 40 miles north of Carrizozo, just south of Corona, USFS Rd 161

and USFS Rd 144 head nine and 11 miles, respectively, to primitive, eight-site **Red Cloud Campground** in the Cibola National Forest (free). This is at 7600 feet on the slopes of isolated **Gallinas Peak** (8637 feet) and there is no drinking water.

Several motels, including the **Four Winds Motel** (☎ 648-2356), offer doubles in the $40s. The rural and peaceful **Oscuro High Desert Hostel** (☎ 648-4007), 1½ miles east of the Hwy 54 mile marker 108, 15 miles south of Carrizozo, has dorm beds for $14 and private rooms for $27. A laundry and a guest kitchen (with tea, coffee and food from the ranch) are all available at no extra charge. The hostel, a pleasant place to hang out in the desert, provides pickup at the bus stop in Carrizozo.

In the search for the best green chile in New Mexico, stop by the recommended **Outpost Bar and Grill** (☎ 684-9994), a great bar in the middle of nowhere. An impressive gun collection and the obligatory selection of stuffed animal heads adorn the walls, and the green chile stew and green chile cheeseburgers are excellent. It is located in town on US 54 S and is open 10 am to 2 am Monday to Saturday and noon to midnight Sunday. For coffee shop fare, try **Carizzozo Joe's** (☎ 648-5639), just north of the Outpost Bar and Grill.

RUIDOSO AREA
☎ 505 • pop 8000 • elevation 7000 feet

The pleasant climate and forested surroundings of the resort town Ruidoso attract people escaping the summer heat of Alamogordo 46 miles to the southwest, and Roswell 71 miles to the east, as well as many visitors from Texas. The lovely Rio Ruidoso, a small creek with good fishing, runs through town.

Orientation
Ruidoso is a very spread-out town, with vacation homes tucked away on narrow streets sprawling into the surrounding mountains. Hwy 48 from the north is the main drag through town. This is called Mechem Dr until the small downtown area where it becomes Sudderth Dr heading east to the Y-intersection with Hwy 70. Six miles north on

Mechem Dr is the community of Alto, with more accommodations. The community of Ruidoso Downs is a separate village just east of Ruidoso on Hwy 70. Both Ruidoso Downs and Alto are included under this Ruidoso section.

Information

Tourist information is available at the chamber of commerce (☎ 257-7395, 800-253-2255), 720 Sudderth Dr. Write to them at Box 698, Ruidoso, NM 88355.
website: www.ruidoso.net

The Lincoln National Forest Smokey Bear Ranger Station (☎ 257-4095) is at 901 Mechem Dr or www.fs.fed.us/r3/lincoln .com. Other services include the library (☎ 257-4335), 107 Kansas City Rd (off the east end of Cree Meadows Dr); the post office (☎ 257-7120), 1090 Meechem Dr; the medical center and hospital (☎ 257-7381), 211 Sudderth Dr; and the police (☎ 258-7365), 1085 Meechem Dr.

Ruidoso Downs Racetrack

Thursday to Sunday from late May to early September, you can come watch all kinds of horse races. The Ruidoso Downs Racetrack (☎ 378-4431), on Hwy 70 about 4½ miles east of downtown, is one of the major racetracks in the Southwest. The All American Futurity is held at the end of the season on Labor Day – this is the world's richest quarterhorse race and is worth over $2,000,000. General admission is free, parking is $3 and grandstand seats and boxes are available for $2.50 to $8.50. A full casino is open year-round.

Hubbard Museum of the American West

This museum (☎ 378-4142, 800-263-5929), just east of the racetrack entrance, has a fine display of more than 10,000 western-related items including Old West stagecoaches, saddles and American Indian pottery, as well as works by Frederic Remington and Charles M Russell. An impressive collection

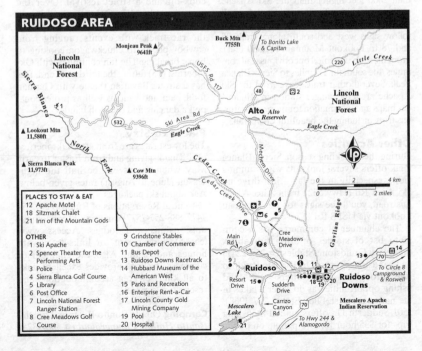

RUIDOSO AREA

Buck Mtn 7755ft
To Bonito Lake & Capitan
Monjeau Peak ▲ 9641ft
Lincoln National Forest
USFS Rd 117
220   Little Creek
Sierra Blanca
48
☐ 2
Lincoln National Forest
532   Ski Area Rd
Alto   Alto Reservoir
Eagle Creek
Eagle Creek
▲ Lookout Mtn 11,580ft
North Fork
Cedar Creek
Mechem Drive
0   2   4 km
0   1   2 miles
▲ Sierra Blanca Peak 11,973ft
▲ Cow Mtn 9396ft
Cedar Creek Drive
Gavilan Ridge
■ 3
❶ 4
☐ 6   ● 5
7 ❶
Cree Meadows Drive
Main Rd
❶ 8
☐ 13 ●   🏛 14
70
To Circle 8 Campground & Roswell
Resort Drive
15 ●
Ruidoso
❶ 11   ☐ 12
16 ●● ☐ ●
17 ●☐ ❶
18 19 ●20
Ruidoso Downs
Sudderth Drive
Mescalero Lake
Carrizo Canyon Rd
70
Mescalero Apache Indian Reservation
❶ 21
To Hwy 244 & Alamogordo

PLACES TO STAY & EAT
12 Apache Motel
18 Sitzmark Chalet
21 Inn of the Mountain Gods

OTHER
1 Ski Apache
2 Spencer Theater for the Performing Arts
3 Police
4 Sierra Blanca Golf Course
5 Library
6 Post Office
7 Lincoln National Forest Ranger Station
8 Cree Meadows Golf Course
9 Grindstone Stables
10 Chamber of Commerce
11 Bus Depot
13 Ruidoso Downs Racetrack
14 Hubbard Museum of the American West
15 Parks and Recreation
16 Enterprise Rent-a-Car
17 Lincoln County Gold Mining Company
19 Pool
20 Hospital

of horse-related displays, including a collection of saddles and the Racehorse Hall of Fame, lures horse-lovers. Hours are 10 am to 5 pm daily and admission is $6.

Ski Apache

The best ski area south of Albuquerque is Ski Apache (☎ 336-4356, 257-9001 snow conditions), 18 miles northwest of Ruidoso on the slopes of beautiful Sierra Blanca Peak (about 12,000 feet). All-day passes are $42/27 for adults/children. Shuttle Ruidoso (☎ 336-1683) will pick you up from seven pickup points every five minutes from 8 to 8:30 am and from 11 to 11:30 am, with a return at 4 pm.
website: www.skiapache.com

Hiking

Hiking is a popular summertime activity, with the 4.6-mile day hike from the Ski Apache area to the summit of Sierra Blanca Peak being especially popular. The summit is more than 2000 feet higher than the Ski Apache parking lot. Take Trail 15 from the small parking area just before the main lot and follow signs west and south along Trails 25 and 78 to Lookout Mountain (11,580 feet). From there an unnamed but obvious trail continues due south for 1¼ miles to Sierra Blanca Peak. Several other trails leave from the Ski Apache area; the ranger station in Ruidoso has maps and information for more adventurous trips, including the beautiful Crest Trail.

Other Activities

During the nonskiing season, Sierra Blanca Peak offers several lookouts with stunning views, especially in the fall – just drive up Ski Area Rd (Hwy 532) from Alto. Along this road, you'll see signs for the Monjeau Lookout via USFS Rd 117.

The chamber of commerce has a complete list of stables offering **horseback riding**; try Grindstone Stables (☎ 257-2241) on Grindstone Resort Dr. The Rio Ruidoso runs through town and offers some good **fishing** opportunities, as do several lakes in the national forest. Flies Etc (☎ 257-4968), 2501 Sudderth Dr, offers guided fly-fishing trips for $35/hour for two people on public

water or $450/day for fishing on private water (only two people allowed at a time).

Try **gold panning** with the Lincoln County Gold Mining Company (☎ 257-4070), 629 Sudderth Dr, which leads two trips each day of the year to a local stream. Cost is $25 per person (including a brief mine tour). Though you can keep the gold you find, don't expect anything even close to the record 61lb nugget found here in 1900.

For information on area parks, contact the Ruidoso Parks & Recreation (☎ 257-5030), 801 Resort Dr.

Special Events

During the last full weekend in July, the top-quality Ruidoso Art Festival attracts thousands of browsing and buying visitors from all over the Southwest and beyond. Up to 30,000 motorcycles ride into town for the Golden Aspen Motorcycle Rally on the third weekend of September. The Aspenfest in the first weekend in October has a chili cook-off and a street festival. Over the second weekend in October, the Lincoln County Cowboy Symposium ($15) is held at the racetrack with events ranging from cowboy poetry to chuckwagon cooking to horse breaking. The fun continues with Oktoberfest ($5) during the third weekend. This has a strong Bavarian theme with German food, beer and wine as well as professional polka dancing and oompah bands.

Places to Stay

The lowest rates are from after Oktoberfest until Thanksgiving and from Easter to early May, when rooms can be half the high-season (June to August) rates given below. Ask about ski packages.

Central Reservations of Ruidoso (☎ 257-7477, 888-257-7577) can arrange condominiums, cabins and lodges. Access www.casasderuidoso.com for links to private homes and casitas. Also, the chamber of commerce website provides excellent links to all kinds of area accommodations and reservation services.

Camping On the Bonito River in Alto, the *Bonito Hollow Campground* (☎ 336-4325) has tent/RV sites for $12/16 as well as bunkhouse rooms and cabins for $25 to $40. In keeping with camping necessities of the 21st century, they offer a laptop modem hookup as well as the usual picnic tables and campfire rings.

The Lincoln National Forest (☎ 257-4095) operates several campgrounds north of Ruidoso. All are open from May to September and none have showers. **South Fork Campground**, near Bonito Lake, has fishing, hiking trails and drinking water ($10). To get to the campground, take Hwy 48, 9 miles north from Ruidoso, to Hwy 37, turn left and a mile down the road is USFS Rd 107. Turn left and go five miles. The **Oak Grove**, **Skyline** and **Monjeau Campgrounds**, at about 9000 feet, have pit toilets but no drinking water and are free. Oak Grove is 5 miles west of Alto on Ski Area Rd. Skyline and Monjeau are 4 and 5 miles along USFS Rd 117, which heads north a mile along Ski Area Rd. Free dispersed camping is also allowed.

Motels & Cabins Seventeen simple but nice rooms with refrigerators and microwaves start at around $50 at the **Sitzmark Chalet** (☎ 257-4140, 800-658-9694, 627 Sudderth Dr). There is a hot tub and you can send free emails and faxes from the office. The small hot tub **Apache Motel** (☎ 257-2986, 800-426-0616, 344 Sudderth Dr) offers basic rooms, some with kitchenettes, from $50.

There are lots of cabin rentals in the area, and some are cramped in town. Most of the newer, spiffier cabins are located in the

Upper Canyon. Generally, cabins have kitchens and grills, and often they have fireplaces and decks. The nicer of the older, less expensive cabins includes **High Country Lodge** (☎ 336-4321, 800-845-7265) on Hwy 48 a little south of the turnoff to Ski Apache. It has 32 basic two-bedroom cabins, each with kitchen, fireplace and porch. There is a pool and hot tub on the grounds. Weekday/weekend rates are $89/119.

The pleasant and friendly **Ponderosa Cabins** (☎ 257-2631, 800-2575865, 104 Laurel Dr), just off Sudderth Dr, has basic cabins starting at $59 for a one-bedroom. Cabins back up against the forested city park, with hiking trails to the river.

Set among the pines on the north side of the river a few blocks off the main drag, **Sierra Blanca Cabins** (☎ 257-2103, 217 Country Club Rd) has nine log cabins, all with fireplaces. Rates start at $72 for two people and go up to $125 for six people. Another good choice is **Ruidoso Lodge Cabins** (☎ 257-2510, 800-950-2510, 300 Main Rd). Nine recently renovated knotty-pine cabins, all with fireplaces and decks, are quietly set in the trees on the river. Rates range from $80 to $150.

The **Dan Dee Cabins** (☎ 257-2165, 310 Main Rd) has 12 cabins spread out over 5 acres. These cabins were constructed at various times beginning in the 1940s and each one is unique. Rates start at $104 for a one-bedroom model.

Hotels Hotels in Ruidoso are often referred to as 'lodges' or 'inns' in keeping with the mountain feel of the resort. They are, however, basically your standard motel.

Nicely situated on the river, the **Pines Motel** (☎ 257-4334, 800-257-4834, 620 Sudderth Dr) has 10 small but spotless rooms, all either recently remodeled or newly built for $50 to $85. One-bedroom suites with equipped kitchens are $78 ($82 with a fireplace) at **Upper Canyon Inn** (☎ 888-257-7577). The **Innsbruck Lodge** (☎ 257-4071, 601 Sudderth Dr) offers pleasant doubles starting at $65.

Convenient to the ski slopes and hugging the forest, the **Best Western Swiss Chalet**

(☎ 258-3333, 1451 Meechem Dr) offers basic rooms from $114, a pool and a restaurant serving German fare. Ask about ski and bike packages.

On the Mescalero Apache Reservation (described later in this chapter), the *Inn of the Mountain Gods* (☎ 257-5141, 800-545-9011) offers a casino, all kinds of activities (including guided fishing and horseback riding) and rooms for about $100. Once a grand hotel, it is getting a little worn looking but it is in a beautiful spot. Wooden balconies and fireplaces (pay for your own wood!) make *Shadow Mountain Lodge* (☎ 257-4886) a good option for adults looking for a quiet getaway. Rates range from $69 to $109.

B&Bs Fifteen miles north of Ruidoso is *Monjeau Shadows* (☎ 336-4191, Bonito Rd). This Victorian-style B&B has six rooms, four with private bath and a pleasant 10-acre garden for walks. Doubles are $75 to $100; dinner can be arranged. It's for sale, however, at the time of this writing, so things may change. The friendly *Park Place B&B* (☎ 257-4638, 800- 687-9050, 137 Reese Dr), a ranch house surrounded by tall pines next to the river, has three rooms from $75/85 weekdays/weekends. Rates include a full hot breakfast.

Places to Eat

Most restaurants are located on Sudderth between Mechem Dr and Carrizo Canyon Rd.

Stop at the *Hummingbird Tearoom* (☎ 257-5100, 2306 Sudderth Dr), in the Village Plaza, for soup, salad and sandwich lunches. Delectable desserts and afternoon tea are served in the afternoon. The *Casa Blanca* (☎ 257-2495, 501 Mechem Dr) serves Mexican food and hamburgers in a renovated Spanish-style house with a pleasant beer garden outside – musicians sometimes provide entertainment and the crowd is lively. Prices for dinner entrées are under $10. *Terraza Campanario* (☎ 257-4227, 1611 Sudderth Dr) is a good spot for Mexican all day.

The *Flying J Ranch* (☎ 336-4330), on Hwy 48 about 1½ miles north of Alto, is a 'Western village' with gunfights, pony rides and a cowboy-style chuckwagon followed by early Western music (open June to September; $16).

Santinos (☎ 257-7540), on Sudderth Dr, has received good reviews for its Northern Italian lunches and dinners. Also good is *Café Rio* (☎ 257-7746, 2547 Sudderth Dr), with well-prepared pizza and international food in a low-key setting. *Pub 48* (☎ 257-9559, 441 Meechem Dr) serves microbeers and pizza, among other things.

Skylights and stained glass, cowboy art and a saloon all contribute to the Western ambiance of the *Incredible Restaurant & Saloon* (☎ 336-4312), on the right side of Hwy 48 in Alto, just before the Ski Apache turnoff. Dinner entrées run from about $8 to $20. The popular Western lounge features live entertainment on some nights.

Call for reservations and directions to one of the busiest and best (though pricey) restaurants in town, *The Texas Club* (☎ 258-3325, 212 Metz Dr). It is open Wednesday to Sunday 5 to 10 pm. For an upscale meal that won't disappoint, try *La Lorraine* (☎ 257-2954, 2523 Sudderth Dr). Excellent French cuisine is served on an outdoor patio in the summer and in the cozy bistro in the winter. Dinner entrées are in the $12 to $22 range. The casino at the Inn of the Mountain Gods (see Places to Stay) offers lunch and dinner buffets; also here is the *Dan-Li-Ka* restaurant, with beautiful views of the Sacramento Mountains and Lake Mescalero.

Entertainment

Numerous bars, coffeehouses and hotel or restaurant lounges offer weekend entertainment. Enjoy a beer and a game of pool while you munch on peanuts (just throw the shells on the ground) at *Farley's Food Fun and Pub* (☎ 258-5676, 1200 Mechem Dr), the most popular hangout in town. Another good spot to relax over a game of pool is *The Quarters* (☎ 257-9535, 2535 Sudderth Dr), with laid-back live music Wednesday to Sunday. You can two-step to country & western music at *Win, Place & Show* (☎ 257-9982, 2516 Sudderth Dr). Also popular for dancing in a Texas décor is *The Texas Club* (see Places to Eat, above).

The *Spencer Theater for the Performing Arts* (☎ 336-4800, 888-818-7872), set in the mountains on Airport Hwy 220 in Alto, hosts theatrical, musical and dance performances for $20 to $40.

See also the *Flying J Ranch* under Places to Eat, above.

Getting There & Around

Mesa Air (☎ 800-637-2247) flies to Alamogordo and Roswell. The nearest major airport is El Paso, 125 miles away.

The bus depot (☎ 257-2660), 138 Service Rd, is just north of the 300 block of Sudderth Dr. TNM&O and Greyhound buses head to Alamogordo ($11, one hour), Roswell ($15.75, 1½ hours) and El Paso, Texas ($27, three hours), several times a day; buses to Carlsbad ($29.40, four hours) leave on weekdays only. Shuttle Ruidoso (☎ 336-1683) goes to Alamogordo by reservation only four times a day ($25/40 one-way/roundtrip), where it connects with a shuttle to El Paso (see Alamogordo's Getting There & Around section).

Enterprise (☎ 257-1154), 643 Sudderth Dr, rents cars. Call Ruidoso Taxi (☎ 378-4848) for a cab.

MESCALERO APACHE INDIAN RESERVATION

The Apaches were a nomadic people who arrived in this area about 800 years ago and soon became the enemies of the local Pueblo Indians. In the 19th century, under pressure from European settlement and with their mobility greatly increased by the introduction of the horse, the Apaches became some of the most feared raiders of the West. Today, about 3000 Native Americans live on the 719-sq-mile reservation, which lies in attractive country south and west of Ruidoso. Despite the name of the reservation, the Apaches here are of three tribes: the Mescalero, the Chiricahua and the Lipan. Residents make a living from logging, ranching and tourism.

The **Mescalero Cultural Center** (☎ 671-9254), on the Chiricahua Plaza off of Hwy 70, has a small but interesting exhibit about the peoples and customs. Also here is the Inn of the Mountain Gods (see Places to Stay in the Ruidoso Area section). The annual Apache Maidens' Puberty Ceremony takes place for about five days around the Fourth of July. Apart from the sacred rites of the Puberty Ceremony, there is a powwow, a rodeo, and arts and crafts demonstrations to which the public is welcome. Contact the Tribal Council (☎ 671-4494), Box 227, Mescalero, NM 88340, for information about dancing and other cultural demonstrations. The village of Mescalero is 17 miles southwest of Ruidoso on Hwy 70.

SMOKEY BEAR HISTORICAL STATE PARK

This three-acre park, set in the village of Capitan (population 800), celebrates the town's one claim to fame: Smokey Bear. Visitors can see the bear's grave and watch audio-visual programs about fire prevention in the visitor center (☎ 354-2748). Day use is $1. Every Fourth of July there is a Smokey Bear Stampede with a parade, a rodeo, cookouts and other festivities.

You can *camp* in the Lincoln National Forest nearby (see the Ruidoso Area's Places to Stay section, earlier in this chapter).

The inexpensive *Smokey Bear Motel* (☎ 800-766-5392) on the main road is the only place to stay. With fantastic green chile salsa and local meat, the family-owned *El Paisano Restaurant* (☎ 354-2206), just east of town, is a good place to eat. Everything is homemade, including the chips and tortillas.

LINCOLN
☎ 505 • pop 55 • elevation 5700 feet

For fans of Western history, a visit to tiny Lincoln (12 miles east of Capitan along the **Billy the Kid National Scenic Byway**), the scene of the gun battle that turned Billy the Kid into a legend, is a must. Modern influences, such as souvenir stands, are not allowed.

The few remaining inhabitants of Lincoln have preserved the buildings of the 1880s and the main street of town has been designated the **Lincoln State Monument** (☎ 653-4372). You can visit the Tunstall Store (with a remarkable display of late-19th-century merchandise), the courthouse where the Kid escaped imprisonment, and Dr Wood's house, an intact turn-of-the-century doctor's home and office. At the **Anderson Freeman Visitors Center and Museum** (☎ 653-4025), exhibits on the Buffalo soldiers, Apaches and the Lincoln County War explain the town's history. Admission to all four sites is $6; the Tunstall Store and Dr Wood's house are closed from March to November.

Old Lincoln Days are held during the first full weekend in August. Musicians and mountain men, doctors and desperadoes wander the streets in period costume, and there are demonstrations of spinning, black-smithing and other common frontier skills. In the evening there is the folk pageant, 'The Last Escape of Billy the Kid.'

Places to Stay & Eat

Accommodations in town are limited. The recommended *Casa de Patrón B&B* (☎ 653-4676, 800-524-5202), is in a house built around 1860 and purportedly slept in by the Kid. Seven rooms, all with private baths, are in either the historic main house, in adjoining casitas or in a newer addition. Rates are $87 to $117, including a full breakfast.

website: www.casapatron.com

Another good spot is the rural **Hurd Ranch Guest Homes** (☎ 653-4331, 800-658-6912) in San Patricio 14 miles south of Lincoln. Six lovely casitas by an apple orchard are $125 to $225 (some sleep up to six). Also here is the Peter Hurd la Rinconada Gallery, an art gallery housed in what was once Peter Hurd's home.

A 19th-century adobe surrounded by grass and filled with antiques, the *Ellis Store Country Inn* (☎ 653-4609, 800-653-6460) offers three rooms for $90 to $110. Four more rooms, in a historic mill on the property, range from $79 to $90. Rates include a full breakfast. A six-course gourmet dinner (about $50, wine is extra), served in the cozy dining room, can be ordered from Wednesday to Saturday. The public is welcome by reservation.

Though they only have seven RV sites and one tent site (or rather, because of this), **Sunset Peak Campground** (☎ 653-4442) is a beautiful spot. Campers have access to the 680-acre ranch and neighboring wilderness area. Toilets but no water are available, and firewood is provided. Tent/RV sites cost $10/20 per day, or $50/100 per week. The campground is located 31 miles east of Lincoln on State Rt 368.

Lincoln County War

In the mid-1870s, Lincoln's 400 inhabitants lived in adobe houses and shopped at Murphy's General Store, the only store in the region. Murphy's made large profits by also providing supplies to nearby Fort Stanton. In 1877, competition arrived in the form of John Tunstall, an English merchant who built another general store.

To say the merchants did not get along is an understatement. Within a year of his arrival, Tunstall was shot dead, allegedly by Murphy and his boys. Supporters of Tunstall wanted revenge, and the entire region erupted in what became known as the Lincoln County War. Tunstall's most famous follower was a wild teenager named Henry McCarty, alias William Bonney, soon to become known as Billy the Kid. Over the next months the Kid and his gang gunned down any of the Murphy faction that they could find, including Sheriff Pat Brady and other lawmen. The Kid was captured or cornered a couple of times but managed some brazen and lucky escapes before finally being shot by Sheriff Pat Garrett near Fort Sumner in 1881.

The story has since been romanticized and retold many times in books, movies and songs. The consummate American outlaw, often portrayed as a gunslinger fighting for what he thought was right rather than as a criminal desperado, Billy the Kid has captured the nation's imagination for more than a century.

For dinner you can head west to Capitan (where there is also an inexpensive motel; see Smoky Bear Historical State Park, earlier in this chapter) or 14 miles east to the town of Tinnie, where the friendly *Silver Dollar* (☎ 653-4425) serves lunch and dinner daily.

ROSWELL

☎ 505 • pop 50,000 • elevation 3649 feet

Roswell stands at the western edge of the dry plains known as the Llano Estacado. If you're driving east on Hwy 70/380 out of the Sacramento Mountains, enjoy the view. These are the last big mountains you'll see for a while.

The 'Staked Plains' extending east through Texas were once home to millions of buffalo and many nomadic Native American hunters. White settlers and hunters moved in throughout the late 19th century, and between 1872 and 1874, some 3,700,000 buffalo were killed, an estimated 3.5 million by whites. Within a few years, the Llano Estacado became desolate and empty, with only a few groups of Comanche mixed with the other tribes roaming the plains, hunting and trying to avoid confinement on reservations. Roswell, founded in 1871, served as a stopping place for cowboys driving cattle.

Today, oddly famous as both the country's largest producer of wool and its UFO capital, Roswell has built a tourist industry around the alleged 1947 UFO crash here (see the boxed text 'Visitors from Afar'). It is the largest town in this part of the state and is the seat of Chaves County. The county has a population of some 64,000, of whom 50,000 live in Roswell, which suggests how empty the surrounding areas are.

Summers are fairly hot, with many 90°F days, but it's a dry heat. Evenings cool down to pleasant temperatures. Winters see an occasional snowfall that rarely lasts more than a day or two.

Orientation & Information

The main west-east drag through town is 2nd St and the main north-south thoroughfare is Main St; their intersection is the heart of downtown. Accommodations are on

ROSWELL

OTHER
1 Del Norte Twin Cinema
2 Eastern New Mexico Medical Center
9 General Douglas L McBride Museum; New Mexico Military Institute
10 Anderson Museum of Contemporary Art
14 TNM&O/Greyhound Bus Depot
15 Roswell Community Little Theater
16 Roswell Museum & Art Center; Goddard Planetarium
18 Post Office
19 Hispano Chamber and Visitors Bureau
20 Library
22 Historical Center for Southeast New Mexico
23 Chamber of Commerce
25 Police
26 International UFO Museum & Research Center

PLACES TO STAY
3 Econo Lodge
4 Best Western El Rancho Palacio
6 Holiday Inn Express
7 Budget Inn North
8 Best Western Sally Port Inn
11 Days Inn
12 Zuni Motel

PLACES TO EAT
6 Nuthin' Fancy Café
13 The Cattle Baron
17 Teresa's
21 Martin's Capitol Café
24 Denny's
27 El Toro Bravo

these two streets. The Hispano Chamber and Visitors Bureau (☎ 624-0889, 888-767-9355), 426 N Main St, can be visited online at www.roswell-usa.com. It and the BLM office (☎ 627-0272), 2909 W 2nd St, are open weekdays. Other services include the main post office (☎ 623-7232), 415 N Pennsylvania Ave; the library (☎ 622-7101), 301 N Pennsylvania Ave; the Eastern New Mexico Medical Center (☎ 622-8170), 405 W Country Club Rd; and the police (☎ 624-6770),128 W 2nd St.

Roswell Museum & Art Center & Goddard Planetarium

The excellent Roswell Museum and Planetarium (☎ 624-6744), 100 W 11th St, deserves a visit. With 17 galleries showcasing Southwestern artists including Georgia O'Keeffe, Peter Hurd and Henriette Wyeth, and an eclectic mix of Native American, Hispanic and Anglo artifacts, there is something here for everyone. A major focus is space research. Robert H Goddard, who launched the world's first successful liquid fuel rocket in 1926, spent more than a decade carrying out rocket research in Roswell. His laboratory has been reconstructed at the museum, and a variety of early rocketry paraphernalia is on display. The museum is open 9 am to 5 pm daily except Sunday, when hours are 1 to 5 pm. Admission is free.

Historical Center for Southeast New Mexico

Housed in the 1910 mansion of local rancher James Phelp White, this museum (☎ 622-8333), 200 N Lea St, is on the National Register of Historic Places. The building is worth seeing; the inside has been carefully restored to its original early-20th-century décor with period furnishings, photographs and art. The museum is open daily and admission is by donation.

General Douglas L McBride Museum

This museum (☎ 624-8220), 101 W College Blvd, is on the campus of the New Mexico Military Institute. The institute was estab-

lished in 1891 and the military Gothic architecture is impressive. The museum has displays on US military history with a focus on the contributions of New Mexicans and alumni. Hours are limited and sporadic, but admission is free.

Anderson Museum of Contemporary Art

This small free museum (☎ 623-5600), 409 E College Blvd, exhibits work by past and present artists-in-residence in Roswell. Hours are 9 am to noon and 1 to 4 pm Monday to Friday.

Spring River Park & Zoo

The zoo (☎ 624-6760), on College Blvd at Atkinson St, is a good place for younger kids. Apart from the animals, there is a petting zoo, prairie-dog town, miniature train, antique carousel and kids' fishing pond. Hours are 10 am until 8 pm daily from June to August (it closes at 5:30 during the rest of the year) and admission is free.

Dexter National Fish Hatchery

The fish hatchery (☎ 734-5910), 20 miles southeast of Roswell on Hwy 2 (take Hwy 285 southbound to Dexter and look for signs), is an interesting sidetrip. A small visitor center explains the hatchery's efforts to study and propagate rare and endangered Southwestern fish species. The hatchery is next to Lake Van, where you can camp.

Bitter Lake National Wildlife Refuge

Wintering water birds gather at the 38-sq-mile Bitter Lake National Wildlife Refuge (☎ 622-6755); in the summer, various birds remain to nest. More than 300 have been recorded. The refuge, open from one hour before sunrise to one hour after sunset, is about 15 miles northeast of Roswell. Follow the signed roads from either Hwy 380 or Hwy 285/70 (free admission).

Special Events

The main annual event is the Eastern New Mexico State Fair (☎ 623-9411), held in early

October, with rodeo, livestock and agricultural competitions and chile-eating contests.

Roswell has a couple quirky festivals worth checking out if you happen to be in the area. One is New Mexico Dairy Day in early June. This features the Great Milk Carton Boat Race on Lake Van, 20 miles south of Roswell, as well as cheese sculpting contests, 36-foot-long ice cream sundaes, games and sporting events. The second is the UFO Encounter, around July 4, with alien-costume competitions and lectures about UFOs.

Places to Stay

On the south end of town is the *Town & Country RV Park (☎ 624-1833, 333 W Brasher Rd)* with tent and RV sites from $11 to $16. Seven popular lakes provide some relief from the summer heat at *Bottomless Lakes State Park (☎ 624-6058)*, which has tent/RV sites for $10/14. Primitive campsites are available. Day use is $4 per car. To get to the park, drive 10 miles east of Roswell on Hwy 380, then 5 miles south on Hwy 409. Also see Dexter National Fish Hatchery.

The following have clean, simple rooms for $25 to $35, and the first two have pools.

Budget Inn North (☎ 623-6050) 2101 N Main St

Budget Inn West (☎ 623-3811) 2200 W 2nd St

Frontier Motel (☎ 622-1400, 800-678-1401) 3010 N Main St

Zuni Motel (☎ 622-1930) 1201 N Main St

Travelers will find plenty of *chain motels*, including Econo Lodge, Days Inn, Best Western Sally Port Inn (Roswell's best) and Holiday Inn Express, lining Main and 2nd Sts.

Visitors from Afar

In July 1947 the Roswell newspaper reported a UFO crash near town. The military quickly closed the area and allowed no more information for several decades (although recently they claimed it was a balloon). Was it a flying saucer? The local convention and visitors bureau suggests that Roswell's special blend of climate and culture attracted touring space aliens who wanted a closer look!

Serious followers of UFO phenomena (not to mention skeptics or the merely curious) will want to check out the **International UFO Museum and Research Center** (☎ 625-9495), 114 N Main St, open 10 am to 5 pm daily. Original photographs and witness statements form the Roswell Incident Timeline and explain the great cover-up. A library with videos, books and magazines claims to be the most comprehensive UFO-related library in the world.

Bruce Rhodes (☎ 622-0628), an expert on the history of the alien incident, guides trips to the original crash sites (there's no wreckage!) with 24-hours notice. The first site is the Ragsdale site, 53 miles west of Roswell. In 1947 Jim Ragsdale and his girlfriend were camping on the edge of the forest when they allegedly saw the crash. One hundred miles northwest of Roswell is the Crona Site (or debris site), a ranch owned by the Fosters in 1947 where WW Brizel picked up the original debris and brought it to the air field in town. A full-day trip to both sites is $150 for up to four people ($40 per person after that); the Ragsdale site alone is $75, plus $25 for each additional person after three.

During the first week of July, Roswell hosts the 'UFO Encounter,' with alien-costume competitions, lectures, films, workshops and other extraterrestrial festivities.

Places to Eat

For diner food, including blue-plate specials, an espresso bar and 14 beers on tap, try the *Nuthin' Fancy Café* (☎ 623-4098, 2103 N Main St) open 6 am to 9 pm.

Several inexpensive New Mexican and Mexican restaurants are good. One of the cheapest is *Martin's Capitol Café* (☎ 624-2111, 110 W 4th St), with dinners for about $5 and breakfast from 6 am. Also try the small *Teresa's* (☎ 623-9691, 505 N Main St) for breakfast or lunch and *El Toro Bravo* (☎ 622-9280, 102 S Main St). For reasonably priced steaks, *The Cattle Baron* (☎ 622-2465, 1113 N Main St) is dependable. The *Pasta Café* (☎ 624-1111) in the Roswell Mall is considered the best Italian restaurant.

If you are hungry at 3:49 am, *Denny's* (☎ 623-5377) at 200 N Main St and 2200 N Main St (☎ 622-9960) is open 24 hours.

Entertainment

The *Roswell Symphony Orchestra* (☎ 623-5882) officially plays from October to April, but additional concerts may be scheduled throughout the year. Performances are held at Pearson Auditorium on the New Mexico Military Institute Campus. The *Roswell Community Little Theater* (☎ 622-1982, 1101 N Virginia Ave) performs several plays throughout its September to June season.

Call ☎ 623-5139 for show times at *Del Norte Twin Cinema* (2800 N Main St); *Cinema 4* in the Roswell Shopping Mall; and *Park Twin* (1717 S Union Ave).

Getting There & Around

Mesa Air (☎ 347-5501, 800-637-2247) flies daily to Albuquerque, Carlsbad, and Dallas, Texas from the Roswell Air Center (☎ 347-5703), at the south end of Main St.

The TNM&O/Greyhound Bus Depot (☎ 622-2510), 1100 N Virginia Ave behind Wendy's, has daily buses to Carlsbad ($20, 1½ hours), Albuquerque ($35, four hours) and beyond. From Tuesday to Saturday a 7 am bus heads to Santa Fe ($42, 5¾ hours); otherwise the daily bus to Santa Fe departs at noon and requires a four-hour layover in Albuquerque. Buses to Texas go to Amarillo, Lubbock and El Paso.

Pecos Trails Transit (☎ 624-6766) runs local buses throughout the city and to/from the airport. Hertz (☎ 347-2211) and Avis (☎ 347-2500) have car rental offices at the airport.

ARTESIA

☎ 505 • pop 1200 • elevation 3380 feet

Artesia, 30 miles north of Carlsbad, is the home of New Mexico's largest petroleum refinery. The landscape east of Artesia is dominated by thousands of small 'grasshopper' oil wells and the electric lines that support them. Each well is located on a patch of bare, bulldozed earth, and the air is thick with the smell of petroleum. Some side roads bear signs reading 'Dangerous Gases May Be Present.'

There isn't really much reason to come here, but if you're driving through, there are *chain motels,* including Motel 6 and Best Western, on the west end of town. The *Heritage Inn B&B* (☎ 748-2552, 209 W Main St) offers kitschy, plush rooms from $60.

The best food and drinks can be found at *The Wellhead* (☎ 740-0640, 332 W Main St), a modern brewpub restaurant and bar with an oil drilling theme housed in a 1905 building.

CARLSBAD

☎ 505 pop 29,000 elevation 3120 feet

On the Pecos River approximately 30 miles north of the Texas state line, Carlsbad is an important destination for travelers in southeastern New Mexico because of its proximity to the world-famous Carlsbad Caverns, about 25 miles away. Ranching and the cultivation of cotton, alfalfa and vegetables were the base of the economy until the discovery of oil and potash (a mineral fertilizer). Carlsbad now produces 85% of the USA's potash. The proclamation of Carlsbad Caverns as a national monument in 1923 attracted a trickle of tourists, which soon became a flood – now hundreds of thousands of visitors come through every year.

Summer temperatures climb over 100°F fairly often, though nights are pleasant. Winters are cool but see little snowfall and only a few freezes. Annual precipitation is about 12 inches.

Orientation

The northern and eastern downtown areas of Carlsbad are bounded by the Pecos River. The main thoroughfare is Hwy 285, entering town from the northwest as Pierce St and then veering south to become Canal St, Carlsbad's main drag. Canal St becomes S Canal, south of Mermod St and then National Parks Hwy at the south end of town.

Information

The chamber of commerce (☎ 887-6516, 800-221-1224), 302 S Canal St, is open 8 am to 5 pm Monday to Friday. Visit online at www.chamber.caverns.com or write to them at PO Box 910, Carlsbad, NM 88220. The National Parks Information Center (☎ 885-8884), 3225 National Parks Hwy, with information on both Carlsbad Caverns National Park and Guadalupe Mountains National Park, and the BLM office (☎ 887-6544), 620 E Green St, are open Monday to Friday. The USFS Lincoln National Forest Guadalupe Ranger Station (☎ 885-4181) is in the federal building at Halagueno and Fox Sts. Other services include the library (☎ 885-6776), 101 S Halagueno St; the post office (☎ 885-5717), 301 N Canyon St; the medical center (☎ 887-4100), 2430 W Pierce St; and the police (☎ 885-2111), 405 S Halagueno St.

Things to See & Do

Spread out over the Ocotillo Hills on the northwestern outskirts of town (on Miehls Dr off Hwy 285), **Living Desert State Park** (☎ 887-5516) exhibits the wildlife of the Chihuahuan Desert. It's a great place to see and learn about cacti, coyotes and wildlife with evocative Southwestern names such as agave, javelina, ocotillo and yucca. It's open daily and admission is $4.

The **Carlsbad Museum & Art Center** (☎ 887-0276), 418 W Fox St, displays Apache artifacts, pioneer memorabilia and art from the Taos school (free admission). Hours are 10 am to 5 pm daily (closed Sunday). The Southwestern touches at the **Eddy County Courthouse** (constructed in 1891 and remodeled in 1939) are worth a look: The cattle brands of the most impor-

CARLSBAD

PLACES TO STAY
8 Parkview Motel
11 Holiday Inn
14 La Fonda Motel
17 Economy Inn
17 Best Western Motel Stevens; Silver Spur Lounge
18 Carlsbad Inn
20 Quality Inn
21 Super 8 Motel

PLACES TO EAT
6 Deluxe Cafe
10 Cortez Cafe
12 Lucy's

OTHER
1 Post Office
2 Eddy County Courthouse
3 Carlsbad Museum & Art Center; Library
4 USFS Ranger Station
5 The Firehouse
7 Chamber of Commerce
9 Police
13 TNM&O/ Greyhound Bus Depot
16 Fiesta Drive-In Theater
19 National Parks Information Center
22 WIPP Visitor Center

tant local ranches are carved into the door frames, and the interior ceilings boast heavy beams and ornate iron chandeliers.

In 1974 the Atomic Energy Commission chose a site 30 miles east of Carlsbad as a potential underground nuclear repository, and in 1999 the controversial **Waste Isolation Pilot Plant** (WIPP) received its first shipment of nuclear waste. Tours descending 2150 feet underground are offered with four weeks advance notice (45 days for foreign visitors). Call ☎ 800-336-9477 for details.

North of Bataan Bridge, a system of dams and spillways on the Pecos River creates the two-mile **Lake Carlsbad**, with various amusements, including a 4½-mile trail along its banks. At the north end of Park Dr, or at the east end of Church St, is **Carlsbad Riverfront Park**, with a beach and swimming area. At nearby **Port Jefferson** (☎ 887-8343), visitors can rent pontoon boats or go on a paddlewheel tour of the river. Boats are available every day from Memorial Day to Labor Day and on weekends from March to October. Call ☎ 885-4993 for more information.

From Thanksgiving to December 31, the riverfront is lit with Christmas lights and boat tours ($7) leave three times an hour from 5:45 to 9:15 pm nightly, except Christmas Eve. Make reservations at the chamber of commerce.

Places to Stay
The nearby national park and mild winters make this a year-round destination, though rooms are a bit more from May to August; always ask for the best rate. On National Parks Hwy, travelers will find plenty of *chain motels*, including Motel 6, Super 8, and Days Inn.

With more than 100 sites, an indoor pool, grocery, laundry, playground and showers, **Carlsbad RV Park & Campground** (☎ 885-6333, 4301 National Parks Hwy) offers tent/RV sites for $14.50/20, cabins for $27 and a teepee with four beds for $22. At **Brantley Lake State Park** (☎ 457-2384), 12 miles north of Carlsbad and 5 miles east of Hwy 285, primitive camping/RV hookups are

$7/11 (day use is $3 per vehicle). For back-country camping, see Carlsbad Caverns.

The following motels offer simple but acceptable rooms in the lower $30s: **La Fonda Motel** (☎ 885-6242, 1522 S Canal St), the **Parkview Motel** (☎ 885-3117, 401 E Greene St) and the recently remodeled **Economy Inn** (☎ 885-4914, 1621 S Canal St).

The **Carlsbad Inn** (☎ 887-1171, 2019 S Canal St) has microwaves and refrigerators in some rooms ($40). Sizable doubles are about $45 at the **Continental Inn** (☎ 887-0341, 3820 National Parks Hwy).

All the better hotels are standard chains; most have pools and provide courtesy transportation to the bus depot or airport.

The **Quality Inn** (☎ 887-2861, 3706 National Parks Hwy) has a lounge with live entertainment and dancing and attractively landscaped grounds with a hot tub ($60s). The similarly priced **Best Western Motel Stevens**(☎ 887-2851, 800-730-2851, 1829 S Canal St) is by far the largest hotel in town, with more than 200 rooms, some with kitchenettes or microwave/refrigerator combos, a restaurant and a lounge. The two-story **Holiday Inn** (☎ 885-8500, 601 S Canal St) is the only full-service hotel downtown. Doubles range from $75 to $100.

Places to Eat
Since 1951 the **Deluxe Cafe** (☎ 887-1304, 224 S Canal St) has been serving American and New Mexican food, and the interior looks about the same as it has for decades. It is open 5 am to 2 pm daily.

For lunch and dinner, there are several homey and good Mexican restaurants. **Lucy's** (☎ 887-7714, 701 S Canal St) is deservedly the most popular and is often packed with both locals and visitors. Apart from a great Mexican menu, Lucy's serves up tasty margaritas and a selection of microbrews. Most everything on the menu is well under $10. Another good choice is the **Cortez Cafe** (☎ 885-4747, 506 S Canal St), a smaller place that has been around since 1937 (a long time for southeastern New Mexico).

Two 24-hour restaurants are **Jerry's** (☎ 885-6793, 3720 National Parks Hwy) and **Denny's** (☎ 885-5600, 810 W Pierce St).

Entertainment

For country music, try the *Silver Spur Lounge* (☎ 887-2851) at the Best Western Motel Stevens or the Quality Inn. If you want to avoid motel lounges, *Lucy's* (see Places to Eat) and *The Firehouse* (☎ 234-1546, 222 W Fox St) have live music of all sorts on weekends.

The *Fiesta Drive-In Theater* (☎ 885-4126, San Jose Blvd) gives you the chance to soak up some nighttime desert air and experience a form of American entertainment that has almost disappeared – the drive-in movie. The concession stand offers a range of fast food (not just candy and popcorn), so you can eat here and make a night of it; prices range from $2 to $8 per car, and it's closed Tuesday to Thursday.

If you would rather see indoor movies, try the *Mall Cinema 3* (☎ 885-0777, 2322 W Pierce St).

The *Carlsbad Community Theater* (☎ 887-3157), on National Parks Hwy about 5 miles south of downtown, offers regular dramatic performances.

Getting There & Around

Carlsbad's City Airport (☎ 887-9008) is about 6 miles south of town. Mesa Air (☎ 885-0245) has a daily flight to Albuquerque. TNM&O/ Greyhound buses leave from the bus depot (☎ 887-1108), 1000 Canyon St, daily to Albuquerque ($47, five hours) and El Paso, Texas ($32, three hours).

Hertz (☎ 887-1500) at the airport, and Enterprise (☎ 887-3039), 1724 S Canal St, rent cars.

WHITE'S CITY

Named after Jim White, the first serious explorer of Carlsbad Caverns, this 'city' is just a Best Western 'old west' complex (☎ 785-2291, 800-228-3767) 7 miles from the entrance to the national park. Carlsbad is 21 miles to the north.

White's City RV Park has about 150 sites, many with RV hookups ($16 for up to six people). The *Best Western Cavern Inn* and the *Best Western Guadalupe Inn* have acceptable rooms for about $90. You are paying for the convenience of staying near the park; rooms in Carlsbad are better and cheaper.

In the hotel complex there's a small grocery store, post office and the kitschy **Million Dollar Museum**, which claims to have 50,000 Western items on display and charges visitors $3 to see them. *Velvet Garden Restaurant & Saloon* has swinging Wild West–style doors you can swagger (stagger?) through en route to a steak or seafood meal.

Be prepared to cheer the heroine, boo the villain and throw your popcorn at the enemy at *Granny's Opera House*; old-fashioned melodrama is presented most nights during the summer.

There are daily buses from Carlsbad or El Paso (Texas) to White's City with TNM&O and a van shuttle to the caverns.

CARLSBAD CAVERNS NATIONAL PARK

Who in their right mind would drive for hours across the desert just to see a cave? Once visitors see the caverns, however, even the most skeptical are impressed. This is one of the greatest cave systems in the world, and a visit is, without a doubt, a highlight of a journey through the Southwest.

The park covers 73 sq miles and includes over 85 caves. A 2-mile subterranean walk from the cave mouth reaches an underground chamber 1800 feet long, 255 feet high and over 800 feet below the surface. Exploration continues at the awe-inspiring **Lechugilla Cave**; with a depth of 1567 feet and a length of about 60 miles, it is the deepest cave and third longest limestone cave in North America (experienced spelunkers only). The park's second attraction is the Mexican free-tail bat colony. More than 300,000 bats roost here from April to October.

The park entrance is 23 miles northeast of Carlsbad. A three-day pass for self-guided tours to the natural entrance and the Big Room (send a postcard from the lunchroom, 829 feet below the surface!) costs $6 for adults, $3 for children and passes are honored. Beyond the self-guided tours, call the park (☎ 785-2232, 800-967-2283) to

Geology of Carlsbad Cavern

Although once touted by geologists as a typical example of how most caves form, the caves in Carlsbad Caverns National Park actually have quite an unusual origin. Caves are normally created when rainwater, made slightly acidic by interaction with atmospheric carbon dioxide, dissolves limestone and widens fractures into long, low, conduit-shaped passages. In contrast, Carlsbad Caverns consists of large, interconnected rooms with high ceilings. These formed as hydrogen sulfide gas from adjacent oil deposits reacted with groundwater to form sulfuric acid, an extremely powerful dissolving agent that quickly (by geologic standards) scoured out huge volumes of bedrock. This occurred within the last 5 to 10 million years.

Another reason for these gigantic rooms is the nature of the rock that hosts the caves. Carlsbad Caverns lies in the Capitan Limestone of the Guadalupe Mountains. About 300 million years ago, the Capitan Limestone was a barrier reef that flourished in a shallow inland sea. Minerals crystallized out of the seawater, cementing the skeletons of the reef coral into thick rock layers that are massive enough to support the rooms, high ceilings and wide expanses of the caverns. Then the sea evaporated, leaving salt and gypsum deposits. Rainwater percolating through the exposed reef gradually dissolved some of the limestone, forming a few small caves.

Once the rooms were no longer submerged by groundwater, the rapid dissolution of limestone ended and speleothems (cave formations) began to grow. Radiometric dating of large speleothems from the Big Room tells us that Carlsbad Cavern (the main tourist cave) was completely drained of water around 600,000 years ago.

While they are found in numerous shapes and sizes, each speleothem is formed by the same basic process. As rainwater enters the cave, carbon dioxide gas escapes from the water, forcing calcium carbonate to crystallize. Stalactites (think 'c' for ceiling) grow downward from drips hanging on the roof, while stalagmites (think 'g' for ground) form upward when drips fall to the floor. Some formations you might see include cave popcorn, cave pearls and helictites (small spiraling stalagmites). The numerous speleothems in Carlsbad Cavern attest to a humid climate in the past, but today, because of the hot, dry Southwestern climate, speleothems grow more slowly.

– Rhawn Denniston, geologist

make the required advance reservations for a spectrum of ranger-led tours and bat flight programs (from $7); if you want to scramble and climb to lesser known areas, ask about the **Wild Cave Tours**.

The visitor center is open daily 8 am to 7 pm from late May to mid-August and 8 am to 5:30 pm the rest of the year, but be warned that ticket sales stop two to 3½ hours before the visitor center closes. There are no accommodations within the park. Backpacking trips into the desert backcountry (33,125 of the 46,766 acres are wilderness) are allowed by permit (free) and topographical maps of the 50-plus miles of hiking trails are available at the visitor center.

Complete information is available at www.nps.gov/cave or write to Carlsbad Caverns National Park, 3225 National Parks Hwy, Carlsbad, NM 88220.

GUADALUPE MOUNTAINS

This southeastern extension of the Sacramento Mountains continues through southeastern New Mexico and across into western Texas.

The northern part of the range is in the Guadalupe District of New Mexico's Lincoln National Forest. South of the Texas state line, these mountains form the Guadalupe Mountains National Park. The eastern foothills of these mountains are in Carlsbad Caverns National Park.

Lincoln National Forest

The Guadalupe District of the Lincoln National Forest encompasses 445 sq miles and ranges in altitude from 3500 to 7600 feet, allowing for a varied wildlife population.

The main attraction is **Sitting Bull Falls**, 50 miles from Carlsbad. Here there are waterfalls and swimming holes but no campground. The area is open from April to November. The falls are reached either by taking Hwy 285 north from Carlsbad for 12 miles and then heading west on Hwy 137 (paved) and 276, or by taking Hwy 62/180 south from Carlsbad for about 10 miles and taking Hwy 408 west to Hwy 137 and 276. These are mostly unpaved roads passable to cars most of the summer.

Hwy 137 continues south to Rim Road 540 and **Five Points Vista** (viewpoint) on the way to the Guadalupe Mountains National Park. Dispersed *camping* is allowed throughout the national forest. Further information and maps are available in Carlsbad at the USFS Ranger Station (☎ 885-4181) or the BLM office (☎ 887-6544).

Guadalupe Mountains National Park (Texas)

Fifty-five miles south of Carlsbad and 110 miles east of El Paso, this national park is in Texas, although the northern boundary is the New Mexico state line and the closest access is from New Mexico. This is a park for the seeker of remote wilderness; 80 miles of steep, rocky trails offer hiking and backpacking. In the fall **McKittrick Canyon**, one of the most scenic hiking areas in the park, brightens to a spectacular red and yellow (day use only).

There is no food or lodging in the park, though two campgrounds have water and restrooms ($8; passes are honored). *Pines Springs Campground* is next to the main visitor center. *Dog Canyon Campground*, at the far north of the park in a forested canyon, can be reached via Hwy 137 from New Mexico, or along Hwy 408 between Carlsbad and White's City. The main visitor center (☎ 915-828-3251), HC 60 Box 400, Salt Flat, Texas 79847, on Hwy 62/180 in the far southeastern corner of the state, is open weekdays and has free backcountry permits.
website: www.nps.gov/gumo/gumo/home.html.

HOBBS

☎ 505 • pop 32,000 • elevation 3615 feet

Hobbs, 69 miles east of Carlsbad and 3 miles from the Texas state line, is the center of New Mexico's largest oil field. The town and the horizontal landscape of the surrounding Llano Estacado is punctuated frequently by the seesaw-like pumpjacks, or 'lufkins,' stolidly forcing oil to the surface.

If you're a soaring enthusiast, Hobbs is worth a visit. Hobbs' weather is ideal for **gliding** and the town is the home of the National Soaring Foundation (☎ 392-6032) and the Soaring Society of America (☎ 392-1177). Call the foundation to arrange a joy ride during the summer.

Closer to earth, nearby Lovington hosts the **Lea County Fair & Rodeo** (☎ 396-5344), one of the state's biggest county fairs and more than 60 years old, during the second week in August.

There isn't much other reason to visit Hobbs, but there are several *inexpensive motels* ($30s); try the Sixpence Inn (☎ 393-0221, 509 N Marland Blvd) and the Western Holiday Motel (☎ 393-6494, 2724 W Marland Blvd). Travelers will also find plenty of *chain motels* on Marland Blvd and Lovington Hwy, including Super 8 and the new Holiday Inn Express. In Lovington, the cheery and unusual *Pyburn House B & B* (☎ 396-3460, 203 N 4th St, Lovington, NM 88260), built of local stone in the '30s, offers several lavishly furnished rooms starting at $55 for a single.

Noah's Restaurant (☎ 393-6614, 701 N Dal Paso St) serves homemade New Mexican food from 11 am to 9 pm Tuesday to Sunday (even the chips are homemade). *Lucy's Mexicali Restaurant* (☎ 392-1802, 4428 Lovington Hwy) is a simple, colorful place that serves good New Mexican food ($4 to $7), beer and wine.

Big Sky Air (☎ 800-237-7788) flies into Hobbs daily from Dallas, Texas.

PORTALES

☎ 505 • pop 12,280 • elevation 4000 feet

This pleasant college town is the home of Eastern New Mexico University (ENMU). With almost 4000 students, the university contributes a great deal to the atmosphere and cultural life of the town. Agriculture and ranching form the base of the economy. Portales produces more Valencia peanuts than does anywhere else in the world – peanut farming and peanut-butter manufacturing are big business and you can buy all kinds of peanut candy at the peanut factories in town.

Orientation

Portales is 19 miles southwest of Clovis and 91 miles northeast of Roswell on Hwy 70 (this parallels the railway; there are no passenger services). Getting around can be confusing. Hwy 70 is a divided road downtown, running southwest to northeast on W 2nd St and northeast to southwest on W 1st. Downtown streets run southwest to northeast, while avenues run southeast to northwest. Things get complicated away from the old downtown, where avenues change to run north-south and streets to east-west.

PORTALES

To Campgrounds, Blackwater Draw Museum & Site & Clovis

To Grulla National Wildlife Refuge

To Hospital & Roswell

Eastern New Mexico University

To Hobbs

PLACES TO STAY & EAT	
1	La Hacienda Restaurant
2	El Rancho Restaurant
6	Roosevelt Restaurant and Bar
9	Morning Star Inn B&B
10	Sands Motel; Mark's Eastern Grill
12	Juanito's Restaurant
17	Classic American Economy Inn
18	Super 8 Motel
19	Wagon Wheel Café

OTHER	
3	Post Office
4	TNM&O Bus Depot
5	Tower Theater
7	Library
8	Chamber of Commerce
11	Roosevelt County Historical Museum
13	Golden Library
14	University Theater
15	Miles Mineral Museum; Natural History Museum
16	Windmill Collection

0   .5   1 km

0   .25   .5 mile

Information

Tourist information is available from the Roosevelt Chamber of Commerce (☎ 356-8541, 800-635-8036), 200 E 7th St, Portales, NM 88130; visit online at www.portales.com. Information about ENMU is available on campus (☎ 562-1011). Other services include the library (☎ 356-3940), 218 S Ave B; the post office (☎ 356-4781), 116 W 1st St (inside, check out *Buffalo Range,* a New Deal mural painted in 1938); the hospital (☎ 359-1800), 42121 US 70; and the police (☎ 356-4404), 1700 N Boston Ave.

Eastern New Mexico University Museums

There are several museums on the campus that don't have fixed hours, so call ahead. With a focus on pioneer and early settlement history, **Roosevelt County Historical Museum** (☎ 562-2592) is a good spot for history buffs. Science-fiction fans will enjoy the **Jack Williamson Science Fiction Collection** in the Golden Library (☎ 562-2624). Williamson used to teach at ENMU and authored dozens of sci-fi novels and stories. His manuscripts and his letters to sci-fi writers Robert Heinlein and Ray Bradbury can be inspected here.

The **Miles Mineral Museum** (☎ 562-2651) south of the library in Roosevelt Hall displays, yes, you guessed it, minerals, and the **Natural History Museum** (☎ 562-2723) focuses on local wildlife.

Blackwater Draw Museum & Site

Arrowheads and other artifacts of Paleo-Indian culture discovered in the 1930s at the Blackwater Draw Archaeological site proved that people were living here at least 11,000 years ago. This led scientists to the realization that people had been living in the Americas several thousand years earlier than previously estimated. The museum (☎ 562-2202), on Hwy 70 about 7 miles northeast of downtown, displays Clovis arrowheads, bones and interpretive dioramas of what prehistoric life was like. From Memorial Day to Labor Day, the museum is open 10 am to 5 pm Monday to Saturday,

noon to 5 pm on Sunday (call for hours during the rest of the year). Admission is $2.

Archaeology buffs can visit the site (☎ 356-5235), which is several miles from the museum (get directions from the museum). Summer hours are the same as the museum's. In spring and fall the site is open on weekends only, weather permitting; it is closed from November to February.

Windmill Collection

A private collection of more than 80 windmills, some of them dating to the 1870s, can be seen in a field off Kilgore St, three-quarters of a mile south of 3rd St at the east end of town. Owned and curated by Bill Dalley (☎ 356-6263), it is one of the largest private windmill collections in the USA.

Grulla National Wildlife Refuge

Although administered from Texas, the Grulla National Wildlife Refuge (☎ 806-946-3341) a wintering site for various waterfowl (including sandhill cranes) is in New Mexico. To get here, drive 16 miles east from Portales on Hwy 88 to the village of Arch, then 3 miles south.

Special Events

The big annual event is the Peanut Valley Festival, usually held around the third or fourth weekend in October. The festival features nutty events such as burying students in a tank full of peanuts (for charity), peanut-cooking and -eating and peanut Olympics.

Places to Stay & Eat

Tent/RV sites go for $14/16 at the *Wagon Wheel Campground* (☎ 356-3700), about 4 miles northeast of downtown on Hwy 70. *Oasis State Park* (☎ 356-5331, 1891 Oasis Rd), a 3-acre lake (the oasis) surrounded by cottonwood trees and sand dunes, offers fishing and tent/RV sites for $10/14. Day use is $4 per car. Get there by taking Hwy 70 for 2 miles northeast from Portales, then Hwy 467 north for about 6 miles.

The *Sands Motel* (☎ 356-4424, 800-956-4424, 1130 W 1st St) and the *Classic American Economy Inn* (☎ 356-6668,

800-901-9466), on Hwy 70 just west of ENMU, have rooms for $35 to $45. A simple B&B option is the ***Morning Star Inn B&B*** *(☎ 356-2994, 620 W 2nd St)*, with basic rooms for $50.

For homemade country-style cooking, try the unpretentious ***Wagon Wheel Café*** *(☎ 356-5036, 521 W 17th St)* open 6 am to 8 pm Monday to Saturday. Another spot for early risers is ***Mark's Eastern Grill*** *(☎ 359-0857, 1126 W 1st St)*, a diner and college-crowd hangout open daily 5 am to 9 pm. ***El Rancho*** *(☎ 359-0098, 101 N Chicago St)*; ***La Hacienda*** *(☎ 359-0280, 909 N Ave K)*; and ***Juanito's*** *(☎ 359-1860, 813 S Ave C)* all serve inexpensive Mexican lunches and dinners.

Built around 1900 and recently renovated (with a pressed-tin ceiling), ***Roosevelt Restaurant & Bar*** *(☎ 356-4000, 107 W 2nd St)*, on the square, is the nicest restaurant in town. There's a pleasant old bar, good steaks ($15) and a decent wine selection.

Entertainment

The College of Fine Arts at ENMU presents theater and symphony events several times a year. Call ENMU information *(☎ 562-1011)* or the ***University Theater*** *(☎ 562-2711)* for more details. ***Tower Twin*** *(☎ 356-6081, 101 N Ave A)* shows movies.

Getting There & Away

The nearest scheduled commercial air service is in Clovis. The bus depot *(☎ 356-6914)* is at 215 E 2nd St. TNM&O has daily buses to Amarillo, Texas ($27, 2½ hours), Roswell ($20, two hours), Ruidoso ($29.40, three hours), Alamogordo ($34.65, 4½ hours), Las Cruces ($56.70, six hours) Albuquerque ($33.60, four hours) and beyond.

CLOVIS

☎ 505 • pop 43,041 • elevation 4260 feet

Although Indians have roamed this area for millennia, there were no permanent Indian settlements here. In 1906, Clovis was founded to serve as a Santa Fe Railroad town. Today, Clovis is the seat of Curry County, the second smallest county in New Mexico. Agriculture, specifically wheat, sorghum grain, alfalfa, corn and peanuts are

important, and livestock and nearby Cannon Air Force Base are fundamental to Clovis' economy. Though not much of a tourist town, archaeology buffs know Clovis as the namesake of the Clovis Points (see Blackwater Draw Museum & Site under Portales) and rock & roll enthusiasts come here to visit the Norman Petty Studios.

Orientation & Information

Mabry Dr (Hwy 60/70/84), the main west-east street, continues to Texas, 9 miles east. Prince St (Hwy 70 southbound and Hwy 209 northbound) is the major north-south street and Main St is the most historic.

The chamber of commerce *(☎ 763-3435, 800-261-7656)*, 215 N Main St, is open weekdays. Other services include the library *(☎ 769-7840)*, 701 N Main St; the post office *(☎ 763-3467)*, on 5th St at Giddings St; the hospital *(☎ 769-2141)*, 2100 N Thomas St; and the police *(☎ 769-1921)*, 300 Connelly St.

Historic Buildings

Sections of Main St are cobbled and have several interesting early buildings on the National Register of Historic Buildings. Some of this street looks like part of a 1940s Western movie set. The nine-story **Hotel Clovis**, topped by statues of Indian heads, is on Main St near the chamber of commerce. When built in 1931, it was New Mexico's tallest building and it retained that status until 1953.

Built in 1919, the **Old Lyceum Theater** *(☎ 763-6085)*, 411 N Main St, has been refurbished and has occasional performances. Tours of its ornate vaudeville interior are available on request; call the barbershop next door at ☎ 683-3773.

Up the street at 122 W 4th St (a block west of Main St) is a 1931 building that was the post office, then the county library and now is an architect's office. The lobby houses a 4-by-9-foot oil mural of Clovis in the 1930s, painted under government New Deal sponsorship. Ask at the architect's office for a free tour – it is pretty cool, with things like spy holes in the ceiling that the postmaster used to spy on employees.

The town's oldest surviving house was built in 1907 and is at the Curry County

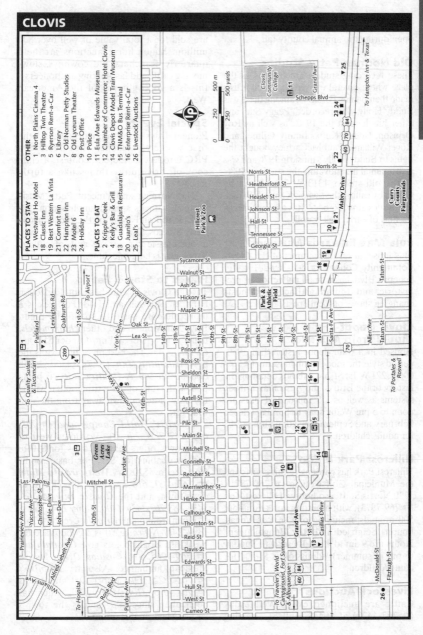

CLOVIS

PLACES TO STAY
17 Westward Ho Motel
18 Classic Inn
19 Best Western La Vista
21 Comfort Inn
22 Hampton Inn
23 Motel 6
24 Holiday Inn

PLACES TO EAT
4 Kripple Creek
4 Kelly's Bar & Grill
13 Guadalajara Restaurant
20 Juanito's
25 Leal's

OTHER
1 North Plains Cinema 4
3 Hilltop Twin Theater
5 Ryerson Rent-a-Car
6 Library
7 Old Norman Petty Studios
8 Old Lyceum Theater
9 Post Office
10 Police
11 Eula Mae Edwards Museum
12 Chamber of Commerce; Hotel Clovis
14 Clovis Depot Model Train Museum
15 TNM&O Bus Terminal
16 Enterprise Rent-a-Car
26 Livestock Auctions

Fairgrounds (☎ 763-6502) at 600 S Norris St. The house contains a small museum that is open during the annual county fair.

Old Norman Petty Studios

These recording studios are famous as the place where several early rock & roll artists made their names. Foremost among these was Buddy Holly, who recorded 'Peggy Sue' and other hits here in the 1950s, as well as Roy Orbison, Buddy Knox, Jimmy Gilmer and Roger Williams. Paul McCartney bought the rights to Buddy Holly's music in 1976 and was instrumental in renovating the studio in 1986.

The old studio, 1313 W 7th St, can be toured by calling the owner, Kenneth Broad, in Portales at ☎ 336-6422. It is a minor mecca for fans of early rock & roll.

Eula Mae Edwards Museum

This museum on the campus of the **Clovis Community College** (☎ 505-769-2811), 417 Schepps Blvd, has a small collection of prehistoric and Indian artifacts and hosts changing shows of local artists.

Clovis Depot Model Train Museum

Housed in a train depot restored in 1950s period style, the model train museum (☎ 762-0066), 221 W 1st St, has exhibits detailing the history of the British and Australian railway systems as well as US railroads. Hours are noon to 5 pm Wednesday to Sunday (closed February and September); admission is $4/2 for adults/children.

Hillcrest Park & Zoo

Hillcrest Park has gardens, tennis courts and the Municipal Golf Course (☎ 769-7871), 1220 Norris St. It also houses Hillcrest Zoo (☎ 769-7873), with a petting zoo and about 500 animals, including one of Las Vegas' famous Seigfried and Roy Bengal tigers. Hours are 9 am to 4 pm Tuesday to Sunday (5 pm in summer); admission is $1/50¢ for adults/children.

Livestock Auctions

Cattle are auctioned every Wednesday (☎ 762-4422) at 504 S Hull St, drawing buyers from Texas, Kansas, Oklahoma and Arizona. In a good year about 70,000 head are sold for a total value of well over $30 million. Major horse auctions are held quarterly. Ranchers and cowboys, slow-moving cattle and fast-talking auctioneers – this is a good glimpse of the American West.

Special Events

Pioneer Days occur annually around the first weekend in June. They feature a PRCA rodeo, a fiddlers' contest, a chile cook-off and quirky things like a turtle race.

The Norman and Vincent Petty Music Festival, with its special emphasis on '50s rock & roll and tours of the old Norman Petty Studios, also features a balloon rally, a '50s classic car parade and, of course, dancing. It is held mid-June.

Places to Stay & Eat

Though Clovis has the best hotel selection between Roswell and I-40, Portales is a more pleasant town to spend the night. Days Inn, Motel 6 and other *chain motels,* many with a pool and most under $50, are on Mabry Dr. The best place in town is the new *Hampton Inn (☎ 763-3300),* with doubles for $69. A *Quality Suites* is being built at the time of this writing, and it will be the only motel in town away from the railroad tracks.

Travelers' World Campground (☎ 763-6360, 4707 W 7th St), 3½ miles west of downtown, offers tent/RV sites for $10/16 and two cabins for $22. For basic rooms from the low $20s, try *Westward Ho Motel (☎ 762-4451, 616 E 1st St),* the closest to downtown, and the *Classic Inn (☎ 763-3439, 888-763-3439, 1400 Mabry Dr).*

Open from 6 am, *Kripple Creek (☎ 762-7399, 2417 N Prince St)* is a good place for breakfast. Bright colors give *Guadalajara (☎ 769-9965, 916 Casillas Dr)* a festive Mexican ambiance. Also try *Juanito's (☎ 762-7822, 1608 Mabry Dr)* and *Leal's (☎ 763-4075, 3100 Mabry Dr),* which has been open since 1957 and is the town's largest Mexican restaurant.

Entertainment

On the weekends, *Kelly's Bar & Grill* (☎ 762-0044, 2208 N Prince St) has dancing and live music. The *North Plains Cinema 4* (☎ 763-7713, 2809 N Prince St) and the *Hilltop Twin Theater* (☎ 763-7876), on Main St at 21st St, screen Hollywood movies.

Getting There & Around

Clovis Airport is 7 miles east of town on 21st St. Mesa Airlines (☎ 389-1230) flies to Albuquerque daily. TNM&O buses pass through the bus terminal (☎ 762-4584), 121 E 2nd St, several times daily on their way to Amarillo, Texas ($24.80, two hours), Ruidoso ($31.50, four hours), Albuquerque ($36, 5½ hours) and beyond.

Clovis City Cab (☎ 742-2100) has cabs from 8 am to midnight. You can rent a car from Enterprise Rent-a-Car (☎ 763-9733), 500 E 1st St, which services the airport, or Ryerson Rent-a-Car (762-4586), 421 Commerce Way.

FORT SUMNER

☎ 505 • pop 1250 • elevation 4030 feet

This village sprang up around old Fort Sumner and is in history books for two reasons: the disastrous Bosque Redondo Indian Reservation (see the 'Bosque Redondo' boxed text) and Billy the Kid's last showdown with Sheriff Pat Garrett. The area is full of Indian and outlaw history, and is the seat of small and sparsely populated De Baca County.

Orientation & Information

Hwy 60 (Sumner Ave) is the main thoroughfare and runs east-west through town; most places of interest lie along it. Fort Sumner is 84 miles north of Roswell, 45 miles southwest of Santa Rosa and 60 miles west of Clovis.

The chamber of commerce (☎ 355-7705, 355-2462), 707 N 4th St, is open weekdays. Other services include the library (☎ 355-2832), 300 W Sumner Ave; the post office

---

Bosque Redondo

With the Union victory at Glorietta Pass in March 1862, the threat of Confederate control of the Southwest ended and the troops turned all their force on the Indians. The battles that followed were cruel and bloody, involving broken treaties and several massacres. Brigadier General James H Carleton directed Kit Carson of the New Mexico volunteers to invade the Mescalero Apaches and Navajos and, despite his initial reluctance to fight Indians, arguing that he had volunteered to fight Confederates, not Indians, and threatening to resign, Carson followed orders. During a cold and snowy March in 1863, Carson marched into Canyon de Chelly, the Navajo stronghold, and destroyed crops, orchards and livestock. Six thousand Navajo surrendered out of starvation, and so began the close to 400 mile 'long walk' from Canyon de Chelly to Bosque Redondo. Hundreds of Navajo died from hunger or the elements before reaching the reservation.

Chiefs Manuelito, Barboncito and Armicjo, refusing to surrender, hid in the mountains with their people. Others escaped the reservation, and Carleton posted guards for forty miles around Fort Sumner. For years, Carleton hunted Navajos, and for years Manuelito and other warriors resisted capture. On September 1, 1866, a worn down Manuelito finally surrendered, and soon after Barboncito, the last of the Navajo chiefs, surrendered.

Carleton had hoped to convert the defeated Indians to Christian farmers, but the land was harsh, and unsuitable for agriculture, and brackish water spurred disease. Eighteen days after Manuelito's surrender, General Carleton was removed from command in New Mexico and for two years officials fromWashington came to assess the situation. In 1868, under the direction of General William Sherman and after four years of starvation and deprivation, the surviving Indians were allowed to return to their homelands. About 3000 had died since their imprisonment at Bosque Redondo.

(☎ 355-2423), 622 N 5th St; the De Baca General Hospital (☎ 355-2414), 500 N 10th St; and the Fort Sumner Sheriff's Office (☎ 355-2405), in the courthouse at 514 Ave C.

Billy the Kid Museum

With more than 60,000 privately owned items on display, the Billy the Kid Museum (☎ 355-2380), 1601 E Sumner Ave, is obviously more than just a museum about the famous outlaw. Indian artifacts and items from late-19th- and early-20th-century frontier life fill the rooms. Hours are 8:30 am to 5 pm daily (shortened summer hours in the winter). The museum is closed the first two weeks of January. Admission is $4/2 for adults/children.

Fort Sumner State Monument

The state monument (☎ 355-2573) is 2 miles east of town on Hwy 60, then 4 miles south on Hwy 272. The original Fort Sumner was built here in 1862 as an outpost to fight the Apache tribe and the Confederate army around the time of the Civil War. After driving the Confederates south, the troops turned all their force on the Indians (see the 'Bosque Redondo' boxed text).

Once the Indians were killed or put on a reservation, the fort was purchased by Lucien Maxwell, one of the richest ranchers of the period, who turned it into a palatial ranch. Maxwell literally owned most of New Mexico north of Fort Sumner and east of the Rockies – the largest spread ever owned by one individual in the United States. His son, Peter, inherited the ranch in 1875. Billy the Kid was visiting here on July 14, 1881, when he was shot and killed by Sheriff Pat Garrett.

Unfortunately, the original fort no longer stands, but a visitor center has interpretive exhibits and historical artifacts. Several trails, including one to Navajo sites and one to the river, leave from the visitor center. Admission is $1.

Old Fort Sumner Museum

This museum (☎ 355-2942), with more local history here and an emphasis on Billy the Kid, is near the state monument. Hours are 10 am to 3 pm daily (extended hours June to September) and admission is $3/2 for adults/children.

Behind the museum are the graves of the Kid and Lucien Maxwell (you can see them for no charge). The Kid's tombstone is protected by an iron cage – 'souvenir hunters' keep stealing it.

Weather Balloon Launches

The unusual atmospheric circulation patterns in the spring and fall bring NASA and international scientists to Fort Sumner to launch weather balloons that carry scientific research instruments 32 miles into the atmosphere. One inflates to the size of the Houston Astrodome at its highest elevation. Ask at the Billy the Kid Country Inn (see below) for timing and directions to the launch site.

Special Events

The second weekend in June sees Old Fort Days, featuring various athletic events. The purse for the winner of the tombstone race, in which contestants must negotiate an obstacle course while lugging an 80lb tombstone, is $1000.

Places to Stay & Eat

Camping is available at **Sumner Lake State Park** (☎ 355-2541), which surrounds an artificial lake made by damming the Pecos River. Primitive sites cost $8, sites with a grill and shelter cost $10 and sites with partial hookups cost $14. There is a day charge of $4 per vehicle. Get there by taking Hwy 84 north for 11 miles, then Hwy 203 west for 6 miles. You can camp for free (no water) near Bosque Redondo Lake, 2 miles south of the east end of town.

The **Billy the Kid Country Inn** (☎ 355-7414, 1700 E Sumner Ave) offers simple but clean rooms and mobile homes with kitchenettes, both for $40. Also on Sumner Ave is the **Coronado Motel** (☎ 355-2466, with doubles for $35, and the **Super 8 Motel** (☎ 355-7888).

The best restaurant is the **Sprouts Café** (☎ 355-7278), located next to the Billy the Kid Country Inn and open 5 am to 8:30 pm.

If passing through and in a hurry, pick up a homemade breakfast burrito for $1 at *Sadie's (☎ 355-1461, 510 Sumner Ave)*; they serve simple but good New Mexican fare. *Two Sisters (☎ 355-3663)* offers American food including pasta, subs, pizza and steaks from the owner's own cows.

Getting There & Away

The Fort Sumner Bus Station (☎ 355-7745), 11th St at Sumner Ave, has a 9:30 pm TNM&O bus to Albuquerque ($25, three hours) and a 10 pm bus to Clovis ($10.50, one hour) and continuing to Lubbock, Texas, and beyond.

Thanks

Many thanks to the travelers who used the last edition and wrote to us with helpful hints, useful advice and interesting anecdotes:

Sara Anderson, Ian Anton, Randy Ballard, David Barkshire, Paul Barron, Mark Beeden, Richard Beeson, Brian & Caryl Bergeron, Franck Bessoles, Norman Broad, Victoria Bulostin, Pierpaola Conte, Sena & Ray Copson, Clive Cornwall, Noah Crescent, Chris Dalton, Gill Darling, Carola Eder, Jennifer Edwards, Patricia Empsall, Linnie Evans, Evan Eyler, Chris Forster-Brown, Hans-Dieter Gleich, Paul Green, Nico Heijnen, JC Henaut, Allan Hoben, Janet Howell, Page Inman, Susanne & Dietmar Kainer, Karles Karwin, Michelle King, Micky Lampe, Staci Lichterman, Gail Lloyd, J McAllister, Anita Morav, Angela Morris, Roberta Murray, Ana Nicolau, Tony Parkinson, Barbara Pieh, Eliose de Paula Piva, Andrea Redman, William Reeves, Elliot & Tey Roberts, Jo Ann Robertson, Jack Rocchio, Melissa Shim, Emily Showalter, George Smith, Anita Spencer, Rob Stevens, Mel Sutherland, Petra Joho Thomma, Joe Vante, Isabelle Verzelen, D van der Waaij, Christine Weber

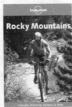

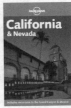

You already know that Lonely Planet produces more than this one guidebook, but you might not be aware of the other products we have on this region. Here is a selection of titles which you may want to check out as well:

Index

Abbreviations

AZ – Arizona   CO – Colorado   NM – New Mexico

NV – Nevada   UT – Utah

Text

A

Abiquiu (NM) 603–4
accommodations 68–73. *See also individual locations*
  B&Bs 70
  camping 69, 81–2
  guest ranches 72
  hostels 69–70
  hotels 70–2
  lodges 72
  motels 70–2
  reservations 72–3
  resorts 72
Acoma Pueblo (NM) 611
activities 80–90. *See also individual activities*
agaves 35–6
agriculture 38, 107, 294
Aguirre Springs National Recreation Area (NM) 649–50
AIDS 44, 58
air travel 91–7, 99
airports 91
Ajo (AZ) 475–6
Alamogordo (NM) 659, **661**
Albuquerque (NM) 521–43, **522, 523, 526–7, 539**
  accommodations 530–2
  activities 529–30
  entertainment 534–6
  history 521
  information 521–3
  organized tours 530
  orientation 521
  places to eat 532–4

Bold indicates maps.

shopping 536
special events 530
spectator sports 536
transportation 536–8
Alpine (AZ) 443
American Automobile Association (AAA) 62, 100, 480
American West Heritage Center (UT) 177
Anasazi Indians. *See* Ancestral Puebloan Culture
Ancestral Puebloan Culture 19–20, 430, 500, 502, 504–5, 506, 521, 572, 598, 656
Ancient Southwestern Cultures **18**
Angel Fire (NM) 589
Angel Peak National Recreation Area (NM) 596
Antelope Island State Park (UT) 141–3
Apache Indians 20, 22, 445–6, 599, 671
  Apache Trail 447–8
  history 292, 439–40, 449–50
Apache Trail 447–8
archaeological sites
  Arizona 389, 390, 409–10, 442, 472
  Colorado 502
  New Mexico 596, 598, 608, 634
  Utah 246, 279
Arches National Park (UT) 256–8, **257**
Arcosanti (AZ) 307, 390
Arizona 289–499, **290–1, 360, 380, 416, 436, 450, 484**

economy 294
information 294–5
recent history 291–4
Arizona State University (ASU) 296–7, 308
Arizona Trail 83
Arizona-Sonora Desert 26, 34–5, 36, 450, 469
Artesia (NM) 676
arts 39–40
  music 40–1
ATMs 48
atomic bombs 517, 550, 606–7
Aztec (NM) 596–7
Aztec Ruins National Monument (NM) 596

B

B&Bs. *See* accommodations
backpacking 81–4. *See also* hiking
  Arizona 332, 347–8, 420, 427, 461, 471
  New Mexico 608
  Utah 193, 231, 239–40, 250, 257–8, 262–4
Bandelier National Monument (NM) 608
bars 77. *See also* drinks
baseball 78, 139, 322, 536, 592–3
basketball 78, 138–9, 322, 536
Bear Lake (UT) 179
Beaver (UT) 211–3
Belen (NM) 542
Benson (AZ) 483, **485**
Bernalillo (NM) 539–40
Betatakin Pueblo (AZ) 430

Bold indicates maps.

Bold indicates maps.

Bold indicates maps.

Bold indicates maps.

Boxed Text

MAP LEGEND

ROUTES

City — Regional

- Freeway
- Toll Freeway
- Primary Road
- Secondary Road
- Tertiary Road
- Dirt Road
- Pedestrian Mall
- Steps
- Tunnel
- Trail
- Walking Tour
- Path

TRANSPORTATION

- Train
- Metro
- Bus Route
- Ferry

HYDROGRAPHY

- River; Creek
- Canal
- Lake
- Spring; Rapids
- Waterfalls
- Dry; Salt Lake

ROUTE SHIELDS

- **80** Interstate Freeway
- **G4** County Road
- **MEX 2** Mexico Highway
- **101** US Highway
- **IR 15** Indian Reservation Road
- **95** State Highway
- **375** Nevada State Highway

BOUNDARIES

- International
- State
- County
- Disputed

AREAS

- Beach
- Building
- Campus
- Cemetery
- Forest
- Garden; Zoo
- Golf Course
- Park
- Plaza
- Reservation
- Sports Field
- Swamp; Mangrove

POPULATION SYMBOLS

- ✪ NATIONAL CAPITAL — National Capital
- ◉ State Capital — State Capital
- ● Large City — Large City
- ● Medium City — Medium City
- ● Small City — Small City
- ○ Town; Village — Town; Village

MAP SYMBOLS

- ■ Place to Stay
- ▼ Place to Eat
- ● Point of Interest

- Airfield
- Airport
- Archeological Site; Ruin
- Bank
- Baseball Diamond
- Battlefield
- Bike Trail
- Border Crossing
- Buddhist Temple
- Bus Station; Terminal
- Cable Car; Chairlift
- Campground
- Castle
- Cathedral
- Cave
- Church
- Cinema
- Dive Site
- Embassy; Consulate
- Footbridge
- Gas Station
- Hospital
- Information
- Internet Access
- Lighthouse
- Lookout
- Mine
- Mission
- Monument
- Mountain
- Museum
- Observatory
- Park
- Parking Area
- Pass
- Picnic Area
- Police Station
- Pool
- Post Office
- Pub; Bar
- RV Park
- Shelter
- Shipwreck
- Skiing - Cross Country
- Skiing - Downhill
- Stately Home
- Surfing
- Synagogue
- Tao Temple
- Taxi
- Telephone
- Theater
- Toilet - Public
- Tomb
- Trailhead
- Tram Stop
- Transportation
- Volcano
- Winery

Note: Not all symbols displayed above appear in this book.

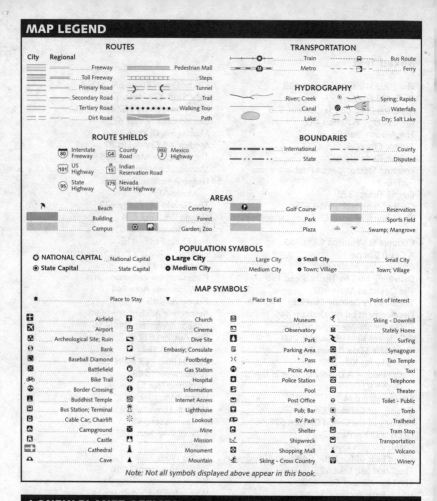

LONELY PLANET OFFICES

Australia
Locked Bag 1, Footscray, Victoria 3011
☎ 03 8379 8000 fax 03 8379 8111
email talk2us@lonelyplanet.com.au

USA
150 Linden Street, Oakland, CA 94607
☎ 510 893 8555, TOLL FREE 800 275 8555
fax 510 893 8572
email info@lonelyplanet.com

UK
10a Spring Place, London NW5 3BH
☎ 020 7428 4800 fax 020 7428 4828
email go@lonelyplanet.co.uk

France
1 rue du Dahomey, 75011 Paris
☎ 01 55 25 33 00 fax 01 55 25 33 01
email bip@lonelyplanet.fr
www.lonelyplanet.fr

World Wide Web: www.lonelyplanet.com *or* AOL keyword: lp
Lonely Planet Images: lpi@lonelyplanet.com.au